Berlitz®

CRUISING
& CRUISE SHIPS

2016

BY DOUGLAS WARD

THE WORLD'S FOREMOST AUTHORITY ON CRUISING

Introduction

Welcome to the 2016 edition of Berlitz Cruising & Cruise Ships – the book's 31st year of continuous publication.

The cruise industry is a fiercely competitive business, and one within which any marketing opportunity is seized upon and hyped to the nth degree. Travel industry awards – often in the form of magazine or online readers' polls – provide a perfect such opportunity and are extremely valuable to the cruise lines.

Yet these polls are only ever as good as the number of people who vote in them, the number of ships, and the criteria established for measuring quality. For example, if a magazine initiates a readers' poll, and no readers have cruised aboard a Spanish-speaking cruise ship, that ship will receive no votes. So, votes go to the most traveled ships, which are not necessarily the best. The magazines never state the criteria for their decisions, and the polls results are therefore unreliable.

At Berlitz, we always state our criteria, clearly and honestly. That's why the Berlitz Cruising & Cruise Ships 2016 is the most authoritative and dependable guide on the market. What's more, this book is totally independent, and unconnected or influenced by sponsorship.

My 6,070-plus days at sea

In welcoming new readers to this edition, I should mention my qualifications for assessing cruise ships on your behalf. I first fell in love with ships when, in 1965, I sailed aboard Cunard Line's 83,673-ton ocean liner RMS *Queen Elizabeth* – at that time the world's largest passenger ship.

To date, I have completed over 6,070 days at sea, participating in more than 1,070 cruises, 158 transatlantic crossings, and countless Panama Canal transits, plus shipyard visits, numerous ship-naming ceremonies, and maiden voyages.

The first edition of this book, reviewing, testing, and evaluating 120 ships, appeared in 1985, when cruising seemed to most people an expensive, rarefied experience. Today, the book is the most highly regarded source of comparative information not only for cruise purchasers, but also for cruise industry executives, travel agents, and crew members.

This book is a tribute to everyone who has made my seafaring experiences possible, especially my mother and father, and I thank the cruise lines for their assistance during the complex scheduling, sailing, inspection, evaluation, and rating processes.

How to use this book

This book is divided into two main parts. The first one – the introductory section – helps you to define what you are looking for in a cruise vacation and advises you on how to find it; it provides a wealth of information, including a look at life aboard ship. Specialist cruises are discussed, too, culminating with that ultimate travel experience: the around-the-world cruise.

The book's main section profiles 275 ocean-going cruise ships. From large to small, from unabashed luxury and exclusivity to ships for the budget-minded, and from new to old, they are all here.

The ratings and evaluations are a painstaking documentation of my personal work. I travel throughout the world, and I am at sea for up to 200 days each year. All evaluations are made objectively, without bias, partiality, or prejudice. In almost all instances, the ships have been visited recently by me or one of my team.

My intention has always been to make this the most informative and useful guidebook of its type, and to help you to make informed decisions about the ship(s) you choose for your next cruise(s).

Although price indicators are supplied for some things such as alternative restaurants, spa treatments,

and other items, prices and price categories may have changed since this book went to press. Check all prices with your cruise line.

Most of the statistical information contained in the ship profiles was supplied by the cruise lines and ship owners. You are welcome to send any errors or updated information to me at: shipratings@hotmail.com.

My constant travel and ship inspection schedule means I am frequently at sea, and I no longer answer mailed letters.

Sign up for Regular Updates

Cruise ships and their facilities are changing constantly. To keep abreast of developments, readers can sign up for our cruise and travel newsletter, distributed by email. This will contain our latest information and insights. To sign up, please email: cruiseletter@berlitzpublishing.com

Table of Contents

Introduction

Beginners Please 7
31 Wonderful Cruise Experiences............. 15
What's Ahead 18
Cruising's Continued Growth..................... 22
Frequently Asked Questions 26
Choosing Your Destination 43
Excursions Ashore..................................... 50

The Cruising Experience

Life Aboard 54
Cuisine... 61
Entertainment 68
Spas and Wellness Facilities...................... 72

Types of Cruising

Cruising for Families 79
Cruising for Seniors................................... 90
Cruising for Romantics 92
Cruising for Solo Travelers........................ 94

Cruising to Suit Special Needs 96
Expedition Cruises 99
Cruising to a Theme 105
Coastal Cruises 110
Transatlantic Crossings............................114
Cruising Under Sail...................................116
Cruising Around-the-World.......................118

Choosing the Right Cruise

Choosing your Ship 122
Choosing your Accommodation...............127
Comparing the Major Cruise Lines..........132
    Carnival Cruise Line..............................132
    Celebrity Cruises...................................136
    Costa Cruises..138
    Cunard Line...141
    Holland America Line 142
    MSC Cruises 144
    Norwegian Cruise Line 146
    P&O Cruises..147
    Princess Cruises....................................148
    Royal Caribbean International 151

The Smaller Operators 154
Living in Luxury 170

Practical Information
What To Do If... 174
Eco Cruising 176
Cruise Ship Safety 178

The Ships and Their Ratings
How We Evaluate the Ships 183
    What the ratings mean 184
    The Criteria 186
What the Descriptions Mean 188
This Year's Star Performers 190

Tables and Charts
New ships to debut 21
Cruise lines: private islands 47
How the major cruise lines score
    on cuisine 67

Hurtigruten ships 112
Comparing coastal ships 113
Around-the-world cruises in 2016 121
Advantages and disadvantages of
    large resort ships 123
Advantages and disadvantages of
    mid-size ships 124
Advantages and disadvantages of
    small ships/boutique ships 125
Comparing the biggest of the big 126
Comparing Luxury Ships 173
Ship Ratings 700

Enjoying a cabin balcony.

Beginners Please

Are you all at sea about cruise vacations, when it seems like everyone around you has taken a cruise, but you haven't? Here are the basics you'll need to know before you first step aboard.

Actually, there are thousands of others like you. It's a bit of an obstacle course, like trying to choose between different models of car and deciding on all the optional extras before actually getting the model you want. About 75 cruise companies operate around 350 ocean-going cruise ships (not to mention over 1,000 river ships) providing cruise vacations.

An ocean cruise can offer variety, great value for money, and a memorable experience, and, with a little planning, it will hopefully all go smoothly. And, after your first cruise, be prepared for the feeling of addiction that so often hits.

You'll need to do a little planning in order to find the right ship and cruise to suit your needs – whether you are a young couple, a family with children, sophisticated and well-traveled seniors, or you want unabashed luxury and total relaxation.

What exactly is a cruise?

A cruise is an escape from everyday life on land. It is a (mostly) pre-paid, hopefully hassle-free and crime-free vacation, where you only have to pack and un-pack once. You seldom have to make blind choices, you sleep in the same bed each night, the ship moves the scenery for you, and organized excursions ashore can add to the sense of discovery.

Everything's close at hand and there are always polite people to help you. You can explore new places, meet new people and make new friends. It can facilitate multi-generational togetherness, solo adventuring, or escapism for couples. And, some of the world's most beautiful places are best seen from the deck of a cruise ship.

What a cruise is not

Some cruises simply aren't relaxing, despite cruise brochure claims that 'you can do as much or as little as you want to.' For example, large resort ships carrying over 2,001 passengers pack lots of people into small cabins and provide almost nonstop activities and entertainment.

Reasons to take a cruise

Value for money. A cruise represents excellent value for money, considering everything that is being provided in the package. As it's mostly pre-paid, you don't have to constantly make financial decisions once you're on your way, either.

Convenience. You can probably drive to your port of embarkation (doorstep cruising). If not, the cruise line can make all the arrangements, including flights, baggage handling, and transfers to and from the ship. And you only have to unpack once during the vacation!

Comfort. A suite or cabin is your home away from home. It can be as small as a tent (at about 60 sq ft/6 sq m) or as large as a villa (at 3,000 sq ft/279 sq m), or anything in between.

Good food. Dining is one of the greatest pleasures of ship life, and all your meals are included from breakfast through to late-night snacks. A cruise is one of the best options if you are looking for a vacation that can easily accommodate specific dietary needs.

Family togetherness. Cruising offers a safe, friendly environment, which is great for families with children. Many ships have well-supervised activities for kids, too. Cruising is also an excellent way for groups of friends to vacation together.

Learning experience. Most cruise ships have guest speakers/lecturers, so you can learn while you cruise.

Royal Court Theatre aboard *Queen Elizabeth*.

Europa 2, by Hapag-Lloyd Cruises.

Adventure. A cruise can be an adventure. It can take you to places that are impossible to reach by almost any other means, such as the Antarctic Peninsula, the Arctic, or to remote islands. A cruise can inspire the explorer in you.
Staying healthy. A cruise allows you to pamper yourself in a spa, although body-pampering treatments are at extra cost. And, with all the available food, learn to pace yourself to stay healthy.
Entertainment. Cruise ships provide a wide range of professional entertainment, from spectacular Vegas-style production shows to intimate piano, guitar, and jazz bars. And during the day, there are activities, fun, and games galore – enough to keep even the most active occupied.

About the price

The amount you are prepared to spend will determine the length of the cruise, plus the size, location, and style of accommodation you get. Be wary of huge discounts – these either mean that the product was unrealistically priced at source or that quality is reduced somewhere.

Will I need a passport?

Yes. You'll need to ensure that any appropriate authorizations and visas are obtained ahead of your cruise. If you already have a valid passport, make sure that you have at least six months left on in at the *end* of the cruise. If you don't have a passport, allow plenty of time to apply for one. Note that in some ports (such as Venice, Italy, and all ports in Russia) you are required to carry your passport when ashore.

10 steps to a good first cruise experience

1. Find a cruise specialist. Although the Internet is a popular research tool, it pays to find a specialist cruise agent as soon as possible (note that some Internet-only 'agencies' with slick websites have been known to disappear without trace – with your money).

Describe your preferences (relaxation, visiting destinations, adventure, activities, entertainment, etc.), so that your agent can suggest what's appropriate. They will then find a cruise that is right for you, for the right reasons, and find the best fares available.

They can guide you through all the important details, such as choice of cabin, dining arrangements, cruise lines, and ships best suited to your needs. They may also have insider tips, knowledge about upgrades, pre- and post-cruise programs, and hotel and other travel arrangements.

2. Where to? Choose where you want to cruise (Bahamas, Bermuda, Caribbean, Alaska, Hawaii, US east coast, the Baltic, Northern Europe, Mediterranean, Indian Ocean, Southeast Asia, Australia/New Zealand, South Africa, South America, South Pacific, etc.). And when you want to cruise (Alaska is only offered by cruise companies in the summertime; the Caribbean may be too hot for you in summer; Northern Europe is best in the summer, although South America and Southeast Asia are best in the winter). If you are interested in a special theme, such as Carnival in Rio or Formula One racing in Monte Carlo, this will determine the time of year.

3. How long? Decide on the length of cruise vacation you can afford to take. Allow traveling time to get to and from your ship, particularly if it is in a region far from home, or during winter. The standard length of cruise in the Caribbean, for example, is seven days, although short-break Bahamas or Mexican Riviera cruises for three or four days are popular, too. In Northern Europe 12–14 days are more typical, while for an around-South America cruise, you'll need 30 days or more. For visiting the Antarctic Peninsula, allow 21 days. Finally, a complete around-the-world cruise will take 90–120 days.

How to get the best deal

Find out what's available by reading newspaper advertising and checking the Internet. Then identify a travel agency that *specializes* in cruises. In some countries, such as the UK, they'll be bonded if they belong to an industry association. A good agent will get you the best price, as well as upgrades and other benefits you won't be able to get elsewhere.

Big travel agency groups and consortiums often reserve large blocks of cabins, while smaller independent agencies can access extensive discounts, upgrades, and other benefits not available on the Internet. The cruise lines consider travel agents as their principal distribution system, so they can provide special discounts and value-added amenities that aren't provided to Internet sites.

4. Choose the right ship. Size matters! Choose the right size ship for your needs. Do you want to be with 100, 200, 500, 1,000, or 5,000-plus others on your vacation? As a rule of thumb, the larger the ship, the more the itinerary focuses on the ship as the destination.

Or perhaps you would like to experience cruising under sail; or with specialist lecturers; or an adventure/expedition cruise; or a coastal and inland waterways cruise; or with a large spa and choice of body-pampering treatments; or aboard a ship with non-stop entertainment and fun activities.

5. Choose the right cabin. For a first cruise, if the budget allows, choose an outside-view cabin. In an interior (no-view) cabin you won't know how to dress when you wake up, because you can't see what the weather is like outside, although interior no-view cabins are good if you like to sleep in a really dark room. If you are concerned about motion sickness (it's not common, but it can happen), choose a cabin in the mid-section of the ship.

The average cabin size aboard a large resort ship is 180–200 sq ft (16.5–18.5 sq m); anything less and you will feel cramped. With limited closet space, you'll need fewer clothes than you might think. The more space you want, the more it will cost. Today, many passengers like to have a private balcony.

6. Dining. If the ship has two seatings for dinner (many large resort ships do), it could be wise to choose the later seating (typically 8:30pm), so that you have enough time ashore on the days the ship is in port without having to rush back to shower and change for the first seating, which is typically at 6:30pm.

Some ships have several dining venues, and you go where and when and with whom you like.

7. Health and fitness. If you are interested in wellness or spa treatments, ask your agent to make sure that your chosen ship has adequate facilities, space, and equipment. Aboard some of the largest ships, you'll need to sign up for many exercise classes, and there may be a 30-minute time limit to use the treadmill or video bike.

It's best to book early for spa treatments, because the appointment times go quickly. Some cruise lines with large resort ships allow you to book online, although this means planning your time in advance.

8. Families. If you are traveling with children, choose a family-friendly ship. While most large resort ships have good facilities to help everything run smoothly with youngsters, mid-size and small ships have more limited facilities. Some have none at all aimed at little ones. Children generally love cruising, finding it educational, fun, safe, and sociable.

Conversely, if you don't want to cruise with lots of children, avoid the main school vacation periods. For those who don't want children around them, there are several child-free ships to choose from.

9. Dress codes. Dress codes today tend to be informal, particularly aboard the large resort ships. In general, no tuxedo is needed, although there are exceptions to this, such as on a transatlantic crossing aboard Cunard Line's *Queen Mary 2*, where dressing more formally is part of the tradition. It sounds obvious, but ships move around, so flat or low-heeled shoes are strongly recommended for women.

Visiting the Norwegian fjords aboard *Balmoral* (Fred. Olsen Cruise Lines).

Relaxing on a deckchair on a transatlantic crossing with Cunard Line.

10. Extra expenses. Finally, you'll need to budget for extra-cost items such as shore excursions, drinks (unless they are included), meals in any 'specialty' dining venue, spa treatments, gaming, and other personal items. Also, allow some additional money to cover souvenirs and other purchases. Last, but not least, make sure you have full insurance cover for your vacation.

Digital details

Today, most passengers use mobiles, tablets, and laptops and expect to be able to use these devices during their cruise.

You can't use your mobile or tablet for embarkation check-in yet, but you can use your device aboard ship – in port. Once you leave port your mobile may automatically lock into the ship's digital network, incurring a charge. At sea, your mobile is out of range with your land-based carrier and locks into a 'mini-cell' aboard ship (Cellular at Sea), controlled by the MTN (Marine Telephone Network).

You will be asked to establish a user name and password before you can access the Internet. Wi-Fi is available aboard most ships – at extra cost – but it's not high speed like on land.

Some mobile phone carriers have a preferred carrier list built into every phone that pre-selects preferred carriers throughout the world with whom they have roaming agreements – at optimum rates.

Note that some ships have notices outside their restaurants prohibiting the use of mobile phones.

Mobile phone tips

Turn off Data Roaming to save data roaming charges. Turn off Location Services to prevent apps from constantly trying to update your location. Turn off Data Push, because some e-mail accounts, including Gmail, push the data to your smartphone, incurring charges even if you don't open any e-mails. Turn off Data Synchronization, because it consumes bandwidth trying to keep your accounts up to date. Better still – have a digital detox!

What to expect

Stepping aboard for the first time? Here is what you need to know about a typical embarkation.

Make sure you have your passport and any visas required. Pack any medication you may need (in original, labeled containers) in your carry-on hand luggage.

You will already have been sent your cruise tickets and other relevant documents (including immigration forms to be completed before you get to your ship), as well as luggage tags, either digitally or as paper copies from the cruise line or your travel agent.

You've arrived at the airport closest to your ship's embarkation point, and retrieved your luggage. There will be a representative from the cruise line waiting, holding aloft a sign with the company's name on it. Your luggage, which you should make sure has your cabin number displayed clearly on it, is placed in a cluster together with that of other passengers. The next time you see your bags should be in your cabin.

You'll find check-in desks in the passenger terminal. If you have suite-grade accommodation, there should be a separate check-in facility. (*Note:* don't buy duty-free liquor to take on board – it will be confiscated.)

Anyone cruising from a US port who is a non-US citizen, or 'resident alien,' is sent to a separate desk to check in. Leave your passport with the check-in personnel, but ask for a receipt. It's advisable to also have a photocopy of the main pages of your passport to keep with you.

Getting aboard

You'll go through security-screening, just as at airports. Then it's a few paces to get to the gangway. This may be a covered, airport-type gangway, or an open one – hopefully with a net underneath it in case you drop something. As you approach the gangway, you will probably be greeted by the ship's snap-happy photographers ready to take your photograph, bedraggled as you may appear after having traveled for hours. Just say no (firmly) if you don't want your photograph taken.

Online check in

Most cruise lines now expect you to check in online to reduce staff numbers at check-in desks in embarkation cruise terminals. Paper cruise tickets and other documents formerly used by most major cruise lines have become collectors' items. You must print your boarding pass at your own cost. It typically takes about 10 minutes, assuming that you have all your booking details to hand.

Depending on the cruise line, there are usually four major steps to complete before you can print your boarding pass.
Step 1: Passenger information.
Step 2: Your onboard expense account information (pre-register your credit card).
Step 3: Cruise ticket contract.
Step 4: Print your boarding pass and baggage tags.

At the ship end of the gangway, you will find the cruise staff will welcome you aboard, although they may or may not guide you to your cabin.

Things to check

Once inside your cabin, look around. Is it clean? Is it tidy? Are the beds properly made? Is there ice in the ice container? Check the bathroom, bathtub – if there is one – or shower. Make sure there are towels and soap. If there are problems, tell your cabin steward.

Memorize the telephone number for the ship's hospital, doctor, or for medical emergencies, just so you know how to call for help of that sort.

Your luggage probably will not have arrived yet – especially if it is a large resort ship carrying more than 2,001 passengers – but don't sit in the cabin waiting for it. Put your hand luggage away, and, deck plan in hand, take a walk. If you're hungry, head to the self-serve buffet – be warned, though, that aboard the large resort ships, it can be a bit of a free-for-all.

Familiarize yourself with the ship's layout. Learn which way is forward, and which way is aft, and how to reach your cabin from the main stairways. This is also a good time to learn how to get from your cabin to the outside decks in an emergency – these are rare, but they do happen.

Control that thirst

Picture the scenario: you're thirsty when you arrive in your cabin. You notice a bottle of water with a tab around its neck. Be sure to read the notice on the tab: 'This bottle is provided for your convenience. If you open it, your account will be charged $4.50.'

On deck, you are greeted by a smiling waiter offering you a colorful, cool drink. But, put your fingers on the glass as he hands it to you and he'll also ask for your cruise card. Bang, you've just paid $6.95 for a drink full of ice worth 5¢.

The cost of drinks soon adds up. Aboard ships operated by Europe-based companies, mixers such as tonic for gin are usually charged separately.

The safety drill

A Passenger Lifeboat Drill will take place before a ship sails from the embarkation port. (This was introduced following the *Costa Concordia* tragedy in 2012.) It is mandatory that you attend the drill, and do pay attention – it could save your life. Directions to your assembly station are posted on the back of the cabin door. By now, your luggage probably will have arrived.

Titanic-style stairway aboard *Insignia*.

TODAY'S ACTIVITIES

6am

6.00am WAKE UP WITH PAUL
TV show with your Entertainment Director, Paul O'Loughlin.
TV Ch. 41 (repeated continuously until 12.00pm)

6.00am DISEMBARKATION TALK
Your Entertainment Director, Paul O'Loughlin, presents the information you need regarding disembarking QUEEN MARY 2 in Southampton.
TV Ch. 44 (repeated continuously all day)

8am

8.00am CANYON RANCH FITNESS◯
Power Deck walk - 1 mile brisk walk & talk. Previous sign-up required.
Meet at the Canyon Ranch SpaClub Gym

8.30am CATHOLIC MASS
Led by Father Robert Allan Jeffers.
Illuminations ⑦, deck 3, A or B stairway (until 9.00am)

9.00am CROSSWORD & QUIZ AVAILABLE◉
Library, deck 8 forward, A stairway

9.00am CANYON RANCH FITNESS◯
Stretch and relax - full body stretch. Previous sign-up required.
Queens Room ⑦, deck 3, D stairway (until 9.30am)

9am

9.30am CHALLENGE YOUR SPORTS DIRECTORS
Hosted by your sports directors.
Sign up at the Fairways, deck 12, B stairway (until 3.00pm)

9.30am BEGINNERS' BRIDGE CLASS - DAY 6
Atlantic Room, deck 11, A stairway (until 10.15am)

9.30am iSTUDY: SEMINAR
Communicating: Skype and WhatsApp!
ConneXions 6, deck 2, A stairway (until 10.15am)

10.00am CANYON RANCH LECTURE◯
Agony of Sore Feet. Find out how knee, hip and back pain can stem from poor biomachanics of the foot.
Winter Garden, deck 7, B stairway (until 10.45am)

10.00am RADA WORKSHOP
Queens Room , deck 3, D stairway (until 10.45am)

10.00am CUNARD INSIGHTS LECTURE
Recorded and broadcast on TV Ch. 42 from 5.00pm onwards
'Measuring the Universe – How do we know it's such a big place?' From the Ancient Greeks to today, understanding the size of the Universe has been an enduring quest. How can astronomers calculate the huge distances involved without leaving earth? Learn how attempts to measure the size of the Universe resulted in Captain Cook landing in Australia and how observing distant stars and galaxies allows us to look back down the corridors of time. Presented by Royal Astronomical Society speaker, Mark Butterworth.
Illuminations ⑦, deck 3, A or B stairway (until 10.45am)

10.00am CANYON RANCH FITNESS◯
Pilates - mat based all levels. Fitness Pass and previous sign-up required.
Knightsbridge Room, deck 1, C stairway (until 10.45am)

10am

10.00am WATERCOLOUR ART CLASS AND EXHIBITION
A one-time fee of $35 for supplies. Numbers are limited to 25 guests. Between 11.30am and 12.00pm the doors will be open for fellow guests to view the work created on this voyage.
Chelsea Room, deck 1, B stairway (until 12.00pm)

10.00am SOCIAL MAHJONG
Outside on the port side of the Royal Court Theatre, deck 2

10.15am ART TALK: THE ART OF SEASCAPES
The Art Gallery, Deck 3L, Starboard, Stairway C or D (until 11.00am)

10.15am CANYON RANCH LECTURE◯
Expert Make-Up Tips for Mature Women. Join our Make-up Artist as she guides you through looking fabulous.
Belgravia Room, deck 1, B stairway (until 10.45am)

10.30am INTERMEDIATE BRIDGE CLASS - DAY 6
Atlantic Room, deck 11, A stairway (until 11.15am)

10.30am MORNING TRIVIA◉
Hosted by the entertainment staff.
Golden Lion Pub, deck 2, C stairway (until 11.15am)

10.30am NAPKIN FOLDING CLASS
With your Social Hostess Imogen.
G32, deck 3, D stairway (until 11.15am)

10am

10.30am SOLO TRAVELLERS' MORNING COFFEE
With your Gentleman Dance Hosts.
Chef's Galley, deck 7, C stairway

11.00am iSTUDY: iPAD WORKSHOP
Using an iPad Part 3: The Next Stage (loan available $5). A $15 fee applies. Bookings welcomed
ConneXions 6, deck 2, A stairway (until 11.45am)

11.00am CUNARD INSIGHTS LECTURE
Recorded and broadcast on TV Ch. 42 from 5.00pm onwards
'Her Majesty's Yacht Britannia. 'A celebration of the Her Majesty The Queen's former floating palace and the many roles that she fulfilled. Presented by Dr Stephen M. Payne OBE.
Illuminations ⑦, deck 3, A or B stairway (until 11.45am)

11am

11.15am FRIENDS OF BILL W.
The Boardroom, deck 9, A stairway (until 12.00pm)

11.15am QUIZZICAL CORNER ◉
Golden Lion Pub, deck 2, C stairway (until 11.45am)

11.15am BALLROOM DANCE CLASS
Jive, with your on board dance couple, Volodymyr and Nadiya.
Queens Room⑦, deck 3, D stairway (until 12.00pm)

11.30am BINGO TICKET SALE
Casino blackjack table outside the Golden Lion Pub (until 1.15pm)

12.00pm EIGHT BELLS
Grand Lobby, deck 3, C stairway

12pm

12.00pm NAVIGATIONAL ANNOUNCEMENT
Public address system.

12.00pm TIME CHANGE
Please be advised that today at midday the ships clocks will be SET FORWARD BY ONE HOUR. Please set your watches FORWARD at 12 noon today, Friday 12 July.

1pm

1.15pm LINE DANCING
Queens Room⑦, deck 3, D stairway (until 2.00pm)

1.15pm DIXIELAND LUNCH
With the Royal Court Theatre Orchestra.
Golden Lion Pub, deck 2, C stairway (until 2.00pm)

1.15pm LUNCHTIME MELODIES
With pianist Geza Torocsik.
Chart Room, deck 3, C stairway (until 2.00pm)

1.30pm POOLSIDE MUSIC WITH XTASEA
Pavilion Pool, deck 12, B stairway (until 2.30pm)

1.45pm DUPLICATE BRIDGE TOURNAMENT◉
Atlantic Room, deck 11, A stairway (until 3.45pm)

2.00pm MASONIC MEETING
The Boardroom, deck 9, A stairway (until 2.30pm)

2.00pm LIVE PLANETARIUM PRESENTATION
Tickets are available from ConneXions, deck 2, A stairway, from 9.00am.
Explore the night sky live in the planetarium with Royal Astronomical Society fellow, Mark Butterworth. Find out what you'll be able to see from the decks of the ship and what treats the heavens have in store for us in the coming months.
Illuminations ⑦, deck 3, A or B stairway (until 2.45pm)

2.00pm CANYON RANCH FITNESS◯
Yoga - Basic Moves. Fitness Pass and previous sign-up required.
Knightsbridge Room, deck 1, C stairway (until 2.45pm)

2pm

2.00pm WATERCOLOUR ART CLASS AND EXHIBITION
A one-time fee of $35 for supplies. Numbers are limited to 25 guests. Between 3.30pm and 4.00pm the doors will be open for fellow guests to view the work created on this voyage.
Chelsea Room, deck 1, B stairway (until 4.00pm)

2.00pm GOLDEN YEARS OF CUNARD SHIPS TRIVIA◉
Hosted by the entertainment staff.
Chart Room, deck 3, C stairway (until 2.30pm)

2.00pm SNOWBALL JACKPOT BINGO
Tickets will be on sale outside the Queens Room port side from 1.30pm to 2.00pm.
Queens Room , deck 3, D stairway (until 2.30pm)

2.30pm SOCIAL NEEDLEWORK & KNITTING
With you rSocial Hostess, Imogen. Please note that this is not a class.
Champagne bar, deck 3, Grand Lobby (until 3.30pm)

This is an example of a full day at sea aboard Cunard Line's *Queen Mary 2*. As you see, there really is plenty of life on a day at sea, and absolutely no time to become bored.

TODAY'S ACTIVITIES

2pm

2.30pm **iSTUDY: NEXT STEPS**
Photoshop Elements: Part 3 Using Layers (Apple or Windows).
A $25 fee applies.
ConneXions 6, deck 2, A stairway (until 3.30pm)

3.00pm **Q&A WITH JUILLIARD**
Join James Burton of the Juilliard School in New York for an informative
Question and Answer session in the Chart Room, hosted by Musical
Director Brad Black.
The Chart Room, deck 3, C stairway (until 3.45pm)

3.00pm **BINGO TICKET SALE**
Outside the Queens Room, port side (until 4.45pm)

3.00pm **DARTS COMPETITION** 🎯
Golden Lion Pub, deck 2, C stairway (until 3.30pm)

3.00pm **WHISKY LOVER'S GET-TOGETHER**
A fee applies, call 29000 to book.
Commodore Club, deck 9, A stairway

3.00pm **INTEREST CORNER**
For those guests who sailed on the Inaugural Transatlantic
aboard QUEEN MARY 2 in April 2004.
ConneXions 3, deck 2, A stairway (until 3.45pm)

3.00pm **CANYON RANCH FITNESS○**
Legs, bums and tums. Previous sign-up required.
Knightsbridge Room, deck 1, C stairway (until 3.45pm)

3pm

3.00pm **TEXAS HOLD'EM TOURNAMENT**
Followed by $1 / $2 No limit cash game.
Empire Casino, deck 2, B or C stairway

3.30pm **CUNARD INSIGHTS LECTURE**
Recorded and broadcast on TV Ch. 42 from 5.00pm onwards
'The Special Relationship: The Intelligence Link Between
10 Downing Street and the White House'. This is the final
presentation by intelligence and espionage expert, Nigel West.
Illuminations 📽, deck 3, A or B stairway (until 4.15pm)

3.30pm **AFTERNOON TEA DANCE**
The Queen's Room Orchestra will be on hand today to
accompany you as you enjoy a classic Cunard afternoon tea.
Queens Room 📽, deck 3, D stairway (until 4.30pm)

3.30pm **BUFFET AFTERNOON TEA**
Kings Court, Lotus, deck 7 (until 4.30pm)

3.30pm **COMPLIMENTARY GOLF COMPETITION◉**
40 yards chipping out of the bunker / rough. Places are limited.
(30 Places Maximum). Sign up is required.
The Fairways, deck 12, B stairway (until 4.15pm)

4.00pm **CANYON RANCH FITNESS○**
Abs Express. Previous sign-up required.
Knightsbridge Room, deck 1, C stairway (until 4.45pm)

4.00pm **iSTUDY: iPAD WORKSHOP**
Using an iPad Part 4: Cameras, Photographs & Movies. A $25
fee applies. Bookings welcomed.
ConneXions 6, deck 2, A stairway (until 4.45pm)

4pm

4.30pm **MEET THE SPEAKERS**
Join us this afternoon for an informal get together with this
voyage's Cunard Insights lecturers. Don't miss this great
opportunity to meet and chat with them.
Chart Room, deck 3, C stairway (until 5.15pm)

4.30pm **AFTERNOON TRIVIA** ◉
Golden Lion Pub, deck 2, C stairway (until 5.00pm)

5.00pm **FINAL SNOWBALL JACKPOT BINGO**
The final bingo session for the voyage, the money must be won!
Queens Room , deck 3, D stairway (until 5.30pm)

5.00pm **FILM: 'BEST EXOTIC MARIGOLD HOTEL'**
Starring Judi Dench, Bill Nighy, Maggie Smith and Celia Imrie.
Directed by John Madden. Rated PG13; 2012.
Illuminations 📽, deck 3, A or B stairway (duration 124 minutes)

5.00pm **'LIVE @ 5' RADIO SHOW WITH DJ CHRIS**
TV Ch. 41 (until 7.00pm Call 23015 for requests and dedications)

5.00pm **JEWISH SABBATH**
ConneXions Rooms 4 & 5, deck 2, A or B stairway (until 5.45pm)

5pm

5.00pm **FRIENDS OF DOROTHY LGBT**
Commodore Club (stbd), deck 9, A stairway (until 5.45pm)

5.15pm **PIANIST RUSSELL HOLMES**
Golden Lion Pub, deck 2, C stairway (until 6.00pm)

5.15pm **SUNRISE STRING QUARTET**
Chart Room, deck 3, C stairway (until 6.00pm)

5.15pm **ACTIVITY STAMP REDEMPTION**
For guests disembarking in Southampton tomorrow, redeem the
stamps you have won at activities. Bring your stamped Activity Reward
Cards to exchange for prizes. Please note: Your stamp log is valid
only for the duration of your voyage and may not be carried forward
after you disembark. We do not accept yellow prize vouchers.
ConneXions Room 3, deck 2, A stairway (until 5.45pm)

6pm

6.30pm **PIANIST RUSSELL HOLMES**
Chart Room, deck 3, C stairway (until 7.15pm)

7.00pm **SHOWTIME: COMEDY JUGGLER JON UDRY**
Jon has been perfecting his skills in juggling and manipulation for
the past 13 years. His show is a fine fusion of technical juggling,
stand up comedy and audience participation. Jon is known to
juggle up to 7 objects, 9 cigar boxes, a bowling ball, a small
child and a chainsaw (one of these may not be true). Jon was
awarded British Young Juggler of the Year in 2006. Jon's show
is a visual feast that will have you on the edge of their seats.
Presented by your Entertainment Director, Paul O'Loughlin.
Royal Court Theatre 📽, decks 2 & 3, B stairway (until 7.45pm)

7pm

7.15pm **PIANIST AND SINGER PETER KOVACS**
Golden Lion Pub, deck 2, C stairway (until 8.00pm)

7.30pm **PIANIST RUSSELL HOLMES**
The Commodore Club, deck 9, A stairway (until 8.30pm)

7.30pm **SUNRISE STRING QUARTET**
Chart Room, deck 3, C stairway (until 8.30pm)

7.45pm **PRE-RECORDED MUSIC**
Queens Room 📽, deck 3, D stairway (until 8.30pm)

8.00pm **FILM: 'BEST EXOTIC MARIGOLD HOTEL'**
Illuminations 📽, deck 3, A or B stairway (duration 124 minutes)

8.30pm **BALLROOM AND LATIN DANCE MUSIC**
With the Queens Room Orchestra under the direction of Maurice
Williams, featuring vocalist Paul Christopher.
Queens Room 📽, deck 3, D stairway (until 11.30pm)

8pm

8.45pm **SHOWTIME: COMEDY JUGGLER JON UDRY**
Jon has been perfecting his skills in juggling and manipulation for
the past 13 years. His show is a fine fusion of technical juggling,
stand up comedy and audience participation. Jon is known to juggle
up to 7 objects, 9 cigar boxes, a bowling ball, a small child and a
chainsaw (one of these may not be true). Jon was awarded British
Young Juggler of the Year in 2006. Jon's show is a visual feast
that will have you on the edge of their seats. Presented by your
Entertainment Director, Paul O'Loughlin.
Royal Court Theatre 📽, decks 2 & 3, B stairway (until 9.30pm)

9.30pm **THE JAZZ CLUB**
Chart Room, deck 3, C stairway (until 12.30am)

9pm

9.30pm **PIANIST AND SINGER PETER KOVACS**
Golden Lion Pub, deck 2, C stairway (until 10.00pm)

9.45pm **INTERNATIONAL BAND, XTASEA**
G32, deck 3, D stairway (until 10.45pm)

10.00pm **PIANIST GEZA TOROCSIK**
Commodore Club, deck 9, A stairway (until 12.00am)

10.00pm **FAREWELL TRIVIA**◉
Golden Lion Pub, deck 2, C stairway (until 10.45pm)

10pm

10.30pm **FILM: 'BEST EXOTIC MARIGOLD HOTEL'**
Illuminations 📽, deck 3, A or B stairway (duration 124 minutes)

10.45pm **ALL REQUEST EXPRESS WITH DJ CHRIS**
G32, deck 3, D stairway (until 11.30pm)

10.45pm **SINGER AND PIANIST PETER KOVACS**
Golden Lion Pub, deck 2, C stairway (until 12.00am)

11.30pm **INTERNATIONAL BAND, XTASEA**
G32, deck 3, D stairway (until 12.30am)

11pm

11.30pm **STRICT TEMPO MUSIC**
Queens Room 📽, deck 3, D stairway (until 12.30am)

12am

12.30am **DJ CHRIS**
G32, deck 3, D stairway (until late)

All times and durations are subject to change. Some durations are dependant on participation.

31 Wonderful Cruise Experiences

During the 31-year lifespan of this book, I have been privileged to enjoy some wonderful experiences aboard cruise ships. Here, in no particular order, are 31 highlights.

Fingal's Cave
Passing within an arm's distance of Fingal's Cave on the uninhabited island of Staffa (one of Scotland's Inner Hebridean Islands), as Felix Mendelssohn's *Hebrides Overture* (inspired by the real molten lava rock cavern) was played on the open back deck of the pocket-sized *Hebridean Princess*. At the time – late one chilly morning in spring– I was sitting wrapped in a tartan blanket under a grey, foreboding sky, enjoying a single malt whisky.

Slice of ice
Watching from the observation deck above the bridge of *Hanseatic*, as the ship sliced slowly through the pack-ice in the incredibly scenic, steep-sided Lamaire Channel in the Antarctic Peninsula.

'Europa's Best'
Tasting some beautiful artisan cuisine prepared by chefs whose restaurants have three Michelin three stars aboard Europa for the annual Europa's Best event in Antwerp. In June 2014 the chefs had 18 Michelin stars between them! Some of the finest cheese and wine producers from Austria, France, Germany, and Switzerland displayed their wares, too. This culinary heaven can be enjoyed by anyone with a ticket.

Culinary tour de force
Enjoying freshly sliced tuna and yellowtail sashimi at Nobu Matsuhisa's Silk Road Sushi Bar aboard *Crystal Serenity*. Not only was this a culinary tour de force, but watching the Japanese chefs was entertaining, too.

Amalfi magic
Sitting on the corner balcony of a Club Suite aboard *Azamara Quest*, admiring the beautiful scenery of Sorrento, Italy, with the ship at anchor off the famed coastline and a Limoncello to hand.

Candles in the wind
Dining by candlelight at the aft terrace café of *Aegean Odyssey* while watching the mesmerising patterns created on the water by a full, seemingly orange moon in Southeast Asia.

Noodles in Alaska
Sitting on my balcony, breathing in the fresh air and enjoying room-service steaming hot udon noodles, while transiting Alaska's Inside Passage aboard *Nippon Maru*.

Sydney sights
Being outside on deck watching as *Queen Mary 2* turned majestically in Sydney Harbour and sidled up to Circular Quay, close to the Sydney Harbour Bridge and Opera House. All this with hundreds of spectators.

Blue lagoon nights
Lying down in the padded 'Blue Lagoon' seating area at the stern of the *Sea Cloud*, watching the sails directing this wonderful tall ship and seeing a shooting star pass quickly overhead – a most serene experience.

Shackleton's grave
One Christmas Day, paying homage in Grytviken – the former Norwegian whaling station in South Georgia – with passengers from the expedition ships *Bremen*

Douglas Ward at Shackleton's grave, South Georgia.

The Blue Lagoon thermal hot spring, Iceland.

and *Hanseatic*. We poured Aquavit on the grave of the explorer Sir Ernest Shackleton to toast the great man.

The green flash
Cruising aboard a *Hurtigruten* ship, near Hammerfest or Honningsvag on the northern coast of Norway in October, and seeing the 'green flash' of the Northern Lights appear on the horizon, as the sun dipped and disappeared.

Under the stars
Standing on deck at the front of the ship, just before bedtime, in one of the wonderfully comfortable cotton sleep suits provided aboard *SeaDream I* and *SeaDream II*. The rhythm of the ship was lulling me to sleep as it sailed to its next destination.

Spiderman
Sitting in the netting hanging at the bowsprit (front) of the sail-cruise ship (tall ship) *Star Flyer* – an exhilarating experience. On this occasion, the ship was gliding gracefully through the water on a perfect, sun-filled day in the azure blue Caribbean Sea.

Misty morning
Standing on the foredeck of a cruise ship entering Halong Bay, a UNESCO-protected World Heritage site close to the Bay on Tonkin in Quang Ning Province in north-eastern Vietnam. Go in the early morning, when the mist is heavy, for an ethereal feeling of calmness. The dramatic limestone karsts (stone islands) surrounding the ship loom up from the sealevel cloud of heavy air.

Queen and country
Taking a bath in Cabin 1066 of the *Queen Elizabeth 2* one evening during a transatlantic crossing, listening to Elgar's *Pomp and Circumstance* on the in-cabin broadcast system and thinking: how incredibly British.

Canal move
Watching as steel-wired electric mules (each costing over $2 million) pull your cruise ship into position in one of the lock chambers at Miraflores Locks, in the Panama Canal.

Bird's-eye view
Being aboard a cruise ship sailing into or out of Venice, gliding past St Mark's Square. It's a view of Venice you only get from the deck (or balcony – if yours is on the correct side) of a waterborne vessel.

Steps away
Being aboard a small cruise ship moored alongside the State Hermitage Museum in St. Petersburg, Russia. This takes you literally just a few steps away from the iconic building – one of the largest and oldest museums in the world, with over 3 million exhibits, including its stunning collection of Fabergé eggs.

Titanic pose
Standing with outstretched arms, just like Kate Winslet in the movie *Titanic*, at the front of *Braemar*, as the ship glided slowly through the Swedish archipelago towards Stockholm.

Bathtub cruising

Staring at the horizon while lying in the bathtub in the 'wet room' (with heated floor) in one of the two Deck 10 Crystal Penthouse suites aboard *Crystal Symphony*, as the ship glides through open water.

Slipping away

Sitting on the deck of a pocket-sized cruise ship in Glacier Bay, Alaska, watching the blue glacial ice calving, making you rock and roll as it slips, slides, and crashes into the water within inches of your body.

Melting away

Sitting in a pool of silica- and sulphur-rich geo-thermal water in Iceland's Blue Lagoon – a man-made outlet close to the Svartsengi power plant and part of the lava field located on the Reykjanes Peninsula. This is offered as part of a tour from your cruise ship.

Surprise, surprise

Meeting someone you never expected to, or thought possible to meet. On cruises over the years, I have been fortunate enough to meet, talk to, and have a drink with some well-known film stars and other personalities including Elizabeth Taylor and Richard Burton, Tippi Hedren, Dame Margot Fonteyn, and the great conductor Leopold Stokowski.

Photo opportunity

Being aboard a photo tender arranged by the cruise line (in my case, this was aboard a tall ship), and taking photographs as the tall ship was under full sail and not slowing down. An exhilarating experience that you can still enjoy.

Passing the lava

Being aboard a cruise ship off the north coast of Sicily, where you pass close to Stromboli in action. The almost constantly erupting volcano bursts into life and emits incandescent lava.

Michelin dining

Dining in the intimate Dieter Mueller At Sea restaurant aboard Hapag-Lloyd Cruises' *Europa*. Mueller – a three Michelin-starred chef – sold his own restaurant and now operates his own seagoing dining venue for six months each year.

Natural wonders

I was on deck aboard an expedition cruise ship in Antarctic waters when a number of killer whales (orcas) began splashing in the water just off the starboard side aft, making the ship roll. They were so close that I could have touched one of their dorsal fins. A spectacular show of nature.

New Year's Eve pyrotechnics

Being aboard ship supping Champagne while enjoying the magnificently colourful New Year's Eve firework display in Funchal, Madeira. A cruise ship offers the very best vantage point for this fantastic display, which lasts around 10 minutes or so and is considered to be one of the most spectacular in the world.

Zip-a-dee-doo-dah

Careening along the zip line strung between rows of cabins high above the deck of *Allure of the Seas*. Quite a surprise to the occupants of those cabins!

Virgin cruise

Enjoying the anticipation and excitement of a maiden voyage aboard a brand new ship – an experience highly prized among cruise collectors. Just be prepared for the fact that it might not all be smooth sailing, and there might be teething troubles.

Happy ever after

Looking for a partner? I met my future wife aboard a Japanese cruise ship some years ago, and we married several years later. You too, could meet the person of your dreams aboard a cruise ship – it happens all the time.

Michelin-starred dining at Dieter Mueller At Sea, aboard *Europa*.

What's Ahead

The race is on, as the three major cruise companies (Carnival Cruise Line, Norwegian Cruise Line, and Royal Caribbean International) battle it out to provide new attractions to woo families and newcomers to cruising.

More than 24 million people took a cruise in 2015, and by the end of the year over 50 ships measuring over 100,000 gross tons were in service, with more on their way. As this book went to press, almost 30 new ships of various sizes were scheduled for delivery between January 2016 and the end of 2020.

In 2016, of the 10 new ships scheduled for delivery, the smallest in capacity is Viking Cruises' engaging 47,000 ton, 930-passenger *Viking Sky*, while the largest is Royal Caribbean International's 227,000 ton, 5,400-passenger *Harmony of the Seas* – this will become the new largest ship in the world. Given the economics of scale and shipbuilding costs, the new 'optimum' size for large resort ships is now about 160,000 tons, with a capacity of 3,500–4,200 passengers.

The titans continue to introduce new attractions for the whole family, cruise pricing is also being simplified, with more and more 'experience (added-value) pricing' introduced. This means that the whole business is more personalized, with add-ons available, so you pay only for what you want – the 'pay-more, get-more' principle.

AIDA Cruises

The 3,286-passenger, *AIDAprima* has an unusual, stark upright bow – a throwback to the early 20th-century ocean liners – and an ultra-efficient hull design that takes advantage of the latest eco-friendly discoveries. The rest of the ship is ultra-contemporary, with all the family-friendly features so popular with its youthful cruise audience. It features a Beach Club for activities day and night, while '4Elements' is all about action and sports for the whole family; oh, and a micro-brewery is on board, too. The ship will be based year-round in Hamburg, Germany, with an epic Maiden Voyage to Hamburg from Yokohama, Japan.

Carnival Cruise Line

To date, Carnival's ships have been almost cookie-cutter duplicates of the same type. But with the

Viking Star in Venice.

4,000-passenger *Carnival Vista*, the company ups the ante. The ship will have the first IMAX theater at sea – a three-deck-high surround experience. Other features include Sky Ride, with recumbent bicycles for passengers to pedal around an arial sport track; a Kaleid-O-Slide water tube attraction (with two-person rafts); a brewery and bar with its own brew (Red Frog) on tap; a New England Seafood Shack; indoor-outdoor seating at several eateries; and several cabins with balconies and hammocks (AIDA Cruises and TUI Cruises have had these for some time).

Holland America Line

Koningsdam (named after the first king of Norway, Willem-Alexander), the company's first 'Pinnacle' class ship, is the largest ship to be built for Holland America Line (founded in 1873. However, the design is simply an evolution of – with the same platform as – *Eurodam*.

The 2,650 passenger vessel continues to honor Dutch traditions, but features more dining and informal eatery choices than any other in the fleet. One standout feature is its 270-degree LED surround stage backdrop in the showlounge.

Norwegian Cruise Line

The 4,266-passenger *Norwegian Escape* arrives in 2016, with three more sister ships scheduled for delivery in 2017, 2018, and 2019. These are *Norwegian Breakaway*-'plus' ships. Norwegian Cruise Line has pushed the choice of entertainment and dining venues to the limit, and introduced sweet bakery products from Buddy Valasco's Carlo's Bakery. These ships cater extremely well to families with children and also feature a number of the popular (capsule-like) 'studio' cabins for solo-occupancy.

Applying the 'pay-more, get-more' principle, the ship also features 'The Haven' exclusive gated community accommodation area, located forward and above the ship's navigation bridge – as aboard *Norwegian Breakaway*, *Norwegian Getaway*, and *Norwegian Epic*.

Regent Seven Seas Cruises

The 750-passenger *Seven Seas Explorer* will become the flagship of this small premium cruise company (with all-inclusive fares), and its largest ship to date. An evolutionary ship, it features the same basic layout and public rooms as *Mariner* and *Voyager*, but in a slightly larger format, and including one stunning multi-room 'Regent Suite', with its own mini-spa with sauna and heated loungers, and several other suites with interconnecting doors (think 'his and hers' bathrooms).

Royal Caribbean International

The second of a pair of 4,180 passenger 'Project Sunshine' ships (each costing over $1 billion), *Anthem of the Seas* arrived in the latter part of 2015 to great

The mini spa in *Seven Seas Explorer*'s Regent Suite.

acclaim for its innovative, trendy, heart-stopping attractions, and a design more akin to the *Voyager*-class ships rather than the larger (spread-superstructure) *Oasis*-class ships.

Third in the trilogy of *Quantum*-class sister ships, the 4,180-passenger *Ovation of the Seas* arrives in 2016. All three vessels feature dodgem cars in the SeaPlex, and a North Star roving cherry-picker capsule that had the wow factor when first introduced, including the Ripcord by iFly sky dive thrill – all this and more aboard these family-friendly 'tech-smart' ships.

Also coming in 2016 is the third *Oasis*-class ship, the 5,496-passenger *Harmony of the Seas*, a family resort that includes some of the *Quantum*-class features and gimmicks such as a Bionic Bar. In addition, it will have a water slide that zooms over the Boardwalk, and, as with the *Oasis*-class ships, there are seven neighborhoods: Central Park, Boardwalk, the Royal Promenade, the Pool and Sports Zone, Vitality at Sea Spa and Fitness Center, Entertainment Place, and Youth Zone.

Seabourn

Next in the series of *Odyssey*-class ships, the latest addition for Seabourn, Seabourn Encore, expands the firm's fleet to five ships, all of which are designated as small ships, carrying around 450 passengers in a high degree of comfort.

Star Cruises

The Hong-Kong based company ordered two 3,305-passenger ships, the first of which arrives in fall 2016, with the first steel being cut in February 2015. The second is scheduled for 2017. The ships are designed for families with children, and are being designed to cater to a wide range of ethnic tastes, particularly with regard to cuisine.

Viking Cruises

In 2015, *Viking Star* was the first of a series of ships for newcomer Viking Cruises (sister company to extremely popular Viking River Cruises), with the sleek design of this 930-passenger mid-sized ship breaking from the somewhat boxy shape of the large resort ships.

With a 360-degree walk-around promenade deck, a Wintergarden, an infinity pool, a choice of several restaurants and eateries (some with al fresco dining), all-outside cabins, and in-depth destination experiences at a modest price point, *Viking Sky* (arrives in 2016) deserves serious consideration. *Viking Sea* will follow in 2017.

Looking ahead

Nine 'new generation' cruise ships have been ordered by the Carnival Corporation for several of its brands. These will be built by Fintactieri (Italy) and Meyer Werft (Germany) for delivery between 2019 and 2022.

Also, the opening of a new shipping lane (due to start operation in early 2016) and the widening of the Panama Canal will provide large resort ships previously unable to transit the waterway between the Atlantic and Pacific oceans with more options for itinerary planners.

The $5.25 billion project, which began in 2007, entailed the widening and deepening of the existing navigational channels in Gatun Lake and the deepening of the Culebra Cut.

Nonstop refurbishment

Ships no longer in the first flush of youth need cosmetic surgery and regular makeovers in order to keep up their appearance. Items such as balcony door frames need replacing, furniture needs refinishing, and navigational, safety, and technical machinery always needs updating.

Cruise lines often add more cabins during refurbishment programs. This brings additional passengers, increasing occupancy levels and revenue, but, of course, decreases the amount of space per passenger (passenger space ratio). Usually, there's no corresponding increase in the number of crew, and so the crew-to-passenger ratio unfortunately decreases.

And, because no new elevators are added, there is more density (less space per passengers) and congestion in the elevators, too, with elevator waiting time increasing.

Recent examples include Royal Caribbean International's *Voyager*-class ships, such as *Adventure of the Seas*, *Explorer of the Seas*, *Mariner of the Seas*, *Navigator of the Seas*, and *Voyager of the Seas* (all 81 interior cabins had 'virtual' balconies added).

Stretch marks

For some cruise companies 'stretching' older ships make sense in light of the enormous cost of a new ship and the typical two-year time frame needed for completion and delivery. Even so, refits are expensive, at around $2 million a day, with that figure being pushed up by material, equipment, and labor costs. MSC Cruises, for example, 'stretched' four of its ships (*MSC Armonia*, *MSC Lirica*, *MSC Opera*, *MSC Sinfonia*) in 2014/2015, by adding a newly built 68-ft (24-m) mid-section in 'cut-and-insert' operations at Fincantieri's shipyard in Palermo.

All change

In late 2015 Holland America Line's 1,266-passenger *Ryndam* and *Statendam* left the company and were moved to Carnival Australia and renamed *Pacific Eden* and *Pacific Aria*, respectively. In 2016, the following ships are scheduled to shift from one company to another: the 688-passenger *Ocean Princess* (Princess Cruises) will move to Oceania Cruises (to be renamed *Serena*) in April 2016; the 1,804-passenger *Splendour of the Seas* (Royal Caribbean International) will pass over to Thomson Cruises in summer 2016, to be renamed *Thomson Discovery*. Finally, as ships start to age increasingly quickly, a growing number will be moved to smaller companies, sold, or scrapped, as cruise lines strive for better fuel economy and greater returns on investment. In other words, watch this space!

The newly 'stretched' *MSC Sinfonia*.

New ships to debut

Cruise line	Ship name	Gross tonnage	Debut date	Cost (approximate)	Length (feet/meters)	Passengers (lower beds)	Builder
AIDA Cruises	AIDAprima	125,000	March 2016	S650 million	984.2/300.0	3,250	Mitsubishi (Japan)
Carnival Cruise Line	Carnival Vista	135,000	April 2016	$780 million	1,054.7/321.5	4,000	Fincantieri (Italy)
Holland America Line	Koningsdam	99,700	April 2016	$518 million	983.5/299.8	2,650	Fincantieri (Italy)
Regent Seven Seas Cruises	Seven Seas Explorer	54,000	Fall 2016	$450 million	731.6/223.0	738	Fincantieri (Italy)
Royal Caribbean International	Harmony of the Seas	227,000	May 2016	$1.03 billion	1,184.3/361.0	5,400	STX (France)
Royal Caribbean International	Ovation of the Seas	167,800	May 2016	$1.03 billion	1,112.2/339.0	4,180	Meyer Werft (Germany)
Seabourn	Seabourn Encore	40,350	Fall 2016	$250 million	295.0–438.1/27.5–133.6	450	Mariotti (Italy)
Star Cruises	TBA	151,000	October 2016	€707.2 million	1,082.6/330.0	3,364	Meyer Werft
TUI Cruises	Mein Schiff 5	99,300	Winter 2016	€390 million	967.8/295.0	2,500	Meyer Turku (Finland)
Viking Cruises	Viking Sky	47,800	May 2016	$400 million	754.4/230.0	928	Fincantieri (Italy)
MSC Cruises	'Seaside' class	154,000	November 2017	€700 million	1,059.7/323.00	5,300	Fincantieri (Italy)
MSC Cruises	MSC Meraviglia	167,600	Spring 2017	€750 million	1,049.8/320.0	4,500	STX (France)
Norwegian Cruise Line	Norwegian Bliss	163,000	Spring 2017	€700 million	1,066.2/325.0	4,200	Meyer Werft (Germany)
Princess Cruises	TBA	143,000	Winter 2017	€600 million	1,082.6/330.0	4,140	Fincantieri (Italy)
Star Cruises	TBA	151,000	October 2017	€697.2 million	1,082.6/330.0	3,364	Meyer Werft
TUI Cruises	Mein Schiff 6	93,300	Winter 2017	€390 million	967.8/295.0	2,500	Meyer Turku (Finland)
Viking Cruises	Viking Sea	47,800	February 2017	$430 million	754.5/230.0	928	Fincantieri (Italy)
Carnival Cruise Line	TBA	133,500	Spring 2018	$730 million	1,054.7/321.5	3,954	Fincantieri (Italy)
Celebrity Cruises	TBA	117,000	Fall 2018	$875 million	984.2/300.00	2,900	STX (France)
MSC Cruises	'Seaside' class	154,000	May 2018	€700 million	1,059.7/323.00	5,300	Fincantieri (Italy)
Norwegian Cruise Line	TBA	164,600	Spring 2018	€800 million	1,066.2/325.0	4,200	Meyer Werft (Germany)
Royal Caribbean International	Oasis-class 4	227,000	Fall 2018	$1.03 billion	1,184.3/360.0	5,400	STX (France)
Seabourn	Seabourn Ovation	40,350	Fall 2018	$250 million	295.0–433.1/27.5–133.6	450	Mariotti (Italy)
TUI Cruises	Mein Schiff 8	TBA	Winter 2018	€390 million	967.8/295.0	2,500	Meyer Turku (Finland)

Cruising's Continued Growth

**When the first jet aircraft made many former
passenger liners redundant, some were scrapped,
but others gave birth to the modern cruise industry.**

Although Bahamas/Caribbean cruises from Miami resurfaced in the 1950s with a ship named *Nuevo Dominicano* (ex-*New Northland*), it was not until the 1960s that cruising was updated and re-packaged for a society that had an increasing amount of leisure time on its hands.

Thirty one years ago, the first edition of this book listed 120 ships, some of which are still operating in one form or another. Today, that number has grown to around 350, including ships operating coastal cruises. Throughout the period, the cruise industry has maintained a global growth rate of over 7 percent each year. But many well-known cruise lines have also gone to the deep blue seabed in the past 31 years. Indeed, since 1990 more than 65 cruise companies have either merged, or been taken over, or simply gone out of business, including such well-liked companies as Chandris Cruises, Epirotiki, Renaissance Cruises, Royal Cruise Lines, Royal Viking Line, and Sun Line Cruises.

Cunard linked up with BOAC in the early 1960s.

Some start-up lines, using older ships and aimed at specific markets, also came and went – companies such as American Family Cruises, Festival Cruises, Fiesta Marina Cruises, Premier Cruise Lines, and Regency Cruises. In came new shiny tonnage, complete with vanity logos and adornments painted on all-white hulls – the attributes of the industry's emerging giants. Fresh thinking transformed the design of accommodation, the use of public spaces, and the growing number of food and entertainment venues.

Yield management, a term purloined from the airline industry, was introduced. These days, company executives think of little else, because running a cruise company is all about economics.

Modern cruising is born

In the early 1960s, passenger-shipping directories listed over 100 passenger lines. Until the mid-1960s, it was cheaper to cross the Atlantic by ship than by plane, but the introduction of the jet aircraft changed that rapidly, particularly with the appearance of the Boeing 747 in the early 1970s. In 1962, more than 1 million people crossed the North Atlantic by ship; in 1970, that number was down to 250,000.

The success of the jumbo jets created a fleet of unprofitable and out-of-work passenger liners that appeared doomed for the scrapyard. Even the famous big 'Queens', noted for their regular weekly transatlantic service, were at risk. Cunard White Star Line's *Queen Mary* (81,237 gross tonnage) was withdrawn in September 1967. Cunard tried to fight back with Cunard-Eagle Airways but then formed a short-lived BOAC-Cunard joint venture with the British Overseas Aircraft Corporation, flying 707s and Super VC10s.

Cunard Line's *Queen Elizabeth*, at 83,673 gross tonnage the largest-ever passenger liner (until 1996), made its final crossing in November 1968.

Who goes cruising

The global cruise industry carried almost 24 million passengers in 2014. The largest concentration of passengers came from the US (13.5 million), followed by Continental Europe (almost 6.4 million, including Germany's 1.77 million, but not including the UK's 1.64 million), or the 300,000 passengers who took a coastal voyage aboard the Hurtigruten (Norwegian Coastal Voyages) ships.

Caribbean cruising as depicted in a 1947 advertisement.

Ships were sold for a fraction of their value. Many lines went out of business, and ships were scrapped. Those that survived attempted to mix transatlantic crossings with voyages south to the sun. The Caribbean (including the Bahamas) became appealing, cruising became an alternative, and an entire new industry was born, with new lines being formed exclusively for cruising.

Then smaller, more specialized ships arrived, capable of accessing the tiny ports of developing Caribbean islands; there were no commercial airlines taking vacationers to the Caribbean then, and few hotels. Instead of cruising long distances south from more northerly ports such as New York, companies established their headquarters in Florida. This avoided the cold weather, choppy seas, and expense of the northern ports and saved fuel costs with shorter runs to the Caribbean.

Cruising was reborn. California became the base for cruises to the Mexican Riviera, while Vancouver was the focus for summer cruises to Alaska.

Flying passengers to embarkation ports was the next logical step, and soon a working relationship emerged between the cruise lines and the airlines. Air/sea and 'sail and stay' packages thrived – joint cruise and hotel vacations with inclusive pricing.

Complaints about ports

Berlitz continues to receive complaints about the forceful tactics of baggage handlers (porters) at the Port of Miami and at Port Everglades (Fort Lauderdale). As passengers alight from airport buses, which often have a sign stating 'Tips Not Included,' the baggage handlers ask passengers to identify their baggage, which they then place into nearby luggage cages. For this 'service,' passengers are asked to tip generously.

So, do the math. If each baggage handler receives the requested $1–2 per bag tip, and the ship carries 5,000 passengers, that's a lot of money. Be smart: don't let them bully you into thinking your luggage won't get to your ship in time for your cruise – a threat often used. They are responsible for making sure that all bags, yours included, do reach the ship on time.

Pier pressure
Bigger ships can mean overcrowded ports. Some large-city ports, such as Barcelona and St. Petersburg, can handle the influx of large resort ships during the busy summer months, helped by the number of shore excursion choices available. However, stretching the cruising season in these areas also helps lessen overcrowding. The most congested ports – where several ships carrying thousands of passengers may be in port at the same time – include the following:
Caribbean/Bahamas: Antigua, Barbados, Grand Cayman, Nassau, St. Maarten, St. Thomas.
Europe/Mediterranean: Barcelona, Civitavecchia (the port for Rome), Kuşadasi, Venice.
Other ports: Cabo San Lucas, Juneau, Ketchikan, Mazatlan, Sydney.

Disney Dream features AquaDuck, the first-ever shipboard water coaster.

Some of the old liners came out of mothballs, purchased by emerging cruise lines and refurbished for warm-weather cruising operations, often with their interiors redesigned and refitted. During the late 1970s, the modern cruise industry grew at a rapid rate.

Cruising today

Today's cruise concept hasn't changed much from that of earlier days, although it has been improved, refined, expanded, and packaged for ease of consumption. Cruising today attracts people of all ages, socio-economic backgrounds, and tastes. It's no longer the shipping business, but the hospitality industry.

New ships are generally larger than their predecessors, yet cabin size is 'standardized' to provide more space for entertainment and other public facilities. Today's ships boast air conditioning to keep out heat and humidity; stabilizers to keep the ship on an even keel; a high level of maintenance, safety, and hygiene; and more emphasis on health and fitness facilities.

Although ships have long been devoted to eating and relaxation in comfort, they now offer a greater number of activities, and more learning and life-enriching experiences than ever. For the same prices as a quarter of a century ago, you can cruise aboard the latest large resort ships that offer ice-skating, rock climbing, golfing, rollerblading, wave surfing, bowling, even 'skydiving,' and so on, as well as dining at fine restaurants that offer varied cuisines, relaxing in luxurious spas, and being entertained by high-quality productions. And there are many more places to visit than ever, from Acapulco to Antarctica, Bergen to Bermuda, Dakar to Dominica, and St Thomas to Shanghai.

The 'small is beautiful' concept has really taken hold in the cruising world, particularly with the more upscale/exclusive brands. Cruise lines with

Ship captains at P&O's 175th birthday celebrations in 2012.

high-quality, low-capacity ships can provide a highly personalized range of services and top-level hospitality. This means better-trained, more-experienced staff serving fewer passengers and higher-quality food, with more meals cooked to order. Small ships can also visit the less-crowded ports.

Some cruise lines have expanded by 'stretching' their ships – accomplished by cutting a ship in half and inserting a newly constructed midsection, thus instantly adding more accommodation and public rooms, while maintaining the same draft.

Ships that have been 'stretched' (with year and length of 'stretch') include: *Albatros* (1983, 91ft/27.7m), *Balmoral* (2007, 98.4ft/30m), *Black Watch* (1981, 91ft/27.7m), *Boudicca* (1982, 91ft/27.7m), *Braemar* (2008, 102.4ft/31.2m), *Enchantment of the Seas* (2005, 72.8ft/22.2m), *Berlin* (1986, 65.6ft/20m), *MSC Armonia* (2014,

82 ft/25m), *MSC Lirica* (2015, 82 ft/25m), *MSC Opera* (2015, 82 ft/25m), *MSC Sinfonia* (2015, 82 ft/25m), *SuperStar Aquarius* (1998, 131.2ft/40m), *SuperStar Gemini* (1998, 131.2ft/40m), *Thomson Dream* (1990, 131.2ft/40m), and *Thomson Majesty* (1999, 98.4ft/30m).

Exclusivity

Exclusive communities at sea are proliferating. These 'gated' areas are for those paying extra to live in a larger suite and gain access to 'private' facilities, concierge lounges, and private sunbathing areas. Ships that have them: *MSC Divina, MSC Fantasia, MSC Preziosa, MSC Splendida, Norwegian Breakaway, Norwegian Epic, Norwegian Getaway, Norwegian Gem, Norwegian Jade*, and *Norwegian Pearl*. Two-class cruising – in some cases, three-class cruising – is back in vogue.

Highlights of the past 20 years

1995 British company Airtours bought *Southward* from Norwegian Cruise Line and *Nordic Prince* from Royal Caribbean Cruises.

1996 Cunard (and parent company Trafalgar House) were bought by Kvaerner.

1997 Carnival Corporation, jointly with Airtours, purchased Costa Cruises. Royal Caribbean International bought Celebrity Cruises.

1998 Kvaerner sold Cunard to Carnival Corporation. Norwegian Cruise Line bought Orient Lines.

1999 Crown Cruise Line was reintroduced as an upscale part of Commodore Cruise Line.

2000 Star Cruises took full control of Norwegian Cruise Line (including Orient Lines) after buying the outstanding shares held by Carnival Corporation. P&O Group separated its cruising activities from the rest of the group. Costa Cruises became wholly owned by Carnival Corporation.

2001 Renaissance Cruises (10 ships) ceased operations after the September 11 terrorist attacks on the US – one of several casualties.

2002 SeaDream Yacht Club began with *SeaDream I* and *SeaDream II*.

2003 NCL America launched its US-flag operation.

2004 Carnival Corporation and P&O Princess PLC merged to become the world's largest cruise company, with 60-plus ships and 13 brands.

2005 Orion Expedition Cruises launched with one ship, *Orion*.

2006 Radisson Seven Seas Cruises became Regent Seven Seas Cruises. Royal Caribbean International bought Pullmantur.

2007 Celebrity Cruises created a sub-brand, Azamara Cruises. *Queen Elizabeth 2* was sold for £50 million ($100 million) to a state investment company in Dubai, to be refitted and become a floating hotel and museum alongside the Palm Jumeirah.

2008 Fred. Olsen Cruise Lines 'stretched' its *Braemar* by 102ft (31.2m). Almost all cruise lines increased fuel surcharges in the face of rising oil prices. Most paddlewheel riverboats ceased operations in the US.

2009 Island Cruises was acquired by TUI Travel's Thomson Cruises division. TUI Cruises started cruising with one ship. Imperial Majesty Cruise Line ceased operations, replaced by Celebration Cruise Line. Azamara Cruises was renamed Azamara Club Cruises.

2010 The Ocean Village brand disappeared; its two ships joined the P&O Cruises (Australia) fleet. Island Cruises became a sub-brand of Thomson Cruises. NCL America was merged into Norwegian Cruise Line (NCL). Cruise West and Delfin Cruises ceased operations. India's Blue Ocean Cruises began operations.

2011 Middle East conflicts forced cruise lines to cancel port calls in Egypt, Libya, and Tunisia. Some cruise lines changed their around-the-world itineraries to avoid Somalia's pirates. Disney Cruise Line introduced the first real water coaster at sea, AquaDuck. Happy Cruises ceased operations.

2012 Three new niche market cruise lines were started in Germany: Ambiente Cruises, FTI Cruises, and Passat Cruises, each with one ship. Delphin Cruises (1 ship) was also resurrected. In June all three Cunard Queens were in Southampton to celebrate the Queen's Diamond Jubilee, and in July P&O Cruises celebrated its 175th anniversary by assembling all seven of its ships in Southampton. Silversea Cruises purchased Galapagos operator Canodros (1 ship). Classic International Cruises went into administration (5 ships) following the death of its founder, George Potamianos. Ola Cruises ceased operation.

2013 Norwegian Cruise Line goes public on the NYSE. *Saga Ruby* (originally *Vistafjord*) was retired. Portuscale Cruises commenced operations, with four ships previously belonging to Classic International Cruises.

2014 Ambiente Cruises, Kristina Cruises, Passat Cruises, and Peter Deilmann Cruises ceased operations. Norwegian Cruise Holdings acquired Prestige Cruises International (parent company of Oceania Cruises and Regent Seven Seas Cruises). The Ibercruceros brand disappears after a merger with Costa Cruises.

2015 Cunard Line celebrated its 175th anniversary.

Frequently Asked Questions

Most cruise brochures are hype over reality. We answer the questions about ocean cruising most frequently asked by those new to this type of vacation and by experienced passengers.

Cruises are packaged vacations, offering overall good value for money, with your accommodation, meals, and entertainment included. But it's the little hidden extras that are not made clear in the brochures that you have to look out for. Some ships have 'drinks-inclusive' fares, while others let you choose from one of several 'beverage packages' on offer.

Here are some of the most commonly asked questions, covering those items that the brochures gloss over.

Is cruising good value?

Yes, it is. In fact, it's never been better, thanks in part to the economic downturn that forced cruise lines to offer more incentives – such as onboard credit, cabin upgrades, and other perks – in an effort to keep their companies afloat and their ships full.

The price of your vacation is protected by advance pricing, so you know before you go that your major outgoings have already been set. A fuel sur-

Hanseatic passengers exploring a new destination.

charge is the only additional cost that may change at the last minute.

Isn't cruising expensive?

Compare what it would cost on land to have all your meals and entertainment provided, as well as transportation to different destinations, fitness and sports facilities, leisure activities, educational talks, parties, and other social functions, and you'll see the remarkable value of a cruise.

What you pay determines the size, location, and style of accommodation. Ships are as individual as fingerprints: each can change its 'personality' from cruise to cruise, depending on the mix of passengers (and crew). The choice ranges from basic to luxury, so give yourself a budget, and ask your professional travel supplier how to make the best use of it.

Although bargains exist, always read the small print and check what's included. A highly discounted fare may apply only to certain dates and itineraries, for example, the eastern Caribbean instead of the more popular western Caribbean. A bargain price may be subject to a booking deadline or may be 'cruise-only', which means you must arrange your own air transportation separately. If air transportation *is* included, changes or deviations may not be possible.

Your accommodation choice, grade, and location may not be available. You could be limited to first seating aboard a two-seating ship for dinner (possibly less convenient, if you are busy with activities or excursions during the day, for example); also, some highly discounted fares may not apply to children. Port charges, handling fees, fuel surcharges, or other taxes may be extra.

Is the brochure price firm?

Cruise brochure prices are set by cruise line sales and marketing departments. It's the price they would like to achieve to cover themselves against currency fluctuations, international bonding schemes, and the like. But discounts attract business, and so there is always some leeway. Also, travel agents receive a commission. As a consumer, always ask for the 'best price', watch for special offers in newspapers and magazines, and talk to your travel agent –they may even rebate some of their commission, something they are not allowed to advertise on their websites.

How do I get the best discount?

Book ahead for the best discounts, as they normally decrease closer to the cruise date. You may reserve a cabin grade, but not a specific cabin – 'TBA' (to be assigned). Some lines will accept this arrangement and may even upgrade you. The first cabins to be sold out are usually those at minimum and maximum prices. Note: premium rates usually apply to Christmas/ New Year cruises. Make sure that all port charges, government fees, and any additional fuel surcharges are included in the quote.

Should I use the Internet or a travel agent?

You've found an attractive price for your cruise on the web – fine. But, if a cruise line suddenly offers special discounts for your sailing, or cabin upgrades, or if things go wrong with your booking, your Internet booking service may prove difficult to access for post-purchase questions. Your travel agent, however, can probably make special discounts work for you and perhaps even provide upgrades.

The Internet may be a useful resource tool, but it is not the place to book your cruise, unless you know exactly what you want, and can plan ahead – and it doesn't work for groups. You can't ask questions, and most of the information provided by the cruise companies is strictly marketing hype. Most websites providing cruise ship reviews have paid advertising, or something to sell, and the sound-bite information can be misleading. Special discounts for senior citizens, military personnel, and alumni groups are not usually available on the web, but only through cruise-booking agencies. Be aware that many Internet booking agents are unlicensed and unregulated, and some add a 'booking fee', which can be substantial.

10 questions to ask a travel agent

1. Is air transportation included in the cabin rate quoted? If not, how much will it be? What other costs will be added – these can include port charges, insurance, gratuities, shore excursions, laundry, and drinks?
2. What is the cruise line's cancellation policy?
3. If I want to make changes to my flight, routing, dates, and so on, are there any extra charges?
4. Does your agency deal with only one, or several different insurance companies?
5. Does the cruise line offer advance booking discounts or other incentives?
6. Do you have preferred suppliers, or do you book any cruise on any cruise ship?
7. Have you sailed aboard the ship I want to book or that you are recommending?
8. Is your agency bonded and insured? If so, by whom?
9. Is insurance included if I book the shore excursions offered by the cruise line?
10. Can I occupy my cabin on the day of disembarkation until I am ready to disembark?

If you do book with an Internet-based cruise agency or wholesaler: 1) Confirm with the cruise line that the booking has been made. 2) Confirm that any payments have been received. 3) Large travel agency groups and consortiums often reserve large blocks of cabins, while smaller independent agencies can access extensive discounts not available on the Internet. Furthermore, cruise lines consider travel agents as their distribution system and provide special discounts and value-added amenities not provided over the Internet.

Do travel agents charge for their services?

Travel agents do not charge for their services, although they earn a commission from cruise lines. Consider a travel agent as your business advisor, not just a ticket agent. He/she will handle all matters relevant to your booking and should have the latest information on changes of itinerary, cruise fares, fuel surcharges, discounts, and any other related items, including travel and cancellation insurance in case you have to cancel prior to sailing – perhaps for medical reasons. Travel agents are linked into cruise company computer systems and have access to most shipboard information.

Your travel agent should find exactly the right ship for your needs and lifestyle. Some sell only a limited number of cruises and are known as 'preferred suppliers,' because they receive 'overrides' on top of their normal commission. (They probably know their limited number of ships well, however.)

If you have chosen a ship and cruise, be firm and book exactly what you want, or change agencies. Look for a CLIA- (Cruise Lines International Association) affiliated agency.

How do I get my tickets?

Most cruise lines have changed to online bookings and check-in. You'll need to print your own boarding passes, travel documents, and luggage tags. If you go through a cruise-travel agent, they can print these for you.

Your printed documents will allow you to pass through the port's security station to get to your ship. Only the more exclusive, upscale cruise lines, expedition companies, and sail-cruise ship lines now provide boxes or wallets packed with documents, cruise tickets, leather (or faux-leather) luggage tags, and colorful destination booklets – cruise lines operating large resort ships have all but abandoned such niceties.

Should I have cancellation insurance?

Yes, if it is not included, as cruises (and air transportation to/from them) must be paid in full before your tickets are issued. Otherwise, if you cancel at the last minute – even for medical reasons – you could lose the whole fare. Insurance coverage can be obtained from your travel agent, from an independent com-

Queen Mary 2 has kennels on board.

pany, or online. Pay by credit card, if you have one – that way you're more likely to get your money back if the agency goes bust.

Note that cancellation insurance offered by a cruise line is a 'one-size-fits-all' product, so personalization is impossible. It covers only the cruise itself but not any add-ons that you may have arranged on your own, such as non-refundable air tickets.

Cruise lines typically accept cancellations more than 30 days before sailing, but all charge full fare if you don't turn up on sailing day. Other cancellation fees depend on the cruise and length of trip. Many lines do not return port taxes, which are not part of the cruise fare.

Note that if the cruise company appears to have gone out of business, some insurance policies will not cover you unless the cruise company declares bankruptcy.

Travel insurance

Cruise lines and travel agents routinely sell travel cover policies that, on close inspection, appear to wriggle out of payment due to a litany of exclu-

sion clauses, most of which are never explained. Examples include pre-existing medical conditions (ignoring this little gem could cost you dearly) and valuables left unattended on a tour bus, even if the guide says it is safe and that the driver will lock the door.

What does a category guarantee mean?

It means you have purchased a specific grade of accommodation (just as in a hotel), although the actual cabin may not have been assigned to your booking yet. Your cabin may be assigned before you go, or when you arrive for embarkation.

Isn't cruising just for old people?

Not at all. The average age of passengers gets lower each year, with the average age of first-timers now well under 40. But retirees do find that cruising is a safe, comfortable way to travel, and many have plenty of get-up-and-go. On a typical cruise you're likely to meet solo travelers, couples, families with children of all ages, honeymooners, groups of friends, and college buddies.

Won't I get bored?

Whether you want to lie back and be pampered, or be active nonstop, you can do it on a cruise. Just being at sea provides an intoxicating sense of freedom that few places on dry land can offer. And, in case you think you may feel cut off without contact, almost all large resort ships (those carrying over 2,001 passengers) have ship-wide Wi-Fi access, Internet access, movies, and digital music libraries.

Why is it so expensive for solo travelers?

Almost all cruise lines base their rates on double occupancy, so, when you travel alone, the cabin portion of your fare reflects an additional supplement. Although most new ships are built with cabins for double occupancy (exceptions include *Anthem of*

---

10 tips to get the best travel insurance

1. Shop around and don't accept the first travel insurance policy you are offered.

2. If you purchase travel cover on the Internet, check the credentials of the company underwriting the scheme. Deal with well-established names instead of automatically taking what appears to be the cheapest deal offered.

3. Read the contract carefully and make sure you know exactly what you are covered for.

4. Beware the 'box ticking' approach to travel cover, which is often done quickly at the booking agent's office in lieu of providing proper advice. Insurers should not, in reality, be allowed to apply exclusions that have not been clearly pointed out to you.

5. Ask for a detailed explanation of all exclusions, excesses, and limitations.

6. If you purchase your own air transportation, check whether

your insurance policy covers you if the airline fails, or if bad weather prevents you from joining your ship on time.

7. Check out the procedure you need to follow if you are the victim of a crime, such as your wallet or camera being stolen while on a shore excursion.

8. If you are a crime victim, obtain a police report as soon as possible. Many insurance policies will reimburse you only for the second-hand value of any lost or stolen items, rather than the full cost of replacement, and you may have to produce the original receipt for any such items claimed.

9. Watch out for exclusions for 'hazardous sports.' These could include activities typically included in shore excursions such as horseback riding, cycling jet skiing, or ziplining.

10. Different countries have different requirements for travel insurance providers. Be sure to check the details in the country where you purchased your policy.

the Seas, Norwegian Breakaway, Norwegian Epic, Norwegian Escape, Norwegian Getaway, Quantum of the Seas), older ships, such as Aegean Odyssey, Hebridean Princess, and Saga Sapphire, have many solo-occupancy cabins. Cruise line special offers are nearly always aimed at double-occupancy passengers first, followed by those for solo travelers.

Are there facilities for solo travelers?

Some ships have dedicated cabins for solo travelers and special add-on rates for solo occupancy of double cabins. Some companies will even find a cabin mate for you to share with, if you so desire. However, in cabins with three or four berths (two beds plus upper berths), personal privacy doesn't exist. Some companies sell two-bed cabins at a special single rate. Also, some companies schedule a solo travelers get-together, usually on the first or second day of a cruise.

How about holiday season cruises?

Celebrating the festive lifestyle is even more special aboard ship, where decorations add to the sense of occasion. However, the large resort ships can be very busy during the main holiday periods. (Don't travel at these busy times, if you want to have the facilities of a large resort ship, but want to be able to relax.)

What about 'Spring Break' cruises?

If you take a cruise aboard one of the large resort ships (the most popular brands for Spring Break cruises are Carnival Cruise Lines, Norwegian Cruise Line, and Royal Caribbean International) during the annual Spring Break (usually in March, but dependent on the decisions of the school-curriculum), you should expect to find hordes of students causing mayhem.

Do cruise lines have loyalty programs?

All of the major cruise lines and several of the smaller ones have loyalty clubs. You can earn credits and onboard benefits unavailable to non-members, although some perks might also be available if you book suite-grade accommodation. Programs are based either on the number of cruises taken, or, probably more fairly, on the number of days sailed. There's no charge to join, but many benefits to gain if you keep cruising with the same line.

Some companies, such as Celebrity Cruises, allow you to transfer point levels to sister a company, Azamara Club Cruises or Royal Caribbean International; multi-cruise line companies, such as Carnival, may also allow this across the company's various brands. There are usually several levels, such as Silver, Gold, Platinum, and Diamond, depending on the cruise line, the number of voyages, or cruises, or cruise days.

Can I pay in cash for purchases on board?

Although few cruise lines accept cash for purchases on board, many older passengers (particularly from countries such as Germany and Japan) do not possess credit cards, and want to pay in cash. Cruise lines need to be more flexible.

Father and son playing table tennis on a Carnival ship.

A birthday aboard a Carnival ship.

Is there enough to keep kids busy?

Most cruises provide families with more quality time than any other type of vacation, and family cruising is the industry's largest growth segment, with activities tailored to various age groups. Responding to this trend, Disney Cruise Line doubled its fleet, from two to four ships, with the introduction of *Disney Dream* in 2011 and *Disney Fantasy* in 2012.

Do we need to take towels and soap?

No. They are provided by the cruise ship. Some ships have individual soaps, and some fit liquid soap and shampoo in wall-mounted dispensers. Towels for the pool deck are provided, either in your cabin or by the pool.

Do cruise ship pools have lifeguards?

In general, no, although the exception to this at present is Disney Cruise Line, which installed lifeguards aboard its four ships in 2013.

Do youth programs operate on port days?

Most cruise lines also operate programs on port days, although they may not be as extensive as on days at sea.

Are there adults-only ships?

Companies that operate small and mid-size adults-only ships include Cruise & Maritime Voyages (*Magellan, Marco Polo*), P&O Cruises (*Adonia, Arcadia, Oriana*), and Saga Cruises (*Saga Pearl II, Saga Sapphire*). The minimum age may be different depending on the company, so do check for the latest information.

How can I celebrate a birthday or anniversary?

If you have a birthday or anniversary or other special occasion to celebrate during your cruise, let the cruise line know in advance. They should be able to arrange a special cake for you, or a special 'Champagne breakfast' in bed. Some cruise lines offer special anniversary packages – for a fee – or a meal in an alternative restaurant, where available.

Can I bring my pet?

Pets are not allowed aboard cruise ships, with one exception: the regular transatlantic crossings aboard Cunard Line's ocean liner *Queen Mary 2*, which has carried more than 500 pet animals since its debut in 2004. It provides air-conditioned kennels and cat containers.

Do cruises suit honeymooners?

Absolutely. A cruise is the ideal setting for romance, for shipboard weddings aboard ships with the right registry (they can also be arranged in some ports, depending on local regulations), receptions, and honeymoons. And for those on a second honeymoon, many ships can perform a 'renewal of vows' ceremony; some will make a charge for this service.

Do some people really live on board?

Yes! There are several 'live aboard' passengers who simply love traveling the world continuously – and why not? They sell their house, put possessions into storage, step on board, and disembark only when the ship has to go into dry dock for refits.

Five rip-offs to watch out for

1. Internet charges. Cruise lines often overcharge for use of the Internet, with connections made via satellite.

2. Currency conversion. Using a foreign credit card to pay your onboard account means you could incur unseen currency conversion charges, known in the trade as dynamic currency conversion (DCC). When you pay your bill, the price quoted is recalculated into a 'guaranteed' price, often higher than the rate quoted by banks or credit card companies.

3. Double gratuities. The major cruise lines typically imprint an additional gratuity line on signable receipts for such things as spa treatments, extra-cost coffees, or other bar charges, despite a 15 percent gratuity having already been added. Example: for an espresso coffee costing $2.80, a 15 percent tip of 40 cents is added, thus making the total cost $3.22. You sign the receipt, but one line above the signature line says 'Additional Gratuity' – thus inviting you to pay a double gratuity.

4. Transfer buses. The cost of airport transfer buses in some ports, such as Athens and Civitavecchia (the port for Rome). A cheaper option is to take the train instead.

5. Mineral water. The cost of bottled mineral water for shore excursions. Example: one cruise line charges $4.50, but then adds another 15 percent gratuity 'for your convenience.' Budget accordingly.

Is a repositioning cruise cheaper?

When ships move from one cruise region to another, it is termed repositioning. When ships move between the Caribbean and Europe, typically in April/May, or between Europe and the Caribbean (typically in October/November), for example, the cruise fares are usually discounted. The ships rarely sail full, and offer excellent value for money.

How inclusive is all-inclusive?

It usually means that transportation, accommodation, food, and entertainment are wrapped up in one neat package. If drinks are included, it's mostly a limited range of low-quality brands, and bartenders tend to be overgenerous with ice for cocktails. While that concept works better aboard small ships (those carrying 251–750 passengers), large resort ships (those carrying more than 2,001 passengers) provide a larger number of facilities and a bigger number of reasons for you to spend money on board. So 'mostly inclusive' might be a better term to use.

Tell me more about extra costs

While cruise lines offer appealingly low fares, most try hard to maintain revenues by increasing the cost of onboard choices (particularly for specialty restaurants), including beverages. Expect to spend at least $25 a day per person on extras, plus $10–12 a day per person in gratuities (unless they are included). Here are the approximate prices per person for a typical seven-day cruise aboard a well-rated midsize or large resort ship, based on an outside-view two-bed cabin:

Cruise fare: $1,000
Port charges: $100 (if not included)
Gratuities: $50
Total cost per person: $1,150

This is less than $165 per person per day, which seems reasonable when you consider all it covers.

However, your seven-day cruise can become expensive when you start adding on any extras. For example, add two flight-seeing excursions in Alaska (at about $250 each), two cappuccinos each a day ($25), a scotch and soda each a day ($35), a massage ($125), 7 mineral waters ($28), 30 minutes' access to the Internet for email ($15), three other assorted excursions ($150), and gratuities ($50). That's an extra $928 – without even one bottle of wine with dinner! So a couple will need to add an extra $1,856 for a seven-day cruise, plus the cruise fare, of course, and the cost of getting to and from your local airport, or ship port.

More examples of extra-cost items (these are provided only as guidelines, and may have changed since this book was completed, so always check with the cruise line, onboard concession, or your travel provider for the latest prices) may include:

Aqua Spa use: $30–35 per day
Babysitting (per hour): $10
Bottled water: $2.50–7 (per bottle)
Cappuccino/espresso: $2.50–$4.50
Cartoon character bedtime 'tuck-in' service: $20–25
Dry-clean dress: $8–10
Dry-clean jacket: $8–10

Outdoor breakfast aboard *Seven Seas Voyager*.

10 money-saving tips

1. Research online, but book through a specialist cruise-travel agency.
2. Cut through the sales hype and get to the bottom line.
3. Make sure that all taxes are included.
4. Book early – the most desirable itineraries go soonest. If air travel is involved, remember that air fares tend to rise in peak seasons.
5. The best cabins also go sooner rather than later, so book early to get the best one of these at the lowest prices.
6. Book a cabin on a lower deck – the higher the deck, the more expensive will it be.
7. An interior (no view) cabin is cheaper, if you can live without natural light.
8. Be flexible with your dates – go off-season, when fares will be lower.
9. Book an older (pre-1990) ship – the newest ships are more expensive.
10. Purchase travel cancellation insurance – your cruise is an investment, after all.

Pool deck on *Seven Seas Voyager.*

Golf simulator: $25 (30 minutes)
Group bicycling class: $11
Hair wash/set: $40–75
Haircut (men): $30
Ice cream: $2.50–4.00
In-cabin (on-demand) movies: $6.95–12.95
Internet connection: $0.50–0.95 per minute
Kick-boxing class: $12 per class
Laundry soap: $1–1.50
Laundry: wash one shirt: $3–4
Massage: $3-plus a minute (plus tip)
Satellite phone/fax: $4.95–9.95 per minute
Shuttle bus in ports of call: $3–6
Sodas (soft fizzy drinks): $2–3
Souvenir photograph (8x6in/20x12cm): $10–12
Souvenir photograph (10x8in/25x20cm): $20–30
Specialty dining (cover charge): $15–100 each
Wine/cheese tasting: $10–25
Wine with dinner: $7–500
Yoga or Pilates class: $12

What are port charges?

These are levied by various ports visited, rather like city taxes imposed on hotel guests. They help pay for the infrastructure required to provide facilities including docks, linesmen, security and operations personnel, and porters at embarkation and disembarkation ports.

Do cruise lines have their own credit cards?

Most don't, but those that do include Carnival Cruise Lines, Celebrity Cruises, Disney Cruise Line, Holland America Line, Norwegian Cruise Line, Princess Cruises, Saga Cruises, and Seabourn. You'll earn credits for any spending charged to the card. If you accrue enough points, you can exchange them for cruises or onboard credit.

Should I take a back-to-back cruise?

If you're considering two seven-day back-to-back cruises, for example eastern Caribbean and western Caribbean, bear in mind that many aspects of the cruise – the seven-day menu cycle, one or more ports, all shows and cabaret entertainment, even the cruise director's jokes and spiel – may be duplicated.

Do ships have different classes?

Gone are the class distinctions and the pretensions of formality of the past. Differences are now found mainly in the type of accommodation chosen, in the price you pay for a larger cabin (or suite), the location of your cabin (or suite), and whether or not you have butler service.

Some cruise lines have a 'concierge lounge' that can be used only by occupants of accommodation designated as suites, thus reviving a two-class system.

Private areas have been created by Cunard Line, MSC Cruises (Yacht Club), and Norwegian Cruise Line (The Haven) for occupants of the most expensive suites, in an effort to insulate their occupants from the masses. The result is like a 'ship within a ship.'

Most companies, however, have in essence, created two classes: (1) Suite-grade accommodation; (2) Standard cabins (either exterior view or interior – no view).

Cunard Line has always had several classes for transatlantic travel (just like the airlines), but the company's three ships (*Queen Elizabeth, Queen Mary 2, Queen Victoria*) are classed according to the restaurant and accommodation grade chosen.

Do ships have deck names or numbers?

Ships can have both names and numbers. Historically, ships used to have only deck names (example: Promenade Deck, 'A' Deck, 'B' Deck, 'C' Deck, Restaurant Deck, and so on). As ships became larger, numbers started appearing, as aboard ferries. Note that some ships don't have a Deck 13 (examples include the ships of AIDA Cruises, Carnival Cruise Line, Celebrity Cruises, and Princess Cruises), or any cabin with the number ending in 13 in it.

Can I eat when I want to?

Most major cruise lines now offer 'flexible dining,' which allows you to choose (with some limitations) when you want to eat, and with whom you dine, during your cruise – or a choice of several restaurants. As with places to eat ashore, reservations may be required, you may also have to wait in line at busy periods, and occupants of the top suites get priority.

Aboard large resort ships (2,001-plus passengers) the big evening entertainment shows are typically staged twice each evening, so you end up with the equivalent of two-seating dining anyway.

15 things not included in 'all-inclusive'

1. Dining in extra-cost restaurants
2. Premium (vintage) wines
3. Specialty ice creams
4. Specialty teas and coffees
5. Wine tastings/seminars
6. Internet and Wi-Fi access
7. Spa treatments
8. Some fitness classes
9. Personal training instruction
10. Use of steam room/saunas
11. Laundry, pressing (ironing), and dry-cleaning
12. Personal shopping
13. Professional souvenir photographs
14. Casino gaming
15. Medical services

What is specialty dining?

Mass-market dining isn't to everyone's taste, so some ships now have alternative dining spots other than the main restaurant. These à la carte restaurants usually cost extra – typically between $15 and $75 a person – but the food quality, preparation, and presentation are decidedly better, as is service and ambience. You may need to make a reservation.

What's the minimum age for drinking alcohol?

Aboard most ships based in the US and Canada, the minimum drinking age is 21. However, for ships based throughout the rest of the world, it is generally 18. But you should always check with your chosen cruise line.

How expensive are drinks?

Most US-based cruise lines see drinks both alcoholic and non-alcoholic as a huge source of revenue. As an example, drinks aboard Royal Caribbean International's *Independence of the Seas* when it is based in the UK during the summer are at least twice the cost of those aboard the UK-based ships of Fred. Olsen Cruise Lines, P&O Cruises, and Saga Cruises.

Are drinks packages good value?

Yes, if you like to drink. Note that they can vary hugely between cruise ships in terms of cost, and some also add a mandatory gratuity.

Can I bring my own booze on board?

No, at least not aboard the major cruise lines, where it will be confiscated. Some smaller lines turn a blind eye if you want to bring your favorite wine or spirit on board for in-cabin consumption.

How about service standards?

You can estimate the standard of service by looking at the crew-to-passenger ratio – provided in the ship profiles in this book. The best service levels are aboard ships that have a ratio of one crew member to every two passengers, or higher. The best ships in the world, from the point of view of crew living and working conditions, also tend to be the most expensive ones – the adage 'you get what you pay for' tends to be all too true.

Do ships have room service?

While most cruise ships provide free 24-hour room service, some ships charge a delivery fee for items such as food and beverages, including tea and coffee (particularly late at night). A room service menu will be in your cabin. Aboard sail-cruise ships such as those of Sea Cloud Cruises or Star Clippers, there's no room service.

If you occupy suite-grade accommodation, you may get additional services such as afternoon tea

Poolside movie screens adorn large resort ships, including *Carnival Sunshine*.

trolley service and evening canapés, at no extra cost. Some ships may offer room service specialties, for example a Champagne breakfast, at an extra cost (Louis Cruises, Princess Cruises, for example).

Should I tip for room service?
No. It's part of the normal onboard duties that the hotel staff are paid to carry out. Watch out for staff aboard the large resort ships saying that they don't always get the tips that are 'automatically added' to onboard accounts – it's a ploy to get you to tip them more in cash.

What does a butler do?
The best ships butlers will have been in private service on land, or will have been trained at one of the accredited specialist schools in London. A good butler should be educated, able to communicate well, provide unobtrusive service, and anticipate what might be required.

They should learn your likes and dislikes, such as how you want your tea, how you like your fresh juice in the morning, or how you want your ties laid out – whether rolled and placed in a drawer, or hung over a tie rack. And a good butler ought to remember your preferences should you return to the same ship.

Do any special food events take place?
In addition to birthdays, anniversaries and other celebrations, special events, or special celebration dinners, or 'foodertainment' event may be featured once each cruise. Examples of this include a Champagne Waterfall (Princess Cruises) and Rijsttafel (pronounced 'rice-taffle'), rice-based Indonesian food to which small items of meat, seafood, and vegetables are added (Holland America Line).

Some cruise lines feature a British Pub Lunch (featuring fish and chips, or sausages and mash) or late-morning 'Frühschoppen' (German sausages, pretzels, and beer). Others still offer an old standby, the

Baked Alaska Parade, also known as 'Flaming Bombé Alaska.' This usually happens on the night before the last night of a typical cruise (also known as 'Comment Form Night'), although some companies have replaced this with a Chef's Parade. Traditionally, February 1 is the official Baked Alaska Day.

Do ships still serve bouillon on sea days?
Some ships carry on the tradition of serving or making bouillon available at 11am each sea day. Examples include the ships of Cunard Line, Fred. Olsen Cruise Lines, Hapag-Lloyd Cruises, Hebridean Island Cruises, P&O Cruises, Phoenix Reisen, Saga Cruises, and Voyages to Antiquity.

Do all ships have proper dance floors?
For social dancing, a properly 'sprung' wood floor is the best for social (ballroom) dancing. However, most of the newest cruise ships have marble floors – if there is any dance space at all, except for a disco. Ships with good, large wooden dance floors include *Asuka II*, *Aurora*, *Britannia*, *Oriana*, *Queen Elizabeth*, *Queen Mary 2*, *Queen Victoria*, and *Saga Sapphire*.

Do all ships have swimming pools?
The largest is the half Olympic size (82ft/25m in length) pool aboard *Mein Schiff 3* and *Mein Schiff 4*. Most, however, are a maximum of just over 56ft (17m) long and 19.6ft (6m) wide. They are usually located on one of the uppermost decks of a ship for stability.

Some ships have multi-pool complexes that include water slides (examples: *Allure of the Seas*, *Carnival Sunshine*, *Norwegian Breakaway*, *Norwegian Epic*, *Norwegian Escape*, *Norwegian Getaway*, and *Oasis of the Seas*). Some ships have 'infinity' pools on an aft deck, so when you swim or take a dip it looks like you're one with the sea (*MSC Divina* and *MSC Preziosa*).

Some ships have completely separate adult-only, family pools, and toddler pools, such as *Disney Dream*, *Disney Fantasy*, *Disney Magic*, and *Disney Wonder*. The family-friendly large resort ships usually have separate pools and tubs for children in differ-

10 things a butler can do
1. Assist with unpacking your suitcase
2. Bring you DVDs, CDs, board games, or a pack of cards
3. Bring you menus for all dining venues and serve course-by-course meals in your suite
4. Arrange a private cocktail party
5. Arrange for laundry/cleaning items
6. Make dining reservations
7. Provide afternoon tea or canapés
8. Book shore excursions
9. Make your spa reservations
10. Shine your shoes

A spot of social dancing aboard *Queen Elizabeth*.

ent age groups located within a children-only zone, or a water park with great water-slide and flume-like experiences.

Some ships (including *Europa* and *Europa 2*) have pools that can be covered by a retractable glass dome – useful in case of inclement weather; other ships only have open-air pools, yet trade in cold weather areas in winter. A few ships have heated pools – examples include *Freedom of the Seas*, *Independence of the Seas*, *Liberty of the Seas*, and *Saga Sapphire*.

While most pools are outside, some ships also have indoor pools set low down in the ship so that the water doesn't move about when sea conditions are unkind. Examples include *Astor* and *Saga Sapphire*.

Some of the smaller ships have only a 'dip' pool – just big enough to cool off in on hot days – while others may have hot tubs and no pool.

Note that when there is inclement weather, swimming pools are emptied to avoid the water sloshing around.

Do all ships have freshwater pools?

All the ships of Disney Cruise Line and most of the large resort ships (such as *Allure of the Seas* and *Oasis of the Seas*) have freshwater pools. Some ships, however, do have saltwater pools with the water for the pools being drawn from the sea, and filtered.

How are swimming pools kept clean?

All shipboard swimming pools have chlorine – a member of the residual halogen group – added (a minimum of 1.0–3.0 ppm in recirculated swimming pools), while some have chemically treated saltwater pools. Pools are regularly checked for water flow rates, pH balance, alkalinity, and clarity – all of which are entered into a daily log.

Do any ships have walk-in pools (instead of steps)?

Not many, because of space considerations, although they can often be useful for older passengers. Some ships do, however, including *Aurora*, *Crystal Serenity*, *Crystal Symphony*, and *Oriana*.

What's the difference between an outside and an interior cabin?

An 'outside' (or 'exterior') cabin has a window (or porthole) with a view of the outside, or there is a private balcony for you physically to be – or look – outside. An 'interior' (or 'inside') cabin means that it doesn't have a view of the outside, but it will have artworks or curtains on one wall instead of a window or patio-like (balcony) door.

Can I visit the bridge?

Usually not – for insurance and security reasons – and never when the ship is maneuvering into and out of port. However, some companies, such as Celebrity Cruises, Cunard Line, NCL, and Princess Cruises, run extra-cost 'Behind the Scenes' tours. The cost varies between $120 and $150 per person.

Can I bring golf clubs?

Yes, you can. Although cruise lines do not charge for carrying them, some airlines (especially budget ones) do, so it's worth checking this if you have to fly to join your cruise, or you may be in for a nasty shock. Some ships cater for golfers with mini-golf courses on deck and electronically monitored practice areas.

Golf-themed cruises are popular, with 'all-in' packages allowing participants to play on some of the world's most desirable courses. Hapag-Lloyd Cruises and Silversea Cruises, for example, operate a number of golf-themed sailings each year, and if you take your own clubs, they will provide storage space and arrange everything.

Do mobile phones work on board?

Most cruise lines have contracts with maritime phone service companies. Mobile phone signals piggyback off systems that transmit Internet data via satellite. When your ship is in port, the ship's network may be switched off, and you will pay the going local (country-specific) rate for mobile calls if you can manage to access a local network.

Keeping in touch with children's whereabouts on a big resort ship can be expensive using mobile phones.

Europa provides free bicycles for passengers.

Instead, use two-way radio transceivers (walkie-talkies); at sea they won't interfere with any public-service radio frequency.

Are there any ships without in-cabin WLAN wiring? I am allergic to it.

The 94-passenger *Sea Cloud II* comes to mind, as well as some of the older ships that have not been retrofitted with WLAN cabling.

Where can I watch movies?

Some – but not many – ships have a dedicated movie theater. The movies are provided by a licensed film distribution or leasing service. Many newer ships have replaced or supplemented the movie theater with TV sets and DVD players in cabins, or with giant poolside screens for 24-hour viewing. Set to sail from April 2016, Carnival's 4,000-passenger *Carnival Vista* will have the first IMAX theater at sea.

Do all cabins have flat-screen TV sets?

No. Some older cruise ships still have bulky CRT sets, but these are replaced when a ship goes for refurbishment. The latest ships have flat-screen TVs.

Are there any ships without televisions?

Yes – the beautiful 64-passenger sailing ship *Sea Cloud*.

Can I take an iron to use in my cabin?

No. However, some ships have self-service launderettes, which include an ironing area. Check with your cruise line.

What is expedition cruising?

Expedition cruises are operated by specialists such as Quark Expeditions, using small ships that have ice-strengthened hulls or with specially constructed ice-breakers that enable them to reach areas totally inaccessible to 'normal' cruise ships. The ships are usually converted to carry passengers in some degree of basic comfort, with comfortable accommodation and a relaxed, informal atmosphere, with expert lecturers and expedition leaders accompanying every cruise.

What is a Panamax ship?

This is one that conforms to the maximum dimensions possible for passage through the Panama Canal – useful particularly for around-the-world voyages. These dimensions are: 965ft (294m) long, with a beam of 106ft (32m). The 50-mile (80-km) canal transit takes from eight to nine hours. Some large resort cruise ships (examples: *Carnival Dream, Celebrity Reflection, MSC Preziosa, Queen Mary 2*, and *Royal Princess*) are too big to go through the Panama Canal, and are classed as 'post-Panamax' ships – at least until early 2016, when the newly widened canal is scheduled to open.

Is there a cruise that skips ports?

Yes, but it isn't really a cruise. It's a transatlantic crossing, from New York to Southampton, England (or vice versa), aboard *Queen Mary 2*.

Can I shop in ports of call?

Many passengers embrace retail therapy when visiting ports of call such as Dubai, Hong Kong, Singapore, St. Maarten, and St. Thomas, among many others. However, it's prudent to exercise self-control. Remember that you'll have to carry those purchases home at the end of your cruise.

Do I have to go ashore in each port?

Absolutely not! In fact, many passengers enjoy being aboard 'their' ships when there are virtually no other passengers aboard. Also, if you have a spa treatment, it could be less expensive during this period than when the ship is at sea; some ships, such as *Queen Mary 2*, have price differentials for sea days and port days.

Do I need to bring my own beach towels?

No. Cruise ships have plenty of towels for both shipboard and shore use – but you'll be charged if you don't return them.

Can I fly in the day before or stay an extra day after the cruise?

Cruise lines often offer pre- and post-cruise stay packages at an additional cost. The advantage is that you don't have to do anything else – all will be taken care of, as they say. If you book a hotel on your own, however, you may have to pay an 'air deviation' fee if you don't take the cruise line's air arrangements or you want to change them.

Should I book early?

The farther ahead you book, the better the discount. You'll get the cabin you want, in the location you want, and you may even be upgraded. When you book close to the sailing date, you may get a low price, but you probably won't get the cabin or location you'd like, or, in ships with two seatings for dinner, you most likely won't be able to choose between early or late seating – you will just get what you are given.

What legal rights do I have?

Almost none! After reading a cruise line's Passenger Ticket Contract, you'll see why. A 189-word sentence in one contract begins 'The Carrier shall not be liable for ...' and goes on to cover the legal waterfront.

What are the downsides to cruising?

Much-anticipated ports of call can be aborted or changed due to poor weather or other conditions. Some popular ports (particularly in the Caribbean) can become extremely crowded – there can be up to

Carnival Paradise in the Panama Canal.

12 ships in St. Thomas, or six in St. Maarten at the same time, disgorging 20,000-plus people.

Many frequent irritations could be fixed if the cruise lines really tried. Entertainment, for instance, whether production shows or cabaret acts, is always linked to dinner times. Also, many aggressive, young, so-called 'cruise directors' insist on interposing themselves into every part of your cruise, day and night, through the public address system.

Where did all the money go?

Apart from the cruise fare itself, incidentals could include government taxes, port charges, air ticket tax, and fuel surcharges. On board, extra costs may include drinks, mini-bar items, cappuccino and espresso coffees, shore excursions (especially those involving flightseeing tours), Internet access, sending or receiving e-mail, beauty treatments, casino gaming, photographs, laundry and dry-cleaning, babysitting services, wine tasting, bottled water placed in your cabin, and medical services.

A cruise aboard a ship belonging to a major cruise line could be compared to buying a car, whereby motor manufacturers offer a basic model at a set price, and then tempt you with optional extras to inflate the cost. Cruise lines say income generated on board helps to keep the basic cost of a cruise reasonable. In the end, it's up to your self-restraint to keep those little extras from mounting up to a very large sum.

Ships with a shallow draft, such as *Hanseatic*, can get surprisingly close to shore.

Does a ship's registry (flag state) matter?

Not really. Some years ago, cruise ships used to be registered in their country of operation, so Italian Line ships (with all-Italian crews) would be registered only in Italy, and Greek ships (with all-Greek crews) would be registered only in Greece, etc. To avoid prohibition, some American-owned ships were re-registered to Panama. Thus was born the flag of convenience, now called the 'Flag State.'

Today's ships no longer have single-nationality crews, however, so where a ship is registered is not of such great importance. Cunard Line and P&O Cruises ships, for example, are now registered in Bermuda, so that weddings can be performed on board.

Today, the most popular flag registries are (in alphabetical order): the Bahamas, Bermuda, Italy, Japan, Malta, Marshall Islands, Panama, and The Netherlands. This fragmented authority means that all cruise ships come under the IMO (International Maritime Organization, within the United Nations) when operating in international waters – 12 nautical miles from shore. A country only has authority over the ship when it is either in one of its own ports or within 12 nautical miles offshore.

How are ships weighed?

They aren't. They are measured. Gross tonnage is a measurement of the enclosed space within a ship's hull and superstructure (1 gross ton = 100 cubic ft).

Is anyone building a cruise ship powered by liquefied natural gas (LNG)?

Not yet, but the possibility of powering a cruise ship using LNG has been under consideration for several years. One or two companies, including AIDA Cruises, are, however, getting close. There's also one nuclear-powered cruise vessel: the Russian Arctic expedition ship *50 Years of Victory*, which debuted in 2008.

Why is a coin laid under the mast of ships as they are built?

According to a 2,000-year old shipbuilding tradition, the coin brings good luck, and also protects the ship's keel.

How long do cruise ships last?

In general, a very long time. For example, during the *QE2*'s almost-40-year service for Cunard Line, the ship sailed more than 5.5 million nautical miles, carried 2.5 million passengers, completed 25 full world cruises, and crossed the Atlantic more than 800 times. But *QE2* was built with a very thick hull, whereas today's thin-hulled cruise ships probably won't last so long. Even so, the life expectancy is typically a healthy 30 years.

Where do old cruise ships go when they're scrapped?

They go to the beach. Actually, they are driven at speed onto a not very nice beach at Alang in India, or to Chittagong in Bangladesh, or to Pan Yo in China – the main shipbreaking places. Greenpeace has claimed that workers, including children, at some sites have to work under primitive conditions without adequate equipment to protect them against the toxic materials that can be released into the environment. In 2009, a new IMO guideline – 'International

Convention for the Safe and Environmentally Sound Recycling of Ships' – was adopted.

Will I get seasick?

Today's ships have stabilizers – large underwater 'fins' on each side of the hull – to counteract any rolling motion, and most cruises are in warm, calm waters. As a result, fewer than 3 percent of passengers become seasick. Yet it's possible to develop some symptoms – anything from slight nausea to vomiting.

Both old-time sailors and modern physicians have their own remedies, and you can take your choice or try them all, as follows:

When you notice the first movement of a ship, walk back and forth on the deck. You will find that your knees will start getting their feel of balance and counteraction.

Get the sea breeze into your face (arguably the best antidote) and, if nauseous, suck an orange or a lemon.

Eat lightly. Don't make the mistake of thinking a heavy meal will keep your stomach anchored. It won't.

When on deck, focus on a steady point, such as the horizon.

Dramamine (dimenhydrinate, an antihistamine and sedative introduced just after World War II) will be available aboard in tablet (chewable) form. A stronger version (Meclazine) is available on prescription (brand names for this include Antivert, Antrizine, Bonine, and Meni-D). Ciba-Geigy's Scopoderm (or Transderm Scop), known as 'The Patch,' contains scopolamine and has proven effective, but possible side effects include dry mouth, blurred vision, drowsiness, and problems with urinating.

If you are really distressed, the ship's doctor can give you, at extra cost, an injection to alleviate discomfort. Note that this may make you drowsy.

A natural preventive for sea-sickness, said to settle any stomach for up to eight hours, is ginger in powder form. Mix half a teaspoon in a glass of warm water or milk, and drink it before sailing.

'Sea Bands' are a drug-free method of controlling motion sickness. These are slim (usually elasticated and available in different colors) bands that slip onto the wrist. They have a circular 'button' that presses against the acupressure point Pericardium 6 (nei kuan) on the lower arm. Attach them a few minutes before you step aboard and wear on both wrists throughout the cruise.

Another drug-free remedy can be found in Reletex, a watch-like device worn on the wrist. First used for patients undergoing chemotherapy, it emits a small neuromodulating current that stops peristaltic waves in the stomach causing nausea and vomiting.

Is having hay fever a problem?

People who suffer from hay fever and pollen allergies benefit greatly from a cruise. Almost all sufferers I have met say that their symptoms simply disappear on a ship – particularly when it is at sea.

Are hygiene standards high enough?

News reports often focus on hygiene and sanitation aboard cruise ships. In the 1980s, the North American cruise industry agreed with the Centers for Disease Control (CDC) that hygiene and sanitation inspections should be carried out once or twice yearly aboard all cruise ships carrying American passengers, and the Vessel Sanitation Program (VSP) was born. The original intention of the VSP was to achieve and maintain a level of sanitation that would lower the risk of gastro-intestinal disease outbreaks and assist the cruise industry to provide a healthy environment for passengers and crew.

It is a voluntary inspection, and cruise lines pay handsomely for each one. For a ship the size of *Queen Mary 2*, for example, the cost would be about $15,000; for a ship the size of *Azamara Journey*, it would be about $7,800. However, the inspection points are accepted by the international cruise industry as a good system. Inspections cover two main areas: 1) Water sanitation, including free chlorine residuals in the potable water system, swimming pool, and hot tub filters; and 2) Food sanitation: food storage, preparation, and serving areas, including bars and passenger service pantries.

The ships score extremely well – the ones that undergo inspections, that is. Some ships that don't call on US ports would possibly not pass the inspections every time. Older ships with outdated galley equipment and poor food storage facilities would have a harder time complying with the United States Public Health (USPH) inspection standards. Some other countries also have strict health inspection standards. However, if the same USPH inspection standards were applied to restaurants and hotels ashore (in the US), it is estimated that at least 95 percent or more would fail.

Gaming table chips.

Helping to stop norovirus.

What about the norovirus?

This temporary but highly contagious condition occurs worldwide. Humans are the only known hosts, and only the common cold is reported more frequently than viral gastroenteritis as a cause of illness in the US. About 23 million Americans each year are diagnosed with the effects of the Norwalk-like virus (NLV gastroenteritis, sometimes known as winter vomiting virus or norovirus). It is more prevalent in adults and older children than in the very young.

Norovirus is part of the 'calicivirus' family. The condition itself is self-limiting, mild, and characterized by nausea, vomiting, diarrhea, and abdominal pain. Although it can be transmitted by person-to-person contact, it is more likely to arrive via contaminated foods and water. Shellfish (most notably clams and oysters), salad ingredients (particular salad dressings), and fruits are the most often implicated in noroviral outbreaks.

A mild and brief illness typically occurs 24 to 48 hours after contaminated food or water has been consumed, and lasts for 24 to 72 hours. If you board a large resort ship after norovirus has struck, bread and bread rolls, butter, and salt and pepper shakers may not be placed on tables, but will be available on request during meals.

When an outbreak occurs, a cruise line will immediately sanitize the entire ship and may confine affected passengers to their cabins to stop the condition spreading. Hand gel dispensers are provided at the entrance to all eateries. Crew members and their livelihoods can also be affected, so they will want any outbreak contained as quickly as possible.

Are incidents on the rise? Yes, but so is the number of cruise ships and riverships. Should cruise lines pay compensation? I don't think so. In my experience, almost all outbreaks have occurred because someone has brought the condition with them from ashore.

How can you avoid the bug? Don't drink from aircraft water dispensers on the way to join your cruise – they are seldom cleaned thoroughly. And always, of course, wash your hands thoroughly after using the toilet, both on the plane and the ship.

Most ships now provide liquid gel dispensers as a preventative – at the gangway and outside the dining venues (especially the self-serve buffets), for example – and it is wise to use them. Ships constructed after October 2011 must provide washbasins in buffets (one per 100 seats) under the United States Public Health's Vessel Sanitation Program. Several cruise lines (with older as well as new ships) now show a 'Wash Your Hands' video at muster stations following the passenger emergency drill.

What do ships do about garbage?

The newest ships are models of recycling and efficient waste handling. Items such as used cooking oil, for example, is turned into biodiesel. Garbage is sorted into dry and wet bins, and the dry garbage is burned on board or compacted for offloading in selected ports. Aluminum cans, for instance, are offloaded for recycling. As for sewage, ships must be three nautical miles from land before they can dump treated sewage and 12 miles for untreated sewage and food waste.

Where is smoking allowed?

A few cruise lines allow smoking in cabins, while others permit it only in cabins with balconies. Some, such as P&O Cruises (Australia), place a notice in each cabin advising passengers, 'A $300 cleaning fee will be added to your onboard account if we find evidence of smoking in your cabin.'

Almost all cruise lines prohibit smoking in restaurants and food service areas; almost no ships have smoking sections in dining rooms. Most ships now allow smoking only on the open decks. But that means when non-smokers are sunbathing on an open deck, the person next to them can light up.

What about cigars?

Cigar-smoking lounges are found aboard many ships, including: *Adventure of the Seas, Amadea,*

Anthem of the Seas, Artania, Asuka II, Brilliance of the Seas, Crystal Serenity, Crystal Symphony, Europa, Europa 2, Explorer of the Seas, Freedom of the Seas, Harmony of the Seas, Independence of the Seas, Liberty of the Seas, Mariner of the Seas, MSC Armonia, MSC Divina, MSC Fantasia, MSC Lirica, MSC Magnifica, MSC Musica, MSC Opera, MSC Orchestra, MSC Poesia, MSC Preziosa, MSC Sinfonia, MSC Splendida, Navigator of the Seas, Norwegian Bliss, Norwegian Breakaway, Norwegian Dawn, Norwegian Epic, Norwegian Escape, Norwegian Gem, Norwegian Getaway, Norwegian Jewel, Norwegian Pearl, Norwegian Star, Norwegian Sun, Queen Elizabeth, Queen Mary 2, Queen Victoria, Radiance of the Seas, Seabourn Odyssey, Seabourn Quest, Seabourn Sojourn, Seven Seas Mariner, Seven Seas Voyager, Silver Shadow, Silver Spirit, Silver Whisper, SuperStar Virgo, and Voyager of the Seas.

Remember that if you smoke a cigar in a ship's dedicated cigar lounge, the air purification system will often not be effective enough if someone comes in to smoke a cigarette, and you may suffer the consequences of inhaling second-hand cigarette smoke.

How about freighter travel?

Slow freighter voyages appeal to independent travelers (about 3,000 passengers annually travel aboard them) who don't require constant entertainment but want comfortable accommodation and the joy of days at sea. For more information, contact the specialists:

www.cruisepeople.co.uk/freighters.htm
www.freightertravel.co.nz
www.freightervoyages.eu
www.travltips.com

Do accidents happen aboard ship?

Broken bones seem to be the most common type of accident on cruises, the result of passengers stumbling on stairways. In 2012, a 47-year-old woman died aboard Royal Caribbean International's *Liberty of the Seas* when she fell down a short flight of stairs. Also in 2012, a 26-year-old man died aboard Carnival Cruise Lines' *Carnival Fantasy*. He fell from an upper level in the ship's nine-deck-high atrium to the lobby floor below while the ship was docked in Nassau late one evening. It was thought he had been trying to jump from one deck to another. Both of these were highly unusual occurrences.

Have there been murders during a cruise?

Violent crime is far less common on a cruise than during land-based vacations, but there have been a few suspicious deaths, and a number of passengers have gone missing, mainly in the Caribbean and on Mexican Riviera cruises. A small number have been thrown over a balcony by another passenger, typically after an alcohol-fueled argument, or dare.

If an alleged crime happens at sea, the jurisdiction responsible for investigating will depend on the ship's registry.

The cigar smokers' lounge aboard *Europa 2*.

the holiday &cruise channel

Watch us on Sky, Freeview & Online ...

www.holidayandcruisechannel.co.uk

Choosing Your Destination

Cruise lines visit around 2,000 destinations, from the
Caribbean to Antarctica, from the Mediterranean to the
Baltic, and from Northern Europe to the South Pacific.

Where can I go on a cruise? As the saying goes:
the world is your oyster. There are more
than 30,000 different cruises to choose from
each year, and about 2,000 cruise destinations in the
world. A cruise can also take you to places inaccessible by almost any other means, such as Antarctica,
the North Cape, or the South Sea islands.

Itineraries vary widely, so make as many comparisons as you can by reading the cruise brochures for
descriptions of the ports. Several ships may offer the
same or similar itineraries simply because these have
been tried and tested. Narrow the choice by noting
the time spent at each destination call (few ships stay
overnight in port) and whether the ship docks in
port or lies at anchor – it can take time to get ashore
by the tender.

Caribbean cruises

There are more than 7,000 islands in the Caribbean
Sea, although many are small or uninhabited. Caribbean cruises are usually destination-intensive, with
three or four ports into one week, depending on
whether you sail from a Florida port or from a port already in the Caribbean, such as Barbados or San Juan.
This means you could be visiting at least one port a
day, with little time at sea for relaxation. Although
you may see several islands in a week, by the end of
the cruise you might need another week to unwind.

From June 10 to November 30 is the official Caribbean Atlantic hurricane season in the Caribbean
(including Bermuda and the Bahamas) and Florida.
Cruise ships can change course quickly to avoid
weather problems, which can also mean a change of
ports or itinerary. When that happens, cruise lines
will generally not offer compensation, nor will travel
insurance providers.

Geographically, the Caribbean region is large
enough to be split into sections: eastern, western,
and southern.

Eastern Caribbean. Cruises sail to the Leeward
and Windward Islands, and might include calls at
Antigua, Barbados, Dominica, Martinique, Puerto
Rico, St. Croix, St. Kitts, St. Maarten, St. Lucia, and
St. Thomas.

Western Caribbean. Cruises sail to the Cayman
Islands, Mexico, and Jamaica, and might call at Calica, Cozumel, Grand Cayman, Grand Turk, Playa del
Carmen, Ocho Rios, and Roatan Island.

Southern Caribbean. Cruises might call at Antigua, the Netherlands Antilles (Aruba, Bonaire,
Curaçao), Barbados, La Guaira (Venezuela), Tortola,
and San Juan.

Cuba, the Caribbean's largest island, holds a
fascination for many. Although several cruise lines
have called there during the past 25 years (examples include Fred. Olsen Cruise Lines, Hapag-Lloyd
Cruises, Phoenix Cruises, Thomson Cruises, and
Transocean Cruises), no American cruise passengers
can visit the island because of the US embargo imposed in the early 1960s restricting trade with Cuba,
including tourism.

This long-standing ban may well be lifted soon –
if it is, American interest in visiting Cuba will soar
and cruise options will follow suit.

Private island beach days

Several cruise lines with Bahamas/Caribbean itineraries feature a 'private island' – also called an 'out-island'. NCL pioneered the trend when it bought a
former military outpost in 1977. So far, it has spent
$22 million upgrading its facilities, with further

Castaway Cay, Disney's private island in the Bahamas.

plans to develop 75 acres across two Belize islands, in a project – called Harvest Caye – costing some $50 million and including a pier for one ship to go alongside. Disney Cruise Line spent $13 million on upgrading and expanding its facilities – Disney's Castaway Cay has separate areas for adults and families with children, and is the only private island that permits its ships can berth alongside, so that passengers do not have to take a tender to go ashore.

These islands, or secure protected beaches, usually leased from the owning governments, have all that's needed for an all-day beach party – water sports, scuba, snorkeling, crystal-clear waters, warm sands, even a hammock or two, and private beach cabanas. There are no reservations to make, no tickets to buy, no hassles with taxis. But you may be sharing your private island with more than 5,000 others from a single large resort ship anchored for a 'beach day.'

Such beach days are not all-inclusive, however, and command premium prices for items such as snorkel gear and mandatory swim vest, rental pleasure craft, 'banana' boat fun rides, floating beach mats, private waterfront cabanas for the day, sunfish sailboat rent-

al, floating foam mattresses, and hammock rental. Rent a cabana (example; Cabanas on the Cay at NCL's Great Stirrup Cay beach day) with deck and sunbeds for the day (around $300), and you even get 'butler' service, with lunch and drinks.

One bonus is that such an island will not be cluttered with hawkers and hustlers, as are so many Caribbean beaches. And, because they are private, there is security, and no fear of being mugged, as occurs in some islands. Reality can intrude, however, as it did in Royal Caribbean International's private resort of Labadee in Haiti, when it narrowly escaped the devastating 2010 earthquake.

Alaska cruises

These are especially popular because Alaska is still a vast, relatively unexplored region. Cruise ships offer the best way to see the state's magnificent shoreline and glaciers. There is a wide range of shore excursions, including many floatplane and helicopter tours, some going to glaciers and salmon fisheries. There are many excursions, including 'dome car' rail journeys to Denali National Park to see North America's highest peak, Mt. McKinley.

Pre- and post-cruise journeys to Banff and Jasper National Parks can be made from Vancouver.

There are two popular cruise routes: **The Inside Passage Route,** a 1,000-mile (1,600-km) stretch of protected waterways carved by Ice Age glaciers. This usually includes visits to tidewater glaciers, such as those in Glacier Bay's Hubbard Glacier or Tracy Arm – just two of the 15 active glaciers along the bay's 60-mile (100-km) coastline. Glacier Bay was established in 1986 as a biosphere reserve, and in 1992 the 3.3-million-acre (1.3-million-hectare) park became a World Heritage Site. Typical ports might include Juneau, Ketchikan, Skagway, and Haines. **The Glacier Route** usually includes the Gulf of Alaska during a one-way cruise between Vancouver and Anchorage. Typical ports might include Seward, Sitka, and Valdez.

Holland America Line and Princess Cruises own many facilities in Alaska (hotels, tour buses, even trains), and between them have invested more than $300 million in the state. Indeed, Holland America Line is Alaska's largest private employer, but both companies take in excess of 250,000 passengers to Alaska each year. Other lines depend on what's left of the local transportation for their land tours.

In ports where docking space is limited, some ships anchor rather than dock. Many cruise brochures do not indicate which ports are known to be anchor (tender) ports.

With slightly under one million cruise passengers a year visiting Alaska and several large resort ships likely to be in port on any given day, there's so much congestion in many of the small ports that avoiding crowded streets can be difficult. Even nature is retreating; with more people around, wildlife is harder

Glacier trekking during an Alaska visit.

to spot. And many of the same shops are now found in Alaska as well as in the Caribbean.

The more adventurous might consider one of the more unusual Alaska cruises to the far north, around the Pribilof Islands (superb for bird-watching) and into the Bering Sea.

Alaska isn't always good-weather cruising – it can be wet and windy, and excursions may be canceled or changed. Even if it's sunny in port, glaciers have their own weather systems and helicopter flightseeing excursions are vulnerable. Take an Alaska cruise in May or August, when it gets darker earlier, for the best chance of seeing the Northern Lights.

Greenland cruises

The world's largest island, the inappropriately named Greenland, in the Arctic Circle, is 82 percent covered with ice – actually compressed snow – up to 11,000ft (3,350m) thick. Its rocks are among the world's oldest, yet its ecosystem is one of the newest.

The glacier at Jacobshavn, also known as Ilulissat, is the world's fastest moving and creates a new iceberg every five minutes. Greenland, which was granted home rule by Denmark in 1978, makes a living from fishing. The island is said to have more dogs than people – its population is 68,400 – and dogs are an important means of transport.

Iceland cruises

Cruising around Iceland, located just south of the Arctic Circle, and her fjords is akin to tracing Viking legends across the land of fire and ice. Geysers, lava fields, ice sheets, hot springs, fjords, inlets, remote coastal stretches, waterfalls, snow-clad peaks, and the towering icebergs of Jökulsárlón can all be part of an Icelandic adventure cruise, as can looking for the Northern Lights (Aurea Borealis) at night.

Canada/New England cruises

These 10–14 day cruises travel between New York or Boston and Montreal (northbound and southbound). Ports may include Boston; Québec City, Québec; Charlottetown, Prince Edward Island; Sydney and Halifax, Nova Scotia; Bar Harbor, Maine; and Saguenay, Québec.

The ideal time to sail is during the fall, when the leaves dramatically change color. Shorter five-to-seven day cruises – usually from New York or Boston – go north to take in the fall foliage.

European and Mediterranean cruises

Traveling within Europe (including the Aegean, Baltic, Black Sea, Mediterranean, and Norwegian fjord areas) by cruise ship makes economic sense. Although no single cruise covers every port, cruise ships do offer a comfortable way of exploring a rich mix of destinations, cultures, history, architecture, lifestyles, and cuisines – without having to pack and unpack each day.

Crystal Serenity in Venice.

European cruises have become increasingly popular because so many of Europe's major cities – Amsterdam, Athens, Barcelona, Copenhagen, Dubrovnik, Genoa, Helsinki, Lisbon, London, Monte Carlo, Nice, Oslo, St. Petersburg, Stockholm, and Venice – are on the water. It is far less expensive to take a cruise than to fly and stay in decent hotels, paying extra for food and transport. You will not have to try to speak or understand different languages when you are aboard ship, as you would ashore – if you choose the right ship. Aboard ship you use a single currency – typically US dollars, British pounds, or euros. A wide variety of shore excursions are offered. Lecture programs provide insights into a culture before you step ashore.

Small ships are arguably better than large resort ships, as they can obtain berthing space – the large resort ships may have to anchor in more of the smaller ports, so it can take time to get to and from shore, and you'll probably have to wait for shore tender tickets. Many Greek islands are accessible only by shore tender. Some companies allow more time ashore than others, so compare itineraries in the brochures; it's probably best to choose a regional cruise line (such as Louis Cruises) for these destination-intensive cruises, for example.

The Baltic and Northern capitals cruises

A Baltic and Northern capitals cruise is an excellent way to see several countries in a week or so, and enjoy different architecture, cultures, cuisines, history, and stunning scenery. The season for most cruises to this region runs from May to September, when the weather really is at its best.

Copenhagen, Stockholm (the entry through the archipelago is awash with islands and country cottages), Helsinki, Tallinn, and an overnight stay in the treasure chest city of St. Petersburg – for many the highlight of the cruise – with its sumptuous architecture, palaces, and, of course, the Hermitage Museum. Most ships include at least one overnight stay, so that you can also take in a ballet or circus performance.

Norwegian fjords cruises

These cruises usually include a visit to Bergen, and

Who goes where

This is a selection of just some of the cruise companies that operate cruises regularly in the world's most popular cruise regions. These are not recommendations but rather suggestions to help you research what's right for you.

Caribbean
Carnival Cruise Line, Celebrity Cruises, Disney Cruise Line, Holland America Line, Norwegian Cruise Line, Oceania Cruises, Princess Cruises, Regent Seven Seas Cruises, Royal Caribbean International, SeaDream Yacht Club, Sea Cloud Cruises, Star Clippers, Windstar Cruises

Alaska
Celebrity Cruises, Crystal Cruises, Disney Cruise Line, Holland America Line, Lindblad Expeditions, InnerSea Discoveries, Norwegian Cruise Line, Oceania Cruises, Princess Cruises, Regent Seven Seas Cruises, Royal Caribbean International, Silversea Cruises, Un-Cruise Adventures

Polar Expeditions (Arctic/Antarctic)
Aurora Expeditions, Gadventures, Hapag-Lloyd Expedition Cruises, Heritage Expeditions, Lindblad Expeditions, Oceanwide Expeditions, Ponant Quark Expeditions, Poseidon Expeditions, Silversea Cruises

Baltic/Northern Europe
Azamara Cruises, Crystal Cruises, Cunard Line, Fred. Olsen Cruise Lines, Hapag-Lloyd Cruises, Holland America Line, Oceania Cruises, P&O Cruises, Phoenix Reisen, Saga Cruises, Swan Hellenic Cruises, Voyages of Discovery

Greenland/Iceland
Fred. Olsen Cruise Lines, Hurtigruten, Lindblad Expeditions, Saga Cruises

Mediterranean
AIDA Cruises, Azamara Club Cruises, Celebrity Cruises, Costa Cruises, Cunard Line, MSC Cruises, Oceania Cruises, P&O Cruises, Ponant, Princess Cruises, Pullmantur Cruises, Regent Seven Seas Cruises, Saga Cruises, SeaDream Yacht Club, Seabourn, Silversea Cruises, Star Clippers, Swan Hellenic Cruises, Thomson Cruises, TUI Cruises, Voyages of Discovery, Windstar Cruises

Greek Islands
Celestyal Cruises, Noble Caledonia, Oceania Cruises, Swan Hellenic Cruises, Voyages to Antiquity

Around Britain
Cunard Line, Fred. Olsen Cruise Lines, P&O Cruises, Saga

Cruises, Seabourn, Silversea Cruises, Voyages of Discovery

Canary Islands
Fred. Olsen Cruise Lines, P&O Cruises, Saga Cruises, TUI Cruises

Middle East
AIDA Cruises, Costa ('neoCollection') Cruises, Hapag-Lloyd Cruises, Noble Caledonia, Phoenix Reisen, Swan Hellenic Cruises, TUI Cruises

Indian Ocean
Hapag-Lloyd Cruises, Phoenix Reisen, Ponant, Voyages to Antiquity

South America
Celebrity Cruises, Costa Cruises, Crystal Cruises, Holland America Line, MSC Cruises, MOPAS, Oceania Cruises, Princess Cruises, Regent Seven Seas Cruises, Silversea Cruises

South America (Amazon)
Azamara Club Cruises, Fred. Olsen Cruise Lines, Hapag-Lloyd Cruises

Great Lakes (US)
Noble Caledonia, Ponant

New England/Canada
Celebrity Cruises, Crystal Cruises, Holland America Line, Oceania Cruises, Princess Cruises, Regent Seven Seas Cruises

Australia/New Zealand
Carnival Cruise Line, Celebrity Cruises, Cunard Line, Lindblad Expeditions, P&O Australia Cruises, Lindblad Expeditions, Princess Cruises, Royal Caribbean International

Southeast Asia
Asuka Cruise, Crystal Cruises, Oceania Cruises, Seabourn, Silversea Cruises, Star Cruises

South Pacific
Oceania Cruises, P&O Cruises (Australia), Paul Gauguin Cruises, Princess Cruises

South Africa
MSC Cruises, plus several cruise lines operating around-the-world cruises

Transatlantic Crossings
Cunard Line

Cruise lines: private islands			
Cruise line	Name of island	Location	First used
Carnival Cruise Line	Amber Cove	Dominican Republic	2015
Celebrity Cruises	Catalina Island	Dominican Republic	1995
Costa Cruises	Serena Cay	Dominican Republic	1996
Disney Cruise Line	Castaway Cay	Bahamas	1998
Holland America Line	Half Moon Cay	Bahamas	1997
MSC Cruises	Cayo Lecantado	Dominican Republic*	2005
Norwegian Cruise Line	Great Stirrup Cay	Bahamas	1977
Norwegian Cruise Line	Harvest Caye	Belize	2015
Princess Cruises	Princess Cays	Eleuthera, Bahamas	1992
Royal Caribbean Int.	Coco Cay	Bahamas	1990
Royal Caribbean Int.	Labadee	Haiti	1986

*Not exactly private, but a fine leased beach/palm tree island.

perhaps a train ride to the peak of Mt. Floyen, and the stunning views over the city and harbor. A highlight could be a visit to Troldhaugen in Bergen – the stunning home (and now a museum) of Edvard Grieg, Norway's most famous composer.

However, it's the sheer scenic beauty of cruising through fjords such as Eidfjord, Geiranger, Hardangerfjord, and Sognefjord that inspires the traveler. Typical stops will be made at Bergen, Flåm, Olden, Ålesund, and Oslo.

Around Britain cruises

Traveling around the British Isles' more than 7,455 miles (12,000km) of coastline by cruise ship provides a unique perspective. The major sights – and some unexpected gems – of England, Scotland, Wales, the Republic of Ireland, and Northern Ireland can be covered in a single cruise that typically lasts 10–14 days. Because the British Isles are compact – Great Britain actually consists of over 1,000 islands – the actual time at sea is short. But the range of experiences is vast: the turquoise waters off the Scilly Isles and the coast of Cornwall in England's southwest; the northern highlights in Scotland's more remote, nature-rich islands; the laid-back lifestyle of Ireland and the charm and distinctive voices of Wales, not to mention towering castles, incredible gardens, the England of Shakespeare, and, of course, the coastline itself.

Canary Islands cruises

The sun-kissed Islas Canarias, a Spanish archipelago and the outermost region of the European Union, are located just off the northwest coast of mainland Africa – they are actually closer to Africa than Europe. With a year-round temperature of 70 degrees Fahrenheit (21 degrees Celsius) the islands provide a fine setting for a winter escape.

The islands of Gran Canaria, Tenerife, La Gomera, Lanzarote, Fuerteventura, La Palma, and Hierro make up the itinerary of some cruises to the region.

A Canary Islands cruise usually includes a call at Funchal on the Portuguese island of Madeira. You should head to Ponta de São Lourenço for some of the island's most stunning views.

Middle East cruises

The Middle East cruise region includes the Arab countries bordering the Arabian and Red seas, and the southeastern Mediterranean. Countries with cruise facilities and places of historic interest are: Bahrain, Egypt, Iran (one of the author's favorite shore excursions was to the ancient site of Persepolis, near Shiraz), Jordan, Oman, Qatar, Yemen, and the seven sheikdoms – the governing bodies of the United Arab Emirates (UAE). You will need to carry your passport with you in almost all these countries – it will be available at the ship's reception desk.

Abu Dhabi and Dubai are fast becoming cruise bases, although cruise terminal and handling facilities are still quite limited. If you visit Dubai, note that displays of affection such as hand-holding or kissing are not permitted in public, and you can't drink alcohol in a public place. If you fly into Dubai with prescription medicines, make sure you have the appropriate, signed prescription.

South Africa and Indian Ocean cruises

Attractions include cosmopolitan cities, wine tours, wildlife safaris, unspoiled landscapes, and uninhabited beaches. Itineraries (usually 10–14 days) include sailings starting and finishing in Cape Town, or from Cape Town to East African ports such as Port Elizabeth, Richards Bay, Durban, Zanzibar, and Mombasa (Kenya).

Queen Mary 2 leaving Sydney harbor.

The Mexican Riviera

These typically sail from Los Angeles or San Diego, along Mexico's west coast, calling at ports such as Cabo San Lucas, Mazatlán, Puerto Vallarta, Ixtapa/Zihuatanejo, Manzanillo, and Acapulco. They usually include a call in the Baja Peninsula, Mexico's northernmost state. Be aware that there has been a considerable amount of crime even in the most visited ports such as Puerto Vallarta and Manzanillo in the past few years. Also, a number of cruise tourists have been caught out by rip tides and rogue waves when swimming in Cabo San Lucas.

Route Canal (Transcanal cruises)

These take you through the Panama Canal, constructed by the US after the failure of a French effort that began in 1882 with a labor force of over 10,000 but was plagued by disease and financial problems – more than 22,000 people died. The US took over the building effort in 1904 and the waterway opened on August 15, 1914, shaving more than 7,900 nautical miles off the distance between New York and San Francisco. The Panama Canal runs from *northwest* to *southeast* (not west to east), covering 51 miles (82km) of locks and gates and

dams. Control of the canal passed from the US to Panama in 2000.

Between the Caribbean and the Pacific, a ship is lifted 85ft (26m) in a continuous flight of three steps at Gatun Locks to Gatun Lake, through which it travels to Gaillard Cut, where the canal slices through the Continental Divide. It is lowered at Pedro Miguel Locks 31ft (9.4m) in one step to Miraflores Lake, then the remaining two steps to sea level at Miraflores Locks before passing into the Pacific.

Ships move through the locks under their own power, guided by towing locomotives. The 50-mile (80-km) trip takes eight to nine hours. All this effort isn't cheap; cruise ships over 30,000 tons pay a fee of $134 per occupied bed. So, a ship with 3,000 passengers would pay a one-way transit fee of $402,000!

Most Panama Canal cruises depart from Fort Lauderdale or San Juan, calling at islands such as Aruba or Curaçao before entering the canal and ending in Acapulco, Los Angeles, or San Francisco. In 2008, the Inter-American Development Bank approved a $400 million loan to help finance the historic Panama Canal Expansion Program. The new three-step locks feature 16 rolling instead of mitre gates, each weighing around 3,300 tons. It becomes operational in 2016.

Panama Canal Locks

While the existing Panama Canal locks measure 963x106ft (293.5x32m), with 39.5ft (12m) maximum draft, the new ones will be 1,200x160ft (366x49m), with 49.9ft (15m) maximum draft. These new locks will allow almost all cruise ships, including the *Oasis of the Seas*-class and *Queen Mary 2*, to pass through, although there is still the problem of a bridge at Panama City not being high enough for them to pass underneath. These ships need more than 200ft (61m) of air draft (height from waterline to topmost part of the ship), but the present limit of the Panama Canal is under 190ft (58m).

Hawaii and its islands

The islands of Hawaii, America's 50th state, are a tropical feast. Although relatively close together, they have many differences. For example, the lush, Garden-of-Eden-like Kauai is a world away from Oahu, with its urban metropolis of ever-busy Honolulu. The two parts of the Big Island, Kona and Hilo, are really opposites.

Although several cruise lines feature Hawaii once or twice a year, usually on Circle Pacific or special Hawaii sailings, only one ship is allowed to cruise in the state year-round: NCL's US-flagged *Pride of America*. Note that anything purchased aboard, including drinks, is subject to Hawaii sales tax, although this doesn't apply to ships registered outside the US.

South America cruises

Cruises around Cape Horn between Santiago or Valparaíso in Chile and Buenos Aires in Argentina are increasingly popular. The optimum season is November to March and most cruises last 14 days. However, operating costs are high, because several countries are involved. Pilotage charges, for example, are among the highest in the world. Chile and Peru require compulsory tugs. Steep charges for provisioning and supplies, visa complexities, and infrastructure issues all push up the cost.

Sailing southbound, ports might include Puerto Montt (Chile), the magnificent Chilean fjords, Punta Arenas (Chile), and Ushuaia (Argentina), the world's southernmost city (pop. 90,000) and the starting point for many cruises to the Antarctic Peninsula.

Coming up the continent's east coast, ports may include Puerto Madryn (Argentina) and Montevideo (Uruguay). Slightly longer itineraries might include a call at Port Stanley in the Falkland Islands.

A number of cruise lines also operate seven-day cruises from Rio de Janeiro, Brazil, mainly for Brazilians – who typically love to dance the night away and don't arise until nearly afternoon. Called 'eat late, sleep late' cruises, these are generally aboard large resort ships chartered to local companies.

Australia and New Zealand

Australia and New Zealand offer a wealth of cruising possibilities, with a growing number of port cities attracting cruise ships. Apart from the major destinations, such as Sydney, Melbourne, Brisbane, and Perth (Australia), and Auckland, Christchurch, and Wellington (New Zealand), there are numerous smaller ports, such as Adelaide, Cairns, and the Great Barrier Reef.

Then there's Tasmania's Hobart and the stunning former penal colony of Port Arthur – Tasmania's official top tourist attraction, renowned for its beautiful grounds. Scenic cruising along Tasmania's coastline is glorious, particularly in the area such as Wineglass Bay and Great Oyster Bay. The best time to go is November to March, ie summer in Australasia.

The extraordinarily beautiful Kimberley region, in Australia's Northwest Territories, essentially in the area between Broome and Darwin, is a must. The best time to go is in April or May, after the rainy season, for the best waterfall action. Landings are by Zodiac inflatable rubber craft or by helicopter for a visit to the sandstone formation of the 350-million years old Bungle Bungle Ranges.

Asia cruises

With such a rich tapestry of different countries, cultures, traditions, food, and sights to see, Asia should be high on the list of places to visit for the inquisitive traveler, and what better way to do this than by cruise ship. Hong Kong, China, Japan, Indonesia, Malaysia, Singapore, Thailand, and Vietnam can all be visited by cruise ship. Indeed, 'marquee' ports such as Singapore, Hong Kong, Yokohama, and Bangkok are all good points from which to join your cruise. The region has so much to offer that it's worth taking a cruise of 14 days or longer to discover many of the fascinating destinations that await you.

South Pacific cruises

The region is large, and so are the distances between island groups. Still, the area has inspired many people to travel to them to discover the unique lifestyle of its indigenous peoples. The region encompasses French Polynesia, the Marquesas, Trobriand, Pitcairn, and Cook island groups, among others – like string of pearls. Some magical names come to mind – Bora Bora, Moorea, Easter Island, Fiji, and Tonga.

The oceans on which we sail...

Oceans – large bodies of saline water – form 71 percent of the surface of the earth and are a major component of its hydrosphere. Some 86 percent of the water we drink comes from oceans, and they absorb 48 percent of the carbon that we humans launch into the atmosphere. The world's oceans form an incredible natural recycling organ.

In addition, there are many seas (smaller branches of an ocean). These are often partly enclosed by land, the largest being the South China Sea, the Caribbean Sea, and the Mediterranean Sea.

In size order, the world's five oceans are:

Pacific Ocean. The planet's largest ocean, the Pacific measures a colossal 60,060,700 sq miles (155,557,000 sq km). That equates to some 28 percent of the earth and means it is equal in size to all of the land area of the earth. It is located between the Southern Ocean, Asia, Australia, and the Western Hemisphere.

Atlantic Ocean. The world's second-largest ocean measures 29,637,900 sq miles (76,762,000 sq km) – a relative puddle compared with the Pacific. Located between Africa, Europe, the Southern Ocean, and the Western Hemisphere, it includes the Baltic Sea, Black Sea, Caribbean Sea, the Gulf of Mexico, the Mediterranean Sea, and the North Sea.

Indian Ocean. Next, at No. 3, is the Indian Ocean, which is just slightly smaller than the Atlantic, at 26,469,900 sq miles (68,566,000 sq km). It is located between Africa, the Southern Ocean, Asia, and Australia.

Southern Ocean. Quite a drop down in size is the world's fourth-largest, and also its newest, ocean, measuring 7,848,000 sq miles (20,327 sq km). The Southern Ocean extends from the coast of Antarctica to 60 degrees south latitude.

Arctic Ocean. Finally, there's the Arctic Ocean, which measures some 5,427,000 sq miles (14,056,000 sq km) – a mere baby compared with its big brothers. What it lacks in size (in ocean terms, that is), it makes up for in terms of outreach, extending between Europe, Asia, and North America. Most of its waters are north of the Arctic Circle.

Excursions Ashore

Escorted tours in ports of call cost extra, but they are often the best way to get a nutshell view of a destination and make the most efficient use of your limited time ashore.

While shore excursions used to be limited to rather cheesy city tours, today's excursions are extraordinarily varied, from crocodile hunting in the Amazon to kayaking in Alaska, and from elephant riding in Thailand, to flying over Moscow in a MiG jet. Most offer good value, but it's easy to spend more on shore excursions than on buying the cruise.

Shore excursions are offered by cruise lines in order to enhance a destination visit. Booking with a cruise line avoids the hassle of arranging your own excursions, and you'll be covered by the cruise line's insurance just in case things do go wrong. General city tours are designed to give you an overview and show you the highlights in a limited time period – typically about 3 hours. Other excursions provide a mind-boggling array of possibilities, including some that may be exclusive to a particular cruise line – even overland tours are part of the excursions available on longer cruises.

Not all tours are by bus. Some may be by bicycle, boat, car, or mini-van. Some cruise lines also offer

Playing with the stingrays in Nassau.

private, tailor-made excursions to suit you, a family, or small group. A private car, with a tour guide who speaks your language, for example, may be a good way for a family to get to know a foreign destination.

To get the most out of your shore visits, doing a little research – particularly if you are visiting foreign countries – will pay dividends. Once on board, attend the shore excursion lectures, or watch destination and shore excursion videos on the television in your cabin.

Once your ship reaches a destination, it must be cleared by local officials before you are free to go ashore. In most ports, this is accomplished speedily. Meanwhile, you may be asked to assemble for your organized tours in one of the ship's public rooms. You'll need to carry the ship's identification card with you (remember to take the ship's telephone number with you, in case of emergencies), to be checked at the gangway, and for when you re-board.

How tiring are excursions?

Most tours will involve some walking; some require extensive walking. Most cruise lines grade their excursions with visual symbols to indicate the level of difficulty, for example in terms of fitness required.

How expensive are they?

For an average three-hour city sightseeing tour, expect to pay $40–100, and for whole-day excursions with lunch, $100–250. Flightseeing or seaplane sightseeing tours will cost $250–350, depending on the location, what is included, and how long they last – the flightseeing itself usually lasts about 30–45 minutes.

What if my first choice is sold out?

Some excursions do sell out, owing to limited space or transport, but there can be last-minute cancellations. Check with the shore excursion manager on board.

What should I take with me?

Only what's necessary; leave any valuables aboard ship, together with any money and credit cards you do not plan to use. Groups of people are often targets

---

A ticket to ride

Many companies with large resort ships charge extra for shuttle buses to take you from the port or other docking area to a local city or town center. The port with the highest charge is Venice, Italy, where the transport is by motorboat, between the cruise terminals and St. Mark's Square.

Shopping on a shore excursion with Norwegian Cruise Line.

for pickpockets in some sightseeing destinations. Also, beware of excursion guides who give you a colored disk to wear for 'identification' – they may be marking you as a 'rich' tourist for local shopkeepers. It's always prudent to wear comfortable rubber-soled shoes, particularly in older ports, where there may be cobblestones or other uneven surfaces.

How can I make a booking?

Several cruise lines allow you to book shore excursions online *before* you cruise, which means that some popular excursions may sell out before you even get to your ship. So book early.

If you need to cancel a shore excursion, you usually need to do so at least 24 hours before its advertised departure time. Otherwise, refunds are at the discretion of the cruise line, and refunds of pre-paid tickets booked over the Internet can take a long time to make and can incur currency exchange losses. You may be able to sell your ticket to another passenger – tickets don't normally have names or cabin numbers on them, except those involving flights or overland arrangements – but check first with the shore excursion manager.

How to tell which excursions are good?

If it's your first cruise, try to attend the shore excursion briefing. Read the excursion literature and circle tours that appeal to you, then go to the shore excursion office and ask any other questions you may have before you book.

Shore excursions are designed for general interest. If you want to see something that isn't described in the excursion literature, skip the excursion. Go on your own or with friends.

Brochure descriptions of shore excursions, often written by personnel who haven't visited the ports of call, can be imprecise. All cruise lines should adopt the following definitions in their descriptive literature, lectures, and presentations: the term 'visit' should mean actually entering the place or building concerned; the term 'see' should mean viewing from the outside – as from a bus, for example.

City excursions are basically superficial. To get to know a city intimately, go alone or with a small group. Go by taxi or bus, or explore on foot.

If you don't want to miss the major sightseeing attractions in each port, organized shore excursions provide a good solution. They also allow you to meet fellow passengers with similar interests.

---

10 destination disappointments

These destinations are lovely places, but watch out for the following nuisances.
1. **Cagliari, Italy.** Poor beaches and staggeringly overpriced shops.
2. **Grenada.** Hawkers on Grand Anse and other beaches.
3. **Gibraltar.** The rock's fine, but that's it – there's nothing else other than duty-free liquor.
4. **Naples, Italy.** Trying to cross the road from the cruise terminals to town can be a nail-biting experience.
5. **Cannes/Nice, France.** There's dog muck all over the sidewalks!
6. **Portofino, Italy.** Several ships disgorging passengers onto the skinniest strip of land in summer.
7. **St. Maarten.** When six large resort ships are docked at the same time.
8. **Ensenada, Mexico.** The poor area surrounding the cruise ship docking area.
9. **Ocho Rios, Jamaica.** Constant hustling to get you to buy something, and the general unsafe feeling.
10. **Juneau, Alaska.** The tacky souvenir shops are overwhelming.

In the Caribbean, many sightseeing tours cover the same ground, regardless of the cruise line you sail with. Choose one and then do something different in the next port. The same is true of the history and archaeology excursions in the Greek islands, where the same ancient gods will put in frequent appearances.

What if I lose my ticket?

Report lost or misplaced tickets to the shore excursion manager. Aboard most ships, excursion tickets, once sold, become the sole responsibility of the buyer, and the cruise line isn't generally able to issue replacements.

Are there private excursions?

Most cruise line-organized excursions work on the 'one-size-fits-all' principle. However, a more personalized alternative exists for anyone looking for privately guided tours and land experiences. Tailor-made 'build-your-own' excursions provide private tours of a destination and its environs, all arranged by a 'travel concierge.' These could include lunch or dinner in a hard-to-book top-class restaurant, a visit to a private museum, or other bespoke requirements for small groups.

The right transportation and private guide will be arranged, and all arrangements taken care of – at a cost, of course. A cruise line destination 'expert' will plan an excursion, arrange the right transportation, and attend to all the other details that make the experience more personal. It's all about exclusivity – at a price.

Shopping aboard

Many ships have designer brands (clothing items, cosmetics and perfume, watches) on board at duty-free prices, so you don't need to spend time shopping ashore. Some ships have private rooms where you can view expensive jewelry or watches in private. Onboard shops are closed while the ship is in port, however, due to international customs regulations. Good discounts are often offered on the last day of the cruise.

Shopping ashore

Aboard ship, a 'shopping lecturer' will give a presentation about shopping in the various ports of call. Many cruise lines operating in Alaska, the Bahamas, the Caribbean, and the Mexican Riviera engage an outside company that provides the services of a 'shopping lecturer.' Most talks are about designer jewelry and watches – high-ticket items that boost commissions to cruise lines. The 'Shopping lecturers' heavily promote 'selected' shops, goods, and services, authorized by the cruise line, which receives a commission. Shopping maps, with 'selected' stores highlighted, are usually placed in your cabin, and

White-water rafting in Costa Rica.

sometimes include a guarantee of satisfaction valid for 30 days.

During organized shore excursions, be wary of stores recommended by tour guides – they may be receiving commissions from the merchants. Shop around before you purchase. When buying local handicrafts, make sure they have indeed been made locally. Be wary of 'bargain-priced' name brands, as they may be counterfeit. For watches, check the guarantee.

Some of the world's shopping havens put serious temptation in the way of cruise passengers. Top of the list are Hong Kong, Singapore, and Dubai (especially in the Mall of the Emirates – a shopping resort rather than a mall – and the Dubai Mall, with over 1,200 shops, including the only Bloomingdale's outside the US).

Shopping tips

Know in advance just what you are looking for, especially if your time is limited; when time is no problem, browsing can be fun.

When shopping time is included in an excursion, be wary of stores repeatedly recommended by tour guides; the guides may be receiving commissions from the merchants.

When shopping for local handicrafts, make sure they have indeed been made locally. It can happen that a so-called local product has in fact been made

Shore excursion to Ephesus, Turkey.

in Taiwan, Hong Kong, or another Far Eastern country. It pays to check.

Be wary of 'bargain-priced' name brands such as Gucci bags and Rolex or Omega watches – they are probably counterfeit. For watches, check the guarantee.

Going ashore independently – and safely

The major advantage of going independently is that you do so at your own pace and see the sights you want to see. If you hire a taxi for sightseeing, negotiate the price in advance, and don't pay until you get back to the ship or to your destination. If you are with friends, hiring a taxi for a full- or half-day sightseeing trip can often work out far cheaper than renting a car – and it's probably safer and more relaxing. Try to find a driver who speaks your language.

Exploring independently is straightforward in the major cruise ports of the Aegean, Alaska, the Bahamas, Bermuda, the Caribbean, the Mexican Riviera, the Canary Islands, the Mediterranean, and the South Pacific's islands. If you don't speak the local language, carry some identification (but not your actual passport, unless required – keep a photocopy with you instead), the name of your ship (and its telephone number, for emergencies), and the area in which it is docked. If the ship is anchored, and you take a launch tender ashore, observe landmarks near the landing place, and write down the location. This will help if you get lost and need to take a taxi back to the launch.

Some small ships provide an identification tag or boarding pass at the reception desk, to be handed in each time you return to the ship. Remember that ships have schedules – and sometimes tides – to meet, and they won't wait for you if you return late. If you are in a launch port and severe weather approaches, the ship's captain could make a decision to depart early to avoid being hemmed in by an approaching storm. Although this is rare, it has happened, especially in the

Caribbean. If it does, in the port, locate the ship's agent, who will try to get you back.

Planning on going to a quiet, secluded beach to swim? First check with the shore excursion manager, as certain beaches may be considered off-limits because of a dangerous undertow, drug pushers, or persistent hawkers. And don't even think of going diving alone – even if you know the area well.

If you explore independently and need medical help, you could risk missing the ship when it sails. Unless the destination is a familiar one, first-time cruisers are probably safer booking excursions organized by the ship and vetted by the cruise line. Also, if you have a problem during a tour, the cruise line should be able to sort it out on the spot.

The main downside of going it alone is the possibility of delay. If your chosen transport has a problem, you could miss the ship as a result. In such a case (it does happen), you are responsible for getting to the ship. This may not be easy if the next port of call is in another country, and you don't have your passport. You should also be aware that cruise lines do change itineraries occasionally, due to weather, or political or other factors. If you book your own tours, and it's a tender port where the ship has to remain at anchor offshore, you may need to wait until passengers on the ship's organized tours have been offloaded. This can take two or more hours aboard some of the large resort ships.

Allow plenty of time to get back to your ship before sailing time – the ship won't wait. Make sure your travel insurance covers you fully.

Life Aboard

This A to Z survey covers the astonishing range of facilities that modern cruise ships offer and tells you how to make the most of them.

Air conditioning
Cabin temperature is regulated by an individually controlled thermostat, so you can adjust it to suit yourself. However, aboard some ships, the cabin air conditioning can't be turned off. Air temperatures in public rooms are often kept relatively cool.

Art auctions
Aboard many large resort ships, art auctions form part of the 'entertainment' program. They may be fun participation events – though the 'free Champagne' given to entice you is usually sparkling wine and not authentic Champagne, while most of the art is rubbish.

Art 'appraisal prices' are done by the art provider, a company that pays a cruise line to be on board. Watch out for 'retail replacement value,' a misleading term used by the art salespeople. Listen for phrases such as 'signed in the stone' – it means that the artists did not sign the work – or *pochoire* (a stencil print less valuable than an original etching or lithograph.)

A beauty treatment aboard *Louis Aura*.

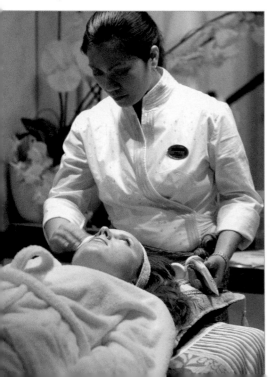

If the auctioneer tries to sell a piece of art (particularly a 'block' print or woodcut/engraving) with an 'authenticated signature,' don't buy it – when it's delivered to your home and you have it appraised, you'll probably find it's not genuine.

Beauty salon/barber shop
Make appointments as soon after boarding as possible, particularly on short cruises. Appointment times fill up rapidly, especially before social events such as a 'Welcome Aboard' cocktail party. Charges are comparable to city prices ashore.

Cashless cruising
You simply settle your account with one payment (by cash or credit card) before disembarking on the last day. An imprint of your credit card is taken at embarkation or when you register online, permitting you to sign for everything. Before the end of the cruise, a detailed statement is delivered to your cabin.

But, beware, because not being able to pay cash for anything can lull you into a false sense of security, because it's easy to overspend. Make a careful note of what you sign for.

Some cruise lines, irritatingly, discontinue their 'cashless' system for the last day of the cruise. Some may add a 'currency conversion service charge' to your credit card account if it is not in the currency of the cruise line.

Casino gaming
Many cruise ships have casinos, where the range of table games includes blackjack or 21, Caribbean stud poker, roulette, craps, and baccarat. Under-18s are not allowed in casinos, and photography is usually banned inside them. Customs regulations mean that casinos generally don't open when the ship is in port.

Gaming casino operations aboard cruise ships are unregulated. However, some companies, such as Celebrity Cruises and Royal Caribbean International, abide by Nevada Gaming Control Board regulations. Most table games have a $5 minimum and $200 maximum – but, for serious players, Carnival Cruise Line's casinos have blackjack tables with a $25 minimum and $500 maximum.

Some cruise lines have 'private gaming club' memberships, with regular rebates and special offers (example: Star Cruises/Genting Hong Kong). Slot ma-

Disembarking from large resort ships can be tedious.

chines are also in evidence and bring in more than half of a casino's profits.

Comment cards

On the last day of the cruise you will be asked to fill out a company 'comment card.' Some lines offer 'incentives' such as a bottle of Champagne. Be truthful, as the form serves as a means of communication between you and the cruise line. Pressure from staff to write 'excellent' for everything is rampant, but, unless you highlight problems you have encountered, things are unlikely to improve.

Disembarkation

This can be the most trying end to any cruise. The cruise director gives an informal talk on customs, immigration, and disembarkation procedures. The night before the ship reaches its destination, you will be given a customs form. Include any duty-free items, whether purchased aboard or ashore. Save the receipts, in case a customs officer asks for them after you disembark.

The night before arrival at your cruise's final destination, place your main baggage outside your cabin on retiring, or before 2am. It will be collected and offloaded on arrival. Leave out fragile items and the clothes you intend to wear for disembarkation and onward travel – it is amazing just how many people pack absolutely everything. Anything left in your cabin will be considered hand luggage.

Before leaving the ship, remember to claim any items placed in your in-cabin safe. Passengers cannot go ashore until all baggage has been offloaded and customs and/or immigration inspections or pre-inspections have been carried out. In most ports, this takes two to three hours after arrival.

On disembarkation day, breakfast will probably be early. It might be better to miss breakfast and sleep later. Even worse than early breakfast is the fact that aboard many ships you will be commanded to leave your cabin early, only to wait in crowded public rooms, sometimes for hours.

Some companies, such as Princess Cruises, offer a more relaxed system that allows you to stay in your cabin as long as you wish, or until your tag color is called, instead of waiting in public areas.

Once off the ship, you identify your baggage on the pier before going through customs inspection. Porters may be there to assist you.

Duty-free liquor

If you buy any 'duty-free' liquor along the way, it will be taken from you at the gangway as you reboard and given back to you the day before you disembark. This is because cruise lines want you to buy your alcohol on board.

Engine room

For insurance and security reasons, visits to the engine room are seldom allowed. Some ships may have a technical information leaflet, with details of what's what in the engine room. Aboard others, a behind-the-scenes video may be shown on the cabin infotainment system. A number of ships do offer 'Behind-the-Scenes' tours, which include the Engine Control Room, at extra cost.

Tenders transport passengers when a ship can't dock, as seen here aboard *Regatta*.

Gratuities/tips

Aboard many large resort ships, tipping seems to be mandatory rather than voluntary. Gratuities, typically of around $12 per person (slightly more for occupants of suite-grade or butler-service accommodation), per day, are added automatically to your shipboard account. These may need to be converted to your credit card currency at the prevailing rate.

Be aware that cabin stewards have been known to scroll through their passengers' on-board account on the infotainment system, so they can tell if you have opted out of the automatic gratuity charge!

Gratuities are included in the cruise fare aboard a small number of ships, mainly those at the luxury ('all-inclusive') end of the market, where no extra tipping is permitted – at least in theory. Even when cruise brochures state 'tipping is not required,' gratuities will usually be expected by the staff. Aboard some ships, subtle suggestions are made regarding tips; in others, cruise directors get carried away and dictate rules.

Here are the accepted industry guidelines: dining room waiter, $3–4 per person, per day; assistant waiter (busboy), $1.50–2 per day; cabin steward or stewardess, $3–3.50 per person, per day; Butler: $5 per person, per day. Tips are normally given on the last evening of a cruise of up to 14 days' duration. For longer cruises, hand over half the tip halfway through and the rest on your last evening.

Aboard many ships, a gratuity (typically of 15 percent) is automatically added to your bar check, whether you get good service or not, and a gratuity (of 15–18 percent) may be added for spa treatments.

Internet access and cell (mobile) phones

Smartphone/cell phone use aboard ships is growing, and most modern cruise ships are wired for Internet access and cell phone use, at a price. You can use your own device, but it must be set for roaming – and extra charges will apply. Before you cruise, check with your phone operator for the international roaming rates applicable to your tariff. All calls (at sea) are handled by a marine satellite provider, which passes on the international roaming charges to your phone operator.

As for Internet use, some ships have a room – often part of the library – with Internet-connect computers. The best-wired ships also have strong signals to cabins and public areas, so you can use your own laptop in the privacy of your cabin or on deck (extra charges apply).

Signal strength can vary substantially from hour to hour. The farther north you get, the closer the tele-communications satellite is to the horizon, so signals tend to fade in and out, and waiting for web pages to appear on your computer screen can be frustrating.

Internet time ranges from about 50¢ to 75¢ a minute. If you think you will use the Internet a lot, perhaps for emails, buy a package of minutes. Expect to pay around $50 for 100 online minutes and $100 for 250 minutes.

Note that attachments usually cannot be downloaded or uploaded.

Launch (shore tender) services

Enclosed or open motor launches ('tenders') are used when your cruise ship is unable to berth at a port or island. In such cases, a regular launch service is operated between ship and shore for the duration of the port call. Aboard the large resort ships, you'll need to obtain a tender ticket, usually given out in one of the lounges, unless you are on an organized excursion, which take priority. The procedure can take a long time.

When stepping on or off a tender, extend 'forearm to forearm' to the person who is assisting you. Do not grip their hands because this has the unintentional effect of immobilizing the helper.

Laundry and dry cleaning

Most ships offer a full laundry and pressing (ironing) service. Some ships may also offer dry-cleaning facilities. A detailed list of services, and prices, will be in your cabin. Your steward will collect and deliver your clothes. Some ships have self-service launderettes, well equipped with washers, dryers, and ironing facilities. There may be a charge for washing powder and for the use of the machines.

Library

Some cruise ships have a library offering a good selection of books, reference material, and periodicals. Aboard small luxury ships, the library is open 24/7. Aboard the large resort ships, the library may be open only a couple of hours a day.

Queen Mary 2, Queen Elizabeth, and *Queen Victoria* have full-time, qualified librarians provided by the dedicated specialist company Ocean Books, which also sells a superb range of specialist maritime books and memorabilia aboard the three Queens.

Aboard the small expedition ships, the library is one of the most important – and most used – facili-ties, and high-quality reference books on all aspects of nature, marine life, and polar exploration are usually provided.

Lido

This is a deck devoted to swimming pools, hot tubs, showers, and general recreation, often with intrusive 'background' music. Aboard most cruise ships, it also includes a self-serve buffet.

Lost property

Contact the reception desk immediately if you lose or find something aboard the ship.

Mail

You can buy stamps and mail letters aboard most ships, at the reception desk. Some ships use the postal privileges and stamps of their flag of registration; others buy local stamps at ports of call. Mail is usually taken ashore by the ship's port agent just before the ship sails.

Medical care

Doctors aboard most cruise ships are required to have current medical licensing, three years of post-medical school clinical practice, certification in emergency medicine, family practice, or internal medicine or experience as a GP or Emergency ward doctor. So, if you have a serious health issue that predates your cruise, or a permanent disability, you need to be upfront about it with your travel agent or the cruise line's reservationist. They may be able to advise you on a ship that best meets your needs.

The Lido Deck aboard *Carnival Magic* is devoted to swimming pools and hot tubs.

Anyone with long-term health issues should get prescriptions made up for the whole period of the cruise, because many places will not process prescriptions from other countries. Take out a travel insurance policy that reimburses you for visits to the onboard medical service, but check the small print. These policies often refuse to pay out if you had a condition you didn't mention when you bought the policy. Most medical care on cruise ships is perfectly adequate. Just in case it isn't, the cruise lines have a clause that says they aren't responsible for the malpractice of a ship's doctors.

News/sports bulletins

Most ships have satellite television for world news and sports coverage. On some, world news and sports results are printed and delivered, or displayed on a bulletin board near the reception desk or in the library. For sports results not listed, ask at the reception desk. A few ships can even print a full-size version of your favorite newspaper.

Photographs

Professional photographers on board take digital pictures of you during embarkation and throughout the cruise. They cover all the main events and social functions, such as a captain's cocktail party. The pictures can be viewed without any obligation to buy, but the prices may surprise.

Postcards/stationery

These are typically available from the reception desk, although some cruise lines now charge for them. If you are in suite-grade accommodation, you may get complimentary stationery personalized with your name and suite number when you embark.

Pre-paid drinks

Most large resort ships offer drinks packages in an effort to 'add value.' However, although these booze-cruise packages mean you don't need to sign each time you order a drink, they really are a temptation to drink more. Some packages include wine, but it's the cruise line's choice – not yours.

Reception desk

This is also known as the purser's office, guest relations, or information desk. Centrally located, it is the nerve center of the ship for general passenger information and problems. Opening hours – in some ships, 24 hours a day – are posted outside the office and given in the 'daily program,' which is delivered to your cabin.

Religious services

Interdenominational services are conducted on board many ships – usually by the captain or staff captain. Costa Cruises' ships have a small private chapel. Denominational services may also be held by clergy traveling as passengers.

The reception desk is the ship's information hub.

Room service
Beverages and snacks are available at most times. Liquor is normally limited to the opening hours of the ship's bars. Some ships charge for room service.

Sailing time
In each port of call, sailing and all-aboard times are posted at the gangway. The all-aboard time is usually half an hour before sailing. If you miss the ship, it's entirely your responsibility to get to the next port of call to rejoin the vessel.

Shipboard etiquette
Two points that are sometimes overlooked:
1) If you take a video camera with you, be aware that international copyright laws prohibit you from recording the professional entertainment shows.
2) It is fine to dress in a casual manner onboard ship, but you must not to enter a ship's dining room in just a bathing suit, or with bare feet.

Swimming pools
Most ships have swimming pools outdoors; some have pools that can be covered by a glass dome in case of inclement weather, while a handful of ships have indoor pools located on the lowest deck. Pools may be closed in port owing to local health regulations or cleaning requirements. Diving is not allowed – pools are shallow.

Parents should note that most ship pools are unsupervised. Some ships use excessive chlorine or bleaching agents, which might cause bathing suits to fade or run.

Telephone calls
Most ships have a direct-dial satellite link; you can call (by satellite) from your cabin to anywhere in the world. All ships have an internationally recognized radio call sign, a combination of letters and digits, for example: C6SE7. Satellite telephone calls cost between US$5 and $12 a minute.

To reach any ship from land, dial the International Direct Dial (IDD) code for the country you are calling from, followed by the ship's telephone number.

Anyone without a direct-dial telephone should call the High Seas Operator – in the US, dial 1-800-SEA-CALL. The operator will need the name of the ship, together with the ocean code: Atlantic East is 871; Pacific is 872; Indian Ocean is 873; Atlantic West/Caribbean/US is 874.

Television
Programming is obtained from a mixture of satellite feeds and onboard videos. Some ships lock on to live international news programs such as CNN or BBC World, or to text-only news services. Satellite television reception can sometimes be poor because ships constantly move out of the narrow beam transmitted from the satellite.

A wine tower aboard *Celebrity Eclipse*.

Valuables
Most ships have a small personal safe in each cabin, but items of special value should be kept in a safety deposit box (accessible during the cruise) at the reception desk.

Water sports
Some small ships have a water sports platform that lowers from the ship's stern or side. These ships usually carry windsurfers, waterski boats, jet skis, water skis, and scuba and snorkel equipment, usually at no extra charge – except for scuba equipment.

Such facilities look good in brochures, but ships are often reluctant to use them. This is because many itineraries have too few useful anchor ports. Also, the sea must be in an almost flat, calm condition – seldom the case. Insurance regulations can be restrictive, too.

Wine and liquor
The cost of drinks on board is generally lower than on land, since ships have access to duty-free liquor. Drinks may be ordered in the dining room, at any of the ship's bars, or from room service. There are usually extensive and reasonably priced wine lists in the dining room.

Some ships sell duty-free wine and liquor to drink in your cabin. You can't normally bring these into the dining room or public rooms, nor any duty-free wine or liquor bought in port. These rules protect bar sales, a substantial source of onboard revenue.

A Carnival chef putting the finishing touches to dessert.

Cuisine

Anyone determined to eat around the clock could do so aboard many ships, but the health-conscious should exercise restraint, especially at self-service buffets.

The dining rooms and restaurants aboard any cruise ship are the collective lifeblood of the entire ship, cruise, and hospitality experience. Except for the facilities and destinations, it's the food that most people remember and talk about.

Cruise lines love to boast about their food – and often with their celebrity TV chefs – who only sail occasionally for a bit of show – but the reality is that most meals aboard most ships are not gourmet affairs. How could they be, when a kitchen has to turn out hundreds of meals at the same time? I've never actually met a passenger able to recite the menu of their most memorable meal (including appetizer, main course/entrée, and dessert) aboard a cruise ship. Why? It's just that most ships simply can't deliver the 'Wow' factor the brochure promises, and so hype about 'gourmet' food is often overstated puffery.

Generally speaking, as in most restaurants on land, you get what you pay for. High-quality ingredients cost money, so it's unrealistic to expect low-cost cruises to offer anything other than low-cost food. Most cruise ship cuisine compares favorably with 'banquet' food in a family restaurant. You can expect a selection of palatable and complete meals served properly in comfortable surroundings. Maybe you will even dine by candlelight – well, battery-powered candlelight – which creates some ambience. Menus are typically displayed outside the dining room each day, so that you can preview each meal. Menus are usually delivered to suite occupants.

The major cruise lines sometimes bulk-purchase food, which means lower-quality ingredients and cheaper cuts of meat and fish, perhaps 'enhanced' with preservatives. That said, cruise lines do sometimes upgrade food items – Carnival Cruise Line and Royal Caribbean International, for example, introduced free-range eggs aboard their ships in 2011.

Fresh versus frozen

Aboard low-priced cruises, you will typically be served portion-controlled frozen food that has been

Dieter Mueller creating an appetizer on *Europa*.

Self-serve buffets

Most ships have self-serve buffets for breakfast and luncheon (some also for dinner). Strangely, passengers don't seem to mind lining up for self-service food in scandalously overcrowded venues. But while buffets look fine when they're fresh, they don't after a few minutes of passengers helping themselves. Self-serve buffets have become more user-friendly by increasing the number of 'active cooking' stations and food islands, which help to break up lines created by typical straight-line buffet counters.

Dare to ask for something that's not on the display, however, and any form of human communication ceases and supervisors become invisible. For example: trying to get a freshly cooked four-minute soft-boiled egg at a breakfast buffet is a major challenge. I am always met with: 'We've only got the ones in the bowl, sir.' But the 'eight-minute' eggs in the bowl have been sitting there since they were boiled at 6:30am before the buffet opened. They're still under the infrared heat lamp at 9:30am! Plus, there are typically no eggcups – or small spoons to eat them with!

Nor can you expect to find the following at the large resort ships' breakfast and lunch buffets: warm plates (for 'hot' food items), fish knives, a smoked salmon omelet, soy milk, brown rice, fresh herbs, loose tea, or freshly grated nutmeg for oatmeal or cream of wheat.

reheated. Fresh fish and the best cuts of meats cost the cruise lines more, and that cost is reflected in the cruise price. Aboard some ships, the 'fresh' fish – often described as 'Catch of the Day' – has clearly had no contact with the sea for quite some time.

Sushi bars are a fashionable addition to some ships. However, as the kitchen facilities on ships are generally inadequate to turn out food something as super-fresh as sushi, the only ships with authentic sushi bars and authentic sushi/sashimi are *Asuka II, Crystal Serenity, MSC Musica, MSC Poesia,* and *Nippon Maru.* Note also that many items of 'fresh' fruit may have been treated with 1-MCP (methylcyclopropene) to make them last longer – apples, for example, may be up to a year old.

Bread and pastry items

While there are exceptions, much of the bread baked aboard cruise ships is unappealing, because, with little time for fermentation of natural yeast, it is made instead with instant dough that contains dried yeast from packets. Many baked goods and pastry items are made mostly from refined flours and sugars.

Specialty restaurants

Most new cruise ships have a number of specialty restaurants and dining venues that provide alternatives to the large main dining rooms. Extra-cost specialty restaurants were pioneered in 1936 by RMS *Queen Mary* (Verandah Grill, for first-class passengers only, at an extra cost of one guinea – one English pound and one shilling) and introduced in modern times by Norwegian Cruise Line in 1988 (The Bistro – an à la carte, extra-cost French dining spot) and Crystal Cruises in 1990. But it was Star Cruises that introduced *multiple* venues – seven of them – aboard *Star Aquarius* in 1993; some were included in the cruise price, others cost extra. Thus was born 'Freestyle Cruising' – or dine where you want, when you want, and with whom you wish.

These specialist restaurants are always smaller, à la carte venues, for which you make a reservation, and pay an extra charge of between $6 and $75 a person. In return, you get better food, wine selection, service, and ambience. Celebrity chefs add to the mix and are asked to establish their own 'at sea' dining venues, or collaborate on menus for shipboard eateries, although they seldom appear on board.

Some specialty restaurants can also be entertaining (think 'eatertainment'), such as the Teppanyaki Grill aboard *Norwegian Breakaway, Norwegian Epic,* Norwegian Escape, and *Norwegian Getaway.*

Special diets

Cruise lines tend to cater to general tastes. If you are allergic to ingredients such as nuts or shellfish, want lactose-free or gluten-free food, or have any other dietary restrictions, let the cruise line know in writing well ahead of time and, once on board, check with the restaurant manager.

If you are vegetarian, vegan, macrobiotic, or counting calories or want a salt-free, sugar-restricted, low-fat, low-cholesterol, or any other diet, advise your travel agent when you book, and get the cruise line to confirm that the ship can meet your needs. Cruise ship food tends to be liberally sprinkled with salt, and vegetables are often cooked with sauces containing dairy products, salt, and sugar.

Most cruise ships don't cope well with those on vegan or macrobiotic diets who regularly need freshly squeezed juices; most large resort ships use commercial canned or bottled juices containing preservatives and aren't able to provide really fresh juices in their bars.

Healthy eating

You can gain weight when cruising, but it's not inevitable. In fact, taking a cruise could be a good reason to get serious about your well-being. Weight- and health-conscious passengers should exercise self-restraint, particularly at self-service buffets.

Many ships' menus include 'heart-healthy' or 'lean and light' options, with calorie-filled sauces replaced by so-called 'spa' cuisine. It may also be wise to choose grilled or poached fish – salmon or sea bass, for example – rather than heavy meat dishes, chicken, or fried food items.

Quality and variety are directly linked to the per-passenger budget set by each cruise line and are dictated by suppliers, regions, and seasons. Companies operating large resort ships buy fruit at the lowest price, which can translate to unripe bananas, tasteless grapes, and hard-as-nails plums. The smaller,

---

Celebrity chefs

Several cruise lines have signed up well-known chefs to devise menus for their alternative dining venues. Celebrity Cruises, for example, worked with three-star Michelin chef Michel Roux from 1989 until 2007. It's worth paying extra because the price is far less than it would be in the celebrity chef's land-based restaurants – there's no extra charge for dining in the Dieter Müller at Sea restaurant aboard *Europa,* for example. Acclaimed chefs have included (in cruise line order) Georges Blanc (Carnival Cruise Line), Elizabeth Blau (Celebrity Cruises), Nobu Matsuhisa (Crystal Cruises), Todd English (Cunard Line), Dieter Müller (Hapag-Lloyd Cruises), Mauro Uliassi (MSC Cruises), Geoffrey Zakarian (Norwegian Cruise Line), Jacques Pépin (Oceania Cruises), Atul Kochhar, James Martin, and Marco Pierre White (P&O Cruises), and Jamie Oliver (Royal Caribbean International).

Most celebrity chefs sail only one or two cruises a year, but Germany's three-star Michelin chef Dieter Müller has set a new benchmark by sailing for up to half a year in order to run his eponymous restaurant aboard Hapag-Lloyd Cruises' *Europa.*

Hebridean Princess provides the antithesis to mass catering.

more upscale ships usually carry better-quality ripe fruits as well as the more expensive varieties such as dragon fruit, carambola (star fruit), cherimoya, cactus pear, guava, kumquat, loquat, passion fruit, persimmon, *physalis* (Cape gooseberry), rambutan, and sharon fruit.

Even some of the large resort ships, such as *Allure of the Seas* and *Oasis of the Seas*, have calorie-control food items at the Solarum Bistro, where no dish is more than 500 calories. Carnival Cruise Line has a Mongolian barbecue on their buffets, where tofu is a regular feature. Crystal Cruises features more grains and fresh fruits on its buffet lines than is standard on a cruise, and you'll find Ayervedic breakfast items in *Europa 2*'s Yacht Club.

Raw food

In 2011, SeaDream Yacht Club introduced 'raw food' dishes. The cruise line tapped into the Hippocrates Health Institute's Life Transformation Program and introduced a complete additional menu. 'Raw' means that ingredients are raw, organic, enzyme-rich, and vegan: no meat, fish, eggs, or dairy items, or nothing heated above 118 degrees Fahrenheit (48 degrees Celsius), to retain as many micronutrients as possible.

Items include fresh sprout and vegetable juices, plant-based protein foods, and items such as pasta made from spinach leaves and coconut meat. Even desserts are created from raw foods including cashews, almond milk, and coconut butter.

Molecular gastronomy

The term, invented in 1992 by the physicist Nicholas Kurti, signals food's collision with science to create molecularly synthesized food. It was first introduced to the cruising industry by Italy's Emilio Bocchia in extra-cost restaurants aboard some Costa Cruises ships. To provide it, kitchens need blast chillers, atomizers, vacuum sealers, a Pacojet (a machine that can turn everyday ingredients into ice cream), liquid nitrogen, thickening gums (such as algin and xantham), malic acid, and flame retardants such as gellan. It also requires a qualification in molecular engineering and pharmaceutical know-how, and access to mountains of gelatin.

The end result equals a plate of colorful toy portions of 'foam food.' It can look pretty, and is reassuringly expensive. In the world of molecular gastronomy, bacon can be made to taste like melon. In the most literal sense, it's a matter of taste.

BBQs and hot rock grills

Although some ships – usually the smaller ones – offer barbecues on deck, some also feature a Hot Rocks Grill. This is for steaks, grilled meats, and seafood presented on a platter that includes a scorchingly hot rock base – so you can cook however little or well you want it done yourself. It makes for a pleasant, refreshing change, all in a casual pool deck environment. Seabourn and Silversea Cruises pioneered this option; more lines will surely follow.

Other casual eating spots include various coffee shops.

Afternoon tea in *Crystal Symphony*'s Palm Court.

The oatmeal factor

One factor that I have found to be quite consistent across most ships is what I call the 'Oatmeal Factor': how various cruise ships provide a basic item such as a bowl of oatmeal.

Standard. Hot oatmeal (supermarket brand oats) mixed with water, with little or no chance of obtaining tahini to add taste to the oatmeal. You get it from a soup tureen at the buffet, and put it into a plastic or inexpensive bowl yourself (or it may be served in the dining room by a waiter/waitress); it is eaten with plastic or basic canteen cutlery.

Premium. Hot oatmeal, water, salt, and a little olive oil; served in a higher-quality bowl, by a waiter or waitress, with hotel-quality (or better) cutlery. It's possible that the ship will have tahini, to add taste and creaminess. It's also possible that the waiter/waitress will ask if you'd like hot or cold milk with your oatmeal. There may even be a doily between the oatmeal bowl and base plate.

Luxury. Hot oatmeal (medium or large flakes), water, salt, tahini, a little (extra virgin) olive oil, and nutmeg, with a dash of blended Scotch (whisky); served in a high-quality brand-name bowl (Versace), with base plate and doily, and Hepp- or Robbe & Berking-quality silverware. The waiter/waitress will ask if you'd like hot or cold milk with your oatmeal.

Incomparable. Hot Scottish (large flakes, hand-ground) oatmeal, water, sea salt, tahini, and nutmeg (grated at the table), high-quality cold-pressed olive oil and a layer of rare single-malt Scotch; served in small-production hand-made china, with base plate and doily, and sterling silver cutlery. The waiter/waitress will ask if you'd like hot or cold milk (or anything else) with your oatmeal.

Service

Aboard many ships today, passengers are often in a hurry (to get to a show or shore excursion) and want service to be as fast as possible. They also don't like seeing empty plates in front of them, and so service speeds up because waiters need to clear the empty plates away as soon as someone has finished eating a particular course. In what is correctly termed European Service, however, there should *always* be a pause between courses, not only for conversation, but to let the appetite and digestive tract recover, and also to anticipate the arrival of the next course.

Plate service versus silver service

Plate service. When the food is presented as a complete dish, as the chef wants it to look. In most cruise ships, 'plate service' is now the norm. It works well and means that most people seated at a table will be served at the same time and can eat together, rather than letting their food become cold.

Silver service. When the component parts are brought to the table separately, so that the diner, not the chef, can choose what goes on the plate and in what proportion. Silver service is best when there is plenty of time, and is rare aboard today's ships. What some cruise lines class as silver service is actually silver service of vegetables only, with the main item, whether it is fish, fowl, or meat, already on the plate.

National differences

Different nationalities tend to eat at different times. North Americans and Japanese, for example, tend to dine early (6–7pm), while many Europeans and South Americans prefer to eat much later (at least 8–11pm). Brazilians traditionally like dinner at midnight. During Ramadan, Muslims cannot eat during the daytime, but can instead order room-service meals during the night.

Beef, lamb, and pork cuts are different on both sides of the Atlantic, so what you ordered may not be the cut, shape, or size you expected. For example, there are 15 British cuts of beef, 17 American cuts, and 24 French cuts. There are six American cuts of lamb, eight British cuts, and nine French cuts. There are eight American cuts of pork, 10 British cuts, and 17 French cuts.

Few large resort ships provide correctly shaped fish knives or the correct soup spoons – oval for thin bouillon-style soups and round for creamy soups.

A typical day

From morning until night, food is offered to the point of overkill, even aboard the most modest cruise ship. Aboard large resort ships, pizzas, hamburgers, hot dogs, ice cream, and frozen yogurt are almost always available. If you're still hungry, there's 24-hour room service, which, aboard some large resort ships, may cost extra. Some ships also have extra-charge bistros, cafés, and patisseries.

If you prefer to eat at set times rather than graze, these are the options:

6am: hot coffee and tea on deck for early risers (or late-to-bed types).

Full breakfast: typically with as many as 60 different items, in the main dining room. For a more casual meal, you can serve yourself buffet-style at an indoor/outdoor deck café, though the choice may be restricted.

Lunchtime: with service in the dining room, buffet-style at a casual café, or at a separate grill for hot dogs and hamburgers, and a pizzeria, where you can watch the cooking.

4pm: afternoon tea, in the British tradition, complete with finger sandwiches and scones. Typically, this is served in a lounge to the accompaniment of live music (it may even be a 'tea-dance') or recorded classical music.

Dinner: the main event of the evening; except for the casualness of the first and last nights, it is generally more formal in style.

Dinner in Manfredi's aboard *Viking Star*.

Light bites: typically served in public rooms late at night. These have mostly replaced the traditional midnight buffet.

Gala midnight buffet: this is almost extinct, but if there is one, it is usually on the penultimate evening of a cruise when the chefs pull out all the stops. It consists of a grand, colorful spread with intricate decoration that can take up to 48 hours to prepare.

Seating

Depending on the size of the ship, it may have single, two, or open seatings:

Open seating. You can sit with whomever you wish at any available table, at any time the restaurant is open.

Single seating. This doesn't mean seating for single passengers. It means you can choose when you wish to eat (within dining room hours), but you will have the same table assigned for the whole cruise.

Two seatings. You are assigned (or choose) one of two seatings: early or late.

Some ships operate two seatings for all meals, and some do so only for dinner. Some ships operate a mix of open seating (dine when you want) or fixed dining times, for greater flexibility. Dinner

Where to find real ale

Most major cruise lines offer mainly canned lagers such as Becks, Budweiser, or Heineken. The best beer from the barrel and bottled beers are stocked by UK-based cruise lines such as Cunard Line, Fred. Olsen Cruise Lines, P&O Cruises, Saga Cruises, and Swan Hellenic Cruises, though the selection is generally unexciting. Many real ales do not travel well. But then, AIDA Cruises has a micro-brewery aboard its newest ships (*AIDAblu, AIDAmar, AIDAprima, AIDAsol,* and *AIDAstella*), as does Carnival Cruise Line (Carnival Vista – coming in 2016).

The iPad menu and wine list at *Celebrity Reflection*'s QSine.

hours may vary when the ship is in port to allow for the timing of shore excursions. Ships that operate in Europe and the Mediterranean or in South America may have later meal times to suit their clientele.

The captain's and senior officers' tables

The captain usually occupies a large table in or near the center of the dining room on 'formal' nights, with senior officers such as the chief engineer and hotel manager hosting adjacent tables. However, this tradition is disappearing, as ship dress codes become more casual. The table usually seats between eight and 12 people picked from the passenger or 'commend' list by the hotel manager. If you are invited to the captain's table (or any senior officer's table), it is gracious to accept; you will have the chance to ask questions about shipboard life.

Dining room and kitchen staff

Although celebrity chefs make the headlines, it's the ship's executive chef who plans the menus, orders the food, organizes and supervises staff, and arranges all the meals.

The restaurant manager, also known as the maître d'hôtel (not to be confused with the ship's hotel manager), is an experienced host, with shrewd perceptions about compatibility. It is his or her responsibility to seat you with suitable companions.

The best waiters are those trained in hotels or catering schools. They provide fine service and quickly learn your likes and dislikes. They normally work aboard the best ships, where dignified professionalism is expected, and living conditions and benefits are good.

Some lines contract the running and staffing of dining rooms to a specialist maritime catering organization. Ships that cruise far from their home country find that professional caterers, such as Hamburg-

---

Douglas Ward's top restaurants

If asked to pick a baker's dozen, my choice would probably be (in alphabetical order by restaurant name):

Dieter Müller at Sea aboard *Europa*
Le Champagne aboard *Silver Spirit*
Le Cordon Bleu aboard *Seven Seas Voyager*
Ocean Grill aboard *Oriana*
Olympic Restaurant aboard *Celebrity Millennium*
Polo Grill aboard *Marina* and *Riviera*
Remy aboard *Disney Dream* and *Disney Fantasy*
Silk Road Sushi Bar aboard *Crystal Serenity* and *Crystal Symphony*
Surf and Turf aboard *Mein Schiff 3* and *Mein Schiff 4*
Tarragon aboard *Europa 2*
Teppanyaki Grill aboard *Norwegian Getaway*
Umihiko aboard *Asuka II*
The Veranda Restaurant aboard *Queen Elizabeth*

How the major cruise lines score on cuisine						
	Dining room/ Cuisine	Buffets/ Informal dining	Quality of ingredients	Afternoon tea/snacks	Wine list	Overall food score
Carnival Cruise Line	5.8	5.9	6	4	5.7	5.48
Celebrity Cruises	7.1	7	7	6.5	7.3	6.98
Costa Cruises	5.9	5.6	6	4.2	5.6	5.46
Cunard Line	7.6	7.0	7.5	7.4	8	7.5
Holland America Line	7.1	6.2	6.6	5.6	6.1	6.32
MSC Cruises	7	6.4	7.5	6.6	7.3	6.96
Norwegian Cruise Line	6	6.2	6.1	4.5	6.2	5.8
P&O Cruises	6.5	6	6.6	6.5	6.7	6.46
Princess Cruises	7.3	6.7	6.8	6.3	6.6	6.74
Royal Caribbean Intl.	5.0	5.8	6.0	4	5.4	5.24
Star Cruises	6	5.7	6.4	5.2	5.5	5.76

Scores out of a maximum of 10. Note that these ratings do not reflect extra-cost 'alternative' restaurants.

based Sea Chefs, do an outstanding job. However, ships that control their own catering staff and food often try very hard for good quality.

Hygiene standards

Galley equipment is in almost constant use, and regular inspections and maintenance help detect potential problems. There is continual cleaning of equipment, utensils, bulkheads, floors, and hands.

Cruise ships sailing from or visiting US ports are subject to in-port sanitation inspections. These are voluntary, not mandatory inspections, carried out by the United States Public Health (USPH) Department of Health and Human Services, under the auspices of the Centers for Disease Control (CDC). Cruise lines pay for each inspection.

A tour of the galley proves to be a highlight for some passengers, when a ship's insurance company permits.

In accordance with international standards, all potable water brought on board, or produced by distillation aboard cruise ships, should contain a free chlorine or bromine residual greater than or equal to 0.2ppm (parts per million). This is why drinking water served in dining rooms may taste of chlorine.

Remy, an exquisite, top-deck restaurant aboard *Disney Dream*.

Entertainment

The bigger the ship, the bigger the show, with tired old song-and-dance routines now being replaced by Broadway hits and Disney musicals.

Cruise lines with large resort ships have upped the ante lately, competing to attract attention by staging super-lavish, high-tech productions that are licensed versions of Broadway shows, with cruise lines signing partnership deals with musical producers, composers, and songwriters.

Large-scale shows: what's playing

Aladdin – A Musical Spectacular (Disney Fantasy)
Believe (Disney Dream)
Chicago (Allure of the Seas)
Hairspray (Oasis of the Seas)
Legally Blonde (Norwegian Getaway)
Mamma Mia (Quantum of the Seas)
Priscilla Queen of the Desert (Norwegian Epic)
Saturday Night Fever (Liberty of the Seas)

These big theater shows, with impressively large casts (except for the Blue Man Group shows), are abridged versions specially adapted to a large resort ships' showroom stage, typically by trimming and fine-tuning them, so that they fit in with the ship's

operational schedule – not to mention dinner.

Also, Royal Caribbean International's *Allure of the Seas* and *Oasis of the Seas* have an outdoor 'Aqua-Theater' (with a part-watery stage), where aquabatics and comedy provide a nighttime entertainment spectacular.

Aboard Norwegian Cruise Line's *Norwegian Epic*, the Blue Man Group present a mime and multi-sensory effects show that is a hit with families, as are *Cirque Dreams & Jungle Dinner (Norwegian Breakaway)*, and The Illusionarium magic show *(Norwegian Getaway)*, both of which are part of a supper club.

Disney Cruise Line also has other fine stage shows taken from its vast array of choices, plus *Believe*, developed specifically for *Disney Dream*. A proven family favorite is *Toy Story – The Musical*. Disney has separate entertainment shows for adults, too.

The good news is you don't pay extra to see the show, except if it's part of a supper club; there are few bad seats in the house; you don't have to find a

Old-style cabaret aboard Celebrity Cruises' *Celebrity Millennium*.

Believe, staged in the Walt Disney Theatre aboard *Disney Dream*.

parking place; or find a restaurant to eat in before or after the show. And there's always a handy bar nearby.

Onboard productions

Colorful, 'one-size-fits-all' Las Vegas–style production shows have evolved enormously aboard the large resort ships, as have the stages, technical equipment, and facilities. Although they still can't match the budgets of Las Vegas, they can certainly beat many shore-side venues. Most shipboard production shows have two things in common: little or no audience contact, and intense volume. With few exceptions, the equation 'volume = ambience' is thoroughly entrenched in the minds of many young, musically challenged audiovisual technicians.

With few exceptions, there's little elegance in most production shows, and all are too long. The after-dinner attention span of most cruise passengers – who are generally not unlike a television studio audience – is about 35 minutes. Most production shows run for about 45 to 50 minutes.

Most production show 'dancing' today consists of stepping in place, while pre-recorded backing tracks are often synthetic and grossly imbalanced.

Some cruise lines have a live showband to back the large-scale production shows. This band plays along with a pre-recorded backing track to create an 'enhanced' or larger sound. Some companies, such as Disney Cruise Line, use only a prerecorded track. This has little 'feel' to it, unlike a live showband that can generate empathy and variation – as well as create work for musicians. Although live music may contain minor imperfections, which some might regard as 'characterful', most passengers would prefer it to canned music.

Great expectations

Many passengers, despite having paid comparatively little for their cruise, expect to see top-notch entertainment, headline cabaret artists, the world's most popular singers, and the most dazzling shows with slick special effects, just as one would find in the best venues in Las Vegas, London, or Paris. There are many reasons why the reality is different. Cruise line brochures tend to over-hype entertainment. International star acts invariably have an entourage that accompanies them to any venue: their personal manager, their musical director (often a pianist or conductor), a rhythm section with bass player and drummer, and even their hairdresser.

On land, one-night shows are possible, but with a ship, an artist cannot always disembark after just one night, especially when it involves moving equipment, costumes, stage props, and baggage. This makes the deal logistically and financially unattractive for all but the very largest ships on fixed itineraries, where a marquee-name act might be a marketing plus.

For their part, most entertainers don't like to be away from their 'home base' for long periods, as they rely on reliable phone and Internet access for managing their careers. Nor do they like the long contracts that most ships must offer in order to amortize the high costs.

Entertaining but predictable

So many acts from one cruise ship to the next are interchangeable with each other. Ever wonder why? It relates to the limited appeal of a cruise ship gig. Entertainers aboard ships have to live with their audiences for several days and perhaps weeks – something unheard of on land – as well as work on stages aboard older ships that weren't designed for live performances.

As for the 'sameness' of so many shows, entertainment aboard large resort ships is directed toward family cruising. This is predominantly a family audience, so the fare must appeal to a broad age range. That partly accounts for the frequency of formulaic Cirque du Soleil-style acrobatic routines and rope climbing. In future, however, more 'branded' shows and entertainment partnerships will prevail, and, no doubt, some will cost extra.

A cruise line with several ships will normally employ an entertainment director and several assistants, and most cruise lines use entertainment agencies that specialize in entertainment for cruise ships. As a result, regular passengers are likely to see the same acts time after time on various ships.

Mistakes do happen. It is no use, for example, booking a juggler who needs a floor-to-ceiling height of 12ft (3.6m) but finds that the ship has a showlounge with a height of just 7ft (2m) – although I did overhear one cruise director ask if the act 'couldn't juggle sideways'; or an acrobatic knife-throwing act (in a moving ship?); or a concert pianist when the ship only has an upright honky-tonk piano; or a singer who sings only in English when the passengers are German-speaking.

Trying to please everyone

The toughest audience is one of mixed nationalities, each of which will expect entertainers to cater exclusively to their particular linguistic group. Given that cruise lines are now marketing to more international audiences in order to fill ever-larger ships, the problem of finding the right entertainment is far more acute – which is why *Queen Mary 2* is to be envied for the visual appeal of its Illuminations Planetarium shows.

The 'luxury' cruise lines (typically those operating small ships) offer more classical music, even some light opera, and more guest lecturers and top authors than the seven-day package cruises heading for the sun.

These performers – and ship entertainers generally – need to enjoy socializing. Successful shipboard acts tend to be good mixers, are presentable when in public, do not do drugs or take excess alcohol, are not late for rehearsals, and must cooperate with the cruise director.

Part of the entertainment experience aboard large resort ships is the glamorous 'production show', the kind of show you would expect to see in any good Las Vegas show palace – think flesh and feathers – with male and female lead singers and Madonna or Marilyn Monroe look-alike dancers, a production manager, lavish backdrops, extravagant sets, grand lighting, special effects, and stunning custom-designed costumes. Unfortunately, most cruise line executives, who know little or nothing about entertainment, still favor plumes and huge feather boas paraded by showgirls who *step*, but don't *dance*. Some cruise ships have coarse shows, and topless performances can be found aboard the ships of Star Cruises/Genting Hong Kong.

Book back-to-back seven-day cruises (on alternating eastern and western Caribbean itineraries, for example), and you'll probably find the same two or three production shows and the same acts on the second week of your cruise. The way to avoid seeing everything twice is to pace yourself.

Other entertainment

Most ships organize acts that, while not nationally known 'names', can provide two or three different

Movies under the stars aboard a Princess Cruises' *Grand*-class ship.

The cost of staging a show

Staging a lavish 50-minute production show can easily cost between $500,000 and $1 million, plus performers' pay, costume cleaning and repair, royalties, and so on. To justify that cost, shows must remain aboard for 18 to 24 months.

Some smaller operators see entertainment as an area for cost-cutting, so you could find yourself entertained by low-budget singers and bands.

shows during a seven-day cruise. These will be singers, illusionists, puppeteers, reality TV show wannabes, hypnotists, and even circus acts, with wide age-range appeal. Also, comedians who perform 'clean' material can find employment year-round on the cruise ship circuit. These popular comics enjoy good accommodation, are mini-stars while on board, and may go from ship to ship on a standard rotation every few days. There are raunchy, late-night 'adults only' comedy acts in some of the ships with younger audiences, but few have enough material for several shows. In general, the larger a ship, the broader the entertainment program will be.

Movies on deck

Showing movies on the open deck has been part of the cruise scene since the 1970s, when they were often classic black-and-white films shown at midnight. In those days, the screens were small, roll-down affairs, and the projectors were set up on makeshift pedestals. The result was often images that vibrated, and sound that quivered.

Speed forward into the 21st century. Many large resort ships now have huge outdoor poolside LED movie screens 300 sq ft (approximately 28 sq m) that cost around $1 million each. The screens are complemented by 50,000 to 80,000-watt sound systems for a complete 'surround the deck' experience.

Princess Cruises started the trend in 2004 aboard *Grand Princess* with its 'Movies Under the Stars' program, but now all companies with large resort ships have them. The experience is reminiscent of the old drive-in movies, the difference being that cruise lines often supply blankets and even popcorn free of charge.

Movies are shown throughout the day and evening. Aboard the family-friendly ships, they may

Illuminations Planetarium, *Queen Mary 2*.

include special films for junior cruisers. Big sports events such as the Super Bowl or World Cup soccer are also presented.

Smaller cruise ships, expedition cruise ships, and sail-cruise ships may have little or no entertainment. Aboard those ships, after-dinner conversation, reading, and relaxation become the entertainment of choice.

What's on

Entertainment onboard is listed in the 'daily program' – a mini-newspaper for the following day that is delivered to your suite/cabin each night when your bed is turned down. Any changes (due to bad weather, for example) are announced over the PA system.

Who's who in shipboard entertainment

Although production companies differ in their approach, the following gives some idea of the various people involved behind the scenes.

Executive producer. Transfers the show's concept from design to reality. First, the brief from the cruise line's director of entertainment might be for a new production show – the average being two major shows per seven-day cruise. After deciding on an initial concept, they then call in the choreographer, vocal coach, and musical arranger.

Choreographer. Responsible for auditioning the dancers and for creating, selecting, and teaching the routines.

Musical director. Coordinates all musical scores and arrangements; trains the singers in voice and microphone techniques, projection, accenting, phrasing, memory, and general presentation; and oversees session singers and musicians for the recording sessions.

Musical arranger. After the music has been selected, the musical arrangements must be made. This is a time-consuming task. Just one song can cost more than $2,000 for a single arrangement for a 12-piece orchestra.

Costume designer. Provides creative original designs for a minimum of seven costume changes in one show lasting 45 minutes. The costumes must also be practical, as they will be used repeatedly.

Costume maker. Buys all materials, and must be able to produce all required costumes in time for a show.

Graphic designer. Provides all the set designs, whether they are physical two- or three-dimensional sets for the stage, or photographic images created on slide film, video, laser disk, or other electronic media.

Lighting designer. Creates lighting patterns and effects for a production show. Sequences and action on stage must be carefully lit to the best advantage. The completed lighting plot is computerized.

Bands/musicians. Before the big production shows and artists can be booked, bands and musicians must be hired, often for long contracts. Big bands are often placed in some of the larger ships for special sailings, or for world cruises, on which ballroom dancing plays a large part. Most musicians work to contracts of about six months.

Spas and Wellness Facilities

The 'feel-good factor' is alive and well aboard the latest cruise ships, which offer a growing array of beauty salons and body-pampering treatments.

Land-based health spas have long provided a range of body treatments and services for those who wanted to escape the bustle of everyday life. Responding to the rise in popularity of 'wellness' breaks, today's cruise ships now have elaborate spas to rival those on land, where, for an extra fee, whole days of almost-continuous treatments are on offer. Once the domain of women, spas now cater almost as equally for men.

A ship's spa will help you to relax and feel pampered. Many people unaccustomed to spas may find some of the terminology daunting: aromatherapy, hydrotherapy, ionithermie, rasul, thalassotherapy. Spa staff will help you choose the massage or other treatment that best suits you and your needs. It's a good idea to visit the spa on embarkation day, when staff will be on hand to show you around, and answer your questions. Some cruise lines let you pre-book spa treatments online before your cruise. But take note of prices, which can quickly add up.

Pampering in *Disney Dream*'s Senses spa.

It's best to avoid booking massage treatments at a time when the ship is about to leave port (usually in the late afternoon/early evening), because there may be interruptive announcements, and noise and vibration from the propulsion machinery, particularly if the spa is located in the aft section of the ship.

Facilities

Large resort ships have a large ocean-view fitness facility; it may include saunas, steam rooms, rasul chamber, several body treatment rooms, thalassotherapy (saltwater) pool, relaxation area, changing/locker rooms, and a beauty salon. Some ships have acupuncture treatment clinics, and some have a built-in juice bar. Some offer a 'couples' experience, complete with 'spa suites' for rent by the day or half-day.

Thermal suites

Thermal suites are private areas that provide a combination of various warm scented rain showers, saunas, steam rooms, and thalassotherapy pools, with relaxation zones offering the promise of ultimate relaxation. Although most ships don't charge for use of the sauna or steam room, some make a per-day charge. Some ships even add a gratuity to a spa day pass, although it's supposed to be included. Some ships limit the number of people that can get a day pass, for example, aboard *Queen Elizabeth* and *Queen Victoria* the limit is 40 persons per day.

Personal spa suites

Each consists of a large room with floor-to-ceiling windows (one-way glass, of course), a heated floor, lots of space (about the size of three or four standard cabins), and plenty of towels. It has a two-person sauna, steam room, shower enclosure, two heated tiled relaxation loungers, two hydraulic massage tables, and, usually in one of its storage cupboards, a choice of massage oils. You can book therapists for treatments such as massage, manicure, pedicure, or facial – all in complete privacy.

A personal spa suite has herbal tea-making facilities and is bookable for a couple of hours, a half-day, or a full day – all at extra cost. Examples include AIDA Cruises and TUI Cruises.

Spa design

Many ship spas have Asian-themed decor, with warm woods and gently flowing water to provide a sooth-

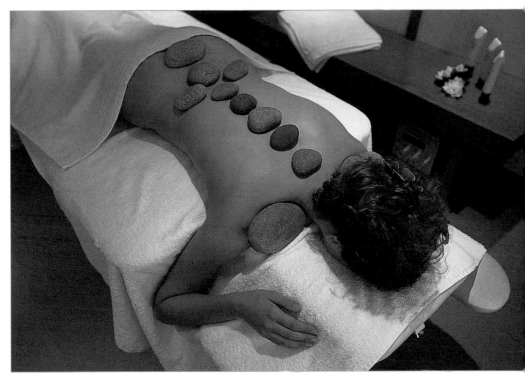

A hot stone massage aboard an AIDA cruise offers complete body relaxation.

ing atmosphere. Unfortunately, the spa reception areas are often a little too bright and in need of dimmers or mood lighting.

Pampering treatments

Stress-reducing and relaxation treatments are offered, combined with the use of seawater, which contains minerals, micronutrients, and vitamins. Massages might include Swedish remedial massage, shiatsu, and aromatherapy oils. You can even get a massage on your private balcony aboard some ships.

Having body-pampering treatments aboard a cruise ship can be wonderful, as the ship can provide a serene environment in itself; when enhanced by a massage or facial, the benefits can be even more therapeutic. Ship interior designers do, however, need to pay more attention not only to lighting dimmers but also to soundproofing, so that facilities can be used at all hours. Examples of poor soundproofing include treatment rooms aboard *Golden Princess* and *Grand Princess*, where they are located directly underneath a sports court. So, before you actually book your relaxing massage, find out whether the treatment rooms are quiet enough.

Unfortunately, treatments are usually available only until about 8pm, whereas some passengers would welcome being able to have a massage late at night before retiring to bed – the problem is that most shipboard spas are run by concessions, with wellbeing treated as a daytime-only event.

Some of the smaller, more upscale ships also offer 'Spa Days' with a whole day of body-pampering treatments, often termed 'wellness packages'. Expect to pay up to $500 a day *in addition to* the basic cruise fare.

Berlitz Tip: Check the daily program for 'port day specials' and packages that make the prices more palatable.

Fitness centers

A typical large resort ship spa will include a gymnasium, probably with ocean-view windows. Virtual-reality exercise machines are found in the techno-gyms aboard most large resort ships, with state-of-the-art muscle-pumping and body-strengthening equipment, universal stations, treadmills, bicycles, rowing machines, and free weights.

Most fitness centers are open only until early evening, although one exception is the Norwegian Cruise Line ships, whose gyms are open 24 hours a day. And if you've forgotten your workout clothes, you can probably purchase new items on board.

Typical exercise classes include aerobics (for beginners, intermediate, and advanced), high-intensity/low-impact aerobics, step aerobics, interval training, stretch and relax, super body sculpting, fab abdominals, sit and be fit, and walk-a-mile.

Group exercycling, kick-boxing, Pilates and yoga classes, body composition analysis, and sessions with a personal trainer will cost extra.

Massage

Having a massage aboard ship can be a real stress-busting experience, although if it's not right it can prove frustrating, and expensive.

Here are some favorite massage moments (always taken in the late afternoon or early evening, preferably just before sundown):

Aboard *Celebrity Constellation, Celebrity Infinity, Celebrity Millennium, Celebrity Summit*, on the balcony of a Sky Suite.

Aboard *Royal Clipper*, in a private massage hut on an outside deck.

Aboard *SuperStar Virgo*, on the floor of a junior suite bedroom.

Inside a beach cabana ashore on Castaway Cay or Half Moon Cay in the Bahamas, or as part of the beach, caviar, and champagne experience of ships such as *SeaDream I* and *II* in the British Virgin Islands.

Make appointments for a massage as soon as possible, so you can obtain the time and day of your choice. The cost averages $2 a minute. In some ships, massage may be available in your cabin (or on your private balcony), if it's large enough to accommodate a portable massage table.

Although it's easy to telephone and make an appointment for a massage or facial or two (some cruise lines let you do this online), do watch the cost. When you charge treatments to your onboard account, remember that gratuities are often added automatically, and these are typically 10–15 percent. Elixirs of youth, lotions and potions, creams, and scrubs – all are sold by therapists, typically at the end of your treatment, for you to use when you get home. But be warned, these are expensive items; beware of falling for subtle and flattering sales talk.

A whole range of treatments and styles has evolved from the standard Swedish Remedial Massage. The most popular are:

Swedish massage. Developed by Swedish physiologist Per Hendrik Ling in the 1830s, this is the most common form of massage today. There are four basic movements: effleurage (the stroking movements that benefit the circulation of lymphatic fluids and drainage), petrissage (the picking, kneading, rolling, and wringing movements), friction (the application of circular pressure), and tapotement (percussive tapping, flicking, and hacking movements that stimulate circulation). Long strokes are employed over your well-oiled body to reduce stress and to provide a feeling of relaxation for sore joints and muscles.

Ayurvedic head massage. Using warmed herbal oils, the therapist applies oil to the scalp, neck, and

A gym with a view on a Celebrity cruise.

Some RCI ships have a full-size boxing ring.

shoulders to stimulate circulation and nourish the hair – you'll need to wash your hair afterward, as it will be extremely oily. Shirodhara is the form of Ayurvedic medicine that involves gently pouring warm oil (made from tulsi, or holy basil) over the forehead. Ayurveda is a compound word meaning life and knowledge.

Chinese Tui Na. This is a therapeutic massage based on a diagnostic evaluation, manipulation of the joints and muscle fibers, and identification and prevention of wrong body postures, habits, and degenerative conditions.

Couples massage. Sometimes known as a 'duet massage', this is typically a 90-minute session for a couple that includes a hands-on lesson from a massage specialist on the art of massaging each other.

Hot stones massage. Between 24 and 36 smooth heated basalt volcanic stones of varying sizes are applied to key energy points of your oiled body to gently massage specific areas and muscles. The stones are then left in place while the therapist works on other parts of the body. The heat from the stones promotes a sense of deep relaxation. Cold stones may be used on the face, for their firming action.

Lomi-Lomi massage. This is a more rhythmic massage inspired by Hawaiian healing traditions that restore the free flow of 'mana' or life force; it is typically given using warm aromatherapy oils, and may be a two-hand or four-hand massage.

Lymphatic massage. This detox massage – developed in France in the 1930s is designed to improve circulation by releasing body toxins and nodes that build up in key lymphatic points. It is usually recommended for those who have poor circulation and can help deliver cellular waste.

Shiatsu massage. Originating in Japan, this means 'finger pressure', applied to the pressure points of the body as a preventative measure. It typically promotes a peaceful awareness of both body and mind, and is administered in a calm environment, without oil.

Sports massage. Typically provided by a male therapist, sports massage is a deep-tissue massage designed to unlock the kinks and knots.

Thai massage. Uses pressure points and stretching techniques employed by the therapist, using both hands and feet, to stretch and relax muscles, improve circulation, and reduce stress. It is usually carried out on a mat or thin mattress, which is laid out on the floor.

Underwater massage. You soak in a large tub of warm water, possibly with rose petals floating around you, while the therapist massages joints and muscles.

Ultimate massage. Two therapists provide a synchronized full body massage, using Swedish massage movements to provide the ultimate in stress-busting relief. However, it can be less than good, if the two therapists are even slightly out of sync.

Bamboo massage for two in the Cloud 9 spa on *Carnival Magic*.

Well-being massage. This puts more emphasis on effleurage movements, the use of complementary, warmed aromatic (aromatherapy) oils, and four-hand massage (two therapists working rhythmically in unison).

Recent variations of massage include a warm candle massage and a bamboo tamping treatment.

Other treatments

Although massage is the most popular shipboard spa treatment, some ships offer other body-pampering treatments such as facials, manicures, pedicures, teeth whitening, and acupuncture. Most are based on holistic Asian therapies. Some examples: *mandi lulur*, a scrub made from herbs, essential oils, and rice to soften the skin; *boreh*, a warm Balinese herb, rice, spice, galangal water, and oil body wrap for detoxification;

The spa will provide towels, robes, and slippers, but it's best to store valuables safely in your cabin prior to your appointment. Some spas offer disposable underwear for body treatments such as a Body Salt Glow or Seaweed Wrap.

Acupuncture. Used to prevent and remedy many maladies, this works by inserting super-fine needles into special points on the skin.

Halotherapy. One of the latest body detox treatments, this uses a Himalayan crystal salt bed for deep relaxation and body detoxing. It involves lying on a bed of 290lbs (130kg) of Himalayan salt crystals heated from 90 to 104 degrees Fahrenheit (32–40 degrees Celsius), and breathing in the salt-infused air. The salt contains 84 essential minerals as fine particles.

Moxibustion. This is a treatment that involves the insertion of hair-thin needles, dipped into mugwort (*Artemisa capillaris*), into one of the body's 1,100-plus acupuncture points. The mugwort may also be rolled into a cigar-shaped stick and burned above acupuncture points.

Body scrub

This treatment cleanses and softens the skin, and draws out impurities using aromatic oils, creams, lotions, and perhaps sea salt, together with exfoliation (removal of dead skin cells).

Body wrap

Often called a body mask, this treatment typically includes the use of algae and seaweeds applied to the whole body. The body is then covered in aluminum foil and blankets. There are many variations on this theme, using mud from the Dead Sea or the Mediterranean, or sea salt and ginger, or cooling cucumber and aloe, or combinations of herbs and oils that leave you with a warm glow. The aim is to detoxify, firm, and tone the skin, and reduce cellulite.

Dry flotation

This involves lying on a plush rubberized warm blanket on water, which gives the sensation of floating without getting wet. A therapist then gently massages your head and neck.

Facials

Aromatherapy facial. This treatment typically uses aromatic oils such as lavender, sandalwood, and geranium, plus a rejuvenating mask and accompanying creams and essences to 'lift' the skin and facial muscles.

Rejuvenation facial. This is typically a classic French facial, which utilizes the latest skin care products that may include essential plant and vitamin-rich oils. This facial aims to reduce lines and wrinkles.

Other popular treatments include eye lifting, volcanic mud masks, and manicures, possibly with a back and neck massage.

Rasul chamber

This is a steam chamber (Hammam) that is typically fully tiled, with a domed roof and Moorish decor. You paste yourself or your partner with three types of mud and sit down while gentle steam surrounds you. The various types of mud become heated and then you're in a mud bath, after which you rub yourself (or perhaps each other) with large crystals of rock salt.

Reflexology

The body's energy meridians exist as reflex points on the soles of the feet. The therapist uses thumb pressure to stimulate these points to improve circulation and restore energy flow throughout the body.

Teeth whitening

This treatment uses one of several methods, including bleaching strips, pen, gel, and laser bleaching. Carbomine peroxide, when mixed with water, forms hydrogen peroxide – the substance most used in teeth-whitening procedures. Power bleaching uses light energy to accelerate the process. Expect to pay about $200.

Thalassotherapy

The use of seawater to promote wellbeing and healing dates back to ancient Greece. Today, shipboard spas have whole bath rituals involving water and flower petals, herbs, or mineral salts.

Sample prices

Prices of body-pampering treatments have escalated recently and are now equal to the prices you would find at land-based spas in the US. You can expect to pay up to:
$200 for a 75-minute Hot stones massage
$125 for a 50-minute Wellbeing massage
$200 for a 75-minute Seaweed wrap
$125 for a 50-minute Reflexology session

Spa cuisine

Originally designed as low-fat, low-calorie meals for weight loss using grains, greens, and sprouts, spa cuisine now includes whole grains, seasonal fruits and vegetables, and lean proteins – ingredients low in saturated fats and cholesterol, low-fat dairy products, and reduced salt. They provide the basis for balanced nutrition and portion sizes, while maintaining some flavor, texture, and taste; foods are grilled rather than baked or fried.

Sports facilities

Sports facilities might include basketball, paddle tennis (a sort of downsized tennis court), and electronic golf simulators. Some boutique/small 'luxury' ships offer kayaking, water-skiing, jet skiing, and wake boarding for no extra charge. In reality, however, the water sports equipment is typically only used on one or two days (or part days) during a seven-day cruise.

Who runs the spas?

Aboard most ships, the spa and fitness areas are operated by a specialist concession, although each cruise line may have a separate name for the spa, such as AquaSpa (Celebrity Cruises), The Greenhouse Spa (Holland America Line), Lotus Spas (Princess Cruises), etc.

Aboard the large resort ships, spa staff tends to be young, enthusiastic 'therapists,' who will try hard to sell you own-brand beauty products, for a commission.

Steiner Leisure is the largest concession, operating spas aboard more than 100 ships. The company, founded in London in 1901 by Henry Steiner, began its ambitious growth in 1926, when Herman Steiner got involved in the family beauty salon on his father's death. He opened salons throughout England, became official cosmetician to the late Queen Elizabeth the Queen Mother, and won his first cruise ship contract in 1956.

The company closed its land-based salons in the 1990s, as its cruise ship business burgeoned. It bought Elemis, a lifestyle range of plant-based beauty products, and acquired Mandara Spas, which it has developed in the US alongside its Elemis Spas. In 2010 it bought The Onboard Spa Company.

Other spa concessions include: Blue Ocean (MSC Cruises); Canyon Ranch At Sea (Celebrity Cruises, Cunard, Oceania Cruises, and Regent Seven Seas Cruises); Carita, Espace Elegance; Flair (Louis, Voyages to Antiquity, Thomson); LivNordic (Viking Cruises); and Ocean Spa (Hapag-Lloyd, Tui Cruises, Voyages of Discovery).

Mini golf on *Norwegian Breakaway*.

Cruising for Families

Cruising can be a great vacation for families, but be sure to choose the right ship for your needs.

More than two *million* under-18s went on a cruise in 2015 – a figures that reflects just how well cruising suits children. Cruise ships provide a virtually crime-free, safe, contained environment, which is great for families. For younger kids, there are so many fun things to keep them entertained, while for the older ones, there's lots to do, plus they can enjoy a certain level of independence – something that always goes down well with teens. Meanwhile, parents can enjoy vacationing together as a family, as well as taking some time out. With everything – dining, entertainment, wellness facilities, etc. – being on tap and hugely accessible, it makes it so much easier to combine those things with parenting. And if the children are old enough to attend children's clubs, the parents really will have the opportunity to enjoy some 'me time.' Planning family vacations can be complicated, with so many things to think about. Here are the key things you need to know.

It goes without saying that you need to choose a family friendly ship. Generally speaking, the newest large resort ships have numerous dedicated spaces for children of all ages, as well as water parks and lots of neat things for active kids. Some cruise lines employ whole teams of counselors, who run special programs off-limits to adults; others may only have token family programs, with limited activities and only a couple of general staff allocated to look after children. Some ships provide children's programs and youth counselors only during the summer holidays, the Christmas holiday season, New Year, and Easter. Check whether the cruise line offers the right facilities for your needs at other times. Also note that although many ships have full programs for children during days at sea, these may be limited when the ship is in port. If the ship has a playroom, find out if it is open and supervised on all days of the cruise.

Cruise companies such as Carnival Cruise Line, Disney Cruise Line, Norwegian Cruise Line, Princess Cruises, and Royal Caribbean International provide pagers for parents; others provide them only for special-needs children. In-cabin telephones aboard some ships can be set to 'in-cabin listening,' allowing parents to call their cabin from any of the ships' telephones, and eavesdrop.

Most cruise lines give children colored bracelets, to be worn at all times. These identify which muster station they belong to in the event of an emergency, as well as showing which children are enrolled in which activity programs.

Some youth programs allow older children (usually 10 and older, but it varies by cruise line) to sign themselves out of youth centers, if authorized to do so by a parent. This makes it easy for children to meet family members somewhere else – by the pool or casual restaurant, for example – or to go back to the cabin. If authorization isn't granted, only designated adults can sign them out of programs, typically by showing some ID or by providing a password created at the beginning of the cruise.

Cruise lines expect parents to watch over their children when using a ship's swimming pools. Lifeguards are not generally provided, but Disney Cruise Line started providing trained lifeguards (not babysitters) at the family pool aboard its four ships during pool opening hours in 2013; perhaps other lines will follow.

Bear in mind that a ship's medical department isn't set up for pediatric services as cruise ship doctors are generalists.

If you book a cruise aboard one of the ships catering to more international passengers, such as Costa

Teaching kids how to draw Disney characters.

Carnival's Seuss-a-palooza parade.

Cruises, MSC Cruises, or Star Cruises, your young-sters may find themselves surrounded by children speaking other languages. This might be a little con-fusing to them at first, but in most cases it will prove to be an adventure in learning and communication that adds immensely to their vacation.

Age groups
Cruise lines generally divide young cruisers into distinct age groups. We put them into four groups: infants (3 months–up to 3 years); children (3–10); pre-teens (11–12); teens (13–17).

Cruising with babies and infants
Many new or recent parents want to take their babies with them when they cruise. Check the minimum age requirements for your chosen cruise line and itinerary; they vary according to the cruise, length, and region. By choosing the right ship, a cruise with baby should hopefully be much more enjoyable than many package holidays on land. The biggest attrac-tions include only having to pack and unpack the baby things only once, plus the convenience of hav-ing everything (food, entertainment, activities, etc.) absolutely on hand. There may also be a crèche/nurs-ery (see below), plus there's always room service, if you prefer to dine in your cabin.

Bottle warmers are available for babies, as are bottle sterilizers – upon request – so there's need to bring your own. Highchairs are also available upon request for meal times. For babies already on solids, menu items can be pureed and blended for them.

Check the ship's itinerary to see whether a ship docks alongside in each port. This is easier than be-ing at anchor, when shore tenders must be used – these may require you to go down a rigged ladder to a small boat waiting to take you ashore, which not so easy with an infant in tow.

Check with the cruise line or your travel agent before you book as to what equipment is avail-able, and whether any of it needs to be pre-booked. Some cruise ships will lend you cribs, strollers (some charge a rental fee), bouncy seats, books, toys, cots, and bed guards.

An inexpensive umbrella-type stroller will prove invaluable in airports, aboard ship (Carnival Cruise Line is one of few operators to offer them for rent aboard ship), and ashore. Small is better because it takes up less space in cabins, elevators, and self-serve buffet areas. It will be easier to maneuver at the cruise terminal, and for negotiating open deck areas aboard ship.

Consider taking a car seat for flights, buses and taxis, and a sling-style baby carrier for hands-free baby carrying when negotiating stairways, and for shore outings.

Request a crib as soon as possible (and book as early as you can), as ships carry only a limited num-ber of them. However, while it's fine to order cribs and camp beds, you'll soon find there's little room to move about, so go for as large a cabin as your budget allows. If you have a non-walker, consider a cabin with a balcony, as this will give more breathing space – you can relax on the balcony, while your infant has a nap in the cabin.

Disposable diapers (nappies), wipes, and sterilizing fluid can be purchased aboard most family-friendly ships, but they are expensive, so it's wise to bring your own supplies. If you are a Disney Cruise Line ship, you can order diapers and other products online at www.babiestravellite.com. These will be delivered to your cabin – so you can save valuable luggage space.

As for laundry, it's best to use the self-service launderette, if your ship has one – not all do, so this is another thing to check out before booking. Pack all-detergent sheets, as they are easier to transport than liquid detergent. Some ships have laundry 'bundles' (either all-you-can-bundle, or a set number of items, depending on the cruise line, into a provided laundry sack) for a special price, typically around $25.

You'll need to look after your child the whole time, unless you choose one of the large resort ships with a proper nursery and qualified staff to look after infants. Ships with a nursery for ages six months to 36 months include: *Allure of the Seas, Anthem of the Seas, Disney Dream, Disney Fantasy, Disney Magic, Disney Wonder, Oasis of the Seas,* and *Quantum of the Seas.* Ships with a free night nursery: *Azura, Britannia, Oceana, Queen Elizabeth, Queen Mary 2,* and *Queen Victoria.*

Children under three years old need to be potty-trained to take part in any group activities. Check with the cruise line whether babies and infants are allowed in paddling and swimming pools, and whether they must wear swim diapers.

Bear in mind that you may have to bathe infants/small children in a cabin with a small shower enclosure, possibly with a fixed-head shower; choosing a cabin with a bathtub makes it easier to do bathtime. Some ships (e.g. those of Costa Cruises) have baby baths available. Make sure you have adequate medical insurance, and take your infant's medical information in case of an emergency.

Minimum age accepted

It's important to check the minimum age requirements for your chosen cruise line and itinerary, because they can vary according to the cruise, length, and region. Here's our list of 12 principal cruise lines and the minimum age allowed for sailing, which was correct at time of going to press.

Carnival Cruise Line
Minimum sailing age: 6 months (12 months on transatlantic, Hawaii, and South America cruises).

Celebrity Cruises
Minimum sailing age: 6 months (12 months for transatlantic and transpacific and some South American cruises).

Costa Cruises
Minimum sailing age: 6 months.

Cunard Line
Minimum sailing age: 6 months (some sailings); 12 months for transatlantic and transpacific crossings, world cruise segments, and Hawaii cruises.

Disney Cruise Line
Minimum sailing age: 3 months.

Suggested packing lists for infants

Travelling by plane? Suggested items for your carry-on bag.
Diapers (or Pull-Ups), and changing pad.
Antibacterial wipes (take plenty).
Snacks.
Drinks (small).
Small toys and books to keep your infant happy.
Pacifiers and bibs (if your child still uses one).
A camera (or smart phone).
Suggested items for your checked luggage
Diapers/Pull-Ups and wipes, if your infant is not potty-trained.
Night-time diapers, if your infant is potty-trained.
Any toiletries your infant may need, including special baby soap and shampoo (these are not provided by cruise lines), lotions, sunscreen, toothbrush, and toothpaste.
Outlet plugs for childproofing.
Clothes.
Bibs.
Pacifiers.
Utensils and sip-cups.
First-aid kit and any medication such as pain relievers, fever reducers, and the name and contact details of your infant's pediatrician (for comfort).

Plastic bags for any snacks for shore excursions.
Ziplock bags – useful for soiled clothing.
Portable potty seat (if your infant is potty-trained).
Disposable diapers, deodorized disposal bags, and wipes.
Swim diapers.
Swim vest: make sure it's of an approved type.
Sunglasses and sun hat (if your cruise is in or to a warm weather area).
Bottles and sip cups: cruise lines don't provide these. They can be washed in your cabin, so a little dish detergent and bottle brush could be useful.
Formula: ready-to-feed variety is convenient but bulky. Or, bring powder and buy bottled mineral water from the ship's bar (a more expensive option).
Medication, such as pain relievers and fever reducers for babies, and the name and contact details of your child's pediatrician – just in case.
Inflatable toys such as beach balls and zoo animals are inexpensive and easy to pack (you won't be able to borrow toys from the ship's playroom).
Picture books to keep baby amused.

Fun design in *Europa 2*'s family apartments.

Holland America Line
Minimum sailing age: 12 months.
MSC Cruises
Minimum sailing age: 3 months.
Norwegian Cruise Line
Minimum sailing age: 6 months.
P&O Cruises
Minimum sailing age: 6 months (12 months for transatlantic cruises) aboard the family-friendly ships *Aurora, Azura, Britannia, Oceania,* and *Ventura*.
Princess Cruises:
Minimum sailing age: 6 months.
Royal Caribbean International:
Minimum sailing age: 6 months for many itineraries; 12 months for any cruises with three or more sea days, and for all transatlantic, transpacific, Hawaii and South Pacific cruises.
Star Cruises
Minimum sailing age: 6 months (note: any child whose travel document is attached to the parent's passport must travel with the accompanying parent).

Babysitting
If you do take baby (or babies) along, and you want some time to yourself, you'll need the services of a babysitter. Some, but not all, ships have babysitting services; some have restricted hours (meaning you'll need to be back by midnight like a grown-up Cinderella); and some have group babysitting, not in-cabin care. In some ships, stewards, stewardesses, and other staff may be available as private babysitters for an hourly charge. For example, *Queen Mary 2* has

children's nurses and English nannies. *Aurora, Azura, Britannia, Oceana,* and *Ventura* have a 'night nursery' for two- to five-year-olds.

Feeding infants under three
Selected baby foods are stocked by ships catering to infants, but ask your booking agent to get confirmation in writing that they'll be provided. Some cruise lines may even mash food up for your child, if you ask. If you need a special brand of baby food, advise your booking agent well in advance, or bring your own. Parents providing organic baby foods, such as those obtained from health food stores, should be aware that cruise lines buy their supplies from major general food suppliers and not from the smaller specialized food houses. You may need to check whether the ship has whole or soy milk available, for example.

Cruising with children ages 3–10
Assuming they don't get seasick, children of this age should love cruising. They love to get involved right from the planning stages, learning how big the ship is, what facilities it has on board, etc. All very exciting.

One thing to note, if your budget allows, and you think your young children will be happy at sea for this long, is that it's best to avoid cruises of fewer than seven days, because they tend to attract the party-going types out for a good time.

Once on board, go to the children's clubs and sign in your youngsters – you need to give their name, cabin number, and details of allergies to any foods or materials (this typically applies up to an age according to cruise line). You'll probably be given a pager in case you need instant contact. Children's activities are mostly about team participation events, so they may seem highly programmed to some youngsters used to getting their own way.

In addition to the clubs, there are plenty of other facilities on deck that will appeal to children of this age, from aqua parks to chill-out rooms to sports activities such as rope courses. Most large resort ships close their pools at 6pm, although those of MSC Cruises are exceptions to this – aboard *MSC Preziosa*, for example, a large, covered family pool is open until 9pm.

Barbie steps aboard
Mattel and Royal Caribbean International offer free Barbie-related activities in the Adventure Ocean youth club (ages four to 11 are the main consumers). There's also a Barbie Premium Experience ($349 per child), complete with special pink cabin decor and a free Barbie doll blanket, tote bag and toothbrush, a special tea with pink cupcakes and dainty dishes, and a mermaid dance class featuring dances from the movie *Barbie in a Mermaid Tale 2;* plus other perks.

Dr. Seuss, steps aboard, too

Not to be outdone – and a better bet for boys – Carnival Cruise Line's 'Seuss at Sea' program has a veritable array of immersive onboard youth, family, dining, and entertainment experiences featuring the amazing world and words of Dr. Seuss. The main dining room aboard each ship features 'The Green Eggs and Ham Breakfast' with the Cat in the Hat and Friends. Children (parents can go too) get to eat the playful foods from Dr. Seuss's imagination, notably green eggs and ham, moose juice and goose juice, fruit and pancake stacks, funky French toast, and more. (Note that traditional breakfast favorites are also available.) The dining room staff wear Dr. Seuss-inspired uniforms, and Dr. Seuss characters such as the Cat in the Hat, Thing One and Thing Two, and Sam join families at their tables for fun interaction and photo opportunities. This takes place on the first sea day of each cruise, and costs $5 per person.

In addition, there are Dr. Seuss-themed toys, games, and arts and crafts activities on board. Some ships have a Dr. Seuss Bookville Seuss-themed play space with iconic decor, colors, shapes, and funky furniture, where families get to relax. And movies such as The Cat in the Hat and Dr. Seuss's How the Grinch Stole Christmas are shown outdoors on Lido Deck Seaside Theater screens.

Carnival also introduced 'Seuss-a-palooza Story Time,' an interactive reading event that brings the colorful world and characters of Dr. Seuss to life for kids of all ages. It usually takes place inside a tent on the main showlounge stage on a sea day each cruise.

There's also a Character Parade and a swirly conga line that includes Dr. Seuss characters along the Promenade. Naturally, Dr. Seuss-themed retail items are also available.

Disney goes cruising

In 1998, Disney Cruise Line introduced the first of two large resort ships to cater for families with children, with cruises of three, four, and seven days. *Disney Magic* and *Disney Wonder* were joined by *Disney Dream* in 2011 and by *Disney Fantasy* in 2012. The casino-free ships have ambitious entertainment programs, with everything centered around Disney and its superb stable of famous characters. Disney has its own Art Deco passenger terminal at Port Canaveral, Florida, plus a fleet of special motorcoaches.

Each ship carries over 40 children's and youth counselors, plus lifeguards at the family pool. Families preparing to sail with toddlers under three can access online service to order baby supplies in advance of their cruise and have them delivered to their cabin. The service, exclusive to Disney Cruise Line, is provided by Babies Travel Lite (www.babiestravellite.com), an online retailer with more than 1,000 brand-name baby products including diapers, baby food, infant formula, and specialty travel items. The ships sail in the Caribbean, the Bahamas, Alaska, the Mediterranean, and the Baltic. Disney calls at its own 1,000-acre (400-hectare) private island on Bahamas and Caribbean cruises – about 50 miles (80km) north of Nassau in the Bahamas, Castaway Cay has its own ship docking pier. Locals say it had a military landing strip that was once used by drug runners. Beaches are divided into family-friendly and adults-only 'quiet' sections.

Why teens love cruising

After talking to teenagers and younger children aboard various cruise ships, I decided it was time to include a couple of quotes about how they enjoy cruising and their experiences.

Tabea M., from Berlin, a teenager travelling with her parents, said that *Sea Cloud II* was her first cruise experience – and a long-time dream for the family.

She said, 'I thought at first that it might be boring, because I am the only non-adult on board, but I found it to be completely the opposite.' What did she like most? Her reply, 'The friendly atmosphere, and the attention and caring service of the crew.' During the cruise (around Sicily and Italy's Aeolian Islands), she saw whales, and the volcano Stromboli erupting.

'The variety of food is amazing, and I enjoyed trying some of the non-alcoholic cocktails, too.'

'My favourite place on board is the Blue Lagoon' (lying down on the blue mattresses at the ship's stern watching the stars at night, or sunbathing during the day). She also loved watching the sailors climbing the masts, unfurling the sails on sea days, and talking to the navigation officers on the bridge. 'I expected to find more electronic machinery, but I was pleasantly surprised to find that a lot of traditional instruments are used.'

Tabea's eyes lit up when I asked her where she would like to go next. Without hesitation, she replied, 'the Caribbean, and through the Panama Canal – aboard *Sea Cloud* or *Sea Cloud II*.'

Jens S. (in his early teens, Jens has sailed for more than 200 cruise days aboard some very nice ships), from Copenhagen, Denmark, says: 'I really like cruise vacations, because they are a lot more fun than staying at a hotel. You get to see several places and nice beaches, and the staff are always kind and smiling.'

'It's exciting to sail, especially when you see dolphins and whales. And in the restaurants you can get all your favorite meals, and desserts, and even extra portions if you want (my favorite dessert is Chocolate Fondant). If you want popcorn or a hamburger – or almost anything – you just order it from room service and it comes free!'

'I have been lucky enough to be invited to the bridge several times – some captains let me sound the horn. Now I have started a collection of plaques from the ships I sail with. My favorite ship is *Silver Wind*, because it sails to so many nice areas of the world, and the captain and I have become good friends. But I also like *SeaDream I*. But my favorite trip of all is a transatlantic crossing aboard *Queen Mary 2*. My ultimate Christmas present, however, is going to be a cruise aboard *Europa 2*. Please, dad…'

Basketball on a Carnival ship.

Cruising with older children (pre-teens 11–12)

Some cruise lines provide extra attention for the 'Tweens.' Supervised group activities and activity/ play centers mean that parents won't have to be concerned, and will be able to enjoy themselves, knowing that their children are in good hands, enrolled in special programs. Activities typically include make-up and cookery classes, arts and crafts projects, group games, interactive computer programs, character parades and scavenger hunts, and watching movies and video wall programming. Then there are the outdoor activities such as water slides, miniature golf, and swimming and other sports events for the pre-teens.

Cruising with teenagers (13–17)

Teens love cruising, too, and many large resort ships have dedicated 'no adults allowed' zones and chill-out rooms. Teens-only activities include deck parties, pool parties, sports tournaments, poolside games, karaoke, discos, dances, computer games, video arcades, activity clubs, and talent shows. Some ships provide musical instruments for jam sessions (Royal Caribbean International, for example). Sports activities include rock-climbing, rollerblading, basketball, and riding the wave surfer.

With some cruise lines the fun can extend ashore, with beach barbecues. There's usually almost unlimited food, too, although some of it may not be very nutritious.

Choosing the right cabin

Cruise lines know that 'families who play together want to stay together.' Although connecting cabins and Pullman beds are nothing new on family-friendly ships, brands such as Disney Cruise Line, Norwegian Cruise Lines, and Royal Caribbean International have taken group-friendly accommodations more seriously than some others.

Families cruising together often find that sharing a confined space causes the most distress. It's best to choose the largest accommodation option you can afford. Before booking, check the size of the cabin and pace it out at home, remembering that the size quoted on ship deck plans includes the bathroom. If you have a large or extended family, cabins with interconnecting doors may be more practical.

Certain ships may work best for certain age groups. For example, multigenerational groups might consider large resort ships such as Royal Caribbean International's *Allure of the Seas* or *Oasis of the Seas* or

Safety tips at sea

In case children get lost or separated from their parents, most cruise lines provide them with colored wristbands, which must be worn at all times. Disney Cruise Line has 'Mickey Bands' – magic bracelets that use radio tracking to locate the exact whereabouts of children at any time.

Young children love to climb, so don't ever leave them on a balcony alone. On the open decks, ships have railings – these are either horizontal bars through which children cannot get their heads, or they are covered in glass/ plexiglass under a thick wooden top rail.

While children find their way around easily, walk with them between the playroom/activity and your cabin, so that all of you are more familiar with the route.

Discuss safety issues with them, and, with children old enough to read, warn them not to walk into 'Crew Only' areas at any time.

Children's lifejackets are available aboard most cruise ships that carry children. However, check your cabin as soon as you embark. If no child's or infant's life vests are provided, see your steward right away.

Disney Cruise Lines ships because of their wide range of facilities and eateries.

If you are a large family, some ships (such as those of Norwegian Cruise Line) have family cabins and suites that can sleep up to 14. Larger cabins or suites simply have more space than standard cabins, and may include sofa beds.

If you are traveling with teens, consider booking them an adjoining cabin or one across the hallway from yours. You get your own space, and your teens will have their own bathroom and privacy. You give them freedom, but at arm's length. If your children are younger, a cabin with an interconnecting door would be a good option, if the budget allows. Many ships have cabins with two lower beds and one or two upper berths. In some cabins, the two lower beds can't be pushed together to form a queen-size bed for parents. This means mom and dad and one or two children all have separate beds. Some ships, such as *Disney Dream, Disney Fantasy, Disney Magic, Disney Wonder,* and *Norwegian Epic,* have cabins with two bathrooms, as well as a privacy curtain to screen off your youngsters.

Dependent on how young your children are (and how safe you feel this would be), you might like to opt for a cabin with a balcony. An interior (no-view) cabin may be adequate for a short cruise, but could be claustrophobic on a longer one. To get access to fresh air without a balcony, you'd have to keep trudging up to the open deck, carrying towels and other paraphernalia. On the other hand, if you don't anticipate spending much time in your cabin, an interior (no-view) cabin is cheaper, but the storage space limitations will probably prove really frustrating.

Try to book an *assigned* cabin rather than a *guaranteed* cabin; the latter means that only the space within a specific category is *guaranteed* for you – the room and bed configuration may not be the one you want.

On the look-out for icebergs.

Children's fares

Children under two travel free on most cruise lines and airlines (aboard MSC Cruises, kids under 12 sail free, paying only port taxes). If they're older, however, you have to pay. Most cruise lines offer special rates for children sharing their parents' cabin. The cost is often lower than third and fourth person share rates.

Although many adult cruise rates include airfare, most children's rates don't. Also, although some lines say children sail 'free,' they must pay port taxes as well as airfare. The cruise line should be able to get the airfare at the best rate.

Dining with children

Flexibility is the key. Coaxing children out of a pool, getting them dressed and ready to sit quietly through a four-course dinner every night can be tough. Work out a compromise by eating dinner together occasionally at the buffet. Most ships offer a tempting

---

Ships that cater well for children

These ships have been selected for the quality of their children's programs and facilities:

Aida Cruises: *AIDAbella, AIDAblu, AIDAluna, AIDAmar, AIDAprima, AIDAsol, AIDAstella*

Carnival Cruise Line: *Carnival Breeze, Carnival Conquest, Carnival Dream, Carnival Freedom, Carnival Glory, Carnival Legend, Carnival Liberty, Carnival Magic, Carnival Pride, Carnival Spirit, Carnival Splendor, Carnival Sunshine, Carnival Triumph, Carnival Valor, Carnival Victory*

Celebrity Cruises: *Celebrity Constellation, Celebrity Eclipse, Celebrity Equinox, Celebrity Infinity, Celebrity Millennium, Celebrity Reflection, Celebrity Solstice, Celebrity Summit*

Costa Cruises: *Costa Atlantica, Costa Deliziosa, Costa Diadema, Costa Fascinosa, Costa Favolosa, Costa Fortuna, Costa Luminosa, Costa Magica, Costa Mediterranea, Costa Pacifica, Costa Serena*

Cunard Line: *Queen Elizabeth, Queen Mary 2, Queen Victoria*

Disney Cruise Line: *Disney Dream, Disney Fantasy, Disney Magic, Disney Wonder*

MSC Cruises: *MSC Divina, MSC Fantasia, MSC Preziosa, MSC Splendida*

Norwegian Cruise Line: *Norwegian Breakaway, Norwegian Epic, Norwegian Getaway, Norwegian Star*

P&O Cruises: *Aurora, Azura, Britannia, Oceana, Ventura*

Princess Cruises: *Crown Princess, Diamond Princess, Emerald Princess, Golden Princess, Grand Princess, Regal Princess, Royal Princess, Ruby Princess, Sapphire Princess, Star Princess*

Royal Caribbean International: *Adventure of the Seas, Allure of the Seas, Anthem of the Seas, Explorer of the Seas, Freedom of the Seas, Independence of the Seas, Liberty of the Seas, Mariner of the Seas, Navigator of the Seas, Oasis of the Seas, Quantum of the Seas, Voyager of the Seas*

Star Cruises: *SuperStar Virgo*

TUI Cruises: *Mein Schiff 1, Mein Schiff 2, Mein Schiff 3, Mein Schiff 4*

menu of children's favorites, and some ships have special mealtimes for children.

Children with special needs

If a child has special needs, advise the cruise line before you book. Children needing one-to-one care or assistance must be accompanied by a parent or guardian when in the children's play center.

Practical matters: passports

Note that separate passports are required for all children traveling internationally. If you have an *adopted* child, you may also need Adoption Placement Papers, as well as the child's Birth Certificate.

Confirming a guardian's identity

A Parent and Guardian Consent Form (PGCSA) will be needed at or before embarkation, if you are a grandparent, parent, or guardian with a passport surname different from that of any child traveling with you. Without this form, which includes passport information of the child's legal parent, you will be denied boarding. Check with your cruise provider if you are unclear.

Single parents

A few cruise lines have introduced their versions of the 'Single Parent Plan' (e.g., Disney Cruise Line, P&O Cruises). This offers an economical way for single parents to take their children on a cruise, with parent and one child, sharing a two-berth cabin, or parent with more children, sharing a three- or four-berth cabin. Reduced rates may apply to children of single parents in the same cabin.

As a single parent with just one child, you may have to pay for two adults (double occupancy), so it's important to check the pricing policy of each cruise line you're interested in. It may also be better to take an adult friend and share the cost (in some cases, your child could travel free).

Family reunions and birthdays

A cruise can provide the ideal place for a family get-together, with or without children, and, because it's an almost all-inclusive vacation, you won't have to haggle about who pays for the extras.

With pricing that includes accommodations, meals, entertainment, use of most of the ship's recreational facilities, and travel from destination to destination, a cruise represents good value for money. Cruise lines also make special offers to groups. Let your travel agent make the arrangements, and ask for a group discount if there are more than 15 of you.

Family groups may have the option to ensure even greater value by purchasing everything in advance, from cruise fares to shore excursions, drinks packages, spa packages, and pre-paid gratuities. Additional savings can be realized through reduced fares for third and fourth passengers in each cabin, and some cruise lines offer 'kids sail free' programs.

Formal nights

Some ships have nights when traditional 'formal attire' is the required dress code. If you don't want

Junior chefs of Princess Cruises.

your children to dress formally (although some children really enjoy getting dressed up – it's a bit like going to a birthday party or prom night), you can opt out of the festivities, and simply head for one of the casual dining options. Or your kids may prefer to opt out and go to the children's clubs or teen rooms and hang out while you go to the captain's cocktail party.

Tips for cruising with children

Take wet wipes for those inevitable clothes stains, and anti-bacterial hand wipes and face wipes to keep you cool when it's hot outside.

Take a highlighter pen – good for marking the daily program and shore excursion literature, so you can focus on what's important to you and the children.

Take an extension cord or power strip (although note that not all cruise lines allow them), because there will be plenty of things to plug in (chargers for games consoles, mobile phone, and iPod/iPad, etc.). Most cabins provide only one electrical outlet.

Use plastic compression bags for packing clothes (squeezing or vacuuming the air out). They help keep clothes fresh, and make it easier to sort out when you return home

Wide-mouth water bottles (empty until you are on board ship) are useful for shore excursions, beach days, and other outings.

A pop-up laundry basket could prove useful for keeping everyone's dirty laundry separate from clean items (really useful in small cabins).

Take lots of high factor sunscreen (SPF50 or above).

A set of walkie-talkie radios can prove useful for keeping track of everyone's whereabouts – if everyone remembers to turn them on!

Glow sticks – kids love them – for use as night lights (they are cheap and come in different colors – one for each night).

Shore excursions

When going ashore, remember that if you want to take your children swimming or to the beach, it is wise to telephone ahead to a local hotel with a beach or pool. Many hotels will be happy to show off their property to you, hoping to gain your future business.

Ropes course on *Norwegian Breakaway*.

Some cruise ships in the Caribbean have the use of a 'private' island for a day, including waterpark areas for children and adults. A lifeguard will be on duty, and there will be water-sports and snorkeling equipment you can rent. Operators take advantage of the

---

Ships that cater well to infants

Disney Cruise Line: *Disney Dream, Disney Fantasy, Disney Magic, Disney Wonder*
P&O Cruises: *Aurora, Azura, Britannia, Oceana, Ventura*
Royal Caribbean International: *Adventure of the Seas, Allure of the Seas, Explorer of the Seas, Freedom of the Seas, Independence of the Seas, Liberty of the Seas, Mariner of the Seas, Navigator of the Seas, Oasis of the Seas, Quantum of the Seas, Voyager of the Seas*
Star Cruises: *SuperStar Virgo*

Cruising when pregnant

In 2010, a 30-year-old passenger on a four-night Baja cruise aboard *Carnival Paradise* gave birth on board to a premature baby. Both mother and baby were transported from the ship to a local hospital near San Diego, and the ship continued to its home port of Long Beach, California.

It can happen. Nevertheless, if your pregnancy is routine and healthy, there's no reason not to go on a cruise, assuming you are within the normal travel limits for pregnant women. Indeed, a cruise could be a great getaway before you deal with the things associated with an upcoming childbirth. First, ask about any restrictions imposed by your chosen cruise line. Some cruise lines may let you sail even in your 27th week of pregnancy, most will not accept you if you have entered your 24th week. You may be required to produce a doctor's note. (You may wish to check with your doctor or midwife that you are safe to travel, prior to sailing, anyway.)

Be sure to purchase travel insurance that will cover you for last-minute cancellation and medical treatment due to pregnancy complications, both on board and in ports of call.

captive market, so rental of beach and water-sports items can be very expensive.

It's best not to book a long shore excursion if you have an infant, unless you know he/she can handle it. Diaper-changing facilities are likely to be limited (and non-existent on buses).

How grandparents can bridge the generation gap

Many children love to go cruising with grandparents, perhaps because they anticipate fewer restrictions than they have at home. And busy parents like the idea, too, particularly if the grandparents make a contribution to the cost.

Having enrolled their grandchildren in age-related groups for daytime activities aboard ship (note the limitations on activities for children under three, as mentioned above), grandparents will be able to enjoy the adults-only facilities, such as the wellness and spa treatments. Not surprisingly, it's the large resort ships that provide the widest choice of facilities for both age groups. For those not averse to ubiquitous cartoon characters, Disney Cruise Line provides some facilities for adults and children in separate areas, but also allows them to mix in others.

Before you leave home

Grandparents should remember that, in addition to their grandchildren's passports, they should also bring along a letter signed by the parent authorizing any necessary medical attention. A Parent and Guardian Consent Form (PGCSA) will be needed at or before embarkation, if you are a grandparent (or parent or guardian) with a passport surname different from that of any child traveling with you. Check with your cruise provider about this.

Ground rules should be established with a child's parent(s) present to avoid potential problems. An important issue is whether a child will be allowed to roam the ship unsupervised, given that some cruise lines allow children as young as eight to sign themselves out of supervised programs. Walkie-talkies are a good solution to this issue. They work well aboard ships, and allow adults and children to stay in constant touch.

On board

Most cruise lines offer scheduled activities from 9am to noon, 2–5pm, and 7–10pm. This means you can drop your grandchild off after breakfast, relax by the pool, go to a lecture, or take part in other activities, and pick them up for lunch. After a couple of hours together, they can rejoin their friends, while you enjoy an afternoon movie or siesta.

Shore excursions

Consider your grandchild's interests before booking expensive shore excursions (example: flightseeing in Alaska). It's also best to avoid long bus rides, shopping trips, and scenic tours, and better to choose excursions that feature water and/or animals. Examples include snorkeling, aquariums, or nature walks. Remember to pack snacks. In some ports, it may be better to explore on your own. If your grandchildren are really young, full-day shore excursions are a probably bad idea.

A family goes snorkeling in the Caribbean.

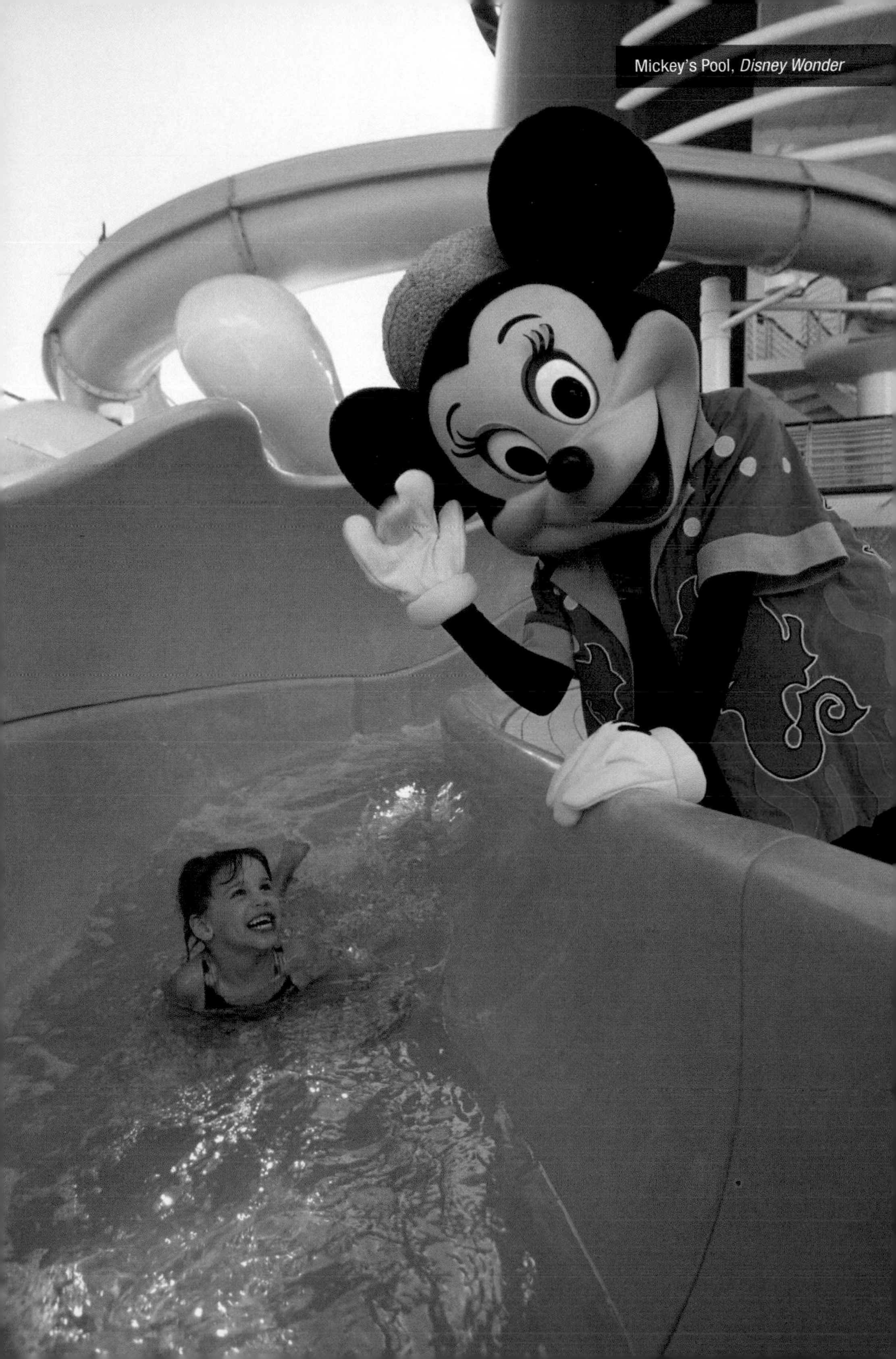

Mickey's Pool, *Disney Wonder*

Cruising for Seniors

People everywhere are living longer and healthier lives, and cruise lines are keen to cater to their particular needs.

Although cruise lines have been striving, with some success, to embrace all age groups, the over-60s remain an important segment of the market. Group cruising for seniors, in fact, is growing in popularity and is a good way for like-minded people to vacation together. Nowhere is this more evident than in Japan's 'Golden Week', a collection of four national holidays within seven days in late April/ early May, when seniors clamor for available cabins.

One trend for seniors is toward longer cruises – even round-the-world cruises, if they can afford them. Some opt for an adults-only ship such as *Magellan* (CMV), *Adonia, Arcadia,* or *Oriana* (P&O Cruises) or *Saga Sapphire* (Saga Cruises), for example. There are bargains to be had, too. Organizations for seniors such as AARP (American Association of Retired Persons) in the US and Saga in the UK often offer discount fares and upgrades.

Some seniors who may have had major surgery or have mobility problems cannot fly, or don't wish to, are helped by the 'Homeland Cruising' trend,

Making new friends aboard *Oasis of the Seas*.

which enables them to embark at and disembark from a nearby port in their home country. In the US, the number of homeland ports increased dramatically following the terrorist attacks of September 2001. In the UK, some cruise ships sail from ports in both the north and south of the country. The same is true elsewhere, as language-specific cruise lines and ships proliferate.

But all is far from perfect. Some cruise lines have yet to recognize that, with seniors as with other groups, one size does *not* fit all. Only a few, for example, take the trouble to provide the kind of items that millions of seniors need, such as large-print editions of daily programs, menus, and other printed matter.

Special diets

While the wide range of cuisine aboard many ships is a big attraction, cruise lines understand that many passengers are on special diets. Lighter menu options are available aboard most ships, as well as vegetarian and vegan choices. Options include low sodium, low fat, low cholesterol, and sugar-free entrées (main courses) and desserts. A booking agent will ensure that special dietary needs are recorded.

Healthier eating

You don't have to put on weight during a cruise. Many health-conscious seniors prefer smaller portions of food with taste and nutritional value rather than the overflowing plates.

Heart-healthy diets are in demand, as are low-fat, low-carbohydrate, salt-free, or low-salt foods. Denture wearers often request food that includes softer items.

Those seeking lighter fare should be aware that most cruise lines have an 'always available' section of heart-healthy items that can be cooked plainly, such as grilled or steamed salmon, skinless chicken breast, lean sirloin steak, or baked potatoes.

Gentlemen hosts

Because more female than male seniors cruise, cruise lines have developed 'gentlemen host' programs. These are gentlemen, typically over 55 years of age, selected for their social skills and competence as dance partners, for dining table conversation, and for accompanying passengers on shore excursions.

Cruise lines with gentlemen hosts include: Celebrity Cruises, Crystal Cruises, Cunard Line, Holland America Line, P&O Cruises, Princess Cruises, Regent Seven Seas Cruises, Seabourn, Silversea Cruises, Swan Hellenic Cruises, Voyages of Discovery Cruises, and Voyages to Antiquity.

Enrichment programs

Many seniors want to learn about a destination's history and culture rather than be told which shops to visit ashore. Lecturers of academic quality are found aboard some smaller ships such as *Aegean Odyssey* (Voyages to Antiquity), *Minerva* (Swan Hellenic Cruises), and *Saga Sapphire* (Saga Cruises). Some lines, such as Crystal Cruises, have special-interest lecturers on topics such as archaeology, food and wine, ornithology, and military history.

Tips for seniors

If you're traveling solo, it's important to check the price of any single supplements.

If you take medication, make sure you have enough with you. Some ships have a dress-up code, while some are casual. Choose a ship according to your own lifestyle and tastes.

If you have mobility difficulties, choose one of the newer ships that have public rooms with an 'open-flow' style of interior design. Examples include *Arcadia, Balmoral, Eurodam, Magellan, Nieuw Amsterdam, Oosterdam, Queen Elizabeth, Queen Mary 2, Queen Victoria, Westerdam,* and *Zuiderdam.* Older ships, such as *Marco Polo,* have 'lips' or doors between public rooms.

Lecture aboard *Minerva.*

Best facilities

Among the cruise lines that provide the facilities and onboard environment that seniors tend to enjoy most are: American Cruise Lines, Azamara Club Cruises, Blount Small Ship Adventures, Crystal Cruises, Fred. Olsen Cruise Lines, Hebridean Island Cruises, Holland America Line, Noble Caledonia, Oceania Cruises, P&O Cruises, Pearl Seas Cruises, Regent Seven Seas Cruises, Saga Cruises, Sea Cloud Cruises, Seabourn, Silversea Cruises, Swan Hellenic Cruises, Voyages of Discovery, and Voyages to Antiquity.

Why seniors like cruising – but can often find it frustrating

Thumbs up

A cruise is an excellent choice for those who like to be independent while having the chance to meet other like-minded people.

Cruising is stress-free and relaxing. You don't have to keep packing and unpacking as you do on a land-based tour.

It's safe. You travel and dine in comfort and safety, while your floating hotel takes you to a choice of around 2,000 destinations all over the world.

Lecturers and lessons in everything from golf to computing provide a chance to learn something new.

There's plenty of entertainment – shows, cinema, casinos, games, dances.

All main and self-serve buffet meals are included in the fare, and those passengers on special diets can be easily accommodated.

Senior singles, in particular, find it easy to meet others in a non-threatening environment. Some ships provide male dance hosts, screened and subject to a strict code of ethics, who can also act as escorts on shore excursions.

Most ships have 24-hour room service and a 24-hour reception desk.

Passengers with disabilities can find ships that cater to their needs.

Ships carry a medical doctor and one or more trained nurses. In an emergency, treatment can be arranged.

Thumbs down

Online check-in procedures, and unreadable Passenger Ticket Conditions and Contracts that are provided only online.

Credit card-size electronic key cards to cabins – it is often unclear with these which end to insert, especially for passengers with poor eyesight.

Booking events and meals via the in-cabin 'interactive' television/keypad system; it is user-unfriendly for many seniors. All services should be readily accessible via the telephone.

Poor, difficult-to-read signage such as 'You are here' deck plans unreadable from farther away than an inch (2.5cm).

Menus with small, hard-to-read typefaces, and daily programs that require a magnifying glass.

Buffets with plates only, requiring several visits, and cutlery too heavy to hold comfortably.

Anything that requires a signature – for example: bar, shore excursions, spa bills with small print.

Libraries with few books, if any, in large-print format – notably recent novels.

The absence of a 'concierge' for seniors.

Public toilets not clearly marked.

The lack of music-free lounges and bars for conversation and drinks.

Cruising for Romantics

No need to worry about getting to the church on time – you can be married at sea, get engaged, renew your vows, or enjoy a second honeymoon.

Two classic TV shows, *The Love Boat* (US) and *Traumschiff* (Germany), boosted the concept of cruising as a romantic vacation, the natural culmination of which would be getting married at sea – the ultimate 'mobile wedding.' Such ceremonies have become such big money-earners that, after 171 years, Cunard Line changed the registry of its three ships in 2011 from its traditional home port of Southampton to Hamilton, Bermuda, partly because its British registry didn't allow it to perform weddings at sea. As a result, couples can now say 'I do' aboard *Queen Mary 2* in the middle of the North Atlantic; the first such wedding was in May 2012.

Saying 'I do' aboard ship

This increasingly popular option includes a honeymoon conveniently in the same location and a 'wedding planner,' who can sort out all the nitty-gritty details such as arranging flights, hotels, transportation, and packages. For the bride, spa and beauty services are immediately on hand, unlike on land, and you literally can sail into the sunset after the reception.

Check first in your country of domicile whether such a marriage is legal, and ascertain what paperwork and blood tests are needed. It is up to you to prove the validity of such a marriage. The captain could be held legally responsible if he has married a couple not entitled to be wed.

It's relatively easy to get wed aboard almost any cruise ship when it's alongside in port. Carnival Cruise Line, Celebrity Cruises, Costa Cruises, Holland America Line, Princess Cruises, and Royal Caribbean International, among others, offer special wedding packages. These include the services of a minister to marry you, wedding cake, Champagne, bridal bouquet and matching boutonnière for the bridal party, a band to perform at the ceremony, and an album of wedding pictures. Note that US citizens and 'green card' residents may need to pay sales tax on wedding packages.

Asuka Cruise, Azamara Club Cruises, Celebrity Cruises, Cunard Line, P&O Cruises, Princess Cruises, Royal Caribbean International, and Sea Cloud Cruises offer weddings aboard their ships. The ceremonies can be performed by the captain, who is certified as a notary, when the ships' registry – Bermuda, Japan, or Malta, for example – recognizes such unions. Japanese citizens can also be married at sea aboard one of the Japan-registered cruise ships such as *Asuka II*.

Expect to pay about $3,000 (Sea Cloud Cruises, from €1,995), plus about $500 for licensing fees. Harbor-side or shore-side packages vary according to the port.

Even if you don't get married aboard ship, you could have your wedding reception aboard one. Contact the director of hotel services at the cruise line. The cruise line will go out of its way to help, especially if you follow the reception with a honeymoon cruise – and a cruise, of course, also makes a fine, worry-free honeymoon.

UK-based passengers should know that P&O Cruises hosts a series of cruises called the 'Red-Letter Anniversary Collection' for those celebrating 10, 15, 20, 25, 30, 35, 40, 45, 50, 55, or 60 years of marriage. The cruise comes with a complimentary gift, such as a brass carriage clock, leather photograph album, or free car parking at Southampton.

Welcome champagne on a Silversea cruise.

Getting married ashore

An alternative is to have a marriage ceremony in an exotic destination with your reception and honeymoon aboard ship afterwards. For example, you could get married on the beach in Barbados or Hawaii; on a glacier in Juneau, Alaska; in a villa in Rome or Venice; in an authentic Tahitian village; in Central Park, New York; or on Disney's Castaway Cay in the Bahamas, with Mickey and Minnie at hand. Note that your marriage license must be from the jurisdiction in which you will be married. If you set your heart on a Bermuda beach wedding, for example, the license to marry must be obtained in Bermuda, no matter what your nationality is.

Carnival Cruise Line's wedding packages, available both aboard ship on embarkation day or in tropical ports of call, are immensely popular, with more than 2,600 ceremonies performed each year. Carnival's packages start at $1,355.

Getting engaged aboard ship

For those who aren't quite ready to tie the knot, Princess Cruises has a special 'Engagement Under the Stars' package that allows you to propose to your loved one in a personal video that is then screened just before an evening movie at a large outdoor screen aboard some of the company's ships. Current cost: $695.

Renewal of vows

Many cruise lines perform 'renewal of vows' ceremonies. A cruise is a wonderful setting for reaffirming to one's partner the strength of commitment. A handful of ships have a small chapel where this ceremony can take place; otherwise, it can be anywhere aboard ship – a most romantic time is at sunrise or sunset on the open deck. The renewal of vows ceremony is conducted by the ship's captain, using a non-denominational text.

Although some companies, such as Carnival Cruise Line, Celebrity Cruises, Cunard Line, Holland America Line, P&O Cruises, and Princess Cruises,

A honeymoon couple enjoy being pampered aboard a MSC Cruises ship.

have complete packages for purchase, which include music, Champagne, hors d'oeuvres, certificate, corsages for the women, and so on, most other companies do not charge – yet.

Cruising for honeymooners

There are many advantages in honeymooning at sea: you pack and unpack only once; it is a hassle-free and safe environment; and you get special attention, if you want it. It is easy to budget in advance, as one price often includes airfare, cruise, food, entertainment, several destinations, shore excursions, and pre- and post-cruise hotel stays. Also, some cruise lines offer discounts if you book a future cruise to celebrate an anniversary.

Although no ship as yet provides real bridal suites, many ships have suites with king- or queen-size beds. Some also provide tables for two in the dining room, should you wish to dine together without having to make friends with others. A variety of honeymoon packages are available; these might include Champagne and caviar for breakfast, flowers in the suite or cabin, a complimentary cake, and a private captain's cocktail party.

Some cruise ships have Sunday departures, so couples can plan a Saturday wedding and reception before traveling to their ship. Pre- and post-cruise hotel accommodation can also be arranged.

Most large resort ships can accommodate honeymoon couples well. However, couples averse to crowds might try one of the smaller cruise ships such as those of Regent Seven Seas Cruises, Seabourn, Sea Cloud Cruises, Silversea Cruises, or Windstar Cruises.

And for quiet moments? The deck to the forward part of a ship, near the bridge, is the most dimly lit part and the quietest – except perhaps for some wind noise.

Practical tips for honeymooners

Remember to take a copy of your marriage license or certificate, for immigration (or marriage) purposes, as your passports will not yet have been amended. Since you may well wish to share a large bed with your partner, check with your travel agent and cruise line to make sure the cabin you have booked has such a bed. Better still, book a suite if you can afford to. It's important to check and double-check to avoid disappointment.

If you plan to combine your honeymoon with getting married along the way – in Hawaii or Bermuda, for example – and need to take your wedding gown aboard, there's usually space to hang it in the dressing room next to the stage in the main showlounge, especially aboard the large resort ships.

Cruising for Solo Travelers

Cruise prices are geared toward couples.
Yet about one in four cruise passengers travels
alone or as a single parent. How do they fare?

Cruising, in general, is designed for couples. Many solo passengers (including GLBT – gay, lesbian, bisexual, and transgender) feel that cruising penalizes them, because most lines charge them a single-occupancy supplement. The reason is that the most precious commodity aboard any ship is space. Since a solo-occupancy cabin is often as large as a double and is just as expensive to build, cruise lines feel the premium price is justified. What's more, because solo-occupancy cabins are at a premium, they are less likely to be discounted. However, it's good to see that companies including Cunard Line and P&O Cruises are building or retrofitting solo-occupancy cabins into their ships.

Single supplements

If you are not sharing a cabin, you'll be asked to pay either a flat rate or a single 'supplement' to occupy a double-occupancy cabin by yourself. Some lines charge a fixed amount – $250, for instance – as a

Cunard Line provides dance hosts.

supplement, no matter what the cabin category, ship, itinerary, or length of cruise. Such rates vary between lines, and sometimes between a particular line's ships. Because there are so few single-occupancy cabins, it's best to book as far ahead as you can.

Cruise lines that charge low single supplements – on selected voyages – include Azamara Club Cruises, Crystal Cruises, Fred. Olsen Cruise Lines, Saga Cruises, Seabourn, Silversea Cruises, and Voyages of Discovery. Note that Saga Cruises has no additional supplements for solo travelers on any cruise, but has special fares built-in. Do watch out for sneaky cruise lines that may try to charge you *twice* for port charges and government taxes by including that non-existent second person in the cabin you occupy as a single, so check your cruise fare invoice carefully.

Other cruise lines, such as MSC Cruises and Norwegian Cruise Line, often have special promotions for solo occupancy of what are normally priced as double-person cabins.

Guaranteed singles rates

Some lines offer singles a set price for a double cabin but reserve the right to choose the cabin. So you could end up with a rotten cabin in a poor location or a wonderful cabin that happened to be unallocated.

Guaranteed share programs

These allow you to pay what it would cost each half of a couple for a double-occupancy cabin, but the cruise line will find another passenger of the same sex (and preferences such as smoking or non-smoking) to share it with you. If the line doesn't find a cabin-mate, the single passenger may get the cabin to themselves at no extra charge. Some cruise lines don't advertise a guaranteed share program in their brochures but will often try to accommodate such bookings at times when demand for space is comparatively light.

Solo dining

A common irritation concerns dining arrangements. Before you take your cruise, make sure that you request a table assignment based on your personal preferences; table sizes are typically for two, four, six, or eight people. Do you want to sit with other singles? Or do you like to sit with couples? Or perhaps with a mixture of both? Or with passengers who may not speak your language?

When you are on board, make sure that you are comfortable with the dining arrangements, particularly in ships with fixed table assignments, or ask the maître d' to move you to a different table. Aboard ships with open seating or with several different dining venues, you can choose which venue you want to eat in, and when; Norwegian Cruise Line (NCL) is an example of this arrangement, with its Freestyle Dining, as is Star Cruises.

Cruising for single women

A cruise ship is at least as safe for single women as any major vacation destination. It may not, of course, be entirely hassle-free, but it is not a 'meat market' that keeps you under constant observation.

If you enjoy meeting other singles, the easiest way is to participate in scheduled activities. However, beware of embarking on an affair with a ship's officer or crew member – it has been known for them to award an imaginary Golden Mattress to whomever can bed the most passengers.

Gentlemen cruise hosts

The female-to-male passenger ratio is typically high, especially among older people, so some cruise lines provide male social hosts. They may host a table in the dining room, appear as dance partners at cocktail parties and dance classes, join bridge games, and accompany women on shore excursions.

These men, usually over 55 and retired, are outgoing, mingle easily, and are well groomed. First introduced aboard Cunard Line's *QE2* in the mid-1970s, gentlemen hosts are now employed by a

A DJ keeps late night clubbers dancing.

number of cruise lines, including Crystal Cruises, Cunard Line, Holland America Line, Regent Seven Seas Cruises, Silversea Cruises, and Voyages to Antiquity.

If you think you'd like such a job, do remember that you'll have to dance for several hours most nights, and be proficient in just about every kind of dance.

Options for GLBT travelers

Several US companies specialize in ship charters or large group bookings for gay and lesbian passengers. These include the California-based Atlantis (www.atlantisevents.com), San Francisco's lesbian specialist Olivia (www.olivia.com), or New York's Pied Piper Travel (http://piedpipertravel.com/gay groupcruises).

One drawback of gay charters is that they're as much as 20 percent more expensive than the equivalent general cruise. Another is that they have been greeted with hostility by church groups on some Caribbean islands such as Grand Cayman, Jamaica, and Bermuda. One Atlantis cruise was even denied the right to dock. But their great advantage is that they provide an accepting environment and gay-oriented entertainment, with some big-name comedians and singers.

Another idea is to join a gay affinity group on a regular cruise at normal prices; these groups may be offered amenities such as private dining rooms and separate shore excursions.

If you are concerned that on a mainstream cruise, you might be seated for dinner with unsympathetic companions, opt for a cruise line offering 'open choice seating' (where you sit where you want, when you want at dinner, and you

can change time you dine), for example Carnival Cruise Line, Celebrity Cruises, Holland America Line, Norwegian Cruise Line, Princess Cruises, and Royal Caribbean International (request this option when you book). That doesn't mean that any of the major cruise companies are not gay-friendly – many hold regular 'Friends of Dorothy' gatherings, sometimes scheduled and sometimes on request – though it would be prudent to realize that Disney Cruise Line, for example, will not really offer the ideal entertainment and ambience. Among the smaller companies, Windstar's sail-powered cruise yachts have a reputation for being gay-friendly.

Gay families are catered to by R Family Vacations (www.rfamilyvacations.com), although it's not essential to bring children. Events may include seminars on adoption and discussion groups for teenagers in gay families. One of the company's founders was the former TV talk show host Rosie O'Donnell.

Transgender passengers may encounter some problems, such as the passport name being of one gender, while appearance and dress suggest another. Ships sometimes encounter problems in some ports when passenger ID cards do not match the gender on the ship's manifest.

Cruising to Suit Special Needs

Cruising for those with physical special needs offers one of the most hassle-free vacations possible. But it's important to choose the right ship and to prepare in advance.

If you are mobility-limited or have any other kind of physical disabilities (this includes sight or hearing impairments), do tell the cruise line (or your travel agent) at the time you book; otherwise, you may legally be denied boarding by the cruise line.

Anyone in a wheelchair but considering a cruise may be nervous at the thought of getting around. However, you'll find that crew members aboard most ships are extremely helpful. Indeed, cruise ships have become much more accessible for people with most types of disabilities. Ships built in the past five to 10 years have the most up-to-date suites, cabins, and accessible shipboard facilities for those with special needs. Many new ships also have text telephones and listening device kits for the hearing-impaired (including showlounges aboard some ships). Special dietary needs can often be met, and many cabins have refrigerators – useful for those with diabetes who need to keep supplies of insulin cool.

Wheelchair users should check in advance what help is available.

Special haemodialysis cruises cater for dialysis patients (check out www.dialysisatsea.com and www.dialysis-cruises.com). Typically, a renal care specialist team consisting of a Nephrologist, dialysis nurses, and certified technicians will be provided. Some ships (examples include Astor, Europa, and Europa 2) have first-class dialysis equipment such as the Fresenius 4008 B and a special dialysis room within the medical center. Expect to pay between $350–650 per session (depening on ship and company).

If you use a wheelchair, take it with you, as ships carry only a limited number for emergency hospital use only. An alternative is to rent an electric wheelchair, which can be delivered to the ship on your sailing date.

Arguably the weakest point of cruising for the mobility-limited is any shore tender operation. Ship tenders simply aren't designed properly for the wheelchair-bound. Also, when you reach the shore, you may find facilities very limited.

Little problems to consider

Unless cabins and bathrooms are specifically designed, problem areas include the entrance, furniture configuration, closet hanging rails, beds, grab bars, height of toiletries cabinet, and wheel-in shower stall. The elevators may present the biggest obstacle, and you may get frustrated at the waiting time involved. In older ships, controls often can't be reached from a wheelchair.

A few ships have access-help hoists installed at swimming pools. These include Celebrity Cruises' *Celebrity Reflection* and *Celebrity Silhouette,* the pool in 'The Haven' aboard Norwegian Cruise Line's *Norwegian Breakaway, Norwegian Epic, Norwegian Getaway,* and *Norwegian Gem,* and P&O Cruises' *Britannia, Oriana* and *Aurora.*

It can be hard to access areas including self-serve buffets, and many large resort ships provide only oval plates (no trays) in their casual eateries. So you may need to ask for help.

Some insurance companies may prohibit smaller ships from accepting passengers with severe disabilities. Some cruise lines will send you a form requesting the dimensions and weight of the wheelchair, stating that it has to fold to be taken inside the cabin.

Note that wheelchairs, mobility scooters, and walking aids must be stored in your cabin – they *cannot* be left in the hallway outside your cabin.

Only five cruise ships have direct access ramps to lifeboats: *Amadea*, *Asuka II*, *Crystal Serenity*, *Crystal Symphony*, and *Europa*.

Avoid pitfalls

Start by planning an itinerary and date, and find a travel agent who knows your needs. But follow up on all aspects of the booking yourself to avoid slip-ups; many cruise lines have a department or person to handle requests from disabled passengers.

Choose a cruise line that lets you select a specific cabin, not just a price category.

If the ship doesn't have any specially equipped cabins, book the best outside cabin in your price range, or choose another ship.

Check whether your wheelchair will fit through your cabin's bathroom door or into the shower area and whether there is a 'lip' at the door. Don't accept 'I think so' as an answer. Get specific measurements.

Choose a cabin close to an elevator. Not all elevators go to all decks, so check the deck plan. Smaller and older vessels may not even have elevators, making access to even the dining room difficult.

Avoid, at all costs, a cabin down a little alleyway shared by several other cabins, even if the price is attractive. It's hard to access a cabin in a wheelchair from such an alleyway. Cabins located amidships are less affected by vessel motion, so choose something in the middle of the ship if you are concerned about possible rough seas. The larger – and therefore more expensive – the cabin, the more room you will have to maneuver in.

Hanging rails in the closets on most ships are positioned too high for someone in a wheelchair to reach – even the latest ships seem to repeat this basic error. Many cruise ships, however, have cabins to suit the mobility-limited. They are typically fitted with roll-in closets and have a pull-down facility to bring your clothes down to any height you want.

Meals in some ships may be served in your cabin, on special request, but few ships have enough space in the cabin for dining tables. If you opt for a dining room with two fixed-time seatings for meals, the second is more leisurely. Alert the restaurant manager in advance that you would like a table that leaves plenty of room for your wheelchair.

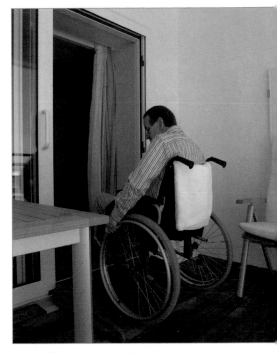

Douglas Ward tests accessibility around a ship.

Hand-carry your medical information. Once on board, tell the reception desk help may be needed in an emergency.

Make sure that the contract specifically states that if, for any reason, the cabin is not available, that you will get a full refund and transportation back home as well as a refund on any hotel bills incurred.

Advise the cruise line of the need for proper transfer facilities such as buses or vans with wheelchair ramps or hydraulic lifts.

If you live near the port of embarkation, arrange to visit the ship to check its suitability – most cruise lines will be accommodating.

Coping with embarkation

The boarding process can pose problems. If you embark at ground level, the gangway may be level or

---

Doors can present a problem for wheelchair users

The design of cruise ships has traditionally worked against the mobility-limited. To keep water out or to prevent water escaping from a flooded area, raised edges (lips) – unfriendly to wheelchairs – are often placed in doorways and across exit pathways. Also, cabin doorways, at a standard 24in (60cm) wide, are not big enough for wheelchairs, for which about 30in (76cm) is needed.

Bathroom doors, whether they open outward or inward, similarly hinder maneuverability (an electrically operated sliding door would be better). Bathrooms in some older ships

are small and full of plumbing fixtures, often at odd angles – awkward for wheelchair movement. Those aboard new ships are much better, but plumbing may be located beneath the complete prefabricated module, making the floor higher than that in the cabin, so a ramp is needed. Some cruise lines will, if given advance notice, remove a bathroom door and hang a fabric curtain in its place, and provide a ramp for the doorway if needed.

Access to outside decks may be through doors that must be opened manually rather than via automatic electric-eye doors.

A cabin number in Braille on *Costa Serena*.

inclined. It will depend on the embarkation deck of the ship and/or the tide in the port.

Alternatively, you may be required to embark from an upper level of a terminal, in which case the gangway could well be of the floating loading-bridge type, like those used at major airports. Some have flat floors; others may have raised lips at regular intervals.

Ship-to-shore launches

Cruise lines should – but don't always – provide an anchor emblem in brochures for those ports of call where a ship will be at anchor instead of alongside. If the ship is at anchor, the crew will lower you and your wheelchair into a waiting tender and then, after a short boat ride, lift you out again onto a rigged gangway or integral platform. If the sea is calm, this maneuver proceeds uneventfully; if the sea is choppy, it could vary from exciting to somewhat harrowing.

This type of embarkation is rare except in a busy port with several ships sailing the same day. Holland America Line is one of the few companies to make shore tenders accessible to the disabled, with a special boarding ramp and scissor lift so that wheelchair passengers can see out of the shore tender's windows.

Help for the hearing-impaired

Difficulties for such passengers include hearing announcements on the public address system, using the telephone, and poor acoustics in key areas such as where shore tenders are boarded.

Some cruise lines have special 'alert kits.' These include 'visual-tactile' devices for those unable to hear a knock on the door, a telephone ringing, or the sound of an alarm clock. Crystal Cruises' *Crystal Serenity* and *Crystal Symphony*, and TUI Cruises' *Mein Schiff 1*, *Mein Schiff 2*, *Mein Schiff 3* and *Mein Schiff 4* have movie theaters fitted with special headsets for those with hearing difficulties.

Finally, when going ashore, particularly on organized excursions, be aware that some destinations are simply not equipped to handle people with hearing impairment.

Cruising for the blind and sight-impaired

Any totally or almost-blind persons must be accompanied by a fully able-bodied person, occupying the same cabin. A few cruise lines will allow seeing-eye dogs (guide dogs).

All elevators and cabins have Braille text. Some large resort ships (examples include *Celebrity Reflection*, *Celebrity Silhouette*, *MSC Divina*, *MSC Fantasia*, *MSC Preziosa*, and *MSC Splendida*) have Braille pads subtly hidden under each lower section of handrail in the main foyers – very user-friendly, and most welcome.

Recent improvements

Many new ships now provide mobility-limited cabin bathrooms with collapsible shower stools mounted on shower walls, and bathroom toilets have collapsible arm guards and lower washbasins. Other cabin equipment may include a vibrating alarm clock, door beacon (with a light that flashes when someone knocks on the door), television with closed-caption decoders, and a flashing light as fire alarm.

Look out, too, for:

Kits for the hearing-impaired, available on request.

Induction systems for the hearing impaired.

Dedicated wheelchair positions in the show-lounge.

Electrical hoist to access pool and hot tubs.

Although public rooms do not have special seating areas, most showlounges do – almost always at the back, adjacent to the elevators – for wheelchair passengers.

Wheelchair accessibility

Each cruise ship reviewed in this book is rated in its data listing for wheelchair accessibility.

Questions to ask before you book
Are any public rooms or public decks inaccessible to wheelchairs?
Will special transportation be provided to transfer you from airport to ship?
Will you need to sign a medical release?
If you need a collapsible wheelchair, can this be provided by the cruise line?
Can the ship supply a raised toilet seat?
Will crew members be on hand to help?
Will you be guaranteed a good viewing place in the showlounge if seated in a wheelchair?
How do you get from your cabin to lifeboats in an emergency, if the elevators are out of action?
Does the cruise line's travel insurance (with a cancellation or trip interruption) cover you for any injuries while you are aboard?
Most disabled cabins have twin beds or one queen-size bed. Anyone with a disabled child should ask whether a suitable portable bed can be installed.

Expedition Cruising

Like sport utility vehicles, some ships have become crossovers, operating as expedition cruise ships but offering a quite plush and comfortable lifestyle.

Expedition cruising is poles apart from all other types of cruising. It is total immersion in nature, wildlife, and discovery, with a sense of pioneering thrown in. Passengers joining cruise expeditions become 'participants' and need to be more self-reliant and more interested in doing or learning than in being entertained. They become 'participants' and take very active roles in almost every aspect of a voyage.

Naturalists, historians, and lecturers (rather than entertainers) are aboard each ship to provide background information and observations about wildlife. Each participant receives a personal logbook, illustrated and written by the wildlife artists and writers who accompany each cruise – a fine souvenir.

About expedition cruises

You can venture to the North Pole, walk on pack ice in the islands and land masses in the Arctic Ocean and Arctic Circle, explore a huge penguin rookery on an island in the Antarctic Peninsula, the Falkland Islands, or South Georgia, or search for 'lost' peoples in Melanesia. Or you can cruise close to the source of the Amazon, gaze at species of flora and fauna in the Galápagos Islands (Darwin's laboratory), or watch a genuine dragon on the island of Komodo – from a comfortable distance, of course.

Great expedition experiences: Aleutian-Pribiloff Islands, Amazon (Manaus-Iquitos), Antarctic Peninsula, Arctic (North Pole), Galápagos Islands, Islands of Micronesia, Northeast Passage, Northwest Passage, Papua New Guinea, and Ross Ice Shelf (Antarctica).

Explore in comfort

Briefings and lectures bring cultural and intellectual elements to expedition cruise vessels. There is no formal entertainment as such; participants enjoy this type of cruise more for the camaraderie and learning experience, and being close to nature. There is no cruise director, rather an experienced expedition leader who works closely with the ship's captain and marine operations department. The ships are designed and equipped to sail in ice-laden waters, yet they have a shallow-enough draft to glide over coral reefs.

Despite being rugged, expedition cruise vessels can provide comfortable and even elegant surroundings for up to 200 participants, as well as offering good food and service. Without traditional cruise ports at which to stop, a ship must be self-sufficient, capable of long-range cruising, and totally environmentally friendly. Although there's no professional entertainment, recaps of the day's experiences usually take place each evening, and, if you're not too tired (expedition cruising can be exhausting), board games and library books are always available.

However, the expedition experience itself really comes alive by the use 'Zodiacs' – inflatable but rigid craft that can seat up to a dozen participants. The feel of sea spray and wind on your face gives you a thrill, and the feeling that this really is something different from any cruising you may have done previously.

How expedition cruising developed

Lars-Eric Lindblad pioneered expedition cruising in 1966. A Swedish-American, he turned travel into adventure by going to parts of the world tourists had not visited. After chartering several vessels for voyages to Antarctica, he organized the design and construction of a small ship capable of going almost anywhere in comfort and safety. In 1969, *Lindblad Explorer* was launched; it soon earned an enviable reputation in adventure travel. Others followed.

Silver Explorer in Antarctica.

MS Hanseatic is equipped with the highest ice class (E4) for passenger ships, enabling it to safely navigate through the ice.

To put together cruise expeditions, companies turn to specialist advisers. Scientific institutions are consulted; experienced world explorers and naturalists provide up-to-date reports on wildlife sightings, migrations, and other natural phenomena. Sea days are usually spent preparing, and participants are kept physically and mentally active. Avoid such an adventure cruise if you are not completely ambulatory, because getting into and out of Zodiacs (inflatable shore landing craft) can be very tricky.

Adventure cruise companies provide expedition parkas and waterproof boots, but you will need to take waterproof trousers for Antarctica and the Arctic.

Antarctica

See the 'Frozen Planet' for yourself. While Arctic ice is only a few feet thick, the ice of Antarctica is thousands of feet thick. The continent was first sighted in 1820 by the American sealer Nathaniel Palmer, British naval officer Edward Bransfield, and Russian captain Fabian Bellingshausen.

For most, it is just a windswept frozen wasteland – it has been calculated that the ice mass contains almost 90 percent of the world's snow and ice, while its treeless land mass is twice the size of Australia. For others, it represents the last pristine place on earth, offering an abundance of marine and bird life.

As many as 36,000 people a year visit Antarctica. In 2014, there were 18,000 expedition cruise visitors to Port Lockroy, the British research station, which has a resident postmaster. There is 24-hour sunshine during the austral summer, but not a single native inhabitant. Its ice is as much as 2 miles (3km) thick, and its total land mass equals more than all the rivers and lakes on earth and exceeds that of China and India combined. Icebergs can easily be the size of Belgium. The region has a raw beauty.

There are two ways to go to the cold continent.

From Ushuaia in Argentina or Punta Arenas in Chile, across the Drake Passage, to the Antarctic Peninsula (the most popular route). The peninsula (sometimes together with South Georgia) is visited by the 'soft' expedition cruise ships and even normal-size cruise ships with ice-hardened hulls. From Ushuaia or Punta Arenas, it takes two days to reach the Antarctic Peninsula, to see the pristine Antarctic ice and observe the wildlife (the best time is mid-November, when penguins come ashore for courtship and nesting). South Georgia is famous, because the explorer Ernest Shackleton is buried in Grytviken – a former Norwegian whaling station.

From Hobart (Australia) or Auckland (New Zealand) to the Ross Ice Shelf, it takes about seven days to reach the eastern side of the continent in the Ross Sea (hence it is more expensive than leaving from Argentina or Chile). This, the more remote 'far side' – the Oates and Scott coasts, McMurdo Sound, and the famous Ross Ice Shelf – can be visited only by genuine icebreakers, as the katabatic winds can easily reach more than 100mph (160kph). However, a highlight will be a visit to Scott's well-preserved hut at Cape Evans on Ross Island. It has been frozen in time since 1912 (with over 8,000 items – including many tins of food). You can also visit Shackleton's hut, at Cape Royds on Ross Island (it contains over 5,000 items), and Mawson's huts at Cape Denison in the eastern sector (a replica of one of Mawson's huts (built by the Mawson's Huts Foundation) opened in December 2013. It sits on the dockside in Hobart, Australia.

The first ship carrying participants on a complete circumnavigation of Antarctica was the 114-passenger *Kapitan Khlebnikov*, operated by Quark Expeditions, in 1996–97.

Only 100 participants *per ship* are now allowed ashore at any given time, so if you cruise aboard one of the larger ships that claim to include Antarctica on their itineraries, it will probably be to view it – but only from the ship. Indeed, since 2011 cruise ships with more than 500 participants have not been allowed to sail in Antarctic waters unless they use lighter-grade distillate fuel. Moreover, the chances of rescue in the event of pack ice crushing a normal cruise ship hull are virtually nil. For real expedition cruising, choose a ship that includes a flotilla of Zodiacs, proper boot washing stations, expedition equipment, experienced expedition leaders, and ice captains. Two companies that stand out from the crowd are Hapag-Lloyd Expedition Cruises and Quark Expeditions.

Most large resort ship operators exited Antarctica in 2011 due to a ban on carrying or burning heavy fuel oil below 60 degree south latitude, leaving travel mainly in the hands of specialist expedition ship operators. 'Antarctic' fuel (lighter-grade distillate fuel) is the world's highest cost fuel for ship use. However, some large resort ships and mid-size ships also carry the special fuel, which allows them to continue traveling to Antarctica – although these are for cruising only, not passenger landings.

Be aware that you can still get stuck even aboard these specialized expedition ships, as did *Nordkapp*, which ran aground near Deception Island in 2007. In the same year, Canadian company GAP Expeditions' (now renamed G Adventures) *Explorer* hit an iceberg in Bransfield Strait off King George Island and sank; all 91 participants, nine expedition staff, and 54 crew members were rescued thanks to the coordination efforts of the British Coast Guard and the Hurtigruten cruise ship *Nordnorge*. In 2008 Antarpply Expeditions' *Ushuaia* was grounded; all 89 participants were rescued by the Chilean navy vessel *Achilles*. In 2009, Quark Expeditions' *Ocean Nova* was grounded, and in 2011 *Polar Star* grounded on an uncharted rock; fortunately there were no injuries to participants or crew.

Tip: Wear an ID bracelet or belt at all times while on an Antarctic expedition cruise, and take thermal underwear. Anyone on a special diet should advise the cruise operator as early as possible, so that any necessary items can be obtained.

Wildlife you may see or come into contact with include orcas, dolphins, the six species of Antarctic seals, penguins, birds, and various species of lichen and flora, depending on the area visited.

Take plastic bags to cover your camera, so that condensation forms inside the bag and not on your camera when changing from the cold of the outside Antarctic air to the warmth of your expedition cruise vessel. Make sure you know how to operate your camera with gloves on – frostbite is a real danger.

The High Arctic

This is an ocean surrounded by continents, whereas Antarctica is an ice-covered continent surrounded by ocean. The Arctic Circle is located at 66 degrees, 33 minutes, 3 seconds North, although this really designates where 24-hour days and nights begin. The High Arctic is best defined as that region north of which no trees grow, and where water is the primary feature of the landscape.

Poseidon Expeditions, an Arctic expedition cruise specialist, operates under the strict guidelines of Arctic Expedition Cruise Operators (AECO), the body committed to minimizing the impact of visit to the Far North. These expeditions to the North Pole (90 degrees North) are undertaken only at the height of the Arctic summer, in June and July, usually aboard the world's most powerful icebreaker – the Russian nuclear-powered *50 Years of Victory* – which can crush ice

up to 10ft (3m) thick. An onboard helicopter whisks participants between the ship and the North Pole.

This really is a once-in-a-lifetime adventure. Only 250 participants visited the North Pole in 2014, and some took the optional excursion in a tethered hot-air balloon.

The Northwest Passage

Passenger ships that have navigated the often-dangerous Northwest Passage linking the Atlantic and Pacific Oceans include *Lindblad Explorer* (1984), *World Discoverer* (1985), *Society Explorer* (1988), *Frontier Spirit* (1992), *Kapitan Khlebnikov* (1994, 1995, 1998, 2006, 2007, 2008), *Hanseatic* (1995, 1996, 1997, 1999, 2007, 2010, 2012), and *Bremen* (2009, 2010). In 2013 and 2015, unusual double crossings took place; *Hanseatic* went east to west, while *Bremen* went west to east.

The Amazon

The River Amazon is long – 4,080 miles (6,566km) from close to its source in the Peruvian Andes, to Belem on South America's Atlantic coast – and contains one fifth of the earth's water supply. Home to a tenth of the planet's animal species and plant life, it has thousands of tributaries, and is often so wide you cannot see the riverbank on the opposite side.

Cruises usually start in the Caribbean from ports such as Barbados and end up in Manaus (or vice versa). Starting in Manaus, with its muddy red-brown water, and ending up in the clear blue waters of the Caribbean may be the more appealing option. Calls along the way may be made in Parintins, Alter do Chão, Santarém, and Belém. Few ships venture far-

The nuclear-powered *50 Years of Victory* at the North Pole.

An excursion in Papua New Guinea.

ther upriver from Manaus to Iquitos; Hapag-Lloyd Expedition Cruises' *Hanseatic* is one that does.

The city of Manaus, 1,000 miles (1,600km) from the ocean, was built by barons of the rubber industry. Today, it really is a gaudy metropolis, but its opera house, built at the end of the 19th century, remains a much-visited icon and still stages concerts.

One must-do shore excursion is a rainforest walk with a knowledgeable Brazilian guide to give you an insight into the richest variety of life on the planet. But make sure you have plenty of insect repellent – more than 200 varieties of mosquito inhabit the Amazon Basin.

The Galápagos Islands

These islands, 600 miles (966km) off the coast of Ecuador in the Pacific Ocean, are a microcosm of our planet. More than 100 islands, plus mineral-rich and lava outcroppings, make up the Galápagos, which are fed by the nutrient-rich Cromwell and Humboldt currents. The fertile waters can be cold, even on the equator.

The Ecuadorians jealously guard their islands and prohibit the movement of almost all non-Ecuador-registered cruise vessels within its boundaries. The best way to follow in the footsteps of Charles Darwin, who visited the islands in 1835 aboard the *Beagle*, is to fly to Quito and cruise aboard an Ecuadorian-registered vessel. Ecological fact: cruising leaves a smaller carbon footprint because it does not contribute to the building of hotels, restaurants, roads, and cars.

The government of Ecuador set aside most of the islands as a wildlife sanctuary in 1934, while uninhabited areas were declared national parks in 1959. The national park includes approximately 97 percent of the islands' landmass, together with 20,000 sq miles (50,000 sq km) of ocean. The Charles Darwin Research Station was established in 1964, and the government created the Galápagos Marine Resources Reserve in 1986.

The Galápagos National Park tax is $100, plus $10 for an Immigration Control Card (this must be obtained before you travel). Smoking is prohibited on the islands, and no more than 50,000 visitors a year are admitted. In 2012 new rules stopped ships from visiting most islands more than once in a 14-day period. Some cruise lines require vaccinations for cruises that include Ecuador, although the World Health Organization does not.

The ships

It's important to explain that few cruise operators, unlike Hapag-Lloyd Cruises and Silversea Cruises, actually own their specialist expedition ships. Most of these vessels are owned by companies formed of investors who charter the ships to cruise operators. Also, ship management and technical operations may be unrelated to the catering company, the marketing company, or the expedition tour operator, making it difficult to guarantee consistency.

Protecting sensitive environments

In the future, only ships capable of meeting new 'zero discharge' standards will be allowed to cross environmentally sensitive areas. Expedition cruise companies are concerned about the environment, and they spend much time and money in educating their crews and participants about safe procedures.

They observe the 'Antarctic Traveler's Code,' based on 1978's Antarctic Conservation Act, designed to protect the region's ecosystem, flora, and fauna.

The Antarctic Treaty Meeting in Kyoto in 1994 made it unlawful, unless authorized by permit, to take native animals, birds, and certain native plants, introduce species, enter certain special protected areas (SPAs), or discharge or dispose of pollutants. The original Antarctic Treaty, signed in 1959 by 12 nations active in the region, defined Antarctica as all of the land and ice shelves south of 60 degrees South latitude. The signatories were Argentina, Australia, Belgium, Chile, France, Japan, New Zealand, Norway, South Africa, the Soviet Union, the UK, and the US. There are now 28 countries comprising

the Antarctic Treaty Consultative committee, and 39 research stations across the continent.

To 'take' means to remove, harass, molest, harm, pursue, hunt, shoot, kill, trap, capture, restrain, or tag any native mammal or bird, or to attempt to do so. Violators face civil penalties, including a fine of up to $10,000 and one-year imprisonment for each violation. A copy of the Act can be found in the library of each adventure or expedition ship that visits the continent.

Ships carrying over 500 participants are not allowed to land and are restricted to 'scenic' cruising, so the likelihood of a large resort ship with 3,000-plus passengers zooming in on the penguins is low. Nor would it be possible to rescue so many passengers (plus crew), in the event of an emergency. Also, large resort ships burn heavy oil rather than the lighter oil used by the specialist expedition ships, which also have ice-strengthened hulls, so the danger of pollution arising from an accident is greater.

Comparing expedition ships

Ship name	Company/operator (1)	Built	Passenger cabins	Tonnage	Registry	Length (m)
50 Years of Victory (1) (2)	Various expedition operators	2007	66	23,439	Russia	159.00
Akademik Ioffe (3)	Various expedition operators	1988	55	6,460	Russia	117.10
Akademik Sergey Vavilov (3)	Various expedition operators	1988	40	6,231	Russia	117.80
Antarctic Dream	Oceanwide Expeditions	1959	39	2,180	Panama	83.00
Bremen	Hapag-Lloyd Cruises	1990	82	6,752	The Bahamas	111.51
Expedition	Gadventures	1972	58	6,336	Liberia	105.00
Hanseatic	Hapag-Lloyd Cruises	1993	92	8,378	The Bahamas	122.80
Marco Polo	Cruise and Maritime Voyages	1965	425	22,080	The Bahamas	176.28
Minerva	Swan Hellenic Cruises	1996	178	12,500	The Bahamas	133.00
National Geographic Endeavour	Lindblad Expeditions	1966	62	3,132	The Bahamas	89.20
National Geographic Explorer	Lindblad Expeditions	1982	81	6,200	The Bahamas	108.60
National Geographic Orion	Lindblad Expeditions	2003	53	4,050	The Bahamas	102.7
Ocean Diamond	Quark Expeditions	1986	112	8,282	The Bahamas	124.00
Ortelius (3)	Oceanwide Expeditions	1989	45	4,575	The Bahamas	89.98
Plancius (3)	Oceanwide Expeditions	1976	53	3,434	Holland	89.00
Polar Pioneer (3)	Various expedition operators	1985	26	2,140	Russia	71.60
Professor Molchanov (3)	Southern Explorations	1983	29	1,753	Russia	71.60
Professor Multanovskiy (3)	Southern Explorations	1983	29	1,753	Russia	71.60
Sea Adventurer	Quark Expeditions	1976	61	5,750	The Bahamas	100.01
Sea Explorer	Various expedition operators	1992	57	4,200	The Bahamas	
Sea Spirit	Various expedition operators	1991	57	4,200	The Bahamas	89.70
Serenissima	Serenissima Cruises	1960	59	2,362	Liberia	84.7
Silver Explorer	Silversea Cruises	1989	66	6,072	The Bahamas	108.20
Spirit of Enderby (3)	Heritage Expeditions	1984	29	6,231	Russia	72.00
Ushuaia (3)	Ushuaia Adventure Corp/Antarpply Expeditions	1970	44	2,903	Argentina	84.73

NOTES
(1) = true expedition (ice-breaker) vessel
(2) = nuclear powered
(3) = built originally as a research vessel

P&O Cruises operates regular *Strictly Come Dancing* cruises.

Cruising to a Theme

A whole world of hobby, special interest, and lifestyle theme cruises awaits your participation.

What's your interest? Think of it and you'll probably find a special cruise dedicated to it. These are the special theme cruises that don't really fit into the normal range of offerings, although they usually follow the same itinerary.

Theme cruises are primarily 'regular' cruises, but with additional programs, linked to personalities and theme subject specialists. With special seminars and hands-on learning sessions, dances or concerts, sports, activities, and leisure on the menu, the possibilities are endless. Also, you'll be traveling with people who have the same hobbies, interests, or passions, or to increase your knowledge of a particular subject. You could also be close to your favorite celebrity and get to talk to them in person.

Music on the high seas

Music has always been a popular feature of shipboard entertainment, and special-interest music festivals, celebrations, and even competitions at sea have been part of the modern-day cruise scene since the 1960s. It's like having a special backstage pass to be up-close-and-personal with world-class musical talent.

Solo instruments are an unusual item for a theme cruise, but in 1986 the first Accordion Festival at Sea – with over 600 accordionists on board competing for financial and other prizes – took place aboard Chandris Fantasy Cruises' *Galileo*. It was not a full ship charter, so the other passengers were fascinated by the richness of performances of this much-misunderstood, but versatile, instrument.

Even before that, however, starting in 1976, a Classical Music Festival At Sea took place annually aboard the Paquet French Cruises' 650-passenger *Mermoz* until the early 1990s (and wine, all other drinks, and shore excursions were included in the fare). The artistic director André Borocz organized the whole event, including booking about 70 musicians who sailed on each of these special cruises (either in the Mediterranean or Caribbean). World-class artists such as James Galway, Barbara Hendricks, Jean-Pierre Rampal, Maurice André, Mstislav Rostropovich, Yo-Yo Ma, Emmanuel Ax, Schlomo Mintz, Bobby McFerrin, and the English Chamber Orchestra sailed aboard the ship, with music concerts performed ashore – usually in the evening – in Caribbean venues such as Papa Doc's Citadel in Haiti, La Popa Monastery in Cartagena, or, in Europe, the ancient Greek theatre at Epidaurus, the Teatro Mercadante in Naples, or the ancient open-air theatre at Xanthos, Turkey.

What was unusual, and fun, was to watch these world-famous artistes rehearsing in the daytime – often in their bathrobes – with passengers (also in bathrobes or casual clothing) attending; then, at around 6pm, everyone donned tuxedos for the evening. The close contact and interaction between performers and the music-loving passengers were wonderful. Suffice it to say that this was indeed a very special theme cruise, unlike any other.

In 1993 Paquet French Cruises was purchased by Costa Cruises, which was itself purchased by the Carnival Corporation in 1996. In 1999 Paquet Cruises was dismantled, and the *Mermoz* was sold to Louis Cruise Lines (the ship was scrapped in 2008).

Today, several cruise lines have taken up the Classical Music Festival at Sea theme, with Hapag-Lloyd's annual Ocean Sun Festival the most prestigious event. It has seen great success each year.

Nestor Torres performs as part of The Grammy Experience on *Norwegian Getaway*.

The company also hosts the annual Stella Maris International Vocal Competition (opera, song, and oratorio) in cooperation with renowned opera houses throughout the world. It is organized under the direction of Canadian tenor Michael Schade aboard *Europa*, with up-and-coming opera singers from around the world competing to win €15,000 and a recording contract with the German classical music record label, Deutsche Grammophon.

Cool jazz

Staying on the music theme, Big Band theme cruises have also always been popular, with bands such as the Glenn Miller Orchestra, Tommy Dorsey Orchestra, Count Basie Orchestra, and the Duke Ellington Orchestra all having been part of the music on the high seas theme. In October 2015, Cunard hosted the first-ever Blue Note-themed crossing, aboard *Queen Mary 2* – showcasing Blue Note's 75th anniversary All Star Band. It featured keyboardist Robert Glasper, trumpeter Keyon Harrold, tenor saxophonist Marcus Strickland, guitarist Lionel Loueke, bassist Derrick Hodge, and drummer Kendrick Scott. Two more special Blue Note-themed crossings are scheduled for 2016.

Jazz greats such as Dizzy Gillespie and Clark Terry (trumpet), Woody Herman (clarinet), Benny Carter, Buddy Tate, Gerry Mulligan (saxophone), Junior Mance, Mel Powell, and Paul Broadnax (piano), Howard Alden (guitar), Keter Betts, Major Holley, Milt Hinton, and Kiyoshi Kitagawa (double bass), Chuck Riggs and Louis Bellson (drums), Mel Tormé (voice), the Harlem Blues and Jazz Band, Joe Williams and the Festival Jazzers have all sailed and played on Norwegian Cruise Line's Floating Jazz Festival cruises aboard the now-scrapped *Norway* and other ships in the fleet (organized by Hank O'Neal).

Today, the Smooth Jazz Cruise (also known as 'The Greatest Party At Sea') has been attracting well-known names such as the jazz violinist Ken Ford, guitarist-vocalist George Benson, bassist Marcus Miller, guitarist Earl Klugh, saxophonists David Sanborn, Mindy Abair, Paul Taylor, and Richard Elliott, and jazz fans – principally aboard Holland America Line ships.

Off your rocker

Today, even rock 'n' roll stars and fans have taken to cruising, with music-themed charters of ships becoming more prevalent. In 2013, Weezer – the LA rockers – took more than 2,500 fans aboard *Carnival Sunshine*, and in the same year, the '70,000 Tons of Metal' theme cruise (almost two dozen heavy metal bands from around the world) took over *Majesty of the Seas*. In 2015, *Norwegian Sky* was billed as the 'loudest boat in the world,' featuring heavy metal bands Anthrax, Motorhead, and Slayer.

In the recent past, the Moody Blues with Peter Dalton, The Zombies, Carl Palmer, The Orchestra with ELO, Starship, Little River Band, and Yes have all featured on cruises.

Not to be left out, 'boy bands,' including the Backstreet Boys and New Kids on the Block, have also been cruising.

Expect more of the same as rock 'n' roll and blues bands go cruising to replace the loss of land-based venues, and revenue (merchandising aboard a cruise ship with a captive audience is a massive incentive).

Although classical music and jazz cruises tend to last 7–14 days, other music themes, such as rock 'n' roll, or heavy metal, tend to be shorter (and less expensive). However, a 5-day Rock Legends Cruise IV is scheduled aboard *Independence of the Seas* in January 2016.

Soul train

Usually a full-ship charter, a re-creation of the popular music show Soul Train includes artists such as Gladys Knight and Earth, Wind and Fire, together with numerous artists that have been part of the television show, created and hosted by Don Cornelius. The artists, dancers, and fans have a blast, and enjoy the close interaction with each other (www.soultraincruise.com).

Going up country

Country and Western and Gospel music theme cruises also pop up occasionally. In fact, in 2013, the country and western band Alabama sailed with a flotilla of some of their biggest fans on a country music festival at sea to celebrate the band's 40th Anniversary of their first show at The Bowery.

In 2014, The 'Best Country Cruise Ever' took place aboard *Norwegian Pearl*. Among the featured artists were: Trace Adkins, Montgomery Gentry, Wynonna, Neal McCoy, Love and Theft, Craig Morgan, and Lonestar, as well as up-and-coming hopefuls. There were also songwriter workshops and, of course, karaoke (judged by the professionals), plus late-night dance parties, and a little unscheduled jammin' along the way.

Meanwhile, in January 2014, Kenny Rogers, Vince Gill, and Larry Gatlin and the Gatlin Brothers performed aboard Holland America Line's *Eurodam*.

Strictly dancing with the stars

Holland America Line (www.hollandamerica.com) has several voyages for followers of TV's *Dancing with the Stars*. TV personality Carson Kressley and show dancers Tristan MacManus and Kym Johnson host each sailing.

Fans of TV's *Strictly Come Dancing* ballroom dancing shows will find special theme cruises throughout the year with P&O Cruises (www.pocruises.com).

Family themes

Aboard the ships of Disney Cruise Line, *everything* is Disney – every song heard, every game played, every participation event, race, or party – it's the complete Disney at sea package.

Norwegian Cruise Line and Royal Caribbean International have their own star themes at sea. Norwegian Cruise Line have teamed up with TV's Nickelodeon to provide cruises with characters SpongeBob, Patrick, Dora the Explorer, and Diego, among others (not all ships).

Aboard some of Royal Caribbean International's ships, the Premium Barbie Experience holds sway; so do characters from the DreamWorks Experience such as Alex from *Madagascar*, Fiona and Puss in Boots from *Shrek*, and Po from *Kung Fu Panda*.

Culinary theme cruises

Food and wine cruises have always attracted interest, although some are better than others. Most have tended to be more like presentation lectures at cooking stations set on a large stage – more show than go – and always seem to leave audiences wanting to ask questions one-on-one rather than as part of a general audience.

Wine-themed cruises are especially popular with oenophiles (wine lovers), who get to meet owners and specialists from various world-famous vineyards with wine talks and wine tasting as part of the pleasure of these special voyages.

Finally, cruises for 'chocaholics' have been a big draw in the past.

Many ships now have culinary classes and demonstration kitchens (those aboard Holland America Line ships are set up in the theatre and are among the best). However, Oceania Cruises' *Marina* and *Riviera* have gone one better; each has 24 individual cooking workstations for classes on days at sea at the Bon Appétit Culinary Center. Hapag-Lloyd Cruises' *Europa 2* and P&O Cruises' *Britannia*, meanwhile, have 12-station Culinary Centers, using appliances that you would find in your own home.

Astronomical events

Total solar eclipse at sea. For the ultimate 'disappearing sun' experience, a cruise ship can represent the ideal place to be. Ships can position themselves – using the latest in weather technologies to avoid cloud banks – in the best location for optimum viewing opportunities.

The author remembers over 600 astronomers aboard one 1,200-passenger ship – you couldn't move on deck because of the tripods, huge telescopes, and long camera lenses. The ship, however, had a deep draft and was hence very stable – good for the photo-snappers!

A total solar eclipse, said to be the eclipse of the decade, took place on March 20, 2015, and the best location to see it was in the Arctic, off the coast of the Faroe Islands – north of Scotland – where the longest duration of totality was two minutes 47 seconds. Another total eclipse will not be seen in the UK until 2090. The next total solar eclipse visible from the US, however, is somewhat sooner, being due to take place on August 21 2017.

Star Wars

For 2016, Disney Cruise Line has designated eight (western Caribbean) sailings aboard Disney Fantasy as *Star Wars* cruises. *Star Wars* films will be shown, and Darth Vader, Chewbacca, Boba Fett, Stormtroop-

Making music aboard *Crystal Serenity*.

Star Wars Day at Sea is coming to Disney cruises in 2016.

ers, and other characters from across the *Star Wars* galaxy will be aboard for meet-and-greet sessions.

A shipboard version of the Jedi Training Academy invites young Jedi hopefuls to learn lightsaber moves from a Jedi master. They can then use 'the force' and face off in a final test against the evil Darth Vader.

Families will participate in *Star Wars* trivia games, while themed arts and crafts, games, and activities will be featured daily.

A Mos Eisley cantina scene will be created in the adults-only nightclub. Characters and cantina music will set the mood, as *Star Wars*-themed specialty cocktails are served.

Sports-theme cruises

In 2014, one fascinating short cruise, aboard *Asuka II* (Asuka Cruise), featured four of the world's top Sumo wrestlers. The world-famous wrestlers – including grand champion Hakuhoh – spent lots of time with passengers, who were thrilled to be so close to them.

Meanwhile, in January 2016 Celebrity Cruises and the Boston Red Sox have teamed up for a 'Take Me Out to the High Seas 2016 Red Sox Fan Cruise'. Onboard will be carry legendary Red Sox players and WEEI radio announcer, Dave O'Brien. Events will feature Hall of Famer Jim Rice, Red Sox Hall of Famer 'El Tiante' Luis Tiant, four-time World Series champion Mike Timlin, 2004 Red Sox World Series closer Keith Foulke, and television analyst Steve Lyons.

Not your regular theme cruise

Other unusual theme cruises include naturist vacations – clothing-free vacations. Bare Necessities has been doing it since 1990, although participants do dress to go to the dining room. The Big Nude Boat

Cruise 2016 takes place aboard *Celebrity Constellation*. Then there's Dream Pleasure Tours (www.dreampleasuretours.com), founded in 2007 for sensual indulgence. This company charters ships for hedonistic lifestyle cruises, including for the gay, lesbian, and swinger communities. A swingers' (adventurous couples) cruise is scheduled for April 2016 aboard *MSC Divina*, with a Bliss Cruise (for couples) in November 2016, aboard *Celebrity Silhouette*.

The Harley-Davidson Motorcycle Rally At Sea has been happening for almost 10 years aboard Celebrity Cruises. Dress code: biker attire. Naturally, there's a belly smacker contest; a treasured chest (women); best beard (men); and a contest for the best tattoo. Speaking of tattoos, a special 'Ink or swim' tattoo-themed cruise was scheduled aboard *Liberty of the Seas* in April 2015.

Some cruises are just magical adventures in themselves. But, in 2013, everyone's favorite wizard, the venerable Harry Potter, took to the seas with his own theme cruise. It's the latest movie-themed voyage to hit the high seas, and follows in the footsteps of recent additions such as the *Saw* film franchise cruise. Other theme vacations include Wellness, Fitness, 'Mind, Body and Spirit', and 'Life Modification' cruises (the first Holistic Health Cruise at sea was aboard *Cunard Countess* in 1976, with the well-known Ida Rolf – creator of the extreme massage technique known as Rolfing – on board). Then there's the Quilting and Girlfriends cruise – for girls who cruise to quilt (www.stitchinheaven.com); castles and gardens cruises (www.hebridean.co.uk); scrapbooking cruises (www.cruiseandcrop.com); a horror theme cruise, with all the thrills of the *Saw* franchise but none of the morbid consequences (www.scare-zone.com); a *Star Trek* cruise – with actors from the cult television show (www.startrekcruise.com); and a baseball giants cruise (MSC Cruises; www.msccruises.com).

In addition, several cruise lines have golf-themed cruises, but perhaps the best packages are put together by companies including Crystal Cruises, Hapag-Lloyd Cruises, Regent Seven Seas Cruises, and SeaDream Yacht Club, all of which operate smaller-size ships for a more personal experience.

Corporate cruising

Corporate incentive organizations and seagoing conferences need to have such elements as accommodation, food, or entertainment for delegates organized as one contract. Cruise companies have specialized departments to deal with all the details. Helpfully, many larger ships have almost identical cabin sizes and configurations.

Once a corporate contract is signed, no refund is possible, so insurance is essential. Although you may need to charter only 70 percent of a ship's capacity for your purposes, you will have to pay for the whole ship if you want an *exclusive* charter.

Although you can contact cruise lines directly, I strongly recommend contacting the professionals at www.seasite.com, which contains all cruise brands designed for event planners by the Miami-based ship charter specialists Landry & Kling (who can also arrange whole-ship charters for theme cruises). You can download a Meeting Planner Guide for ships from their website, http://landrykling.com/.

Maiden and inaugural voyages

It can be fun to take part in the maiden voyage of a new cruise ship. Or you could join an inaugural voyage aboard a refurbished, reconstructed, or stretched ship. However, you'll need a degree of tolerance – and be prepared for some inconveniences, such as slow or non-existent service in dining venues.

One thing is certain: any maiden voyage is a collector's item, but Murphy's Law – 'If anything can go wrong, it will' – can prevail. Service aboard new or recently refurbished ships (or a new cruise line) is likely to be uncertain and could be a disaster. An existing cruise line may use experienced crew from its other vessels to help 'bring out' a new ship, but they may be unfamiliar with the ship's layout and may have problems training other staff.

Plumbing and electrical items tend to cause the most problems, particularly aboard reconstructed and refurbished vessels. Examples: toilets that don't flush or don't stop flushing; faucets incorrectly marked, where 'hot' really means 'cold'; and 'automatic' telephones that refuse to function.

In the entertainment department, items such as spare spotlight bulbs may not be in stock. Or what if the pianos arrive damaged, or audio-visual materials for the lecturers haven't been delivered? Manuals for high-tech sound and lighting equipment may be in a foreign language.

Items such as menus, postcards, writing paper, or TV remote control units, door keys, towels, pillowcases, glassware, and even toilet paper may be lost in the bowels of the ship, or simply not ordered.

The galley (kitchen) of a new ship is in trouble if the right supplies don't turn up on time.

If you feel any of these mishaps might spoil your cruise, it would probably be better to wait until the ship has been in service for at least three months.

Taking part in a culinary class aboard *Riviera*.

Coastal Cruises

Being all at sea doesn't appeal? You can stay close to dry land by journeying round the coasts of Australia, Europe, and North and South America.

The marine wonderland of the Great Barrier Reef, a World Heritage Site off the northeast coast of Australia, is the earth's largest living coral reef – it actually consists of more than 2,800 individual coral reefs. It is visited by around 70 local Australian boutique ship operators, who mostly offer one- to four-night cruises to the reefs and Whitsunday Islands. The area is excellent for scuba diving and snorkeling.

June through September is humpback whale-watching season; the Reef shelters the young whales, while the adults nurture them in the shallow waters. Note that the Australian government levies an environmental charge of A\$5 on everyone over four years of age visiting the Great Barrier Reef and its environs.

Norway

An alternative to traditional cruise ships can be found in the year-round coastal cruising along the shores of Norway to the Land of the Midnight Sun

A scuba diving lesson at the Great Barrier Reef with Princess Cruises.

aboard the ships of the Hurtigruten Group, formerly known as Norwegian Coastal Voyages. The fleet consists of small, comfortable, working express coastal vessels and contemporary cruise vessels that deliver mail, small packaged goods, and foodstuffs, and take passengers to the communities spread on the shoreline.

Invariably dubbed 'the world's most beautiful voyage,' this is a 1,250-mile (2,000-km) journey from Bergen in Norway to Kirkenes, close to the Russian border (half of which is north of the Arctic Circle) and takes 12 days. The service started in 1893 to provide connection to communities when there were no roads, and the name Hurtigruten – meaning 'fast route' – reflects the fact that this coastal express was once the most reliable communication link between southern Norway and its remote north. Today the company carries more than 300,000 passengers a year. It's a good way to meet Norwegians, who treat the service like a bus.

You can join it at any of the 34 ports of call and stay as long as you wish because the vessels, being working ships, sail every day of the year (some port calls are of only one hour or so – enough to get off and on and unload freight). Most ports are repeated on the return journey, but stop at different times, so you may get a different feeling for a place, even if you've also visited it.

Note that double beds are available only in suite-grade accommodation (other cabins are dimensionally challenged, with sparse decor, furnishings, and minimal luggage storage space); many of the beds are fixed in an L-shape, or in a bed and sofa/bed combination. Note that most of the ships do not have stabilizers, and there is no doctor on board, nor indeed any medical facilities, but all gratuities are included in the fare.

At the height of summer, north of the Arctic Circle, there are almost 24 hours of daylight (there is no sunset between April 19 and August 23). Between November and February, the northern lights – if the atmospheric conditions are right – create spectacular arcs across the sky. Some specialist voyages are aimed at wildlife, birdwatchers, astronomy, and others, while onboard concerts and lectures celebrate the work of Norwegian composer Edvard Grieg.

The ships can accommodate between 144 and 652 passengers. The newest ships have an elevator that can accommodate a wheelchair passenger, but, otherwise, they are fairly plain, basic, practical vessels, with food that is more bistro than restaurant. A 24-hour restaurant provides items at extra cost. Note that the price of alcoholic drinks is extremely high (you can take your own on board), as it is throughout Norway, and that the currency is the Norwegian krone.

Archipelago hopping can be done along Sweden's eastern coast, too, by sailing in the daytime and staying overnight in one of the many small hotels en route. One vessel sails from Norrtalje, north of Stockholm, to Oskarshamn, near the Baltic island of Öland, right through the spectacular Swedish archipelago.

The Hurtigruten Group also operates utilitarian ships for expeditions to the Arctic, Antarctic, and Greenland.

Scotland

The fishing town of Oban, two hours west of Glasgow by road, is the base for one of the world's finest cruise experiences. *Hebridean Princess* is a real gem, with Laura Ashley-style interiors – posh enough to have been chartered by Queen Elizabeth II for a family-only celebration of her 80th birthday in 2006. The food is excellent, and includes locally sourced Scottish beef, local seafood, and seasonal vegetables. There's fine personal service.

This ship, owned by Hebridean Island Cruises, carries up to 50 passengers around some of Scotland's most magnificent coastline and islands. If you cruise from Oban, you can be met at Glasgow airport or rail station and taken to the ship by motor coach. Take lots of warm clothing, however (layers are best), as the weather can be changeable and often inclement.

There's also the 54-passenger *Lord of the Glens*, operated by the Magna Carta Steamship Company and with many of its fittings taken from famous ocean liners and trains of yesteryear. It cruises in style through Scotland's lakes and canals, although it's not a steamship but a modern deluxe vessel. Some high-season sailings are accompanied by historians and guest lecturers. Note that the cuisine is not up to the standard of Hebridean Princess, and drinks are very expensive.

North America

Coastal cruise ships flying the American flag offer a complete change of style from the large resort cruise ships. They are American-owned and American-crewed, and very informal. Being US-registered, they can start from and return to a US port without being required to call at a foreign port along the way – which a foreign-flagged cruise ship must do.

Accommodating up to 200 passengers, the ships are more like private family affairs, and are rarely out of sight of land. These cruises are low-key, low-pace, and not for active, adventurous types. Their operators seek out lesser-known areas, offering in-depth visits to destinations inaccessible to larger ships, along

Hebridean Princess in the Scottish islands.

both the eastern and western seaboards of the US, including Alaska.

Most passengers are of senior years. Many prefer not to fly, and wherever possible drive or take a train to join their ship. During the summer, you might see a couple of children on board, but in general small kids are not allowed. There are no facilities for them, and no staff to look after them.

Destinations. Eastern US and Canadian seaboard cruises include the St. Lawrence River, Atlantic Coastal Waterways, New England (good for fall cruises), Cape Cod and the Islands – and Cape Cod Canal, the Great Lakes – and Welland Canal, the Colonial Deep South, and Florida waterways.

Western seaboard cruises cover Alaska, the Pacific Northwest, California Wine Country, and Baja California/Sea of Cortés. Cruises focus on historically relevant destinations, nature and wildlife spotting, and coastal viewing. On some cruises, these boutique ships can dock adjacent to a town, allowing easy access on foot.

The ships. These 'D-class' vessels are less than 2,500 gross tonnage, and are subject neither to bureaucratic regulations nor to union rules. They are restricted to cruising no more than 20 miles (32km) offshore, at a comfortable 12 knots (13.8mph). Public room facilities are limited. Because the vessels are US-registered, there is no casino. They really are ultra-casual, no-frills ships with the most basic of facilities, no swimming pools, little artwork, and no glitz in terms of the interior decor. They usually have three or four decks and, except for the ships of American Cruise Lines and sister company Pearl Seas Cruises, no elevator. Stairs can be steep and are not recommended for people with walking difficulties. Because of this, some ships have an electric chairlift on indoor or outdoor stairways.

Cabins. Accommodation is in outside-view cabins, some opening directly onto a walking deck, which is inconvenient when it rains. Each has a pic-

Swimming from *Wilderness Adventurer* in Alaska.

Hurtigruten ships			
Ship	Tonnage	Built	Berths
Finnmarken	15,000	2002	638
Fram *	12,700	2007	328
Kong Harald	11,200	1993	490
Lofoten	2,621	1964	147
Midnatsol	16,053	2003	652
Nordkapp	11,386	1996	464
Nordlys	11,200	1994	482
Nordnorge	11,386	1997	455
Nordstjernen **	2,621	1956	114
Polar Star **	4,998	1969	100
Polarlys	12,000	1996	479
Richard With	11,205	1993	483
Trollfjord	15,000	2002	648
Vesteralen	6,261	1983	316

* for expedition voyages only
** for 'soft' expedition-style cruises

ture window and small bathroom. They are basic, with very limited closet space – perhaps just a curtain across a space with a hanging rod for clothes. Many don't have a television set or telephone. There's no room service, and you may have to turn your own bed down. Cabins are closer to the engines and generators than aboard the large resort ships, so the humming noise of the generator can be disturbing at night. The quietest cabins are at the bows – although there could be noise, if the ship is equipped with a bow thruster – and most cruising is done in the early morning, so that passengers can sleep better at night.

Tall passengers should note that the overall length of beds rarely exceeds 6ft (1.8m). Although soap is provided, it's best to bring your own shampoo, conditioner, and other toiletries. The ships of Blount Small Ship Adventures do not have cabin keys.

Although some of the older ships are very basic, the latest, particularly those of American Cruise Lines and Pearl Seas Cruises, are quite comfortable. Because they are not classified for open-water cruising, they don't have to conform to the same rigorous shipbuilding standards that larger ocean-going cruise ships do. Hot and cold water lines may run close to each other in your bathroom, delivering neither really hot nor really cold water. Sound insulation could be almost non-existent.

Activities. The main evening event is dinner in the dining room, with one seating. This can be a family-style affair, with passengers at long tables, and the food passed around.

The cuisine is decidedly American, with fresh local specialties. Menus aboard the ships of Alaskan Dream Cruises and Blount Small Ship Adventures are quite limited, while those aboard the ships of American Cruise Lines offer slightly more variety, including seasonal items. You'll probably be asked in the morning to choose which of the two main courses you'd like for dinner.

Evening entertainment consists mainly of after-dinner conversation. Most vessels are in port during the time, so you can easily go ashore for the local nightlife, although most passengers simply go to bed early.

The cost. These cruises are expensive, with an average daily rate of $400–800 a person. Suggested gratuities are high – typically about $125 per person, per seven-day cruise – but they are shared by all personnel.

Coastal cruise lines in North America

There are several small ship cruise companies: Alaskan Dream Cruises, American Cruise Lines, Blount Small Ship Adventures, Lindblad Expeditions, Pearl Seas Cruises, and Un-Cruise Adventures.

What differentiates them? American Cruise Lines, Pearl Seas Cruises, and Un-Cruise Adventures provide better food and service than the others. American Cruise Lines' and Pearl Seas Cruises' ships have larger cabins, and more public rooms. Drinks are included aboard the ships of American Cruise Lines only.

American Cruise Lines, Blount Small Ship Adventures, and Pearl Seas Cruises operate on the US East Coast; Lindblad Expeditions and Un-Cruise Adventures operate on the US West Coast and Alaska.

Comparing coastal ships

Ship name	Cruise line	Passengers	Region	Length (m)
Admiralty Dream	Alaskan Dream Cruises	78	Alaska	50.5
Alaskan Dream	Alaskan Dream Cruises	40	Alaska	31.6
American Glory	American Cruise Lines	54	US Coastal Cruises	53
American Spirit	American Cruise Lines	100	US Coastal Cruises	67
American Star	American Cruise Lines	104	US Coastal Cruises	67
Aranui 5	Campagnie Polynesienne de Transport Maritime	228	Tahiti/Marquesas	124.0
Baranof Dream	Alaskan Dream Cruises	78	Alaska	47.5
Celebrity Xpedition	Celebrity Cruises	96	Galapagos Islands	88.5
Coral Princess II	Captain Cook Cruises	50	Australia (Great Barrier Reef)	35
Emeraude	Emeraude Classic Cruises	76	Halong Bay (Vietnam)	56
Fiji Princess	Blue Lagoon Cruises	68	Yasawa Islands (Fiji)	60
Grande Caribe	Blount Small Ship Adventures	96	US Coastal Cruises	55.7
Grande Mariner	Blount Small Ship Adventures	100	US Coastal Cruises	55.7
Independence	American Cruise Lines	104	US Coastal Cruises	67.9
Lord of the Glens	Magna Carta Cruises	54	Scotland	45.7
Mare Australis	Cruceros Australis	128	Chilean Fjords (Patagonia)	71.83
Mystique Princess	Blue Lagoon Cruises	72	Yasawa Islands (Fiji)	56
National Geographic Endeavour	Lindblad Expeditions	96	Various regions	89.2
National Geographic Explorer	Lindblad Expeditions	162	Various regions	112
National Geographic Islander	Lindblad Expeditions	48	Galapagos Islands	50
National Geographic Sea Bird	Lindblad Expeditions	70	Alaska, Baja	46.3
National Geographic Sea Lion	Lindblad Expeditions	70	Alaska, Baja	46.3
Oceanic Discoverer	Coral Princess Cruises	72	Australia	63
Pearl Mist	Pearl Seas Cruises	206	US Coastal Cruises	102.1
Safari Endeavour	Un-Cruise Adventures	86	Alaska	70.7
Safari Explorer	Un-Cruise Adventures	36	Alaska/Mexican Coast	44.1
Safari Legacy	Un-Cruise Adventures	96	Alaska/Pacific Northwest	58.2
Safari Quest	Un-Cruise Adventures	22	Alaska/Mexican Coast	36.5
Saint Laurent	Haimark Line	220	US/Canada	91.4
Sea Voyager	Sea Voyager Expeditions	60	Central America	53
Silver Explorer	Silversea Cruises	114	Galapagos Islands	108.2
True North	North Star Cruises	36	Australia (west coast)	50
Tu Moana	Bora Bora Cruises	40	Tahitian Islands	69.1
Via Australis	Australis	136	Chilean Fjords (Patagonia)	72.3
Wilderness Adventurer	Un-Cruise Adventures	60	Alaska	47.7
Wilderness Discoverer	Un-Cruise Adventures	76	Alaska	51.5
Wilderness Explorer	Un-Cruise Adventures	76	Alaska	56.5

Transatlantic Crossings

You may be facing some unpredictable weather, but there's something romantic and adventurous about this classic ocean voyage.

This should be one of life's essential travel experiences. Crossing the 3,000 miles (4,800km) of the North Atlantic by ship is a great way to avoid the hassles of airports. I have done it 158 times and always enjoy it immensely – and unlike flying, there's no jet lag. Yet the days when ships were built specifically for crossings are almost gone. The only one offering a regularly scheduled service is Cunard Line's *Queen Mary 2 (QM2)*, built with a thick hull designed to survive the worst weather the North Atlantic has to offer.

It's a leisurely seven-day voyage, on five of which the clocks will be advanced (eastbound) or put back (westbound) by one hour. You can take as many bags as you want, and even your pets – *QM2*'s 12 kennels are overseen by a full-time kennel master, and there is an outdoor walking area. Book well in advance, if you want to travel with your dog, however, as there are limited numbers.

The 2,620 passenger *QM2* is the largest ocean liner ever built, and a destination on its own. New in 2004, it measures 148,528 gross tons. It has a wide walk-around promenade deck outdoors, and its forward section is under cover from the weather or wind (three times around is 6,102 ft/1,860 m, or 1.1 miles/1.6km).

By comparison, *QM2*'s smaller half-sisters *Queen Elizabeth* and *Queen Victoria* both measure about 90,000 gross tons. The *QE2*, which was retired in 2008, measured 70,327 gross tons – the ill-fated *Titanic* measured a mere 46,328 gross tons. The difference is that *QM2* is a real, thick-hulled ocean liner, designed to withstand the pressures of the North Atlantic and its unpredictable weather.

The North Atlantic can be as smooth as glass or as rough as old boots, although in my experience it's rare for the weather to be bad for an entire crossing. But when it *is* a bit choppy, its heavy beauty really is mesmerizing – never, ever boring. However, make sure you always use the handrails when you move around, and use the elevators rather than the stairs.

When the ship is under way at high speed (above 25 knots – about 30 land miles per hour) on a windy day, a cabin balcony is pretty useless, and the promenade deck is a challenging place to be – if you can even get outside, that is! Sometimes, visibility is low (think pea soup fog), and you'll hear the ship's horn – a powerful, haunting sound – bellowing every two minutes.

If you can, book a balcony cabin on the port side on westbound crossings, and on the starboard side on eastbound crossings – if the weather is kind and the sun is shining, you'll be in the sun this way.

During the crossing

Once *Queen Mary 2* has left port, and settled down at sea on the second day, the natural rhythm of

Queen Mary 2 leaving New York City.

life slows down, and you begin to understand that time spent at sea, with few distractions, is special indeed, and completely different from any 'normal' cruise. It allows you some well-earned 'me' time – to pamper yourself in the Canyon Ranch Spa, to attend a lecture by a well-known author or other personality, or simply to relax and read a book from the wonderful library on board. Cunard has a list of '101 Things To Do On A *Queen Mary 2* Transatlantic Crossing' – just in case you really do want to be active.

Apart from distinguished guest speakers, QM2 has a wide variety of leisure facilities, including a superb planetarium (several different shows, for which you'll need to make a reservation) and a 1,094-seat theater. There are acting classes, bridge (the card-playing kind) groups, big-band-style dance sessions, movies, exercise, cooking, and computer classes, so you'll never be bored in mid-ocean. There are now usually three formal (tuxedo) nights and four informal nights during a 7-night crossing, when an outbreak of elegance prevails. The gentlemen dance hosts are always kept busy by the number of solo female passengers who love to go dancing.

One of its most used facilities is the ship's outstanding library and bookshop – it offers over 8,000 books in 132 cabinets that have to be locked by hand – central locking was never part of the ocean liner setup – in several languages and staffed by full-time librarians from maritime library specialists Ocean Books. The bookstore not only sells books, but also Cunard memorabilia and souvenirs.

There's always a cozy chair to curl up on to read, or just admire the sea, and, if the weather's decent, you can even swim outside; this, however, tends to be rare –except in the height of summer – because of the ship's speed and wind speed.

One of the classic things to do is to enjoy the typically British afternoon teatime, complete with cakes, scones, pastries, and finger sandwiches – all served by a rather hurried white-gloved staff – together with tea, and accompanied by live, light classical music.

The problem is that you'll find there simply isn't enough time to do everything, and there's no way you'll ever get bored aboard this ship – the archetypal ocean liner.

You can also get married in mid-Atlantic during a crossing. Cunard Line started its now immensely popular 'Weddings At Sea' program in 2012. The first couple to be married by the ship's captain was Dr. William DeLuca (from the US) and Kelly Lewis (from the UK). They couldn't decide whether to marry in the UK or the US, so they chose halfway between the two (it was their first crossing, and, indeed, their first-ever vacation at sea). The couple chose Cunard Line because of the company's 'distinguished history of transatlantic crossings.' Note that only one wedding per day can be arranged, with a time of 11am or 3.30pm. Ceremonies take place only on days at sea, and every detail is planned by an onboard wedding coordinator. The cost starts at $2,500.

A memorable arrival

The day before you arrive in New York, Southampton, or (occasionally) in Hamburg, Germany, the disembarkation procedures will arrive in your suite or cabin. If you are in a hurry to disembark, you can opt to carry your own bags by registering for 'Express Disembarkation.'

Arriving in New York is one of cruising's iconic experiences, but you'll need to be up early. You'll see the lights of Long Island on your starboard side at about 4:30am, while the Verrazzano Narrows suspension bridge, at the entrance to New York harbor, will be dead ahead. QM2 usually passes the State of Liberty at about 6am – when a cabin with a balcony on the port side will give you the best views – and then makes a right turn opposite the statue towards the Brooklyn Cruise Terminal. On the occasions when the ship berths at Pier 90 in Manhattan at the Passenger Terminal, it will turn left towards the Hudson River – you'll get the best views of the Manhattan skyline at this point from a cabin with balcony on the starboard side. Arrival always creates a sense of anticipation of what lies ahead, and the feeling that, after a week of being cosseted, you will be thrust back into the fast lane with full force.

Leaving New York/arriving in Southampton

If you sail from Red Hook Point in Brooklyn, the last thing you'll notice before entering the ship is the overhead banner that declares: 'Leaving Brooklyn? Fuhgeddaboudit!' And that, dear reader, is *precisely* what a transatlantic crossing will have you do.

For arrival in Southampton, QM2 will usually round the Isle of Wight at about 4:30am, and be berthed alongside in Southampton by around 6:30am. Immigration is upon arrival in either New York or Southampton.

Repositioning crossings

Other cruise ships crossing the Atlantic are really little more than repositioning cruises – a way of moving ships that cruise the Mediterranean in summer to the Caribbean in winter, and vice versa, usually in spring and fall. Most of these ships cross the Atlantic using the sunny southern route, departing from southern ports such as Fort Lauderdale, San Juan, or Barbados, and ending the journey in Lisbon, Genoa, or Copenhagen via the Azores or the Canary Islands, off the coast of northern Africa.

These repositioning trips take longer – between eight and 12 days – but they do offer an alternative way of experiencing the romance and adventure of a crossing – with a number of sea days for total relaxation. Note that when the weather is not so good, the outdoor swimming pools will probably be out of use on repositioning crossings.

Cruising Under Sail

Want to be free as the wind? Think about cruising under sail, with towering masts, the creak of the deck, and gleaming white sails to power the ship along.

There's simply nothing that beats the thrill of being aboard a multi-mast tall ship, sailing under thousands of square feet of canvas through waters that mariners have sailed for centuries. This is cruising in the traditional manner of seafaring, aboard authentic sailing ships, contemporary copies of clipper ships, or high-tech cruise-sail ships, which provides a genuine sailing experience, while keeping creature comforts.

Mealtimes apart, there are no rigid schedules, so life aboard can be liberatingly unstructured. Weather conditions may often dictate whether a scheduled port visit will be made or not, but passengers sailing on these vessels are usually unconcerned. They would rather savor the feeling of being at one with nature, albeit in a comfortable, civilized setting, and without having to do the work themselves. The more luxurious sailing ships are the closest most people will get to owning their own mega-yacht.

Real sail-cruise ships

While we have all been dreaming of adventure, a pocketful of designers and yachtsmen committed pen to paper, hand in pocket and rigging to mast, and came up with a potpourri of stunning vessels to delight the eye and refresh the spirit. Examples are *Royal Clipper, Sea Cloud, Sea Cloud II, Star Clipper,* and *Star Flyer* – all of which have beautiful retro decor to convey the feeling of yesteryear and a slower pace of life.

Of these, *Sea Cloud,* built in 1931, restored in 1979, and adapted to satisfy the latest safety regulations of the International Convention for the Safety of Life at Sea (SOLAS), is the most romantic sailing ship afloat. It operates under charter for part of the year, and sails in both the Caribbean and the Mediterranean. A kind of stately home afloat, *Sea Cloud* remains one of the finest and most exhilarating travel experiences in the world.

A real steering wheel aboard *Sea Cloud.*

How to measure wind speeds

Understanding wind patterns is important to sailing ships, but the numbering system for wind velocity can confuse. There are 12 velocities, known as 'force' on the Beaufort scale, devised in 1805 by Sir Francis Beaufort, an Irish-born hydrographer and officer in Britain's Royal Navy. It was adopted internationally in 1874 as the official means of recording wind velocity. They are as follows, with descriptions of the ocean surface:

Force 0 (0–1mph): Calm; glassy (like a mirror).
Force 1 (1–3mph): Light wind; rippled surface.
Force 2 (4–7mph): Light breeze; small wavelets.
Force 3 (8–12mph): Gentle breeze; large wavelets, scattered whitecaps.
Force 4 (13–18mph): Moderate breeze; small waves, frequent whitecaps.
Force 5 (19–24mph): Fresh breeze; moderate waves, numerous whitecaps.
Force 6 (25–31mph): Strong breeze; large waves, white foam crests.
Force 7 (32–38mph): Moderate gale; streaky white foam.
Force 8 (39–46mph): Fresh gale; moderate waves.
Force 9 (47–54mph): Strong gale; high waves.
Force 10 (55–63mph): Whole gale; very high waves, curling crests.
Force 11 (64–73mph): Violent storm; extremely high waves, froth and foam, poor visibility.
Force 12 (73+mph): Hurricane; huge waves, thundering white spray, visibility nil.

The beautiful *Sea Cloud*.

The activities are few, so relaxation is the key, in a stylish but unpretentious setting. The food and service are good, as is the interaction between the 69 passengers and 60 crew members, many of whom have worked aboard the ship for many years. One bonus is the fact that a doctor is available on board at no charge for emergencies or seasickness medication.

A modern interpretation of the original *Sea Cloud*, a second ship, named *Sea Cloud II*, was built and introduced in 2001.

Contemporary sail-cruise ships

To combine sailing with push-button automation, try *Club Med 2* (Club Méditerranée) or *Wind Surf* (Windstar Cruises) – with five tall aluminum masts, they are the world's largest sail-cruise ships – and *Wind Spirit* and *Wind Star* (Windstar Cruises), with four masts. Not a hand touches the sails; they are computer-controlled from the navigation bridge.

The traditional sense of sailing is almost absent in these ocean-going robots, because the computer keeps the ship on an even keel. Also, some people find it hard to get used to the whine of the vessels' generators, which run the lighting and air-conditioning systems 24 hours a day.

From a yachtsman's viewpoint, the sail-to-power ratio is poor. That's why these cruise ships with sails have engine power to get them into and out of port. The *Sea Cloud* and *Star Clipper* ships do it by sail alone, except when there is no wind, which doesn't happen all that often.

On some itineraries, when there's little wind, you could be motor-powered for most of the cruise, with only a few hours under sail. The three Windstar Cruises vessels and one Club Med ship are typically under sail for about 40 percent of the time.

The Windstar ships carry mainly North Americans and the Club Med vessel mainly French speakers.

Another slightly smaller vessel is the chic *Le Ponant*. This three-mast ship caters to just 64 French-speaking passengers in elegant, yet casual, high-tech surroundings, advancing the technology of the original Windstar concept. The ship made news in 2008, when its crew was held to ransom by pirates off the Somali coast; no passengers were on board at the time.

When the engine cuts in

So, do you get to cruise under sail most of the time? Not really. Aboard the ships of Sea Cloud Cruises and Star Clippers, because they are real sailing ships, you could be under sail for most of the night when the ships are under way, as long as there is wind, of course, and on the days or part days at sea.

The ship's small engine is used for maneuvering in and out of port. In the Caribbean, for example, the trade winds are good for most of the year, but in the Mediterranean the winds are not so potent.

Aboard the ships of Windstar Cruises, however, the itineraries are so port-intensive that the computer-controlled sails are hardly ever used today – so the experience can be disappointing.

Cruising Around-the-World

They are a great way to roam the world without
having to pack and unpack constantly. But choose
carefully: some ships spend very little time in ports.

Since Cunard operated its first world cruise aboard the *Laconia* in 1922, this has become the ultimate classic journey – more a voyage of discovery than a cruise. It is defined as the complete circumnavigation of the earth in a continuous one-way voyage, typically including both the Panama and the Suez Canals. Ports of call are carefully planned for their interest and diversity, and the entire voyage can last six months or longer.

Galas, themed balls (for example, Cunard's Black & White Ball and Royal Ascot Ball), special social events, top entertainers, and, typically, well-known lecturers are all part of the package. It's a great way of exchanging the northern winter for the southern sun in a grand voyage that is over 32,000 nautical miles long, following in the wake of Ferdinand Magellan, who led his round-the-world voyage in 1519–22, although he himself was killed en route.

Around-the-world cruises generally pursue the sun in a westbound direction, which gives the added bonus of gaining an hour each time a ship goes

Aurora transiting the Panama Canal.

into the next time zone. Travel in an eastbound direction – between, for example, Europe and Australia – and you lose an hour each time. A few ships that include an around-South America voyage will generally travel in a southbound, then westbound, direction.

A world cruise aboard means enjoying stabilized, air-conditioned comfort in luxury cabins, combined with extraordinary sightseeing and excursions on shore and overland. It is all about exchanging familiar environments with new ones, glamorous evening soirées, special social parties, themed balls, and entertainment that ranges from intimate recitals to large-scale shows and headline cabaret specialty acts. Best of all: you need pack and unpack just once during a three-month circumnavigation.

It generally appeals to retirees, anyone who simply wants to escape the winter, and those who delight in roaming the world in search of new experiences, sights, sounds, cultures, and aromas. There'll be lots of sea days, during which your suite or cabin can be a private refuge, so it's worth choosing the best you can afford.

There are four aspects to a good world cruise: itinerary, ship, price, and the cruise line's experience. Some of the most ambitious itineraries are those operated by German cruise lines such as Hapag-Lloyd Cruises and Phoenix Reisen (whose itineraries usually feature more than 60 ports of

Planning

For passengers, one of the most important decisions to make will be about what clothes to pack for different climates and conditions. What's really good is that once you have boarded the ship, you need unpack only once. Also, you can take as much luggage as you wish; if you need to fly to join the cruise, you can send your luggage on ahead with a courier service. Although all ships have laundries, some also have self-service launderettes (the place to go for all the inside gossip), so you can clean small items that you need to reuse quickly.

For an operator, planning a world cruise involves daunting organization. For example, more than 700,000 main meals will be prepared during a typical world cruise aboard *Queen Mary 2*. A ship of its size needs two major crew changes during a three-month-long voyage. Hundreds of professional entertainers, lecturers, bands, and musicians must be booked a year in advance.

Crystal Serenity in French Polynesia.

call, compared to the average 35). Staying overnight in several ports of call means that you can plan to meet friends, go out for dinner, and enjoy nights out on the town. But check cruise line websites and brochures and itineraries carefully, because some ships spend surprisingly little time in port.

World cruise segments

If you want to experience all the extra things that around-the-world cruises provide but don't have the three months needed, most lines offer the cruise in several 'segments.' This way you can try the ship and service levels before investing the time and money needed for a full circumnavigation. Europa offers nine segments on its 155-day around-the-world cruise. The most popular length for a segment is around 18 days.

'Segmenters,' as they are known, typically add on a stay pre- or post-cruise in a destination combining a cruise 'n' stay vacation. In this way, they can visit exotic destinations such as China, the South Pacific, the Indian Ocean, or South America, while also enjoying the elegance, comfort, splendid food, and good company of their cruise ship.

Bear in mind that you get what you pay for. Ships rated at four stars or more will probably include shuttle buses from your ship to town centers; ships rated three stars or less will not.

Ships that roam worldwide during the year offer the most experienced world cruises or segments. In August 2016, for example, Europa 2 will operate a world voyage lasting 337 days, divided into three routes and more than 20 segments,

What's the cost

Prices for a full world cruise vary depending on the cruise line, ship, and accommodation chosen. The following examples are taken from 2015/16 world cruise brochures; per person rates are quoted, based on double occupancy for an interior (no view) cabin. Single-occupancy rates are available on request:

Amsterdam (116 days, from $13,598.85)
Insignia (180 days, from £39,999)
Queen Mary 2 (121 days, from £12,799)
Silver Whisper (115 days, from $59,950)

Substantial discounts and special incentives are offered by many cruise lines, particularly if you book early. The lowest-grade cabins tend to sell out fastest, so book as soon as you can to secure one of these. Some cruise lines quote only a 'from' price as a lead-in rate, and provide the price for the largest suites only upon application.

Passengers booking a full world cruise may enjoy a pre-cruise five-star hotel stay and extravagant dinner with the cruise line's top executives, onboard credit, plus other special events during the cruise (not avail-

Queen Mary 2 leaving Sydney.

able to 'segmenters'). Note that some cruise lines reserve the right to add a surcharge if the NYNEX oil price exceeds $70 a barrel – read the fine print in the brochure. Also, the lowest prices may not include the airfare, if any is required.

Some ships include alcoholic drinks and wine in their cruise fares (examples include *Crystal Serenity*, *Seabourn Quest, Seven Seas Voyager*, and *Silver Spirit*), but most do not. There will inevitably be the question of gratuities to staff, which are included aboard some ships. Factor in about $10 per person, per day to your budget for these. On a 90-day world cruise, that's a whopping $1,800. If you are in one of the largest suites, it would be considerably more – allow about $3,000 per couple.

Shore excursions

Part of the excitement of an around-the-world voyage is the anticipation of seeing new destinations, and planning how best to use your time. This is where the expertise of cruise line shore excursion departments and concierges can prove worthwhile.

Aboard some ships, tailor-made excursions are always available, as are extras including arranging private cars with a driver and guide for a few hours or a whole day.

Overland tours lasting from one to five days are sometimes featured. Here, you leave the ship in one

port and rejoin in another a few days later – for example, leave the ship in Mumbai, fly to Agra to see the Taj Mahal, and perhaps ride aboard the Maharaja Express train, then fly to another port to rejoin the ship. Depending on the 'overland' country, you may need to apply for a visa before your voyage.

Helicopter or seaplane flightseeing tours, typically costing around $300, are always popular.

One problem is the lack of port information for independent passengers not wishing to join organized excursions. The answer is to do the research yourself. Books in the ship's library should help if you haven't done your homework before embarking, as, of course, will information available over the Internet.

Extra baggage

One of the nice things about an around-the-world cruise is that if you buy big or heavy items along the way, the ship can store the item on board for you. If you only take a segment (Southampton to Sydney, say), you may be able to collect the items when the ship completes its voyage at its home port. Not all cruise lines offer this service.

Celebrations at sea

On around-the-world cruises, special dates for English-speaking passengers are usually observed with decorations, dinners, dances, teas, and menus that reflect the occasion. Examples include: Burns Night, Valentine's Day, Australia Day, April Fool's Day, May Day, etc.

Jan 25: Robert Burns Night (Burns Dinner).
Jan 26: Australia's National Constitution Day.
Feb 6: New Zealand (Waitangi) Day.
Feb 14: St. Valentine's Day.
Mar 1: St. David's Day (patron saint of Wales).
Mar 17: St. Patrick's Day (patron saint of Ireland – think green beer).
Apr 1: April Fools' Day (a morning of jokes and tricks to be played before midday).
Apr 23: St. George's Day (patron saint of England).
May 1: May Day (traditional Morris dancing).

Two special ceremonies form part of the passenger participation events on a traditional around-the-world cruise:

Crossing the Equator, when King Neptune (Neptunus Rex, the old man of the sea), his wife Amphitrite, and the Royal Court initiate those crossing the line for the first time (called pollywogs). An old naval tradition, it is usually conducted at the poolside – with inevitable results.

Crossing the International Date Line, where you gain or lose a day, depending on whether you're traveling eastbound or westbound. The imaginary line, at approximately 180 degrees longitude, isn't straight but zigzags to avoid splitting countries apart. Although it was established with international agreement, there are no formal treaties or

Flowers on Valentine's Day

conventions. It has confused explorers, navigators, and travelers ever since man began circumnavigating the globe 500 years ago. In Jules Verne's *Around the World in 80 Days* Phileas Fogg and his crew returned to London one day late (or so they thought), but it was the extra day gained by crossing the International Date Line that enabled them to win their wager.

Around-the-world cruises in 2015							
Ship	Company	Days	Date (start)	Start	End	No. of ports
Albatros	Phoenix Reisen	128s	December 22, 2015	Genoa	Genoa	68
Amadea	Phoenix Reisen	136	December 20, 2015	Villefranche (Nice)	Hamburg	66
Amsterdam	Holland America Line	116	January 5, 2016	Ft. Lauderdale	Ft Lauderdale	42
Arcadia	P&O Cruises	116	January 11, 2016	Southampton	Southampton	32
Artania	Phoenix Reisen	138	December 21, 2015	Genoa	Venice	70
Aurora	P&O Cruises	115	January 2, 2016	Southampton	Southampton	38
Black Watch	Fred. Olsen Cruise Lines	116	January 8, 2016	Southampton	Southampton	41
Costa Luminosa	Costa Cruises	109	January 6, 2016	Savona	Savona	37
Costa Luminosa	Costa Cruises	97	September 16, 2016	Savona	Savona	36
Europa	Hapag-Lloyd Cruises	155	December 1, 2015	Dubai	Hamburg	63
Insignia	Oceania Cruises	180	January 4, 2016	Miami	Miami	91
Pacific Princess	Princess Cruises	111	January 3, 2016	Ft Lauderdale	Ft Lauderdale	35
Queen Mary 2	Cunard Line	120	January 10, 2016	Southampton	Southampton	38
Queen Victoria	Cunard Line	120	January 10, 2016	Southampton	Southampton	39
Sea Princess	Princess Cruises	105	May 15, 2016	Sydney	Sydney	119
Silver Whisper	Silversea Cruises	116	January 5, 2016	Ft. Lauderdale	Venice	51

Choosing Your Ship

What's the difference between large and small ships? Are new ships better than older ones? Here is the latest to make sure you select the right ship on which to sail away.

There's something to suit virtually all tastes when it comes to which ship to choose. Ships are measured (not weighed) in gross tonnage (GT) and come in four principal size categories:

Large resort ships: for 2,001–6,500 passengers (typically measure 50,000–220,000 gross tonnage). *Think:* double-decker bus (with some seats that are better than others).

Mid-size ships: for 751–2,000 passengers (typically 25,000–50,000 gross tonnage). *Think:* long-distance coach (comfortable seats).

Small ships: for 251–750 passengers (typically 5,000–25,000 gross tonnage). *Think:* mini-van (some are executive types; some are more mainstream).

Boutique ships: 50–250 passengers (typically 1,000–5,000 gross tonnage). *Think:* private car (luxury, mid-range, or compact).

Small luxury ship *Silver Cloud*.

Space

For an idea of the amount of the space around you (I call it the 'crowd factor'), check the 'Passenger Space Ratio' given for each ship in the listings section (gross tonnage divided by the number of passengers, based on two lower beds per cabin, plus single-occupancy cabins).

Passenger space ratio:
50 and above: outstanding
30 to 50: very spacious
20 to 30: not very spacious
20 and under: very cramped

Large resort ships (2,001–6,500 passengers)

Choose a large resort ship if you like being with lots of other people in a big-city environment, you enjoy being sociable, and you want to have lots of entertainment and dining (well, eating) options. These balcony-rich ships provide a well-packaged standard or premium vacation, usually in a seven-day cruise. It is the interaction between passengers and crew that determines the quality of the on-board experience.

Large resort ships have extensive facilities and programs for families with children of all ages. But if you meet someone on the first day and want to see them again, make sure you appoint a very specific place and time – apart from the size of the ship, they may be at a different meal seating. These ships have a highly structured array of activities and passenger participation events each day, together with large entertainment venues, and the most lavish production shows at sea.

It is the standard of service, entertainment, lecture programs, level of communication, and finesse in dining services that really can move these ships into high rating categories, but they must be exceptional to do so. Choose higher-priced suite accommodation, and the service improves. In other words: pay more, get more.

Large resort ships are highly programmed. It is difficult, for example, to go swimming in the late evening – the decks are cleaned and pools are often netted over by 6pm. Having Champagne delivered to outdoor hot tubs late at night is virtually impossible. The flexibility for which cruise ships were once known has been lost here, with the cruise lines becoming victims of company 'policy' and insurance regulations. There can be a feeling

Advantages and disadvantages of large resort ships	
Advantages	**Disadvantages**
They have the widest range of public rooms and facilities, often a walk-around promenade deck outdoors, and more space (but more passengers).	The itineraries may be limited by ship size, and there may be tender ports where you need to take a number, sit in a lounge, and wait… and wait.
They generally have more dining options.	Room-service breakfast is not generally available on the day of disembarkation.
The newest ships have state-of-the-art electronic interactive entertainment facilities – good if you like computers and high-tech gadgetry.	They are floating hotels – with many announcements – and many items cost extra. They are like retail parks surrounded by cabins.
There are more facilities and activities for people of all ages, particularly for families with children.	Finding your way around the ship can be frustrating, and signage is often confusing.
Children of all ages will have a whale of a time.	There will be a lack of available elevators at peak times.
They generally sail well in open seas in bad weather.	You may have to use a sign-up sheet to use gym equipment such as treadmills or exercise bikes.
Announcements could be in several languages.	The restaurant service staff is trained to provide fast service, so it's almost impossible to dine in leisurely fashion.
The large choice of rooms is likely to mean a large range of price points.	Food may well be bland – cooking for 5,000 is not quite the same as cooking for a dinner party of eight.
There will be a huge variety of passengers on board – great for socializing.	Telephoning room service can be frustrating, particularly in ships with automatic telephone answering systems.
There is a wide choice of shopping opportunities for clothing, watches, and jewelry.	There will be lots of lines to wait in: for embarkation, reception, elevators, buffet meals, shore excursions, security checkpoint, and disembarkation.
The newest ships have large spas with numerous exercise and body pampering facilities.	In the early evening, the deckchairs are taken away, or strapped up, so they can't be used.
There are usually more outdoor aqua park facilities.	The in-cabin music aboard the latest ships is supplied through the television set; it may be impossible to turn off the picture while listening.
There should be larger casino and gaming facilities.	Some large resort ships have only two main passenger stairways.

of 'conveyor-belt' cruising, with cultural offerings scarcely extending beyond rap, rock, alcohol, and gambling.

Mid-size ships
(751–2,000 passengers)

These suit the smaller ports of the Aegean and Mediterranean, and are more maneuverable than larger ships. Several operate around-the-world cruises and other long-distance itineraries to exotic destinations not really feasible aboard many small ships or large resort ships.

There is a big difference in the amount of space available. Accommodation varies from large 'penthouse suites' complete with butler service to tiny interior (no-view) cabins. These ships will generally be more stable at sea than 'small ships,' due to their increased size and draft. They provide more facilities, more entertainment, and more dining options than smaller ships. Of course, there is some entertainment and more structured activities than aboard small ships, but less than aboard large resort ships.

Formal dining aboard Cunard's *Queen Victoria*.

Advantages and disadvantages of mid-size ships	
Advantages	Disadvantages
They are neither too large, nor too small; their size and facilities often strike a happy balance.	Few have large showlounges for large-scale production shows, so entertainment tends to be more of the cabaret variety.
It is easy to find one's way around.	They don't offer as wide a range of public rooms and facilities as the large resort ships.
They generally sail well in bad weather, being neither high-sided like the large resort ships, nor of too shallow draft like some of the small ships.	Most activities will be geared to couples, and single travellers might feel left out.
Lines seldom form, except on ships approaching 1,600 passengers.	Aboard some ships bathrooms may be small and cramped.
They appear more like traditional ships than most of the larger vessels, which tend to be more 'boxy' in shape and profile.	There are fewer opportunities for social gatherings.

Small ships (251–750 passengers) and boutique ships (50–250 passengers)

Choose a small or boutique ship for an intimate cruise experience and a small number of passengers. Some of the world's most exclusive cruise ships belong in this group – but so do most of the coastal vessels with basic, unpretentious amenities, sail-cruise ships, and the expedition-style cruise vessels that take passengers to see natural wonders.

Select this size of ship if you don't need much entertainment, large resort ship facilities, gambling casinos, several restaurants, and if you don't like to wait in lines for anything. If you want to swim in the late evening, or have Champagne in the hot tub at

midnight, it's easier aboard boutique or small ships than aboard larger ships, where more rigid programs lead to inflexible, passenger-unfriendly thinking.

What about age?

A ship's condition depends on the level of maintenance it has received, and whether it has operated on short or longer cruises – short cruises get more passenger throughput and wear and tear. Many passengers like older ships, as they tend to have fewer synthetic materials in their interior decor. It's inevitable that most of the older tonnage won't match the latest high-tech hardware, but today's ships aren't built with the same loving care as in the past.

Casual lunch aboard a large resort ship.

Most cruise advertising you'll see revolves around the newer, larger ships, but some older ships have much to offer if you don't want the latest trendy facilities and city high street feel. Indeed, some of the older, smaller ships have adequate facilities, tend to have more character, and provide a more relaxing vacation experience than the go-go contemporary ships, where you're just one of a large crowd.

Ships under 10 years old: advantages
Newer ships typically incorporate the latest in high-tech equipment in advanced ship design and construction; they also meet the latest safety and operating regulations.

Many new ships have 'pod' propulsion systems, which have replaced conventional propeller shafts, propellers, and rudders, resulting in little or no vibration, and greater fuel efficiency.

Although the trade-off is debatable, more recent ships have been built with more space given over to the interior public rooms, and less to the topside pool deck so there's less space for sunbathing.

Newer ships have design advantages as well, including: a shallower draft, which makes it easier for them to enter and leave ports; bow and stern thrusters, so they seldom require tug assistance in many ports, which reduces operating costs; and many have the latest submersible lifeboats, creating a safer operating environment.

An illustrated nature talk aboard *National Geographic Explorer*.

Ships under 10 years old: disadvantages
Recent design changes mean that newer ships have thin hulls and do not withstand the bangs and dents as well as older, more heavily plated vessels.

The interior decor is made mostly from synthetic materials, due to stringent regulations, and could cause problems for passengers sensitive to such materials. Cabin windows are usually sealed, and not portholes that can be opened. Most egregiously, newer ships almost always have toilets of the powerful vacuum suction, which I call the 'barking dog' type, due to the noise they make when flushed.

Advantages and disadvantages of small ships/boutique ships	
Advantages	**Disadvantages**
Most provide 'open seating' in the dining room; this means that you can sit with whomever you wish, whenever you wish, for all meals.	They don't have the bulk, length, or beam to sail well in open seas in inclement weather conditions.
They provide a totally unstructured lifestyle, offering a level of service not found aboard most of the larger ships, and no – or almost no – announcements.	They don't have the range of public rooms or open spaces that the large resort ships can provide.
They are at their best in warm-weather areas.	Options for entertainment are more limited than on larger ships.
They are capable of offering true culinary excellence, with fresh foods cooked to order.	The cost – this is the upper end of the market, and doesn't come cheap.
They're more like small inns than mega-resorts.	The size of cabin bathrooms (particularly the shower enclosures) is often disappointing.
It's easy to find your way around, and signage is usually clear and concise.	The range of shore excursion opportunities is more limited.
They provide an 'open bridge' policy, allowing passengers to visit the navigation bridge when it is safe to do so.	Swimming pools will be very small; in fact, they are more like 'dip' pools.
Some small ships have a hydraulic marina water-sports platform at the stern and carry equipment such as jet skis and scuba/snorkeling gear.	Many of the smaller ships do not have balcony cabins, simply because the accommodation decks are too close to the waterline.
They can visit the more off-beat ports of call that larger ships can't.	
When the ship is at anchor, going ashore is easy and speedy, with a continuous tender service and no lines. Access to these less-crowded ports means more exclusivity.	

Comparing the biggest of the big				
Ship name	Cruise line	Gross tonnage	No. of passengers	Year built
Harmony of the Seas	Royal Caribbean International	227,700	5,496	2016
Allure of the Seas	Royal Caribbean Int.	225,282	5,400	2010
Oasis of the Seas	Royal Caribbean Int.	225,282	5,400	2009
Anthem of the Seas	Royal Caribbean Int.	168,666	4,180	2015
Quantum of the Seas	Royal Caribbean Int.	168,666	4,180	2014
Norwegian Escape	Norwegian Cruise Line	163,000	4,200	2015
Freedom of the Seas	Royal Caribbean Int.	154,407	3,634	2006
Independence of the Seas	Royal Caribbean Int.	154,407	3,634	2008
Liberty of the Seas	Royal Caribbean Int.	154,407	3,634	2007
Norwegian Epic	Norwegian Cruise Line	153,000	4,200	2010
Queen Mary 2	Cunard Line	148,528	2,620	2004
Norwegian BBreakawayBreakaway	Norwegian Cruise Line	145,655	3,998	2013
Norwegian Getaway	Norwegian Cruise Line	145,655	3,998	2014
Royal Princess	Princess Cruises	141,200	3,600	2013
Regal Princess	Princess Cruises	141,200	3,600	2014
Britannia	P&O Cruises	141,000	3,638	2015
MSC Preziosa	MSC Cruises	140,000	3,502	2013
MSC Divina	MSC Cruises	139,400	3,502	2012
MSC Fantasia	MSC Cruises	137,936	3,274	2008
MSC Splendida	MSC Cruises	137,936	3,274	2009
Explorer of the Seas	Royal Caribbean Int.	137,308	3,634	2000
Voyager of the Seas	Royal Caribbean Int.	137,280	3,634	1999
Adventure of the Seas	Royal Caribbean Int.	137,276	3,634	2001
Mariner of the Seas	Royal Caribbean Int.	137,276	3,634	2004
Navigator of the Seas	Royal Caribbean Int.	137,276	3,634	2003
Costa Diadema	Costa Cruises	132,500	3,700	2014
Disney Dream	Disney Cruise Line	129,690	2,500	2011
Disney Fantasy	Disney Cruise Line	129,690	2,500	2012
Carnival Breeze	Carnival Cruise Line	128,251	3,646	2012
Carnival Dream	Carnival Cruise Line	128,251	3,646	2009
Carnival Magic	Carnival Cruise Line	128,251	3,646	2011
AIDAprima	AIDA Cruises	125,000	3,286	2015
Celebrity Reflection	Celebrity Cruises	122,210	2,852	2012
Celebrity Silhouette	Celebrity Cruises	122,210	2,852	2011
Celebrity Eclipse	Celebrity Cruises	121,878	2,852	2010
Celebrity Equinox	Celebrity Cruises	121,878	2,852	2009
Celebrity Solstice	Celebrity Cruises	121,878	2,852	2008
Ventura	P&O Cruises	116,017	3,092	2008
Diamond Princess	Princess Cruises	115,875	2,674	2004

Choosing Your Accommodation

Does cabin size count? Are suites sweeter
than cabins? How desirable is a balcony?
What about location?

Ideally, you should feel at home when at sea, so it is important to choose the right accommodation, even if most of your time in it is spent with your eyes shut. Accommodation sizes range from a whopping 4,390 sq ft (407 sq m) to a minuscule 60 sq ft (5.5 sq m). Choose wisely (dependent on your budget, of course), for if you find that your cabin (incorrectly called a 'stateroom' by some companies) is too small when you get to the ship, it may be impossible to change it, as the ship could be full.

Cruise lines designate cabins only when deposits have been received – they may, however, guarantee the grade and rate requested. If this isn't done, or if you find a disclaimer such as 'All cabin assignments are confirmed upon embarkation of the vessel,' get a guarantee in writing that your cabin will *not* be changed on embarkation.

There are three main types of accommodation: suites, outside-view cabins, and interior cabins. But there are many variations on each type, as detailed below.

The suite life

Suites are the most luxurious and spacious of all shipboard accommodation, and typically come with butler service. A suite (in the sense of a 'suite of rooms') should comprise a lounge or sitting room separated from a bedroom by a solid door (not just a curtain), a bedroom with a large bed, one or more bathrooms, and an abundance of closet, drawer, and other storage space. The best suites have the most desirable position, privacy, good views, and quality bed linen. Many cruise lines inaccurately describe some accommodation as suites, when they are nothing more than a large cabin with a curtain that divides sitting and sleeping areas.

Be aware that, although the large resort ships may devote a whole deck or two to penthouses and suites, you will have to share the rest of the ship with those in lower-priced accommodation. That means there is no preferential seating in the showroom, dining rooms, or on sunbathing decks. You may get separate check-in facilities and preferential treatment upon disembarkation, but your luggage will be lumped with everyone else's.

'Spa suite' accommodation

Spa suites – not to be confused with the 'thermal spa suites' (comprising sauna, steam room, and herbal showers), which are found in the on-board spa – are usually located adjacent to or near the ship's spa. They often have 'spa-added' features such as a bath-room with window into the sleeping area, bathtub, and mood lighting, and perhaps special health teas or herbal infusions. Some cruise lines may even include a spa treatment such as a massage or facial, in the 'spa suite' package, plus unlimited access to the actual spa.

Examples with spa suites include *Celebrity Reflection*, *Costa Deliziosa*, *Costa Fascinosa*, *Costa Favolosa*, *Costa Luminosa*, *Costa Pacifica*, *Costa Serena*, *Europa*, *Europa 2*, *MSC Divina*, *MSC Fantasia*, *MSC Preziosa*, and *MSC Splendida*. Some ships also have a special spa-food-menu-only restaurant; examples include *Celebrity Eclipse*, *Celebrity Equinox*, *Celebrity Reflection*, *Celebrity Silhouette*, *Celebrity Solstice*, *Costa Deliziosa*, *Costa Fascinosa*, *Costa Favolosa*, and *Costa Serena*.

Are balconies worth it?

Romeo and Juliet thought so. And they're addictive, too. A private balcony (or veranda, terrace, or lanai), for which you pay a premium, is just that. It is a mini-terrace adjoining your cabin where you can sit, enjoy the

The lavish Reflection Suite bathroom on *Celebrity Reflection*.

View from a Carnival balcony.

private view, smell the sea, dine, or even have a massage.

Some private balconies aren't so private, though. Balconies not separated by full floor-to-ceiling partitions don't quite cut it (examples include *Carnival Sunshine, Carnival Triumph, Carnival Victory, Maasdam, Oriana, Queen Mary 2, Pacific Aria, Pacific Eden, Seven Seas Mariner, Seven Seas Voyager,* and *Veendam*). You could be disturbed by noise or (worse still) smoke from your neighbor.

Many large resort ships have balconies that are too small to accommodate even two reclining chairs, and they may have plastic matting or plain painted-steel decking instead of traditional, more expensive hardwood. The average size of a cabin balcony aboard large resort ships is about 9 by 6ft (2.7x1.8m) or about 55 sq ft (5.2 sq m), but they can measure as much as 30 times that.

Suites with forward-facing private balconies may not be so good, as the wind speed can make them all but unusable. Ships with balconies of this kind include *Silver Cloud, Silver Shadow, Silver Spirit, Silver Whisper, Silver Wind, Star Legend, Star Pride,* and *Star Spirit*. And when the ship drops anchor in ports of call, the noise pollution can be irritating – as on *Silver Cloud* and *Silver Wind*, for example.

For the best in privacy, a balcony suite at a ship's stern is hard to beat, and some of the largest afloat can be found there – sheltered from the wind, such as aboard *Marina* and *Riviera* (Oceania Cruises).

Installing a balcony means that space is often taken away from either the cabin or the bathroom, which is why today's bathrooms are smaller and almost none have tubs.

All private balconies have railings to lean on, but some have solid steel plates between the railing and deck, so you can't look out to sea when seated (*Costa neoClassica, Costa neoRomantica, Dawn Princess, Oceana, Sea Princess,* and *Sun Princess*). Better are ships whose balconies have clear glass (*Aurora, Brilliance of the Seas, Empress, Mein Schiff 1, Mein Schiff 2, Mein Schiff 3, Mein Schiff 4, Radiance of the Seas,* and *Serenade of the Seas*) or horizontal bars.

Balcony doors can be quite heavy and difficult to open. Many ships have doors that slide open (examples: *Crystal Serenity, Grand Princess, Norwegian Gem*); a few have doors that open inward (examples: *Silver Cloud, Silver Wind, Star Breeze, Star Legend, Star Pride*); some have doors that open outward (examples: *Eurodam, Legend of the Seas, Queen Elizabeth, Queen Victoria*).

French balconies

A 'French' balcony (also called a 'Juliet' or 'Juliette' balcony) is neither French, nor a balcony as such. It is a full floor-to-ceiling sliding door with a tiny ledge (not really a balcony) that allows you to stick out your toes and smell the fresh air, and railings for safety.

Interior-view balconies

Aboard Royal Caribbean International's *Allure of the Seas, Harmony of the Seas* and *Oasis of the Seas*, 'interior' balcony cabins are novel. They overlook one of two 'neighborhoods': Central Park, with its trees and plants, or The Boardwalk, at the stern of the ship. However, these really are classed as outside balcony cabins – if it rains, your balcony *can* get wet, but it's unlikely. Also, people scream as they career along the Zipline above the Boardwalk balconies (aboard *Harmony of the Seas* it's a waterslide), so they can be really noisy by day. And, when no one is zipping, you may have a view of the sea (and perhaps the excellent acrobatic AquaShow) at the ship's stern.

Balconies that lack privacy

If you choose a Riviera Deck (Deck 14) balcony cabin aboard *Azura* or *Ventura*, for example, you can oversee many balconies on the decks below yours – particularly those on C Deck and D Deck – because they are built right out to the ship's sides. If you have such a cabin, it would be unwise to sunbathe or sit naked on your balcony. Not only that, but almost *all* balcony cabins can be seen from the navigation bridge, where the staff is equipped with binoculars (for lookout purposes).

Interior 'virtual' balconies

For the latest in interior design, there's the 'virtual' balcony. Royal Caribbean International's *Anthem of the Seas* and *Quantum of the Seas* have them, and so do 81 interior cabins retrofitted to Navigator of the Seas. They give the cabins an 'outside' feel, and feature 6ft 7in (2m) 'screens' with a live video feed from cameras mounted on the front and aft of the ship fed through the ship's computer server and fibre-optic cables. With curtains on either side of the (almost) floor-to-ceiling wall 'screen' (which you can turn off), the 'balcony' is positioned on a forward- or aft-facing cabin wall. Naturally, these cabins command a premium price.

Balconies to covet

Some of my favorite large balcony suites and cabins include Celebrity Cruises' *Celebrity Constellation, Celebrity Infinity, Celebrity Millennium,* and *Celebrity Summit* (6147, 6148, 9096, 9098, 9156, 9197); Cunard Line's *Queen Mary 2* (9069, 9078, the Balmoral and Sandringham duplexes at the stern); Hapag-Lloyd Cruises' *Europa 2* (the two owner's suites 1001, 1002); Oceania Cruises' *Insignia, Nautica* and *Regatta* (6088, 6091, 7114, 7119, 8064, 8067), *Marina and Riviera* (8143, 9147, 10111 – these suites span the ship's entire beam, although the balcony is actually split into two); *P&O Cruises Britannia* (A726, A727; B725, B726; C736, C737; D738, D739; E742, E743; F730, F731; G732, G733); Regent Seven Seas Cruises' *Seven Seas Mariner* (780, 781, 8100, 8101, 988, 989, 1080, 1081), and *Seven Seas Voyager* (673, 674, 781, 782, 970, 971).

Upstairs and downstairs

Allure of the Seas, Anthem of the Seas, Aurora, Oasis of the Seas, Quantum of the Seas, and *Queen Mary 2* have 'loft'-style or 'duplex' accommodation, with a living room downstairs and bedroom upstairs.

How much?

Accommodation cost is directly related to size, location, facilities, and services. Each line implements its own system according to ship size, age, construction, and profit potential. It may be better to book a low-grade cabin on a good ship than a high-grade cabin on a poor ship, if your budget forces you to choose between the two. If you are in a party of three or more and don't mind sharing a cabin, you'll save a lot per person, so you may be able to afford a higher-grade cabin.

Cabin numbers

Nautical tradition aboard ocean-going ships dictates that even-numbered cabins should be on the port side (the same as the lifeboats), and most companies follow this rule.

Some companies – including Celebrity Cruises, MSC Cruises, and TUI Cruises – have odd-numbered cabins on the port side. Strangely, *Costa neoClassica, Costa neoRiviera, Costa neoRomantica,* and *Costa Victoria* also have odd-numbered cabins on the port side, although other, newer, Costa ships follow nautical tradition. Meanwhile, aboard Royal Caribbean International's *Freedom of the Seas, Independence of the Seas,* and *Liberty of the Seas,* outside cabins have even numbers, and interior cabins have odd numbers. But AIDA Cruises places both even- and odd-numbered cabins on the same side, whether port or starboard side. The admiralty would never approve!

Cabin sizes

Cabins provide more or less the same facilities as hotel rooms, except space. Most cruise companies favor providing large public rooms over large cabins. In some smaller interior (no-view) and outside cabins, changing clothes can be a challenge.

The latest ships have more standardized cabin sizes, because they are made in modular form. I consider 180 sq ft (16.7 sq m) to be the *minimum* acceptable size for a 'standard' cabin today.

Cabin location

I recommend an 'outside-view' cabin for your first cruise; an 'interior' cabin has no portholes or windows, making it more difficult to get oriented or to gauge the weather or time.

Cabins in the center of a ship are more stable and tend to be quieter and vibration-free. Ships powered by diesel engines (i.e., the most modern vessels) create and transmit some vibrations at the stern.

Take into account personal habits when choosing your cabin location. If you like to go to bed early, avoid a cabin close to the disco. If you have trouble walking, choose a cabin close to the elevator.

Generally, the higher the deck, the higher the cabin price, and the better the service. This is an inheritance from transoceanic times, when upper-deck cabins and suites were sunnier and warmer.

Cabins at the front of a ship are slightly crescent-shaped, given that the outer wall follows the curvature of the ship's hull. But they can be exposed to early-morning noises, such as the anchor being dropped at ports where the ship is too big to dock.

Cabins with interconnecting doors are fine for families or close friends, but the dividing wall may be so thin that you can hear the conversation next door.

10 reasons why people like balconies

1. You can get fresh air.
2. You can listen to the waves.
3. You get the maximum amount of natural light.
4. You can have tea/coffee or breakfast outside.
5. You can see what the weather is like, to decide how to dress.
6. You may see the stars (and shooting stars) at night.
7. You can sunbathe in private – assuming that the ship is in the right position and your balcony isn't overlooked.
8. You can escape from the noise of the entertainment areas.
9. You can take pictures of the sea from within your cabin.
10. You can boast about it to your friends.

Allure of the Seas' Royal Loft Suite.

Many brochures indicate cabins with 'obstructed views.' Cabins on lower decks are closer to engine noise and heat, especially at the stern of the vessel and around the engine casing. In many older ships, elevators may not operate to the lowermost decks.

And so to bed

Aboard ship, the bed frames are usually made of steel or tubular aluminum for fire protection purposes, although some older ships may have (flame-retardant) wood frames. Some have rounded edges, while others have square edges (watch your legs on these), particularly when the mattress is contained within the bed frame.

Some beds have space underneath for your luggage, while others have drawers fitted for additional storage space, so your luggage has to be stored elsewhere in the cabin.

Mattresses

Mattresses can be hard, semi-hard, or soft. If your mattress is not to your liking, ask your cabin steward if it can be changed – most ships have spare mattresses, and, to make the bed firmer, bed boards.

Some cruise lines provide simple foam mattresses, while others place more emphasis on providing extra comfort. Regent Seven Seas Cruises, for example, provides a custom-designed 'Suite Slumber Bed' – a plush euro-top mattress capped with a double layer of memory foam and dressed in the finest linens to assure a refreshing sleep.

Ultra-expensive Tempur-Pedic memory foam mattresses can be found aboard the tiny coastal boutique-size cruise ships of Un-Cruise Adventures ships (*Safari Endeavor, Safari Explorer, Safari Legacy,* and *Safari Quest*).

There are differences between mattress sizes in the UK, US, and Europe, depending on which supplier a cruise line specifies when a ship is outfitted or when bed frames and mattresses are replaced.

Duvets

Down duvets, fine bed linens, and plush mattresses are what superior sleeping environments are all about. Duvets are usually goose down or cotton filled, and range from 3.5 togs (thin) to 13.5 togs (thick), the tog rating being the warmth rating. Anyone with allergies should try a spundown duvet, which is filled with non-allergenic polyester microfiber.

Duvet covers can be for single, double, queen-, or king-size mattresses. If you request a queen-size bed configuration when you book your cruise, request an overlay, otherwise there will be a crack between the beds. Not all ships have them but the luxury/premium grade ships, and ships with suite-grade accommodation, should.

Duvet covers and sheets of 100 percent cotton (up to 400 thread count) are best, but may be more difficult for a ship's laundry to handle. But they do provide those wonderful moments when you slip into bed.

Pillows

Many ships have a 'pillow menu' in suite-grade accommodation. This gives you a choice of several different pillow types, including hop-filled or hypoallergenic, goose down, Hungarian goose down (considered the best), silk-filled, body pillow (as long as an adult body, providing full support at to the head and neck at the top and, lower down, to legs and knees), Tempur-Pedic, isotonic or copycat memory foam.

Facilities

The standard is a private bathroom (generally small) with shower, washbasin, and toilet. Higher-grade cabins and suites may have full-size bathtubs. Some have a whirlpool bath and/or bidet, a hairdryer, and more space. Most cabins come with the following: flat-screen television 'infotainment' system or regular television (regular satellite channels or closed circuit); two beds (possibly, another one or two upper berths), or a double, queen- or king-size bed (some twin beds can be pushed together to form a double/queen). Depending on cabin size, they should also have: a chair, or chair and table, or sofa and table, or, in higher grades, even a separate lounge/sitting area; telephone (for inter-cabin or ship-to-shore calls); refrigerator/wet bar (higher grades); electrical outlets for personal appliances, usually 110 and 220 volts, vanity/desk unit with chair or stool, safe; closet space, drawer space, plus under-bed storage for suitcases; bedside night stand/table unit.

Some older ships may have upper and lower berths. A 'berth' is a nautical term for a bed held in a wooden or metal frame. A 'Pullman berth' tucks away out of sight during the day, usually into the bulkhead or ceiling. You climb up a short ladder at night to get into an upper berth.

Stateroom vs cabin explained

In the 1830s, the steamer George Washington had 26 cabins, and since there were then 26 states in the United States union, each room was given the name of a state. Since that time, US-based companies have called their cabins 'staterooms.' In most other countries, 'stateroom' means 'rooms of state.'

Typical Cabin Layouts

The following rates are typical of those you can expect to pay for **Ⓐ** a seven-day and **Ⓑ** a 10-day Caribbean cruise aboard a modern cruise ship. The rates are per person and include free round-trip airfare or low-cost air add-ons from principal North American gateways

Luxury outside-view suite with private veranda, separate lounge area, vanity area, extra-large double or queen-size bed, bathroom with tub, shower, and extensive closet and storage space.
Ⓐ $1,750 Ⓑ $3,000

Luxury outside-view suite with private veranda, separate lounge, vanity area, king- or queen-size bed, bathroom with full-sized tub and separate shower, and extensive walk-in closet and storage space (plus a guest bathroom). Typical size: 550 sq. ft (50 sq. meters).
Ⓐ $2,000 Ⓑ $3,000

Note that in some ships, third- and fourth-person upper berths are available for families or friends wishing to share. The upper Pullman berths, not shown on these cabin layouts, are recessed into the wall or ceiling above the lower beds.

Large outside-view double with bed and convertible daytime sofabed, bathroom with shower, and good closet and drawer space. Typical size: 270 sq.ft (23 sq. meters).
Ⓐ $1,000 Ⓑ $2,000

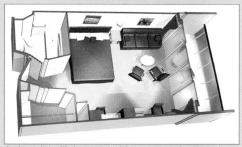

Junior suite with lounge, double or queen-size beds, bathroom with tub, shower, and ample closet and storage space. Typical size: 375 sq.ft (35 sq.meters).
Ⓐ $1,500 Ⓑ $2,000

Junior suite with lounge, double or queen-size beds, bathroom with tub, shower, and ample closet and storage space. Typical size: 375 sq.ft (35 sq.meters).
Ⓐ $1,500 Ⓑ $2,000

Comparing the Major Cruise Lines

We compare what the world's 10 largest – or best-known – cruise companies, reviewed in alphabetical order, have to offer when it comes to facilities, cuisine, service, and ambience.

The major cruise lines today are global in scale. Although the industry may appear diverse, it is dominated by just a few conglomerates, principally the Carnival Corporation, Norwegian Crise Line Holdings, and Royal Caribbean Cruises Ltd. Dig deeper and you'll find, for example, that two Carnival subsidiaries, Holland America Line and Princess Cruises, virtually control large resort ship cruising in Alaska, where they own hotels, lodges, tour companies, and much land-based transportation (other operators have to buy these services).

What they have in common

All offer one thing: a well-packaged cruise vacation, generally lasting seven days, typically with a mix of days at sea and days in port, plenty of food, reasonable service, large-scale production shows, and trendy cabaret acts, plus large casinos, shopping malls, and extensive, busy spa and fitness facilities.

Their ships have a lot in common, too. Except for MSC Cruises, all have art auctions, bingo, horse rac-

White star service aboard *Queen Mary 2*.

ing, shopping talks for ports of call, facilities and programs for children and teens, wedding vows/renewal programs, and Wi-Fi or Internet connect centers. All are dedicated to generating higher revenue returns ('pay more, get more').

Standing in line for embarkation, disembarkation (and shore tenders, shore excursion and shuttle buses in ports of call), and for self-serve buffet meals is inevitable aboard most large resort ships and the larger mid-size ships. But the ships differ in their characters, facilities, space, crew-to-passenger ratio, food and service, and crew training. You'll be escorted to your cabin aboard the ships of Cunard Line (Queen Grill-grade accommodation only) and MSC Cruises (Yacht Club-grade only). Aboard other lines, the minimal number of staff at the ship-side of the gangway simply point you in the right direction – even if you have heavy carry-on luggage – and gangway staff may even try to give you a daily program, or spa details, or shop specials. In other words, there's too much paper, even before you've reached the cabin.

What makes them different

Ships belonging to the major companies may look similar, but they differ not only in their layout, decor, and passenger flow but also in small details. Even towel sizes can vary widely.

Carnival Cruise Line

Ships

Carnival Breeze (2012), *Carnival Conquest* (2002), *Carnival Dream* (2009), *Carnival Ecstasy* (1991), *Carnival Elation* (1998), *Carnival Fantasy* (1990), *Carnival Fascination* (1994), *Carnival Freedom* (2007), *Carnival Glory* (2003), *Carnival Imagination* (1995), *Carnival Inspiration* (1996), *Carnival Legend* (2002), *Carnival Liberty* (2005), *Carnival Magic* (2011), *Carnival Miracle* (2004), *Carnival Paradise* (1998), *Carnival Pride* (2002), *Carnival Sensation* (1993), *Carnival Spirit* (2001), *Carnival Splendor* (2008), *Carnival Sunshine* (1996), *Carnival Triumph* (1999), *Carnival Valor* (2004), *Carnival Victory* (2000), *Carnival Vista* (2016)

About the company

Israel-born Ted Arison (born Theodore Arisohn), whose ambition was to be a concert pianist, founded Carnival Cruise Line, the world's largest and most successful single cruise line, in 1972, with one ship,

Mardi Gras (formerly *Empress of Canada*). Carnival wanted to be different, and developed the 'fun ship' concept. It worked, appealing to people of all ages and backgrounds.

The company's first new ship, *Tropicale*, debuted in 1982. In 1984 Carnival started advertising on television, introducing a wider public to the idea of cruising. It introduced the first cruise ship measuring over 100,000 gross tons – *Carnival Destiny* (now named *Carnival Sunshine*) – in 1996.

Today, the Carnival Corporation, parent company of Carnival Cruise Line, is run by Ted Arison's son, Micky Arison, who is chairman of the board – and owns the NBA's Miami Heat basketball team. Over 20 new ships have been introduced since the line was founded in 1972.

What is it really like?

Carnival's 'fun' style of cruising is good for families with children and teens (anyone under 21 must be

---

Which cruise line does what best

 Carnival Cruise Line is for all-round fun, activities, and casinos for the lively, no-sleep-needed youth market – although many passengers are over 45. Carnival doesn't sell itself as a 'luxury' or 'premium' cruise line, which it certainly isn't. It consistently delivers exactly the well-packaged cruise vacation its brochures promise, for which there is a huge demand. Its ships have good entertainment facilities and features, and some include extra-cost dining spots for the more discerning passenger. Carnival is all about 'participatory fun.'

 Celebrity Cruises has perhaps the best food variety of the major cruise lines, plus the most elegant ships and spas. Although it advertises itself as a 'premium' line offering 'modern luxury,' some aspects are not premium – for example, recorded 'music' blaring over pool decks 24 hours a day is not relaxing. But the term still sums up Celebrity reasonably well.

 Costa Cruises has the edge on quasi-Italian style and lively ambience, with a mix of passengers of several nationalities, but the swimming pools are full of noisy children, especially in peak holiday periods. Costa provides first-time cruise passengers with a packaged holiday that is a mix of contemporary surroundings and basic fare, accompanied by loud everything. Most passengers are Italian.

 Cunard Line has one real ocean liner *(Queen Mary 2)* that provides a regular transatlantic service, while its other two ships are more about regular cruising, albeit in ocean liner style. All three are best suited to a wide range of seasoned and well-traveled couples and solo travelers who enjoy the cosmopolitan setting of an ocean liner. Dressing formally for dinner is encouraged, although – with the exception of the grill rooms – the cuisine is largely of mass-market quality, with many traditional British favorites and extensive French dishes.

Holland America Line has all the right touches for seniors and retirees: smiling service staff, lots of flowers, traditions of the past, good cooking demonstrations, and specialty grill rooms. The ships are best suited to older couples and solo travelers who like to mingle in a large ship, in an unhurried setting, with fine-quality surroundings. There's plenty of eclectic antique artwork, decent – though not gourmet – food, and service from a smiling crew (many of whom are Indonesian/Filipino), who don't quite have the finesse many expect from a 'premium' product.

 MSC Cruises – which, unusually, is a real family-owned company – tailors its onboard product mostly to pan-European passengers of all ages (its name, after all, is Mediterranean Shipping Company). The firm displays fine Italian and pan-European flair, with a high level of service and hospitality training from a friendly, multilingual crew. It has evolved quickly as the 'new kid on the block.' Of all the major cruise lines, it's also the cleanest. Bed linen and towels are changed every third day, and bathrobes in suites daily, unlike most other brands listed here.

 Norwegian Cruise Line is a really good choice for a first cruise for families with children, with a great choice of eateries, great entertainment, and friendly service staff. Its ships are best suited to first-time youthful, single passengers, children, and teenagers who want upbeat, color-rich surroundings, plenty of entertainment lounges and bars, and high-tech sophistication – all in one programmed, well-packaged vacation.

 P&O Cruises operates mainly ex-UK cruises for its predominantly UK-based passengers, with very good facilities for families with children, as well as adults-only ships (minimum age 18). The company specializes in providing all the little things that British passengers have come to expect, including tea/coffee-making sets in all cabins (not all ships), and a choice of Indian food.

 Princess Cruises has consistent product delivery, although the ships have somewhat restrained decor. Choose Princess Cruises if you enjoy being with families and fellow passengers of mid-50s and upwards, who want a well-organized cruise experience with unpretentious middle-of-the-road cuisine, a good range of entertainment, and an excellent shore excursion program – arguably the best-run of any of the major cruise lines.

 Royal Caribbean International is really good for the Caribbean (naturally), especially for first-time cruisers and families. Its latest ships are stunning, and filled with high-tech gismos, plus there's an excellent variety of entertainment including scaled-down versions of well-known Broadway shows. The ships are liked by active, young-minded couples and solo cruisers of all ages, and families with toddlers, children, and teenagers who enjoy mingling in a large ship setting with plenty of life, and bright lighting everywhere. The food is more about quantity than quality – unless you pay extra for dining in a 'specialty' restaurant (not all the ships have them). There's background music everywhere.

accompanied by a parent, relative, or guardian) and youthful adults. The glitzy ships are also well suited to multi-generational groups, and for family reunions. Typically, about half of Carnival's passengers are taking their first cruise. About 30 percent are under the age of 35.

The dress code is ultra-casual – indeed, the waiters are better dressed than most passengers – particularly during youth-heavy holiday seasons and spring breaks. Carnival is all about 'happy' and 'fun' – cruise directors actually tell passengers to 'make some noise,' so Camp Carnival is for adults as well as children. But it's a very impersonal cruise experience, and solo travelers can get lost in the crowds of doubles. It's all about towels shaped like animals, scheduled participation activities, yelling and screaming, and having fun.

Perhaps this doesn't matter too much, because this will be a first cruise for most passengers. Repeat customers, however, have a distinct sense of déjà vu, but carry a Gold or Platinum card for better recognition from 'service' staff.

The ships are clean and well maintained – if you don't look too closely. Open deck space may look adequate when you board, but on days at sea you can expect your plastic deck chair (if you can find one that's

Enjoying the splash park aboard a Carnival Cruise Line ship.

free) to be kissing its neighbor, and probably even tied to it. There are no cushioned pads, and these seats are uncomfortable to sit on for any length of time.

The decibel level is high: it is almost impossible to escape from noise and loud music, and 'background' music is played in cabin hallways and elevators 24/7. There are libraries, but with few books, and the bookshelves are locked by 6pm, because you are expected to be out in the (revenue-earning) public areas. If you enjoy casino gaming at sea, joining Carnival's Ocean Players Club brings benefits to frequent players, depending on your skill level.

Accommodation: Note that balconies in many cabins with 'private' balconies aren't so private – most can be overlooked from other cabins located on the deck above and from various public locations. You may have to carry a credit card to operate the personal safes, which can be inconvenient. High-quality mattresses and bed linen, also available for sale, have been fitted to all beds.

Passenger niggles: The most consistent complaints are that most activities are geared around trying to sell you something. Intrusive photographers are almost impossible to escape. The smell of cigarette smoke from smokers in the casino invades other adjacent areas. There's no listing of the free in-cabin TV movies – only those that are pay-per-view. Non-stop recorded poolside music is intrusive. *Carnival Capers*, the ship's daily program, is mostly devoted to persuading you to spend money.

Cuisine/dining

Carnival ships have one or two main dining rooms, and its 'Your Choice Dining' program offers three dinner seating options, including 'Your Time' open seating. Dining assignments are confirmed at time of booking. Menus are standardized across the fleet; all dining venues are non-smoking.

Don't even think about a quiet table for two, or a candlelight dinner on deck – it's not Carnival's style – unless you pay extra at a 'specialty' restaurant. Dining aboard a Carnival ship is all about table mates, social chat, lively meals, fast eating, and fast service.

Tables are, however, nicely set with tablecloths, plenty of silverware, and iced water/iced tea whenever you want it.

The main dining rooms marry food and show business. Waiters sing and dance, and there are constant waiter parades with flashing lights in an attempt to create excitement (or take your mind off the food).

Taste-filled food is not the company's strong point, although consultant chef Georges Blanc has created daily 'Georges Blanc Signature' menu items. The actual food delivered is simply speedy banquet-style catering, with its attendant standardization and production cooking. Although meats are of a decent quality, poultry, fish, seafood, and desserts can be disappointing. Sauces and gravies are used well as disguises, and there are few garnishes. The selection of fresh green vegetables, breads, rolls, cheese, and ripe fruit could be better. Bakery items are thawed and heated from frozen. There is much use of canned fruit and jellied desserts, not to mention packets of jam, marmalade, butter, sugar – the same things you'd find in a diner or family eatery in the US.

'Spa Carnival Fare' was introduced to provide a healthier food option; vegetarian and children's menus are also available for all meals, but they wouldn't get a generous score for their nutritional content. The wine list is poor, and there are no wine waiters or decent-size wine glasses.

Specialty dining venues: *Carnival Breeze, Carnival Conquest, Carnival Dream, Carnival Freedom, Carnival Glory, Carnival Liberty, Carnival Miracle, Carnival Splendor, Carnival Sunshine, Carnival Triumph, Carnival Valor, Carnival Vista.*

Extra-cost steak houses have nicer table settings, china and silverware, and leather-bound menus. Favorites include prime American steaks such as filet mignon (9oz), porterhouse steak (24oz), and New York strip loin (shown to you at your table before you order), broiled lobster tail, and stone crab claws from Joe's Stone Crabs of South Miami Beach.

Reservations are necessary, and a cover charge applies. The food is good, and the ambience is reasonably quiet.

Casual eateries: All ships also have large food court-style spaces for casual food, grilled and fried fast-food 'chowdown' items, pizzas (each ship serves over 800 pizzas in a typical day), stir-fry, sushi, deli, and salad items. There are also self-help beverage stands, coffee that looks like rusty water, and tea in paper cups with a teabag, plastic or wooden stirrers (no teaspoons or saucers), and packets of chemical 'milk' or creamer.

Guy Fieri's Burger Joints have appeared aboard Carnival's ships for good reason – television's Food Network audience is typical of Carnival's 'chowdown' clientele. So you can get a Plain Jane, Straight

Carnival Liberty calls at Roatán in Honduras Bay.

Up, Pig Patty, Chilius Maximus, or The Ringer burger, all served with hand cut fries and Guy's signature seasoning.

Late-night 'snacks' consist of fast-food items instead of healthy alternatives such as light fruit bites, and are often the same every night. Breakfast buffets are as repetitive as canned laughter on television.

The coffee/tea factor: Regular coffee is very weak, scoring 1 out of 10 (paper/foam cups in buffet areas), unless you pay extra in the coffee shops.

For children

Carnival is a family-friendly cruise line, carrying more than 700,000 children a year, and 'Camp Carnival,' the line's extensive child/youth program, is well organized. There are five age groups: Toddlers (ages two to five), Juniors (six to eight), Intermediate (nine

The big players: who owns whom

Carnival Corporation

AIDA Cruises	Carnival Cruise Line	Costa Cruises	Cunard Line	Holland America Line	P&O Cruises	Princess Cruises	Seabourn

P&O Cruises (Australia)

Royal Caribbean Cruises — **Apollo Management** — **Genting Hong Kong**

Azamara Club Cruises	Celebrity Cruises	Pullmantur Cruises	Royal Caribbean International	Norwegian Cruise Line	Oceania Cruises	Regent Seven Seas Cruises	Crystal Cruises	Norwegian Cruise Line	Star Cruises

CDF Croisières de France

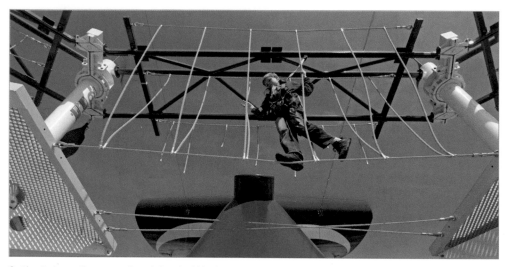

Getting to know the ropes aboard *Carnival Magic.*

to 11), Tweens (12–14, Circle C), and Late Teens (15–17, with Club 02). Even the under-twos can be catered to, with special programs aboard each ship. Soft-drinks packages can be bought for children (adults, too). Note that a babysitting service is not generally available after 10pm.

In 2014 Carnival partnered with children's specialist Dr. Seuss to create 'Seuss at Sea' – a program for immersive onboard youth, family, dining and entertainment experiences featuring the world and words of Dr. Seuss.

Best ships for children: *Carnival Breeze, Carnival Conquest, Carnival Dream, Carnival Freedom, Carnival Glory, Carnival Legend, Carnival Liberty, Carnival Miracle, Carnival Pride, Carnival Spirit, Carnival Splendor, Carnival Sunshine, Carnival Triumph, Carnival Valor, Carnival Victory,* and *Carnival Vista.*

Entertainment

The ships have big showlounges featuring loud, large-scale, skimpy-costumed flesh-and-feather Las Vegas-style production shows. On a typical cruise, there will be one or two shows, with male and female lead singers and a clutch of dancers backed by a live show-band supported by pre-recorded backing tracks.

Specialty acts take center stage on nights when there's no production show. There's also live music in just about every bar and lounge, and smutty late-night adults-only comedy. Each ship has karaoke nights, and a disco with ear-splitting volumes.

Celebrity Cruises

Ships

Celebrity Constellation (2002), *Celebrity Eclipse* (2010), *Celebrity Equinox* (2009), *Celebrity Infinity* (2001), *Celebrity Millennium* (2000), *Celebrity Reflection* (2012),
Celebrity Silhouette (2011), *Celebrity Solstice* (2008), *Celebrity Summit* (2001), *Celebrity Xpedition* (2001)

About the company

Celebrity Cruises was the brainchild of Harry H. Haralambopoulos, and brothers John and Michael Chandris, London-based Greek cargo ship owners and operators of the former Chandris Lines and Chandris Cruises. In 1989, as the cruise industry was gaining momentum, they were determined to create a newer, better cruise line, with new ships, larger, more standard cabins, and greater focus on food and service in the European tradition.

Its image as a 'premium' line is justified because the product delivery on board is superior to that of

---

Celebrity's classy approach

There really are four 'classes' aboard Celebrity ships: accommodation designated as suites; those in standard (exterior-view) and interior (no-view) cabins; a third that comes between the two, known as Concierge Class; and Aqua (Spa) Class.

Concierge Class brings added value to passengers with enhanced facilities including priority embarkation, disembarkation, priority tender tickets, specialty dining, and spa reservations; European duvet; double-bed overlay (no more falling 'between the cracks' for couples); choice of four pillows (goose down pillow, isotonic pillow, body pillow, conformance pillow); eight-vial flower vase on vanity desk; throw pillows on sofa; fruit basket; binoculars; golf umbrella; leather telephone notepad; larger beach towels; hand-held hairdryer. Balconies get better furniture. In the bathrooms: Frette bathrobe; larger towels; flower in silver vase in bathroom.

Aqua Class accommodation occupants get priority access to spa treatments, and have special 'uprated' spa amenities.

its parent company, Royal Caribbean International, which bought it in 1997 for $1.3 billion. The ships are recognizable by a large 'X' on the funnel denoting the third letter from the end of the Greek alphabet, the Greek 'chi' or 'Ch' in English, for Chandris, the founding family.

In 2007 Celebrity Cruises created the sub-brand Azamara Cruises (now Azamara Club Cruises), with two small ships: *Azamara Journey* (2000) and *Azamara Quest* (2000). These focus on lesser-visited destinations, and offer a more personal cruise experience. All hotel services and cruise operations are, however, operated by Celebrity Cruises.

What is it really like?

The ships are very clean and well maintained. There are always lots of flowers and flower displays – some ships have flower shops, where you can buy fresh blooms for special occasions.

Celebrity provides some extras that other lines have long forgotten, such as water spritzes on the pool deck. On sea days in warm-weather areas, if you are sunbathing on deck, someone will bring you a cold towel, and a sorbet, iced water, or iced tea.

Celebrity Cruises delivers a well-defined North American cruise experience at a modest price. If the budget allows, book a suite-category cabin for the extra benefits it brings – it's worth it. Strong points include the many European staff and the higher standard of service, good spas with a wide range of facilities and treatments, and a 'zero announcement policy.' Such touches differentiate Celebrity Cruises

from its competitors. Celebrity Cruises also has some of the most eclectic sculptures and original artwork, from Picasso to Warhol, found at sea.

The ships have more staff than other ships of comparable size and capacity, especially in the housekeeping and food and beverage departments. However, the company has seen fit to take away some items, such as personalized stationery (from some accommodation grades), it has substituted cloth napkins with paper ones, and has reduced the amount and quality of fresh flower displays.

You can book spa, salon, and personal fitness appointments, make main (Celebrity Select) and specialty dining reservations, and book shore excursions online before you cruise – so planning ahead can pay off (exception: *Celebrity Xpedition*).

Unfortunately, background music is played almost everywhere, and any lounge designated as 'music-free' is typically full of activities and participation events, so it's hard to find a quiet corner to sit and read.

So, what are the differences between Celebrity Cruises and its parent, Royal Caribbean International? Here are a few food-related examples:

RCI

Café: Seattle Coffee Company (extra cost) coffee, in paper cups.

Dining room: no tables for two.

In the Windjammer Café, plastic plates are used (there are no trays); cutlery is wrapped in paper napkins; melamine mugs are used for coffee/tea; the tea selection is poor, and it is impossible to get hot water.

Celebrity Equinox leaves Istanbul.

The Lawn Club aboard *Celebrity Silhouette*.

Celebrity Cruises:
Café el Bacio: Extra-cost coffees/teas served in china cups and saucers, with a chocolate.
Dining room: The food is of good quality and attractively presented. Tables for two are available.
Lido Café: Real china, white cloth napkins, polished cutlery, and a decent selection of teas are provided.

Cuisine/dining
Table settings are very good, with fine-quality linen, china, and glassware. Tables for two are available. What sets Celebrity apart is the superior training and supervision of dining room waiters and service staff.

The food represents a range of culinary influences; it is based loosely on classic French cuisine, modified to appeal to North Americans and Europeans alike. Menus are standardized across the fleet and have recently been dumbed down. Meatloaf, spaghetti, and striploin for dinner are pathetic excuses for what is supposed to be a 'premium' product. Items that can be made at home cannot be considered as acceptable. For better quality, Celebrity Cruises wants you to pay extra to eat in its specialty venues. Full service in-cabin dining is also available for all meals, including dinner.

The food is made from good-quality ingredients. Take croissants, for example: those found aboard Celebrity ships are made fresh each morning (but made from frozen dough), while aboard most competitors' ships they are purchased ashore.

Celebrity Cruises also has good wine waiters. *Celebrity Eclipse, Celebrity Equinox, Celebrity Reflection, Celebrity Silhouette*, and *Celebrity Solstice* have special wine rooms for tastings. *Celebrity Constellation, Celebrity Infinity, Celebrity Millennium*, and *Celebrity Summit* have wine rooms in one of the 'specialty' restaurants.

Suite occupants eat in a dedicated restaurant Luminae, while Aqua-class occupants eat in either Blu or Luminae.
Casual eateries. There are casual self-serve buffets aboard all Celebrity Cruises' ships. Except for *Celebrity Eclipse, Celebrity Equinox, Celebrity Reflection, Celebrity Silhouette*, and *Celebrity Solstice*, most are laid out in congestion-causing straight lines. Celebrity tries to be more creative with these buffets, and, like other cruise lines, has stations for pasta, faux sushi, salads, grill/rotisserie items, and hot-food items. A bar trolley service for drinks and wines is provided at lunchtime, and staff are on hand to take wine orders for dinner.
The coffee/tea factor. Regular (free) coffee is weak and poor. Score: 2 out of 10. Espresso/cappuccino coffees in the dining room incur a charge, because they are treated as a bar item.
Café el Bacio. The cafés are in prominent locations and provide an agreeable setting for those who like decent (extra cost) Italian coffees, pastries, and cakes.

For children
Junior passengers are divided into Shipmates (three to six years), Cadets (seven to nine), Ensigns (10–12), Teens (13–17).
Best ships for children. *Celebrity Eclipse, Celebrity Equinox, Celebrity Reflection, Celebrity Silhouette, Celebrity Solstice*.

Entertainment
Some shows are decent, with good costumes and lighting, while others are dated and lack storyline, flow, or connectivity. Each ship carries its own resident troupe of singers/dancers and audiovisual support staff. Bar service, available throughout shows, disrupts concentration.

Celebrity ships have a variety of bands and small musical units, although there is little music for social dancing, other than disco and pop music. (Recorded music is played constantly in hallways and on the pool deck.) Then there are the summer camp-style audience-participation events, and games that don't sit well with Celebrity's quality of food and service. There are also the inevitable country line dances and playschool routines.

On days at sea the program is crammed with things to do, though the emphasis is on revenue-enhancing activities such as art auctions, bingo, and horse racing.

Costa Cruises

Ships
Costa Atlantica (2000), *Costa Deliziosa* (2010), *Costa Diadema* (2014), *Costa Fascinosa* (2012), *Costa Favolosa* (2010), *Costa Fortuna* (2003), *Costa Luminosa* (2009), *Costa Magica* (2004), *Costa Mediterranea* (2003), *Costa neoClassica* (1992), *Costa neoRiviera* (1999), *Costa neo-*

Romantica (1993), *Costa Pacifica* (2009), *Costa Serena* (2007), *Costa Victoria* (1996)

About the company

Costa Cruises traces its history back to 1860, when Giacomo Costa started an olive oil business. The first ship, in 1924, transported that oil. After he died in 1924, his sons, Federico, Eugenio, and Enrico, inherited the business. First they bought *Ravenna*, a cargo ship, to cut transport costs for their olive oil empire. In 1948, Costa's first passenger ship, the *Anna 'C'*, carried passengers in style from Genoa to South America. In 1997, Costa Cruises was bought by the US's Carnival Corporation and UK's Airtours plc. Three years later Carnival took full control.

Costa specializes in cruises for Europeans or passengers with European tastes – particularly Italians – during the summer. It has initiated an aggressive newbuild policy in recent years, in order to modernize the company's aging fleet of different-size ships. The ships operate in three main markets: the Mediterranean, the Caribbean, and South America.

Most ships are well maintained, although there are inconsistencies throughout the fleet. The same is true of cleanliness – some ships are very clean, while others are a little dusty around the edges, as are its shore tenders. The company's safety procedures came under scrutiny when *Costa Concordia* struck rocks and capsized off the Italian island of Giglio in January 2012.

In 2013 the company started a sub-brand called Costa neoCollection, and the two ships in this branding feature longer cruises at slower speeds, in order to provide a better onboard experience (ships: *Costa neoClassica*, *Costa neoRiviera*, *Costa neoRomantica*).

What is it really like?

Costa is noted for its lively 'Italian' ambience. There are few Italian crew members, however, although many officers are Italian. The dress code is casual, even on formal nights.

One night at the end of each cruise may be reserved for a 'Roman Bacchanal,' when passengers dress up toga-style for dinner and beyond. This is a cruise line for those who like to party. If you want quiet, take earplugs – good ones.

On European and Mediterranean cruises, English will be the language least spoken, as most passengers will be Italian, Spanish, French, or German. On Caribbean itineraries, a high percentage of passengers will speak Spanish, as the ships carry passengers from Latin American countries in addition to passengers from North America.

Expect to cruise with a lot of children of all ages if you book for peak holiday cruises – and remember that in Europe at certain times (such as Easter) schoolchildren have longer vacations. On some European itineraries, passengers embark and disembark in almost every port along the way, which makes for a disjointed cruise experience, since there's almost no start or end to the cruise. There is almost no information for passengers who want to be independent in ports of call, and not take the ship's organized general excursions.

There is extensive smoking on board. No-smoking zones and signs are often ignored to the frustration of non-smoking passengers, and ashtrays are moved at whim; many of the officers and crew also smoke, even when moving through public rooms, so they don't bother to enforce the no-smoking zones.

Cabins tend to be small, but the decor is fresh, and the bathrooms are very practical. Some ships have cabin bathrooms with sliding doors – an excellent alternative to inward-openers that use up space.

Costa neoClassica, *Costa neoRiviera*, *Costa neoRomantica*, and *Costa Victoria* have a very European feel. They are lively without being too much, or pastel-toned without being boring, while all the other, newer ships have an in-your-face brashness similar to Carnival's ships, with grainy and unflattering digital

Making a celebrity-style entrance down the Grand Foyer aboard a Millennium-class ship.

artwork on walls and panels, and even inside elevators.

Cuisine/dining

If you expect to be served by jovial Italian waiters, you'll be disappointed – although the restaurant managers might be Italian. All ships have two seatings for dinner. Dining times on Europe/Mediterranean and South America cruises are usually later than those in the Caribbean (Europeans and Latin passengers tend to eat later). Few tables for two are available, most being for four, six, or eight.

The cuisine is best described as Continental, with many regional Italian dishes and much emphasis on pasta: 50 pasta dishes per cruise. Except for pasta dishes and cream sauces, presentation and food quality are unmemorable, and the subject of many negative passenger comments. Meat is so-so, and often disguised with gravies and rich sauces. Fish and seafood tend to lack taste, and are often overcooked. Green vegetables are hard to come by, but rice is used as a plate-filler.

The decorative Pantheon Atrium aboard *Costa Serena*.

Breads and bread rolls are usually good, but the desserts are of supermarket quality and lack taste.

There is a wine list but no wine waiters; table waiters are expected to serve both food and wine, which does not work well. Almost all wines are young – very young.

Specialty dining venues. If you opt for one of the specialty restaurants aboard the larger ships, note that a cover charge applies.

Casual eateries. All ships have self-serve lido buffets. In most, you have to move along with your tray. The newer ships have more active stations and individual islands. The items available are basic.

The coffee/tea factor. Regular coffee: decent and quite strong. Score: 5 out of 10. Extra cost espresso/cappuccino coffees (illy) are among the best served by the major cruise lines.

For children

Junior passengers are in three groups: Kids Club (ages three to six); Junior Club (seven to 12); and Teen Club (13–17). The program varies by ship, itinerary, and season. Group babysitting is available 6:30–11pm. During port days, babysitting is available generally 8:30am–12:30pm and 2:30–6:30pm.

Best ships for children. *Costa Atlantica, Costa Diadema, Costa Deliziosa, Costa Fascinosa, Costa Fortuna, Costa Favolosa, Costa Luminosa, Costa Magica, Costa Mediterranea, Costa Pacifica, Costa Serena*.

Entertainment

Each ship carries a resident troupe of singers/dancers and audiovisual support staff, but Costa Cruises is not known for the quality of its entertainment. What it does present is of the 'no finesse' variety, with revue-style shows that have little storyline, poor choreography and execution, but plenty of fast-moving action – more stepping in place than dancing – and lots of volume. It's entertainment to pass the time rather than remember.

Cabaret acts – typically singers, magicians, comedy jugglers, ventriloquists, and so on – are entertaining but rather ho-hum. Most passenger participation activities include poolside games such as a 'Belly Flop' competition, election of the 'Ideal Couple', and other juvenile games – but some families love them. There are also dance classes, and the inevitable 'Fine Art Auction'.

Costa Cruises

Costa ships are best suited to young couples, singles, and families with children who enjoy big-city life, a multicultural social mix, outdoor cafés, constant activity, eating late, loud entertainment, and food more notable for quantity than quality. All printed materials (room service folio, menus, etc.) are in six languages: Italian, English, French, German, Portuguese, and Spanish. Announcements are made in at least four languages.

Cunard Line

Ships:
Queen Elizabeth (2010), *Queen Mary 2* (2004), *Queen Victoria* (2007).

About the company
Cunard Line celebrated its 175th anniversary in 2015. The company was established in 1839, as the British and North American Royal Mail Steam Packet Company, to carry the Royal Mail and passengers from the Old World to the New. Its first ship, *Britannia*, sailed on its maiden voyage on American Independence Day in 1840. The author Charles Dickens crossed the Atlantic aboard the ship in 1842 together with 62 other passengers, 93 crew members, one cow, and, most important, Her Majesty's mails and dispatches. Since 1840, Cunard Line has always had ships built to sail across the North Atlantic. From 1850 until the arrival of *QE2* in 1969, all of the line's ships and those of White Star Line (with which Cunard merged in 1934) had several classes. Your luggage label, therefore, declared not only your name but also what you could afford. Today, there's no class distinction, other than by accommodation grade.

But one is still reminded of the company's illustrious history. For example, Cunard Line was the first company to take passengers on regularly scheduled transatlantic crossings. It introduced the first passenger ship to be lit by electricity (*Servia*, 1881) and the first steam turbine engines in an ocean liner (*Carmania*, 1905), had the first ship to have an indoor swimming pool aboard a ship (*Aquitania*, 1914), and pioneered the around-the-world cruise (*Laconia*, 1922). Cunard has held the record for the largest passenger ship ever built (*Queen Elizabeth*, between 1940 and 1996), and is presently the only company to sail regularly scheduled year-round transatlantic crossings (*Queen Mary 2*). Samuel Cunard was from Halifax, Nova Scotia' he established the company in Liverpool. Today, the company is owned by American company the Carnival Corporation), the three Queens were built in France and Italy, registered in Hamilton, Bermuda, with a home port of Southampton, England, while the onboard currency is the US dollar!

Cunard has four distinct accommodation classes, each linked to a specific restaurant: Queens Grill, Princess Grill, Britannia Club, and Britannia.

What is it really like?
Sailing with Cunard Line is quite different from being aboard a standard cruise ship. The ships incorporate a lot of maritime history and the grand traditions of ocean liners – as opposed to the other ships, with their tendency toward tacky high-street trappings.

A transatlantic crossing is supremely civilized, particularly if you can enjoy being cosseted in accom-

Best foot forward beside a Costa funnel.

modation that allows you to dine in the 'grill'-class restaurants with their fine cuisine and presentation. There's less pressure from staff to get you to buy drinks than with other lines, and the itineraries are well spaced and not so hectic.

Cunard Line's three vessels are best suited to a wide range of seasoned and well-traveled couples and solo passengers who enjoy the cosmopolitan setting of an ocean liner, with their extensive array of facilities, public rooms, dining rooms, and lecture programs. Cunard Line is the only cruise line that lets you take your dog or cat with you (*Queen Mary 2* transatlantic crossings only). Also, one of its most successful formulas is its adherence to formal dress codes – in contrast to the downward sartorial spiral of most cruise lines. All three ships have Art Deco decor, fine wood mosaics, and many attributes of the old ocean liners, albeit in a more modern, contemporary setting.

Cuisine/dining
Cunard Line uses good-quality ingredients, sourced in Europe and the US. The cuisine is still of a mass-market standard – some venues have butter in packets. However, in self-serve buffets, salt and pepper are usually provided on each table. Espressos and cappuccinos are available in the dining rooms, and at extra cost in many bars.

All three ships have 'grill rooms' as well as traditional large restaurants and casual self-service eateries. Grill rooms are more exclusive, and some have à la carte menus, while the main restaurants have fixed menus. The grill rooms have seating dining at assigned tables, when you wish, while the main Britannia restaurants in all ships have two seatings.

The cuisine includes many traditional British favorites, together with extensive French dishes as well as regional specialties from around the world, nicely presented on Wedgwood porcelain.

For children

Children's facilities are best aboard *Queen Mary 2*, although not as extensive as aboard the former *Queen Elizabeth 2*. Youngsters are supervised by real English nannies. Note that seasickness is more of an issue on a transatlantic crossing than on a standard cruise, which may be a problem for children who don't travel well.

Entertainment

Production shows are colorful and visual, with prerecorded backing tracks supplementing a showband. Other shows consist of cabaret acts – typically singers, magicians, mime artists, comedy jugglers, and, occasionally, comedians – doing the cruise ship circuit. A number of bands and small musical units provide live music for dancing and listening.

Holland America Line

Ships

Amsterdam (2000), *Eurodam* (2008), *Koningsdam* (2016), *Maasdam* (1993), *Nieuw Amsterdam* (2010), *Noordam* (2006), *Oosterdam* (2003), *Prinsendam* (1988),

The Retreat aboard *Eurodam*.

Rotterdam (1997), *Veendam* (1996), *Volendam* (1999), *Westerdam* (2004), *Zaandam* (2000), *Zuiderdam* (2002)

About the company

Holland America Line was founded in 1873 as the Netherlands-America Steamship Company, shipping immigrants to the New World from Rotterdam. It moved its headquarters to New York in 1971. It bought into Alaskan hotels and transportation when it acquired Westours in 1983, and is one of the state's biggest employers. In 1989, it was acquired by Carnival Cruise Line, but retained its Seattle-based headquarters.

HAL carries both traditional cruise passengers (senior citizens, alumni groups) and multi-generational families. It tries hard to keep its Dutch connections, with antique artifacts and traditional decor, as well as Indonesian stewards. It rents a private island, Half Moon Cay, in the Bahamas.

What is it really like?

Management with updated ideas, the line's 'Signature of Excellence' program, the food variety, and creativity have all improved the HAL experience. The ships benefit from lots of fresh flowers and museum-quality art pieces.

The brand encompasses basically two types of ship. Younger families with children and grandchildren are best suited to the newer, larger vessels such as *Eurodam*, *Nieuw Amsterdam*, *Noordam*, *Oosterdam*, *Westerdam*, and *Zuiderdam*, whereas those of senior years – HAL's traditional audience of repeat passengers from alumni groups – are best suited to ships that are smaller and less glitzy (*Amsterdam*, *Maasdam*, *Prinsendam*, *Rotterdam*, *Veendam*, and *Zaandam*). All ships have teakwood outdoor promenade decks, whereas most rivals have artificial grass or some other form of indoor-outdoor carpeting. Explorations Cafés have been built into its ships recently.

Holland America Line has its own training school in Jakarta, Indonesia, and pre-trains crew members who have never been to sea before. Many crew members have been promoted to supervisory positions due to a host of new ships introduced, but few of those promoted have the formal training, professional, or management skills required for those positions. Internal promotion is fine, but decreased professionalism is not the price that passengers should pay.

HAL is one of only three major cruise lines with cinemas built into its ships. It also operates many theme-related cruises, and has an extensive program of life-enrichment lecturers. The cinemas also have full demonstration kitchens built in for a 'Culinary Arts' program that includes celebrity chefs and interactive cooking demos.

HAL has established smoking and no-smoking areas aboard its ships, but there are many more smokers than you might expect, depending on ship and itinerary.

Queen Elizabeth and *Queen Mary 2* rendezvous in Sydney.

As part of its Signature of Excellence refurbishment program, its ships received 'Mix' – a 'lifestyle' facility – an open area with three themed specialty bars: Champagne (serving Champagne and sparkling wines from around the world), Martinis (martinis in individual shakers), and Spirits & Ales (a sports bar).

Cuisine/dining

For dinner, Holland America Line features both open seating (on one level) or assigned tables (at fixed times, on the other level) in its two-deck dining rooms; it's called 'As You Wish' dining. For breakfast and lunch in the main dining room, an open-seating policy applies. All dining venues are non-smoking.

Some tables for two are available, but most are for four, six, eight, or 10. The larger tables are ideal for

HAL's 'signature of excellence'

Between 2004 and 2006, improvements were introduced at a cost of $225 million. These covered dining, service, accommodation, and activities, and included premium mattresses, cotton bed linens or duvets (top suites only), massage showerheads, fruit baskets, and DVD players. Elemis personal bathroom amenities are provided for all passengers (these are better than Celebrity's present bathroom amenities, for example). Suite occupants also have access to a Neptune Lounge (with concierge services), thus in effect creating a two-class system that appeals to suite occupants. Bathrobes and a range of personal toiletries are provided for all passengers, and hot hors d'oeuvres and canapés are part of the pre-dinner cocktail scene.

multi-generational families. Fine Rosenthal china and cutlery are used. Live music is provided for dinner. 'Lighter option' meals are always available for nutrition- and weight-conscious passengers.

Holland America Line food was upgraded slightly, when master chef Rudi Sodamin arrived in 2005 as a consultant; he introduced his 'Wild about Salmon' and other creative ideas, and the Culinary Arts Center (with its own dedicated live interactive demonstration kitchen and guest chef program) has been a success story. The company now includes more regional cuisine and local ingredients. The main course portions are small, which is better for passengers of senior years.

However, while the USDA beef is very good, poultry and most fish tend to be overcooked (except when the ships are in Alaska, where the halibut and salmon are excellent). Note that 'downmarket' packets of sugar and packets (instead of glass jars) of supermarket-brand breakfast jams, marmalade, honey, sugar, and butter are the norm. Also, coffees and teas are poor-quality, except in the extra-charge Explorations Café. Dessert and pastry items are good, but canned fruit and jellied desserts are much in evidence. Most of the 'international' cheeses are highly colored, processed cheese (cruises in Europe have access to European cheeses).

HAL offers complimentary ice cream during certain hours of the day, as well as hot hors d'oeuvres in all bars – something other major lines seem to have dropped. Cabin service breakfasts are really basic, with only Continental breakfast available and almost no hot food choice.

HAL can provide kosher meals, however. The ships don't have kosher kitchens, so these are prepared

MSC crews typically operate in five languages.

ashore, frozen, and brought to your table (warm) sealed in containers.

The wine list relies heavily on wines from California and Washington State, with few decent French or German wines, other than those found in a typical supermarket ashore. A Connoisseur List is available in the Pinnacle Grill.

Specialty dining venues. All HAL ships have specialty spots called Pinnacle Grill (or Pinnacle Grill at the Odyssey Restaurant), specializing in Pacific Northwest cuisine. Items include an array of premium-quality steaks, presented tableside prior to cooking. These are more intimate restaurants, with tablecloths, linen napkins, and decent-size wine glasses. The food is better than in the main dining rooms. There is a cover charge, and reservations are required. Bulgari china, Frette linens, and Reidel glasses are part of this dining experience.

Casual eateries. All ships have a Lido Deck self-serve buffet. Most have lines you move along with your tray, although the newest ships have more 'active' stations (examples: omelets and pasta cooked to order) and individual islands. There are decent salad bars, dessert bars, regional specialties, and grilled fast-food items such as hamburgers, salmon burgers, hot dogs, and French fries. These venues become overcrowded during breakfast and lunch.

Regular coffee is half-decent, but weak. Score: 3 out of 10. Extra cost espresso/cappuccino coffees (Dutch) are better, served in proper china, but not quite up to the standard of Celebrity or Costa. Score: 6 out of 10.

For children

Club HAL: Junior passengers are divided into three age groups: three to eight, nine to 12, and teens. Programming is based on the number of children booked on any given sailing, and children's counselors are provided accordingly. HAL's children's programs are not as extensive as those of Carnival Cruise

Line, for example, although they are improving with the latest ships.

Best ships for children. *Eurodam, Koningsdam, Nieuw Amsterdam, Noordam, Oosterdam, Westerdam, Zaandam, Zuiderdam.*

Entertainment

Holland America Line is not known for lavish entertainment (the budgets aren't high enough). The production shows, while a good attempt, fall short on storyline, choreography, and performance, while colorful costuming and lighting hide the weak spots. Each ship carries its own resident troupe of singers and dancers and audio-visual support staff. HAL also offers a consistently good, tried-and-tested array of cabaret acts that constantly pop up on the cruise ship circuit.

A number of bands, a string ensemble, and solo musicians present live music for dancing and listening in many of the lounges and bars. Each ship has a Crow's Nest Lounge (by day an observation lounge) for social dancing, and there is always serenading string music in the Explorer's Lounge and dining room.

MSC Cruises

Ships

MSC Armonia (2001), *MSC Divina* (2012), *MSC Fantasia* (2008), *MSC Lirica* (2003), *MSC Magnifica* (2010), *MSC Musica* (2006), *MSC Opera* (2004), *MSC Orchestra* (2007), *MSC Poesia* (2008), *MSC Preziosa* (2013), *MSC Sinfonia* (2005), *MSC Splendida* (2009)

About the company

The HQ of the world's largest privately owned cruise line is in Geneva, Switzerland, home of parent company Mediterranean Shipping Company, the world's second-biggest container shipping company. Operations and marketing are based in Genoa, Italy. The firm started in the passenger shipping business by acquiring the Italian company Star Lauro in 1995, together with two older ships, *Monterey* and *Rhapsody*. It expanded with the purchase of *Melody*, followed by almost new ships bought from bankrupt Festival Cruises.

MSC Cruises has grown incredibly fast and is owned by a shipping-based family, not a faceless corporation. In 2014, MSC Cruises a $273-million program 'chopped and stretched' four ships to update them and accommodate more passengers (*MSC Armonia, MSC Lirica, MSC Opena,* and *MSC Sinfonia*). But new ships are coming, starting in 2017. These are expected to be stunning vessels with an array of facilities that promise outstanding attention to detail. Watch this space.

What is it really like?

MSC Cruises' ships are suited to adult couples and solo travelers, and families with children. They are good for those who enjoy big-city life, a multicultural atmosphere, outdoor cafés, and constant activity accompanied by plenty of live music and late nights. Foodie passengers should note that the food ranges from adequate to very good.

MSC Cruises uses the most environmentally friendly detergents and cleaning materials in its housekeeping department and laundries. It has drastically reduced its onboard use of plastic items and is aiming to eliminate them entirely. The larger ships (*MSC Divina, MSC Fantasia, MSC Preziosa*, and *MSC Splendida*) have an exclusive Yacht Club lounge for suite-grade passengers, and MSC Preziosa has a separate dining room for Yacht Club occupants. This provides exclusive open-seating dining, a private sun deck oasis area, access to the well-run Aurea Spa, priority embarkation, and butler service.

The ships typically operate in five languages, with embarkation-day announcements in English, French, German, Italian, and Spanish. During the cruise, there are, however, few announcements. Given this multilingual emphasis, production shows and other major entertainment displays are more visual than verbal. For the same reason, the ships don't generally carry lecturers.

Cigar lovers will find a selection of Cuban (including Cohiba, Montecristo, Romeo e Julieta, Partagás), Dominican (Davidoff), and Italian (Toscano) smokes in the cigar lounges. The decor is decidedly European/Mediterranean, with much understated elegance and really high-quality soft furnishings and other materials such as Italian marble, and Swarovski glass stairways. The latest ships are much brighter and more contemporary, albeit with restraint.

Cuisine/dining

MSC Cruises provides better-quality ingredients, almost all sourced in Europe, than some other major cruise lines. The cuisine is still mainstream – you'll find butter in packets, for example. But, at the self-serve buffets, salt and pepper are typically provided on each table, not in packets as on most major cruise lines. Espressos and cappuccinos (Segafredo brand Italian coffee) are available in the dining rooms, at extra cost, and in almost all bars – which also have coffees from Brazil, Costa Rica, and Peru.

Aboard the newer ships, MSC Cruises has introduced the Italian 'slow food' concept. Items that are always available include spaghetti, chicken breast, salmon fillet, and vegetables of the day. Refreshingly, the company spotlights regional Italian cuisine and wine, so daily dining room menus feature food from regions including Calabria, Piedmont, Lazio, Puglia, and Sicily.

All pizza dough is made on board, and risotto is a daily signature item for MSC Cruises and something that the ships do really well; each ship also makes one type of pasta almost daily. Spaghetti is always available, with a tomato sauce freshly made each day. Several varieties of Italian breads such as bruschetta, focaccia, and panettone are provided.

Specialty dining venues. The newest ships have specialty restaurants. *MSC Divina, MSC Fantasia*, and *MSC Splendida* all have Eataly, serving Italian bistro fare. Aboard *MSC Musica* and *MSC Poesia*, there is Kaito, an authentic Japanese restaurant and sushi bar with an extensive menu. Aboard *MSC Magnifica* and *MSC Orchestra*, there is Shanghai, a Chinese restaurant with real wok cooking, dim sum, and other Chinese and Asian specialties. The quality is high, and

MSC Fantasia's Top Sail Lounge.

The Ocean Place complex on *Norwegian Getaway*.

it really is worth having at least one meal in these venues; the à la carte prices are very reasonable.
Room service. Continental breakfast is complimentary from 7:30 to 10am; room service snacks can be bought at any other time. A basket of fruit is provided to all cabins at embarkation, and replenished daily for suite-grade accommodation.

For children
Up to three children over two and under 12 cruise free (paying only port dues) when sharing a cabin with two adults paying full fares. Children are divided into three age groups, with facilities to match: Mini Club (ages three to nine); Junior Club (10–13); Teenagers Club (over 14, a pre-paid Teen Card is available). While the facilities and play areas aren't as extensive as those aboard some other major lines, a 'baby parking' service is useful when parents want to go ashore on excursions. MSC Cruises' mascot is Do-Re-Mi – the von Trapp family of *Sound of Music* fame would no doubt be delighted.
Best ships for children. *MSC Divina, MSC Fantasia, MSC Magnifica, MSC Musica, MSC Opera, MSC Orchestra, MSC Poesia, MSC Preziosa, MSC Splendida*.

Entertainment
Because of the multilingual passenger mix, production shows are colorful and visual, particularly aboard the newest ships. Other shows consist of unknown cabaret acts such as singers, magicians, mime artists, and comedy jugglers doing the cruise ship circuit. The ship carries a number of bands and small musical units that provide live music for dancing or listening, but there is no showband, and production shows use pre-recorded backing tracks.

Norwegian Cruise Line

Ships
Norwegian Breakaway (2013), *Norwegian Dawn* (2002), *Norwegian Epic* (2010), *Norwegian Escape* (2015), *Norwegian Gem* (2007), *Norwegian Getaway* (2014), *Norwegian Jade* (2006), *Norwegian Jewel* (2005), *Norwegian Pearl* (2006), *Norwegian Spirit* (1998), *Norwegian Star* (2002), *Norwegian Sun* (2001), *Pride of America* (2005), *Norwegian Sky* (1999),

About the company
Norwegian Cruise Line, the originator of contemporary cruising, was founded in 1966 by three Norwegian shipping companies as Klosters Sunward Ferries and was renamed Norwegian Caribbean Line in 1967. It was bought by Star Cruises in 2000, and has been replacing its older, smaller ships with brand new, larger vessels. NCL also operates one ship with a mostly American crew and a base in Hawaii.

Freestyle Cruising is how NCL describes its operation – although it's hard to detect style in the onboard product (I call it American Bistro-style). Its fleet is diverse, so the cruise experience can vary, although this makes for interesting character variation between the various ship categories. There is more standardization aboard the larger, newer ships. The senior officers are the only thing that's Norwegian.

Most standard cabins are extremely small, though they are laid out in a practical manner.

What is it really like?
If this is your first cruise, you should enjoy a good overall vacation in a lively, upbeat setting. The lifestyle is contemporary, fresh, creative, and sporty, with a casualness typical of youthful city dwellers, and with its 'eat when you want' philosophy, the shipboard ambience is ultra-casual. The dress code is, too – indeed, the waiters are probably better dressed than many passengers. The staff members are generally congenial, and you'll find a high percentage of women in cabin and restaurant service departments – more than most major cruise lines.

There's plenty of lively music, constant activity, entertainment, and food that's mainstream and acceptable, but nothing more – unless you pay extra to eat in the specialty dining spots. All this is delivered by a smiling, very friendly service staff, who can lack polish, but are obliging. In the latest wheeze to extract revenue, NCL is offering extra-cost 'Backstage Tours.'

Cuisine/dining
NCL has recognized the increasing trend away from formal restaurants (purpose: dining) toward bistros (purpose: eat-faster venues). For cruising, NCL has championed more choices in dining than any other cruise line, except sister company Star Cruises, which started 'Freestyle Dining.'

This allows you to try different types of cuisine, in different settings, when you want. In practice, however, it means that you have to make reservations, which can prove frustrating at times, and getting it just right takes a little planning and, often, waiting. Food in the main dining rooms is poor to average and marginally better in the extra-charge venues.

On production show nights, most people want to eat at the same time in order to see a show, causing prime-time congestion, slow service, and frustration; pagers are given out for anyone waiting for a table. The ships have plasma screens or touch screens in various locations, so you can make reservations when you want, and view the waiting times for a table.

After-dinner espressos/cappuccinos are available in the dining rooms at no extra charge – a nice feature. The wine list is quite good, with many excellent wines in the $20–30 range. But the wine is typically served by table waiters, whose knowledge of wines tends to be limited. Once each cruise, there's a Chocoholics Buffet, with paper plates and plastic cutlery.

Cabin service breakfasts are basic, with only Continental breakfast available and no hot food items – for those, you'll need to go to a restaurant or self-serve buffet. The non-breakfast Room Service menu has only two hot items available throughout the day: Oriental soup and pizza – the rest is cold (salads and sandwiches).

The coffee/tea factor. Regular coffee: weak and poor. Score: 2 out of 10. Iced tea: pitifully weak. Espresso/cappuccino coffees score 4 out of 10. Some bars have (extra-cost) espresso/cappuccino machines. **NCL's Private Island (Great Stirrup Cay).** Only coffee and iced water are free (there's no iced tea), all other drinks are charged.

For children

The Splash Academy and Entourage programs divide children into several age groups: Guppies (ages 6 months to three years); Junior sailors (three to five); First Mates (six to eight); Navigators (nine to 12); and two Teens groups (13–14 and 15–17). The kids and teens programming was developed in conjunction with UK-based King's Foundation and Camps, a charity that provides quality sports and activity programs. There's also programming for babies and toddlers ages six months to three years (Guppies). Group babysitting services are also available, at an extra change. Special price packages are available for soft drinks.

Best ships for children. *Norwegian Bliss, Norwegian Breakaway, Norwegian Epic, Norwegian Escape, Norwegian Getaway.*

Entertainment

NCL has exciting shows that really are entertaining, particularly aboard *Norwegian Bliss, Norwegian Breakaway, Norwegian Epic, Norwegian Escape,* and *Norwegian Getaway.*

P&O Cruises

Ships

Adults-only ships. *Adonia* (2001), *Arcadia* (2005), *Oriana* (1995)

Family-friendly ships. *Aurora* (2000), *Azura* (2010), *Britannia* (2015), *Oceana* (2000), *Ventura* (2008)

About the company

P&O's full name is the Peninsular and Oriental Steam Navigation Company, though none of its ships is powered by steam turbines. Based in Southampton, England, it was founded in 1837, just before Samuel Cunard established his company, and was awarded a UK government contract in 1840 to carry the mail from Gibraltar to Alexandria.

Bold hull design for *Norwegian Breakaway.*

An outside single stateroom aboard *P&O Azura*.

P&O Cruises acquired Princess Cruises in 1974, Swan Hellenic in 1982, and Sitmar Cruises in 1988. In 2000 it demerged from its parent to establish itself as P&O Princess plc. It was bought by the Carnival Corporation in 2003, and celebrated its 175th anniversary on July 3, 2012, when all seven ships assembled in Southampton.

What is it really like?

P&O Cruises has always been a traditional British cruise company, never quite matching the quality aboard the Cunard Line ships (whose onboard currency is, strangely, the US dollar), which have more international passengers. With P&O having British captains and navigation officers and Indian/Goanese service staff, the British traditions of unobtrusive service are preserved and well presented. British food favorites (considered bland by some) provide the real comfort factor in a single-language setting that provides a home from home on ships for families with children, or on adults-only ships.

The company targets British passengers who want to sail from a UK port – except for winter Caribbean cruises from Barbados. But now it's also known for having adults-only ships, and so the two products differ widely in their communal spaces. It also makes an effort to provide theme cruises – on antiques, art appreciation, classical music, comedy, cricket, gardening and horticulture, jazz, Scottish dance, etc. The ships usually carry ballroom dance instructors. Bed linen is changed twice a week – not as often as on some lines, such as MSC Cruises, where it is changed every two days. The décor is a mix of British 'traditional' (think comfy, dated armchairs and wood paneling – all non-glitzy). British artists are featured aboard all ships – *Ventura*, for example, displays works by more than 40 of them.

Cuisine/dining

The cuisine is straightforward, no-nonsense British food, reasonably well presented on nice Wedgwood china. But it tends to be rather bland and uninspiring. It is typical of mass-banquet catering with standard fare comparable to that found in a family hotel in a classic English seaside town.

The ingredients of many meals are disguised by gravies and sauces, as in Indian curries – but well liked by most British passengers. Bread, desserts, and cakes are made well, and there is a wide variety. P&O Cruises always carries a decent selection of British, and some French, cheeses.

Most of the dining room staff are from India and provide warm and friendly service. Wine service is amateurish, and the lack of knowledge on wines is lamentable.

Specialty dining venues. Extra-cost restaurants with menus designed by some of Britain's well-known television celebrity chefs such as Marco Pierre White and Atul Kochhar, have their own eateries aboard the ships. These are a mix of trendy bistro-style venues and restaurants with an Asia-Pacific theme.

Casual eateries. The self-serve buffets suffer from having cramped facilities and countless concession staff who take over the tables there and congregate in groups. In other words, the buffets are too small to accommodate the needs of most passengers today.

The coffee/tea factor. Regular coffee: weak and poor. Score: 3 out of 10. Good-quality tea- and coffee-making facilities are provided in all cabins. Self-serve beverage stations are provided at the buffets, but it's often difficult to find proper teaspoons – often only wooden stirrers are available. Espresso/cappuccino coffees in the extra-charge venues are slightly better, but not as good as aboard the ships of Costa Cruises or MSC Cruises.

For children

Aboard *Aurora, Azura, Britannia, Oceana* and *Ventura*, there are children's areas and child-friendly pools, and dedicated clubs for children. Splashers is for two to four year olds; Surfers is for five to eight year olds; Scubas is for nine to 12 year olds; and H2O is for 13 to 17 year olds. There is also a Night Nursery for toddlers from six months to four years old (and it's free).

Entertainment

P&O Cruises has always been known for its traditional British-style entertainment, with lots of pub-like sing-along sessions for the masses. These have been augmented with in-house production shows that provide lots of color, costume changes, and high-tech lighting. Each ship carries its own resident troupe of singers and dancers, called Headliners.

P&O Cruises does a good job of providing guest lecturers with varying themes, as well as occasional after-dinner speakers such as well-known television personalities and book authors.

Princess Cruises

Ships

Caribbean Princess (2004), *Coral Princess* (2002), *Crown Princess* (2006), *Dawn Princess* (1997), *Diamond Prin-*

cess (2004), *Emerald Princess* (2007), *Golden Princess* (2001), *Grand Princess* (1998), *Island Princess* (2003), *Ocean Princess* (1999), *Pacific Princess* (1999), Regal Princess (2014), *Royal Princess* (2013), *Ruby Princess* (2008), *Sapphire Princess* (2005), *Sea Princess* (1998), *Star Princess* (2002), *Sun Princess* (1995)

About the company

Princess Cruises was founded by Stanley McDonald in 1965 with one ship, the former passenger ferry *Princess Patricia,* for cruises along the Mexican Riviera. In 1974, the company was bought by the UK's Peninsular and Oriental Steam Navigation Company (P&O), and in 1988 P&O/Princess Cruises merged with the Italian line Sitmar Cruises. In 2000, Carnival Corporation and Royal Caribbean Cruises fought a protracted battle to buy Princess Cruises. Carnival won.

Princess Cruises provides comfortable mainstream cruising aboard a fleet of mainly large resort ships (plus two small ships), and covers the world. The ships have a higher-than-average Passenger Space Ratio than competitors Carnival or RCI, and the service is friendly without being showy. In 2010 the company converted to fully digital travel documents, so there are no more ticket document wallets, and everything is online.

What is it really like?

Ships in both the small and large resort categories are clean and always well maintained, and the open promenade decks of some ships have teak deck lounge chairs – others have plastic ones. Only *Coral Princess* and *Island Princess* have full walk-around open promenade decks; aboard all other Princess ships you can't walk completely around the ship. The line also has a nice balance of officers, staff, and crew members, and its British connections help it to achieve the feeling of calmness aboard its ships that some other lines lack. Note that there is no Deck 13 aboard any of the ships, which is good news for superstitious passengers.

There are proper cinemas aboard most ships, as well as outdoor poolside mega-screens for showing evening 'movies under the skies.'

Lines form at peak times at the information office, and for open-seating breakfast and lunch in the main dining rooms. Passengers receive turndown service and a pillow chocolate each night, bathrobes (on request), and toiletry kits – larger ones for suite/mini-suite occupants – typically including soap, shampoo, conditioner, and hand/body lotion. A hairdryer is provided in all cabins, sensibly located at a vanity desk unit in the lounge area. In 2012, smoking was prohibited in cabins and on cabin balconies.

The dress code is either formal – usually one formal night per seven-day cruise – or smart casual, the latter interpreted by many as jeans or tracksuits and trainers.

All Grand-class ships include an adults-only area called 'The Sanctuary,' an extra-cost retreat at the top of the ship, forward of the mast. This provides a 'private' place to relax and unwind and includes attendants to provide chilled face towels and deliver light bites. It has thickly padded sunloungers both in the sun and in the shade, a swim-against-the-current pool, and there are also two outdoor cabanas for massages. I recommend The Sanctuary as a retreat from the busyness of the rest of the ship. It's worth the extra cost.

P&O Cruises Britannia's Maiden Voyage.

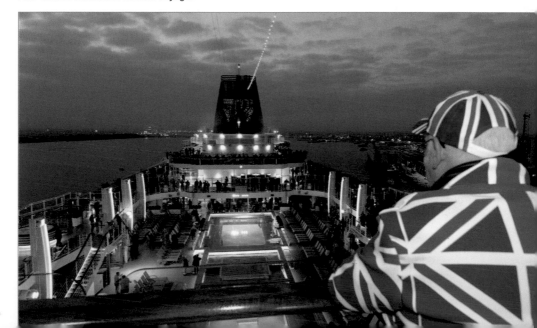

Playing air hockey in a Princess Cruises' teen centre.

Princess's onboard product, especially food and entertainment, is well established and geared to the North American market. But British and other European nationalities should feel at ease, safe in the knowledge that this is all about highly organized, packaged cruising, food, and service. There is, however, an increasing emphasis on onboard revenue, so you can expect to be subjected to daily advertising of art auctions and 'designer' watches.

Princess Cruises' ships are best suited to couples, families with children and teenagers, and older solo travelers who like to mingle in a large ship setting with sophisticated surroundings and lifestyle, and reasonably good entertainment. They offer fairly decent food and service, packaged affordably.

Shipboard hospitals have live SeaMed tele-medicine link-ups with specialists at the Cedars-Sinai Medical Center in Los Angeles for emergency help – useful mainly for passengers who reside in the US.

Princess Cays is the company's own 'private island' in the Caribbean. It's all yours (along with a couple of thousand other passengers) for a day. However, it's a tender ride away from the ship, so getting to it can take some time.

If Carnival's ships have the brightest decor imaginable, the decor aboard Princess Cruises' ships is the opposite – perhaps a little bland in places, with much use of neutral tones, calm colors, and pastels.

Cuisine/dining

Although portions are generous, the food and its presentation are disappointing. Fish is often disguised by a crumb or batter coating, the selection of fresh green vegetables is limited, and few garnishes are used. However, do remember that this is big-ship banquet catering, with all its attendant standardization and production cooking. Meats are of a decent quality, although often disguised by gravy-based sauces. The pasta dishes are acceptable (though voluminous), and are typically served by section headwaiters, who may also make 'something special just for you' – in search of favorable comments and gratuities.

If you like desserts, order a sundae at dinner, as most other sweets are just so-so. Ice cream, when ordered in the dining room, is included, but costs extra elsewhere (Häagen-Dazs can be found at the poolside).

Specially designed dinnerware and good-quality linens and silverware are used, such as Dudson of England dinnerware, Frette Egyptian cotton table linens, with silverware by Hepp of Germany.

An extra-cost ($75 per person) Chef's Table Dinner is an indulgent, three-hour 'foodertainment' event, at which the ship's executive chef interacts with diners; appetizers and cocktails in the galley are followed by a multi-course tasting dinner with wines paired to the meal. The wine list is fair (not good). There are no dedicated wine waiters (waiters serve it).

Balcony-grade accommodation occupants can enjoy a full-service Balcony Dinner for two at $50 per person extra, plus wine, and a truly indulgent Balcony Champagne Breakfast – it's good value.

Casual eateries. For casual eating, each ship has a Horizon Buffet (open almost round the clock), and, at night, it provides an informal dinner setting with sit-down waiter service. A small, limited bistro menu is also available. Buffet displays are mostly repetitious, but there is no finesse in presentation, as plastic plates are provided instead of trays. The cabin service menu is quite limited, and the presentation of food items is uninspiring.

The coffee/tea factor. Regular coffee: weak and poor. Score: 2 out of 10. Except for the beverage station at the serve-yourself buffets, coffees/teas in bars cost extra.

For children

Children are divided into three age groups: Princess Pelicans (ages three to seven); Shockwaves (eight to

---

How to get hitched at sea

Princess Cruises has possibly the most extensive wedding program of any of the major lines, with its 'Tie the Knot' wedding packages. The ship's captain can legally marry American couples at sea aboard its Bermuda-registered ships. This is by special dispensation, and should be verified when in the planning stage, since it may vary according to where you reside.

The basic wedding at sea package includes a personal wedding coordinator. Live music, a candlelit celebration officiated by the captain, Champagne, fresh floral arrangements, a bridal bouquet, boutonnière, a photographer, and a wedding cake can all be laid on, depending on the cruise line and package, with the wedding do in an exclusive wedding chapel (or other location).

You'll also get keepsake Champagne flutes, and a keepsake wedding certificate. Tuxedo rental is available. Harborside or shore-side packages vary according to the port. For the latest rates, see Princess Cruises' website or your travel agent.

12); and Off-Limits or Remix (13–17). The groups are split into age-related activities, and Princess Cruises has good children's counselors and supervised activities.

Best ships for children. *Caribbean Princess, Coral Princess, Crown Princess, Dawn Princess, Diamond Princess, Emerald Princess, Golden Princess, Grand Princess, Island Princess, Ruby Princess, Sapphire Princess, Sea Princess, Star Princess, Sun Princess.*

Entertainment

The company prides itself on its glamorous all-American shows, and they should not disappoint. For variety, there are typically two or three shows during each seven-day cruise. Each ship has a resident troupe of singers and dancers.

Participation events (some more successful than others) are put on by members of the cruise staff. Most lounges and bars have live music. Musical units range from solo pianists to string quartets, from a cappella singers to bands that can provide music for ballroom dancing. The company also provides a number of male hosts as dance partners for women traveling alone.

Royal Caribbean International

Ships

Adventure of the Seas (2001), *Allure of the Seas* (2010), *Anthem of the Seas* (2015), *Brilliance of the Seas* (2002), *Enchantment of the Seas* (1997), *Explorer of the Seas* (2000), *Freedom of the Seas* (2006), *Grandeur of the Seas* (1996), *Harmony of the Seas* (2016), *Independence of the Seas* (2008), *Jewel of the Seas* (2004), *Legend of the Seas* (1995), *Liberty of the Seas* (2007), *Mariner of the Seas* (2004), *Navigator of the Seas* (2003), *Oasis of the Seas* (2009), *Ovation of the Seas* (2016), *Quantum of the Seas* (2014), *Radiance of the Seas* (2001), *Rhapsody of the Seas* (1997), *Serenade of the Seas* (2003), *Splendour of the Seas* (1996), *Vision of the Seas* (1998)

About the company

Royal Caribbean Cruise Line was set up by three Norwegian shipping company dynasties in 1969: Arne Wilhelmsen, I.M. Skaugen, and Gotaas-Larsen (who was more of a sleeping partner). Its first ship, *Song of Norway*, debuted in 1970, followed by *Nordic Prince* and *Sun Viking (all now scrapped)*. Royal Caribbean was different from Carnival and NCL in that it launched its cruise operations with brand new ships, whereas the others had only older, pre-owned tonnage. In 1978 the cruise industry's first 'chop-and-stretch' operation enlarged *Song of Norway* (now scrapped), and 1988 saw the debut of the first large cruise ship, *Sovereign of the Seas*.

In 1997, Royal Caribbean International bought Celebrity Cruises for $1.3 billion and in 2006 acquired Pullmantur Cruises for $889.9 million. In 2007 the company created a new cruise line, Azamara Cruises, with two ships (in essence operated by Celebrity Cruises). In 2007 RCI established CDF Croisières de France with one ship, diverted from the Pullmantur Cruises fleet.

What is it really like?

RCI, which has carried over 50 million passengers since its founding in 1970, provides a well-integrated, fine-tuned, and comfortable cruise experience, but there's nothing royal about it except the name. The product is consistent but homogeneous. This is cruising for mainstream America. The ships are all quite pleasing, and some have really comfortable public rooms, lounges, bars, and innovative gimmicks. For example, the Bionic Bar aboard Anthem of the Seas and Quantum of the Seas, where two robots make, mix, and serve drinks.

RCI's largest ships are termed *Oasis*-class, *Freedom*-class, *Quantum*-class, and *Voyager*-class. They differ from other ships in the fleet, mainly in the internal layout, by having a large mall-like high street – the focal point for most passengers. Many public rooms, lounges, and bars are located as adjuncts to the mall. Indeed, it's rather like a mall with a ship built around it. Also, in placing so much emphasis on 'active' outdoors areas,

Some balconies can be overlooked from above, as aboard *Ruby Princess*.

space has been taken away from the pool areas, leaving little room left just to sit and relax or sunbathe.

The ships in the next group *(Brilliance of the Seas, Jewel of the Seas, Radiance of the Seas, Serenade of the Seas)* have lots of balcony cabins, and large expanses of glass. *Enchantment of the Seas, Grandeur of the Seas, Legend of the Seas, Rhapsody of the Seas, Splendour of the Seas,* and *Vision of the Seas* also have lots of glass in the public areas, but fewer balcony cabins. *Freedom of the Seas* pioneered a concierge lounge available only to suite-grade occupants.

All ships have a rock-climbing wall with several separate climbing tracks. You'll need to plan what you want to take part in wisely, as almost everything requires you to sign up in advance.

Almost everywhere has intrusive background music, played even in elevators and all passenger hallways. Bars also have very loud music. There are many, many unwelcome announcements for activities that bring revenue, such as art auctions and bingo.

Standing in line for embarkation, the reception desk, disembarkation, for port visits, shore tenders, and for the self-serve buffet stations in the Windjammer Café is an inevitable aspect of cruising aboard most large resort ships. It's often hard to escape the ship's photographers – they're everywhere. Budget extra for all the additional-cost items. Expect to be subjected to a

The FlowRider aboard one of the Royal Caribbean International ships.

stream of flyers advertising promotions, while 'artwork' for auction is strewn throughout the ship, and frosted drinks in 'souvenir' glasses are pushed to the hilt. There are no cushioned pads for the deck lounge chairs.

Service personnel are friendly. The elevators talk to you, though 'going up/going down' is informative but monotonous. However, the signage and illuminated picture displays of decks are all good, particularly aboard the Oasis-class ships.

Occupants of the Presidential Family Suite, Royal Suite, Royal Family Suite, Owner's Suite, and Grand Suite get a dedicated security line, where available. Royal and Presidential Family Suite occupants are welcomed by a senior officer and escorted aboard. Those in Grand Suites and higher categories get gold SeaPass cards for better recognition and goodies including free bottled water, fruit plates, slippers, spa bathrobes, better bathroom amenities, and Ghirardelli chocolates or petits fours at turndown. Free 24-hour room service, coffee, and tea are provided, along with the option of ordering from the main dining room's full breakfast, lunch, and dinner menus. There's also free garment pressing on 'formal' evenings, plus other perks. The interior decor is bright and contemporary, but not as neon-intensive and glitzy as Carnival's ships. There is a strong Scandinavian design influence, with some eclectic sculpture and artwork. The 'you are here' signage and deck plans are excellent. The furniture in public lounges tends to include small 'tub' chairs, which are not that robust.

Cuisine/dining

Most ships have large dining halls that are two or three decks high, giving a sense of space and grandeur. Few tables for two are available, most being for four, six, or eight people. All dining rooms and eateries are non-smoking. The efficient dining operation emphasizes highly programmed, extremely hurried service that many find insensitive. There are no fish knives.

'My Time Dining' (rolled out in 2009) means you can choose either a fixed dining time or any time you want. For this option, you pre-pay gratuities and enroll either on board or in advance through www.royalcaribbean.com or by asking your travel agent to arrange it via the reservations system.

The cuisine in the main dining rooms is typical of mass banquet catering, with mediocre standard fare. The food costs per passenger are below those for sister companies Azamara Club Cruises and Celebrity Cruises, so don't expect the same food quality. Menu descriptions sound tempting, but the food, although well-enough prepared, is unmemorable. A decent selection of light meals is provided; vegetarian and children's menus are also available.

The quality of meat, particularly the beef, is poor – unless you pay extra for a 'better-quality' sirloin steak, cooked to order. Other meats are often disguised with gravies or heavy sauces. Most fish (except salmon) and seafood items tend to be overcooked and lack taste. Green vegetables are scarce – they're provided basically for decoration – but salad items are plentiful. Rice is often used as a source of carbohydrates, potatoes being more expensive.

Breads and pastry items are generally good, although some items, such as croissants, may not be made on board. The selection of breads, rolls, and fruit could be better. Dessert items are standardized and lack flavor, and the cheese and cracker selections are poor.

Specialty dining venues. Most ships have one, two or more additional dining venues (a cover charge applies), including Royal Caribbean favorites Chops Grille Steakhouse (for premium veal chops and steaks, cover charge $35 – and that doesn't include lobster and dry-aged meat) and Portofino (for Italian-American cuisine). Reservations are required in both venues. Be prepared to eat Texas-sized portions, presented on large plates. Note that menus do not change throughout the cruise. *Oasis-* and *Quantum-*class ships also have more extra-cost dining venues. Many ships have plasma screens or touch screens in various locations, so you can make reservations at will, and see at a glance the waiting times for a table.

Specialty dining packages are available, with cost savings compared to the sum of the individual restaurants' cover charges.

Casual eateries. All ships have informal venues called Windjammer Café or Windjammer Marketplace for fast food, salads, and the like. Some are of the single-line (move-along-with-your-plate) type, while the newer ships have individual islands for more variety and fewer lines. However, the actual quality of cooked food items is nutritionally poor, as are the tacky salad dressings.

Breakfast buffet items are repetitive – the same is true of lunchtime salad items. The beverage stations have only the most basic items. Hamburgers and hot dogs in self-serve buffet locations are generally displayed in steam dishes (they are steamed rather than grilled, although you can ask for one to be grilled in front of you). Trays are not provided – only oval plates; if you are disabled or have mobility difficulties, do ask for help. Also, because the plates are plastic, it's impossible to get your food on a heated plate.

Almost all ships also have Johnny Rockets 1950s-style diners (extra charge, per person, whether you eat in or take out, and, while the food is included, shakes and drinks cost extra). These serve hamburgers, hot dogs, desserts, and sodas, although the typical waiting time is about 30 minutes – pagers are provided, allowing you to wander off in the meantime.

Drinks packages are available in bars, in the form of cards or stickers, so that you can pre-pay for a selection of soft drinks and alcoholic drinks. However, the rules for using the pre-paid packages are a bit cumbersome. There is a $3.95 charge for cabin service deliveries midnight–5am.

The coffee/tea factor. Regular coffee: weak, poor quality. Score: 1 out of 10. Extra-cost espressos/cap-

Oasis of the Seas' Central Park.

puccinos (Seattle's Best brand) score 4 out of 10, but they come in paper cups.

For children

RCI's youth programs include 'My Family Time' dining and extra-cost packages such as a supervised 'Lunch and Play' option. An extra-cost in-cabin babysitting service is available.

Adventure Ocean is RCI's 'edutainment' area, while aboard *Oasis-* and *Freedom-*class ships, there's also The H2O Zone. Children and teens are divided into seven age-appropriate groups: Royal Babies (six to 18 months); Royal Tots (18–36 months); Aquanauts (three to five years); Explorers (six to eight years); Voyagers (nine to 12 years); Navigators (12–14 years); and Teens (15–17 years).

An unlimited soda and juice package for the under-17s is available. There are lots of activities, and a host of children's counselors is aboard each ship.

Best ships for children. *Adventure of the Seas, Allure of the Seas, Anthem of the Seas, Explorer of the Seas, Freedom of the Seas, Harmony of the Seas, Independence of the Seas, Liberty of the Seas, Mariner of the Seas, Navigator of the Seas, Oasis of the Seas, Ovation of the Seas, Quantum of the Seas, Voyager of the Seas.*

Entertainment

The entertainment is upbeat and plentiful, similar to what you would find in a resort hotel in Las Vegas. The scaled-down version of big-hit Broadway shows such as Chicago, Hairspray, and Saturday Night Fever are excellent. Other production shows are colorful, fast-paced, high-volume razzle-dazzle spectaculars, but with little or no storyline, poor linkage between themes and scenes, and basic choreography. The live band is augmented by pre-recorded backing tracks to make them sound like a big, professional orchestra. Each ship has its resident troupe of singers and dancers.

There are also some silly audience participation events (summer camp-style, but often funny) and activities – something RCI has always done well.

The Smaller Operators

While the major cruise lines dominate the mass market, dozens of smaller companies cater for more specialist tastes and can offer some exotic destinations.

The international cruise industry comprises around 75 companies with oceangoing cruise ships providing vacations to over 23 million passengers a year. Most major cruise lines are owned and operated by large corporations, although one large cruise line (MSC Cruises) is family-owned. There are also some small cruise lines, with just a couple of compact-size ships. Some companies don't own their own ships, but charter them from ship-owning and ship-management companies for year-round or seasonal operation (Thomson Cruises, for example).

The following smaller companies are listed in alphabetical order.

AIDA Cruises

The former East German shipping company Deutsche Seereederei (DSR) and its marketing arm Seetours (Deutsche Seetouristik) were assigned the traditional cruise ship *Arkona* as part of the 1985 East–West integration, which included a contractual

Germany-based AIDA Cruises is one of the Carnival brands.

agreement with the Treuhandanstalt (the agency that privatized East German enterprises) to build a new ship. It did this in 1996 with the newly built *Aida*, designed to appeal to young, active German-speaking families. The concept was to create a seagoing version of the popular Robinson Clubs – a sort of German Club Med concept. When *Aida* first debuted, there were almost no passengers, and the company struggled.

In 1998 the company was sold to Norwegian Cruise Line, which sold it back to its original Rostock-based owners. P&O acquired it in 1999, and it is now a very successful multi-ship brand belonging to the Carnival Corporation, under the direct control of its Costa Cruises division. AIDA Cruises, Germany's largest cruise line, is known for its über-casual cruising, with main self-serve buffet restaurants instead of the traditional waiter service.

AIDA Cruises has now grown up and no longer focuses on summer-camp-style participation events. The ships have become more sophisticated entertaining venues, and the *animateurs* – members of staff who specialize in entertainment – have grown up and morphed into what are known as Club Teams. They, along with other staff, interact with passengers throughout the ship. AIDA Cruises has its own training schools in several countries, plus a recognized training academy in Rostock.

Alaskan Dream Cruises

Allen Marine Tours is an operator of local day vessels in Alaska, operating only in Alaska and family-owned by members of the Kaagwaantaan Clans of the Tlingit people. It formed a new micro-cruise company, Alaskan Dream Cruises, in 2010, after buying two Cruise West 78-passenger vessels when Cruise West declared insolvency and ceased operations. *Spirit of Columbia* and *Spirit of Alaska* were converted into *Admiralty Dream* and *Baranhof Dream* in 2011. Gratuities are not included in the cruise fare.

American Cruise Lines

ACL was originally formed in 1974, at the beginning of American coastal passenger shipping, but it went bankrupt in 1989, the ships were sold off, and the company lay dormant. The original owner, Charles Robertson, a renowned yachtsman who used to race 12-meter (39-ft) America's Cup yachts, resurrected it in 2000, and built its own ships in its own small shipyard in Salisbury, Maryland, on the Chesapeake Bay.

Azamara Journey cruising the Norwegian fjords.

ACL's ships *(American Glory, American Spirit, American Star, Independence)* ply the inter-coastal waterways and rivers of the North American East Coast, and provide an up-close, intimate experience for passengers who don't need luxury or much pampering but do like American history and culture, as well as service from an all-American college-age staff. The 'D-class' vessels are less than 2,500 gross tonnage, and are subject neither to bureaucratic regulations nor to union rules.

In 2011, the company also started operating *Queen of the West*, a 120-passenger paddlewheel (replica steamboat) on rivers in the US Pacific Northwest. In 2012 it introduced the brand new *Queen of the Mississippi*, a replica steamboat, for Mississippi River cruises. Gratuities are not included in the cruise fare. The company's sister brand is Pearl Seas Cruises.

Antarpply Expeditions

Based in Ushuaia, Argentina, this company specializes in inexpensive Antarctic expedition cruises, including the Falkland Isles, Shetland Isles, and South Georgia, during the Austral summer. It has one expedition ship, *Ushuaia*, but the quality of its voyages and operation is not as high as that of the better-run, more experienced European companies. Gratuities are not included in the fare.

Aurora Expeditions

This Australian company was founded in 1993 by Australian Mount Everest veteran and geologist Greg Mortimer and adventure travel specialist Margaret Werner. The company, which specializes in small-group expeditions, uses the chartered expedition ship *Polar Pioneer* for its Antarctic expedition cruise programs. Other destinations include Papua New Guinea, Australia's Kimberley region, and the Russian Far East, for which the ship is the chartered

Russian expedition vessel *Akademik Shokalskiy*. Gratuities are not included in the fare.

Australis

This company, based in Santiago, Chile, operates cruise ships on 'soft' expedition cruises to the Chilean fjords, Patagonia, and Tierra del Fuego – some of the world's most fascinating but hostile environments. Catering increasingly to an international clientele, with Spanish as the official onboard language (English is also spoken). Don't expect high standards aboard its two ships, but the service is very friendly, and the organization and operations are extremely good.

The company introduced a brand new ship in 2010, the 210-passenger *Stella Australis*. The other two ship is the 136-passenger *Via Australis*. Its cruises are 'all-inclusive', with an open bar for all beverages, including wine and gratuities. In 2013 the company shortened its name, from Cruceros Australis to, simply, Australis.

Azamara Club Cruises

This company, formerly Azamara Cruises, is an off-shoot of Celebrity Cruises, and was created in 2007. Having started with little direction, the company was revitalized in 2009–10 by new president Larry Pimentel. It operates two 700-passenger ships, taking people to smaller ports that some of the large resort ships can't get into.

The company specializes in providing high-quality dining, and the ships try to give a floating 'country club' experience. They are in direct competition with the ships of Oceania Cruises – except that Oceania doesn't charge extra to dine in its specialty restaurants. But Azamara has longer port stays and more overnight port stays than Oceania – a bonus during longer itineraries.

Asuka II leaving port.

The onboard experience is similar to that aboard the ships of parent company Celebrity Cruises (including rather tacky art auctions), but modified to suit those who want a more personal and sophisticated cruise experience aboard smaller ships. Its strengths are the food and European-style service, and each ship has two extra-charge restaurants in addition to the main dining venues. Included in the fare are gratuities to dining and housekeeping staff, wine with lunch and dinner, coffee and tea 24 hours a day, and shuttle buses in ports of call, where needed. Complimentary standard spirits, wines, and international beers throughout the ship during bar opening hours were introduced in March 2013. One area where Azamara Club Cruises tries to differentiate itself from its competitors is by providing long-stay port days – including several overnight stays – as well as the company's 'AzAmazing Evenings' cultural excursion programs. Both ships will undergo a major refurbishment early in 2016.

Bahamas Paradise Cruise Line

This one-ship company is owned by Celebration Cruise Holdings, which also owned the now-defunct Imperial Majesty Cruise Line, whose reputation suffered from high-pressure telemarketing campaigns. Its *Grand Celebration* (originally built for Carnival Cruise Line) operates two-night cruises from the Port of Palm Beach, in Florida, to the Bahamas.

Despite the company's claims to 'international gourmet dining,' the ship provides a highly programmed but absolutely basic party getaway cruise with very standard food, and with much pressure for onboard revenue from its dining, casino, and shore excursion operations. Both ships will undergo a major refurbishment early in 2016.

Blount Small Ship Adventures

This company was founded in 1966 by the late Luther H. Blount, an engineer and inventor of the American steam trawler, who built his cruise vessels in his own shipyard in Warren, Rhode Island, and it started as a family-run venture. Today, as the oldest US-flag cruise line still operating, it is run by Luther's daughter, Nancy Blount.

Cruises are operated like private family outings, using two unpretentious ships that have been specially constructed to operate in close-in coastal areas and inland waterways of the eastern US seaboard, with forays to the Bahamas and Caribbean during the winter. The onboard experience is strictly no-frills cruising in really basic, down-to-earth surroundings that have a 1950s feel.

Its early-to-bed passengers – average age 72 years – are typical of those who don't like glitz or all things trendy. Gratuities are not included in the cruise fare. Blount Small Ship Adventures introduced select beers and house wines with lunch and dinner on cruises in 2013.

CDF Croisières de France

Founded and wholly owned by Royal Caribbean Cruise Line (RCCL), CDF Croisières de France was created in 2007. The brand is under the overall control of Pullmantur Cruises (who provide the back office and crewing requirements), which is also owned by RCCL. The company devotes all its resources to cruising for French-speaking passengers, with two ships *Horizon and Zenith (originally built for Celebrity Cruises)*. The emphasis is on fine French cuisine and all-inclusive pricing. Gratuities are included in the fare.

Celestyal Cruises

Established in 2014, Celestyal Cruises is a sub-brand of Louis Cruises. It has two all-white ships, the 966-passenger Louis Crystal and the 1,450-passenger Louis Olympia, both of which are dedicated to cruising in the Greek isles, Croatia, and Turkey – destinations with which the company's Cyprus-based parent company (Louis Cruises) has many years of experience.

Club Med Cruises

Club Med became renowned for providing hassle-free vacations for the whole family. The first Club Med village was started in 1950 on the Spanish island of Majorca, but the concept became so popular that it grew to more than 100 vacation villages throughout the world.

Club Med Cruises, an offshoot of the French all-inclusive vacation clubs, introduced its first ocean-going cruise vessel in 1990, the computer-controlled sail-cruise ship *Club Med II* (extensively refurbished in 2008). Aboard the all-inclusive ship, the so-called *gentils ordinaires* serve as both super-cruise staff and 'rah-rah' cheerleaders, carrying out entertainment and activity programs, for the mainly French-speaking passengers. *Club Med II* has a sister ship, Windstar Cruises' *Wind Surf*, which also provides a relaxed onboard experience. Gratuities are included in the fare.

CMV (Cruise and Maritime Voyages)

This UK-based company (with 50 percent owned by Greece's Maritime Group) existed for many years as a sales and marketing organization representing several small cruise lines. It now charters and operates three ships owned by other companies. The firm, some of whose owners originally worked for long-defunct CTC Cruises, specializes in adults-only (16 and over) cruises from regional UK ports, and provides traditional cruise features such as mid-morning bouillon, and captain's welcome and farewell dinners. The onboard product, particularly the food, is at the lower end of the market. *Magellan* and *Marco Polo* are ships operated for ex-UK cruises. Gratuities are not included in the cruise fare.

Crystal Cruises

Crystal Cruises was founded in 1988 by Nippon Yusen Kaisha (NYK), the world's largest cargo ship and transportation logistics company, with a fleet of more than 700 ships. The American-managed company is based in Century City, Los Angeles. *Crystal Harmony*, the company's first ship, was built in Japan, and debuted in New York in May 1990 to great acclaim. Meanwhile, Crystal Cruises introduced two new ships, *Crystal Symphony* in 1995, and *Crystal Serenity* in 2000, one built in Finland, the other in France.

In 2006 *Crystal Harmony* was transferred to parent company NYK as *Asuka II* for its Asuka Cruise division, for Japanese speakers. Crystal Cruises continues to provide excellent food and service aboard its two spacious ships (*Crystal Serenity* and *Crystal Symphony*), including an excellent Nobu sushi/sashimi bar aboard *Crystal Serenity*.

The ships operate worldwide itineraries with flair. Both ships are superbly maintained, and passengers who seek fine food in a sophisticated setting should be delighted with their choice of ship and company. Open-seating dining was introduced in January 2011 for the first time, but passengers can still opt for fixed-time dining. In spring 2012 Crystal Cruises adopted all-inclusive pricing, with drinks, wines, and gratuities included in the fare. In 2015 the company was acquired by Genting Hong Kong (owner of Star Cruises and a major shareholder of Norwegian Cruise Line).

Disney Cruise Line

It was Lawrence (Larry) P. Murphy, executive vice-president of the Walt Disney Company, who was the guiding light in the early 1990s behind the expansion of the company into the cruise business. Previously, Disney had flirted with cruising by participating in a licensing agreement with a Florida-based cruise line, the now-defunct Premier Cruise Lines, with three vintage ships based in Port Canaveral. Murphy and other Disney executives explored the possibility of creating their own ships when the licensing agreement ran out. They concluded that pairing with an established cruise line wouldn't work because of Disney's policy of generous spending on the guest experience.

The solution: create a new cruise line, wholly owned and controlled by Disney and to be known as Disney Cruise Line. The company committed an astonishing $1 billion to the project.

Its two mid-size ships, *Disney Magic* (1998) and *Disney Wonder* (1999), the first cruise ships since the 1950s to be built with two funnels, cater to loyal Dis-

Crystal Serenity alongside in Malta

Disney takes its brand to Alaska.

ney followers, and everything aboard the ships is Disney – every song, every piece of artwork, every movie and production show – and Mickey's ears adorn the ships' funnels. But there's no casino and no library. However, its 'rotation dining' concept proved to be completely Disneylogical; you move, together with your waiter, to each of three identically sized restaurants – each with different decor – in turn.

One new, larger ship, *Disney Dream*, joined the fleet in 2011, and sister ship *Disney Fantasy* arrived in 2012.

Disney, of course, is all about families with children, and the ships cater to both. You can buy a package combining a short stay at a Disney resort and a cruise. Gratuities are not included in the cruise fare. Disney has its own cruise terminal at Port Canaveral, Florida, its design being an imaginative but close copy of the Ocean Terminal in Southampton, UK, frequented by yesteryear's ocean liners but little used today. The terminal and pier were extended in 2010 and connected to a new parking garage.

Etstur Cruises
Based in Istanbul, this company (Ets Ersoy Turistik Servisieri) – the largest tourism group for domestic travel, vacations, and cruises in Turkey – was founded in 1991 by two brothers. It charters the *Aegean Paradise* (formerly *Delphin Voyager* – sister to *Pacific Venus*) from the ship's Greek owners. Operations and marine catering are outsourced to specialist companies. Etstur also sells other ocean and river cruise lines' products, including river cruises, to its Turkish clientele base.

fathom
fathom is a new brand established by Carnival Corporation for 'social impact' cruises, initially to benefit the Dominican Replubic. It is similar to the 'volunteer vacations' operated by non-profit groups such as GlobeAware. Included in the cruise fare are three 'social impact activities' ashore. Participants teach English to children in the destination, and

assist in programs to help the local population. A portion of the cruise fare goes directly to fathom partner organizations to cover on-the-ground activities and support their missions.

The 710-passenger *Adonia* will be staffed and operated by P&O Cruises (as a business venture) for these one-week cruises.

Fred. Olsen Cruise Lines
This Norwegian family-owned and family-run company was founded in Hvitstein, a town on Oslofjord, Norway, in 1848. Today, a fifth-generation Olsen, Fred Jr, runs the company from its headquarters in Suffolk, England. The group also has interests in hotels, aviation, shipbuilding, ferries, and offshore industries. The company specializes in cruises for adults, who are usually retired and of senior years – typically over 65.

Aboard the ships, interior design reflects traditional design features, and dressing for dinner is expected on four nights during a two-week cruise. Many theme cruises, such as gardening and horticulture, and Scottish country dancing, hosted by recognized television celebrities, are regular features. The company welcomes solo passengers as well as couples and delivers a quintessentially 'British' cruise experience, albeit by a mainly Filipino hotel service staff.

The first ship dedicated exclusively to cruising debuted in 1987, and now ships cruise year-round out of UK ports such as Dover, Southampton, Liverpool, Newcastle, Greenock, Leith, Belfast, and Dublin (ideal for anyone based in the UK to join one of the ships without having to fly), with some ships operating fly-cruises from Canary Island ports, or Caribbean ports such as Barbados in winter.

Coffee- and tea-making facilities are provided in each cabin. Smoking is allowed only on the open decks, and nowhere inside the ships. Gratuities are not included in the cruise fare, but are automatically charged to your onboard account. Drink prices are extremely reasonable aboard the company's ships, where the social scene is courteous, friendly, and warm, and gentlemen hosts are onboard each cruise for unaccompanied women who would like dancing partners.

FTI Cruises
This company, part of the Munich-based FTI Touristik (founded in 1983), bought its only ship from Saga Cruises in 2011 and started its cruise operations in May 2012 for the German-speaking market. The ship, *Berlin*, is well known in Germany for low-cost, good-value cruising for passengers not expecting luxury.

G Adventures
This Canadian company, based in Toronto, was founded in 1990 as GAP Adventures by Bruce Poon Tip, using funds from his own personal credit cards

only. The company has a grassroots approach to travel and operates its own ship – the 140-passenger MS *Expedition* – on polar expedition cruises.

Galápagos Cruises

Metropolitan Touring, Ecuador's foremost tour and travel company is based in Quito and sells its cruises through general sales agents such as the North American Dallas-based Adventure Associates. Its pocket-size ships, the well-run *Isabella* and *Santa Cruz*, visit the Galápagos Islands with all-Ecuadorean crew and food. Go for the destination, not for the ships, which are old and have few facilities. Gratuities are not included in the fare.

Grand Circle Cruise Line

Ethel Andrus, a retired teacher, wanted to share her vision of helping Americans lead more vital, challenging, and politically active lives. She founded the American Association of Retired Persons (AARP) in 1958. The company has exclusive charters for its small group travel (the company's foundation has donated more than $91 million to cultural, educational, and humanitarian organizations since 1992). For many years, this Boston-based travel company (its brands are Grand Circle Travel, Overseas Adventure Travel, and Grand Circle Cruise Line) has chartered riverships and small ocean-going vessels. The firm has three custom-designed sea-going ships (*Arethusa*, *Artemis*, and *Athena*) for coastal cruise tours for two groups of 25 persons each, and in May 2016 will aquire *Tere Moana* from Paul Gaugin Cruises. However, general cruise/travel agents cannot easily book into the company's cruise programs.

Hapag-Lloyd Cruises

Germany's two most famous ocean liner companies, the Bremen-based Norddeutscher Lloyd (founded in 1847) and the Hamburg-based Hamburg America Line (founded in the same year), merged in 1970 to become Hapag-Lloyd. The company no longer operates regularly scheduled transatlantic crossings, but promotes instead four ships in three different market segments.

Two small ships are in the specialized expedition cruise market: the 164-passenger *Bremen* and the 184-passenger *Hanseatic* (run by Hapag-Lloyd Expedition Cruises); and two (the more formal 400-passenger *Europa* and the more informal 516-passenger *Europa 2* – for international travellers and families with children) are in the luxury market. All provide destination-intensive cruises aimed at the German-speaking market, with an increasing number of dual-language cruises for English-speakers.

The staff on board makes all its own breads, soups, pâtés, jams, and preserves from scratch.

Hapag-Lloyd Cruises also supports the annual Stella Maris Vocal Competition, which allows up-and-coming vocalists from around the world to compete for the Young Talent Development Prize and a contract with the prestigious Deutsche Grammophon record label.

Hapag-Lloyd Expedition Cruises

The company operates two specialist expedition cruise ships, the 164-passenger *Bremen* and the 184-passenger *Hanseatic*. There are occasional dual-language cruises for the English-speaking market, but all the crew members speak English anyway.

Both ships carry a fleet of Zodiac inflatable rubber craft for shore landings in the polar region and other destinations with no pier facilities. They have excellent cuisine, proper boot-washing and storage stations, lecture rooms, extensive libraries, and other expedition facilities to suit adventurous itineraries, plus some of the world's best expedition leaders.

Hapag-Lloyd Expedition Cruises is a member of IAATO (International Association of Antarctica Tour Operators), a body committed to the highest standards of responsible tourism to Antarctica and to operating its ships in the most environmentally

Hapag-Lloyd's *Bremen* in the Corinth Canal, Greece.

friendly manner, accompanied by the very best expedition leaders in the business.

Hapag-Lloyd publishes its own excellent handbooks (in both English and German) on expedition regions such as the Arctic, Antarctica, Amazonia, and the South Sea Islands, as well as exclusive maps. Gratuities are not included in the fare.

Hebridean Island Cruises

The company (formerly Hebridean International Cruises) was set up in 1989 under the Thatcher government's British Enterprise Scheme, and has its headquarters in Skipton, Yorkshire. It operates one all-inclusive boutique ship, *Hebridean Princess*, which conveys the atmosphere of English country-house life – think Laura Ashley fabrics and soft furnishings – and specializes in cruises for mature adults. Gratuities and all port taxes are included, as are most excursions. The ship runs cruises around the Scottish islands. There are occasional sailings to English ports, the Channel Islands, and Norway. Each cabin has coffee- and tea-making facilities. Gratuities are included in the fare. The Queen granted Hebridean Island Cruises a royal warrant in her jubilee year.

Heritage Expeditions

This youth-minded adventure travel company, based in Christchurch, New Zealand, focuses on expedition-style cruising for small groups, specifically to Antarctica, the Sub-Antarctic and Russian Far East. The company was founded in 1985 by biologist Rodney Russ who worked for the New Zealand Wildlife Service for many years. The company's single ship, *Spirit of Enderby* was formerly *Professor Khromov*, a small Russian oceanographic research vessel.

HNA Tourism Cruises

HNA Tourism Cruises is owned by the HNA Group (Hainan), a multi-enterprise industry group that covers air transportation (Hainan Air), airport management, hotel (this division provided the accommodations for the 16th Asian Games in 2010), logistics, real estate, tourism, and other related businesses. It has five airlines, including Grand China Express – among the largest regional airlines in China. In 2012, the company purchased the former *Pacific Sun* (originally Carnival Cruise Line's *Jubilee*) from P&O Cruises Australia and became the first mainland China-based company to own and operate a cruise ship for its domestic market. *Henna* (the ship's present name) started operations in January 2013, with voyages between Sanya and Tianjin. Star Cruises operates the ship on behalf of HNA Tourism.

Hurtigruten

The company is an amalgamation of two shipping companies (OVDS and TVDS) and provides year-round service along the Norwegian coast, calling at 33 ports in 11 days. Hurtigruten, formerly known as the Norwegian Coastal Voyage, has also recently developed expedition-style cruises, albeit aboard ships that have been converted for the purpose, rather than specifically built for expedition cruises. So, as long as you think utilitarian and modest decor, you'll get the idea of life aboard one of the Hurtigruten ships, which are practical rather than beautiful. Even aboard the newest ships, the food and service are

At the captain's reception aboard *Europa*.

Louis Aura in the Mediterranean.

fairly basic – there's a lack of green vegetables – but the ships provide a great way to see many, many ports along the coast of Norway in a comfortable manner.

Norway's Crown Princess Mette-Marit was the godmother of the newest ship, *Fram*, a 318-berth expedition-style vessel built for polar and Greenland cruising.

Island Cruises

Island Cruises was founded as a joint venture between Royal Caribbean Cruises and the British low-cost tour operator First Choice Holidays. Its first ship started operations in 2002. However, in 2007, First Choice merged with Germany's largest travel company TUI, to become TUI Travel. Its *Island Escape* is presently operated as a sub-brand of Thomson Cruises.

It provides its mainly British passengers (some with a reputation for being lager louts) with an 'all-inclusive' cruise experience in ultra-casual surroundings. Its self-serve, self-carry buffet meals from an always-busy, congested café are the mainstay of the 'culinary' offerings, although slightly better food can be had in a smaller extra-cost dining venue. Gratuities are not included in the fare.

Lindblad Expeditions

Lars-Eric Lindblad started the whole concept of expedition cruising with a single ship, *Lindblad Explorer*, in 1969, taking adventurous travelers to remote regions of the world. Today, his son, Sven-Olof Lindblad, runs the company, but with an array of small ships. It's all about nature, wilderness, wildlife, off-the-beaten-path adventures, and learning. Zodiac inflatable craft are used to ferry participants ashore in remote Arctic and Antarctic polar regions.

The ships carry excellent lecturers, who are more academic than entertaining. In partnership with the National Geographic Society, the company operates the wholly owned *National Geographic Endeavour* and *National Geographic Explorer* (both with ice-strengthened hulls), together with two small ships (*National Geographic Sea Bird* and *National Geographic Sea Lion*) for coastal or 'soft' expedition-style cruising in, for example, Alaska. National Geographic photographers take part in all cruises. Zodiac inflatable craft are often used for shore landings, and the ships have extensive libraries. Gratuities are not included in the fare.

The National Geographic Society celebrated its 125th anniversary in 2013, when the company purchased Orion Expedition Cruises, based in Sydney, Australia. Orion Expedition's ship, also called *Orion*, was renamed *National Geographic Orion*, when the ship was transferred from Orion Expeditions to the Lindblad fleet in March 2014. Built in Germany, this ship is a little gem, with handcrafted cabinetry in every cabin, together with marble bathrooms and a health spa and gymnasium.

Louis Cruises

In the 1930s and 1940s, Louis Loizou became the undisputed father of tourism in Cyprus. His venture into sea tourism started with the charter of ships transferring immigrants from Cyprus to other continents. His son, Costakis Loizou, who took over the running of the company after Louis's death in 1971,

The horseshoe staircase aboard Oceania's *Marina*.

started organizing short cruises from Cyprus. In 1986 Louis Cruises was officially founded with the acquisition of the company's first fully owned ship, *Princesa Marissa*.

Today, Louis Group owns almost two dozen hotels in the Greek islands and Cyprus, together with a multi-ship fleet of mainly older, small and mid-size ships, which operate principally from Greece and ports in the Mediterranean. Louis Cruises charters two of its ships to TUI Travel's UK-based Thomson Cruises and has over the years chartered some of its ships to many major UK and European tour operators. The company's sub-brand, created in 2014, is Celestyal Cruises.

MOPAS
Osaka Shosen Kaisha was founded in 1884 in Osaka, Japan. In 1964 it merged with Mitsui Steamship, to become Mitsui OSK Passenger Line (MOPAS). It is now one of the oldest and largest shipping companies in the world.

It entered cruise shipping in 1989 with *Fuji Maru*, the first cruise ship in the Japanese-speaking domestic market (now no longer in service). The company specialized in incentive meetings and groups at sea rather than cruising for individuals. But the company steadily changed to more cruises for individuals. The company operates a single ship, the very comfortable *Nippon Maru* (extensively refurbished in 2010), based in Japan for Japanese-speaking passengers. Gratuities are included in the cruise fare.

Noble Caledonia
London-based Noble Caledonia, established in 1991, operates three boutique-size sister ships, *Caledonian Sky*, *Hebridean Sky*, and *Island Sky*, each carrying around 100 passengers. It also sells cruises aboard a wide range of small-ship and expedition cruise companies as well as river cruises. It markets to British passengers of mature years, and operates cruises, generally in sheltered water areas, with cultural interest themes, and so is not recommended for children.

The company, whose financial partners include Sweden's Salen family, who were very involved with expedition cruising in the past, has an excellent reputation for well-organized cruises and tours, accompanied by good lecturers. It specializes in itineraries that would be impossible to operate aboard larger ships. A Commodore Club gives repeat passengers advance information about new voyages and special offers. Gratuities are not generally included in the fare, unless otherwise stated in the brochures.

NYK Cruises
Nippon Yusen Kaisha, the world's largest shipping company, owns the well-known US-based upscale brand Crystal Cruises. It created its own NYK Cruise division – today branded as Asuka Cruise – in 1989 with one Mitsubishi-built ship, *Asuka*, for Japanese-speaking passengers. In 2006, the company sold the original *Asuka* to Germany's Phoenix Reisen, and the former *Crystal Harmony* was transferred from Crystal Cruises to become *Asuka II*. The ship, known for its excellent Japanese and western food, operates an annual around-the-world cruise, plus a wide array of both short and long cruises in the Asia-Pacific region. Coffee- and tea-making facilities are provided in each cabin, as is a large selection of personal toiletries. Gratuities are included in the cruise fare.

Oceania Cruises
The company's ships provide faux English charm in a country-club atmosphere ideal for middle-aged and older couples seeking relaxation. Cruises are usually 10–14 days. Its trademarks are comfortable cabins, warm and attentive service, and fine dining combining French culinary expertise and top-quality ingredients. Breads and baked goods, such as Poilâne-quality croissants, are outstanding.

In 2006, Oceania Cruises was bought by Apollo Management, a private equity company that owns Regent Seven Seas Cruises, and 50 percent of NCL. The brand was placed under the umbrella of Apollo's cruise brand, Prestige Cruise Holdings. With *Insignia*, *Nautica* and *Regatta* now well established (sister ship *Sirena* joins the fleet in April 2016) and with two newer, larger and faster ships – the 1,250-passenger *Marina* (2011) and *Riviera* (2012) – the company is set to grow even more.

With multiple-choice dining at no extra cost, the 700- and 1,250-passenger ships suit anyone who prefers small and mid-size ships to large resort vessels. Bottled mineral water, soft drinks, and beer are included in the price. Gratuities are added at $10.50 per person, per day, and butler-service suites have an additional charge of $3 per person. Bar drinks and spa treatments have 15–18 percent added.

Oceanwide Expeditions
Founded in 1961 as the Dutch 'Plancius Foundation' to operate cruises around Spitzbergen (Norway), the

company changed its name in 1996 to Oceanwide Expeditions in order to offer adventures farther afield. It specializes in small group polar expedition voyages and active shore visits rather than employing experienced lecturers. It operates two expedition ships, *Ortelius* and *Plancius*, and charters others as needed.

One Ocean Expeditions
Based in Toronto, Canada, this small company was founded by Andrew Prossin. It doesn't own any expedition ships itself, but charters them from the Russian pool of specialist vessels. Environmental responsibility is a key ingredient for its staff, all of whom are personable and very customer-oriented. The company operates two sister specialist polar expedition ships, *Akademik Ioffe* and *Akademik Sergey Vavilov*, on Arctic and Antarctic programs.

P&O Cruises (Australia)
Founded in 1932, this Australian division of P&O Cruises provides fun entertainment for the beer-and-bikini brigade and their families, and specializes in cruises in the Pacific and to New Zealand. The line is maturing, though, becoming more of a mainstream operator – particularly so with its latest ships, which are larger, more contemporary hand-me-down vessels (*Pacific Dawn, Pacific Jewel, Pacific Pearl* from P&O Cruises and Princess Cruises; and Pacific Aria and Pacific Eden from Holland America Line), from companies that are part of the Carnival Corporation. The ships have open-seating dining and specialty restaurants such as Australian celebrity chef, Luke Mangan's 'Salt Grill.' Gratuities are not included in the fare.

Paul Gauguin Cruises
Created by the Boston-based tour operator Grand Circle Travel, Paul Gauguin Cruises took over the marketing and operation of *Paul Gauguin* in 2009 from Regent Seven Seas Cruises, which had operated the ship since its inception. Also in 2009, the ship was bought by the Tahiti-based investor Richard Bailey and his company Pacific Beachcomber, which owns Polynesian resort hotels (including four Inter-Continental Hotels). Gratuities are not included in the cruise fare.

Pearl Seas Cruises
Founded in 2007 by Charles Robertson, Pearl Seas Cruises is now a sister company to American Cruise Lines. It has a single ship (a second ship order was canceled), *Pearl Mist*, which was the subject of poor shipbuilding and contract arguments in its early days. *Pearl Mist* was rejected as not fit for purpose by the owner, but was finally completed and debuted in 2014. It has a loyalty club called the Oyster Society.

Phoenix Reisen
Based in Bonn, Germany, the company for many years operated low-budget, tour-operator-style destination-intensive cruises for German speakers. It now has a loyal, widespread audience and more contemporary ships, with better food and service, particularly aboard *Amadea* and *Artania*.

To keep costs down, Phoenix charters its ships for long periods. It is consistently praised for its extremely good itineraries, particularly on world cruises, its pre- and post-cruise programs, and its excellent value for money. The wonderfully comprehensive Phoenix

The *Paul Gauguin* was built specifically to navigate the islands of French Polynesia.

brochure provides photographs of its captains and cruise director, as well as bar lists and drink prices – a refreshing change from the brochures provided by most cruise companies. Single-seating dining is standard, as are low drink prices, and there is no constant pushing for onboard revenue – again different from their rivals.

Phoenix acquired *Artania* (formerly P&O Cruises' *Artemis* and originally *Royal Princess*, named by Princess Diana) in 2011, and also operates the lower-priced *Albatross* (originally *Royal Viking Sea*). Gratuities are included in the fare.

Plantours Cruises

This company, based in Bremen, Germany, provides low-budget cruises for German speakers aboard its single small, chartered cruise ship, *Hamburg*, which was formerly Hapag-Lloyd Cruises' original *Columbus*. The company also sells cruises on the rivers of Europe and Russia. Gratuities are not included in the cruise fare.

Ponant

This company was founded in 1988 by Philippe Videau and Jean-Emmanuel Sauvé. It started life as La Compagnie des Iles du Ponant, and was a subsidiary of the state-owned CMA CGM (Compagnie Maritime d'Affrètement/Compagnie Générale Maritime), until its acquisition by Bridgepoint Capital, a private equity company (who also own the Pret chain of cafés and Leeds Bradford International airport), in 2012.

The cruise company, whose head office is in Marseille, France, operates one boutique-size high-tech sail ship, *Le Ponant*. In 2004, the company bought the Paris-based tour operator Tapis Rouge International, which specializes in upscale travel. Three new small ships – *Le Boréal*, introduced in 2010, *L'Austral*, introduced in 2011, and *Le Soleal*, introduced in 2013 – provide more space and more options for passengers, with a fourth (*Le Lyrial*), introduced in 2015. Ponant increasingly markets cruises in both English and French to international passengers, and onboard announcements are made in both languages. Gratuities are not included in the fare.

Pullmantur Cruises

The company was set up as part of Pullmantur, the Spain-based holiday tour operator founded in 1971. Its cruising division was established in 2000 when it bought *Oceanic* (then known as the Big Red Boat) from the defunct Florida operator Premier Cruise Lines. In 2006, Pullmantur Cruises was bought by Royal Caribbean Cruises. The company, mainly serving the Spanish-speaking market, operates all-inclusive cruises for families with children to the Caribbean and Europe and, during the South American summer, serves the Brazilian market. Although most passengers are Spanish, the company now also markets heavily to US and other cruise goers. Gratuities are included in the fare.

Quark Expeditions

The company was founded in 1991 by Lars Wikander, Mike McDowell, and silent partner the Salen family (formerly of Salen-Lindblad Cruises). Based in Seattle, Washington (US), Quark specializes in providing

Pacific Pearl entering Hobart, Tasmania.

up-close-and-personal Arctic and Antarctic expedition cruises.

In 2007, it was sold to the UK's First Choice Holidays (founded in 1973), merged with Peregrine Shipping, and then in 2007 was bought, along with First Choice, by the German travel company TUI AG.

Cruising with Quark Expeditions is all about being close to nature, wilderness, wildlife, off-the-beaten-path adventures, and learning. The company, an associate member of IAATO (International Association of Antarctica Tour Operators), specializes in chartered Russian icebreakers, the most powerful in the world, to provide participants with truly memorable expedition experiences. This is adventure cruising for toughies. Gratuities are not included in the cruise fare.

A penthouse suite aboard *Seven Seas Explorer*.

Regent Seven Seas Cruises

This company has a complicated history. It was born out of Seven Seas Cruises, which was originally based in San Francisco to market the cruise ship *Song of Flower* (belonging to 'K'-Line, a cargo operator based in New Jersey), as well as expedition cruises aboard the chartered *Hanseatic* (then belonging to Hanseatic Tours). The lyre, logo of that ship, became RSSC's logo.

For many years, the company was part of the Carlson group, and operated as Radisson Seven Seas Cruises. Carlson Hospitality Worldwide ventured into cruising via its Radisson Hotels International division – hence, Radisson Diamond Cruises (when Radisson Diamond joined in 1992). In 1994 Radisson Diamond Cruises and Seven Seas Cruise Line merged to become Radisson Seven Seas Cruises, and in 2007 it became Regent Seven Seas Cruises.

It strives to pay close attention to detail and provide high-quality service aboard its fleet of four small cruise ships – *Seven Seas Explorer (set to debut in 2016), Seven Seas Mariner, Seven Seas Navigator*, and *Seven Seas Voyager* – operating worldwide itineraries.

In 2007 the company was bought by US-based investment group Apollo Management, and, together with Oceania Cruises, was placed under the umbrella of its Prestige Cruise Holdings. The company spent $40 million to refurbish its three ships in 2009–10.

It provides drinks-inclusive cruising, which means that beverages and gratuities are included in the fare, as are shore excursions – even delicious *illy* coffees are included. Passengers pay extra only for laundry services, beauty services, casino, and other personal items.

Saga Cruises

Saga, based in Folkestone, England, was created by Sydney de Haan as a company offering financial services and holidays to an over-60s clientele. As the company's success grew, it reduced this limitation in 1995 to the over-50s and allowed companions older than 40. Its popular travel flourished because it was good at providing personal attention and had competent staff. Instead of sending passengers to ships operated by other companies, it decided to buy its own ships and market its own product under the Saga Holidays brand.

Saga Shipping (Saga Cruises), the cruising division of Saga Holidays, was set up in 1997 when it purchased *Saga Rose* (formerly *Sagafjord*), followed soon after by *Saga Ruby* (formerly *Vistafjord*) and, in 2010, *Saga Pearl II* (formerly *Astoria*). *Saga Sapphire* (ex-Europa) arrived in 2012.

Another brand, Spirit of Adventure, was added in 2006, the year that parent company Saga and Britain's Automobile Association merged. The 'Adventure' cruise brand ended in November 2013, when *Quest for Adventure* became *Saga Pearl II* again.

The cruise company emphasizes British seamanship and training, and its fleet manages to retain the feel of traditional, elegant, adults-only cruising aboard *Saga Pearl II* and *Saga Sapphire*. Saga Cruises offers open-seating dining, friendly, attentive service from a mainly Filipino hotel service crew, and its ships have many single-occupancy cabins. It takes care of the many little details that other lines have long forgotten.

All gratuities are included in the fare. Coffee- and tea-making facilities are provided in each cabin on *Saga Pearl II*.

Sea Cloud Cruises

This company was founded in 1979 by a consortium of ship-owners and investors known as the Hansa Treuhand (active in commercial vessel management, engineering, and construction), with headquarters in Hamburg, Germany. It owns and operates two genuine tall ships (cruise-sail vessels), the legendary *Sea Cloud* (built in 1931 for the cereal heiress Marjorie Merriweather Post), and the 1990-built *Sea Cloud II*.

The company has many corporate clients who charter the two tall ships, while a number of luxury cruise and travel specialist companies sell cruises to individuals. The onboard style and product delivery are something special, with elegant retro decor and

Relaxed life aboard *SeaDream I*.

fine food and service. Gratuities are not included in the cruise fare.

Seabourn

Originally founded in 1986 as Signet Cruise Line, the company, then owned by Norwegian industrialist Atle Brynestad, had to change its name in 1988 as a result of a lawsuit brought by a Texas ferry company that had already registered the name Signet Cruise Lines (no ships were ever built for cruising, however).

In 1998, a consortium, which included the Carnival Corporation and Norwegian investors, bought Seabourn Cruise Line and merged its operations into Cunard Line, which was acquired from Kvaerner. The fleet then included three ships plus *Seabourn Goddess I* and *Seabourn Goddess II* (bought by SeaDream Yacht Cruises in 2002 and named *SeaDream I* and *SeaDream II*) and *Seabourn Sun* (now Holland America Line's *Prinsendam*). The Carnival Corporation acquired 100 percent of Seabourn Cruise Line in 1999.

Three new, larger ships joined the company between 2009 and 2011. All three have an aft watersports platform, as well as a wider number of dining and spa options, a greater amount of space, and more passengers. Seabourn Cruise Line was briefly rebranded as The Yachts of Seabourn in 2009–10, but then became simply Seabourn. The company is managed from within the Holland America Line headquarters in Seattle, US. Gratuities are included in the fare.

In February 2013, the three smaller ships were sold to Xanterra Parks & Resorts, parent company of Windstar Cruises. *Seabourn Pride* was delivered in mid-2014; *Seabourn Legend* and *Seabourn Spirit* were delivered in April and May 2015, respectively. Two new ships are on order, for delivery in 2016 and 2018.

SeaDream Yacht Club

Larry Pimentel, an American, and his Norwegian business partner Atle Brynestad, founder of Seabourn Cruise Line (now called, simply, Seabourn), jointly created the company by buying the former Sea Goddess Cruises' ships. They introduced them in 2002 to an audience anxious for exclusivity, personal pampering, and cuisine prepared to order.

The two ships, *SeaDream I* and *SeaDream II*, have been refreshed several times – although *SeaDream I* is in a better shape than *SeaDream II* – and are often chartered by companies or private individuals who appreciate the refined, elegant, but casual atmosphere on board. The 100-passenger ships operate year-round in the Caribbean and Mediterranean, and provide all-inclusive beverages and open-seating dining at all times, and a high degree of personalized service, all in a cozy, club-like atmosphere, with great attention to detail and personal idiosyncrasies. Atle Brynestad is the company's chairman and sole owner, while Larry Pimentel is now with Azamara Cruises. Gratuities are included in the fare.

Serenissima Cruises

Vladimir Esakov, the owner/operator of the Russian rivership *Volga Dream*, purchased the former *MS Andrea* (a Hurtigruten vessel) in 2012, renamed it *Serenissima* and formed Serenissima Cruises to market the ship. The company has a long-standing association with the UK's Noble Caledonia.

Silversea Cruises

Silversea Cruises is a mostly privately owned cruise line. It was founded in 1992 by the Lefebvre D'Ovidio family from Rome (previously co-owners of Sitmar Cruises; 90 percent partners are the Lefebvre D'Ovidios, 10 percent by V-Ships) and is based in Monaco.

Antonio Lefebvre D'Ovidio was a maritime lawyer and professor of maritime law before acquiring and operating cargo ships and ferries in the Adriatic. He took his family into partnership with Boris Vlasov's Vlasov Group (V-Ships) to co-own Sitmar Cruises, until that company merged with Princess Cruises in 1988.

Silversea Cruises has generated tremendous loyalty from its frequent passengers, who view the ships as their own. All seven Silversea ships have teak verandas and all-inclusive beverages. Open-seating dining prevails at all times, and the company is known for its partnership with the hospitality organization Relais & Châteaux. A new, larger, 540-passenger all-suite luxury ship, *Silver Spirit*, debuted at the end of 2009, while *Silver Whisper* and *Silver Shadow* were refurbished in 2010 and 2011. Silversea Cruises has three specialist ships for expedition cruising (*Silver Explorer*, *Silver Galapagos* and *Silver Discoverer*, added in 2008, 2013 and 2014, respectively). Gratuities are included in the fare for all ships as part of the company's 'all-inclusive' culture.

SkySea Cruises

This new entrant in the China domestic cruise market is owned by partners Ctrip (which has the world's largest reservations and booking platform in the Chinese language), and Royal Carribean Cruises Ltd, each of which has a 35 percent holding, as well as China's Stone Capital, which holds 30 percent. The ship is the ex-*Celebrity Century*, which debuted in May 2015 as SkySea Golden Era, with direct digital (internet) bookings only.

Star Clippers

Swedish-born yachtsman Mikhail Krafft founded Star Clippers in 1991 with *Star Flyer* and then *Star Clipper*, both true tall ships. The company went on to build the largest tall ship presently sailing, the five-mast *Royal Clipper*, a truly stunning ship under sail. Friendly service in a casual, extremely laid-back setting, under the romance of sail (when there is enough wind) is what Star Clippers is all about, and the food variety, creativity, and quality are all extremely good.

These real tall (sail-cruise) ships sail in the Caribbean, Baltic, and Mediterranean. Gratuities are not included in the fare.

Star Cruises

Presently part of the world's third-largest cruise operator, the company was incorporated in 1993 as a subsidiary of Malaysia's Genting Berhad, set up in 1965 by the late Tan Sri Dr Lim Goh Tong as an Asian multinational corporation. Today, Star Cruises is formally known as Star Cruises/Genting Hong Kong but still comes under the umbrella of Genting Berhad. The group's various business include palm oil production, power generation, property development, biotechnology, and oil and gas production, together with leisure activities including resort hotels

Seabourn Odyssey's watersports platform.

The main pool on *Viking Star* when the roof is closed.

and casino/entertainment complexes in Malaysia, Manila, and Singapore, and cruise ships. Almost single-handedly, Star Cruises opened up the Asia-Pacific cruise region (except for Japan).

Genting Hong Kong operates ships dedicated to specific markets. Its brands include Crystal Cruises, Star Cruises and Norwegian Cruise Line (jointly owned with Apollo Management).

Star Cruises also owns the pier facility in Langkawi. Its marketing base is in Hong Kong. Its ships are *MegaStar Aries* (1991), *Star Pisces* (1990), *SuperStar Aquarius* (1993), *SuperStar Libra* (1988), and *SuperStar Virgo* (1999). A new large resort ship is scheduled for delivery in 2016, with another one set for 2017. Gratuities are included in all fares.

Swan Hellenic Cruises

Founded in 1954 By R.K. Swan, this company chartered small cruise ships for years. It was bought by P&O Cruises in 1982, then it changed hands when Carnival Corporation merged with P&O in April 2004. In 2007, the Carnival Corporation disbanded Swan Hellenic, and its single ship (*Minerva II*) was transferred to the Princess Cruises fleet to become *Royal Princess* (now P&O Cruises' *Adonia*). Some months later, a semi-retired Lord Sterling purchased the brand from the Carnival Corporation and joined forces with the UK's Voyages of Discovery (part of All-Leisure) to operate as a separate brand. So, the 'Swanners,' as its clever passengers are called, now have their own ship (*Minerva*).

The company's strengths are its program of highly academic lecturers and speakers, in a small-ship setting that is unpretentious but comfortable, and includes gratuities, drinks (on Antarctic voyages), tailor-made shore excursions, and entrance fees to museums and places of interest. The company operates special-interest themes such as archaeology, history, nature, and wildlife. Coffee- and tea-making facilities are provided in each cabin. Gratuities are included in the fare.

Thomson Cruises

Thomson Cruises' first foray into cruising was in 1973 when it chartered two ships, *Calypso* and *Ithaca*, from the Greek-owned Ulysses Line. It was a disaster, and the company withdrew from cruising two years later (Ulysses Line became known as Useless Line).

The company started again in 2002 after seeing rival tour operator Airtours run ships successfully. Thomson Cruises charters its ships, preferring instead to leave ship operations, management, and catering to specialist maritime companies. The company offers cruises for the whole family aboard its ships – *Thomson Dream*, *Thomson Majesty*, and *Thomson Spirit* – catering principally to the British market, but also to the Scandinavian market. Basic gratuities are included in the price

Thomson Cruises operates sub-brand Island Cruises, with just one ship, *Island Escape*, for the ultra-casual market. The company owns its own airline, Thomson Airlines, part of the TUI Travel group.

TUI Cruises

The German-owned TUI Group has several divisions, but started its own cruise line in 2009 with *Mein Schiff 1*, a mid-size ship (formerly *Celebrity Galaxy*) that underwent a huge reconstruction program. *Mein Schiff 2* (formerly *Celebrity Mercury*) was added in 2011. Two new ships – *Mein Schiff 3* debuted in spring 2014, and *Mein Schiff 4* in 2015. Two further ships are on order, due in 2016 and 2017.

Aboard all TUI Cruises ships, all cabins have their own espresso machines, and there is a wide choice of dining venues and food styles, with an emphasis on healthy eating. Much stress is placed on the extensive wellness facilities aboard the ships, which are all geared to family cruising. Gratuities are included in the 'all-inclusive' fare.

Un-Cruise Adventures

This micro-cruise line was founded in 1997 as American Safari Cruises. It was bought in 2008 by InnerSea Discoveries, owned by the former chief executive officer of American Safari Cruises, Dan Blanchard. ASC It bought the website and database files of now-defunct Cruise West in order to expand its reach to small-ship enthusiasts, and has a fleet of very small motor yacht-type vessels for six to 86 passengers taking expensive cruises in Alaska and the Pacific Northwest. While the vessels are decent, the onboard facilities are few, and the one-seat dining experience is quite casual. However, they all have superb Tempur-Pedic mattresses. The advantage of these intimate vessels is that they really can take you up close to fascinating parts of Alaska that larger ships can't reach. Gratuities are not included. InnerSea Discoveries changed its name to Un-Cruise Adventures in 2013.

Venus Cruise

Founded in 1988, Venus Cruise, which was first known as Japan Cruise Line, is owned by four ferry companies: Shin Nipponkai Ferry, Kyowa Shoji, Hankyu Ferry, and Kanko Kisen. Its headquarters are in Osaka, Japan. As Japan Cruise Line, the company at first operated company and incentive charter cruises before branching out into cruises for individuals. The firm caters exclusively to Japanese speakers and has a single ship, *Pacific Venus*, which operates an annual around-the-world cruise as well as shorter Asia-Pacific cruises. Gratuities are included in the cruise fare.

Viking Cruises

A sister company to the long-established Viking River Cruises, this new company aims to provide both oceangoing and river cruises to the same market segment – a unique approach in the cruise industry. Its chairman is Torstein Hagen, originally a major shareholder owner of the long-defunct but much-respected Royal Viking Line.

At time of printing, a sneak preview of one of three 928-passenger, mid-size ships on order for Viking revealed that, for their size, the vessels would offer an outstanding array of public rooms and dining options, and they would stay longer in ports – including overnight stays, so that passengers could take in the nightlife and cultural attractions of some destinations. The first ship, *Viking Star*, debuted in spring 2015, with *Viking Sky* and *Viking Sea* to follow in 2016 and 2017, respectively.

Voyages of Discovery

UK-based Roger Allard and Dudley Smith jointly founded the company to offer low-cost cruises aboard comfortable and roomy but older small ships, to UK passengers, but with good food and service. The company's *Discovery* is one of the former 'Love Boats' of US television fame, but is now operated by Cruise & Maritime Voyages. It was replaced by *Voyager* in late 2013. Voyages of Discovery went public in 2006 and, with the help of Lord Sterling of Plaistow, purchased Swan Hellenic Cruises. It now operates both brands from its HQ in the south of England, and also owns the premium brand Hebridean Island Cruises.

Voyages to Antiquity

Founded in 2007 by Gerry Herrod, who formerly created the now-defunct Ocean Cruise Lines, the company has just one ship, *Aegean Odyssey*, painstakingly converted into a comfortable cruise ship with a fairly handsome profile. It operates seven- and 14-day cruises to ancient lands, specializing in the Aegean and Mediterranean regions and Asia. The cruises are aimed at British and American passengers who seek educational experiences. Gratuities to dining and housekeeping staff are included, as are most shore excursions and wines with lunch and dinner.

Windstar Cruises

Founded by New York-based Karl Andren in 1984 as Windstar Sail Cruises, the company built high-class sail-cruise ships with computer-controlled sails, outfitting them in a contemporary decor designed by Marc Held. The first ship, *Wind Star*, debuted in 1986 to much acclaim, and was followed by *Wind Spirit* (1988) and *Wind Surf* (1990).

Windstar Cruises was sold to Holland America Line in 1988. The company, with headquarters in Seattle, US, was sold again in 2007 to the Ambassadors Cruise Group, wholly owned by Ambassadors International. It was purchased again in 2011 by Xanterra Parks & Resorts.

The style is casual and unregimented, but smart, with service by Indonesian and Filipino crew members. The ships carry a variety of water-sports equipment, accessed from a retractable stern platform. Itineraries include off-the-beaten-track ports not frequented by large resort ships. The onboard product is decidedly American ultra-casual, with unfussy bistro-style cuisine, and service that lacks the finesse and the small details that could make it a much better experience overall. Gratuities are not included in the fare.

In 2014, Windstar took delivery of the former Seabourn Pride, now renamed Star Pride. By mid-2015, Windstar Cruises will have taken delivery of the other two Seabourn ships – *Seabourn Legend* (now renamed *Star Legend*), and *Seabourn Spirit* (now renamed *Star Breeze*).

Sea lion with *Silver Galapagos* in the distance.

Living in Luxury

Of the 70-plus cruise lines operating internationally, only a handful provide the kind of stylish ships aboard which the word 'no' is virtually unheard.

Luxury (elegant, sumptuous) cruises versus standard (large resort ship) cruises are like the difference between a Bentley automobile and a motor scooter. 'Luxury cruising' should be a flawless combination of ship, facilities, understated decor, food, culinary excellence, and service – and arriving in style. Unfortunately, the word has been degraded through overuse by marketing people and advertising agencies, but the accompanying panel tells you what the term ought to mean in a cruise ship.

Little and large

Size is important. Boutique and small ships (characterized by Berlitz as having 50–250 and 251–750 passengers, respectively) can get into ports that larger ships can't. They can also get closer to the center of large cities. For example, in St. Petersburg, Russia, large and mid-size ships (such as those of Crystal Cruises and Regent Seven Seas Cruises) dock about one hour from the city center, while boutique/small ships such as those of Hapag-Lloyd Cruises, Silversea

Butler service aboard Silversea Cruises.

Cruises, or Seabourn can dock right next to the Hermitage Museum in the heart of the city.

One area where 'luxury' ships differ least from large resort ships is in shore excursions, particularly in the Caribbean and Alaska, where almost all cruise operators are obliged to use the same specialist tour operators ashore – simply because 'luxury' is virtually unknown in these regions, and local tour operators consider all cruise passengers to be the same.

Large resort ships (carrying 2,001–6,500 passengers) simply cannot provide the kind of personal service and attention to detail that the boutique/small ships can (although the 'Yacht Club' of MSC Cruises is an example of the excellent personal service that can be provided aboard large resort ships). Although you can book one of the largest suites afloat aboard a large ship and have a really good cruise, once you leave your 'private living space,' you mix with everyone else, particularly if you want to go to a show, have an informal alfresco meal or coffee in the café, disembark at ports of call (think: lines at gangway security checkpoints), or go on organized shore excursions. That's when you appreciate the fact that smaller may suit you better.

These are ships suited to those not seeking the active, family-friendly, and entertainment-driven cruise experiences that large resort ships offer, and they provide fa-

---

The crème de la crème

These 25 ships (listed alphabetically, by company) belong to eight cruise lines and are the cream of the cruise industry in terms of style, finesse, staff training, cuisine, service, hospitality, and finesse. Their individual facilities are fully reviewed in the ratings section of this book, with Berlitz scores awarded for accommodation, food, service, entertainment, the cruise experience, and so on, indicating their particular strengths.

Crystal Cruises: *Crystal Serenity, Crystal Symphony*
Hapag-Lloyd Cruises: *Europa, Europa 2*
Oceania Cruises: *Marina, Riviera*
Paul Gauguin Cruises: *Paul Gauguin*
Regent Seven Seas Cruises: *Seven Seas Mariner, Seven Seas Navigator, Seven Seas Voyager*
Sea Cloud Cruises: Sea Cloud, Sea Cloud II
Seabourn: *Seabourn Odyssey, Seabourn Quest, Seabourn Sojourn*
SeaDream Yacht Club: *SeaDream I, SeaDream II*
Silversea Cruises: *Silver Cloud, Silver Shadow, Silver Spirit, Silver Whisper, Silver Wind*
Windstar Cruises: *Star Breeze, Star Legend, Star Pride* (formerly *Seabourn Spirit, Seabourn Legend, Seabourn Pride*).

cilities and service levels hard to find elsewhere. While most of them boast about being the best, or boast the awards they receive annually from various magazines (whose respondents are almost never global in scope), not all provide the same degree of luxury, and there *are* differences in the cruise product delivered.

What are the differences?

Luxury varies by degrees. Once you know the main differences, you'll be better equipped to choose the right cruise line and ship to provide the level of food and service you're looking for. Although most of the differences are immediately noticeable when you sail aboard (and compare) them all, some of the variations in style and service are more subtle. One thing is certain: the word 'no' will be virtually unheard.

Some have more crew members per passenger. Some have more public space per passenger. Some have more highly trained crew members. Some have better food and service. Some have entertainment, some don't. Some have more fresh flowers in public areas than others – they're very evident aboard the ships of Hapag-Lloyd Cruises but not aboard Silversea Cruises' ships, for instance (where Prosecco – sparkling wine and not Champagne – is provided on embarkation).

Crystal Cruises, for example, has an excellent program of cultural lecturers, professional bridge (the card game, not the navigation bridge) instructors, together with its Yamaha 'Passport to Music' program on each cruise, whereas others (SeaDream, Regent, Seabourn, and Silversea) don't. Hapag-Lloyd has excellent lecturers, and a PGA golf professional aboard every cruise.

Also, the following facilities, services, and approaches are found and experienced aboard the ships of Hapag-Lloyd Cruises, SeaDream Yacht Club, and Seabourn, but not aboard the ships of Crystal Cruises, Regent Seven Seas Cruises, or Silversea Cruises:

Anticipation – more widely practiced by better-trained staff, who are also more adept at passenger recognition (remembering your name).

Waiters/waitresses escort guests to the dining table and to the dining room exit after meals.

Relaxed embarkation/disembarkation at your leisure.

Cabin stewardesses leave handwritten notes.

There are no announcements, and no background music plays in public rooms, accommodation hallways, or elevators.

The chef invites passengers to accompany him/her on visits to local food markets.

More space, better service

These ships have an excellent amount of open deck and lounging space, and a high passenger space ratio when compared to large resort ships (which are typically under 35 gross tonnage per passenger), the two SeaDreams being the exception.

Almost all have a better crew to passenger ratio than the large resort ships. In warm-weather areas, the ships of SeaDream Yacht Club and Seabourn, all of which have fold-down platforms at the stern, provide jet skis, kayaks, snorkeling gear, windsurfers, and the like, at no extra cost, typically for one day each cruise (the others do not).

Hapag-Lloyd's *Europa* (space ratio: 70.4) and *Europa 2* (space ratio: 83.0) both have a fleet of Zodiac rigid inflatable craft for in-depth exploration and shore adventures, plus an ice-hardened hull and crew members who understand the *culture* of their passengers. And mattresses that are 7ft (2.1m) long.

A good night's sleep

These ships feature premium-quality mattresses and bed linen (all of 100 percent cotton, with a thread count of 300 or more). There's always a little brand-consciousness going on, and some may be better than others.

Crystal Cruises, for example, features Bellora, from Milan (made in India using Egyptian cotton). Silversea Cruises features Egyptian cotton sheets, pillowcases, and duvet covers by Pratesi, founded in 1860, whose custom-made linens come from Tuscany, Italy – the company is known for supplying the Italian and other European aristocracy.

Good pillows are also important for a good night's sleep. You may be able to choose one of several different shapes and fillings. Crystal Cruises' pillow menu, for example, offers a choice of seven, including Side Sleeper Pillow (down or down alternative); Back Sleeper Pillow (down or down alternative); Stomach Sleeper Pillow (down or down alternative); and Body Pillow (down alternative).

Depending on the cruise line, other choices might include hypoallergenic, hop-filled, or lavender-scented pillows.

A good night's sleep – outside

For something quite different, SeaDream Yacht Club has indulgent 'Balinese Dream Beds' for sleeping under the stars (in a secluded area at the front of the ship on the uppermost open deck), a delightful idea for honeymooners or anyone celebrating a special occasion. Custom-made pajamas are supplied, and you can take them home with you. Hapag-Lloyd's *Europa 2* also has 12 Balinese beds.

Creative cuisine

Fine dining is the highlight of ships in this category and is more of an entertainment feature than these ships' entertainment shows – if there are any. Good company and conversation are crucial. You can expect to find plenty of tables for two, a calm refined dining atmosphere, open or one-seating dining, by candlelight (when permitted), with high-quality china and silverware, large wine glasses, fresh flowers, a connoisseur wine list, and sommeliers who can discuss fine wines. Service should be unhurried (not like the two-seating ships, where meals tend to be served as speed trials by waiters), well paced, and unobtrusive.

The spacious lido deck on *Europa*.

It's really about non-repetitive, highly creative menus, high-quality ingredients, moderate portions, and attractive presentation, with fresh local fish provided (when available) and cooked to order (not in batches), and meat of the highest grade. Caviar, foie gras, black/white truffles and other exotic foods, and fresh green vegetables (instead of frozen or canned vegetables) are among the products that feature. Caviar aboard *Europa* and *Europa 2* is typically from farmed sturgeon, and is excellent, while caviar aboard most other ships in this category is from the American farmed hackleback variety of sturgeon, or paddlefish 'caviar' (calling it 'caviar' is stretching it). The caviar (from Uruguay) aboard the Seabourn ships is quite good, however.

Most of the ships provide silver covers for main courses, creating extra 'wow' effect. Passengers may also be invited to visit local markets with the chef aboard the ships of Hapag-Lloyd Cruises, Seabourn, and SeaDream Yacht Club.

Some luxury ships provide even more special touches. *Europa and Europa 2*, for example, make their own breakfast preserves and ice cream, as well as fresh-pressed or freshly squeezed juices (most others provide pasteurized juices from concentrate) on board. *Europa* uses only loose tea (over 30 types), while all the others use teabags of varying quality. All (except Hapag-Lloyd) provide 'free' bottled mineral water.

Lunch and dinner menus may be provided in your suite/cabin in advance, and special orders are often possible. Room service menus are extensive, and meals can be served in your suite/cabin (either on the balcony or inside on portable tables). It is also possible to have a special dinner setup on deck – wonderful in the right location.

Drinks: included or not?

Crystal Cruises, Regent Seven Seas Cruises, Seabourn, SeaDream Yacht Club, and Silversea Cruises provide wine with dinner (Crystal Cruises, Seabourn, and Silversea also include wine with lunch), although the wines are typically young, and not from first-class houses. Real premium brands and classic vintage wines cost extra.

Hapag-Lloyd Cruises charges for all alcoholic beverages (beer and soft drinks are provided in each cabin/suite). Crystal Cruises and Regent Seven Seas Cruise Line provide an all-inclusive product, including gratuities. Crystal, Regent, Seabourn, SeaDream, and Silversea include all drinks, but only standard brands and limited included wines that may not be to your taste. Hapag-Lloyd Cruises doesn't include alcoholic drinks, because those favored by its discerning passengers tend to be far above the level of standard brands carried by the other companies mentioned here (as an example, Hapag-Lloyd Cruises carries over 40 types of premium gins aboard *Europa* and *Europa 2*). In addition, this gets around the problem of passengers who don't drink alcohol not liking to subsidize those that do.

Other differences

Aboard the ships of Regent Seven Seas Cruises and Seabourn, white plastic deck lounge chairs are provided. Aboard the ships of SeaDream Yacht Club these chairs are made of teak (or other hardwood). Aboard Hapag-Lloyd Cruises' *Europa* and *Europa 2* they are made of aluminum and wood, while aboard the ships of Silversea Cruises they are made of faux-wicker or aluminum.

Crystal Serenity, Crystal Symphony, Europa, Europa 2, Seven Seas Mariner, Seven Seas Navigator, and *Seven Seas Voyager* include entertainment featuring multi-cast shows and cabaret acts; the Hapag-Lloyd, Seabourn and Silversea Cruises ships also do this, but to a lesser extent. The others do not have entertainment as such, but instead rely on their intimacy and friendliness, and promote after-dinner conversation, or, aboard the ships of Silversea Cruises, individual specialist cabaret acts.

20 things to expect

1. Flawless (or close to) service and attention to detail.
2. Genuine (not faux) Champagne at embarkation.
3. Personalized stationery.
4. A crew that anticipates your needs, responds quickly to your requests, and doesn't say 'no' or 'impossible.'
5. No announcements (except for emergencies).
6. No background music in public rooms, hallways, and elevators.
7. High passenger space ratio (35 to 83 gross tonnage per passenger).
8. High crew to passenger ratio (1.5 to 1.0 or better).
9. Finest-quality bed linens, duvets, towels, and bathrobes.
10. Pillow menu.
11. High-quality toiletries (Aveda, Bulgari, for example).
12. Gratuities included in the fare.
13. No extra charge for on-demand movies or music.
14. No machinery vibration (engines/propulsion equipment).
15. No lines anywhere.
16. More overnight port stays.
17. Separate gangway for passengers and crew (if possible).
18. Shoeshine service.
19. No signing for drinks or other items.
20. Highly experienced hotel service crew.

Comparing Luxury Ships

Ship name	Company	Size	Pod propulsion	Passenger space ratio	Crew to passenger ratio	Largest suite (m²)	Smallest cabin (m²)	Watersports toys	Hand-held showers	Personal bathroom amenities
Crystal Serenity	Crystal Cruises	Mid-size	Yes	62.6	1.7	125	21	No	Yes	Aveda
Crystal Symphony	Crystal Cruises	Mid-size	No	53.1	1.7	91.2	18.7	No	Yes	Aveda
Europa	Hapag-Lloyd Cruises	Small	Yes	69.6	1.5	85	33	No	Yes	Own brand
Europa 2	Hapag-Lloyd Cruises	Small	Yes	83.0	1.3	114	35	No	Yes	Own brand
Marina	Oceania Cruises	Mid-size	No	51.6	1.5	185	16	No	Yes	L'Occitane
Riviera	Oceania Cruises	Mid-size	No	51.6	1.5	185	16	No	Yes	L'Occitane
Seven Seas Mariner	Regent Seven Seas Cruises	Mid-Size	Yes	67.8	1.6	142	28	No	Yes	Canyon Ranch
Sea Cloud	Sea Cloud Cruises	Boutique	No	39.5	1.1	38.0	9.5	No	Yes	Own brand
Sea Cloud II	Sea Cloud Cruises	Boutique	No	40.9	1.6	30.0	20	No	Yes	Own brand
Seven Seas Navigator	Regent Seven Seas Cruises	Mid-Size	No	58.2	1.5	109	28	No	Yes	Canyon Ranch
Seven Seas Voyager	Regent Seven Seas Cruises	Mid-Size	Yes	59	1.3	130	33	No	Yes	Canyon Ranch
Seabourn Odyssey	Seabourn	Small	No	71.1	1.3	133.6	27.5	Yes	Yes	Therapies (Molton Brown)
Seabourn Quest	Seabourn	Small	No	71.1	1.3	133.6	27.5	Yes	Yes	Therapies (Molton Brown)
Seabourn Sojourn	Seabourn	Small	No	71.1	1.3	133.6	27.5	Yes	Yes	Therapies (Molton Brown)
SeaDream I	SeaDream Yacht Club	Boutique	No	39.4	1.2	45.5	18.1	Yes	Yes	Bulgari
SeaDream II	SeaDream Yacht Club	Boutique	No	39.4	1.2	45.5	18.1	Yes	Yes	Bulgari
Silver Cloud	Silversea Cruises	Small	No	57.1	1.4	122	22.2	No	No	Bulgari and Ferragamo
Silver Shadow	Silversea Cruises	Small	No	72.8	1.3	133.3	26.6	No	No	Bulgari and Ferragamo
Silver Spirit	Silversea Cruises	Small	No	66.6	1.4	150	29	No	No	Bulgari and Ferragamo
Silver Whisper	Silversea Cruises	Small	No	72.8	1.3	133.3	26.6	No	No	Bulgari and Ferragamo
Silver Wind	Silversea Cruises	Small	No	57.1	1.4	122	22.2	No	No	Bulgari and Ferragamo
Star Breeze	Windstar Cruises	Boutique	No	46.9	1.3	53.4	25.7	Yes	Yes	Therapies (Molton Brown)
Star Legend	Windstar Cruises	Boutique	No	46.9	1.3	53.5	25.7	Yes	Yes	Therapies (Molton Brown)
Star Pride	Windstar Cruises	Boutique	No	46.9	1.3	53.4	25.7	Yes	Yes	L'Occitane

What To Do If ...

Twenty practical tips for a good cruise experience, and advice on what to do if you have a problem.

1. Your luggage does not arrive at the ship

If you booked as part of the cruise line's air/sea package, the airline is responsible for locating your luggage and delivering it to the next port. If you arranged your own air transportation, it is wholly *your* problem. Always have easy-to-read name and address tags *inside* as well as *outside* your luggage. Keep track of claim documents, and give the airline a detailed itinerary and list of port agents.

2. You miss the ship

If you miss the ship's departure at the port of embarkation, and you are traveling on an air/sea package, the airline will arrange to get you to the ship, possibly at the next port of call. If you are traveling 'cruise-only', however, then you are responsible for flights, hotel stays, and transfers. If you arrive at the port just as your ship is pulling away, see the ship's port agent immediately.

One answer to lack of storage space aboard *Queen Elizabeth*.

If you miss the ship in a port of call, it is up to you to get back to the ship before its appointed sailing time, unless you are participating in a ship-organized shore excursion. Miss the ship and you'll need to get to its next port at your own cost. *Always* take a copy of your passport with you, just in case.

Ships have also been known to leave port early because of impending inclement weather conditions or natural disasters. If this happens, the ship's port agent should be on the dockside to assist you. Always take the port agent's name and telephone contact details with you.

3. Your cabin is too small

Almost all cruise ship cabins are too small. When you book a cruise, you pay for a certain category and type of cabin, but you have little or no control over which one you actually get. Go to the reception desk as soon as possible and explain what is wrong with the cabin. If the ship is full, it may be difficult to change.

4. Your cabin has no air conditioning, it is noisy, or there are plumbing problems

If there is anything wrong in your cabin, or with your bathroom plumbing, tell your cabin steward immediately. If nothing is done, complain at the reception desk. Some cabins, for example, are located above the ship's laundry, generator, or galley; others may be above the disco. If the ship is full, it may be difficult to change.

5. You have noisy cabin neighbors

First, politely tell your neighbors that you can hear them brushing their hair as the cabin walls are so thin, and would they please not bang the drawers shut at 2am! If that does not work, complain to the hotel manager, and ask them to attend to the problem.

6. You have a problem with a crew member

Go to the ship's hotel manager and explain the problem. Insist on a full written report of the incident, which must be entered into the ship's daily log by the staff captain (deputy captain).

7. You have small children and the brochure implied that the ship had special programs for them, but when aboard you find out it is not a year-round program

In this instance, either the brochure was misleading, or your travel agent did not know enough about the ship. If you have genuine cause for complaint, then see your travel agent when you get home. Most ships will try to accommodate your young ones, but they may not be covered by their insurance for looking after them throughout the day. Check thoroughly with your travel agent *before* you book.

8. You don't like your dining room seating
Most large resort ships operate two seatings for dinner. When you book your cruise, you are asked whether you want the first or second seating. The line will make every attempt to please you. But if you want second seating and are given first seating, there may be little the restaurant manager can do, if the ship is full.

9. You want a table for two and are put at a table for eight
See the restaurant manager and explain why you are not satisfied. A little gratuity should prove helpful.

10. You cannot communicate with your waiter
Dining room waiters might be of a nationality and language completely foreign to yours, with limited fluency in your particular language. This could prove frustrating for a whole cruise, especially if you need something out of the ordinary. See the restaurant manager, and tell him/her you want a waiter with whom you can communicate better.

11. The food is definitely not the gourmet cuisine portrayed in the brochure
If the food is not as described (for example, whole lobster in the brochure, but only cold lobster salad once during the cruise, or the 'fresh squeezed' orange juice on the breakfast menu is anything but), do inform the restaurant manager of the problem.

12. A large group has taken over the ship
Sometimes, large groups have pre-booked several public rooms for meetings – seemingly every hour on the hour in the rooms you want to use. Make your displeasure known to the hotel manager immediately, tell your travel agent, and write a follow-up letter to the line when you get home.

13. A port of call is deleted from the itinerary
If you only plan on taking a cruise because the ship goes to a place you have wanted to go to for years, then read the fine print in the brochure *before* you book. A cruise line is under no obligation to perform the stated itinerary. For whatever reason – political unrest, weather, mechanical problems, no berth space, safety, etc. – the ship's captain has the ultimate say.

14. You leave personal belongings on a tour bus
If, when you're back on board your ship, you find you've left something on a tour bus, the first thing to do is tell the shore excursion staff. The tour operator ashore will then be contacted to see whether any items have been handed in to their office.

15. You are unwell aboard ship
There will be a qualified doctor (who generally operates as a concession) and medical facilities, including a small pharmacy. You will be well taken care of. Although there are charges for medical services, almost all cruise lines offer insurance packages that include medical coverage for most eventualities. It is wise to take out this insurance when you book.

16. The cruise line's air arrangements have you flying from Los Angeles via Timbuktu to get to your cruise ship
Most cruise lines with low rates also use the cheapest air routing to get you to your ship. That could mean flights from a central hub. Be warned: you get what you pay for. Ask questions *before* you book.

17. You fly internationally to take a cruise
If your cruise is a long distance away from your home, then it usually makes good sense to fly to your cruise embarkation point and stay for at least a day or two before the cruise. You will be better rested and able to adjust to any time changes. You will step aboard your ship ready for a vacation. As a bonus, you will get to know the port of departure.

18. The ship's laundry ruins your clothes
If any of your clothing is ruined or discolored by the ship's laundry, first tell your cabin steward(ess), and then follow up by going to the reception (purser's office) and getting it registered as a proper complaint. Take a copy of the complaint with you, so you can follow up when you get home. Unfortunately, you will probably find a disclaimer on the laundry list saying something to the effect that liability is limited to about $1 per item.

19. You have extra charges on your bill
Check your itemized bill carefully, then go to the reception (purser's office) and ask them to show you the charge slips. Finally, make sure you are given a copy of your bill *after* any modifications have been made.

20. You're unhappy with your cruise experience
If your ship does not meet your specific lifestyle and interests, or delivers less well than the brochure promises, then let your travel agent and the cruise line know immediately. If your grievance is valid, many cruise lines will offer a credit toward a future cruise.

Eco Cruising

The good: traveling by sea produces an
estimated 36 times less carbon dioxide than
flying. The bad: that's still not good enough.

Although marine vessels are responsible for almost 3 percent of the world's greenhouse gases, the world's fleet of around 350 oceangoing cruise ships produces just 0.1 percent of those emissions.

Eco diligence

Cruise companies try hard to achieve an integrated, industry-wide approach to reduce pollution and noxious air emissions, provide more fuel-efficient ships, and retrofit older ships with more efficient replacement machinery. New ships benefit from better hydrodynamic hull design, and advanced hull coatings can also improve efficiency. Careful handling of solid and liquid waste results in lower fuel consumption, and, therefore, CO_2 emissions. Flue gas from shipboard incinerators is recycled and wastewater treated according to the toughest legal and eco-friendly standards. Energy recovery (waste-heat recovery) is what is being built into the latest ships.

Since 2011, new diesel ship engines have had to comply with MARPOL Annex VI Tier II standards, requiring more efficient technology, including engine timing and cooling, and advanced monitoring and computer control. The result is a generous reduction in NOx – the term for a group of highly reactive gases, all of which contain nitrogen and oxygen in varying amounts. In 2016, new ship engines must comply with very strict Tier III standards. This means using high-efficiency emissions control technology such as selective catalytic converters to further reduce NOx.

The first cruise ship to be equipped with an SCR-catalytic converter, which reduces nitrogen oxides (including including nitrogen dioxide) by almost 95 percent, is *Europa 2*. Other eco-friendly examples include *MSC Fantasia*-class ships, which use only low-sulfur fuels worldwide, while each *Celebrity Solstice*-class ship's 80 solar panels help power the elevators. Some ship hulls are treated with 'foul release' paint with fluoropolymers or glass-flake vinyl ester resins – non-toxic substances that help reduce CO_2 emissions by using less fuel. But ships that have switched from heavy fuel oil to low-sulfur fuels have experienced greater fuel pump wear when switching over, thereby adding to maintenance, operational, and replacement costs.

Solar panels on *Celebrity Solstice*.

Norwegian Breakaway, which debuted in 2013, was the first cruise ship to take advantage of MARPOL rule MEPC.1/Circ.642 – permitting the recovery and re-use of the HFO fraction of waste oil as fuel for the diesel engines. This is called 'scrubber' technology and is now used by many cruise lines to meet the low sulfur emission requirements that came into effect in January 2015. The ship's waste oil separator system has only two moving parts and leaves only non-pumpable 'super-dry' solids for landing as dry waste. Waste oil volumes are reduced by 99 percent, with around 11–33lbs (5–15kg) per day of solids left for disposal ashore. The separated water, with an oil content of less than 1,000ppm, is pumped to the bilge-water tank as part of an integrated waste oil and bilge-water handling system.

Other measures

Other eco-friendly measures include the use of LED lighting rather than fuel-guzzling halogen lighting and cabin lights and other electrical devices that function only when a cabin key card is in a card device inside the cabin. Motion-activated lighting in closets is also an eco-friendly option. There is also the replacement of single-use plastic cups by melamine and/or porcelain, the use of permanent dispensers instead of plastic single-use soap/shampoo packs, and the replacement of plastic laundry bags with re-washable cotton bags.

High-tech tunnel washers can be fitted into laundries to save water, and dry-cleaning chemicals can be replaced by fruit-based washing chemicals. Water flow reducers can be fitted to faucets (taps) and showers, and paper towels can be made from recycled paper. Other eco-friendly measures include the use of darkness-activated sensors that switch on the ship's external lights at dusk and the use of chilled river rocks that retain low temperatures for buffet items, rather than ice. Then there are heat-deflecting window coatings and the latest wastewater treatment technology.

As far as waste items are concerned, they are sorted by cabin attendants and other cleaning staff, with final sorting conducted in a garbage room. The resulting trash is either incinerated or else off-loaded ashore to be managed by reputable waste management companies. While all these measures help, they must be weighed against the costs of implementing them.

Emissions Control Areas

In 2009 the British Isles introduced the first Emissions Control Areas (ECA) around its shores and in the English Channel. They were followed by 10 countries in the Baltic and North Sea region. The International Maritime Organization (IMO) formally established a North American Emission Control Area in August 2012, an area ringing the US/Canada (including Alaska) coast with a 200-mile (320-km) exclusion zone. The IMO's global air emissions standards called for a progressive reduction of SOx – sulfur dioxide – emissions from 3.5 percent in January 2012, to 0.5 percent by January 2020, subject to a review to be completed by 2018.

When the North American Emission Control Area was implemented in August 2012, fuel costs rose 10 percent to 15 percent. When the sulfur limit dropped to 0.1 percent in January 2015 (under MARPOL Annex VI, Reg. 14), those costs rose again. At present, no technological solution exists.

Wastewater discharge

The IMO also introduced an International Convention on the Management of Ballast Water and Sediments (wastewater discharge) in 2010. By the end of 2010, MSC Cruises, for example, had almost eliminated the use of plastics, and no chemical detergents were being used in its shipboard laundries.

Cold ironing

This means plugging a ship into a land-based energy supply capable of running its essential functions while in port. The procedure only makes sense in areas where electricity can be generated from renewable sources through a national grid, and allows the cruise ship to turn off its generators, thus reducing emissions. So far, cold ironing has been introduced in Halifax, Juneau, Los Angeles, San Diego, Seattle, San Francisco, and Vancouver. Other ports are looking into its possibilities, although it costs about $5 million to install.

LNG

In future, cruise ships will probably be built with the ability to use LNG (liquefied natural gas) fuel to avoid running the diesel generators in port. (It's worth noting, however, that the storage tanks for LNG require 3.5 times the space of conventional fuel tanks, so retrofitting existing ships would be impractical.) An LNG-based power barge could possibly generate and supply electricity while in port, which would reduce CO_2 emissions considerably, and produce almost no SOx, NOx, or particle emissions. This could be a better solution than 'bridge' (interim solution) technology cold ironing, in which power is simply generated in the normal manner and made available to a ship in port.

What is MARPOL?

Short for 'Marine Pollution,' the International Convention for the Prevention of Pollution from Ships (MARPOL73/78 – the dates refer to its adoption) is the convention to which all member countries of the UN specialized agency the International Maritime Organization (IMO) subscribe. It was designed to minimize pollution of the oceans and seas, including dumping, and pollution by oil and exhaust gases, whether by operational or accidental causes. The original MARPOL Convention was signed on February 17, 1973, but did not come into force then. The Convention took effect on October 2, 1983. Presently, some 146 countries, representing 98 percent of the world's shipping tonnage, are signatories to the Convention. Ships flagged under these countries are subject to its requirements, regardless of where they sail.

Cruise Ship Safety

How likely is an accident at sea? What if there's a fire? Can you fall overboard? How good are medical facilities aboard?

When Costa Cruises' 3,800-passenger *Costa Concordia* capsized off the coast of Tuscany in January 2012 with the loss of 32 lives, questions of safety at sea inevitably arose. But this tragedy was entirely avoidable: if *Costa Concordia*'s captain hadn't deviated from his computer-set course to sail too close to the island of Giglia, it could have been just another uneventful Mediterranean cruise. The company was so fortunate in its crew, who did a wonderful job of evacuating more than 3,000 passengers from the stricken ship, in what were rather chaotic circumstances.

Other losses over the past 25 years include *Jupiter* in 1988 and *Royal Pacific* in 1992, both following collisions; *Explorer*, which struck an iceberg near Antarctica in 2007; and *Sea Diamond*, which foundered on a reef off the Greek island of Santorini in 2007. Given that more than 23 million people take a cruise every year, the number of serious incidents is considerably lower than one might expect. After 50 years of sea travel, during which I have experienced minor fires and groundings, I have no doubt that cruising

Cabins are checked during passenger emergency drill.

remains one of the safest forms of transportation.

Evacuations are, fortunately, rare events. At the time of the *Costa Concordia* calamity, the IMO (International Maritime Organization) was bringing in new regulations requiring all new cruise ships to be designed with the capability of making the nearest port in the event of a major casualty, fire, or loss of power.

Safety measures

New safety procedures have been implemented since the *Costa Concordia* incident in 2012.

All cruise ships built after 2010 with a length of 394ft (120m) or greater, or with three or more main vertical zones, must have two engine rooms, so that, in the event that one is flooded or rendered unusable, a ship can safely return to port without requiring passengers to evacuate the ship. This requirement (contained in the 2009 SOLAS – Safety of Life at Sea – treaty) came about due to the growth in size of today's cruise ships, and the fact that several ship fires and loss of propulsion/steering have occurred in the past few years.

Other safety measures introduced include muster drills, bridge access and procedures, life jacket availability and location, lifeboat loading drills, recording of passenger nationalities for on-shore emergency services personnel, and securing of heavy objects.

International regulations require all crew to undergo basic safety training *before* being allowed to work aboard any cruise ship (on-the-job training is no longer enough). All safety regulations are governed by the international SOLAS convention, introduced in 1914 in the aftermath of *Titanic*'s sinking in 1912. A mandatory passenger muster drill prior to departure from the port of embarkation is part of the SOLAS Convention. Passengers who don't attend may be disembarked prior to sailing.

All cruise ships built since 1986 must have either totally or partially enclosed lifeboats with diesel engines that will operate even if the lifeboat is inverted.

Since October 1997, cruise ships have had: all stairways enclosed as self-contained fire zones; smoke detectors and smoke alarms fitted in all passenger cabins and all public spaces; low-level lighting showing routes of escape (such as in corridors and stairways); all fire doors throughout the ship controllable from the ship's navigation bridge; all fire doors that can be opened from a remote location; and emergency alarms made audible in all cabins.

Since 2002, all ocean-going cruise ships on international voyages have had to carry voyage data

Demonstraing how to get in and out of shore tenders.

recorders (VDRs), similar to black boxes carried by aircraft, and, since October 2010, new SOLAS regulations have prohibited the use of combustible materials in all new cruise ships.

Crew members attend frequent emergency drills, the lifeboat equipment is regularly tested, and the fire-detecting devices, and alarm and fire-fighting systems are checked. Any passengers spotting fire or smoke are encouraged to use the nearest fire alarm box, alert a member of staff, or contact the bridge.

Take a small flashlight, in case an emergency arises during a blackout or during the night. I have strongly recommended that all cruise lines fit rechargeable flashlights under each passenger bed (this recommendation was forwarded to the IMO).

Is security good enough?

Cruise lines are subject to stringent international security regulations. Passengers and crew can embark or disembark only by passing through a security checkpoint. Cruise ships maintain zero tolerance for onboard crime or offenses against the person, and trained security professionals are employed aboard all cruise ships.

It is recommended that you keep your cabin locked at all times when you are not there. All new ships have encoded plastic key cards that operate a lock electronically; doors on older ships work with real metal keys. Cruise lines do not accept responsibility for any money or valuables left in cabins and suggest that you store them in a safety deposit box at the purser's office, or, if one is provided, in your in-cabin personal safe.

You will be issued with a personal boarding pass when you embark. This typically includes your photo, lifeboat station, restaurant seating, and other pertinent information, and serves as identification to be shown at the gangway each time you board. You may also be asked for a government-issued photo ID, such as a passport.

Passenger lifeboat drill

A passenger lifeboat drill, announced publicly by the captain, must be held for embarking passengers *before* the ship departs the port of embarkation. This rule was adopted by the global cruise industry following the *Costa Concordia* accident and improved on the existing SOLAS regulations, which require a drill to be held within 24 hours of departure.

Attendance is compulsory. Learn your boat station or assembly point and how to get to it in an emergency. Note your exit and escape pathways and learn how to put on your lifejacket correctly. The drill takes no more than 20 minutes and is a good investment – the 600-passenger *Royal Pacific* took fewer than 20 minutes to sink after its collision in 1992.

General emergency alarm signal

In the event of a real emergency, you'll hear the ship's general emergency alarm signal. This consists of seven short blasts followed by one long blast on the ship's whistle and public address system.

On hearing the signal, go directly to your assembly station. Follow the direction signs and arrows and the directions of crew members or those given over the public address system.

Don't search for others in your party (the assembly station is the meeting point).

Don't use the elevators.

If the nearest exit is blocked, use an alternative exit as marked in the plan (usually shown as a dotted arrow).

Low location lighting

In an emergency, a light strip in the floor will lead to an exit. If there is smoke in the corridor, keep close to the floor and crawl if necessary to avoid breathing the smoke and to be able to see more clearly (smoke typically rises).

Assembly stations

The assembly station is where you assemble in an emergency. They are marked by a sign on the plan on the back of your cabin door. Follow the instructions of crew members, and remain calm. You will be provided with a lifejacket (and with children's lifejackets), if you do not already have one.

Can you accidentally fall overboard?

Of course, cruise lines can't always stop passengers having too much to drink and falling over balconies. But all cruise ships have railings at least 3ft 7in (1.1m) high to protect you and your children.

Medical services

Except for ships registered in the UK or Norway, there are no mandatory international maritime requirements for cruise lines to carry a licensed physician or to have hospital facilities aboard. However, in general, all ships carrying over 50 passengers do have medical facilities and at least one doctor.

The standard of medical care and of the doctors themselves may vary from line to line. Most shipboard doctors are generalists; there are no cardiologists or neurosurgeons. Doctors are typically employed as outside contractors and will charge for use of their services, including seasickness shots.

Regrettably, some cruise lines make medical services a low priority. Most shipboard physicians are not certified in trauma treatment or medical evacuation procedures, for example. However, some medical organizations, such as the American College of Emergency Physicians, have a special division for cruise medicine. Most ships catering to North American passengers carry doctors licensed in the US, Canada, or Britain, but doctors aboard many other ships come from a variety of countries and disciplines.

Cunard Line's *Queen Mary 2*, with 4,344 passengers and crew, has a fully equipped hospital with one surgeon, one doctor, a staff of six nurses, and two medical orderlies; contrast this with *Carnival Paradise*, which carries up to 3,514 passengers and crew, with just one doctor and two nurses.

Ideally, a ship's medical staff should be certified in advanced cardiac life support. The equipment should include an examination room, isolation ward/bed, X-ray machine (to verify fractures), cardiac monitor (EKG) and defibrillator, oxygen-saturation monitor, external pacemaker, oxygen, suction and ventilators, hematology analyzer, culture incubator, and a mobile trolley intensive care unit.

Existing health problems requiring treatment on board must be reported when you book. Aboard some ships, you may be charged for filling a prescription as well as for the cost of prescribed drugs. There may also be a charge if you have to cancel a shore excursion and need a doctor's letter to prove that you are ill.

Fire drill aboard *Hanseatic*.

Shipboard injury

Slipping, tripping, and falling are the major sources of shipboard injury. Here are some things you can do to minimize the chance of injury.

Aboard many ships, raised thresholds separate a cabin's bathroom from the sleeping area. Mind your step to avoid a stubbed toe or banged head.

Don't hang anything from the fire sprinkler heads on the cabin ceilings.

On older ships, note how the door lock works. In some cases, a key is required on the inside in order for the door to be unlocked. Leave the key in the lock, so that in the event of a real emergency, you don't have to hunt for the key.

Aboard older ships, take care not to trip over raised thresholds in doorways leading to the open deck.

Walk with caution when the outer decks are wet. This applies especially to solid steel decks – falling on them is really painful.

Do not throw a lighted cigarette or cigar butt, or knock out your pipe, over the ship's side. They can easily be sucked into an opening in the ship's side or onto an aft open deck area and cause a fire.

Surviving a shipboard fire

Shipboard fires can generate an incredible amount of heat, smoke, and often panic. In the unlikely event that you are in one, try to remain calm and think logically and clearly.

When you first get to your cabin, check the way to the nearest emergency exits. Count the number of cabin doorways and other distinguishing features

Testing lifeboats on *Voyager of the Seas*.

to the exits in case you have to escape without the benefit of lighting. All ships provide low location lighting systems.

Exit signs are normally located just above your head – this is virtually useless, as smoke and flames rise. Note the location of the nearest fire alarm and know how to use it in case of dense smoke. In future, it is likely that directional sound evacuation beacons will be mandated; these will direct passengers to exits, escape-ways, and other safe areas, and may be better than the present inadequate visual aids.

If you are in your cabin, and there is fire in the passageway outside, put on your lifejacket. If the cabin's door handle is hot, soak a towel in water and use it to turn the handle. If a fire is raging in the passageway, cover yourself in wet towels if you decide to go through the flames.

Check the passageway. If there are no flames, walk to the nearest emergency exit or stairway. If there is smoke in the passageway, crawl to the nearest exit. If the exit is blocked, go to an alternate one. It may take considerable effort to open a heavy fire door to the exit. Don't use the elevators.

If there's a fire in your cabin or on the balcony, report it immediately by telephone. Then get out of your cabin, close the door behind you, sound the alarm, and alert your neighbors.

Piracy in the Gulf of Aden

The UN Security Council has renewed its authorization for countries to use military force against the pirates operating off Somalia who have been sabotaging one of the world's busiest shipping lanes. There were scores of pirate attacks in Somali waters in 2010, with nearly 40 cargo ships, several fishing vessels, one yacht, and one cruise ship attacked or hijacked.

The pirates usually seem to aim to take hostages and demand a ransom from a ship's owners. Cruise ships are not immune from attack, particularly smaller ones. But *MSC Melody*, carrying 1,500 passengers, was attacked in 2009; its crew repelled the pirates by firing in the air and spraying water on them. *Oceanic*, a Maltese-flagged educational cruise ship attacked with grenades in 2010, escaped by blasting the pirates with high-pressure water hoses.

In 2008, the US Navy created a special unit, called Combined Task Force 150, to combat piracy in the Gulf of Aden.

In February 2009 the Maritime Security Patrol Area, introduced by coalition navies in 2008 as a safe passage corridor, was replaced by two separate 5-mile-wide (8-km-wide) eastbound and westbound strips, separated by a 2-mile (3.2-km) buffer – this was to help prevent collisions. Today, passengers aboard ships in areas of potential piracy are usually given a briefing before entering the area.

Britannia Restaurant aboard *Queen Elizabeth*.

How We Evaluate the Ships

Ships and their facilities count, of course, but just as important are the factors and standards relating to food, service, staff training, and hospitality. This section explains how the Berlitz points system works.

I have been evaluating and rating cruise ships and the onboard product professionally since 1980. I also receive reports from my small team of trained assessors. The Berlitz ratings are conducted with *total objectivity*, from a set of predetermined criteria, using a modus operandi designed to work across the entire spectrum of oceangoing cruise ships, in all segments of the marketplace.

There really is no 'best cruise line in the world' or 'best cruise ship' – only the ship and cruise that is right for you. After all, it's the overall enjoyment of a cruise as a vacation that's really important. Therefore, different criteria are applied to ships of different sizes, styles, and market segments throughout the world (vacationers of different nationalities are looking for different things).

The evaluation and rating of cruise ships is about as contrary to soccer as you can get. In soccer, the goalposts are always in the same place. But with cruise ships, they keep changing, as the industry evolves and matures.

This section includes 275 oceangoing cruise ships in service (or due to enter service) and chosen by the author for inclusion when this book was completed. Almost all except the very latest ships have been carefully evaluated, taking into account around 400 separate items based on personal cruises, visits, and revisits to ships. In the scoring room, these are channeled into 20 major areas, each with a possible 100 points. The maximum possible score for any ship is therefore 2,000 points.

For user-friendliness and reasons of space, scores are further channeled into five main sections: Ship, Accommodation, Food, Service, and Cruise Operation.

Cruise lines, ship owners, and operators should note that the ratings may be adjusted annually as a result of increased competition, the introduction of newer ships with better facilities, and other market- or passenger-driven factors.

The ratings more reflect the standards of the cruise product delivered to passengers (the software: the dining experience, the service, and the hospitality aspects of the cruise), and less the physical plant (the hardware). Thus, although a ship may be the latest, most stunning vessel in the world in terms of design and decor, if the 'software' (including food) and onboard product delivery are not so good, the scores and ratings will reflect these aspects more clearly.

The stars beside the name of the ship at the top of each page indicate the 'Overall Rating.'

The highest number of stars awarded is five stars (★★★★★), and the lowest is one star. This system is universally recognized throughout the global hospitality industry. A plus (+) indicates that a ship deserves just that little bit more than the number of stars attained. However, it is the number of points achieved rather than the number of stars attained that perhaps is more meaningful when comparing ships.

The star system

★★★★★+ 1,851–2,000 points
★★★★★ 1,701–1,850 points
★★★★+ 1,551–1,700 points
★★★★ 1,401–1,550 points
★★★+ 1,251–1,400 points
★★★ 1,101–1,250 points
★★+ 951–1,100 points
★★ 801–950 points
★+ 651–800 points
★ 501–650 points

Douglas Ward at work.

What the ratings mean

1,851–2,000 points ★★★★★+

You can expect an outstanding, top-class cruise experience – it doesn't get any better than this. It should be truly memorable, and with the highest attention to detail, finesse, and personal service – how important you are made to feel is critical. The decor must be elegant and tasteful, measured by restraint and not flashiness, with fresh flowers and other decorative touches in abundance. The layout of the public rooms might well follow *feng shui* principles.

Any ship with this rating must be just about unsurpassable in the cruise industry, and it has to be very, very special, with service and hospitality levels to match. There must be the very highest-quality surroundings, comfort, and service levels, the finest and freshest quality foods, including all breads and rolls baked on board. Highly creative menus, regional cuisine, and dining alternatives should provide maximum choice and variety, and special orders will be part of the dining ritual.

Dining room meals (particularly dinners) are expected to be memorable affairs, correctly served on the finest china, with a choice of wines of suitable character and vintage available, and served in the correct-sized sommelier glasses of the highest quality (Reidel or Schott).

The service staff will take pleasure in providing you with the ultimate personal, yet unobtrusive, attention with the utmost of finesse, and the word 'no' should not be in their vocabulary. This is the very best of the best in terms of refined living at sea, but it is seriously expensive.

1,701–1,850 points ★★★★★

You can expect a truly excellent, memorable cruise experience, with the finesse and attention to detail commensurate with the amount of money paid. The service and hospitality levels will be extremely high from all levels of officers and staff, with strong emphasis on fine hospitality training – all service personnel members must make you feel important.

The food will be commensurate with the high level expected from what is virtually the best possible at sea, with service that should be very attentive yet unobtrusive. The cuisine should be memorable, with ample taste. Special orders should never be a problem. There must be a varied selection of wines, which should be served in glasses of the correct size.

Entertainment is expected to be of prime quality and variety. Again, the word 'no' should not be in the vocabulary of any member of staff aboard a ship with this rating. Few things will cost extra once you are on board, and brochures should be more 'truthful' than those for ships with a lower rating.

1,551–1,700 points ★★★★+

You can expect to have a high-quality cruise experience that will be memorable, and just a little short of being excellent in all aspects. Perhaps the personal service and attention to detail could be slightly better, but, nonetheless, this should prove to be a fine all-round cruise experience, in a setting that is extremely clean and comfortable, with few lines anywhere, a caring attitude from service personnel, and a good standard of entertainment that appeals to a mainstream market.

The cuisine and service will be carefully balanced, with mostly fresh ingredients and varied menus that

Balinese day beds aboard *Europa 2*.

should appeal to almost anyone, all served on high-quality china.

This should prove to be an extremely well-rounded cruise experience, probably in a ship that is new or almost new. There will probably be fewer 'extra-cost' items than ships with a slightly lower rating.

1,401–1,550 points ★★★★

You can expect to have a very good quality all-round cruise experience, most probably aboard a modern, highly comfortable ship that will provide a good range of facilities and services. The food and service will be quite decent overall, although decidedly not as 'gourmet' and fanciful as the brochures with the always-smiling faces might have you believe.

The service on board will be well-organized, if a little robotic and impersonal at times, and only as good as the cruise line's training program allows. You may notice a lot of things cost extra once you are on board, although the typically vague brochure tells you that these things are 'available' or are an 'option.' However, you should have a good time, and your bank account will be only moderately damaged.

1,251–1,400 points ★★★+

You can expect to have a decent-quality cruise experience, aboard a ship where the service levels should be good, but perhaps without the finesse that could be expected from a more upscale environment. The crew aboard any ship achieving this score should reflect a positive attitude with regard to hospitality, and a willingness to accommodate your needs, up to a point. Staff training will probably be in need of more attention to detail and flexibility.

Food and service levels in the dining venues should be reasonably good, although special or unusual orders might prove more difficult to accommodate. There will probably be a number of extra-cost items you thought were included in the price of your cruise – although the brochure typically is vague and states that the things are 'available' or are an 'option.'

1,101–1,250 points ★★★

You can expect a reasonably decent, middle-of-the-road cruise experience, with a moderate amount of space and quality in furnishings, fixtures, and fittings. The cabins are likely to be a little on the small side. The food and service levels will be quite acceptable, although not at all memorable, and somewhat inflexible with regard to special orders, as almost everything is standardized.

The level of hospitality will be moderate but little more, and the entertainment will probably be weak. This is a good option, however, for those looking for the reasonable comforts of home without pretentious attitudes, and little damage to your bank statement.

951–1,100 points ★★+

You can expect an average cruise experience in terms of accommodation (typically with cabins that are di-mensionally challenged), the quality of the ship's facilities, food, wine list, service, and hospitality levels, in surroundings that are unpretentious. In particular, the food and its service might be disappointing.

There will be little flexibility in the levels of service, hospitality, and staff training and supervision, which will be no better than poor in comparison with that of ships of a higher rating. Thus, the overall experience will be commensurate with the comparatively small amount of money you paid for the cruise.

801–950 points ★★

You can expect to have a cruise experience of modest quality aboard a ship that is probably in need of more attention to maintenance and service levels, not to mention hospitality. The food may be quite lacking in taste, homogenized, and of low quality, and service is likely to be mediocre at best. Staff training is likely to be minimal, and turnover may be high. The 'end-of-pier' entertainment could well leave you wanting to read a good book.

651–800 points ★+

You can expect to have only the most basic cruise experience, with little or no attention to detail, from a minimally trained staff that is probably paid low wages and to whom you are just another body. The ship will, in many cases, probably be in need of much maintenance and upgrading, and will probably have few facilities. Dismal entertainment is also likely. On the other hand, the price of a cruise is probably alluringly low.

501–650 points ★

You can expect to have a cruise experience that is the bottom of the barrel, with little in terms of hospitality or finesse. Forget about attention to detail – there won't be any. This would equal a stay in the most basic motel on land, with few facilities, a poorly trained, uncaring staff, and a ship that needs better maintenance.

The low cost of a cruise aboard a ship with this rating should provide a strong clue to the complete absence of any quality, particularly for food, service, and entertainment. You might remember this cruise, but for all the wrong reasons.

Distribution of points

These are the percentage of the total points available that are allocated to each of the main areas evaluated:
The ship: 25 percent
Accommodation: 10 percent
Food: 20 percent
Service: 20 percent
Entertainment: 5 percent
Cruise Experience: 20 percent
The categories 'Entertainment' (including lecturers and expedition staff) and 'Cruise Experience' may be combined for boutique ships, tall ships, and expedition ships.

Criteria

The ship

Hardware/maintenance/safety. This score reflects the general profile and condition of the ship (hardware), its age and maintenance, exterior paint, decking and caulking, swimming pool and surrounds, deck furniture, shore tenders, lifeboats, and other safety items. It also reflects interior cleanliness (public restrooms, elevators, floor and wall coverings, stairways, passageways, and doorways), food preparation areas, refrigerators, garbage handling, compacting, incineration, and waste-disposal facilities.

Outdoor facilities/space. This score reflects the overall space per passenger on open decks, congestion, swimming pools/whirlpools and their surrounds, number and type of deck lounge chairs (with or without cushioned pads) and other deck furniture, sports facilities, shower enclosures and changing facilities, towels, and quiet (no music) areas.

Interior facilities/space/flow. This score reflects the use of common interior public spaces, including enclosed promenades; flow and congestion points; ceiling height; lobby, stairways, and hallways; elevators; public restrooms and facilities; signage, lighting, air conditioning, and ventilation; and degree of comfort and density.

Decor/furnishings/artwork. This score reflects the overall interior decor (decoration and colors); soft furnishings; paneling; carpeting (color, pattern, and practicality); chairs (comfort); ceilings and treatments; artwork (paintings, sculptures, and atrium centerpieces); and lighting.

Spa/fitness facilities. This score reflects the health spa, wellness center, and fitness facilities: location, accessibility, lighting and flooring materials; fitness machines and fitness programs; sports facilities and equipment; indoor pools; hot tubs; grand baths; hydrotherapy pools; saunas; steam rooms; treatment rooms; changing facilities; jogging and walking tracks; and open promenades.

Accommodation

Cabins: suites and cabins. This score reflects the design and layout of all suite- and deluxe grade cabins, private balconies (whether full floor-to-ceiling partition or part partitions). Also: beds/berths, cabinetry, and other fittings; hanging and drawer space, and bedside tables; vanity unit, bathroom facilities, cabinets, and toiletries storage; lighting, air conditioning, and ventilation; audio-visual facilities; artwork; insulation, noise, and vibration. Suites should not be so designated unless the sleeping room is completely separated from the living area.

Also, soft furnishings, cabin service directory of services, interactive TV; paper, postcards, and personalized stationery; telephone information; laundry lists; tea- and coffee-making equipment; flowers; fruit; bathroom personal amenities kits, bathrobes, slippers, and the size and quality of towels.

Cuisine

Cruise lines put maximum emphasis on promising passengers how good their food will be, often to the point of overstatement. There are, of course, at least as many different tastes as there are passengers. The standard market cruise companies cater to a wide range of tastes, while the more exclusive ones offer better-quality food, mostly cooked individually to your taste. As in any good restaurant, you generally get what you pay for.

Dining venues/cuisine. This score reflects the physical structure of dining rooms, layout, seat-

Balcony cabins at the aft (back) of *Costa Serena*.

ing, and waiter stations; lighting and ambience; table setups; linen, china, and cutlery quality and condition; and table centerpieces (flowers). Also: menus, food quality, presentation, combinations, culinary creativity, appeal, taste, texture, freshness, color, balance; garnishes and decorations; appetizers, soups, pastas, tableside cooking (if any); fresh fruit and cakes; the wine list (and connoisseur wine list), price range, and wine service. Specialty dining venues are also checked for menu variety, food and service quality, decor, seating, noise levels, china, cutlery, and glassware.

Informal eateries/buffets. This score reflects hot and cold display units, sneeze guards, 'active' stations, tongs, ice containers, ladles, and serving utensils; buffet displays (most are disappointing and institutionalized); trays; plates; food temperatures; food labeling; deck buffets; late-night snacks; decorative elements; and staff service and communication.

Quality of ingredients. This score reflects the quality of ingredients, taste, consistency, and portion size; grades of meat, fish, and fowl; and the price paid by the cruise line for food per passenger per day. It is the quality of ingredients that most dictates the presentation and taste of the finished product.

Tea/coffee/bar snacks. This score reflects the quality and variety of teas and coffees available, including afternoon teas/coffees and their presentation; whether mugs or cups and saucers are used; whether milk is served in the correct open containers or in sealed individual packets; whether self-service or served. It also reflects the quality of such items as cakes, scones, and pastries, as well as bar/lounge snacks, hot and cold canapés, and hors d'oeuvres.

Service

Dining room. This score reflects staff professionalism: the maître d'hôtel, under managers, section headwaiters, waiters and assistants (busboys), sommeliers and wine waiters; place settings, cutlery, and glasses; and proper service (serving, taking from the correct side), communication skills, attitude, flair, uniform, appearance, and finesse. Waiters should note whether passengers are right- or left-handed and, when tables are assigned, make sure that cutlery and glasses are placed on the side of preference.

Bars. This score reflects the lighting and ambience; seating, noise levels; communication skills; the staff's attitude, personality, flair, and service finesse; correct use of glasses (and correct size of glasses).

Cabins. This score reflects the cleaning and housekeeping staff, butlers (for penthouse and suite passengers), cabin stewards/stewardesses, supervisory staff, attention to detail and cleanliness, linen and bathrobe changes, and language and communication skills.

Open decks. This score reflects the service for beverages and food items; placement and replacement of towels on deck lounge chairs, towel supply, emptying

of used towel bins; and general tidiness of all associated deck equipment.

Entertainment

The score reflects the overall entertainment program, which needs to appeal to passengers of many ages and types. Included is the physical plant (stage/bandstand) of the main show lounge; technical support, lighting, set/backdrop design; sound systems; pre-recorded tracks and special effects; large-scale production shows (story, plot, content, cohesion, costumes, quality, choreography, and vocal content); cabaret acts; and bands and solo musicians.

Aboard specialist ships such as those offering expedition cruises, or tall ships (sailing ships such as *Sea Cloud*), where entertainment is not a feature, it is the lecture program, library, movies on demand, videos and CDs, and use of watersports items such as jet skis, windsurfers, kayaks, and snorkeling gear (items that the large resort ships usually charge extra for), etc.

The cruise experience

Activities program. This score reflects the daytime activities and events; cruise director and staff (visibility and professionalism), participation games, special-interest programs, port shopping, and enrichment lecturers. Also, watersports equipment, instruction, staff supervision, marina or retractable watersports platforms, and enclosed swimming area.

Movies/television program. This score reflects movies screened in theaters and on poolside screens; picture and sound quality; videos and other programming on the cabin infotainment system, and audio channels.

Hospitality standard. This score reflects the hospitality and professionalism of officers, middle management, supervisors, cruise staff, and crew; social contact; appearance and dress codes; motivation; and communication skills.

Overall product delivery. This score reflects the quality of the overall cruise as a vacation – what the brochure states and promises, and the onboard hospitality and service.

Notes on the rating results

Cruise ship evaluations and ratings have become ever more complex. Although a ship may be the newest, with all the latest facilities possible, it is the onboard food and service that often disappoint, as well as standing in lines and signing up for activities. It's about delivering a cohesive, consistent onboard product.

Cruise companies state that food quality is a trade-off against lower prices. However, this implies a downward spiral that affects the food quality as well as the service, the quality of the personnel, crew training, safety, and maintenance.

In the final analysis, it is the little things that add to points lost on the great scorecard.

What the Descriptions Mean

Each of the following ship reviews is preceded by a panel providing basic data on the ship's size and facilities. Here we explain how to interpret the categories.

Ship size
Large resort ship: 2,001–6,500 passengers
Mid-size ship: 751–2,000 passengers
Small ship: 251–750 passengers
Boutique ship: 50–250 passengers

Lifestyle
Designated as Standard, Premium, or Luxury, according to a general classification into which segment of the market the ship falls. This should help you choose the right size ship and cruise experience to fit your lifestyle.
Standard. The least expensive, offering the basic amenities, food, and service.
Premium. More expensive than Standard, has generally better food, service, facilities, and amenities, more attention to detail, and greater differentiation of suites (with butler service) than standard accommodation.
Luxury. More expensive than Premium or Standard, provides more personal comfort, space, open or one-seating dining, much better food (no processed

The bow of *Queen Mary 2*.

items, more menu creativity, and everything made as freshly as possible), and highly trained staff.

Cruise line
The cruise line and the operator may be different if the company that owns the vessel does not routinely market and operate it. Tour operators often charter ships for their exclusive use (for example Thomson Cruises).

IMO numbers
Each ocean-going ship must have an IMO (International Maritime Organization) number clearly displayed on a ship's hull. This was agreed after the terrorist attacks of September 11, 2001, so that any ship could be clearly identified.

Entered service
Where two dates are given, the first is for the ship's maiden (paid) passenger voyage, and the second is the date it began service for the current operator.

Propulsion
The type of propulsion is given (gas turbine, diesel, diesel-electric, nuclear, or steam turbine), together with the output (at 100 percent), expressed as kW (kilowatts) generated.

Propellers
This heading refers to the number of propellers or fixed or azimuthing pods.

The favored drivers are now eco-friendly diesel-electric or diesel-mechanical propulsion systems that propel ships at speeds of up to 28 knots (32mph). Only Cunard Line's *QM2*, with a top speed of more than 30 knots (34.8mph), is faster.

More than 60 cruise ships are now fitted with the pod propulsion system, first introduced in 1990. It resembles a huge outboard motor fitted below the waterline. It replaces the long-used conventional rudder, shaft, and propeller mechanisms, saves valuable machinery space, and makes stern thrusters redundant.

The pods are compact, self-contained units powered by internal electric propulsion motors. They are turned by the hydraulic motors of the steering gear, and can turn through 360 degrees (azimuthing). This allows even the largest ships to maneuver into tight spaces without help from tugs.

Most ships have two pods, although some have three (*Allure of the Seas, Oasis of the Seas*) or even four units

Lines are inevitable aboard large resort ships.

(*Queen Mary 2*). Each pod weighs about 170 tons, but the four pods attached to *Queen Mary 2* weigh 250 tons each – more than an empty Boeing 747 jumbo jet; two are fixed, two are of the azimuthing variety. Although they are at the stern, pods pull, rather than push, a ship through the water, thanks to their forward-facing propellers; this provides greater maneuverability.

Ships with pod propulsion systems should have no noticeable vibration or engine noise at the stern, unlike ships with conventional propulsion systems. Competing manufacturers have different names for their pod systems – examples: Azipod, Dolphin, Mermaid.

Some ships may be fitted with 'Becker' rudders, which is one where the main body has a hinged, second part. This second, or aft, section can be pointed in a different direction from the main body, so that more control over waterflow can be achieved.

Passenger capacity
This is based on two lower beds/berths per cabin, plus all cabins for single occupancy.

Passenger space ratio (gross tonnage per passenger)
Achieved by dividing the gross tonnage by the number of passengers (lower bed capacity including single-occupancy cabins).

Passenger to crew ratio
Achieved by dividing the number of (lower-bed) passengers by the number of crew.

Cabin size range
From the smallest cabin to the largest suite (including 'private' balconies/verandas), provided in square feet and square meters and rounded up to the nearest whole number.

Wheelchair-accessible ratings
Cabins designed to accommodate passengers with limited mobility. There are four wheelchair accessibility ratings:
Best. The ship is recommended as being most suitable for wheelchair passengers.
Good. Reasonably accessible.
Fair. Moderately accessible.
None. The ship is not suitable.

Dedicated cinema
A 'yes' means that there is a separate cinema dedicated solely to showing large-screen movies. This is distinct from a showlounge that may be used to screen movies during the day and for live shows in the evening, or from poolside movie screens.

About prices
Some price examples may be given throughout the ship reviews. Note that these are provided *only* as a guideline and may have changed since publication. Always check with the cruise line, the onboard concession, or your travel provider for the latest prices.

Footnote to the silhouettes
You may wonder why we do not use color photos of ships, so I thought you might like to know that when the book was first published, I asked a charming lady named Susan Alpert to draw the ship silhouettes. She did a great job. However, she died of ovarian cancer at the age of 33. Afterward I decided to honor her memory by using hand-drawn silhouettes.

This Year's Star Performers

Having reviewed the following 275 cruise ships, Berlitz names the top-rated ships in their size categories for 2016.

Despite constant claims by cruise companies that their ship has been named 'Best Cruise Line' or 'Best Cruise Ship' by this or that magazine or online readers' poll, there really is no such thing – there is only the ship that is right for you. Few operators can really deliver a ship, product, and crew worthy of the highest Berlitz star rating – it's all about excellence, and passion.

For this 2016 edition, just two ships have achieved the score required for them to be awarded membership in the most exclusive 'five-stars-plus' category:

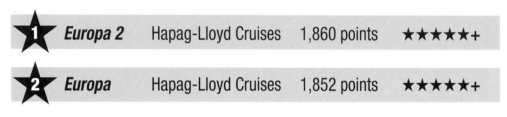

| ★1 | *Europa 2* | Hapag-Lloyd Cruises | 1,860 points | ★★★★★+ |
| ★2 | *Europa* | Hapag-Lloyd Cruises | 1,852 points | ★★★★★+ |

These are both beautiful ships to sail aboard, with an outstanding amount of space per passenger, passageways with high ceilings, a superb range of dining venues and types of cuisine, and attentive, friendly, yet unobtrusive personal service.

We have also compiled a selection of the best cruise ships in each category, the winners and runners-up denoted by the number of points scored overall.

The christening ceremony for *Europa 2* in Hamburg, in 2013.

And the winner is...

The top 5 large resort ships

Mein Schiff 4. This stylish, family-friendly large resort ship has fine contemporary, non-glitzy interior design, a half Olympic-size pool, and a wide choice of dining venues.

(2,0001–6,500 passengers)

Mein Schiff 4	1,698	★★★★+
Mein Schiff 3	1,697	★★★★+
Queen Mary 2	1,675	★★★★+
Britannia	1,656	★★★★+
Queen Elizabeth	1,583	★★★★+

The top 5 small ships

Europa 2. The world's highest scoring ship overflows with contemporary interior design, style, and finesse in food and service for sophisticated international travelers.

(251–750 passengers)

Europa 2	1,860	★★★★★+
Europa	1,852	★★★★★+
Silver Whisper	1,743	★★★★★
Silver Shadow	1,741	★★★★★
Silver Spirit	1,735	★★★★★

The top 5 mid-size ships

Viking Star. This premium ship has many elegant touches; enjoy the tactile comforts of home, Nordic history, excellent inclusive value, and unfussy cuisine.

(751–2,000 passengers)

Viking Star	1,698	★★★★+
Crystal Serenity	1,693	★★★★+
Crystal Symphony	1,684	★★★★+
Riviera	1,682	★★★★+
Marina	1,679	★★★★+

The top 5 boutique ships

Hanseatic. This high-class expedition ship is for adventurous travelers who want style, fine food and service, creature comforts, and top expedition equipment.

(50–250 passengers)

Hanseatic	1,758	★★★★★
SeaDream I	1,756	★★★★★
SeaDream II	1,752	★★★★★
Sea Cloud	1,706	★★★★★
Sea Cloud II	1,701	★★★★★

Europa and *Europa 2* really are exclusive, high-priced ships, so we have also included a top 5 ships in various popular categories to highlight the best in class (in alphabetical order by cruise line or ship name).

Note that some sister ships in the same series with identical, or close to identical, features and facilities have also been included for guidance.

5 best ships for families

These ships have been chosen for their choice of family-friendly facilities, activities, and entertainment.

Allure of the Seas/Oasis of the Seas
Disney Dream/Disney Fantasy
Mein Schiff 3/Mein Schiff 4
MSC Divina/MSC Preziosa
Norwegian Breakaway/Norwegian Escape/Norwegian Getaway

5 best cruise lines for teenagers

Teenagers like space away from adults to hang out, meet others, and simply chill. Some ships get it, and some don't.

Disney Cruise Line *(Disney Dream/Disney Fantasy)*
Norwegian Cruise Line *(Norwegian Breakaway/Norwegian Epic/Norwegian Escape/Norwegian Getaway)*
MSC Cruises *(MSC Divina/MSC Preziosa)*
Royal Caribbean International *(Anthem of the Seas/Quantum of the Seas)*
TUI Cruises *(Mein Schiff 3/Mein Schiff 4)*

5 best splash-tastic water slides

Water slides are always a highlight for youngsters, who can't wait to go for a ride once they are on board.

DrainPipe (Carnival Cruise Line)
Aquaduck (Disney Cruise Line)
Vertigo (MSC Cruises)
Epic Plunge (Norwegian Cruise Line)
Parthenon Slide (Star Cruises)

5 most luxurious suites

Suites are not just about size and space (relative to the ship), but also the furnishings, service, and all those little details.

Royal Loft *Allure of the Seas, Oasis of the Seas* (Royal Caribbean International)
Crystal Penthouse *Crystal Serenity* (Crystal Cruises)
Owner's Suite *Europa 2* (Hapag-Lloyd Cruises)
Owner's Suite *Marina, Riviera* (Oceania Cruises)
Sandringham Suite *Queen Mary 2* (Cunard Line)

5 best cruise ship spas

Wellness and pampering have become major attractions for people who want to take care of their bodies even when on vacation.

AIDA Cruises *(AIDAprima)*
Cunard Line *(Queen Mary 2)*
Hapag-Lloyd Cruises *(Europa 2)*
MSC Cruises *(MSC Divina/MSC Fantasia/MSC Preziosa/MSC Splendida)*
Viking Cruises *(Viking Star)*

5 best ships for child-free cruising

I have chosen one ship from each of five companies that are marketed as, or are best for, child-free cruising.

Adonia (P&O Cruises)
Grande Mariner (Blount Small Ship Adventures)
Island Sky (Noble Caledonia)
Minerva (Swan Hellenic Cruises)
Saga Sapphire (SAGA Cruises)

5 best cruise lines for foodies

These cruise lines have been chosen for the quality and variety of ingredients, their creativity, and presentation.

Crystal Cruises
Hapag-Lloyd Cruises
Oceania Cruises
SeaDream Yacht Club
Silversea Cruises

Welcome to the spa aboard *MSC Fantasia*.

Adonia
★★★★

Size:	Small Ship	Passenger/Crew Ratio (lower beds):	1.8
Tonnage:	30,277	Cabins (total):	355
Lifestyle:	Standard	Size Range (sq ft/m):	145.3–968.7/13.5–90.0
Cruise Line:	P&O Cruises	Cabins (for one person):	0
Former Names:	*Royal Princess, Minerva II, R8*	Cabins (with private balcony):	258
IMO Number:	9210220	Cabins (wheelchair accessible):	4
Builder:	Chantiers de l'Atlantique (France)	Wheelchair accessibility:	Good
Original Cost:	$150 million	Cabin Current:	110 and 220 volts
Entered Service:	Feb 2001/May 2011	Elevators:	4
Registry:	Bermuda	Casino (gaming tables):	No
Length (ft/m):	592.0/180.4	Slot Machines:	No
Beam (ft/m):	83.5/25.4	Swimming Pools:	1
Draft (ft/m):	19.5/6.0	Hot Tubs (on deck):	3
Propulsion/Propellers:	diesel/2	Self-Service Launderette:	Yes
Passenger Decks:	9	Dedicated Cinema/Seats:	No
Total Crew:	293	Library:	Yes
Passengers (lower beds):	710	Onboard currency:	UK£
Passenger Space Ratio (lower beds):	42.6		

This adults-only, friendly ship is suited to British tastes

OVERVIEW. There may not be marble bathroom fittings or other expensive niceties, but *Adonia* provides cruises and programs that are geared specifically to more mature-age British passengers.

THE SHIP. *Adonia*, the last in a series of eight almost identical ships originally built for the defunct Renaissance Cruises in 2001, has the feel of an informal old-world British country hotel – warm, comfortable, cosseting, and friendly. P&O's trademark buff-colored funnel balances the ship's all-white hull and superstructure. An outside lido deck has a swimming pool and good sunbathing space.

The ship is small but well proportioned. Although there is no walk-around promenade deck outdoors, there is a small jogging track above the perimeter of the swimming pool, and you can stroll on open decks on the port and starboard sides. There are no wooden decks outdoors; they are covered by a sand-colored rubberized material.

The interior decor, designed by a Scotsman, John McNeece, is quite elegant, a throwback to the heavy hardwood style of the ocean liners of the 1920s and '30s. It includes detailed ceiling cornices, real and faux wrought-iron staircase railings, wood- and leather-paneled walls, trompe l'oeil ceilings, rich carpeting in hallways, and many other interesting and expensive-looking decorative touches.

The public rooms are basically spread over three decks. The reception hall has a staircase with intricate, real wrought-iron railings (a copy of the staircase

Berlitz's Ratings		
	Possible	Achieved
Ship	500	398
Accommodation	200	154
Food	400	275
Service	400	285
Entertainment	100	71
Cruise Experience	400	293
OVERALL SCORE		
1476 points out of 2000		

aboard SS *Titanic*), but these are cleverly painted on plexiglas panels on the stairways on other decks.

The real social hub of the ship, Raffles Lounge and Bar, is a delightful wood-paneled lounge with a fireplace, a long bar with sit-up bar stools, and the feel of a proper, traditional London club.

The Library is a beautiful, restful room – perhaps the nicest public room – designed in the Regency style. It has a fireplace, a high, indented, trompe l'oeil ceiling, and a collection of about 2,000 books, plus comfortable wingback chairs with footstools, and sofas to fall asleep on.

A Crow's Nest Lounge sits high atop the ship, with great views from its floor-to-ceiling windows. The room has a long bar which faces forward – the barmen actually have the best view – and very comfortable seating. There is a small central bandstand and wooden dance floor forward of the bar.

The Cabaret Lounge is used mainly for evening theatrical shows and musical performances. There are several bars, including one in each of the restaurant entrances.

In April 2016, will *Adonia* transfer to a new Carnival Corporation brand called 'fathom,' for 'social impact' cruises to the Dominican Republic.

ACCOMMODATION. There are six basic cabin size categories, but in many price categories (14 for double occupancy and six for solo occupancy). Some cabins have interconnecting doors, and 18 cabins on Deck 6 have lifeboat-obstructed views. All grades have tea/coffee-making facilities. There are two interior accommodation passageways.

Standard outside-view and interior cabins. These are compact units, and tight for two persons, particularly for cruises longer than five days. They have twin beds or a queen-size bed, with good under-bed storage, personal safe, vanity desk with large mirror, reasonable closet and drawer space in rich, dark woods, TV, and cotton bathrobe. TV sets carry major news channels, where obtainable, plus sport and several movie channels.

Cabins with private balcony. Cabins with private balconies – about 66 percent of all cabins – have partial, and not full, balcony partitions, sliding glass doors and, thanks to good design and layout, only 14 cabins on Deck 6 have lifeboat-obstructed views. The tiled-floor, plain wall bathrooms are compact units, and include a shower stall with a removable hand-held shower unit, wall-mounted hairdryer, 100 percent cotton towels, toiletries storage shelves, and retractable clothesline.

Owner's Suites/Master Suites. The six Owner's Suites and four Master Suites provide abundant space and are worth the extra cost. They are large living spaces located in the forward-most and aftmost sections of the ship. Particularly nice are those that overlook the stern, on Decks 6, 7, and 8. They have more extensive private balconies that really are private and cannot be overlooked by anyone on the decks above. There is an entrance foyer, living room, bedroom (the bed faces the sea), audio unit, bathroom with Jacuzzi tub, and small guest bathroom.

DINING. There are three proper restaurants, plus a casual self-serve buffet-style venue and an outdoor grill: the Pacific Restaurant, in the aft section, is the most formal, with 338 seats and a raised central section. It has large ocean-view windows on three sides, and several prime tables overlook the stern. Dining is at assigned tables, in two seatings. The menu changes daily for lunch and dinner. The noise level can be high, the result of a single-deck-height ceiling and noisy waiter stations. Adjacent to the restaurant entrance (it actually forms part of it) there's a Club Bar – a cozy, open lounge and bar, with an attractive fireplace. The food is rather bland, and quite standardized, more suited to those of a certain age.

Other dining options. Ocean Grill, by Marco Pierre White, has ocean-view windows along one side and aft. The menu is small, and concentrates on steak (including a superb Casterbridge 28-day dry-aged filet steak) and seafood dishes. There is a cover charge to eat here, and reservations are needed. A second reservations-only venue, the Sorrento Restaurant, offers rather pleasant Italian cuisine; a cover charge applies. Both of these L-shaped venues are the same size, and have ocean-view windows along two sides and at the stern. Tables are mostly for four or six.

The Conservatory, with both indoor and outdoor seating, is the ship's casual dining spot, in a self-serve style. It is open for breakfast, lunch, and casual theme-night dinners. The selection and quality of items presented is average, so don't expect haute cuisine.

There is also a Poolside Grill, which provides casual fast food and grilled food fare to accompany those sunbathing moments.

Also, Raffles Lounge and Bar is *the* social hub of the ship.

ENTERTAINMENT. The Curzon Lounge is the venue for all main entertainment events, and occasional social functions. It is a single-level room, with a large bar set at the back – the bartender probably has the best views of the stage and acts. The entertainment consists mainly of cabaret and small group shows.

There's also a Crow's Nest Lounge, which sits atop the ship at the front. It has good forward views, includes a dance floor and live music, and has lots of seating alcoves to the port and starboard sides of the room. However, from most of these seats you don't have a view of the live band or dance floor.

SPA/FITNESS. The Oasis Spa has a gymnasium with some muscle-toning equipment, a large hot tub, steam rooms for men and women (there are no saunas), several treatment rooms, and a beauty salon. A spa concession provides beauty and wellness treatments, as well as exercise classes – some of which may cost extra. Out on deck, there are a small swimming pool, two hot tubs, a jogging track, a golf practice net, and shuffleboard courts.

Adventure of the Seas
★★★+

Size:	Large Resort Ship
Tonnage:	137,276
Lifestyle:	Standard
Cruise Line:	Royal Caribbean International
Former Names:	none
IMO Number:	9167227
Builder:	Kvaerner Masa-Yards (Finland)
Original Cost:	$500 million
Entered Service:	Nov 2001
Registry:	Bahamas
Length (ft/m):	1,020.6/311.1
Beam (ft/m):	155.5/47.4
Draft (ft/m):	28.8/8.8
Propulsion/Propellers:	diesel-electric (75,600kW)/ 3 pods (2 azimuthing, 1 fixed)
Passenger Decks:	14
Total Crew:	1,185
Passengers (lower beds):	3,114

Passenger Space Ratio (lower beds):	44.0
Passenger/Crew Ratio (lower beds):	2.6
Cabins (total):	1,557
Size Range (sq ft/m):	151.0–1,358.0/14.0–126.1
Cabins (for one person):	0
Cabins (with private balcony):	765
Cabins (wheelchair accessible):	26
Wheelchair accessibility:	Best
Cabin Current:	110 volts
Elevators:	14
Casino (gaming tables):	Yes
Slot Machines:	Yes
Swimming Pools:	3
Hot Tubs (on deck):	6
Self-Service Launderette:	No
Dedicated Cinema/Seats:	No
Library:	Yes
Onboard currency:	US$

A large ship that's big on things to do for the whole family

OVERVIEW. *Adventure of the Seas* is a large, floating leisure resort. It provides a host of facilities, rather like a small town, yet offers a healthy amount of space per passenger.

THE SHIP. A four-deck-high Royal Promenade is the main interior focal point; it's a good place to hang out, or to arrange to meet someone. The length of two American football fields, it has two internal lobbies rising through 11 decks. Cafés, shops, and entertainment locations front this winding street and interior 'with-view' bay window cabins look into it from above.

The long super-atrium houses a 'traditional' pub. There's also a Champagne Bar, a Sidewalk Café (for Continental breakfast, all-day pizzas, specialty coffees, and desserts), Sprinkles (for round-the-clock ice cream and yogurt), and a sports bar. There are also several shops – for jewelry, gifts, liquor, perfumes, and souvenirs. Comedy art has its place here, too, for example in the trompe l'oeil painter climbing up the walls.

Arched across the promenade is a captain's balcony, and in the center of the promenade a stairway connects you to the deck below, where you'll find the Schooner Bar (a piano lounge common to all Royal Caribbean International – RCI – ships) and the flashy Casino Royale. Gaming includes blackjack, Caribbean stud poker, roulette, and craps, plus 300 slot machines.

Other facilities include a regulation-size ice-skating rink (Studio B), with real ice, with 'bleacher' seating for up to 900 and broadcast facilities, and a

Berlitz's Ratings

	Possible	Achieved
Ship	500	390
Accommodation	200	141
Food	400	222
Service	400	268
Entertainment	100	76
Cruise Experience	400	264
OVERALL SCORE		
1361 points out of 2000		

stunning two-deck library, open 24 hours a day. There's also $12 million worth of artwork.

Other drinking places include the intimate Champagne Bar, Crown & Anchor Pub, and Connoisseur Club – for cigars and cognacs. Lovers of jazz might appreciate Blue Moon, an intimate room for cool music atop the ship in the Viking Crown Lounge. Golfers might enjoy the 19th Hole, a golf bar, as they play the Adventure Links.

FAMILIES. Facilities for children and teenagers are quite extensive. Aquanauts is for three- to five-year-olds; Explorers is for six- to eight-year-olds; Voyagers is for nine- to 12-year-olds. Optix is a dedicated area for teenagers, including a daytime club with several computers, a soda bar, and a dance floor. Challenger's Arcade has an array of video games. Paint and Clay is an arts and crafts center for younger children. Adjacent is Adventure Beach, an area for all the family to enjoy; it includes swimming pools, a water slide, and outdoor game areas.

ACCOMMODATION. There is a wide range of cabin price grades, in four major groupings: premium ocean-view suites and cabins, interior (atrium-view) cabins, ocean-view cabins, and interior cabins. Many cabins are of a similar size – good for incentives and large groups – and 300 have interconnecting doors (good for families).

Some 138 interior cabins have bay windows that look into the interior horizontal atrium – the Royal

Promenade – a cruise industry first when the ship originally debuted. Regardless of what cabin grade you choose, all except for the Royal and Owner's Suites have twin beds that convert to a queen-size unit, TV set, radio and telephone, personal safe, vanity unit, hairdryer, and private bathroom. However, you'll need to keep the curtains closed in the bay windows if you wear little clothing – you can be seen easily from adjacent bay window cabins.

Royal Suite (Deck 10). At around 1,146 sq ft (107 sq m), the Royal Suite is the largest private living space, located almost at the top of the Centrum lobby on the port side. It is a nicely appointed penthouse suite, whose occupants, sadly, must share the rest of the ship with everyone else, except for access to their own exclusive concierge club. It has a king-size circular bed in a separate large bedroom that can be fully closed off; a living room with an additional queen-size sofa bed, baby grand piano, refrigerator/wet bar, dining table and four chairs, expansive entertainment center, and a reasonably large bathroom.

Royal Family Suites. Each of the four Royal Family Suites (two aft on Deck 9, two aft on Deck 8; each measure around 574 sq ft/53 sq m) has two separate bedrooms. These suites, at the stern, have large balconies with views over the ship's wash.

Owner's Suites. Ten desirable Owner's Suites (around 468 sq ft/43 sq m) are in the center of the ship, on both port and starboard sides, adjacent to the Centrum lobby on Deck 10. There's also a small private balcony.

Standard outside-view and interior cabins. All cabins have a private bathroom, as well as interactive TV and pay-per-view movies. The bathrooms are compact, but do have a proper shower enclosure instead of a shower curtain.

The balcony decking is made of a sort of rubberized sand – and not wood, though the balcony rail is of wood. If you have a cabin with a connecting door to another cabin, be aware that you'll probably be able to hear everything your next-door neighbors say and do. Bathroom toilets are noisy, based on the vacuum system. Cabin bath towels are small and skimpy. Note that room service food menus are very basic.

DINING. The main dining room has a total capacity of 1,919, and consists of three levels, each named after a famous composer: Mozart, Strauss, and Vivaldi. The menu is the same on all three levels. A dramatic staircase connects all three levels, and huge, fat support pillars obstruct sight lines from a number of seats. However, the ambience is good and there's always a good buzz when the ship is full and dinner is in progress.

Two small private wings serve private groups: La Cetra and La Notte, each with 58 seats. When you book, choose one of two seatings, or 'My Time Dining' (eat when you want during dining room hours). Tables are for four, six, eight, 10, or 12. The place settings, china, and cutlery are of good quality.

Other dining options. Portofino is the ship's upscale Euro-Italian restaurant. It's open for dinner only, reservations are required, and there's a cover charge. The food and its presentation are better than the food in the dining room, although the restaurant isn't large enough for all passengers to try even once during a cruise. Choices include antipasti, soup, salad, pasta, main dish, dessert, cheese, and coffee.

Casual and informal meals at all hours can be taken at:

Windjammer Café: this is a really large, sprawling venue for casual buffet-style, self-help breakfast (this tends to be the busiest time of the day), lunch, and light dinners (but not on the last night of the cruise); it's often difficult to find a table, and, by the time you do, your food could be cold.

The Island Grill (it's actually a section inside the Windjammer Café), for casual dinner (no reservations needed), with a grill and open kitchen.

Johnny Rockets, a retro 1950s all-day, all-night diner-style eatery, has hamburgers, malt shakes (at extra cost), and jukebox hits, with both indoor and outdoor seating.

Promenade Café: for Continental breakfast, all-day pizzas, and specialty coffees – which are provided in paper cups.

Sprinkles, located on the Royal Promenade, is for round-the-clock ice cream and yogurt, pastries, and coffee.

ENTERTAINMENT. The 1,350-seat Lyric Theater, the principal showlounge, is a stunning room located at the forward end of the ship. It has Art Nouveau-themed decor, spans the height of five decks, with only a few slim pillars and almost no disruption of sight lines. Production shows are presented here by a large cast and a live band.

SPA/FITNESS. The ShipShape health spa is reasonably large, and measures 15,000 sq ft (1,400 sq m). It includes an aerobics room, fitness center (with all the usual muscle-training equipment), treatment rooms, and men's and women's sauna/steam rooms. Another 10,000 sq ft (930 sq m) of space is devoted to a Solarium (with sliding glass-dome roof) to relax in after you've exercised.

On the back of the funnel is a 32.8ft (10m) rock-climbing wall, with five climbing tracks. It's a great buzz being 200ft (60m) above the ocean while the ship is moving. Other sports facilities include a roller-blading track, a dive-and-snorkel shop (with equipment for rent), a full-size basketball court, and a nine-hole, par 26 golf 'course.'

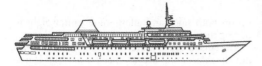

Aegean Odyssey
★★★+

Size:	Small Ship
Tonnage:	12,094
Lifestyle:	Standard
Cruise Line:	Voyages to Antiquity
Former Names:	Aegean I, Aegean Dolphin, Dolphin, Alkyon, Narcis
IMO Number:	7225910
Builder:	Santierul N. Galatz (Romania)
Original Cost:	n/a
Entered Service:	1972/May 2010
Registry:	Malta
Length (ft/m):	460.9/140.5
Beam (ft/m):	67.2/20.5
Draft (ft/m):	20.3/6.2
Propulsion/Propellers:	diesel (10,296kW)/2
Passenger Decks:	8
Total Crew:	200
Passengers (lower beds):	408
Passenger Space Ratio (lower beds):	29.6
Passenger/Crew Ratio (lower beds):	1.8
Cabins (total):	216
Size Range (sq ft/m):	130.0–550.0/12.0–51.0
Cabins (for one person):	26
Cabins (with private balcony):	42
Cabins (wheelchair accessible):	2
Wheelchair accessibility:	Fair
Cabin Current:	220 volts
Elevators:	2
Casino (gaming tables):	No
Slot Machines:	No
Swimming Pools:	1
Hot Tubs (on deck):	0
Self-Service Launderette:	No
Dedicated Cinema/Seats:	No
Library:	Yes
Onboard currency:	US$

Cultural exploration and learning are the big draw

OVERVIEW. *Aegean Odyssey* will appeal to couples and solo travelers looking for a life-enrichment experience in a smart, yet somewhat traditional classic ship environment. The credo is based on history, ancient civilizations, and learning, and the main appeal is the quality of the excursions and lecturers.

THE SHIP. Although this isn't a new ship by any stretch of the imagination, it has been tastefully and skillfully converted to provide an extremely comfortable environment. Its profile is quite smart, with a well-shaped funnel that balances a rather angular stern – the result of a $26 million 'chop-and-stretch' operation some years ago. The present operator, Voyages to Antiquity, bought the ship in December 2007, then set about a painstaking refit and refurbishment program that ended up more like a complete rebuild, because the ship now looks much nicer, and has a pleasing profile.

Originally built to carry munitions, the ship's hull is really strong. The passenger capacity was significantly reduced – from 650 to 378, with a subsequent increase in the passenger/space ratio – in a well thought-out conversion. As a result, the open deck space, covered in teak, is extremely good, and measures 37,674 sq ft (3,500 sq m) – a lot for a small ship.

The Promenade Deck houses most of the public rooms. There is a forward observation lounge, with many windows providing plenty of natural light. The Charleston Lounge – actually a large lounge with a large dance floor and bar – is quite stunning, and sports a classy black and red decor.

Berlitz's Ratings

	Possible	Achieved
Ship	500	348
Accommodation	200	139
Food	400	270
Service	400	291
Entertainment	100	68
Cruise Experience	400	277
OVERALL SCORE		
1393 points out of 2000		

Some materials in public rooms are held together by the 'patch-and-fix' method, but subtle, pleasing, warm color combinations – most with earth tones – help to create a spacious, light, and open feel.

Excellent academic-style lecturers are an intrinsic part of the cruises, which are typically 14 days long, and a good-size library is an important facility. Itineraries include several port overnights.

Gratuities to dining and cabin staff are included in the fare, together with selected wines with dinner (or beer/soft drinks); for non-included drinks, a 12.5 percent service charge is added to bar accounts. Most shore excursions are also included (together with bottled mineral water for the included excursions).

Despite the shakes and rattles of the ship's interior fittings when going at maximum speed, it's the character of the ship, its generous open deck space (and gorgeous thick, highly polished handrails), and an excellent lecture and enrichment program that all help to nudge the final score higher than one might normally expect for a 1970s-built ship.

ACCOMMODATION. There are now many different cabin price grades (six of which are for solo-occupancy cabins), with about half designated as Balcony Class. The accommodation numbering system is nautically incorrect, however, with even-numbered cabins on the starboard side instead of on the port, or left, side of the ship, although the lifeboat numbering is correct. Most cabins have an outside view, with similar sizes and configuration. All have a small refrigerator.

They are reasonably spacious, considering the ship's size, and pleasantly decorated, although closet, drawer, and luggage storage space for two is limited in the lower-grade cabins, particularly for longer cruises. Most bathrooms are partly tiled, with decent storage space for toiletries.

Solo travelers have a choice of 36 single-occupancy cabins (in 6 different grades), most of which are quite spacious.

Two Owner's Suites are located forward on Sun Deck. These are rather nice and have forward ocean views over the bow, and include a narrow balcony on either the port or starboard side. They have a separate bedroom, a walk-in closet, and a bathroom with a tub-shower combination.

DINING. The Marco Polo Restaurant is the ship's main dining room. It is located on the lowest passenger deck (so it's very stable when the ship is at sea). It has a restful color scheme, and a high ceiling. Seating is mostly at large tables – there are no tables for two – in an open-seating arrangement that allows you to dine when you want and with whom you want. The amount of space around each table is good. Portholes, rather than windows, are set high up on both sides, and allow some natural light in during the day.

The cuisine is a mixture of Continental and Asian, but the selection of breads, cheeses, and fruit is limited. Meats, fish, and poultry items are not of a high quality, although they are decent enough for most passengers. For casual meals, self-serve breakfast and lunch buffets are available at the Terrace Café, aft on the Promenade Deck, with indoor-outdoor seating that includes a Tapas Bar each evening ('Tapas on the Terrace'), and daily grilled specialties.

ENTERTAINMENT. The Ambassador Lounge is a single-level showlounge that has a bar at one end, and seating that is mainly in tub-style chairs or old-style banquette seating. The sight lines to the 'stage' from many seats are obstructed, however, because of several support pillars. This room principally serves as a presentation room for the specialist lecturers, and for classical concerts.

SPA/FITNESS. A new indoor wellness centre was built in 2012. It is an attractive facility, and includes a separate male sauna, female wet sauna (steam 'pods'), and a changing area for males and females, two body treatment rooms, plus a beauty salon, and a good-size fitness area.

AIDAaura
★★★+

Size:	Mid-size Ship
Tonnage:	42,289
Lifestyle:	Standard
Cruise Line:	AIDA Cruises
Former Names:	none
IMO Number:	9221566
Builder:	Aker MTW (Germany)
Original Cost:	$350 million
Entered Service:	Apr 2003
Registry:	Italy
Length (ft/m):	665.5/202.8
Beam (ft/m):	92.2/28.1
Draft (ft/m):	20.3/6.2
Propulsion/Propellers:	diesel-electric (27,150kW)/2
Passenger Decks:	10
Total Crew:	389
Passengers (lower beds):	1,266
Passenger Space Ratio (lower beds):	33.4
Passenger/Crew Ratio (lower beds):	3.0
Cabins (total):	633
Size Range (sq ft/m):	145.3–344.4/13.5–32.0
Cabins (for one person):	0
Cabins (with private balcony):	60
Cabins (wheelchair accessible):	4
Wheelchair accessibility:	Good
Cabin Current:	110 and 220 volts
Elevators:	6
Casino (gaming tables):	No
Slot Machines:	No
Swimming Pools:	2
Hot Tubs (on deck):	5
Self-Service Launderette:	Yes
Dedicated Cinema/Seats:	No
Library:	Yes
Onboard currency:	Euros

This upbeat, family-friendly ship is for casual, no-frills cruising

OVERVIEW. An AIDA Cruise is for youthful German-speaking couples, solo travellers, and families seeking good value for money in a party-like environment, with decent entertainment. It's all about über-casual cruising for urbanites, with two main self-serve buffet restaurants, tablecloth-free eating, and little contact with relatively few staff.

THE SHIP. The ship has a smartish profile, with a swept-back funnel and wedge-shaped stern. The bows display the red lips, as well as the blue eyes, of *Aida* (from Verdi's opera, written to commemorate the opening of the Suez Canal in 1871). AIDA Cruises, Germany's largest cruise line, is part of Costa Cruises – itself part of Carnival Corporation.

There are three pricing levels – Aida Premium, Aida Vario, and Just Aida – depending on what you want to be included, plus differences in price according to accommodation size and grade, and the itinerary. Opt for the basic, price-driven Just Aida package, and the cruise line chooses the ship, itinerary, and accommodation for you – sort of a pot-luck cruise, based on or close to the dates you choose.

The dress code is simple: casual (no ties) at all times – there are no formal nights on board. All port taxes and gratuities are included in all packages, and, with very attractive rates, a cruise provides much better value than almost any land-based vacation.

FAMILIES. This is a family-friendly ship. Children are split into five age groups: Seepferdchen ('Seahorses,'

Berlitz's Ratings		
	Possible	Achieved
Ship	500	360
Accommodation	200	131
Food	400	245
Service	400	264
Entertainment	100	71
Cruise Experience	400	276
OVERALL SCORE		
1347 points out of 2000		

for 4–6 years), Delfine ('Dolphins,' for 7–9), Sharks (10–11), Orcas (12–13), and Teens (14–17). Each has its own play area. There is a diverse selection of children's and youth programs, and special Club Team members dedicated to making sure that everyone has a good time.

ACCOMMODATION. There are several grades, from deluxe suites to interior (no-view) cabins, depending on the ship, which keeps your cabin choice simple.

Contrary to maritime tradition (even-numbered cabins on the port side, odd-numbered cabins on the starboard side), cabin numbers progress numerically (example: 8201–8276 on the port side; 8101–8176 on the starboard side). All suites and cabins have two beds (convertible to queen-size bed). Some cabins also have two extra beds/berths for children, and some cabins have interconnecting doors – useful for families.

The decor is bright, youthful, minimalist, even whimsical, and accented with multi-patterned fabrics, wood-trimmed cabinetry (with nicely rounded edges), and rattan or wood-look furniture. Beds have duvets and a colorful Arabian-style fabric canopy from headboard to ceiling. Windows have full pull-down blackout blinds (useful in destinations with long daylight hours). Lifeboats may obstruct views in some cabins in the ship's center.

Bathrooms are compact, practical units, with a shower enclosure, small washbasin, and small toilet. Only a wall-mounted body wash/shampoo dispenser is provided, so take your own conditioner, hand lotion, and other toiletries you need.

Thick, 100 percent cotton bathrobes are provided for suite-grade accommodation, although non-suite grade passengers can obtain one from the spa. Two towels are provided – a face towel and a 'bath' towel. The 'bath' towels are not very large, at 54 by 27 inches – compared to 72 by 36 inches aboard the P&O Cruises' *Ventura*, for example. Although the bathrooms do not have a hairdryer, one is located in the vanity unit in the cabin. Unusually, night-time turndown service is not provided (there is no cabin service after 3pm).

Cabins with balconies have a sliding door that's easy to open and doesn't impinge on balcony space, a small drinks table and two small, light chairs are provided. Balconies on the lowest deck can be overlooked by anyone on a balcony on the decks above. Cabins Nos 5103, 5104, 5105, 5106, 5203, 5204, 5206 (on Deck 5 forward) have an outside view (well, outside light), but they are totally obstructed by steel bulkheads that form the front section of the ship.

Suite-grade accommodation offers more space, including more drawer and storage space, better-quality furniture and furnishings, a larger lounge area, and a slightly larger bathroom with a tub – and a larger balcony (those at the front and stern of the ship have the best views).

DINING. Two eateries are included in the cruise fare; these are the Markt and Karibik self-serve buffet-style restaurants, with open seating at tables of four, six, or eight. Cutlery hangs in a rack (unhygienic because it can be touched by many fingers); there are no soup spoons, only dessert spoons. It's very casual and easy-going mass catering – think food court eating, not formal dining.

When the ship is full, it is challenging to find a seat, not to mention a clean table, and, because it's a buffet venue, you'll be sitting with different people for each meal – which could be a good way to make new friends.

Several food islands and active stations cut down on the waiting time for food. There is always a big selection of breads, cheeses, cold cuts, fruits, and make-your-own coffee and teas – with a choice of loose-leaf regular and herbal teas.

Beer is available at the push of a button or a pull of the tap, and table wine – of the sort that would make a good drain cleaner – is provided in carafes set on tables for lunch and dinner. The beverage stations open only during restaurant opening hours, unless you go to the extra-cost coffee bar (Café Mare). Vending machines dispense out-of-hours snacks.

Other dining options. The small Rossini Restaurant has a quieter, more intimate atmosphere. Open for dinner only, it has a set five- or six-course menu (plus daily specials). An extra charge applies to additional items from an à la carte menu (such as châteaubriand, rib-eye steak), wine, or other drinks. Reservations are needed, tablecloths are provided, the food is good, and the service is friendly.

Vinotheque, a wine bar, located in front of the Weide Welt (Wide World) Restaurant, has a good list of premium wines, and Davidoff cigars (although you can't smoke them at the bar – or anywhere inside the ship).

Pizzeria Mare provides ever-popular pizzas.

ENTERTAINMENT. The Theater (Das Theater) is the venue for shows and most cabaret acts, and is two decks high. It has a raised stage, and amphitheater-style bench seating on all levels. The benches have back rests, and are quite comfortable, and sight lines are good from most seats, with the exception of port and starboard balcony sections, where sight lines are interrupted by thick safety railings.

The trendy, upbeat shows are produced by AIDA Cruises' in-house department in a joint venture with SeeLive (Hamburg's Schmidt's Tivoli Theater). Vocals in the shows are performed live, to pre-recorded backing tracks that mix recorded live music and synthesized sound.

SPA/FITNESS. The Body and Soul Spa, is located forward on Deck 11. It measures 11,840 sq ft (1,100 sq m), and contains two saunas (one dry, one wet, both with seats for more than 20 persons, and glass walls that look onto the deck), massage and other treatment rooms, and a large lounging area. There are also showers, and two 'ice walls' (simply lean into the ice wall for maximum effect). Forward and outside the wellness center is an FKK (Freikoerperkultur) nude sunbathing deck, on two levels.

Sport biking is part of the line's youthful image, with three different levels of cycling to suit differing fitness levels. 'Sport bikes' (mountain bikes with tough front and rear suspension units) are provided for conducted biking excursions in each port of call by a concession run by Austrian downhill champion skier Erwin Resch. You can also book diving and golfing excursions (golf-theme packages include playing at notable courses in many ports of call), play golf in the electronic golf simulator, try billiards, volleyball, or squash – or go jogging.

AIDAbella
★★★+

Size:	Large Resort Ship	Passenger/Crew Ratio (lower beds):	3.1
Tonnage:	69,203	Cabins (total):	1,025
Lifestyle:	Standard	Size Range (sq ft/m):	145.3–473.2/13.5–44
Cruise Line:	AIDA Cruises	Cabins (for one person):	0
Former Names:	none	Cabins (with private balcony):	480
IMO Number:	9362542	Cabins (wheelchair accessible):	11
Builder:	Meyer Werft (Germany)	Wheelchair accessibility:	Good
Original Cost:	$390 million	Cabin Current:	110 and 220 volts
Entered Service:	Apr 2008	Elevators:	10
Registry:	Italy	Casino (gaming tables):	Yes
Length (ft/m):	826.7/252.0	Slot Machines:	No
Beam (ft/m):	105.6/32.2	Swimming Pools:	3
Draft (ft/m):	24.6/7.5	Hot Tubs (on deck):	0
Propulsion/Propellers:	diesel-electric (36,000 kW)/2	Self-Service Launderette:	Yes
Passenger Decks:	13	Dedicated Cinema/Seats:	No
Total Crew:	646	Library:	Yes
Passengers (lower beds):	2,050	Onboard currency:	Euros
Passenger Space Ratio (lower beds):	33.7		

This upbeat, family-friendly ship is for no-frills cruising

OVERVIEW. An AIDA Cruise is for youthful German-speaking couples, solo travellers, and particularly families seeking good value for money in a party-like environment, with excellent entertainment. This is all about über-casual cruising, with two main self-serve buffet restaurants instead of the traditional waiter service. It's tablecloth-less eating, and there is little contact with staff.

Berlitz's Ratings		
	Possible	Achieved
Ship	500	393
Accommodation	200	135
Food	400	250
Service	400	269
Entertainment	100	71
Cruise Experience	400	278
OVERALL SCORE		
1396 points out of 2000		

THE SHIP. The ship has a smart, contemporary profile, with a swept-back funnel and wedge-shaped stern. The bows display the red lips, as well as the blue eyes, of *Aïda* (from Verdi's opera, written to commemorate the opening of the Suez Canal in 1871). AIDA Cruises, Germany's largest cruise line, is part of Costa Cruises, which is itself part of Carnival Corporation.

The open deck space is rather limited, but sunbathing space includes some reasonably quiet space above the navigation bridge. Dip pools and hot tubs, plus seating areas, are provided in a cascading, tiered setting on the pool deck, providing a reasonable amount of sunbathing space. It's all designed to be in a 'beach-like' environment, with splash and play areas.

Several decks of public rooms and facilities are positioned above the accommodation decks, and many of the public room names are common aboard all the ships in the fleet: Aida Bar, for example, the main social gathering place, where the principal feature is a star-shaped bar (its combined length is among the longest at sea), with many tables for standing drinkers.

A small casino features blackjack, roulette and poker gaming tables, and there are also several slot machines. There's also a 'no music' observation lounge, and an art gallery. The embarkation entryway is innovative, has a bar/coffee counter and a lookout 'balcony,' and is cheerfully painted to look like a street scene. It is quite different from the utilitarian gangway entry areas found aboard most cruise ships and provides a welcoming environment.

There are three pricing levels – Aida Premium, Aida Vario, and Just Aida – depending on what you want to be included, plus differences in price according to accommodation size and grade, and the itinerary. Opt for the basic, price-driven 'Just Aida' package, and the cruise line chooses the ship, itinerary, and accommodation for you – sort of a pot-luck cruise, based on or close to the dates you choose.

The dress code is simple: casual (no ties) at all times.

FAMILIES. *AIDAbella* really is a family-friendly ship. Children are split into five age groups: Seepferdchen (4–6 years), Delfine (7–9), Sharks (10–11), Orcas (12–13), and Teens (14–17). Each has its own play area. There is a diverse selection of children's and youth programs in a holiday camp atmosphere, and special Club Team members dedicated to making it all happen. Supervised by a chef, children can make their own menus for the week, and visit the galley to make cookies and other items – a novel idea more cruise lines could adopt.

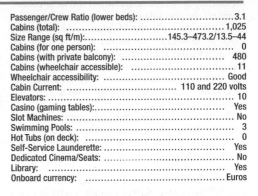

ACCOMMODATION. There are eight or nine grades, from deluxe suites to interior (no-view) cabins, depending on the ship, which keeps your cabin choice simple.

Contrary to maritime traditions (even-numbered cabins on the port side, odd-numbered cabins on the starboard side – like the lifeboats), cabin numbers progress numerically (example: 8201–8276 on the port side; 8101–8176 on the starboard side). All suites and cabins have two beds (convertible to queen-size bed). Some cabins also have two extra beds/berths for children, and some cabins have interconnecting doors – useful for families.

The decor is bright, youthful, minimalist, and slightly whimsical, accented with multi-patterned fabrics, wood-trimmed cabinetry (with nicely rounded edges), and rattan or wood-look furniture. Beds have duvets and a colorful Arabian-style fabric canopy from the headboard to the ceiling. The windows have full pull-down blackout blinds (useful in destinations with long daylight hours).

The bathrooms are compact, practical units, with a shower enclosure, small washbasin, and small toilet. Only a wall-mounted body wash/shampoo dispenser is provided, so take your own conditioner, hand lotion, and other toiletries you may need.

Thick cotton bathrobes are provided, as are a face towel and a 'bath' towel. The 'bath' towels are not large, at 54 by 27 inches – compared to 72 by 36 inches aboard P&O Cruises' *Ventura*, for example. The bathroom does not have a hairdryer, but one is located in the vanity unit in the cabin. Note that the usual night-time turndown service provided aboard most ships is not provided, and there is no cabin service after 3pm.

Cabins with balconies have a sliding door that's easy to open and doesn't impinge on balcony space; a small drinks table and two small, light chairs are provided. Balconies on the lowest deck can be overlooked by anyone on a balcony on the decks above. Balcony cabins have a hammock as standard, but it's just for one (slim) person. Some cabins (forward on Deck 5 – Nos 5103, 5104, 5105, 5106, 5203, 5204, 5206) have cabins with an outside view (well, outside light), but they are obstructed by steel bulkheads.

DINING. There are three self-serve eateries: Markt (Market), Bella Vista (for Italian cuisine), and Weite Welt (Wide World) restaurants. Additionally, there's a Buffalo Steakhouse (which serves excellent steaks), an à la carte Rossini Restaurant with waiter and sommelier service, a Sushi Bar, a Pizzeria Mare, and a Café Mare.

In the three self-serve restaurants, the meal concept is simple: main meals are taken when you want them in one of the large self-serve buffet-style restaurants, with open seating at tables of four, six, or eight. Cutlery can be found hanging in a rack (but this is rather unhygienic because many fingers can touch it); there are no soup spoons, only dessert spoons.

The many food islands and active stations cut down on the waiting time for food. There is always a good selection of breads, cheeses, cold cuts, fruits, and coffee and teas – with a choice of more than 30 types of loose-leaf regular and herbal teas. More than 1,200 items of food are offered, and the fish section has its own fish-smoking unit.

Beer is available at the push of a button or a pull of the tap, and table wine is usually provided in carafes on each table for lunch and dinner. Note that the beverage stations open only during restaurant opening hours, unless you go to the extra-cost coffee bar (Café Mare). Vending machines dispense out-of-hours snacks.

Other dining options. The Rossini Restaurant, with mostly high-back seats, has an intimate atmosphere. It is open for dinner only, and has a set five- or six-course menu, plus daily 'specials.' There is no cover charge, but an extra charge applies to additional items from the à la carte menu, and wines. Reservations are needed. Tablecloths are provided, the food is good, and service is sound.

The Buffalo Steakhouse has an open 'display' kitchen, and offers various steak cuts and sizes – Delmonico, New York Strip Loin, Porterhouse, and Filet, plus bison steaks – and roast lamb rack. There's a daily special – a prix-fixe meal (example: a 180g fillet steak, house salad, and dessert). It's like going out to eat in a decent restaurant ashore – but there are no tablecloths. Wine and any other drinks are extra.

A 12-seater sushi counter is for Japanese-style sushi and sashimi dishes. The Pizzeria Mare provides a small selection of ever popular pizzas.

ENTERTAINMENT. The Theatrium (theater) is in the center of the ship. It is open to the main foyer and other public areas, on three levels (Decks 9, 10, and 11), and topped by a glass dome. Amphitheater-style seating is on three decks (the bench seating on the two upper levels has back supports, but not on the lower level), plus standing tables, although sight lines to the raised thrust stage area are less than good from many of the seats.

SPA/FITNESS. The Body and Soul wellness/oasis area is located on two decks (connected by a stairway) and encompasses some 24,750 sq ft (2,300 sq m). There is also an open-air wellness FKK deck for relaxation/nude sunbathing in an area just forward of the ship's mast. There are saunas and steam rooms, and 14 rooms for massage and other treatments (most named after places associated with the design theme), a fitness room with high-tech machines, neat showers, funky changing rooms, and a tropical garden with real (waxed) palm trees and relaxation loungers. Sport enthusiasts can also play billiards, volleyball or squash – or go jogging.

AIDAblu
★★★+

Size:	Large Resort Ship
Tonnage:	71,100
Lifestyle:	Standard
Cruise Line:	AIDA Cruises
Former Names:	none
IMO Number:	9398888
Builder:	Meyer Werft (Germany)
Original Cost:	€350 million
Entered Service:	Apr 2010
Registry:	Italy
Length (ft/m):	831.1/253.3
Beam (ft/m):	105.6/32.2
Draft (ft/m):	24.6/7.5
Propulsion/Propellers:	diesel-electric (36,000 kW)/2
Passenger Decks:	14
Total Crew:	646
Passengers (lower beds):	2,194
Passenger Space Ratio (lower beds):	34.4

Passenger/Crew Ratio (lower beds):	3.1
Cabins (total):	1,096
Size Range (sq ft/m):	145.3–473.2/13.5–44
Cabins (for one person):	0
Cabins (with private balcony):	491
Cabins (wheelchair accessible):	11
Wheelchair accessibility:	Good
Cabin Current:	110 and 220 volts
Elevators:	10
Casino (gaming tables):	Yes
Slot Machines:	No
Swimming Pools:	3
Hot Tubs (on deck):	0
Self-Service Launderette:	Yes
Dedicated Cinema/Seats:	No
Library:	Yes
Onboard currency:	Euros

An upbeat, family-friendly ship for no-frills cruising

OVERVIEW. AIDA Cruises is for youthful German-speaking couples, solo travellers, and particularly families seeking good value for money in a party-like environment, with excellent entertainment. This is all about über-casual cruising, with two main self-serve buffet restaurants instead of the traditional waiter service.

THE SHIP. The ship has a smart, contemporary profile, with a swept-back funnel and wedge-shaped stern. The bows display the red lips, as well as the blue eyes, of *Aida* (from Verdi's opera, written to commemorate the opening of the Suez Canal in 1871). AIDA Cruises, Germany's largest cruise line, is part of Costa Cruises, which is itself part of Carnival Corporation.

Several decks of public rooms and facilities are positioned above the accommodation decks, and *AIDAblu* shares public room names common to all the ships in the fleet: Aida Bar, for example, the main social gathering place, where the principal feature is a star-shaped bar (it's among the longest at sea), with many tables for standing drinkers.

A small casino features blackjack, roulette and poker gaming tables, and there are also a number of slot machines. There is also a separate aft sports deck, a 'no music' observation lounge, and an 'art' gallery. The embarkation entryway is innovative, has a bar and a lookout 'balcony', and is cheerfully painted to look like a street scene in a city such as Copenhagen. A welcoming environment, it helps to calm tempers after waiting in a line to go through the security process for embarkation or in ports of call.

Berlitz's Ratings		
	Possible	Achieved
Ship	500	393
Accommodation	200	135
Food	400	251
Service	400	269
Entertainment	100	71
Cruise Experience	400	278
OVERALL SCORE		
1397 points out of 2000		

There are three pricing levels – Aida Premium, Aida Vario, and Just Aida – depending on what you want to be included, plus differences in price according to accommodation size and grade, and the itinerary. Opt for the basic, price-driven 'Just Aida' package, and the cruise line chooses the ship, itinerary, and accommodation for you – sort of a pot-luck cruise, based on or close to the dates you choose.

The dress code is simple: casual (no ties) at all times, and there are no 'formal' dress-up nights on board. All port taxes and gratuities are included in all cruises.

FAMILIES. *AIDAblu* really is family-friendly. Children are split into five age groups: Seepferdchen (4–6 years), Delfine (7–9), Sharks (10–11), Orcas (12–13), and Teens (14–17). Each has its own play area. There is a diverse selection of children's and youth programs in a holiday camp atmosphere, and special Club Team members dedicated to making it all happen. Supervised by a chef, children can make their own menus for the week, and visit the galley to make cookies and other items – a novel idea more cruise lines could adopt.

ACCOMMODATION. There are several price grades, from deluxe suites to interior (no-view) cabins, so cabin choice is simple.

Contrary to maritime traditions (even-numbered cabins on the port side, odd-numbered cabins on the starboard side), cabin numbers progress numerically (example: 8201–8276 on the port side; 8101–8176 on the starboard side). All suites and cabins have two beds (convertible to queen-size bed). Some cabins also have two extra beds/berths for children, and some cabins have interconnecting doors.

The decor is bright, youthful, rather minimalist, and slightly whimsical. All are accented with multi-patterned fabrics, wood-trimmed cabinetry, and rattan or wood-look furniture. Beds have duvets and a colorful canopy from headboard to ceiling. The windows have full pull-down blackout blinds (useful in destinations with long daylight hours).

Bathrooms are compact, practical units; they have a shower enclosure, small washbasin, and small toilet. As in most basic hotels and motels, only a wall-mounted body wash/shampoo dispenser is provided, so take your own conditioner, hand lotion, and any other toiletries you may need.

Thick cotton bathrobes are provided, as are two towels – a face towel and a 'bath' towel, in two different colors. The 'bath' towels are not large, at 54 by 27 inches – compared to 72 by 36 inches aboard P&O Cruises' *Ventura*, for example. The bathroom does not have a hairdryer (it's located in the vanity unit in the cabin). There is no night-time turndown service and no cabin service after 3pm.

Cabins with balconies have a sliding door that's easy to open and doesn't impinge on balcony space; a small drinks table and two small, light chairs are provided. Note that balconies on the lowest deck can be overlooked by anyone on a balcony on the decks above. Balcony cabins have a hammock as standard, although it only accommodates one (thin) person. Some cabins (forward on Deck 5 – Nos 5103, 5104, 5105, 5106, 5203, 5204, 5206) have cabins with an outside view (well, outside light), but they are obstructed by steel bulkheads.

Naturally, suite-grade accommodation offers more space, including more drawer and storage space, better-quality furniture and furnishings, a larger lounge area, and a bathroom with a tub – and a larger balcony (those at the front and stern of the ship are the most desirable).

DINING. There are three self-serve eateries: Markt (Market), Bella Vista (for Italian cuisine), and Weite Welt (Wide World) restaurants. The opening times for lunch and dinner are typically 12.30–2pm and 6.30–9pm respectively. Additionally, there's a Buffalo Steakhouse (which serves excellent steaks), an à la carte Rossini Restaurant with waiter and sommelier service, a Sushi Bar, a Pizzeria Mare, and a Café Mare. These venues are open at set times (there are no 24-hour-a-day outlets, because there is little demand for them), although the Pizzeria typically is open until midnight.

In the three self-serve restaurants, the meal concept is simple: main meals are taken when you want them in one of the large self-serve buffet-style restaurants, with open seating at tables of four, six, or eight. Cutlery hangs in a rack (a rather unhygienic arrangement), and there are no soup spoons, only dessert spoons.

The many food islands and active stations cut down on the waiting time for food. There is always a big selection of breads, cheeses, cold cuts, fruits, and make-your-own coffee and teas – with a choice of more than 30 types of loose-leaf regular and herbal teas. More than 1,200 items of food are offered, and the fish section has its own fish-smoking unit.

Beer is available at the push of a button or a pull of the tap, and table wine is usually provided in carafes on each table for lunch and dinner. Note that the beverage stations open only during restaurant opening hours, unless you go to the extra-cost coffee bar (Café Mare). In case you want something to nibble on, vending machines dispense out-of-hours snacks.

Other dining options. The Rossini Restaurant, with mostly high-back seats, is small and intimate. It is open for dinner only, and has a set five- or six-course menu, plus daily 'specials.' There is no cover charge, but an extra charge applies to additional items from the à la carte menu (such as caviar, châteaubriand, rib-eye steak), and wines. Reservations are needed. Tablecloths are provided, the food is rather good, and service is sound.

The Buffalo Steakhouse has an open 'display' kitchen, and offers various steak cuts and sizes – Delmonico, New York Strip Loin, Porterhouse, and Filet, plus bison steaks – and roast lamb rack. There's a daily special – a prix-fixe meal (example: a 180g fillet steak, house salad, and dessert). It's like going out to eat in a decent restaurant ashore – but there are no tablecloths. Wine or any other drinks cost extra.

A 12-seater sushi counter is for Japanese-style sushi and sashimi dishes, at extra cost.

A wine bar, Vinotheque, located in front of the Weide Welt (Wide World) Restaurant, has a list of premium wines, and Davidoff cigars (although you can't smoke them at the bar – or anywhere inside the ship).

ENTERTAINMENT. The Theatrium (theater) is in the center of the ship. It is open to the main foyer and other public areas, on three levels (Decks 9, 10, and 11), and topped by a glass dome. Amphitheater-style seating is on three decks (the bench seating on the two upper levels has back supports, but not on the lower level), plus standing tables, although sight lines to the raised thrust stage area are less than good from many of the seats.

SPA/FITNESS. The spa, fitness, and sports programming is extensive. The Body and Soul wellness/oasis area is located on two decks (connected by a stairway) and encompasses 24,750 sq ft (2,300 sq m). There is also an open-air wellness FKK deck for relaxation/nude sunbathing in an area forward of the ship's mast.

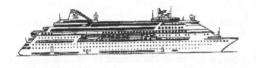

AIDAcara
★★★+

Size:	Mid-size Ship	Passenger/Crew Ratio (lower beds):	3.1
Tonnage:	38,557	Cabins (total):	590
Lifestyle:	Standard	Size Range (sq ft/m):	145.3–376.7/13.5–35.0
Cruise Line:	AIDA Cruises	Cabins (for one person):	0
Former Names:	Aida, Das Clubschiff	Cabins (with private balcony):	48
IMO Number:	9112789	Cabins (wheelchair accessible):	6
Builder:	Kvaerner Masa-Yards (Finland)	Wheelchair accessibility:	Good
Original Cost:	DM300 million	Cabin Current:	110 and 220 volts
Entered Service:	Jun 1996	Elevators:	5
Registry:	Italy	Casino (gaming tables):	No
Length (ft/m):	634.1/193.3	Slot Machines:	No
Beam (ft/m):	90.5/27.6	Swimming Pools:	1
Draft (ft/m):	19.6/6.0	Hot Tubs (on deck):	2
Propulsion/Propellers:	diesel(21,720kw)/2	Self-Service Launderette:	Yes
Passenger Decks:	9	Dedicated Cinema/Seats:	No
Total Crew:	370	Library:	Yes
Passengers (lower beds):	1,180	Onboard currency:	Euros
Passenger Space Ratio (lower beds):	32.6		

This is a busy, family-friendly ship for a frugal cruise

OVERVIEW. *AIDAcara* is for youthful and young-at-heart German-speaking couples, solo travellers, and particularly families seeking good value for money in a party-like environment, with good entertainment. This is über-casual cruising, with two main self-serve buffet restaurants instead of traditional waiter service. It's tablecloth-less eating, a bit like camping at sea, with little contact with the relatively few staff.

Berlitz's Ratings		
	Possible	Achieved
Ship	500	340
Accommodation	200	131
Food	400	244
Service	400	262
Entertainment	100	68
Cruise Experience	400	270
OVERALL SCORE		
1315 points out of 2000		

THE SHIP. The ship has a modern profile, with a swept-back funnel and wedge-shaped stern. The bows display the red lips and blue eyes, of *Aida* (from Verdi's opera, written to commemorate the opening of the Suez Canal in 1871). AIDA Cruises, Germany's largest cruise line, is part of Costa Cruises, which is itself part of the giant Carnival Corporation.

The open deck space is pretty tight, but sunbathing space includes some rather pleasant, reasonably quiet space above the navigation bridge. Dip pools and hot tubs, plus seating areas, are provided in a cascading, tiered setting atop the ship on the pool deck, providing a decent amount of sunbathing space. It's all designed to be in a 'beach-like' environment, with splash and play areas.

Some decks of public rooms and facilities are positioned above the accommodation decks. Public rooms that have become common aboard all the ships include Aida Bar, the main social gathering place, where the principal feature is a star-shaped bar (whose combined length per ship probably makes them the longest at sea), with many tables for standing drinkers.

Other facilities include a shore excursion counter, library, seminar rooms, duty-free shop, several bars and lounges, and eateries.

There are three pricing levels – Aida Premium, Aida Vario, and Just Aida – depending on what you want to be included, plus differences in price according to accommodation size and grade, and the itinerary. Opt for the basic, price-driven 'Just Aida' package, and the cruise line chooses the ship, itinerary, and accommodation for you – sort of a pot-luck cruise, based on or close to the dates you choose.

The dress code is simple: casual (no ties) at all times – there are no formal nights on board. All port taxes and gratuities are included in all packages, and, with very attractive rates, a cruise provides much better value than almost any land-based vacation.

FAMILIES. *AIDAcara* is a family-friendly ship. Children are split into five age groups: Seepferdchen (4–6 years), Delfine (7–9), Sharks (10–11), Orcas (12–13), and Teens (14–17). Each has its own play area. There is a selection of children's and youth programs in a holiday camp atmosphere, and special Club Team members dedicated to making it all happen. Supervised by a chef, children can make their own menus for the week, and visit the galley to make cookies and other items.

ACCOMMODATION. There are several grades, from deluxe suites to interior (no-view) cabins, which makes cabin choice simple.

Contrary to maritime tradition (even-numbered cabins on the port side, odd-numbered cabins on the starboard side), cabin numbers progress numerically (example: 8201–8276 on the port side; 8101–8176 on the starboard side). All suites and cabins have two beds (convertible to queen-size bed). Some cabins also have two extra beds/berths for children, and some cabins have interconnecting doors – useful for families.

The decor is bright, youthful, minimalist, and slightly whimsical. All are accented with multi-patterned fabrics, wood-trimmed cabinetry (with nicely rounded edges), and rattan or wood-look furniture. Beds have duvets and a colorful Arabian-style fabric canopy from the headboard to the ceiling. The windows have full pull-down blackout blinds (useful in destinations with long daylight hours). Lifeboats may obstruct views in some cabins in the ship's center.

The bathrooms are compact, practical units; they have a shower enclosure, small washbasin, and small toilet. As in the most basic hotels and motels, only a wall-mounted body wash/shampoo dispenser is provided, so take your own conditioner, hand lotion, and other toiletries you may need.

Thick cotton bathrobes are provided for suite-grade accommodation only, although non-suite grade passengers can obtain one from the spa. Two towels are provided – a face towel and a 'bath' towel, in two different colors. The 'bath' towels are not very large, at 54 by 27 inches – compared to 72 by 36 inches aboard P&O Cruises' *Azura*, for example. Although the bathrooms do not have a hairdryer, one is located in the vanity unit in the cabin. Nighttime turndown service is not provided, and there is no cabin service after 3pm.

Cabins with balconies have a sliding door that's easy to open and doesn't impinge on balcony space; a small drinks table and two small, light chairs are provided. Note that balconies on the lowest deck can be overlooked by anyone on a balcony on the decks above. Naturally, suite-grade accommodation offers more space, including more drawer and storage space, better-quality furniture and furnishings, a larger lounge area, and a slightly larger bathroom with a tub – and a larger balcony (those at the front and stern of the ship have the best).

DINING. Two eateries are included in the cruise fare: the self-serve Markt and Karibik restaurants. The opening times for lunch and dinner are 12.30–2pm and 6.30–9pm respectively. There's also Rossini, a decent enough à la carte (extra-charge) tablecloth dining spot that serves good-quality meals cooked à la minute, and has friendly waiter service.

Main meals are taken when you want them in one of the large self-serve buffet-style restaurants, with open seating at tables of four, six, or eight. Cutlery

hangs in a rack, but there are no soup spoons, only dessert spoons.

The tables are almost all large, and, when the ship is full, it can prove challenging to find a seat, not to mention service personnel to clean the tables.

The standard of food at the self-serve buffet islands ranges from adequate to quite good, with creative displays and presentation, and table-clearing service that is sometimes efficient, but mostly not.

The many food islands and active stations cut down on the waiting time for food. There is always a big selection of breads, cheeses, cold cuts, fruits, and make-your-own coffee and teas – with a choice of more than 30 types of loose-leaf regular and herbal teas. In all, over 1,200 items of food are offered.

Beer is available at the push of a button or a pull of the tap, and table wine – of the sort that would make a good drain cleaner – is usually provided in carafes on each table for lunch and dinner. Note that the beverage stations open only during restaurant opening hours, unless you go to the extra-cost coffee bar (Café Mare). Vending machines dispense out-of-hours snacks.

Other dining options. The Rossini Restaurant (à la carte), with mostly high-back seats, has an intimate atmosphere. Open for dinner only, it has a set five- or six-course menu (plus daily specials). There is no cover charge, but an extra charge applies to everything on the à la carte menu (such as chateaubriand, rib-eye steak), and for wines. Reservations are needed, tablecloths are provided, the food is good, and waiter and sommelier service are quite friendly.

ENTERTAINMENT. The Theater, the main venue for all shows and most cabaret, is two decks high, with a raised stage, and amphitheater-style bench seating on all levels. The benches have back rests, and are quite comfortable, and sight lines are good from most seats, with the exception of port and starboard balcony sections, where sight lines are interrupted by thick safety railings.

In addition, there is a live band in the Aida Bar, the only room with a large dance floor (except for the disco).

SPA/FITNESS. The Body and Soul Spa, is located forward on Deck 11, measures 11,840 sq ft (1,100 sq m), and contains two saunas (one dry, one wet, both with seats for more than 20 persons and glass walls that look onto the deck), body treatment rooms, and lounging area. There are also showers, and two whole 'ice walls' to use adjacent to the saunas (simply lean into the ice wall for maximum effect). Forward, and outside the wellness center, is an FKK (Freikoerperkultur) nude sunbathing deck, on two levels. A beauty and hair salon is located separately just behind the balcony level of the showlounge.

AIDAdiva
★★★+

Size:	Large Resort Ship	Passenger/Crew Ratio (lower beds):	3.1
Tonnage:	69,203	Cabins (total):	1,025
Lifestyle:	Standard	Size Range (sq ft/m):	145.3–473.2/13.5–44
Cruise Line:	AIDA Cruises	Cabins (for one person):	0
Former Names:	none	Cabins (with private balcony):	480
IMO Number:	9334856	Cabins (wheelchair accessible):	11
Builder:	Meyer Werft (Germany)	Wheelchair accessibility:	Good
Original Cost:	$390 million	Cabin Current:	110 and 220 volts
Entered Service:	Apr 2007	Elevators:	10
Registry:	Italy	Casino (gaming tables):	Yes
Length (ft/m):	830.0/253.3	Slot Machines:	No
Beam (ft/m):	105.6/32.2	Swimming Pools:	3
Draft (ft/m):	24.6/7.5	Hot Tubs (on deck):	0
Propulsion/Propellers:	diesel-electric (36,000 kW)/2	Self-Service Launderette:	Yes
Passenger Decks:	13	Dedicated Cinema/Seats:	No
Total Crew:	646	Library:	Yes
Passengers (lower beds):	2,050	Onboard currency:	Euros
Passenger Space Ratio (lower beds):	33.7		

Try this large family-friendly ship for a good-time experience

OVERVIEW. An *AIDAdiva* cruise is for youthful German-speaking couples, solo travelers, and families seeking a fun-filled environment, with good entertainment. This is all about über-casual cruising, with two main self-serve buffet restaurants and tablecloth-less eating.

THE SHIP. The ship has a contemporary profile, swept-back funnel, and wedge-shaped stern, and the red lips (on the bows) and blue eyes of *Aïda* (from Verdi's opera, written to commemorate the opening of the Suez Canal in 1871). AIDA Cruises, Germany's largest cruise line, is part of Costa Cruises, itself part of Carnival Corporation.

Several decks of public rooms and facilities are positioned above the accommodation decks, and *AIDAdiva* shares public room names that are common aboard all the ships in the fleet: Aida Bar, for example, the main social gathering place, where the principal feature is a star-shaped bar (whose combined length makes it among the longest at sea), with many tables for standing drinkers. There's also a 'no music' observation lounge, and an 'art' gallery.

A small casino features blackjack, roulette, and poker tables, and there are also a number of slot machines. The embarkation entryway is innovative; it has a bar and a lookout 'balcony,' and is cheerfully painted to look like a street scene in a city such as Copenhagen. Different from the utilitarian gangway entry areas found aboard most cruise ships, it is a welcoming environment.

Berlitz's Ratings		
	Possible	Achieved
Ship	500	377
Accommodation	200	135
Food	400	249
Service	400	269
Entertainment	100	68
Cruise Experience	400	277
OVERALL SCORE		
1375 points out of 2000		

There are three pricing levels – Aida Premium, Aida Vario, and Just Aida – depending on what you want to be included, plus differences in price according to accommodation size and grade, and the itinerary. Opt for the basic, price-driven 'Just Aida' package, and the cruise line chooses the ship, itinerary, and accommodation for you – sort of a pot-luck cruise, based on or close to the dates you choose.

The dress code is simple: casual (no ties) at all times, and no 'formal' dress-up nights on board. Port taxes and gratuities are included.

FAMILIES. *AIDAdiva* really is a family-friendly ship. Children are split into five age groups: Seepferdchen (4–6 years), Delfine (7–9), Sharks (10–11), Orcas (12–13), and Teens (14–17). Each has its own play area. There is a diverse selection of children's and youth programs in a holiday camp atmosphere, and special Club Team members dedicated to making it all happen. Supervised by a chef, children can make their own menus for the week, and visit the galley to make cookies and other items – a novel idea more cruise lines could adopt.

ACCOMMODATION. There are several grades, from deluxe suites to interior (no-view) cabins, depending on the ship, which keeps your cabin choice simple.

Contrary to maritime traditions (even-numbered cabins on the port side, odd-numbered cabins on the starboard side), cabin numbers progress numerically (example: 8201–8276 on the port side;

8101–8176 on the starboard side). All suites and cabins have two beds (convertible to queen-size bed). Some cabins also have two extra beds/berths for children, and some have interconnecting doors – useful for families.

The decor is bright, youthful, rather minimalist, and slightly whimsical. All are accented with multi-patterned fabrics, wood-trimmed cabinetry, and rattan or wood-look furniture. Beds have duvets and a colourful canopy from headboard to ceiling, and windows have full pull-down blackout blinds (useful in destinations with long daylight hours).

The bathrooms are compact, with a shower enclosure, small washbasin, and toilet. Only a wall-mounted body wash/shampoo dispenser is provided, so take your own conditioner, hand lotion, and other toiletries you may need.

Thick cotton bathrobes are provided for all grades of accommodation, as are two towels – a face towel and a 'bath' towel. The 'bath' towels are not large, at 54 by 27 inches – compared to 72 by 36 inches aboard P&O Cruises' Ventura, for example. The bathroom does not have a hairdryer – it's located in the vanity unit in the cabin. There is no cabin service after 3pm, and no night-time turn-down service.

Cabins with balconies have a sliding door that's easy to open and doesn't impinge on balcony space; a small drinks table and two small, light chairs are provided. Note that balconies on the lowest deck can be overlooked by anyone on a balcony on the decks above. Balcony cabins have a hammock as standard (for one thin person).

Some cabins (forward on Deck 5 – Nos 5103, 5104, 5105, 5106, 5203, 5204, 5206) have cabins with an outside view (well, outside light), but they are obstructed by steel bulkheads that form the front section of the ship.

Naturally, suite-grade accommodation offers more space, including more drawer and storage space, better-quality furniture and furnishings, a larger lounge area, and a slightly larger bathroom with a tub – and a larger balcony (those at the front and stern of the ship are the best and most desirable).

DINING. There are three self-serve eateries: Markt (Market), Bella Vista (for Italian cuisine), and Weite Welt (Wide World) restaurants. The opening times for lunch and dinner are 12.30–2pm and 6.30–9pm respectively. Additionally, there's a Buffalo Steakhouse (which serves excellent steaks), an à la carte Rossini Restaurant with waiter and sommelier service, a Sushi Bar, a Pizzeria Mare, and a Café Mare. These venues are open at set times (there are no 24-hour-a-day outlets, because there is little demand for them), although the Pizzeria typically stays open until midnight.

In the three self-serve restaurants, the meal concept is simple: main meals are taken when you want them in one of the large self-serve buffet-style restaurants, with open seating at tables of four, six, or eight. Cutlery hangs in a rack (a somewhat unhygienic arrangement), but there are no soup spoons, only dessert spoons.

The many food islands and active stations help reduce the waiting time for food. There is always a good selection of breads, cheeses, cold cuts, fruits, and make-your-own coffee and teas.

Beer is available at the push of a button or a pull of the tap, and table wine – of the sort that would make a good drain cleaner – is usually provided in carafes on each table for lunch and dinner. Note that beverage stations open only during restaurant opening hours, unless you go to the extra-cost coffee bar (Café Mare).

Other dining options. The Rossini Restaurant, with mostly high-back seats, has an intimate atmosphere, and tablecloths. It is open for dinner only, and has a set five- or six-course menu, plus daily 'specials.' There is no cover charge, but an extra charge applies to additional items from the à la carte menu (such as caviar, châteaubriand, rib-eye steak), and wine or any other drinks. Reservations are needed.

The Buffalo Steakhouse has an open 'display' kitchen, and offers various prime steak cuts and sizes – Delmonico, New York Strip Loin, Porterhouse, and Filet, plus bison steaks – and roast lamb rack. It's like going out to eat in a decent restaurant ashore. Wine or any other drinks cost extra.

A 12-seater sushi counter is for Japanese-style sushi and sashimi dishes. The Pizzeria Mare provides a small selection of ever-popular pizzas.

ENTERTAINMENT. The Theatrium (theater) is in the center of the ship. It is open to the main foyer and other public areas, on three levels (Decks 9, 10, and 11), and topped by a glass dome. Amphitheater-style seating is on three decks (the bench seating on the two upper levels has back supports, but not on the lower level), plus standing tables, although sight lines to the raised thrust stage area are less than good from many of the seats.

The shows (each is just 30 minutes long) are produced by AIDA Cruises' in-house department in a joint venture with SeeLive (Hamburg's Schmidt's Tivoli Theater), and consist of around 12 performers. Show vocals are performed live to pre-recorded backing tracks that provide a mix of recorded live music and synthesized sound (there's no live band on stage). The shows are trendy, upbeat, fun, and very entertaining.

SPA/FITNESS. The spa, fitness, and sports programming is extensive. The Body and Soul wellness/oasis area is located on two decks (connected by a stairway) and encompasses some 24,750 sq ft (2,300 sq m). There is also an open-air wellness FKK deck for relaxation/nude sunbathing (atop the ship forward of the ship's mast).

AIDAluna
★★★+

Size:	Large Resort Ship	Passenger/Crew Ratio (lower beds):	3.1
Tonnage:	69,203	Cabins (total):	1,025
Lifestyle:	Standard	Size Range (sq ft/m):	145.3 –473.2/13.5–44
Cruise Line:	AIDA Cruises	Cabins (for one person):	0
Former Names:	none	Cabins (with private balcony):	480
IMO Number:	9334868	Cabins (wheelchair accessible):	11
Builder:	Meyer Werft (Germany)	Wheelchair accessibility:	Good
Original Cost:	$390 million	Cabin Current:	110 and 220 volts
Entered Service:	Apr 2009	Elevators:	10
Registry:	Italy	Casino (gaming tables):	Yes
Length (ft/m):	831.1/253.3	Slot Machines:	No
Beam (ft/m):	105.6/32.2	Swimming Pools:	3
Draft (ft/m):	24.6/7.5	Hot Tubs (on deck):	0
Propulsion/Propellers:	diesel-electric (36,000 kW)/2	Self-Service Launderette:	Yes
Passenger Decks:	13	Dedicated Cinema/Seats:	No
Total Crew:	646	Library:	Yes
Passengers (lower beds):	2,050	Onboard currency:	Euros
Passenger Space Ratio (lower beds):	33.7		

Upbeat, family-friendly, and cheerful, but there's little finesse

OVERVIEW. An *AIDAluna* cruise is for youthful German-speaking couples, solo travellers, and families seeking a party-like environment, with excellent entertainment. This is all about über-casual cruising, with two main self-serve buffet restaurants instead of the traditional waiter service. It's tablecloth-free eating, with few staff.

THE SHIP. The ship has a modern profile, with a swept-back funnel and wedge-shaped stern. The bows display the red lips and blue eyes of *Aïda* (from Verdi's opera, written to commemorate the opening of the Suez Canal in 1871). AIDA Cruises is part of Costa Cruises, itself part of the giant Carnival Corporation.

Several decks of public rooms and facilities are positioned above the accommodation decks, and *AIDAluna* shares public room names that are common aboard all the AIDA Cruises ships: Aida Bar, for example, the main social gathering place, where the principal feature is a star-shaped bar (its combined length makes it among the longest at sea), with many tables for standing drinkers.

There is a separate aft sports deck, a 'no music' observation lounge, an art gallery, plus a small casino featuring blackjack, roulette, and poker gaming tables, and a number of slot machines. The embarkation entryway has a bar and a lookout 'balcony,' and is cheerfully painted to look like a waterside street scene. A welcoming environment, it helps to calm tempers after waiting in a line to go through the security check for embarkation or in ports of call.

Berlitz's Ratings

	Possible	Achieved
Ship	500	378
Accommodation	200	135
Food	400	250
Service	400	269
Entertainment	100	71
Cruise Experience	400	277
OVERALL SCORE		
1380 points out of 2000		

There are three pricing levels – Aida Premium, Aida Vario, and Just Aida – depending on what you want to be included, plus differences in price according to accommodation size and grade, and itinerary.

The dress code is simple: casual (no ties) at all times. All port taxes and gratuities are included.

FAMILIES. *AIDAluna* is a family-friendly ship. Children are split into five age groups: Seepferdchen (4–6 years), Delfine (7–9), Sharks (10–11), Orcas (12–13), and Teens (14–17). Each has its own play area. There is a wide selection of children's and youth programs in a holiday camp atmosphere, and special Club Team members dedicated to making it all happen. Supervised by a chef, children can make their own menus for the week, and visit the galley to make cookies and other items – a novel idea more cruise lines could adopt.

ACCOMMODATION. There are eight or nine grades, from deluxe suites to interior (no-view) cabins, depending on the ship, which keeps your cabin choice simple.

Contrary to maritime tradition (even-numbered cabins on the port side, odd-numbered cabins on the starboard side), cabin numbers progress numerically (example: 8201–8276 on the port side; 8101–8176 on the starboard side). All suites and cabins have two beds (convertible to queen-size bed). Some cabins also have two extra beds/berths for children, and some cabins have interconnecting doors – useful for families.

The decor is bright, youthful, minimalist, and slightly whimsical. All rooms are accented with multi-patterned fabrics, wood-trimmed cabinetry (with nicely rounded edges), and rattan or wood-look furniture. Beds have duvets and a colorful Arabian-style fabric canopy that goes from the headboard to the ceiling. The windows have full pull-down blackout blinds (useful in destinations with long daylight hours).

The bathrooms are compact, practical units, with shower enclosure, small washbasin, and small toilet. As in the most basic hotels and motels, only a wall-mounted body wash/shampoo dispenser is provided, so take any personal toiletries you may need.

Thick cotton bathrobes are provided for everyone, as are two towels – a face towel and a 'bath' towel, in two different colors. The 'bath' towels are not large, at 54 by 27 inches – compared to 72 by 36 inches aboard P&O Cruises' *Ventura*, for example. The bathroom does not have a hairdryer, but one is located in the vanity unit in the cabin. Note that the usual night-time turndown service provided aboard most ships is not provided, and there is no cabin service after 3pm.

Cabins with balconies have an easy-open sliding door that doesn't impinge on balcony space, a small drinks table and two small, light chairs. Note that balconies on the lowest deck can be overlooked by anyone on a balcony on the decks above. Balcony cabins have a hammock as standard, although it only accommodates one (slim) person. Some cabins (forward on Deck 5 – Nos 5103, 5104, 5105, 5106, 5203, 5204, 5206) have cabins with an outside view (well, outside light), but they are obstructed by steel bulkheads that form the front section of the ship.

DINING. There are three self-serve eateries: Markt (Market), Bella Vista (for Italian cuisine), and Weite Welt (Wide World) restaurants. Additionally, there's a Buffalo Steakhouse (which serves excellent steaks), an à la carte Rossini Restaurant with waiter and sommelier service, a Sushi Bar, a Pizzeria Mare, and a Café Mare. These venues are open at set times (there are no 24-hour-a-day outlets, because there is little demand for them), although the Pizzeria typically stays open until midnight.

In the three self-serve restaurants, the meal concept is simple: main meals are taken when you want them in one of the large self-serve buffet-style restaurants, with open seating at tables of four, six, or eight. Cutlery can be found hanging in a rack (this is thought to be somewhat unhygienic), but there are no soup spoons, only dessert spoons.

The many food islands and active stations cut down on the waiting time for food. There is always a big selection of breads, cheeses, cold cuts, fruits, and make-your-own coffee and teas – with a choice of more than 30 types of loose-leaf regular and herbal teas. More than 1,200 items of food are offered. The fish section has its own fish-smoking unit (it resembles a wine cabinet).

Beer is available at the push of a button or a pull of the tap, and table wine – of the sort that would make a good drain cleaner – is usually provided in carafes on each table for lunch and dinner. It's simply casual and easy-going mass catering, so think food court eating – it certainly can't be called dining, but is more like camping at sea. The beverage stations open only during restaurant opening hours, unless you go to the extra-cost coffee bar. Vending machines dispense out-of-hours snacks.

Other dining options. The à la carte Rossini Restaurant, with mostly high-back seats, has an intimate atmosphere. It is open for dinner only, and has a set five- or six-course menu, plus daily 'specials.' There is no cover charge, but everything on the à la carte menu (such as caviar, châteaubriand, rib-eye steak), and wines, costs extra. Reservations are needed. Tablecloths are provided, the food is very good, and service is sound.

The Buffalo Steakhouse has an open 'display' kitchen, and offers various steak cuts and sizes – Delmonico, New York Strip Loin, Porterhouse, and Filet, plus bison steaks – and roast lamb rack. It's like going out to eat in a decent restaurant ashore, without tablecloths. Wine or any other drinks cost extra.

There is a 12-stool counter for Japanese-style sushi and sashimi dishes.

A wine bar, Vinotheque, located in front of the Weide Welt (Wide World) Restaurant, has a list of premium wines, and Davidoff cigars (although you can't smoke them at the bar – or anywhere inside the ship).

The Pizzeria Mare provides a small selection of ever-popular pizzas.

ENTERTAINMENT. The Theatrium (theater) is in the center of the ship. It is open to the main foyer and other public areas, on three levels (Decks 9, 10, and 11), and topped by a glass dome. Amphitheater-style seating is on three decks (the bench seating on the two upper levels has back supports, but not on the lower level), and standing tables, although sight lines to the raised thrust stage area are poor from many seats.

SPA/FITNESS. The spa, fitness, and sports programming are extensive. The Body and Soul wellness/oasis area is located on two decks (connected by a stairway) and encompasses 24,750 sq ft (2,300 sq m). There is also an open-air wellness deck for FKK relaxation/nude sunbathing in an area atop the ship forward of the ship's mast. In keeping with the times, all the trendy treatments are featured in an appealing contemporary setting.

AIDAmar
★★★+

Size:	....	Large Resort Ship
Tonnage:	....	71,304
Lifestyle:	....	Standard
Cruise Line:	....	AIDA Cruises
Former Names:	....	*none*
IMO Number:	....	9490052
Builder:	....	Meyer Werft (Germany)
Original Cost:	....	€350 million
Entered Service:	....	Apr 2012
Registry:	....	Italy
Length (ft/m):	....	831.1/253.3
Beam (ft/m):	....	105.6/32.2
Draft (ft/m):	....	24.6/7.5
Propulsion/Propellers:	....	diesel-electric (36,000 kW)/2
Passenger Decks:	....	14
Total Crew:	....	646
Passengers (lower beds):	....	2,194
Passenger Space Ratio (lower beds):	....	34.6

Passenger/Crew Ratio (lower beds):	....	3.1
Cabins (total):	....	1,097
Size Range (sq ft/m):	....	145.3–473.2/13.5–44
Cabins (for one person):	....	0
Cabins (with private balcony):	....	491
Cabins (wheelchair accessible):	....	11
Wheelchair accessibility:	....	Good
Cabin Current:	....	110 and 220 volts
Elevators:	....	10
Casino (gaming tables):	....	Yes
Slot Machines:	....	No
Swimming Pools:	....	3
Hot Tubs (on deck):	....	0
Self-Service Launderette:	....	Yes
Dedicated Cinema/Seats:	....	No
Library:	....	Yes
Onboard currency:	....	Euros

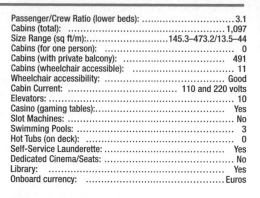

This family-friendly large ship is for lively, casual cruises

OVERVIEW. *AIDAmar* is for youthful German-speaking couples, solo travellers, and families seeking a vacation in a fun party-like environment, with plenty of good entertainment. This is all about über-casual cruising, with two main self-serve buffet restaurants instead of the traditional waiter service. It's tablecloth-free eating.

THE SHIP. The ship's profile is contemporary, quite well proportioned, and the swept-back funnel has a wedge-shaped stern. The bows display the bright red lips, as well as the blue eyes, of *Aïda* (from Verdi's opera, written to commemorate the opening of the Suez Canal in 1871). AIDA Cruises is part of Costa Cruises, itself part of Carnival Corporation.

There are three pricing levels – Aida Premium, Aida Vario, and Just Aida – depending on what you want to be included, and according to accommodation size and grade and itinerary. Opt for the basic, price-driven 'Just Aida' package and the cruise line chooses the ship, itinerary, and accommodation for you – sort of a potluck cruise, based on or close to the dates you choose.

Several decks of public rooms and facilities are positioned above the accommodation decks, and *AIDAmar* shares public room names common to all AIDA Cruises ships: Aida Bar is the main social gathering place; it features a star-shaped bar (whose combined length makes it among the longest at sea), with many tables for standing drinkers.

A small casino features blackjack, roulette, and poker gaming tables, and slot machines. There is a

Berlitz's Ratings	Possible	Achieved
Ship	500	393
Accommodation	200	135
Food	400	250
Service	400	269
Entertainment	100	71
Cruise Experience	400	278
OVERALL SCORE		
1396 points out of 2000		

separate aft sports deck, a 'no music' observation lounge, and an art gallery. Note that there is room service.

FAMILIES. *AIDAmar* really is a family-friendly ship. Children are split into five age groups: Seepferdchen (4–6 years), Delfine (7–9), Sharks (10–11), Orcas (12–13), and Teens (14–17). Each has its own play area. There is a diverse selection of children's and youth programs in a holiday camp atmosphere, and special Club Team members dedicated to making it all happen. Supervised by a chef, children can make their own menus for the week, and visit the galley to make cookies and other items – a novel idea more cruise lines could adopt.

ACCOMMODATION. There are eight or nine grades, from deluxe suites to interior (no view) cabins, depending on the ship, which keeps your cabin choice simple.

Contrary to maritime tradition (even-numbered cabins on the port side, odd-numbered cabins on the starboard side), cabin numbers progress numerically (example: 8201–8276 on the port side; 8101–8176 on the starboard side). All suites and cabins have two beds (convertible to queen-size bed). Some cabins also have two extra beds/berths for children, and some cabins have interconnecting doors – useful for families.

The decor in is bright, youthful, rather minimalist, and slightly whimsical, and accented with multi-patterned fabrics, wood-trimmed cabinetry (with nicely rounded edges), and rattan or wood-look furniture.

Beds have duvets and a colorful Arabian-style fabric canopy from the headboard to the ceiling. Windows have full pull-down blackout blinds (useful in destinations with long daylight hours).

Bathrooms are compact, practical units, with a shower enclosure, small washbasin, and toilet. As in the most basic hotels and motels, only a wall-mounted body wash/shampoo dispenser is provided (take your own preferred personal toiletries).

Thick cotton bathrobes are provided for all grades of accommodation, as are two towels – a face towel and a 'bath' towel, in two different colors. The 'bath' towels are not large, at 54 by 27 inches – compared to 72 by 36 inches aboard P&O Cruises' *Ventura*, for example. The bathroom does not have a hairdryer, but one is located in the vanity unit in the cabin. Note that the usual night-time turndown service provided aboard most ships is not provided, and there is no cabin service after 3pm.

Cabins with balconies have an easy-open sliding door (it doesn't impinge on balcony space), plus a small drinks table and two small, light chairs are provided (balconies on the lowest deck can be overlooked by anyone on a balcony on the decks above). Balcony cabins have a hammock as standard, although it only accommodates one (slim) person. Some cabins (forward on Deck 5 – Nos 5103, 5104, 5105, 5106, 5203, 5204, 5206) have cabins with an outside view (well, an outside light), but they are obstructed by steel bulkheads that form the front section of the ship.

DINING. There are three self-serve eateries: Markt (Market), Bella Vista (for Italian cuisine), and Weite Welt (Wide World) restaurants. The opening times for lunch and dinner are 12.30–2pm and 6.30–9pm respectively. Additionally, there's a Buffalo Steakhouse (which serves excellent steaks), an à la carte Rossini Restaurant with waiter and sommelier service, a Sushi Bar, a Pizzeria Mare, and a Café Mare. These venues are open at set times, although the Pizzeria typically stays open until midnight.

In the three self-serve restaurants, the meal concept is simple: main meals are taken when you want them in one of the large self-serve buffet-style restaurants, with open seating at tables of four, six, or eight. Cutlery can be found hanging in a rack, but there are no soup spoons, only dessert spoons.

The standard of food at the self-serve buffet islands ranges from adequate to quite good, with creative displays and presentation, and table-clearing service that is sometimes efficient, but mostly not.

The many food islands and active stations cut down on the waiting time for food. There is always a good selection of breads, cheeses, cold cuts, fruits, and make-your-own coffee and teas – with a choice of more than 30 types of loose-leaf regular and herbal teas. More than 1,200 items of food are offered. The fish section has its own fish-smoking unit (which resembles a wine cabinet).

Beer is available at the push of a button or a pull of the tap, and table wine – of the sort that would make a good drain cleaner – is usually provided in carafes on each table for lunch and dinner. Note that the beverage stations open only during restaurant opening hours, unless you go to the extra-cost coffee bar (Café Mare). Vending machines dispense out-of-hours snacks.

Other dining options. The (no cover charge) Rossini Restaurant, with mostly high-back seats, has an intimate atmosphere. It is open for dinner only, and has a set menu, plus daily 'specials.' An extra charge applies to everything on the à la carte menu (such as châteaubriand, rib-eye steak), and for wines. Reservations are needed. Tablecloths are provided, the food is good, and service is sound.

Buffalo Steakhouse has an open 'display' kitchen, and offers various steak cuts and sizes – Delmonico, New York Strip Loin, Porterhouse, and Filet, plus bison steaks, and roast lamb rack. There's a daily special – a prix-fixe meal (example: a 180g fillet steak, house salad, and dessert). It's like going out to eat in a restaurant ashore – minus tablecloths. Wine or any other drinks cost extra.

There's a 12-stool sushi counter for (extra cost) Japanese-style sushi and sashimi dishes.

A wine bar, Vinotheque, located in front of the Weide Welt (Wide World) Restaurant, has a list of premium wines, and Davidoff cigars (although you can't smoke them at the bar – or anywhere inside the ship).

The pizzeria Mare provides a small selection of ever-popular pizzas.

ENTERTAINMENT. The Theatrium (theater) is in the center of the ship. It is open to the main foyer and other public areas, on three levels (Decks 9, 10, and 11), and topped by a glass dome. Amphitheater-style seating is on three decks (the bench seating on the two upper levels has back supports, but not on the lower level), plus standing tables, although sight lines to the raised thrust stage area are less than good from many of the seats.

SPA/FITNESS. The spa, fitness, and sports programming is extensive.

The Body and Soul wellness/oasis area is located on two decks (connected by a stairway) and encompasses some 24,750 sq ft (2,300 sq m). There is also an open-air wellness deck for FKK relaxation/nude sunbathing atop the ship forward of the ship's mast. In keeping with the times, all the treatments are provided in an appealing contemporary setting.

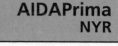

AIDAPrima
NYR

Size:	Large Resort Ship	Passenger/Crew Ratio (lower beds):	3.6/1
Tonnage:	125,000	Cabins (total):	1,643
Lifestyle:	standard	Size Range (sq ft/m):	139.9–1,345.5/13.0–125.0
Cruise Line:	AIDA Cruises	Cabins (for one person):	0
Former Names:	none	Cabins (with private balcony):	1,133
IMO Number:	9636955	Cabins (wheelchair accessible):	12
Builder:	Mitsubishi Heavy Industries (Japan)	Wheelchair accessibility:	Good
Original Cost:	€455 million	Cabin Current:	110 and 120 volts
Entered Service:	Oct 2015	Elevators:	18
Registry:	Italy	Casino (gaming tables):	Yes
Length (ft/m):	984.2/300.0	Slot Machines:	Yes
Beam (ft/m):	123.3/37.6	Swimming Pools:	6
Draft (ft/m):	26.5/8.1	Hot Tubs (on deck):	6
Propulsion/Propellers:	diesel-electric/2 azimuthing pods	Self-Service Launderette:	Yes
Passenger Decks:	16	Dedicated Cinema/Seats:	No
Total Crew:	900	Library:	Yes
Passengers (lower beds):	3,286	Onboard currency:	Euros
Passenger Space Ratio (lower beds):	37.8		

Stunning family-friendly ship for year-round cruises from Hamburg

OVERVIEW. *AIDAprima* is bright, contemporary, and full of facilities and amenities that youthful travelers and families with children can enjoy.

THE SHIP. *AIDAprima* has an unmistakable stark upright bow (unusual for a cruise ship, and a throwback to the early 20th-century ocean liners, although it is expected that this design will provide more of a 'cutting-edge' slicing effect through the water, giving greater speed), together with the familiar pursed red lips from Verdi's opera *Aida*, the company's whimsical logo. It is the first ship in the cruise industry to be fitted with a dual-fuel propulsion system (this includes the possibility to switch to LNG fuel, when available). The ship also has an exhaust-gas treatment system and a Mitsubishi Air Lubrication System.

The ship has three more decks than the newest smaller ships *AIDAblu*, *AIDAmar*, *AIDAsol*, and *AIDAstella*, but its layout is quite logical.

The ship's outdoor pools, located on Lanai Deck, can be used during the warmer summer season, when the water slide (which starts at the funnel and courses through the colorful Beach Club) and a rock-climbing wall can be used.

A private Patio-Bereich is an adults-only retreat with its own pool, lounge areas, and bar – the first aboard an AIDA ship.

Below the apartment-blocks of balcony cabins, just above the safety (lifeboat) deck, outdoor eateries and hot tubs provide the setting for an outdoor lifestyle enjoyed by many. The eateries are not well

Berlitz's Ratings		
	Possible	Achieved
Ship	500	NYR
Accommodation	200	NYR
Food	400	NYR
Service	400	NYR
Entertainment	100	NYR
Cruise Experience	400	NYR
OVERALL SCORE		
NYR points out of 2000		

protected from wind and rain, however, so they may prove to be under-used during the cold winter months.

Inside, there's a two-decks-high AIDA Beach Club, located aft of the almost mid-ship-placed funnel; this can be covered by a large glass roof, which helps to bring the outside inside during the winter cruises in the cold weather regions of Europe, although it takes away some open deck space.

Other features include spacious glass panoramic elevators and a skywalk. The all-white Champagne Bar is cool. One bar has a sort of ultra-Batman feel to it (I couldn't, however, find any gargoyles). There are 17 other bars, (both indoor and outdoor, including a Brauhaus – for onboard-brewed beer), a cooking studio, library, biking station, shops, and an art gallery.

Overall, this is all about cruising for youthful, laid-back, German-speaking families, and for anyone who doesn't mind busy places and lines. An AIDA cruise isn't cheap, but you get lots of high-tech entertainment, fun activities, and there's always plenty of food. The ship's year-round schedule sails from its home-port of Hamburg to Rotterdam, Zeebrugge, Le Havre, and Southampton (the ship is rather large to be able to get into some of the small European ports). Port taxes and gratuities are included in all cruises.

FAMILIES. *AIDAprima* is a family-friendly ship. Children are divided into five age groups: Seepferdchen (4–6 years), Delfine (7–9), Sharks (10–11), Orcas (12–13), and Teens (14–17); each has its own play area. Additionally, a Mini-Club caters to babies and toddlers as young as six months. There is a diverse selection of children's and youth programs, and special Club Team members who are dedicated to making all the activities happen. Children can also make their own menus for the week (under a chef's supervision), and visit the galley to make cookies and other items.

ACCOMMODATION. Modern, colourful, and minimalist best describes the accommodation, which ranges from small interior cabins to large two-bedroom suites.

Some 32 suites range in size from 344.4–882.6 sq ft (32–82 sq m), but most cabins are much more compact, starting at 129.1 sq ft (12 sq m). These offer more space, including more drawer and storage space, better-quality furniture and furnishings, a larger lounge area, and a slightly larger bathroom with a tub – and a larger balcony. Those at the front and stern of the ship are the best and most desirable.

Balcony cabins feature beds adjacent to the floor-to ceiling door that slides open to access the balcony. Panorama cabins can be found on Patio Deck. All cabins with balconies have an easy-open sliding door that doesn't impinge on balcony space.

Thick cotton bathrobes are provided in all accommodation grades, as are two towels – a face towel and a 'bath' towel, in two different colors.

DINING. AIDA Cruises has included more dining choices for this new ship (13 dining venues and eateries in all – some with waiter service, some at extra cost, some include drinks like beer and wine), including the company's signature self-serve food outlet Markt (Market) Restaurant. Here the chairs don't have armrests – they are uncomfortable so you won't want to stay a long time – like shopping mall food court eateries ashore. The decor is, however, pleasingly bright – yellows and oranges to stimulate the senses (plus a little cream to calm them), with Moroccan-style lampshades hanging from a plain ceiling over tables. The food displays are very attractive, and designed with families in mind. Beer is available at the push of a button or a pull of the tap, and table wine is provided in carafes on each table for lunch and dinner.

There's also Bella Donna Restaurant, East Restaurant, and California Grill.

For something different, French Kiss is a casual French-style brasserie (the first of its type aboard an AIDA Cruises ship), with red/black chairs and the red lips of *Aïda* the central decor theme; there's also a Chef's Kitchen (part of the Cooking School), and even a Scharfe Ecke for the ever-popular Currywurst.

Casa Nova is an elegant (extra-cost) Venice-inspired restaurant with elegant surroundings, offering a white tablecloth setting for dinners (although the chairs are not very comfortable and lack armrests).

Buffalo Steakhouse has an open 'display' kitchen, and features various prime steak cuts and sizes – Delmonico, New York Strip Loin, Porterhouse, and Filet, plus bison steaks – and roast lamb rack.

Reservations are required in Buffalo Steakhouse, Casa Nova Restaurant, Brasserie French Kiss, and Rossini-Gourmet Restaurant. Drinks are included in: Bella Donna, East Restaurant, French Kiss, Fuego Family Restaurant, Markt Restaurant, Scharfe Ecke, and the Weite Welt Restaurant.

ENTERTAINMENT. The Theatrium acts (no pun intended) as the main showlounge; its location is in the middle of the ship and it spans three levels. It has an LED stage backdrop, but there is no bandstand. The shows are produced by AIDA Cruises' in-house department in a joint venture with SeeLive (Hamburg's Schmidt's Tivoli Theater), and consist of around 12 performers. All vocals in the shows are performed live to pre-recorded backing tracks (because there's no live band on stage).

SPA/FITNESS. The ship has a very expansive Body and Soul Organic Spa, with multiple body treatments rooms, saunas (at extra cost), steam rooms, thalassotherapy bath, changing rooms, and a beauty salon, plus manicure and pedicure salons. Extra-cost private 'wellness suites' are bookable (good for couples who want wellness treatments in total privacy).

Body and Soul sports activities include indoor cycling. Electric bicycles and Segways are also available (at extra cost) at the Biking Station, and there's a 2,152 sq ft (200 sq m) floating ice-rink on the Sports Deck (winter season only).

AIDAsol
★★★+

Size:	Large Resort Ship
Tonnage:	71,304
Lifestyle:	Standard
Cruise Line:	AIDA Cruises
Former Names:	none
IMO Number:	9490040
Builder:	Meyer Werft (Germany)
Original Cost:	€350 million
Entered Service:	Apr 2011
Registry:	Italy
Length (ft/m):	831.1/253.3
Beam (ft/m):	105.6/32.2
Draft (ft/m):	24.6/7.5
Propulsion/Propellers:	diesel-electric (36,000 kW)/2
Passenger Decks:	14
Total Crew:	646
Passengers (lower beds):	2,194
Passenger Space Ratio (lower beds):	34.6

Passenger/Crew Ratio (lower beds):	3.1
Cabins (total):	1,097
Size Range (sq ft/m):	145.3–473.2/13.5–44
Cabins (for one person):	0
Cabins (with private balcony):	491
Cabins (wheelchair accessible):	11
Wheelchair accessibility:	Good
Cabin Current:	110 and 220 volts
Elevators:	10
Casino (gaming tables):	Yes
Slot Machines:	No
Swimming Pools:	3
Hot Tubs (on deck):	0
Self-Service Launderette:	Yes
Dedicated Cinema/Seats:	No
Library:	Yes
Onboard currency:	Euros

This contemporary, casual, no-frills cruising is for families

OVERVIEW. *AIDAsol* is for youthful German-speaking couples, solo travelers, and families seeking a party-like environment, and good entertainment. This is all about über-casual (tablecloth-free) cruising, with two main self-serve buffet restaurants instead of waiter service.

THE SHIP. The ship has a well-proportioned, contemporary profile with a swept-back funnel. The bows display the bright red lips, as well as the blue eyes, of *Aïda* (from Verdi's opera, written to commemorate the opening of the Suez Canal in 1871). AIDA Cruises, Germany's largest cruise line, is part of Costa Cruises, itself part of Carnival Corporation.

Open deck space is rather limited, but sunbathing space includes some reasonably quiet space above the navigation bridge. Dip pools and hot tubs, plus seating areas, are provided in a cascading, tiered setting atop the ship on the pool deck, providing a decent amount of sunbathing space.

The dress code is simple: casual (no ties) at all times. Port taxes and gratuities are included.

Several decks of public rooms and facilities are positioned above the accommodation decks, and public room names that are common aboard all the ships in the fleet are used: Aida Bar, for example, the main social gathering place, with a star-shaped bar (whose combined length makes it among the longest at sea), and many adjacent tables for standing drinkers. There are several other bars to choose from, plus a 'no music' observation lounge, an art gallery,

Berlitz's Ratings

	Possible	Achieved
Ship	500	393
Accommodation	200	135
Food	400	250
Service	400	269
Entertainment	100	71
Cruise Experience	400	278
OVERALL SCORE		
1396 points out of 2000		

and a small casino (for blackjack, roulette, and poker gaming tables), and slot machines.

FAMILIES. *AIDAsol* is a family-friendly ship, with children divided into five age groups: Seepferdchen (4–6 years), Delfine (7–9), Sharks (10–11), Orcas (12–13), and Teens (14–17). Each has its own play area. There is a diverse selection of children's and youth programs in a holiday camp atmosphere, and special Club Team members dedicated to making it all happen. Supervised by a chef, children can make their own menus for the week, and visit the galley to make cookies and other items.

ACCOMMODATION. There are several grades, from deluxe suites to interior (no-view) cabins.

Contrary to maritime tradition (even-numbered cabins on the port side, odd-numbered cabins on the starboard side), cabin numbers progress numerically (example: 8201–8276 on the port side; 8101–8176 on the starboard side). All suites and cabins have two beds (convertible to queen-size bed). Some cabins also have two extra beds/berths for children, and some cabins have interconnecting doors – useful for families.

The decor is bright, youthful, and minimalist, and accented with multi-patterned fabrics, wood-trimmed cabinetry (with nicely rounded edges), and rattan or wood-look furniture. Beds have duvets and a colorful Arabian-style fabric canopy goes from the headboard to the ceiling. The windows have full pull-down blackout blinds (useful in destinations with long daylight hours).

The bathrooms are compact, practical units; they have a shower enclosure, small washbasin, and small toilet. As in the most basic hotels and motels, only a wall-mounted body wash/shampoo dispenser is provided, so take your own conditioner, hand lotion, and other toiletries you may need.

Thick cotton bathrobes are provided for all grades of accommodation, as are two towels – a face towel and a 'bath' towel, in two different colors. The 'bath' towels are not large, at 54 by 27 inches – compared to 72 by 36 inches aboard P&O Cruises' *Ventura*, for example. The bathroom does not have a hairdryer, but one is located in the vanity unit in the cabin. Note that there is no cabin service after 3pm.

Cabins with balconies have a sliding door that's easy to open and doesn't impinge on balcony space; a small drinks table and two small, light chairs are provided. Note that balconies on the lowest deck can be overlooked by anyone on a balcony on the decks above. Balcony cabins have a hammock as standard, although it only accommodates one (slim) person. Some cabins (forward on Deck 5 – Nos 5103, 5104, 5105, 5106, 5203, 5204, 5206) have cabins with an outside view (well, outside light), but they are obstructed by steel bulkheads that form the front section of the ship.

DINING. There are three self-serve eateries: Markt (Market), Bella Vista (for Italian cuisine), and Weite Welt (Wide World) restaurants. The opening times for lunch and dinner are 12.30–2pm and 6.30–9pm respectively. Additionally, there's a Buffalo Steakhouse (which serves excellent steaks), an à la carte Rossini Restaurant with waiter and sommelier service, a Sushi Bar, a Pizzeria Mare, and a Café Mare. These venues are open at set times (there are no 24-hour-a-day outlets, because there is little demand for them), although the Pizzeria stays open until midnight.

In the three self-serve restaurants, the meal concept is simple: main meals are taken when you want them in one of the large self-serve buffet-style restaurants, with open seating at tables of four, six, or eight. Cutlery can be found hanging in a rack (a bit unhygienic), but there are no soup spoons, only dessert spoons.

The many food islands and active stations cut down on the waiting time for food. There is always a big selection of breads, cheeses, cold cuts, fruits, and make-your-own coffee and teas – with a choice of more than 30 types of loose-leaf regular and herbal teas. More than 1,200 items of food are offered. The fish section has its own fish-smoking unit (which resembles a wine cabinet).

Beer is available at the push of a button or a pull of the tap, and table wine – of the sort that would make a good drain cleaner – is usually provided in carafes on each table for lunch and dinner. Note that the beverage stations open only during restaurant opening hours, unless you go to the extra-cost coffee bar (Café Mare). Vending machines dispense out-of-hours snacks.

Other dining options. The Rossini Restaurant, with mostly high-back seats, has an intimate atmosphere. It is open for dinner only, and has a set five- or six-course menu, plus daily 'specials.' There is no cover charge, but an extra charge applies to everything on the à la carte menu (such as caviar, chateaubriand, rib-eye steak), and for wines. Reservations are needed. Tablecloths are provided, the food is very good, and service is sound.

The Buffalo Steakhouse has an open 'display' kitchen, and offers various steak cuts and sizes – Delmonico, New York Strip Loin, Porterhouse, and Filet, plus bison steaks – and roast lamb rack. There's a daily special – a prix-fixe meal (example: a 180g fillet steak, house salad, and dessert). It's like going out to eat in a decent restaurant ashore – but there are no tablecloths. Wine or any other drinks cost extra.

There's a 12-seater sushi counter for extra cost Japanese-style sushi and sashimi dishes.

Vinotheque, a wine bar located in front of the Weide Welt (Wide World) Restaurant, has a list of premium wines, and Davidoff cigars (although you can't smoke them anywhere inside the ship).

The Pizzeria Mare provides a small selection of ever-popular pizzas.

ENTERTAINMENT. The Theatrium (theater) is in the center of the ship. It is open to the main foyer and other public areas, on three levels (Decks 9, 10, and 11), and topped by a glass dome. Amphitheater-style seating is on three decks (the bench seating on the two upper levels has back supports, but not on the lower level), plus standing tables, although sight lines to the raised thrust stage area are less than good from many of the seats.

SPA/FITNESS. The spa, fitness, and sports programming are extensive. The Body and Soul wellness/oasis area is located on two decks (connected by a stairway) and encompasses some 24,750 sq ft (2,300 sq m). There is also an open-air wellness deck for FKK relaxation/nude sunbathing forward of the ship's mast.

AIDAstella
★★★+

Size:	Large Resort Ship	Passenger/Crew Ratio (lower beds):	3.1
Tonnage:	71,304	Cabins (total):	1,097
Lifestyle:	Standard	Size Range (sq ft/m):	145.3–473.2/13.5–44
Cruise Line:	AIDA Cruises	Cabins (for one person):	0
Former Names:	none	Cabins (with private balcony):	722
IMO Number:	9601132	Cabins (wheelchair accessible):	11
Builder:	Meyer Werft (Germany)	Wheelchair accessibility:	Good
Original Cost:	€350 million	Cabin Current:	110 and 220 volts
Entered Service:	Mar 2013	Elevators:	10
Registry:	Italy	Casino (gaming tables):	Yes
Length (ft/m):	831.1/253.3	Slot Machines:	No
Beam (ft/m):	105.6/32.2	Swimming Pools:	3
Draft (ft/m):	24.6/7.5	Hot Tubs (on deck):	0
Propulsion/Propellers:	diesel-electric (36,000 kW)/2	Self-Service Launderette:	Yes
Passenger Decks:	14	Dedicated Cinema/Seats:	No
Total Crew:	646	Library:	Yes
Passengers (lower beds):	2,194	Onboard currency:	Euros
Passenger Space Ratio (lower beds):	34.6		

A large family-friendly resort ship for basic, but fun cruising

OVERVIEW. *AIDAstella* is for youthful German-speaking couples, solo travellers, and families seeking an urban party-like environment, with very good entertainment. It's all about über-casual cruising, with two main self-serve tablecloth-free buffet restaurants instead of waiter service.

THE SHIP. The ship has a smart profile that is quite well proportioned, with a swept-back funnel and wedge-shaped stern. On the bows are the bright red lips and blue eyes of *Aïda* (from Verdi's opera, which was written to commemorate the opening of the Suez Canal in 1871). AIDA Cruises, Germany's largest cruise line, comes under Costa Cruises, itself part of Carnival Corporation.

Open deck space is rather limited, but sunbathing space includes some reasonably quiet space above the navigation bridge. Dip pools and hot tubs, plus seating areas, are provided in a tiered setting atop the ship on the pool deck, providing a decent amount of sunbathing space. It's all designed as a 'beach-like' environment, with splash and play areas.

Overall, this really is cruising for youthful German-speaking families, and for anyone who likes lots of liveliness around them. An AIDA cruise isn't cheap, but you get lots of high-tech entertainment, and there's always plenty of food. Some frustration can occur when shore excursions sell out, when lines form after shore excursion buses return to the ship and you have to go through the slow security check, and for shore tenders.

Berlitz's Ratings		
	Possible	Achieved
Ship	500	393
Accommodation	200	135
Food	400	250
Service	400	269
Entertainment	100	71
Cruise Experience	400	278
OVERALL SCORE		
1396 points out of 2000		

There are three pricing levels – Aida Premium, Aida Vario, and Just Aida – depending on what you want to be included, plus differences in price according to accommodation size and grade, and itinerary. Opt for the basic, price-driven 'Just Aida' package and the cruise line chooses the ship, itinerary, and accommodation for you – sort of a pot-luck cruise, based on or close to the dates you choose.

The dress code is simple: casual (no ties) at all times. Port taxes and gratuities are included in all cruises.

Several decks of public rooms and facilities are positioned above the accommodation decks, and *AIDAstella* shares public room names that are common aboard all the ships in the fleet: Aida Bar, the main social gathering place, for example, where the principal feature is a star-shaped bar (its combined length makes it one of the longest at sea), with many tables for standing drinkers.

A small casino features blackjack, roulette and poker gaming tables, as well as slot machines. There are many balcony cabins, a separate aft sports deck, a 'no music' observation lounge, and an art gallery.

FAMILIES. *AIDAstella* really is a family-friendly ship. Children are split into five age groups: Seepferdchen (4–6 years), Delfine (7–9), Sharks (10–11), Orcas (12–13), and Teens (14–17). Each has its own play area. There is a diverse selection of children's and youth programs in a holiday camp atmosphere, and special Club Team members dedicated to making it all happen. Supervised by a chef, children can make their own menus for the week, and visit the galley to make cookies and other items.

ACCOMMODATION. There are several cabin grades, from deluxe suites to interior (no-view) cabins.

Contrary to maritime tradition (even-numbered cabins on the port side, odd-numbered cabins on the starboard side), cabin numbers progress numerically (example: 8201–8276 on the port side; 8101–8176 on the starboard side). All suites and cabins have two beds (convertible to queen-size bed). Some cabins also have two extra beds/berths for children, and some have interconnecting doors – useful for families.

The decor is bright, youthful, minimalist, and slightly whimsical. All rooms are accented with multi-patterned fabrics, wood-trimmed cabinetry (with rounded edges), and rattan or wood-look furniture. Beds have duvets and a colorful Arabian-style fabric canopy that goes from headboard to the ceiling. Windows have full pull-down blackout blinds (useful in destinations with long daylight hours).

Bathrooms are compact, practical units; they have a shower enclosure and small washbasin and toilet. As in the most basic hotels and motels, only a wall-mounted body wash/shampoo dispenser is provided, so take your own conditioner, hand lotion, and other toiletries you may need.

Thick cotton bathrobes are provided for all grades of accommodation, as are two towels – a face towel and a 'bath' towel, in two different colors. The bathroom does not have a hairdryer, but one is located in the vanity unit in the cabin. Note that the usual night-time turndown service provided aboard most ships is not provided, and there is no cabin service after 3pm.

Cabins with balconies have an easy-open sliding door that doesn't impinge on balcony space; a small drinks table and two small, light chairs are provided. Balconies on the lowest deck can be overlooked by anyone on a balcony on the decks above. Balcony cabins have a one-person hammock. Some cabins (forward on Deck 5 – Nos 5103, 5104, 5105, 5106, 5203, 5204, 5206) have cabins with an outside view (well, outside light), but they are obstructed by steel bulkheads that form the front section of the ship.

DINING. There are three self-serve eateries: Markt (Market), Bella Vista (for Italian cuisine), and Weite Welt (Wide World) restaurants. The opening times for lunch and dinner are 12.30–2pm and 6.30–9pm respectively. Additionally, there's a Buffalo Steakhouse (which serves fine steaks), an à la carte Rossini Restaurant with waiter and sommelier service, a Sushi Bar, a Pizzeria Mare, and a Café Mare. These venues are open at set times (there are no 24-hour-a-day

outlets – there is little demand for them), although the Pizzeria typically stays open until midnight.

The meal concept is simple: main meals are taken when you want them in one of the large self-serve buffet-style restaurants, with open seating at tables of four, six, or eight.

The many food islands and active stations cut down on waiting time for food. There is always a selection of breads, cheeses, cold cuts, fruits, and make-your-own coffee and teas – with a choice of more than 30 types of (weak) loose-leaf regular and herbal teas. The fish section has its own fish-smoking unit (which resembles a wine cabinet).

Beer is available at the push of a button or a pull of the tap, and table wine is provided in carafes on each table for lunch and dinner. Beverage stations open only during restaurant opening hours, unless you go to the extra-cost coffee bar (Café Mare). Vending machines dispense out-of-hours snacks.

Other dining options. The Rossini Restaurant, with mostly high-back seats, has an intimate atmosphere. It is open for dinner only, and has a set five- or six-course menu, plus daily 'specials'. There is no cover charge, but an extra charge applies to everything on the à la carte menu and for wines. Reservations are needed, tablecloths are provided, the food is good, and service is sound.

Buffalo Steakhouse has an open 'display' kitchen, and offers various premium steak cuts and sizes, plus bison steaks, and roast lamb rack. It's like going out to eat in a restaurant ashore – without tablecloths. Wine or any other drinks cost extra.

There is a 12-seater sushi counter with stools, and two low-slung tables.

A wine bar, Vinotheque, located in front of the Weide Welt (Wide World) Restaurant, has a list of premium wines, and Davidoff cigars (although you can't smoke them at the bar – or anywhere inside the ship).

The Pizzeria Mare provides a small selection of popular, basic pizzas.

ENTERTAINMENT. The Theatrium (theater) is in the center of the ship. It is open to the main foyer and other public areas, on three levels (Decks 9, 10, and 11), and topped by a glass dome. Amphitheater-style seating is on three decks (the bench seating on the two upper levels has back supports, but not on the lower level), plus standing tables, although sight lines to the raised thrust stage area are less than good from many of the seats.

SPA/FITNESS. The Body and Soul wellness/oasis area is located on two decks (connected by a stairway) and encompasses some 24,750 sq ft (2,300 sq m). There is also an open-air wellness FKK deck for relaxation/nude sunbathing (forward of the ship's mast).

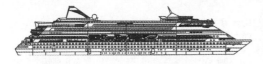

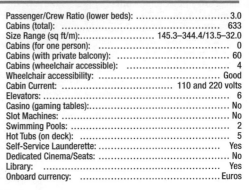

AIDAvita
★★★+

Size:	Mid-size Ship	Passenger/Crew Ratio (lower beds):	3.0
Tonnage:	42,289	Cabins (total):	633
Lifestyle:	Standard	Size Range (sq ft/m):	145.3–344.4/13.5–32.0
Cruise Line:	AIDA Cruises	Cabins (for one person):	0
Former Names:	none	Cabins (with private balcony):	60
IMO Number:	9221554	Cabins (wheelchair accessible):	4
Builder:	Aker MTW (Germany)	Wheelchair accessibility:	Good
Original Cost:	$350 million	Cabin Current:	110 and 220 volts
Entered Service:	Apr 2002	Elevators:	6
Registry:	Italy	Casino (gaming tables):	No
Length (ft/m):	666.5/202.8	Slot Machines:	No
Beam (ft/m):	92.2/28.1	Swimming Pools:	2
Draft (ft/m):	20.7/6.3	Hot Tubs (on deck):	5
Propulsion/Propellers:	diesel-electric/2	Self-Service Launderette:	Yes
Passenger Decks:	10	Dedicated Cinema/Seats:	No
Total Crew:	389	Library:	Yes
Passengers (lower beds):	1,266	Onboard currency:	Euros
Passenger Space Ratio (lower beds):	33.4		

An upbeat, family-friendly ship for vibrant, busy, cruising

OVERVIEW. Any AIDA Cruise is for youthful German-speaking couples, solo travellers, and families looking for good value for money in a party-like environment, with excellent entertainment. This is all about über-casual cruising, with two main self-serve buffet restaurants instead of the traditional waiter service. It's tablecloth-less eating, and there is little contact with the relatively few staff.

THE SHIP. *AIDAvita* has a smart profile, with a swept-back funnel and wedge-shaped stern. The bows display the red lips and blue eyes of *Aida* (from Verdi's opera, written to commemorate the opening of the Suez Canal in 1871). AIDA Cruises, Germany's largest cruise line, is part of Costa Cruises, which is itself part of Carnival Corporation.

Open deck space is tight, but sunbathing space includes some rather pleasant, reasonably quiet space above the navigation bridge. Dip pools and hot tubs, plus seating areas, are provided in a cascading, tiered setting atop the ship on the pool deck, providing a decent amount of sunbathing space. It's all designed to be in a 'beach-like' environment, with splash and play areas.

Other facilities include a shore excursion counter, library, seminar rooms, duty-free shop, several bars and lounges, a small casino with blackjack, roulette, and poker gaming tables, and slot machines.

There is an aft sports deck, a 'no music' observation lounge, and an art gallery. The embarkation

Berlitz's Ratings	Possible	Achieved
Ship	500	355
Accommodation	200	134
Food	400	245
Service	400	263
Entertainment	100	68
Cruise Experience	400	275
OVERALL SCORE		
1340 points out of 2000		

entryway is really innovative, has a bar and a lookout balcony, and is cheerfully painted to look like a city street scene. It is different from the utilitarian gangway entry areas found aboard most cruise ships. A welcoming environment, it helps to calm tempers after waiting in a line to go through the security process for embarkation or in ports of call.

There are three pricing levels – Aida Premium, Aida Vario, and Just Aida – depending on what you want to be included, plus differences in price according to accommodation size and grade, and the itinerary. See the cruise line's brochure for details.

The dress code is simple: casual (no ties) at all times – there are no formal nights on board. All port taxes and gratuities are included in all packages, and, with very attractive rates, a cruise provides much better value than almost any land-based vacation.

Several decks of public rooms and facilities are positioned above the accommodation decks, and *AIDAvita* shares public room names that are common aboard all the ships in the fleet: Aida Bar, for example, the main social gathering place, where the principal feature is a star-shaped bar (whose combined length makes it among the longest at sea), with many tables for standing drinkers.

FAMILIES. This is a family-friendly ship. Children are split into five age groups: Seepferdchen (4–6 years), Delfine (7–9), Sharks (10–11), Orcas (12–13), and Teens (14–17). Each has its own play area.

ACCOMMODATION. There are several grades, from deluxe suites to interior (no-view) cabins.

Contrary to maritime tradition (even-numbered cabins on the port side, odd-numbered cabins on the starboard side), cabin numbers progress numerically (example: 8201–8276 on the port side; 8101–8176 on the starboard side). All suites/cabins have two beds (convertible to queen-size bed). Some cabins have two extra beds/berths for children; some have interconnecting doors – practical for families.

The decor is bright, youthful, minimalist, and slightly whimsical. The rooms are accented with multi-patterned fabrics, wood-trimmed cabinetry (with nicely rounded edges), and rattan or wood-look furniture. Beds have duvets and a colorful Arabianstyle fabric canopy from headboard to the ceiling. The windows have full pull-down blackout blinds (useful in destinations with long daylight hours). Lifeboats may obstruct views in some cabins in the ship's center.

Bathrooms are compact, practical units; they have a shower enclosure, small washbasin, and small toilet. As in the most basic hotels and motels, only a wall-mounted body wash/shampoo dispenser is provided, so take your own conditioner, hand lotion, and other toiletries you may need.

Thick cotton bathrobes are provided for suitegrade accommodation (non-suite grade passengers can obtain one from the spa). A face towel and a 'bath' towel are provided. The 'bath' towels are not very large, at 54 by 27 inches – compared to 72 by 36 inches aboard the P&O Cruises' Azura, for example. A hairdryer is located in the vanity unit in the cabin. Unusually, night-time turndown service is not provided (there is no cabin service after 3pm).

Cabins with balconies have an easy-open sliding door that doesn't impinge on balcony space; a small drinks table and two small, light chairs are provided. Note that balconies on the lowest deck can be overlooked by anyone on a balcony on the decks above. Some cabins (forward on Deck 5 – Nos. 5103, 5104, 5105, 5106, 5203, 5204, 5206) have an outside view (well, outside light), but they are totally obstructed by steel bulkheads that form the front section of the ship.

DINING. Two eateries are included in the cruise fare; these are the Markt and Karibik self-serve buffet-style restaurants. The opening times for lunch and dinner are (typically) 12.30–2pm and 6.30–9pm respectively.

The meal concept is simple: main meals are taken when you want them in one of the large self-serve buffet-style restaurants, with open seating at tables of four, six, or eight. Cutlery hangs in a rack (considered unhygienic), and there are no soup spoons, only

dessert spoons. It's very casual and easy-going mass catering, so think food court eating, not dining.

There is always a decent selection of breads, cheeses, cold cuts, fruits, and make-your-own coffee and teas – with a choice of more than 30 types of looseleaf regular and herbal teas.

You can sit where you want, when you want, and with whom you want, so eating is a socially interactive occasion. In fact, it's hard to be an unsociable couple and have a table for only two. At peak times, the venues may remind you of noisy roadside cafés. Because of the large buffet rooms and self-serve concept, the crew to passenger ratio is poor; this is because there are no waiters as such (except in à la carte venues), only staff for clearing tables.

Beer is available at the push of a button or a pull of the tap, and table wine – of the sort that would make a good drain cleaner – is usually provided in carafes on each table for lunch and dinner. Note that the beverage stations open only during restaurant opening hours, unless you go to the extra-cost coffee bar. Vending machines dispense out-of-hours snacks.

Other dining options. The Rossini Restaurant has a quiet, intimate atmosphere. It is open for dinner only, and has a set five- or six-course menu (plus daily specials). There is no cover charge, but an extra charge applies to everything on the à la carte menu, and for wines. Reservations are needed, tablecloths are provided, the food is good, and the waiter and sommelier service are friendly.

The wine bar, Vinotheque, located in front of the Weide Welt Restaurant, has premium wines and Davidoff cigars (smoking is only allowed in designated spaces on outside decks).

ENTERTAINMENT. The Theater (Das Theater), the main venue for all shows and most cabaret, is two decks high, with a raised stage, and amphitheaterstyle bench seating on all levels. The benches have back rests, and are quite comfortable, and sight lines are good from most seats, with the exception of port and starboard balcony sections, where sight lines are interrupted by thick safety railings.

SPA/FITNESS. The Body and Soul Spa, is located forward on Deck 11. It measures 11,840 sq ft (1,100 sq m), and contains two saunas (one dry, one wet, both with seats for more than 20 persons, and glass walls that look onto the deck), massage and other treatment rooms, and a large lounging area. There are also showers, and two whole 'ice walls' to use when you come out of the saunas (simply lean into the ice wall for maximum effect). Forward and outside the wellness center, is an FKK (Freikoerperkultur) nude sunbathing deck, on two levels.

Albatros
★★★

Size:	Mid-size Ship	Passenger Space Ratio (lower beds):	32.5
Tonnage:	28,078	Passenger/Crew Ratio (lower beds):	2.5
Lifestyle:	Standard	Cabins (total):	449
Cruise Line:	Phoenix Reisen	Size Range (sq ft/m):	123.7– 679.2/11.8–63.1
Former Names:	Crown, Norwegian Star I, Royal Odyssey, Royal Viking Sea	Cabins (for one person):	12
		Cabins (with private balcony):	15
IMO Number:	5347245	Cabins (wheelchair accessible):	0
Builder:	Wartsila (Finland)	Wheelchair accessibility:	Fair
Original Cost:	$22.5 million	Cabin Current:	110 and 220 volts
Entered Service:	Nov 1973/Apr 2004	Elevators:	5
Registry:	Bahamas	Casino (gaming tables):	No
Length (ft/m):	674.2/205.5	Slot Machines:	No
Beam (ft/m):	82.0/25.0	Swimming Pools:	1
Draft (ft/m):	23.9/7.3	Hot Tubs (on deck):	1
Propulsion/Propellers:	diesel (15,840 kW)/2	Self-Service Launderette:	Yes
Passenger Decks:	8	Dedicated Cinema/Seats:	Yes/156
Total Crew:	340	Library:	Yes
Passengers (lower beds):	862	Onboard currency:	Euros

This ship is good for low-price, no-frills long cruises

OVERVIEW. *Albatros* appeals to mature German-speaking adults and families seeking a low-budget, good-value vacation in a comfortable (but not new) ship.

THE SHIP. *Albatros*, built for long-distance cruising for the long-defunct Royal Viking Line, was nicely (and expensively) refurbished in 2014. There is plenty of open deck and sunbathing space, although the popular aft pool area can become crowded.

The ship has a good array of public rooms, including several lounges and bars, most of which are sort of old-world elegant, and have high, indented ceilings. The Observation Lounge is a particularly pleasant place to spend time. Wide stairways and foyers give a sense of space, even when the ship is full. The atmosphere is very casual, as is the dress code. A low 7 percent gratuity is added to bar accounts, and drink prices are very reasonable.

The Phoenix cruise staff is always bright, bubby and friendly, and the shore excursion team is knowledgeable and helpful.

ACCOMMODATION. There are more than 20 price grades, from expansive suites with private balcony to standard outside-view cabins and small interior cabins. A Captain's Suite is located at the front, directly under the navigation bridge, with fine forward-facing views. Nine other Penthouse Suites include a private balcony (with separate bedroom and living area). Most other cabins have an outside view and

Berlitz's Ratings

	Possible	Achieved
Ship	500	310
Accommodation	200	128
Food	400	211
Service	400	237
Entertainment	100	60
Cruise Experience	400	251
OVERALL SCORE		
1197 points out of 2000		

are quite well appointed, and there is a good amount of storage space; however, some bathrooms in the lower categories have awkward access. All cabins have a TV, bathrobe, and personal safe. Suites and 'comfort cabins' also have a minibar. Occupants of eight (mostly suite) accommodation grades receive 'Phoenix VIP' service.

DINING. There are two dining rooms (Mowe and Pelikan); both have high ceilings, and are spacious. Dining is in one seating at assigned tables for two, four, six, or eight. Breakfast and lunch can be taken in the dining room or outdoors in a self-service buffet. Mid-morning bouillon is a Phoenix seagoing tradition, as is a Captain's Dinner (formal night), and a Buffet Magnifique.

The service is friendly and attentive, although there is little finesse, and the food itself (recently upgraded) is quite acceptable (although not as good as *Amadea* or *Artania*). Decent table wines are included for lunch and dinner, but even better-quality wines can also be purchased.

ENTERTAINMENT. The Pacific Lounge is the ship's showlounge. It seats about 500, but several pillars obstruct the sight lines for some. Small-scale production shows are presented by a small team of resident singers/dancers.

SPA/FITNESS. There are a gymnasium and sauna, two steam rooms, body treatment rooms, and a beauty salon.

Allure of the Seas
★★★★

Size:	Large Resort Ship
Tonnage:	225,062
Lifestyle:	Standard
Cruise Line:	Royal Caribbean International
Former Names:	none
IMO Number:	9383948
Builder:	Aker Yards (Finland)
Original Cost:	$1.5 billion
Entered Service:	Dec 2010
Registry:	Bahamas
Length (ft/m):	1,181.1/360.0
Beam (ft/m):	216.5 /66.0
Draft (ft/m):	30.0/9.1
Propulsion/Propellers:	diesel-electric (97,200kW)/3 pods
	(2 azimuthing, 1 fixed)
Passenger Decks:	16
Total Crew:	2,164
Passengers (lower beds):	5,408

Passenger Space Ratio (lower beds):	41.6
Passenger/Crew Ratio (lower beds):	2.4
Cabins (total):	2,704
Size Range (sq ft/m):	150.6–1,523.1/14.0–141.5
Cabins (for one person):	0
Cabins (with private balcony):	1,956
Cabins (wheelchair accessible):	46
Wheelchair accessibility:	Good
Cabin Current:	110 volts
Elevators:	24
Casino (gaming tables):	Yes
Slot Machines:	Yes
Swimming Pools:	3
Hot Tubs (on deck):	10
Self-Service Launderette:	No
Dedicated Cinema/Seats:	No
Library:	Yes
Onboard currency:	US$

This is a mega-large, family-friendly, multi-choice ship

OVERVIEW. This stunning ship provides a fine cruise experience and wide range of choices for youthful adults and families with children. It's packed with innovative design elements such as Central Park, taking urban greenery to sea.

THE SHIP. When it debuted in 2010, *Allure of the Seas* qualified as the world's largest cruise ship – by less than 2in (5cm) longer than sister, *Oasis of the Seas,* the world's first cruise ship measuring over 200,000 tons, which debuted in 2009. However, the ships are pretty much identical. When it debuts in 2016, the 227,700-ton *Harmony of the Seas* will become the new 'largest cruise ship in the world.'

Built as a 'Moveable Resort Vacation' for families with children, this ship is credit to Royal Caribbean International's (RCI's) design team. A lot of outdoor and indoor/outdoor space is devoted to aqua-bathing and sports, but there's little space for sunbathing. If all 5,400 passengers want a sunlounger at the same time, forget it! Anyone able to secure one will find them so tightly packed together that there's little space to put any belongings. There are several swimming pools, three of which – 'main,' 'beach,' and 'sports' – are positioned high on Deck 15 (Pool and Sports Zone) of the 16 passenger decks, as is an H2O Zone. Two large hot tubs extend over the ship's side (the water for the swimming pools alone weighs 2,300 tons).

The ship incorporates the facilities that young families seek for action-packed cruise vacations. There

Berlitz's Ratings		
	Possible	Achieved
Ship	500	409
Accommodation	200	148
Food	400	234
Service	400	291
Entertainment	100	88
Cruise Experience	400	296
OVERALL SCORE		
1466 points out of 2000		

are 37 bars and over 20 places to eat or snack. And the latest technology means that *Allure* and *Oasis* are 30 percent more energy-efficient than even the *Freedom*-class ships.

Public spaces are arranged as seven 'neighborhoods': Central Park, the Boardwalk, the Royal Promenade, the Pool and Sports Zone, Vitality at Sea Spa/Fitness Center, Entertainment Place, and Youth Zone. The most popular are the Boardwalk and Central Park, both open to the air, and the indoor Royal Promenade.

The Boardwalk. An echo of Coney Island, the Boardwalk – which is open to the skies – contains shops (naturally) and an art gallery.

Eateries include a Boardwalk Donut Shop; Johnny Rockets, a burger/milk shake diner; and a covered Seafood Shack for fish and seafood. If you are in a Central Park cabin, you'll need to take the elevator to get to the closest pool – it's like going to the top of a building for a dip. Let's hope the pool volleyball game doesn't end up with the ball being tossed into the park – or onto someone's balcony while they're having coffee.

Central Park. This is 328ft (100m) long, with real vegetation, including 27 trees, almost 12,000 plants, and a vertical 'living' plant wall. But, unlike its New York inspiration, it includes, at its lower level, a 'town center.' At night, it's a quiet and serene area. Vintages wine and tapas bar is a chill-out venue, and there are several reservations-required, extra-charge dining venues; arguably the best is 150 Central Park, while Chops Grille and Giovanni's Table have become favorites.

The Royal Promenade is the equivalent of a floating shopping mall, with casual food eateries (including Starbucks, located at the forward end and open 7am–11pm daily), shops with all kinds of merchandise, video screens, and changing color lights at every step. It's all a bit surreal – like being in a circus at sea, with something going on every minute. But one thing not to be missed is the 'Move On! Move On!' parade, a delightful circus-like extravaganza that includes characters from DreamWorks Animation's Madagascar. Interior-view promenade cabins have balconies that look down onto the action in Central Park. A hydraulic, oval-shaped Rising Tide Bar moves slowly through three decks linking the double-width Royal Promenade with Central Park.

The Pool and Sports Zone forward of the twin funnels is a real adventurous fun place for families. An adults-only open-air solarium and rentable cabanas are part of the outdoor scene today, and Oasis provides several. Two Flow-Riders (surf simulators) are part of the sports line-up; these are located atop the ship around the aft exhaust mast, together with basketball courts and golf. The ship also has an extremely large jogging track.

The Solarium is a welcoming large, light-filled, restful (despite the background music) space. High atop ship, it is frequented by few children – so adults can 'escape' the Las Vegas-like atmosphere of other areas. On the subject of casinos, the roulette tables are stunning – all electronic, with touch buttons. There's also blackjack, craps, Caribbean Stud Poker, and 450 slot machines, plus a player's club and poker room – but this really can be a smoke-filled place, even in the 'no-smoking' area. The casino entrance features a display of gaming history.

Sadly, exterior wooden railings have mostly been replaced by fibreglass railings – it's particularly noticeable on cabin balconies.

Standing in line to make reservations for the main shows can be time-consuming and frustrating (the reservation booth is in the middle of the Royal Promenade). You could make them online before your cruise – good for families that like to plan their vacations together – but making changes can prove frustrating.

Ordering room service is complicated, and you can only do it via the interactive touch-screen television in your suite/cabin. Getting reservations in one of the specialty restaurants takes a bit of effort, unless you are in suite-grade accommodation. Smoking is permitted in several bars and lounges, and the smell of stale smoke permeates several areas. Cigar smokers will probably be underwhelmed by the cigar lounge.

Allure of the Seas operates from the purpose-built $75 million Terminal 18 in Port Everglades (Fort Lauderdale), whose restroom facilities are minimal.

Disembarkation. When the two 'flybridge' gangways are working, disembarkation is relatively speedy, but when only one is working, a line forms in the Royal Promenade, in which case it's better to sit somewhere until the line gets shorter. Disembarkation for non-US citizens can be appallingly slow.

ACCOMMODATION. There are a mind-boggling number of accommodation price grades, reflecting the choice of location and size. Suite occupants can access a concierge lounge and associated services. There are many family-friendly cabins, but no solo-occupancy cabins. The cabin numbering system is a bit awkward to get used to. Cabin doors open outwards (towards you), as in many European hotels. In many lower-grade rooms, closet access is awkward – often with a small sofa in the way. Most standard cabins are dimentionally challenged.

Many suite-grade cabins have bathrooms with granite-look washbasin counter tops, and two washbasins. Some have bidets, Jacuzzi tubs, and a separate shower enclosure. Some Family Suite grades have a separate, small room with bunk beds; some, but not all, have curtains to separate them. Some '395' interior balcony cabins have either Central Park or Royal Promenade views from their curved interior balconies (four are wheelchair-accessible), plus 80 cabins with windows (no balconies) and views of Central Park. Noise could be generated along the inner promenades, particularly late at night with street parades and non-stop music.

Loft Suites. Although ships such as the now-withdrawn *Queen Elizabeth 2*, *Saga Rose*, and *Saga Ruby* had upstairs/downstairs suites, RCI introduced 'loft' suites to the *Oasis*-class ships. These offer fine ocean views from floor-to-ceiling, double-height windows. Each has a lower living area plus a private balcony with sun chairs, and a stairway that connects to the sleeping area overlooking the living area; there are good ocean views. Modern designs are dotted with abstract, modern art pieces.

There are 28 Loft Suites – 25 measure 545 sq ft (51 sq m); three others (called Royal Loft Suites) measure 1,524 sq ft (141 sq m). Each sleeps up to six and each has a baby grand piano, indoor and outdoor dining areas, wet bar, library, and large 843-sq-ft (78.3-sq-m) balcony with flat-screen TV, entertainment area, and Jacuzzi. Two large Sky Loft Suites measure 722 sq ft (67 sq m) and 770 sq ft (71 sq m), and a 737-sq-ft (68-sq-m) Crown Accessible Loft Suite includes an elevator to aid disabled passengers.

Standard cabins (balcony and non-balcony class). Electrical sockets are located below the vanity desk (user-unfriendly). Also, it's difficult to watch television from the bed.

Washbasins in non-suite grade cabins are low, at just 30.5ins (77.5cm) above the floor, and tiny. Be careful – it's easy to hit your head on the mirror above. Small soap bars are provided, while shampoo is in a dispenser in the shower enclosure. Unfortunately, the shower head is fixed, making it difficult to wash yourself thoroughly. Although there is no soap dish or indentation in the washbasin surround for soap, one useful touch is a blue ceiling bathroom nightlight.

Cabins are exposed to noise and whatever is happening on the Boardwalk, including rehearsals and sports activities in the aft Aqua Theater, bells from the carousel forward (its 18 sculptured wooden animal figures took six weeks to carve), rowdy revelers on the Boardwalk late at night, plus screaming zi-plining participants during the day, not to mention loud music from bands playing poolside, and cruise director announcements repeating what's printed in the daily program!

If you have a Boardwalk-view balcony cabin, you'll need to close your curtains for privacy at times. However, the curved balconies – good for storing luggage to free up space inside the cabin – connect you with the open air. Almost all have sea views aft (just); those close to the aft Aqua Theater can use their balconies for a great view of any shows. The lowest deck of Boardwalk-view cabins has windows but no balcony (actually the view is mainly of the top of things such as the carousel). The best Boardwalk balcony cabins are, in my view, located on decks 8–12. For more privacy, however, it might be best to book a sea-facing balcony cabin, not one that overlooks the Boardwalk.

DINING. Spanning three decks, Opus (formerly the main dining room) was split into three different venues in 2015, when 'Dynamic Dining' (eat when you want within restaurant hours) was introduced. Each venue has its own menu: American Icon Grill, Silk (for Asian fusion cuisine), and The Grande (for a more formal dining and dressy experience).

Other dining options (some at extra cost). 150 Central Park, the most exclusive restaurant, combines haute-cuisine with interesting design. A kitchen observation window allows passers-by to watch the chefs (open for dinner only).

Chef's Table, on the upper level of the Concierge lounge, is available to all, and features a six-course meal with wine. It is hosted by the executive chef, but, with just 14 seats, getting a reservation can be difficult.

Giovanni's Table: this casual Italian-influenced dining spot has a rustic feel. It features toasted herb breads, pizzas, salads, pastas, sandwiches, braised meat dishes, and stews (it's worth the price if you're hungry).

Izumi Hibachi & Sushi offers Japanese-style cuisine, including a Teppanyaki menu.

Sabor Taquería & Tequila Bar is for modern tastes of Mexico, while Wonderland Imaginative Cuisine features imaginative fare.

Vintage is a wine bar with a robust selection of wines, accompanied by cheese and tapas (with an à-la-carte item charge).

Central Park Café, a casual deli-style spot with much variety and flexibility, is an indoor/outdoor food market with line-up counters and limited waiter service. Items include freshly prepared salads, made-to-order sandwiches, panini, crêpes, and hearty soups.

Other Boardwalk snacking spots: Donut Shop (for hot dogs, Wieners, Bratwurst, and other sausages), and an Ice Cream Parlor.

Elsewhere, eateries include Sorrento's Pizzeria; Park Café (for salads and light bites); and the Wipe Out Café.

ENTERTAINMENT. The 1,380-seat main show-lounge spans three decks, and stages the musical Chicago – an excellent, 90-minute-long production, just like the Broadway show (performed four times each cruise). Also, Frozen in Time is a stunning, must-see ice show at the ice-skating rink.

There's no charge for any show, and bookings can be made at www.royalcaribbean.com up to three months before your cruise, although reservations are not required. It is, however, quite difficult to change any reservations.

The 750-seat AquaTheater, outside at the ship's stern (with some overhang) has a 6,000-sq-ft (560-sq-m) stage, is a combination show theatre, sound stage, and events space (some great viewing places can be found high in the aft wings of the ship on both sides). A DreamWorks Animation aquatic acrobatic and dive show is also presented.

DreamWorks Animation Studios provides interactive shows featuring characters from *Shrek*, *Kung Fu Panda*, *Madagascar*, and *How to Train Your Dragon*.

SPA/FITNESS. The Vitality at Sea Spa includes a Vitality Café for extra-cost health drinks and snacks. The fitness center includes 158 cardio and resistance machines. An extra-cost thermal suite includes saunas, steam rooms, and heated tiled loungers. You can't just take a sauna for 10 minutes without paying for a one-day pass.

It's not that large. Try not to book a massage when the ship is due to arrive or leave an anchor port – some treatment rooms experience immense vibration when the anchor chain is in use. Steiner Leisure provides the staff and treatments.

Sports facilities include two (Surfrider) surfboard pools, golf putting course, ziplining (screaming mandatory), and an ice-skating rink – it's amazingly popular for kids.

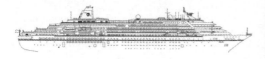

Amadea
★★★★

Size:	Small Ship	Passenger/Crew Ratio (lower beds):	2.0
Tonnage:	28,856	Cabins (total):	297
Lifestyle:	Standard	Size Range (sq ft/m):	182.9–649.0/17.0–60.3
Cruise Line:	Phoenix Reisen	Cabins (for one person):	0
Former Names:	Asuka	Cabins (with private balcony):	122
IMO Number:	8913162	Cabins (wheelchair accessible):	2
Builder:	Mitsubishi Heavy Industries (Japan)	Wheelchair accessibility:	Fair
Original Cost:	$150 million	Cabin Current:	110 volts
Entered Service:	Dec 1991/Mar 2006	Elevators:	5
Registry:	Bahamas	Casino (gaming tables):	No
Length (ft/m):	632.5/192.8	Slot Machines:	No
Beam (ft/m):	81.0/24.7	Swimming Pools:	1
Draft (ft/m):	21.6/6.6	Hot Tubs (on deck):	1
Propulsion/Propellers:	diesel (17,300kW)/2	Self-Service Launderette:	Yes
Passenger Decks:	8	Dedicated Cinema/Seats:	Yes/97
Total Crew:	292	Library:	Yes
Passengers (lower beds):	594	Onboard currency:	Euros
Passenger Space Ratio (lower beds):	48.5		

A stylish, spacious ship with fine food and service

OVERVIEW. *Amadea* is best suited to German-speaking couples, solo travelers, and families with children, who enjoy cruising in very comfortable surroundings aboard a contemporary ship. Because it absorbs people well, there is never any feeling of crowding.

THE SHIP. When introduced in 1991 as *Asuka*, this was the first all-new ship specially designed and built in Japan for the domestic market. It was sold to Phoenix Reisen and, as *Amadea*, started cruising for German-speaking passengers in 2006.

The ship, a more upscale vessel than other ships in the Phoenix Reisen fleet, has pleasing exterior styling and a contemporary profile, with a large, rounded, but squat funnel. There is a generous amount of open deck and sunbathing space, plus a wide walk-around teakwood promenade deck outdoors, good for strolling.

The 'cake-layer' stacking of the public rooms does hamper passenger flow and makes it a little disjointed, but this is because the public rooms are separated from the accommodation areas. There are many intimate public rooms, plenty of space, and lots of natural light.

The interior decor is understated but elegant, with pleasing color combinations, quality fabrics, and fine soft furnishings. There's some fascinating Japanese artwork, including Noriko Tamura's *Song of the Seasons*, a four-deck-high mural on the wall of the main foyer staircase – in many shades of pink and red.

Berlitz's Ratings

	Possible	Achieved
Ship	500	394
Accommodation	200	156
Food	400	319
Service	400	310
Entertainment	100	76
Cruise Experience	400	291
OVERALL SCORE		
1546 points out of 2000		

The delightfully relaxing Vista Lounge, the ship's observation lounge and bar, is also used for afternoon tea service.

Harry's Bar is a bar and lounge decorated in the style of a contemporary gentleman's club, complete with wood-paneled walls and burgundy leather chairs. This popular drinking spot has a light, airy feel. Located in a quiet area is the ship's library, with deeply comfortable armchairs, and a fireplace with electric fire. Cigar smokers will find the Havanna Bar a cozy little hideaway.

As for the dress code, there is a mix of formal and informal nights, while during the day attire is very casual. There is a self-service launderette with eight washing machines – useful for long voyages. Overall, the ship provides an extremely comfortable and serene cruising environment. All gratuities are included.

ACCOMMODATION. There are several price categories, although in reality there are just five types of suites and cabins. Three decks (8, 9, and 10) have suites and cabins with a private balcony (but no outside light)

Suites and cabins in all grades have ocean views, although some are slightly obstructed by the ship's gangway when it is in the raised (stowed) position.

In all grades, cherry wood cabinetry, which is in beautiful condition, has nicely rounded edges. Cabin soundproofing is excellent, and there is a good amount of closet and drawer space (including lockable drawers), refrigerator, and personal safe.

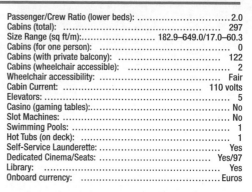

Most grades have bathrooms with bathtubs (and cabins available with shower), and all have a tiled floor and bath/shower area. While the suite bathrooms are generously proportioned, the 'standard' bathrooms are practical but small.

Two suites provide the largest accommodation; these are larger versions of the 'A' grade cabins. Each has a separate bedroom, with walk-in closet that includes a luggage deck, and twin beds that convert to a queen-size bed, sofa, two chairs and coffee table, large vanity desk, plenty of drawer space, and large TV. The marble-clad bathroom is large and has a whirlpool tub set alongside large ocean-view windows overlooking the private balcony, and twin washbasins set in a marble surround. There is a living room and separate guest bathroom. The private balcony is quite large and features a tropical plant set in a glass display enclosure.

In 2009, the company added two Spa Junior Suites; each has a private balcony with whirlpool tub, and good closet and drawer space.

The top grade cabins are very good living spaces and have twice the size and space of the standard cabins. Nicely decorated and outfitted, they have twin beds (convertible to a queen-size bed), sofa, two chairs and coffee table, large vanity desk, plenty of drawer space, and large color TV. However, when in its twin-bed configuration, the room's feng shui is poor, as one of the beds faces a large mirror at the writing/vanity desk – a negative for some people.

Many cabins have a private balcony with full floor-to-ceiling partition and a green synthetic turf floor (but no outside light) with floor-to-ceiling sliding door – and awkward door handles.

There's also an illuminated walk-in closet with long hanging rail and plenty of drawer space. The bathrooms, partly tiled and generously proportioned, include a plastic, glass-fronted toiletries cabinet, and two washbasins set in a thick marble surround.

DINING. There are two main restaurants, both with open seating for all meals. The Four Seasons has two sections; there are ocean-view windows along one side of the aft section, and along two sides of the forward section. The Amadea Restaurant is located on a higher deck, with ocean view windows on two sides. The cuisine is the same in both venues. For casual breakfasts and lunches, there's an informal self-serve Lido Café with plenty of outdoor seating, adjacent to a small pool and hot tub.

With this ship, Phoenix Reisen has taken its cuisine and service to a much higher level than that aboard its other ships (except *Artania*), by spending more money per passenger per day (this is also reflected in the cruise fare).

ENTERTAINMENT. The Atlantic Lounge is the venue for most entertainment events, including shows, social functions, and lectures. The room spans two decks, with seating on both main and balcony levels, and an extra-large wooden dance floor is provided for social dancing.

SPA/FITNESS. There is a spacious wellness center. It has large ocean-view windows, two baths, one hot tub, two saunas, steam room with wooden floor, several shower enclosures, a changing area with vanity counter, and a gymnasium. There are also five body treatment rooms, plus a relaxation area. Sports facilities include a golf court, driving cage, and putting green.

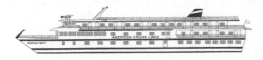

American Star
★★+

Size:	Boutique Ship	Passenger/Crew Ratio (lower beds):	3.4
Tonnage:	2,000	Cabins (total):	48
Lifestyle:	Standard	Size Range (sq ft/m):	204.0–240.0/18.9–22.2
Cruise Line:	American Cruise Lines	Cabins (for one person):	2
Former Names:	none	Cabins (with private balcony):	27
IMO Number:	9427615	Cabins (wheelchair accessible):	1
Builder:	Chesapeake Shipbuilding (USA)	Wheelchair accessibility:	Fair
Original Cost:	n/a	Cabin Current:	110 volts
Entered Service:	Jun 2007	Elevators:	1
Registry:	USA	Casino (gaming tables):	No
Length (ft/m):	220.0/67.0	Slot Machines:	No
Beam (ft/m):	46.0/14.0	Swimming Pools:	0
Draft (ft/m):	8.2/2.5	Hot Tubs (on deck):	0
Propulsion/Propellers:	diesel/2	Self-Service Launderette:	No
Passenger Decks:	4	Dedicated Cinema/Seats:	No
Total Crew:	27	Library:	Yes
Passengers (lower beds):	94	Onboard currency:	US$
Passenger Space Ratio (lower beds):	21.2		

A small US coastal cruising ship with limited facilities

OVERVIEW. *American Star* suits mature couples and solo travelers sharing a cabin and wishing to cruise in an all-American environment where the destinations are more important than food, service, or entertainment.

THE SHIP. This is one of three coastal cruise ships in the fleet of American Cruise Lines, which has its own shipyard in Chesapeake, Maryland. It is the company's nicest ship by far. *American Star* (sister ships: *American Glory* and *American Spirit*) is built for coastal and inland cruising to destinations unreachable by large cruise ships. The uppermost deck is open (good for views) behind a forward windbreaker; many sunloungers are provided, as is a small golf putting green.

Inside the ship, the public rooms include an observation lounge, with views forward and to port and starboard side (complimentary cocktails and hors d'oeuvres are offered before dinner); a library/lounge; a small midships lounge; and an elevator that goes to all decks, including the outdoor sun deck.

Cruises are typically of seven to 14 days' duration. The ship docks in town centers, or within walking distance of most towns and ports. The dress code is 'no ties casual.' It is extremely expensive for what you get. There are no additional costs, except for gratuities and port charges, because it's all included.

ACCOMMODATION. There are five cabin price grades (four are doubles, one is for singles). All cab-

Berlitz's Ratings

	Possible	Achieved
Ship	500	278
Accommodation	200	125
Food	400	236
Service	400	187
Entertainment	100	40
Cruise Experience	400	147
OVERALL SCORE		
1006 points out of 2000		

ins have twin beds, convertible to a king-size bed, a small desk with chair, satellite-feed flat-screen TV, DVD player and Internet access, clothes hanging space, and a modular bathroom with separate shower, washbasin, and toilet (no cabin has a bathtub), and windows that open. Accommodation/rooms incorrectly designated as suites (23) also have a private balcony each; although narrow, these do have two chairs and a small drinks table.

DINING. The dining salon, in the rear third of the vessel, has large, panoramic picture windows on three sides. Everyone dines at a single, open seating. The cuisine is all-American, and its 'Cruise Local. Eat Local' program includes sourcing produce, fish, and meats as near as possible to each cruise, and supporting local markets and small American businesses. There is no wine list, although basic white and red table wines are included.

Note: on the last morning of each cruise, only Continental breakfast is available (no hot food).

ENTERTAINMENT. There is no formal entertainment, although dinner and after-dinner conversation with fellow passengers in the ship's lounge/bar really becomes the entertainment each evening. Otherwise, take a good book.

SPA/FITNESS. There is a tiny fitness room with a few bicycles and other exercise machines.

Amsterdam
★★★★

Size:	Mid-size Ship
Tonnage:	62,735
Lifestyle:	Premium
Cruise Line:	Holland America Line
Former Names:	none
IMO Number:	9188037
Builder:	Fincantieri (Italy)
Original Cost:	$400 million
Entered Service:	Oct 2000
Registry:	The Netherlands
Length (ft/m):	780.8/238.0
Beam (ft/m):	105.8/32.2
Draft (ft/m):	25.5/7.8
Propulsion/Propellers:	diesel-electric (37,500kW)/ 2 azimuthing pods
Passenger Decks:	12
Total Crew:	600
Passengers (lower beds):	1,380

Passenger Space Ratio (lower beds):	45.4
Passenger/Crew Ratio (lower beds):	2.3
Cabins (total):	690
Size Range (sq ft/m):	184.0–1,124.8/17.1–104.5
Cabins (for one person):	0
Cabins (with private balcony):	172
Cabins (wheelchair accessible):	20
Wheelchair accessibility:	Good
Cabin Current:	110 and 220 volts
Elevators:	12
Casino (gaming tables):	Yes
Slot Machines:	Yes
Swimming Pools:	2 (1 w/ sliding glass dome)
Hot Tubs (on deck):	2
Self-Service Launderette:	Yes
Dedicated Cinema/Seats:	Yes/235
Library:	Yes
Onboard currency:	US$

Dutch-style decor and friendly service for mature cruisers

OVERVIEW. *Amsterdam* is extremely comfortable, with fine, elegant, and luxurious decorative features. On the negative side, the quality of food and service is poor and there's a lack of understanding of what it really takes to make a 'luxury' cruise experience, despite what is touted in Holland America Line's (HAL's) brochures.

THE SHIP. *Amsterdam*, a close sister ship to *Rotterdam*, has a nicely raked bow, as well as the familiar interior flow and design style. It was the first ship in the HAL fleet to feature an azimuthing pod propulsion system. The pods are powered by a diesel-electric system.

The decor retains much of the traditional ocean liner detailing so loved by frequent passengers, with some use of medium and dark wood paneling. However, some color combinations – particularly for the chairs and soft furnishings – are rather wacky. Much of the artwork reflects the line's glorious past, as well as items depicting the city of Amsterdam's history.

The interior focal point is a three-deck-high atrium, in an oval, instead of circular, shape. A whimsical 'Astrolabe' is the featured centerpiece in this atrium. Also clustered in the atrium lobby are the reception desk, shore excursion desk, photo shop, and photo gallery.

The ship has three principal passenger stairways – so much better than two from the viewpoint of safety, flow, and accessibility. There is a glass-covered pool on the Lido Deck between the mast and the twin funnels, watched over by a sculpture of a brown bear catching salmon.

Berlitz's Ratings

	Possible	Achieved
Ship	500	397
Accommodation	200	150
Food	400	261
Service	400	268
Entertainment	100	73
Cruise Experience	400	285
OVERALL SCORE		
1434 points out of 2000		

The casino, in the middle of a major passenger flow on one of the entertainment decks, has blackjack, roulette, poker, and dice tables alongside the requisite rows of slot machines.

HAL provides cappuccino and espresso coffees and free ice cream at certain times, as well as hot hors d'oeuvres in all bars – something other major lines have dropped, or charge extra for.

The charge to use the washing machines and dryers in the self-service launderette is irritating.

Perhaps the ship's best asset is its friendly and personable Filipino and Indonesian crew, although communication (in English) can prove frustrating at times, particularly in the dining room and informal buffet areas. The room service menu is limited, and room service is very basic.

FAMILIES. There are children's and teens' play areas – token gestures by a company that traditionally does not cater well to children. Popcorn is available at the Wajang Theater for moviegoers, while adjacent is the popular Java Café.

ACCOMMODATION. This is spread over five decks (some cabins have full or partially obstructed views), in 16 grades: 11 with outside views, and five interior grades (no view). There are four Penthouse Suites, and 50 suites – 14 more than aboard sister ship *Rotterdam*. With one whole deck of suites (and a dedicated, private Concierge Lounge, with preferential passenger treatment), the company has in effect created a two-class ship. No cabin is more than 130ft (40m) from a stairway, which makes it very easy to find your way from your cabin to the public rooms. Although 81 percent of cabins have outside views, only 25 percent of those have balconies.

All of the 'standard' interior and outside-view cabins are tastefully furnished, and have twin beds that convert to a queen-size bed – but the space is a little tight for walking between beds and the vanity unit. There is a decent amount of closet and drawer space, although this will be tight for longer voyages. The fully tiled bathrooms are disappointingly small, particularly on long cruises, the shower tubs are very small, and the storage for toiletries is quite basic. There is little detailing to distinguish the bathrooms from those aboard the Statendam-class ships. All cabin TV sets carry CNN and TNT, as well as movies, and ship information and shopping channels.

There are 50 Verandah Suites and four Penthouse Suites on Navigation Deck; all share a private Concierge Lounge, with a concierge to handle such things as special dining arrangements, shore excursions, and special requests. Strangely there are no butlers for these suites, as aboard ships with similar facilities. The lounge, with its wood detailing and private library, is accessible only by private key-card.

Four Penthouse Suites each have a separate steward's entrance, plus a separate bedroom with king-size bed, vanity desk, large walk-in closet with excellent drawer and hanging space, living room, dining room (seating up to eight), wet bar, and pantry. The bathroom is large, and has a big oval Jacuzzi tub, separate shower enclosure, two washbasins, and separate toilet and bidet. A guest bathroom has a toilet and washbasin. There is a good-size private balcony. Suite occupants get personal stationery, complimentary laundry and ironing, cocktail-hour hors d'oeuvres and other goodies, as well as priority embarkation and disembarkation.

DINING. The La Fontaine Dining Room seats 747, spans two decks, and has a huge stained-glass ceiling measuring almost 1,500 sq ft (140 sq m), with a floral motif and fiber-optic lighting. There are tables for two, four, six, or eight, but few tables for two. Both open seating and fixed (assigned tables and times) seating are available, while breakfast and lunch are open seating (you'll be seated by restaurant staff when you enter). Rosenthal china and fine cutlery are provided.

Other dining options. The 88-seat Pinnacle Grill is available to all passengers on a reservation-only basis, with priority reservations given to those in suite grades. There is a cover charge, but there's better food and presentation than in the main dining room (it's open for lunch and dinner, reservations required). The whimsically surreal artwork features scenic landscapes. The cuisine is California-Italian in style, with small portions and few vegetables. The wine list is good, and wines are served in the correct stemware.

Another venue, the Lido Buffet Restaurant, is open for casual dinners on all except the last night of each cruise, in an open-seating arrangement. Tables are set with crisp linens, flatware, and standard stemware. A set menu includes a choice of four entrées (main courses).

For casual breakfasts and lunches, the Lido Buffet Restaurant provides old-style, stand-in-line serve-yourself canteen food – adequate for anyone used to TV dinner food, but most definitely not as lavish as the brochures claim. Although the salad items appear adequate when displayed, they are too cold and quite devoid of taste. The constant supply of iceberg lettuce doesn't seem to go away, but there is little choice of other, more suitable, lettuces and greens.

Also, a poolside 'Dive-In at the Terrace Grill' features signature burgers (Dive-In sauce), hot dogs, and fries.

ENTERTAINMENT. The 577-seat Queen's Lounge is the venue for all production shows, strong cabaret, and other entertainment. It is two decks high, with main and balcony level seating. The stage has hydraulic lifts and three video screens, and closed-loop system for the hearing-impaired.

While HAL is not known for its fine entertainment (the budgets aren't high enough), what the line does offer is a consistently good, tried-and-tested array of cabaret acts. The production shows, while a decent attempt, fall short on storyline, choreography, and performance, with colorful costuming and lighting hiding the weak spots.

A number of bands, a string ensemble, and solo musicians present live music for dancing and listening in many of the lounges and bars. There's dancing in the Crows Nest (atop the navigation bridge) and serenading string music in the Explorer's Lounge, among other venues.

SPA/FITNESS. The Ocean Spa is located one deck above the navigation bridge at the very forward part of the ship. It includes a gymnasium with all the latest muscle-pumping exercise machines, including an abundance of treadmills. It has forward views over the ship's bows. There's an aerobics exercise area, large beauty salon with ocean-view windows to the port side, several treatment rooms, and men's and women's saunas, steam rooms, and changing areas.

The spa is operated by Steiner, a specialist concession, whose young staff will try to sell you Steiner's own-brand Elemis beauty products. Some fitness classes are free. Massage facials, pedicures, and beauty salon treatments cost extra.

For the sports-minded, two paddle-tennis courts are located at the aft of the Sports Deck.

Anthem of the Seas
★★★★

Size:	Large Resort Ship	Passenger Space Ratio (lower beds):	40.3	
Tonnage:	168,666	Passenger/Crew Ratio (lower beds):	3.2	
Lifestyle:	Standard	Cabins (total):	2,090	
Cruise Line:	Royal Caribbean International	Size Range (sq ft/m):	101.1–799.7/9.4–74.3	
Former Names:	none	Cabins (for one person):	34	
IMO Number:	9656101	Cabins (with private balcony):	1,571	
Builder:	Meyer Werft (Germany)	Cabins (wheelchair accessible):	34	
Original Cost:	$1.03 billion	Wheelchair accessibility:	Good	
Entered Service:	Mar 2015	Cabin Current:	Meyer Werft (Germany)	
Registry:	Bahamas	Elevators:	16	
Length (ft/m):	1112.2/339.0	Casino (gaming tables):	Yes	
Beam (ft/m):	134.5/41.0	Slot Machines:	Yes	
Draft (ft/m):	27.8/8.5	Swimming Pools:	3	
Propulsion/Propellers:	diesel-electric (41,000kW)/ 2 azimuthing pods	Hot Tubs (on deck):		
		Self-Service Launderette:	No	
Passenger Decks:	16	Dedicated Cinema/Seats:	No	
Total Crew:	1,300	Library:	Yes	
Passengers (lower beds):	4,180	Onboard currency:	US$	

A high-tech, high-energy, gizmo-filled family-friendly resort

OVERVIEW. *Anthem of the Seas* is the sister ship to *Quantum of the Seas*, which debuted in 2014. It incorporates all of the latest tech-intensive bling and entertaining features.

THE SHIP. The ship's exterior design (it was built in several huge sections and joined together) looks somewhat like a 'stretched' version of the slender *Celebrity Reflection* and employs the latest in hydrodynamics, hull shape, low emissions, and, importantly, low fuel consumption. The stern slopes nicely – it looks like it could be the front!

Aft is Two70 – an innovative multi-level venue that is a casual living area by day, and a stunning, high-energy entertainment venue by night, with dynamic robotic screens complementing its huge video wall.

Several novel attractions have been incorporated. North Star – quite the engineering marvel – is a 14-person (including an operator) glass capsule that lifts you off from the ship's uppermost deck for a bird's-eye view of all below you, as it moves around. It's like a posh giant 'cherry picker' with attitude, and, with an outreach of almost 135ft (41m), is quite a ride! Located in the front section, just behind the ship's mast, it is complimentary (and wheelchair-accessible), but only operates at sea. A charge applies for booking for weddings and other romantic occasions.

The second stunner is RipCord by iFly – a simulated skydiving experience in a two-storey vertical wind tunnel that lets you experience the thrill of skydiving in a safe, controlled environment. The unit uses a powerful air flow to keep you up – like a giant hairdryer

Berlitz's Ratings		
	Possible	Achieved
Ship	500	431
Accommodation	200	142
Food	400	298
Service	400	286
Entertainment	100	88
Cruise Experience	400	287
OVERALL SCORE		
1528 points out of 2000		

underneath you! It is located aft of the ship's funnel housing, and accommodates 13 persons for each 75-minute class, including two 'hovering in the air' experiences, instruction and gear. You can book both attractions with interactive digital kiosks (adjacent to elevators) and tablets in public areas.

A brain-teasing team challenge can be had in a special puzzle room called Escape from the Future; collectively, the team will need to solve brainteasers within an hour in order to 'get out' – and you thought this was a vacation!

Meanwhile, a SeaPlex complex – located between the two funnels under the North Star – features a circus 'school' and adrenalin-boosting bumper-car rides, and acts as a roller-skating rink and basketball court. It's a veritable interactive sporting venue that replaces the ice rinks of most other RCI ships. Other facilities include a rock-climbing wall, and a Flow-Rider surfing simulator.

The decor is ultra-contemporary, rainbow colorful, and jazzy to boot. The interior focal point is the three-storey-high Royal Esplanade, which includes Michael's Genuine Pub, Sorrento's pizza outlet, a Bionic Bar, Music Hall (a two-deck-high entertainment venue), plus several shops, the Schooner Bar, Boleros (Latin bar), Izumi (for Japanese-style cuisine), and the American Icon Grill.

This ship should be a fabulous cruise experience for the whole family, but, be warned: it's all about making reservations – lots of them – if you want to be sure not to miss out. High-speed wi-fi is extremely expensive, but all cabins come equipped with a USB socket for charging your digital devices.

What this ship does superbly well is entertain you, and I highly recommended it for a first cruise, because of the excellent range of activities, the entertainment, and some very good dining experiences.

FAMILIES. For children and teenagers, the facilities on Decks 11 and 12 are extensive – part of the Adventure Ocean program. Royal Babies and Tots Nursery is for the really young ones; Aquanauts is for 3–5-year-olds; Explorers is for 6–8-year-olds; Voyagers is for 9–12-year-olds. Optix is the chill-out zone for teenagers. There's also Adventure Beach, an area for all the family, which includes swimming pools, a water slide and game areas outdoors in the AquaPark. DreamWorks events and entertainment are featured, with live character appearances from *Shrek*, *Kung Fu Panda* and *Madagascar* – not to mention *Barbie*. Unfortunately, the kids' pool is adjacent to a smoking area.

ACCOMMODATION. There are many different accommodation price grades and categories, with the price dependent on size and location. Every cabin has a view, whether real or virtual. 'Virtual' balconies – first introduced aboard *Navigator of the Seas* in 2013 – are a neat feature of the interior cabins; they can provide real-time ocean views, but you *can* turn them off. Optional wrist-bands (with RFID technology) provide access to your cabin, and act as your charge card (you have to take it off in order to give to the bartender), but they are uncomfortable to wear.

Several new accommodation categories and types have been introduced aboard this ship. Standard cabins are about nine percent larger than those aboard the *Oasis*-class ships. Suite-grade occupants can eat all their meals in the exclusive Coastal Kitchen.

Loft cabins (including a 975 sq ft/90.5 sq m Owner's Loft) vary in size, but measure about 502 sq ft (46.6 sq m) and are located at the ship's stern.

Inter-connecting family cabins are great for multi-generational groups. The 15 units consist of a junior suite, balcony cabin, and interior studio connected through a shared vestibule. Together they can create 575.8 sq ft (53.5 sq m) of living space with three bedrooms and a 216-sq-ft (20-sq-m) balcony.

There are 34 'studio' cabins (12 have balconies; all have wall beds) for solo occupancy. As there's no solo supplement, they are priced in a new category.

Even the smallest bathroom is well designed, with touches such as a night light, and shower and vanity hooks, while cabins have ample storage space.

Negatives include the fact that tablet-based infotainment systems don't answer questions, and the room service menu for breakfast is poor.

DINING. There are 18 restaurant and eatery choices (there's no single main dining room as such). You can go for the same table each night, if you choose the 'classic' option, part of the line's Dynamic Dining (a concept first introduced by Star Cruises). The 'classic' option means that you (together with your waiter) will rotate each night between the four principal (free) restaurants). Overall, however, meals are hit and miss, with extra charges for some dishes.

Some extra-cost restaurants require reservations, which can prove frustrating. Note that the menus are the same each night in most extra-cost restaurants, and service can be slow (there are no assistant waiters).

The following are complimentary (with tablecloths for dinner):

The Grande: with 432 seats, the ship's most elegant restaurant (think Southern mansion hospitality) features classic dishes reminiscent of the days of grand ocean liners. Chic: this 434-seat restaurant features 'contemporary' cuisine and sauces made from scratch. Silk: this 434-seat restaurant features pan-Asian cuisine. American Icon Grill: this 430-seat restaurant features many of America's favorite 'comfort food' dishes.

Extra-cost venues:

Wonderland: based on the four (real and imagined) elements Fire, Ice, Water, Earth, and Dreams, this surreal 62-seat Alice in Wonderland-inspired venue offers food with a quirky touch, including several superb dishes using liquid nitrogen for smoke-infused specialties. It's really worth paying extra for.

Jamie's Italian: it's a 132-seat reservations-required tablecloth-free Euro-Italian bistro – and British celebrity chef Jamie Oliver's first restaurant at sea. Chops Grille: for premium-quality steaks and grilled seafood. Chef's Table: this exclusive 16-seat venue (located within Chops Grille) is good for private parties, with wine-and-food pairing the specialty. Izumi: a 44-seat Japanese-Asian fusion cuisine venue including hot-rock tableside cooking, sashimi, sushi, and sake. Johnny Rockets: a retro 1950s all-day, all-night diner-style eatery (near the main pool) for hamburgers, extra-cost malt shakes, and jukebox hits (all tables feature a mini-jukebox). A-la-carte pricing applies.

For really casual meals at no extra cost, the 860-seat Windjammer Marketplace is a self-serve buffet-style eatery. Other casual (no-extra-cost) spots include: The Café at Two70o; SeaPlex Dog House, Sorrento's – for pizza slices and calzones, and Café Promenade.

ENTERTAINMENT. The Royal Theater spans three decks and is the principal showlounge for 'booked' shows and large-scale production shows by a resident troupe of singers and dancers (reservations advised).

There's also entertainment by night at Two70o and in the Music Hall (DJs and theme nights).

SPA/FITNESS. The Vitality at Sea Spa facilities include a thermal suite (at extra cost), beauty salon, barber shop, and gymnasium with Technogym equipment. Massage and other body-pampering treatments take place in 19 treatment rooms.

Arcadia
★★★★

Size:	Mid-size Ship
Tonnage:	82,972
Lifestyle:	Standard
Cruise Line:	P&O Cruises
Former Names:	none
IMO Number:	9226906
Builder:	Fincantieri (Italy)
Original Cost:	$400 million
Entered Service:	Apr 2005
Registry:	Bermuda
Length (ft/m):	936.0/285.3
Beam (ft/m):	105.0/32.0
Draft (ft/m):	25.5/7.8
Propulsion/Propellers:	diesel-electric (34,000kW)/ 2 azimuthing pods
Passenger Decks:	10
Total Crew:	886
Passengers (lower beds):	1,994

Passenger Space Ratio (lower beds):	37.4
Passenger/Crew Ratio (lower beds):	2.3
Cabins (total):	1,000
Size Range (sq ft/m):	170–516.6/15.7–48
Cabins (for one person):	6
Cabins (with private balcony):	684
Cabins (wheelchair accessible):	30
Wheelchair accessibility:	Good
Cabin Current:	110 and 220 volts
Elevators:	14
Casino (gaming tables):	Yes
Slot Machines:	Yes
Swimming Pools:	2
Hot Tubs (on deck):	5
Self-Service Launderette:	Yes
Dedicated Cinema/Seats:	Yes
Library:	Yes
Onboard currency:	UK£

A very British, contemporary, adults-only ship

OVERVIEW. *Arcadia* is a modern cruise ship based in Southampton, England – so UK passengers can avoid airports. It is for couples and solo travelers looking for a large, adults-only ship, with entertainment geared to British tastes, an informal setting, and with plenty of public rooms to experience.

THE SHIP. *Arcadia*, originally intended to be Cunard Line's *Queen Victoria*, was transferred to the P&O Cruises brand (both companies are owned by the giant Carnival Corporation).

Outdoors facilities include a walk-around promenade deck (the ship's forward section is covered), with plenty of sunloungers and cushioned pads. A large Lido Deck pool has a moveable glass-domed cover – useful in poor weather. Panoramic exterior glass-wall elevators grace the central foyer to port and starboard and travel between all 10 passenger decks. Pod propulsion is provided, so there's no vibration.

The layout provides a decent horizontal flow, with most public rooms, shops, bars, and lounges set open-plan style on two principal decks, so finding your way around is relatively easy, except that the layout of upper public room decks is disjointed. The interior decor is geared towards those with youthful, contemporary tastes. It is, however, restrained, but lacking any connection to the more traditional features that P&O Cruises is known for. There are 3,000 works of art by British artists, costing $4 million. Although *Arcadia* is one of the Carnival Corporation's Vista-class ships, the decor is perhaps the most subtle of them

Berlitz's Ratings		
	Possible	Achieved
Ship	500	397
Accommodation	200	144
Food	400	255
Service	400	285
Entertainment	100	73
Cruise Experience	400	269
OVERALL SCORE		
1423 points out of 2000		

all, and both passenger flow and signage are generally good.

Facilities include a forward-facing Crow's Nest observation lounge high atop the ship (in a contemporary setting nicely refurbished in 2013); a florist, a gift shop arcade, a Monte Carlo casino, a library (with leather armchairs and a Waterstone's section for paperback sales), a 30-seat boutique screening room, and The Retreat (a good place to meet and chill out). The 14 bars include the Spinnaker Bar (good for ship buffs, with its display of ship models), a 'traditional' English pub (The Rising Sun, with Boddington's draught beer), plus a bar overlooking a modest three-deck-high atrium lobby. The ship really lacks a 'soul', because there is no central meeting point – no atrium lobby as such to act as a social centre – quite different to *Oceana*, for example.

Arcadia blends time-honored British cruising with contemporary facilities, but it is completely different from other more traditional ships in the fleet. It is registered in Bermuda, so UK and US passport holders can be legally married by the ship's captain (check with P&O Cruises for the latest requirements). You can also renew your vows in a special ceremony. The ship underwent a refurbishment program in 2013, in which one new suite, and 23 new cabins were added (including 6 for singles) in a new structure aft of the Crow's Nest, plus a new Harrods store (and revitalized shopping area), and an extra-cost East Restaurant, which replaced the former Orchid Restaurant.

A New Horizons lecture program provides an array of lectures on a range of subjects (introductory sessions at no charge; more in-depth subject matter study in smaller groups, at an additional cost).

Many extra onboard revenue centers have appeared aboard P&O Cruises' ships, including *Arcadia* – such as paying for lectures and thalassotherapy pool use. Smoking is permitted only on cabin balconies and in designated spots on the open decks.

Passenger niggles: there is no room for card games such as bridge; dance floor space is pitiful; and the embarkation system keeps people waiting in a lounge after lines at the check-in desks and security until boarding card letters are called. The small public toilets are missing touches such as flowers and hand towels; there are no poolside towels (you must take them from your cabin); poolside gala receptions lack atmosphere; and pre-dinner announcements are robotic. The often-noisy air conditioning cannot be turned off in cabins or bathrooms.

ACCOMMODATION. While there are plenty of price grades, there are really only five types of accommodation: suites, mini-suites, cabins with private balcony, and twin-bedded cabins with or without a window.

All cabin doors and elevators also have numbers in Braille. All accommodation has duvets (or blankets and pillows if you prefer), flat-screen TVs (the audio channels are also on the television, but you can't turn the picture off), tea/coffee-making sets with Tetley teabags and long-life milk, small refrigerator, vanity/writing desk, personal safe, hairdryer; bathrooms have half-size tubs/shower/washbasin, and toilet. Personal toiletries are by Temple Spa, with larger bottles and more selection choice provided for suite occupants.

Also standard are stylish bed runners, Slumberland eight-inch sprung mattresses, 10.5 tog duvets (blankets and pillows if you prefer), Egyptian cotton towels and robes, improved tea/coffee-making facilities with specialty teas (long-life is provided), as well as in-cabin toning and fitness facilities for passengers who would prefer to exercise in private.

In twin-bedded cabin grades (approximately 170 sq ft/16 sq m), when the beds are pushed together, there's little room to maneuver.

Accommodation designated as suites (approximately 516 sq ft/48 sq m, including balcony) and mini-suites (approximately 384 sq ft/36 sq m, including balcony) benefit from more space (some are really just the size of two cabins), king-size bed, trouser press, ironing board and iron, three-seat sofa (suites) or two-seat sofa (mini-suites), wall clock, and binoculars. The bathrooms are larger, and include an aquajet tub, two washbasins, toilet, and separate shower (suites only).

So-called 'butler' service is provided, but, unlike most lines with these kinds of grades, bottled water costs extra, as do soft drinks.

Passenger niggles include the space-hogging tea/coffee-making set on the small vanity desk in the standard cabin grades, although the set itself is good. Other gripes about standard cabins include: closets with hanging space too narrow for the width of a jacket; little drawer space; poor-quality plastic hangers; and no hooks for belts.

DINING. The Meridian Restaurant, located aft, is on two decks, connected by a spiral staircase; it features 11 fine glass fiber-optic ceiling chandeliers created by Neil Wilkin. A podium with grand piano graces the upper level, which is for Freedom Dining – you can go anytime between 6.30pm and 9.30pm. There are two seatings (called Club Dining) in the lower level restaurant only, and tables are for two to eight people. Note that the glasses for both red and white wines are small.

Other dining options. Ocean Grill, by Marco Pierre White, specializes in prime steaks and seafood – with lots of taste. East Restaurant (on Deck 11) has fine panoramic views, Asian-fusion (spice-heavy) cuisine created by Michelin-starred chef Atul Kochhar, and its own bar. Reservations are required in both venues, and a cover charge applies.

For casual meals and snacks, there's a self-serve 24-hour eatery (The Belvedere), a section of which becomes another dining venue at night, serving Indian cuisine. There's also an open-deck Neptune Grill and Caffè Vivo (indoors, adjacent to the library).

ENTERTAINMENT. The Palladium show lounge is an entertainment palace with three seating tiers and excellent high-tech staging, lighting, and sound systems. Seating is in both banquette-style and individual tub chairs, and the sight lines to the stage are generally good. There are several major production shows.

Late-night party types can dance and scream in The Globe. Classical concerts may also be scheduled for many cruises.

Professional dance hosts and teachers are usually carried (but ballroom dance aficionados should note that there are few wooden dance floors).

SPA/FITNESS. The Ocean Spa includes a gymnasium with good forward ocean views, 10 body-pampering treatment rooms, a thermal suite that incorporates a hydrotherapy pool, sauna and steam room, and two small unisex saunas at no charge, but in a location that discourages their use (the thermal suite is better). While the tiny sauna is free, there's a charge to use the Aqua Pool. To get from the changing room to the sauna you must walk across a carpeted foyer.

Additionally, The Retreat is a cool space for relaxation, and for calming classes such as tai chi and yoga. The spa is operated by the UK-based Harding Brothers. Sports facilities include a sports court for racquet or football games, a golf driving range, and the traditional shuffleboard and ringtoss.

Artania
★★★★

Size:	Mid-size Ship
Tonnage:	44,348
Lifestyle:	Standard
Cruise Line:	Phoenix Reisen
Former Names:	*Royal Princess*
IMO Number:	8201480
Builder:	Wartsila (Finland)
Original Cost:	$165 million
Entered Service:	Nov 1984/Apr 2011
Registry:	Bahamas
Length (ft/m):	754.5/230.0
Beam (ft/m):	95.8/29.2
Draft (ft/m):	25.5/7.8
Propulsion/Propellers:	diesel (29,160kW)/2
Passenger Decks:	9
Total Crew:	520
Passengers (lower beds):	1,176
Passenger Space Ratio (lower beds):	37.7
Passenger/Crew Ratio (lower beds):	2.2
Cabins (total):	588
Size Range (sq ft/m):	186.0–1,126.0/17.2–104.5
Cabins (for one person):	0
Cabins (with private balcony):	273
Cabins (wheelchair accessible):	4
Wheelchair accessibility:	Good
Cabin Current:	110 and 220 volts
Elevators:	6
Casino (gaming tables):	No
Slot Machines:	No
Swimming Pools:	2
Hot Tubs (on deck):	2
Self-Service Launderette:	Yes
Dedicated Cinema/Seats:	Yes/150
Library:	Yes
Onboard currency:	Euros

A comfortable, spacious ship for mature-age cruisers

OVERVIEW. *Artania* should provide a fine experience in spacious, reserved contemporary surroundings, at a decent price. It is best suited to German-speaking couples and solo travelers seeking to cruise in a modern, but unpretentious, mid-size ship.

THE SHIP. There's a traditional walk-around teak deck, and the ship has extensive outdoor deck and sunbathing space, plus a wave-action swimming pool.

The interior décor reflects the feeling of space, openness, and light; the passenger flow is good. There are several nicely appointed public rooms, bars, and lounges, plus wide passageways and three spacious stairways (with slightly different carpet colors).

A Pacific Lounge, set around the funnel base, has fine views and a peaceful environment during the day; each evening it becomes a lively nightclub. Around the central stairway foyer, is the popular Harry's Bar; there's also a Bodega (tavern) for food and drinks. A 7 percent gratuity is added to bar accounts.

ACCOMMODATION. The all-outside view cabins (270 with private balcony) represent just four accommodation types (including suites), although there are 21 price categories. All of the cabins (most of which have twin beds convertible into a queen-size bed) are comfortable and well appointed.

All have a large shower enclosure, color TV, hairdryer, personal safe, and European two-pin sockets. Also standard are stylish bed runners,

Berlitz's Ratings

	Possible	Achieved
Ship	500	382
Accommodation	200	153
Food	400	319
Service	400	308
Entertainment	100	74
Cruise Experience	400	285
OVERALL SCORE		
1521 points out of 2000		

high-quality sprung mattresses, European duvets, and cotton towels. L'Occitane personal toiletries are provided, as are chocolates on your pillow each night. Prompt, attentive room service is provided 24 hours a day.

Some cabins on both Apollo Deck and Orion Deck have full or partial lifeboat- and safety equipment-obstructed views, and some cabins have extra sofa beds fitted, which is good for families during the busy summer and school-holiday months.

The 12 largest suites are attractive, but, with the exception of the Royal Suite, are not large, and the balconies are small, although all have teak decking. Suite occupants get an expanded range of toiletries and complimentary mineral water.

DINING. The Vier Jahreszeiten (Four Seasons) restaurant is set low down in the ship, conveniently adjacent to the lobby. One deck above is the Artania Restaurant, with adjacent bar. Casual meals can be taken in the indoor-outdoor Lido Restaurant.

ENTERTAINMENT. The Atlantik Showlounge hosts shows, drama, and cabaret acts. Volume is normally kept to an acceptable level.

SPA/FITNESS. The Artania Spa contains a gym with muscle-toning equipment, saunas and changing rooms. There's also a steam bath, ice-fountain, and salon. For the sports-minded, there's table tennis, table-soccer, shuffleboard, and darts.

Artemis
★★★+

Size:	Boutique Ship	Passenger/Crew Ratio (lower beds):	2.3
Tonnage:	1,206	Cabins (total):	26
Lifestyle:	Premium	Size Range (sq ft/m):	140.0–210.0/13.0–19.5
Cruise Line:	Grand Circle Cruise Line	Cabins (for one person):	2
Former Names:	none	Cabins (with private balcony):	18
IMO Number:	9398010	Cabins (wheelchair accessible):	0
Builder:	Brodogaliste Shipyard (Croatia)	Wheelchair accessibility:	None
Original Cost:	n/a	Cabin Current:	110 volts
Entered Service:	Jun 2009	Elevators:	1
Registry:	Malta	Casino (gaming tables):	No
Length (ft/m):	196.8/60.0	Slot Machines:	No
Beam (ft/m):	36.0/11.0	Swimming Pools:	1
Draft (ft/m):	9.8/3.0	Hot Tubs (on deck):	0
Propulsion/Propellers:	diesel/2	Self-Service Launderette:	No
Passenger Decks:	4	Dedicated Cinema/Seats:	No
Total Crew:	21	Library:	No
Passengers (lower beds):	50	Onboard currency:	US$
Passenger Space Ratio (lower beds):	50.0		

A cute pocket-sized ship for in-depth cultural voyages

OVERVIEW. *Artemis* is one of three fully owned sister ships (the others are *Arethusa* and *Athena*) for Grand Circle Cruise Line.

THE SHIP. *Artemis* is a cute little ship, with a dark blue hull, built specifically for in-depth coastal cruising. The lobby is reminiscent of those found aboard the company's riverships.

The outdoor aft deck area has a bar and canopy cover (which can be removed for warm climate cruising) inboard from two lifeboats that also act as shore tenders.

ACCOMMODATION. The cabins, though small, each have a bed that can be used as a sofa during the day, flat-screen TV with CNN, telephone, personal safe, mini-fridge, individually controlled air condi-

Berlitz's Ratings	Possible	Achieved
Ship	500	327
Accommodation	200	132
Food	400	254
Service	400	258
Entertainment	100	62
Cruise Experience	400	263
OVERALL SCORE		
1296 points out of 2000		

tioning, hair dryer, and dual electrical outlets.

The 18 cabins on Upper Deck have en-suite bathrooms with showers (no cabins have bathtubs), and large sliding glass doors that open onto private balconies. The six cabins on Main Deck have portholes that can be opened, while the two solo traveler-occupancy cabins have portholes that cannot be opened.

DINING. The Restaurant seats all passengers in a single seating.

ENTERTAINMENT. The entertainment is strictly limited to conversation with fellow travelers.

SPA/FITNESS. It's such a small ship, there are no facilities for this.

Astor
★★★+

Size:	Small Ship	Passenger/Crew Ratio (lower beds):	1.9
Tonnage:	20,606	Cabins (total):	295
Lifestyle:	Standard	Size Range (sq ft/m):	140.0–280.0/13.0–26.0
Cruise Line:	CMV/Transocean Cruises	Cabins (for one person):	0
Former Names:	Fedor Dostoyevskiy, Astor (II)	Cabins (with private balcony):	0
IMO Number:	8506373	Cabins (wheelchair accessible):	0
Builder:	Howaldtswerke Deutsche Werft (Germany)	Wheelchair accessibility:	Fair
Original Cost:	$65 million	Cabin Current:	220 volts
Entered Service:	Feb 1987/Apr 1997	Elevators:	3
Registry:	The Bahamas	Casino (gaming tables):	Yes
Length (ft/m):	579.0/176.5	Slot Machines:	Yes
Beam (ft/m):	74.1/22.6	Swimming Pools:	2
Draft (ft/m):	20.0/6.1	Hot Tubs (on deck):	1
Propulsion/Propellers:	diesel (15,400kW)/2	Self-Service Launderette:	No (ironing room only)
Passenger Decks:	7	Dedicated Cinema/Seats:	No
Total Crew:	300	Library:	Yes
Passengers (lower beds):	590	Onboard currency:	Euros
Passenger Space Ratio (lower beds):	34.9		

Traditional style and restful decor for mature-age cruisers

OVERVIEW. *Astor* caters for couples and solo travelers of mature years and provides a degree of traditional style and comfort in a relaxed, spacious environment. It offers a good-value-for-money vacation, with appealing itineraries and destinations, adequate but uninspiring food, and friendly service.

THE SHIP. This is an attractive modern-ish ship with a raked bow, a large square funnel, and a nicely balanced almost contemporary profile. It has been well maintained and refurbished over the years. Introduced by Transocean Tours (as it then was called) in 1997, this ship was placed under a long-term charter agreement from its present owner, Premicon (which also owns a number of fine riverships).

Astor was the original name for this ship, the larger of two vessels bearing the same name in the 1980s, originally built for long-defunct Astor Cruises. Its previous owners, the also defunct AquaMarin Cruises, brought back the ship's name to *Astor* from another previous identity as *Fedor Dostoyevskiy*.

This ship represents a good mix of traditional and modern styling, with restful decor that doesn't jar the senses in any way – though some say it's a little too dark. Its high standard of German construction can be seen in the fine teakwood decking, polished wood railings and interior fittings, much of it refurbished in 2010.

There is an excellent amount of open deck and sunbathing space, plus cushioned pads for the sun-loungers. There is a basketball court for active pas-

Berlitz's Ratings		
	Possible	Achieved
Ship	500	346
Accommodation	200	138
Food	400	254
Service	400	286
Entertainment	100	62
Cruise Experience	400	274
OVERALL SCORE		
1360 points out of 2000		

sengers, as well as a large deck-chess game on an aft deck, and shuffleboard courts.

The public rooms and conference facilities are supremely comfortable and varied, most with high ceilings. Apart from a showlounge, there's a Captain's Club lounge, a library and card room, and two large boutiques. The wood-paneled Hanse Bar, with good German lager on draft, is a fine retreat; it has an outdoor area, too, and is popular as a late-night hangout. There is no crowding anywhere and no annoying background music in hallways or elevators.

Transocean Cruises has interesting and well-designed destination-intensive worldwide itineraries, and cruises are provided at a very attractive price. The mainly European hotel staff members are friendly without being obtrusive.

Transocean Cruises staff can be found aboard every cruise, some of which are designated as special-theme cruises. Port taxes, insurance, and gratuities to staff are all included in the fare. The drinks prices are inexpensive, particularly when compared to land-based prices.

A service provided by ABX Logistics can collect your luggage from your house, and transport it to the ship for you; when you return, the service will collect it from the ship and bring it to your house – all for a nominal fee.

Astor is now operated under charter to the UK's Cruise & Maritime Voyages, and cruises in Australasian waters during its summers. The ship will also continue to be marketed by Transocean Tours.

ACCOMMODATION. The accommodation, spanning numerous price categories, is spread over three decks, and comprises 32 suites and 263 outside-view and interior (no-view) cabins. No matter what grade of accommodation is chosen, rosewood cabinetry and plain beige walls are the norm – a restful environment. All suites and cabins with outside-view windows have blackout blinds – good for cruises to the land of the midnight sun.

Astor Suite. This suite measures approximately 635 sq ft (59 sq m) and includes a private balcony, with a separate bedroom and living room. The large bathroom has a tub, separate shower enclosure, dual washbasins, and a separate toilet with washbasin.

Senator Suites. These two suites (516.6 sq ft/48 sq m) are tastefully decorated in pastel colors, and have wood cabinetry and accents. Each has a separate bedroom, lounge/living room, private balcony, and a French balcony. The bathroom has decent-size storage cabinets for toiletries, as well as a tub, separate shower enclosure, toilet, and dual washbasins. A wide range of bathroom amenities is provided.

Outside-view and interior cabins. These cabins (139.9 sq ft/13 sq m) are well appointed and tastefully decorated in fresh pastel colors, and have dark wood accents and cabinetry, making them very restful. There is plenty of closet and drawer space, as well as some under-bed storage space for luggage. The bathrooms are very practical, and each has a decent-size cabinet for toiletries, as well as all the necessary fittings, including a white enamel washbasin.

Suite 105, facing the piano in the conference room opposite, is subject to the sound of musical rehearsals. In standard cabins, many day sofas convert to beds. Twin beds cannot be pushed together.

Outside-view family cabins. These large, four-berth cabins (258.3 sq ft/24 sq m) have two lower beds, one upper berth and one sofa bed – good for families with children. The tiled bathroom has a shower enclosure, white enamel washbasin and toilet.

All grades have a minibar and personal safe, European duvets, 100 percent cotton towels and bathrobe, soap, shampoo, shower cap, sewing kit, and a basket of fruit. The bathroom towels, however, are small.

The cabin service menu is limited, although German-speaking passengers in general seldom use room service for food items. There is an extra charge for sandwiches, and little else is available. However, there is plenty of food elsewhere around the ship. There is an extra charge for freshly squeezed orange juice, as aboard all ships in the German-speaking market.

DINING. The Waldorf Dining Room is reasonably elegant, well laid-out, and operates two seatings. It also has one small wing – good for groups of up to 30. The service throughout is friendly and unpretentious, and the food quality and presentation has received some attention from the food caterer, although remember that you get what you pay for, and food is not a particularly high priority for Transocean Cruises.

The menus are reasonably attractive, and both quality and presentation are acceptable standard fare, but nothing special – there's certainly no 'wow' factor. In addition to the regular entrées (typically three entrées for dinner), there may also be a pasta dish and a vegetarian specialty dish. The wine list contains a decent selection of wines from many regions, and all at inexpensive to moderate price levels, but wine glasses are small.

Other dining options. Two small specialty dining venues (one serving Italian cuisine, the other a 'romantic dinner') are reservations-only, extra-cost dining spots for those wanting something a little more special and as an alternative to the main dining room. Larger wine glasses are provided.

Casual breakfast and lunch buffets (both in the restaurant and another lounge) are reasonably well presented, and constantly refreshed, although they tend to be somewhat repetitive; the choice of foods is limited, and there is room for improvement. In typical German style, a Frühschoppen with the appropriate music, Bavarian sausages, and complimentary beer, is presented on the open lido deck once each cruise and is not to be missed.

ENTERTAINMENT. The Showlounge is a single-level room, but 14 pillars obstruct the sight lines. The venue is better suited to cabaret and mini-concerts than large-scale staged productions. The stage itself is also the dance floor, and cannot be raised for shows. The entertainment possibilities, therefore, are limited, with singers, magicians, and other visual acts providing the bulk of the shows.

SPA/FITNESS. The Wellness Oasis, located on the lowest passenger deck, contains a sauna, steam room, solarium, indoor swimming pool, beauty salon, treatment rooms, and changing areas. Massage, facials, manicures, and pedicures are some of the services offered. A separate fitness center, equipped with techno-machinery and exercycles, is located on an upper deck (Bridge Deck), complete with ocean views.

Asuka II
★★★★+

Size:	Mid-size Ship	Passenger/Crew Ratio (lower beds):	1.7
Tonnage:	50,142	Cabins (total):	462
Lifestyle:	Luxury/Premium	Size Range (sq ft/m):	198.1–949.4/18.4–88.2
Cruise Line:	NYK Cruises	Cabins (for one person):	0
Former Names:	*Crystal Harmony*	Cabins (with private balcony):	260
IMO Number:	8806204	Cabins (wheelchair accessible):	4
Builder:	Mitsubishi Heavy Industries, Japan	Wheelchair accessibility:	Best
Original Cost:	$240 million	Cabin Current:	115 and 220 volts
Entered Service:	Jul 1990/May 2006	Elevators:	8
Registry:	Japan	Casino (gaming tables):	Yes
Length (ft/m):	790.5/240.9	Slot Machines:	Yes
Beam (ft/m):	97.1/29.60	Swimming Pools:	1
Draft (ft/m):	24.6/7.50	Hot Tubs (on deck):	1
Propulsion/Propellers:	diesel-electric (32,800kW)/2	Self-Service Launderette:	Yes
Passenger Decks:	8	Dedicated Cinema/Seats:	Yes/263
Total Crew:	470	Library:	Yes
Passengers (lower beds):	800	Onboard currency:	Japanese Yen
Passenger Space Ratio (lower beds):	52.0		

An elegant, spacious ship with fine food, for Japanese cruisers

OVERVIEW. *Asuka II* is best suited to Japanese-speaking travelers, typically over 60, seeking a sophisticated ship with fine-quality fittings and furnishings, a wide range of public rooms and facilities, and excellent food and service from a well-trained staff. It is the attention to detail that makes this ship so pleasant, such as almost no announcements and little background music.

Berlitz's Ratings

	Possible	Achieved
Ship	500	414
Accommodation	200	160
Food	400	338
Service	400	331
Entertainment	100	83
Cruise Experience	400	337
OVERALL SCORE		
1663 points out of 2000		

THE SHIP. Although now over 20 years old, *Asuka II*, formerly *Crystal Harmony*, underwent a four-month-long drydocking and refit in 2005–6, and further refurbishment in 2009. It is a handsome, well-balanced contemporary ship with raked clipper bow, sleek lines, and Nippon Yusen Kaisha (NYK) Line's double red band on the funnel. There is almost no sense of crowding anywhere, and the fact that form follows function means that comfort is built in. There is a wide wraparound teakwood deck for walking, and an abundance of open deck space.

Inside, the layout is completely different from the previous *Asuka* in that there is a horizontal flow through the public rooms, as opposed to the previous vertical arrangement, and this better suits the age range of NYK's typical passengers. The design combines some large ship facilities with the intimacy of rooms found aboard many smaller ships. There is a wide assortment of public entertainment lounges and small intimate rooms, and passenger flow is excellent. Fine-quality fabrics and soft furnishings, china, flatware, and silver are used throughout.

Outstanding are the Vista (observation) Lounge and the tranquil, elegant Palm Court, one of the nicest rooms afloat, while adjacent are an Internet room and a Chashitsu (Japanese 12-tatami mat room). Other public spaces and facilities include the Mariner's Club Lounge (piano bar/lounge), Cigar Bar, Bistro Café, Casino Corner, Mahjong Room with eight tables, Compass Room (meeting and activities room), a book/video library, and Stars karaoke bar. The theater is a dedicated room with high-definition video projection. There is a self-service launderette on each deck – practical for long voyages.

Asuka II is a relaxing, grand hotel afloat – approximately the equivalent of Tokyo's Imperial Hotel – and provides abundant choices and flexibility. It has just about everything for the discerning traveler prepared to pay for high style, space, and the comfort and the facilities of a mid-size vessel capable of long voyages. The company pays attention to its repeat passengers, particularly those in Deck 10 penthouses and suites.

Unfortunately, dining is in two seatings, which makes its timing highly structured – there are two shows, because the showlounge can't seat everyone at once. This works well in the Japanese market, and you can always choose to eat in a specialty dining venue, but the arrangement detracts from the otherwise fine setting of the ship and the professionalism of its staff. All gratuities are included.

ACCOMMODATION. There are five categories of suites and cabins (including four Royal Suites with private balcony; 26 Asuka Suites with balcony; 32 suites with balcony; 202 cabins with balcony; 172 cabins without balcony). Regardless of the category, duvets and down pillows are provided, as are lots of other niceties. All cabins have a color TV, DVD player, mini-refrigerator, personal safe, small couch and coffee table, excellent soundproofing, a refrigerator and minibar, full tea-making set, satellite-linked telephone, hairdryer, and slippers. A full range of toiletries (including Shiseido shampoo, hair rinse, shower cap, soap, cotton pads, razor set, hairbrush, and more) is provided, and cotton towels are plentiful.

Deck 10 penthouses. Four Royal Suites, whose entrance doorway has a door phone and camera, measure 949.4 sq ft (88.2 sq m) and have a large private balcony and lounge with elegant walnut furniture, new soft furnishings, and audio-visual entertainment center (Bose audio system, Blu-Ray player); separate master bedroom with twin beds (flat-screen TV); and large walk-in closets. The excellent ocean-view Japanese-style bathrooms, with German quality fittings that include a large overhead shower, come with jet bathtub, two washbasins, and plenty of storage space for toiletries (a range of L'Occitane toiletries is provided). These fine, private, pampered living spaces at sea were totally refurbished in 2010, and include perks such as priority service, free laundry service, a wide variety of alcoholic beverages, and many other goodies.

Other Deck 10 suites. These are worth the asking price. All have a private balcony, with outside light, and plenty of space including a lounge with large couch, coffee table and chairs, large TV set, and a separate sleeping area that can be curtained off with thick drapes that allow you to sleep totally in the dark. The bathrooms are quite large and extremely well appointed. All Deck 10 suites/cabins are attended by social officers, and complimentary in-room dining service is offered.

Deck 9/8/7/5 cabins. Many of the cabins have a private balcony (in fact, half of all cabins have private balconies, with outside lights) and are extremely comfortable. But they are a little tight for space, with one-way traffic past the bed. There is a reasonable amount of drawer and storage space, although the drawers are small and the closet hanging space and the storage space for shoes are very limited for long voyages. Some cabins have lifeboat-obstructed views, so it's best to check the deck plan carefully.

Although well appointed, the bathrooms (except for those in Deck 10 accommodation) are of the 'you first, me next' variety – and size. But they do come with generously sized toiletries and amenities, and all bathrooms are fitted with electric 'washlet' high-cleanse toilets.

DINING. There are several choices. The non-smoking Four Seasons Dining Room is quite elegant, and has a raised central section. There is plenty of space around each table, well-placed waiter service stations and a number of tables for two, as well as tables for four, six, or eight.

Dinner in the main dining room is in two seatings, with no set table assignments. Afternoon tea and coffee can be taken in the Vista Lounge, a restful venue.

Other dining options. Umihiko is a Japanese extra-charge restaurant, complete with a wholly authentic sushi bar and live fish tanks for absolutely fresh sashimi. It specializes in sushi and authentic sashimi dishes, and provides a refined, intimate dining experience with fine ocean views. Reservations are required.

Prego, which has 40 seats with ocean views to starboard and aft, is for occupants of the Royal Suites and Asuka Suites. The menu is the same as the main dining room, but with more intensive waiter service.

For casual meals, beverages, and ice cream, the Lido Café, which was completely reconstructed in the refit, has an extensive self-serve buffet area; it is located high up in the ship and has ocean views from large picture windows. For casual meals, there is also a Lido Garden Grill, a large area with wooden tables and chairs, and bar.

Additionally, The Bistro, located on the upper level of the two-deck-high lobby, is a casual spot for coffees and pastries, served in the style and atmosphere of a European street café.

ENTERTAINMENT. The Galaxy Lounge, the ship's showlounge, is a large room on one level, with a sloping floor. The sight lines are good from most seats, although a few pillars obstruct the view from some seats. Both banquette-style and individual seating is available.

SPA/FITNESS. The Grand Spa includes a large Grand Bath/cleansing center (one for men, one for women), with integral sauna and steam room. Other facilities include five treatment rooms (longevity, water, wind, prosperity, harmony) including one for couples. There's a separate sauna, steam rooms, changing rooms for men and women, a beauty salon, and a relaxation area. Another part of the spa houses the gymnasium, with ocean-view windows on one side.

The Asuka Aveda Salon and Spa offers a wide range of body pampering treatments using Aveda brand products. The spa also offers a kimono dressing service, which costs ¥12,600 (about $110).

There is an excellent amount of open deck space, including a swimming pool that's one of the longest aboard any cruise ship. Sports facilities include a full-size paddle tennis court, putting green, and golf driving range.

Aurora
★★★★

Size:	Mid-size Ship
Tonnage:	76,152
Lifestyle:	Standard
Cruise Line:	P&O Cruises
Former Names:	none
IMO Number:	9169524
Builder:	Meyer Werft (Germany)
Original Cost:	$375 million
Entered Service:	May 2000
Registry:	Great Britain
Length (ft/m):	885.8/270.0
Beam (ft/m):	105.6/32.2
Draft (ft/m):	25.9/7.9
Propulsion/Propellers:	diesel-electric (40,000kW)/2
Passenger Decks:	10
Total Crew:	816
Passengers (lower beds):	1,868
Passenger Space Ratio (lower beds):	40.7

Passenger/Crew Ratio (lower beds):	2.2
Cabins (total):	934
Size Range (sq ft/m):	150.6–953.0/14.0–88.5
Cabins (for one person):	0
Cabins (with private balcony):	406
Cabins (wheelchair accessible):	22
Wheelchair accessibility:	Good
Cabin Current:	110 and 220 volts
Elevators:	10
Casino (gaming tables):	Yes
Slot Machines:	Yes
Swimming Pools:	3 (1 w/ sliding glass dome)
Hot Tubs (on deck):	5
Self-Service Launderette:	Yes
Dedicated Cinema/Seats:	Yes/200
Library:	Yes
Onboard currency:	UK£

A traditional British-style ship with facilities for the whole family

OVERVIEW. *Aurora* is suited to adults of all ages (although most cruises attract the over-50s) and families with children, who want a cruise that starts and ends in the UK, aboard a mid-size ship with all the facilities of a small resort, with food and service that come with a sense of British-ness.

THE SHIP. *Aurora*, which underwent an extensive make-over in 2014–15, was built specifically for Britain's traditional cruise market. It has larger cabins and suites and more dining options and choice of public areas than older sister *Oriana*.

As cruise ships evolve, slight differences in layout occur, as is the case with *Aurora* compared to *Oriana*. One example is a large, glass-domed indoor/outdoor swimming pool – good in all weathers for families with children. The stern superstructure is nicely rounded and has several tiers that overlook the aft decks, pool, and children's outdoor facilities. There is good sunbathing space and an extra-wide walk-around outdoor promenade deck, with plenty of white plastic sunloungers (cushioned pads are available).

Aurora is a ship for all types, with specific areas designed for different age groups and lifestyles. The focal point is a four-decks-high atrium lobby and a dramatic 35ft- (10.6m-) high, Lalique-style fiberglass sculpture of two mythical figures behind a veil of water.

Other features include a virtual reality games room, 12 lounges/bars (among the nicest are Anderson's (similar to Anderson's aboard *Oriana*, with a fireplace and mahogany paneling), and the Crow's

Berlitz's Ratings		
	Possible	Achieved
Ship	500	386
Accommodation	200	158
Food	400	254
Service	400	299
Entertainment	100	76
Cruise Experience	400	287
OVERALL SCORE		
1460 points out of 2000		

Nest – complete with a lovely one-sided model of a former P&O liner: *Strathnaver* of 1931 (scrapped in Hong Kong in 1962). A cinema also doubles as a concert and lecture hall.

FAMILIES. There are various clubs for different age groups (two to five, six to nine, 10 to 13, and 14 to 17). An entire deck includes swimming pools and whirlpools just for youngsters. Children can be entertained until 10pm, giving parents time to have dinner and go dancing. All cabins also have a baby-listening device. A night nursery for children aged two to five is available (6pm–midnight, no charge; from midnight to 2am a fee applies), as well as slumber parties for 6–9-year-olds. Sixteen passenger cabins have interconnecting doors – good for families. At peak holiday times (summer, Christmas, Easter) there could be 400 or more children on board. However, the ship absorbs them well, and there's a lot to keep them occupied.

ACCOMMODATION. There are five main grades in numerous price categories. Included are two two-level penthouses, 10 suites with balconies, 18 mini-suites with balconies, 368 cabins with balconies, 225 standard outside-view cabins, 16 interconnecting family cabins, and 279 interior cabins.

All grades, from the largest to the smallest, provide polished cherry wood laminate cabinetry, full-length mirror, personal safe, refrigerator, television, individually controlled air conditioning; twin beds that convert to a queen-size double bed, sofa, and coffee table. Also standard are stylish bed runners, Slumberland eight-inch sprung mattresses, duvets, Egyptian cotton towels and robes, and tea/coffee-making facilities with specialty teas (long-life milk is provided).

There are four decks of cabins with private balconies (about 40 percent of all cabins); these have easy-to-open sliding glass floor-to-ceiling doors; the partitions are of the almost full floor-to-ceiling type – so they really are quite private and cannot be overlooked from above.

Cabin insulation could be better, and the magnetic catches in drawers and on closet doors are noisy. Although most doorways are 26ins (66cm) wide, the actual access is 2ins (5cm) less because of the doorframe; however, some doorways are only 21.5ins (55cm) wide.

Penthouse Suites. Library Suite and Piano Suite each measure 953 sq ft (88.5 sq m) and have forward-facing views, being located directly underneath the navigation bridge (the blinds must be drawn at night so as not to affect navigation). Each is spread over two decks in height, and connected by a curved wooden staircase. One suite has a baby grand piano, which can be played manually or electronically; the other has a private library. The living area on the lower deck (Deck 10) incorporates a dining suite (a first for a P&O ship) and small private balcony. The bedroom (upstairs) has a walk-in closet, with a bathroom of porcelain and polished granite, twin washbasins, bathtub, separate shower enclosure, and a small private balcony.

Suites. The 10 suites measure about 445 sq ft (41.3 sq m) and have a separate bedroom with two lower beds that convert to a queen-size bed, walk-in dressing area and closet, with plenty of drawer space, trouser press, and ironing board. The lounge has a sofa, armchairs, dining table and chairs, writing desk, television, and audio system. The marble-clad bathroom has a whirlpool bath, shower, and toilet. The balcony has two sunloungers, plus two chairs and two tables.

Mini-suites. These measure 325 sq ft (30.1 sq m) and have a separate bedroom area with two lower beds that convert to a queen-size bed. There are one double and two single closets, a good amount of drawer space, binoculars, a trouser press, and an ironing board. Each private balcony has a blue plastic deck covering, one deck lounge chair, one chair and table, and exterior light.

Standard outside-view/interior cabins. These measure about 175 sq ft (16.2 sq m) and have two lower beds that convert to a queen-size bed, sitting area with a sofa and table, a vanity table/writing desk, a private balcony with blue deck covering, two chairs (with a small recline), and a small table. A 110-volt

(American) socket is located underneath the vanity desk drawer – a difficult-to-access position.

Outside-view or interior cabins. These have two lower beds that convert to a queen-size bed, closet (but few drawers), and are 150 sq ft (14 sq m). The bathroom has a mini-bath/shower and toilet, or shower and toilet.

There are 22 wheelchair-accessible cabins, well outfitted for the physically challenged passenger and almost all within easy access to lifts. However, one cabin (D165 on Deck 8) is located between forward and mid-ships stairways, and it is difficult to access the public rooms on Deck 8 without first going to the deck below, due to several steps and tight corners. All other wheelchair-accessible cabins are well positioned, and eight have a private balcony.

DINING. The two main dining rooms (each seats about 525) have tables for two, four, six, eight, and 10. The midships Medina has a vaguely Moorish theme, and features 'Freedom Dining' – open seating for dinner – with Marco Pierre White dishes on gala evenings, while Alexandria, with windows on three sides, has an Egyptian theme (and two seatings for dinner). Both have more tables for two than in the equivalent restaurants aboard close sister ship *Oriana*. The china is Wedgwood, and the silverware is by Elkington.

Other dining options. You can also dine in The Glasshouse restaurant and wine bar (selected by Olly Smith); or Sindhu (on the upper deck of the atrium lobby), for an Indian-fusion menu designed by Atul Kochhar. Both are extra-cost venues and reservations are required.

Casual, self-serve breakfasts and lunches can be taken from the buffet in The Orangery, which has fine ocean views. Other casual dining spots include the Sidewalk Café (for fast-food items poolside), The Beach House (for lava-rock sizzle food), Champagne bar, and Raffles coffee and chocolate bar (but without the ceiling fans).

ENTERTAINMENT. There is a wide variety of mainly British entertainment, from production shows to top British 'name' (and lesser) cabaret acts.

SPA/FITNESS. The Oasis Spa is amidships on Lido Deck – almost at the top of the ship, just forward of the Crystal swimming pool. Facilities include a gymnasium with the latest high-tech muscle-pumping equipment. There is also a sauna and steam room (both unisex, so take a bathing suit), a beauty salon, a spiral staircase, and a relaxation area overlooking the forward Riviera swimming pool.

Azamara Journey
★★★★+

Size:	Small Ship	Passenger/Crew Ratio (lower beds):	1.6
Tonnage:	30,277	Cabins (total):	338
Lifestyle:	Premium	Size Range (sq ft/m):	151.0–818.0/14.0–76.0
Cruise Line:	Azamara Club Cruises	Cabins (for one person):	0
Former Names:	Blue Star, Blue Dream, R6	Cabins (with private balcony):	249
IMO Number:	9200940	Cabins (wheelchair accessible):	6
Builder:	Chantiers de l'Atlantique (France)	Wheelchair accessibility:	Fair
Original Cost:	$150 million	Cabin Current:	110 and 220 volts
Entered Service:	Feb 2000/May 2007	Elevators:	4
Registry:	Malta	Casino (gaming tables):	Yes
Length (ft/m):	591.8/180.4	Slot Machines:	Yes
Beam (ft/m):	95.1/29.0	Swimming Pools:	1
Draft (ft/m):	19.85/6.0	Hot Tubs (on deck):	3
Propulsion/Propellers:	diesel (18,600kW)/2	Self-Service Launderette:	Yes
Passenger Decks:	9	Dedicated Cinema/Seats:	No
Total Crew:	407	Library:	Yes
Passengers (lower beds):	676	Onboard currency:	US$
Passenger Space Ratio (lower beds):	42.7		

An informal ship with country-house decor and fine food

OVERVIEW. The *Azamara Journey*, virtually identical to *Azamara Quest* in features and fittings, suits mature couples seeking to get away from the crowds aboard a contemporary, mid-size ship with a wide range of bars and lounges, at a slightly lower cost than the luxury lines.

THE SHIP. The ship has a deep blue hull and white superstructure topped by a large, square blue funnel. A lido deck has a tiny swimming pool, and good sunbathing space. There is no outdoor walk-around promenade deck, although a short jogging track encircles the pool deck (one deck above it). The uppermost outdoors deck includes a golf driving net and shuffleboard court. There are no wooden decks outdoors, but they are covered by a sand-colored rubberized material.

The interior decor is in good taste, and is a throwback to ship decor of the ocean liners of the 1920s and '30s. The public rooms are spread over three decks. The reception hall has a staircase with intricate wrought-iron railings. A large observation lounge (The Looking Glass) is high atop the ship. This has a long bar with forward views – for the barmen, that is, as passengers sitting at the bar face aft. There's a bar in each of the restaurant entrances, as well as a Martini Bar. There's also a Mosaic Café, a Luxe Casino, and a shop (Boutique C).

The Drawing Room (the ship's library) is a beautiful, restful room, designed in the Regency style. It has a fireplace, a high, indented, trompe l'oeil ceiling, and a good selection of books, comfortable wingback

Berlitz's Ratings		
	Possible	Achieved
Ship	500	408
Accommodation	200	156
Food	400	295
Service	400	320
Entertainment	100	78
Cruise Experience	400	298
OVERALL SCORE		
1555 points out of 2000		

chairs with footstools, and sofas. Smoking is permitted only in designated spots on the open decks.

Standard drinks and wines are included (premium brands cost extra). Gratuities to housekeeping and dining staff are included in the fare. Shuttle buses are provided free when needed in ports of call. Note that an 18 percent gratuity applies to spa treatments. Big niggle: art auctions simply don't belong to a nice product like this!

In 2016, this ship will undergo a major refurbishment program to refresh all accommodation and public areas.

ACCOMMODATION. There are several suite and cabin price grades. The price you pay reflects the size and location of your chosen accommodation. All have so-called butler service (but they are simply better-dressed cabin stewards). All of the standard interior and outside-view cabins (the lowest four grades) are extremely compact units. *Azamara Journey* calls them staterooms, but they are simply cabins – and rather tight for two persons, particularly during cruises longer than seven days. The bathrooms are postage-stamp-sized and you'll be fighting with the shower curtain, as well as storage space for toiletries. The standard cabins cannot, in any sense, be considered luxury, and even premium is stretching it a bit.

All cabins have two lower beds that can be converted to a (sleep together) queen-sized bed, good under-bed storage areas, flat-screen TV, good closet space, thermostat-controlled air conditioning, hair-dryer, direct-dial telephone and voicemail, and 100 percent cotton towels. Most cabins also have a personal safe, and refrigerator with minibar.

For the extra cost, it's wise to choose a suite or cabin with a balcony. Some cabins have interconnecting doors, while 18 cabins on Deck 6 have lifeboat-obstructed views.

Deluxe ocean-view cabins with balcony. Approximate size: 215 sq ft (20 sq m); balcony 38 sq ft (3.5 sq m).

Sunset verandah cabins. Approximate size: 215 sq ft (20 sq m); balcony 154 sq ft (14 sq m).

Sky Suites and superior exterior-view cabins with balcony. Approximate size: 323 sq ft (30 sq m); balcony 57 sq ft (3.3 sq m).

Royal Suites (Decks 6, 7). In reality these are large cabins, as the sleeping and lounge areas are not divided. Approximate size: 538 sq ft (50 sq m); balcony 173 sq ft (16 sq m).

Penthouse Deluxe Suites with balcony. Providing the most spacious accommodation, these are fine, large living spaces in the forward-most and aft-most sections of the accommodation decks (particularly nice are those overlooking the stern, on decks 6, 7, and 8). Approximate size: 603 sq ft (56 sq m); balcony 215 sq ft (20 sq m). Suite occupants get priority boarding, tender service, specialty dining venue reservations, light bites at 4pm, in-suite spa treatments, in-suite portrait sitting, free espressos/cappuccinos, bottled water, and silk-wrapped hangers. Note that suites/cabins located at the stern can suffer from vibration and noise, particularly when the ship is proceeding at or close to full speed, or maneuvering in port.

DINING. Discoveries, the main dining room, has around 340 seats, a raised central section (conversation at these tables may be difficult, due to its low ceiling height), and open-seating dining. There are large ocean-view windows on three sides, several prime tables overlooking the stern, and a small bandstand for live dinner music. Menus change daily for lunch and dinner, and wine is included. Adjacent to the restaurant is a Martini Bar, with a cozy fireplace.

Other dining options. Aqualina Restaurant is at the aft of the ship on the port side of Deck 10; it has 96 seats, windows along two sides, and serves Mediterranean cuisine. A $70 per person Tasting Menu includes wine pairing.

Prime C is located at the aft of the ship on the starboard side of Deck 10, and features premium-quality steaks and grilled seafood items. It has 98 seats, windows along two sides, and a set menu.

Both Aqualina and Prime C incur a $25 cover charge (no charge for occupants of top-grade suites).

The Windows Café has indoor and outdoor seating (combined, for just over 150, not really enough when cruising in cold areas or in the winter months). It is open for breakfast, lunch, and casual dinners, and incorporates a small Sushi Café.

All dining venues have open-seating dining, although reservations are needed in the Aqualina Restaurant and Prime C, where there are mostly tables for four or six (there are few tables for two). Suite-grade occupants get unlimited access. All cappuccino and espresso coffees cost extra.

The Mosaic Café serves Italian coffees, as well as teas and pastries (no extra cost). Additionally, a Poolside Grill provides fast-food items (some items are grilled to order). A self-serve soft ice cream machine is located adjacent to its beverage station. Coffee and tea are free 24 hours a day.

ENTERTAINMENT. Celebrity Cabaret, located forward, is the venue for all main entertainment events. Evening entertainment consists of a mix of classical concerts, revues, comedy, and drama.

SPA/FITNESS. The Astral Spa has a gymnasium with some high-tech muscle toning equipment, an extra-cost thalassotherapy pool, and several treatment rooms. The spa is staffed and operated by Steiner Leisure. An 'Acupuncture at Sea' clinic provides treatments that are operated independently of the spa (but also as a concession). Outside on the Lido Deck, there are a small swimming pool, two hot tubs, and a jogging track (one deck above the pool).

Azamara Quest
★★★★+

Size:	Small Ship	Passenger/Crew Ratio (lower beds):	2.3
Tonnage:	30,277	Cabins (total):	358
Lifestyle:	Premium	Size Range (sq ft/m):	156.0–484.3/14.5–45.0
Cruise Line:	Azamara Club Cruises	Cabins (for one person):	0
Former Names:	Blue Moon, Delphin Renaissance, R7	Cabins (with private balcony):	232
IMO Number:	9210218	Cabins (wheelchair accessible):	4
Builder:	Chantiers de l'Atlantique (France)	Wheelchair accessibility:	Fair
Original Cost:	$150 million	Cabin Current:	110 and 220 volts
Entered Service:	Oct 2000/Oct 2007	Elevators:	4
Registry:	Malta	Casino (gaming tables):	No
Length (ft/m):	591.8/180.4	Slot Machines:	No
Beam (ft/m):	83.3/25.4	Swimming Pools:	1
Draft (ft/m):	19.0/5.8	Hot Tubs (on deck):	3
Propulsion/Propellers:	diesel (18,600kW)/2	Self-Service Launderette:	Yes
Passenger Decks:	9	Dedicated Cinema/Seats:	No
Total Crew:	306	Library:	Yes
Passengers (lower beds):	716	Onboard currency:	US$
Passenger Space Ratio (lower beds):	42.2		

This small ship reminds you of an elegant country club

OVERVIEW. Like its sister, *Azamara Journey*, this ship has the ambience of an old-world country club. Passengers should be pleased with its tasteful, traditional-style interiors.

THE SHIP. *Azamara Quest* was originally *R7*, one of a series of eight almost identical ships in the long-defunct Renaissance Cruises fleet (when it was in operation, between 1998 and 2001, it was the cruise industry's only totally no-smoking cruise line). It was purchased by Pullmantur in 2006, but transferred in 2007 to Celebrity Cruises' then new small-ship brand, Azamara Cruises (renamed Azamara Club Cruises in 2009). Before entering service, the ship underwent an almost $20 million make-over. The hull is deep blue, while the superstructure is white.

An outdoors lido deck has a swimming pool and good sunbathing space, while one of the aft decks has a thalassotherapy pool. The exterior decks are covered by a rubber and sand-like surface. The uppermost outdoors deck includes a golf driving net and shuffleboard court. The interior decor is elegant, in the style of the ocean liner decor of the 1920s.

Standard drinks and wines are included (premium brands cost extra). Note that an 18 percent gratuity applies to spa treatments. Big niggle: art auctions simply don't belong to a nice product like this!

In 2016, *Azamara Quest* will undergo a major refurbishment program that will see all accommodation and public areas refurbished.

Berlitz's Ratings

	Possible	Achieved
Ship	500	408
Accommodation	200	156
Food	400	295
Service	400	320
Entertainment	100	78
Cruise Experience	400	297
OVERALL SCORE		
1554 points out of 2000		

ACCOMMODATION. There are several suite and cabin price grades. The price you pay reflects the size and location of your chosen accommodation. All have so-called butler service (but they are simply better-dressed cabin stewards). All of the standard interior and outside-view cabins (the lowest four grades) are extremely compact units. *Azamara Quest* calls them staterooms, but they are simply cabins – and rather tight for two persons, particularly during cruises longer than seven days. The bathrooms are postage-stamp-sized and you'll be fighting with the shower curtain and limited with storage space for toiletries. The standard cabins cannot, in any sense, be considered luxury, and even premium is stretching it a bit.

All cabins have two lower beds that can be converted to a (sleep-together) queen-sized bed, good under-bed storage areas, flat-screen TV, good closet space, thermostat-controlled air conditioning, hairdryer, direct-dial telephone and voicemail, and 100 percent cotton towels. Most cabins also have a personal safe, and refrigerator with minibar.

For the extra cost, it's wise to choose a suite or cabin with a balcony. Some cabins have interconnecting doors while 18 cabins on Deck 6 have lifeboat-obstructed views.

Deluxe ocean-view cabins with balcony. Approximate size: 215 sq ft (20 sq m); balcony 38 sq ft (3.5 sq m).

Sunset verandah cabins. Approximate size: 215 sq ft (20 sq m); balcony 154 sq ft (14 sq m).

Sky Suites and superior exterior-view cabins with balcony. Approximate size: 323 sq ft (30 sq m); balcony 57 sq ft (3.3 sq m).

Royal Suites (Decks 6, 7). In reality these are large cabins, as the sleeping and lounge areas are not divided. Approximate size: 538 sq ft (50 sq m); balcony 173 sq ft (16 sq m).

Penthouse Deluxe Suites with balcony. Providing the most spacious accommodation, these are fine, large living spaces in the forward-most and aft-most sections of the accommodation decks (particularly nice are those overlooking the stern, on decks 6, 7, and 8). Approximate size: 603 sq ft (56 sq m); balcony 215 sq ft (20 sq m). Suite occupants get priority boarding, tender service, specialty dining venue reservations, light bites at 4pm, in-suite spa treatments, in-suite portrait sitting, free espressos/cappuccinos, bottled water, and silk-wrapped hangers. Note that suites/cabins located at the stern can suffer from vibration and noise, particularly when the ship is proceeding at or close to full speed, or maneuvering in port.

DINING. Discoveries, the main dining room, has around 340 seats, a raised central section (conversation at these tables may be difficult, due to its low ceiling height), and open-seating dining. There are large ocean-view windows on three sides, several prime tables overlooking the stern, and a small bandstand for live dinner music. The menu changes daily for lunch and dinner, and wine is included. Adjacent to the restaurant is a Martini Bar, with a cozy fireplace.

Other dining options. Aqualina Restaurant is at the aft of the ship on the port side of Deck 10; it has 96 seats, windows along two sides, and serves Mediterranean cuisine. A $70 per person Tasting Menu includes wine.

Prime C is located at the aft of the ship on the starboard side of Deck 10, and features premium-quality steaks and grilled seafood items. It has 98 seats, windows along two sides, and a set menu.

Both Aqualina and Prime C incur a $25 cover charge (no charge for occupants of top-grade suites).

The Windows Café has indoor and outdoor seating (combined, for just over 150, not really enough when cruising in cold areas or in the winter months). It is open for breakfast, lunch, and casual dinners, and incorporates a small Sushi Café.

All dining venues have open-seating dining, although reservations are needed in the Aqualina Restaurant and Prime C, where there are mostly tables for four or six (there are few tables for two). Suite-grade occupants get unlimited access. All cappuccino and espresso coffees cost extra.

The Mosaic Café serves Italian coffees, as well as teas and pastries (no extra cost). Additionally, a Poolside Grill provides fast-food items (some items are grilled to order). A self-serve soft ice cream machine is located adjacent to its beverage station. Coffee and tea are free 24 hours a day.

ENTERTAINMENT. Celebrity Cabaret, located forward, is the venue for all main entertainment events. Evening entertainment consists of a mix of classical concerts, revues, comedy, and drama.

SPA/FITNESS. The Astral Spa has a gymnasium with some high-tech muscle toning equipment, an extra-cost thalassotherapy pool (outside, forward on deck), and several treatment rooms. The spa is staffed and operated by Steiner Leisure. An 'Acupuncture at Sea' clinic provides treatments that are operated independently of the spa (but also as a concession). Spa treatments are possible in your suite, too. Outside on the Lido Deck, there are a small swimming pool, two hot tubs, and a jogging track (one deck above the pool).

Azura
★★★★

Size:	Large Resort Ship	Passenger/Crew Ratio (lower beds):	2.4
Tonnage:	115,055	Cabins (total):	1,557
Lifestyle:	Standard	Size Range (sq ft/m):	134.5–534.0/12.5–49.6
Cruise Line:	P&O Cruises	Cabins (for one person):	18
Former Names:	none	Cabins (with private balcony):	910
IMO Number:	9424883	Cabins (wheelchair accessible):	25
Builder:	Fincantieri (Italy)	Wheelchair accessibility:	Good
Original Cost:	€535 million	Cabin Current:	110 and 220 volts
Entered Service:	Apr 2010	Elevators:	12
Registry:	Bermuda	Casino (gaming tables):	Yes
Length (ft/m):	951.4/290.0	Slot Machines:	Yes
Beam (ft/m):	118.1/36.0	Swimming Pools:	3
Draft (ft/m):	27.8/8.5	Hot Tubs (on deck):	6
Propulsion/Propellers:	diesel-electric (42,000kW)/2	Self-Service Launderette:	Yes
Passenger Decks:	14	Dedicated Cinema/Seats:	No
Total Crew:	1,239	Library:	Yes
Passengers (lower beds):	3,096	Onboard currency:	UK£
Passenger Space Ratio (lower beds):	37.2		

A large ship with sedate decor that suits British tastes

OVERVIEW. *Azura* is best suited to families with children and adult couples who are seeking a big-ship environment with comfortable, unstuffy surroundings, lots of options, and a distinctly British flavor.

THE SHIP. *Azura* and sister ship *Ventura*, which debuted in 2008, are P&O's version of Princess Cruises' *Grand*-class ships. With its flat, upright stern, *Azura* looks a bit like a giant hatchback, although the ship's side profile is softer and more balanced. Promenade walking decks are to the port and starboard sides, underneath the lifeboats. You can't walk completely around; it's also narrow in some places, with deck lounge chairs in the way.

There are three main pools: two on the pool deck, one at the stern. There's not a lot of outdoor deck space – unless you pay extra to go into a covered, adults-only zone called The Retreat, with its faux-grass floor, private cabanas, and personal waiter service. What's new is a huge open-air movie screen, the aptly named SeaScreen, forward of the funnel by the Aqua Pool.

Inside, a three-deck atrium, with integral dance floor, is the focal social point, like a town center at sea. Four large, three-deck-high black granite archways provide 'gateways' to the center. It's the place to see and be seen – as are the specialty dining venues. Also in the atrium is a smallish open-plan library (that isn't at all intimate or good for reading in when noisy events are staged in the atrium) including computers for Internet access. There's also the Java Café for extra-cost coffees, teas, cakes, pastries, and snacks.

Berlitz's Ratings

	Possible	Achieved
Ship	500	399
Accommodation	200	154
Food	400	249
Service	400	287
Entertainment	100	77
Cruise Experience	400	301
OVERALL SCORE		
1467 points out of 2000		

Other rooms, bars and lounges include a casino; The Exchange, an urban 'warehouse' bar; the Blue Bar, the ship's social hub; Brodies, a 'traditional' British pub (named after Brodie McGhie Wilcox, P&O's co-founder); and the Planet Bar, set high in the ship, featuring a video wall.

The upper-deck public room layout means you can't easily go from one end of the ship to the other without first going down, along, and up. Anyone with mobility problems will need to plan their journey and use the most appropriate of three elevator banks.

Gratuities are optional, unless you choose Freedom Dining, when they are automatically applied to your onboard account. Smoking is permitted only on cabin balconies and in designated spots on the open decks.

FAMILIES. *Azura* is really child-friendly, with clubs for the under-twos up to 17 years, plus a rock 'n' roll school. There's a Night Nursery for under-fives. Youngsters can also enjoy a dedicated Wii room, Scalextric at sea with a Grand Prix-style track, a 3D cinema, and interactive classes. Family shore programs include aqua and 'theme parks.'

ACCOMMODATION. There are 27 price grades, but really just five types of accommodation: suite with balcony; family suite with balcony; outside-view twin/queen with balcony; outside-view twin/queen; interior cabin. Although there are more balconies than aboard *Ventura*, more than a third of all cabins have no outside view. Some have extra third/fourth berths that fold down from the ceiling.

Most welcome are 18 solo-occupancy cabins, a first for P&O Cruises, located in a small section on the port side. Also new are spa cabins, with added amenities and direct access to the ship's spa, and two large suites for large groups.

While the suites are small when compared to those of lines such as Celebrity Cruises or Norwegian Cruise Line, whose top suites are four or five times the size, they are intelligently laid out, and feel spacious.

Standard in all cabins: bed runners, 10.5 tog duvets, Slumberland eight-inch sprung mattresses, and Egyptian cotton towels. Tea/coffee-making facilities are adequate, but with UHT rather than fresh milk. Bathrobes are provided only for passengers occupying grades A, B, and D accommodation. There are UK three-pin sockets, plus US-style 110-volt sockets for electrical devices.

Open closets provide easy access, but the 'no trust' attached hangers can bang against the wall when the ship is 'moving'. Balcony cabins have wooden railings atop glass dividers, green plastic floors, a couple of small chairs and drinks table, and an outside light. Most cabin bathrooms are small, as are the shower enclosures.

Wheelchair-accessible cabins, which have a large, user-friendly shower enclosure, are mostly located in the front section of the ship, but one of the main restaurants is aft. So be prepared for lots of wheeling time, and waiting time at the elevators.

There is no room service breakfast on disembarkation day, when you must vacate your cabin early.

DINING. P&O's marketing blurb claims that there are 10 restaurants. There aren't. There are five genuine restaurants (Peninsular, Oriental, Meridian, Sindhu, and Seventeen); the others are bistro-style eateries or fast-food joints.

The three main dining rooms, Peninsular, Oriental, and Meridian, share the same menus. Peninsular and Oriental offer fixed seating dining with assigned tables (typical seating times: 6:30pm or 8:45pm). In the Meridian restaurant, you can dine when you want, with whomever you want, between 6pm and 10pm – P&O calls it 'Freedom Dining', although at peak times there can be a bit of a wait, and it's not open for breakfast or lunch. Occasionally, special dinners are served in the main dining rooms, one of which is a Chaîne des Rôtisseurs event.

Wheelchair users should note that breakfast in the fixed dining restaurants typically ends at 9:30am on sea days and 9am on port days. To take breakfast in the self-serve casual eatery, you may need to wheel across the decks containing the forward and midship pools and a sea of deck chairs – not easy. Alternatively, you can order room service breakfast – typically cold items only.

Other dining options. Sindhu is an Indian-themed restaurant (reservation-only, extra-charge). It is overseen by Michelin-star chef Atul Kochhar, whose specialty is British and Indian fusion cuisine. The food is cooked to order, unlike in the three main dining rooms. Table seating includes several alcove-style areas that make it impossible for waiters to serve food correctly without reaching across others at the same table.

For the Glass House, TV wine expert Olly Smith has helped create a 'Select Dining' restaurant and wine bar. The venue offers seafood and grilled items, paired with wines chosen by Smith. You can also, of course, have a glass of wine, without food.

Seventeen is a reservations-only, extra-charge, à la carte restaurant in a quiet setting, with plenty of space around tables for waiters to serve correctly. The venue also features an outdoor terrace for warm-weather areas.

Venezia is the ship's large, casual, self-serve buffet eatery/food court, open almost around the clock, with a large indoor-outdoor seating area. The buffet layout is confined, and can get congested. On the same deck, adjacent to the forward pool, are a poolside grill and pizzeria. Verona is a family-friendly self-service eatery.

In addition, 24-hour room service is available in cabins.

ENTERTAINMENT. The 800-seat Playhouse theater spans two decks and is located at the front of the ship. It is the venue for shows; with two large video screens on either side of the stage; the sight lines are very good from all seats.

The Manhattan Lounge, a multi-function social/entertainment venue, hosts family shows and cabaret acts, and is a late-night disco. Malabar, another night venue, has decor based on the hotels on Marine Drive, Mumbai. Cabaret, live bands, and dancing are featured here. Meanwhile, the Planet Bar, a nightclub and entertainment venue is an activities room by day and a club by night.

SPA/FITNESS. The Oasis Spa – located forward, almost atop the ship – has a gymnasium, aerobics room, beauty salon, separate men's and ladies' sauna and steam rooms (no charge), and 11 treatment rooms. An internal stairway connects to the deck below, which contains an extra-charge Thermal Suite (there's a cost per person, per day, or a composite price per cruise).

Balmoral
★★★+

Size:	Mid-size Ship
Tonnage:	43,537
Lifestyle:	Standard
Cruise Line:	Fred. Olsen Cruise Lines
Former Names:	*Norwegian Crown, Crown Odyssey*
IMO Number:	5034927
Builder:	Meyer Werft (Germany)
Original Cost:	$178 million
Entered Service:	Jun 1988/Jan 2008
Registry:	The Bahamas
Length (ft/m):	715.2/218.1
Beam (ft/m):	92.5/28.2
Draft (ft/m):	23.8/7.2
Propulsion/Propellers:	diesel (21,330kW)/2
Passenger Decks:	10
Total Crew:	471
Passengers (lower beds):	1,747
Passenger Space Ratio (lower beds):	24.9

Passenger/Crew Ratio (lower beds):	3.0
Cabins (total):	828
Size Range (sq ft/m):	153.9–613.5/14.3–57.0
Cabins (for one person):	91
Cabins (with private balcony):	121
Cabins (wheelchair accessible):	9
Wheelchair accessibility:	Good
Cabin Current:	110 and 220 volts
Elevators:	4
Casino (gaming tables):	Yes
Slot Machines:	No
Swimming Pools:	2
Hot Tubs (on deck):	4
Self-Service Launderette:	Yes
Dedicated Cinema/Seats:	No
Library:	Yes
Onboard currency:	UK£

A well-designed ship with a very British ambience

OVERVIEW. *Balmoral* is best suited to British couples and solo travelers wanting destination-intensive cruising in a ship that has European quality, style, and character, a sense of space, comfortable surroundings, decent facilities, and realistic pricing, and that provides good value for money.

THE SHIP. *Balmoral*, formerly *Norwegian Crown*, is a well-designed and built ship, originally constructed for the long defunct Royal Cruise Line. Norwegian Cruise Line then operated the ship for many years, before it was transferred to Orient Lines in 2000, and then back to Norwegian Cruise Line in September 2003.

Fred. Olsen Cruise Lines bought the ship in 2007 and gave it a major refurbishment, including a 'chop and stretch' operation involving the addition of a 99ft (30.2m) midsection. Although the company's logo includes the Norwegian flag, the ship is registered in the Bahamas.

The all-white ship has a relatively handsome, nicely balanced exterior profile, and one of its plus features is its full, walk-around teak promenade deck outdoors, although it becomes a little narrow in the forward section of the vessel. There are many nicely polished wood railings on balconies and open decks, and there is a jogging track on the uppermost deck outdoors. Atop the ship is the Observatory Lounge, with fine ocean views, central dance floor, and bar. Out on deck, there is a heated salt-water pool, but little shade (no glass dome for inclement weather).

The main public room spaces are on Lounge

Berlitz's Ratings

	Possible	Achieved
Ship	500	369
Accommodation	200	148
Food	400	258
Service	400	263
Entertainment	100	64
Cruise Experience	400	271
OVERALL SCORE		
1373 points out of 2000		

Deck. At the front of the ship is the Neptune Lounge, the main showlounge, with an integral bar at the back of the room; the raised stage and wood dance floor are surrounded by amphitheater-style seating in banquettes with small drinks tables. To its aft are the shops – a curved staircase connects this deck with the reception lobby on the deck below.

Next is the Braemar Lounge, alongside a lifestyle area that includes an Internet center with good separation for privacy; there are also a library and a separate card room. Aft of the Braemar Lounge is the Morning Light Pub (named after the very first Fred. Olsen ship, *Morning Light*). This venue is more like a lounge than a real pub, although it does have draft beers. Aft is the Palms Café, the ship's casual self-service buffet-style café.

The high lobby has a large gold sculpture in the shape of a globe of the world by the famous sculpture artist Arnaldo Pomodoro (called Microcosm, Macrocosm); it used to revolve.

Balmoral offers a wide range of itineraries, which keeps people coming back to this very comfortable ship; passengers also receive a log of each cruise to take home. Niggles include an inflexible bed layout in some cabins, and dated decor in some older cabins.

Port taxes are included for UK passengers. Gratuities of £4 ($6) per passenger, per day, are suggested. The drinks prices are very reasonable, but laundry/dry-cleaning prices are quite high. The mostly Filipino/Thai crew is warm and friendly, and should help make your cruise enjoyable.

ACCOMMODATION. There are 21 price categories; typically, the higher the deck, the higher the price. Most cabins are of the same size and layout, have blond wood cabinetry and accents, an abundance of mirrors, and closet and drawer space, and are very well equipped. All accommodation grades have a color TV, a hairdryer, music console (plus a button that can be used to turn announcements on or off), personal safe, and private bathroom with shower (many upper-grade cabins have a good-size tub).

All towels are 100 percent cotton, and quite large; a soap and shampoo dispenser is mounted on the shower wall and a shower cap is provided. Duvets (single) are standard, blankets and bed linen are available on request, as are double-bed-size duvets. On-demand movies are £2.95 from the in-cabin Infotainment System.

The soundproofing is generally good. Some cabins have interconnecting doors, so that they can make a two-room suite – good for families with children.

The largest accommodations are the suites on Highland Deck 10. They are quite spacious units, and provide a sleeping area and separate living room, including some nicely finished wood cabinetry and a large amount of closet and drawer space, together with a large, white marble-clad bathroom with a full-size tub and integral shower. There is a large private balcony, although some balconies can be overlooked from the deck above.

There are nine wheelchair-accessible cabins; these provide plenty of space to maneuver, and all include a bathroom with roll-in shower. But wheelchair accessibility in some ports on the many itineraries operated by this ship – particularly in Europe – may prove quite frustrating and wheelchair-accessible transportation may be limited.

Cabins in the new midsection have attractive, light, airy, contemporary decor. Some on the upper decks (Decks 8 and 9) have bathrooms with a vertical window with a direct view from the large shower enclosure through the sleeping space to the outside, providing an enhanced feeling of spaciousness. Bathrooms have shower enclosures rather than tub/shower combinations (some have two washbasins), and enough storage space for toiletries.

DINING. The Ballindalloch Restaurant, in the aft third section of the ship, is the main dining room. It has ocean-view windows on port and starboard sides, and operates two seatings. It has comfortable seating at tables for two to eight. However, the waiter stations are exposed and can be extremely noisy; indeed, the noise level in this main restaurant is high, so trying to hold a conversation can be frustrating.

Other dining options. The Avon Restaurant and Spey Restaurant, both named after rivers, are located aft on Highland Deck 10 – the deck that contains the higher-priced suites. The floor-to-ceiling windows provide lots of light. The decor is contemporary and minimalist, and the noise level is low, which makes for comfortable conversation. However, these venues also operate two seatings.

The 70-seat Palms Café is an alternative, more intimate venue for informal self-serve buffet meals. All venues have open seating for breakfast and lunch.

ENTERTAINMENT. The Neptune Lounge is the setting for all entertainment shows, cabaret acts, lectures, and some social functions. It is a single-level room with tiered seating levels. Sight lines are generally good, but could be better.

Revue-style production shows are staged by a resident troupe of singers and dancers, and there are cabaret acts. The quality of the shows, however, is average. Cabaret acts – typically singers, magicians, ventriloquists, comedy jugglers, and comedians – perform individually or as part of the revues.

A piece of trivia for ship buffs: a bar at the back of the showlounge was originally named Theo's bar after one of the former Royal Cruise Line's most popular bartenders.

SPA/FITNESS. There is a reasonably decent – but not large enough – indoor wellness facility, with a fitness room with great forward ocean views, plenty of muscle-pumping equipment, and several body treatment rooms.

Berlin
★★★

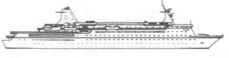

Size:	Small Ship
Tonnage:	9,570
Lifestyle:	Standard
Cruise Line:	FTI Cruises
Former Names:	FTI Berlin, Spirit of Adventure, Berlin, Princess Mahsuri, Berlin
IMO Number:	7904889
Builder:	Howaldtswerke Deutsche Werft (Germany)
Original Cost:	n/a
Entered Service:	Jun 1980/May 2012
Registry:	The Bahamas
Length (ft/m):	457.0/139.3
Beam (ft/m):	57.5/17.52
Draft (ft/m):	15.7/4.8
Propulsion/Propellers:	diesel (7,060kW)/2
Passenger Decks:	7
Total Crew:	168
Passengers (lower beds):	412
Passenger Space Ratio (lower beds):	23.2
Passenger/Crew Ratio (lower beds):	2.4
Cabins (total):	206
Size Range (sq ft/m):	92.5–191.6/8.6–17.8
Cabins (for one person):	0
Cabins (with private balcony):	0
Cabins (wheelchair accessible):	2
Wheelchair accessibility:	None
Cabin Current:	220 volts
Elevators:	1
Casino (gaming tables):	No
Slot Machines:	No
Swimming Pools:	2
Hot Tubs (on deck):	0
Self-Service Launderette:	Yes
Dedicated Cinema/Seats:	No
Library:	Yes
Onboard currency:	Euros

A small, comfortable ship for 'destination-a-day' cruising

OVERVIEW. This ship is best suited to German-speaking couples and solo travelers seeking a vacation in a ship that is unpretentious and provides a reasonable standard.

THE SHIP. *Berlin (formerly FTI Berlin)*, a somewhat angular ship, has an all-white ice-strengthened hull and a profile made more balanced by a thin blue line. It starred for many years in the long-running German TV show *Traumschiff* (Dream Ship). FTI Cruises bought the ship from previous owners Saga Cruises in 2011.

The interiors are crisp, contemporary and well appointed, with tasteful European decor and furnishings. The Library occupies an expansive space; Internet access is provided at four computer stations.

The swimming pool, located aft, is just a 'dip' pool. The surrounding open-deck and sunbathing space is cramped, because it's in the same area as the outdoor seating for the Verandah Restaurant. There is only one elevator and it doesn't go to the two topmost decks or to the Spa Aquarius on the lowermost deck. The passenger accommodation hallways are rather narrow.

ACCOMMODATION. There are four types: Superior Suite, Junior Suite, standard outside-view, and standard interior cabins, in 12 price categories. Most of the cabins are small, but comfortable enough for short cruises. There are no balcony cabins. While most cabins have fixed twin beds, more than 60 cabins do have double beds. The bathrooms have

Berlitz's Ratings		
	Possible	Achieved
Ship	500	290
Accommodation	200	120
Food	400	248
Service	400	247
Entertainment	100	62
Cruise Experience	400	252
OVERALL SCORE		
1219 points out of 2000		

showers but no tubs, and storage space for toiletries is really limited. All cabins have a refrigerator and TV/DVD player. Cabins nearest the engine room suffer from more noise.

The largest accommodation is in two Owner's Suites (Rhapsody and Sonata); both have a double bed, lounge area, extra closet and drawer space, larger bathroom, binoculars, and shoe horn/clothes brush.

DINING. The 280-seat Restaurant has large, ocean-view picture windows, and dark wood accents. There are tables for four or six, and dining is in one seating.

Casual breakfasts, lunches and dinners can be taken in the Verandah Restaurant, a self-serve buffet-style venue with both indoor and outdoor seating areas. A variety of well-prepared, attractively presented items is the norm, with of cold cuts, cheeses, bread, and pastry items.

ENTERTAINMENT. The 250-seat Main Lounge is a single-level venue designed for cabaret performances, but used mainly for concerts, lectures, and guest speakers. The Yacht Club Lounge/Bar is the evening/late-night gathering place.

SPA/FITNESS. Spa Aquarius is the indoor health spa; it includes a shallow swimming pool, small fitness area, massage room, sauna, and relaxation room. A beauty salon is adjacent to the Library.

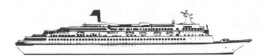

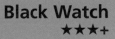

Black Watch
★★★+

Size:	Mid-size Ship		Passenger/Crew Ratio (lower beds):	2.2
Tonnage:	28,613		Cabins (total):	421
Lifestyle:	Standard		Size Range (sq ft/m):	135.6–819.1/12.6–76.1
Cruise Line:	Fred. Olsen Cruise Lines		Cabins (for one person):	38
Former Names:	*Star Odyssey, Westward, Royal Viking Star*		Cabins (with private balcony):	70
IMO Number:	7108930		Cabins (wheelchair accessible):	4
Builder:	Wartsila (Finland)		Wheelchair accessibility:	Fair
Original Cost:	$22.5 million		Cabin Current:	110 and 220 volts
Entered Service:	Jun 1972/Nov 1996		Elevators:	4
Registry:	The Bahamas		Casino (gaming tables):	Yes
Length (ft/m):	674.1/205.4		Slot Machines:	No
Beam (ft/m):	82.6/25.2		Swimming Pools:	2
Draft (ft/m):	24.7/7.5		Hot Tubs (on deck):	3
Propulsion/Propellers:	diesel (13,400kW)/2		Self-Service Launderette:	Yes
Passenger Decks:	8		Dedicated Cinema/Seats:	Yes/156
Total Crew:	350		Library:	Yes
Passengers (lower beds):	804		Onboard currency:	UK£
Passenger Space Ratio (lower beds):	35.5			

This ship provides good value for mature-age cruisers

OVERVIEW. *Black Watch* is a comfortable but not luxurious ship best suited to the older traveler seeking a British cruise environment, where relatively formal attire is the norm. Cruises are well organized, with interesting itineraries and free shuttle buses in many ports of call.

THE SHIP. The ship's name is taken from the famous Scottish Black Watch regiment. There is a good amount of open deck and sunbathing space, and a decent health and fitness area high atop the ship, as well as a wide walk-around teakwood promenade deck with wind-breaker on the aft part of the deck.

The interior decor is quiet and restful, with wide stairways and foyers, soft lighting and no glitz anywhere, though many passengers find the artwork a little drab. In general, good materials, fabrics (including the use of the Black Watch tartan), and soft furnishings give a pleasant ambience and comfortable feeling to the public rooms. Most of these are quite spacious, with high ceilings, and located on one deck in a user-friendly horizontal layout.

An observation lounge, The Observatory, displays nautical memorabilia and has commanding views. Draft beers are available in all bars. The whole ship indoors is a smoke-free zone.

There is a good cinema (few ships today have a dedicated cinema) with a steeply tiered floor.

A popular meeting place is the Braemar Room, a large lounge close to the restaurant; it has a self-help beverage corner for coffees and teas (open 24

Berlitz's Ratings		
	Possible	Achieved
Ship	500	324
Accommodation	200	130
Food	400	252
Service	400	254
Entertainment	100	62
Cruise Experience	400	259
OVERALL SCORE		
1281 points out of 2000		

hours a day, although it becomes overly busy during afternoon tea time), comfortable chairs, and large ocean-view windows along one side. The Library and Card Room is a very pleasant facility with an adjacent room containing two computer terminals for Internet access. There is a self-serve launderette, useful on the longer cruises, with washing machines, dryers, and irons.

Although it is being well maintained, this ship is now 40 years old, which means that little problems such as gurgling plumbing, creaking joints, and other idiosyncrasies can occur, and air conditioning may not be all that it should be in some cabins. But the ship still looks good, and is very comfortable. The company suggests gratuities of £4 per passenger per day.

Black Watch offers a moderate standard of service from a friendly, mostly Filipino staff that provides decent, though not faultless, service. There is ample space per passenger, even when the ship is full. Port taxes are included for UK passengers.

The National Express bus operator works in conjunction with Fred. Olsen Cruise Lines to provide a dedicated Cruiselink service via London's Victoria Coach Station to the UK departure ports of Dover or Southampton.

Passenger niggles include: noticeable cutbacks in food variety and quality; packets of butter, margarine, and preserves; very poor coffee; long lines at the cramped buffet; poor wine service; and too few staff for the increased passenger numbers following the addition of more cabins.

ACCOMMODATION. There are many cabin price categories (plus one for the Owner's Suite, whose price is not listed in the brochure). These include four grades of cabin, spread around most of the decks, for solo travelers. The wide range of cabins provides something for everyone, from spacious suites with separate bedrooms, to small, no-view cabins. While most cabins are for two, some can sleep up to five people. Some 27 balconies were added to cabins on Lido Deck in a 2015 refit.

In all accommodation, hairdryers, and duvets are provided, as are 100 percent cotton towels, and wall-mounted soap and shampoo dispensers in the bathrooms. Suite-grade occupants also get a cotton bathrobe and cold canapés each evening, plus priority seating in the dining rooms.

The suites and cabins on decks 7, 8, and 9 are quiet units. A number of cabins in the aft section of decks 3, 4, and 5 can be uncomfortable, with noise from the generators, particularly in the cabins adjacent to the engine casing. The room service menu is limited.

Outside-view and interior cabins. Spread across decks 3, 4, 5, 7, and 8, all cabins are quite well equipped, and there is plenty of good (illuminated) closet, drawer, and storage space. Some bathrooms have awkward access, and insulation between some of the lower grade cabins could be better. The bathrooms are of a decent size. Some cabins have a small bathtub; others have only a shower.

Deluxe/Bridge/Junior Suites. These suites, on decks 7 and 8, have a large sleeping area and lounge area with ocean-view picture windows and refrigerator, plenty of hooks for hanging bathrobes, outerwear, and luggage; and a bathroom with tub and shower (cabin 8019 is the exception, with a shower only).

Marquee Suites. These suites have a large sleeping area and lounge area with bigger ocean-view picture windows and a refrigerator, more hooks for hanging bathrobes, outerwear, and luggage; and a bathroom with tub and shower.

Premier Suites. Each of these nine suites is named after a place: Amalfi (9006), Lindos (9002), and Nice (9004), each measuring 547.7 sq ft/50.8 sq m; Seville (9001), Singapore (9003), Carmel (9005), Bergen (9007), and Waterford (9009), each measuring 341.7 sq ft/31.7 sq m; and Windsor (9008), measuring 574.8 sq ft/53.4 sq m. Each has a separate bedroom with ample closet and other storage space, a lounge with large windows (with large television and video, refrigerator, and minibar), and bathroom with full-size tub and shower, and separate toilet.

Owner's Suite. Measuring 819.1 sq ft/76.1 sq m, it includes a large balcony, and consists of a foyer leading into a lounge, with sofa, table and chairs, audio center (TV/audio system), refrigerator, and minibar. A separate bedroom has a double bed, and ample closet and drawer space. A second bedroom has two bunk beds – good for families with children. The bathroom is large and has a full-size tub, separate shower, toilet, and two washbasins. The balcony has space enough for a table and six chairs, plus a couple of sunloungers. It is located just aft of the navigation bridge on the starboard side of the ship.

DINING. The Glentanar Dining Room has a high ceiling, a white sail-like focal point at its center, and ample space at each table. The chairs have armrests, and are quite comfortable. The Orchid Room is a smaller offshoot of the dining room, which can be reserved for more intimate, quieter dining. While breakfast and lunch are typically in an open-seating arrangement, there are two sittings for dinner. Passengers help themselves from two cold food display counters during breakfast and lunch.

The Garden Café is a small, more casual dining spot with a light, breezy decor. It sometimes has themed dinners, such as French, Indian, or Thai. There is a self-help salad bar and hot food display. This is also the place for late-night snacks.

Fred. Olsen Cruise Lines has above-average cuisine that is attractively presented, with a good range of fish, seafood, meat, and chicken dishes, and has a good selection of cheeses, plus vegetarian options. There is a decent range of wines, at really moderate prices, but few of the stewards have much knowledge of wines. Coffee and tea are always available in the Braemar Room, next to the Glentanar Restaurant.

An 80-seat poolside Grill Restaurant costs extra for dinner, but menu items include premium steaks and lobster, and the surroundings are pleasant.

ENTERTAINMENT. The Neptune Lounge, the ship's showlounge, seats about 400, although some sight lines are obstructed by pillars. The entertainment mainly consists of small-scale production shows presented by a small team of resident singers/dancers, and cabaret acts. Standards are quite poor though, to be fair, passengers who cruise aboard this ship are not especially looking for first-rate entertainment, but rather something to fill the time after dinner. There is plenty of live music in several lounges, and good old British singalongs.

SPA/FITNESS. The spa/fitness facilities are located at the top and front of the ship – inaccessible for wheelchair users. There is a combined gymnasium/aerobics room, while a door provides access to steam rooms, saunas, and changing rooms. Some fitness classes are free, while some, such as yoga and kick-boxing, cost extra. It's prudent to make appointments as early as possible. Sports facilities include a large paddle tennis court, golf practice nets, shuffleboard, and ringtoss.

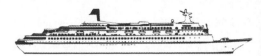

Boudicca
★★★+

Size:	Mid-size Ship	Passengers (lower beds):	839
Tonnage:	28,388	Passenger Space Ratio (lower beds):	33.8
Lifestyle:	Standard	Passenger/Crew Ratio (lower beds):	2.3
Cruise Line:	Fred. Olsen Cruise Lines	Cabins (total):	437
Former Names:	Grand Latino, SuperStar Capricorn,	Size Range (sq ft/m):	135.6–579.1/12.6–53.8
	Hyundai Keumgang, SuperStar, Capricorn,	Cabins (for one person):	35
	Golden Princess, New Sunward, Birka Queen,	Cabins (with private balcony):	64
	Sunward, Royal Viking Sky	Cabins (wheelchair accessible):	4
IMO Number:	7218395	Wheelchair accessibility:	Fair
Builder:	Wartsila (Finland)	Cabin Current:	110 and 220 volts
Original Cost:	$22.5 million	Elevators:	5
Entered Service:	Jun 1973/Feb 2006	Casino (gaming tables):	Yes
Registry:	The Bahamas	Slot Machines:	No
Length (ft/m):	674.1/205.4	Swimming Pools:	2
Beam (ft/m):	82.6/25.2	Hot Tubs (on deck):	2
Draft (ft/m):	24.7/7.5	Self-Service Launderette:	Yes
Propulsion/Propellers:	diesel (13,400kW)/2	Dedicated Cinema/Seats:	No
Passenger Decks:	8	Library:	Yes
Total Crew:	320	Onboard currency:	UK£

An older-style ship with a traditional British ambience

OVERVIEW. This ship appeals to British couples and solo travelers seeking a sense of space, comfortable surroundings with decent facilities, realistic, good value-for-money pricing, with British food and entertainment.

THE SHIP. Acquired by Fred. Olsen Cruise Lines in 2005, this well-proportioned ship, originally built for long-distance cruising for the now-defunct Royal Viking Line (it was built for one of the three original shipping partners who formed the line – Bergenske Dampskibsselskab), has a sharply raked bow and a sleek appearance. The ship was 'stretched' in 1982 with the addition of a 91ft (28m) midsection.

The outer styling is quite handsome for an early 1970s-built vessel. The single funnel bears the company's starfish logo and balances the profile of this attractive (now contemporary-classic) ship. The name *Boudicca* comes from the Queen of the Iceni tribe that occupied England's East Anglia, who led a dramatic revolt against the Romans in AD 61; her body is supposedly buried under Platform 10 of King's Cross Station in London.

The ship has a good amount of open deck and sunbathing space; in fact, there is plenty of space everywhere and little sense of crowding because the ship absorbs passengers well. There is a complete walk-around teak promenade deck outdoors.

The interior decor is restful, with a mix of English and Norwegian styles (particularly the artwork) with wide stairways and foyers, good passenger flow,

Berlitz's Ratings		
	Possible	Achieved
Ship	500	324
Accommodation	200	130
Food	400	252
Service	400	254
Entertainment	100	62
Cruise Experience	400	258
OVERALL SCORE		
1280 points out of 2000		

soft lighting, and no glitz. In general, good materials, fabrics, and soft furnishings add to a pleasant ambience and comfortable feeling experienced throughout the public rooms, most of which are quite spacious and have high, indented ceilings.

There are lots of (small) public rooms, bars, and lounges, unlike the newer (larger) ships built today, including a delightful observation lounge, a small casino, card room, large library, and the Secret Garden Lounge.

Boudicca is an extremely comfortable ship in which to cruise, with a moderate standard of food and service from a friendly, mostly Filipino staff, featuring extremely good value for money cruises in a relaxed environment that provides passengers with many of the comforts of home.

Although the ship has benefited from an extensive refit and refurbishment, it will soon be 40 years old, which means that little problems such as gurgling plumbing, creaking joints, and other idiosyncrasies can occur, and air conditioning may not be all that it should be. Port taxes are included for UK passengers. Gratuities of £4 ($6) per passenger, per day, are suggested.

Passenger niggles include: noticeable cutbacks in food variety and quality; an increased use of packets of butter, margarine, and preserves; the lack of choice of sugar; very poor coffee; long lines at the cramped buffet; and too few wine waiters.

For the ship's mainly British passengers, the National Express bus operator works in conjunction with Fred. Olsen Cruise Lines to provide a dedicated Cruiselink service via London's Victoria Coach Station to the UK departure ports of Dover or Southampton.

ACCOMMODATION. There is something for every taste and wallet, from spacious family suites to small interior cabins. While most cabins are for two persons, some can accommodate a third, fourth, or even a fifth person. There are 20 price categories of cabins (plus one for the Owner's Suite, whose price isn't listed in the brochure), including four grades of cabin for those traveling solo (these are spread across most of the cabin decks, and not just the lower decks, as is the case with some cruise lines), and three of these have a private balcony. While most cabins have bathtubs, some lower grades have only a shower enclosure.

Some of the quietest cabins are those located just under the navigation bridge, on Lido Deck, as well as those suites and cabins on Bridge Deck. In the refit, a vacuum toilet system was fitted.

In all grades, duvets are provided, the bathroom towels are 100 percent cotton and are quite large, a hairdryer is provided, as is a shower wall-mounted soap and shampoo dispenser. Occupants of suite grades also get a cotton bathrobe and cold canapés each evening, and priority seating in the dining rooms.

The room service menu is quite limited and could be improved, although there is an abundance of food available at most times of the day. All cabins have had a facelift. Only a few suites have private balconies.

Outside-view/inside cabins. These are quite well equipped, and there is plenty of good (illuminated) closet, drawer, and storage space, but insulation between some of the lower grade cabins could be better. While most cabin bathrooms are of a decent size, some have awkward access. Some have a small tub, although many have only a shower enclosure.

Deluxe/Bridge/Junior Suites. These suites, on decks 7 and 8, have a large sleeping area and lounge area with ocean-view picture windows and refrigerator, plenty of hooks for hanging bathrobes, outerwear, and luggage; and a bathroom with bathtub and shower.

Marquee Suites. These suites have a large sleeping area and lounge area with bigger ocean view picture windows and a refrigerator, more hooks for hanging bathrobes, outerwear, and luggage; and a bathroom with tub and shower.

Premier Suites. Anyone wanting the most space should consider one of these suites (each is named after a place). These have a separate bedroom with ample closet and other storage space, a lounge with large windows (with large television and refrigerator/minibar), and bathroom with full-size tub and shower, and a separate toilet.

DINING. The main dining room is divided into three venues: Heligan, Tintagel, and Four Seasons; each has a high ceiling, and ample space at each table. Although the decor is reserved, the chairs, which have armrests, are comfortable. Window-side tables for two are the most sought after, naturally.

Breakfast and lunch are in an open-seating arrangement, with two seatings for dinner. Cold food display counters are provided for passengers to help themselves to breakfast and lunch items.

Fred. Olsen Cruise Lines has above-average cuisine that is attractively presented and includes a good range of fish, seafood, meat, and chicken dishes, plus vegetarian options, and a wide selection of cheeses to suit most British tastes. You'll also find popular British pub standards such as bangers and mash, toad in the hole, and spotted dick. Breakfast buffets tend to be repetitive, although they appear to satisfy most passengers. There is a reasonably decent range of wines, at unpretentious prices.

Coffee and tea are available in the Secret Garden Café (part of the Secret Garden Lounge), just aft of the main dining venues – but, sadly, not round-the-clock, although there are late-night 'supper club' snacks.

Casual self-serve deck buffets are provided outdoors at the Poolside Café. An 80-seat poolside Grill Restaurant costs extra for dinner, but menu items include premium steaks and lobster, and the surroundings are pleasant.

ENTERTAINMENT. The Neptune Lounge is the venue for shows, cabaret acts, and lectures. It is a large room that seats about 400, although some pillars obstruct sight lines from some seats. The entertainment consists of small-scale production shows presented by a small team of resident singers/dancers, and cabaret acts (these typically rotate around many cruise ships of the same standard).

There is plenty of live music for social dancing (many of the musicians are Filipino) and listening in several lounges, and good British singalongs are a feature on each cruise.

SPA/FITNESS. A decent amount of ocean-view space is given to providing health and fitness facilities, which include sauna/steam rooms, gymnasium/aerobics room, changing rooms, while the beauty salon is located in a window-less area.

Some fitness classes are free, while some, such as yoga and kick-boxing, cost extra.

It's best to make appointments as early as possible, as treatment time slots go quickly. Sports facilities include golf practice nets, shuffleboard, and ringtoss.

Braemar
★★★+

Size:	Mid-size Ship
Tonnage:	24,344
Lifestyle:	Standard
Cruise Line:	Fred. Olsen Cruise Lines
Former Names:	*Norwegian Dynasty, Crown Majesty,*
	Cunard Dynasty, Crown Dynasty
IMO Number:	9000699
Builder:	Union Navale de Levante (Spain)
Original Cost:	$100 million
Entered Service:	Jul 1993/Aug 2001
Registry:	The Bahamas
Length (ft/m):	639.7/195.0
Beam (ft/m):	73.8/22.5
Draft (ft/m):	17.7/5.4
Propulsion/Propellers:	diesel (13,200kW)/2
Passenger Decks:	7
Total Crew:	371
Passengers (lower beds):	930

Passenger Space Ratio (lower beds):	25.9
Passenger/Crew Ratio (lower beds):	2.3
Cabins (total):	484
Size Range (sq ft/m):	139.9–349.8/13.0–32.5
Cabins (for one person):	38
Cabins (with private balcony):	79
Cabins (wheelchair accessible):	4
Wheelchair accessibility:	Fair
Cabin Current:	110 and 220 volts
Elevators:	5
Casino (gaming tables):	Yes
Slot Machines:	No
Swimming Pools:	2
Hot Tubs (on deck):	2
Self-Service Launderette:	Yes
Dedicated Cinema/Seats:	No
Library:	Yes
Onboard currency:	UK£

A smart-looking ship with decor suited to casual cruisers

OVERVIEW. This handsome-looking mid-size ship suits middle-aged and older UK and Scandinavian passengers who want to cruise in a casual, unstuffy environment, in a ship with British food and entertainment. It's a refreshing change for those who don't enjoy larger, warehouse-size ships. But it does roll somewhat, probably because of its shallow draft design, meant for warm-weather cruise areas.

Berlitz's Ratings

	Possible	Achieved
Ship	500	326
Accommodation	200	128
Food	400	240
Service	400	251
Entertainment	100	62
Cruise Experience	400	268

OVERALL SCORE
1275 points out of 2000

THE SHIP. *Braemar* has attractive exterior styling, and a lot of glass space. There is a good amount of open deck and sunbathing space for its size, and this includes two outdoor bars – one aft and one midships adjacent to the two swimming pools and paddling pool – that have Boddington's and Stella Artois keg beers. Four open decks, located aft of the funnel, provide good, quiet places to sit and read.

The teak promenade deck is a complete walk-around deck, wrapping around Lounge Deck. Passengers can go right to the ship's bow – good for those 'Titanic' pose photographs. Faux teak floor covering is used on the pool deck, which has two pools; it looks tacky, but works well in warm-weather areas.

Inside, there is a pleasant five-deck-high, glass-walled atrium on the starboard side. Off-center stairways add a sense of spaciousness to a clever interior design that surrounds passengers with light. The interior decor in public spaces is warm and inviting, with contemporary, but not brash, Art Deco color combinations. The artwork is colorful and pleasant, in the Nordic manner.

The Morning Light Club is an open-plan lounge, with its own bar, split by a walkway that leads to the showlounge (forward), a lifestyle lounge (incorporating the library, Internet center, and Café Venus), a card room/arts and crafts centre, and a boutique (midships). Despite being open, it has cozy seating areas and is very comfortable, with a tartan carpet. A model of the first Fred. Olsen ship named Braemar (4,775 gross tonnage) is displayed in the center of the room, as is a large carved wood plaque bearing the name of the Scottish Braemar Castle.

The mostly Filipino staff is attentive, and the hospitality factor is good. The company has come a long way from its humble beginnings, and now offers extremely good value for money cruises in a relaxed, welcoming environment that provides passengers with many of the comforts of home. The dress code is casual.

In 2008, a 102ft (31m) midsection extension was added, providing additional cabins and balcony 'suites.' Facilities added or changed include a second swimming pool and more sunbathing space, an observatory lounge, a new restaurant, and a pub-style bar.

There can be a bit of a wait for shore tenders and for the few elevators aboard this ship. British passengers should note that no suites or cabins have bathtubs.

Passenger niggles include: lines at the cramped self-service buffet; poor wine service (not enough wine waiters); an increase in the use of packets of butter, margarine, and preserves; the lack of choice of sugar; weak coffee; and badly worn bathroom fittings. There is a self-service launderette (£2 for wash and dry) – and the company may charge for shuttle buses in some ports of call.

ACCOMMODATION. There are several cabin price categories; the higher the deck, the higher the price. All grades have a small television and hairdryer (some are awkward to retract from their wall-mount holders), plus European-style duvets. The large bathroom towels are cotton (bathrobes are available upon request in suite-grade cabins). There is no separate audio system in the cabin, but music can be obtained from one of the TV channels, although you'll have to leave the picture on. Suites, however, do have a CD music system.

Standard (outside-view)/inside cabins. Almost all are the same size – which is really small – although they are nicely furnished. Most have broad picture windows, but some deluxe cabins on decks 6 and 7 have lifeboat-obstructed views. They are practical and comfortable, with blond wood-trimmed accents and multi-colored soft furnishings, but there is very little drawer space, and hanging space is extremely limited (the ship was purpose-built originally for seven-day cruises). So take only the clothing you think necessary. Each outside-view cabin on Deck 4 has a large picture window, while those on the lower decks 2 and 3 have a porthole. They are quite well equipped, with a small vanity desk unit, minimal drawer space, curtained windows, and personal safe (hard to reach).

Each cabin has a private bathroom (of the 'me first, you next' variety) with a tiled floor, small shower enclosure, toiletries cupboard, washbasin, and low-height toilet of the 'barking dog' vacuum variety. There is some under-basin storage space, and an electrical socket for shavers.

When Fred. Olsen Cruise Lines bought the ship, it converted a number of cabins from double-occupancy units to solo traveler cabins.

Some cabins suffer from inadequate soundproofing; passengers in cabins on Deck 4 in particular are disturbed by anyone running or jogging on the promenade deck above. Cabins on the lowest deck (Deck 2) in the ship's center are subject to noise from the adjacent engine room.

Suites. While they are not large, the suites do have a sleeping area that can be curtained off from the living area. All suites are decorated in individual styles, but with contemporary decor.

DINING. There are two restaurants (Thistle, and Grampian: assigned according to your accommodation grade). The Thistle Restaurant is a pleasing and attractive venue, with large ocean-view windows on three sides; its focal point is a large oil painting on a wall behind a buffet food display counter. However, space is tight, and tables are extremely close together, making proper service difficult. There are tables for two, four, six, or eight; the Porsgrund china has a Venus pattern.

There are two seatings for dinner, and an open seating for breakfast and lunch. The menu is varied. Salad items are quite poor and very basic, with little variety, although there is a decent choice of dessert items. For breakfast and lunch the dual food counters are functional, but the layout is not ideal and at peak times they create much congestion. The Grampian Restaurant is located aft at the top of the ship, with fine aft views. Service is attentive (if hurried) in both venues.

Other dining options. Casual breakfasts and luncheons can also be taken in the self-service buffet located in the Palms Café, although these tend to be repetitive and poorly supervised, with dishes not replaced or refreshed properly. There is indoor and outdoor seating. Although it is the casual dining spot, tablecloths are provided. The indoor flooring is wood, which makes it rather a noisy room, and some tables adjacent to the galley entrance are to be avoided at all costs.

Out on the pool deck, there is a barbecue grill, for casual eating – welcome when the ship is in warm-weather areas.

ENTERTAINMENT. The Neptune Showlounge sits longitudinally along one side of the ship, with amphitheater-style seating in several tiers, but its layout is less than ideal for either shows or cocktail parties. There is often congestion between first- and second-seating passengers at the entrance.

Unfortunately, 15 pillars obstruct sight lines to the stage, and the banquet and individual tub chair seating arrangement is quite poor.

The entertainment mainly consists of small-scale production shows and mini-musicals presented by a small troupe of resident singers/dancers, and cabaret acts. They are rather amateurish, but enjoyable.

SPA/FITNESS. The health spa facilities are limited. The spa includes a combined gymnasium/aerobics room, and a separate room for women and men, with sauna, steam room, and small changing area. Spa Rituals treatments are provided by Steiner. Some fitness classes are free; others, such as yoga and kickboxing, cost extra.

Bremen
★★★★+

Size:	Boutique Ship
Tonnage:	6,752
Lifestyle:	Premium
Cruise Line:	Hapag-Lloyd Expedition Cruises
Former Names:	*Frontier Spirit*
IMO Number:	8907424
Builder:	Mitsubishi Heavy Industries (Japan)
Original Cost:	$42 million
Entered Service:	Nov 1990/Nov 1993
Registry:	The Bahamas
Length (ft/m):	365.8/111.5
Beam (ft/m):	55.7/17.0
Draft (ft/m):	15.7/4.8
Propulsion/Propellers:	diesel (4,855kW)/2
Passenger Decks:	6
Total Crew:	94
Passengers (lower beds):	164
Passenger Space Ratio (lower beds):	41.1

Passenger/Crew Ratio (lower beds):	1.7
Cabins (total):	82
Size Range (sq ft/m):	174.3–322.9/16.2–30.0
Cabins (for one person):	0
Cabins (with private balcony):	18
Cabins (wheelchair accessible):	2
Wheelchair accessibility:	None
Cabin Current:	110 and 220 volts
Elevators:	2
Casino (gaming tables):	No
Slot Machines:	No
Swimming Pools:	1
Hot Tubs (on deck):	0
Self-Service Launderette:	No
Dedicated Cinema/Seats:	Yes/164
Library:	Yes
Onboard currency:	Euros

A fine, strong expedition ship for in-depth discovery

OVERVIEW. This ship is for anyone who enjoys the natural world, and traveling to remote, unspoiled areas. Venturing on the wild side of cruising, *Bremen* has some superb destination-intensive itineraries, with a good degree of comfort and useful documentation, including port information and maps. It's a charming, very friendly ship with a homely, welcoming ambience that's hard to beat.

THE SHIP. This purpose-built all-white expedition vessel, equipped with 12 Zodiac inflatable craft and a helicopter pad, has a handsome, wide, squat, contemporary profile and good equipment. Its wide beam provides good stability and the vessel's long cruising range and ice-hardened hull allows it access to remote destinations. The ship carries the highest ice classification for passenger vessels.

Sustainable tourism is the norm. Zero-discharge of waste matter is fiercely practiced; this means that absolutely nothing is discharged into the ocean that does not meet with the international conventions on ocean pollution (MARPOL). Equipment for in-depth marine and shore excursions is provided, including a boot-washing station with three water hoses and boot-cleaning brushes.

There is almost a walk-around deck – you have to go up and down steps at the front of the deck to complete the 'walk.' A large open deck aft of the mast provides a good viewing platform that's also useful for sunbathing on warm-weather cruises.

The ship has a good number of public rooms for its size, including a forward-facing observation

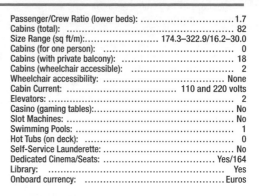

Berlitz's Ratings		
	Possible	Achieved
Ship	500	365
Accommodation	200	155
Food	400	312
Service	400	320
Entertainment	100	81
Cruise Experience	400	322
OVERALL SCORE		
1555 points out of 2000		

lounge/lecture room, and a main lounge (The Club) with a high ceiling, bandstand, dance floor and large bar, and an adjacent library with 12 bookcases (most books are in German).

Bremen is a practical expedition cruise vessel, nicely refurbished in 2009, when flat-screen TVs were placed in all cabins, and the number of Internet-connect computers was increased to four. Arguably, it is a better expedition vessel than *Hanseatic*, and, although not quite as luxurious in its interiors and appointments, the ship has a loyal following. Its cruises will provide you with a fine learning and expedition experience, particularly its Antarctic cruises. All shore landings and tours are included, as is seasickness medication. There's a fine array of expert lecturers, and a friendly crew. The ship has two microscopes, and a plankton-collection net for in-depth studies.

The onboard ambience is completely casual, cozy, unstuffy (no dressy clothes needed), and very accommodating. Also, there is no music in hallways or on open decks. The reception desk is open 24 hours a day, and there's an 'invitation to the bridge' policy.

Arctic/Antarctic Cruises. Parkas (waterproof outdoor jackets) and tough 'snow-grip' boots are supplied, but you should take strong waterproof trousers and thick socks, plus thermal underwear. Each of the fleet of 12 Zodiacs (rubber-inflatable landing craft) is named after a place or region: Amazon, Antarctic, Asmat, Bora Bora, Cape Horn, Deception, Jan Mayen, Luzon, Pitcairn, San Blas, Spitzbergen, and Ushuaia.

On Arctic and Antarctic cruises, it is particularly pleasing to go to the bridge wings late at night to stargaze under pollution-free skies – the watch officers will be pleased to explain star formations.

Special sailings may be under the auspices of various tour operators, although the ship is operated by Hapag-Lloyd Expedition Cruises. Thus, your fellow expedition voyagers may well be from many different countries. Insurance, port taxes, and all staff gratuities are typically included in the cruise fare, and a logbook is provided at the end of each expedition cruise for all participants – a reminder of what's been seen and done during the course of the adventure.

There's no 'bulbous bow' and so the ship can pitch in some more challenging sea conditions; but it does have stabilizers. The swimming pool is small, as is the open deck space around it, although there are both shaded and open areas. In-cabin announcements cannot be turned off (on cruises in the Arctic and Antarctic regions, announcements are often made at or before 7am on days when shore landings are permitted). Sadly, the ship was not built with good cabin soundproofing.

Hapag-Lloyd publishes its own excellent handbooks, in both English and German, on expedition regions such as the Arctic, Antarctica, Amazonia, and the South Sea Islands, as well as exclusive maps.

ACCOMMODATION. There are just four different configurations. All cabins have an outside view – those on the lowest deck have portholes, and the others have good-size picture windows. All are well equipped for the size of the vessel. Each has wood accenting, a color TV and DVD player, telephone, refrigerator (soft drinks are provided free and replenished daily), vanity desk with 220-volt European-style electrical sockets, sitting area with small drinks table, and wireless access.

Cabins have either twin beds (convertible to a queen-size bed, but with individual European cotton duvets) or double bed, according to location, plus bedside reading lights and alarm clock. There is a small indented area for outerwear and rubber boots, while a small drawer above the refrigerator unit provides warmth when needed for such things as wet socks and gloves.

Each cabin has a private bathroom (totally replaced in 2010) with a tiled floor, shower enclosure with curtain, toiletries shelf, washbasin and low-height toilet (vacuum type), a decent amount of under-basin storage space, and an electrical socket for shavers. Large towels and 100 percent cotton bathrobes are provided, as is a range of Crabtree & Evelyn toiletries (shampoo, body lotion, shower gel, soap, and shower cap).

Each cabin has a moderate amount of illuminated closet space (large enough for two weeks for two persons, but tight for longer cruises), although the drawer space is limited – suitcases can be stored under the beds. Some Sun Deck and Bridge Deck cabins also have a small balcony (*Bremen* was the first expedition cruise vessel to have these) with blue plastic, easily cleanable decking and wooden handrail, but no exterior light. The balconies have two teak chairs and a small drinks table, but are small and narrow, with partial partitions and doors that open outwards onto the balcony, taking up space.

Two Sun Deck suites have a separate lounge area with sofa and coffee table, bedroom with wall clock, large walk-in closet, and marble bathroom with tub and basin.

DINING. The dining room has open seating when operating for mixed German and international passenger cruises, and open seating for breakfast and lunch, with one sitting for dinner (assigned seats) when operated solely as a German-speaking cruise. It is fairly attractive, with pleasing decor and pastel colors; it has big picture windows and 12 pillars placed in inconvenient positions – the result of old shipbuilding techniques.

The food, made with high-quality ingredients, is extremely good. Although the portions are small, the presentation is appealing to the eye – and you can always ask for more. There is an excellent choice of freshly made breads and pastries, and a good selection of cheeses and fruits.

Dinner typically includes a choice of two appetizers, two soups, an in-between course, two entrées (mains), and two or three desserts, plus a cheese board (note that Europeans typically have cheese before dessert). There is always a vegetarian specialty, as well as a healthy-eating option. The service is good, with smartly dressed, bilingual (German- and English-speaking) waiters and waitresses.

As an alternative to the dining room, breakfast and luncheon buffets are available in The Club, or outside on the Lido Deck (weather permitting), where the Starboard Bar/Grill provides grilled food.

ENTERTAINMENT. The Club is the main lounge, used as a gathering place after meals and before expedition landings ashore. There is no formal entertainment as such. At the end of each cruise, the ship's chart is auctioned off one evening to the highest bidder, with profits donated to charity.

SPA/FITNESS. There is a small fitness room, a large sauna, and beauty salon with integral massage table. Out on the open deck is a small swimming pool, which is heated when the ship is sailing in cold-weather regions such as the Arctic or Antarctica.

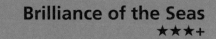

Brilliance of the Seas
★★★+

Size:	Large Resort Ship
Tonnage:	90,090
Lifestyle:	Standard
Cruise Line:	Royal Caribbean International
Former Names:	none
IMO Number:	9195200
Builder:	Meyer Werft (Germany)
Original Cost:	$350 million
Entered Service:	Jul 2002
Registry:	The Bahamas
Length (ft/m):	961.9/293.2
Beam (ft/m):	105.6/32.2
Draft (ft/m):	27.8/8.5
Propulsion/Propellers:	gas turbine/2 azimuthing pods
Passenger Decks:	12
Total Crew:	869
Passengers (lower beds):	2,112
Passenger Space Ratio (lower beds):	42.6

Passenger/Crew Ratio (lower beds):	2.5
Cabins (total):	1,056
Size Range (sq ft/m):	165.8–1,216.3/15.4–113.0
Cabins (for one person):	0
Cabins (with private balcony):	577
Cabins (wheelchair accessible):	24
Wheelchair accessibility:	Good
Cabin Current:	110 and 220 volts
Elevators:	9
Casino (gaming tables):	Yes
Slot Machines:	Yes
Swimming Pools:	2
Hot Tubs (on deck):	3
Self-Service Launderette:	No
Dedicated Cinema/Seats:	Yes/40
Library:	Yes
Onboard currency:	US$

This ship has modern decor for youthful families

OVERVIEW. This ship was constructed for longer itineraries, with more space and comfortable public areas, larger cabins, and more dining options. For sporty passengers, there is activity galore – including a 30ft (9m) rock-climbing wall with five separate climbing tracks.

THE SHIP. *Brilliance of the Seas* is a streamlined contemporary ship, built in 66 blocks. Along the port side, a central glass wall protrudes, giving great views (cabins with balconies occupy the space directly opposite on the starboard side). The gently rounded stern has a nicely tiered appearance, giving the ship a well-balanced look. As is common aboard all Royal Caribbean International ships, the navigation bridge is of the fully enclosed type – good for cold-weather areas, and one of two swimming pools can be covered by a large glass dome for use as an all-weather indoor/outdoor pool. The interior decor is modern and quite elegant. While not as large as some of the newer ships in the fleet, *Brilliance of the Seas* is perhaps best suited to couples and families with children – those who don't need all those bells and whistles, but want to cruise with up-to-date facilities and have multiple dining choices for more convenience. In 2013 the company added some of the dining options found on the larger ships, and enhanced the overall onboard experience by adding, for example, ship-wide Wi-Fi (it costs extra if you use it), flat-screen televisions in all cabins, and finger-touch digital 'wayfinder' direction screens.

A nine-deck-high atrium lobby called the Centrum is the real focal point within the ship, and *the* social

Berlitz's Ratings		
	Possible	Achieved
Ship	500	371
Accommodation	200	141
Food	400	242
Service	400	279
Entertainment	100	73
Cruise Experience	400	270
OVERALL SCORE		
1376 points out of 2000		

meeting place. In the 2013 makeover, the whole area was revamped, and new features were added. On its various levels, it houses an R Bar (for some creative cocktails), several passenger service counters, art gallery, and Café Latte-tudes (for coffee). Aerial entertainment happens in the Centrum, too. Close by is the decidedly flashy Casino Royale (for table gaming and slot machines), the popular Schooner Bar, with its nautical-theme decor and maritime art, the Centrum shops, and the library.

At the top of the ship and you'll find a Viking Crown Lounge set around the ship's funnel. This functions as a sort of observation lounge during the day; in the evening, it becomes a high-energy dance club. Gratuities are automatically charged to your onboard account.

FAMILIES. Youth facilities include Adventure Ocean, an 'edutainment' area with four separate age-appropriate sections for junior passengers: Aquanaut Center (for ages 3–5); Explorer Center (6–8); Voyager Center (9–12); and the Optix Teen Center (13–17). Adventure Beach includes a splash pool with water slide. Surfside has computer stations with entertaining software. Ocean Arcade is a video games hangout.

The largest family-friendly cabins consist of a suite with two bedrooms. One bedroom has twin beds (convertible to a queen-size bed), while a second has two lower beds and two upper Pullman berths, a combination that can sleep up to eight persons – good for large families.

ACCOMMODATION. A wide range of suites and standard outside-view and interior cabins comes in several categories and price groups. Except for the six largest suites (called Owner's Suites), which have king-size beds, almost all other cabins have twin beds that convert to queen-size beds. There are 14 wheelchair-accessible cabins, 8 of which have a private balcony.

All cabins have rich (faux) wood cabinetry, including a vanity desk (with hairdryer), faux wood drawers that close silently (hooray), television, personal safe, and three-sided mirrors. Some cabins have ceiling-recessed, pull-down berths for third and fourth persons, although closet and drawer space would be extremely tight for four persons (even if two are children), and some have interconnecting doors. Audio channels are available through the TV set, so if you want to go to sleep with soft music playing you'll need to put a towel over the television screen.

Most bathrooms have tiled accenting and a terrazzo-style tiled floor, and a rather small half-moon shower enclosure, 100 percent Egyptian cotton towels, a small cabinet for toiletries, and a shelf.

Occupants of cabins designated as suites get the use of a private Concierge Lounge, where priority dining room reservations, shore excursion bookings, and beauty salon/ spa appointments can be made.

Many 'private' balcony cabins are not very private, as they can be overlooked from the port and starboard wings of the Solarium, and from other locations.

DINING. Minstrel, the main dining room, spans two decks (the upper deck level has floor-to-ceiling windows, while the lower deck level has windows). It seats 1,104, and has music of the Middle Ages as its decorative theme. There are tables for two, four, six, eight, or 10 in two seatings for dinner. Two small private dining rooms (Zephyr, with 94 seats, and Lute, with 30 seats) are located off the main dining room.

Choose one of two seatings, or 'My Time Dining' (eat when you want during dining room hours) when you book. Minstrel is closed for lunch on most days, which leaves passengers scrambling for food and seating in the Windjammer Café – an awful prospect after passengers return from morning excursions.

The cuisine in the main dining room is typical of mass banquet catering that offers standard fare comparable to that found in American family-style restaurants ashore – mostly disappointing and without much taste (a vegetarian menu is available).

The descriptions on the menu make the food sound better than it is, and the selection of breads, rolls, fruit, and cheese is poor. Overall, meals are rather hit and miss – unmemorable, in fact. Also, if you want lobster or a decent filet mignon (steak), you will be asked to pay extra.

Other dining options. There are two specialty alternative dining spots: Portofino, with 112 seats, has Italian-American cuisine (choices include antipasti, soup, salad, pasta, main dish, dessert, cheese, and coffee); and Chops Grille Steakhouse, with 95 seats and an open (show) kitchen, which has premium veal chops and steaks (New York Striploin Steak, Filet Mignon, Prime Rib of Beef). There is a per-person cover charge for both, and reservations are required.

Added in 2013 were Giovanni's Table (an Italian trattoria), Izumi (for Asian cuisine), Rita's Cantina, a Chef's Table, and a Park Café (deli-style venue). Some venues incur a cover charge, and some food items have à la carte pricing.

Casual meals (for breakfast, lunch, and dinner) can be taken in the self-serve, buffet-style Windjammer Café, which can be accessed directly from the pool deck. It is impossible to get a hot plate for hot food because the plates are plastic, so things go cold quickly.

Rita's Cantina, set along the port side of the Windjammer Café, caters to families by day, and adults by night. It features Mexican-style cuisine, and à la carte menu pricing applies.

Additionally, the Seaview Café is open for lunch and dinner. Choose from the self-serve buffet, or from the menu for fast-food seafood items, hamburgers, and hot dogs. The decor, naturally, is marine-, and ocean-related.

ENTERTAINMENT. The Pacifica Theatre, the main showlounge, is three decks high, has 874 seats, including 24 stations for wheelchairs, and good sight lines from most seats.

The entertainment is always lively and upbeat. There is even background music in all corridors and elevators, and constant music outdoors on the pool deck.

SPA/FITNESS. The Vitality at Sea Spa and Fitness Center has themed decor. It includes a 10,176-sq-ft (945-sq-m) solarium with whirlpool and counter current swimming under a retractable glass roof, a gymnasium with cardiovascular machines, an aerobics room, sauna and steam rooms, and therapy treatment rooms. All are on two of the uppermost decks.

Sports facilities include a 30ft (9m) rock-climbing wall, golf course, jogging track, basketball court, a nine-hole miniature golf course with novel decorative ornaments (Fairways of Brilliance), an indoor/outdoor country club with golf simulator, and an exterior jogging track.

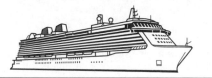

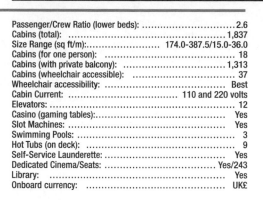

Britannia
★★★★+

Size:	Large Resort Ship	Passenger/Crew Ratio (lower beds):	2.6
Tonnage:	143,000	Cabins (total):	1,837
Lifestyle:	Standard	Size Range (sq ft/m):	174.0-387.5/15.0-36.0
Cruise Line:	P&O Cruises	Cabins (for one person):	18
Former Names:	None	Cabins (with private balcony):	1,313
IMO Number:	9614036	Cabins (wheelchair accessible):	37
Builder:	Fincantieri (Italy)	Wheelchair accessibility:	Best
Original Cost:	€775 million	Cabin Current:	110 and 220 volts
Entered Service:	Mar 2015	Elevators:	12
Registry:	Great Britain	Casino (gaming tables):	Yes
Length (ft/m):	1,082.6/330.0	Slot Machines:	Yes
Beam (ft/m):	125.9/38.4	Swimming Pools:	3
Draft (ft/m):	27.2/8.3	Hot Tubs (on deck):	9
Propulsion/Propellers:	diesel-electric (62,400kW/2	Self-Service Launderette:	Yes
Passenger Decks:	14	Dedicated Cinema/Seats:	Yes/243
Total Crew:	1,400	Library:	Yes
Passengers (lower beds):	3,737	Onboard currency:	UK£
Passenger Space Ratio (lower beds):	38.2		

This floating 'little Britain' has all the right family-friendly trimmings

OVERVIEW. *Britannia* features the rising sun as its logo on its two funnels (it's the only P&O Cruises ship with two funnels), while along the side of the hull there's no mistaking the Union Jack – at 94m (308.3ft) long, it's a big, bold British statement.

THE SHIP. Modeled loosely on the *Royal Princess* platform, *Britannia* – named by Queen Elizabeth II and bearing the same name as her former (slightly smaller) Royal Yacht Britannia – is a thoroughly British ship, and incorporates the classic features of ships such as *Aurora* and *Oriana* into a design that is contemporary but not brash. The stern of the ship is nicely tiered, and slightly reminiscent of the back of an American Airstream trailer (caravan), but the bow (the front) is extremely short. Sadly, there is no open walk-around promenade deck; there's no Deck 13 either.

On the open (family-friendly) deck are two main swimming pools (Lido and Riviera) and several hot tubs (close by is a Pizzeria, Lido Grill, and Grab & Go ice cream bar). Some nights may feature sound-and-light shows performed by the ship's resident dance and vocal troupe. To escape the general noise and hubbub of the family-friendly pools and water splash features, it's worth paying extra to use the adults-only Retreat (just forward of the mast on Deck 17), with its own serenity pool and two hot tubs.

Unusually for P&O Cruises, this ship's interiors were created by a single designer, and the consistently simple, uncluttered yet superb modern design

Berlitz's Ratings		
	Possible	Achieved
Ship	500	581
Accommodation	200	158
Food	400	257
Service	400	282
Entertainment	100	82
Cruise Experience	400	296
OVERALL SCORE		
1656 points out of 2000		

is evident throughout. The interior focal point – and its real social hub – is a spacious and charming three-deck-high atrium lobby, which has curved staircases, four panoramic elevators, and a fascinating starburst mirrored central lighting chandelier. Most of the interior decor is nicely restrained, with a color palette of chocolate, brown, beige, and gray (rather like *Europa 2*), together with occasional bursts of blue and purple. As this is intended to be a ship for all types of passenger, specific areas have been designed to attract different age groups and lifestyles.

On the lower level of the atrium (Deck 5) is Market Café, which features some delightful (extra-cost) patisserie items by Eric Lanlard as well as coffees, cakes, and pastries, a gelateria, and Blue Bar. Also close by is The Limelight Club (a specialty dining venue that is like a supper club). On the other levels you'll find a range of shops and a comfortable (extra-cost) Java Café.

On the middle level (Deck 6) you'll find Brodies (another rather comfortable place for lounging and drinking – named after Brodie Wilcox, co-founder of the Peninsular & Oriental Steam Navigation Company), a small-ish casino (with gaming tables and slot machines, and several shops. On the upper level (Deck 7) is the comfortable Java Café, for extra-cost Costa coffees, and The Glass House extra-cost restaurant.

In all, there are 13 restaurants and eateries, and 13 bars to choose from (one of the favorites will probably be the Blue Bar in the atrium lobby). Atop the ship is the Crow's Nest Bar – always a popular feature aboard P&O ships. Like a large London club, with panoramic views, this is always a good meeting place for pre-dinner cocktails and after-dinner lounging; it has a selection of 20 British artisan gins (also on board – more than 70 different bottled beers and ales). Adjacent are two meeting rooms, the Marlow Suite, and the Ivory Suite; both are on the port side, while the Library is located on the starboard side.

Niggles include the fact that although there are elevators in the center of the ship, there are no stairs between Decks 7 and 16.

FAMILIES. The ship has age-specific clubs and play areas called The Reef for the under-18s (the various rooms are named Surfers, Splashers, Scubas, and H20), a night nursery for toddlers aged 2–5, and a pool and sun deck just for teenagers (a first on any P&O Cruises ship). Access to these areas is best from the aft stairway. At peak holiday times (summer, Christmas, Easter) there could be 400 or more children on board, but this ship should absorb them well, and there's plenty to keep them occupied.

ACCOMMODATION. This comes designated in five categories: suites; deluxe balcony cabins; outside and balcony cabins; interior (no view) cabins; single inside cabins (and very pleasant single cabins with balcony); and wheelchair-accessible cabins (roll-in shower only – no bathtubs). All of the outside suites and cabins have private balconies (the best are those on the port and starboard side corners aft – with numbers A726, A727, B725, B726, C736, C737, D738, D739, E742, E743, F730, F731, G732, and G733). The decor is delightfully contemporary but restrained – somewhat akin to that of a designer boutique hotel, featuring colors such as chocolate, beige, and cream. All shower enclosures are glazed (no shower curtains, thank goodness). Suite-grade occupants are given bathrobes, 'butler' service, and chic bathroom toiletries, but note that many suite-grade balconies are disappointingly small and narrow.

All accommodation grades feature a large flat-screen TV for movies on demand, as well as products from The White Company, and tea/coffee-making facilities (if you want fresh milk, ask your room steward). Balcony cabins have rubberized (not wood) decking, sliding glass doors, and low-grade chairs. Note that balcony cabins with a sofa are more comfortable than those without. Cabins for passengers with disabilities are fitted with roll-in showers.

DINING. The three principal dining rooms are Meridian, Oriental, and the Peninsular. While Oriental features fixed dining times for dinner, Meridian and Peninsular are for 'Freedom Dining,' so you choose the seating time to suit (early one evening, late the next, for example). Well-known celebrity chef Marco Pierre White has created special dishes to be featured in the main dining rooms on gala evenings.

Extra-cost dining options: The Epicurean Restaurant (adjacent to Reception on Deck 5) has a setting of understated glamor, and features arguably the best cuisine on board, especially the cheese selection. The white individual chairs, however, have only curved half armrests that are uncomfortable.

The Glass House offers trendy light cuisine, with wine and food pairings by Olly Smith.

Sindhu features Indian cuisine, with menus designed by Michelin-starred Atul Kochhar, who also has restaurants aboard *Azura* and *Ventura*.

The Limelight Club is a rather like a supper club, so it's all about dinner with a (little) show.

Casual eateries: Horizon Restaurant is the main self-serve buffet-style eatery (open 24/7); it has several 'active' stations (pancakes, omelettes, quiches, noodles are examples), as well as 'grab and go' sandwiches, filled rolls, and deli-style food – most of which has little taste, because almost nothing is made to order. There's also a grill for fast-food items such as hamburgers and hot dogs, and pizzas at poolside grill stations.

In the atrium lobby, the Market Café features (extra-cost) charcuterie, gelateria, and patisserie items by master patissier Eric Lanlard, plus John Turnbull's premium cheese selection, and premium coffees and teas. Java (featuring extra-cost Costa coffees) is more like a 'lifestyle' lounge, with an oceanview terrace.

Just in case you want to hone your culinary skills, a 24-station culinary kitchen – part of the James Martin Cookery Club – can be found aft on Deck 17. Various celebrity chefs (including 'Food Heroes' James Martin, Marco Pierre White, and Atul Kochhar) and other invited chefs may take part and host masterclasses throughout the year – at extra cost.

ENTERTAINMENT. The 936-seat Headline's Theatre is the principal venue for colorful large-scale productions and top cabaret entertainment. The room has gently tiered seating (with good stage views from almost all seats), and an LED stage backdrop provides great sets and lighting effects.

Live Lounge. This room hosts live music, cabaret acts, and comedy, but late at night it morphs into a disco/late-night spot, with bar.

The Crystal Room. This room features a large wooden dance floor, grand piano, and dance hosts to help you dance better or teach you something new.

The Studio. This is a multi-function venue for talks, films, cooking and other demonstrations, recitals, game shows, and conferences.

SPA/FITNESS. Larger than anything (and with more facilities) than on any previous P&O ship, the Oasis Spa is designed to help you relax, be pampered, and achieve serenity. It includes a thermal suite, thalassotherapy pool, treatment rooms, salon, and a rentable 'private spa villa' for couples, plus a spa shop.

Sports facilities include a 'short' tennis court, and an Arena Sports area that includes a combined football/basketball/cricket court, and other deck games, plus a gymnasium and aerobics room (on Deck 17).

Caledonian Sky
★★★★+

Size:	Boutique Ship
Tonnage:	4,200
Lifestyle:	Premium
Cruise Line:	Noble Caledonia
Former Names:	*Sunrise, Hebridean Spirit, Sun Viva 2, MegaStar Capricorn, Renaissance VI*
IMO Number:	8802870
Builder:	Nuovi Cantieri Apuania (Italy)
Original Cost:	$25 million
Entered Service:	Mar 1991/Jul 2012
Registry:	Great Britain
Length (ft/m):	297.2/90.6
Beam (ft/m):	50.1/15.3
Draft (ft/m):	13.7/4.2
Propulsion/Propellers:	diesel (5,000kW)/2
Passenger Decks:	5
Total Crew:	74
Passengers (lower beds):	114

Passenger Space Ratio (lower beds):	36.8
Passenger/Crew Ratio (lower beds):	1.5
Cabins (total):	57
Size Range (sq ft/m):	215.0–365.9/20.0–34.0
Cabins (for one person):	0
Cabins (with private balcony):	23
Cabins (wheelchair accessible):	0
Wheelchair accessibility:	None
Cabin Current:	110 and 220 volts
Elevators:	1
Casino (gaming tables):	No
Slot Machines:	No
Swimming Pools:	0
Hot Tubs (on deck):	0
Self-Service Launderette:	No
Dedicated Cinema/Seats:	No
Library:	Yes
Onboard currency:	UK£

Delightful country inn afloat for educated, seasoned travelers

OVERVIEW. The delightful pocket-sized *Caledonian Sky* is best suited to couples and singles who enjoy learning about the natural sciences, geography, history, gardening, art, and architecture, and want to be aboard a very small ship with little or no entertainment. This is ideal for those who abhor big-ship cruising. In addition, the crew is extremely personable.

THE SHIP. This ship has a neat, modern look, coupled with a traditional single funnel and a navigation bridge in a well-rounded half-moon design. It was one of a series of eight similar vessels originally built for the long-defunct Renaissance Cruises, and acquired by Noble Caledonia in 2011, after being in the possession of a private Abu-Dhabi-based individual for use as his private yacht.

The exterior design has been altered somewhat with the addition of an enclosed lounge deck forward of the funnel. There are teakwood walking decks outdoors, and a very reasonable amount of open deck space. All of the deck furniture – the tables and chairs – are made of teak or hardwood and sunloungers have thick cushioned pads. All exterior handrails are of beautifully polished wood. There is also a teakwood water sports platform at the stern of the ship. The ship carries 10 Zodiac landing craft for up-close-and-personal coastal excursions or wet landings (where necessary).

You'll find elegant interior design and the touches reminiscent of a small, lavish country house hotel. The lounge has the unmistakable feel of a British traditional drawing room; it includes a large, white Bath stone

Berlitz's Ratings		
	Possible	Achieved
Ship	500	402
Accommodation	200	163
Food	400	318
Service	400	313
Entertainment	100	70
Cruise Experience	400	325
OVERALL SCORE		
1591 points out of 2000		

fireplace with an imitation log fire (safety regulations prohibit a real one) and is the focal point for all social activities and cocktail parties. There is also a good travel library/reading room. Inspector Hercule Poirot would be very much at home here, as it is rather like a small, exclusive club. The fact that the ship doesn't have photographers and other trappings found aboard larger ships doesn't matter one bit.

Although the dress code is casual and comfortable, most passengers tend to dress nicely for dinner. The service is friendly but unobtrusive; the atmosphere is quiet (no music in passageways or elevator) and refined, and the ship is well run by a crew proud to provide the kind of personal service expected by intelligent, well-traveled passengers. In fact, unobtrusive service from a Filipino and East European crew are hallmarks of a cruise aboard this ship. The fare includes gratuities, transfers, and shore excursions, plus house wine, beer, and soft drinks during lunch and dinner.

Although several pillars, needed for structural support, are obstructions in some public rooms and hallways, and the interior decor consists of wood laminates instead of real wood, the ambience is warm.

The ship's itineraries take participants mostly to quiet, off-the-beaten-track ports not often visited by larger cruise ships. Destination lecturers accompany each cruise.

ACCOMMODATION. There are several grades of double or twin-bedded cabins and four grades of cabins for single travelers, priced by grade, size, and location. The cabins are quite spacious, measuring 215–365 sq ft (20–34 sq m), including bathrooms and balconies – generous for such a small ship. All have outside views, and most feature wallpapered walls, lighted closets, full-length mirror, dressing table with three-sided vanity mirrors, tea/coffee-making equipment, large-screen TV, refrigerator/minibar (always stocked with fresh milk and mineral water), direct-dial satellite telephone, personal safe, ironing board, and electric trouser press. However, there is no switch to turn announcements off in your cabin. There are two suites that provide lots of extra space, and several other cabins have an additional sofa bed.

The bathrooms are of a decent size, and marble-clad; towels and thick, plush bathrobe are 100 percent cotton, as is the bed linen, but note that there is a small step between bedroom and bathroom.

DINING. The Restaurant has ocean-view portholes, and operates with table assignments for dinner, in a single sitting, and an open-seating arrangement for breakfast and lunch. It is a very elegant and pleasant room, with wood paneling, fine furnishings, subtle lighting, and plenty of space around each table. A mix of chairs with and without armrests is provided. There are many tables for two, but also for four, six, and eight. Breakfast is buffet-style, while lunch and dinner are served.

Fresh ingredients are often bought locally when possible – a welcome change from the mass catering of many ships today, and the desserts are worth saving space for.

Breakfasts and lunches can also be taken outdoors at the alfresco café, particularly when the ship is operating in warm-weather areas. Morning coffee and afternoon tea can be taken in the lounge areas or, weather permitting, on the open decks.

ENTERTAINMENT. The Club Lounge is the room for social gatherings and talks. Passengers particularly like the fact that there is no formal entertainment or forced parlor games – just good company and easy conversation.

SPA/FITNESS. The Asian-style spa, at the aft end of Promenade Deck, is a peaceful place. It contains a hairdressing salon, gymnasium, steam room shower, and a relaxation area.

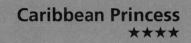

Caribbean Princess
★★★★

Size:	Large Resort Ship
Tonnage:	112,894
Lifestyle:	Standard
Cruise Line:	Princess Cruises
Former Names:	None
IMO Number:	9215490
Builder:	Fincantieri (Italy)
Original Cost:	$500 million
Entered Service:	Apr 2004
Registry:	Bermuda
Length (ft/m):	951.4/290.0
Beam (ft/m):	118.1/36.0
Draft (ft/m):	28.3/8.6
Propulsion/Propellers:	diesel-electric (42,000kW)/2
Passenger Decks:	15
Total Crew:	1,163
Passengers (lower beds):	3,114
Passenger Space Ratio (lower beds):	36.2

Passenger/Crew Ratio (lower beds):	2.6
Cabins (total):	1,557
Size Range (sq ft/m):	163–1,279/15.1–118.8
Cabins (for one person):	0
Cabins (with private balcony):	881
Cabins (wheelchair accessible):	25
Wheelchair accessibility:	Good
Cabin Current:	110 volts
Elevators:	14
Casino (gaming tables):	Yes
Slot Machines:	Yes
Swimming Pools:	3
Hot Tubs (on deck):	9
Self-Service Launderette:	Yes
Dedicated Cinema/Seats:	No
Library:	Yes
Onboard currency:	US$

A multi-choice large ship for informal family cruising

OVERVIEW. The ship is a grand resort. Princess Cruises delivers a consistent, well-packaged vacation at an attractive price. If you're not used to large ships, it'll take you some time to find your way around this one, despite the company's claim that it offers a 'small ship feel, big ship choice.'

THE SHIP. *Caribbean Princess* has the same profile as its half-sisters *Golden Princess*, *Grand Princess*, and *Star Princess*. However, it carries 500 more passengers, thanks to an extra accommodation deck (Riviera Deck). Despite its greater capacity, the outdoor deck space remains the same, as do the number of elevators – so there's a longer wait during peak usage.

There is a good sheltered faux teak promenade deck – it's actually painted steel – which almost wraps around the ship (three times around equals one mile). The outdoor pools have various beach-like surroundings. 'Movies Under the Skies' and major sporting events are shown on a 300-sq-ft (28-sq-m) poolside movie screen.

Unlike the outside decks, there is plenty of space inside, and a wide array of public rooms, with many intimate areas. The passenger flow is good, and there is little congestion, except the wait for elevators at peak times.

High atop the stern is a ship-wide glass-walled disco pod with spectacular views from the extreme port and starboard side windows.

The interior decor is attractive, with mainly earth tones. An extensive collection of artworks comple-

Berlitz's Ratings		
	Possible	Achieved
Ship	500	370
Accommodation	200	145
Food	400	254
Service	400	290
Entertainment	100	78
Cruise Experience	400	293
OVERALL SCORE		
1430 points out of 2000		

ments the interior design and colors well. *Caribbean Princess* also has a Wedding Chapel. The captain can legally marry American couples, thanks to the ship's Bermuda registry. The 'Hearts & Minds' chapel is also useful for renewal of vows ceremonies.

The Grand Casino has over 260 slot machines, and blackjack, craps, and roulette tables, plus games such as Let It Ride Bonus, Spanish 21, and Caribbean Draw Progressive. But the highlight could be the specially linked slot machines that provide a combined payout.

Other facilities include a small library and Internet-connect room. A wood-paneled Wheelhouse Bar is finely decorated with memorabilia and ship models tracing part of parent company P&O's history. Churchill's cigar/sports bar has several TV screens. A high-tech hospital has SeaMed tele-medicine link-ups to specialists at the Cedars-Sinai Medical Center in Los Angeles.

FAMILIES. Children's facilities include a large playroom, a teens-only room, and a host of youth counselors. Children have their own pools, hot tubs, and open deck area at the stern of the ship. There are good netted-in areas; one section has a dip pool, while another has a mini-basketball court. Two family suites consist of two suites with an interconnecting door, plus a large balcony.

ACCOMMODATION. There are six principal types of cabins and configurations: (a) grand suite, (b) suite, (c) mini-suite, (d) outside-view double cabins with balcony, (e) outside-view double cabins, and (f) interior double cabins. These come in many different price categories. The choice is quite bewildering for both travel agents and passengers; pricing depends on two things: size and location.

Cabin bath towels are small, and drawer space is limited. Even the top-grade suites are not really large in comparison to similar suites aboard some other ships. Cabin attendants have too many cabins to look after (typically 20), which does not translate to fine personal service.

Occupants of suite-grade accommodation receive more attention, including priority embarkation, disembarkation, and shore tender ticket privileges.

The largest, most lavish suite is the Grand Suite, at the stern. It has a large bedroom with queen-size bed, large walk-in (illuminated) closets, two bathrooms, a lounge with fireplace and sofa bed with wet bar and refrigerator, and a large private balcony on the port side - with a hot tub that can be accessed from both balcony and bedroom.

Suites (with a semi-private balcony) have a separate living room (with sofa bed) and bedroom, both with a TV set. The bathroom is quite large and has both a tub and shower stall. Mini-suites also have a private balcony, and separate living and sleeping area, with a TV set in each.

Both interior and outside-view cabins – 80 percent of the latter have a private balcony – are functional, although almost no drawers are provided. They are quite attractive, with warm, pleasing decor and fine soft furnishing fabrics. Interior cabins measure 163 sq ft (15.1 sq m).

The 28 wheelchair-accessible cabins have no mirror for dressing, and no full-length hanging space.

All cabins receive turndown service and chocolates on pillows each night, bathrobes (on request), and toiletry kits. A hairdryer is provided in all cabins. All bathrooms have tiled floors, and there is a decent amount of open shelf storage space for toiletries, although the plain beige decor is basic and unappealing.

Most outside-view cabins on Emerald Deck have views obstructed by lifeboats. There are no cabins for solo travelers.

Some cabins can accommodate a third and fourth person in upper berths. However, in such cabins, the lower beds cannot then be pushed together to make a queen-size bed.

Almost all balcony suites and cabins can be overlooked both from the navigation bridge wing and from sections of the discotheque. Passengers in some the most expensive suites with balconies at the stern may experience some vibration during certain ship manoeuvers.

DINING. The three principal dining rooms for formal dining are Coral, Island, and Palm. The Palm Dining Room has traditional two seating dining, while Coral and Island have 'anytime dining'. All are split into multi-tier sections in a non-symmetrical design that breaks what are quite large spaces into smaller sections for better ambience. Each dining room has its own galley. While four elevators go to Fiesta Deck, where the Coral and Island restaurants are located, only two go to Plaza Deck 5, where the Palm Restaurant is located. Note that 15 percent is added to all beverage bills, including wines.

Other dining options. Sabatini's Trattoria features Italian-style pizzas and pastas, with a variety of sauces, as well as Italian entrées including tiger prawns and lobster tail (reservation only; cover charge).

Sterling Steakhouse is located in a somewhat open area, to tempt you as you pass by, with people walking through as you eat – not a particularly comfortable arrangement. There is a cover charge.

Casual eateries include a poolside hamburger grill and pizza bar (no additional charge), while extra charges do apply if you order items to eat at the coffee bar/patisserie, or the caviar/Champagne bar. Other casual meals can be taken in the Horizon Court, open 24 hours a day.

For something different, try an 'Ultimate Balcony Dinner' – an all-inclusive evening, featuring cocktails, fresh flowers, Champagne, and a deluxe four-course meal including Caribbean lobster tail – or an 'Ultimate Balcony Breakfast'. There's 24-hour room service – but some room service menu items are unavailable during early morning hours.

ENTERTAINMENT. The Princess Theater, the main showlounge, spans two decks and has comfortable seating on both main and balcony levels. It has $3 million worth of sound and light equipment, plus a nine-piece orchestra; a scenery loading bay connects it from stage to a hull door for direct transfer to the dockside. The ship carries a resident troupe of singers and dancers.

Club Fusion, located aft, has cabaret spots at night, and lectures, bingo, and horse racing during the day. Explorers also hosts cabaret acts and dance bands. Other lounges and bars have live music, and Princess Cruises employs dance hosts.

SPA/FITNESS. The Lotus Spa is located forward on Sun Deck – one of the uppermost decks. Facilities include a sauna, steam room, and changing rooms; common facilities include a relaxation/waiting zone, body-pampering treatment rooms, and a gymnasium with packed with high-tech muscle-pumping, cardio-vascular equipment, and ocean views.

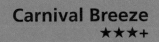

Carnival Breeze
★★★+

Size:	Large Resort Ship
Tonnage:	128,251
Lifestyle:	Standard
Cruise Line:	Carnival Cruise Line
Former Names:	none
IMO Number:	9555723
Builder:	Fincantieri (Italy)
Original Cost:	$740 million
Entered Service:	Jun 2012
Registry:	Panama
Length (ft/m):	1,004.0/306.0
Beam (ft/m):	158.0/48.0
Draft (ft/m):	26.2/8.0
Propulsion/Propellers:	diesel-electric (75.600kW)/2
Passenger Decks:	13
Total Crew:	1,386
Passengers (lower beds):	3,690
Passenger Space Ratio (lower beds):	34.7

Passenger/Crew Ratio (lower beds):	2.6
Cabins (total):	1,845
Size Range (sq ft/m):	185.0–430.5/17.1–40.0
Cabins (for one person):	0
Cabins (with private balcony):	905
Cabins (wheelchair accessible):	35
Wheelchair accessibility:	Good
Cabin Current:	110 volts
Elevators:	20
Casino (gaming tables):	Yes
Slot Machines:	Yes
Swimming Pools:	2
Hot Tubs (on deck):	7
Self-Service Launderette:	Yes
Dedicated Cinema/Seats:	No
Library:	Yes
Onboard currency:	US$

An ultra-fun, Vegas-style water park of a ship for the whole family

OVERVIEW. *Carnival Breeze* is a big floating playground, carrying almost 5,000 passengers when full. It has lots of facilities for young families with children, who will love the outdoor pool deck and its facilities. Serenity is an adults-only, extra-charge retreat, with two large hot tubs on deck.

THE SHIP. This ship and its sisters, *Carnival Dream* and *Carnival Magic*, are the largest 'fun ships' yet for Carnival. Although its bows (front part) are short, the ship's profile is quite well balanced, with a rakish front and more rounded stern than most other Carnival ships.

A WaterWorks pool deck has lots of water and sports amusements – not to mention a really long orange multi-deck 'Twister Water Slide' and the catch-you-off-guard 'Power Drencher'. There's also a large Seaside Theater LED screen for poolside movies and a laser light show at night. The general open deck space is nowhere near large enough for the number of passengers. The ship has a full walk-around open promenade deck lined with deck chairs. Also along the outdoor promenade, four 'scenic whirlpools' are cantilevered over the water, and provide fine sea views.

On a lower deck, The Ocean Plaza, with around 190 seats, is a comfortable place by day and a trendy entertainment venue by night. Its indoor/outdoor café and live music venue has a bandstand and a large circular dance floor.

The Caribbean-themed interior decor is bright, but well executed. Many of the public rooms, lounges, bars, and nightspots are located on two main public

Berlitz's Ratings

	Possible	Achieved
Ship	500	377
Accommodation	200	144
Food	400	220
Service	400	260
Entertainment	100	77
Cruise Experience	400	260
OVERALL SCORE		
1338 points out of 2000		

room/entertainment decks. These can be accessed via an 11-deck-high atrium lobby, whose ground level has a cantilevered bandstand atop a massive dance floor.

Jackpot is the colorful, large, and always lively casino. Other rooms include The Song (Jazz Bar), and Ocean Plaza, a sort of quiet area during the day, but lively at night with live entertainment. Three dozen Internet terminals are scattered around the ship, although most have no privacy. There's a 232-capacity conference room. The Library has a bar, board games, and even a few books.

FAMILIES. Youngsters have their own play areas, with children's programs divided into five age-specific groups under Camp Ocean (ages 2–11 – with children ages 2–5 called 'Penguins'; 6–8-year-olds called 'Sting Rays'; and 9–11-year-olds called 'Sharks'). Tweens have 'Circle C', while teenagers have their own 'Club O2' – a chill-out (no adults allowed) room/disco. Also, soft-drinks packages can be purchased for children (and adults).

Kids also get their own restaurant towards the top of the atrium. Carnival WaterWorks, the expansive aqua park offering exhilarating multi-deck tunnel water slides and various water spray apparatus, is a big hit with the active kids.

At the end of 2015, the world of Dr. Seuss was added as part of the children's program (check before you sail) – from 'green eggs and ham' for breakfast, served by waiters in Dr. Seuss-inspired uniforms, and characters such as the Cat in the Hat, Thing One and

Thing Two, and Sam attending, to special showings of movies such as *The Cat in the Hat* and *How the Grinch Stole Christmas* (shown outdoors on the poolside Seaside Theater screen on Lido Deck).

ACCOMMODATION. There are numerous cabin price categories, priced by size, grade and location. Whether you go for high end or low end, all include plush mattresses, good-quality duvets, linens, pillows, and tropical decor (even cabin doors have cabana-style slats to get the mood going). The suites are not large, although they are laid out in a practical manner, while some of the standard cabins are fine for two but become crowded for three or more.

The decor is a mix of light browns and nautical blues, but accommodation deck hallways are bright, even at night.

There are a lot of interior cabins. All in all, the cabins to go for are those at the very stern of the ship, with great rearward ocean views, on decks 6, 7, 8, and 9.

'Deluxe' ocean-view cabins, with two bathrooms, provide comfort and convenience for families. In addition to twin beds that convert to a king, decent closet space and elegant decor, the two-bathroom configuration includes one full bathroom and a second bathroom containing a small tub with shower and sink.

Some cabins can sleep five persons – useful for families. There's a wide selection of balcony cabins and suites (not really suites because they don't have separate sleeping and living quarters).

Adjacent to the Cloud 9 Spa are 50 spa cabins, designated as no-smoking; these come with a number of 'exclusive' amenities and privileges. All have direct access to the spa. Note that cabins on Deck 12 are subject to lots of noise from kids having fun on the deck above – so forget the afternoon nap.

DINING. There are two main dining rooms: the Sapphire (midships) and the smaller Blush (aft). Each has a main and balcony level (stairways connect them). There are also two small restaurant annexes, which can be reserved by small groups as a private dining room. Choose either fixed time dining (6pm or 8.15pm) or flexible dining (any time between 5.45pm and 9.30pm). Although the menu choice looks good, the cuisine delivered is simply adequate, but unmemorable. Note that the two main dining rooms are not open for lunch on port days.

Other dining options. Fahrenheit 555 Steakhouse (and bar) has an à la carte menu. It has good table settings, china and silverware, and leatherbound menus. The specialties are premium-quality steaks and grilled seafood items. It's worth paying the cover charge for food that is cooked to order.

The Lido Marketplace – a direct copy of the name used aboard the AIDA Cruises ships – is a large, self-serve buffet facility, with indoor/outdoor seating areas on a lower (main) level and indoor-only seating on an upper level. A number of designated areas serve different types of ethnic cuisine (including 'Comfort Kitchen,' for Americana favorites), although it gets congested at peak times – the worst is during breakfast – especially around the beverage stands. Go off-peak, and it's much better. The venue includes a Mongolian Wok and Pasta Bar on the upper level, open 6–9pm for tablecloth-free, candle-less buffet dinners. Outside and aft you'll find the deli and tandoor.

Forward of the Lido Marketplace, adjacent to the 'beach pool' you'll find Guy's Burger Joint. There's also BlueIguana Cantina for Tex-Mex fast-food items including burritos (good for breakfast), tacos, and enchiladas.

Down on Promenade Deck on the starboard (right) side is Fat Jimmy's C-Side BBQ – always a hit. Reminiscent of a backyard barbeque, it features grilled items like kielbasa, grilled chicken breast, and the venue's signature item – pulled pork sandwiches.

Inside on Promenade Deck is Bonsai Sushi – Carnival's first full-service sushi restaurant, with decor by graffiti artist Erni Vales, and sushi, sashimi, and bento boxes by Carnival.

Cucina del Capitano is an Italian extra-charge eatery, located on the upper level of the Lido Marketplace, with pasta served at lunchtime, and 'authentic' Italian specialties at night (now you know where the ship's navigation officers go).

ENTERTAINMENT. The 1,964-seat Ovation Showlounge spans three decks at the front of the ship, with seating set in a horseshoe shape around a large proscenium arched stage; the sight lines are generally good, except from some of the seats at the back of the lowest level. Large-scale production shows, with lots of feathers and skimpy costumes, are staged, together with snappy cabaret acts, all accompanied by a live showband.

The Limelight, aft (the showlounge is at the front), seats 425, and has a stage, dance floor, and large bar. For late-night raunchy adult comedy, it becomes the Punchline Comedy Club.

For an active movie experience, check out the Thrill 5D Theater, where the seats really move you.

SPA/FITNESS. The expansive 23,750-sq-ft (2,206-sq-m) Cloud 9 Spa is positioned over three decks in the front section of the ship. The uppermost deck includes indoor/outdoor private spa relaxation areas, at extra cost. A spiral staircase connects the two decks.

The spa offers a wide range of treatments. There are 10 treatment rooms, including a VIP room, a large massage room for couples, and a Rasul mud treatment room, plus two dry flotation rooms. An extra-charge Thermal Suite features the sensory-enhanced soothing heated chambers: Laconium, Tepidarium, Aroma, and Oriental steam baths.

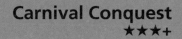

Carnival Conquest
★★★+

Size:	Large Resort Ship	Passenger/Crew Ratio (lower beds):	2.5
Tonnage:	110,239	Cabins (total):	1,487
Lifestyle:	Standard	Size Range (sq ft/m):	179.7–482.2/16.7–44.8
Cruise Line:	Carnival Cruise Line	Cabins (for one person):	0
Former Names:	none	Cabins (with private balcony):	574
IMO Number:	9198355	Cabins (wheelchair accessible):	25
Builder:	Fincantieri (Italy)	Wheelchair accessibility:	Good
Original Cost:	$500 million	Cabin Current:	110 volts
Entered Service:	Dec 2002	Elevators:	18
Registry:	Panama	Casino (gaming tables):	Yes
Length (ft/m):	951.4/290.0	Slot Machines:	Yes
Beam (ft/m):	116.4/35.5	Swimming Pools:	2 (1 w/ sliding glass dome)
Draft (ft/m):	27.0/8.2	Hot Tubs (on deck):	7
Propulsion/Propellers:	diesel-electric (63,400kW)/2	Self-Service Launderette:	Yes
Passenger Decks:	13	Dedicated Cinema/Seats:	No
Total Crew:	1,160	Library:	Yes
Passengers (lower beds):	2,974	Onboard currency:	US$
Passenger Space Ratio (lower beds):	37.0		

This is a vivid, fun-filled ship for ultra-casual family cruising

OVERVIEW. This is quite a stunning ship, built to impress at every turn. The layout is quite logical, so finding your way around is easy. The decor features great Impressionist painters, and

THE SHIP. *Carnival Conquest* has the same well-balanced profile as its close sisters: *Carnival Sunshine*, *Carnival Freedom*, *Carnival Glory*, *Carnival Liberty*, *Carnival Triumph*, and *Carnival Victory*.

Amidships on the open deck is a long water slide (200ft/60m long), as well as tiered sunbathing decks positioned between two swimming pools, several hot tubs, and a giant poolside movie screen (Seaside Theater). It's all about imagination and sensorial fantasy, but it's really more reserved than Carnival's *Fantasy*-class ships.

There are three decks full of lounges, several bars, and lots of rooms to enjoy. There are two atriums: the largest, the forward, glass-domed Artists Atrium spans nine decks, while the aft atrium goes through just three decks.

The ship's interior decor is all about the Impressionist painters such as Degas, Toulouse Lautrec, Gauguin, Cézanne, and others, while Murano glass flowers on antiqued brass stems are displayed in several public areas.

The Tahiti casino is large and action-packed, with over 320 slot machines alongside all the popular gaming tables. There are several other nightspots for just about every musical taste (except for opera, ballet, and classical music lovers), such as the Degas

Berlitz's Ratings

	Possible	Achieved
Ship	500	366
Accommodation	200	144
Food	400	218
Service	400	259
Entertainment	100	77
Cruise Experience	400	258
OVERALL SCORE		
1322 points out of 2000		

Lounge, Vincent's Piano Bar, Henri's Dance Club, and Gauguin's Bar.

Carnival Conquest is a floating playground for the young and young-at-heart, and anyone who enjoys constant stimulation and lots of participation events, together with the three 'Gs' – glitz, glamour, and gambling. This is cruising Vegas style – and an all-American fun experience. Because it's a large resort ship, there will be lines for things such as shore excursions and security control when re-boarding.

Forget fashion, a Carnival cruise is all about having fun. While the cuisine is just so-so, the real fun begins at sundown when Carnival really excels in sound, lights, razzle-dazzle shows, and late-night high volume sounds.

Niggles include: a large number of dining room pillars, which make it difficult for proper food service by the waiters; public toilets that are somewhat utilitarian and could do with some cheering up. It is impossible to escape from noise and loud music (it's even played in cabin hallways and lifts), not to mention smokers, and people walking around in unsuitable clothing, clutching plastic sport drinks bottles, at any time of the day or night. You have to carry a credit card to operate the personal safes, which is inconvenient.

The ship underwent an extensive refurbishment program in 2012 to modernize it and give it a facelift. This included the addition of Guy's Burger Joint (in partnership with Guy Fieri of Food Network) for burgers, hand-cut fries, and assorted toppings, a poolside RedFrog Rum Bar (including ThirstyFrog

Red – Carnival's private-label draft brew) and BlueI-guana Tequila Bar (for Mexican-themed frozen cocktails and Tequila), and a Sports Bar (an interactive venue with video games and a 24/7 sports ticker). Meanwhile, Cherry on Top is a sweet-tooth shop full of bins of – you guessed it – bulk candy, as well as novelty gift items.

FAMILIES. Youngsters have their own play areas, with children's programs divided into five age-specific groups under Camp Ocean (ages 2–11 – with children ages 2–5 called 'Penguins'; 6–8-year-olds called 'Sting Rays'; 9–11-year-olds called 'Sharks'). Tweens have 'Circle C', while teenagers have their own 'Club O2' – a chill-out (no adults allowed) room/disco. Also, soft-drinks packages can be purchased for children (and adults).

By the end of 2015, the world of Dr. Seuss was rolled out as part of the children's program – from 'green eggs and ham' for breakfast, served by waiters in Dr. Seuss-inspired uniforms, and characters such as the Cat in the Hat, Thing One and Thing Two, and Sam attending, to special showings of movies such as *The Cat in the Hat* and *How the Grinch Stole Christmas* (shown on the poolside Seaside Theater screen on Lido Deck).

ACCOMMODATION. There are numerous cabin-price categories, in seven different grades: suites with private balcony; deluxe outside-view cabins with private balcony; outside-view cabins with private balcony; outside-view cabins with window; cabins with a porthole instead of a window; interior cabins; and interior cabins with upper and lower berths. The price reflects the grade, location, and size.

Five decks of cabins have private balconies – over 150 more than *Carnival Triumph* or *Carnival Victory*, for example. But many are not so private, and can be overlooked from various public locations.

There are 18 spa cabins, located directly around and behind the Spa Carnival, so you can get out of bed and go straight to the treadmill without having to go through any of the public rooms first!

The standard cabins are of good size and are equipped with all the basics, although the furniture is rather angular, with no rounded edges. Three decks of cabins (eight on each deck, each with private balcony) overlook the stern. Most cabins with twin beds can be converted to a queen-size bed format. A gift basket is provided in all grades of cabin; it includes aloe soap, shampoo, conditioner, deodorant, breath mints, candy, and pain relief tablets (all in sample sizes).

Note: If you book one of the Category 11 or 12 suites you get 'Skipper's Club' priority check-in at any US homeland port – useful for getting ahead of the crowd.

DINING. There are two principal dining rooms: the 744-seat Renoir Restaurant, and the larger 1,044-seat Monet Restaurant. Both are two decks high, and both have a balcony level for diners (the balcony level in the Monet Restaurant is larger). Cassat and Pissaro, two additional wings in the Renoir Restaurant, can accommodate large groups in a private dining setting. There's a choice of either fixed time dining or flexible dining (any time between 5.45pm and 9.30pm). Although the menu choice looks varied, the cuisine delivered is usually unmemorable but adequate. Note that the two main dining rooms are not open for lunch on port days, so you will need to go to the serve-yourself buffet – or order room service.

Other dining options. The Steakhouse is the reservations-only, extra-cost, specialty dining spot. The decor includes wall murals in the style of Seurat's famous Le Cirque (The Circus). There are fine table settings, china, and silverware, as well as leather-bound menus (steaks and seafood are featured).

The Cézanne Restaurant is a casual self-serve 'international' food court-style lido deck eatery, with a capacity for over 1,200. Its decor reflects the style of a 19th-century French café. It has two main serving lines, is adjacent to the aft pool, and can be covered by a glass cover in poor weather. Included are Paul's Deli, PC's Wok (Chinese cuisine, with wok preparation), a 24-hour pizzeria, and a patisserie (there's an extra charge for pastries, however). There's also Guy's Burger Joint (created in partnership with Guy Fieri), for hamburgers, hot dogs, and hand-cut fries, and BlueIguana Cantina – a Mexican-themed taco and burrito joint with a self-serve salsa and toppings bar.

At night, the Cézanne Restaurant becomes the Seaview Bistro, providing a casual alternative to eating in the main restaurants. It features pasta, steaks, salads, and desserts, typically between 6pm and 9pm.

ENTERTAINMENT. The Toulouse-Lautrec Show-lounge is a multi-deck showroom seating 1,400. It has a revolving stage, hydraulic orchestra pit, superb sound, and seating on three levels (the upper levels being tiered through two decks). A proscenium over the stage acts as a scenery loft.

Hasbro, The Game Show (added in 2012) includes audience participation, as competitive interpretations of the larger-than-life board games.

SPA/FITNESS. SpaCarnival is a fairly large health, fitness, and spa complex. You'll find it directly above the navigation bridge in the forward part of the ship and it is accessed from the forward stairway. Facilities include a gymnasium (packed with muscle machines and exercise equipment), body treatment area, sauna and steam rooms for men and women, and a beauty salon.

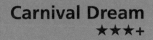

Carnival Dream
★★★+

Size:	Large Resort Ship
Tonnage:	128,251
Lifestyle:	Standard
Cruise Line:	Carnival Cruise Line
Former Names:	none
IMO Number:	9378474
Builder:	Fincantieri (Italy)
Original Cost:	$740 million
Entered Service:	Sep 2009
Registry:	Panama
Length (ft/m):	1,004.0/306.0
Beam (ft/m):	158.0/48.0
Draft (ft/m):	26.2/8.0
Propulsion/Propellers:	diesel-electric (75,600kW)/2
Passenger Decks:	13
Total Crew:	1,367
Passengers (lower beds):	3,646
Passenger Space Ratio (lower beds):	35.1

Passenger/Crew Ratio (lower beds):	2.6
Cabins (total):	1,823
Size Range (sq ft/m):	185.0–430.5/17.1–40.0
Cabins (for one person):	0
Cabins (with private balcony):	887
Cabins (wheelchair accessible):	35
Wheelchair accessibility:	Good
Cabin Current:	110 volts
Elevators:	20
Casino (gaming tables):	Yes
Slot Machines:	Yes
Swimming Pools:	2
Hot Tubs (on deck):	7
Self-Service Launderette:	Yes
Dedicated Cinema/Seats:	No
Library:	Yes
Onboard currency:	US$

Fun for a first cruise, with a splash-tastic water-slide

OVERVIEW. *Carnival Dream*, whose sister ships are *Carnival Breeze* and *Carnival Magic*, operates year-round Caribbean cruises from Florida. There are ample facilities for children, who particularly enjoy the outdoor waterpark and pool facilities. There's also a Serenity adults-only, extra-charge retreat as well as a sports activity area on deck.

THE SHIP. Although the ship's bows are short, the ship's profile is nicely balanced, with a rakish front and more rounded stern than some other ships in the Carnival fleet.

WaterWorks – on the pool deck – has lots of water and sports amusements, not to mention a really long orange multi-deck 'Twister Water Slide' and popular 'Power Drencher'. However, the general open deck space is really not enough for the number of passengers carried, so the sunbed loungers are packed in tightly.

There is a full walk-around open promenade deck, lined with deck chairs, so it can be difficult to navigate your way through them. Along the outdoor promenade, four 'scenic whirlpools' are cantilevered over the water and provide fine sea views. Higher up, Lido Deck 10 offers the best open-deck area of any Carnival ship with a tropical, resort-style main pool complete with a giant Seaside Theater LED screen for outdoor movies. *Carnival Dream* was the first Carnival ship to have a laser light show outdoors.

The interior decor is bright (take sunglasses), but well executed. Most public rooms, lounges, and bars are on Dream Street or Upper Dream Street. The stunning Dream Lobby is the connection point for

Berlitz's Ratings

	Possible	Achieved
Ship	500	377
Accommodation	200	144
Food	400	218
Service	400	260
Entertainment	100	77
Cruise Experience	400	261
OVERALL SCORE		
1337 points out of 2000		

ship functions and people. Take the glass-walled elevators for a neat view. There are three main elevator towers: forward, amidships, and aft.

Many lounges, bars, and night-spots – including a dance club with a twist, offering indoor/outdoor access – are accessible via an 11-deck-high atrium, the ground level of which has a neatly cantilevered bandstand atop a large dance floor. The Page Turner (great name) is the library, while Jackpot is – you guessed it – the colorful, large, and lively casino. Other rooms include The Song (Jazz Bar), and Ocean Plaza, a sort of quiet area during the day, but lively at night with live entertainment. Three dozen Internet terminals are scattered around the ship, although most have no privacy. There's a 232-capacity conference room, The Chambers.

The indoor/outdoor Ocean Plaza, with around 190 seats, is a comfortable spot for people-watching by day and becomes a trendy entertainment venue by night, with its own dance floor and bandstand.

Although passenger flow is generally sound, the ship's layout is rather disjointed. Just before the second seating, there is much congestion on Upper and Lower Dream Streets, both located on the starboard side. Congestion also appears around the photo gallery in the atrium lobby. Passenger niggles highlight the barely warm food in the two main dining rooms, lines for self-serve food items, and congestion in the public areas just before the second seating for dinner. Gratuities are automatically charged to your onboard account.

FAMILIES. Youngsters have their own play areas, with children's programs divided into five age-specific groups under Camp Ocean (ages 2–11 – with children ages 2–5 called 'Penguins'; 6–8-year-olds called 'Sting Rays'; 9–11-year-olds called 'Sharks'). Tweens have 'Circle C', while teenagers have their own 'Club O2' – a chill-out (no adults allowed) room/disco. Also, soft-drinks packages can be purchased for children (and adults).

Carnival WaterWorks, an aqua park offering exhilarating multi-deck tunnel slides and various water spray apparatus, is also a huge hit with the kids.

At the end of 2015, the world of Dr. Seuss was added as part of the line's children's program – from 'green eggs and ham' for breakfast, served by waiters in Dr. Seuss-inspired uniforms, and characters such as the Cat in the Hat, Thing One and Thing Two, and Sam attending, to special showings of movies such as *The Cat in the Hat* and *How the Grinch Stole Christmas* (these will be shown outdoors on the poolside Seaside Theater screen on Lido Deck).

ACCOMMODATION. There are several cabin price categories, in just six cabin types. The price depends on the accommodation grade and location you choose. Whether you go for high end or low end, all accommodation includes the Carnival Comfort Bed with plush mattresses, good-quality duvets, linens, and pillows. However, the straight accommodation deck hallways create rather a cell-block look – and they are bright, very bright, even at night. There are also lot of interior cabins. The cabins to go for are those at the stern: they are quieter and offer great rearward ocean views on decks 6, 7, 8, and 9.

'Deluxe' ocean-view cabins, with two bathrooms, provide comfort and convenience for families. In addition to twin beds that convert to a king, decent closet space, and elegant decor, the two-bathroom configuration includes one full bathroom and a second bathroom containing a small tub with shower and washbasin.

Some cabins can accommodate five persons – useful for families. There is a wide selection of balcony cabins and suites, including 'Cove Balcony' cabins that are the closest to the waterline.

Additionally, adjacent to the Serenity Spa are 65 'Cloud 9' spa cabins. They include a number of amenities and privileges. Twenty of these are positioned directly aft of the lower level of the spa, with direct access to it.

DINING. There are two main restaurants: the 1,180-seat Crimson (midships) and the smaller 828-seat Scarlet (aft). Each has two levels: main and balcony (stairways connect both levels), with the galley on the lower level. Forward of Crimson are two small restaurant annexes; these can be reserved by small groups as private dining rooms. Choose either fixed-time dining (typically 6pm or 8.15pm) or flexible dining (any time between 5.45 and 9.30pm). Note that the two main dining rooms are not open for lunch on port days.

The Gathering is the ship's Lido Deck self-serve buffet facility, with indoor/outdoor seating areas on the lower (main) level, and indoor-only seating on the upper level. A number of designated areas serve different types of ethnic cuisine, although it does become very congested at peak times – especially breakfast – especially around the beverage stands. Go off-peak and it's much better. The venue includes a Mongolian Wok and Pasta Bar on the upper level, open 6–9pm.

Outside, aft is where the deli and tandoor (Indian food) counters can be found, for snacks, while forward of the self-serve buffet, and outdoors, is a fast-food grill and pizzeria.

Other dining options. The Chef's Art Supper Club (and bar) seats 139 and has great views to port and starboard from its aft location high on Spa Deck 12, and an à la carte menu. It has fine table settings, china, and silverware. The specialties are steaks and seafood items. It's worth paying the cover charge to get a taste of what Carnival can deliver. On Promenade Deck you'll find Wasabi, the ship's tribute-to-sushi venue.

ENTERTAINMENT. The 1,964-seat Encore Showlounge spans three decks at the front of the ship, with seating set in a horseshoe shape around the stage; the sight lines are generally good, except from some of the seats at the back of the lowest level. Large-scale production shows, with lots of feathers and skimpy costumes, are staged, together with snappy cabaret acts, all accompanied by a live showband.

The 425-seat Burgundy Lounge, at the aft end of the ship (opposite to the showlounge, at the front), has a stage, dance floor, and large bar, and is the venue for late-night in-your-face, smutty 'adult comedy'. Caliente, the ship's nightclub, provides loud Latin dance music.

SPA/FITNESS. The expansive 23,750-sq-ft (2,206-sq-m) Cloud 9 Spa is Carnival's largest and most elaborate health and wellness center to date. It is positioned over three decks in the front section of the ship. The uppermost deck includes indoor/outdoor private spa relaxation areas, at extra cost. A spiral staircase connects the two decks.

There are 10 body treatment rooms, including a VIP room, a large massage room for couples, and a Rasul mud treatment room, plus two dry flotation rooms. An extra-charge 'Thermal Suite' comes with the typical sensory-enhanced soothing heated chambers: Laconium, Tepidarium, Aroma, and Oriental steam baths.

Carnival Ecstasy
★★★

Size:	Large Resort Ship
Tonnage:	70,526
Lifestyle:	Standard
Cruise Line:	Carnival Cruise Line
Former Names:	*Ecstasy*
IMO Number:	8711344
Builder:	Kvaerner Masa-Yards (Finland)
Original Cost:	$225 million
Entered Service:	Jun 1991
Registry:	Panama
Length (ft/m):	855.8/263.6
Beam (ft/m):	103.0/31.4
Draft (ft/m):	25.9/7.9
Propulsion/Propellers:	diesel-electric (42,240kW)/2
Passenger Decks:	10
Total Crew:	920
Passengers (lower beds):	2,056
Passenger Space Ratio (lower beds):	34.4

Passenger/Crew Ratio (lower beds):	2.2
Cabins (total):	1,026 or 1,028
Size Range (sq ft/m):	173.2–409.7/16.0–38.0
Cabins (for one person):	0
Cabins (with private balcony):	52
Cabins (wheelchair accessible):	22
Wheelchair accessibility:	Fair
Cabin Current:	110 volts
Elevators:	14
Casino (gaming tables):	Yes
Slot Machines:	Yes
Swimming Pools:	3
Hot Tubs (on deck):	6
Self-Service Launderette:	Yes
Dedicated Cinema/Seats:	No
Library:	Yes
Onboard currency:	US$

A floating fun palace for ultra-casual first-time cruisers

OVERVIEW. *Carnival Ecstasy* is the second in a series of eight almost identical ships in Carnival's *Fantasy*-class ships. Although externally angular and not at all handsome, this is nonetheless a popular ship – aimed at anyone taking their first cruise.

THE SHIP. *Carnival Ecstasy* – now well over 20 years old and looking tired – has open deck space that is inadequate when the ship is full. The aft decks tend to be less noisy, whereas all the activities are focused around the main swimming pool and hot tubs (one with a thatched shade). There's also a topless sunbathing area, as well as Serenity – an adult-only 'quiet' lounging space on Deck 9 aft. There is no walk-around open promenade deck, although there is a short jogging track atop ship. The lifeboats, six of which double as shore tenders, are positioned high in the ship.

The interior spaces are well utilized and the general passenger flow is good. The interior design – the work of Miami-based creative genius Joe Farcus – is clever, functional, and extremely colorful. He calls it 'entertainment architecture.' The ship's interior design theme is mythical muses and music. You'll find a rather nice Rolls-Royce car (and coffee shop) located on the indoor promenade.

The interior focal point is an 'open' atrium lobby, with a balconied shape that recalls some of the world's great opera houses; styled to impress, it spans six decks, and is topped by a large glass dome. The lowest level of the atrium lobby is where you'll find the purser's desk and shore excursion desk, together

Berlitz's Ratings

	Possible	Achieved
Ship	500	309
Accommodation	200	138
Food	400	212
Service	400	256
Entertainment	100	73
Cruise Experience	400	244
OVERALL SCORE		
1232 points out of 2000		

with a popular Atrium Bar (with live music), as well as a small sushi bar off to one side.

There are public entertainment lounges, bars, and clubs galore, with something for everyone (except quiet space). The public rooms, connected by a double-width promenade called City Highlights Boulevard, combine a colorful mix of classic and contemporary (think garish) design elements. Most public rooms and attractions lead off from this boulevard – a sort of shipboard Main Street, which runs between the showlounge (forward) and the Starlight Aft Lounge/nightclub. Gamers and slot players alike will enjoy the almost non-stop action in the Crystal Palace Casino. There is also a fine-looking library and reading room, but few books, and a 1,200-sq-ft (111-sq-m) conference room.

Carnival Ecstasy is a floating playground for the young and young-at-heart, and anyone who enjoys constant stimulation and lots of participation events. Because it's a large resort ship, there will be lines for the likes of shore excursions, security control when re-boarding, and disembarkation, as well as sign-up sheets for fitness equipment.

Forget fashion – a Carnival cruise is all about having fun. While the cuisine is just so-so, the real fun begins at sundown when Carnival really excels in sound, lights, and shows. From venues such as the Stripes Dance Club/Disco to the Society Cigar Bar, the ship's interior decor will certainly entertain you.

Carnival Ecstasy, however, is not for those who want a quiet, relaxing cruise experience. There are simply too many annoying announcements, and a great deal of hustling for drinks. Shore excursions are booked via the in-cabin 'Fun Vision' television system, so obtaining advice and suggestions is not easy. The art in the Art Gallery is rather tacky, to say the least!

FAMILIES. Youngsters have their own play areas, with children's programs divided into five age-specific groups under Camp Ocean (ages 2–11 – with children ages 2–5 called 'Penguins'; 6–8-year-olds called 'Sting Rays'; 9–11-year-olds called 'Sharks'). Tweens have 'Circle C', while teenagers have their own 'Club O2' – a chill-out (no adults allowed) room/disco. Also, soft-drinks packages can be purchased for children (and adults).

By the end of 2015, the world of Dr. Seuss was added as part of the children's program – from 'green eggs and ham' for breakfast, served by waiters in Dr. Seuss-inspired uniforms, and characters such as the Cat in the Hat, Thing One and Thing Two, and Sam attending, to special showings of movies such as *The Cat in the Hat* and *How the Grinch Stole Christmas* (shown on the poolside Seaside Theater screen on Lido Deck).

ACCOMMODATION. There are several types of accommodation and prices, according to facilities, size, and location. The standard outside-view and interior cabins have decor that is rather plain and unmemorable. They are marginally comfortable, yet are spacious enough and practical (most are of the same size and appointments), with good storage space and practical, well-designed no-nonsense bathrooms. However, if you have a queen-bed configuration instead of the standard twin-bed layout, note that one person has to clamber over the bed, which can be an ungainly exercise.

Anyone booking an outside suite will find more space, whirlpool bathtubs, and some rather eclectic decor and furniture. These are mildly attractive, but so-so, and they are much smaller than those aboard ships of a similar size of competing companies. A small gift basket of toiletry samples is provided in all grades.

Book a Category 11 or 12 suite and you get Skipper's Club priority check-in at any US homeland port – useful for getting ahead of the crowd.

Room service items are available 24 hours a day, although in standard-grade cabins, only cold food is available, while occupants of suite-grade accommodation have a greater range of items (both hot and cold) to choose from.

DINING. The two large main dining rooms, Wind Star and Wind Song, are located amidships and aft. They have ocean-view windows and are noisy, but

the decor is attractive, although extremely bright. Choose either fixed-time dining (6pm or 8.15pm) or flexible dining (any time between 5.45 and 9.30pm).

The food is so-so. Presentation is simple, and few garnishes are used. Many meat and fowl dishes are disguised with gravies and sauces. The selection of fresh green vegetables, breads, rolls, cheeses, and fruits is limited, and there is much use of canned fruit and jellied desserts. There's a decent wine list, but no wine waiters. The waiters sing and dance, and there are constant parades – so it's really more about 'eatertainment' than food quality. Remember, however, that this is standard banquet catering. If you want something really simple, there's an 'always available' (when the dining rooms are open) list of 'Carnival Classics' including mahi mahi (fish), baby back ribs (beef), and grilled chicken. Note that the two main dining rooms are not open for lunch on port days.

Other dining options. A Lido café (Panorama Bar & Grill), features the usual casual self-serve buffet eats. The venue includes a deli counter and pizzeria. At night, the venue morphs into the Seaview Bistro, a casual alternative to the main dining rooms, for pasta, steaks, salads, and desserts. Outside on deck is a Mongolian Rotisserie Grill.

A patisserie offers specialty coffees and sweets (extra charge), and a so-called sushi bar off to one side of the atrium lobby bar on Promenade Deck is open prior to dinner; if you know anything about sushi, don't expect authenticity.

There is no specialty (extra-charge) restaurant, as aboard some of the larger ships in the Carnival fleet.

ENTERTAINMENT. The 1,010-seat Blue Sapphire Showlounge is the venue for large-scale production shows and major cabaret acts – although 20 pillars obstruct some views. During a typical cruise, there will be one or two high-energy production shows, with a cast of two lead singers and a clutch of dancers, backed by a large live band.

SPA/FITNESS. SpaCarnival is a large, glass-wrapped health, fitness, and spa complex located on the uppermost interior deck, forward of the ship's mast, and is typically open from 6am to 8pm daily. It consists of a gymnasium with ocean-view windows that look out over the bow and the latest in muscle-pumping electronic machines, an aerobics exercise room, men's and women's changing rooms, sauna and steam rooms, beauty salon, and body treatment rooms. Some fitness classes incur an extra charge. A common complaint is that there are not enough staff to keep the area clean and tidy.

Sporty types can also play basketball, volleyball, or table tennis, go jogging, or play mini-golf.

Carnival Elation
★★★

Size:	Large Resort Ship
Tonnage:	70,390
Lifestyle:	Standard
Cruise Line:	Carnival Cruise Line
Former Names:	*Elation*
IMO Number:	9118721
Builder:	Kvaerner Masa-Yards (Finland)
Original Cost:	$225 million
Entered Service:	Mar 1998
Registry:	Panama
Length (ft/m):	855.8/263.6
Beam (ft/m):	103.0/31.4
Draft (ft/m):	25.9/7.9
Propulsion/Propellers:	diesel-electric (42,842kW)/ 2 azimuthing pods
Passenger Decks:	10
Total Crew:	920
Passengers (lower beds):	2,056

Passenger Space Ratio (lower beds):	34.4
Passenger/Crew Ratio (lower beds):	2.2
Cabins (total):	1,026 or 1,028
Size Range (sq ft/m):	173.2–409.7/16.0–38.0
Cabins (for one person):	0
Cabins (with private balcony):	152
Cabins (wheelchair accessible):	22
Wheelchair accessibility:	Fair
Cabin Current:	110 volts
Elevators:	14
Casino (gaming tables):	Yes
Slot Machines:	Yes
Swimming Pools:	3
Hot Tubs (on deck):	6
Self-Service Launderette:	Yes
Dedicated Cinema/Seats:	No
Library:	Yes
Onboard currency:	US$

This floating fun palace is for ultra-casual family cruising

OVERVIEW. *Carnival Elation* is the seventh in a series of eight almost identical ships in Carnival's *Fantasy*-class (sister ships: *Carnival Ecstasy*, *Carnival Fantasy*, *Carnival Fascination*, *Carnival Imagination*, *Carnival Inspiration*, *Carnival Paradise*, and *Carnival Sensation*), all of which have extremely short bows. The ship has an angular exterior profile and is not very handsome. *Carnival Elation* is nonetheless a popular ship – aimed at anyone taking a first cruise.

Berlitz's Ratings		
	Possible	Achieved
Ship	500	309
Accommodation	200	138
Food	400	212
Service	400	262
Entertainment	100	73
Cruise Experience	400	243
OVERALL SCORE		
1237 points out of 2000		

THE SHIP. *Carnival Elation* is one of only two ships in the series of eight (the other is *Carnival Paradise*) with a 'pod' propulsion system, which gives a vibration-free ride, rather than the traditional propeller shaft and rudder system. The open deck space, however, gets really crowded when the ship is full and everyone wants to be out on deck. The aft decks tend to be less noisy, whereas all the activities are focused around the main swimming pool and hot tubs (one with a thatched shade). There's also a topless sunbathing area, as well as Serenity – an adult-only 'quiet' lounging space on Deck 9 aft. There is no walk-around open promenade deck, although there is a short jogging track atop ship. The lifeboats, six of which double as shore tenders, are positioned high in the ship.

The interior spaces are well utilized. The general passenger flow is good, and the interior design – the work of Miami-based creative genius Joe Farcus – is clever, functional, and extremely colorful. The interior decor theme is mythical muses, and composers and their compositions.

The interior focal point is an 'open' atrium lobby, whose balconied shape recalls some of the world's great opera houses; styled to impress, it spans six decks, and is topped by a large glass dome. The lowest level of the atrium lobby is where you'll find the purser's desk and shore excursion desk, together with a popular Atrium Bar (with live music), as well as a small sushi bar off to one side; it's a good central meeting place.

There are public entertainment lounges, bars, and clubs galore, with something for everyone (except quiet space). The public rooms, connected by a double-width Elation's Way and Promenade, combine a colorful mix of classic and contemporary design elements. Most public rooms and attractions lead off from this boulevard – a sort of shipboard Main Street, which runs between the showlounge (forward) and the Cole Porter lounge/nightclub aft. Gamers and slot players alike will enjoy the almost non-stop action in the Casablanca Casino. There is also a fine-looking library and reading room, but few books, and a 1,200-sq-ft (111-sq-m) conference room.

While the cuisine is just so-so, the real fun begins at sundown when Carnival really excels in sound, lights, razzle-dazzle shows, and late-night high volume sounds. From venues such as the Jekyll & Hyde Dance Club/Disco to Gatsby's Great Cigar Bar, the ship's interior decor will certainly entertain you.

Carnival Elation is a floating playground for the young and young-at-heart. It really is cruising Splash Vegas style – an all-American experience. Because it's a large resort ship, expect lines for shore excursions, security control when re-boarding, and disembarkation, as well as sign-up sheets for fitness equipment.

A Carnival cruise is all about having fun, and not for those who want a quiet, relaxing cruise experience. There are simply too many annoying announcements, and a great deal of hustling for drinks. Shore excursions are booked via the in-cabin 'Fun Vision' television system, so obtaining advice and suggestions is not easy.

FAMILIES. Youngsters have their own play areas, with children's programs divided into five age-specific groups under Camp Ocean (ages 2–11 – with children ages 2–5 called 'Penguins'; 6–8-year-olds called 'Sting Rays'; 9–11-year-olds called 'Sharks'). Tweens have 'Circle C', while teenagers have their own 'Club O2' – a chill-out (no adults allowed) room/disco. Also, soft-drinks packages can be purchased for children (and adults).

By the end of 2015, the world of Dr. Seuss was rolled out as part of the line's children's program – from 'green eggs and ham' for breakfast, served by waiters in Dr. Seuss-inspired uniforms, and characters such as the Cat in the Hat, Thing One and Thing Two, and Sam attending, to special showings of movies such as *The Cat in the Hat* and *How the Grinch Stole Christmas* (shown on the poolside Seaside Theater screen on Lido Deck).

ACCOMMODATION. There are 13 grades of accommodation, ranked by facilities, size, and location. The standard outside-view and interior cabins have decor that is rather plain and unmemorable. They are marginally comfortable, yet spacious enough and practical (most are of the same size and appointments), with good storage space and practical, well-designed no-nonsense bathrooms. However, if you have a queen-bed configuration instead of the standard twin-bed layout, note that one person has to clamber over the bed – an ungainly exercise.

Anyone booking an outside suite will find more space, whirlpool bathtubs, and some rather eclectic decor and furniture. These are mildly attractive, but they are much smaller than those aboard ships of a similar size of competing companies. Room service items are available 24 hours a day, although in standard-grade cabins, only cold food is available; occupants of suite-grade accommodation have more items (both hot and cold) to choose from.

DINING. There are two large main dining rooms, Imagination and Inspiration, located amidships and aft. They have ocean-view windows and are noisy, but the decor is attractive, bright and colorful. Choose either fixed-time dining (6pm or 8.15pm) or flexible dining (any time between 5.45 and 9.30pm).

The food is so-so. Presentation is simple, and few garnishes are used. Many meat and fowl dishes are disguised with gravies and sauces. There's a decent wine list, but no wine waiters. The waiters sing and dance, and there are constant waiter parades – so it's really more about 'foodertainment' than food quality. If you want something really simple, there's an 'always available' (when the dining rooms are open) list of 'Carnival Classics' that includes mahi mahi (fish), baby back ribs (beef), and grilled chicken. Note that the two main dining rooms are not open for lunch on port days.

Other dining options. A Lido café (Tiffany's Lido Restaurant) features the usual casual self-serve buffet eats, but most are non-memorable. The venue includes a deli counter and pizzeria. At night, the venue morphs into the Seaview Bistro, and is a casual alternative to the main dining rooms, for pasta, steaks, salads, and desserts. Outside on deck is a Mongolian Rotisserie Grill.

There is no specialty (extra-charge) restaurant, as aboard some of the larger ships in the fleet.

ENTERTAINMENT. The Mikado Showlounge is the venue for large-scale production shows and major cabaret acts – although 20 pillars obstruct some views. During a typical cruise, there will be one or two high-energy production shows, with a cast of two lead singers and a clutch of dancers, backed by a large live band.

SPA/FITNESS. SpaCarnival is a large, glass-wrapped health, fitness, and spa complex located on the uppermost interior deck, forward of the ship's mast, and is typically open from 6am to 8pm daily. It consists of a gymnasium with ocean-view windows that look out over the bow and the latest in muscle-pumping electronic machines, an aerobics exercise room, men's and women's changing rooms, sauna and steam rooms, beauty salon, and body treatment rooms. Some fitness classes incur an extra charge. A common complaint is that there are not enough staff to keep the area clean and tidy.

Sporting types can play basketball or volleyball, or table tennis. There is also a banked jogging track on the deck above the spa, and a mini-golf course.

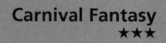

Size:		Large Resort Ship
Tonnage:		70,367
Lifestyle:		Standard
Cruise Line:		Carnival Cruise Line
Former Names:		*Fantasy*
IMO Number:		8700773
Builder:		Kvaerner Masa-Yards (Finland)
Original Cost:		$225 million
Entered Service:		Mar 1990
Registry:		Panama
Length (ft/m):		855.8/263.6
Beam (ft/m):		103.0/31.4
Draft (ft/m):		25.9/7.9
Propulsion/Propellers:		diesel-electric (42,240kW)/2
Passenger Decks:		10
Total Crew:		920
Passengers (lower beds):		2,056
Passenger Space Ratio (lower beds):		34.4

Passenger/Crew Ratio (lower beds):		2.2
Cabins (total):		1,026 or 1,028
Size Range (sq ft/m):		173.2–409.7/16.0–38.0
Cabins (for one person):		0
Cabins (with private balcony):		152
Cabins (wheelchair accessible):		22
Wheelchair accessibility:		Fair
Cabin Current:		110 volts
Elevators:		14
Casino (gaming tables):		Yes
Slot Machines:		Yes
Swimming Pools:		3
Hot Tubs (on deck):		6
Self-Service Launderette:		Yes
Dedicated Cinema/Seats:		No
Library:		Yes
Onboard currency:		US$

This is ultra-casual cruising for the whole family

OVERVIEW. *Carnival Fantasy* is the first (in a series of eight almost identical ships) in the *Fantasy*-class. *Carnival Fantasy* has always been a popular ship – good for anyone taking a first cruise.

THE SHIP. The ship, now 25 years old, sports the company's trademark red, white, and blue wing-tipped funnel. The open deck space is inadequate when the ship is full and the weather's nice. A Carnival WaterWorks – complete with long (about 300ft/90m) and short water slides and water-burst fountains – is a popular and very active area for children. There's also a topless sunbathing area, while Serenity is an adult-only 'quiet' lounging space on Deck 9 aft.

Although there is no walk-around open promenade deck, there is a short jogging track atop ship. The lifeboats, six of which double as shore tenders are positioned high in the ship.

The interior spaces are well utilized. The general passenger flow is good, and the interior design – the work of Miami-based creative genius Joe Farcus – is clever, functional, and extremely colorful. The ship's interior design theme is inspired by the ancient city of Pompeii, and includes a colorful mix of classic and contemporary.

The interior focal point is an 'open' atrium lobby. It has a balconied shape, and is styled to impress. Spanning six decks, it is topped by a large glass dome. The lowest level of the atrium lobby is where you'll find the purser's desk and shore excursion desk, together with a popular Atrium Bar (with live music),

Berlitz's Ratings

	Possible	Achieved
Ship	500	308
Accommodation	200	138
Food	400	212
Service	400	256
Entertainment	100	73
Cruise Experience	400	244
OVERALL SCORE		
1231 points out of 2000		

as well as a small sushi bar off to one side; it's a good central meeting place.

There are public entertainment lounges, bars, and clubs galore, with something for everyone (except quiet space). The public rooms, connected by a double-width Via Marina Promenade, combine a colorful mix of classic and contemporary design elements. Most public rooms and attractions lead off from this boulevard – a sort of shipboard Main Street, which runs between the showlounge (forward) and The Forum aft lounge. Gamers and slot players alike will find almost non-stop action in the Club 21 Casino. There is also a nice-looking library and reading room, but few books.

Carnival Fantasy is a floating playground for the young and young-at-heart, and anyone who enjoys constant stimulation and lots of participation events. Because it's a large resort ship, there will be lines for the likes of shore excursions, security control when re-boarding, and disembarkation, as well as sign-up sheets for fitness equipment.

While the cuisine is just so-so, the vibe gets going at sundown when Carnival really excels in volume, lights, and shows. From venues such as the Electricity Dance Club/Disco to the Majestic Cigar Bar, the ship's bars and lounges will certainly entertain you.

Carnival Fantasy is not for anyone seeking a quiet, relaxing cruise experience. There are many annoying revenue announcements, and a never-ending hustling to get you to buy drinks and other things. Also, shore excursions are booked via the in-cabin 'Fun Vision' television system, so obtaining advice and suggestions is not easy.

FAMILIES. Youngsters have their own play areas, with children's programs divided into five age-specific groups under Camp Ocean (ages 2–11 – with children ages 2–5 called 'Penguins'; 6–8-year-olds called 'Sting Rays'; 9–11-year-olds called 'Sharks'). Tweens have 'Circle C', while teenagers have their own 'Club O2' – a chill-out (no adults allowed) room/disco. Also, soft-drinks packages can be purchased for children (and adults).

By the end of 2015, the world of Dr. Seuss was added as part of the children's program – from 'green eggs and ham' for breakfast, served by waiters in Dr. Seuss-inspired uniforms, and characters such as the Cat in the Hat, Thing One and Thing Two, and Sam attending, to special showings of movies such as *The Cat in the Hat* and *How the Grinch Stole Christmas* (these will be shown outdoors on the poolside Seaside Theater screen on Lido Deck).

ACCOMMODATION. There are several accommodation price grades. What you pay will depend on the size, and location. The standard outside-view and interior cabins have decor that is rather plain and unmemorable. They are marginally comfortable, yet spacious enough and practical (most are of the same size and appointments), with good storage space and practical, well-designed no-nonsense bathrooms. However, if you have a queen-bed configuration instead of the standard twin-bed layout, note that one person has to clamber over the bed, which can be awkward.

Anyone booking a suite gets more space, whirlpool bathtubs, and some rather eclectic decor and furniture.

Some 50 cabins feature inter-connecting doors, which is good for families with children – they can be close, but not too close.

Room service items are available 24 hours a day, although in standard-grade cabins, only cold food is available, while occupants of suite-grade accommodation have a greater range of items (both hot and cold) from which to choose.

DINING. The two large main dining rooms, Celebration and Jubilee, are located amidships and aft.

Both have ocean-view windows and attractive, but very bright decor, but they are noisy. Choose either fixed-time dining (6pm or 8.15pm) or flexible dining (any time between 5.45 and 9.30pm).

The food is unmemorable, with simple presentation and few garnishes. Many dishes are disguised with gravies and sauces. The selection of fresh green vegetables, breads, rolls, cheeses, and fruits is limited, and there is much use of canned fruit and jellied desserts. The waiters sing and dance, so it's really more about 'foodertainment' than food quality. If you want something really simple, there's an 'always available' list of 'Carnival Classics' that includes mahi mahi (fish), baby back ribs (beef), and grilled chicken. Note that the two main dining rooms are not open for lunch on port days.

Other dining options. A Lido café, the Paris Lido restaurant, features the usual casual self-serve buffet eats, most of which are very basic. The venue includes a deli counter and pizzeria. At night, the venue morphs into the Seaview Bistro, and provides a casual alternative to the main dining rooms, for pasta, steaks, salads, and desserts. A patisserie offers specialty coffees and sweets (extra charge), and a so-called sushi bar off to one side of the atrium lobby bar on Promenade Deck is open prior to dinner; if you know anything about sushi, don't expect authenticity.

There is no specialty (extra-charge) restaurant, as aboard some of the larger ships in the Carnival fleet.

ENTERTAINMENT. The Universe Showlounge is the venue for colourful production shows and major cabaret acts, although 20 pillars obstruct some views. During a typical cruise, there will be one or two high-energy production shows, with a cast of two lead singers and a clutch of dancers, backed by a large live band.

SPA/FITNESS. SpaCarnival is a glass-wrapped health, fitness, and spa complex located on the uppermost interior deck, forward of the ship's mast. It consists of a gymnasium with ocean-views over the bow, high-tech muscle-pumping machines, an aerobics room, men's and women's changing rooms, sauna and steam rooms, beauty salon, and body treatment rooms. Some fitness classes may incur an extra charge.

Sporting types can play basketball, volleyball, table tennis, or mini-golf, or go jogging.

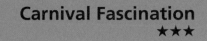

Carnival Fascination
★★★

Size:	Large Resort Ship	Passenger/Crew Ratio (lower beds):	2.2
Tonnage:	70,538	Cabins (total):	1,026 or 1,028
Lifestyle:	Standard	Size Range (sq ft/m):	173.2–409.7/16.0–38.0
Cruise Line:	Carnival Cruise Line	Cabins (for one person):	0
Former Names:	*Fascination*	Cabins (with private balcony):	250
IMO Number:	9041253	Cabins (wheelchair accessible):	22
Builder:	Kvaerner Masa-Yards (Finland)	Wheelchair accessibility:	Fair
Original Cost:	$225 million	Cabin Current:	110 volts
Entered Service:	Jul 1994	Elevators:	14
Registry:	The Bahamas	Casino (gaming tables):	Yes
Length (ft/m):	855.8/263.6	Slot Machines:	Yes
Beam (ft/m):	103.0/31.4	Swimming Pools:	3
Draft (ft/m):	25.9/7.9	Hot Tubs (on deck):	6
Propulsion/Propellers:	diesel-electric (42,240 kW)/2	Self-Service Launderette:	Yes
Passenger Decks:	10	Dedicated Cinema/Seats:	No
Total Crew:	920	Library:	Yes
Passengers (lower beds):	2,056	Onboard currency:	US$
Passenger Space Ratio (lower beds):	34.4		

This is a vibrant, floating movie set for casual family cruising

OVERVIEW. *Carnival Fascination* is the fourth in a series of eight almost identical *Fantasy*-class ships. It's all about partying and having fun – for the whole family.

THE SHIP. *Carnival Fascination*'s open deck space is really inadequate when the ship is full and everyone wants to be out on deck. The aft decks, however, tend to be less noisy, because all the activities are focused around the main swimming pool and hot tubs (one with a thatched shade). For anyone who prefers European-style sunning, there's also a topless sunbathing area, as well as Serenity – an adult-only 'quiet' lounging space on Deck 9 aft. While there isn't a walk-around open promenade deck, there is a short jogging track atop ship. The lifeboats, six of which double as shore tenders, are positioned high in the ship – this wouldn't be acceptable in new ships today.

The interior spaces are well utilized. The general passenger flow is good, and the interior design – the work of Miami-based creative genius Joe Farcus – is clever, functional, and extremely colorful, and includes plenty of neon and glitz. He calls it 'entertainment architecture' and considers every part of a ship as a piece of a giant jigsaw puzzle. The ship's interior design theme is all about Hollywood and the movies. There are great photo opportunities with some 24 life-like figures from the movies.

The interior focal point is an 'open' atrium lobby, with a balconied shape and styled to impress. It spans six decks, and is topped by a large glass dome. The

Berlitz's Ratings		
	Possible	Achieved
Ship	500	309
Accommodation	200	138
Food	400	212
Service	400	262
Entertainment	100	73
Cruise Experience	400	245
OVERALL SCORE		
1239 points out of 2000		

lowest level of the atrium lobby is where you'll find the purser's desk and shore excursion desk, together with a popular Atrium Bar (with live music), as well as a small sushi bar off to one side; it's a good central meeting place.

There are public entertainment lounges, bars, and clubs galore, with something for everyone (except quiet space). The public rooms, connected by a double-width Via Marina Promenade, combine a colorful mix of classic and contemporary design elements. Most public rooms and attractions lead off from this boulevard – a sort of shipboard Main Street, which runs between the showlounge (forward) and the Puttin' on the Ritz aft lounge. Gamers and slot players alike will enjoy the almost non-stop action in the Club 21 Casino. There is also a nice-looking library and reading room, but few books, and there's also a 1,200-sq-ft (111-sq-m) conference room. As for the 'art' in the Art Gallery it's rather tacky, to say the least!

Forget fashion – a Carnival cruise is all about having fun. While the cuisine is just so-so, the real fun begins at sundown when Carnival really excels in sound, lights, and shows. From venues such as the Diamonds are Forever Dance Club/Disco to the Beverly Hills Cigar Bar, the ship's interior decor will certainly entertain you.

Carnival Fascination is a floating playground for the young and young-at-heart. Because this is a large resort ship, there will be lines for the likes of shore excursions and re-boarding at ports of call.

Carnival Fascination, however, is not for those seeking a quiet, relaxing cruise experience. There are many annoying announcements, and never-ending hustling to get you to buy drinks and many other things. Also, shore excursions are booked via the in-cabin 'Fun Vision' television system, so obtaining advice and suggestions is not easy.

FAMILIES. Youngsters have their own play areas, with children's programs divided into five age-specific groups under Camp Ocean (ages 2–11 – with children ages 2–5 called 'Penguins'; 6–8-year-olds called 'Sting Rays'; 9–11-year-olds called 'Sharks'). Tweens have 'Circle C'; while teenagers have their own 'Club O2' – a chill-out (no adults allowed) room/disco. Also, soft-drinks packages can be purchased for children (and adults).

By the end of 2015, the world of Dr. Seuss was added as part of the children's program – from 'green eggs and ham' for breakfast, served by waiters in Dr. Seuss-inspired uniforms, and characters such as the Cat in the Hat, Thing One and Thing Two, and Sam attending, to special showings of movies such as *The Cat in the Hat* and *How the Grinch Stole Christmas* (shown outdoors on the poolside Seaside Theater screen on Lido Deck)

ACCOMMODATION. There are several grades of accommodation, priced by facilities, size, and location. Standard outside-view and interior cabins have decor that is rather plain and unmemorable. They are fairly comfortable and spacious enough (most are of the same size and appointments), with good storage space and well-designed bathrooms. However, in a queen-bed configuration instead of a twin-bed layout, note that one person has to clamber over the bed.

Anyone booking an outside suite will find more space, whirlpool bathtubs, and some eclectic decor and furniture. These are mildly attractive, but so-so, and they are much smaller than those aboard ships of a similar size of competing companies. A small basket of toiletry samples is provided in all grades.

Book a Category 11 or 12 suite and you get Skipper's Club priority check-in at any US homeland port – useful for getting ahead of the crowd.

Room service items are available 24 hours a day, although in standard cabins, only cold food is available; anyone in suite-grade accommodation gets a greater range of items (both hot and cold) from which to choose.

DINING. The two large main dining rooms, Sensation and Imagination, are located midships and aft. Both have ocean-view windows and attractive, but very bright decor, but they are noisy. Choose either fixed-time dining (6pm or 8.15pm) or flexible dining (any time between 5.45 and 9.30pm).

The food is not very inspiring (it's banquet-style production catering, after all). The selection of fresh green vegetables, breads, rolls, cheeses, and fruits is limited, and there is much use of canned fruit and jellied desserts. There are no wine waiters. The waiters sing and dance – so 'service' is more 'foodertainment' than service finesse.

A Lido café, called Coconut Grove Bar & Grill, features the usual casual self-serve buffet eats. The venue includes a deli counter and pizzeria. At night, the venue morphs into the Seaview Bistro, and provides a casual alternative to the main dining rooms, for pasta, steaks, salads, and desserts.

A patisserie offers specialty coffees and sweets (extra charge), and a so-called sushi bar off to one side of the atrium lobby bar on Promenade Deck is open prior to dinner; if you know anything about sushi, don't expect authenticity.

There is no specialty (extra-charge) restaurant, as aboard some of the larger ships in the Carnival fleet.

ENTERTAINMENT. The Palace Showlounge is the venue for large-scale production shows and major cabaret acts – although 20 pillars obstruct some views. During a typical cruise, there will be one or two high-energy production shows, with a cast of two lead singers and a clutch of dancers, backed by a large live band.

SPA/FITNESS. SpaCarnival is a large, glass-wrapped health, fitness, and spa complex located on the uppermost interior deck, forward of the ship's mast; it is typically open from 6am to 8pm daily. It consists of a gymnasium with ocean-view windows that look out over the bow and the latest in muscle-pumping electronic machines, an aerobics exercise room, men's and women's changing rooms, sauna and steam rooms, beauty salon, and body treatment rooms. Some fitness classes (such as kick-boxing or yoga) may incur an extra charge. A common complaint is that there are not enough staff to keep the area clean and tidy, and used towels are often strewn around the changing rooms.

Sporting types can play basketball, volleyball, or table tennis. There is also a banked jogging track outdoors on the deck above the spa, and a mini-golf course.

Carnival Freedom
★★★+

Size:	Large Resort Ship	Passenger/Crew Ratio (lower beds):	2.5
Tonnage:	110,320	Cabins (total):	1,487
Lifestyle:	Standard	Size Range (sq ft/m):	179.7–484.2/16.7–44.8
Cruise Line:	Carnival Cruise Line	Cabins (for one person):	0
Former Names:	none	Cabins (with private balcony):	574
IMO Number:	9333149	Cabins (wheelchair accessible):	25
Builder:	Fincantieri (Italy)	Wheelchair accessibility:	Good
Original Cost:	$500 million	Cabin Current:	110 volts
Entered Service:	Feb 2007	Elevators:	20
Registry:	Panama	Casino (gaming tables):	Yes
Length (ft/m):	951.4/290.0	Slot Machines:	Yes
Beam (ft/m):	105.6/32.2	Swimming Pools:	2 (1 w/ sliding glass dome)
Draft (ft/m):	27.2/8.3	Hot Tubs (on deck):	7
Propulsion/Propellers:	diesel-electric (63,400kW)/2	Self-Service Launderette:	Yes
Passenger Decks:	13	Dedicated Cinema/Seats:	No
Total Crew:	1,150	Library:	Yes
Passengers (lower beds):	2,974	Onboard currency:	US$
Passenger Space Ratio (lower beds):	37.0/29.7		

A fun-filled ship that comes alive at night

OVERVIEW. *Carnival Freedom* shares the same generally balanced profile as its sisters *Carnival Conquest, Carnival Glory, Carnival Liberty, Carnival Sunshine, Carnival Triumph, Carnival Valor,* and *Carnival Victory.* Immediately recognizable is the trademark swept-back wingtip funnel.

THE SHIP. Carnival's Seaside Theater for movies on an upper outside deck recalls those classic drive-in movie theaters, with seating in tiered rows and the screen in front. The ship has bow-to-stern (extra-cost) Wi-Fi Internet access, including all passenger cabins. Also outside is Serenity, an adult-only quiet spot at the top and front of the ship – a nice escape from all of the hubbub on the open decks below.

Inside, the interior decor really is a kaleidoscopic blend of colors (most of which are a mix of dark and gaudy) that stimulate and excite the senses, and is dedicated to time and the decades. The deck and public room layout is fairly logical (except for getting from the aft-placed Posh Dining Room to the showlounge, because you have to go up and down a deck or two). Most of the public rooms are located on one deck off a main interior boulevard, above a deck containing the two main dining rooms (Chic and Posh). Public rooms include the Babylon Casino with gaming tables and over 300 slot machines, a fine Havana Cigar Bar, Monticello Library (with few books), Conference Center, Scott's Piano Bar, Swingtime Bar, and a popular Wine Bar, among others.

Carnival Freedom is a large floating playground

Berlitz's Ratings		
	Possible	Achieved
Ship	500	375
Accommodation	200	144
Food	400	218
Service	400	260
Entertainment	100	77
Cruise Experience	400	258
OVERALL SCORE		
1332 points out of 2000		

for the young and young-at-heart, and anyone who enjoys constant stimulation and lots of participation events, together with the three 'Gs' – glitz, glamour, and gambling. This really is cruising Splash Vegas style – and a fun, all-American experience. Because it's a large resort ship, expect lines for shore excursions, security control when reboarding, and disembarkation.

Forget fashion – the *sine qua non* of any Carnival cruise is having fun. While the cuisine is just so-so, the real fun begins at sundown when Carnival really excels in sound, lights, razzle-dazzle shows, and late-night high-volume reverie.

Minor niggles include the fact that many pillars obstruct passenger flow, particularly in the dining room, where they make it difficult for the waiters to serve food properly; also the non-stop infomercials on the in-cabin infotainment system (you can, however, turn it off).

FAMILIES. Youngsters have their own play areas, with children's programs divided into five age-specific groups under Camp Ocean (ages 2–11 – with children ages 2–5 called 'Penguins'; 6–8-year-olds called 'Sting Rays'; 9–11-year-olds called 'Sharks'). Tweens have 'Circle C'; while teenagers have their own 'Club O2' – a chill-out (no adults allowed) room/disco. Also, soft-drinks packages can be purchased for children (and adults).

Dr. Seuss has arrived, with Bookville, a play space that features iconic decor, colors, shapes, and quirky furniture inspired by the whimsical world of Seuss; it was installed in a 2014 makeover.

ACCOMMODATION. There are numerous cabin price categories, in several different suite/cabin types, sizes, and grades. These include suites with private balcony; deluxe outside-view cabins with private balcony; outside-view cabins with private balcony; outside-view cabins with window; cabins with a porthole instead of a window; interior cabins; and interior with upper and lower berths.

There are five decks of cabins with private balconies. Standard cabins are of good size and come equipped with all the basics, although the furniture is rather square and angular, with no rounded edges. However, there's plenty of drawer space, as well as space for toiletries in bathrooms. Three decks of cabins (eight on each deck, each with private balcony) overlook the stern. Most cabins have twin beds that can be converted to a queen-size bed format.

Book a suite (Category 11 or 12 in the Carnival Cruise Lines brochure), and you'll get Skipper's Club priority check-in at any US homeland port – useful for getting ahead of the crowd, as well as other perks.

There are also 'spa' cabins aboard this ship – a grouping of 18 cabins located directly around and behind SpaCarnival; so fitness devotees can get out of bed and go straight to the treadmill without having to go through any of the public rooms first.

A gift basket of toiletries is provided in all grades of cabins; it typically includes aloe soap, shampoo, conditioner, deodorant, breath mints, candy, and pain relief tablets (all in sample sizes – and most in paper packets that are difficult to open).

DINING. There are two principal dining rooms (Chic, located midships, seating 744; and Posh, aft, seating 1,122). Both are two decks high and have a balcony level (the balcony level in Posh is larger than the one in Chic). There's a choice of either fixed-time dining (6pm or 8.15pm) or flexible dining (any time between 5.45pm and 9.30pm). Note that they are not open for lunch on port days.

There are few tables for two, but among my favorites are two tables for two right at the very back of the restaurant, with ocean views astern.

Other dining options. The (reservations required) Sun King Supper Club has fine table settings, china, and silverware, and features prime dry-aged steaks and grilled seafood items. It's worth paying the cover charge to get a taste of what Carnival can really deliver in terms of food that's of better quality than what's served in the main dining rooms.

The Freedom Restaurant, a casual self-serve international food court-style lido deck eatery, has two main serving lines. Included are a deli, an Asian eatery with wok preparation (and sushi), a 24-hour pizzeria, a fish 'n' chippery (on the upper level), and a grill for fast foods such as hamburgers and hot dogs. Each night the Freedom Restaurant morphs into the Seaview Bistro and provides a dress-down alternative to eating in the main dining rooms, serving pasta, steaks, salads, and desserts (typically 6–9pm).

For a special celebration, you might like the Chef's Table experience – a multi-course 'dégustation' dinner for up to 12 persons. It costs $75 per person and usually takes place in a small, quiet spot such as the Monticello Library, Dynasty Conference room, or other secluded venue.

ENTERTAINMENT. The Victoriana Theater (named after England's Queen Victoria) is the ship's multi-deck showlounge, seating up to 1,400 and staging colorful Las Vegas-style production shows and major cabaret acts. It has a revolving stage, hydraulic orchestra pit, superb sound, and seating on three levels (the upper levels being tiered through two decks). A proscenium arch acts as a scenery loft. The decor is medieval – drinks tables look like shields, and coats of armor and towers with stained-glass windows flank the stage.

An alternative entertainment venue is the aft lounge, which seats 425 and typically features live music and late-night cabaret acts including smutty adult comedy.

Body-throbbing loud music sensations can be found in the ship's discotheque; it includes a video wall with live projections from the dance floor. Meanwhile piano bar lovers should enjoy the 100-seat Scott's Piano Bar.

SPA/FITNESS. SpaCarnival has a total area of approximately 13,300 sq ft/1,235 sq m, is located above the navigation bridge, and accessed from the forward stairway. Facilities include a solarium, eight treatment rooms, lecture rooms, sauna and steam rooms for men and women, a beauty parlor, a large gymnasium with floor-to-ceiling windows including forward-facing ocean views, and an aerobics room with instructor-led classes (some at extra cost) for which you'll need to sign up.

Carnival Glory
★★★+

Size:	Large Resort Ship
Tonnage:	110,239
Lifestyle:	Standard
Cruise Line:	Carnival Cruise Line
Former Names:	none
IMO Number:	9198367
Builder:	Fincantieri (Italy)
Original Cost:	$500 million
Entered Service:	Jul 2003
Registry:	Panama
Length (ft/m):	951.4/290.0
Beam (ft/m):	116.4/35.5
Draft (ft/m):	27.0/8.2
Propulsion/Propellers:	diesel-electric (63,400kW)/2
Passenger Decks:	13
Total Crew:	1,160
Passengers (lower beds):	2,974
Passenger Space Ratio (lower beds):	37.0

Passenger/Crew Ratio (lower beds):	2.5
Cabins (total):	1,487
Size Range (sq ft/m):	179.7–482.2/16.7–44.8
Cabins (for one person):	0
Cabins (with private balcony):	590
Cabins (wheelchair accessible):	25
Wheelchair accessibility:	Good
Cabin Current:	110 volts
Elevators:	14
Casino (gaming tables):	Yes
Slot Machines:	Yes
Swimming Pools:	2 (1 w/ sliding glass dome)
Hot Tubs (on deck):	7
Self-Service Launderette:	Yes
Dedicated Cinema/Seats:	No
Library:	Yes
Onboard currency:	US$

This is an ultra-casual, fun-filled ship for first-time cruisers

OVERVIEW. Like its sisters – *Carnival Conquest*, *Carnival Freedom*, *Carnival Liberty*, *Carnival Sunshine*, *Carnival Triumph*, Carnival Valor, and *Carnival Victory* – this ship has three decks full of public lounges, bars, and lots of rooms to play in, together with good facilities and programs for children.

THE SHIP. *Carnival Glory* is a large floating playground for the young and young-at-heart, and for anyone who likes constant stimulation, lots of participation events, and gaming casino. This really is cruising Splash Vegas style – and a fun, all-American experience.

A much-needed makeover in 2012 added two half-decks at the front of the ship, extended two other decks at the aft, added 182 cabins (but no extra elevators), several new, much revamped eateries. These include an Alchemy Bar – for good cocktails created by a 'mixologist' (bartender); a (music-free) Library Bar; a Sports Bar (interactive, and with results on the 24/7 sports ticker); and an art gallery.

Amidships on the open deck is a water slide (200ft/60m long), as well as tiered sunbathing decks positioned between two swimming pools, several hot tubs, and a giant poolside movie screen (Seaside Theater). For adults who want to escape most of the outdoor activities and noise, however, there is Serenity – an (extra-cost) adults-only area for relaxation – located on two decks at the top, forwardmost part of the ship.

The ship's interior decor is a fantasyland of colors, with every hue of the rainbow represented. Most

Berlitz's Ratings		
	Possible	Achieved
Ship	500	363
Accommodation	200	144
Food	400	218
Service	400	259
Entertainment	100	76
Cruise Experience	400	255
OVERALL SCORE		
1315 points out of 2000		

public rooms are located off the Kaleidoscope Boulevard, which is the main interior promenade – great for strolling and people-watching. The larger of two atriums, The Colors Lobby spans nine decks in the forward third of the ship. Check out the interpretative paintings of US flags at the Color Bar. The smaller aft atrium goes through three decks.

Forget fashion – the *sine qua non* of a Carnival cruise is all about having fun. While the cuisine is just so-so, the real fun begins at sundown when Carnival really excels in sound, lights, razzle-dazzle shows, and late-night high-volume sounds. There are nightspots and watering holes for just about every musical taste (except opera, ballet, and classical music lovers), such as the Ivory Club Bar, Ebony Aft Cabaret Lounge, Cinn-a-Bar (Piano Bar), White Heat Dance Club, and Bar Blue.

Niggles: the modifications and additions, while good, have also created a more crowded and congested feeling throughout the ship. Also, the open deck space is poor considering the increase in the number of passengers. The pool deck really becomes cluttered, and there are no cushioned pads for the deck chairs. Also, the Photo Gallery, adjacent to the atrium/purser's office, becomes congested when photos are on display. There is constant hustling for drinks. Because it's a large resort ship, there will be lines for the likes of shore excursions, security control when re-boarding, and disembarkation, as well as sign-up sheets for fitness equipment.

FAMILIES. Youngsters have their own play areas, with children's programs divided into five age-specific groups under Camp Ocean (ages 2–11 – with children ages 2–5 called 'Penguins'; 6–8-year-olds called 'Sting Rays'; 9–11-year-olds called 'Sharks'). Tweens have 'Circle C', while teenagers have their own 'Club O2' – a chill-out (no adults allowed) room/disco. Also, soft-drinks packages can be purchased for children (and adults).

Also, soft-drinks packages can be purchased for children (and adults).

By the end of 2015, the world of Dr. Seuss was rolled out as part of Carnival's children's program – from 'green eggs and ham' for breakfast, served by waiters in Dr. Seuss-inspired uniforms, and characters such as the Cat in the Hat, Thing One and Thing Two, and Sam attending, to special showings of movies such as *The Cat in the Hat* and *How the Grinch Stole Christmas* (shown on the poolside Seaside Theater screen on Lido Deck).

ACCOMMODATION. There are numerous cabin price categories, in seven different grades: suites with private balcony; deluxe outside-view cabins with private balcony; outside-view cabins with private balcony; outside-view cabins with window; cabins with a porthole instead of a window; interior cabins; and interior cabins with upper and lower berths. The price reflects the grade, location, and size.

Several decks of cabins have a private balcony – but many are not quite so private, and can be overlooked from various public locations.

During the makeover, a large number of Spa Cabins were added over three decks in the front of the ship, adjacent to the Carnival Spa and Serenity adult-only area; these have all the usual fittings, plus special spa-like extras, and access to the spa.

The standard cabins are of good size and are equipped with all the basics, although the furniture is rather angular, with no rounded edges. Three decks of cabins (eight on each deck, each with private balcony) overlook the stern. Most cabins with twin beds can be converted to a queen-size bed format. A gift basket is provided in all grades of cabin; it includes aloe soap, shampoo, conditioner, deodorant, breath mints, candy, and pain relief tablets (all in sample sizes).

Note: If you book one of the Category 11 or 12 suites, you get 'Skipper's Club' priority check-in at any US homeland port – useful for getting ahead of the crowd.

DINING. The two main dining rooms, Golden and Platinum, are two decks high, with seating on both levels. The decor includes wall coverings featuring a pattern of Japanese bonsai trees. Choose either fixed-time dining (6pm or 8.15pm) or flexible dining (any time between 5.45 and 9.30pm).

Other dining options. Several dining options and new eateries were added (or existing ones changed) during an extensive 2014 makeover, providing you with more choice. These include:

Guy's Burger Joint, a complimentary poolside venue offering fresh-made burgers, hand-cut fries and toppings and condiments created by Food Network personality and chef Guy Fieri.

The BlueIguana Cantina, a (no-charge) Mexican cantina featuring tacos and burritos, with a salsa and toppings counter.

For something a little more exclusive, it's worth booking a table in the (extra-cost) Emerald Room Steakhouse, which serves (large) prime steaks and grilled seafood and has lighting fixtures that look like giant emeralds.

There is also a casual self-serve food court-style lido deck eatery, the two-level Red Sail Restaurant, which includes a Mexican counter for burritos and tacos, a deli, and on the upper level, a fish 'n' chippery (there is seating on both levels).

ENTERTAINMENT. The Amber Palace Showlounge is a multi-deck showroom seating 1,400. It has a revolving stage, hydraulic orchestra pit, superb sound, and seating on three levels (the upper levels being tiered through two decks). A proscenium over the stage acts as a scenery loft.

Hasbro, The Game Show was added in 2012; the show includes audience participation, as competitive interpretations of the larger-than-life board games.

Jazz lovers could head for the Bar Blue, while the Cinn-A-Bar is a piano bar, with curved aluminum walls – so 'bending' notes should be easy.

SPA/FITNESS. SpaCarnival is a fairly large health, fitness, and spa complex. You'll find it directly above the navigation bridge in the forward part of the ship and is accessed from the forward stairway.

Facilities include a gymnasium (packed with muscle machines and exercise equipment), body treatment area, sauna and steam rooms for men and women, and a beauty salon.

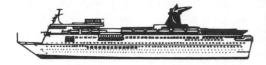

Carnival Imagination
★★★

Size:	Large Resort Ship	Passenger/Crew Ratio (lower beds):	2.2
Tonnage:	70,367	Cabins (total):	1,028
Lifestyle:	Standard	Size Range (sq ft/m):	173.2–409.7/16–38
Cruise Line:	Carnival Cruise Line	Cabins (for one person):	0
Former Names:	*Imagination*	Cabins (with private balcony):	152
IMO Number:	9053878	Cabins (wheelchair accessible):	22
Builder:	Kvaerner Masa-Yards (Finland)	Wheelchair accessibility:	Fair
Original Cost:	$330 million	Cabin Current:	110 volts
Entered Service:	Jul 1995	Elevators:	14
Registry:	The Bahamas	Casino (gaming tables):	Yes
Length (ft/m):	855.0/260.6	Slot Machines:	Yes
Beam (ft/m):	103.0/31.4	Swimming Pools:	3
Draft (ft/m):	25.9/7.9	Hot Tubs (on deck):	6
Propulsion/Propellers:	diesel-electric (42,240kW)/2	Self-Service Launderette:	Yes
Passenger Decks:	0	Dedicated Cinema/Seats:	No
Total Crew:	920	Library:	Yes
Passengers (lower beds):	2,056	Onboard currency:	US$
Passenger Space Ratio (lower beds):	34.4		

This fun ship is for high-energy family cruisers

OVERVIEW. *Carnival Imagination* is the fifth in a series of eight almost identical *Fantasy*-class ships. This has always been a popular ship, aimed at anyone taking a first cruise.

THE SHIP. The open deck space is really inadequate when the ship is full and everyone wants to be out on deck. The aft decks used to be less noisy when all the activities were focused around the main swimming pool and hot tubs, but now that a Carnival WaterWorks – with long (about 300ft/90m) and short water slides and water-burst fountains – has been added, it's now a loud, active area.

There's also a topless sunbathing area, as well as Serenity – an adult-only 'quiet' lounging space on Deck 9 aft. There is no walk-around open promenade deck, although there is a short jogging track atop ship. The lifeboats, six of which double as shore tenders, are positioned high in the ship.

The interior spaces are well utilized. The general passenger flow is good and the interior design – the work of Miami-based creative genius Joe Farcus – is clever, functional, and extremely colorful. The interior design theme is all about the legendary symbols of antiquity (think winged deities and beings).

The interior focal point is an 'open' atrium lobby, with a balconied shape, styled to impress. It spans six decks, and is topped by a large glass dome. The lowest level of the atrium lobby is where you'll find the purser's desk and shore excursion desk, together with a popular Atrium Bar (with live music), as well as a small sushi bar off to one side.

Berlitz's Ratings

	Possible	Achieved
Ship	500	309
Accommodation	200	138
Food	400	212
Service	400	262
Entertainment	100	73
Cruise Experience	400	241
OVERALL SCORE		
1235 points out of 2000		

There are public entertainment lounges, bars, and clubs galore, with something for everyone (except quiet space). The public rooms, connected by a double-width Via Marina Promenade, combine a colorful mix of classic and contemporary design elements. Most public rooms and attractions lead off from this boulevard – a sort of shipboard Main Street, which runs between the showlounge (forward) and Xanadu aft lounge. Gamers and slot players alike will enjoy the almost non-stop action in the El Dorado Casino. There is also a nice-looking library and reading room, but few books, and there's also a 1,200-sq-ft (111-sq-m) conference room.

Forget fashion – the *sine qua non* of a Carnival cruise is all about having fun. While the cuisine is just so-so, the real fun begins at sundown when the ship really excels in lights, volume, and show. From venues such as the Illusions Dance Club/Disco to the Pinnacle Cigar Bar, the ship's interior decor will certainly entertain you.

Carnival Imagination is a floating playground for the young and young-at-heart, and anyone who enjoys constant stimulation and lots of participation events. This really is cruising Splash Vegas style. Because it's a large resort ship, there will be lines for the likes of shore excursions, security control when re-boarding, and disembarkation.

However, this is not for those seeking a quiet, relaxing cruise experience. There are many annoying announcements, and the never-ending hustling to get you to buy drinks and many other things. Also, shore excursions are booked via the in-cabin 'Fun Vision' television system, so obtaining advice and suggestions is not easy.

FAMILIES. Youngsters have their own play areas, with children's programs divided into five age-specific groups under Camp Ocean (ages 2–11 – with children ages 2–5 called 'Penguins'; 6–8-year-olds called 'Sting Rays'; 9–11-year-olds called 'Sharks'). Tweens have 'Circle C', while teenagers have their own 'Club O2' – a chill-out (no adults allowed) room/disco. Also, soft-drinks packages can be purchased for children (and adults).

By the end of 2015, the world of Dr. Seuss was added as part of the children's program – from 'green eggs and ham' for breakfast, served by waiters in Dr. Seuss-inspired uniforms, and characters such as the Cat in the Hat, Thing One and Thing Two, and Sam attending, to special showings of movies such as *The Cat in the Hat* and *How the Grinch Stole Christmas* (shown on the poolside Seaside Theater screen on Lido Deck).

ACCOMMODATION. There are several grades of accommodation, ranked by facilities, size, and location. The standard outside-view and interior cabins have decor that is rather plain and unmemorable. They are marginally comfortable, but practical (most are of the same size and appointments), with good storage space and practical, well-designed no-nonsense bathrooms. However, if you have a queen-bed configuration instead of the standard twin-bed layout, note that one person has to clamber over the bed – an ungainly exercise.

Anyone booking an outside suite will find more space, whirlpool bathtubs, and some rather eclectic decor and furniture. These are mildly attractive, but so-so, and they are much smaller than those aboard ships of a similar size of competing companies. A small gift basket of toiletry samples is provided in all grades.

Book a Category 11 or 12 suite and you get Skipper's Club priority check-in at any US homeland port – useful for getting ahead of the crowd.

Families now have 50 connecting cabins to choose from – good if you have children and want them close by, but not *that* close.

Room service items are available 24 hours a day, although in standard cabins, only cold food is available, while those in suite-grade accommodation get a greater range of items (both hot and cold) to choose from.

DINING. The two large main dining rooms, Pride and Spirit, are located amidships and aft. Both have ocean-view windows and attractive, but very bright decor, but they are noisy. Choose either fixed-time dining (6pm or 8.15pm) or flexible dining (any time between 5.45 and 9.30pm). Note that the two main dining rooms are not open for lunch on port days.

The food is really unmemorable, with simple presentation, and little use of garnishes. Remember, however, that this is bog-standard catering – with all its attendant standardization and production cooking. For something simple, a selection of always available (when the dining rooms are open) 'Carnival Classics' includes mahi mahi (fish), baby back ribs (beef), and grilled chicken. Note that the two main dining rooms may not be open for lunch on port days.

Waiters are almost more about entertaining than serving food with any finesse.

Other dining options. The Horizon Bar & Grill acts as a Lido café, and features casual self-serve buffet eats, most of which are non-memorable. The venue includes a deli counter and pizzeria. At night, the venue morphs into the Seaview Bistro, and provides a casual alternative to the main dining rooms, for pasta, steaks, salads, and desserts – it typically operates only between 6pm and 9pm. The food selection, though limited, makes a change from the large, crowded and noisy main dining rooms.

A patisserie offers specialty coffees and sweets (extra charge), and a so-called sushi bar off to one side of the atrium lobby bar on Promenade Deck is open prior to dinner; if you know anything about sushi, don't expect authenticity.

There is no specialty (extra-charge) restaurant, as aboard some of the larger ships in the fleet.

ENTERTAINMENT. The Universe Showlounge is the venue for the large-scale production shows and major cabaret acts – although 20 pillars obstruct the views from some seats. During a typical cruise, there will be one or two shows, with a cast of two lead singers and a clutch of dancers, backed by a large live band.

SPA/FITNESS. SpaCarnival is a large, glass-wrapped health, fitness, and spa complex. It is located on the uppermost interior deck, forward of the ship's mast, and is typically open from 6am to 8pm daily. It consists of a gym with windows that look out over the bow and the latest in machines, an aerobics room, changing rooms, sauna and steam rooms, beauty salon, and body treatment rooms. A common complaint is that there is not enough staff to keep the area clean and tidy.

Sporting types can play basketball or volleyball, table tennis, go jogging, or play mini-golf.

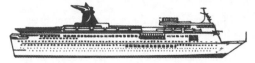

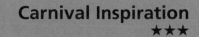

Carnival Inspiration
★★★

Size:	Large Resort Ship
Tonnage:	70,367
Lifestyle:	Standard
Cruise Line:	Carnival Cruise Line
Former Names:	*Inspiration*
IMO Number:	9047489
Builder:	Kvaerner Masa-Yards (Finland)
Original Cost:	$270 million
Entered Service:	Apr 1996
Registry:	The Bahamas
Length (ft/m):	855.0/260.6
Beam (ft/m):	103.0/31.4
Draft (ft/m):	25.9/7.9
Propulsion/Propellers:	diesel-electric (42,240kW)/2
Passenger Decks:	10
Total Crew:	920
Passengers (lower beds):	2,056
Passenger Space Ratio (lower beds):	34.4

Passenger/Crew Ratio (lower beds):	2.2
Cabins (total):	1,028
Size Range (sq ft/m):	173.2–409.7/16–38
Cabins (for one person):	0
Cabins (with private balcony):	152
Cabins (wheelchair accessible):	22
Wheelchair accessibility:	Fair
Cabin Current:	110 volts
Elevators:	14
Casino (gaming tables):	Yes
Slot Machines:	Yes
Swimming Pools:	3
Hot Tubs (on deck):	6
Self-Service Launderette:	Yes
Dedicated Cinema/Seats:	No
Library:	Yes
Onboard currency:	US$

This ultra-colorful ship is good for a first casual cruise

OVERVIEW. *Carnival Inspiration* is the sixth in a series of eight almost identical *Fantasy*-class ships. It is a well-liked ship – and is ideally suited to anyone taking a first cruise.

THE SHIP. The open deck space is quite inadequate when the ship is full and everyone wants to be out on deck. However, the aft decks tend to be less noisy because all the activities are focused around the main swimming pool and hot tubs (one has a thatched shade). There's also a top-less sunbathing area, as well as Serenity – an adult-only 'quiet' (extra-cost) lounging space on Deck 9 aft that you need to be over 21 to use. Sadly, there is no walk-around open promenade deck, although there is a short jogging track atop ship. The lifeboats, six of which double as shore tenders are positioned high in the ship.

The interior of the ship is well designed. The general passenger flow is good, and the interior design – the work of creative genius Joe Farcus – is clever, functional, and extremely colorful. The underlying decor theme is the arts (in an Art Nouveau style) and literature. It includes a colorful mix of classic and contemporary design elements.

The interior focal point is an 'open' atrium lobby, with a balconied shape and styled to impress (including with decoration resembling the necks and heads of violins). The lobby spans six decks, has a marble staircase, and is topped by a large glass dome. The purser's desk and shore excursion desk occupy the lowest level, together with a popular Atrium Bar

Berlitz's Ratings

	Possible	Achieved
Ship	500	309
Accommodation	200	138
Food	400	212
Service	400	262
Entertainment	100	73
Cruise Experience	400	242

OVERALL SCORE
1236 points out of 2000

with live music, and a small sushi bar off to one side; it's a good central meeting place.

There are public entertainment lounges, bars, and clubs galore, with something for everyone (except quiet space). The public rooms, connected by a double-width Inspiration Boulevard, feature many contemporary design elements. Most public rooms and attractions lead off from this boulevard – a sort of shipboard Main Street, which runs between the showlounge (forward) and the Candlelight aft lounge. Gamers and slot players alike will enjoy the almost non-stop action in the Monte Carlo Casino. The Shakespeare Library is a rather stately room, and 25 of his quotations adorn the oak veneer walls, but, sadly, there are few books. One of the most dazzling rooms is the Rock and Roll Discotheque, with its guitar-shaped dance floor, video dance club, and dozens of video monitors. There's also a 1,200-sq-ft (111-sq-m) conference room for meetings and group use.

Forget fashion – a Carnival cruise is all about having fun. While the cuisine is just so-so, the real fun begins at sundown when Carnival really excels in sound, lights, and shows. From venues such as the Rock and Roll Dance Club/Disco to the Chopin Cigar Bar, the ship's interior decor will certainly entertain you.

This is a floating playground for the young and young-at-heart. Because it's a large resort ship, there will be lines for the likes of shore excursions, security control when re-boarding, and disembarkation, as well as sign-up sheets for fitness equipment.

The ship is not for those seeking a quiet, relaxing cruise experience. There are many annoying announcements, and the never-ending hustling to get you to buy drinks and many other things. Also, shore excursions are booked via the in-cabin 'Fun Vision' television system, so obtaining advice and suggestions is not easy.

FAMILIES. Youngsters have their own play areas, with children's programs divided into five age-specific groups under Camp Ocean (ages 2–11 – with children ages 2–5 called 'Penguins'; 6–8-year-olds called 'Sting Rays'; 9–11-year-olds called 'Sharks'). Tweens have 'Circle C', while teenagers have their own 'Club O2' – a chill-out (no adults allowed) room/disco. Group babysitting is also available.

Also, an expansive children's water park is a lot of fun as an outdoor play area.

ACCOMMODATION. There are several accommodation grades, ranked by facilities, size, and location. The standard outside-view and interior cabins have decor that is rather plain and unmemorable. They are marginally comfortable, yet spacious enough and practical (most are of the same size and appointments), with good storage space and practical, well-designed no-nonsense bathrooms. However, if you have a queen-bed configuration instead of the standard twin-bed layout, note that one person has to clamber over the bed – an ungainly exercise.

Choose a suite and you get more space, whirlpool bathtubs, and some rather eclectic decor and furniture. These are mildly attractive, but so-so, and they are much smaller than those aboard ships of a similar size of competing companies. A small gift basket of toiletry samples is provided in all grades.

Room service items are available 24 hours a day, although in standard cabins, only cold food is available, while those in suite-grade accommodation get a greater range of items (both hot and cold) to choose from.

DINING. The two large main dining rooms, Mardi Gras and Carnivale (the names given to Carnival's first two ships), are located amidships and aft, respectively. Both have ocean-view windows and attractive, but very bright decor, but they are noisy. Choose either fixed-time dining (6pm or 8.15pm) or flexible dining (any time between 5.45 and 9.30pm). For something really simple, there's an 'always available' (when the dining room is open) list of 'Carnival

Classics' including mahi mahi (fish), baby back ribs (beef), and grilled chicken. Note that the two main dining rooms are not open for lunch on port days.

Remember, however, that this is standard catering, with all its attendant standardization and production cooking; it is, therefore, difficult to obtain anything unusual or 'off-menu'. The selection of fresh green vegetables, breads, rolls, cheeses, and fruits is limited, and there is much use of canned fruit and jellied desserts. The waiters sing and dance, and there are constant waiter parades – so it's really more about 'foodertainment' than food quality.

Other dining options. A Lido café, called the Brasserie Bar & Grill, features the usual casual self-serve buffet eats, most of which are non-memorable. The venue includes a deli counter and pizzeria. At night, the venue morphs into the Seaview Bistro, and provides a casual alternative to the main dining rooms, for pasta, steaks, salads, and desserts – it typically operates only between 6pm and 9pm. The food selection, though limited, makes a change from the large, crowded and noisy main dining rooms. Outside on deck is a Mongolian Rotisserie Grill.

A patisserie offers specialty coffees and sweets (extra charge), and a so-called sushi bar off to one side of the atrium lobby bar on Promenade Deck is open prior to dinner only; the sushi is just so-so.

There is no specialty (extra-charge) restaurant, as aboard some of the larger ships in the Carnival fleet.

ENTERTAINMENT. Paris Main Lounge is the principal showlounge – the venue for large-scale production shows and major cabaret acts – although 20 pillars obstruct some views. The resident troupe includes two lead singers and a clutch of dancers, backed by a large live band.

SPA/FITNESS. SpaCarnival is a large, glass-wrapped health, fitness, and spa complex. It is located on the uppermost interior deck, forward of the ship's mast, and is typically open from 6am to 8pm daily. It consists of a gymnasium with ocean-view windows that look out over the bow and the latest in muscle-pumping machines, an aerobics room, changing rooms, sauna and steam rooms, beauty salon, and body treatment rooms. Some fitness classes may incur an extra charge.

Sporting types can play basketball volleyball, table tennis, mini-golf, and go jogging on the banked track on the deck above the spa.

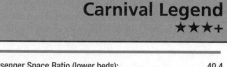

Carnival Legend
★★★+

Size:	Large Resort Ship	Passenger Space Ratio (lower beds):	40.4
Tonnage:	85,942	Passenger/Crew Ratio (lower beds):	2.2
Lifestyle:	Standard	Cabins (total):	1,062
Cruise Line:	Carnival Cruise Line	Size Range (sq ft/m):	185–490/17.1–45.5
Former Names:	none	Cabins (for one person):	0
IMO Number:	9224726	Cabins (with private balcony):	750
Builder:	Kvaerner Masa-Yards (Finland)	Cabins (wheelchair accessible):	16
Original Cost:	$375 million	Wheelchair accessibility:	Good
Entered Service:	Aug 2002	Cabin Current:	110 volts
Registry:	Panama	Elevators:	15
Length (ft/m):	959.6/292.5	Casino (gaming tables):	Yes
Beam (ft/m):	105.6/32.2	Slot Machines:	Yes
Draft (ft/m):	25.5/7.8	Swimming Pools:	2
Propulsion/Propellers:	diesel-electric (62,370kW)/ 2 azimuthing pods	Hot Tubs (on deck):	5
		Self-Service Launderette:	Yes
Passenger Decks:	12	Dedicated Cinema/Seats:	No
Total Crew:	1,030	Library:	Yes
Passengers (lower beds):	2,124	Onboard currency:	US$

A ship for a fun-filled family cruise in a contemporary setting

OVERVIEW. *Carnival Legend* is sister to *Carnival Miracle*, *Carnival Pride*, and *Carnival Spirit*, and shares the same layout and configuration. The ship is designed for families with children, and for entertainment, but has been modified to suit Australasian tastes.

THE SHIP. The open deck and sunbathing space is not extensive, but there are two swimming pools, one of which can be covered by a sliding glass dome in case of inclement weather. A Water Park and Kids Splash Zone was installed in time for the ship's first cruise season from Sydney, Australia, with water wheels, spraying jets, water blasters, pull ropes, two Mini Racer slides, and more (watch out for the giant water bucket). But the really big attraction is Green Thunder, a thrill ride that starts 100ft (30m) above sea level. The floor suddenly drops out of the platform, and you plummet in a near-vertical drop at about 23ft (7m) a second. When you hit the water in the fast water slide, you twist and turn through a transparent tube that extends over the side of the ship. Kids love it. The open deck space is a bit tight when the ship sails full in warm-weather areas.

Meanwhile, an extra-charge, adults-only area, Sanctuary, has its own bar, pool, hot tub and other facilities. Located at the ship's stern, it is good for anyone seeking a quieter space for sunbathing and relaxation.

The interior decor is dedicated to the world's great legends, from the heroes of antiquity to 20th-century jazz masters and athletes – an eclectic mix that somehow works.

Berlitz's Ratings		
	Possible	Achieved
Ship	500	361
Accommodation	200	143
Food	400	223
Service	400	249
Entertainment	100	76
Cruise Experience	400	262
OVERALL SCORE		
1314 points out of 2000		

Most bars and lounges are on two entertainment/public room decks, the upper featuring an exterior promenade deck. A walkway, named Hollywood Boulevard, connects many of the major public rooms on Atlantic Deck, one deck above Promenade Deck, which also sports a number of public rooms, including a large Club Merlin Casino (you have to walk though it to get to the main level of the showlounge from the restaurant, which is located aft). In a 2014 makeover, a Red Frog Pub (featuring Carnival's own ThirstyFrog Red draft brew), Bonsai Sushi (a sushi venue with Asian-style decor and food items), and Cherry on Top candy store were added.

The colorful atrium lobby spans eight decks; its wall decorations are best seen from any of the viewing balconies on any deck above the main lobby level. Take a drink from the lobby bar and look upwards – the surroundings are stunning, the focal point being a mural of the Colossus of Rhodes.

The ship's most dramatic room is the Follies Showlounge. Spanning three decks in the forward section, it recalls a 1920s movie palace.

A small wedding chapel is forward of the uppermost level of the two main entertainment decks, adjacent to the library. Other facilities include a shopping street with boutique stores, photo gallery, and an observation balcony in the center of the vessel, at the top of the multi-deck atrium.

While the cuisine is just so-so, the real fun begins at sundown when Carnival really excels in sound, lights, razzle-dazzle shows, and loud, late-night music.

Niggles include the small reception desk in the atrium lobby, which is often congested. Many pillars also obstruct passenger flow – the ones in the dining room, for example, make it difficult for proper food service by the waiters. Books and computers are cohabitants in the ship's Holmes library/Internet center, but anyone wanting a book has to lean over others who may be using a computer, which is an awkward arrangement.

FAMILIES. Youngsters have their own play areas, with children's programs divided into five age-specific groups under Camp Ocean (ages 2–11 – with children ages 2–5 called 'Penguins'; 6–8-year-olds called 'Sting Rays'; 9–11-year-olds called 'Sharks'). Tweens have 'Circle C', while teenagers have their own 'Club O2' – a chill-out (no adults allowed) room/disco. Also, kids will just love the 187-ft-long (57m) Green Thunder and 214-ft-long (65m) Twister water slides in the WaterWorks Aqua Park.

By the end of 2015, the world of Dr. Seuss was rolled out as part of the children's program (check before you sail) – from 'green eggs and ham' for breakfast, served by waiters in Dr. Seuss-inspired uniforms, and characters such as the Cat in the Hat, Thing One and Thing Two, and Sam attending, to special showings of movies such as *The Cat in the Hat* and *How the Grinch Stole Christmas* (shown on the poolside Seaside Theater screen on Lido Deck).

ACCOMMODATION. There are numerous cabin categories, priced by grade, location, and size, including suites (with private balcony), outside-view cabins with private balcony, 68 ocean-view cabins with French doors (pseudo balconies that have doors that open, but no balcony to step onto), and a healthy proportion of standard outside-view to interior cabins.

All cabins have spy-hole doors, twin beds that can be converted into queen-size beds, individually controlled air conditioning (it can't be switched off), TV, and telephone. A number of cabins on the lowest deck have lifeboat-obstructed views. Some cabins can accommodate a third and fourth person, but there's little closet space, and only one personal safe – still, these are useful if you have small children.

Among the most desirable suites and cabins are those on five of the aft-facing decks; these have balconies overlooking the stern and ship's wash. There's no vibration – a bonus provided by the pod propulsion system.

DINING. This ship has a single, large, two-deck-high, 1,300-seat main dining room, Truffles Restaurant,

with seating on both upper and main levels. Its huge ceiling has large murals of a Royal Copenhagen china pattern, and there are wall-mounted glass cases displaying fine china. Small rooms on both upper and lower levels can be booked for groups of up to 60. Choose either fixed-time dining (6pm or 8.15pm) or flexible dining (between certain hours). Note that the main dining room is not open for lunch on port days.

The Unicorn Café (Lido restaurant) is an extensive self-serve buffet-style casual eatery that forms the aft third of Deck 9 (part of it wraps around the upper section of the huge atrium). It includes a central area with a deli sandwich corner, Asian corner, rotisserie, and international (Taste of the Nations) counter. There are salad and dessert counters, and a 24-hour pizzeria counter, with both indoor and outdoor seating. Movement around the buffet area is slow, and you have to stand in line for everything. Each night, the Unicorn Café becomes Seaview Bistro, for serve-yourself dinners (typically 6pm–9.30pm).

Other dining options. The Steakhouse is an extra-cost dining spot atop the ship, with 156 seats and a show kitchen, featuring prime steaks and grilled seafood. Reservations are required. The decor features the Greek legend of Jason and the Argonauts (the bar has a large sculpture of the Golden Fleece). Decent table settings, china, and silverware are provided.

ENTERTAINMENT. The four-deck-high, 1,170-seat Follies Showlounge is the main venue for large-scale production shows and cabaret shows. Shows are best seen from the upper three levels. Directly underneath the showlounge is the Firebird lounge and bar.

Almost every lounge/bar, including Billie's Bar (a piano lounge) and Satchmo's Club (a nightclub with bar and dance floor), has live music in the evening. Finally, for the very lively, there's the disco; and there's always karaoke!

SPA/FITNESS. SpaCarnival spans two decks above the bridge in the forward part of the ship; it has 13,700 sq ft (1,272 sq m) of space. Lower level facilities include a solarium, several treatment rooms, sauna and steam rooms for men and women, and beauty salon. The upper level consists of a gymnasium with floor-to-ceiling ocean-view windows, and an aerobics room.

There are two centrally located swimming pools outdoors: one can be used in inclement weather due to its retractable glass dome. Adjacent are two whirlpool tubs. Another smaller pool is for children. An outdoor jogging track is located around the mast and the forward part of the ship; it doesn't go around the whole ship, but it's long enough for some serious walking.

Carnival Liberty
★★★+

Size:	Large Resort Ship	Passenger/Crew Ratio (lower beds):	2.5
Tonnage:	110,320	Cabins (total):	1,487
Lifestyle:	Standard	Size Range (sq ft/m):	179.7–482.2/16.7–44.8
Cruise Line:	Carnival Cruise Line	Cabins (for one person):	0
Former Names:	none	Cabins (with private balcony):	574
IMO Number:	9278181	Cabins (wheelchair accessible):	25
Builder:	Fincantieri (Italy)	Wheelchair accessibility:	Good
Original Cost:	$500 million	Cabin Current:	110 volts
Entered Service:	Jul 2005	Elevators:	18
Registry:	Panama	Casino (gaming tables):	Yes
Length (ft/m):	951.4/290.0	Slot Machines:	Yes
Beam (ft/m):	116.4/35.5	Swimming Pools:	3 (1 w/ sliding glass dome)
Draft (ft/m):	27.0/8.2	Hot Tubs (on deck):	7
Propulsion/Propellers:	diesel-electric (63,400kW)/2	Self-Service Launderette:	Yes
Passenger Decks:	13	Dedicated Cinema/Seats:	No
Total Crew:	1,160	Library:	Yes
Passengers (lower beds):	2,974	Onboard currency:	US$
Passenger Space Ratio (lower beds):	37.0		

This ultra-colorful ship is good for first-time cruisers

OVERVIEW. *Carnival Liberty* shares the same fairly well-balanced profile as sisters *Carnival Conquest, Carnival Freedom, Carnival Glory, Carnival Sunshine, Carnival Triumph, Carnival Valor,* and *Carnival Victory.* A giant Seaside Theater LED movie screen adorns the open pool deck, and a Serenity area provides an adults-only escape.

THE SHIP. The decor in the public rooms, hallways, and atrium adopts a design theme saluting master trades such as ironwork, masonry, pottery, and painting. The layout is logical, so finding your way around is easy. Most public rooms are located off a main boulevard (an interior promenade that is great for strolling and people-watching – particularly from the Jardin Café or Promenade Bar). Other hangouts and drinking places include The Stage (live music/karaoke lounge), the Flower Bar (main lobby), Gloves Bar (sports bar), Paparazzi (wine bar), and The Cabinet.

Amidships on the open deck is a long water slide (200ft/60m long), plus tiered sunbathing decks positioned between two swimming pools, several hot tubs, and a large poolside (Seaside Theater) movie screen. It's all about imagination and sensorial fantasy.

There are two atriums: the largest, in the forward third of the ship spans nine decks (the Grand Villa Garden Atrium combines all four of the design themes), while a small aft atrium spans three decks. The large Czar's Palace Casino, with its Russian motifs and theme, is action-packed, with more than 320 slot machines.

Berlitz's Ratings

	Possible	Achieved
Ship	500	361
Accommodation	200	144
Food	400	218
Service	400	252
Entertainment	100	76
Cruise Experience	400	254
OVERALL SCORE		
1305 points out of 2000		

This is a veritable floating playground for the young and young-at-heart, and anyone who enjoys constant stimulation and lots of participation events, together with the three 'Gs' – glitz, glamour, and gambling. This really is cruising Splash Vegas style – a fun, all-American experience. Because it's a large resort ship, there will be lines for the likes of shore excursions, security control when re-boarding, and disembarkation, as well as sign-up sheets for fitness equipment.

Forget fashion – the *sine qua non* of a Carnival cruise is all about having fun. While the cuisine is just so-so, the real fun begins at sundown, when it excels in terms of sound, lights, razzle-dazzle shows, and late-night high-volume sounds.

Niggles include: many pillars in the dining room make it difficult for proper food service by the waiters; public toilets that are utilitarian and need some cheering up. It is impossible to escape from noise and loud music (it's even played in cabin hallways and lifts), not to mention smokers, and people walking around in unsuitable clothing, clutching plastic sport drinks bottles, at any time of the day or night. You have to carry a credit card to operate the personal safes, which is inconvenient.

FAMILIES. Youngsters have their own play areas, with children's programs divided into five age-specific groups under Camp Ocean (ages 2–11 – with children ages 2–5 called 'Penguins'; 6–8-year-olds called 'Sting Rays'; 9–11-year-olds called 'Sharks').

Tweens have 'Circle C', while teenagers have their own 'Club O2' – a chill-out (no adults allowed) room/disco.

By the end of 2015, the world of Dr. Seuss was rolled out as part of Carnival's children's program – from 'green eggs and ham' for breakfast, served by waiters in Dr. Seuss-inspired uniforms, and characters including the Cat in the Hat, Thing One and Thing Two, and Sam attending, to special showings of movies such as *The Cat in the Hat* and *How the Grinch Stole Christmas* (shown on the poolside Seaside Theater screen on Lido Deck).

ACCOMMODATION. There are numerous cabin price categories, in seven different grades: suites with private balcony; deluxe outside-view cabins with private balcony; outside-view cabins with private balcony; outside-view cabins with window; cabins with a porthole instead of a window; interior cabins; interior cabins with upper and lower berths. The price reflects the grade, location, and size.

Five decks of cabins have a private balcony – over 150 more than *Carnival Sunshine*, *Carnival Triumph*, or *Carnival Victory*, for example. But many are not so private, and can be overlooked from various public locations.

There are 18 'fitness' cabins, located directly around and behind the SpaCarnival. This gives fitness devotees an opportunity to get out of bed and head straight to the treadmill without having to go through any of the public rooms first.

The standard cabins are of good size and are equipped with all the basics, although the furniture is angular (no rounded corners). Three decks of cabins (eight on each deck, each with private balcony) overlook the stern. Most cabins with twin beds can be converted to a queen-size bed format. A gift basket is provided in all grades of cabin; it includes aloe soap, shampoo, conditioner, deodorant, breath mints, candy, and pain relief tablets (all in sample sizes).

DINING. There are two main dining rooms, Golden Olympian Restaurant, forward, seating 744, and Silver Olympian Restaurant, aft, seating 1,122. Two additional wings (the Persian Room and Satin Room) can accommodate large groups.

Other dining options. There is a casual self-serve international food court-style Lido Deck eatery, the two-level Emile's, which morphs into the Seaview Bistro in the evening to provide a casual alternative to the main dining rooms. The specialty dining venue is The Steakhouse, for prime meats and seafood.

ENTERTAINMENT. The Venetian Palace Showlounge is a 1,400-seat multi-deck showroom for large-scale Las Vegas-style production shows and major cabaret acts. The Victoria Lounge, located aft, seats 425 and typically features live music and late-night cabaret acts, including adult comedy. The Tattooed Lady Dance Club is the ship's discotheque; it includes a video wall with projections live from the dance floor. Piano bar lovers should enjoy the 100-seat Piano Man piano bar.

SPA/FITNESS. SpaCarnival is a large health, fitness, and spa complex that spans two decks (the walls display hand-painted reproductions of the artist's poster work). It is directly above the navigation bridge in the forward part of the ship and is accessed from the forward stairway.

Facilities on the lower level include a solarium, eight treatment rooms, lecture rooms, sauna and steam rooms for men and women, and a beauty parlor. The upper level consists of a large gymnasium with floor-to-ceiling windows on three sides, including forward-facing ocean views, and an aerobics room with instructor-led classes, some at extra cost.

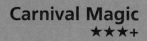

Carnival Magic
★★★+

Size:	Large Resort Ship	Passenger/Crew Ratio (lower beds):	2.6
Tonnage:	128,048	Cabins (total):	1,823
Lifestyle:	Standard	Size Range (sq ft/m):	185.0–430.5/17.1–40.0
Cruise Line:	Carnival Cruise Line	Cabins (for one person):	0
Former Names:	none	Cabins (with private balcony):	887
IMO Number:	9378486	Cabins (wheelchair accessible):	35
Builder:	Fincantieri (Italy)	Wheelchair accessibility:	Good
Original Cost:	$740 million	Cabin Current:	110 volts
Entered Service:	Jun 2011	Elevators:	20
Registry:	Panama	Casino (gaming tables):	Yes
Length (ft/m):	1,004.0/306.0	Slot Machines:	Yes
Beam (ft/m):	158.0/48.0	Swimming Pools:	2
Draft (ft/m):	26.2/8.0	Hot Tubs (on deck):	7
Propulsion/Propellers:	Diesel-electric (75,600kW)/2	Self-Service Launderette:	Yes
Passenger Decks:	13	Dedicated Cinema/Seats:	No
Total Crew:	1,367	Library:	Yes
Passengers (lower beds):	3,646	Onboard currency:	US$
Passenger Space Ratio (lower beds):	35.1		

The whole family will enjoy this high-energy floating resort

OVERVIEW. *Carnival Magic* is a sister ship to *Carnival Dream*, introduced in 2010, and both are 13 percent larger than earlier close sister *Carnival Splendor*. One thing that stands out is a long Twister Water Slide, part of The WaterWorks on pool deck, which is lots of fun for kids. An extra-charge retreat called Serenity is for adults only.

THE SHIP. Although the ship's bows are short, its profile is nicely balanced, with a rakish front and a more rounded stern. The ship is based on the original design for *Carnival Sunshine*, and includes some of the design flaws of the *Sunshine*-class, with a passenger capacity increase of over 1,000. Strangely, the cabin numbering system – even numbers on the starboard (right) side and odd numbers on the port (left) side – goes completely against the maritime tradition that places even-numbered cabins on the port side and odd-numbered cabins starboard.

A WaterWorks pool deck has lots of water and sports amusements – not to mention a really long orange multi-deck 'Twister Water Slide' and 'Power Drencher'. However, there simply isn't enough open deck space for the number of passengers the ship carries, so sunbed loungers are tightly packed together.

There is a full walk-around open promenade deck, lined with deck chairs. Four 'scenic hot tubs' are cantilevered over the sea and provide fine views, but they do get crowded, and rowdy. Higher up, Lido Deck 10 offers a good open-deck area, with small pool and

Berlitz's Ratings

	Possible	Achieved
Ship	500	369
Accommodation	200	144
Food	400	218
Service	400	256
Entertainment	100	76
Cruise Experience	400	254
OVERALL SCORE		
1317 points out of 2000		

a large Seaside Theater LED movie screen and laser light show.

The interior decor is vivid – really vivid. The main lobby is the connection point for ship functions and for meeting people. Take the glass-walled elevators for a neat view, though you may need sunglasses. It's good to see three main elevator towers: forward, amidships, and aft, unlike larger ships such as *Oasis of the Seas*, which, although it carries many more passengers, has only two such towers.

The Ocean Plaza is a comfortable area by day and an entertainment venue by night. The indoor/outdoor café and live music venue has a bandstand where a variety of musical genres are showcased, a large circular dance floor, and around 190 seats. A floor-to-ceiling curved glass wall separates the room, dividing indoor and outdoor seating areas. An adjacent bar offers coffee, ice creams, and pastries. The Page Turner (great name) is the ship's library, while Jackpot is – you guessed it – the colorful, large, lively casino, with gaming tables and slot machines.

Other rooms include The Song (Jazz Bar) and Ocean Plaza (a sort of quiet area during the day, but busy at night with live entertainment); Internet-connect computer terminals are scattered throughout the ship, but few have much privacy. There's also a 232-capacity conference room called The Chambers. This was the first Carnival ship to have a pub, the RedFrog Pub, with its own-label beer, ThirstyFrog Red.

FAMILIES. Youngsters have their own play areas, with children's programs divided into five age-specific groups under Camp Ocean (ages 2–11 – with children ages 2–5 called 'Penguins'; 6–8-year-olds called 'Sting Rays'; 9–11-year-olds called 'Sharks'). Tweens have 'Circle C', while teenagers have their own 'Club O2' – a chill-out (no adults allowed) room/disco.

Also, all kids love Carnival WaterWorks, an outdoor aqua park with exhilarating water slides.

At the end of 2015, the world of Dr. Seuss was rolled out as part of Carnival's children's program – from 'green eggs and ham' for breakfast, served by waiters in Dr. Seuss-inspired uniforms, and characters such as the Cat in the Hat, Thing One and Thing Two, and Sam attending, to special showings of movies such as *The Cat in the Hat* and *How the Grinch Stole Christmas* (shown on the poolside Seaside Theater screen on Lido Deck).

'Deluxe' ocean-view cabins, with two bathrooms, provide comfort and convenience for families. In addition to twin beds that convert to a king, decent closet space, and elegant decor, the two-bathroom configuration includes one full bathroom and a second bathroom containing a small tub with shower and sink. Some cabins can accommodate five people.

ACCOMMODATION. There are many different cabin price categories, but just six cabin types. All accommodation includes the Carnival Comfort Bed with plush mattresses, good-quality duvets, linens, and pillows. However, the straight accommodation deck hallways create rather a cell-block look – and they are bright, very bright, even at night. There are also lot of interior cabins. The cabins to go for are those at the stern, with great rearward ocean views on decks 6, 7, 8, and 9.

Apart from the Deluxe cabins, there is a wide selection of balcony cabins and suites, including 'Cove Balcony' cabins that are the closest to the waterline. Adjacent to the Cloud 9 Spa are 'Cloud 9' spa cabins. They provide a number of 'exclusive' amenities and privileges.

DINING. There are two main restaurants: Northern Lights, a 1,180-seat amidships dining room, and a smaller 828-seat aft dining room, Southern Lights. Each has two levels: main and balcony, with the galley set on the lower level. Two small restaurant annexes can be reserved by small groups as a private dining room. Expect all-singing, all-dancing waiters to entertain you, while you search for the elusive green vegetables. Choose either fixed-time dining (6pm or 8.15pm) or flexible dining (any time between 5.45 and 9.30pm). Note that the two main dining rooms are not open for lunch on port days.

Other dining options. The Lido Marketplace, the ship's large (but not large enough) self-serve buffet facility, has indoor/outdoor seating areas on the lower (main) level and indoor-only seating on the upper level. A number of designated areas serve different types of ethnic cuisine. It gets seriously congested – particularly for breakfast – and the food is pretty basic, but it works… just. The venue includes a Mongolian Wok and Pasta Bar on the upper level, open 6–9pm for tablecloth-free buffet dinners.

Forward of the buffet venue, and adjacent to the 'beach pool' is a pizzeria and fast-food grill. Aft on the same deck is a tandoor (Indian), and a deli counter (for sandwiches and wraps).

An extra-charge, reservations required Prime Steakhouse and bar seats 139. Located on Promenade Deck aft, it features an à la carte menu, fine table settings, and china and silverware. It's worth paying the cover charge to get a taste of what Carnival can deliver. There's a sushi venue, too, called Sushi and More, on Promenade Deck, close to the RedFrog Pub.

ENTERTAINMENT. The 1,964-seat Showtime Theater spans three decks at the front of the ship, with seating set in a horseshoe shape around a large proscenium arched stage; the sight lines are generally good, except from some of the seats at the back of the lowest level. Large-scale production shows with lots of feathers and skimpy costumes are staged, together with snappy cabaret acts, all with a live showband.

The 425-seat Spotlight Lounge, at the aft end of the ship, has a stage, dance floor, and large bar, and is a comedy venue, including late-night 'adult comedy'. Caliente is the ship's loud, Latin nightclub.

SPA/FITNESS. The expansive 23,750-sq-ft (2,206-sq-m) Cloud 9 Spa is a large and elaborate health and wellness center. The uppermost deck includes indoor/outdoor private spa relaxation areas, at extra cost.

There are 10 treatment rooms, including a VIP room, a large massage room for couples, and a Rasul mud treatment room, plus two dry flotation rooms. An extra-charge 'Thermal Suite' comes with the typical sensory-enhanced soothing heated chambers: Laconium, Tepidarium, Aroma, and Oriental steam baths. There are two steam rooms, one each for men and women, and a small unisex sauna with a floor-to-ceiling window on its starboard side.

A large outdoor SportsSquare for adults is a fenced area for basketball, football, and volleyball. Then there's an outdoor weight-training circuit (SkyFitness), and the cutely named Turf on Surf miniature golf course. Perhaps the highlight is SkyCourse, a 230ft (70m) -long outdoor ropes course, suspended above the uppermost deck. After all those activities, you'll need a cruise to relax.

Carnival Miracle
★★★+

Size:	Large Resort Ship	Passenger Space Ratio (lower beds):	40.4
Tonnage:	85,942	Passenger/Crew Ratio (lower beds):	2.2
Lifestyle:	Standard	Cabins (total):	1,062
Cruise Line:	Carnival Cruise Line	Size Range (sq ft/m):	185.0–490.0/17.1–45.5
Former Names:	none	Cabins (for one person):	0
IMO Number:	9237357	Cabins (with private balcony):	750
Builder:	Kvaerner Masa-Yards (Finland)	Cabins (wheelchair accessible):	16
Original Cost:	$375 million	Wheelchair accessibility:	Good
Entered Service:	Apr 2004	Cabin Current:	110 volts
Registry:	Panama	Elevators:	15
Length (ft/m):	959.6/292.5	Casino (gaming tables):	Yes
Beam (ft/m):	105.6/32.2	Slot Machines:	Yes
Draft (ft/m):	25.5/7.8	Swimming Pools:	3 (1 w/ sliding glass dome)
Propulsion/Propellers:	diesel-electric (62,370kW)/	Hot Tubs (on deck):	5
	2 azimuthing pods	Self-Service Launderette:	Yes
Passenger Decks:	13	Dedicated Cinema/Seats:	No
Total Crew:	961	Library:	Yes
Passengers (lower beds):	2,124	Onboard currency:	US$

This fun-filled, family-friendly ship is for high-energy cruising

OVERVIEW. *Carnival Miracle* is sister to *Carnival Legend*, *Carnival Pride*, and *Carnival Spirit, and* shares the same layout and configuration. It is good for the whole family. It was built in 100 blocks, each weighing up to 450 tons, and assembled in the shipyard.

THE SHIP. The open deck and sunbathing space is not extensive, but there are two swimming pools, one of which can be covered by a sliding glass dome in case of inclement weather. An extra-charge, adults-only area, Sanctuary, has its own bar, pool, hot tub, and other facilities. Located at the aft of the ship on Lido Deck, it is a good area for anyone wanting to have a quieter space for sunbathing and relaxation.

Inside, the decor is dedicated to 'fictional icons,' including the Phantom of the Opera, Sherlock Holmes, Philip Marlowe, and Captain Ahab. Bronze statues of Orpheus and Ulysses adorn the swimming pools.

There are two entertainment/public room decks, the upper with an exterior promenade deck. A walkway, named the Yellow Brick Road, connects many of the major public rooms on Atlantic Deck, one deck above Promenade Deck, which also sports a number of public rooms, including a large Club Merlin Casino.

The colorful atrium lobby spans eight decks and has wall decorations best seen from any of the multiple viewing balconies on any deck above the main lobby level. Take a drink from the lobby bar and look upwards – the surroundings are visually stunning.

Berlitz's Ratings

	Possible	Achieved
Ship	500	361
Accommodation	200	143
Food	400	223
Service	400	249
Entertainment	100	76
Cruise Experience	400	265
OVERALL SCORE		
1317 points out of 2000		

Perhaps the most dramatic large room is the Phantom Showlounge, which spans three decks in the forward section. Directly underneath is the Firebird Lounge, which has a bar in its starboard aft section.

A small wedding chapel is located forward of the uppermost level of the two main entertainment decks, adjacent to the Raven Library and Internet center. Other facilities include a shopping street, with boutique stores, photo gallery, and an observation balcony in the center of the vessel, at the top of the multi-deck atrium. The large Mr Lucky's Casino invites wishful gamers and slot players.

Niggles include the small reception desk in the atrium lobby, which can become very congested. Many private balconies are not so private and can be overlooked from public locations. You need a credit card to open the personal safe in your cabin – inconvenient if your credit cards and wallet are inside the safe! In 2015, some facilities were added or changed. These include a RedFrog Pub (it dispenses Carnival's own brew, Thirsty Frog Red), an Alchemy Bar (for vintage pharmacy-inspired cocktails), four new production shows (*88 Keys*; *80s Pop to the Max*; *Getaway Island*; and *Heart of Soul*), and Hasbro, *The Game Show* (live versions of favorite games).

Niggles: Many pillars obstruct passenger flow – the ones in the dining room, make it difficult for proper food service by the waiters, for example. Books and computers cohabit the ship's Holmes library/Internet center, but anyone wanting a book has to lean over others who may be using a computer, which is an awkward arrangement.

FAMILIES. Youngsters have their own play areas, with children's programs divided into five age-specific groups under Camp Ocean (ages 2–11 – with children ages 2–5 called 'Penguins'; 6–8-year-olds called 'Sting Rays'; 9–11-year-olds called 'Sharks'). Tweens have 'Circle C', while teenagers have their own 'Club O2' – a chill-out (no adults allowed) room/disco.

In 2015, the world of Dr. Seuss were added as part of the line's children's program – from 'green eggs and ham' for breakfast, served by waiters in Dr. Seuss-inspired uniforms, and characters such as the Cat in the Hat, Thing One and Thing Two, and Sam attending, to special showings of movies such as *The Cat in the Hat* and *How the Grinch Stole Christmas* (shown on the poolside Seaside Theater screen on Lido Deck).

ACCOMMODATION. There are many cabin categories, priced by grade, location, and size. The range of cabins includes suites (with private balcony), outside-view cabins with private balcony, ocean-view cabins with French balconies (pseudo balconies that have doors that open, but no balcony to step out onto), and a healthy proportion of standard outside-view to interior cabins.

All cabins have spy-hole doors, twin beds that can be converted into a queen-size bed, individually controlled air conditioning, TV set, and telephone. A number of cabins on the lowest deck have views that are obstructed by lifeboats. Some cabins can accommodate a third and fourth person, but have little closet space, and there's only one personal safe. There is no separate radio in each cabin – instead, audio channels are provided on the in-cabin TV system, but you can't turn the picture off. Nor can you turn off the air conditioning in cabins or bathrooms.

Among the most desirable suites and cabins are those on five aft-facing decks, with private balconies overlooking the stern. You might think that these units would suffer from vibration, but they don't – a bonus provided by the 'pod' propulsion system.

For extra space, it's worthwhile booking one of the larger deluxe balcony suites on Deck 6, with private teakwood balcony. These tend to be quiet suites, with a lounge and sleeping area, a good-size bathroom with twin washbasins, toilet and bidet, and whirlpool tub. They have twin beds convertible to a queen-size bed, three (illuminated) closets, and a huge amount of drawer space. The balcony has an outside light and a wide teakwood deck with smoked glass and wood railing (you could easily seat 10 people).

DINING. The Bacchus Dining Room is the 1,300-seat main restaurant; it spans two decks, with seating on both upper and main levels. Its ceiling features large murals. The galley is underneath the restaurant, with escalator access. Tables are for two to eight; small rooms on both upper and lower levels can be booked for groups of up to 60. Choose either fixed-time dining (6pm or 8.15pm) or flexible dining (between 5.45pm and 9.30pm). Note that the dining room is not open for lunch on port days.

Other dining options. For casual eaters, Horatio's Lido Restaurant is an extensive self-serve buffet-style eatery that forms the aft third of Deck 9 (part of it wraps around the upper section of the atrium). Unicorn murals are everywhere. It includes a central area with a deli sandwich corner, Asian corner, rotisserie, salad bar, international (Taste of the Nations) counter, a dessert counter, and a 24-hour pizzeria counter; with both indoor and outdoor seating. Movement around the buffet area is slow, and you have to stand in line for everything. Each night, the venue morphs into the Seaview Bistro, for casual, serve-yourself-style dinners (typically 6pm–9.30pm).

Nick & Nora's Steakhouse is a more upscale dining spot atop the ship, with just 156 seats and a show kitchen. It is located on two of the uppermost decks of the ship, above Horatio's Lido Restaurant, with great views over the atrium lobby.

ENTERTAINMENT. The 1,170-seat Phantom Showlounge is the ship's principal venue for large-scale production shows and cabaret shows. Spiral stairways at the back of the lounge connect all three levels. Shows are best seen from the upper three levels. Directly underneath the showlounge is the Mad Hatter's Ball Lounge, which has a bar in its starboard aft section.

Almost every lounge/bar, including Sam's Piano Bar, the Jazz Lounge, and Jeeves Lounge, has live music in the evening. Finally, for the very lively, there's the disco; and there's always karaoke.

SPA/FITNESS. SpaCarnival, spanning two decks, is located directly above the navigation bridge in the forward part of the ship and has 13,700 sq ft (1,272 sq m) of space. Lower level facilities: a solarium, eight treatment rooms, lecture rooms, sauna and steam rooms for men and women, and a beauty parlor. Upper level facilities: a large gymnasium with floor-to-ceiling windows on three sides, including forward-facing ocean views, and an aerobics room.

There are two centrally located swimming pools outdoors, and one can be used in inclement weather due to its retractable glass dome. Adjacent are two whirlpool tubs, and a smaller children's pool. Aft is a winding water slide two decks high. An outdoor jogging track is located around the ship's mast; it doesn't go around the whole ship, but it's long enough for some serious walking.

Carnival Paradise
★★★

Size:	Large Resort Ship	Passenger Space Ratio (lower beds):	34.2
Tonnage:	70,390	Passenger/Crew Ratio (lower beds):	2.2
Lifestyle:	Standard	Cabins (total):	1,026
Cruise Line:	Carnival Cruise Line	Size Range (sq ft/m):	173.2–409.7/16–38
Former Names:	*Paradise*	Cabins (for one person):	0
IMO Number:	9120877	Cabins (with private balcony):	152
Builder:	Kvaerner Masa-Yards (Finland)	Cabins (wheelchair accessible):	22
Original Cost:	$300 million	Wheelchair accessibility:	Fair
Entered Service:	Nov 1998	Cabin Current:	110 volts
Registry:	Bahamas	Elevators:	14
Length (ft/m):	855.0/260.6	Casino (gaming tables):	Yes
Beam (ft/m):	103.3/31.5	Slot Machines:	Yes
Draft (ft/m):	25.9/7.9	Swimming Pools:	3
Propulsion/Propellers:	diesel-electric (42,842kW)/ 2 azimuthing pods	Hot Tubs (on deck):	6
		Self-Service Launderette:	Yes
Passenger Decks:	10	Dedicated Cinema/Seats:	No
Total Crew:	920	Library:	Yes
Passengers (lower beds):	2,052	Onboard currency:	US$

This family-friendly ship is for ultra-casual cruising

OVERVIEW. *Carnival Paradise* is the eighth in a series of eight almost identical *Fantasy*-class ships. *It has always been a popular, fun ship for anyone taking a first cruise.*

THE SHIP. *Carnival Paradise* is one of only two ships in the series of eight (the other is *Carnival Elation*) with a 'pod' propulsion system; this provides a vibration-free ride. While the open deck space is reasonable, it is inadequate when the ship is full and everyone wants to be out on deck. The aft decks tend to be less noisy, whereas all the activities are focused around the main swimming pool and hot tubs (one with a thatched shade). There's a topless sunbathing area, as well as Serenity – an adults-only 'quiet' lounging space on Deck 9 aft. There is no walk-around open promenade deck. The lifeboats (six double as shore tenders) are positioned high in the ship, rather than lower down, as in Carnival's newer ships.

The interior design is the work of Miami-based creative genius Joe Farcus; it's clever, functional, and extremely colorful, with a theme of yesteryear's ocean liners.

The interior focal point is an 'open' atrium lobby, with a balconied shape; styled to impress, it spans six decks and is topped by a large glass dome. The lowest level of the atrium lobby is where you'll find the purser's desk and shore excursion desk, together with a popular Atrium Bar with live music, as well as a small sushi bar off to one side; it's a good central meeting place.

Berlitz's Ratings

	Possible	Achieved
Ship	500	309
Accommodation	200	138
Food	400	212
Service	400	257
Entertainment	100	76
Cruise Experience	400	242
OVERALL SCORE		
1234 points out of 2000		

There are many public entertainment lounges, bars, and clubs, with something for everyone (except quiet space). Most of the public rooms, connected by a double-width Carnival Boulevard Promenade and lead off from this boulevard – a sort of shipboard Main Street, which runs between the showlounge (forward) and the Queen Mary Lounge aft. Gamers and slot players alike will enjoy the serious action in the Majestic Casino, with its blackjack and roulette tables, and an array of slot machines. The Blue Riband library is a pleasant room; although it has only a few books, there are several models of ocean liners. Another dazzling room is the Rock and Roll Discotheque, with its guitar-shaped dance floor, video dance club, and dozens of video monitors.

Carnival Paradise is a floating playground for the young and young-at-heart. This really is cruising Splash Vegas style. Because it's a large resort ship, there will be lines for things such as shore excursions, security control when re-boarding, and disembarkation.

The *sine qua non* of a Carnival cruise is all about having fun. While the cuisine is just so-so, the real fun begins at sundown, when the ship excels in sound, lights, and high-volume shows. Venues from the Rex Dance Club/Disco to the Rotterdam Cigar Bar will certainly keep you occupied.

This ship, however, is not for those seeking a quiet, relaxing cruise experience. Niggles include annoying announcements, and the never-ending hustling to get you to spend money. Also, shore excursions are booked via the in-cabin 'Fun Vision' television system, so obtaining advice and suggestions is not easy.

FAMILIES. Youngsters have their own play areas, with children's programs divided into five age-specific groups under Camp Ocean (ages 2–11 – with children ages 2–5 called 'Penguins'; 6–8-year-olds called 'Sting Rays'; 9–11-year-olds called 'Sharks'). Tweens have 'Circle C', while teenagers have their own 'Club O2' – a chill-out (no adults allowed) room/disco.

By the end of 2015, the world of Dr. Seuss was rolled out as part of the line's children's program – from 'green eggs and ham' for breakfast, served by waiters in Dr. Seuss-inspired uniforms, and characters such as the Cat in the Hat, Thing One and Thing Two, and Sam attending, to special showings of movies such as *The Cat in the Hat* and *How the Grinch Stole Christmas* (shown on the poolside Seaside Theater screen on Lido Deck).

ACCOMMODATION. There are numerous price grades for accommodation, by facilities, size, and location. The standard outside-view and interior cabins have decor that is rather plain (uninspiring). They are fairly comfortable, yet spacious enough and practical (most are of the same size and appointments), with good storage space and practical, well-designed, no-nonsense bathrooms. With a queen-bed configuration instead of the standard twin-bed layout, note that one person has to clamber over the bed, which can be awkward.

Choose a suite and you get more space, whirlpool bathtubs, and some rather eclectic decor and furniture. These are mildly attractive, but so-so, and they are much smaller than those aboard ships of a similar size of competing companies. A small gift basket of toiletry samples is provided in all grades.

Room-service items are available 24 hours a day, although in standard cabins, only cold food is available. Those in suite-grade accommodation are able to choose from a greater range of both hot and cold items.

DINING. The two large main dining rooms, Elation and Destiny, are located amidships and aft. Both have ocean-view windows and attractive, but very bright decor, but they are noisy. Choose either fixed-time dining (6pm or 8.15pm) or flexible dining (any time between 5.45 and 9.30pm).

The food is best described as uneventful, with simple presentation and little in the way of garnishes. The selection of fresh green vegetables, breads, rolls, cheeses, and fruits is quite unimaginative, and there is too much use of canned fruit and jellied desserts. There's a decent wine list, but no wine waiters. The waiters sing and dance, so it's really more about 'eatertainment' than food quality. For something really simple, there's an 'always available' list of 'Carnival Classics' including mahi mahi (fish), baby back ribs (beef), and grilled chicken. Note that the two main dining rooms are not open for lunch on port days.

Other dining options. A Lido café, called the Brasserie Bar & Grill, features the usual casual self-serve buffet eats, most of which are non-memorable. The venue includes a deli counter and pizzeria. At night, the venue morphs into the Seaview Bistro, and provides a casual alternative to the main dining rooms, for pasta, steaks, salads, and desserts. The food variety, though limited, makes a change from the large, crowded main dining rooms.

A patisserie offers specialty coffees and sweets (extra charge), and a so-called sushi bar off to one side of the atrium lobby bar on Promenade Deck is open prior to dinner only; the sushi could not be called authentic.

There is no specialty (extra-charge) restaurant, as aboard some of the larger ships in the fleet.

ENTERTAINMENT. The 1,010-seat Normandie Main Lounge is the showlounge, and the venue for large-scale production shows and major cabaret acts – although 20 pillars obstruct some views. During a typical cruise, there will be one or two high-energy production shows, with a cast of two lead singers and a clutch of dancers, backed by a large live band.

SPA/FITNESS. SpaCarnival is a large, glass-wrapped health, fitness, and spa complex. It is located on the uppermost interior deck, forward of the ship's mast, and is typically open from 6am to 8pm daily. It consists of a gymnasium with windows that look out over the bow and the latest in electronic machines, an aerobics room, changing rooms, sauna and steam rooms, beauty salon, and body treatment rooms. Some fitness classes may incur an extra charge.

Sporting types can play basketball or volleyball, or table tennis. There is also a banked jogging track outdoors on the deck above the spa, and a mini-golf course.

Carnival Pride
★★★+

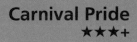

Size:	Large Resort Ship
Tonnage:	85,920
Lifestyle:	Standard
Cruise Line:	Carnival Cruise Line
Former Names:	none
IMO Number:	9223954
Builder:	Kvaerner Masa-Yards (Finland)
Original Cost:	$375 million
Entered Service:	Jan 2002
Registry:	Panama
Length (ft/m):	959.6/292.5
Beam (ft/m):	105.6/32.2
Draft (ft/m):	25.5/7.8
Propulsion/Propellers:	diesel-electric (62,370kW)/ 2 azimuthing pods
Passenger Decks:	12
Total Crew:	1,029
Passengers (lower beds):	2,124

Passenger Space Ratio (lower beds):	40.4
Passenger/Crew Ratio (lower beds):	2.2
Cabins (total):	1,062
Size Range (sq ft/m):	185.0–490.0/17.1–45.5
Cabins (for one person):	0
Cabins (with private balcony):	750
Cabins (wheelchair accessible):	16
Wheelchair accessibility:	Good
Cabin Current:	110 volts
Elevators:	15
Casino (gaming tables):	Yes
Slot Machines:	Yes
Swimming Pools:	3 (1 w/ sliding glass dome)
Hot Tubs (on deck):	5
Self-Service Launderette:	Yes
Dedicated Cinema/Seats:	No
Library:	Yes
Onboard currency:	US$

Try this ship for a fun-filled, contemporary family-friendly cruise

OVERVIEW. *Carnival Pride* is sister to *Carnival Legend*, *Carnival Miracle*, and *Carnival Spirit*, and shares the same layout and configuration. It was designed with families in mind, and there are plenty of entertainment facilities, so kids should have a great time.

THE SHIP. While the open deck and sunbathing space is not extensive, there are two swimming pools: one can be covered by a sliding glass dome in case of inclement weather; another smaller pool is for children. An extra-charge, adults-only area, Sanctuary, has its own bar, pool, hot tub, and other facilities. Located at the aft on Lido Deck, it is good for anyone wanting quieter sunbathing space.

Inside, the interior decor is very artistic – with art being the theme (including nude figures – reproductions from the Renaissance period). Even the elevator doors and interiors contain reproductions (blown-up, grainy photographic copies) of some the great masters such as Gauguin, Matisse, and Jacopo Vignali.. It's all a bit of an eclectic mix. Somehow, it all works – well, sort of!

An interior walkway, named the Yellow Brick Road, connects many of the major public rooms on Atlantic Deck, one deck above Promenade Deck, which also sports a number of public rooms, located aft.

The colorful atrium lobby, which spans eight decks, has wall decorations best seen from any of the viewing balconies on any deck above the main lobby level. Take a drink from the lobby bar and look upwards – the surroundings are visually stunning, and

Berlitz's Ratings		
	Possible	Achieved
Ship	500	361
Accommodation	200	143
Food	400	223
Service	400	251
Entertainment	100	76
Cruise Experience	400	270
OVERALL SCORE		
1324 points out of 2000		

include a 37ft (11m) -tall reproduction of Raphael's *Nymph Galatea*.

A small wedding chapel is located forward of the uppermost level of two main entertainment decks, adjacent to the Nobel Library and Internet center. Other facilities include a shopping street with boutique stores, photo gallery, video games room, and an observation balcony in the center of the vessel, at the top of the multi-deck atrium. A large Winner's Club Casino (you have to walk though it to get to the main level of the showlounge from the restaurant) invites hopeful gamers and slot players.

Carnival Pride is a floating playground for the young and young-at-heart, and anyone who enjoys constant stimulation and lots of participation events, together with the three 'Gs' – glitz, glamour, and gambling. This really is cruising Splash Vegas style – a fun, all-American experience. Because it's a large resort ship, there will be lines for the likes of shore excursions, security control when re-boarding, and disembarkation, as well as sign-up sheets for fitness equipment.

This ship is not for anyone seeking a quiet, relaxing cruise experience. Niggles include many annoying announcements, and constant hustling to get you to buy drinks, jewelry, and trinkets. Also, shore excursions are booked via the in-cabin 'Fun Vision' television system, so obtaining advice and suggestions is not easy. The small reception desk in the atrium lobby is almost always congested. It's hard to escape from noise and loud music (even in cabin hallways and lifts), and masses of people walking around day and night. Many private balconies can be overlooked from public locations. You need a credit card to open the personal safe in your cabin, which is inconvenient if you want to store credit cards and wallet inside the safe!

FAMILIES. Youngsters have their own play areas, with children's programs divided into five age-specific groups under Camp Ocean (ages 2–11 – with children ages 2–5 called 'Penguins'; 6–8-year-olds called 'Sting Rays'; 9–11-year-olds called 'Sharks'). Tweens have 'Circle C', while teenagers have their own 'Club O2' – a chill-out (no adults allowed) room/disco.

By the end of 2015, the world of Dr. Seuss was rolled out as part of the children's program – from 'green eggs and ham' for breakfast, served by waiters in Dr. Seuss-inspired uniforms, and characters such as the Cat in the Hat, Thing One and Thing Two, and Sam attending, to special showings of movies such as *The Cat in the Hat* and *How the Grinch Stole Christmas* (shown on the poolside Seaside Theater screen on Lido Deck).

ACCOMMODATION. There are many cabin categories, priced by grade, location, and size. The range includes suites (with private balcony), outside-view cabins with private balcony, 68 ocean-view cabins with French doors (pseudo balconies that have doors which open, but no balcony to step out onto), and a healthy proportion of standard outside-view to interior cabins.

All cabins have spy-hole doors, twin beds that can be converted into a queen-size bed, individually controlled air conditioning, television, and telephone. A number of cabins on the lowest deck have views that are obstructed by lifeboats. Some cabins can accommodate a third and fourth person, but have little closet space, and there's only one personal safe.

Among the most desirable suites and cabins are those on five of the aft-facing decks; these have private balconies overlooking the stern and ship's wash. You might think that these units would suffer from vibration, but they don't – a bonus of the pod propulsion system.

For extra space (if the budget allows), it's worthwhile booking one of the larger deluxe balcony suites on Deck 6, with private teakwood balcony. These tend to be quiet suites, with a lounge and sleeping area, a good-size bathroom with twin washbasins, toilet and bidet, and whirlpool tub. They have twin beds convertible to a queen-size bed and a huge amount of storage space. The balcony has a wide teakwood deck with smoked glass and wood railing (you could easily seat 10 people).

DINING. The 1,300-seat Normandie Restaurant is the main restaurant, with seating on two levels. Small rooms can be closed off for groups of up to 60. Choose either fixed-time dining (6pm or 8.15pm) or flexible dining (between 5.45pm and 9.30pm). Note that the dining room is not open for lunch on port days.

Other dining options. For casual eaters, there's Mermaid's Grill Lido Restaurant – it's a fancy name for a self-serve buffet-style eatery. It's located in the aft third of Deck 9. The venue includes a central area with a deli sandwich corner, Asian corner, rotisserie, salad bar, dessert counter, and a 24-hour pizzeria, all of which offer both indoor and outdoor seating. Movement around the buffet area is slow, and lines form for everything. Each night, the venue morphs into the Seaview Bistro, for serve-yourself dinners (typically 6pm–9.30pm).

There's also David's Steakhouse, an upscale dining spot atop the ship, with just 156 seats and a show kitchen. There are great views over the atrium lobby and fine table settings, with proper china and silverware. Reservations are required and a cover charge applies.

ENTERTAINMENT. The glamorous 1,170-seat Taj Mahal Showlounge is the principal venue for large-scale production shows and cabaret shows. Spiral stairways at the back of the lounge connect all three levels. Shows are best seen from the upper three levels. Directly underneath the showlounge is the Butterflies lounge and bar.

Almost every lounge/bar, including the Ivory Piano Bar, the Starry Night Jazz Club, and the Florentine Lounge, has live music in the evening. Finally, for the very lively, there's the Beauties Dance Club for thump music; and there's always karaoke.

SPA/FITNESS. SpaCarnival, spanning two decks, is located directly above the navigation bridge in the forward part of the ship. Facilities on the lower level include a solarium, eight treatment rooms, lecture rooms, sauna and steam rooms for men and women, and a beauty parlor. The upper level consists of a large gymnasium with forward-facing ocean views, and an aerobics room.

An outdoor jogging track is located around the ship's mast and the forward third of the ship, close to a basketball court and mini-golf.

Carnival Sensation
★★★

Size:	Large Resort Ship	Passenger/Crew Ratio (lower beds):	2.2
Tonnage:	70,536	Cabins (total):	1,020
Lifestyle:	Standard	Size Range (sq ft/m):	173.2–409.7/16.0–38.0
Cruise Line:	Carnival Cruise Line	Cabins (for one person):	0
Former Names:	Sensation	Cabins (with private balcony):	152
IMO Number:	8711356	Cabins (wheelchair accessible):	20
Builder:	Kvaerner Masa-Yards (Finland)	Wheelchair accessibility:	Fair
Original Cost:	$300 million	Cabin Current:	110 volts
Entered Service:	Nov 1993	Elevators:	14
Registry:	The Bahamas	Casino (gaming tables):	Yes
Length (ft/m):	855.0/260.6	Slot Machines:	Yes
Beam (ft/m):	104.0/31.4	Swimming Pools:	3
Draft (ft/m):	25.9/7.9	Hot Tubs (on deck):	6
Propulsion/Propellers:	diesel-electric (42,240kW)/2	Self-Service Launderette:	Yes
Passenger Decks:	10	Dedicated Cinema/Seats:	No
Total Crew:	920	Library:	Yes
Passengers (lower beds):	2,040	Onboard currency:	US$
Passenger Space Ratio (lower beds):	34.4		

This ultra-colorful, casual ship is good for a first cruise

OVERVIEW. *Carnival Sensation* is the third in a series of eight almost identical *Fantasy*-class ships (sister ships: *Carnival Ecstasy*, *Carnival Elation*, *Carnival Fantasy*, *Carnival Fascination*, *Carnival Imagination*, *Carnival Inspiration*, and *Carnival Paradise* – all with extremely short bows). *Carnival Sensation* is well liked, and good for families and party types taking a first cruise.

THE SHIP. While the open deck space is reasonable, it is inadequate when the ship is full and everyone wants to be out on deck. The aft decks used to be less noisy when all the activities were focused around the main swimming pool and hot tubs, but now that the WaterWorks – with long and short water slides and water-burst fountains – has been added, it's the active area.

There's also a topless sunbathing area, as well as Serenity – an adult-only 'quiet' lounging space on Deck 9 aft. There is no walk-around open promenade deck, although there is a short jogging track atop ship. The lifeboats, six of which double as shore tenders, are positioned high in the ship (they are located much lower aboard Carnival's newer ships).

The interior of the ship is well designed and the general passenger flow is good. The interior design – the work of creative genius Joe Farcus – is clever, functional, and colorful, and includes plenty of glitz. He calls it 'entertainment architecture' and considers every part of a ship as a piece of a giant jigsaw puzzle. The underlying decor theme is the arts (in a sort of Art Nouveau style) and literature. It includes a color-

Berlitz's Ratings

	Possible	Achieved
Ship	500	314
Accommodation	200	138
Food	400	212
Service	400	250
Entertainment	100	73
Cruise Experience	400	242
OVERALL SCORE		
1229 points out of 2000		

ful mix of classic and contemporary design elements.

The interior focal point is an 'open' atrium lobby, with a balconied shape; it spans six decks, and is topped by a large glass dome. The lowest level of the atrium is where you'll find the purser's and shore excursion desks, an Atrium Bar (with live music), plus a small sushi bar off to one side; it's a good central meeting place.

There are public entertainment lounges, bars, and clubs galore, with something for everyone (except quiet space). Most public rooms and attractions lead off from Sensation Boulevard – a shipboard Main Street, which runs between the showlounge (forward) and the Plaza Aft lounge, with Joe's Café a popular spot for coffees and teas. Gamers and slot players alike will surely enjoy the almost non-stop action in the Club Vegas Casino close by.

The Oak Room Library is a stately reading room, but there are few books. Meanwhile, the Kaleidoscope Discotheque, with its dozens of video monitors and dance floor, hits you with a dazzling variety of stimulating, electric colors. There's also a 1,200-sq-ft (111-sq-m) conference room.

This ship is definitely not for anyone seeking a quiet, relaxing cruise experience. Niggles include the many annoying announcements, and the never-ending hustling to incite you to buy drinks, jewelry, and trinkets. Also, shore excursions are booked via the in-cabin 'Fun Vision' television system, so obtaining advice and suggestions is not easy.

FAMILIES. Youngsters have their own play areas, with children's programs divided into five age-specific groups under Camp Ocean (ages 2–11 – with children ages 2–5 called 'Penguins'; 6–8-year-olds called 'Sting Rays'; 9–11-year-olds called 'Sharks'). Tweens have 'Circle C', while teenagers have their own 'Club O2' – a chill-out (no adults allowed) room/disco. Also, soft-drinks packages can be purchased for children (and adults).

Also, a water park is always a lot of fun as an outdoor play area. For really young ones, group babysitting is available.

By the end of 2015, the world of Dr. Seuss was rolled out as part of the children's program – from 'green eggs and ham' for breakfast, served by waiters in Dr. Seuss-inspired uniforms, and characters such as the Cat in the Hat, Thing One and Thing Two, and Sam attending, to special showings of movies such as *The Cat in the Hat* and *How the Grinch Stole Christmas* (shown on the poolside Seaside Theater screen on Lido Deck).

ACCOMMODATION. There are many different accommodation price grades, ranked by facilities, size, and location. The standard outside-view and interior cabins have decor that is rather plain. They are fairly comfortable, yet spacious enough and practical (most are of the same size and appointments), with good storage and no-nonsense bathrooms. However, if you have a queen-bed configuration instead of the standard twin-bed layout, note that one person has to clamber over the bed – a potentially ungainly exercise.

Choose a suite and you get more space, whirlpool bathtubs, and rather eclectic decor and furniture. These are reasonably attractive, but much smaller than those aboard ships of a similar size of competing companies. Some 50 cabins have interconnecting doors – good for families with children.

Room service items are available 24 hours a day, although in standard cabins, only cold food is available, while those in suite-grade accommodation get a greater range of items (both hot and cold) to choose from.

DINING. The two large main dining rooms, Fantasy and Ecstasy, are located amidships and aft. Both have ocean-view windows and attractive, but very bright decor, and they are noisy – full of anticipatory excitement. Choose either fixed-time dining (6pm or 8.15pm) or flexible dining (any time between 5.45 and 9.30pm).

The food is really not memorable, with simple presentation and few garnishes used. Meat and fowl main courses are often disguised with gravies and sauces. The selection of fresh green vegetables, breads, rolls, cheeses, and fruits is limited, and there is much use of canned fruit and jellied desserts. There's a decent wine list, but no wine waiters. The waiters sing and dance, and there are constant waiter parades – so it's more about 'eatertainment' than food quality.

This is, however, basic catering – with all its attendant standardization and production cooking, which makes it difficult to obtain anything unusual or 'off-menu'. For something simple, there's an 'always available' list of 'Carnival Classics' that includes mahi mahi (fish), baby back ribs (beef), and grilled chicken (when the dining rooms are open). The two main dining rooms are not open for lunch on port days.

Other dining options. The Seaview Bar & Grill is like a lido cafe, and features casual self-serve buffet eats, most of which are non-memorable. The venue includes a deli counter and pizzeria. At night, the venue morphs into the Seaview Bistro, and provides a casual alternative to the main dining rooms, for pasta, steaks, salads, and desserts – it typically operates only between 6pm and 9pm. The food selection, though limited, makes a change from the large, crowded and noisy main dining rooms. Outside on deck is a Mongolian Rotisserie Grill.

A patisserie offers specialty coffees and sweets (extra charge), and a so-called sushi bar on Promenade Deck is open prior to dinner only.

There is no specialty (extra-charge) restaurant, as aboard some of the larger ships in the Carnival fleet.

ENTERTAINMENT. The Fantasia Lounge is the ship's principal showlounge, and the venue for large-scale production shows and major cabaret acts. However, some 20 pillars obstruct the views from several seats. During a typical cruise, there will be one or two high-energy production shows, backed by a large live band.

SPA/FITNESS. SpaCarnival is a large, glass-wrapped health, fitness, and spa complex, located on the uppermost interior deck, forward of the ship's mast. It consists of a gymnasium with ocean-view windows and the latest muscle-pumping equipment, an aerobics exercise room, sauna and steam rooms, beauty salon, and body treatment rooms. Some fitness classes (such as kick-boxing or yoga) may incur an extra charge. A common complaint is that the area is not kept clean and tidy, and used towels are often strewn around the changing rooms.

Sporting types can play basketball, volleyball, table tennis, mini-golf, or go jogging (on a banked course).

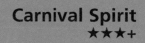

Carnival Spirit
★★★+

Size:	Large Resort Ship	Passenger Space Ratio (lower beds):	40.4
Tonnage:	85,920	Passenger/Crew Ratio (lower beds):	2.2
Lifestyle:	Standard	Cabins (total):	1,062
Cruise Line:	Carnival Cruise Line	Size Range (sq ft/m):	185.0–490.0/17.1–45.5
Former Names:	none	Cabins (for one person):	0
IMO Number:	9188647	Cabins (with private balcony):	750
Builder:	Kvaerner Masa-Yards	Cabins (wheelchair accessible):	16
Original Cost:	$375 million	Wheelchair accessibility:	Good
Entered Service:	Apr 2001	Cabin Current:	110 volts
Registry:	Malta	Elevators:	15
Length (ft/m):	959.6/292.5	Casino (gaming tables):	Yes
Beam (ft/m):	105.6/32.2	Slot Machines:	Yes
Draft (ft/m):	25.5/7.8	Swimming Pools:	3 (1 w/sliding glass dome)
Propulsion/Propellers:	diesel-electric (62,370kW)/ 2 azimuthing pods	Hot Tubs (on deck):	5
		Self-Service Launderette:	Yes
Passenger Decks:	12	Dedicated Cinema/Seats:	No
Total Crew:	930	Library:	Yes
Passengers (lower beds):	2,124	Onboard currency:	US$

Good for a fun-filled cruise in a contemporary setting

OVERVIEW. *Carnival Spirit* is a sister ship to *Carnival Legend*, *Carnival Miracle*, and *Carnival Pride*, and shares the same layout and configuration. It was built in 100 blocks, each weighing up to 450 tons, and assembled in the shipyard. In 2012, the ship was moved to Sydney, Australia, for year-round fun-in-the-sun cruises.

THE SHIP. It's all about active entertainment. Following a 2012 refurbishment before the ship's Australia deployment, much of its outdoor deck space was designated a Water Park and Splash Zone, with water wheels, spraying jets, water blasters, pull ropes, two Mini Racer slides, and more.

Then there's the really big attraction, Green Thunder, a thrill ride that starts 100ft (30m) above sea level. The floor suddenly drops out of the platform, and you plummet in a near-vertical drop at about 23ft (7m) a second. When you hit the water in the fast water slide, you twist and turn through a transparent tube that extends over the side of the ship. Kids will love it, but need to be 42ins (1.1m) tall to be able to experience it. The open deck space is a bit tight when the ship sails full in warm-weather areas.

An extra-charge, adults-only area, Sanctuary has its own bar, pool, hot tub, and other facilities. Located at the aft of the ship on Lido Deck, it is a pleasant area for anyone seeking a quieter space for sunbathing and relaxation – and to escape the many children on board during the major holidays.

Berlitz's Ratings		
	Possible	Achieved
Ship	500	361
Accommodation	200	143
Food	400	223
Service	400	252
Entertainment	100	76
Cruise Experience	400	265
OVERALL SCORE		
1320 points out of 2000		

An interior walkway, named the Fashion Boulevard, connects many of the major public rooms on Atlantic Deck, one deck above Promenade Deck, which is also home to a number of public rooms, including a large Louis XIV Casino.

The colorful atrium lobby, which spans eight decks, has wall decorations best seen from any of the multiple viewing balconies on any deck above the main lobby level. Take a drink from the lobby bar and look upwards – the surroundings and artwork are visually stunning.

Perhaps the most dramatic room is the Pharaoh's Palace Showlounge, which spans three decks in the forward section. Directly underneath is the Versailles Lounge, which has a bar in its starboard aft section.

A small wedding chapel is located forward of the uppermost level of the two main entertainment decks, adjacent to the Nobel Library and Internet center. Other facilities include a winding shopping street with boutique stores, photo gallery, video games room, and an observation balcony in the center of the vessel, at the top of the multi-deck atrium. The large Winner's Club Casino invites hopeful gamers and slot players alike.

You need a credit card to open the personal safe in your cabin – somewhat inconvenient, if you want to store all your credit cards and your wallet inside the safe!

FAMILIES. Youngsters have their own play areas, with children's programs divided into five age-specific groups under Camp Ocean (ages 2–11 – with children ages 2–5 called 'Penguins'; 6–8-year-olds called 'Sting Rays'; 9–11-year-olds called 'Sharks'). Tweens have 'Circle C', while teenagers have their own 'Club O2' – a chill-out (no adults allowed) room/disco. Also, soft-drinks packages can be purchased for children (and adults).

At the end of 2015, the world of Dr. Seuss was rolled out as part of the children's program – from 'green eggs and ham' for breakfast, served by waiters in Dr. Seuss-inspired uniforms, and characters such as the Cat in the Hat, Thing One and Thing Two, and Sam attending, to special showings of movies such as *The Cat in the Hat* and *How the Grinch Stole Christmas* (shown on the poolside Seaside Theater screen on Lido Deck).

ACCOMMODATION. There are many different cabin categories, priced by grade, location, and size. The range includes suites (with private balcony), outside-view cabins with private balcony, 68 ocean-view cabins with French doors (pseudo balconies that have doors which open, but no balcony to step out onto), and a healthy proportion of standard outside-view to interior cabins.

Among the most desirable suites and cabins are those on five of the aft-facing decks; these have private balconies overlooking the stern and ship's wash. You might think that these units would suffer from vibration, but they don't – a bonus provided by the pod propulsion system.

For extra space, book one of the larger deluxe balcony suites on Deck 6, with private teakwood balcony. These tend to be quiet, with a lounge and sleeping area, a good-size bathroom with twin washbasins, toilet and bidet, and whirlpool tub; twin beds convert to a queen-size bed, and there's a huge amount of storage space. The balcony has a wide teakwood deck with smoked glass and wood railing (you could easily seat 10 people).

Even the largest suites are quite small compared with suites aboard other ships of a similar size – for example, Celebrity Cruises' *Celebrity Constellation*, *Celebrity Infinity*, *Celebrity Millennium*, and *Celebrity Summit*, where penthouse suites measure up to 2,530 sq ft (235 sq m).

DINING. The Empire Restaurant is the large, two-deck-high, 1,250-seat main restaurant. Small rooms on both upper and lower levels can be closed off for groups of up to 60. Choose either fixed-time dining or flexible dining. The restaurant is not open for lunch on port days.

Other dining options. La Playa Grille Lido Restaurant is the large casual self-serve buffet-style eatery on Lido Deck aft. It includes a central area with a deli sandwich corner, Asian corner, rotisserie, salad bar, an international (Taste of the Nations) counter, and a 24-hour pizzeria counter. Both indoor and outdoor seating is available. In a 2015 refit, Guy's Burger Joint (for burgers and hot dogs), BlueIguana Cantina were added, as was a special brew – the ThirstyRed Frog Summer Ale – at various bars. There's also Fat Jimmy's C-Side BBQ on Sun Deck.

Nouveau Steakhouse is a premium (reservations-required) dining spot atop the ship, with 156 seats and a show kitchen. It is located on two of the uppermost decks of the ship, above the Lido Restaurant, in the lower, forward section of the funnel housing, with neat views over the colorful atrium lobby (actually, the four-person tables tucked beneath the overhang of the upper level are cozy and have ocean views). Fine table settings, china, and silverware are provided, a cover charge applies, and reservations are needed.

ENTERTAINMENT. The glamorous 1,167-seat Pharaoh's Palace is the ship's principal venue for large-scale production shows and cabaret shows. Shows are best seen from the upper three levels. Directly underneath the showlounge is the Versailles Lounge and bar.

Almost every lounge/bar, including the Shanghai Piano Bar, the Club Cool Jazz Club, and the Artists' Lobby Lounge, has live music in the evening. Finally, for the very lively, there's the Dancin' Dance Club for thump thump music; and there's always karaoke.

SPA/FITNESS. SpaCarnival spans two decks; it is located directly above the navigation bridge in the forward part of the ship and has 13,700 sq ft (1,272 sq m) of space. Facilities on the lower level include a solarium, eight treatment rooms, lecture rooms, sauna and steam rooms for men and women, and a beauty parlor. The upper level consists of a large gymnasium with floor-to-ceiling windows on three sides, including forward-facing ocean views, and an aerobics room with instructor-led classes.

There are two centrally located pools outdoors, one with a retractable glass dome cover. An outdoor jogging track is located around the ship's mast and the forward third of the ship; it doesn't go around the whole ship, but it's long enough for some serious walking.

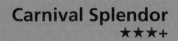

Carnival Splendor
★★★+

Size:	Large Resort Ship	Passenger/Crew Ratio (lower beds):	2.5
Tonnage:	113,323	Cabins (total):	1,487
Lifestyle:	Standard	Size Range (sq ft/m):	179.7–484.2/16.7–44.8
Cruise Line:	Carnival Cruise Line	Cabins (for one person):	0
Former Names:	none	Cabins (with private balcony):	574
IMO Number:	9333163	Cabins (wheelchair accessible):	25
Builder:	Fincantieri (Italy)	Wheelchair accessibility:	Good
Original Cost:	$500 million	Cabin Current:	110 volts
Entered Service:	July 2008	Elevators:	18
Registry:	Panama	Casino (gaming tables):	Yes
Length (ft/m):	951.4/290.0	Slot Machines:	Yes
Beam (ft/m):	105.6/32.2	Swimming Pools:	3
Draft (ft/m):	27.2/8.3	Hot Tubs (on deck):	7
Propulsion/Propellers:	diesel-electric (63,400kW)/2	Self-Service Launderette:	Yes
Passenger Decks:	13	Dedicated Cinema/Seats:	No
Total Crew:	1,150	Library:	Yes
Passengers (lower beds):	2,974	Onboard currency:	US$
Passenger Space Ratio (lower beds):	37.0		

This family-friendly, fun-filled ship has a great water-slide

OVERVIEW. *Carnival Splendor* shares the same generally balanced profile as sisters *Carnival Conquest*, *Carnival Freedom*, *Carnival Glory*, *Carnival Liberty*, *Carnival Sunshine*, *Carnival Triumph*, *Carnival Valor*, and *Carnival Victory*, although it was originally designated as a ship for the Costa Cruises brand. The interior decor displays a vivid palette of colors that excite the senses.

THE SHIP. The deck and public room layout is logical, so finding your way around is relatively easy. Most of the public rooms are located on one deck off a main interior boulevard, above a deck that contains the two main dining rooms.

Public rooms include a large Royal Flush Casino. Gaming includes blackjack, craps, roulette, three-card poker, Caribbean Stud poker, Face Up, Let it Ride, Bonus, and Wheel of Madness, and an array of more than 300 slot machines.

Recalling the drive-in movie theaters of the 1950s, the Seaside Theater shows movies, and sports features on deck, with seating in tiered rows and the screen facing forward (popcorn obligatory, of course). The ship has bow-to-stern Wi-Fi Internet access (for a fee), and this includes all passenger cabins.

Carnival Splendor is a floating playground for the young and young-at-heart, and anyone who enjoys constant stimulation and lots of participation events, together with the three 'Gs' – glitz, glamour, and gambling. This really is cruising Splash Vegas style – a fun, all-American experience. Because it's a large resort ship, there will be lines for the likes of shore

Berlitz's Ratings		
	Possible	Achieved
Ship	500	369
Accommodation	200	144
Food	400	218
Service	400	255
Entertainment	100	77
Cruise Experience	400	258
OVERALL SCORE		
1321 points out of 2000		

excursions, security control when re-boarding, and disembarkation, as well as sign-up sheets for fitness equipment.

Forget fashion – the *sine qua non* of a Carnival cruise is all about having fun. The cuisine is just so-so, but the real fun begins at sundown, with sound, lights, razzle-dazzle shows, and late-night high-volume sounds.

Minor niggles include the fact that many pillars obstruct passenger flow, particularly in the dining rooms, where they make it difficult for the waiters to serve properly, and the food itself (particularly the bakery items).

FAMILIES. Youngsters have their own play areas, with children's programs divided into five age-specific groups under Camp Ocean (ages 2–11 – with children ages 2–5 called 'Penguins'; 6–8-year-olds called 'Sting Rays'; 9–11-year-olds called 'Sharks'). Tweens have 'Circle C', while teenagers have their own 'Club O2' – a chill-out (no adults allowed) room/disco. Also, soft-drinks packages can be purchased for children (and adults).

By the end of 2015, the world of Dr. Seuss was rolled out as part of the children's program – from 'green eggs and ham' for breakfast, served by waiters in Dr. Seuss-inspired uniforms, and characters including the Cat in the Hat, Thing One and Thing Two, and Sam attending, to special showings of movies such as *The Cat in the Hat* and *How the Grinch Stole Christmas* (shown on the poolside Seaside Theater screen on Lido Deck).

ACCOMMODATION. There are many different cabin price categories, in seven suite/cabin types, sizes, and grades. These include suites with private balcony; deluxe outside-view cabins with private balcony; outside-view cabins with private balcony; outside-view cabins with window; cabins with a porthole instead of a window; interior cabins; and interior cabins with upper and lower berths (good for families with very small children). There are five decks of cabins with private balconies.

The standard cabins are of good size and come equipped with all the basics, although the furniture is angular, with no rounded edges. Three decks of cabins (eight per deck, each with private balcony) overlook the stern. Most cabins with twin beds convert to a queen-size bed format. Book one of the suites (Category 11 or 12 in the Carnival brochure) and you'll get Skipper's Club priority check-in at any US homeland port – useful for getting ahead of the crowd.

There are even 'spa' cabins – a grouping of 18 cabins located directly around and behind SpaCarnival; fitness devotees can get out of bed and go straight to the treadmill without having to go through any of the public rooms first.

A basket of small sample toiletries is provided in all cabins, although it's better to take your own preferred brands.

DINING. There are two principal dining rooms, the 744-seat Black Pearl – located amidships, and the 1,122-seat Gold Pearl, located aft. Both are two decks high and include a balcony level – Gold Pearl is the larger of the two balconies. There's a choice of either fixed-time dining (6pm or 8.15pm) or flexible dining (any time between 5.45pm and 9.30pm). There are few tables for two, but my favorites are the two tables for two, right at the very back of the Gold Pearl restaurant, with ocean views astern. Note that the two main dining rooms are not open for lunch on port days.

Other dining options. The Steakhouse has fine table settings, china, and silverware, and leatherbound menus. The specialties are USDA dry-aged prime steaks and seafood items. It's worth paying the cover charge to get a taste of what Carnival can deliver in terms of food that is of better quality than what

is served in the main dining rooms. Reservations are required, and a cover charge applies.

The Lido Restaurant is a casual self-serve international food court-style eatery. It has two main serving lines and several stand-alone sections. Included in this eating mall are a New York-style deli, a 24-hour pizzeria, and a grill for fast foods such as hamburgers and hot dogs; one section has a tandoori oven for Indian-theme items.

Each night, this venue morphs into Seaview Bistro to provide a dress-down alternative the main dining rooms, serving pasta, steaks, salads, and desserts (typically between 6pm and 9pm). An upstairs rotisserie offers chicken.

ENTERTAINMENT. The large, multi-deck Spectacular Showlounge seats 1,400, and hosts colorful large-scale entertainment including Las Vegas-style production shows (think girls, feathers and flesh) and major cabaret acts. It has a revolving stage, hydraulic orchestra pit, excellent sound, and seating on three levels. The upper levels are tiered through two decks.

An alternative entertainment venue is the El Morocco, a 425-seat lounge located aft; this typically features live music and late-night cabaret acts including smutty adult comedy. Adjacent is the Grand Piano Lounge/Bar.

SPA/FITNESS. The Cloud 9 Spa spans two decks (with a total area of around 40,000 sq ft/3,715 sq m, including the 16 spa suites – or 13,000 sq ft/1,235 sq m, excluding them). Located directly above the navigation bridge in the forward part of the ship, it is accessed from the forward stairway.

Facilities on the lower level include a gymnasium, solarium, a thermal suite (a number of saunas and steam rooms – some infused with herbal aromas), thalassotherapy pool (check out the huge Chinese dogs), and a beauty salon. The upper level houses 17 massage/body treatment rooms, including two VIP suites (one for couples, one configured for wheelchair access), Rasul (Mediterranean mud treatment – best for couples) chamber, floatation therapy room, treatment rooms, and outdoor relaxation areas on both port and starboard sides with integrated massage cabana. To use the thermal suite, there's an extra cost.

Carnival Sunshine
★★★+

Size:	Large Resort Ship
Tonnage:	102,853
Lifestyle:	Standard
Cruise Line:	Carnival Cruise Line
Former Names:	*Carnival Destiny*
IMO Number:	9070058
Builder:	Fincantieri (Italy)
Original Cost:	$400 million
Entered Service:	Nov 1996
Registry:	The Bahamas
Length (ft/m):	892.3/272.0
Beam (ft/m):	116.0/35.3
Draft (ft/m):	27.0/8.2
Propulsion/Propellers:	diesel-electric (63,400kW)/2
Passenger Decks:	12
Total Crew:	1,150
Passengers (lower beds):	3,006
Passenger Space Ratio (lower beds):	34.2

Passenger/Crew Ratio (lower beds):	2.6
Cabins (total):	1,503
Size Range (sq ft/m):	179.7–482.2/16.7–44.8
Cabins (for one person):	0
Cabins (with private balcony):	418
Cabins (wheelchair accessible):	25
Wheelchair accessibility:	Good
Cabin Current:	110 volts
Elevators:	18
Casino (gaming tables):	Yes
Slot Machines:	Yes
Swimming Pools:	3 (1 w/sliding glass dome)
Hot Tubs (on deck):	7
Self-Service Launderette:	Yes
Dedicated Cinema/Seats:	No
Library:	Yes
Onboard currency:	US$

This vibrant ship is good for first-time cruisers

OVERVIEW. *Carnival Sunshine* (formerly *Carnival Destiny*) was the first cruise ship with a gross tonnage that exceeded 100,000. After a lengthy refurbishment, the ship shouts 'Party, party, party!' It's a good ship for families with children.

THE SHIP. The ship has short bows and a distinctive, large, swept-back wing-tipped funnel. Tiered sunbathing decks positioned between small swimming pools, several hot tubs, and a large poolside movie screen have transformed the area into a relaxation zone, complete with a small waterfall feature.

Also, on the open deck and aft of the funnel is WaterWorks, including a 334ft (101.8m) Twister water slide (the longest in the fleet), and Speedway Splash slide – so you and a competitor race down the Twister to a splashy finish.

The interior decor is a sensory wonderland. There are three decks full of lounges and bars, lots of rooms to play in, and a double-width indoor promenade. A glass-domed rotunda Sunshine Atrium lobby – with bar, two panoramic elevators and dual stairway – is nine decks high. An always-busy Sunshine Casino has ample gaming tables for serious gamers (poker, craps, blackjack, and roulette), and over 320 slot machines.

In spring 2013 a much-needed makeover (costing $155 million) lasted almost three months and added two half-decks at the front of the ship, extended two other decks aft, added 182 cabins (but no extra elevators), and several new and other revamped eateries. Public rooms include Piano Bar 88 (named for the

Berlitz's Ratings

	Possible	Achieved
Ship	500	372
Accommodation	200	144
Food	400	226
Service	400	254
Entertainment	100	74
Cruise Experience	400	261
OVERALL SCORE		
1331 points out of 2000		

88 keys on a grand piano); Alchemy Bar, for 'mixologist' cocktails; a (music-free) Library Bar; a Sports Bar (interactive, with results on a 24/7 sports ticker); and an art gallery.

FAMILIES. Youngsters have their own play areas, with children's programs divided into five age-specific groups under Camp Ocean (ages 2–11 – with children ages 2–5 called 'Penguins'; 6–8-year-olds called 'Sting Rays'; 9–11-year-olds called 'Sharks'). Tweens have 'Circle C', while teenagers have their own 'Club O2' – a chill-out (no adults allowed) room/disco. Also, soft-drinks packages can be purchased for children (and adults).

There are lots of sporty things for kids to do, too, including taking the adventure course, with its tightropes, nets, and swinging planks, not to mention the real 'wow' – the two water slides in the Waterpark.

ACCOMMODATION. There are several accommodation categories (Captain's Suite, Grand Suite, Ocean Suite, Premium Balcony Cabin, Scenic Oceanview Cabin, Oceanview Cabin, Interior Cabin, and Small Interior), and a multitude of different price grades, depending on size and location. Over half of all cabins have ocean views, and, at 225 sq ft/21 sq m, they are a decent size. The cabins, spread over four decks, have private balconies with glass rather than steel balustrades for better, unobstructed ocean views; balconies have bright fluorescent lighting. However, there are many, many interior (no-view) cabins.

During the 2013 refit, 95 Cloud 9 Spa Cabins were added over three decks in the front of the ship, adjacent to the Cloud 9 Spa and Serenity adult-only area; these have all the usual fittings, plus special spa-like extras, and access to the Cloud 9 Spa.

Standard cabins are of an adequate size and come equipped with all the basics, although the furniture is angular (think Ikea flatpack), with no rounded corners – in other words, nothing is superfluous. Three decks of cabins (eight on each deck, each with private balcony) overlook the stern.

Eight penthouse suites each have a large private balcony. Although they are quite well appointed, they are really modest when compared to the good-sized suites even in many smaller ships. Other suites each feature a decent-size bathroom and lounge space.

In cabins with balconies, the partition between each balcony is open at top and bottom, so you can hear noise from neighbors. Three categories of cabins, both outside and interior, have upper and lower bunk beds, which is useful for families with small children.

The cabins have a pastel color scheme and soft furnishings. Interactive 'Fun Vision' technology lets you choose movies on demand, for a fee (although the television screen is not very large). The bathrooms, which have good-size showers, have adequate storage space in the toiletries cabinet. A gift basket is provided in all grades; it includes aloe soap, shampoo, conditioner, deodorant, breath mints, candy, and pain relief tablets – albeit all in sample sizes.

Book one of the suite-grades and you get 'Skipper's Club' priority check-in at any US homeland port. Note that the soundproofing between cabins is poor and the cabin doors have (non-closable) vents – so any noise from the hallway filters through.

DINING. There are two main restaurants: the Sunrise Forward Dining Room, with windows on two sides; and the Sunrise Aft Dining Room, with windows on three sides). Each is a single deck high and has bright, modern design and decor.

The Sunset dining room has a wall of glass overlooking the stern. There are tables for four, six, and eight and even a few tables for two – nice for honeymooners. Choose either fixed-time dining (6pm or 8.15pm) or flexible dining (any time between 5.45 and 9.30pm). Although menu choices look good, the actual cuisine delivered is adequate, but unmemorable. Still, the waiters try to impress with lots of dancing on tables and other hoopla, telling everyone they're having fun. Note that the two main dining rooms are not open for lunch on port days.

Other dining options. Fahrenheit 555 Steakhouse is an extra-cost, reservations-required dining spot for fine steaks (worth the extra money) and grilled seafood dishes. There are many tables for two

(although they are quite close together), as well as larger tables, and the seating is comfortable.

For casual eats, there's the Ocean Plaza (Lido Market Place), a large international food court-style self-serve eatery. It's open for breakfast and lunch, and there are plenty of food displays (it's a copy of the self-serve Markt Restaurants aboard AIDA Cruises' ships). It includes a 24-hour pizzeria (Pizzeria del Capitano). Self-serve beer is available (charged automatically to your account swipe card). There's no bar in the venue itself – but there are several on the adjacent pool deck.

A JavaBlue Café with 'comfort' snacks was introduced into the Fun Hub Internet-connect area. A Havana Bar was also added (within the Market Place), as was a RedFrog Pub, pouring Carnival's own tasty house brew, ThirstyFrog Red. Adjacent, but outside, are Cucina del Capitano (for Italian cuisine, with made-to-order pasta dishes); the BlueIguana Cantina Mexican-style street eatery (for tacos and burritos); Ji Ji's Asian Kitchen, which features lunchtime stir-fry dishes, while (extra-cost) dinners include more exotic favorites; a 24-hour pizzeria; a patisserie (extra charge for pastries); a car-culture-inspired Guy's Burger Joint for fast foods including burgers and hot dogs; and a RedFrog Rum Bar.

For something more unusual, or to celebrate, you can also choose to eat at the Chef's Table (it's reserved for only 12 hungry diners, at $75 each), which includes a look into the galley when it's in full operation, followed by a specially prepared multi-course dinner.

ENTERTAINMENT. The two-level Liquid Lounge – the ship's showlounge which seats 800 and is the setting for high energy production legs and feathers shows and large-scale cabaret acts – is quite stunning. It has a revolving stage, hydraulic orchestra pit, good sound, and seating on three levels (the upper levels being tiered through two decks). A proscenium over the stage acts as a scenery loft.

Other entertainment options include a Hasbro Game Show and the Punchliner Comedy Club presented by George Lopez, and, the Liquid Lounge for those high-volume disco sounds.

SPA/FITNESS. Cloud 9 Spa spans two decks, and encompasses 13,700 sq ft/1,272 sq m. It is located above the navigation bridge, and is accessible via the forward stairway. Lower level facilities include a solarium, body treatment rooms, sauna and steam rooms for men and women, and a beauty salon; the upper level consists of a large gymnasium with floor-to-ceiling windows on three sides, with ocean views, and an aerobics room for instructor-led classes (some at extra cost).

SportSquare is an outdoor recreation area with a suspended ropes course (and some great views), for activity fans.

Carnival Triumph
★★★+

Size:	Large Resort Ship
Tonnage:	101,509
Lifestyle:	Standard
Cruise Line:	Carnival Cruise Line
Former Names:	none
IMO Number:	9138850
Builder:	Fincantieri (Italy)
Original Cost:	$420 million
Entered Service:	Oct 1999
Registry:	The Bahamas
Length (ft/m):	893.0/272.2
Beam (ft/m):	116.0/35.3
Draft (ft/m):	27.0/8.2
Propulsion/Propellers:	diesel-electric (34,000kW)/ 2 azimuthing pods
Passenger Decks:	13
Total Crew:	1,100
Passengers (lower beds):	2,758

Passenger Space Ratio (lower beds):	36.8
Passenger/Crew Ratio (lower beds):	2.3
Cabins (total):	1,379
Size Range (sq ft/m):	179.7–482.2/16.7–44.8
Cabins (for one person):	0
Cabins (with private balcony):	508
Cabins (wheelchair accessible):	25
Wheelchair accessibility:	Good
Cabin Current:	110 volts
Elevators:	18
Casino (gaming tables):	Yes
Slot Machines:	Yes
Swimming Pools:	3 (+1 with sliding glass dome)
Hot Tubs (on deck):	7
Self-Service Launderette:	Yes
Dedicated Cinema/Seats:	No
Library:	Yes
Onboard currency:	US$

A floating fun palace for ultra-casual family cruising

OVERVIEW. *Carnival Triumph* is a contemporary ship, with extremely short bows (the pointy bit at the front). It is designed specifically for families with children, who will probably not want to leave when the cruise is over.

THE SHIP. The ship underwent quite an extensive facelift in 2013, which added new facilities and eating options.

Outside on Lido Deck, there is one small pool (with adjacent hot tubs – although the whole area is extremely cluttered and congested), and one aft pool (with retractable glass roof for use in poor weather conditions). Note that there are no cushioned pads for the sunloungers, but there is a large poolside movie screen.

Also outside is a 200 ft (60m) -long water slide, which travels from just aft of the ship's mast.

Inside, the decor is quite tasteful, and is themed around great European cities including Rome and Paris. The layout is fairly logical and it's quite easy to find one's way around. There are basically three decks full of bars and lounges to enjoy.

The interior focal point is a main (atrium) lobby, which is nine decks high, and is topped by a glass-domed roof. The lowest deck features a square-shaped bar, facing forward to the glass-walled lifts.

Carnival Triumph is a floating playground for the young and young-at-heart, and anyone who enjoys constant stimulation and participation events, together with the three 'Gs' – glitz, glamour, and gambling. This really is cruising Splash Vegas style – a fun, all-

Berlitz's Ratings

	Possible	Achieved
Ship	500	359
Accommodation	200	144
Food	400	218
Service	400	254
Entertainment	100	76
Cruise Experience	400	251
OVERALL SCORE		
1302 points out of 2000		

American experience. Because it's a large resort ship, expect lines for the likes of shore excursions, security control when re-boarding, and disembarkation, plus sign-up sheets for fitness equipment. Getting away from people and noise is difficult.

FAMILIES. Youngsters have their own play areas, with children's programs divided into five age-specific groups under Camp Ocean (ages 2–11 – with children ages 2–5 called 'Penguins'; 6–8-year-olds called 'Sting Rays'; and 9–11-year-olds called 'Sharks'). Tweens have 'Circle C', while teenagers have their own 'Club O2' – a chill-out (no adults allowed) room/disco. Also, soft-drinks packages can be purchased for children (and adults).

By the end of 2015, the world of Dr. Seuss was rolled out as part of the line's children's program – from 'green eggs and ham' for breakfast, served by waiters in Dr. Seuss-inspired uniforms, and characters such as the Cat in the Hat, Thing One and Thing Two, and Sam attending, to special showings of movies such as *The Cat in the Hat* and *How the Grinch Stole Christmas* (shown on the poolside Seaside Theater screen on Lido Deck).

ACCOMMODATION. There are numerous price categories, depending on the grade, location and size you choose. Over half of all cabins are outside and, at 225 sq ft/21 sq m, are among the largest in the standard market. They are spread over four decks and have private balconies extending from the ship's side; these have glass rather than steel balustrades for unobstructed ocean views, as well as bright fluorescent lighting. The standard cabins are of good size and have all the basics, although the furniture is angular, with no rounded edges. Three decks of cabins – eight per deck, each with private balcony – overlook the stern.

Many cabins have upper and lower bunk beds – good for families with small children. The cabins have a light color scheme. Interactive 'Fun Vision' technology includes movies on demand, for a fee. The bathrooms, which have good-size showers, have good storage space for toiletries.

Book one of the suites, and you get Skipper's Club priority benefits and other little perks.

DINING. There are two main dining rooms, one forward (London) with windows on two sides and 706 seats, and the other (Paris) aft with windows on three sides and 1,090 seats. Each spans two decks, and incorporates a dozen domes and chandeliers. The aft dining room has a two-deck-high wall of glass aft. Tables are for four to eight customers, with even a few tables for two. The dining room entrances have comfortable drinking areas for pre-dinner cocktails.

You can choose either fixed-time dining (6pm or 8.15pm), or flexible dining (any time between 5.45pm and 9.30pm). This gives you very little time to 'dine' – although it should give you some idea of what to expect from your dining experience. Although the menu choice looks good, the actual cuisine delivered is adequate, but quite unmemorable. Note that the two main dining rooms are not open for lunch on port days.

Other dining options. The Steakhouse is a reservations-required extra-cost dining venue (serving prime steaks and grilled seafood). It has fine table settings, china, and silverware, as well as leatherbound menus, and a design theme set around Scarlett O'Hara, the heroine of Margaret Mitchell's classic novel *Gone With the Wind*.

In 2013, the ship underwent an extensive facelift. This included the debut of Guy's Burger Joint (in partnership with Guy Fieri of Food Network) for burgers, hand-cut fries, and assorted toppings. A BlueIguana Cantina also made its debut. New and revamped bars include a poolside RedFrog Rum Bar (where you can also get ThirstyFrog Red – Carnival's private-label draft brew), BlueIguana Tequila Bar (for frozen Mexican-style cocktails and tequila), and a Sports Bar (an interactive venue, which includes video games and a 24/7 sports ticker). For ultra-casual eating, go to the Lido Deck self-serve buffet area. There are several sections (the ship's decor theme is, after all, international) including a deli, and an Asian section. Outside on deck and adjacent is a pizzeria, Guy's Burger Joint, and BlueIguana Cantina. The buffet itself is congested for much of the time, particularly for breakfast (my advice would be to go to one of the main dining rooms for a more relaxed breakfast).

ENTERTAINMENT. The three-level Rome Main Lounge is quite a stunning room, with a revolving stage, hydraulic orchestra pit, good (but loud) sound, and seating on three levels, the upper levels being tiered through two decks. A proscenium over the stage acts as a scenery loft.

SPA/FITNESS. SpaCarnival spans two decks, and is located directly above the navigation bridge in the forward part of the ship; it is accessed from the forward stairway. Facilities on the lower level include a solarium, massage/body treatment rooms, lecture rooms, sauna and steam rooms for men and women, and a beauty parlor; the upper level consists of a large gymnasium with floor-to-ceiling windows on three sides, including forward-facing ocean views, and an aerobics room with instructor-led classes, some at extra cost.

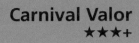

Carnival Valor
★★★+

Size:	Large Resort Ship	Passenger/Crew Ratio (lower beds):	2.3
Tonnage:	110,239	Cabins (total):	1,487
Lifestyle:	Standard	Size Range (sq ft/m):	179.7–482.2/16.7–44.8
Cruise Line:	Carnival Cruise Line	Cabins (for one person):	0
Former Names:	none	Cabins (with private balcony):	574
IMO Number:	9236389	Cabins (wheelchair accessible):	25
Builder:	Fincantieri (Italy)	Wheelchair accessibility:	Good
Original Cost:	$500 million	Cabin Current:	110 volts
Entered Service:	Dec 2004	Elevators:	18
Registry:	Panama	Casino (gaming tables):	Yes
Length (ft/m):	951.4/290.0	Slot Machines:	Yes
Beam (ft/m):	116.0/35.3	Swimming Pools:	3 (1 w/ sliding glass dome)
Draft (ft/m):	27.0/8.2	Hot Tubs (on deck):	7
Propulsion/Propellers:	diesel-electric (34,000kW)/2	Self-Service Launderette:	Yes
Passenger Decks:	13	Dedicated Cinema/Seats:	No
Total Crew:	1,160	Library:	Yes
Passengers (lower beds):	2,974	Onboard currency:	US$
Passenger Space Ratio (lower beds):	37.0		

This floating fun palace is good for the whole family

OVERVIEW. *Carnival Valor* is one of a series of look-alike ships; the others are *Carnival Conquest, Carnival Freedom, Carnival Glory, Carnival Liberty, Carnival Splendor, Carnival Sunshine, Carnival Triumph, Carnival Valor, and Carnival Victory.* It is built to impress.

THE SHIP. A terraced pool deck is cluttered, particularly when the ship is full at sea, and there are no cushioned pads for the deck chairs.

There are three decks full of lounges, 10 bars, and lots of rooms to play in. Inside, the public rooms are given a visual theme, and, on *Carnival Valor*, this is famous personalities, including the dancer and singer Josephine Baker and the aviator Charles Lindbergh. The layout is fairly logical and easy to navigate.

There is a double-width indoor promenade, and an atrium lobby that spans nine decks, topped by a glass dome. Amidships on the open deck is a long water slide. At 200ft (60m) long, it travels from just aft of the ship's mast. Tiered sunbathing decks are positioned between two small swimming pools and several hot tubs.

A square-shaped bar sits on the lowest deck of the atrium, and faces forward towards panoramic glass-walled elevators. A sports bar has tables displaying sports memorabilia.

The ship is a floating playground for the young and young-at-heart, and anyone who enjoys constant stimulation and participation events, together with the three 'Gs' – glitz, glamour, and gambling. This really is cruising Splash Vegas style – a fun, all-Ameri-

Berlitz's Ratings

	Possible	Achieved
Ship	500	359
Accommodation	200	144
Food	400	218
Service	400	254
Entertainment	100	76
Cruise Experience	400	250
OVERALL SCORE		
1301 points out of 2000		

can experience. Because it's a large resort ship, you can expect lines for the likes of shore excursions, security control when re-boarding, and disembarkation, as well as sign-up sheets for fitness equipment.

Forget fashion, a Carnival cruise is all about having fun. While the cuisine is just so-so, the real fun begins at sundown, when Carnival really excels in lights, razzle-dazzle shows, and late-night high volume sounds. Getting away from people and noise is difficult, however.

FAMILIES. Youngsters have their own play areas, with children's programs divided into five age-specific groups under Camp Ocean (ages 2–11 – with children ages 2–5 called 'Penguins'; 6–8-year-olds called 'Sting Rays'; 9–11-year-olds called 'Sharks'). Tweens have 'Circle C'; while teenagers have their own 'Club O2' – a chill-out (no adults allowed) room/disco. Also, soft-drinks packages can be purchased for children (and adults).

By the end of 2015, the world of Dr. Seuss was added as part of the children's program – from 'green eggs and ham' for breakfast, served by waiters in Dr. Seuss-inspired uniforms, and characters such as the Cat in the Hat, Thing One and Thing Two, and Sam attending, to special showings of movies such as *The Cat in the Hat* and *How the Grinch Stole Christmas* (shown on the poolside Seaside Theater screen on Lido Deck).

ACCOMMODATION. There are numerous price categories, depending on grade, location and size.

Over half of all cabins are outside and, at 225 sq ft/21 sq m, are among the largest in the standard market. They are spread over four decks and have private balconies extending from the ship's side; these have glass rather than steel balustrades for unobstructed ocean views, as well as bright fluorescent lighting. The standard cabins are of good size and have all the basics, although the furniture is angular, with no rounded edges. Three decks of cabins – eight per deck, each with private balcony – overlook the stern.

There are eight penthouse suites, each with a large private balcony. Although quite decent in their appointments, at only 483 sq ft (44.8 sq m), they are really quite small when compared to the best suites even in many smaller ships. There are also 40 other suites that are nothing special, although each has a decent-size bathroom and a good amount of lounge space.

In cabins with balconies, the partition between each balcony is open at top and bottom, so you may well hear noise from neighbors. It is disappointing to see three categories of cabins (both outside and interior) with upper and lower bunk beds – lower beds are far more preferable, but this is how the ships absorb hundreds of extra passengers over and above the lower bed capacity.

The cabins have soft color schemes and more soft furnishings in more attractive fabrics than other ships in the fleet. Interactive 'Fun Vision' technology lets you choose movies on demand, for a fee. The bathrooms, which have good-size showers, have good storage space for toiletries. All grades get a gift basket of toiletry samples.

Book one of the suites, and you get Skipper's Club priority check-in at any US homeland port.

DINING. The ship has two main dining rooms, one forward (Lincoln) with windows on two sides and 706 seats, and the other (Washington) aft with windows on three sides and 1,090 seats. Each spans two decks, and incorporates a dozen domes and chandeliers. Washington has two-deck-high glass walls overlooking the stern. Tables are for four, six, and eight. There are even a few tables for two – good for honeymooners who want to be by themselves.

Choose either fixed-time dining (6pm or 8.15pm), or flexible dining (any time between 5.45pm and 9.30pm). This gives you little time to 'dine' – al-

though perhaps it gives you an idea about what to expect from your dining experience. Although the menu choice looks good, the actual cuisine delivered is quite unmemorable. Note that the two main dining rooms are not open for lunch on port days.

The dining room entrances have comfortable drinking areas for pre-dinner cocktails. There are also many options for casual dining, particularly during the day.

Other dining options. An informal international self-serve buffet-style eatery has seating on two levels. Included in this eatery are a New York-style deli (open 11am–11pm), a Chinese restaurant with wok preparation, and a 24-hour pizzeria, which typically serves an average of more than 800 pizzas every day.

At night, the Seaview Bistro provides a casual alternative to the main dining rooms, serving pasta, steaks, salads, and desserts. There is also a barbecue for fast grilled foods such as chicken, hamburgers and hot dogs, and a salad bar. Additionally, there is a self-serve ice cream and frozen yoghurt station, at no extra charge. If you want to eat 24 hours a day, you can.

The Steakhouse is a reservations-only, extra-cost dining spot. It features prime USDA steaks and grilled seafood. The restaurant has fine table settings, china, and silverware, as well as leather-bound menus, and a design theme set around Scarlett O'Hara, the heroine of Margaret Mitchell's classic novel *Gone With the Wind*. It's worth the extra cost, if you like really good steaks.

ENTERTAINMENT. The three-level Ivanhoe showlounge is stunning; it has a revolving stage, hydraulic orchestra pit, superb sound, and seating on three levels, the upper levels being tiered through two decks. A proscenium over the stage acts as a scenery loft.

SPA/FITNESS. SpaCarnival spans two decks, and measures 13,700 sq ft/1,272 sq m. It is located above the navigation bridge, and accessed from the forward stairway. Facilities on the lower level include a solarium, eight treatment rooms, lecture rooms, sauna and steam rooms for men and women, and a beauty parlor; the upper level consists of a large gymnasium with floor-to-ceiling windows on three sides, including forward-facing ocean views, and an aerobics room with instructor-led classes, some at extra cost.

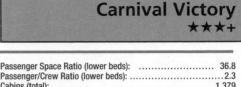

Carnival Victory
★★★+

Size:	Large Resort Ship
Tonnage:	101,509
Lifestyle:	Standard
Cruise Line:	Carnival Cruise Line
Former Names:	none
IMO Number:	9172648
Builder:	Fincantieri (Italy)
Original Cost:	$410 million
Entered Service:	Aug 2000
Registry:	Panama
Length (ft/m):	893.0/272.2
Beam (ft/m):	116.0/35.3
Draft (ft/m):	27.0/8.2
Propulsion/Propellers:	diesel-electric (34,000kW)/ 2 azimuthing pods
Passenger Decks:	13
Total Crew:	1,100
Passengers (lower beds):	2,758

Passenger Space Ratio (lower beds):	36.8
Passenger/Crew Ratio (lower beds):	2.3
Cabins (total):	1,379
Size Range (sq ft/m):	179.7–482.2/16.7–44.8
Cabins (for one person):	0
Cabins (with private balcony):	508
Cabins (wheelchair accessible):	25
Wheelchair accessibility:	Good
Cabin Current:	110 volts
Elevators:	18
Casino (gaming tables):	Yes
Slot Machines:	Yes
Swimming Pools:	3 (1 w/ sliding glass dome)
Hot Tubs (on deck):	7
Self-Service Launderette:	Yes
Dedicated Cinema/Seats:	No
Library:	Yes
Onboard currency:	US$

Fun ship for a family-friendly first cruise adventure

OVERVIEW. *Carnival Victory's sister ships are* Carnival Conquest, *Carnival Freedom,* Carnival Glory, *Carnival Liberty,* Carnival Sunshine *(originally* Carnival Destiny), *Carnival Valor, and* Carnival Victory. The ship has extremely short bows (the front), but still looks balanced overall.

THE SHIP. Amidships on the exterior open deck is a water slide, about 200ft (60m) long; it travels from just aft of the ship's mast. Tiered sunbathing decks are positioned between two small swimming pools and several hot tubs.

The terraced pool deck is cluttered, and there are no cushioned pads for the deck chairs. Although the outdoor deck space has been improved, there is still much crowding when the ship is full and at sea.

Inside, the decor is quite tasteful, with the design in the public rooms themed around the oceans of the world, with seahorses, corals, and shells prominent throughout. The layout is logical and fairly easy to navigate.

There are three decks full of lounges, 10 bars, and lots of rooms to play in. The ship has a double-width indoor promenade, nine decks high, with statues of Neptune at both ends, and a glass-domed rotunda atrium lobby. On the lowest deck of the atrium lobby is a square-shaped bar, which faces forward to glass-walled panorama elevators and sits under a 10-deck-high dome. A sports bar has tables with sports memorabilia.

From a safety viewpoint, passengers can embark directly into the lifeboats from their secured position without having to wait for them to be lowered, thus

Berlitz's Ratings		
	Possible	Achieved
Ship	500	359
Accommodation	200	144
Food	400	218
Service	400	246
Entertainment	100	76
Cruise Experience	400	252
OVERALL SCORE		
1295 points out of 2000		

saving time in the event of a real emergency.

Carnival Victory is a floating playground for the young and young-at-heart, and those who enjoy constant stimulation and lots of participation events, together with the three 'Gs' – glitz, glamour, and gambling. This is cruising Splash Vegas style – a fun, all-American experience. Niggles include lines for the likes of shore excursions, security control when re-boarding, and disembarkation, and well as for filling in sign-up sheets for fitness equipment.

Forget fashion, this is all about having fun. While the cuisine is just so-so, the real fun begins at sundown when lights, razzle-dazzle shows, and late-night high volume sounds are the norm, and getting away from people and noise is difficult.

FAMILIES. Youngsters have their own play areas, with children's programs divided into five age-specific groups under Camp Ocean (ages 2–11 – with children ages 2–5 called 'Penguins'; 6–8-year-olds called 'Sting Rays'; 9–11-year-olds called 'Sharks'). Tweens have 'Circle C', while teenagers have their own 'Club O2' – a chill-out (no adults allowed) room/disco. Also, soft-drinks packages can be purchased for children (and adults).

By the end of 2015, the world of Dr. Seuss was rolled out as part of the children's program – from 'green eggs and ham' for breakfast, served by waiters in Dr. Seuss-inspired uniforms, and characters such as the Cat in the Hat, Thing One and Thing Two, and

Sam attending, to special showings of movies such as *The Cat in the Hat* and *How the Grinch Stole Christmas* (shown on the poolside Seaside Theater screen on Lido Deck).

ACCOMMODATION. There are a number of different price categories. The price you pay depends on the grade, location and size you choose. Over half of all cabins have outside views and, at 225 sq ft/21 sq m, are quite large. They are spread over four decks and have private balconies extending from the ship's side; these have glass rather than steel balustrades for unobstructed ocean views, as well as bright fluorescent lighting. The standard cabins are of good size and have all the basics, although the furniture is angular, with no rounded edges. Three decks of cabins – eight per deck, each with private balcony – overlook the stern.

Eight penthouse suites each have a large private balcony. Although quite smart in their appointments, at only 483 sq ft (44.8 sq m), they are small when compared to the best suites even in many smaller ships. There are also other suites that are nothing special, although each has a decent-size bathroom and a good amount of lounge space.

In cabins with balconies, the partition between each balcony is open at top and bottom, so you will hear noise from neighbors or smell their cigarettes, if smokers. It is disappointing to see three categories of cabins (both outside and interior) with upper and lower bunk beds – lower beds are more preferable, but this is how the ships absorb hundreds of extra passengers over and above the lower bed capacity.

DINING. The ship has two main dining rooms, the Atlantic – forward – with windows on two sides and 706 seats, and the Pacific – aft – with windows on three sides and 1,090 seats. Each spans two decks, and incorporates a dozen domes and chandeliers. Tables are for four to eight, and even a few tables for two (good for romantic couples). The dining room entrances have comfortable drinking areas for pre-dinner cocktails.

Choose either fixed-time dining (6pm or 8.15pm) or flexible dining (any time between 5.45 and 9.30pm. This gives you little time to 'dine' – although it should give you some idea of what to expect from your dining experience. Although the menu choice looks good, the actual cuisine delivered is adequate, but quite unmemorable. Note that the two main dining rooms are not open for lunch on port days.

Other dining options. An informal 'international' self-serve buffet-style eatery (the rather fancily named Mediterranean Lido Restaurant) has seating on two levels. Included in this eatery are a New York-style deli, a Yangtze Wok (for wok stir-fry preparation), an East Close deli, a Mississippi BBQ, and a 24-hour pizzeria (Pizzeria Arno), which typically serves an average of more than 800 pizzas every day. The restaurant is open at night for casual eats. A Sushi Bar (on Promendade Deck) is close to Coral Seas Café and South China Sea Club Casino.

The one reservations-only, extra-cost dining spot is The Steakhouse. It features prime USDA steaks and grilled seafood items (it's worth paying the extra cost). It has fine table settings, china, and silverware, as well as leather-bound menus, and a design theme set around Scarlett O'Hara, the heroine of Margaret Mitchell's classic novel *Gone With the Wind*.

ENTERTAINMENT. The three-level Caribbean Main Lounge, the showlounge, is a stunning room, with a revolving stage, hydraulic orchestra pit, superb sound, and seating on three levels, the upper levels being tiered through two decks. A proscenium over the stage acts as a scenery loft. Other entertainment spots include the Club Arctic (disco), Adriatic Aft Lounge, and the Irish Sea Piano Bar.

SPA/FITNESS. SpaCarnival spans two decks, with a total area of 13,700 sq ft/1,272 sq m, and is located directly above the navigation bridge in the forward part of the ship and accessed from the forward stairway. Facilities on the lower level include a solarium, body treatment rooms, sauna and steam rooms for men and women, and a beauty parlor; the upper level consists of a large gymnasium with floor-to-ceiling windows on three sides, including forward-facing ocean views, and an aerobics room with instructor-led classes, some at extra cost.

Carnival Vista
NYR

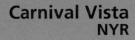

Size:	Large Resort Ship	Passenger/Crew Ratio (lower beds):	2.7
Tonnage:	135,000	Cabins (total):	2,000
Lifestyle:	Standard	Size Range (sq ft/m):	161.4-344.4/15.0-32.0
Cruise Line:	Carnival Cruise Line	Cabins (for one person):	0
Former Names:	none	Cabins (with private balcony):	887
IMO Number:	9614141	Cabins (wheelchair accessible):	25
Builder:	Meyer Werft (Germany)	Wheelchair accessibility:	Good
Original Cost:	$780 million	Cabin Current:	110 volts
Entered Service:	May 2016	Elevators:	16
Registry:	Panama	Casino (gaming tables):	Yes
Length (ft/m):	1,054.7/321.5	Slot Machines:	Yes
Beam (ft/m):	101.7/31.0	Swimming Pools:	3
Draft (ft/m):	27.0/8.2	Hot Tubs (on deck):	6
Propulsion/Propellers:	diesel-electric/2 azimuthing pods	Self-Service Launderette:	No
Passenger Decks:	15	Dedicated Cinema/Seats:	No
Total Crew:	1,450	Library:	Yes
Passengers (lower beds):	4,000	Onboard currency:	US$
Passenger Space Ratio (lower beds):	33.7		

A ship for family fun and cardio-active outdoor facilities

OVERVIEW. There's more connection to the ocean than aboard previous Carnival ships – this is essentially a vessel built around its Waterworks aqua park – plus it has numerous other sporting attractions to keep you occupied. Carnival Vista is all about the fun of the fair at sea.

THE SHIP. Although the ship's design itself is quite old – based mostly on *Carnival Destiny* of 1996, the (*Carnival Breeze*-plus) ship is evolutionary in that it provides an array of activity-fuelled fun for the family.

So, it's time to get on your bike to pedal the suspended track of Sky Ride – maybe cycle yourself to the next port! Other attractions include the large WaterWorks aqua park, which includes Kaleid-O-Slide, a twisting, turning waterslide adventure with kaleidoscopic effects.

Considering the number of passengers carried, the swimming pools are small, and open deck space is limited because of all the activity features crammed in. The general open deck space is nowhere near large enough for the number of passengers.

The ship has a full walk-around open promenade deck lined with deck chairs. Also at the aft, two 'scenic whirlpools' are cantilevered over the water (as part of the Havana Outside area), with fine sea views.

Inside, facilities include an IMAX Theater (for blockbuster movies and documentary content), a large Vista Casino (adjacent to the atrium), a Thrill Theater (for a 4-D moving experience), and many oth-

Berlitz's Ratings

	Possible	Achieved
Ship	500	NYR
Accommodation	200	NYR
Food	400	NYR
Service	400	NYR
Entertainment	100	NYR
Cruise Experience	400	NYR
OVERALL SCORE		
NYR points out of 2000		

er lounges and bars, although the ship's layout is a little disjointed.

The main social center of the ship is the atrium, with large LED screens to provide mood-changing backdrops. Counters for guest services and shore excursions are just off the atrium, while aft of the lobby is the Reflections Dining Room.

Many of the public rooms, lounges, bars, and nightspots are located on two main public room/entertainment decks. These can be accessed via an 11-deck-high atrium lobby, with a cantilevered bandstand atop a massive dance floor on the ground level.

The myriad bars include a sports bar, a trendy Havana Bar, Alchemy Bar (for 'mixologist' cocktails, and a RedFrog Pub (with Carnival's own brew the ThirstyFrog Red).

An adults-only (extra-cost) Serenity area atop the ship at the front provides a beach-like escape from the noisy family-filled decks below, with hot tubs, sunloungers, a bar, and other 'take a break' facilities, including massage 'huts.'

Families with children are well catered for, not only with hyper-activity sporty areas outdoors, but also play rooms for kids and teens (in several different locations), and plenty of youth counselors to take charge, so parents and carers can get some 'me' time, too.

What Carnival does well is to provide lots of almost non-stop excitement, and entertainment fun, and this ship provides the right setting for it all. While the cuisine is just so-so, the real fun will begin at sundown, when the entertainment kicks in.

FAMILIES. Youngsters have their own play areas, with children's programs divided into five age-specific groups under Camp Ocean (ages 2–11, with children aged 2–5 called 'Penguins', 6–8-year-olds called 'Sting Rays', and 9–11-year-olds called 'Sharks'). Tweens have 'Circle C', while teenagers have their own 'Club O2' – a chill-out (no adults allowed) room/disco. Also, soft-drinks packages can be purchased for children (and adults).

Kids also get their own restaurant towards the top of the atrium. Carnival WaterWorks, the expansive aqua park, offering exhilarating multi-deck tunnel water slides and various water spray apparatus, is a huge hit with the kids.

Dr. Seuss is also on board as part of the children's program, including a 'green eggs and ham' for breakfast, served by waiters in Dr. Seuss-inspired uniforms, and characters such as the Cat in the Hat, Thing One and Thing Two, and Sam attending. Movies such as *The Cat in the Hat* and *How the Grinch Stole Christmas* are also shown outdoors on the poolside Seaside Theater screen on Lido Deck.

ACCOMMODATION. The range of cabin sizes, locations, grades and prices includes 'Family Harbor' – family cabins that can sleep up to five. Whether you go for high end or low end, all include plush mattresses, good-quality duvets, linens, pillows, and tropical decor (even cabin doors have cabana-style slats to get the mood going). The suites are not large, although they are laid out in a practical manner, while some of the standard cabins are fine for two but become crowded for three or more.

All cabins have spy-hole doors, twin beds that can convert into queen-size beds, individually controlled air conditioning, TV set, and telephone. Some cabins can accommodate a third and fourth person, but have little closet space, and there's only one personal safe. A number of cabins on Deck 3 have views that are obstructed by lifeboats.

Among the most desirable suites and cabins are those on five of the aft-facing decks; these have private balconies overlooking the stern and ship's wash. You might think that these units would suffer from vibration, but they don't – a bonus provided by the pod propulsion system.

CUISINE. There are more restaurant and eatery choices than on any other Carnival ship – so you'll never go hungry. The two main dining rooms – Horizons and Reflections – are for served meals (breakfast, lunch and dinner) in two seatings. Horizons Restaurant includes some tables at the stern with fine views (on both main and balcony levels – although the upper level has a low ceiling height), plus a bar – a good meeting place for pre-dinner cocktails. You can (at extra cost) also have selections from the steakhouse menu.

Lido Marketplace is the self-serve, buffet-style casual restaurant, while close by are other laid-back (free) eateries, including the popular Guy's Burger Joint, BlueIguana Cantina, and Pizzeria del Capitano (where you can 'toss it, stretch it and cheese it – according to Carnival). There's also Fat Jimmy's C-Side BBQ – oh, and you can get some light bites at The Taste Bar, hot dogs at SeaDogs in SportSquare, sandwiches at the Carnival Deli, and frozen yoghurt at Swirls.

Other dining spots include Farhenheit 555, an extra-cost all-American steakhouse (for prime meats and grilled seafood), Bonsai Sushi Restaurant, for (extra-cost) Japanese-style cuisine (both with indoor and outdoor seating), and Seafood Shack, a New England-style indoor-outdoor eatery for steamed lobster, crab cakes, and fried shrimp. Plus there's Cucina del Capitano (for Italian-style cuisine), and Ji-Ji Asian Kitchen (for Asian fusion cuisine), both on the upper level of Lido Marketplace. Families with youngsters might like to indulge in a Green Eggs and Ham breakfast, while Chef's Table (for foodies) includes a little show business from the chef for a small number of diners (at extra cost).

ENTERTAINMENT. Liquid Lounge is the ship's showlounge; it spans two decks and is the venue for Carnival's Vegas-style feather and skin production shows and 'A'-list cabaret acts.

A second entertainment lounge is the Limelight Lounge (for adult comedy), while a Piano Bar offers lighter fare.

The IMAX Theater has a three-deck high screen, while adjacent is a multi-dimensional, special-effects experience in the Thrill Theater. Both are located on the interior of the forward section of Upper Promenade Deck. Extra-cost popcorn and movie snacks are available, of course. Next door is a video arcade.

SPA/FITNESS. The Cloud 9 Spa is on two levels, with treatment rooms, men's and women's infrared saunas and hamam (slow steam and mud room – good for couples), relaxation lounger, fitness center, and 'pay more' thermal suites, plus a VIP treatment room for Spa Suite occupants.

Activity/sports facilities include an outdoor Sky-Course suspended ropes course (always fun on a moving ship), Sky Gardens mini-golf course, and a Skycourt (for baseball). The Clubhouse at SportSquare includes mini-bowling, ping-pong, arcade basketball, and video games.

Celebrity Constellation
★★★★

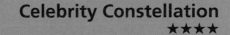

Size:	Large Resort Ship
Tonnage:	90,940
Lifestyle:	Premium
Cruise Line:	Celebrity Cruises
Former Names:	*Constellation*
IMO Number:	9192399
Builder:	Chantiers de l'Atlantique (France)
Original Cost:	$350 million
Entered Service:	May 2002
Registry:	Malta
Length (ft/m):	964.5/294.0
Beam (ft/m):	105.6/32.2
Draft (ft/m):	26.2/8.0
Propulsion/Propellers:	gas turbine/2 azimuthing pods
Passenger Decks:	11
Total Crew:	999
Passengers (lower beds):	2,170
Passenger Space Ratio (lower beds):	44.6

Passenger/Crew Ratio (lower beds):	2.0
Cabins (total):	1,085
Size Range (sq ft/m):	165.1–2,530.0/15.34–235.0
Cabins (for one person):	0
Cabins (with private balcony):	569
Cabins (wheelchair accessible):	26
Wheelchair accessibility:	Best
Cabin Current:	110 and 220 volts
Elevators:	12
Casino (gaming tables):	Yes
Slot Machines:	Yes
Swimming Pools:	3 (1 w/ sliding glass dome)
Hot Tubs (on deck):	4
Self-Service Launderette:	No
Dedicated Cinema/Seats:	Yes/368
Library:	Yes
Onboard currency:	US$

Understated decor provides a stylish setting for families

OVERVIEW. A cruise aboard a large resort ship provides a wide range of choices and possibilities. Travel in one of the suites, and the benefits include the best personal service levels. One thing really is certain: this relatively hassle-free environment is hard to beat no matter how much or how little you pay.

THE SHIP. *Celebrity Constellation* is a sister ship to *Celebrity Infinity*, *Celebrity Millennium*, and *Celebrity Summit*, the line's *Millennium*-class ships.

Unfortunately, there is no walk-around wooden promenade deck outdoors. Inside, the ship has an understated elegance, with the same high-class decor and materials – including lots of wood, glass, and marble – and public rooms that have made other ships in the fleet so popular. The atrium, with a separately enclosed room for shore excursions, is four decks high and houses the reception desk, tour operator's desk, and bank. Four glass-walled elevators travel through 10 passenger decks, including the tender stations – a nice ride.

New AquaClass veranda staterooms and Blu, a Mediterranean-themed specialty restaurant exclusively for AquaClass passengers, were added in a 'Solsticizing' of the ship in 2013. Also added were a Celebrity iLounge (for the latest Apple products, computer classes, and Internet connection), a Martini Bar with frosted countertop, a delightful Cellar-Masters wine bar (good for wine-tasting), QSine (an extra-cost fine dining venue with iPad menus), and a Bistro on Five (a crêperie).

Berlitz's Ratings		
	Possible	Achieved
Ship	500	387
Accommodation	200	160
Food	400	285
Service	400	298
Entertainment	100	74
Cruise Experience	400	287
OVERALL SCORE		
1491 points out of 2000		

FAMILIES. Families with children will appreciate the Fun Factory (for children) and The Tower (for teenagers). Children's counselors and youth activities staff provide a wide range of supervised activities.

ACCOMMODATION. There are many price grades from which to choose, depending on your preference for the size and location. Almost half of the ship's accommodation features a 'private' balcony. The cabins are extremely comfortable, regardless of which grade you choose. If you choose a balcony cabin on one of the upper decks, note that could be shaded under the pool deck, which extends over the ship's side.

Penthouse Suites (2). These, on Penthouse Deck, each occupy one half of the beam (width) of the ship, overlooking the stern. Each measures a huge 2,530 sq ft (235 sq m), with 1,431.6 sq ft (133 sq m) of living space, plus a huge wraparound terrace measuring 1,098 sq ft (102 sq m) with 180-degree views, a wet bar, hot tub, and whirlpool tub – but much of it can be overlooked by anyone on the decks above. Features include a marble foyer, separate living room (with ebony baby grand piano and formal dining room), master bedroom with walk-in closet, dressing room with vanity desk, exercise equipment, marble-clad bathroom with twin washbasins, whirlpool tub, separate shower, toilet and bidet areas, flat-screen infotainment systems electronically controlled drapes, and a butler's pantry (with separate entry door). An interconnecting door can be opened into the adjacent suite (useful for multi-generation families).

Royal Suites. These measure 733 sq ft (68 sq m) and are located towards the aft. Each has a living room with dining and lounge areas, a separate bedroom, and a large walk-in closet with vanity desk. The marble-clad bathroom has a whirlpool bathtub with integral shower, and separate shower enclosure, two washbasins, and toilet. The teakwood-decked balcony is large enough for on-deck massage and also has a hot tub.

Celebrity Suites. Each measures 467 sq ft (44 sq m) and has floor-to-ceiling windows, a separate living room with dining and lounge areas, two flat-screen infotainment systems, and a walk-in closet with vanity desk. The marble-clad bathroom has a whirlpool tub with integral shower (a window with movable blinds lets you look out through the lounge to the large ocean-view windows). Interconnecting doors allow two suites to be used as a family unit (there is no balcony). The suites are located opposite a group of glass-walled lifts and provide stunning ocean views from the glass-walled sitting/dining area, which extends out from the ship's side.

Sky Suites. Each measures 308 sq ft (28.6 sq m), including a private balcony (some balconies are larger than others, depending on the location). Although designated as suites, they are just larger cabins with a marble-clad bathroom and bathtub/shower combination. They have a larger lounge area (than standard cabins) and sleeping area.

Concierge Class. Positioned between the top-grade suites and standard cabin grades, you get priority embarkation, disembarkation, tender tickets, specialty dining, spa reservations, double bed overlay (no more 'falling between the cracks' for couples), throw pillows on sofas, fruit basket, binoculars, golf umbrella, leather telephone notepad, larger beach towels, and hand-held hairdryer. In the bathrooms: plush Frette bathrobes, large towels, and a flower in a silver vase. It adds up to fine value for money for anyone who appreciates the little extras.

AquaClass. 'AquaClass' occupants get spa-healthy dining in the exclusive Blu restaurant, and complimentary access to the Persian Garden (thermal suite) and Relaxation Room in the spa, plus daily delivery of bottled water and herbal teas (infusions), and some spa-related personal amenities.

Standard outside-view/interior (no-view) cabins. Facilities include a sitting area with sofa or convertible sofa bed, sleeping area with twin beds that convert to a double bed, good closet and drawer space, personal safe, minibar/refrigerator (extra cost), interactive television, and bathroom with a decent-sized shower enclosure. There is none of the boxy feel of cabins in many ships, due to the angled placement of vanity and infotainment consoles.

Wheelchair-accessible suites/cabins. Wheelchair accessibility is provided in several grades. They are located close to elevators for good accessibility – all have wheelchair-accessible doorways and showers. Some cabins have extra berths for up to four.

DINING. The 1,198-seat San Marco Restaurant is the main dining room. Two decks high, with a grand connecting staircase (a musicians' gallery is on the upper level), and a huge glass wall overlooks the sea aft (electrically operated blinds provide several different backdrops). There are two seatings for dinner (with open seating for breakfast and lunch), at tables for two–10. The dining room, like all large dining halls, can be extremely noisy.

The menu variety is good, and the food is tasty and attractively presented and served in a well-orchestrated operation with European traditions and training. In-cabin dining is also available for all meals, including dinner.

Suite occupants can dine in the exclusive setting of 'Luminae', which features tableside preparation of signature dishes, an eclectic menu, and a selection of over 400 wines.

Blu, located on the port side on upper level entrance of the San Marco dining room, is provided exclusively for occupants of AquaClass accommodation.

Other dining options. Ocean Liners Restaurant is a reservations-required, extra-cost venue; it is adjacent to the main lobby. The decor includes some lacquered paneling from the famed 1920s French ocean liner *Ile de France*. Tableside preparation and classic French cuisine are featured. This is a room that is not merely for dinner, and features the French culinary arts of découpage and flambé. However, there are just 115 seats, so it's best to make reservations as soon as possible. A wine cellar houses more than 200 labels from around the world.

QSine, with menus and wine list on iPads, is another extra-cost, fine-dining venue. Reservations are required (the food is funky and tasty, and it comes in small bite-sized portions).

The Seaside Café & Grill is a casual self-serve buffet area, with six principal serving lines, and around 750 seats, grill and pizza bar. Each evening, casual meals feature tablecloths and a modicum of service. Reservations are needed, although there's no additional charge.

Café al Bacio and Gelateria is located on the uppermost (third) level of the atrium lobby, it's the place to see and be seen, for (extra-cost) coffees, pastries, cakes, and ice creams, in a trendy setting.

ENTERTAINMENT. The 900-seat Celebrity Theater is the venue for the ship's production shows and major cabaret acts. Spanning three decks, it is located in the forward part of the ship, with seating on the main level and two balcony levels.

SPA/FITNESS. A large SpaClub measures 24,219 sq ft (2,250 sq m) and is operated by Canyon Ranch.

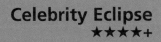

Celebrity Eclipse
★★★★+

Size:	Large Resort Ship	Passenger/Crew Ratio (lower beds):	2.3
Tonnage:	121,878	Cabins (total):	1,426
Lifestyle:	Premium	Size Range (sq ft/m):	182.9–1,668.4/17.0–155.0
Cruise Line:	Celebrity Cruises	Cabins (for one person):	0
Former Names:	none	Cabins (with private balcony):	1,216
IMO Number:	9404314	Cabins (wheelchair accessible):	30
Builder:	Meyer Werft (Germany)	Wheelchair accessibility:	Best
Original Cost:	$641 million	Cabin Current:	110 and 220 volts
Entered Service:	Jun 2010	Elevators:	12
Registry:	Malta	Casino (gaming tables):	Yes
Length (ft/m):	1,033.4/315.0	Slot Machines:	Yes
Beam (ft/m):	120.7/36.8	Swimming Pools:	3
Draft (ft/m):	27.2/8.3	Hot Tubs (on deck):	6
Propulsion/Propellers:	diesel (67,200kW)/2 azimuthing pods	Self-Service Launderette:	No
Passenger Decks:	14	Dedicated Cinema/Seats:	No
Total Crew:	1,210	Library:	Yes
Passengers (lower beds):	2,852	Onboard currency:	US$
Passenger Space Ratio (lower beds):	42.7		

A large, stylish, premium ship for family-friendly cruising

OVERVIEW. This slimline ship is a sister to *Celebrity Equinox* (2009), *Celebrity Reflection* (2012), *Celebrity Silhouette* (2011), and *Celebrity Solstice* (2008).

THE SHIP. *Celebrity Eclipse* has a steeply raked stern, which includes a mega-yacht-style ducktail platform above the ship's propulsion pods; it is attractive, and nicely balances the ship's contemporary profile.

Behind the two smallish funnels is a real grass outdoor area, the Lawn Club. This is the authentic stuff – not green fake turf – and it seems to like the salty air. The club is open to all, so you can putt, play croquet or bocce ball (like bowling or French boules), picnic on the grass, or perhaps sleep on it. Several pool and water-play areas are found on Resort Deck: one in a glass-roofed solarium, a sports pool, a family pool, and a wet zone. The deck space around the two pools, however, isn't large enough for the number of passengers carried.

The interior spaces are well designed, with most of the entertainment rooms positioned forward, and dining venues located in the aft section. There's a wine bar with a sommelier; a cocktail lounge that reflects the jazz age of the 1930s and '40s; a bar with the look of an ocean-going yacht; Quasar, a bar with designs from the 1960s and '70s and large screens that create a nightly light show synchronized to music; and an observation lounge with a dance floor.

Celebrity's signature Martini Bar, with its frosted bar and more than 100 varieties of vodka as well as martinis, has a small alcove called Crush with an ice-

Berlitz's Ratings		
	Possible	Achieved
Ship	500	413
Accommodation	200	165
Food	400	295
Service	400	306
Entertainment	100	77
Cruise Experience	400	297
OVERALL SCORE		
1553 points out of 2000		

filled table where you can participate in caviar and vodka tasting, or host a private party. It's noisy and congested.

An innovative Hot Glass Show, housed in an outdoor studio on the open deck as part of the Lawn Club and created in collaboration with Corning Museum of Glass, includes demonstrations and a narrated performance of glass-blowing. Resident glass-blowing artists also host workshops.

An Apple 'iLounge' is equipped with 26 Apple MacBook Pro work stations (you can also buy Apple products). Also, the elevator call buttons are located in a floor-stand 'pod' and, when the elevator arrives, a glass panel above it turns from blue to pink.

Gratuities are automatically charged to your onboard account.

FAMILIES. Play areas include the Fun Factory (for 3–12-year-olds, featuring Leapfrog Schoolhouse's educational programs); and 'X Club' – a high-tech teens-only chill-out room with coffee bar and a night-time dance club.

ACCOMMODATION. From suite-grade Penthouse Suites to non-suite-grade interior cabins, the accommodation is both practical and comfortable. There are numerous price grades, depending on size and location. In non-suite-grade cabins there is little space between the bed and the wall, and usable drawer space is limited. So, if your budget allows, book a suite-category cabin for all the extra benefits – and a lot more drawer space.

About 90 percent of cabins have an outside view, and many have a balcony. Due to the ship's pencil-slim width, there are few interior cabins. The suite-grade categories are: Royal Suite, Celebrity Suite, Sky Suite, and Penthouse Suite.

All accommodation grades include: twin beds convertible to a queen- or king-size bed, sitting area, vanity desk with hairdryer, but there's almost no drawer space. Also standard in all cabins: 32-ins flat-screen TVs (larger in suites), Wi-Fi Internet access (for a fee), and premium bedding. Although the closets have good hanging space, other storage space is limited. Bathrooms have a shower enclosure, toilet, and tiny washbasin. Suites have more space, plus larger balconies with good-quality sunloungers, and more personal amenities.

AquaSpa cabins incorporate select spa elements into the cabins, and allow for specialized access to the AquaSpa's Thermal Relaxation Room and Persian Garden (with aromatherapy/steam rooms) on the same deck. Features include: a choice of four pillows (conformance, body, goose, Isotonic); express luggage delivery; shoeshine; Frette bathrobes; dining and seating preferences in specialty dining venues; and early embarkation and disembarkation. Bathrooms have a decent amount of space, and a large shower enclosure. Occupants also get assigned seating at the exclusive 130-seat Restaurant Blu.

Other accommodation grades are named Veranda Class, Sunset Veranda Class, Concierge Class, Family Ocean View with veranda, Deluxe Ocean View with veranda, Standard Ocean View, and Standard Interior cabins.

Cabins 1551–1597 on the port side and 1556–1602 on the starboard side on Penthouse Deck (Deck 11) suffer from 'aircraft carrier' syndrome because they are directly under the huge overhanging Resort Deck. They have little exposure to sun or light, so sunbathing is out of the question. Many thick supporting struts ruin the view from these cabins, which are otherwise pleasant enough.

DINING. Moonlight Sonata is the 1,430-seat two-deck main dining room (included in the cruise price). It has ocean views on the port and starboard sides, and to the stern (aft). The design is stunning and contemporary. At the forward end, a two-deck-high wine tower provides an eye-catching focal point.

Suite occupants can dine in the exclusive setting of 'Luminae,' which features tableside preparation of signature dishes, an eclectic menu, and a selection of over 400 wines.

Blu is a 130-seat specialty restaurant just for the occupants of AquaClass cabins. The room has a pleasing, but rather cool, blue decor.

Other dining options. The following dining spots provide an alternative to the main dining room, good for special occasions or just for something different.

Murano is an extra-cost, reservations-required venue offering high-quality traditional dining with a French flair and exquisite table settings, including large Reidel wine glasses. Food and service are very good.

The Tuscan Grille, an extra-cost venue, serves Kobe beef and premium-quality steaks, and has beautifully curved archways – it's like walking into a high-tech winery. There are great views from huge aft-view windows.

Qsine is an extra-cost, 90-seat reservations-required, tablecloth-less 'fun-food' restaurant, with trendy interactive iPad food and wine menus that include cute foodie video snaps. The food consists of multi-flavored, multi-colored, quirky small-bite items that provide you with a selection to tease your taste buds. The food is presented in many unusual ways – even on sticks. It's a delightful experience that I can recommend.

For snacks and less ambitious meals, the options are:

Bistro on Five (Deck 5, that is) for coffee, cakes, crêpes, pastries, and more. It gets busy at times, and the serving counter is small, so it's a congested area.

Café al Bacio & Gelateria, a coffeehouse serving Lavazza Italian coffee. It is on one side of the main lobby, but it's small and lines quickly form at peak times. The seating is mostly in large, very comfortable armchairs.

Oceanview Café and Grill, a large, tray-free, casual self-serve buffet venue, which includes a number of food 'islands,' and good signage. However, it's impossible to get a warm plate for so-called hot food items.

The AquaSpa Café for light, healthier options (solarium fare), but the selections are not exactly thrilling.

The Mast Bar Grill and Bar, an outside venue offering fast food.

ENTERTAINMENT. The 1,115-seat Eclipse Theater (the main showlounge) stages three circus-themed production shows featuring in-your-face, formulaic acrobatics.

Colorful theme nights are held in the Observation Lounge (whose bland daytime decor comes alive at night thanks to mood lighting effects). The 200-seat Celebrity Central, hosts stand-up comedy, cooking demonstrations, enrichment lectures, and feature films. Quasar is a high-volume nightclub.

An Entertainment Court showcases street performers, psychics, and caricaturists, and is in the center of the ship. There's also a big-band-era cocktail lounge with live jazz-styled music, set adjacent to the Murano, the specialty restaurant.

SPA/FITNESS. The Canyon Ranch SpaClub is laid out over two decks. A large fitness center includes kinesis (pulleys against gravity) workout equipment, plus all the familiar gym machinery.

An extra-cost, unisex thermal suite features several steam and shower mist rooms and a glacial ice fountain, plus a calming relaxation area with heated tiled beds, and an acupuncture center.

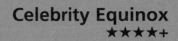

Celebrity Equinox
★★★★+

Size:	Large Resort Ship
Tonnage:	122,000
Lifestyle:	Premium
Cruise Line:	Celebrity Cruises
Former Names:	none
IMO Number:	9372456
Builder:	Meyer Werft (Germany)
Original Cost:	$641 million
Entered Service:	Aug 2009
Registry:	Malta
Length (ft/m):	1,033.4/315.0
Beam (ft/m):	120.7/36.8
Draft (ft/m):	27.2/8.3
Propulsion/Propellers:	diesel (67,200kW)/2 azimuthing pods
Passenger Decks:	14
Total Crew:	1,210
Passengers (lower beds):	2,852
Passenger Space Ratio (lower beds):	42.7
Passenger/Crew Ratio (lower beds):	2.3
Cabins (total):	1,426
Size Range (sq ft/m):	182.9–1,668.4/17.0–155.0
Cabins (for one person):	0
Cabins (with private balcony):	1,216
Cabins (wheelchair accessible):	30
Wheelchair accessibility:	Best
Cabin Current:	110 and 220 volts
Elevators:	12
Casino (gaming tables):	Yes
Slot Machines:	Yes
Swimming Pools:	3
Hot Tubs (on deck):	6
Self-Service Launderette:	No
Dedicated Cinema/Seats:	No
Library:	Yes
Onboard currency:	US$

This large ship has contemporary style, for the well traveled

OVERVIEW. This is a sister ship to *Celebrity Eclipse*, *Celebrity Reflection*, *Celebrity Silhouette*, and *Celebrity Solstice*. The steeply sloping stern, with its mega-yacht-style ducktail platform above the propulsion pods, is very attractive, and nicely balances the ship's contemporary profile. The bows are rounded to accommodate a helipad.

THE SHIP. Two rather slim funnels, set one behind the other, distinguish *Celebrity Equinox* from previous single-funnel Celebrity ships. Between the two funnels is a grass outdoor area, the Lawn Club. This grass is real, and seems to like the salty air. The Lawn Club is open to all, so you can go putting, play croquet or bocce ball (like bowling or boules), or have a picnic on the grass.

There are several pool and water-play areas on Resort Deck: one in a solarium (with glass roof), a sports pool, a family pool, and a wet zone. However, the deck space around the two pools is not large enough for the number of passengers carried.

The interior decor is elegant, yet contemporary. Michael's Club is an intimate, quiet lounge with classic English leather chairs, a dramatic black glass chandelier, a grand fireplace, and some contemporary artwork. Rich furnishings help create a warm atmosphere, amidst a backdrop of piano and jazz music, plus single malt Scotch and cognacs for tastings.

Other attractions include a Gastropub; a cocktail lounge with jazz; a bar with the look of an ocean-going yacht; Quasar, a bar with large screens that create a nightly light show synchronized to music; and an ob-

Berlitz's Ratings		
	Possible	Achieved
Ship	500	413
Accommodation	200	165
Food	400	295
Service	400	306
Entertainment	100	77
Cruise Experience	400	297
OVERALL SCORE		
1553 points out of 2000		

servation lounge with dance floor.

Celebrity's signature Martini Bar, which has a frosted bar, includes a small alcove called Crush with an ice-filled table for caviar and vodka tastings.

Fortunes Casino has 16 gaming tables and 200 slot machines. There's a two-deck library, but the books on the upper shelves are impossible to reach. An innovative Hot Glass Show, created in collaboration with Corning Museum of Glass, includes demonstrations and a narrated performance of glass-blowing, housed in an outdoor studio on the open deck as part of the Lawn Club.

Passenger niggles include poor drawer space in cabins; inadequate children's facilities and staff; congestion when you exit the showlounge; and noise in all areas of the lobby when the Martini Bar is busy.

Good points include elevator call buttons located in a floor-stand 'pod'; when an elevator arrives, a glass panel above it turns from blue to pink. Also, the ship has a good collection of designer chairs and sunloungers in various locations.

Gratuities are charged to your onboard account. A refurbishment in 2014 added more branded merchandise for shops, changed Cellar Masters into a Gastrobar featuring more than 40 craft beers and 'comfort food,' and online@Celebrity into the Celebrity iLounge (a swish computer room, equipped with Apple macs).

ACCOMMODATION. From suite-grade Penthouse Suites to non-suite-grade interior cabins, the accommodation is practical and comfortable. There are many price grades, depending on size and location. In standard Interior and Ocean View cabins, there is little space between the bed and the wall, and usable drawer space is poor. So, if your budget allows, book a suite-category cabin for all the extra benefits – and much more drawer space.

About 90 percent of the cabins have an outside view, and many of these have a balcony; due to the ship's pencil-slim width, there are few interior cabins. The suite-grade categories are: Royal Suite, Celebrity Suite, Sky Suite, and Penthouse Suite.

All accommodation grades include: twin beds convertible to a queen-size bed, sitting area, vanity desk with hairdryer, but there's almost no drawer space. Also standard in all cabins: 32-ins flat-screen TVs (larger screens in suites), Wi-Fi Internet access (for a fee), and premium bedding. However, although the closets have good hanging space, other storage space is limited. The bathrooms have a shower enclosure, toilet, and tiny washbasin, although the faucet gets in the way when washing your face or brushing your teeth, there's no retractable clothesline for washed small items, and the two hooks on the back of the bathroom door are tiny. In suite-grade accommodation there is more space, larger balconies with good-quality sunloungers, and more personal amenities.

Some 130 AquaSpa-class cabins incorporate select spa elements into the cabins, and allow for specialized access to the Thermal Relaxation Room and Persian Garden (with aromatherapy/steam rooms) on the same deck. Features include: a choice of four pillows (conformance, body, goose, Isotonic); express luggage delivery; shoeshine; Frette bathrobes; dining and seating preferences in other specialty dining venues; and early embarkation and disembarkation. Bathrooms have a decent amount of space, and a large shower enclosure. Occupants also get assigned seating at the exclusive 130-seat Restaurant Blu.

Other accommodation grades are Veranda Class, Sunset Veranda Class, Concierge Class, Family Ocean View with veranda, Deluxe Ocean View with veranda, Standard Ocean View, and Standard Interior cabins.

Cabins 1551–1597 on the port side and 1556–1602 on the starboard side on Penthouse Deck (Deck 11) suffer from 'aircraft carrier' syndrome because they are directly under the huge overhanging Resort Deck. They have little exposure to sun or light, so private balcony sunbathing is out of the question. Many thick supporting struts ruin the view from these cabins, which are otherwise pleasantly fitted out.

DINING. Silhouette, the ship's balconied main dining room (included in the cruise price), has ocean views on the port and starboard sides. The contemporary design is stunning. At the forward end, a two-deck-high wine tower provides an eye-catching focal point. As for the food, it's a bit of a let down – the decreased quality is all too obvious to repeat Celebrity passengers.

Suite occupants can dine in the exclusive setting of 'Luminae,' which features tableside preparation of signature dishes, an eclectic menu, and a selection of over 400 wines. Blu is a 128-seat specialty restaurant designated just for the occupants of AquaClass cabins. The room has pleasing, but rather cold, blue decor.

Other dining options. Murano is an extra-cost, reservations-required venue offering high-quality traditional dining with a French flair and exquisite table settings, including large Reidel wine glasses. Food and service are very good.

The Tuscan Grille, an extra-cost venue, serves Kobe beef and premium quality steaks, and has beautifully curved archways – it's like walking into a high-tech winery. There are great views from huge aft-view windows.

QSine is an extra-cost, reservations-required quirky fine-dining venue, with iPad menus.

Bistro on Five (Deck 5, that is) is for coffee, cakes, crêpes, pastries, and more. It can get busy at times, and the serving counter is small.

The Café al Bacio & Gelateria coffee lounge serves Lavazza Italian coffee. It is on one side of the main lobby, but it's small and lines form at peak times. The seating is mostly in large, very comfortable armchairs.

Oceanview Café and Grill is the expansive, tray-free, casual self-serve buffet venue. There are a number of food 'islands' rather than those awful straight buffet counters, and good signage. However, it's impossible to get a warm plate for so-called hot food items, and condiments are hard to find.

The AquaSpa Café is for light, healthier options (solarium fare), but the selections are bland and boring.

The Mast Bar Grill and Bar is an outside venue offering fast food.

ENTERTAINMENT. The 1,115-seat Equinox Theater, the ship's showlounge, has a main level and two balconied sections positioned amphitheater-style around a stage with music lofts set on either side. Three circus-themed production shows highlight in-your-face, formulaic acrobatics.

Colorful theme nights are held in the Sky Observation Lounge, where the daytime decor comes alive at night thanks to mood lighting. The 200-seat Celebrity Central hosts comedy, cooking demonstrations, enrichment lectures, and feature films. An Entertainment Court showcases street performers, psychics, and caricaturists, and is in the center of the ship, linked to the Quasar nightclub. The Ensemble Lounge is a big-band-era cocktail lounge with live jazz, next to the Murano restaurant.

SPA/FITNESS. This is a large, two-deck Canyon Ranch SpaClub at Sea. The fitness center includes kinesis (pulleys against gravity) workout equipment, plus cardio-vascular machinery. An extra-cost, unisex thermal suite features steam and shower mist rooms, and a glacial ice fountain, plus a calming relaxation area with heated tiled beds, and an acupuncture center.

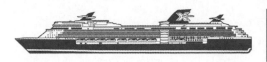

Celebrity Infinity
★★★★

Size:	Large Resort Ship
Tonnage:	90,940
Lifestyle:	Premium
Cruise Line:	Celebrity Cruises
Former Names:	*Infinity*
IMO Number:	9189421
Builder:	Chantiers de l'Atlantique (France)
Original Cost:	$350 million
Entered Service:	Mar 2001
Registry:	Malta
Length (ft/m):	964.5/294.0
Beam (ft/m):	105.6/32.2
Draft (ft/m):	26.2/8.0
Propulsion/Propellers:	gas turbine (39,000kW)/2 azimuthing pods
Passenger Decks:	11
Total Crew:	999
Passengers (lower beds):	2,170
Passenger Space Ratio (lower beds):	41.9

Passenger/Crew Ratio (lower beds):	2.1
Cabins (total):	1,085
Size Range (sq ft/m):	165.1–2,530.0/15.34–235.0
Cabins (for one person):	0
Cabins (with private balcony):	606
Cabins (wheelchair accessible):	26 (17 with private balcony)
Wheelchair accessibility:	Best
Cabin Current:	110 and 220 volts
Elevators:	12
Casino (gaming tables):	Yes
Slot Machines:	Yes
Swimming Pools:	3 (1 w/sliding glass dome)
Hot Tubs (on deck):	4
Self-Service Launderette:	No
Dedicated Cinema/Seats:	Yes/368
Library:	Yes
Onboard currency:	US$

This is a family-friendly, modern resort ship with style

OVERVIEW. The ship provides a wide range of choices and possibilities. Travel in one of the suites and you will receive the highest level of personal service, while cruising in non-suite accommodation is much like any large ship. It all depends how much you are willing (and able) to pay. The two-seating dining and two shows nightly detract from an otherwise excellent product.

THE SHIP. *Celebrity Infinity* is a sister ship to *Celebrity Constellation*, *Celebrity Millennium*, and *Celebrity Summit*. Famous mega-yacht designer Jon Bannenberg created the exterior.

The atrium is the interior focal point; three decks high, it houses the reception desk, tour desk, and bank. Four glass-walled elevators travel through the ship's exterior (port) side, connecting the atrium with another seven decks, thus traveling through 10 passenger decks, including the tender stations – a nice ride.

Michael's Club (which was a cigar smoker's haven, when the ship was new) is now a pleasant, comfortable lounge/piano bar.

Gaming sports include the ship's overly large Fortunes Casino, with blackjack, roulette, and slot machines, and lots of bright lights and action. A 15 percent gratuity is added to bar and wine accounts.

FAMILIES. The Fun Factory is designed for young children and The Tower caters to teenagers. Children's counselors and youth-activities staff provide a wide range of supervised activities.

Berlitz's Ratings

	Possible	Achieved
Ship	500	388
Accommodation	200	160
Food	400	285
Service	400	296
Entertainment	100	74
Cruise Experience	400	286

OVERALL SCORE
1489 points out of 2000

ACCOMMODATION. There are many grades from which to choose, depending on your preference for the size and location of your living space, in either suite-grade or non-suite-grade. Almost half feature a 'private' balcony; approximately 80 percent are ocean-view suites and cabins, and the rest are interior cabins. All the accommodation is extremely comfortable, but suites, naturally, have more space. If you choose a balcony cabin on one of the upper decks, note that it could be shaded under the pool deck, which extends over the ship's side – and by many balconies (so, not good for private sunbathing).

Penthouse Suites (2). These are like apartments. Each occupies one half of the width of the ship at the stern. Each is a huge 2,530 sq ft (235 sq m): 1,432 sq ft (133 sq m) of living space, plus a huge wraparound balcony of 1,098 sq ft (102 sq m), including a wet bar, hot tub, and whirlpool tub; but much of this terrace can be overlooked from other decks above.

Royal Suites (8). Located towards the aft (four each on the port and starboard sides), each measures 733 sq ft (68 sq m) and has a separate living room with dining and lounge areas (with refrigerator, minibar, and Bang & Olufsen audio system) and a bedroom and a large walk-in closet with vanity desk. The marble-clad bathroom has a whirlpool tub with integral shower, and there is also a separate shower enclosure, plus two washbasins, and toilet. The teakwood balcony is extensive – large enough for on-deck massage – and has a hot tub.

Celebrity Suites (8). These measure 467 sq ft (44 sq m) and have floor-to-ceiling windows, a separate living room with dining and lounge areas, two flat-screen infotainment centers and a walk-in closet with vanity desk. The marble-clad bathroom has a whirlpool tub with integral shower; a window with movable shade lets you look out of the bathroom through the lounge to the large ocean-view windows, and balcony.

Sky Suites (30). Each is 308 sq ft (29 sq m), including the private balcony – some balconies may be larger than others, depending on the location. Although these are designated as suites, they are really just larger cabins that have a marble-clad bathroom with tub/shower combination. They have an infotainment system and a larger lounge area and sleeping area than standard cabins.

Butler service. This is provided in all suite-grade accommodation, and includes full breakfast, lunch and dinner service, afternoon tea, evening hors d'oeuvres, complimentary espresso and cappuccino, daily news delivery, and shoeshine.

Concierge Class. Positioned between the top-grade suites and standard cabin grades, this class adds value, as do 'AquaClass' cabins, added in 2012, with perks including spa-healthy dining in the smaller Blu restaurant. Other extras include complimentary access to the thermal suite and relaxation room in the spa, plus bottled water daily and herbal teas (infusions), and spa-related personal amenities.

Enhanced facilities include priority embarkation, disembarkation, tender tickets, specialty dining, and spa reservations. Concierge Class cabin occupants get double bed overlay (no more 'falling between the cracks' for couples); choice of four pillows (goose down, Isotonic, body, conformance); eight-vial flower vase on vanity desk; throw pillows on sofa; fruit basket; binoculars; golf umbrella; leather telephone notepad; larger beach towels; and hand-held hairdryer. The balcony gets better furniture. In the bathrooms: plusher Frette bathrobes; larger towels; and a flower in silver vase. It all adds up to excellent value for money.

Standard outside-view/interior cabins. All other outside-view and interior cabins have a lounge area with sofa or convertible sofa bed, sleeping area with twin beds convertible to a double bed, good closet and drawer space, personal safe, minibar/refrigerator (extra cost), interactive television, and private bathroom.

Wheelchair-accessible accommodation. This is available in various grades and practical locations, close to elevators. Cabin and bathroom doorways and showers are wheelchair-accessible. Some cabins have extra berths for third or third and fourth occupants. There is only one safe for personal belongings, which must be shared.

DINING. The 1,170-seat Thellis Restaurant is the main dining room. It is two decks high; a grand staircase connects the two levels. A huge glass wall overlooks the sea at the stern (electrically operated shades provide several different backdrops), and a musicians' gallery on the upper level. There are two seatings for dinner (open seating for breakfast and lunch), at tables for two–10. The dining room, like all large dining halls, can be extremely noisy. Menu variety is good, the food has taste, and it is attractively presented and served in an orchestrated fashion with European traditions and training. Full service in-cabin dining is also available for all meals, including dinner.

Suite occupants can dine in the exclusive setting of 'Luminae,' which features tableside preparation of signature dishes, an eclectic menu, and a selection of over 400 wines.

Blu, located on the port side of the upper level entrance of The Thellis dining room, is exclusively for the use of occupants of AquaClass accommodation.

Other dining options. The 134-seat United States Restaurant is adjacent to the main lobby. It has the actual glass paneling from the former United States Lines liner *United States*, which in 1952 made the fastest transatlantic crossing by a passenger ship, taking the famed Blue Riband from Cunard's *Queen Mary*.

A team of chefs prepares the cuisine exclusively for this restaurant. Fine French-style tableside preparation is the attraction. This is haute cuisine at the height of professionalism, for this is a room for a full dégustation, and not just for dinner. Reservations are necessary, and a per-person cover charge applies. There's a dine-in wine cellar and a demonstration galley.

QSine, with menus and wine list on iPads, is another extra-cost, fine-dining venue (added in 2011, it replaced the former Conservatory); reservations are required.

Las Olas Café and Grill is a casual self-serve buffet area, with six principal serving lines, and seating for 754; there is also a grill and pizza bar.

For Champagne and caviar lovers, not to mention Martinis, Carlisle's is the place to see and be seen.

Café al Bacio and Gelateria, on the third level of the atrium lobby, is the place to see and be seen, for (extra-cost) coffees, pastries, cakes, and ice creams, in a trendy setting. Bistro on Five is a new crêperie.

ENTERTAINMENT. The 900-seat Celebrity Theater is the venue for production shows and major cabaret acts. Spanning three decks in height, it is located in the forward part of the ship; seating is on main, and two balcony levels, and the large stage has a full fly loft behind its proscenium.

SPA/FITNESS. The Canyon Ranch SpaClub at Sea measures 24,219 sq ft (2,250 sq m). It includes a large thalassotherapy pool under a solarium glass dome, complete with health bar for light breakfast and lunch items and fresh squeezed fruit and vegetable juices.

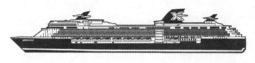

Celebrity Millennium
★★★★

Size:	Large Resort Ship	Passenger/Crew Ratio (lower beds):	2.1
Tonnage:	90,940	Cabins (total):	1,079
Lifestyle:	Premium	Size Range (sq ft/m):	170.0–2,350.0/15.7–235.0
Cruise Line:	Celebrity Cruises	Cabins (for one person):	0
Former Names:	*Millennium*	Cabins (with private balcony):	606
IMO Number:	9189419	Cabins (wheelchair accessible):	26
Builder:	Chantiers de l'Atlantique (France)	Wheelchair accessibility:	Best
Original Cost:	$350 million	Cabin Current:	110 and 220 volts
Entered Service:	Jun 2000	Elevators:	12
Registry:	Malta	Casino (gaming tables):	Yes
Length (ft/m):	964.5/294.0	Slot Machines:	Yes
Beam (ft/m):	105.6/32.2	Swimming Pools:	3 (1 w/ sliding glass dome)
Draft (ft/m):	26.2/8.0	Hot Tubs (on deck):	4
Propulsion/Propellers: gas turbine (39,000kW)/2 azimuthing pods		Self-Service Launderette:	No
Passenger Decks:	11	Dedicated Cinema/Seats:	Yes/368
Total Crew:	999	Library:	Yes
Passengers (lower beds):	2,158	Onboard currency:	US$
Passenger Space Ratio (lower beds):	42.1		

This mid-size, family-friendly ship has a touch of class

OVERVIEW. *Celebrity Millennium* delivers a well-defined North American cruise vacation at a modest price. A zero-announcement policy means there is little intrusion. Although two-seating dining and two nightly shows detract from an otherwise good product, this ship (like sisters *Celebrity Constellation*, *Celebrity Infinity*, and *Celebrity Summit*) provides a 'premium' cruise experience.

THE SHIP. Unfortunately, there is no walk-around wooden promenade deck outdoors. There are cushioned pads for poolside deck lounge chairs only, but not for chairs on other outside decks. Passenger participation activities are mostly amateurish.

Inside, the ship has an understated elegance, with the same high-class decor and materials (lots of wood, glass, and marble) and a four-deck-high atrium. It houses the reception desk, tour operator's desk, and bank. Four glass-walled elevators travel through 10 passenger decks (including the tender stations).

Located directly in front of the main funnel, and with glass walls overlooking the ship's side, is a 70-person-capacity sports bar, Extreme; somehow, however, it just doesn't belong.

Gaming sports include the ship's overly large Fortunes Casino, with blackjack, roulette, and slot machines, bright lights, and action. New AquaClass veranda cabins and Blu, a Mediterranean-themed specialty restaurant exclusively for AquaClass passengers, were added in a 'Solsticizing' of the ship in 2012. Also added were a Celebrity iLounge (for Apple products, computer classes, and Internet connection); a Martini Bar with

Berlitz's Ratings

	Possible	Achieved
Ship	500	388
Accommodation	200	160
Food	400	285
Service	400	298
Entertainment	100	74
Cruise Experience	400	287
OVERALL SCORE		
1492 points out of 2000		

a frosted bar top; a Cellar-Masters wine bar; QSine, an extra-cost fine-dining venue with iPad menus; and a Bistro on Five crêperie.

FAMILIES. The Fun Factory is designed for young children, and The Tower caters to teenagers. Children's counselors and youth activities staff provide a wide range of supervised activities. Interconnecting doors in two Celebrity Suites allow them to be used as one unit; as there is no balcony, they are ideal for those with small children.

ACCOMMODATION. Choose from either suite-grade or non-suite-grade accommodation, depending on your preference for the size and location. Suites, naturally, have more space, butler service, and more amenities. If you can afford it, book a suite-category cabin for its many extra benefits. Occupants in Penthouse, Royal, Celebrity, and Sky Suites are also given welcome Champagne; a full personal computer in each suite, including a printer and Internet access (on request in the Sky Suites); a choice of films from a video library; personalized stationery; tote bag; priority dining room seating preferences; private portrait sitting; and bathrobe; and in-suite massage service. Note that if you choose a balcony cabin on one of the upper decks, it may well be shaded under the pool deck, which extends over the ship's side – and by many balconies (so, not good for private sunbathing).

Penthouse Suites. On Penthouse Deck, these are the largest suites. Each occupies one half of the ship's beam, and overlooks the stern. Each measures a huge

2,530 sq ft (235 sq m): 1,432 sq ft (133 sq m) of living space, plus a huge wraparound balcony measuring 1,098 sq ft (102 sq m) with 180° views plus a wet bar, hot tub, and whirlpool tub. Much of this terrace, however, can be overlooked by passengers on decks above.

Royal Suites. These suites, each 733 sq ft (68 sq m), are located towards the ship's aft (four each on the port and starboard sides). The decor in each is different and is geographically themed: Africa, China, Mexico, France, India, Italy, Morocco, and Portugal. Each has a separate living room with dining and lounge areas (with refrigerator, minibar, and Bang & Olufsen audio system). There are two entertainment centers with DVD players, and TVs in the living area and bedroom, and a large walk-in closet, with vanity desk. The marble-clad bathroom has a whirlpool tub with integral shower, and there is also a separate shower enclosure, two washbasins, and toilet. The teak balcony is extensive – large enough for on-deck massage – and also has a whirlpool hot tub.

Celebrity Suites. These measure 467 sq ft (44 sq m), have floor-to-ceiling windows, a separate living room with dining and lounge areas, two flat-screen infotainment centers, and a walk-in closet with vanity desk. The marble-clad bathroom has a whirlpool tub with integral shower – a window with movable shade lets you look out of the bathroom through the lounge to the large ocean-view windows.

Sky Suites. Each is 308 sq ft (28.6 sq m), including the private balcony – some balconies may be larger than others, depending on location. Although designated as suites, they're just large cabins with a marble-clad bathroom with tub/shower combination. The suites have a TV set, and a larger lounge area than standard cabins, and separate sleeping area.

Butler service, in all suite-grade accommodation, includes full breakfast, in-suite lunch and dinner service (as required), afternoon tea service, evening hors d'oeuvres, free espresso and cappuccino, daily news delivery, shoeshine, and other personal touches.

Concierge Class. Concierge Class offers added value to these 'middle-class' cabins, as does 'AquaClass', added in 2012, with spa-healthy dining in Blu Restaurant, and complimentary access to the Persian Garden (thermal suite) and Relaxation Room in the spa, plus daily delivery of bottled water and herbal teas (infusions), and a host of spa-related personal amenities.

Standard outside-view/interior cabins. All outside-view and interior cabins have a lounge area with sofa or convertible sofa bed, sleeping area with twin beds that convert to a double, good closet and drawer space, personal safe, minibar/refrigerator (all items cost extra), interactive television, and bathroom. Even the smallest interior cabin has a good-size bathroom.

Wheelchair-accessible accommodation. These are located in the most practical parts of the ship, close to elevators for good accessibility. All have doorways and bathroom doorways and showers that are wheelchair-accessible.

DINING. The 1,224-seat Metropolitan Restaurant is the main dining room. Two decks high, it has a grand staircase connecting the two levels, a huge glass wall aft overlooking the sea, and a small 'musicians' gallery' on the upper level. There are two dinner seatings (open seating for breakfast and lunch), at tables for two–10. Menu variety is good, the food has taste, and it is attractively presented. Full service in-cabin dining is also available, with dinner menu items from the Metropolitan Restaurant.

Suite occupants can dine in the exclusive setting of 'Luminae', which features tableside preparation of signature dishes, an eclectic menu, and a selection of over 400 wines.

Blu, located on the port side of the upper level entrance of the Metropolitan dining room, is exclusively for the use of occupants of AquaClass accommodation.

Other dining options. Celebrity Cruises created its first 'alternative' restaurant aboard this ship. The Olympic Restaurant is named after White Star Line's transatlantic ocean liner (sister ship to *Titanic*, *Olympic* sailed between 1911 and 1935). It is adjacent to the atrium lobby, and its dining lounge contains figured French walnut wood paneling from the à la carte dining room of the S.S. *Olympic*, which was decorated in Louis XVI splendor.

Classic French cuisine and service are provided. This is, indeed, a room for a full degustation, and not just a dinner. The wine list is extensive, but the real treat is an additional list of rare vintage wines. However, with just 134 seats, it's best to make reservations early (a cover charge applies). There's also a dine-in wine cellar and a demonstration galley.

QSine, which features its menus and wine list on iPads, is another extra-cost, fine-dining venue (added in 2010), and reservations are required.

Ocean Café is a self-serve 754-seat buffet-style eatery. At the aft end of the Ocean Buffet, a separate pasta bar, sushi counter, grill/rotisserie, and pizza station provide freshly made items. Pizzas are made on board from pizza dough and do not come ready made for reheating, as with many cruise lines. There is also an outdoor grill, adjacent to the swimming pool, for fast-food items.

Café al Bacio and Geleteria, located on the third level of the atrium lobby, is the place to see and be seen, for extra-cost coffees, pastries, cakes, and gelato all in a trendy setting.

ENTERTAINMENT. The 900-seat Celebrity Theater is a three-deck-high showlounge for production shows and major cabaret acts. It is located forward, with seating on all levels. The stage is equipped with a full fly loft behind its proscenium.

SPA/FITNESS. Canyon Ranch SpaClub at Sea measures 24,219 sq ft (2,250 sq m). It features a large thalassotherapy pool under a large solarium dome, with a health bar for light breakfast and lunch items and fresh squeezed fruit and vegetable juices.

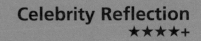

Celebrity Reflection
★★★★+

Size:	Large Resort Ship		Passenger/Crew Ratio (lower beds):	2.3
Tonnage:	125,366		Cabins (total):	1,523
Lifestyle:	Premium		Size Range (sq ft/m):	182.9–1,668.4/17.0–155.0
Cruise Line:	Celebrity Cruises		Cabins (for one person):	0
Former Names:	none		Cabins (with private balcony):	1,216
IMO Number:	9506459		Cabins (wheelchair accessible):	30
Builder:	Meyer Werft (Germany)		Wheelchair accessibility:	Best
Original Cost:	$641 million		Cabin Current:	110 and 220 volts
Entered Service:	Oct 2012		Elevators:	12
Registry:	Malta		Casino (gaming tables):	Yes
Length (ft/m):	1,047.2/319.2		Slot Machines:	Yes
Beam (ft/m):	120.7/36.8		Swimming Pools:	3
Draft (ft/m):	27.2/8.3		Hot Tubs (on deck):	6
Propulsion/Propellers:	diesel (70,500kW)/2 azimuthing pods		Self-Service Launderette:	No
Passenger Decks:	14		Dedicated Cinema/Seats:	No
Total Crew:	1,271		Library:	Yes
Passengers (lower beds):	3,046		Onboard currency:	US$
Passenger Space Ratio (lower beds):	41.1			

A premium-quality ship for stylish, family-friendly cruising

OVERVIEW. *Celebrity Reflection* is a sleek-looking ship, with two slim funnels. It is a close sister ship to *Celebrity Eclipse* (2010), *Celebrity Equinox* (2009), *Celebrity Silhouette* (2011), and *Celebrity Solstice* (2008). Behind the two funnels, the ship recreates the great outdoors with a Lawn Club, with real Bermudan (not fake) grass. You can go putting, play croquet or bocce ball (similar to boules), picnic on the grass, or walk barefoot.

THE SHIP. *Celebrity Reflection* has a steeply sloping stern with a mega-yacht-style ducktail platform above the propulsion pods. It's attractive, and nicely balanced (the hull is two feet wider, and has an additional deck, although the ship's superstructure is the same width, than *Celebrity Silhouette*). On the open deck, 'The Alcoves' are extra-cost 'private' Wi-Fi-equipped cabanas ($149 per day on sea days and $99 on port days).

Celebrity Reflection is a close sister to *Celebrity Silhouette*, but it has an additional deck (with 78 more suites, and additional seating in the showlounge, main dining room, and other venues. With a larger number of passengers (but the same number of elevators), the passenger/space ratio is therefore reduced. The ship's name is positioned directly under the navigation bridge and not forward on the bows (for space reasons), and the rounded bows accommodate a helicopter winch pad.

Several pool and water-play areas are on Resort Deck: one under a glass-roofed solarium (with Aqua

Berlitz's Ratings		
	Possible	Achieved
Ship	500	414
Accommodation	200	165
Food	400	298
Service	400	307
Entertainment	100	80
Cruise Experience	400	298
OVERALL SCORE		
1562 points out of 2000		

Café for light healthy bites). There's a sports pool, a family pool, and a wet zone. The open deck and sunning space around the main pool, however, isn't large enough for the number of passengers carried, although there are several other outdoor areas, including a music-free Solstice Deck high atop the ship – a nice space in which to relax.

The interior spaces are well designed, and the passenger flow is good; most of the entertainment rooms are positioned forward, while dining venues are located in the aft of the ship.

Celebrity's signature Martini Bar has a frosted bar and carries over 100 varieties of vodka, as well as Martinis. It's lively (noisy) and can get congested, but it can be a lot of fun, as can the Molecular Bar, with its special mixologist concoctions, including fruits and ingredients, aided by liquid nitrogen.

Cellar Masters, which is hosted by a sommelier, provides a cozy space for drinking wines. Its wine list is extensive, and Riedel glasses are featured. The room has several hideaway alcoves.

A two-deck library is a delightful open-ended space (operated on an 'honor' system – so you can check out a book 24/7), though books on the upper of 12 shelves are impossible to reach (they are just for show).

Fortunes Casino is a non-smoking gaming room with multiple tables for serious players, and 235 slot machines. It is open sided, so anyone passing is subject to noise from the slot machines.

Elevator call buttons are in a floor-stand 'pod,' and, when an elevator arrives, a glass panel above it turns from blue to pink – neat! Also notable is a collection of designer chairs and sunloungers in various locations, although some are on the impractical side of comfort.

Public rooms include an Art Studio, for the budding artist in you (classes and projects are at extra cost).

And speaking of art, when on board, take a look along the 'dining walkway', where several specialty restaurants are located. Two pieces of art stand out: one a delightful total optical illusion, by Anthony James (Kiln-dried birch trees, glass and steel mirrors 2,350 x 1,680 x 279mm); the other is a fascinating video art piece that tells a story about a man, his flashlight, a forest, and things that happen in the forest – I won't tell you more – you'll simply have to experience it for yourself. Gratuities are automatically charged to your onboard account.

Passenger niggles include lack of usable drawer space in standard-grade cabins; congestion when exiting the showlounge after a show; and the noise level in all areas of the lobby (which has a marble dance floor), particularly when the Martini Bar on the deck above is busy.

FAMILIES. Play areas include the Fun Factory (for 3–12-year-olds, featuring Leapfrog Schoolhouse's educational programs; and video game room; and 'X' Club – a teens-only chill-out room with a night-time dance club. Plenty of additional counsellors are provided during peak holiday periods.

ACCOMMODATION. From suite-grade Penthouse Suites to non-suite-grade interior cabins, the accommodation is practical and comfortable, with prices that depend on size and location. A wide range of accommodation includes a Reflection Suite (not aboard other *Solstice*-class ships). Suite-grade occupants get small bottles of Bulgari toiletries; everyone else doesn't.

About 90 percent of the accommodation is in outside-view cabins. Of these, 85 percent have a balcony – due to its slender width, there are very few interior cabins. There are seven suite-grade categories (compared to five aboard other Solstice-class ships): Reflection, Signature, Aqua, Penthouse, Royal, Celebrity, and Sky.

In the standard Interior and Ocean View cabins, there is little space between the bed and the wall, and the usable drawer space is poor. If you can afford it, book suite-grade accommodation for extra benefits.

All accommodation grades include: twin beds convertible to a queen-size bed, sitting area, and vanity desk with hairdryer, but almost no drawer space. Also standard: 32-ins flat-screen infotainment TVs (larger screens in suites), Wi-Fi Internet access (for a fee), premium bedding. Although the closets have good hanging space, there are no shelves on which to place folded items, and drawers in the vanity desk can't accommodate these. The bathroom has a shower enclosure, toilet, and tiny washbasin but no soap dish, and the faucet gets in the way when washing your face or

brushing your teeth; there's no retractable clothesline for washed small items; and two hooks on the back of the bathroom door are tiny. In suite-grade accommodation there is more space, larger balconies with good-quality sunloungers, and more personal amenities.

For the ultimate accommodation, book the Reflection Suite. It is a stunning, high-ceilinged abode with two separate bedrooms, large balcony along the port side. Creams, beiges, and chocolate colors dominate, and the furniture is large and extremely comfortable, but it's the high ceiling, and infusion of natural light and location, that make one feel special. The suite – together with five Signature-class suites – is located in a key-card access-only area next to the Sky Observation Lounge – the ship's disco at night. However, some noise can intrude from the basketball court on the deck above when it's in use.

DINING. Meals in Opus, the ship's expansive two-level, 1,454-seat principal dining room, are included in the cruise price. It has ocean views on the port and starboard sides, and two seating times, and anyone choosing 'Celebrity Select Dining' is usually assigned to the upper level, which helps to keep the dining room running smoothly. The design is contemporary, and, despite its size it's very comfortable. A two-deck-high wine tower – located towards the aft of the room is a great focal point.

Other dining options. Celebrity Cruises features cuisine that is creative, trendy, and slightly more health-oriented (ie less reliance on salt and food modifiers). If you like to eat in different venues instead of the main dining room, different dining packages are available, so you can 'dine around.' The following venues provide options that are good for special occasions or for something different (including the self-serve casual eatery, Oceanview Café).

Murano is an extra-cost, 72-seat, reservations-required dinner venue (with tablecloths), offering high-quality traditional dining with a real French flair and fine table settings, including large Reidel wine glasses. The food, its preparation and presentation, and the service are excellent.

Suite occupants can dine in the exclusive setting of 'Luminae', which features tableside preparation of signature dishes, an eclectic menu, and a selection of over 400 wines.

Blu is a 156-seat specialty restaurant, with tablecloths, designated exclusively for occupants of Aqua-Class suites/cabins, with cool ice white décor; the cuisine focuses slightly more on nicely presented healthy combinations.

Tuscan Grille is a 146-seat, extra-cost no tablecloth informal restaurant, for both traditional and trendy fare with an Italian focus, but includes Kobe beef, premium quality steaks, and seafood. Its entrance is barrel-shaped, with curved archways – it's like walking into a high-tech winery. Large aft-facing windows offer a great view.

Qsine is an extra-cost, 92-seat reservations-required, tablecloth-less 'fun-food' restaurant, with trendy interactive iPad food and wine menus that include cute foodie video snaps. The food consists of multi-flavored, multi-colored, quirky small-bite items that provide you with a selection to tease your taste buds. The food is presented in many unusual ways – even on sticks – sort of 'lollipop' or 'circus' cuisine.

A wine-tasting and enjoyment lounge, the 72-seat Cellar Masters features several alcoves for intimate discussions about wine. A wide choice is available, and a sommelier will make suggestions (about wine).

Bistro on Five (Deck 5, that is) is for coffee, cakes, crêpes, pastries, and more – it's a sort of French-style bistro-crêperie. It gets busy at times and the serving counter is small, so it can become congested, but the seating is comfortable.

Café al Bacio & Gelateria is a coffeehouse serving (extra cost) Lavazza Italian coffees, teas, and herbal infusions. It is on one side of the main lobby, with seating mostly in large, comfortable armchairs.

For something different: the Lawn Club. This patio-style outdoors (glass-covered) lean-to-style venue that overlooks the lawn and reserveable cabanas), and it's *the* place to go for beautifully grilled steaks, lamb chops, and seafood dishes. You can even grill the food to your liking – with a chef at your side, of course, just in case you burn your fingers!

Close by is The Porch, another enclosed venue, on the starboard side, with 48 seats, for paninis and light bites throughout the day (including breakfast, with delightful fruit muffins and pastry items).

Oceanview Café and Grill is an expansive, tray-less, casual self-serve buffet venue. A number of food 'islands' help to prevent lines, and the flow is good; the signage is clear and concise. A wide variety of food items is available, and plates are available at each of the 'islands' and cooking stations (such as 'Eggs and More' for breakfast). However, it *is* challenging to get a warm plate for hot food items.

The AquaSpa Café is for lighter options – low-salt solarium dishes, including a choice of salad items – and even a few sprouts, together with grilled items such as salmon and chicken, all attractively presented.

The Mast Bar Grill, an outside venue above the main pool deck, provides comfort fast food items including burgers.

Do try the Elegant Champagne High Tea in Murano. Presented only once each cruise (usually on a sea day), it comes with a choice of seven teas and tisanes, a three-tier stand full of finger sandwiches and pastry items, plus scones and real clotted cream, and a glass of Perrier Jouet Champagne.

ENTERTAINMENT. The 1,160-seat Reflection Theater, the ship's main showlounge, has a main level and two balconied sections positioned amphitheater-style around the stage.

Colorful nights are held in the Sky Observation Lounge, where the minimalist decor (relaxing by day) comes alive at night thanks to mood lighting.

Meanwhile, the 200-seat Celebrity Central hosts adult-only stand-up comedy, cooking demonstrations, enrichment lectures, and feature films.

Ensemble Lounge is a big-band-era-style cocktail lounge with live jazz-styled music, and is located close to specialty restaurant, Murano.

SPA/FITNESS. The Canyon Ranch SpaClub at Sea is laid out over two decks. A large fitness center includes kinesis equipment, plus all the familiar muscle-pumping machinery.

An extra-cost (free to occupants of AquaSpa-grade accommodation) unisex thermal suite contains several steam and shower mist rooms, and a glacial ice fountain, plus a calming relaxation area with heated tiled beds.

Additionally a small fitness 'suite' (for two), each with a selection of cardio-vascular machines, treadmills, etc., can be rented, so you can exercise in privacy.

Celebrity Silhouette
★★★★+

Size:	Large Resort Ship
Tonnage:	122,210
Lifestyle:	Premium
Cruise Line:	Celebrity Cruises
Former Names:	none
IMO Number:	9451094
Builder:	Meyer Werft (Germany)
Original Cost:	$641 million
Entered Service:	Jul 2011
Registry:	Malta
Length (ft/m):	1,047.2/319.2
Beam (ft/m):	120.7/36.8
Draft (ft/m):	27.2/8.3
Propulsion/Propellers:	diesel (70,500kW)/2 azimuthing pods
Passenger Decks:	14
Total Crew:	1,210
Passengers (lower beds):	2,886
Passenger Space Ratio (lower beds):	42.3

Passenger/Crew Ratio (lower beds):	2.3
Cabins (total):	1,443
Size Range (sq ft/m):	182.9–1,668.4/17.0–155.0
Cabins (for one person):	0
Cabins (with private balcony):	1,216
Cabins (wheelchair accessible):	30
Wheelchair accessibility:	Best
Cabin Current:	110 and 220 volts
Elevators:	12
Casino (gaming tables):	Yes
Slot Machines:	Yes
Swimming Pools:	3
Hot Tubs (on deck):	6
Self-Service Launderette:	No
Dedicated Cinema/Seats:	No
Library:	Yes
Onboard currency:	US$

Premium large ship with contemporary decor and style

OVERVIEW. *Celebrity Silhouette* is quite a sleek-looking ship, with two slim funnels. Behind them is the great outdoors, with the Lawn Club, an area with real Bermudan (not fake) grass, where you can go putting, play croquet or bocce ball (like boules), picnic on the grass, and just enjoy walking around barefoot.

THE SHIP. *Celebrity Silhouette* is sister to *Celebrity Eclipse, Celebrity Equinox, Celebrity Reflection* and *Celebrity Solstice.* Resort Deck is where you'll find several water-play areas, one within a glass-roofed solarium. However, the deck space around the two pools isn't large enough for the number of passengers carried. For open deck privacy, try 'The Alcoves'; these are garden cabanas for two to four persons, positioned on the lawn. They cost $149 per day on sea days and $99 on port days.

A favorite spot is Michael's Club, an intimate lounge with classic English leather club chairs and a handsome fireplace, plus more than 50 types of beer, whiskies, and cognacs.

Part of the Lawn Club is an interactive Lawn Club Grill, while The Porch is a 48-seat eatery overlooking the lawn, for complimentary breakfast and lunches, plus specialty coffees, wine, and beer (at extra cost).

Near the Lawn Club entrance is the Art Studio, for art demonstrations and classes on various topics. Some are free; others cost extra.

Most of the entertainment rooms are positioned forward, while dining venues are located aft. There's a wine bar with a sommelier; a jazz-age cocktail

Berlitz's Ratings

	Possible	Achieved
Ship	500	413
Accommodation	200	165
Food	400	297
Service	400	307
Entertainment	100	78
Cruise Experience	400	298

OVERALL SCORE
1558 points out of 2000

lounge; a bar with the look of an ocean-going yacht; Quasar, a bar with a nightly light show synchronized to music; and an observation lounge with a dance floor.

The two-deck library is a delightful open-ended space. The card room – located, unusually, in the center of the ship, with no ocean-view windows to distract players – is open, and attracts noise from adjacent areas, so it's almost useless as a serious card playing room. Fortunes Casino (non-smoking) has 16 gaming tables and 200 slot machines.

Celebrity's signature Martini Bar carries over 100 varieties of vodka, as well as Martinis. There's also a small alcove called Crush with an ice-filled table where you can participate in caviar and vodka tasting, or host a private party. It's very noisy and congested, but can be a lot of fun.

Passenger niggles include lack of usable drawer space in cabins; inadequate children's facilities and staff in school holidays; congestion when you exit the showlounge; and noise in all areas of the lobby when the Martini Bar is busy.

Gratuities are charged to your onboard account.

FAMILIES. Play areas include the Fun Factory (for 3–12-year-olds, featuring Leapfrog Schoolhouse's educational programs); and 'X Club' – a high-tech teens-only chill-out room with coffee bar and dance club.

ACCOMMODATION. From suite-grade Penthouse Suites to non-suite-grade interior cabins, the accommodation is practical and comfortable, with price depending on size and location. In standard Interior and Ocean View cabins, there is little space between the bed and the wall, and usable drawer space is poor. So, if your budget allows, book a suite-category cabin for all the extra benefits – and a lot more drawer space.

The suite-grade categories are: Royal Suite, Celebrity Suite, Sky Suite, and Penthouse Suite. Most of the balcony cabins on Penthouse Deck and Sky Deck suffer from permanent shade because they are just under the wide deck overhang – the large suites surrounding the aft elevator foyers get much more sunlight.

All grades of accommodation include: twin beds convertible to a queen-size bed, sitting area, vanity desk with hairdryer. Also standard in all cabins: 32-ins flat-screen TVs (larger screens in suites), Wi-Fi Internet access (for a fee), and premium bedding. However, although the closets have good hanging space, other storage is limited. The cramped bathroom has a shower enclosure, toilet, and tiny washbasin. In suite-grade accommodation there is more space, larger balconies and more personal amenities.

Some 130 'AquaSpa'-class cabins incorporate spa elements into the cabins, and allow access to the AquaSpa's Thermal Relaxation Room and a Persian Garden (with aromatherapy/steam rooms) on the same deck, and other spa amenities. Occupants get assigned seating in Blu Restaurant. Facilities include: a choice of four pillows (conformance, body, goose, Isotonic); express luggage delivery; shoeshine; Frette bathrobes; dining and seating preferences in other specialty dining venues; and early embarkation and disembarkation. Bathrooms include a tub plus a separate shower.

Other accommodation grades are Veranda Class, Sunset Veranda Class, Concierge Class, Family Ocean View with veranda, Deluxe Ocean View with veranda, Standard Ocean View, and Standard Interior cabins.

DINING. Grand Cuvée is the ship's 1,430-seat main dining room – included in the cruise price – is spread over two decks and has ocean views on the port and starboard sides and at the stern. The design is stunning and contemporary. Towards the aft section, a two-deck-high wine tower provides an eye-catching focal point (I'd like to have dinner inside it!).

Suite occupants can dine in the exclusive setting of 'Luminae', which features tableside preparation of signature dishes, an eclectic menu, and a selection of over 400 wines.

Blu is a 128-seat specialty restaurant, with tablecloths, exclusively for the occupants of AquaClass cabins. The room has pleasing, but rather cool decor.

Other dining options. Murano is an extra-cost, reservations-required, 70-seat dinner venue (with tablecloths), offering high-quality traditional dining with a French flair and gorgeous table settings. The cuisine and service are extremely good.

The 144-seat Tuscan Grille, an extra-cost, tablecloth-less venue, for Italian cuisine, Kobe beef and premium quality steaks. It has nicely curved archways – like a high-tech winery. Large aft-facing windows offer a great view.

Qsine is a 90-seat 'fun-food' venue. The food consists of multi-flavored, multi-colored, quirky small-bite items. The food is presented in quirky fashion – even on sticks – sort of 'lollipop' cuisine. It's a delightful experience.

Bistro on Five (Deck 5, that is) is for coffee, cakes, crêpes, pastries, and more. The serving counter becomes congested at busy times.

Café al Bacio & Gelateria is a coffeehouse featuring Lavazza Italian coffee, situated on one side of the main lobby.

Oceanview Café and Grill is a tray-less, casual self-serve buffet venue. There are a number of food 'islands' and the signage is reasonable.

The AquaSpa Café is for light, healthier options (solarium fare), but the selections are uninspiring.

The Mast Bar Grill and Bar is an outside fast-food venue.

ENTERTAINMENT. The 900-seat Celebrity Theater is the three-deck-high venue for production shows and major cabaret acts.

Colorful theme nights are held in the Observation Lounge (whose daytime bland and minimalist decor comes alive at night). The 200-seat Celebrity Central hosts comedy, cooking demonstrations, lectures, and films.

An Entertainment Court showcases street performers, psychics, and caricaturists, and is in the center of the ship, linked to Quasar, a high-pulse, high-volume nightclub. The Ensemble Lounge is a big-band-era cocktail lounge with live music.

SPA/FITNESS. The Canyon Ranch SpaClub at Sea measures 24,219 sq ft (2,250 sq m). It includes a large thalassotherapy pool under a solarium glass dome, complete with health bar for light food and fresh squeezed juices.

Facilities include 25 treatment rooms, including one designed for wheelchair passengers. There's also an aerobics room, a gymnasium, large men's and women's saunas with a sizable ocean-view window, and a beauty salon.

An extra-cost (free to occupants of AquaSpa-grade accommodation) unisex thermal suite contains several steam and shower mist rooms and a glacial ice fountain, plus a calming relaxation area with heated tiled beds.

Celebrity Solstice
★★★★

Size:	Large Resort Ship
Tonnage:	121,878
Lifestyle:	Premium
Cruise Line:	Celebrity Cruises
Former Names:	none
IMO Number:	9362530
Builder:	Meyer Werft (Germany)
Original Cost:	$641 million
Entered Service:	Nov 2008
Registry:	Malta
Length (ft/m):	1,033.4/315.0
Beam (ft/m):	120.7/36.8
Draft (ft/m):	27.2/8.3
Propulsion/Propellers:	diesel (67,200kW)/2 azimuthing pods
Passenger Decks:	14
Total Crew:	1,210
Passengers (lower beds):	2,852
Passenger Space Ratio (lower beds):	42.7
Passenger/Crew Ratio (lower beds):	2.3
Cabins (total):	1,426
Size Range (sq ft/m):	182.9–1,668.4/17.0–155.0
Cabins (for one person):	0
Cabins (with private balcony):	1,216
Cabins (wheelchair accessible):	30
Wheelchair accessibility:	Best
Cabin Current:	110 and 220 volts
Elevators:	12
Casino (gaming tables):	Yes
Slot Machines:	Yes
Swimming Pools:	3
Hot Tubs (on deck):	6
Self-Service Launderette:	No
Dedicated Cinema/Seats:	No
Library:	Yes
Onboard currency:	US$

Really elegant, understated decor in a premium setting

OVERVIEW. *Celebrity Solstice* is a sleek-looking ship, with two slim funnels.

THE SHIP. The vessel has a steeply sloping stern, which includes a mega-yacht-style ducktail platform above the propulsion pods, and is quite attractive. The ship's name is positioned directly under the navigation bridge and not forward on the bows (for space reasons). An unusual feature is an outdoor grass area (Lawn Club); it's open to all, so you can go putting, play croquet or bocce ball, or have a picnic on the grass, or walk barefoot.

Several pool and water-play areas are on Resort Deck; one within a glass-roofed solarium, a sports pool, a family pool, and a fun wet zone. The deck space around the two pools, however, isn't large enough for the number of passengers carried.

The interior spaces are well designed, and the decor is elegant yet contemporary. Most of the entertainment rooms are positioned forward, with dining venues mostly located aft.

There's a wine bar with a sommelier; a pre-dinner cocktail lounge that reflects the jazz age of the 1930s and '40s; a bar with the look of an ocean-going yacht; Quasar, a retro bar with large screens that create a nightly light show synchronized to music; and an observation lounge with a dance floor.

Celebrity's signature Martini Bar has over 100 varieties of vodka, as well as Martinis. There's also a small alcove called Crush with an ice-filled table where you can participate in caviar and vodka

Berlitz's Ratings	Possible	Achieved
Ship	500	403
Accommodation	200	165
Food	400	295
Service	400	306
Entertainment	100	78
Cruise Experience	400	297
OVERALL SCORE		
1544 points out of 2000		

tasting, or host a private party. It's noisy and congested, but can be a lot of fun.

A two-deck library is a delightful open-ended space, though books on the upper shelves are impossible to reach. The card room – located in the center of the ship, with no ocean view windows to distract players – is open to noise from adjacent areas, so it's useless as a serious card playing room. Fortunes Casino (non-smoking) has 16 gaming tables and 200 slot machines.

A Hot Glass Show, housed in an outdoor studio on the open deck as part of the Lawn Club and created in collaboration with Corning Museum of Glass, includes a novel glass-blowing show.

Public rooms include an Art Studio, for your artistic needs. Meanwhile The Alcoves are extra-cost 'private' Wi-Fi-equipped cabanas on deck ($149 per day on sea days and $99 on port days).

Passenger niggles include lack of usable drawer space in cabins; inadequate children's facilities and staff during school holidays; congestion when you exit the showlounge; and noise in the lobby when the Martini Bar is busy.

Gratuities are automatically charged to your onboard account.

FAMILIES. Play areas include the Fun Factory (for 3–12-year-olds, featuring Leapfrog Schoolhouse's educational programs); and 'X Club' – a high-tech teens-only chill-out room with coffee bar and a night-time dance club.

ACCOMMODATION. From suite-grade Penthouse Suites to non-suite-grade interior cabins, the accommodation is practical and comfortable, and comes in numerous price grades, depending on size and location. In standard Interior and Ocean View cabins, there is little space between the bed and the wall, and usable drawer space is poor. So, if your budget allows, book a suite-category cabin for all the extra benefits – and a lot more drawer space.

About 90 percent of the accommodation is in outside-view cabins. Of these, 85 percent have a balcony, and, due to the ship's slender width, there are few interior cabins. There are four suite-grade categories: Royal Suite, Celebrity Suite, Sky Suite, and Penthouse Suite.

All accommodation grades include: twin beds convertible to a queen-size bed, sitting area, vanity desk with hairdryer, but almost no drawer space. Also standard in all cabins: 32-ins flat-screen TVs (larger screens in suites), Wi-Fi Internet access (for a fee), premium bedding. Although the closets have good hanging space, storage space is limited. The bathroom is small, with a shower, toilet, and tiny washbasin, and there's no retractable clothesline.

AquaSpa-class cabins share the relaxation room of the AquaSpa itself, incorporate select spa elements into the cabins, and allow for specialized access to the Thermal Relaxation Room and Persian Garden (with aromatherapy/steam rooms) on the same deck. Features include: a choice of four pillows (conformance, body, goose, Isotonic); express luggage delivery; shoeshine; Frette bathrobes; dining and seating preferences in dining venues; and early embarkation and disembarkation. In suite-grade accommodation there is more space, larger balconies and bathrooms, and more personal amenities. Occupants also get assigned seating at the exclusive 130-seat Restaurant Blu.

Other accommodation grades are Veranda Class, Sunset Veranda Class, Concierge Class, Family Ocean View with veranda, Deluxe Ocean View with veranda, Standard Ocean View, and Standard Interior cabins.

Cabins 1551–1597 on the port side and 1556–1602 on the starboard side on Penthouse Deck (Deck 11) suffer from 'aircraft carrier' syndrome because they are directly under the huge overhanging Resort Deck. They have little exposure to sun or light, and thick supporting struts ruin the view from these cabins, which are otherwise pleasantly fitted out.

DINING. Grand Epernay, the principal dining room (included in the cruise price), is located towards the aft, and has ocean views on both sides. The design is contemporary; however, the almost-backless tub-style chairs are uncomfortable. At the forward end, a two-deck high wine tower provides a fine talking point. The food is disappointing; the decreased quality all too obvious to repeat Celebrity passengers.

Suite occupants can dine in the exclusive setting of 'Luminae', which features tableside preparation of signature dishes, an eclectic menu, and a selection of over 400 wines.

Blu is a 130-seat specialty restaurant designated for occupants of AquaClass cabins. The room has pleasing (but rather cold) blue decor. The ambience is cool.

Other dining options. Murano is an extra-cost, reservations-required venue offering high-quality traditional dining with a French flair and fine table settings.

The Tuscan Grille, an extra-cost, reservations-required venue, serves Kobe beef and premium quality steaks.

Silk Harvest is a Southeast Asian extra-cost dining venue serving unmemorable pan-Asian fusion cuisine.

Bistro on Five (Deck 5, that is) is for coffee, cakes, crêpes, pastries, and more. It gets busy at times and the serving counter is small, so it's a congested area.

Café al Bacio & Gelateria is a small coffeehouse serving Lavazza Italian coffee, situated on one side of the main lobby; lines quickly form at peak times.

Oceanview Café and Grill is the expansive, trayless, casual self-serve buffet venue. It has a number of food 'islands' rather than those awful straight buffet counters. The signage is reasonable, but condiments are hard to find.

The AquaSpa Café is for light, healthier options (solarium fare), but the selections need improvement.

ENTERTAINMENT. The 1,115-seat Solstice Theatre, the main showlounge, stages three circus-themed production shows. Colorful theme nights are held in the Observation Lounge. The 200-seat Celebrity Central hosts comedy, cooking demonstrations, enrichment lectures, and feature films. Quasar is a high-pulse, high-volume nightclub. An Entertainment Court showcases street performers. The Ensemble Lounge is a big-band-era cocktail lounge with live jazz, next to the Murano restaurant.

SPA/FITNESS. The large Canton Ranch SpaClub at Sea is laid out over two decks. A large fitness center includes kinesis (pulleys against gravity) workout equipment, plus all the familiar muscle-pumping cardio-vascular machinery. An extra-cost, unisex thermal suite features several steam and shower mist rooms with fragrances such as chamomile, eucalyptus, and mint, and a glacial ice fountain, plus a calming relaxation area with heated tiled beds, and an acupuncture center.

Celebrity Summit
★★★★

Size:	Large Resort Ship
Tonnage:	90,940
Lifestyle:	Premium
Cruise Line:	Celebrity Cruises
Former Names:	*Summit*
IMO Number:	9192387
Builder:	Chantiers de l'Atlantique (France)
Original Cost:	$350 million
Entered Service:	Oct 2001
Registry:	Malta
Length (ft/m):	964.5/294.0
Beam (ft/m):	105.6/32.2
Draft (ft/m):	26.2/8.0
Propulsion/Propellers:	gas turbine (39,000kW)/2 azimuthing pods
Passenger Decks:	11
Total Crew:	999
Passengers (lower beds):	2,158
Passenger Space Ratio (lower beds):	42.1

Passenger/Crew Ratio (lower beds):	2.1
Cabins (total):	1,079
Size Range (sq ft/m):	165.1–2,530.0/15.34–235.0
Cabins (for one person):	0
Cabins (with private balcony):	606
Cabins (wheelchair accessible):	26 (17 with private balcony)
Wheelchair accessibility:	Best
Cabin Current:	110 and 220 volts
Elevators:	12
Casino (gaming tables):	Yes
Slot Machines:	Yes
Swimming Pools:	3 (1 w/ sliding glass dome)
Hot Tubs (on deck):	4
Self-Service Launderette:	No
Dedicated Cinema/Seats:	Yes/368
Library:	Yes
Onboard currency:	US$

A premium-quality large resort ship for family-friendly cruising

OVERVIEW. *Celebrity Summit* is a sister ship to *Celebrity Constellation*, *Celebrity Infinity*, and *Celebrity Millennium*. The accommodation is extremely comfortable in all grades, and only the two sittings for dining and for the nightly shows detract from an otherwise excellent product.

THE SHIP. Mega-yacht designer Jon Bannenberg was responsible for the exterior, with its royal blue-and-white hull, but it actually looks rather ungainly. In early 2012, the ship underwent a 'Solsticizing' program, which added more cabins, more facilities and more dining options to match the newer ships in the fleet.

Inside, the ship has a similar standard of decor and materials, and public rooms that make ships in the fleet so user-friendly. The atrium is three decks high and houses the reception desk, tour operator's desk, and bank. Four dramatic glass-walled elevators travel through the ship's exterior (port) side, connecting the atrium with another seven decks, thus traveling through 10 passenger decks, including the tender stations – a nice ride.

Facilities include a combination Cinema/Conference Center, an expansive shopping arcade with 14,447 sq ft (1,300 sq m) of retail store space (with brand name labels such as Fendi, Fossil, Hugo Boss, and Versace), a lavish four-deck-high showlounge with high-tech sound and lighting, a two-level library (one level for English-language books; a second for other languages and reference material), card room, music listening room, and an observation lounge/discotheque with fine views.

Berlitz's Ratings		
	Possible	Achieved
Ship	500	387
Accommodation	200	160
Food	400	285
Service	400	290
Entertainment	100	74
Cruise Experience	400	288
OVERALL SCORE		
1484 points out of 2000		

Michael's Club, formerly a cigar smoker's haven, is now a rather nice lounge/piano bar offering over 50 craft beers plus fine whiskies and cognacs. An Internet café has almost 20 computers and extra-cost Internet connectivity.

Gaming sports include the ship's overly large Fortunes Casino, with lots of bright lights and action. Families with children will appreciate the Fun Factory (for children) and The Tower (for teenagers). Children's counselors and youth activities staff provide a wide range of supervised activities.

ACCOMMODATION. From suite-grade to non-suite-grade, the choice depends on your preference for the size and location. Almost half feature a 'private' balcony; approximately 80 percent are ocean-view suites and cabins, and the rest are interior cabins. All the accommodation is extremely comfortable. Suites, naturally, have more space, butler service (whether you want it or not), more and better amenities, and a greater degree of personal service than standard grades. Note that if you choose a balcony cabin on one of the upper decks, it could be shaded under the pool deck, which extends over the ship's side – as well as by many balconies (so, not good for private sunbathing).

Penthouse Suites (2). These Penthouse Deck suites are like apartments. Each occupies one half of the width of the ship, overlooking the stern. Each is a huge 2,530 sq ft (235 sq m): 1,432 sq ft (133 sq m) of living space, plus a huge wraparound balcony of 1,098 sq ft (102 sq m), which includes a wet bar, hot tub, and whirlpool tub (but much of this terrace can be overlooked from other decks above).

Royal Suites (8). These are located towards the aft (four each on the port and starboard sides). Each measures 733 sq ft (68 sq m) and has a separate bedroom, dining and lounge areas (with refrigerator, minibar, and Bang & Olufsen audio system). There are two flat-screen infotainment centers, and a large walk-in closet with vanity desk. The marble-clad bathroom has a whirlpool tub with integral shower, and there are also a separate shower enclosure, two washbasins, and toilet. The teakwood balcony is extensive – large enough for on-deck massage – and has a hot tub.

Celebrity Suites (8). These measure 467 sq ft (44 sq m) and have floor-to-ceiling windows, a separate living room with dining and lounge areas, two entertainment centers with flat-screen TVs in both living room and bedroom, and a walk-in closet with vanity desk. The marble-clad bathroom has a whirlpool tub with integral shower; a window with movable shade lets you look out through the lounge to the ocean-view windows. Balconies were added in a 2011 refit.

Sky Suites (30). Each is 308 sq ft (29 sq m), including the private balcony – some balconies may be larger than others, depending on the location. Although these are designated as suites, they are really just larger cabins that have a marble-clad bathroom with tub/shower combination.

Butler service. Provided in all suite accommodation, this service includes full breakfast, in-suite lunch and dinner (as required), afternoon tea, evening hors d'oeuvres, complimentary espresso and cappuccino, daily news delivery, and shoeshine.

Concierge Class. In 2003, Celebrity Cruises added a third service 'class' to the accommodation grades. Positioned between the top-grade suite grades and standard cabin grades, Concierge Class offers added value to these 'middle-class' cabins, as does a new 'AquaClass,' added in 2012, with spa-healthy dining in the exclusive Blu Restaurant, and complimentary access to the Persian Garden (thermal suite) and Relaxation Room in the spa, plus daily delivery of bottled water and herbal teas, and spa-related personal amenities.

Standard outside-view/interior cabins. All other outside-view and interior cabins have a lounge area with sofa or convertible sofa bed, sleeping area with twin beds that can convert to a double bed, ample closet and drawer space, personal safe, minibar/refrigerator (extra cost), and interactive TV. The cabins are nicely decorated with warm wood-finish furniture, and there is none of the boxy feel of cabins in so many ships, due to the angled placement of vanity and audio-video consoles. Even the smallest cabin has a good-size bathroom and shower.

Wheelchair-accessible accommodation. This is available in various grades and practical locations, close to elevators. All doorways and bathroom doorways and showers are wheelchair-accessible. Some cabins have extra berths for third or third and fourth occupants.

DINING. The Cosmopolitan Restaurant is a 1,170-seat main dining room. It is two decks high and has a grand staircase connecting the two levels, a huge glass wall overlooking the sea at the stern of the ship (electrically operated shades provide several different backdrops), and a musicians' gallery on the upper level, typically for a string quartet or quintet. As a tribute to the French Line ship *Normandie*, a statue (called *La Normandie*) that was created by Leon-Georges Baudry and once overlooked the ship's grand staircase (and for the past approximate half a century graced Miami's Fontainebleau Hotel) was bought for $250,000 and can now be seen here. There are two seatings for dinner (it's an open seating for breakfast and lunch), at tables for two, four, six, eight, or 10.

Suite occupants can dine in the exclusive setting of 'Luminae,' which features tableside preparation of signature dishes, an eclectic menu, and a selection of over 400 wines.

Blu, located on the port side of the upper level entrance to the Cosmopolitan dining room, is exclusively for the use of occupants of AquaClass accommodation. Other dining options.The extra-cost, reservations-only specialty dining option is the 134-seat Normandie Restaurant, with gold-lacquered paneling from the smoking room of the original French Line ship.

A team of chefs prepares the cuisine exclusively for this restaurant. Fine tableside preparation is the attraction and both the classic French cuisine and service are good. This is haute cuisine, and for a full dégustation, and not just a dinner, but with just 134 seats, it's best to book early (there is a cover charge). A dine-in wine cellar is located at one end of the restaurant, and a demonstration galley is at the other.

QSine, which features its menus and wine list on iPads, is another extra-cost, fine-dining venue, and reservations are required.

There are several options in more casual settings. The Waterfall Café and Grill is a casual self-serve buffet area, with six serving lines, and seating for 754; there is also a grill and pizza bar. For Champagne and caviar lovers, Carlisle's is the place to go.

Café al Bacio and Gelateria, on the third level of the atrium lobby, is the place for coffees, pastries, cakes, and gelato, in a trendy setting. Meanwhile, Bistro on Five is a popular French crêperie.

ENTERTAINMENT. The 900-seat Celebrity Theater is the three-deck-high venue for the ship's production shows and major cabaret acts. It is located in the forward part of the ship, with seating on main, and two balcony levels. The large stage is equipped with a full fly loft behind its traditional proscenium.

SPA/FITNESS. A large Canyon Ranch SpaClub at Sea measures 24,219 sq ft (2,250 sq m). It has a large thalassotherapy pool under a solarium dome, complete with health bar for fresh squeezed fruit and vegetable juices.

Celebrity Xpedition
★★★+

Size:	Boutique Ship	Passenger/Crew Ratio (lower beds):	1.4
Tonnage:	2,842	Cabins (total):	45
Lifestyle:	Premium	Size Range (sq ft/m):	156.0–460.0/14.5–42.7
Cruise Line:	Celebrity Cruises	Cabins (for one person):	0
Former Names:	Sun Bay	Cabins (with private balcony):	8
IMO Number:	9228368	Cabins (wheelchair accessible):	0
Builder:	Cassens-Werft (Germany)	Wheelchair accessibility:	None
Original Cost:	DM 35 million	Cabin Current:	220 volts
Entered Service:	Jun 2001/Jun 2004	Elevators:	0
Registry:	The Bahamas	Casino (gaming tables):	No
Length (ft/m):	290.3/88.5	Slot Machines:	No
Beam (ft/m):	45.9/14.0	Swimming Pools:	No
Draft (ft/m):	11.4/3.5	Hot Tubs (on deck):	1
Propulsion/Propellers:	diesel (3,000kW)/2	Self-Service Launderette:	No
Passenger Decks:	4	Dedicated Cinema/Seats:	No
Total Crew:	64	Library:	Yes
Passengers (lower beds):	90	Onboard currency:	US$
Passenger Space Ratio (lower beds):	31.5		

A comfortable ship for exploring the Galápagos Islands

OVERVIEW. This was the first specialist boutique ship for Celebrity Cruises and is like a small private club for Galápagos ecotourism. It will suit mature adults who want an intimate and casual cruise experience, and, of course, to see the famous Galápagos Islands.

THE SHIP. There is a surprisingly good amount of open deck space – much of it with teakwood decking, as well as teak sunloungers and patio furniture. Although there is no swimming pool, there is a whirlpool tub. Stabilizers were installed in 2004.

All accommodation is located forward half, with public rooms aft. The ambience is unhurried, yet subtly elegant. Except for the dining room, which can double as a conference room, there is only one public room: the main lounge, complete with bar, dance floor, and bandstand.

Shore excursions by Zodiac inflatable boats are in small groups led by Ecuadorian guides. On your return, waiters greet you with refreshing drinks and towels. Included in the fare: excursions, gratuities to shipboard staff, beverages including house wine, Champagne, liquor, beer, and soda.

ACCOMMODATION. There are four price categories in two cabin types: nine Suites measuring 247 sq ft (23 sq m); 34 Comfort Cabins, 172 sq ft (16 sq m); and three Comfort Cabins, 156 sq ft (14.5 sq m). All suites and cabins have twin beds (four comfort cabins have double beds), TV, sofa, drinks

Berlitz's Ratings

	Possible	Achieved
Ship	500	334
Accommodation	200	140
Food	400	265
Service	400	279
Entertainment	100	62
Cruise Experience	400	251
OVERALL SCORE		
1331 points out of 2000		

table, vanity desk with hairdryer, minibar/refrigerator, and personal safe. Bathrooms all have a good-size shower enclosure (there are no tubs) with soap/shampoo dispenser, black granite washbasin, and white marble-clad walls.

The largest accommodation is in nine suites, each with a private balcony. One suite is located forward, with forward-facing views, and has a sloping ceiling with character. Balcony partitions are almost private; the balcony deck is teak covered. Two of the suites can be joined together. One bedroom has two pull-down Murphy beds.

DINING. The Darwin Dining Room operates on an open-seating basis. A self-serve buffet offers salads, cold cuts, and cheeses. House wines and beer are included in the fare; a few better wines can be bought. The cuisine depends on local suppliers; fish seafood and fruits are good, but vegetables are inconsistent. The casual, self-serve Seagull Buffet is just behind the main lounge, with teak tables and chairs.

ENTERTAINMENT. Dinner and after-dinner conversation with fellow passengers is the main entertainment.

SPA/FITNESS. There is a small fitness room, and adjacent unisex sauna located inside on the uppermost deck, while a small beauty salon is located on the lowest deck.

Celestyal Cristal
★★★

Size:	Mid-size Ship		Passenger Space Ratio (lower beds):	26.5
Tonnage:	25,611		Passenger/Crew Ratio (lower beds):	2.4
Lifestyle:	Standard		Cabins (total):	483
Cruise Line:	Celestyal Cruises		Size Range (sq ft/m):	107.6–462.8/10.0–43.0
Former Names:	Louis Crystal, Silja Opera, SuperStar Taurus,		Cabins (for one person):	0
	Leeward, Sally Albatross, Viking Saga		Cabins (with private balcony):	10
IMO Number:	n/a		Cabins (wheelchair accessible):	6
Builder:	Wartsila (Finland)		Wheelchair accessibility:	None
Original Cost:	n/a		Cabin Current:	110 and 220 volts
Entered Service:	1980/Jul 2007		Elevators:	Yes
Registry:	Malta		Casino (gaming tables):	Yes
Length (ft/m):	530.5/161.7		Slot Machines:	Yes
Beam (ft/m):	100.0/30.5		Swimming Pools:	1 (indoors)
Draft (ft/m):	20.1/6.1		Hot Tubs (on deck):	0
Propulsion/Propellers:	diesel (19,120kW)/2		Self-Service Launderette:	No
Passenger Decks:	7		Dedicated Cinema/Seats:	Yes
Total Crew:	400		Library:	Yes
Passengers (lower beds):	966		Onboard currency:	Euros

Note: IMO Number shown as 7827213 in source.

A casual ship with a friendly crew for port-intensive cruises

OVERVIEW. *Celestyal Cristal* should appeal to anyone who simply wants to cruise the Greek Islands in a modicum of comfort, and at a very modest price. The dress code is casual throughout, with no formal nights.

THE SHIP. *Celestyal Cristal* has undergone several name changes during its busy life. Originally built as a Viking Line ferry, it was extensively reconstructed in 1995, after which it operated under charter to Norwegian Cruise Line as *Leeward*.

The ship has a smart wedge-shaped profile with a squared-off stern and short, stubby bows, and the enclosed bridge looks like it's really one deck lower than it should be. But *Celestyal Cristal* does benefit from a good, walk-around teak promenade deck. The pool deck is very cramped, although the pool itself can be covered by a sliding glass dome. There is no forward-facing observation lounge atop the ship, but the accommodation hallways are wide. There is a reasonable array of public rooms: lounges, bars, a casino with gaming tables and slot machines, a convenience store, duty-free shop, and internet center (Wi-Fi costs extra). The ship operates 3-, 4- and 7-day cruises (many of them with themes including history, food, and health). Drinks-inclusive packages are available. Note that gratuities are not included in the fare.

ACCOMMODATION. There are three suite categories (Imperial, Balcony, and Junior), and a mix of outside-view cabins (some of which have balconies) and interior cabins in 19 price grades.

Berlitz's Ratings		
	Possible	Achieved
Ship	500	322
Accommodation	200	133
Food	400	230
Service	400	246
Entertainment	100	65
Cruise Experience	400	243
OVERALL SCORE		
1239 points out of 2000		

The top-grade suites have neatly-angled private balconies and provide a decent amount of space for short cruises; the bathrooms have a tub, separate shower, and good storage facilities for toiletries. Most of the standard cabins and bathrooms are really very small, and in need of updating and better soundproofing. Note that some cabins have views obstructed by safety equipment.

DINING. Olympus Restaurant is the ship's main dining room, but there are also a number of other dining spots and casual eateries. There are two seatings for dinner on most nights (typically an open seating for the first night), and open seating for breakfast and lunch. Seating and table assignments for dinner are made by the maître d' during embarkation.

Celestyal Cruises specializes in Greek regional cuisine, as well as some international favorites. All tables are laid with crisp white linen. Spa and vegetarian dishes are available on lunch and dinner menus. Celestyal Cruises (a sub-brand of Louis Cruises) makes its own breads, soups, pâtés, jams, pizzas, and burgers on board.

Amalthia is a self-serve buffet restaurant for casual meals and snacks, with some excellent views. Other casual eateries include Aura and Leda Casual Dining.

ENTERTAINMENT. Muses Lounge is the ship's show-lounge, with tiered seating and decent sight lines.

SPA/FITNESS. Sana Beauty center facilities include a beauty salon, fitness room, and men's and women's saunas and steam rooms.

Celestyal Odyssey
★★★+

Size:	Small ship
Tonnage:	24,318
Lifestyle:	Standard
Cruise Line:	Celestyal Cruises
Former Names:	*Explorer, Olympia Explorer*
IMO Number:	9183518
Builder:	Blohm & Voss (Germany)
Original Cost:	$175 million
Entered Service:	May 2001/Jun 2015
Registry:	Malta
Length (ft/m):	590.5/180.0
Beam (ft/m):	83.6/25.5
Draft (ft/m):	23.9/7.3
Propulsion/Propellers:	diesel/2
Passenger Decks:	8
Total Crew:	230
Passengers (lower beds):	840
Passenger Space Ratio (lower beds):	28.9
Passenger/Crew Ratio (lower beds):	3.6
Cabins (total):	420
Size Range (sq ft/m):	139.9-376.7/13.0-35.0
Cabins (for one person):	0
Cabins (with private balcony):	12
Cabins (wheelchair accessible):	4
Wheelchair accessibility:	Fair
Cabin Current:	110 volts
Elevators:	4
Casino (gaming tables):	Yes
Slot Machines:	Yes
Swimming Pools:	1
Hot Tubs (on deck):	0
Self-Service Launderette:	No
Dedicated Cinema/Seats:	No
Library:	Yes
Onboard currency:	Euros

A good water taxi for Greek island-hopping in style

OVERVIEW. *Celestyal Odyssey* is best suited to couples and solo travelers who want to experience multiple Greek islands, in contemporary, comfortable, but not luxurious surroundings, and with food and a level of service that are quite acceptable, but nothing special.

THE SHIP. *Celestyal Odyssey* was the second of a pair ordered by the long-defunct, financially troubled Royal Olympia Cruises, which was forced to sell the ship at auction in 2003–4. The ship was purchased by Stellar Maritime (V-Ships), and chartered to Semester at Sea (administered by the University of Virginia) for 15 years. The ship has a compact outer design, with a slender, indigo blue, fast naval frigate-like hull. However, it is a high-density ship.

There are two engine rooms (forward and amidships), capable of providing a 27-knot service speed, and a streamlined, swept-back funnel.

If the ship is not full, there is a reasonable amount of open deck space, but there are few deck lounge chairs. All exterior railings are stainless steel (topped with thick, beautifully polished wood). A sea-water swimming pool is located aft, but it's really just a dip pool; adjacent are two shower enclosures.

The interior design combines contemporary conveniences with understated European decor reminiscent of the Mediterranean region, with warm colors, blond woods, and opaque glass paneling.

The most striking, but subtle, features in terms of design and decoration can be found in the artwork. Of particular note are two poems by writers from

Berlitz's Ratings

	Possible	Achieved
Ship	500	299
Accommodation	200	144
Food	400	277
Service	400	294
Entertainment	100	64
Cruise Experience	400	269
OVERALL SCORE		
1347 points out of 2000		

Greece and Cyprus etched in backlit, opaque-glass panels on the stairways; to read them, you'll need to walk down the complete stairway.

Most of the public rooms are located on one principal deck in a horizontal-flow layout that makes it easy to quickly find your way around, with a slightly winding open passageway linking several leisure lounges in one neat 'street scene,' showcasing more artworks, in this case valuable rocks and gems from Greece and the islands.

There's also a large library, housed in the former casino, with several internet-connect computer terminals, and a piano lounge (Turquoise Piano Lounge – although the only thing turquoise are the table tops), with bar.

Complementing each cruise is a good program of special-interest lectures, on topics including destinations, culture, or lifestyle.

There is a good degree of warmth and friendliness throughout the ship – a factor that so many cruise lines seem to have neglected. Although there is no full walk-around outdoor promenade deck, you can walk around parts of the ship. No public toilet is accessible by wheelchair passengers.

ACCOMMODATION. The accommodation, which is available at several price grades, consists of 12 Sky Suites (with large balcony), 12 Balcony Cabins (with a covered roof over the balcony, and a full partition, so you can't hear your neighbor or smell any smoke from smokers), 20 Junior Suites, 292 cabins (double occupancy), 72 cabins (two lower beds and a third, upper berth), 4 cabins (two lower beds, two upper berths), and 4 wheelchair-accessible cabins (with spacious bathrooms and roll-in showers). The price you pay will depend on the grade, location, and size you choose.

Standard cabins: The standard interior (no-view) and outside-view cabins are quite compact, although some interior cabins are larger than others. They are practically laid-out, and the decor includes warm blond-wood cabinetry, accents, and facings, and pleasing soft furnishings. The bathrooms are small, but have decent-sized shower enclosures, and storage facilities for personal toiletry items. All cabins include a television (with pay-per-view movies), hairdryer, mini-bar/refrigerator, and personal safe. The Junior Suites simply have a little more room than the standard cabins.

Sky Suites: The largest accommodation can be found in 12 Sky Suites, located high atop the ship and in the forward-most section. Their names are: Aghioklima, Begonia, Elia, Filoria, Gazia, Itia, Kiparissi, Lemonia, Margarita, Mouria, Pefko, and Violetta. They have large private balconies (some are more like large terraces), floor-to-ceiling windows, limited butler service, and 24-hour dining service. Elia, Gazia, Kiparissi, and Margarita have large structures above their balconies – these constitute the port side and starboard side gangway-lowering mechanism, so they can be noisy in ports of call and anchor ports, and the balconies cannot be considered very private. Some of the suites have walk-in closets, while others have closets facing the entranceway; all, however, have an abundance of drawer and hanging space, and chrome pullout shoe racks. The bathroom has a combination tub/shower (although the sit-in bathtub is small), and a retractable clothesline. All suites have wood-paneled walls with mirrored vanity desk (however, from a feng shui viewpoint, the mirror is directly opposite the bed, which is a negative), mini-bar/refrigerator, sofa, coffee table (fixed), and sleeping area partly separated from the lounge by a wood/glass divider. Also, you should note that when the ship is traveling at speed, considerable wind sweeps across the balconies, rendering them all but useless. The balconies have (expensive) stainless-steel railings instead of glass topped with a thick wooden rail.

Deluxe (Balcony) Suites: Twelve cabins with private balconies have electric sliding doors to the balconies (operated by compressed air filling a 'skirt'

around the door frame to keep them airtight and soundproof). Facilities include wood-paneled walls with vanity desk, mini-bar/refrigerator, sofa, and drinks table (fixed). There is a separate sleeping area (with twin or queen-sized bed), and vanity/make-up desk with a good amount of drawer space. There is a decent amount of closet space and an abundance of drawer and hanging space, and chrome pullout shoe rack baskets. The bathroom has a combination sit-in bathtub/shower and a retractable clothesline.

DINING. The 470-seat Aqua Marine Dining Room is located aft, one deck below the main 'street' of public rooms and thus out of the main flow. It has picture windows on three sides and a semi-circular walkway, with minimalist decor, as its entrance. The decor in the dining room itself is warm, welcoming, and tasteful. There are tables for two, four, six, or eight, but the chairs do not have armrests. A few tables close to the entrance to the galley's escalators suffer from traffic from the service area, and, because of the single-deck height ceiling and open waiter stations, the noise level can be considerable at times.

Other dining options. For casual breakfast and self-service lunch buffets, the Topaz Garden Lounge is a pleasant, but very basic, room, with large picture windows and an open feel. There is seating for 210 indoors and about 200 outdoors, and there is an outdoor bar with sailcloth-style cover. The layout of the two buffet counter lines is unfortunately poor, and causes congestion – a testament to poor design.

Additional munching outlets include a pizza-serving area, small salad bar, and an ice cream bar.

ENTERTAINMENT. The Amber Main Lounge is the venue for entertainment events. It is a single-level room with 420 seats, although many pillars obstruct the sightlines from about 40 percent of the seats. There is a sound system in one of the lounges and bars, and a disco is also available for the young-at-heart (and hard of hearing).

SPA/FITNESS. The spacious Sana Spa has facilities including a hydrotherapy bath, mosaic tiled steam room and sauna (both are unisex, so a swimming costume is required), and several treatment rooms. The area is secluded from the main passenger flow, although non-spa passengers have a habit of opening doors and walking through the area.

Celestyal Olympia
★★★

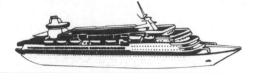

Size:	Mid-size Ship	Passenger Space Ratio (lower beds):	26.0
Tonnage:	37,773	Passenger/Crew Ratio (lower beds):	2.6
Lifestyle:	Standard	Cabins (total):	725
Cruise Line:	Celestyal Cruises	Size Range (sq ft/m):	118.4–425.1/11.0–39.5
Former Names:	Louis Olympia, Thomson Destiny, Sunbird, Song of America	Cabins (for one person):	0
		Cabins (with private balcony):	9
IMO Number:	8814744	Cabins (wheelchair accessible):	0
Builder:	Wartsila (Finland)	Wheelchair accessibility:	Fair
Original Cost:	$140 million	Cabin Current:	110 volts
Entered Service:	Dec 1982/May 2012	Elevators:	7
Registry:	Malta	Casino (gaming tables):	Yes
Length (ft/m):	705.0/214.8	Slot Machines:	Yes
Beam (ft/m):	93.1/28.4	Swimming Pools:	2
Draft (ft/m):	22.3/6.8	Hot Tubs (on deck):	0
Propulsion/Propellers:	diesel (16,480kW)/2	Self-Service Launderette:	No
Passenger Decks:	11	Dedicated Cinema/Seats:	No
Total Crew:	540	Library:	Yes
Passengers (lower beds):	1,450	Onboard currency:	Euros

A comfortable family-friendly ship for casual cruising

OVERVIEW. *Celestyal Olympia* is best suited to adult couples and singles taking their first or second cruise, and families with children, all seeking a modern but not glitzy ship with a wide array of public lounges and bars, a middle-of-the-road lifestyle, and decent food and service. It operates in the Greek Islands and Mediterranean.

THE SHIP. Originally built for Royal Caribbean International, the all-white ship is smart looking, with nicely rounded lines, sharply raked bow, and a single funnel with a cantilevered, wraparound lounge – a fine place from which to observe the world around and below you.

There's a decent amount of open deck and sunbathing space, but it gets crowded when the ship sails full, which is most of the time. There are some nicely polished wooden decks and rails and two swimming pools – the aft one designated for children, the forward one for adults.

The interior decor is bright and breezy. There's a good array of public rooms, most with high ceilings. All are located one deck above the dining room and include the main showlounge, casino, and nightclub. There's also a small conference center for meetings, as well as an Internet café with several computer terminals.

There are no cushioned pads for the sunloungers. Standing in line for embarkation, disembarkation, shore tenders, and for self-serve buffet meals is an inevitable aspect of cruising aboard all large ships. Passenger niggles include the dated look of the ship's interiors.

Berlitz's Ratings

	Possible	Achieved
Ship	500	310
Accommodation	200	118
Food	400	242
Service	400	251
Entertainment	100	63
Cruise Experience	400	262
OVERALL SCORE		
1246 points out of 2000		

The best part of cruising aboard *Celestyal Olympia* lies in the destinations, and not the ship – although it is perfectly comfortable, and Celestyal Cruises provides a consistent, well-tuned, and well-packaged product.

ACCOMMODATION. This is provided in several categories and price bands: interior cabins (parallel or L-shaped bed arrangement), outside-view cabins (parallel or L-shaped bed arrangement), deluxe cabins (with parallel twin beds that can convert to a queen-size bed), suites, and Grand Suites.

Most cabins are of a similar size – dimensionally challenged when compared to today's newer ships – and insulation between them is poor. The cabins also have mediocre closets and little storage space, yet somehow everyone seems to manage. They are just about adequate for a one-week cruise, as you'll require only a small selection of mainly casual clothes. You'll probably need to store your shoes and luggage under the bed.

Most bathrooms contain a washbasin, toilet, and shower, with very little space for toiletries. Although they are reasonably cheerful, the shower enclosure is small, and has a curtain that you might end up fighting with.

In some cabins, twin beds are fixed in a parallel mode – some are moveable and can be made into a queen-size bed – while others may be in an L-shape. In almost all cabins there is a threshold of about 9ins (23cm) at the bathroom door to step over.

You can get more space and a larger cabin if you book one of the 21 slightly more expensive deluxe-grade cabins on Promenade Deck. These have twin beds that convert to a queen-size bed, set diagonally into a sleeping area adjacent to outside-view windows. There's more drawer space, more closet space, and the bathroom has a half-size tub and shower combination. Bathrobes are also provided. The largest of these deluxe-grade cabins is Cabin 7000.

For even more exclusivity, you can book one of nine suites. All are located in a private area, have fine wood paneling and trim, and come with additional space and better, more personalized service.

The additional space includes a lounge area with sofa (this converts to a double bed – making it ideal for families with children), coffee table and two chairs, a vanity desk, combination TV/DVD, an abundance of drawers, illuminated closets with both hanging space and several shelves, excellent storage space, king-size bed, and bathrobes. The bathroom is fully tiled and has a full-size enamel tub (rare in ships today) with shower, pink granite-look washbasin, and plenty of storage space for toiletries.

Suite occupants also get a semi-private balcony – with a door that is extremely heavy and hard to open – with drinks table and two teak chairs. Book one of the two Grand Suites, and you'll get even more room – plus views over the bows and a larger balcony (these can be overlooked from the open deck above), more floor space, and a walk-in closet. Missing are a bedside telephone and a bathroom telephone.

The accommodation deck hallways are also very narrow on some decks.

DINING. The Seven Seas Restaurant, a large room, consists of a central main section and two long, narrow wings – the Magellan Room and Galileo Room – with large, ocean-view windows. The low ceiling creates a high level of ambient noise. There are two seatings. There are tables for two (but only 14), four, six, or eight, and window tables are for two or six.

If you enjoy eating out adventurously, you could be disappointed. The menus are standard and deviation is difficult. Bottled water costs extra. There is an adequate wine list. Wine prices are quite modest, as are the prices for most alcoholic drinks.

Other dining options. For casual, self-serve breakfasts and lunches, the Veranda Café is the alternative choice, although the tables and seats outdoors are of metal and plastic, and the buffets are basic and old-fashioned. The low cruise fare dictates the use of plastic cups and plastic stirrers – teaspoons are unheard of. At night you can 'dine' under the steel and canvas canopy, where the café becomes a pleasant, outdoors alternative to the dining room – and includes waiter service.

The excellent Italian illy coffee brand is featured aboard this ship, together with a selection of fine teas, in several bars and lounges.

ENTERTAINMENT. The Can Can Lounge, the venue for all entertainment events and social functions, has a stage and hardwood dance floor. It is a single-level room, designed more for cabaret acts than for large-scale production shows. The revue-style shows are typically of the end-of-pier variety type, with an energetic, well-meaning cast of young people who also double as cruise staff during the day, together with some professional cabaret acts.

Another, smaller room, the Oklahoma Lounge, has a stage and dance floor, and is often used to present late-night comedy and other acts.

SPA/FITNESS. Although the Sana Spa facilities are not exactly generous, there is a gymnasium, sauna but no steam room, changing rooms for men and women, and a beauty salon. You can book a massage, an aromatherapy facial, manicure, and pedicure, among other treatments. Sports facilities include basketball, badminton, and table tennis.

Club Med 2
★★★+

Size:	Small Ship
Tonnage:	14,983
Lifestyle:	Premium
Cruise Line:	Club Med Cruises
Former Names:	none
IMO Number:	9007491
Builder:	Ateliers et Chantiers du Havre
Original Cost:	$125 million
Entered Service:	Dec 1992
Registry:	Wallis & Fortuna
Length (ft/m):	613.8/187.1
Beam (ft/m):	65.6/20.0
Draft (ft/m):	16.4/5.0
Propulsion/Propellers:	diesel (9,120kW)/2
Passenger Decks:	8
Total Crew:	200
Passengers (lower beds):	394
Passenger Space Ratio (lower beds):	38.0

Passenger/Crew Ratio (lower beds):	1.9
Cabins (total):	197
Size Range (sq ft/m):	193.8–322/18–30
Cabins (for one person):	0
Cabins (with private balcony):	0
Cabins (wheelchair accessible):	0
Wheelchair accessibility:	None
Cabin Current:	110 and 220 volts
Elevators:	2
Casino (gaming tables):	No
Slot Machines:	No
Swimming Pools:	2
Hot Tubs (on deck):	0
Self-Service Launderette:	No
Dedicated Cinema/Seats:	No
Library:	Yes
Onboard currency:	Euros

The ship's French ambience and style puts wind in your sails

OVERVIEW. This ship appeals best to youthful French-speaking couples and solo travelers who want contemporary facilities and water sports in a casual but chic setting that's different from 'normal' cruise ships, with good food and service, and little or no entertainment.

THE SHIP. *Club Med 2* is one of a pair of the world's largest high-tech sail-cruisers (the other is *Wind Surf*), part-cruise ship, part-yacht. Five huge masts rise 221ft (67.5m) above sea level; they carry seven triangular, self-furling Dacron sails with a total surface area of 26,881 sq ft (2,497 sq m). No human hands touch the sails, as everything is controlled by computer from the bridge. This also keeps the ship on an even keel via the movement of a hydraulic ballast system, so there is no rolling over 6°. When the ship is not using the sails, four diesel-electric motors propel it at up to 12 knots. The ship was refurbished in 2008, when 10 new cabins were added.

An array of water sports facilities is provided (all except scuba gear are included in the cruise fare), and equipment on the aft marina platform includes 12 windsurfers, three sailboats, two waterski boats, several kayaks, 20 single scuba tanks, snorkels, and four motorized water sport boats. There are two small saltwater swimming pools (really 'dip' pools).

Inside, facilities include a main lounge, meeting room, and an extra-charge golf simulator, plus a fitness and beauty center, and piano bar. No gratuities are expected.

Berlitz's Ratings

	Possible	Achieved
Ship	500	372
Accommodation	200	150
Food	400	272
Service	400	274
Entertainment	100	67
Cruise Experience	400	260
OVERALL SCORE		
1395 points out of 2000		

ACCOMMODATION. There are five suites and 192 standard cabins, all of equal size. All cabins are nicely equipped and very comfortable, and have an inviting decor that includes much blond wood cabinetry. They have a minibar/refrigerator, 24-hour room service (but you pay for food), a personal safe, color television, plenty of storage space, bathrobes, and a hairdryer. There are six four-person cabins, and some 35 doubles are fitted with an extra Pullman berth.

DINING. The two main dining rooms are Le Mediterranée and Le Magellan. Both have tables for two, four, six, or eight. There is open seating, so you can sit with whom you wish. The Grand Bleu Restaurant has a delightful open terrace for informal meals. Complimentary wines and beers are available with lunch and dinner; there is also an à la carte wine list, at a price. Afternoon tea is a delight. The cuisine provides French, Continental, and Japanese specialties, and the creativity and presentation are good.

ENTERTAINMENT. Apart from occasional cabaret acts, there is live music each evening.

SPA/FITNESS. The Health Spa has a sauna, beauty salon, and treatment rooms for massage, facials, and body wraps. There is also a decent fitness room and a beauty salon, but spa facilities are split over three separate decks.

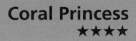

Size:	Mid-size Ship	Passenger/Crew Ratio (lower beds):	2.1
Tonnage:	91,627	Cabins (total):	987
Lifestyle:	Standard	Size Range (sq ft/m):	156–470.0/14.4–43.6
Cruise Line:	Princess Cruises	Cabins (for one person):	0
Former Names:	none	Cabins (with private balcony):	727
IMO Number:	9229659	Cabins (wheelchair accessible):	20
Builder:	Chantiers de l'Atlantique (France)	Wheelchair accessibility:	Good
Original Cost:	$360 million	Cabin Current:	110 volts
Entered Service:	Dec 2002	Elevators:	14
Registry:	Bermuda	Casino (gaming tables):	Yes
Length (ft/m):	964.5/294.0	Slot Machines:	Yes
Beam (ft/m):	105.6/32.2	Swimming Pools:	2
Draft (ft/m):	26/7.9	Hot Tubs (on deck):	5
Propulsion/Propellers:	gas turbine + diesel (40,000kW)/2	Self-Service Launderette:	Yes
Passenger Decks:	11	Dedicated Cinema/Seats:	No
Total Crew:	900	Library:	Yes
Passengers (lower beds):	1,974	Onboard currency:	US$
Passenger Space Ratio (lower beds):	46.4		

A comfortable mid-size ship for mature-age cruisers

OVERVIEW. The layout is quite user-friendly, and less disjointed than on many ships of a similar size. In a 2009 refit, an adults-only 'Sanctuary' area was added to provide a quiet zone, with comfortable, padded sunloungers, and 'Serenity' steward service. Although there's a daily fee, it's worth it.

THE SHIP. *Coral Princess* (sister to *Island Princess*) has an instantly recognizable funnel due to two jet engine-like pods that sit high up on its structure, but these really are mainly for decoration. Four diesel engines provide the generating power. Electrical power is provided by a combination of four diesel and one gas turbine (CODAG) unit; the diesel engines are located in the engine room, while the gas turbine unit is located in the ship's funnel housing.

The interior layout is similar to that of the *Grand*-class ships, but with two decks full of public rooms, lounges, and bars instead of just one. Sensibly, it has three major stair towers. There's a large Movies Under the Stars screen in the second pool area just forward of the funnel. Unlike many modern ships, *Coral Princess* has a walk-around open promenade deck, a feature much appreciated by many.

Adjacent is a Wedding Chapel, from which a live web-cam can relay ceremonies via the Internet. The ship's captain can legally marry (American) couples, thanks to the ship's registry and a special dispensation – though this may depend on where you live and should be verified when in the planning stage. The

Berlitz's Ratings		
	Possible	Achieved
Ship	500	378
Accommodation	200	146
Food	400	256
Service	400	290
Entertainment	100	77
Cruise Experience	400	292
OVERALL SCORE		
1439 points out of 2000		

Wedding Chapel can also host renewal of vows ceremonies, for a fee.

This ship has lots of nooks and crannies, so you can hide away and just read a book if you want to. Also, at the forward end of decks 10 and 11, doors open onto a large observation terrace. There are also several self-service launderettes; these are much appreciated during longer cruises.

Niggles include the fact that the forward elevators go between Decks 15 and 7, but you need to change elevators to get down to the dining rooms on Deck 5.

ACCOMMODATION. With many different price categories, there's a wide choice: 16 Suites with balcony (470 sq ft/43.6 sq m); 184 Mini-Suites with balcony (285–302 sq ft/26.4–28.0 sq m); eight Mini-Suites without balcony (300 sq ft/27.8 sq m); 527 Outside-View Cabins with balcony (217–232 sq ft/ 20–21.5 sq m); 144 Standard Outside-view Cabins (162 sq ft/15 sq m); plus 108 Interior Cabins (156 sq ft/144.5 sq m). There are 20 wheelchair-accessible cabins (217–374 sq ft/20–34.7 sq m). All measurements are approximate. Almost all outside-view cabins have private balconies. Some cabins can accommodate a third, or third and fourth person, which is good for families with children. Some cabins on Emerald Deck (Deck 8) have a view obstructed by lifeboats.

Suites. There are just 16 suites and, although none is really large when compared to those on such ships as *Norwegian Dawn* and *Norwegian Star* (where the largest suites measure a whopping 5,350 sq ft/497 sq m, for example), each has a private balcony. All are named after islands – mostly coral-based islands in the Indian and Pacific oceans. All suites are located on either Deck 9 or Deck 10, but there are no suites or cabins with a view over the stern. There are also four Premium Suites, located sensibly in the ship's center, adjacent to a bank of six elevators. Six other suites, called Verandah Suites, are located further aft.

All suites and cabins are equipped with a refrigerator, personal safe, interactive TV, hairdryer, satellite-dial telephone, and twin beds that convert to a queen-size bed (there are a few exceptions). All accommodation has a bathroom with shower enclosure and toilet. Accommodation designated as suites and mini-suites (there are seven price categories) has a bathtub and separate shower enclosure, and two TV sets.

All passengers receive turndown service and chocolates on pillows nightly, bathrobes on request, and toiletries (larger kits, naturally, for suite/mini-suite occupants). Cabin attendants have many cabins to look after – typically 20 – which does not translate to fine personal service.

DINING. The two main dining rooms, Bordeaux and Provence, are in the forward part of the ship on the two lowest passenger decks. The galley is all the way forward, so it doesn't intersect public spaces. Both are almost identical in design and layout. The ceilings are quite low and make the rooms appear confined. They have plenty of intimate alcoves, and tables are for two, four, six, or eight. There are two seatings for dinner (or you can opt for 'Anytime Dining' in the Bordeaux Restaurant), while breakfast and lunch are on an open-seating basis; you may have to wait for some while at peak times, just as in many large restaurants ashore.

Other dining options. Horizon Court, a casual 24-hour eatery, is located in the forward section of Lido Deck, with superb ocean views. Several self-serve counters provide an array of food for breakfast and lunch buffets, and offer bistro-style casual dinners in the evening. The venue is a bit short on seating, however.

There are two specialty dining rooms: Sabatini's and the Bayou Café. Both cost extra. Sabatini's is an Italian eatery, with colorful tiled Mediterranean-style decor; it is named after Trattoria Sabatini, the 200-year-old institution in Florence. It has Italian-style pizzas and pastas, with a variety of sauces, as well as Italian-style entrées (mains) – all provided with flair and entertainment by the waiters. The food is both creative and tasty, with seriously sized portions. Sabatini's is by reservation only, and there's a cover charge.

The Bayou Café (reserve for this too), open for lunch and dinner, has a cover charge that includes a Hurricane cocktail. It evokes the charm of New Orleans' French Quarter, with wrought-iron decoration, and features Cajun/Creole cuisine. Platters include Peel 'n' Eat Shrimp Piquante, Sausage Grillades, Oysters Sieur de Bienville. Popular entrées include premium steaks (the Porterhouse and New York Strip are good), Seafood Gumbo, and Chorizo Jambalaya, plus Alligator Ribs, Corn Meal Fried Catfish, Chicken Brochette, and Red Pepper Butter Broiled Lobster. Desserts include sweet potato pie and banana whiskey pound cake. The venue has a small stage with baby grand piano, and live jazz is part of the evening dining scenario.

ENTERTAINMENT. The Princess Theater is two decks high, and, unusually, there is much more seating in the upper level than on the main floor below. There are typically two production shows on a seven-day cruise, and three on a 10-day cruise. These are colorful, glamorous shows with well-designed costumes and good lighting.

A second entertainment lounge (Universe Lounge) is designed more for cabaret-style features. It also has two levels – a first for a Princess Cruises ship – and three separate stages, enabling nonstop entertainment to be provided without constant set-ups. The room, which has a full kitchen set, is also used for cooking demonstrations and other life-enrichment participation activities. There is a good mix of music in the various bars and lounges.

For self-improvement, Princess Cruises' Scholar Ship@Sea program offers about 20 courses each cruise. Although introductory classes are free, there's a charge if you want to continue any chosen subject in a smaller setting.

SPA/FITNESS. The Lotus Spa is located aft on one of the uppermost decks. It contains men's and women's saunas, steam rooms, changing rooms, relaxation area, beauty salon, an aerobics exercise room and gymnasium with ocean views and the latest high-tech muscle-pumping, cardio-vascular equipment. There are several large rooms for individual treatments.

Sports enthusiasts will find a nine-hole golf putting course, two computerized golf simulators, and a sports court.

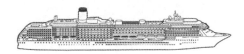

Costa Atlantica
★★★+

Size:	Large Resort Ship
Tonnage:	85,700
Lifestyle:	Standard
Cruise Line:	Costa Cruises
Former Names:	none
IMO Number:	9187796
Builder:	Kverner Masa-Yards (Finland)
Original Cost:	$335 million
Entered Service:	Jul 2000
Registry:	Italy
Length (ft/m):	959.6/292.5
Beam (ft/m):	105.6/32.2
Draft (ft/m):	25.5/7.8
Propulsion/Propellers:	diesel-electric (34,000kW)/ 2 azimuthing pods
Passenger Decks:	12
Total Crew:	920
Passengers (lower beds):	2,112
Passenger Space Ratio (lower beds):	40.5
Passenger/Crew Ratio (lower beds):	2.3
Cabins (total):	1,056
Size Range (sq ft/m):	161.4–387.5/15.0–36.0
Cabins (for one person):	0
Cabins (with private balcony):	742
Cabins (wheelchair accessible):	8
Wheelchair accessibility:	Good
Cabin Current:	110 volts
Elevators:	12
Casino (gaming tables):	Yes
Slot Machines:	Yes
Swimming Pools:	2 (1 w/sliding glass dome)
Hot Tubs (on deck):	4
Self-Service Launderette:	No
Dedicated Cinema/Seats:	No
Library:	Yes
Onboard currency:	Euros

A contemporary Italian ship with volume everywhere

OVERVIEW. This ship is designed to wow the trendy as well as pay homage to many of Italy's great art and past masters. *Costa Atlantica* is aimed at young (and young-at-heart) couples and solo travelers plus families with children who enjoy big-city life. The international clientele are offered constant activity accompanied by Italian ambience and loud entertainment.

THE SHIP. *Costa Atlantica* is a sister (or close sister) to *Costa Deliziosa*, *Costa Favolosa*, *Costa Fascinosa*, *Costa Luminosa*, and *Costa Mediterranea*. It has two centrally located swimming pools outdoors, one with a retractable glass dome cover that can be used in poor weather conditions. A bar abridges two adjacent hot tubs. There's also a smaller pool for children, and a winding water slide spanning two decks in height.

The deck names are inspired by Federico Fellini movies (Roma Deck, Le Notte di Cabiria, La Voce della Luna, La Strada, La Luci del Varieta). One deck is named after a Fellini TV movie, *Ginger and Fred*. The interior design is bold and brash – a mix of classical Italy and contemporary features. Good points include the fact that the interior design allows efficient passenger flow from one public space to another, and there are several floor spaces for dancing, and a wide range of bars and lounges for socializing.

The colorful lobby spans eight decks. Take a drink from the lobby bar and look upwards – the surroundings are visually stunning.

Berlitz's Ratings

	Possible	Achieved
Ship	500	371
Accommodation	200	142
Food	400	241
Service	400	264
Entertainment	100	61
Cruise Experience	400	262
OVERALL SCORE		
1341 points out of 2000		

A small chapel is located forward of the uppermost level. Other facilities include a winding shopping street with boutique stores (Fendi, Gianni Versace, Paul & Shark Yachting – as well as a shop that sells Caffè Florian products), a photo gallery, a video games room, an observation balcony, a casino, and a library with Internet access.

Niggles! Several pillars obstruct passenger flow and sight lines throughout the ship. The fit and finish of some interior decoration is quite poor, and the decor is a bit overdone. Note that *Costa Atlantica* is now based year-round in Shanghai, China, for short cruises. The cuisine has been modified to accommodate Chinese preferences, and announcements are made in Mandarin.

ACCOMMODATION. There are many different price categories, and a healthy (78 percent) proportion of outside-view to interior cabins. All cabins have twin beds that can be converted into a queen-size bed, individually controlled air conditioning (but it can't be turned off), TV set, and telephone. Many cabins have views obstructed by lifeboats on Deck 4 (Roma Deck), the lowest of the accommodation decks, as well as some cabins on Deck 5. Some cabins have pull-down (Pullman-style) berths that are fully hidden in the ceiling when not in use. There is much use of fluorescent lighting in the suites and cabins, and the soundproofing could be much better. Some bathroom fixtures – bath and shower taps in particular – are frustrating to use at first.

Some of the most desirable suites and cabins are those with private balconies on five aft-facing decks (Decks 4, 5, 6, 7, and 8) with views overlooking the stern and ship's wash. Other cabins with private balconies will find the balconies not so private – the partition between one balcony and the next is not a full partition – so you might be able to hear your neighbors.

However, balcony occupants all have good views through glass and wood-topped railings, and the deck is made of teak. The cabins are well laid out, typically with twin beds that convert to a queen-size bed, vanity desk with built-in hairdryer (but you'll need to hold down the on button continuously), large TV set, and personal safe. One closet has moveable shelves, providing more space for storing luggage. However, the lighting is fluorescent, and much too harsh. The bathroom is a simple, modular unit that has shower enclosures with soap dispenser.

The largest suites are designated Penthouse Suites, although they are really quite small when compared with suites aboard other ships of a similar size. However, they do at least offer more space to move around in, and a slightly larger, better bathroom.

DINING. The 1,320-seat Tiziano Dining Room is in the aft section of the ship on two levels, with a spiral stairway between them. There are two seatings, with tables for two, four, six, or eight. Dinner on European cruises is typically scheduled at 7pm and 9pm to accommodate the typically later eating habits of Continental Europeans. Themed evenings are a part of the Costa Cruises tradition, and three different window blinds help create a different feel. However, the artwork is placed at table height, so the room seems more closed-in than it should. Some tables have a less than comfortable view of the harsh lighting of the escalators between the galley and the two decks of the dining room. This cuisine is traditional cruise fare that is best described as banquet-style food. Note that there are no real sommeliers, so the waiters (who are young) serve the wine (which is also young). They also dance at the tables during the cruise – it's a little bit of show business.

Other dining options. A reservations-only 125-seat dinner venue, Ristorante Club Atlantica, with menus by Gualtiero Marchesi, has a cover charge, but suite-grade occupants get a free pass for one evening. It's a smaller, quieter venue, and the food, though nothing special, is cooked to order and is decidedly better than in the main dining room.

Casual breakfast and luncheon self-serve buffet-style meals can be taken in the Botticelli Buffet Restaurant, adjacent to the swimming pools, with seating both indoors and outdoors. A grill (for hamburgers and hot dogs) and a pasta bar are conveniently adjacent to the second pool, while indoors is the Napoli Pizzeria. Excellent (illy brand) cappuccino and espresso coffees are always available in various bars around the ship, served in the right-sized china cups.

One place to see and be seen is in the informal Caffè Florian – a replica of the famous indoor/outdoor café that opened in 1720 in Venice's St Mark's Square. There are four separate salons (Sala delle Stagioni, Sala del Senato, Sala Liberty, and Sala degli Uomini Illustri) and the same fascinating mosaic, marble and wood floors, opulent ceiling art, and special lampshades. Even the espresso/cappuccino machine is a duplicate of the one found in the real thing. The only problem is that the chairs are much too small.

ENTERTAINMENT. A three-deck-high, 949-seat showlounge (Caruso Theater) is an imposing room, with just over 1,000 seats. Spiral stairways at the back of the lounge connect all levels. Stage shows are best seen from the upper three levels, from where the sight lines are reasonably good.

Directly underneath the showlounge is the large Coral Lounge, complete with its own bar. An on-board resident troupe of singers and dancers provides the cast members for colorful, high-energy production shows – though these shows are loud and poor. For nights when there are no big shows, the showlounge presents cabaret acts such as singers, comedy jugglers, magicians, and ventriloquists.

A number of bands and small musical units provide a variety of live music in many lounges and bars, and there is a discotheque.

SPA/FITNESS. The Ischia Spa spans two decks. Facilities include a solarium, eight treatment rooms, lecture rooms, sauna and steam rooms for men and women, and a beauty parlor. A large gymnasium has floor-to-ceiling windows on three sides, including forward-facing ocean views, and an aerobics room with instructor-led classes. There is a jogging track outdoors.

The spa is operated by Steiner, a specialist concession, whose young staff will try to sell you Steiner's own-brand Elemis beauty products. Some fitness classes are free, while some (yoga, for example) cost extra.

Massages (including exotic massages such as Aroma Stone massage, and other wellbeing massages), facials, pedicures, and beauty salon treatments are at extra cost.

Costa Deliziosa
★★★+

Size:	Large Resort Ship	Passenger Space Ratio (lower beds):	41.0/32.7
Tonnage:	92,700	Passenger/Crew Ratio (lower beds):	2.1
Lifestyle:	Standard	Cabins (total):	1,130
Cruise Line:	Costa Cruises	Size Range (sq ft/m):	134.5–534.0/12.5–49.6
Former Names:	none	Cabins (for one person):	0
IMO Number:	9398917	Cabins (with private balcony):	772
Builder:	Fincantieri (Italy)	Cabins (wheelchair accessible):	12
Original Cost:	€548 million	Wheelchair accessibility:	Good
Entered Service:	Mar 2010	Cabin Current:	110 and 220 volts
Registry:	Italy	Elevators:	12
Length (ft/m):	958.0/292.0	Casino (gaming tables):	Yes
Beam (ft/m):	111.5/34.0	Slot Machines:	Yes
Draft (ft/m):	26.2/8.0	Swimming Pools:	2 (1 w/sliding glass dome)
Propulsion/Propellers:	diesel-electric (42,000kW)/ 2 azimuthing pods	Hot Tubs (on deck):	4
		Self-Service Launderette:	No
Passenger Decks:	13	Dedicated Cinema/Seats:	No
Total Crew:	1,050	Library:	Yes
Passengers (lower beds):	2,260	Onboard currency:	Euros

It's Italy afloat aboard this casual, contemporary big ship

OVERVIEW. This ship, sister to *Costa Luminosa*, was named in Dubai, the first new cruise ship to be named in an Arab city (instead of Champagne a bottle of fig juice was used for the ceremony). Most passengers will be Italian, with a sprinkling of other nationalities.

THE SHIP. *Costa Deliziosa* has a nicely balanced profile and a single large funnel in the Costa colors of yellow and blue. A two-deck midships Lido area swimming pool can be covered with a sliding glass roof in poor weather. A large 194-sq-ft (18-sq-m) poolside movie screen often plays lots of Costa Cruises commercials as well as feature films.

The interior decor, which includes marble and gold, pays tribute to the senses, although sensory overkill might be a better description; in any event, it's a lot of overdone bling. The focal point (and always a good meeting place) is the atrium lobby, which features a large sculpture, *Sphere*, by Arnaldo Pomodoro.

The public rooms include 11 bars (one of the largest is Grand Bar Mirabilis), a large casino (Casino Gaius, for table gaming and slot machines), lots of lounges and entertainment venues to enjoy, including a piano bar (Excite), card room, a small screening room (Cinema Etoiles – a 4D cinema highlights sound and lighting effects, with scent pumped in to heighten the experience), a cigar lounge (Tabac Blonde), and a shopping arcade (Galleria Shops).

Gratuities are charged to your onboard account. Although Costa Cruises is noted for its 'Italian' style, ambience and spirit, there are few Italian crew members

Berlitz's Ratings		
	Possible	Achieved
Ship	500	388
Accommodation	200	143
Food	400	246
Service	400	271
Entertainment	100	65
Cruise Experience	400	270
OVERALL SCORE		
1383 points out of 2000		

on board. Although many officers are Italian, most of the crew members, particularly the dining room and housekeeping staff, are from the Philippines. But the lifestyle on board is perceived to be Italian – lively, noisy, with lots of love for life and a love of all things casual, even on so-called formal nights.

All printed material – room service folio, menus, etc. – will typically be in six languages. During peak European school holiday periods, particularly Christmas and Easter, you can expect to be cruising with a lot of children of all ages.

As aboard other Costa ships, note that for embarkation, few staff members are on duty at the gangway when you arrive; they merely point you in the direction of your deck, or to the ship's elevators and do not escort you to your cabin. Also, note that 'wallpaper' music is played 24 hours a day in all accommodation hallways and elevators, so you may well hear it if you are a light sleeper. Expect lots of announcements – especially for revenue activities such as art auctions, bingo, horse racing – and much hustling for drinks.

ACCOMMODATION. About 68 percent of all accommodation suites and cabins have an ocean view, and there are 772 balcony cabins. Four suites and 52 Samsara Spa cabins are adjacent to (and considered part of) the designated wellness area. Samsara suite/cabin occupants get unlimited access to the spa plus two treatments and fitness or meditation lessons as part of their package, and dine in one of the two Samsara restaurants.

A pillow menu, with five choices, is available to suite-grade occupants, who also get bathrobes, better amenities, a shaving mirror, and walk-in closets. Background music is played 24 hours a day in all hallways and elevators, so you may well be aware of it if you are a light sleeper.

DINING. The 1,264-seat Albatros Restaurant is the ship's large, main dining hall. It is located at the aft of the ship and you eat at one of two seatings for dinner, at tables for two to eight assigned according to your grade of accommodation. This dining room offers traditional cruise fare that is best described as banquet-style food that shows little finesse. Note that there are no real sommeliers, so the waiters, who are young, serve the wine, which is also young. They also dance at the tables during the cruise – it's a little bit of show business.

A 68-seat Samsara Restaurant is adjacent to the Albatros Restaurant; it is a smaller venue that is more intimate and much quieter. It features healthier food with reduced calories, fat, and salt content. Menu creations are under the direction of dietary consultant and Michelin-starred chef Ettore Boccia, known for molecular Italian cuisine. The venue is open for lunch and dinner to those in Samsara-grade suites and cabins, and to anyone else for dinner only at an extra daily or weekly charge.

Other dining options. The Restaurant Club Deliziosa is a reservations-only, specialty restaurant with 182 seats that features à la carte dining with a pristine show kitchen. The food is cooked à la minute and so it is fresher, looks better, and has more taste than food served in the main dining room. Menus are under the direction of Italy's molecular cooking master, Ettore Bocchia, Costa's consulting chef.

Buffet Muscadins is the self-serve casual eatery, but its disjointed layout invites congestion. While there appears to be a decent choice of food, it is extremely repetitive (particularly for breakfast), and a major source of passenger complaints. Also, after it closes in the afternoon, only slices of pizza are available.

One event not to be missed, however, is an 'Elegant Teatime,' during which rather nice cakes and sandwiches are served, together with a choice of teas or tisanes, in one of the lounges.

Espresso/cappuccinos coffees (illy brand) are available in the Atrium Bar – a good place to sit and be seen, and to observe others.

ENTERTAINMENT. The Theater Duse, with over 800 seats, spans three decks (with seating on all three levels) and is the ship's main showlounge, with the latest computer-controlled lighting and high-volume sound equipment. High-energy production shows are performed here, with Costa's own song and dance troupe.

SPA/FITNESS. The Samsara Spa area occupies some 37,674 sq ft (3,500 sq m) of space, and spans two decks in height. Facilities include a large fitness room (with all the techno gym muscle-pumping equipment you could ever want), separate saunas, steam rooms, UVB solarium, changing rooms for men and women, and 10 private massage/body treatment rooms. Two VIP treatment rooms, available to couples as a half-day rental, are located on the upper level.

The facilities are staffed and operated by Steiner Leisure, a specialist spa/beauty concession. Some fitness classes are free, while some, such as Pathway to Yoga, and Pathway to Pilates, cost extra. It's wise to make any treatment appointments early as time slots can go quickly.

You can buy a day pass in order to use the sauna/steam rooms, thermal suite and relaxation area, at a cost of €35 per person. However, there's an additional free (no charge) sauna for men and women, but to access it you must walk through an active fitness area, maybe with your bathrobe on – not comfortable for everyone, especially women.

For the sports-minded, a Grand Prix Formula One simulator is housed in a glass enclosure close to the spa. A golf simulator provides a choice of 37 18-hole courses.

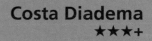

Costa Diadema
★★★+

Size:	Large Resort Ship	Passenger/Crew Ratio (lower beds):	2.9
Tonnage:	132,500	Cabins (total):	1,854
Lifestyle:	Standard	Size Range (sq ft/m):	125.9–554.3/11.7–51.5
Cruise Line:	Costa Cruises	Cabins (for one person):	0
Former Names:	none	Cabins (with private balcony):	913
IMO Number:	9636888	Cabins (wheelchair accessible):	8
Builder:	Fincantieri (Italy)	Wheelchair accessibility:	Good
Original Cost:	€550 million	Cabin Current:	110 and 220 volts
Entered Service:	Nov 2013	Elevators:	19
Registry:	Italy	Casino (gaming tables):	Yes
Length (ft/m):	1,003.9/306.0	Slot Machines:	Yes
Beam (ft/m):	122.0/37.2	Swimming Pools:	2 (1 w/sliding glass dome)
Draft (ft/m):	27.2/8.3	Hot Tubs (on deck):	8
Propulsion/Propellers:	diesel-electric (42,000kW)/2	Self-Service Launderette:	No
Passenger Decks:	14	Dedicated Cinema/Seats:	No
Total Crew:	1,253	Library:	Yes
Passengers (lower beds):	3,708	Onboard currency:	Euros
Passenger Space Ratio (lower beds):	35.7		

This sparkly, family-friendly Italian ship is more water taxi than cruise ship

OVERVIEW. *Costa Diadema* is the newest, largest, and grandest ship in the growing Costa Cruises fleet of family-friendly ships, and it's now the company's flagship. This is all about casual cruising for a youthful clientele who enjoy the Italian flair for life.

THE SHIP. The ship (whose name means 'tiara') has a well-proportioned profile with a rounded front, bolt-upright Costa yellow funnel, and nicely tiered aft decks. The lifeboats are mounted lower down; this position gives a sense of balance to the ship's towering superstructure. *Costa Diadema* is equipped with a cold ironing facility, allowing it to plug into shore-side electric power, and all solid waste is collected for recycling. All exterior decks are covered in a rubberized material (no teak anywhere), but the railings are made of hardwood. A nice feature is the outdoor 1,640-ft (500-m) walk-around promenade deck.

The interior decor is best decribed as glowing, very bright, and ultra-bold, The central focal point is an (enlarged) atrium lobby (Atrio Eliodoro), with four panoramic elevators. Look upwards from the floor of the lobby and you'll see the inner part of the multi-deck atrium studded with diamonds – well, blue diamond-look lighting (you'll find it on the ceilings of other public areas, too). In fact, you'll see diamonds in the artworks throughout the ship. The reception desk and shore excursion desk (called the Costa Travel Office) are located to one side, while comfortable seating is set around the lobby and adjacent areas.

Berlitz's Ratings		
	Possible	Achieved
Ship	500	391
Accommodation	200	143
Food	400	246
Service	400	268
Entertainment	100	65
Cruise Experience	400	264
OVERALL SCORE		
1377 points out of 2000		

There are seven restaurants and eateries (four of these are at extra cost) and 15 bars to enjoy including a Birreia La Flamma pub (with several draft beers/lagers).

A whole shopping street awaits you in the form of the Portobello Market Piazza – filled with designer stores within its 11,840-sq-ft (1,100-sq-m) area. Other public rooms include a 4D racing car experience, and a chapel – a Costa Cruises must-have.

Niggles include the fact that, in common with many large resort ships today, there is little open space on the upper decks, so be prepared to hunt for seating around the main swimming pool/water park area. You'll need to take a towel from your cabin, as they are not provided at the pool. Note that passengers embark and disembark at each port of call, so a cruise is more like a water taxi; this means there is little communication between staff and passengers. This is also a high-density ship, with the lowest number of crew per passengers of all the ships in the Costa Cruises fleet.

For families with children, there are several age-divided playrooms and indoor-outdoor areas overseen by youth counselors, plus video gaming rooms.

ACCOMMODATION. The accommodation configuration consists of 12 Grand Suites, 49 Suites, 14 Mini-Suites, 795 Balcony Cabin, 110 Cove Balcony, 240 Oceanview Cabins, and 666 Interior Cabins. The Grand Suites are not true suites (there's no completely separate bedroom), and are small when compared to many other ships; they measure 554.3 sq ft (51.5 sq m), including balcony.

Some 130 of these are designated Samsara Spa-grade suites/cabins, whose occupants eat in the intimate Samsara Restaurant.

While suites have larger bathrooms (some with a tub/shower), surprisingly, many cabins have a shower curtain, instead of a proper glazed door, and a shower head that is fixed (no flexible shower hose except in high-grade accommodation).

DINING. Restaurant Sissi is the cavernous main dining room; located aft, it is two decks high, with bright decor. Seating, which is allocated according to your accommodation grade and location, is at banquettes and individual chairs without armrests.

A second dining room, the single-deck Scudo Rosso Restaurant, is located in the center of the ship.

Samsara Restaurant is a smaller, more intimate venue for occupants of Samsara-grade accommodation. The cuisine focuses more on healthy items, with reduced calories and less fat and salt.

The self-serve Corona Blu Restaurant (a buffet on the Lido Deck) has tacky (AIDA-style), unhygienic cutlery stands on tables.

Costa has introduced some more ethnic-centric eating areas (some at extra cost), such as a Vinoteca, Proseccherria, a Bavarian Bierkeller, a Japanese Tavola Teppanyaki Grill, an extra-cost pizzeria (it's in the Piazza, so it's called the Pizzeria in Piazza Pizza – now there's a mouthful!), and a Gelateria. This gives you a choice of different venues and food styles, plus illy brand espresso/cappuccino from extra-cost coffee bars.

The Club Diadema restaurant is an extra-cost, reservations-required dining spot, and delivers more upscale cuisine. It's worth it if you are celebrating something special, or for something a little different to the noisy main dining room.

ENTERTAINMENT. The Emerald Theater – the ship's showlounge – is spread over three decks and has over 1,500 seats (with tables for drinks), many of which have upright backs, a large stage with proscenium arch, and the latest in LED lighting technology. Costa Cruises' revue-style shows – performed by a troupe of resident onboard singers/dancers – are all about color, lights, high-energy action, and volume.

A Country Rock Club is something new for Costa Cruises; it's an upbeat venue for listening to country-rock crossover music.

SPA/FITNESS. Measuring some 780 sq m (8,396 sq ft), Samsara Spa is a large facility, spread over three decks. It includes a large gymnasium with the latest in muscle-training equipment, saunas, steam rooms, a thermal area, and several massage/body treatment rooms. VIP treatment rooms are also available to couples for half-day rentals. You'll need to purchase a day pass in order to use the sauna/steam rooms, thermal suite and relaxation area. Some fitness classes are free, while others cost extra.

Costa Fascinosa
★★★+

Size:	Large Resort Ship
Tonnage:	114,500
Lifestyle:	Standard
Cruise Line:	Costa Cruises
Former Names:	none
IMO Number:	9479864
Builder:	Fincantieri (Italy)
Original Cost:	€510 million
Entered Service:	May 2012
Registry:	Italy
Length (ft/m):	952.0/290.2
Beam (ft/m):	116.4/35.5
Draft (ft/m):	26.9/8.2
Propulsion/Propellers:	diesel-electric (75,600kW)/2
Passenger Decks:	13
Total Crew:	1,090
Passengers (lower beds):	3,016
Passenger Space Ratio (lower beds):	38.0

Passenger/Crew Ratio (lower beds):	2.7
Cabins (total):	1,508
Size Range (sq ft/m):	179.7–482.2/16.7–44.8
Cabins (for one person):	0
Cabins (with private balcony):	650
Cabins (wheelchair accessible):	12
Wheelchair accessibility:	Good
Cabin Current:	110 and 220 volts
Elevators:	14
Casino (gaming tables):	Yes
Slot Machines:	Yes
Swimming Pools:	2
Hot Tubs (on deck):	5
Self-Service Launderette:	No
Dedicated Cinema/Seats:	No
Library:	Yes
Onboard currency:	Euros

Upbeat Italian decor and style, for trendy family cruising

OVERVIEW. Costa Cruises is for those who want to enjoy the casual life to the full. It does a good job of providing first-time cruise passengers with a packaged seagoing vacation – particularly for families with children – that's a mix of sophistication and chaos, accompanied by loud music everywhere.

THE SHIP. With an instantly recognizable single, large yellow funnel, *Costa Fascinosa* is a sister to *Costa Favolosa*, *Costa Fortuna*, *Costa Magica*, *Costa Pacifica*, and *Costa Serena*. On the open decks, two pool areas can be covered with retractable glass domes – useful for inclement weather conditions; one pool has a long water slide, much liked by children; there is also a large poolside movie screen. However, the open deck space is pretty cramped when the ship is full, the plastic sunloungers are crammed together, and do not have cushioned pads.

With three decks packed with 13 bars and lounges and other public rooms, there's a place for all tastes. The decor throughout is on the wild side. The focal social point is a three-deck-high atrium lobby, with four glass panoramic elevators providing a neat view over the lobby bar – a good place for espresso/cappuccino and people-watching. The Casino is large and very colorful, but the slot machines occupy a separate area from the gaming tables, so serious gamers can concentrate. Other public rooms include a small library, an Internet-connection center, 4D cinema, card room, art gallery, and video game room, plus a chapel – a standard aboard all Costa Cruises' ships.

Berlitz's Ratings

	Possible	Achieved
Ship	500	381
Accommodation	200	143
Food	400	246
Service	400	269
Entertainment	100	65
Cruise Experience	400	260
OVERALL SCORE		
1364 points out of 2000		

Families like Costa Cruises for its perceived 'Italian' style, ambience and spirit, and most passengers will be Italian, with a sprinkling of other European nationals. However, you won't find many Italian hotel service staff on board – although many of the officers are Italian, most crew members, particularly the dining room and housekeeping staff, are from the Philippines. But the lifestyle on board is decidedly Italian – lively, noisy, and full of sparkle. Naturally, during peak European school-holiday periods, especially during Christmas and Easter, you can expect to be cruising with a lot of children of all ages.

Printed material such as the cabin service folio and menus, are provided in six languages – Italian, English, French, German, Portuguese, and Spanish – and announcements are also made in several languages.

As aboard other Costa ships, few staff members are on duty at the gangway when you arrive for embarkation; they merely point you in the direction of your deck, or to the ship's elevators and do not escort you to your cabin.

ACCOMMODATION. There are many accommodation price grades, from two-bed interior cabins to grand suites with private balcony, although in reality there are only three different sizes: suites with 'private' balcony – which are really not particularly large in comparison with some other large ships; two- or four-bed outside-view cabins; and two- or four-bed interior cabins. Fortunately, no cabins have views obstructed by lifeboats or other safety equipment views, and, in most cabins, twin beds can be changed to a double/queen-bed configuration.

Eight Grand Suites, in the center of the ship on one of the uppermost decks, comprise the largest accommodation. They have a queen-size bed and larger living area with vanity desk; the bathrooms have a tub and two washbasins.

A total of 103 Samsara Spa Suites are designated as Samsara-grade. Occupants get unlimited spa access plus two treatments, and fitness or meditation lessons as part of the package. These grades have an Oriental decorative theme, special Samsara bathroom personal amenities, and can eat in one of two designated Samsara Restaurants.

Suite-grade occupants get bathrobes and better amenities, shaving mirror, a pillow menu, and walk-in closets – although the hangers are plastic. Music is played 24 hours a day in all accommodation hallways and elevators, so you may well hear it if you are a light sleeper.

DINING. There are two principal dining rooms, Il Gattopardo and Otto e Mezza. One is aft, the other in the ship's center. Tables for two to eight are allocated according to your accommodation grade and location, in one of two seating times. These dining rooms offer traditional cruise fare that is best described as banquet-style food. Note that there are no real sommeliers, so the waiters serve the wine. They also dance at the tables during the cruise – for a bit of show business.

Two Samsara Restaurants – open for lunch and dinner to those in Samsara-grade suites and cabins, and to anyone else for dinner only at an extra charge – have separate entrances. While the two main restaurants offer traditional cruise fare, these 'spa cuisine' spots feature healthier food – reduced calories, fat, and salt, with menu creations under the direction of dietary consultant and Michelin-star chef Ettore Boccia.

Other dining options. A reservations-required, extra-cost restaurant, Club Fascinosa, has fine table settings and leather-bound menus. The self-serve, buffet-style eatery, Tulipano Nero Buffet, is open for breakfast, lunch, afternoon pizzas, and coffee or tea at any time. A balcony level provides additional seating, but you'll need to carry your own food plates because there are no trays, which makes it difficult to carry both food and a beverage at the same time. The food in this venue is extremely repetitive, and a major source of passenger complaints.

Additionally, a venue called Caffeteria is the place to go for decent, extra-cost illy-brand coffees and Italian sweet pastries.

ENTERTAINMENT. The Fascinosa Showlounge seats over 800. It's three decks high and is the venue for all production shows and large-scale cabaret acts, with a revolving stage, hydraulic orchestra pit, good sound, and seating on three levels, the upper levels being tiered through two decks.

High-energy revue-style shows are performed by a small troupe of resident onboard singers/dancers, with fast-moving action and busy lighting and costume changes.

SPA/FITNESS. The Samsara Spa is a large facility occupying some 64,585 sq ft (6,000 sq m) of space, including relaxation areas, spread over two decks. It has a large fitness room, separate saunas, steam rooms, UVB solarium, changing rooms for men and women, and 10 body treatment rooms. Two VIP treatment rooms, available to couples for half-day rentals, are located on the upper level.

The Spa/fitness facilities are staffed and operated by Steiner Leisure, a specialist spa/beauty concession. Some fitness classes are free, while some, such as Pathway to Yoga, Pathway to Pilates, and Pathway to Meditation, cost extra. It's wise to make appointments early as time slots can go quickly.

You can buy a day pass in order to use the sauna/steam rooms, thermal suite and relaxation area, at a cost of €35 per person. However, there's an additional no-charge sauna for men and women, but to access it you must walk through an active fitness area, maybe with your bathrobe on – not comfortable for everyone.

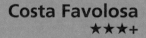

Costa Favolosa
★★★+

Size:	Large Resort Ship
Tonnage:	114,500
Lifestyle:	Standard
Cruise Line:	Costa Cruises
Former Names:	none
IMO Number:	9479852
Builder:	Fincantieri (Italy)
Original Cost:	€510 million
Entered Service:	Jul 2011
Registry:	Italy
Length (ft/m):	952.0/290.2
Beam (ft/m):	116.4/35.5
Draft (ft/m):	26.9/8.2
Propulsion/Propellers:	diesel-electric (75,600kW)/2
Passenger Decks:	13
Total Crew:	1,110
Passengers (lower beds):	3,012
Passenger Space Ratio (lower beds):	38.0
Passenger/Crew Ratio (lower beds):	2.7
Cabins (total):	1,506
Size Range (sq ft/m):	179.7–482.2/16.7–44.8
Cabins (for one person):	0
Cabins (with private balcony):	579
Cabins (wheelchair accessible):	12
Wheelchair accessibility:	Good
Cabin Current:	110 and 220 volts
Elevators:	14
Casino (gaming tables):	Yes
Slot Machines:	Yes
Swimming Pools:	2
Hot Tubs (on deck):	5
Self-Service Launderette:	No
Dedicated Cinema/Seats:	No
Library:	Yes
Onboard currency:	Euros

Upbeat Italian decor and style, for family cruising

OVERVIEW. Costa Cruises is a line for those who like lively atmosphere. It does a good job of providing first-time cruise passengers with a packaged seagoing vacation – particularly for families with children – that is a mix of sophistication and chaos, accompanied by loud music everywhere. Most passengers are Italian, with a sprinkling of other European nationals.

THE SHIP. Displaying a single, large funnel, *Costa Favolosa* is a close sister to *Costa Serena*. Two pool areas can be covered with retractable glass domes – useful in case of bad weather. One has a long water slide, which is great for kids. There is a large poolside movie screen and, on one of the upper decks, a Grand Prix simulator. However, the open deck space can be pretty cramped when the ship is full, so the sunloungers, which don't have cushioned pads, will be crammed together.

There are three decks full of bars and lounges plus many other public rooms. This ship has a glass-domed rotunda atrium lobby that is nine decks high, with excellent upward views from the lobby bar, as well as from its four glass panoramic elevators.

The Casino is large and glitzy, but always lively and entertaining – slot machines occupy a separate area to gaming tables, so serious gamers can concentrate. There's a very small library, an Internet center, card room, art gallery, 4D cinema (Belphegor), and a video game room, plus a small chapel – a standard aboard all Costa Cruises' ships.

Berlitz's Ratings

	Possible	Achieved
Ship	500	382
Accommodation	200	143
Food	400	246
Service	400	269
Entertainment	100	65
Cruise Experience	400	262
OVERALL SCORE		
1367 points out of 2000		

Although Costa Cruises is noted for its 'Italian' style, ambience and spirit, there are few Italian crew members on board. Although many officers are Italian, most of the crew members, particularly the dining room and housekeeping staff, are from the Philippines. But the lifestyle on board is perceived to be Italian – lively, noisy, with lots of love for life and a love of all things casual, even on so-called formal nights.

All printed material – room service folio, menus, etc. – will typically be in six languages: Italian, English, French, German, Portuguese, and Spanish. During peak European school holiday periods, particularly Christmas and Easter, you can expect to be cruising with a lot of children of all ages.

As aboard other Costa ships, note that for embarkation, few staff members are on duty at the gangway when you arrive; they merely point you in the direction of your deck, or to the ship's elevators and do not escort you to your cabin. Also, note that 'wallpaper' music is played 24 hours a day in all accommodation hallways and elevators, so you may well hear it if you are a light sleeper.

ACCOMMODATION. There are numerous accommodation price grades, from two-bed interior cabins to grand suites with private balcony although in reality there are only three different sizes: suites with 'private' balcony – which are really not particularly large in comparison with some other large ships; two- or four-bed outside view cabins; and two- or four-bed interior cabins. Fortunately, no cabins have views obstructed by lifeboats or other safety equipment views, and, in most cabins, twin beds can be changed to a double/queen-bed configuration.

Two Grand Suites comprise the largest accommodation, and include a large balcony with hot tub. They have a queen-size bed and larger living area with vanity desk; the bathrooms have a tub and two washbasins.

If you are into wellness treatments, there are 12 Samsara Spa Suites just aft of the spa itself, although 99 cabins, including the 12 suites, are designated as Samsara-grade. Samsara suite/cabin occupants get unlimited access to the spa plus two treatments and fitness or meditation lessons as part of their package, and dine in one of the two Samsara restaurants. All Samsara-designated accommodation grades have an Oriental decorative theme, and special Samsara bathroom personal amenities.

A pillow menu, with five choices, has been introduced in all suite-grade accommodation. Only suite grades get bathrobes and better amenities, shaving mirror, and walk-in closets – although the hangers are plastic. Music is played 24 hours a day in all hallways and elevators, so you may well hear it if you are a light sleeper.

DINING. There are two principal dining rooms, Duke of Burgundy and Duke of Orleans. One is aft, the other in the ship's center. Tables for two to eight are allocated according to your accommodation grade and location, in one of two seating times. These dining rooms offer traditional cruise fare that is best described as banquet-style food. Note that there are no real sommeliers, so the waiters serve the wine. They also dance at the tables during the cruise – it's a little bit of show business.

Two 100-seat Samsara Restaurants (spa cuisine spots) are provided with separate entrances. These are for those seeking healthier food with reduced calories, fat, and salt content. Menu creations are under the direction of dietary consultant and Michelin-starred chef Ettore Boccia, known for his molecular Italian cuisine. These venues are open for lunch and dinner to those in Samsara-grade suites and cabins, and to anyone else for dinner only at an extra daily or weekly charge.

Other dining options. The intimate Favolosa Club Restaurant sits under a huge glass dome and Murano-glass decorative elements. Fine table settings, china,

silverware and leather-bound menus are provided. There's a cover charge and reservations are required.

The self-service Ca' d'Oro buffet restaurant offers breakfast, lunch, afternoon pizzas, and coffee and tea at any time. A balcony level provides additional seating, but you'll need to carry your own food plates since there are no trays. The food in this venue is extremely repetitive, and a major source of passenger complaints.

Additionally, the Caffeteria is a good place to go for decent (extra-cost) coffees and Italian pastries, but all bars have coffee machines (featuring illy brand coffees), at extra cost.

ENTERTAINMENT. The Favolosa showlounge, which seats more than 800, utilizes the latest in LED technology. Three decks high, it is decorated in a Baroque style, with warm colors and a Murano-glass chandelier. It is the venue for all production shows and large-scale cabaret acts, is stunningly glitzy, and has a revolving stage, hydraulic orchestra pit, superb sound, and seating on three levels – the upper levels are tiered through two decks.

Revue-style shows are performed by a small troupe of resident onboard singers and dancers. Their fast-moving action, busy lighting and costume changes all add up to a high-energy performance.

SPA/FITNESS. The Samsara Spa is a large facility that occupies 23,186 sq ft (2,154 sq m), spread over two decks. It includes a large fitness room, separate saunas, steam rooms, UVB solarium, changing rooms for men and women, and 10 body treatment rooms. Two VIP treatment rooms, available to couples as a half-day rental, are located on the upper level.

The Spa/fitness facilities are staffed and operated by Steiner Leisure, a specialist spa/beauty concession. Some fitness classes are free, while some, such as Pathway to Yoga, Pathway to Pilates, and Pathway to Meditation, cost extra. It's wise to make appointments early as time slots can go quickly.

You can buy a day pass in order to use the sauna/steam rooms, thermal suite and relaxation area, at a cost of €35 per person. However, there's an additional no-charge sauna for men and women, but to access it you must walk through an active fitness area, maybe with your bathrobe on, which might not be comfortable for everyone.

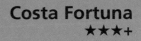

Costa Fortuna
★★★+

Size:	Large Resort Ship
Tonnage:	102,587
Lifestyle:	Standard
Cruise Line:	Costa Cruises
Former Names:	none
IMO Number:	9239783
Builder:	Cantieri Sestri Navale (Italy)
Original Cost:	$381 million
Entered Service:	Nov 2003
Registry:	Italy
Length (ft/m):	892.3/272.0
Beam (ft/m):	124.6/38.0
Draft (ft/m):	27.2/8.3
Propulsion/Propellers:	diesel-electric (34,000kW)/ 2 azimuthing pods
Passenger Decks:	13
Total Crew:	1,068
Passengers (lower beds):	2,716

Passenger Space Ratio (lower beds):	37.7
Passenger/Crew Ratio (lower beds):	2.5
Cabins (total):	1,358
Size Range (sq ft/m):	179.7–482.2/16.7–44.8
Cabins (for one person):	0
Cabins (with private balcony):	522
Cabins (wheelchair accessible):	8
Wheelchair accessibility:	Good
Cabin Current:	110 and 220 volts
Elevators:	14
Casino (gaming tables):	Yes
Slot Machines:	Yes
Swimming Pools:	2
Hot Tubs (on deck):	6
Self-Service Launderette:	No
Dedicated Cinema/Seats:	No
Library:	Yes
Onboard currency:	Euros

A large, colorful family-friendly Italian-style ship

OVERVIEW. *Costa Fortuna* – now over 10 years old – was built to impress trendy city-dwellers at every turn. It absorbs passengers quite well, with a good passenger/space ratio. While a variety of nationalities are carried, most of the passengers are Italian, so the ship is lively but quite noisy, with lots of children running around, particularly during the main European school holiday periods.

THE SHIP. The ship's name is an interesting one: in Greek mythology, Fortuna is the daughter of Poseidon (God of the sea), as well as being associated with the Temple Fortuna, located along one of Pompeii's conserved streets.

The aft decks are well tiered, with cut-off quarters that make the ship's stern look a little less square than it otherwise would. There are three pools, one of which can be covered by a sliding glass dome in case of inclement weather, while one pool (Barcelona Pool) features a long water slide. There is not a lot of open deck space considering the number of passengers carried, so sunloungers tend to be crammed together (there's a lack of small tables for drinks – or for somewhere to place those small items you always take to the pool), and they lack cushioned pads.

The interior decor focuses on the Italian passenger ships of yesteryear, so much of the finishing detail replicates the Art Deco interiors fitted aboard ocean liners such as the *Conte de Savoia*, *Michelangelo*, *Neptunia*, *Rafaello*, *Rex*, etc., although in the kind of contemporary colors not associated with

Berlitz's Ratings

	Possible	Achieved
Ship	500	380
Accommodation	200	143
Food	400	246
Service	400	268
Entertainment	100	64
Cruise Experience	400	261
OVERALL SCORE		
1362 points out of 2000		

such ships, whose interiors were rather subdued.

The deck names are those of major cities in Europe and North and South America (Barcelona, Buenos Aires, Caracas, Lisbon, Genoa, Miami). The passenger flow is generally good, with few congestion points.

There are three decks full of lounges, and 11 bars to enjoy, and almost all have espresso coffee machines – a must for Italians – featuring the illy brand. The interior focal point is a nine-deck high, glass-domed atrium lobby: it houses a Costa Bar on the lower level, a bank of four glass-walled (panoramic) elevators, and, in a tribute to ship buffs, 26 models of Italian ships past and present are glued upside down on the ceiling – it's a bit of a strange feeling to look at them and then look at your feet. The lowest three decks connect the public rooms, the upper levels being mainly for accommodation (plus the pool deck).

For gamers, the Neptunia 1932 Casino is the place to go (if you want to get from the center to the aft lounges you have to walk through it). There are plenty of gaming tables plus an array of slot machines to entertain you. There's also a chapel – standard aboard Costa ships – and a small library that's a bit of a token gesture, an Internet center, card room, art gallery, and video games room.

Although Costa Cruises is noted for its 'Italian' style, ambience and spirit, there are few Italian crew members on board. Although many officers are Italian, most of the crew members, particularly the dining room and housekeeping staff, are from the

Philippines. But the lifestyle on board is perceived to be Italian – lively, noisy, with lots of love for life and a love of all things casual, even on so-called formal nights.

All printed material – room service folio, menus, etc. – will typically be in six languages: Italian, English, French, German, Portuguese, and Spanish. During peak European school-holiday periods, particularly Christmas and Easter, you can expect to be cruising with a lot of children of all ages.

As aboard other Costa ships, note that for embarkation, few staff members are on duty at the gangway when you arrive; they merely point you in the direction of your deck, or to the ship's elevators and do not escort you to your cabin. Also, note that 'wallpaper' music is played 24 hours a day in all accommodation hallways and elevators, so you may well hear it if you are a light sleeper. Niggles include the drinks package and its rules.

ACCOMMODATION. There are 15 price grades, from two-bed interior cabins to grand suites with private balcony, although in reality there are only three different sizes: suites with balcony, two- or four-bed outside-view cabins (some 335 of which have portholes rather than windows), and two- or four-bed interior cabins. There are also two cabins for solo travelers. In an example of good design, no cabins have lifeboat-obstructed views; this is something not easy to design in large ships such as this.

The largest accommodation can be found in eight Grand Suites, located in the center of the ship on one of the higher decks. They have a queen-size bed; bathrooms have a tub and two washbasins.

Note that 12 of the most desirable (outside-view) wheelchair-accessible cabins are rather idiotically located a long way from elevators, while eight interior cabins are located close to elevators.

DINING. There are two dining rooms: the 1,046-seat Michelangelo 1965 Restaurant (aft), whose ceiling features frescoes by the Great Masters, and the 664-seat Rafaello 1965 Restaurant (midships); both two decks high and have two seatings. Note that dinner on European cruises is typically scheduled at 7pm and 9pm. Costa Cruises prides itself on the more than 50 types of pasta it uses during a typical one-week cruise. There is a wine list, although there are no wine waiters, and nearly all the wines (mostly Italian) are really very young.

Other dining options. The 94-seat Conte Grande 1927 Club is the more intimate upscale dining venue with seating for around 150 under a huge glass dome – if the lights were turned out, you might be able to see the stars. In its show kitchen, chefs can be seen preparing their masterpieces. Fine table settings, china, silverware, and leather-bound menus are used. Reservations are required, and there is a cover charge.

The Christoforo Columbus 1954 Buffet Restaurant is a self-serve eatery for breakfast, lunch, afternoon pizzas, and beverages at any time. The food in this venue is repetitive, and a major source of passenger complaints. Also, good cappuccino and espresso coffees are always available in the various bars.

ENTERTAINMENT. The Rex 1932 Theater spans three decks in the ship's forward-most section. It is a stunning setting for all production shows and large-scale cabaret acts, and has a revolving stage, hydraulic orchestra pit, excellent (but usually loud) sound system, and seating on three levels – the upper levels being tiered through two decks.

Typical fare consists of revue-style shows performed by a small troupe of resident singers/dancers, with fast-moving action and busy lighting and costume changes that all add up to a high-energy performance.

SPA/FITNESS. Facilities in the two-deck high Saturnia Spa 1927, and measures about 14,424 sq ft (1,340 sq m), includes a large solarium, eight private massage/body treatment rooms, sauna and steam rooms for men and women, and a beauty parlor. A gym has floor-to-ceiling windows on three sides, including forward-facing ocean views, and there's an aerobics section with instructor-led classes (some, such as yoga, cost extra). The spa/fitness facilities are staffed and operated by Steiner Leisure, a specialist spa/beauty concession. Some fitness classes are free; others, such as Pathway to Yoga, and Pathway to Pilates, cost extra. Make appointments early, as time slots can go quickly. If you like being near the spa, note that there are 18 two-bed cabins with ocean-view windows, located adjacent (just aft of it).

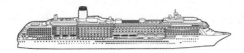

Costa Luminosa
★★★+

Size:	Large Resort Ship	Passenger Space Ratio (lower beds):	41.0
Tonnage:	92,700	Passenger/Crew Ratio (lower beds):	2.1
Lifestyle:	Standard	Cabins (total):	1,130
Cruise Line:	Costa Cruises	Size Range (sq ft/m):	134.5–534.0/12.5–49.6
Former Names:	none	Cabins (for one person):	0
IMO Number:	9398905	Cabins (with private balcony):	772
Builder:	Fincantieri (Italy)	Cabins (wheelchair accessible):	12
Original Cost:	€420 million	Wheelchair accessibility:	Good
Entered Service:	Jun 2009	Cabin Current:	110 and 220 volts
Registry:	Italy	Elevators:	12
Length (ft/m):	958.0/292.0	Casino (gaming tables):	Yes
Beam (ft/m):	111.5/34.0	Slot Machines:	Yes
Draft (ft/m):	26.2/8.0	Swimming Pools:	2
Propulsion/Propellers:	diesel-electric (42,000kW)/	Hot Tubs (on deck):	4
	2 azimuthing pods	Self-Service Launderette:	No
Passenger Decks:	13	Dedicated Cinema/Seats:	No
Total Crew:	1,050	Library:	Yes
Passengers (lower beds):	2,260	Onboard currency:	Euros

A vessel with bold decor and big-ship facilities that is good for families

OVERVIEW. While several nationalities are carried, most passengers are Italian, so the ship is lively and noisy, with lots of children running around, particularly during school holidays.

THE SHIP. *Costa Luminosa* was constructed as what is termed a Vista-class ship – although it is slightly larger than close sisters *Costa Atlantica* and *Costa Mediterranea*. The ship's two-deck midships Lido area swimming pool can be covered with a sliding glass roof. There's also a large 194-sq-ft (18-sq-m) poolside movie screen.

The interior decor, which includes marble, wood, and mother of pearl, pays tribute to light and lighting – hence the name *Costa Luminosa*, so it feels like you are cruising in a stunning special-effects bubble, with reflections everywhere.

Public rooms include 11 bars, a large Vega Casino (with gaming tables and slot machines), and lots of lounges and entertainment venues. Sony PlayStation fans can enjoy PlayStation World. PlayStations are also available in cabins, on the pool-deck movie screen, and in the children's and teens' clubs. A 4D cinema highlights sound and lighting effects, with scent pumped in to heighten the experience. One thing you won't miss is a fascinating – and rather large, at 11ft long (almost 3.5m) – *Reclining Woman 2004* bronze sculpture by Fernando Bolero, in the Atria Supernova, the atrium lobby. Weighing 2,000lbs (910kg), the suntanned, rather voluminous woman is depicted staring into the atrium space, with her legs in a dynamic position of movement.

Berlitz's Ratings

	Possible	Achieved
Ship	500	381
Accommodation	200	143
Food	400	242
Service	400	268
Entertainment	100	65
Cruise Experience	400	263
OVERALL SCORE		
1362 points out of 2000		

Although Costa Cruises is noted for its 'Italian' style, ambience, and spirit, there are few Italian crew members on board. Although many officers are Italian, most of the service crew, particularly the dining room and housekeeping staff, are from the Philippines. But the lifestyle on board is perceived to be Italian – lively, noisy, with lots of love for life and a love of all things casual, even on so-called formal nights.

All printed material – room service folio, menus, etc. – is usually available in six languages: Italian, English, French, German, Portuguese, and Spanish. During peak European school-holiday periods, particularly Christmas and Easter, you can expect to be cruising with a lot of children of all ages.

As aboard other Costa ships, note that for embarkation, few staff members are on duty at the gangway when you arrive; they merely point you in the direction of your deck, or to the ship's elevators and do not escort you to your cabin. Also, note that 'wallpaper' music is played 24 hours a day in all accommodation hallways and elevators – you may well hear it, if you are a light sleeper.

ACCOMMODATION. There are numerous price grades. About 68 percent of all accommodation suites and cabins have an ocean view. Four suites and 52 Samsara Spa cabins are located adjacent to (and considered part of) the designated wellness area. As part of their package, Samsara accommodation occupants get unlimited access to the spa plus two treatments and fitness or meditation lessons, Samsara bathroom amenities, and can dine in one of the two Samsara restaurants.

A pillow menu, with five choices, is available to suite-grade occupants, who also get bathrobes, better amenities than standard-grade cabin occupants, a shaving mirror, and walk-in closets – although the hangers are plastic.

All cabins have twin beds that can be converted into a queen-size bed, individually controlled air conditioning, television, and telephone. Some cabins have views obstructed by lifeboats – on Deck 4 and Deck 5. Some cabins have pull-down Pullman berths that are fully hidden in the ceiling when not in use.

Some of the most desirable suites and cabins are on aft-facing decks 4, 5, 6, 7, and 8, with private balconies and views overlooking the stern. In most other cabins with balconies are not as private – the partition between adjacent cabins is not a full partition, so you will be able to hear your neighbors. However, these balcony occupants all have good views through glass and wood-topped railings, and the deck is made of teak.

The cabins are practically designed, typically with twin beds that convert to a queen-size bed, vanity desk with built-in hairdryer, large TV set, personal safe, and one closet that has moveable shelves – thus providing useful space for storing luggage.

The largest suites are the Penthouse Suites, although they are really quite small when compared with suites aboard other ships of a similar size. However, they do at least offer more space to move around in, and a slightly larger, better bathroom.

DINING. The Taurus Restaurant is the large, main restaurant. It is located at the aft of the ship. There are two seatings, with assigned tables for two to eight, according to your chosen accommodation grade. Dinner on European cruises is typically scheduled at 7pm and 9pm. Some tables have an unwelcome view of the harsh lighting of the escalators between the galley and the two decks of the dining room. Also, a number of support pillars provide something of an obstacle course for the waiters.

A Samsara Restaurant is for occupants of the Samsara-grade cabins, and is located adjacent to the Taurus Restaurant; because it's small, it provides a quieter

environment in which to dine. Healthier food with reduced calories, fat, and salt content is featured.

Other dining options. The Club Restaurant is a reservations-only, intimate restaurant that features à la carte dining with a pristine show kitchen as part of the venue. The food is cooked to order and so it is better than food in the main dining room. The menus are under the direction of Italy's molecular cooking master, Ettore Bocchia, Costa's consulting chef. It's a good idea to go for a meal in this venue, particularly to celebrate a special occasion, because it's different, and portions are small.

The Andromeda Buffet is the self-serve casual eatery. While there appears to be a decent choice of food, it is extremely repetitive (particularly for breakfast), and is a major source of passenger complaints. Its layout invites congestion because of some narrow passageways between the indoor seating and the food dispensing areas.

Extra-cost coffee bars throughout the ship feature illy-brand espressos and cappuccinos.

ENTERTAINMENT. The Phoenix Theater, with over 800 seats, spans three decks and is the ship's main showlounge. It appears as if it is illuminated by a rainbow of effects, using the latest computer-controlled lighting. Typical fare consists of revue-style shows performed by a small troupe of resident on-board singers/dancers, with fast-moving action and busy lighting and costume changes that all add up to a high-energy performance.

SPA/FITNESS. This area contains 37,700 sq ft (3,500 sq m) of Samsara Spa space. Included are a Venus beauty salon, saunas for men and women, several private massage/body treatment rooms, a fitness center, and a relaxation area.

The spa/fitness facilities are staffed and operated by Steiner Leisure, a specialist spa/beauty concession. Some fitness classes are free, while some, such as Pathway to Yoga, Pathway to Pilates, and Pathway to Meditation, cost extra. It's wise to make appointments early, as time slots can go quickly.

Close by, a Grand Prix Formula One simulator is housed in a glass enclosure. For tee-time, a golf simulator provides a choice of 37 18-hole courses. Other sporting facilities include a roller-skating track.

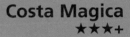

Costa Magica
★★★+

Size:	Large Resort Ship	Passenger Space Ratio (lower beds):	37.7
Tonnage:	102,587	Passenger/Crew Ratio (lower beds):	2.5
Lifestyle:	Standard	Cabins (total):	1,359
Cruise Line:	Costa Cruises	Size Range (sq ft/m):	179.7–482.2/16.7–44.8
Former Names:	none	Cabins (for one person):	0
IMO Number:	9239795	Cabins (with private balcony):	522
Builder:	Fincantieri (Italy)	Cabins (wheelchair accessible):	8
Original Cost:	$418.5 million	Wheelchair accessibility:	Good
Entered Service:	Nov 2004	Cabin Current:	110 and 220 volts
Registry:	Italy	Elevators:	14
Length (ft/m):	893.3/272.3	Casino (gaming tables):	Yes
Beam (ft/m):	124.6/38	Slot Machines:	Yes
Draft (ft/m):	27.2/8.3	Swimming Pools:	2
Propulsion/Propellers:	diesel-electric (34,000kW)/	Hot Tubs (on deck):	6
	2 azimuthing pods	Self-Service Launderette:	No
Passenger Decks:	13	Dedicated Cinema/Seats:	No
Total Crew:	1,068	Library:	Yes
Passengers (lower beds):	2,718	Onboard currency:	Euros

This is a family-friendly large ship with bright Italian decor

OVERVIEW. *Costa Magica* is a ship that is built to impress, with decks named after famous Italian artists. The ship is designed to suit upbeat and active families with children. It is, after all, very Italian, and there are lots of loud announcements.

THE SHIP. There is not a lot of open deck space considering the number of passengers carried, so sunloungers tend to be crammed together.

Inside, the decor is quite chic, and not overly glitzy, as aboard some of the other ships in the fleet. There are three decks full of lounges and 11 bars to choose from, including a very pleasant Piano Bar Capo Colunna. A nine-deck-high, glass-domed atrium lobby houses a Costa Bar on its lowest level (you'll find good extra-cost illy-brand coffees here), and panoramic elevators provide pleasant views of the atrium. In the Sicilia Casino, some 65 sculptured soldier puppets oversee the venue, which also has gaming tables and slot machines.

ACCOMMODATION. There are numerous price grades, and accommodation ranges from two-bed interior cabins to grand suites with private balcony. There are two solo-occupancy cabins (unusual for a large ship). No cabins have lifeboat-obstructed views, due to the smart design.

The largest accommodation can be found in eight Grand Suites, in the center of the ship on Perugino Deck 7. These feature a queen-size bed, while the bathrooms have a tub, two washbasins, and more storage space for personal toiletry items. Note that 12

Berlitz's Ratings		
	Possible	Achieved
Ship	500	380
Accommodation	200	143
Food	400	245
Service	400	266
Entertainment	100	64
Cruise Experience	400	262
OVERALL SCORE		
1360 points out of 2000		

of the most desirable (outside-view) wheelchair-accessible cabins are located a long way from elevators.

DINING. The two main dining rooms are Costa Smeralda Restaurant (aft) and the Portofino Restaurant (midships); both span two decks and feature two seatings, with dinner on European cruises typically scheduled at 7pm and 9pm at assigned tables.

Other dining options. The intimate Club Vincenza is a more intimate dining spot with seating for around 150. There is a cover charge, and reservations are required, but it's worth booking to get a sample of what Costa can do when food is cooked to order. The Bellagio Buffet Restaurant is a self-serve eatery for breakfast, lunch, afternoon pizzas, and beverages at just about any time. The food here is extremely repetitive, however.

ENTERTAINMENT. The Urbino Theater spans three decks in the forward-most section of the ship. It is the setting for all production shows and large-scale cabaret acts, is quite stunning, and has a revolving stage, hydraulic orchestra pit, excellent (but overly loud) sound, and seating on three levels. In the ship's aft section is the Salon Capri – a dancing lounge and nightclub – always popular with Europeans.

SPA/FITNESS. Facilities in the two-deck high Saturnia Spa include a large solarium, eight treatment rooms, sauna and steam rooms for men and women, and a beauty parlor.

Costa Mediterranea
★★★+

Size:	Large Resort Ship	Passenger Space Ratio (lower beds):	40.5
Tonnage:	85,700	Passenger/Crew Ratio (lower beds):	2.2
Lifestyle:	Standard	Cabins (total):	1,056
Cruise Line:	Costa Cruises	Size Range (sq ft/m):	161.4–387.5/15.0–36.0
Former Names:	none	Cabins (for one person):	0
IMO Number:	9237345	Cabins (with private balcony):	742
Builder:	Kvaerner Masa-Yards (Finland)	Cabins (wheelchair accessible):	8
Original Cost:	$335 million	Wheelchair accessibility:	Good
Entered Service:	May 2003	Cabin Current:	110 and 220 volts
Registry:	Italy	Elevators:	12
Length (ft/m):	959.6/292.5	Casino (gaming tables):	Yes
Beam (ft/m):	105.6/32.2	Slot Machines:	Yes
Draft (ft/m):	25.5/7.8	Swimming Pools:	3 (1 w/ sliding glass dome)
Propulsion/Propellers:	diesel-electric (34,000kW)/ 2 azimuthing pods	Hot Tubs (on deck):	4
		Self-Service Launderette:	No
Passenger Decks:	11	Dedicated Cinema/Seats:	No
Total Crew:	920	Library:	Yes
Passengers (lower beds):	2,112	Onboard currency:	Euros

Upbeat Italian decor and style, suitable for families

OVERVIEW. The interior design is bold and brash – a mix of Classical Italy and contemporary features. There is good passenger flow, several spaces for dancing, and a range of bars and lounges for socializing. The appeal is to young and young-at-heart couples and solo travelers, plus families with children, who enjoy big-city life, loud entertainment, and an international mix of passengers.

THE SHIP. *Costa Mediterranea* is one of a series of ships with the same layout and design, the others are: *Costa Atlantica*, *Costa Deliziosa*, *Costa Fascinosa*, *Costa Favolosa*, and *Costa Luminosa*). There are two centrally located swimming pools outdoors, one with a retractable glass dome – so it can be covered in poor weather conditions or when it's cold. Two hot tubs are adjacent. Another smaller pool is for children. There is a winding water slide spanning two decks in height, starting on a platform bridge well aft of the funnel.

The main interior focal point is a dramatic eight-deck atrium lobby, with two grand stairways. It features a stunning wall decoration, which consists of two huge paintings and *Danza*, a 25-piece wall sculpture by Gigi Rigamonte – best seen from any of the multiple viewing balconies on the decks above the main lobby-floor level. The squid-shaped wall-lighting sconces are neat, too.

The decor itself is inspired by many Italian palaces (some well known, many less so) and by a love of art and architecture. It is extremely upbeat, bright, glitzy, and quite in-your-face. I was amused by one of three

Berlitz's Ratings		
	Possible	Achieved
Ship	500	372
Accommodation	200	142
Food	400	240
Service	400	268
Entertainment	100	64
Cruise Experience	400	264
OVERALL SCORE		
1350 points out of 2000		

larger-than-life digital faces of Dionisio in the Dionisio Lounge, with a door handle sticking out of his mouth - in a style recalling Monty Python rather than an Italian palace!

A small chapel is located forward of the uppermost level. Other facilities include a winding shopping street with some of the fashionable brand name stores such as Fendi, Fossil, and Paul & Shark Yachting. There's also a photo gallery, video games room, observation balcony, a large Grand Canal Casino with gaming tables, as well as an array of slot machines – and a rarely open library with Internet access, but not many books. Printed material such as room service folio and menus are in six languages (Italian, English, French, German, Portuguese, Spanish).

Expect lots of announcements – especially for revenue activities such as art auctions, bingo, and horse racing – and much hustling for drinks.

ACCOMMODATION. There are several different price grades; this includes a healthy 78 percent proportion of outside-view to interior cabins. All cabins have twin beds that convert into a queen-size bed, individually controlled air conditioning, TV set, and telephone. Some cabins have views obstructed by lifeboats – on Deck 4 (Roma Deck), the lowest of the accommodation decks, as well as some cabins on Deck 5. Some cabins have pull-down Pullman berths that are fully hidden in the ceiling when not in use.

There is too much use of fluorescent lighting in the suites and cabins, and the soundproofing could be better. Some of the bathroom fixtures such as the bath and shower taps can be frustrating to use at first.

Some of the most desirable suites and cabins are those with private balconies on the five aft-facing decks (Decks 4, 5, 6, 7, and 8) with views overlooking the stern and ship's wash. Those in other cabins with 'private' balconies will find the balconies not so private – the partition between them is not a full partition, so you'll be able to hear your neighbors (and smell their smoke, if they are smokers, or hear their mobile phone conversations).

However, these balcony occupants all have good views through glass and wood-topped railings, and the deck is teak. The cabins are well laid out, typically with twin beds that convert to a queen-size bed, vanity desk (with built-in hairdryer), large television, personal safe, and one closet with moveable shelves – to provide more space for storing luggage. However, the lighting is fluorescent and too harsh. The bedside control is for a master switch only – other lights cannot be controlled.

The bathroom is a simple, modular unit (it's a little on the bland, minimalist side) that has shower enclosures with soap dispenser; there is a good amount of stowage space for personal toiletries.

The largest suites are the Penthouse Suites, although they are small when compared with suites aboard other ships of a similar size. At least they do offer more space to move around in, and a slightly larger, better bathroom.

In 2008, some 44 cabins were converted to become Samsara Spa cabins. Occupants get special spa amenities and access to the spa. You pay a little extra for these cabins, but you get more, and it may be worth it if you want to spend time in wellness moments.

DINING. The 1,320-seat Ristorante degli Argentiere, the ship's main dining room, is a very large venue. It is located in the aft section of the ship on two levels with a spiral stairway between them. There are two seatings, with assigned tables for two, four, six, or eight. Dinner on European cruises is typically scheduled at 7pm and 9pm. Some tables have a less-than-comfortable view of the harsh lighting of the escalators between the galley and the two decks of the dining room. Also, a number of support pillars provide a bit of an obstacle course for waiters.

Other dining options. The Club Medusa is a more upscale dining spot that spans two of the uppermost decks under a large glass dome that is adjacent to the ship's funnel. It seats around 125 and has a menu by Zeffirino, a well-respected restaurant in Genoa. An open kitchen provides a view into the cooking area, so you can watch the chefs preparing their masterpieces. Fine table settings, china, and silverware are used, and menus are leather-bound. Reservations are needed and there's a cover charge, although you may think it's worth it in order to have dinner in a setting that's quieter and much more refined than the main dining room.

The Perla del Lago Buffet is an extensive eatery forming the aft third of Deck 9, with part of it wrapping around the upper section of the multi-deck atrium. It includes a central area with several small buffet counters; there are salad counters, a dessert counter, and a 24-hour Posillipo Pizzeria counter, all creating a large eatery with both indoor and outdoor seating. Movement around the buffet area is very slow, and requires you to stand in line for everything. Venture outdoors and you'll find a grill for hamburgers and hot dogs, and a pasta bar, both conveniently located adjacent to the second of two swimming pools on the Lido Deck.

The place most people will want to see and be seen is the ultra-casual Oriental Café; it features four separate 'salons,' which provide intimate spaces for drinks, conversation, and people-watching.

Excellent illy brand Italian cappuccino and espresso coffees are always available in various bars around the ship, and these are always served in the right-sized china cups.

ENTERTAINMENT. The 949-seat Osiris Theater is the venue for the Splash Vegas-style production shows and major cabaret acts. It spans three decks, with seating on all three levels. Sight lines to the stage are, however, a little better from the second and third levels. Curving stairways at the back of the showlounge connect all levels.

SPA/FITNESS. The expansive Ischia Spa spans two decks, is located directly above the navigation bridge in the forward part of the ship (accessed by the forward stairway elevators), and has around 13,700 sq ft (1,272 sq m) of space. Lower-level facilities include a solarium, eight private massage/body treatment rooms, sauna and steam rooms for men and women, and a beauty parlor. The upper level has a large gymnasium with floor-to-ceiling windows on three sides, and an aerobics room with instructor-led classes (some, such as yoga, may cost extra).

For sporty types, there's a jogging track outdoors, around the ship's mast and the forward third of the ship, as well as a multi-purpose court for basketball, volleyball and deck tennis.

Costa neoClassica
★★★

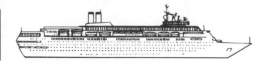

Size:	Mid-size Ship	Passenger/Crew Ratio (lower beds):	2.0
Tonnage:	52,950	Cabins (total):	654
Lifestyle:	Standard	Size Range (sq ft/m):	185.1–430.5/17.2–40.0
Cruise Line:	Costa Cruises	Cabins (for one person):	0
Former Names:	Costa Classica	Cabins (with private balcony):	10
IMO Number:	8716502	Cabins (wheelchair accessible):	6 (interior)
Builder:	Fincantieri (Italy)	Wheelchair accessibility:	Good
Original Cost:	$287 million	Cabin Current:	110 and 220 volts
Entered Service:	Jan 1992	Elevators:	8
Registry:	Italy	Casino (gaming tables):	Yes
Length (ft/m):	718.5/220.6	Slot Machines:	Yes
Beam (ft/m):	98.4/30.80	Swimming Pools:	2
Draft (ft/m):	25.0/7.60	Hot Tubs (on deck):	4
Propulsion/Propellers:	diesel (22,800kW)/2	Self-Service Launderette:	No
Passenger Decks:	10	Dedicated Cinema/Seats:	No
Total Crew:	650	Library:	Yes
Passengers (lower beds):	1,308	Onboard currency:	Euros
Passenger Space Ratio (lower beds):	40.4		

An elegant Italian-style ship for mature passengers

OVERVIEW. This ship, which brought Costa into the mainstream of cruising Italian-style, has a modern-ish design and styling best described as befitting European tastes. It attracts a multinational group of young (and young-at-heart) couples and solo travelers who enjoy big-city life with constant activity and lots of noise.

THE SHIP. *Costa neoClassica* (in December 2014 its name was changed from *Costa Classica*) is an all-white ship, now over 20 years old, with a slab-sided unflattering profile, topped by an unmistakable trio of tall yellow funnels. Lifeboats positioned in an upper location make the high-sided ship look ungainly.

The interior design, however, incorporates much use of circles – large portholes instead of windows can be found in cabins on lower decks, and in the dining room, self-serve buffet area, coffee bar (for illy-brand espressos and cappuucinos), and discotheque, for example. There is an excellent range of public rooms, lounges, and bars.

Some fascinating artwork includes six hermaphrodite statues in one lounge. The multi-level atrium is stark, angular, and cold. The marble-covered staircases look pleasant, but are uncarpeted and a little dangerous if water or drinks are spilled on them when the ship is moving.

Perhaps the interior is best described as an innovative design project that almost works. A forward observation lounge/nightclub sits atop ship like a lump of cheese, and, unfortunately, fails to work well as a

Berlitz's Ratings		
	Possible	Achieved
Ship	500	331
Accommodation	200	133
Food	400	214
Service	400	257
Entertainment	100	60
Cruise Experience	400	234
OVERALL SCORE		
1229 points out of 2000		

nightclub. Internet access is available from one of several computer terminals in an Internet café.

Gratuities are charged to your onboard account. Although Costa Cruises is noted for its 'Italian' style, ambience and spirit, there are few Italian crew members on board. Although many officers are Italian, most of the crew, particularly the dining room and housekeeping staff, are from the Philippines. But the lifestyle on board is perceived to be Italian – lively, noisy, with lots of love for life and a love of all things casual, even on so-called formal nights.

Note that all printed material – room service folio, menus, etc. – will typically be in six languages: Italian, English, French, German, Portuguese, and Spanish. During peak European school holidays, particularly Christmas and Easter, you can expect to be cruising with a lot of children of all ages.

As aboard other Costa ships, few staff members are on duty at the gangway when you arrive for embarkation; they merely point you in the direction of your deck, or to the ship's elevators and do not escort you to your cabin. Also, note that 'wallpaper' music is played 24 hours a day in all accommodation hallways and elevators, so you may well hear it if you are a light sleeper.

Niggles include the fact that there is no walk-around promenade deck outdoors. The ship's rather slow service speed (19.5 knots) means that itineraries have to be carefully chosen, as the ship cannot compete with the newer ships with faster speeds. Also, the air-conditioning system in the Tivoli Dining

Room is noisy. There are too many loud, repetitious, and irritating announcements.

ACCOMMODATION. There are several categories. These include 10 suites, while other cabins are fairly standard in size, shape, and facilities, a higher price being asked for cabins on the highest decks. All suites and cabins have twin lower beds, color TV set, telephone, illy coffee-pod machine, and Elemis toiletries.

Suites. The 10 suites, located in the center of Portofino Deck, have a private rounded balcony, marble-clad bathroom with Jacuzzi tub, and separate shower enclosure. There is plenty of space in the living and sleeping areas, and for storing luggage.

Standard outside-view/interior cabins. In general, the cabins are of a fairly generous size, and are laid out in a practical manner. They have cherry wood veneered cabinetry and accenting, and include a vanity desk unit with a large mirror. There are useful (unusual, for a cruise ship) sliding doors to the bathroom and closets, but the cabin soundproofing is poor. The soft furnishings are of good quality, but the room service menu is disappointing. The suites have more space – although they are not large by any means – and hand-woven bedspreads.

Some cabins have one or two extra pull-down (Pullman-style) berths – useful for families with small children.

DINING. The Tivoli Dining Room has an indented, clean white ceiling. Open seating is the norm for all meals, and there are now more tables for two and four (plus some larger tables) than before. Changeable wall panels help create a European Renaissance atmosphere, albeit at the expense of blocking off windows – but during dinner, it's dark outside anyway unless you're in the far North.

The cuisine is traditional cruise fare that is best described as banquet-style food. Note that there are no real sommeliers, so the young waiters serve the (mostly Italian) wine (which is also young). They also dance at the tables during the cruise – it's a little bit of show business that you get caught up in – whether you like it or not.

Other dining options. For casual outdoor eating, the Alfresco Café has teak decking and traditional canvas sailcloth awning. Breakfast and luncheon buffets are repetitious and uncreative, and the source of many passenger complaints. However, after a recent refit, the venue presents its new 'green' image.

Excellent (extra-cost) Italian illy-brand cappuccino and espresso coffees are always available in various bars around the ship, served in the right-sized china cups.

ENTERTAINMENT. The Colosseo Theater, the main showlounge, has an interesting amphitheater-like design. However, the seats are bolt upright, and quite uncomfortable for any length of time. A Galileo disco is located atop the ship, for the young-at-heart (and hard of hearing).

SPA/FITNESS. The Caracalla Spa, on one of the uppermost decks, contains a gymnasium with good forward-facing views over the ship's bows and high-tech muscle-pump machines, an aerobics exercise area, two hot tubs, Roman bath, health bar, sauna and steam rooms, and beauty salon. The spa is operated by Steiner, a specialist concession, whose young staff will try to sell you Steiner's own-brand Elemis beauty products.

Some fitness classes are free, while some, such as yoga and kick-boxing, cost extra. Massage, facials, pedicures, and beauty salon treatments cost extra. It's best to make appointments as early as possible as time slots can go quickly.

Costa neoRiviera
★★★

Size:	Mid-size Ship	Passenger/Crew Ratio (lower beds):	2.0
Tonnage:	48,200	Cabins (total):	624
Lifestyle:	Standard	Size Range (sq ft/m):	139.9–236.8/13.0–22.0
Cruise Line:	Costa neoCollection	Cabins (for one person):	0
Former Names:	Grand Mistral, Mistral	Cabins (with private balcony):	90
IMO Number:	9172777	Cabins (wheelchair accessible):	2
Builder:	Chantiers de l'Atlantique (France)	Wheelchair accessibility:	Fair
Original Cost:	$245 million	Cabin Current:	110 and 220 volts
Entered Service:	Jul 1999/Nov 2013	Elevators:	6
Registry:	Marshall Islands	Casino (gaming tables):	Yes
Length (ft/m):	709.9/216.4	Slot Machines:	Yes
Beam (ft/m):	94.6/28.8	Swimming Pools:	2
Draft (ft/m):	22.4/6.8	Hot Tubs (on deck):	2
Propulsion/Propellers:	diesel-electric (31,680kW)/2	Self-Service Launderette:	No
Passenger Decks:	8	Dedicated Cinema/Seats:	No
Total Crew:	600	Library:	Yes
Passengers (lower beds):	1,248	Onboard currency:	Euros
Passenger Space Ratio (lower beds):	38.6		

Family-friendly, casual 'slow-cruising' for Europeans

OVERVIEW. *Costa neoRiviera* (formerly *Grand Mistral*) is best suited to mature couples, solo travelers, and families with children – those who enjoy big-city life and outdoor cafés, constant activity accompanied by lots of noise, late nights, loud entertainment, and food that focuses more on seasonal and regional cuisine.

THE SHIP. *Costa neoRiviera* is part of a new sub-brand of Costa Cruises, called Costa neoCollection – a strange name – which operates slower, longer cruises than Costa's other brands. The vessel's profile is similar to that of most new cruise ships, although the built-up stern makes it look bulky and is less than handsome.

The lido deck surrounding the small outdoor swimming pool has two whirlpool tubs, and a large canvas-covered bandstand. There is no full walk-around promenade deck outdoors, although there is a partial walking deck on port and starboard sides under the lifeboats, plus an oval jogging track atop ship.

The interior layout and general passenger flow is good, as are the 'you are here' deck signs, and the ship absorbs passengers quite well. It is light and cheerful without being glitzy in any way – there's not even a hint of colored neon – and there's much use of blonde/cherry wood paneling and rich, textured soft furnishings.

Public rooms include six lounges and bars, with names inspired by European places or establishments such as Saint Maxime Casino, St. Paul de Vence Lounge, the San Marco Lounge, plus a Library

Berlitz's Ratings	Possible	Achieved
Ship	500	341
Accommodation	200	132
Food	400	217
Service	400	255
Entertainment	100	58
Cruise Experience	400	241
OVERALL SCORE		
1244 points out of 2000		

(Biblioteca Conca dei Marini, with real writing desks, something most ships no longer have).

Atop the ship is an observation lounge with a twist – it faces aft, instead of forward; it doubles as a disco for the late nighters. There's a video games room for teens, and a small children's center (Squok Club). A conference center provides facilities for meetings.

Although Costa Cruises is noted for its 'Italian' style, ambience, and spirit, there are few Italian crew members on board. Although many officers are Italian, most of the crew, particularly the dining room and housekeeping staff, is from the Philippines. But the lifestyle on board is perceived to be Italian – lively, noisy, with lots of love for life. Gratuities are charged to your onboard account.

ACCOMMODATION. There are three basic cabin types, in several different price grades. These include 80 'suites' (each with a private balcony, although partitions are of the partial, and not the full type), ocean-view standard cabins, and interior standard cabins. The price you pay will depend on grade, size and location.

Note that cabins on Deck 10 are subject to noise from the Lido Deck above. Good planning and layout means that no outside-view cabins have lifeboat-obstructed views, but there are many, many interior (no-view) cabins. The cabin numbering system goes against maritime tradition, where even-numbered cabins are on the port side and odd-numbered cabins on the starboard; aboard this ship, the opposite is the case.

All cabins have twin beds that convert to a queen-size unit, bold, colorful bedspreads (with blankets and sheets, not duvets), a personal safe, a flat-screen television, and a good amount of closet and drawer space for a one-week cruise. The bathrooms, although not large, do have a good-size shower enclosure, and there is a decent amount of stowage space for toiletries.

Accommodation designated as suites – which are really only larger cabins and not suites, as there is no separation of lounge and sleeping space – have more space, larger (walk-in) closets, more drawers and better storage space, plus a two-person sofa, coffee table and additional armchair, vanity desk, floor-to-ceiling mirrors, and hairdryer; bathrooms have a tub/shower combination.

Six Grand Suites are well-designed units that have a separate bedroom with flat-screen TV, bedside tables, vanity desk, floor-to-ceiling windows, and door to balcony; the lounge has an audio-visual center, sofa, dining table, and lots of space, plus a balcony door. A large bathroom has contemporary styling, two washbasins, dark hardwood storage cabinets, large Jacuzzi tub, separate shower enclosure (hand-held shower), and bathrobes.

In addition, there are two interior wheelchair-accessible cabins for the handicapped, which provide more spacious interiors than standard cabins.

DINING. There are two dining rooms (and two seatings for meals, with dinner at 6.30pm and 9pm), which can be configured in several different ways. Both have ocean-view windows. The principal 612-seat Restaurant Cetara has round tables for two, four, six, or eight, and a small podium with baby grand piano.

Restaurant Saint Tropez, a second dining venue seating 274 in chairs with no armrests, is on a different deck. Smaller and more intimate, it is for passengers occupying Deck 10 accommodation; it has tables for two, four, or six, and ocean-view windows.

The food is quite sound, and, with varied menus and decent presentation, should prove a highlight for most passengers. The wine list features a fair variety of standard wines at reasonable prices, but almost all are young.

The casual Vernazza Buffet is for alfresco self-serve breakfasts and lunches; it has ocean-view windows, but the flow is awkward and cramped. Additionally, there's an outdoor pool bar pizzeria and a grilled food counter (for burgers and hot dogs). Also, there's a pleasant little coffee bar (Café Eze – for excellent illy-brand coffees) on the upper level of the two-deck high lobby, which, unfortunately, has lifeboat-restricted ocean views.

ENTERTAINMENT. The Teatro Ravello, the show-lounge, spans two decks, has a sloping floor, and good sight lines from most seats (the seating is in banquettes), and there is a small balcony level at the rear. Sadly, the designer forgot to include space for a live band (so all shows are performed to pre-recorded backing tracks), and the lighting facilities are anything but high-tech. Entertainment is, without doubt, a weak link in the chain for passengers.

SPA/FITNESS. The Santai Spa health/fitness facilities, located forward of the mast, are quite decent. Included is a gymnasium with high-tech muscle-pump equipment, lifecycles, and life-rowing machines and a view over the bow of the ship through large floor-to-ceiling windows.

Other facilities include a thalassotherapy room, and beauty salon, six rooms for massage and other body treatments, as well as a sauna each for men and women, plus an aerobics exercise room. It's best to make appointments early, as the best time slots can go fairly quickly.

Costa neoRomantica
★★★

Size:	Mid-size Ship
Tonnage:	57,150
Lifestyle:	Standard
Cruise Line:	Costa neoCollection
Former Names:	*Costa Romantica*
IMO Number:	8821046
Builder:	Fincantieri (Italy)
Original Cost:	$325 million
Entered Service:	Nov 1993/Nov 1993
Registry:	Italy
Length (ft/m):	718.5/220.6
Beam (ft/m):	98.4/30.8
Draft (ft/m):	25.0/7.6
Propulsion/Propellers:	diesel (22,800kW)/2
Passenger Decks:	10
Total Crew:	662
Passengers (lower beds):	1,578
Passenger Space Ratio (lower beds):	36.2

Passenger/Crew Ratio (lower beds):	2.3
Cabins (total):	789
Size Range (sq ft/m):	185.1–430.5/17.2–40.0
Cabins (for one person):	0
Cabins (with private balcony):	74
Cabins (wheelchair accessible):	6
Wheelchair accessibility:	Good
Cabin Current:	110 and 220 volts
Elevators:	8
Casino (gaming tables):	Yes
Slot Machines:	Yes
Swimming Pools:	2
Hot Tubs (on deck):	2
Self-Service Launderette:	No
Dedicated Cinema/Seats:	No
Library:	Yes
Onboard currency:	Euros

An elegant Italian-style ship for a mature audience

OVERVIEW. Being Italian, this ship is chic and very tasteful, and will appeal to the sophisticated. The layout and flow are somewhat disjointed, however. The ship's multi-level atrium is open and spacious, and has a revolving mobile sculpture as its focal point. The decor is contemporary and minimalist in style.

THE SHIP. *Costa neoRomantica* (a play on the ship's original name of *Costa Romantica*) is now over 20 years old, and, although not very handsome, it is easily recognizable by its cluster of three upright yellow funnels. There is, however, no walk-around promenade deck outdoors, so contact with the sea is minimal, although there's some good open space on several of the upper decks.

In 2011–12, the ship was given an extensive €90 million refit, refurbishment and renewal program that added more public rooms, two half-deck extensions, 111 new cabins, 120 suites and cabins with balcony, wine and cheese bar, a chocolate confectionary bar, new Pizzeria Capri (with its black-and-white tiled decor), a cabaret lounge and nightclub, and LED lighting. However, no additional elevators were installed for the additional growth in passenger numbers, and the very small swimming pool remains very small.

Facilities also include a Monte Carlo Lido indoor/outdoor bar; Vienna cabaret lounge; Piazza Italia Grand Bar (arguably the best place to see and be seen); a new atrium (with minimalist design features); a new neoRomantica Club Restaurant; Casino Excelsior; a wine and cheese bar, coffee and chocolate bar for excellent illy brand coffees), and a Caffeteria that forms part of the Via Condotti shopping area. Out on the pool deck (Lido Saint-Tropez) several 'private' cabanas, adjacent to the pool, can be rented.

Berlitz's Ratings		
	Possible	Achieved
Ship	500	333
Accommodation	200	135
Food	400	214
Service	400	260
Entertainment	100	60
Cruise Experience	400	237
OVERALL SCORE		
1239 points out of 2000		

Although Costa Cruises is noted for its 'Italian' style, ambience, and spirit, there are few Italian crew members on board. Although many officers are Italian, most of the crew, particularly the dining room and housekeeping staff, is from the Philippines. But the lifestyle on board is perceived to be Italian – lively, noisy, with lots of love for life and a love of all things casual, even on so-called formal nights.

All printed material – room service folio, menus, etc. – will typically be in six languages: Italian, English, French, German, Portuguese, and Spanish. During peak European school holidays, particularly Christmas and Easter, you can expect to be cruising with a lot of children of all ages.

As aboard other Costa ships, note that for embarkation, few staff members are on duty at the gangway when you arrive; they merely point you in the direction of your deck, or to the ship's elevators and do not escort you to your cabin. Also, note that 'wallpaper' music is played 24 hours a day in all accommodation hallways and elevators, so you may well hear it if you are a light sleeper. Gratuities are automatically charged to your onboard account.

ACCOMMODATION. There are several different price categories. These include 16 suites, 10 of which have a private semi-circular balcony, while six suites command views over the ship's bows. The other cabins are fairly standard in size, shape, and facilities; the ones on the highest decks cost more.

A whole 'wedge' of cabins with half-moon-shaped balconies, as well as normal balconies, has been added in the mid-section of the ship.

Samsara Suites/Cabins. Occupants of these 6 suites and 50 cabins have access to the Samsara Spa and its facilities, located at the front of the ship. Samsara accommodation provides organic cotton bedlinen, purifying shower filter, and a selection of Ayurvedic teas.

Suites/Mini-Suites. The suites (with floor-to-ceiling windows) and mini-suites are quite pleasant, except for the rounded balconies of the suites on Madrid Deck, where a solid steel half-wall blocks the view. A sliding door separates the bedroom from the living room, and bathrooms are of a decent size. Cherry wood walls and cabinetry help make these suites warm and attractive.

The six suites at the forward section of Monte Carlo Deck are the largest, and have huge glass windows with commanding forward views, but no balconies.

Standard outside-view/interior cabins. All other cabins are of a moderately generous size, and all have nicely finished cherry wood cabinetry and walls. However, the cabin bathrooms and shower enclosures are quite small. There are a good number of triple and quad cabins, ideal for families with children. The company's in-cabin food service menu is extremely basic.

DINING. The 738-seat Botticelli Restaurant is of a fine design. There are tables for two to eight persons, and it's an open-seating ('My Time') arrangement for all meals. Romantic candlelight dining is typically featured on 'formal' night. Traditional cruise fare is served, and best described as banquet-style food. Note that there are no real sommeliers, so the waiters are expected to serve the wine. They also dance in the restaurant during the cruise – an example of Costa Cruises' penchant for show business.

Other dining options. The 72-seat Samsara Restaurant is the venue for occupants of Samsara-grade accommodation. The restaurant is located at the aft of the ship on the port side of Vienna Deck. The cuisine is more health-oriented, and the venue is quieter and more intimate than the main dining room.

Club neoRomantica Restaurant is an extra-cost, reservations-required, à la carte, cozy, 90-seat venue. While the banquette seating is unbecoming of 'fine' dining, it's a rather pleasant spot for an intimate dinner, and features contemporary French and Italian fare that is worth the extra cost.

For casual meals and snacks, the self-serve Giardino Buffet is a small, cramped buffet. The buffet food items are very much standard fare (repetitive breakfast items are a major source of passenger complaints), with the exception of some good commercial pasta dishes. One would expect Italian waiters, but most hail from elsewhere.

Pizzeria Capri has something unusual for any cruise ship – a real wood-burning oven – used for making 'genuine' Neapolitan-style pizzas (the venue makes 15 different ones).

Enoteco Verona is a wine and cheese bar that features more than 100 different wines, and 80 cheeses from around the world. Italian coffee machines are provided in all bars (coffees are at extra cost, however), so there's never a shortage of espressos and cappuccinos.

ENTERTAINMENT. Cabaret Vienna is the ship's main showlounge. It is an interesting amphitheater-like design that spans two decks, with seating on both levels. However, the seats are quite upright and uncomfortable, and 10 large pillars obstruct the sight lines from many seats. Typical fare consists of revue-style shows performed by a small troupe of resident singers/dancers, with fast-moving action and busy lighting and costume changes that all add up to a high-energy performance.

SPA/FITNESS. A Samsara Spa spans two decks in the forward section of the ship. It contains a gymnasium with some high-tech muscle-pump machines, an aerobics exercise area, thalassotherapy pool, Turkish baths, health bar, sauna and steam rooms, a solarium, and a beauty salon. Occupants of the 56 adjacent Samsara Spa cabins also have a private, dedicated, intimate Samsara Restaurant featuring slightly lighter fare.

The spa/fitness facilities are staffed and operated by Steiner Leisure, a specialist spa/beauty concession. Some fitness classes are free, while some, such as Pathway to Yoga, Pathway to Pilates, and Pathway to Meditation, cost extra. It's wise to make appointments early, as time slots can go quickly.

Costa Pacifica
★★★+

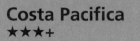

Size:	Large Resort Ship
Tonnage:	114,500
Lifestyle:	Standard
Cruise Line:	Costa Cruises
Former Names:	none
IMO Number:	9378498
Builder:	Fincantieri (Italy)
Original Cost:	€510 million
Entered Service:	Apr 2009
Registry:	Italy
Length (ft/m):	952.0/290.0
Beam (ft/m):	116.4/35.5
Draft (ft/m):	27.2/8.3
Propulsion/Propellers:	diesel-electric (34,000kW)/ 2 azimuthing pods
Passenger Decks:	13
Total Crew:	1,110
Passengers (lower beds):	3,012

Passenger Space Ratio (lower beds):	38.0
Passenger/Crew Ratio (lower beds):	2.7
Cabins (total):	1,506
Size Range (sq ft/m):	179.7–482.2/16.7–44.8
Cabins (for one person):	0
Cabins (with private balcony):	579
Cabins (wheelchair accessible):	12
Wheelchair accessibility:	Good
Cabin Current:	110 and 220 volts
Elevators:	14
Casino (gaming tables):	Yes
Slot Machines:	Yes
Swimming Pools:	2
Hot Tubs (on deck):	5
Self-Service Launderette:	No
Dedicated Cinema/Seats:	No
Library:	Yes
Onboard currency:	Euros

This is a large, colorful, family-friendly, Italian-style ship

OVERVIEW. Costa Cruises provides first-time cruisers with a well-packaged holiday, particularly families with children. It's a mix of semi-sophistication and chaos, accompanied by loud music. This ship has a musical design theme featuring 'greatest hits'. The lobby, for example, is covered in musical symbols and instruments.

THE SHIP. Sporting a single, large funnel, *Costa Pacifica* is a sister to the popular *Costa Serena*, which now operates short Asia cruises from its year-round base in Shanghai, China. Two pool areas can be covered with retractable glass domes – good in case of poor weather – and one of the pools has a water slide that's great for kids. There is also a huge screen for poolside movies. A Grand Prix simulator is positioned on one of the upper decks.

However, the open deck space is cramped when the ship is full, so sunloungers tend to be crammed together, and they don't have cushioned pads.

There are three decks full of bars and lounges plus many other public rooms. The glass-domed atrium lobby is nine decks high, with great upward views from the lobby bar, as well as from its four glass panoramic elevators. The passenger flow inside is quite good, and the ship absorbs passengers reasonably well. It also provides a decent passenger/space ratio, which means that it won't feel too crowded.

The Flamingo Casino is large and glitzy, but always lively and entertaining; slot machines occupy a separate area from gaming tables, so that serious gamers can concentrate. There's also a very small li-

Berlitz's Ratings

	Possible	Achieved
Ship	500	380
Accommodation	200	143
Food	400	242
Service	400	266
Entertainment	100	65
Cruise Experience	400	259
OVERALL SCORE		
1355 points out of 2000		

brary, an Internet-connection center, card room, art gallery, and video game room, together with several other bars and lounges. A chapel is a standard aboard all Costa ships.

Children are divided into three age groups. They have their own swimming pool in an area called Lido La Bamba, while other facilities include playrooms and video games rooms.

Although Costa Cruises is noted for its 'Italian' style, ambience and spirit, there are few Italian crew members on board its ships. While many of the officers are Italian, most of the crew – particularly the dining room and housekeeping staff – is from the Philippines. The lifestyle on board is, however, perceived to be Italian – lively, noisy, and embracing a casual lifestyle – even on so-called formal nights. Most passengers will be Italian, with a sprinkling of other European nationals.

Printed material such as room service folio and menus will typically be in six languages (Italian, English, French, German, Portuguese, and Spanish). During peak European school holidays, particularly Christmas and Easter, expect to be cruising with a lot of children of all ages. Sony PlayStation fans can enjoy PlayStation World. PlayStations are also available in cabins, in the children's and teens' clubs, and can be used with the poolside movie screen.

As aboard other Costa ships, few staff members are on duty at the gangway when you embark; they merely point you in the direction of your deck, or to the ship's elevators and do not escort you to your cabin. Gratuities are automatically added to your onboard account.

ACCOMMODATION. There are numerous price grades, from two-bed interior cabins to grand suites with private balcony, although in reality there are only three different sizes: suites with 'private' balcony (which are not large when compared with many other large ships), two- or four-bed outside view cabins, and two- or four-bed interior cabins. No cabins have views obstructed by lifeboats or other safety equipment, and, in all cabins, twin beds can be changed to a double/queen-bed configuration.

A total of eight Grand Suites comprise the largest accommodation. These are in the center of the ship on one of the uppermost decks. They have a queen-size bed and larger living area with vanity desk; the bathrooms have a tub and two washbasins.

If you like wellness treatments, 12 Samsara Spa Suites are located just aft of the spa – although 91 cabins, including the suites, are designated as Samsara-grade. Samsara suite/cabin occupants get unlimited access to the spa plus two treatments and fitness or meditation lessons as part of their package, and dine in one of the two Samsara restaurants. All Samsara-designated accommodation grades have an Oriental decorative theme, and special Samsara bathroom amenities.

A pillow menu, with five choices, is available in all suite accommodation grades. Only suite grades get bathrobes and better amenities, shaving mirror, and walk-in closets – although the hangers are plastic. Music is played 24 hours a day in all hallways and elevators, so you may well hear it, if you are a light sleeper.

DINING. There are two main dining rooms (the 1,036-seat New York, New York, and the 752-seat My Way), allocated according to your accommodation grade and location. There are two seatings in each for dinner.

Two 84-seat Samsara Restaurants have separate entrances, located adjacent to the My Way restaurant. Unlike the main restaurants that offer traditional cruise fare, these provide more health-conscious fare – this means reduced calories and less fat and salt in the cooking, with menus created under the direction of dietary consultant and Michelin-star chef Ettore Boccia and his molecular Italian cuisine. These dining venues are open for lunch and dinner for occupants of Samsara-grade suites and cabins, and to anyone else (for dinner only) for an extra charge.

Other dining options. The 118-seat Club Restaurant Blue Moon (reservations required) is an elegant, intimate venue with seating under a huge glass dome. Fine table settings, china, silverware and leather-bound menus are provided. A cover charge applies, for service and a gratuity.

La Paloma Buffet Restaurant is a self-serve eatery for breakfast, lunch, afternoon pizzas, and coffee and tea at any time. A balcony level provides additional seating. You'll need to carry your own food plates – there are no trays. High-quality illy-brand cappuccino and espressos are always available in various bars, at extra cost, including the Caffeteria Rondo.

ENTERTAINMENT. The Stardust Theater seats more than 800 and utilizes the latest in LED technology. It is three decks high and is decorated in a Baroque style, with warm colors and a Murano-glass chandelier. It is the venue for all production shows and large-scale cabaret acts, is quite stunningly glitzy, and has a revolving stage, hydraulic orchestra pit, superb sound, and seating on three levels (the upper levels are tiered through two decks).

Typical fare consists of revue-style shows performed by a small troupe of resident onboard singers/dancers, with fast-moving action and busy lighting and costume changes that all add up to a high-energy performance.

SPA/FITNESS. The Samsara Spa is a large facility that occupies 23,186 sq ft (2,154 sq m) of space, spread over two decks. It includes a large fitness room, separate saunas, steam rooms, UVB solarium, changing rooms for men and women, and 10 body treatment rooms. On the upper level, two VIP treatment rooms are available to couples for half-day rentals.

The spa/fitness facilities are staffed and operated by Steiner Leisure, a specialist spa/beauty concession. Some fitness classes are free; others, such as Pathway to Yoga, and Pathway to Pilates, cost extra. Make appointments early, as time slots can go quickly.

You can buy a day pass in order to use the sauna/steam rooms, thermal suite, and relaxation area, at a cost of €35 per person. However, there's an additional no-charge sauna for men and women, but to access it you must walk through an active fitness area, perhaps wearing your bathrobe – an arrangement with which some people may not feel particularly comfortable.

Costa Serena
★★★+

Size:	Large Resort Ship
Tonnage:	114,147
Lifestyle:	Standard
Cruise Line:	Costa Cruises
Former Names:	none
IMO Number:	9343132
Builder:	Fincantieri (Italy)
Original Cost:	€475 million
Entered Service:	May 2007
Registry:	Italy
Length (ft/m):	952.0/290.2
Beam (ft/m):	116.4/35.5
Draft (ft/m):	27.2/8.3
Propulsion/Propellers:	diesel-electric (34,000kW)/ 2 azimuthing pods
Passenger Decks:	13
Total Crew:	1,090
Passengers (lower beds):	3,000
Passenger Space Ratio (lower beds):	38.0
Passenger/Crew Ratio (lower beds):	2.7
Cabins (total):	1,500
Size Range (sq ft/m):	482.2–179.7/44.8–16.7
Cabins (for one person):	0
Cabins (with private balcony):	575
Cabins (wheelchair accessible):	12
Wheelchair accessibility:	Good
Cabin Current:	110 and 220 volts
Elevators:	14
Casino (gaming tables):	Yes
Slot Machines:	Yes
Swimming Pools:	2
Hot Tubs (on deck):	5
Self-Service Launderette:	No
Dedicated Cinema/Seats:	No
Library:	Yes
Onboard currency:	Euros

Really upbeat Italian decor and style, for family cruising

OVERVIEW. Costa Cruises does a good job of providing first-time cruise passengers with a well-packaged holiday that is a mix of sophistication and basic fare.

THE SHIP. *Costa Serena* absorbs passengers well and won't feel too crowded, except on the open decks. The delightful interior design is themed around the heavens and astrology.

There are three decks full of bars and lounges plus lots of other public rooms. This ship has a nine-deck-high glass-domed atrium lobby with four panoramic elevators providing great views. The Casino is large and glitzy, but always lively and entertaining; slot machines occupy a separate area from gaming tables, which helps to reduce the noise level. There's also a small library, an Internet center, card room, art gallery, and video game room.

As aboard other Costa ships, few staff members are at the gangway when you embark; they point you in the direction of your deck and do not escort you.

In April 2015 *Costa Serena* started sailing year-round from Shanghai, China, with an increasing number of Chinese passengers (and announcements in Mandarin to suit the domestic market).

Gratuities are automatically charged to your onboard account.

ACCOMMODATION. There are numerous price grades, from two-bed interior cabins to grand suites with private balcony, although in reality there are only three different sizes: suites with balcony and two- or four-bed outside-view or interior cabins. Eight Grand

Berlitz's Ratings

	Possible	Achieved
Ship	500	380
Accommodation	200	143
Food	400	245
Service	400	266
Entertainment	100	64
Cruise Experience	400	257
OVERALL SCORE		
1355 points out of 2000		

Suites comprise the largest accommodation.

DINING. There are two main dining rooms: the 1,125-seat Ceres, located aft, and the 775-seat Vesta, amidships. Tables for two to eight are allocated according to your accommodation grade, in two seatings. The food is best described as banquet-style.

Two 84-seat Samsara Restaurants are for those seeking spa food with reduced calories, fat, and salt. Menu creations are under the direction of dietary consultant and Michelin-starred chef Ettore Boccia, known for his molecular Italian cuisine. This venue is open for lunch and dinner to those in Samsara-grade suites and cabins, and to anyone else for dinner only at an extra charge.

Other dining options. The 90-seat Bacco Club Restaurant is an upscale, intimate, extra-cost, reservations-required restaurant. The Promotea Buffet Restaurant is a self-serve eatery. The food in this venue is repetitive, and a source of passenger complaints. The Caffeteria is the place to go for excellent illy-brand Italian coffees and Italian pastries (extra cost).

ENTERTAINMENT. The three-deck-high 1,287-seat Giove Theater is the venue for all production shows and large-scale cabaret acts. Typically, it presents revue-style shows performed by a troupe of resident artists.

SPA/FITNESS. Samsara Spa occupies 23,186 sq ft (2,154 sq m) of space, spread over two decks. It includes a fitness room, saunas, steam rooms, UVB solarium, changing rooms, and treatment rooms.

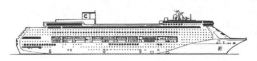

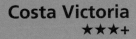

Costa Victoria
★★★+

Size:	Mid-size Ship	Passenger/Crew Ratio (lower beds):	2.4
Tonnage:	75,200	Cabins (total):	964
Lifestyle:	Standard	Size Range (sq ft/m):	120.0–430.5/11.1–40.0
Cruise Line:	Costa Cruises	Cabins (for one person):	0
Former Names:	none	Cabins (with private balcony):	246
IMO Number:	9109031	Cabins (wheelchair accessible):	6
Builder:	Bremer Vulkan (Germany)	Wheelchair accessibility:	Good
Original Cost:	$388 million	Cabin Current:	110 and 220 volts
Entered Service:	Jul 1996	Elevators:	12
Registry:	Italy	Casino (gaming tables):	Yes
Length (ft/m):	823.0/251.0	Slot Machines:	Yes
Beam (ft/m):	105.5/32.2	Swimming Pools:	3
Draft (ft/m):	25.6/7.8	Hot Tubs (on deck):	4
Propulsion/Propellers:	diesel (30,000kW)/2	Self-Service Launderette:	Yes
Passenger Decks:	10	Dedicated Cinema/Seats:	No
Total Crew:	800	Library:	Yes
Passengers (lower beds):	1,928	Onboard currency:	Euros
Passenger Space Ratio (lower beds):	39.0		

Sedate decor in an Italian setting for Asia cruises

OVERVIEW. Where this vessel differs from many other ships is in its distinct interior decor, with styling that is decidedly Italian, and quite cozy.

THE SHIP. *Costa Victoria* features an outdoor walk-around promenade deck, although it tends to be full of sunloungers. Inside is a charming four-deck-high observation lounge with a glass elevator; in the center is a cone-shaped waterfall. A seven-deck-high 'planetarium' atrium is the ship's focal point. The uppermost level of the atrium is the deck where two outdoor swimming pools are located, together with four blocks of showers, a grill, and an ice cream bar.

Note that Costa Victoria now cruises year-round from Shanghai, China, with the Italian food slightly modified to accommodate Chinese cuisine preferences.

ACCOMMODATION. There are 13 price categories. The six large Panorama Suites (each with third/fourth Pullman berths in tiny compartments, like those on a train) and 14 mini-suites have butler service; 65 percent of all other cabins have outside views (portholes and not windows), but they are extremely small for two persons. While the suites aren't large, all other cabins are of mean dimensions. Only 16 of the interior cabins accommodate four people, while all other cabins are for two or three.

All cabins have wood cabinetry, minibar/refrigerator, and electric blackout window blind, but the storage space is very limited. The ocean-view cabins have large picture windows. Bathrooms are small but quite well appointed.

Berlitz's Ratings

	Possible	Achieved
Ship	500	339
Accommodation	200	132
Food	400	219
Service	400	262
Entertainment	100	62
Cruise Experience	400	247
OVERALL SCORE		
1261 points out of 2000		

DINING. This ship has two main dining rooms: the 594-seat Sinfonia Restaurant and the 506-seat Fantasia Restaurant. There are two seatings, with assigned tables for two to eight, according to your chosen accommodation grade. Some tables have a less-than-comfortable view of harsh lighting of the escalators between the galley and the two decks of the restaurant. Also, a number of support pillars provide an obstacle course for the waiters.

Other dining options. Ristorante Magnifico by Zeffirino (reservations only, service charge added). Suite occupants receive a free pass for one evening. Buffet Bolero is a self-serve cafeteria for casual eats, although the food displays and variety are poor (and a source of passenger complaints). Outdoors is a Pizzeria and Tavernetta, while extra-cost illy-brand coffees are available at various bars.

ENTERTAINMENT. The entertainment consists of revue-style shows performed by a small troupe of resident onboard singers/dancers in the Festival Theatre, which has both a main and balcony level, and is located at the back of the ship.

SPA/FITNESS. The congested spa/fitness area, on a lower deck, is much too small for the size of the ship. It has a beauty salon, tiny indoor swimming pool, treatment rooms, sauna, and steam room, but cramped changing areas. Sporting facilities include a covered walking/jogging track and a tennis court.

Crown Princess
★★★★

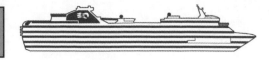

Size:	Large Resort Ship	Passenger/Crew Ratio (lower beds):	2.6
Tonnage:	116,000	Cabins (total):	1,557
Lifestyle:	Standard	Size Range (sq ft/m):	163–1,279/15.1–118.8
Cruise Line:	Princess Cruises	Cabins (for one person):	0
Former Names:	none	Cabins (with private balcony):	881
IMO Number:	9293399	Cabins (wheelchair accessible):	25
Builder:	Fincantieri (Italy)	Wheelchair accessibility:	Best
Original Cost:	$500 million	Cabin Current:	110 volts
Entered Service:	May 2006	Elevators:	14
Registry:	Bermuda	Casino (gaming tables):	Yes
Length (ft/m):	951.4/290.0	Slot Machines:	Yes
Beam (ft/m):	118.1/36.0	Swimming Pools:	3
Draft (ft/m):	26.2/8.0	Hot Tubs (on deck):	9
Propulsion/Propellers:	diesel-electric/2 azimuthing pods	Self-Service Launderette:	Yes
Passenger Decks:	15	Dedicated Cinema/Seats:	No
Total Crew:	1,163	Library:	Yes
Passengers (lower beds):	3,114	Onboard currency:	US$
Passenger Space Ratio (lower beds):	37.2		

A large ship with comfortable, sedate decor

OVERVIEW. Princess Cruises delivers a consistently fine, well-packaged product, always with a good degree of style, at a competitive price. With many choices and 'small' rooms (a relative term) to enjoy, the ship has been extremely well designed, and the odds are that you'll have an enjoyable vacation.

THE SHIP. If you are not used to large ships, it may take some time to find your way around, despite the company's claim that it offers passengers a 'small ship feel, big ship choice.' One nice feature is The Sanctuary, an extra-cost adults-only retreat located forward on the uppermost deck.

Outdoors, there is a good sheltered teakwood promenade deck, which almost wraps around, and a walkway that leads to the enclosed bow of the ship. The outdoor pools have quasi-beach-like surroundings, while 'Movies Under the Skies' and major sporting events are shown on a 300-sq-ft (28-sq-m) movie screen located at the pool in front of the large funnel.

Just aft of the funnel is Skywalkers nightclub/disco. The interior decor is attractive, with lots of earth tones. An extensive collection of artworks complements the interior design and colors well.

Crown Princess also includes a Wedding Chapel with live web-cam, which is used to relay ceremonies via the Internet (the ship's captain can legally marry American couples, thanks to the ship's Bermuda registry and a special dispensation).

A large Gatsby's Casino has more than 260 slot machines, and blackjack, craps, and roulette tables,

Berlitz's Ratings

	Possible	Achieved
Ship	500	372
Accommodation	200	145
Food	400	251
Service	400	289
Entertainment	100	78
Cruise Experience	400	292
OVERALL SCORE		
1427 points out of 2000		

plus games such as Let It Ride Bonus, Spanish 21, and Caribbean Draw Progressive.

Other facilities include a decent library/computer room. Ship lovers should enjoy the wood-paneled Wheelhouse Bar, finely decorated with memorabilia and ship models tracing part of parent company P&O's history.

The dress code is either formal or smart casual. Gratuities are automatically charged to your onboard account (gratuities for children are at the same daily rate).

FAMILIES. There is a two-deck-high playroom, teen room, and a host of trained counselors. Children have their own pools, hot tubs, and open deck area at the stern, thankfully away from adult areas. There are good netted-in areas; one section has a dip pool, while another has a mini-basketball court. There's a video games arcade, too.

Two family suites consist of two suites with an interconnecting door, plus a large balcony. These sleep up to 10 (if at least four are children) or up to eight adults.

ACCOMMODATION. There are six principal types of cabins and configurations: (a) grand suite, (b) suite, (c) mini-suite, (d) outside-view double cabins with balcony, (e) outside-view double cabins, and (f) interior double cabins. These come in a bewildering choice of 35 different brochure price categories.

Some 28 wheelchair-accessible cabins measure 250–385 sq ft (23.2–35.7 sq m); surprisingly, there is no mirror for dressing, and no full-length hanging space.

Cabin bath towels are small, and drawer space is very limited. There are no butlers, even for top-grade suites. Cabin attendants have many cabins to look after (typically 20), which does not translate to fine personal service. All cabins receive toiletry kits and include a hairdryer.

Most outside-view cabins on Emerald Deck have views obstructed by lifeboats. There are no cabins for solo travelers. There is 24-hour room service, but some items on the room service menu are not available during early morning hours.

Some cabins can accommodate a third and fourth person in upper berths. However, in some cabins, the lower beds cannot then be pushed together to make a queen-size bed.

Almost all balcony suites and cabins can be overlooked both from the navigation bridge wing, as well as from the port and starboard sections of the ship's discotheque – high above the ship at the stern. Cabins with balconies on Dolphin, Caribe, and Baja decks can also be overlooked.

Perhaps the least-desirable balcony cabins are eight located forward on Emerald Deck, as the balconies do not extend to the side of the ship and can be passed by walkers and gawkers on the adjacent Upper Promenade walkway, so occupants need to keep their curtains closed most of the time. Passengers occupying some of the most expensive suites with balconies at the ship's stern may experience considerable vibration during certain maneuvers.

DINING. Of the three principal formal dining rooms (Botticelli, Da Vinci, and Michaelangelo), one has traditional two-seating dining, while the other two offer 'anytime dining.' All are no-smoking and split into multi-tier sections in a non-symmetrical design that breaks what are quite large spaces into smaller sections. While six elevators go to Fiesta Deck, where two of the restaurants are located, only four go to Plaza Deck 5, where the Michelangelo Restaurant is located – this can lengthen waits at peak times, particularly for those in wheelchairs.

Other dining options. Sabatini's and Crown Grill are both are open for dinner on days at sea. Sa-

batini's has Italian-style pizzas and pastas, with a variety of sauces, as well as Italian-style entrées including tiger prawns and lobster tail – all provided with flair and entertainment from by the staff of waiters. Reservations are needed, and there's a cover charge for lunch or dinner.

The 160-seat Crown Grill (a steakhouse, for premium-quality steaks, grilled meat, and seafood items), also with cover charge, is in a wide promenade area, to tempt you as you pass by – it's worth the extra cost to get food cooked to order.

Casual eateries include a poolside hamburger grill and pizzeria. Some items cost extra at the International Café coffee bar/patisserie in the atrium lobby.

Vines, in the atrium lobby, features sushi and cheese at no extra charge, and extra-cost wine. Other casual meals can be taken in the Horizon Court, open 24 hours a day, with ocean views.

For something different, however, you could try a private dinner on your balcony ('Ultimate Balcony Dinner'), an all-inclusive evening featuring cocktails, fresh flowers, Champagne, and a deluxe four-course meal including Caribbean lobster tail; or an 'Ultimate Balcony Breakfast.'

ENTERTAINMENT. The Princess Theater spans two decks and has comfortable seating on both main and balcony levels. It has $3 million worth of sound and light equipment, plus a nine-piece orchestra. The ship carries a resident troupe of almost 20 singers and dancers.

Club Fusion, a second entertainment lounge located aft, features cabaret acts at night, and lectures, bingo, and horse racing by day. Explorers, a third entertainment lounge, can also host cabaret acts and dance bands. A variety of other lounges and bars have live music, and a number of male dance hosts act as partners for women traveling alone.

SPA/FITNESS. The Lotus Spa has separate facilities for men and women, including a sauna, steam room, and changing rooms; common facilities include a relaxation/waiting zone, body-pampering treatment rooms, and a gymnasium with great ocean views and the latest high-tech equipment. Some fitness classes are free, others cost extra.

Crystal Serenity
★★★★+

Size:	Mid-size Ship	
Tonnage:	68,870	
Lifestyle:	Luxury/Premium	
Cruise Line:	Crystal Cruises	
Former Names:	*none*	
IMO Number:	9243667	
Builder:	Chantiers de l'Atlantique (France)	
Original Cost:	$350 million	
Entered Service:	Jun 2003	
Registry:	The Bahamas	
Length (ft/m):	820.2/250.0	
Beam (ft/m):	111.5/34.0	
Draft (ft/m):	24.9/7.6	
Propulsion/Propellers:	diesel/2 azimuthing pods	
Passenger Decks:	9	
Total Crew:	650	
Passengers (lower beds):	1,090	
Passenger Space Ratio (lower beds):	62.6	
Passenger/Crew Ratio (lower beds):	1.7	
Cabins (total):	545	
Size Range (sq ft/m):	226–1,345.5/21–125	
Cabins (for one person):	0	
Cabins (with private balcony):	465	
Cabins (wheelchair accessible):	8	
Wheelchair accessibility:	Best	
Cabin Current:	110 and 220 volts	
Elevators:	8	
Casino (gaming tables):	Yes	
Slot Machines:	Yes	
Swimming Pools:	2 (1 w/sliding glass dome)	
Hot Tubs (on deck):	2	
Self-Service Launderette:	Yes	
Dedicated Cinema/Seats:	Yes/202	
Library:	Yes	
Onboard currency:	US$	

This elegant, spacious ship has very good food and service

OVERVIEW. *Crystal Serenity* is best suited to sophisticated travelers, typically over 50, who seek contemporary ship surroundings, with fine-quality fittings and furnishings, a wide range of public rooms and facilities, and excellent food and service from a well-trained staff. This ship has just about everything for its target clientele, including an excellent program of guest lecturers.

THE SHIP. *Crystal Serenity* is the slightly larger but still mid-size close sister ship to *Crystal Symphony*, with a similar look and profile. While some might not like the exterior's 'apartment-block' look, it is in fashion today. The ship was given an extensive multi-million dollar refit and refurbishment in 2013 and looks almost new again.

The ship has an excellent amount of open deck, sunbathing space, and sports facilities. The aft of two outdoor swimming pools can be covered by a retractable glass dome in poor weather. There is no sense of crowding anywhere, although the self-service buffet can get very busy. There is also a really wide walk-around teakwood deck for walking, and it's pleasingly uncluttered by sunloungers.

Elegant public rooms include Palm Court, evoking images of a Colonial-style grand hotel lounge; the Avenue Saloon, a favorite watering hole of late-nighters and a throwback to traditional gentlemen's clubs; the Connoisseur Club, for cigar and cognac enthusiasts; and the Stardust Club, a lounge/nightclub. There are new shops and a private jewelry room, a computer-learning center with 24 terminals, and an Internet

Berlitz's Ratings

	Possible	Achieved
Ship	500	429
Accommodation	200	164
Food	400	340
Service	400	337
Entertainment	100	83
Cruise Experience	400	340
OVERALL SCORE		
1693 points out of 2000		

center. One neat feature is a Vintage Room, a private dining room where 12 invited diners can enjoy exclusive vintages, paired with food, in special wine-tasting dinners. Another is a Yamaha keyboard learning center for the excellent 'Passport to Music' program, which gives you a chance to learn how to play a keyboard instrument (and you get to take home a manual, so you can carry on learning); the program is free – great value indeed.

Crystal Serenity is an all-inclusive ship, so the fare includes all gratuities, decent wines for lunch and dinner, and bar drinks.

ACCOMMODATION. This consists of: four Crystal Penthouse Suites with large balcony. Other accommodation: penthouse-grade with balcony; superior outside-view cabins with balcony; outside-view cabins with balcony; and 84 outside-view cabins without balcony. All the best accommodation is on Decks 11 and 10; all other accommodation is located on Decks 7, 8, and 9. Each has an electronic 'Do Not Disturb'/doorbell system.

All accommodation has duvets, down pillows, a refrigerator and mini-bar, flat-screen infotainment TV (close-captioned videos are available for the hearing-impaired), data laptop socket, satellite-linked telephone, and hairdryer. There's a range of Aveda toiletries (suite-grade occupants get personalized stationery on request, plus a larger list of 'inclusive' brands to choose from), a plush, cotton bathrobe, and plenty of cotton towels, the largest a generous

70 by 34ins (180 by 85cm). The air conditioning in bathrooms and walk-in closets is quite noisy and cannot be turned off.

Butlers provide good service in all the top-category suites on Decks 10 and 11, where room service food arrives on silver trays. Afternoon tea trolley service and evening hors d'oeuvres are delivered in butler-service suites.

Crystal Penthouses (with balcony). There are four, each 1,345 sq ft (125 sq m), and ideally located in the center of the ship on Penthouse Deck 11. Each has a large private balcony with outside light, a lounge, separate master bedroom with king-size bed and electric curtains, large walk-in closets, and large vanity desk. Marble-clad bathrooms have ocean views; they feature a whirlpool tub and shower, two washbasins, separate shower enclosure, bidet and toilet, and ample storage space. They were completely redesigned and rebuilt in 2013.

Penthouse-grade (with balcony). These measure 538 sq ft (50 sq m), on Penthouse Deck 11, and each has a separate bedroom and walk-in closet.

Penthouse-grade (with balcony). Located on Penthouse Decks 10 and 11, these measure 404 sq ft (38 sq m). Note that eight of these located at the aft of Deck 11 have larger balconies.

Deluxe outside-view cabins (with balcony). Measuring 269 sq ft (25 sq m), these are larger than the standard outside-view cabins aboard many ships.

Deluxe outside-view cabins (with balcony). These measure 269 sq ft (25 sq m). These are about the same size and shape as the 'Deluxe' version but are on a 'superior' deck (Penthouse Deck 10), and are longer than cabins that don't have a private balcony.

Deluxe outside-view cabins (no balcony). These have a window that looks onto a walk-around promenade deck outside each cabin. They measure 226 sq ft (21 sq m).

Wheelchair-accessible accommodation. This is spread over several different grades and locations.

DINING. There is one main dining room (the Crystal Dining Room) and two specialty, reservations-required restaurants. The Crystal Dining Room is quite elegant, with a crisp, clean style that includes plenty of space around each table. It is well laid-out and has a raised, circular central section, although it is noisy at times and not conducive to a fine-dining experience. There are tables for two, many positioned adjacent to large ocean-view windows, and for four, six, or eight.

Other dining options. There are two, one Italian and one Asian, both requiring reservations but without any extra charge. They are aft on Deck 7, with ocean-view windows. Prego is for Italian food from a menu created by Piero Selvaggio; it offers Italian wines, and the service has flair.

Silk Road has Asian-California 'fusion' food. Although there is no extra charge, a small 'gratuity' is suggested. The alternative dining spots provide an excellent standard of culinary fare with food cooked to order. A semi-separate sushi bar with counter stools is part of Silk Road, which features items selected by superb Los Angeles-based Japanese super-chef Nobuyuki 'Nobu' Matsuhisa, and skillfully prepared on board by Nobu-trained chefs; the high-cost ingredients are flown regularly to the ship. Note that to eat in a Nobu restaurant ashore would cost a considerable amount of money, but aboard the ship, this outstanding food is free.

The Bistro, located on the upper level of the two-deck-high lobby, is the casual spot for coffees and pastries, with the atmosphere of a European street café. For informal eats, the Lido Café has an extensive self-serve buffet area. It's high up in the ship, with great views from its large picture windows. For casual meals, Tastes features regional cuisine and family-style service, and four vertical 'living walls' of greenery. There's also an ice cream/frozen yoghurt counter (no extra charge), and a Chinese street food zone (for steamed dumplings).

ENTERTAINMENT. The Galaxy Lounge (show-lounge) has a high ceiling, with a sloping floor for good sight lines from almost all seats (both banquette and individual seating is provided). The stage, lighting, and sound equipment are all first rate.

SPA/FITNESS. Crystal Spa is located aft on an uppermost deck. Facilities include men's and women's changing rooms with sauna (with a large porthole-shaped window), steam rooms, gymnasium with high-tech muscle-pumping equipment, an aerobics exercise area, and a reception/relaxation area.

Crystal Symphony
★★★★+

Size:	Mid-size Ship	
Tonnage:	51,044	
Lifestyle:	Luxury/Premium	
Cruise Line:	Crystal Cruises	
Former Names:	none	
IMO Number:	9066667	
Builder:	Masa-Yards (Finland)	
Original Cost:	$300 million	
Entered Service:	Mar 1995	
Registry:	The Bahamas	
Length (ft/m):	777.8/237.1	
Beam (ft/m):	98.0/30.2	
Draft (ft/m):	24.9/7.6	
Propulsion/Propellers:	diesel-electric (33,880kW)/2	
Passenger Decks:	8	
Total Crew:	545	
Passengers (lower beds):	960	
Passenger Space Ratio (lower beds):	53.1	

Passenger/Crew Ratio (lower beds):	1.7
Cabins (total):	480
Size Range (sq ft/m):	201.2–981.7/18.7–91.2
Cabins (for one person):	0
Cabins (with private balcony):	276
Cabins (wheelchair accessible):	7
Wheelchair accessibility:	Best
Cabin Current:	110 and 220 volts
Elevators:	8
Casino (gaming tables):	Yes
Slot Machines:	Yes
Swimming Pools:	2 (1 w/sliding glass dome)
Hot Tubs (on deck):	2
Self-Service Launderette:	Yes
Dedicated Cinema/Seats:	Yes/143
Library:	Yes
Onboard currency:	US$

A highly comfortable ship with elegant, refined decor

OVERVIEW. *Crystal Symphony* is best suited to discerning adult travelers, typically over 50, who seek contemporary ship surroundings, with fine-quality fittings and furnishings, a wide range of public rooms and facilities, and excellent food and service.

THE SHIP. *Crystal Symphony* has, over the years, had a number of refurbishments that have made the ship more modern.

Crystal Symphony has a nicely raked clipper bow and well-balanced lines. While some might not like the 'apartment-block' look of its exterior, it is the contemporary look, balconies having become standard aboard almost all new cruise ships. This one has an excellent amount of open deck, sunbathing space, and sports facilities. The aft of two outdoor pools can be covered by a glass dome in poor weather. There is no sense of crowding anywhere. It combines big-ship facilities with the intimacy of rooms found aboard many small vessels. There is a wide walk-around teakwood deck for strolling, and it's pleasantly uncluttered by lounge chairs.

The Palm Court, an observation lounge with forward-facing views over the ship's bows, is tranquil; one of the nicest rooms afloat, it is larger than its equivalent aboard sister ship, *Crystal Serenity*.

There is an excellent library, combined with a business center. The cinema has high-definition video projection and headsets for the hearing-impaired. Useful self-service launderettes are provided on each deck.

Berlitz's Ratings		
	Possible	Achieved
Ship	500	424
Accommodation	200	163
Food	400	340
Service	400	337
Entertainment	100	83
Cruise Experience	400	340
OVERALL SCORE		
1687 points out of 2000		

The Connoisseurs Club, adjacent to the Avenue Saloon, serves fine premium brands of liquor and cigars. The Computer Learning Center, with more than 20 stations, is a popular venue (private lessons are available, but expensive).

The ship achieves a high rating because of its fine facilities, space, service, and crew. It is the extra attention to detail that really counts. Crystal Cruises also provides impressive, cultural lecturers, and the 'Passport to Music' keyboard learning center is excellent. The passenger mix is approximately 85 percent North American (typically half will be from California) and 15 percent other nationalities.

In March 2012, *Crystal Symphony* became an 'all-inclusive' ship, with gratuities to staff, decent wines for lunch and dinner, and bar drinks included – so, no more signing or paying extra for drinks, which makes for a more enjoyable cruise experience. In 2014, *Crystal Symphony* eliminated smoking from all indoor areas, except for the Connoisseur Lounge (cigar lounge), but maintained designated smoking areas on open decks. This is announcement-free cruising in a well-tuned, very professionally run, service-oriented ship.

ACCOMMODATION. There are eight categories, with the most expensive suites located on the highest accommodation deck (Deck 10). There are two Crystal Penthouses with private balcony; 18 Penthouse Suites with private balcony; 44 Penthouse Cabins with balcony; 214 cabins with balcony; 202 cabins without balcony. Some cabins have obstructed views. Except for the suites on Deck 10, most other cabin bathrooms are compact, but very comfortable. Interconnecting doors were added to 18 in 2013 – good for families with children.

Duvets and down pillows are provided in all cabins, as are lots of other niceties, together with a data socket for connecting a computer. All accommodation has a refrigerator and minibar, TV set, satellite-linked telephone, and hairdryer. A full range of Aveda toiletries is provided, plus a plush cotton bathrobe and plenty of cotton towels, the largest of which measures a generous 70 by 34ins (180 by 85cm). Suite-grades get a larger choice of drinks as well as personalized stationery on request. Excellent in-cabin television programming, including CNN, is transmitted, as well as close-captioned videos for the use of the hearing-impaired.

Deck 10 penthouses. Two delightful Crystal Penthouses measure 982 sq ft (91 sq m) and have a huge private balcony, a lounge with audio-visual entertainment center, separate master bedroom with king-size bed and electric curtains, large walk-in closets, and stunning ocean-view marble bathrooms with a Philippe Starck whirlpool tub. These really are among the best in fine, private, pampered living spaces at sea, and come with all the best perks, including laundry service.

Other Deck 10 suites. All of the other suites on this deck have plenty of space and a private balcony. They have a lounge with large sofa, coffee table and chairs, a sleeping area, and walk-in closet. Rich wood cabinetry provides a warm decor. The bathrooms are extremely well appointed, with full-size tub and separate shower, two washbasins, bidet, and toilet.

Five butlers provide the best in personal service in all the top-category suites on Deck 10 (with a total of 132 beds). Afternoon tea and evening hors d'oeuvres are standard, and the food arrives on silver trays.

Decks 5/6/7/8/9. More than 50 percent of all cabins have private balconies. All cabins are well equipped and extremely comfortable, with excellent sound insulation. The balcony partitions, however, do not go from floor to ceiling, so you can hear your neighbors. Even in the lowest category of standard cabins, there is plenty of drawer space, but the closet hanging space is limited. European stewardesses provide excellent service and attention.

DINING. The Crystal Dining Room is quite elegant, with crisp design and plenty of space around each table, although it can be noisy at times.

The food, which is of a high standard, is always attractively presented and well served, using a mix of plate service and silver service. European dishes are predominantly featured, but in an American style. The menus include a fine selection of meat, fish, and vegetarian dishes. Off-menu orders are available, as is caviar.

Kosher meals are also available (frozen when brought on board); Kosher pots, pans, and utensils are sterilized in salt water, and all plates used during service are hand-washed.

Overall, the food is really good for the size of ship, and, with the choice of the two specialty dining spots, receives high praise. Dining is in two seatings, unless you choose the more flexible 'open dining by reservation' option, whereby you can dine at different or set times each evening. While the early seating may be too rushed for many, with two specialty restaurants, off-menu choices, a hand-picked European staff and excellent service, dining is often memorable. Dessert flambé specialties are made at the table each day by accommodating headwaiters.

Other dining options. Prego is a 75-seat restaurant, featuring fine Italian cuisine created by Piero Selvaggio, with good Italian wines, and service with flair.

Silk Road features Asian-California 'fusion' food provided by Nobu Matsuhisa-trained chefs. The high-cost ingredients are flown regularly to the ship. To eat in a Nobu restaurant ashore costs a considerable amount; aboard the ship, this outstanding food is free.

Afternoon tea in the Palm Court is a pleasant, civilized daily event, but do try the 'Mozart Teatime', in which the waiters all dress in period costume.

For informal eats, the Lido Café has great views from its large windows. For casual poolside lunches, there is also Trident Bar & Grill, as well as an ice cream/frozen yoghurt counter (no extra charge). A Chinese street food zone has favorites such as steamed dumplings.

ENTERTAINMENT. The Galaxy Lounge is quite large, with a high ceiling, but it's on one level with a tiered floor, for good visibility. A few pillars obstruct sight lines from some seats. Both banquette and individual seating is provided. The stage, lighting, and sound equipment are all excellent.

The shows are elegant, with excellent costuming and scenery, but they are too long, and too familiar to Crystal Cruises' many repeat passengers. On the plus side, the cabaret acts are of a good caliber, and constantly changing. The bands are also good, and there's plenty of music for social dancing. The ship also provides male hosts for solo travelers.

SPA/FITNESS. Facilities include one room for yoga and Pilates (no extra charge), an aerobics/exercise room, plus sauna and steam rooms. There are seven treatment rooms and a beauty salon.

Dawn Princess
★★★★

Size:	Mid-size Ship	Passenger/Crew Ratio (lower beds):	2.1
Tonnage:	77,499	Cabins (total):	975
Lifestyle:	Standard	Size Range (sq ft/m):	135.0–635.0/12.5–59.0
Cruise Line:	Princess Cruises	Cabins (for one person):	0
Former Names:	none	Cabins (with private balcony):	446
IMO Number:	9103996	Cabins (wheelchair accessible):	19
Builder:	Fincantieri (Italy)	Wheelchair accessibility:	Good
Original Cost:	$300 million	Cabin Current:	110 and 220 volts
Entered Service:	May 1997	Elevators:	11
Registry:	Bermuda	Casino (gaming tables):	Yes
Length (ft/m):	857.2/261.3	Slot Machines:	Yes
Beam (ft/m):	105.6/32.2	Swimming Pools:	3
Draft (ft/m):	26.5/8.1	Hot Tubs (on deck):	5
Propulsion/Propellers:	diesel-electric (46,080kW)/2	Self-Service Launderette:	Yes
Passenger Decks:	10	Dedicated Cinema/Seats:	No
Total Crew:	900	Library:	Yes
Passengers (lower beds):	1,950	Onboard currency:	US$
Passenger Space Ratio (lower beds):	39.7		

This mid-size ship has warm decor for mature-age cruisers

OVERVIEW. *Dawn Princess*, like sister ships *Sea Princess* and *Sun Princess*, is dedicated to the Australian cruise region. As aboard most ships, if you live in the top suites, you'll be well cared for; if not, you'll just be one of a crowd. The collection of artwork is good, and helps make the ship feel smaller than it is.

THE SHIP. *Dawn Princess*, an all-white ship, has a decent contemporary profile balanced by a large funnel containing a deck tennis/basketball/volleyball court in its sheltered aft base. There is a wide, teak walk-around promenade deck outdoors, some real teak steamer-style deck chairs complete with royal blue cushioned pads, and 93,000 sq ft (8,640 sq m) of space outdoors. A great amount of glass area on the upper decks provides plenty of light and connection with the outside world. There's a large poolside movie screen and an adults-only Sanctuary relaxation area.

The interiors are pretty and warm, with attractive colors, and the welcoming decor includes some attractive wall murals and other artwork. The signage could be better, however. There are a number of dead ends in the interior layout, so it's not as user-friendly as a ship this size could be. The cabin numbering system is illogical, with numbers going through several hundred series on the same deck.

The wide range of public rooms includes several intimate rooms, so that you don't get the feel of being overwhelmed by large spaces. The interior focal point is a four-deck-high atrium lobby with winding,

Berlitz's Ratings		
	Possible	Achieved
Ship	500	376
Accommodation	200	148
Food	400	247
Service	400	278
Entertainment	100	77
Cruise Experience	400	283
OVERALL SCORE		
1409 points out of 2000		

double stairways, and two panoramic glass-walled elevators.

There are two showlounges, one at each end of the ship; one is a 550-seat, theater-style space that also screens movies, and the other is a 480-seat cabaret-style lounge, with bar.

The library, a warm room with ocean-view windows, has six large butter-colored leather chairs for listening to audio discs. There is a conference center for up to 300, as well as a business center with computers and copiers. The casino, while large, is not really in the main passenger flow and so doesn't generate the 'walk-through' factor found aboard so many ships.

The most traditional room is the Wheelhouse Lounge/Bar, decorated in the style of a late 19th-century gentleman's club, with wood paneling and comfortable seating. The focal point is a large ship model, *Kenya*, from the P&O collection archives.

The captain's cocktail party is typically held in the four-deck-high main atrium so that you can come and go as you please. Cruising aboard ships such as this one has become increasingly an onboard revenue-based product. In-your-face art auctions are overbearing, and the paintings, lithographs, and framed pictures strewn throughout the ship clash irritatingly with the interior decor. This is an annoying intrusion into what should be a vacation, not a cruise inside a floating 'art' emporium. Also, bazaar-like tables filled with trinket junk clutter the area outside the shops.

The swimming pools are small, given the number of passengers, and the pool deck is cluttered with white, plastic sunloungers, without cushioned pads. Waiting for tenders in anchor ports can prove irritating, but is typical of large ship operations. Charging for use of the machines and washing powder in the self-service launderette is trifling.

ACCOMMODATION. There are many, many different cabin price grades. Although the standard cabins are a little small, they are well designed and functional in layout; they are decorated in earth tones, accentuated by splashes of color from the bedspreads. Proportionately, there are a lot of interior cabins. Many outside-view cabins have private balconies, and all seem to be quite well soundproofed, although the balcony partition is not the floor-to-ceiling type, so you can hear your neighbors clearly, or smell their smoke, if they are smokers. The balconies are very narrow, only just large enough for two small chairs, and there is no dedicated lighting.

All cabins have a reasonable amount of closet and abundant drawer and shelf space – adequate for a seven-night cruise – plus a TV set and refrigerator. The bathrooms are practical, although they really are tight spaces, which are best described as one-person-at-a-time units. But they do have a decent shower enclosure, a small amount of shelving for toiletries, real (not plastic) glasses, a hairdryer, and a bathrobe.

The largest accommodation is in six suites, two on each of three decks located at the stern; these measure 536–754 sq ft (49.8–21.3 sq m), including a private balcony. They are well laid out, and have large bathrooms with two washbasins, a Jacuzzi tub, and a separate shower enclosure. The bedroom has generous amounts of wood accenting and detailing, indented ceilings, and TV sets in both bedroom and lounge areas. The suites also have a dining room table and four chairs.

Some 32 mini-suites (374–536 sq ft/34.7–49.7 sq m) typically have two lower beds that convert to a queen-size bed. There is a separate bedroom/sleeping area with vanity desk, and a lounge with sofa and coffee table, indented ceilings with generous amounts of wood accenting and detailing, walk-in closet, and larger bathroom with Jacuzzi bathtub and separate shower enclosure.

There are 19 wheelchair-accessible cabins, which measure 213–305 sq ft (19.7–28.2 sq m) and are a mix of seven outside-view and 12 interior cabins.

DINING. There are two main dining rooms of asymmetrical design, Florentine and Venetian, each with about 500 seats. They are located adjacent to the two lower levels of the atrium lobby. Each has its own galley and is split into multi-tier sections, which help create a feeling of intimacy, although there is noise from the waiter stations adjacent to many tables. Breakfast and lunch are provided in an open-seating arrangement, while dinner is in two seatings. The wine list is reasonable, but there are no wine waiters. Note that 15 percent is added to all beverage bills, including wines.

Other dining options. The Horizon Buffet is open 24 hours a day, and, at night, has an informal dinner setting with sit-down waiter service; a small bistro menu is also available. The buffet displays are, for the most part, repetitious, but better than they have been in the past. There is no real finesse in presentation, however, as oval plastic plates are provided, instead of trays. The cabin service menu is limited, and presentation of the food items featured is poor (except for a rather nice, extra-cost Champagne Breakfast).

For some good meat, try the Sterling Steakhouse; it's for those who want to taste four different cuts of Angus beef from the popular 'Sterling Silver' brand of USDA prime meats – Filet Mignon, New York Strip, Porterhouse, and Rib-Eye – all presented on a silver tray. There is also a barbecue chicken option, plus baked potato or French fries as accompaniments. This is available as an alternative to the dining rooms, between 6.30pm and 9.30pm only, at extra cost. However, it is not, as you might expect, a separate, intimate dining room, but is located in a section of the Horizon Buffet, with its own portable bar and some decorative touches to set it apart from the regular buffet.

There is also a patisserie for cappuccino/espresso coffees and pastries, a wine/caviar bar, and a pizzeria with cobblestone floors, wrought-iron decorative features, and a choice of six excellent pizzas.

ENTERTAINMENT. There are two showlounges, both theatre and cabaret style. The main one, Princess Theater, has a sloping floor, with aisle-style seating (as found in shoreside movie theaters) that is well tiered, and with good sight lines to the raised stage from most of the 500 seats.

A second showlounge, Vista Lounge, located at the aft end of the ship, is for cabaret, as well as for lectures and other presentations. Princess Cruises has a good stable of regular cabaret acts to draw from, so there should be something for most tastes.

SPA/FITNESS. A glass-walled health spa complex located high atop the ship includes a gymnasium with the latest high-tech machines. One swimming pool is 'suspended' aft between two decks. There are two other pools, although they are not large for the size of the ship.

Sports facilities are located in an open-air sports deck positioned inside the funnel and adaptable for basketball, volleyball, badminton, or paddle tennis. Joggers can exercise on the walk-around open Promenade Deck.

Diamond Princess
★★★★

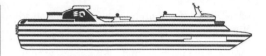

Size:	Large Resort Ship	Passenger/Crew Ratio (lower beds):	2.4
Tonnage:	115,875	Cabins (total):	1,351
Lifestyle:	Standard	Size Range (sq ft/m):	168–1,329.3/15.6–123.5
Cruise Line:	Princess Cruises	Cabins (for one person):	0
Former Names:	none	Cabins (with private balcony):	750
IMO Number:	9228198	Cabins (wheelchair accessible):	28
Builder:	Mitsubishi Heavy Industries (Japan)	Wheelchair accessibility:	Good
Original Cost:	$400 million	Cabin Current:	110 volts
Entered Service:	Feb 2004	Elevators:	14
Registry:	Great Britain	Casino (gaming tables):	Yes
Length (ft/m):	951.4/290.0	Slot Machines:	Yes
Beam (ft/m):	123.0/37.5	Swimming Pools:	3
Draft (ft/m):	26.4/8.0	Hot Tubs (on deck):	9
Propulsion/Propellers:	diesel-electric (42,000kW)/2	Self-Service Launderette:	Yes
Passenger Decks:	13	Dedicated Cinema/Seats:	No
Total Crew:	1,100	Library:	Yes
Passengers (lower beds):	2,702	Onboard currency:	US$
Passenger Space Ratio (lower beds):	42.8		

This large ship has relaxing decor, for mature-age cruisers

OVERVIEW. If you are not used to large ships, it may take you some time to find your way around *Diamond Princess*. The passenger flow has been well thought-out aboard this ship, and works with little congestion. The decor is attractive, with lots of earth tones.

THE SHIP. *Diamond Princess*, sister to *Sapphire Princess* (both built in Japan), has an instantly recognizable funnel due to two jet engine-like pods that sit high up on its structure but really are mainly for decoration.

Four areas focus on swimming pools. One has a giant poolside movie screen, and another is two decks high and is covered by a retractable glass dome, itself an extension of the funnel housing. One pool lies within The Sanctuary – an adults-only, extra-cost (it's worth it) relaxation area. There's also a children's pool.

There is plenty of space inside the ship – but there are also plenty of passengers – and a wide array of public rooms, with many 'intimate' – this being a relative word – spaces and places to enjoy. The passenger flow is well thought-out, and there is little congestion anywhere, except perhaps for waiting for elevators at peak times (usually each evening, before dinner).

The interior focal point is a piazza-style atrium lobby, with Vines (wine bar), an International Café (for coffee, pastries, panini sandwiches, etc.) library/Internet-connect center, and Alfredo's sit-down pizzeria.

A Wedding Chapel has a web-cam that can relay ceremonies via the Internet. The ship's captain can legally marry American couples, due to the ship's Ber-

Berlitz's Ratings		
	Possible	Achieved
Ship	500	384
Accommodation	200	147
Food	400	251
Service	400	293
Entertainment	100	78
Cruise Experience	400	295
OVERALL SCORE		
1448 points out of 2000		

muda registry and a special dispensation (which should be verified when in the planning stage, according to where you reside). Princess Cruises offers three wedding packages – Pearl, Emerald, Diamond; the fee includes registration and official marriage certificate. The Hearts & Minds chapel is useful for renewal of vows ceremonies.

The large Grand Casino has more than 260 slot machines; there are blackjack, craps, and roulette tables, plus other table games. Linked slot machines provide a combined payout.

Other facilities include a library/computer room and a card room. Ship lovers should enjoy the wood-paneled Wheelhouse Bar, housing memorabilia and ship models tracing part of parent company P&O's history. Aft of the International Dining Room is the Wake View Bar, with a spiral stairway leading down to a great viewing spot for watching the ship's wake; it is reached from the back of Club Fusion, on Promenade Deck. Skywalkers Nightclub is set around the base of the funnel structure and has a view overlooking the aft-facing cascading decks and children's pool.

There are many extra-charge items such as ice cream, and freshly squeezed orange juice. There's an hourly charge for group babysitting services and a charge for using the washers and dryers in the self-service launderettes.

In 2014 the ship underwent a $30 million refit that included the addition of 14 cabins, and the installation of Izumi, an 8,800-sq-ft (817.5-sq-m) onsen-style Japanese bath and garden area on Deck 15 aft (including gender-separated indoor and outdoor Cypress baths, and Stone baths with adjacent Utaseyu hot water cascades), in what was formerly part of the youth area.

Diamond Princess operates cruises from Yokohama during the summer, with extra Japanese-speaking staff employed in key positions. During the Northern Hemisphere winter (Australia's summer), the ship operates in Australasian waters.

FAMILIES. Facilities are extensive, and include a two-deck-high playroom, teen chill-out room, and a host of specially trained counselors. Children have their own pools, hot tubs, and open deck area at the stern of the ship (away from adult areas).

ACCOMMODATION. All cabins receive turndown service and pillow chocolates each night, as well as bathrobes on request and toiletry kits (larger for suite/mini-suite occupants). A hairdryer is located at the vanity desk unit in the living area. The tiled bathrooms have a decent amount of open shelf storage space for toiletries. Princess Cruises has BBC World, CNN, CNBC, ESPN, and TNT on the in-cabin TV system (when available, depending on cruise area).

Many outside cabins on Emerald Deck have views obstructed by the lifeboats. There are no cabins for solo travelers. Your name is typically placed outside your suite or cabin – making it simple for delivery service personnel, but limiting your privacy. There is 24-hour room service, but some items on the room service menu are not available during early morning hours. Most balcony suites and cabins can be overlooked from the navigation bridge wing. Cabins with balconies on Baja, Caribe, and Dolphin decks are also overlooked by passengers on balconies on the deck above.

Note that the bath towels are small, and drawer space is limited. The top-grade suites are not really large in comparison to similar suites aboard some other ships of a similar size.

DINING. There are five principal dining rooms with themed decor and cuisine – International (the largest, located aft, with two seatings and 'traditional' cuisine), Savoy, Vivaldi, and Pacific Moon. These offer a mix of two sittings, with seating assigned according to your cabin location, and 'anytime dining', where you choose when and with whom you want to eat.

All main dining rooms are split into sections in a non-symmetrical design that breaks what are quite large spaces into many smaller sections, for more intimate ambience and less noise pollution. Specially designed dinnerware and good-quality linens and silverware are used: Dudson of England (dinnerware), Frette Egyptian cotton table linens, and Hepp silverware.

Other dining options. Sabatini's (on Deck 7) is an informal eatery (reservations needed, and a cover charge applies). It serves a multi-course meal, including Italian-style pizzas and pastas with a variety of sauces, and entrées (mains), all provided with flair and entertainment by the waiters. The cuisine here is better than in the other dining rooms, with better-quality ingredients and items cooked to order.

Next door is Kai Sushi – a 66-seat restaurant (added in 2014) with its own integral sushi bar. The venue features à-la-carte, extra-cost sushi (for items such as maki, nigiri, and sashimi), a noodle bar, regional tea tastings, and a special sake menu.

Sterling Steakhouse (on the starboard side aft of the Horizon Court on Deck 14) is an extra-cost (reservations-required) venue for prime steaks and grilled meats and seafood items, with everything freshly cooked to order.

A poolside hamburger grill and a pizza bar (no additional charge) are additional eateries for casual bites, while extra charges will apply if you order items to eat at the Lobby bar/patisserie.

Other casual meals can be taken in the Horizon Court, open 24 hours a day, with large ocean-view on port and starboard sides and direct access to the two main swimming pools and Lido Deck. There is little presentation finesse, and oval-shaped plastic plates, not trays, are provided.

ENTERTAINMENT. The Princess Theater spans two decks and has comfortable seating on both main and balcony levels. Princess Cruises prides itself on its glamorous production shows, performed by its resident troupe of singers/dancers.

A second large entertainment lounge, Club Fusion, presents cabaret acts at night, lectures, bingo, and other activities during the day. A third entertainment lounge can also host cabaret acts and dance bands. Many other lounges and bars have live music, and a number of male dance hosts act as partners for women traveling alone.

SPA/FITNESS. The Lotus Spa complex (on Deck 15 forward), with Japanese-style decor, surrounds a lap pool – you can have a massage or other spa treatment in an ocean-view treatment room. Facilities include a beauty salon, male and female saunas and changing rooms, and an aerobics room and gymnasium.

Activities such as yoga, group exercise bicycling, and kick-boxing classes cost extra. For exercise, there is a good sheltered faux teak promenade deck (it's actually painted steel), which almost wraps around the ship (three times around equals one mile).

Disney Dream
★★★★

Size:	Large Resort Ship		Passenger/Crew Ratio (lower beds):	1.7
Tonnage:	129,690		Cabins (total):	1,250
Lifestyle:	Standard		Size Range (sq ft/m):	169–1,781/15.7–165.5
Cruise Line:	Disney Cruise Line		Cabins (for one person):	0
Former Names:	none		Cabins (with private balcony):	901
IMO Number:	9434254		Cabins (wheelchair accessible):	37
Builder:	Meyer Werft (Germany)		Wheelchair accessibility:	Good
Original Cost:	€600 million		Cabin Current:	110 volts
Entered Service:	Jan 2011		Elevators:	14
Registry:	The Bahamas		Casino (gaming tables):	No
Length (ft/m):	1,113.8/339.5		Slot Machines:	No
Beam (ft/m):	120.7/36.8		Swimming Pools:	3
Draft (ft/m):	26.0/7.9		Hot Tubs (on deck):	4
Propulsion/Propellers:	diesel-electric (42,000kW)/2		Self-Service Launderette:	No
Passenger Decks:	14		Dedicated Cinema/Seats:	No
Total Crew:	1,458		Library:	No
Passengers (lower beds):	2,500		Onboard currency:	US$
Passenger Space Ratio (lower beds):	51.8			

This is the ultimate family-friendly floating theme park

OVERVIEW. *Disney Dream* is ideal for families with children or grandchildren. Couples and solo travelers are also welcome, though there are few activities for couples in the daytime, and enough entertainment at night. You will, however, need to be a real Disney fan, as everything revolves around Disney characters and the family theme.

THE SHIP. Made of pieces of steel and pixie dust, the ships' exterior is about 40 percent larger than the first two Disney ships, *Disney Magic* and *Disney Wonder*. It also has two extra decks, although the design is similar – a tribute to the grand ocean liners of the 1930s. Like all Disney ships, there are two large funnels. The bows have handsome gold scrollwork more typically seen adorning yesteryear's tall ships (the stern is reminiscent of one of those lovely Airstream trailers). The ship's exterior colors are also those of Mickey himself: red, white, yellow, and black. The lifeboats are yellow, and not the normal orange, by special dispensation.

The biggest outdoor 'wow' factor is definitely going to be the AquaDuck, a 765ft (233m) shipboard 'watercoaster' spanning four decks in height – two-and-a-half times the length of a football field. It's pure Disney, really splash-tastic, and beyond anything aboard any other cruise ship dedicated to family cruising.

Disney whimsy and Art Deco style are the hallmarks of the stunning interior decor, too. In the main three-deck-high lobby stands a bronze statue of none other than Admiral Donald (Duck). The decor

Berlitz's Ratings		
	Possible	Achieved
Ship	500	422
Accommodation	200	159
Food	400	220
Service	400	293
Entertainment	100	91
Cruise Experience	400	335
OVERALL SCORE		
1520 points out of 2000		

is enhanced by original paintings, statues, and woodwork all bearing the characteristic Disney attention to detail.

Most public rooms have high ceilings, and the Art Deco theme of the old ocean liners or New York's Radio City Music Hall has been tastefully carried out. Have a look at the stainless steel/pewter Disney detailing on the handrails and balustrades in the atrium lobby. Other facilities include a digital photo kiosk.

Grown-ups can inhabit their own area of the ship – away from the kids. Known as The District, it includes five different adults-only venues, including Evolution (a lounge with dance floor and bar), a cozy Skyline Lounge, Pink, 687 Lounge, and District Lounge. There's also a centrally located Concierge Lounge, for occupants of accommodation designated as Concierge Class, all on Deck 12, plus a dedicated private sundeck for Concierge-class occupants.

Other venues include: Mickey's Mainsail, Sea Treasure, Whitecaps, and Whozits and Whatsits (retail shops); District Bar, Pink Champagne Bar, Skyline Bar, Waves Bar, Bon Voyage, Meridian Bar, 687 (sports bar), Currents Bar, and Arr-cade. The best place for a quiet drink, however, is in the ship's delightful Observation Bar.

During the winter, *Disney Dream* sails on three- and four-day cruises to the Bahamas as part of a seven-night vacation package that includes a three- or four-day stay at a Walt Disney World resort hotel in Orlando; the cruise then forms the second half of the vacation. The ship calls at Castaway Cay, Disney's excellent private beach island, whose facilities are constantly being enhanced. American Express cardholders get special treatment and extra goodies. Members of Disney's Vacation Club can exchange points for cruises.

Gratuities are extra, and 15 percent is added to all bar/drinks purchases.

FAMILIES. Almost one entire deck is devoted to catering for children and teens. With names of places to play in including Animator's Studio and Nemo's, it's no wonder that kids have a great time.

It's a Small World Nursery is for children aged from three months to three years. The Oceaneer Lab and Oceaneer Club both have an interactive play floor – a sort of down-to-earth Wii, where team actions translate to movement, a novel idea.

'Edge' is for 11–13-year-olds, a tween pad inside the forward funnel that's a chill-out zone including karaoke with green-screen technology. 'Vibe' is for the real teens, an indoor/outdoor space for 14–17s that is almost 9,000 sq ft (830 sq m), accessed by a teen-only swipe card.

ACCOMMODATION. There are nine types of suites and cabins, but many more price grades, depending on the size and location of the accommodation.

Interior cabins have a virtual porthole that gives you the feeling that you are in an outside cabin. It's done with high-definition cameras positioned on the outside decks to feed live video to each virtual porthole. You almost expect one or more Disney characters to pop by your porthole.

One feature that's different to *Disney Magic* and *Disney Wonder*: all bathrooms have round tubs with a pull-down seat and hand-held shower hose – practically perfect for washing babies and small children. The bed frames have been elevated so that luggage can easily be stored underneath.

The largest accommodation can be found in the Concierge Royal Suite (1,781 sq ft/166 sq m, including balcony), with hot tub. It can sleep five and has one master bedroom with a large walk-in closet, a living room (with one additional pull-down wall double bed and one pull-down single bed), two bathrooms (one has two washbasins), dining room, media library, pantry, and wet bar, plus a large balcony. These suites are located in the best possible position in the ship, with great ocean views.

If you opt for one of the 21 Concierge Class suites, you'll get higher-quality bed linen (Frette 300-thread count Egyptian cotton), feather and down duvets, cotton bathrobe, and H2O Plus bath and spa products.

DINING. There are three main dining rooms, each with a different decor. Passengers rotate through all three, together with their regular waiter (server in Disney-speak).

Expect to see the surfer-dude sea turtle from *Finding Nemo* swimming around Animator's Palate, making special appearances and interacting with passengers; the room transforms into a coral reef during dinner. It's all about 'foodertainment,' which Disney does well, but the noise level can sometimes be a little intense.

Royal Palace has decor inspired by the classic Disney films *Cinderella*, *Snow White and the Seven Dwarfs*, *Beauty and the Beast*, and *Sleeping Beauty*.

The Enchanted Garden is a whimsical main dining room inspired by the gardens of Versailles, near Paris, and the lighting magically transforms from day to night (the central glass panel ceiling is almost covered in what can only be magical foliage).

Other dining options. Cabanas is open to all. At night, it becomes another restaurant where meals from the main dining room menu are available in an even more casual setting but with waiter service.

For something different, and as an escape from the big dining rooms, Remy is an upscale French-style restaurant with menus created by Michelin-starred French chef Arnaud Lallement from L'Assiette Champenoise, close to Reims in France, in conjunction with Scott Hunnel from Victoria & Albert's at Walt Disney World. An extra-cost, reservations-only venue, it offers leisurely European-style dining – ideal for an evening out (without the kids, of course), but at $75 a head for dinner (plus wine) it's not cheap. The design is rather ratty, too (think Disney's *Ratatouille*); in fact, rats are everywhere in the 'fine-dining' venue – though not on your plate. A new seasonal tasting menu was added in 2015.

Palo is an Italian-cuisine themed adults-only restaurant, with à-la-carte items cooked to order. On days at sea, high tea is also served here, and there's a cover charge.

ENTERTAINMENT. Live shows are presented at the Walt Disney Theater, the ship's 1,340-seat showlounge. It has a star-studded ceiling and proscenium arch stage.

Villains Tonight, which premiered in 2010 aboard *Disney Dream* and features the baddies in Disney's films, is one of the shows being presented, along with other Disney favorites.

The Buena Vista Theater – which is not to be confused with the Walt Disney Theater – is the ship's movie house, with 399 seats.

There's live evening entertainment on deck including a Pirate Night, with visual and lighting effects, and live fireworks. Everyone's favorite Disney characters will be on board in many different locations, so make sure you have your camera with you (there are lots of photo opportunities).

SPA/FITNESS. Senses Spa and Salon has 17 treatment rooms and private outdoor verandahs. Rainforest features steam heat, misty showers, and hydrotherapy for relaxation. Teens can also have specially tailored spa treatments in their own chill-out zone.

Disney Fantasy
★★★★

Size:	Large Resort Ship		Passenger/Crew Ratio (lower beds):	1.7
Tonnage:	129,690		Cabins (total):	1,250
Lifestyle:	Standard		Size Range (sq ft/m):	169–1,781/15.7–165.5
Cruise Line:	Disney Cruise Line		Cabins (for one person):	0
Former Names:	none		Cabins (with private balcony):	901
IMO Number:	9445590		Cabins (wheelchair accessible):	37
Builder:	Meyer Werft (Germany)		Wheelchair accessibility:	Good
Original Cost:	€600 million		Cabin Current:	110 volts
Entered Service:	Apr 2012		Elevators:	14
Registry:	The Bahamas		Casino (gaming tables):	No
Length (ft/m):	1,113.8/339.5		Slot Machines:	No
Beam (ft/m):	120.7/36.8		Swimming Pools:	3
Draft (ft/m):	26.0/7.9		Hot Tubs (on deck):	4
Propulsion/Propellers:	diesel-electric (42,000kW)/2		Self-Service Launderette:	No
Passenger Decks:	14		Dedicated Cinema/Seats:	No
Total Crew:	1,458		Library:	No
Passengers (lower beds):	2,500		Onboard currency:	US$
Passenger Space Ratio (lower beds):	51.8			

An excellent family-friendly floating theme park

OVERVIEW. *Disney Fantasy* is ideal for families with children or grandchildren. Couples and solo travelers are also welcome, though there are few activities for couples in the daytime, and enough entertainment at night.

THE SHIP. Made of pieces of steel and pixie dust, the ships' exterior is about 40 percent larger than the first two Disney ships, *Disney Magic* and *Disney Wonder*. It also has two extra decks, although the design is similar – a tribute to the grand ocean liners of the 1930s. Like all Disney ships, there are two large funnels. The bows have handsome gold scrollwork more typically seen adorning yesteryear's tall ships (the stern is reminiscent of one of those lovely Airstream trailers). The ship's exterior colors (red, white, and black) are also those of Mickey himself. The lifeboats are yellow, and not the normal orange, by special dispensation.

No doubt the biggest outdoor 'wow' factor is AquaDuck, a 765ft (233m) AquaDuck shipboard 'watercoaster' spanning four decks in height – two-and-a-half times the length of a football field.

Disney whimsy and Art Deco style are the hallmarks of the stunning interior decor, too. In the main three-deck-high lobby stands a bronze statue of none other than Admiral Donald (Duck). A chandelier is the atrium's focal point. The Art Nouveau decor is enhanced by original paintings, statues, and woodwork all bearing the characteristic Disney attention to detail.

Berlitz's Ratings		
	Possible	Achieved
Ship	500	422
Accommodation	200	159
Food	400	220
Service	400	294
Entertainment	100	91
Cruise Experience	400	336
OVERALL SCORE		
1522 points out of 2000		

Most public rooms have high ceilings, and the Art Nouveau theme has been tastefully carried out. All the artwork in public areas comes from Disney films or animation features.

Grown-ups inhabit their own area of the ship, in an area known as The District. It includes five different adults-only venues, including The Tube (lounge with dance floor and bar), a cozy Skyline Lounge, O'Gill's Pub, La Piazza, and Ooh La La. There's also a centrally located Concierge Lounge, for occupants of accommodation designated as Concierge Class, all on Deck 12, plus a dedicated private sundeck for Concierge-class occupants.

Other venues include: Mickey's Mainsail, Sea Treasure, Whitecaps, and Whozits and Whatsits (retail shops); District Bar, Pink Champagne Bar, Skyline Bar, Waves Bar, Bon Voyage, Meridian Bar, 687 (sports bar), Currents Bar, and Arr-cade. The best place for a quiet drink, however, is in the ship's delightful Observation Bar.

Disney has its own private island, Castaway Cay, where the facilities are constantly being enhanced. American Express cardholders get special treatment and extra goodies. Members of Disney's Vacation Club can exchange points for cruises.

At Port Canaveral, the Disney terminal was inspired by the original Ocean Terminal in Southampton, England, from which the famous ocean liners *Queen Elizabeth*, *Queen Mary*, and the ill-fated *Titanic* once sailed.

Gratuities are extra, and 15 percent is added to all bar/drinks purchases.

FAMILIES. Almost one entire deck is devoted to catering for children and teens. With names of places to play in including Animator's Studio and Nemo's, it's no wonder that kids have a great time.

It's a Small World Nursery is for children aged from three months to three years. The Oceaneer Lab and Oceaneer Club both have an interactive play floor – a sort of down-to-earth Wii, where team actions translate to movement, a novel idea.

'Edge' is for 11–13-year-olds, a tween pad inside the forward funnel that's a chill-out zone including karaoke with green-screen technology. 'Vibe' is for the real teens, an indoor/outdoor space for 14–17s that is almost 9,000 sq ft (830 sq m), accessed by a teen-only swipe card.

ACCOMMODATION. There are nine types of suites and cabins, but many more price grades, depending on the size and location of the accommodation.

Interior cabins have a virtual porthole that gives you the feeling that you are in an outside cabin. It's done with high-definition cameras positioned on the outside decks to feed live video to each virtual porthole. You almost expect one or more Disney characters to pop by your porthole.

One feature that's different from *Disney Magic* and *Disney Wonder*: all bathrooms have round tubs with a pull-down seat and hand-held shower hose – great for washing babies and small children. The bed frames have been elevated, so that luggage can easily be stored underneath.

The largest accommodation can be found in the Concierge Royal Suite (1,781 sq ft/166 sq m, including balcony), with hot tub. It can sleep five and has one master bedroom with a large walk-in closet, a living room (with one additional pull-down wall double bed and one pull-down single bed), two bathrooms (one has two washbasins), dining room, media library, pantry, and wet bar, plus a large balcony. These suites are located in the best possible position in the ship, with great ocean views.

If you opt for one of the 21 Concierge Class suites, you'll get higher-quality bed linen (Frette 300-thread count Egyptian cotton), feather and down duvets, cotton bathrobe, and H2O Plus bath and spa products.

DINING. There are three main dining rooms, each with a different decor. Passengers rotate through all three, together with their regular waiter (server in Disney-speak).

Expect to see the surfer-dude sea turtle from *Finding Nemo* swimming around Animator's Palate, making special appearances and interacting with passengers; the room transforms into a coral reef during dinner. It's all about 'foodertainment', which Disney does well, but the noise level can sometimes be a little intense.

Royal Court has decor inspired by the classic Disney films *Cinderella*, *Snow White and the Seven Dwarfs*, *Beauty and the Beast*, and *Sleeping Beauty*.

The Enchanted Garden is a whimsical main dining room inspired by the gardens of Versailles, near Paris, and the lighting magically transforms from day to night (the central glass panel ceiling is almost covered in what can only be magical foliage).

Other dining options. Cabanas, is open to all. At night, it becomes another restaurant where meals from the main dining room menu are available in an even more casual setting but with waiter service.

As an escape from the big, lively dining rooms, try Remy. It's an upscale French-style restaurant with menus created by Michelin-starred French chef Arnaud Lallement from L'Assiette Champenoise, close to Reims in France, in conjunction with Scott Hunnel from Victoria & Albert's at Walt Disney World. An extra-cost, reservations-only venue, it offers leisurely European-style dining – ideal for an evening out (without the kids, of course), but at $75 a head for dinner (plus wine) it's not cheap. The design is rather ratty, too (think Disney's Ratatouille); in fact, rats are everywhere in the 'fine-dining' venue – though not on your plate. A new seasonal tasting menu was added in 2015.

Palo is an Italian-cuisine themed adults-only restaurant, with à-la-carte items cooked to order. On days at sea, high tea is also served here, and there's a cover charge.

ENTERTAINMENT. Live shows are presented at the Walt Disney Theater, the ship's 1,340-seat showlounge, which has a star-studded ceiling and proscenium arch stage.

Villains Tonight, which premiered in 2010 aboard *Disney Dream* and features the baddies in Disney's films, is one of the shows being presented, along with other Disney favorites.

The Buena Vista Theater – which is not to be confused with the Walt Disney Theater – is the ship's movie house, with 399 seats.

There's live evening entertainment on deck including a Pirate Night, with visual and lighting effects, and live fireworks. Everyone's favorite Disney characters will be on board in many different locations, so make sure you have your camera with you (there are lots of photo opportunities).

SPA/FITNESS. Senses Spa and Salon has 17 treatment rooms and private outdoor verandahs. Rainforest features steam heat, misty showers, and hydrotherapy for relaxation. Teens can also have specially tailored spa treatments in their own chill-out zone.

Disney Magic
★★★★

Size:	Mid-size Ship	Passenger/Crew Ratio (lower beds):	1.8
Tonnage:	83,338	Cabins (total):	875
Lifestyle:	Standard	Size Range (sq ft/m):	180.8–968.7/16.8–90.0
Cruise Line:	Disney Cruise Line	Cabins (for one person):	0
Former Names:	none	Cabins (with private balcony):	388
IMO Number:	9126807	Cabins (wheelchair accessible):	12
Builder:	Fincantieri (Italy)	Wheelchair accessibility:	Good
Original Cost:	$350 million	Cabin Current:	110 volts
Entered Service:	Jul 1998	Elevators:	12
Registry:	The Bahamas	Casino (gaming tables):	No
Length (ft/m):	964.5/294.0	Slot Machines:	No
Beam (ft/m):	105.7/32.2	Swimming Pools:	3
Draft (ft/m):	26.2/8.0	Hot Tubs (on deck):	6
Propulsion/Propellers:	diesel-electric (38,000kW)/2	Self-Service Launderette:	Yes
Passenger Decks:	11	Dedicated Cinema/Seats:	Yes/270
Total Crew:	945	Library:	No
Passengers (lower beds):	1,750	Onboard currency:	US$
Passenger Space Ratio (lower beds):	47.6		

Ultra family-friendly cruising in a casual, big ship setting

OVERVIEW. *Disney Magic* is like a floating version of Disney's incredibly popular theme parks – a seagoing Never-Never Land. In reality, it provides a highly programmed, well-organized, and regimented onboard experience, with tickets, lines, and reservations necessary for almost everything. Children of all ages (minimum 12 weeks old) will have a great time aboard this ship.

Berlitz's Ratings		
	Possible	Achieved
Ship	500	397
Accommodation	200	155
Food	400	201
Service	400	287
Entertainment	100	88
Cruise Experience	400	317
OVERALL SCORE		
1445 points out of 2000		

THE SHIP. Disney Cruise Line's first ship's profile is sleek, and combines streamlining with tradition and nostalgia, a black hull, and two large red-and-black funnels reminiscent of the ocean liners of the past – *Disney Magic* was the first cruise ship built with two funnels since the 1950s. The forward funnel is a dummy containing various public spaces, including a teen center, Aloft.

There are two outdoor pools: one pool for adults only (in theory), and one for families. One has a large poolside movie screen. In a 2013 makeover, a super-popular AquaDunk water-slide experience was added.

Inside, the ship is quite stunning. Most public rooms have high ceilings, and the Art Deco theme of the old ocean liners or New York's Radio City Music Hall has been tastefully carried out. Have a look at the stainless steel/pewter Disney detailing on the handrails and balustrades in the three-deck-high lobby. The lobby provides a real photo opportunity, with a 6ft (1.8m) bronze statue of Mickey Mouse in the role of a ship's helmsman.

A highlight for most is a day spent on Disney's private island, Castaway Cay in the Bahamas. It is an outstanding private island – perhaps the benchmark for all private islands for families with children. It has its own pier, so that the ship can dock alongside. Water sports equipment – floats, paddle-boats, kayaks, hobie cats, aqua fins, aqua trikes, and snorkels – can be rented.

Take mainly casual clothing, although there are two 'formal' nights on the seven-day cruises. Gratuities are extra, suggested at about $10 per person, per day, and 15 percent is added to all bar/beverage/wine and spa accounts.

FAMILIES. The ship has three main zones: one for adults only, one for families with children, and one for families or single parents with toddlers. Each group has its own swimming pool and open deck/sunbathing areas – adults only at the front of the ship. A 24 x 14ft (7 x 4m) Goofy Pool Jumbo Screen is positioned by the family pool area, just behind the forward funnel; it shows classic Disney animated and live-action movies, TV shows, and sporting events.

A child drop-off service is available in the evenings, and private babysitting services are available at around $11 an hour, as are character 'tuck-ins' for children, and character breakfasts and lunches – all at extra cost. Free strollers are available, and parents can be provided with beepers in order to enjoy their time alone, away from their offspring for much of the day.

ACCOMMODATION. There are just six different cabin layouts, in several price grades; the price will depend on the grade, size, and location chosen, and is linked to the resort accommodation for those taking a combined resort/cruise vacation. Spread over six decks, all have been designed for practicality and have space-efficient layouts.

Most cabins have common features such as a neat vertical steamer trunk for clothes storage, illuminated closets, a hairdryer located at a vanity desk or in the bathroom, and bathrobes for all passengers. Many cabins have third and fourth pull-down berths that rise and are totally hidden in the ceiling when not in use, but the standard interior and outside cabins, while acceptable for two, are extremely tight with three or four. Some cabins can also accommodate a fifth person. Cabins with refrigerators can have them stocked, at extra cost, with one of several drinks/soft drinks packages.

Bathrooms, although compact due to the fact that the toilet is separate, are really functional units, designed with split-use facilities so that more than one person can use them at the same time – good for families. Many have bathtubs, which are really shower tubs.

Accommodation designated as suites offers much more space, and extra goodies including CD and DVD players, big-screen TVs, and extra beds (useful for larger families). Some suites are beneath the pool deck, teen lounge, or informal café, so there could be noise as the ceiling insulation is poor – although cabin-to-cabin insulation is good.

Wheelchair-bound passengers have a variety of cabin sizes and configurations, including suites with a private balcony – unfortunately you can't get a wheelchair through the balcony's sliding door – and over-sized bathrooms with excellent roll-in showers, and good closet and drawer space. Almost all the vessel is accessible. For the sight-impaired, cabin numbers and elevator buttons are braille-encoded.

DINING. There are three main dining rooms – non-smoking of course – each with over 400 seats, two seatings, and unique themes. Lumiere's (in the center of the ship on Deck 3) has Beauty and the Beast; Parrot Cay (Deck 4) has a tacky, pseudo-Caribbean theme; also on Deck 4 aft, with great ocean views over the stern, is Animator's Palate, the most visual of the three, with food and electronic art that makes the evening decor change from black and white to full-color (this author's signature is on a hidden wall panel in this venue – it was done in the shipyard at Disney Cruise Line's invitation).

You eat in all three dining rooms in rotation – twice per seven-day cruise – and move with your assigned waiter and assistant waiter to each dining room in turn, thus providing the variety of different decor and different menus. It's a great concept – and unique in the cruise industry. As you will have the same waiter in each of the three restaurants, any gratuities go only to 'your' waiter. Parrot Cay and Lumiere's have open seating for breakfast and lunch, but the lunch menu is pitiful.

Other dining options. Palo is a 140-seat reservations-only alternative restaurant with a small cover/gratuity charge, serving Italian cuisine. It has a 270-degree view and is for adults only; the à-la-carte cuisine is cooked to order, and the wine list is good, although prices are high. Make your reservations as soon as you board or you will miss out on the ship's only decent food. Afternoon High Tea is presented here, on days at sea.

Topsider's (incorporating Beach Blanket Buffet) is an indoor/outdoor café serving low-quality self-serve breakfast and lunch buffets with limited choice and presentation, and a buffet dinner, consisting mostly of fried foods, for children. But the venue is often overcrowded at lunchtime, so it may be better to go to the Parrot Cay dining room, which offers breakfast and lunch buffet, too. A poolside Goofy's Galley has grilled panini and wraps, and soft drinks are complimentary.

Scoops, an ice cream and frozen yogurt bar, opens infrequently; other fast-food outlets include Pluto's for hamburgers, hot dogs, and Pinocchio's, which is open all day but not in the evening, for basic pizza and sandwiches.

On one night, there is also an outdoor self-serve Tropicalifragilisticexpialidocious buffet.

A casual Outlook Café, installed in 2010, has fine views from Deck 10, just forward of the first funnel housing. Vegetarians and those looking for light cuisine will be underwhelmed by the lack of green vegetables. Guest chefs from Walt Disney World Resort prepare signature dishes each cruise, and also host cooking demonstrations.

ENTERTAINMENT. The entertainment and activities programs for families and children are extremely good. There are three big stage shows in the stunning 977-seat showlounge, presenting original Disney musicals and the latest comedy productions, bring together a cast of Disney baddies from many Disney films. Sadly, there is no live orchestra, although the lighting, staging, and technical effects are excellent. There is also a Disney-themed Trivia Game Show.

SPA/FITNESS. The Vista Spa is the ship's fitness/wellbeing complex measuring 10,700 sq ft/994 sq m. The fitness/workout room, with high-tech Cybex muscle-toning equipment, has ocean-view windows overlooking the navigation bridge one deck below. There are 11 rooms for spa/beauty treatments – but note 192.168.254.22 that the pounding from the basketball court on the sports deck directly overhead makes spa treatments less than relaxing.

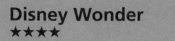

Disney Wonder
★★★★

Size:	Mid-size Ship	Passenger/Crew Ratio (lower beds):	1.8
Tonnage:	85,000	Cabins (total):	875
Lifestyle:	Standard	Size Range (sq ft/m):	180.8–968.7/16.8–90.0
Cruise Line:	Disney Cruise Line	Cabins (for one person):	0
Former Names:	none	Cabins (with private balcony):	388
IMO Number:	9126819	Cabins (wheelchair accessible):	12
Builder:	Fincantieri (Italy)	Wheelchair accessibility:	Good
Original Cost:	$350 million	Cabin Current:	110 volts
Entered Service:	Aug 1999	Elevators:	12
Registry:	The Bahamas	Casino (gaming tables):	No
Length (ft/m):	964.5/294.0	Slot Machines:	No
Beam (ft/m):	105.7/32.2	Swimming Pools:	3
Draft (ft/m):	26.2/8.0	Hot Tubs (on deck):	6
Propulsion/Propellers:	diesel-electric (38,000kW)/2	Self-Service Launderette:	Yes
Passenger Decks:	11	Dedicated Cinema/Seats:	Yes/270
Total Crew:	945	Library:	No
Passengers (lower beds):	1,750	Onboard currency:	US$
Passenger Space Ratio (lower beds):	48.5		

This is good theme-park, casual cruising for the whole family

OVERVIEW. *Disney Wonder* is like a floating version of Disney's incredibly popular theme parks – a seagoing Never-Never Land. In reality, the ship provides a highly programmed, well-organized, strictly timed, and regimented cruise experience, with tickets, lines, and reservations necessary for almost everything. But for children of all ages (minimum 12 weeks old), it's hard to beat Disney's entertainment.

THE SHIP. *Disney Wonder* is the second of an identical pair of ships (the first was the 1998-built *Disney Magic*). The ship's profile is sleek, and combines streamlining with tradition and nostalgia, a black hull and two large red-and-black funnels designed to remind you of the ocean liners of the past – *Disney Magic* was the first cruise ship built with two funnels since the 1950s. One funnel is a dummy containing various public spaces, including a teen center, Aloft.

There are three outdoor pools: one pool for adults only (in theory), one for families, and one for children. One has a large poolside movie screen, and you can guess which one has Mickey's face and ears painted into the bottom.

Inside, the ship is quite stunning. Most public rooms have high ceilings, and the Art Deco theme of the old ocean liners or New York's Radio City Music Hall has been tastefully carried out. Have a look at the stainless steel/pewter Disney detailing on the handrails and balustrades in the three-deck-high lobby.

Apart from the ports of call, the highlight for most is a day spent on Disney's private island, Castaway

Berlitz's Ratings

	Possible	Achieved
Ship	500	397
Accommodation	200	155
Food	400	201
Service	400	287
Entertainment	100	88
Cruise Experience	400	319
OVERALL SCORE		
1447 points out of 2000		

Cay in the Bahamas. It is an outstanding private island for families.

Take mainly casual clothing. Gratuities are extra, suggested at about $10 per person, per day, and 15 percent is added to all bar/beverage/wine and spa accounts.

FAMILIES. The ship has three main zones: one for adults only, one for families with children, and one for families or single parents with toddlers. Each group has its own swimming pool and open deck/sunbathing areas – adults only at the front of the ship. A 24 x 14ft (7 x 4m) Goofy Pool Jumbo Screen is positioned by the family pool area, just behind the forward funnel; it shows classic Disney animated and live-action movies, TV shows, and sporting events.

A child drop-off service is available in the evenings, and private babysitting services are available at around $11 an hour, as are character 'tuck-ins' for children, and character breakfasts and lunches – all at extra cost. Free strollers are available, and parents can be provided with beepers in order to enjoy their time alone, away from their offspring for much of the day.

ACCOMMODATION. There are 12 grades, but just six different cabin layouts; the price will depend on the grade, size, and location chosen, and are linked to the resort accommodation for those taking a combined resort/cruise vacation. Spread over six decks, all suites and cabins have been designed for practicality and have space-efficient layouts.

Most cabins have common features such as a neat vertical steamer trunk for clothes storage, illuminated closets, a hairdryer located at a vanity desk or in the bathroom, and bathrobes for all passengers. Many cabins have third and fourth pull-down berths that rise and are totally hidden in the ceiling when not in use, but the standard interior and outside cabins, while acceptable for two, are extremely tight with three or four. Some cabins can also accommodate a fifth person. The cabin decor is practical, creative, and colorful, with lots of neat styling touches. Cabins with refrigerators can have them stocked, at extra cost, with one of several drinks/soft drinks packages.

Bathrooms, although compact due to the fact that the toilet is separate, are really functional units, designed with split-use facilities, so that more than one person can use them at the same time – good for families. Many have bathtubs, which are really shower tubs.

Accommodation designated as suites offers much more space, and extra goodies such as CD and DVD players, big-screen TVs, and extra beds (useful for larger families). Some suites are beneath the pool deck, teen lounge, or informal café, so there could be noise as the ceiling insulation is poor – although cabin-to-cabin insulation is good.

The two largest suites, the Walter E. Disney Suite and the Roy O. Disney Suite, are located beside the central bank of elevators. These are luxurious living spaces, each with two bedrooms, and all the Disney trimmings you'd expect.

Wheelchair-bound passengers have a variety of cabin sizes and configurations, including suites with a private balcony – unfortunately you can't get a wheelchair through the balcony's sliding door – and extra-large bathrooms with excellent roll-in showers, and good closet and drawer space. Almost all the vessel is accessible. For the sight-impaired, cabin numbers and elevator buttons are braille-encoded.

A 24-hour room service is available, and suites also get 'concierge service.' But the room service and cabin breakfast menu are limited. A 15 percent service charge applies to beverage deliveries, including tea and coffee.

DINING. There are has three main dining rooms, all non-smoking, each with over 400 seats, two seatings, and unique themes. Lumiere's (in the center of the ship on Deck 3) has Beauty and the Beast; Parrot Cay (Deck 4) has a tacky, pseudo-Caribbean theme; also on Deck 4 aft, with great ocean views over the stern, is Animator's Palate, the most visual of the three with food and electronic art that makes the evening decor change from black and white to full-color.

You will eat in all three dining rooms in rotation – twice per seven-day cruise – and move with your assigned waiter and assistant waiter to each dining room in turn, thus providing the variety of different decor and different menus. It's a great concept – and unique in the cruise industry. As you will have the same waiter in each of the three restaurants, any gratuities go only to 'your' waiter. Parrot Cay and Lumiere's have open seating for breakfast and lunch, but the lunch menu is pitiful.

Other dining options. Palo is a 140-seat reservations-only restaurant with a cover/gratuity charge, for Italian cuisine. It has a 270-degree view and is for adults only; the à-la-carte cuisine is cooked to order, and the wine list is good, although prices are high. Make reservations as soon as you board or you will miss out on the ship's only decent food. Afternoon High Tea is presented here, on days at sea.

Topsider's (incorporating Beach Blanket Buffet) is an indoor/outdoor café serving low-quality self-serve breakfast and lunch buffets with limited choice and presentation, and a buffet dinner, consisting mostly of fried foods, for children. But the venue is often overcrowded at lunchtime, so it may be better to go to the Parrot Cay dining room, which offers breakfast and lunch buffet, too. A poolside Goofy's Galley has grilled panini and wraps, and soft drinks are complimentary.

Scoops, an ice cream and frozen yogurt bar, opens infrequently; other fast-food outlets include Pluto's for hamburgers, hot dogs, and Pinocchio's, which is open all day but not in the evening, for basic pizza and sandwiches.

On one night, there is also an outdoor self-serve Tropicalifragilisticexpialidocious buffet.

A casual Outlook Café, installed in 2010, has fine views from Deck 10, just forward of the first funnel housing. Vegetarians and those looking for light cuisine will be underwhelmed by the lack of green vegetables. Guest chefs from Walt Disney World Resort prepare signature dishes each cruise, and also host cooking demonstrations.

ENTERTAINMENT. The entertainment and activities programs for families and children are superb. There are three large-scale stage shows in the stunning 977-seat showlounge, presenting original Disney musicals and comedy productions, bringing together a cast of Disney baddies from many Disney films. Sadly, there is no live orchestra, although the lighting, staging, and technical effects are excellent. There is also a Disney-themed Trivia Game Show.

SPA/FITNESS. The Vista Spa is a fitness/wellbeing complex measuring 10,700 sq ft/994 sq m. The fitness/workout room, with high-tech Cybex muscle-toning equipment, has ocean-view windows overlooking the navigation bridge one deck below. There are 11 rooms for spa/beauty treatments – but note that the pounding from the basketball court on the sports deck directly overhead makes spa treatments less than relaxing.

Emerald Princess
★★★★

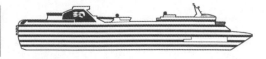

Size:	Large Resort Ship
Tonnage:	113,561
Lifestyle:	Standard
Cruise Line:	Princess Cruises
Former Names:	none
IMO Number:	9333151
Builder:	Fincantieri (Italy)
Original Cost:	$500 million
Entered Service:	May 2007
Registry:	Bermuda
Length (ft/m):	951.4/290.0
Beam (ft/m):	118.1/36.0
Draft (ft/m):	26.2/8.0
Propulsion/Propellers:	diesel-electric (42,000kW)/2
Passenger Decks:	15
Total Crew:	1,200
Passengers (lower beds):	3,114
Passenger Space Ratio (lower beds):	36.2

Passenger/Crew Ratio (lower beds):	2.5
Cabins (total):	1,557
Size Range (sq ft/m):	163–1,279/15.1–118.8
Cabins (for one person):	0
Cabins (with private balcony):	881
Cabins (wheelchair accessible):	25
Wheelchair accessibility:	Good
Cabin Current:	110 volts
Elevators:	14
Casino (gaming tables):	Yes
Slot Machines:	Yes
Swimming Pools:	3
Hot Tubs (on deck):	9
Self-Service Launderette:	Yes
Dedicated Cinema/Seats:	No
Library:	Yes
Onboard currency:	US$

This is a very comfortable, family-oriented large resort ship

OVERVIEW. The ship is a fine resort playground in which to roam when you are not ashore, and Princess Cruises consistently delivers a well-packaged cruise, always with a good degree of style, at an attractive, highly competitive price. With many choices and 'small' rooms to enjoy, the ship has been extremely well designed, and you should have an enjoyable time.

Berlitz's Ratings		
	Possible	Achieved
Ship	500	382
Accommodation	200	147
Food	400	250
Service	400	285
Entertainment	100	80
Cruise Experience	400	298
OVERALL SCORE		
1442 points out of 2000		

THE SHIP. *Emerald Princess* has the same profile as sister *Crown Princess* (similar to half-sisters *Diamond Princess*, *Golden Princess*, *Grand Princess*, *Ruby Princess*, *Sapphire Princess*, and *Star Princess*). Although the ship takes over 500 more passengers than the half-sisters, the outdoor deck space remains the same, as do the number of elevators, so waiting time will increase at peak periods. The Passenger Space Ratio is also considerably reduced.

One nice feature worth booking on days at sea is The Sanctuary, an extra-cost adults-only retreat located forward on the uppermost deck. It provides a 'private' place to relax and unwind and includes attendants to provide chilled face towels and deliver light bites; there are also two outdoor cabanas for massages. It's worth the extra charge, calculated by the half-day.

There is a good sheltered faux teak promenade deck – it's actually painted steel – which almost wraps around (three times round is equal to one mile) and a walkway, which goes to the enclosed, protected bow of the ship. The outdoor pools have various beach-like surroundings, and Movies Under the Skies and major sporting events are shown on a 300-sq-ft (28-sq-m) movie screen at the pool in front of the large funnel structure.

Unlike on the outside decks, there is plenty of space inside – but there are also plenty of passengers – and a wide array of public rooms, with many 'intimate' (this being a relative term) spaces and places to play. The passenger flow has been well thought-out, and there is little congestion.

Just aft of the funnel housing is a ship-wide glass-walled disco called Skywalkers; it's in a lower position than in some of the half-sister ships, but still has fine views from port and starboard side windows – it would make a great penthouse.

The interior decor is attractive, with lots of earth tones. An extensive collection of artworks complements the interior design and colors well. If you see something you like, you may be able to purchase it.

Emerald Princess also has a Wedding Chapel, with a live web-cam to relay ceremonies via the Internet. The captain can legally marry (American) couples, thanks to the ship's Bermuda registry and a special dispensation (which should be verified when in the planning stage, according to where you reside). But getting married and taking close family members and entourage with you on your honeymoon may prove expensive. The Hearts & Minds chapel is also useful for renewal of vows ceremonies.

Gamers should enjoy the large Gatsby's Casino, with more than 260 slot machines, and blackjack, craps, and roulette tables, plus games such as Let It Ride Bonus, Spanish 21, and Caribbean Draw Progressive. But the highlight could be the linked slot machines that provide a combined payout.

Other features include a small library, and a decent Internet-connect room. Ship lovers should enjoy the wood-paneled Wheelhouse Bar (a good place for cocktails and beer), finely decorated with memorabilia and ship models tracing part of parent company P&O's history. A sports bar has two billiard tables, and several television screens.

As with any large resort ship it will take you some time to find your way around, despite the company's claim that it offers passengers a 'small ship feel, big ship choice.' There are several points of congestion, particularly outside the shops, when bazaar tables are set up outside on the upper level of the atrium lobby.

FAMILIES. There's a two-deck-high playroom, teens' chill-out room, and a host of trained counselors. Children have their own pools, hot tubs, open deck, and sports court area at the stern of the ship, away from the adults.

ACCOMMODATION. There are six main types of cabins and configurations: (a) grand suite, (b) suite, (c) mini-suite, (d) outside-view double cabins with balcony, (e) outside-view double cabins, and (f) interior double cabins. These come in many price categories (the choice is bewildering), depending on size and location.

For further information on the facilities available in each type of cabin, see the entry for *Crown Princess*.

DINING. Of the three main dining rooms – Botticelli, Da Vinci, and Michelangelo – one has two-seating dining and the other two have 'anytime dining' that allows you to choose when and with whom you want to eat. All three are split into multi-tier sections in a non-symmetrical design that breaks what are quite large spaces into smaller sections for better ambience.

While four elevators go to the deck where two of the restaurants are located, only two go to Plaza Deck 5, where the Michelangelo Dining Room is located – this causes waiting problems at peak times, particularly for anyone in a wheelchair.

Specially designed dinnerware, high-quality linens and silverware, Frette Egyptian cotton table linens, and Hepp silverware are used in the main dining rooms. Note that 15 percent is added to all beverage bills, including wines.

Other dining options. There are two extra-cost venues: Sabatini's and Crown Grill. Both are open for lunch and dinner on days at sea. Sabatini's is an Italian eatery located on a high deck aft of the funnel

housing, with colorful tiled Mediterranean-style decor; it is named after Trattoria Sabatini, the 200-year-old institution in Florence. It includes Italian-style multi-course antipasti and pastas and Italian-style entrées, including tiger prawns and lobster tail, all provided with flair and entertainment by the waiters. It's by reservation only and has a cover charge.

The Crown Grill, located aft on Promenade Deck, is a reservation-only, extra-cost steakhouse, offering premium-quality American steaks and seafood.

Others include a poolside hamburger grill and pizza bar (no additional charge), while extra charges apply if you order items to eat either at the International Café (a coffee bar/patisserie) or in Vines seafood/wine bar in the atrium lobby. Other casual meals can be taken in the Horizon Court (open 24 hours a day). It has large ocean-view on port and starboard sides and direct access to the two principal swimming pools and Lido Deck. Although there is a wide variety of food, there is no finesse in presentation as plastic plates are provided.

For something different, you could try a private dinner on your balcony, an all-inclusive evening featuring cocktails, fresh flowers, Champagne, and a deluxe four-course meal including Caribbean lobster tail – all served by a waiter on your balcony. Of course, it costs extra.

ENTERTAINMENT. The 800-seat Princess Theater is the main entertainment venue; it spans two decks and has comfortable seating on both main and balcony levels. It has $3 million worth of sound and light equipment, plus a nine-piece orchestra. The ship has a resident troupe of almost 20 singers and dancers.

A second entertainment lounge, Club Fusion, is located aft. It features cabaret acts and karaoke contests at night, and lectures, bingo, and horse racing during the day. The Explorer's Lounge, a third entertainment lounge, can also host cabaret acts and dance bands.

A variety of other lounges and bars feature live music, including a string quartet, and 'street performers' in the main atrium lobby.

SPA/FITNESS. The Lotus Spa is located forward on Sun Deck, one of the uppermost decks. Separate facilities for men and women include a sauna, steam room, and changing rooms; common facilities include a relaxation/waiting zone, body-pampering treatment rooms, and a gymnasium with packed with the latest high-tech muscle-pumping, cardiovascular equipment, and great ocean views. Some fitness classes are free, while others cost extra.

Empress
★★★

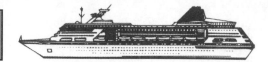

Size:	Mid-size Ship
Tonnage:	48,563 tons
Lifestyle:	Standard
Cruise Line:	Pullmantur Cruises
Former Names:	Empress of the Seas, Nordic Empress
IMO Number:	8716899
Builder:	Chantiers de l'Atlantique (France)
Original Cost:	$170 million
Entered Service:	Jun 1990/May 2008
Registry:	The Bahamas
Length (ft/m):	692.2/211.0
Beam (ft/m):	100.7/30.7
Draft (ft/m):	24.9/7.6
Propulsion/Propellers:	diesel (16,200kW)/2
Passenger Decks:	9
Total Crew:	685
Passengers (lower beds):	1,600
Passenger Space Ratio (lower beds):	30.2

Passenger/Crew Ratio (lower beds):	2.3
Cabins (total):	800
Size Range (sq ft/m):	117.0–818/10.8–76
Cabins (for one person):	0
Cabins (with private balcony):	69
Cabins (wheelchair accessible):	4
Wheelchair accessibility:	Fair
Cabin Current:	110 volts
Elevators:	7
Casino (gaming tables):	Yes
Slot Machines:	Yes
Swimming Pools:	1
Hot Tubs (on deck):	4
Self-Service Launderette:	No
Dedicated Cinema/Seats:	No
Library:	No
Onboard currency:	Euros

A dated but family-friendly ship for Spanish speakers

OVERVIEW. *Empress* is best suited to youthful Spanish-speaking couples and solo travelers seeking an all-inclusive cruise, and anyone wanting a good basic first getaway cruise aboard a ship that offers some good drinking places.

THE SHIP. This fairly modern ship has a polished wood walk-around promenade deck outdoors. The two swimming pools are very small for the number of passengers, and there's little open deck space, so sunloungers are crammed together.

A nine-deck-high atrium is the focal point of the interior design, which has many Scandinavian influences. Passenger flow is generally good. A three-level casino has a sailcloth ceiling, but it is a noisy room. The Viking Crown Lounge, aft of the funnel, is a two-level nightclub-disco.

Empress is a fairly smart ship with a high passenger density, so you won't be bored, but you may be overwhelmed by the public spaces, and underwhelmed by the size of the cabins.

ACCOMMODATION. There are several price categories. The largest accommodation, the Royal Suite, has a queen-size bed, walk-in closet, separate living area with bar, refrigerator, entertainment center, and private balcony; the bathroom has a whirlpool tub and vanity dressing area.

Nine cabins have private balconies overlooking the stern; these consist of two large owner's suites

Berlitz's Ratings	Possible	Achieved
Ship	500	312
Accommodation	200	117
Food	400	215
Service	400	248
Entertainment	100	61
Cruise Experience	400	236
OVERALL SCORE		
1189 points out of 2000		

and seven 'superior' ocean-view cabins. Other cabins with private balconies also have a decent amount of living space, small sofa, coffee table and chair, and vanity desk. Almost all other cabins are really small, but adequate, with twin beds that convert to a queen-size configuration. The bathrooms are nicely laid-out.

DINING. The Miramar Restaurant is two decks high, but it really is a noisy room. There are two seatings, at tables for four, six, eight, or 10. The cuisine is typical of mass banquet catering that offers standard fare.

There is one à-la-carte extra-charge restaurant, where reservations are required. Its intimacy makes it a romantic place, with a good number of tables for two.

For casual breakfasts and lunches, the Panorama Buffet provides an alternative to the dining room.

ENTERTAINMENT. The two-level Broadway Showroom has poor sight lines in the upper lateral balconies. The sight lines from the balcony are ruined by railings. The entertainment throughout is upbeat – in fact, it is difficult to get away from music. There is even background music in all corridors and lifts, and constant music on the pool deck.

SPA/FITNESS. A gymnasium has some good equipment. Sports fans will like the climbing wall at the stern of the ship.

Enchantment of the Seas
★★★+

Size:	Large Resort Ship	Passenger/Crew Ratio (lower beds):	2.6
Tonnage:	81,500	Cabins (total):	1,126
Lifestyle:	Standard	Size Range (sq ft/m):	158.2–1,267.0/14.7–117.7
Cruise Line:	Royal Caribbean International	Cabins (for one person):	0
Former Names:	none	Cabins (with private balcony):	248
IMO Number:	9111802	Cabins (wheelchair accessible):	20
Builder:	Kvaerner Masa-Yards (Finland)	Wheelchair accessibility:	Good
Original Cost:	$300 million	Cabin Current:	110 and 220 volts
Entered Service:	Jul 1997	Elevators:	9
Registry:	The Bahamas	Casino (gaming tables):	Yes
Length (ft/m):	990.1/301.8	Slot Machines:	Yes
Beam (ft/m):	105.6/32.2	Swimming Pools:	3 (1 w/sliding glass dome)
Draft (ft/m):	25.5/7.6	Hot Tubs (on deck):	4
Propulsion/Propellers:	diesel-electric (50,400kW)/2	Self-Service Launderette:	No
Passenger Decks:	11	Dedicated Cinema/Seats:	No
Total Crew:	840	Library:	Yes
Passengers (lower beds):	2,252	Onboard currency:	US$
Passenger Space Ratio (lower beds):	36.1		

A fine resort ship with elegant decor, for savvy families

OVERVIEW. This ship has quite attractive interiors and will provide you with a good cruise vacation. It is good particularly for first-time passengers seeking comfortable surroundings similar to those in a Hyatt Hotel, with fabrics and soft furnishings that blend together. This company provides a well-organized but rather homogenous cruise experience, with the same decades old passenger participation activities and events.

Berlitz's Ratings

	Possible	Achieved
Ship	500	374
Accommodation	200	141
Food	400	240
Service	400	262
Entertainment	100	75
Cruise Experience	400	273

OVERALL SCORE
1365 points out of 2000

THE SHIP. *Enchantment of the Seas*, sister to *Grandeur of the Seas*, has a fairly sleek profile, with a single funnel located well aft – almost a throwback to the designs of the 1950s, and a nicely rounded stern. There is a walk-around promenade deck outdoors, but no cushioned pads for the plastic sunloungers.

A large Viking Crown Lounge, a trademark lounge aboard all Royal Caribbean International ships, sits between the funnel and mast at the top of the atrium lobby, and overlooks the forward section of the swimming pool deck, with access provided from a stairway off the central atrium.

In 2005, a $60 million 'chop-and-stretch' exercise added a 72.8ft (22.2m) mid-section, increasing its overall length to 990.1ft (301.8m) and upping its gross tonnage. It added 151 passenger cabins, including two 'family' cabins that can sleep six. The pool deck was given more space plus soaring 'suspension' bridges. Special lifts were provided for the two pools, as was a new Splash Deck (kids love the 64 water jets). While not as large as some of the newer ships in the fleet, *Enchantment of the Seas* is perhaps more suited to couples and families with children that don't need all those bells and whistles, but want to cruise with up-to-date facilities and have multiple dining choices for more convenience. Between 2011 and 2014 the company added some of the dining options found on the larger ships, and enhanced the overall onboard experience by adding, for example, ship-wide (extra-cost) Wi-Fi, flat-screen televisions in all cabins, and finger-touch digital 'wayfinder' direction screens.

The principal interior focal point (and the social hub of the ship) is a seven-deck-high Centrum (atrium lobby). On its various levels, it houses an R Bar (for some creative cocktails), several passenger service counters, art gallery, and Café Latte-tudes (for coffee). Aerial entertainment happens in the Centrum, too. Close by is the decidedly flashy Casino Royale (for table gaming and slot machines – and interesting exhibits under glass floor panels), the popular Schooner Bar, with its nautical-theme decor and maritime art, Boleros (for Latin sounds and dancing), Centrum shops, and the library.

There's a varied collection of artworks, including several sculptures, principally by British artists; much of it is on the themes of classical music, ballet, and theater. There are also huge murals of opera scenes on several stairways. There is a good use of tropical plants throughout the public rooms, which helps to counteract the plain, clinical pastel wall colors.

ACCOMMODATION. There are multiple price grades, with location and grade perhaps the most important determining factor, given that so many of the cabins are of the same or very similar size. All suite and cabin grades are provided with a hairdryer. The room service menu has only the most basic selection.

Royal Suite. The largest accommodation, which contains a baby grand piano, is the Royal Suite, located directly aft of the ship's navigation bridge on the starboard side. It has a separate bedroom with king-size bed, walk-in closet and vanity dressing area, living room with queen-size sofa bed, refrigerator and wet bar, dining table, entertainment center, and large private balcony. The bathroom has a whirlpool tub, separate shower enclosure, two washbasins, and toilet.

Owner's Suites. The Owner's Suites are at the forward end of the ship, just behind the navigation bridge, close to the Royal Suite. They have a queen-size bed, separate living area with queen-size sofa bed, vanity dressing area, refrigerator, and wet bar. The bathroom has a full-size tub, separate shower enclosure, toilet, and two washbasins.

Royal Family Suites. These suites have two bedrooms with twin beds that convert to queen-size beds, living area with double sofa bed and Pullman bed, refrigerator, two bathrooms (one with tub), and private balcony. This suite can accommodate eight and might suit families.

Grand Suites. Features of these suites include twin beds that convert to a queen-size bed, vanity dressing area, lounge area with sofa bed, refrigerator, and a bathroom with tub. There's also a private balcony.

Superior Suites. Features of these suites, which include two superior suites for the disabled, have twin beds that convert to a queen-size bed, vanity dressing area, lounge area with sofa bed, refrigerator, a bathroom with tub, and private balcony. Although these are called suites, they really are little more than a larger standard cabin with balcony.

Other grades. Standard cabins have twin beds that convert to a queen-size bed, ample closet space for a one-week cruise, and a good amount of drawer space, although under-bed storage space is not good for large suitcases. The bathrooms have nine mirrors. Plastic buckets are provided for Champagne/wine and are really tacky.

DINING. The 1,365-seat My Fair Lady Dining Room spreads over two decks, connected by a grand, sweeping staircase. When you book, choose one of two seatings, or 'My Time Dining' (eat when you want, during dining hours). The food is not as good as the menu makes it sound, and the selection of breads, rolls, fruit, and cheese is poor. Overall, meals are rather hit and miss – in fact it's unmemorable. Also, if you want lobster or a decent filet mignon (steak) you'll need to pay extra.

Other dining options. Extra-cost, reservations-needed Chops Grille Steakhouse is an à-la-carte steakhouse serving prime steaks and veal chops. Aft is the Park Café: an indoor/outdoor deli for salads, sandwiches, soups, and pastries.

Casual, self-serve breakfasts and luncheons can be taken in the 790-seat informal Windjammer Marketplace. It has a great expanse of ocean-view glass windows, the decor is bright and cheerful, and buffet 'islands' contain food from around the world.

ENTERTAINMENT. The 875-seat Orpheum Theater, the main showlounge, is a grand room at the forward part of the ship. This is where the big production shows are staged, as well as the major cabaret acts.

A second showlounge, the 575-seat Carousel Lounge, is located aft, and is for smaller shows and adult cabarets, including late-night adults-only comedy. A variety of other lounges and bars have almost constant live music; in fact, there's no bar without music to have a quiet drink in. There's even background music in all corridors and elevators, and constant music outdoors on the pool deck. If you want a quiet relaxing holiday, choose another ship.

SPA/FITNESS. The Vitality at Sea Spa is aft of the funnel and spans two decks. Facilities include a gymnasium (with the latest techno- and cardio muscle pumping machines), aerobics room, sauna and steam rooms, a beauty salon, and 13 private massage/body treatment rooms, including a couples' massage room.

The Spa and fitness facilities are staffed and operated by Steiner Leisure, a specialist spa/beauty concession. Some fitness classes are free, while some, such as Pathway to Yoga, and Pathway to Pilates, cost extra.

Eurodam
★★★★

Size:	Large Resort Ship
Tonnage:	86,273
Lifestyle:	Premium
Cruise Line:	Holland America Line
Former Names:	none
IMO Number:	9378448
Builder:	Fincantieri (Italy)
Original Cost:	$450 million
Entered Service:	Jul 2008
Registry:	The Netherlands
Length (ft/m):	935.0/285.0
Beam (ft/m):	105.6/32.2
Draft (ft/m):	25.5/7.8
Propulsion/Propellers:	diesel-electric (34,000kW)/ 2 azimuthing pods
Passenger Decks:	12
Total Crew:	929
Passengers (lower beds):	2,104

Passenger Space Ratio (lower beds):	41.0
Passenger/Crew Ratio (lower beds):	2.2
Cabins (total):	1,052
Size Range (sq ft/m):	170.0–1,318.6/15.7–122.5
Cabins (for one person):	0
Cabins (with private balcony):	708
Cabins (wheelchair accessible):	30
Wheelchair accessibility:	Good
Cabin Current:	110/220 volts
Elevators:	14
Casino (gaming tables):	Yes
Slot Machines:	Yes
Swimming Pools:	2 (1 w/sliding glass dome)
Hot Tubs (on deck):	5
Self-Service Launderette:	No
Dedicated Cinema/Seats:	Yes/170
Library:	Yes
Onboard currency:	US$

A large, spacious ship with family-friendly Dutch-style interiors

OVERVIEW. The ship has a bright interior decor designed to appeal to younger, more vibrant, multigenerational holidaymakers. In keeping with the traditions of Holland America Line (HAL), a large collection of artwork is a standard feature, and pieces reflect the former Dutch East Indies.

THE SHIP. *Eurodam* has two funnels, positioned close together – one behind the other instead of side by side – the result of the machinery configuration because the ship has, in effect, two engine rooms – one with three diesels, and one with two diesels. A pod propulsion system is provided, so there's virtually no vibration.

There are 22 rent-by-the-day cabanas, with goodies such as Champagne, chocolate strawberries, an iPod pre-stocked with music, bathrobes, fresh fruit, and chilled towels. These are designed for two adults and two children, so they may not be the promised 'quiet' spaces, after all. They are located in an area on observation deck and around the Lido Pool.

There is a complete walk-around exterior teak promenade deck, real teak steamer-style sunloungers, and a jogging track around the forward third of the ship.

There are two centrally located swimming pools outdoors, one of which has a retractable glass roof, plus a children's pool.

The lobby spans three decks. Adjacent are interior and glass-walled elevators with fine ocean views through 11 decks. The information desk (on the lobby's lowest level) is small and somewhat removed

Berlitz's Ratings		
	Possible	Achieved
Ship	500	394
Accommodation	200	150
Food	400	270
Service	400	272
Entertainment	100	71
Cruise Experience	400	290
OVERALL SCORE		
1447 points out of 2000		

from the main passenger flow on the two decks above it.

There are two decks of public rooms. Perhaps the most dramatic is the showlounge, spanning four decks in the forward section. Other facilities include a winding shopping street with several boutique stores, card room, an art gallery, photo gallery, and several meeting rooms; a casino is large and equipped with gaming tables and slot machines. One of the most popular public rooms is Explorations – a combination coffee bar (drinks are at extra cost), lounge, library, and Internet center, all in one attractive, open 'lifestyle' environment, adjacent to a Crow's Nest Lounge.

On other decks (lower down), you'll find a Queen's Lounge (this acts as a lecture room), a Culinary Arts Center, where cooking demonstrations and classes are held, and a number of other bars and lounges. The ship also has a small movie screening room – a nice feature.

Gratuities are automatically added to your onboard account. Passenger niggles include noisy cabin air conditioning (the flow can't be turned off, the only regulation being for temperature control), and the many pillars that obstruct passenger flow and lines of sight throughout the ship.

FAMILIES. For families with children, Club HAL's KidZone provides a whole area dedicated to children's facilities and extensive programming for different age groups (five to 17), with one counselor for every 30 children. Ice cream is free at certain hours.

There are no self-service launderettes – something many families with children miss, although special bulk laundry packages are available.

ACCOMMODATION. There are numerous price categories. Most of the suites/cabins have an outside-view or 'private' balcony. Note that many of the cabins on Upper Promenade Deck have lifeboat- or safety equipment-obstructed views. Avoid cabins directly under the aft pool deck because deck chair dragging noises can be really irritating.

Some cabins that can accommodate a third and fourth person have very little closet space, and only one personal safe. Occupants of suites get exclusive use of the Neptune Lounge and concierge service, priority embarkation and disembarkation, and other benefits. In many of the suites/cabins with private balconies, the balconies can be overlooked from various public locations.

Penthouse Verandah Suites. These offer the largest accommodation (1,318 sq ft/123 sq m, including balcony) and include a separate bedroom with a king-size bed, walk-in closet, dressing room, living room, dining room, butler's pantry, minibar and refrigerator, and balcony. The main bathroom has a large whirlpool tub, and two washbasins. Personalized stationery and free dry cleaning are included, as are hot hors d'oeuvres and other goodies daily.

Deluxe Verandah Suites. These suites measure 563 sq ft (53 sq m). They have twin beds that convert to a king-size bed, vanity desk, lounge area, walk-in closet, minibar and refrigerator, and bathroom with full-size tub, washbasin, and toilet. Personalized stationery and complimentary dry cleaning are included, as are hot hors d'oeuvres and other perks.

Verandah Suites. Actually they are cabins, not suites, and measure 284 sq ft (26 sq m). Twin beds can convert to a queen-size bed. There is also a lounge area, minibar, and refrigerator, while the bathroom has a tub, washbasin, and toilet. Floor-to-ceiling windows open onto a private balcony.

Outside-view cabins. Standard outside cabins (197 sq ft/18 sq m) have twin beds that can convert to a queen-size bed. There's a small sitting area, while the bathroom has a tub/shower combination. The interior cabins are slightly smaller (183 sq ft/17 sq m).

Some 37 cabins have interconnecting doors. All balconies have solid steel lower sections instead of glass – so your view is a little restricted when seated.

All suites/cabins have 'Signature of Excellence' premium amenities: plush Mariner's Dream beds, waffle/terry cloth robes, Egyptian cotton towels, flat panel TVs, DVD players, make-up mirrors with halo lighting, massage shower heads, large hairdryers, fresh flowers, and fruit baskets.

DINING. The bi-level Rembrandt Dining Room – a stunning room – is at the stern. Both open seating (you may have to wait a considerable time for a table) and fixed (assigned tables and times) seating are available. It provides a traditional HAL dining experience, with friendly service from Indonesian and Filipino stewards.

The waiter stations in the dining room can be noisy for anyone seated adjacent to them. Live music is provided for dinner each evening. Once each cruise, there's a Dutch Dinner (hats are provided), and an Indonesian Lunch. 'Lighter-option' meals are always available. HAL can provide kosher meals, although these are prepared ashore, frozen, and brought to your table sealed in their original containers.

Other dining options. The 130-seat Pinnacle Grill is a more upscale, more intimate restaurant, with higher-quality ingredients and better presentation than in the larger main dining room. It is on Lower Promenade Deck and fronts onto the second level of the atrium lobby. Pacific Northwest cuisine is featured, plus an array of premium-quality steaks. There are fine table settings, china and silverware, and leather-bound menus. The wine bar offers mostly American wines. Reservations are required, and there's a cover charge (but the premium-quality steaks are worth it).

There's also Tamarind, a 144-seat pan-Asian (fusion cuisine) restaurant; there's no charge for lunch, but there is a cover charge for dinner.

For casual eats, there's an extensive Lido Café. It includes a pizzeria/Italian specialties counter, a salad bar, Asian stir-fry counter, deli sandwiches, and desserts. Movement through the buffet area can be very slow. In the evenings, one side of this venue is turned into an extra-cost Canaletto Restaurant – a quasi-Italian informal eatery with waiter service.

Also, a poolside 'Dive-In at the Terrace Grill' features multi-choice signature burgers (and special Dive-In sauce), hot dogs, and fries.

An extra-cost Windsurf Café in the atrium lobby (open 20 hours a day) serves coffee and snacks.

ENTERTAINMENT. Theater-style seating is provided in The Mainstage Showlounge, the venue for colourful Las Vegas-style revues and major cabaret shows. Stage shows are best seen from the upper levels, from where the sight lines are quite good.

SPA/FITNESS. The Greenhouse Spa, the largest yet for HAL, includes a thermal suite, hydropool, several private rooms for body pampering treatments, and a large fitness center. Sports enthusiasts can enjoy a basketball court, volleyball court, and a golf simulator.

Europa
★★★★★+

Size:	Small Ship
Tonnage:	28,890
Lifestyle:	Luxury
Cruise Line:	Hapag-Lloyd Cruises
Former Names:	none
IMO Number:	8224432
Builder:	Kvaerner Masa-Yards (Finland)
Original Cost:	DM260 million
Entered Service:	Sep 1999
Registry:	The Bahamas
Length (ft/m):	651.5/198.6
Beam (ft/m):	78.7/24.0
Draft (ft/m):	20.0/6.1
Propulsion/Propellers:	diesel-electric (21,600kW)/ 2 azimuthing pods
Passenger Decks:	7
Total Crew:	280
Passengers (lower beds):	408

Passenger Space Ratio (lower beds):	70.4
Passenger/Crew Ratio (lower beds):	1.4
Cabins (total):	204
Size Range (sq ft/m):	355.2-914.9/33.0-85.0
Cabins (for one person):	0
Cabins (with private balcony):	168
Cabins (wheelchair accessible):	2
Wheelchair accessibility:	Good
Cabin Current:	110 and 120 volts
Elevators:	4
Casino (gaming tables):	No
Slot Machines:	No
Swimming Pools:	1 (1 w/ sliding glass dome)
Hot Tubs (on deck):	2
Self-Service Launderette:	No
Dedicated Cinema/Seats:	Yes/60
Library:	Yes
Onboard currency:	Euros

A truly sophisticated ship for formal, longer cruising

OVERVIEW. *Europa* is the most luxurious of all the smaller formal cruise ships, and for the German-speaking market (the crew also speaks English), nothing else comes close. Combined with an enthusiastic, well-trained, well-dressed crew, the tradition of luxury cruising is taken to its highest expression, with superb food and culinary diversity, and a wide range of creature comforts.

Berlitz's Ratings		
	Possible	Achieved
Ship	500	471
Accommodation	200	183
Food	400	373
Service	400	360
Entertainment	100	91
Cruise Experience	400	373
OVERALL SCORE		
1852 points out of 2000		

THE SHIP. *Europa* has a really sleek appearance, a graceful profile, and Hapag-Lloyd's signature orange-and-blue funnel. The stern is rounded and gracefully shaped. It is a very stable ship at sea, with no vibration or noise – thanks partly to its pod propulsion system and excellent build quality. Europa carries 14 Zodiac landing craft for close-up coastal shore excursions; boot-washing areas are also provided. Over 20 bicycles are available free for use ashore and are offloaded on to the dock in each port (where possible).

There is an outdoor walking/jogging area with rubberized deck (plus a walk-around teak promenade deck), and a small FKK (Frei-KörperKultur) deck for nude sunbathing. Sunloungers have thick pads.

There is one long, rectangular swimming pool outdoors (half indoors, and half outdoors). While not the widest, it is longer than the pools aboard most other cruise ships, at 56.7 by 16.8ft (17.3 by 5.15m). Movies are screened poolside on selected evenings, and themed social events are held here.

Most of *Europa's* hotel service crew understand the culture and can talk in depth about German, Swiss, and Austrian life.

Europa is one of the world's most spacious purpose-built cruise ships – an exquisite retreat, an intensely welcoming world of stylish cruising, with painstakingly accomplished service. The space per passenger is high, there is never a hint of a line, and both restaurant and show lounge seat a full complement of passengers. Only the best-quality soft furnishings are used, blending traditional with modern designs and materials. Most public rooms and hallways have extremely high ceilings, providing an enhanced sense of space and grandeur. The interior decor colors are light and contemporary.

The central interior focal point is a seven-deck-high central atrium; included are two glass-walled elevators (these are operated by 'piccolos' on embarkation day). The lower level features a white Steinway grand piano and a Piano Bar, reception desk, concierge desk, and shore excursion desk. It's a cozy, open space for social parties, particularly on nights designated as 'formal,' with passengers dressed accordingly. In the ship's 2013 refurbishment, plush new chairs and sofas were added, in plum and wine colors. Tucked away in one corner is a business center – good for small group meetings.

Forward of the atrium lobby is the Europa Lounge, with U-shaped seating configuration and a raised stage, although several pillars obstruct sight lines.

Several public rooms are located along a curved 'street' leading aft from the atrium, including the Clipper Lounge/Bar, which has an extremely high ceiling. This room is a multi-function room, with a small stage and wooden dance floor.

What was originally designed to be a casino is now a multi-function space for small cocktail parties, and also serves as a high-class art gallery showcasing German culture artists.

Supremely comfortable, the sidewalk Havana Bar cigar lounge is a clubby room (with armchairs and a huge photograph of Che Guevara), with three large glass-fronted, conditioned humidor cabinets, and an extensive range of cigars. Those stocked include a range (from 102mm to 232mm) of top (mostly Cuban) brands. The bar also serves a fine range of armagnacs, calvados, and cognacs, all poured tableside, plus Cuban beer. A wall-mounted digital MP3 jukebox has a push-button selection of thousands of songs and instrumental music. I recommend an Irish Coffee, correctly made with the glass rotated while sugar is blended with the alcohol, and heated gently over a candle flame. Adjacent is the ship's jeweler/clothing boutique (Wempe).

On a higher deck, Club Belvedere is the place for afternoon tea (there's a choice of over 30 teas – mostly loose-leaf ones) and intimate music recitals. It is simply a lovely room, with its own bar. There are also several types of coffee and impeccably made liqueur coffees, and a superb selection of cakes, made fresh daily.

The library, which is home to an illuminated globe of the world and numerous bookcases, is open 24 hours a day. Opposite is a small cinema/meeting room.

There are also dedicated rooms for hobbies (arts and crafts). For wheelchair-bound passengers, a special ramp is provided from the outdoor lido/pool deck down to where the lifeboats are located; only three other ships have such a ramp (*Asuka II*, *Crystal Serenity*, and *Crystal Symphony*).

Although a children's playroom is provided, *Europa* really is best for adults seeking a quiet, refined setting.

ACCOMMODATION. This is provided in five configurations and several price categories. It consists of all-outside-view suites: two Penthouse Grand Suites (Hapag and Lloyd) and 10 Penthouse Deluxe Suites (Bach, Beethoven, Brahms, Handel, Lehár, Haydn, Mozart, Schubert, Strauss, Wagner; each suite contains a large framed picture of the composer), 156 suites with private balcony, and 36 standard suites. There are two suites (with private balcony) for passengers with disabilities, and eight suites with interconnecting doors.

Almost all suites have a private balcony with wide teak deck and lighting, and a smoked glass screen topped by a teak rail. The 12 suites overlooking the stern are among the most sought-after accommodation – six on each of two decks, each suite having a balcony with canvas 'ceiling' for shade and privacy.

General information. Each suite has a sleeping area with twin beds convertible to a queen-size bed and two bedside tables with lamps and drawers. There is a separate lounge area with curtain divider and bird's-eye maple wood cabinetry with rounded edges. Facilities include a refrigerator/mini-bar (beer and

soft drinks are supplied at no extra charge), writing desk, and couch with large table in a separate lounge area. An illuminated walk-in closet provides ample hanging space, six drawers, personal safe that can be opened with a credit card, umbrella, and clothes brush. European duvets are provided, as is a full-color free daily newspaper (there's a wide choice). Almost all suites have totally unobstructed views and excellent soundproofing. All passengers receive a practical shoulder travel bag, an insulated lunch bag for shore excursions, and leather keycard holder.

A Media4Cruises infotainment system includes 24 hours per day video and audio on-demand. This includes a large flat-screen television and Internet connection via a wireless keyboard. A dedicated email address is provided with your tickets and other documentation in a leather document holder; there is no charge for incoming or outgoing emails. A data socket is provided, should you decide to bring your own laptop (the ship has a small number of laptops you can borrow).

Western European butlers and cabin stewardesses are employed (butlers for the 12 premium suites on Deck 10, cabin stewardesses for all other suites).

The white/gray/sea green marble-tiled bathrooms are very well designed, have light decor, and include two good-size cabinets for toiletries. Each has a full bathtub plus an integral shower, retractable clothesline, and separate glass-fronted shower enclosure. Thick cotton bathrobes are provided, as are slippers and an array of personal amenities. Parents with babies get a video baby phone (camera via PDA with vibration alarm, and wireless access).

Penthouses (Deck 10). There are two Penthouse Grand suites, redesigned in 2011, and 10 Penthouse Deluxe suites, refurbished in 2009, when electronically adjustable beds and Nespresso coffee machines were installed. A teakwood entrance hall opens into a spacious living room with full-size dining table and four chairs, fully stocked drinks cabinet with refrigerator and complimentary bar set-up, laundry and ironing service, priority spa reservations, caviar or other canapés daily before dinner, hand-made chocolates, petit-fours, and other niceties. Balconies have teakwood decking, and white canvas ceiling shades. For the ultimate in exclusivity, the two Penthouse Grand suites have even larger bathrooms (each with a private sauna and specially angled bathtubs and delightful heated floor), and extensive forward views from their prime, supremely quiet location, plus a large wraparound private balcony; they also have larger walk-in closets (with a window), large flat-screen TVs, and Robbe and Berking silver Champagne goblets. Well-trained butlers provide the highest level of unobtrusive service.

Spa suites. Four 'spa suites' are located adjacent to the Futuresse Spa. These incorporate a large private teak-decked balcony; twin or queen-size bed; walk-in closet; dark wood cabinetry housing a refrigerator stocked with fruit juices and different mineral waters; and bar set-up. There's a flat-screen TV, and storage space including a jewelry drawer, with pull-around doors that can close off everything to view, a writing/vanity desk, and floor-to-ceiling windows. There is a large window between the living/sleeping area and the bathroom, which has warm Asian-style decor, underwater lighted Jacuzzi bath, separate large shower enclosure (with rain shower), gold, thick-glass washbasin, hairdryer, and ample storage space. Special teas and other services are provided by spa personnel.

Suites for the Disabled (Deck 7). These spacious suites have one electronically operated bed with hydraulic elevator plus one regular bed, and a closet with drawers (this replaces the walk-in closet in all other suites). The bathroom has a roll-in shower area; all fittings are at the appropriate height, and there are several grab handles, plus an emergency call-for-help button. Wheelchair-accessible public toilets are provided on the main restaurant/entertainment deck.

DINING. With over 5,000 separate food ingredients carried, the executive chef can produce menus that don't repeat even for around-the-world voyages. The cuisine is outstanding, and full of surprises. Seasonal and regional ingredients are featured, with much totally fresh fish and seafood as standard. Plated presentation of food is provided for entrées with silver service for additional vegetables, plus tableside flambé dishes. Portion size is sensible, never overwhelming.

The Europa Restaurant is a beautiful, formal dining room that can accommodate all passengers in one seating; tables are assigned for dinner only (breakfast and lunch are open seating), so you keep your waiter for dinner throughout each cruise. In common with most German ships, a small smoking section is provided. There are many tables for two, four, six, or eight. For superb service, there is a *chef de rang* and an assistant waiter system, so that the *chef de rang* is always at the station, with the assistant waiter acting as runner.

On days at sea, in addition to the regular, extensive breakfast, a Gourmet Breakfast menu includes items such as beef tartare, carpaccio of smoked tuna with wasabi cream, gooseliver tureen with orange confit, and other specialties rarely found aboard cruise ships today. A Cuisine Légère menu provides light, healthy, but tasty spa cuisine.

Table settings include Dibbern china, Robbe & Berking silverware, and Riedel wine glasses. The cuisine includes German favorites and regional dishes from around the world. Top-grade Ossetre caviar is on the dinner menu at least once each week, and is always available on request, at extra cost.

An extensive wine list includes a good selection of vintage French wines, as well as a well-balanced selection of Austrian, German, and Swiss wines.

Other dining options. In a first for the cruise industry, three Michelin-starred chef Dieter Müller has his Dieter Müller at Sea Restaurant, a pocket-sized 26-seat intimate restaurant featuring a personally designed five-course menu (three courses for lunch). The menu changes three times during a world cruise, and seasonally during the rest of the year. Müller participates in about 15 cruises a year – about half of *Europa*'s annual program. The restaurant – open for dinner nightly and for lunch on sea days – can be reserved once per cruise by all passengers, and there's no extra charge.

Venezia is much loved for its fine Italian cuisine – and for its variety of olive oils and grappa. It is open for lunch and dinner, at no extra charge. Both venues are by the main restaurant, and provide the setting for an intimate dining experience (reservations required).

The elegant Lido Café is the casual eatery for serve-yourself breakfasts (the ship even makes its own preserves), luncheons, and dinners, with both indoor and outdoor seating (under heat lamps, when needed) and adjacent indoor/outdoor bar. Themed evening dining is also featured, with full waiter service. There is a wide variety of food, and many special lunch buffets have a number of popular themes and regional specialties.

Above the Lido Café is the popular indoor/outdoor chill-out Sansibar, with great aft-facing views.

Europa is known for its real German sausages, available in the Clipper Bar and at a typical Bavarian Frühschoppen (featured once each cruise in the Lido Café). Also, 'light bites,' beautifully presented on silver trays, are taken around the various bars and lounges nightly.

Nautical tradition is maintained with bouillon service each morning at sea, and other daily niceties include waffles and ice cream poolside each afternoon.

ENTERTAINMENT. The Europa Lounge, where the decor is a rich red, is a traditional showlounge; it has a sloping floor, providing good sight lines from most seats. The ship excels in its intellectual entertainment program – tailored to the theme of the cruise – including a constant supply of high-quality classical and contemporary musical artistes, a variety of cabaret acts, as well as a programme of expert lecturers and poetry readers. There's the occasional colorful production show, plus local shows brought on board in port.

A smaller, more intimate Clipper Lounge is for late-night cabaret. The ship carries a main showband, plus small musical units to provide live music (for listening and dancing to). Classical concerts and recitals are provided in the Belvedere Lounge.

SPA/FITNESS. Ocean Spa has a wide range of beauty services and treatments, including an array of rejuvenating treatments, and full-day spa packages.

Facilities include a steam room and sauna (mixed), two shower enclosures and foot-washing stations, a relaxation room with hot tiled beds, three wicker relaxation beds, and a beauty salon. Treatment rooms have music menus. The gymnasium is located one deck above the swimming pool, and includes a 'miha' bodytec training machine and personal trainer.

An electronic golf simulator room complements a golf driving range; a PGA golf pro is carried on all cruises. There are shuffleboard courts on the deck.

Europa 2
★★★★★+

Size:	Small Ship	Passenger Space Ratio (lower beds):	83.0
Tonnage:	42,830	Passenger/Crew Ratio (lower beds):	1.3
Lifestyle:	Luxury	Cabins (total):	258
Cruise Line:	Hapag-Lloyd Cruises	Size Range (sq ft/m):	376.7-1,227.1/35.0-114.0
Former Names:	none	Cabins (for one person):	0
IMO Number:	9616230	Cabins (with private balcony):	258
Builder:	STX France	Cabins (wheelchair accessible):	2
Original Cost:	$360 million	Wheelchair accessibility:	Best
Entered Service:	May 2013	Cabin Current:	110 volts
Registry:	Malta	Elevators:	4
Length (ft/m):	739.5/225.4	Casino (gaming tables):	No
Beam (ft/m):	87.5/26.7	Slot Machines:	No
Draft (ft/m):	20.6/6.3	Swimming Pools:	1 (1 w/ sliding glass dome)
Propulsion/Propellers:	diesel-electric (24,000kW)/ 2 azimuthing pods	Hot Tubs (on deck):	2
		Self-Service Launderette:	No
Passenger Decks:	8	Dedicated Cinema/Seats:	Yes/75
Total Crew:	370	Library:	Yes
Passengers (lower beds):	516	Onboard currency:	Euros

A stunningly elegant, spacious, informal ship for stylish internationals

OVERVIEW. *Europa 2* is the superb, elegant, contemporary but informal sister to the much-acclaimed Europa. This all-suite, all-balcony ship, currently with the highest passenger/space ratio in the cruise industry, is the ultimate space ship – the benchmark in contemporary cruising, and no bling, but rather an impressive culinary diversity. It is for youthful, but sophisticated, cosmopolitan travelers and their families, and operates in English and German.

THE SHIP. *Europa 2* has a sleek profile and appearance, balanced by Hapag-Lloyd's signature orange-and-blue funnel. Look down from an upper aft deck and you'll see a fine rounded stern.

The ship has one additional deck than its close sister *Europa*, but 40 percent more space. In fact, it's the spaciousness and natural light that is so evident. There is a complete walk-around deck – wide enough to walk around even with deck lounge chairs inhabiting the space – an unusual feature for a ship of this size. Teak decking is everywhere (no artificial turf anywhere), as are teak handrails on all balconies and outdoor stairways.

The two-level pool deck is a stunning space, with a 49-ft (15-m) rectangular heated saltwater pool with a large moveable glass roof that can completely cover the area in cool or inclement weather conditions (when closed the area is like a cozy winter garden). Five Balinese sleep beds inhabit the upper level (another seven can be found on a secluded aft deck), contemporary sun beds and drinks tables, as well as

Berlitz's Ratings

	Possible	Achieved
Ship	500	476
Accommodation	200	185
Food	400	373
Service	400	360
Entertainment	100	91
Cruise Experience	400	375
OVERALL SCORE		
1860 points out of 2000		

a bar, separate food bar (think waffles and ice cream made on board in the afternoon), and removable movie screen (you can lie down in the Balinese beds in the upper section and watch movies).

A fleet of 12 Zodiacs – all named after Hamburg suburbs – is carried for landings in small harbors and isolated bays away from more familiar routes, as well as 20 bicycles for passenger use (at no charge).

Europa 2 is beautifully appointed, with a high-quality fit and finish. Interior designers PartnerShipDesign have created something really contemporary and slightly edgy in a ship that also includes some traditional Hapag-Lloyd characteristics from yesteryear – such as the indented handrails in the main stairways – yet is completely different to the more formal *Europa*, with a museum-quality art collection that is breathtaking.

The atrium lobby has chic gray, black and chrome decor, armchair-style seating, a long bar, and a specially commissioned gray Steinway grand piano. A high ceiling sets it all off, together with what look like four huge gray and black distillery still-like features, and a long reception desk. A glass viewing wall in the centre on both sides of the main elevator foyer provides multi-deck contact with the sea outside, and lets natural outside light flood in, providing a connection with the sea (isn't this why people go cruising, after all?). Adjacent to the atrium is a large, upscale Wempe boutique and jewelry store, and, along the walls, some rather expensive pieces of art (including a Gerhard Richter).

There are seven restaurants (plus an extra-cost 16-seat venue with nautical decor – good for private family functions), two lounges, and six bars – some with familiar names carried over from the tradition of *Europa*, (Club Belvedere and Sansibar). Like her sister ship, Europa 2 has several public rooms located off a main high-ceilinged hallway, connecting at the central atrium lobby.

The L-shaped, but elegant, Club Belvedere provides a refined setting for chamber concerts and poetry readings, and is a relaxing venue for afternoon tea (it incorporates a pastry and cake counter, and a bar).

Herrenzimmer is a cigar lounge with three large glass-fronted, temperature-controlled cigar cabinets. The bar features a wide range of armagnacs, calvados, and cognacs, all poured tableside, plus Cuban beer, and the largest collection of premium and trendy multi-country artisan gins of any cruise ship – over 40.

Sansibar, a firm favorite with many regulars, is a sea-going outpost of the fashionable seafood/wine restaurant on the north German island of Sylt. This popular aft hangout has indoor seating, a dance floor, and plenty of seating outdoors (the room's floor-to-ceiling windows open to the outside). It has an à-la-carte menu, tapas-style nibbles, wine selections, and a great club-like atmosphere. It's now the 'in' place to be at night. It also offers a 'late riser's breakfast.'

The Jazz Club is a trendy dedicated lounge featuring live (modern) jazz (a seven-piece band plus two vocalists when I last sailed), soul music, and other artistic presentations. There's also an auditorium with a stage for presentations as well as 3D movies, a library full of fiction, reference and destination books, and a Miele Culinary Arts School.

Europa 2 and *Europa* are vastly different ships – and cater to a very different set of passengers. *Europa 2* features shorter-length cruises for the time-challenged (including 7-day cruises, with different itineraries combinable into a longer cruise). Europa 2 has even more delightful dining venues than its sister ship, and even more exclusive features.

There's no traditional captain's dinner, because the ship is for a more youthful clientele seeking high quality in a relaxed, but refined setting, although senior officers do dine occasionally with passengers in varying venues. Detail matters here: examples include leather-covered tissue boxes, different-sized spoons for small or large coffees in your suite. This really is a lusciously contemporary interpretation of the company's renowned and highly rated *Europa* – and then some. This ship exudes quality discreetly, without shouting about it, and delivers it all with a smile.

FAMILIES. There are three special areas for kids and teens: a Knopf Club (a new 'Cap'n Knopf' bear was created specially by Steiff – and available for sale in the shop – only aboard *Europa 2*) for children aged from two to three; a Kids' Club for 4- to 10-year-olds; and a separate Teens' Club for 11–15s – with iPod chairs,

table football, and chill-out area. Special (parent-free) shore excursions for children are also available.

ACCOMMODATION. There are 13 price categories and eight accommodation grades (sizes given include balcony).

There are two Owner's Suites (1,227 sq ft/114 sq m); two Grand Penthouses (947 sq ft/88 sq m); 16 Spa Suites (560 sq ft/52 sq m); 24 Grand Suites (559.7 sq m/52s sq m), including two for the disabled; 59 Ocean Suites; seven Family Apartments (581 sq ft/54 sq m); and 141 Ocean Suites (376.7 sq ft/35 sq m). Even the smallest balcony measures 75.3 sq ft/7 sq m, and all except the 'Family Apartments' have Jacuzzi bathtubs. All Penthouse Deck suite occupants can choose their favorite bottles of spirits at no extra cost; they also come with butler service.

The two Owner's Suites are truly luxurious apartments (like a villa, with a hotel attached), with double-wide balconies, and a beautiful piece of butterfly art by Damien Hirst. The standout feature, though, is a huge ocean-view wet room (bathroom) with a private steam sauna, large 'rain' shower with built-in chromo-therapy lighting, and a separate hand held shower hose; plus separate circular whirlpool tub for two, window-side daybed, two large washbasins, and floor-to-ceiling windows. The spacious living area has walk-in closets to die for, a fully stocked refrigerator, full dining table and chair set, butler service, and an Eames lounge chair. There are multiple TV sets, including one integrated in a bathroom mirror adjacent to the whirlpool bath.

Spa Suites have a rain-shower/steam sauna combination, whirlpool bathtub, and a large window between sleeping/living area and bathroom (with a wooden blind for complete privacy), and separate toilet. There's also a television screen integrated into the bathroom mirror.

Two specially outfitted suites for the disabled each has a large bathroom with roll-in shower, three washbasins, and an integrated 'mirror' TV.

Facilities in even the smallest standard suite (28 sq m/301 sq ft plus 75.3 sq ft/7.0 sq m balcony) are excellent, and the layout is both well designed and practical. The overall decor is relaxing but not boring, with brown, beige, and cream the underlying colors, and beautiful custom-made deep-pile carpets. The beds have an adjustable torsion arrangement, so that you can vary it from hard to soft. Both head and body/foot sections can be raised electrically for optimum comfort.

A wide choice of large-size, full-color daily newspapers is available (at extra cost except for Penthouse Deck 10 suites); all accommodation grades feature a Nespresso coffee machine and associated items. An interactive TV can be positioned for viewing from the bed or lounge seating area. Other practical features include a 'butler's pantry'-like refrigerator/minibar cabinet (beer and soft drinks are supplied at no extra charge) with several 'quiet-close' integral storage trays for glasses, cups, and other wet bar amenities – all contained in a superbly designed anti-rattle cabinet. There's also a writing/vanity desk, and couch with large table in a separate lounge area, and a leather keycard holder (the door unlocks when you touch the keycard against the lock).

An integrated color TV/computer monitor and Media4Cruises infotainment system includes 24 hours per day video and audio on-demand, and internet connection via a wireless keyboard or tablet. There is no charge for incoming or outgoing emails, only for attachments and general Internet access. A data socket is provided, should you decide to bring your own laptop computer, and the ship is Wi-Fi enabled throughout.

DINING. *Europa 2* really is all about an elegant, but utterly relaxed, lifestyle and a huge choice when it comes to food, dining experiences, and culinary adventures. The open-seating concept in all restaurants makes it easy for families with children to choose when to eat. Dibbern china and Schott Zwiesel glassware are provided. What's nice is that (unusually for a ship of this size) some 40 percent of all tables are for two – the others are for four, six or eight. What makes most of these double-deck height restaurants special is their decor, individuality, and the different cuisines featured.

Weltmeere: This 266-seat restaurant (its huge, pink 'octopus' tentacle-like glass chandeliers are whimsical) features a wide range of international cuisine favorites, and the contemporary chairs have armrests. Open for breakfast, lunch, and dinner.

Other dining options. Yachtclub: this 276-seat (142 indoor and 134 outdoor seats) restaurant is open for breakfast, lunch, and dinner. It includes a self-serve multi-section buffet (including an Ayurvedic 'bio-food' section), rotisserie and two active cooking stations – plus a wonderful manual Berkel meat-slicing machine for wafer-thin cold cuts. Outside is an excellent Pasta Bar (several types of pasta are made on board, as are six different sauces daily), and a separate Grill Bar (featuring several types of fish). A canvas-like canopy incorporates heaters for cool-weather areas or conditions.

Tarragon: this extremely chic, tile-floored 44-seat French-style bistro restaurant specializes in tableside carvings (the steak tartare – prepared tableside – is exceptional, and you can choose the accompanying ingredients), regional/seasonal food, and a focus on fresh herbs. It is open for dinner (and on selected days for lunch). Reservations are required.

Grand Réserve: this 12-seat wine bar/dining venue features special tasting events. Reservations are required. It is adjacent to Tarragon, and open only for dinner.

Serenissima: this 56-seat Italian restaurant has open seating for lunch and dinner (reservations are required for dinner). The large white columns add to the feeling of grandeur.

Elements is a reservations-required 48-seat pan-Asian food themed restaurant, open for lunch and dinner.

Sakura is a 58-seat sushi restaurant (part of the Yacht Club, but open only for dinner) featuring Japanese cuisine (a favorite here is the 'Black Spider Man' – tempura soft shell crab with avocado – and other ingredients); it incorporates a sit-up sushi counter. Reservations are required.

Speisezimmer is a 16-seat dining venue for private dining. It has nautically themed decor, costs €1,500, and can be reserved for breakfast, lunch, or dinner.

Although reservations are required for dinner in several venues, there's no extra cost in any of them (unlike the specialty dining venues aboard many other ships). Hapag-Lloyd Cruises has long been known for its culinary creativity and extremely high quality of food and service. This ship won't disappoint those who seek the best.

Sansibar is a trendy indoor-outdoor venue featuring special drinks and items from the venue of the same name in Sylt. It features special wines, has an à-la-carte late-riser's breakfast, and constantly changing tapas-style eats. It has a dance floor, and is the champion late-night disco-style venue, and is a great place to see and be seen.

ENTERTAINMENT. The Theater is the ship's two-level showlounge, with good sightlines from almost all seats. It has LED lighting for superb show backdrops and scenery changes, and a thrust stage for cabaret acts, or concerts. Multi-faceted entertainment is provided by the company's own production team, with 16 different shows scheduled each year – each designed to be highly visual to accommodate the bilingual, international clientele.

Live music can be found around the ship, but the Jazz Club is a standout venue for the cool stuff (and its long drinks list). Meanwhile light classical and chamber concerts take place in various venues throughout the ship.

SPA/FITNESS. The Ocean Spa is to die for. It is, without doubt, the largest wellness and spa zone for this size of ship, with indoor and outdoor zones measuring a combined 10,764 sq ft (1,000 sq m) that does justice to the trend for combining holidays and wellbeing.

The calming, beautifully crafted wellness facilities are outstanding, and include a beauty salon, eight massage/body treatment rooms; a dry-ice wall; a steam sauna and three dry saunas with differing temperatures (Finnish, Herbal, and Bio), one of which overlooks the stern; two foot-washing stations (with different temperatures), two relaxation rooms (one with three hot, tiled beds), men's and women's changing/dressing rooms, showers, and two Dr Kneipp basins for foot baths and water walks.

For golfers, almost 700 sq ft (65 sq m) is devoted to two electronic golf simulators. *Europa 2* is the first ship to combine state-of-the-art golf-simulator with a full-body video analysis – and a golf driving range. There's also a golf club storage room.

Explorer of the Seas
★★★+

Size:	Large Resort Ship
Tonnage:	137,308
Lifestyle:	Standard
Cruise Line:	Royal Caribbean International
Former Names:	none
IMO Number:	9161728
Builder:	Kvaerner Masa-Yards (Finland)
Original Cost:	$500 million
Entered Service:	Oct 2000
Registry:	The Bahamas
Length (ft/m):	1,020.6/311.1
Beam (ft/m):	155.5/47.4
Draft (ft/m):	28.8/8.8
Propulsion/Propellers:	diesel-electric (75,600kW)/3 pods (2 azimuthing, 1 fixed)
Passenger Decks:	14
Total Crew:	1,181
Passengers (lower beds):	3,114
Passenger Space Ratio (lower beds):	44.0
Passenger/Crew Ratio (lower beds):	2.6
Cabins (total):	1,557
Size Range (sq ft/m):	151.0–1,358.0/14.0–126.1
Cabins (for one person):	0
Cabins (with private balcony):	757
Cabins (wheelchair accessible):	26
Wheelchair accessibility:	Best
Cabin Current:	110 volts
Elevators:	14
Casino (gaming tables):	Yes
Slot Machines:	Yes
Swimming Pools:	3
Hot Tubs (on deck):	6
Self-Service Launderette:	No
Dedicated Cinema/Seats:	No
Library:	Yes
Onboard currency:	US$

A large resort ship to entertain the whole family

OVERVIEW. This is a large, family-friendly ship, with cabin hallways that are warm and attractive, and artworks and wavy lines to break up the monotony.

THE SHIP. *Explorer of the Seas* is sister to *Adventure of the Seas*, *Mariner of the Seas*, *Navigator of the Seas*, and *Voyager of the Seas*. It provides an abundance of facilities and options, yet it has a healthy amount of space per passenger. One neat feature is an outdoors observation deck at the bows (good for photos, if you face aft, with most of the ship behind you).

A four-deck-high Royal Promenade, 394ft (120m) long and the main interior focal point, is the place to hang out or to arrange to meet someone. Two American football fields long, it has two internal lobbies that rise up to 11 decks high. Eateries and shops, and entertainment locations front this street, and interior 'with-view' cabins look into it from above. Guest reception and shore excursion counters are located at the aft end of the promenade, as is an ATM machine. Look up: you'll see a large moving, asteroid-like sculpture (constantly growing and contracting). Entertaining street parades take place here.

Arched across the promenade is a captain's balcony. A stairway in the center of the promenade connects you to the deck below, where you'll find Schooner Bar (a piano lounge that's a feature of all Royal Caribbean International ships) the colorful Casino Royale, and several shops. At times, street entertainers appear, and parades happen.

Berlitz's Ratings

	Possible	Achieved
Ship	500	392
Accommodation	200	142
Food	400	222
Service	400	266
Entertainment	100	74
Cruise Experience	400	264
OVERALL SCORE		
1360 points out of 2000		

There is an ice-skating rink (Studio B), with real ice, and seating for up to 900. Slim pillars obstruct clear-view arena stage sight lines, however. If ice-skating in the Caribbean doesn't appeal (it has actually become extremely popular), perhaps you'd like reading in the two-deck library, open 24 hours a day.

Drinking places include an Aquarium Bar, with 50 tons of glass and water in four large aquariums (no swimming!), a Champagne Bar, Crown & Kettel Pub, a Café Promenade (for Continental breakfast, pizzas, coffee, and desserts), Weekend Warrior (a sports bar), and a Connoisseur Club (for cigars and cognacs). Jazz fans will head for Dizzy's, an intimate room within the Viking Crown Lounge, or the Schooner Bar piano lounge. Golfers might also enjoy the 19th Hole, a golf bar, as they play the Explorer Links.

Passenger gripes include cabin bath towels and noisy (vacuum) toilets; there are also few quiet places to sit and read – almost everywhere there is intrusive background music (particularly on the pool deck). And if you have a cabin with an interconnecting door to another cabin, be aware that you'll be able to hear everything your next-door neighbors say and do.

In spring 2015, the ship underwent an extensive refurbishment; it now features some new dining options, a Flowrider surf simulator, 'virtual' balconies for interior cabins, and a 3D cinema. The new dining venues (most at an extra cost) include: Chops Grille (open for lunch and dinner, this steakhouse features prime steaks, other meats, and grilled seafood items); Giovanni's Table (open for lunch and dinner, this tratto-ria features Italian classics served family-style); Izumi Asian Cuisine (open for lunch and dinner, includes a sushi bar and sizzling hot-rock cooked items); Chef's Table (open for dinner only, this 'private' experience is co-hosted by the executive chef and sommelier and features a wine pairing dinner of five courses); Park Café (open for breakfast, lunch and dinner, this in-door/outdoor deli is for salads, sandwiches, soups, and pastries). All except Park Café incur a cover charge.

FAMILIES. Facilities for children and teenagers are good. Aquanauts is for 3–5s; Explorers (6–8); and Voyagers (9–12). Optix is a dedicated area for teenag-ers, including a daytime club with computers, soda bar, and disco. Challenger's Arcade has the latest vid-eo games. Paint and Clay is an arts-and-crafts center for younger children. Adjacent to these indoor areas is Adventure Beach, an area for all the family to enjoy.

ACCOMMODATION. There are numerous cabin categories, in four major groupings: premium ocean-view suites and cabins, promenade-view (interior-view) cabins, ocean-view cabins, and interior cabins. Many cabins are of a similar size – good for incen-tives and large groups – and 300 have interconnect-ing doors, which is good for families.

Some 138 interior cabins have bay windows look into a central shopping plaza – and into your neigh-bor's cabin, unless you keep the curtains closed. All cabins except for the Royal Suite and Owner's Suite have twin beds that convert to a queen-size unit, TV set, radio and telephone, personal safe, vanity unit, minibar, hairdryer, and bathroom.

The largest accommodation includes luxurious Penthouse Suites; occupants have sole access to a concierge club. The grandest is the Royal Suite, on the port side of the ship, and measures 1,146 sq ft (107 sq m). It has a king-size bed in a large bedroom, a living room with an additional queen-size sofa bed, baby grand piano, refrigerator/wet bar, dining table, entertainment center, and large bathroom.

There are similar facilities in the slightly smaller, but still highly desirable Owner's Suites – all 10 are in the center of the ship, on both port and starboard sides, each measuring 468 sq ft (43 sq m). There are also four Royal Family Suites, each measuring 574 sq ft (53 sq m), with two bedrooms (including one with third/fourth upper Pullman berths) apiece. They are located at the stern and have fine views over the ship's wake.

All cabins have a private bathroom with shower enclosure (towels are 100 percent cotton), plus inter-active television and pay-per-view movies. Note that cabins with 'private' balconies aren't so private, be-cause the partitions are only partial.

DINING. The huge main dining room is set on three levels, and each is named after an explorer: Colum-bus, Da Gama, and Magellan. All three have the same menus. Choose one of two seatings, or My Time Din-ing (eat when you want, during dining room hours), when you book.

Place settings, china, and cutlery are of good qual-ity. However, the menu descriptions make the food sound better than it is, and the selection of breads, rolls, fruit, and cheese is poor. Overall, meals are rath-er hit and miss – in fact, it's unmemorable. Also, if you want lobster or a decent filet mignon (steak) you will be asked to pay extra.

Other dining options. Portofino, an upscale Eu-ro-Italian restaurant, is open for dinner only; reser-vations are required, and there's a cover charge. The food and its presentation are better than the food in the dining room.

Windjammer Café: this is a really large, sprawling venue for buffet-style, self-help breakfast (this tends to be the busiest time of the day), lunch, and light dinners (but not on the last night of the cruise); it's often difficult to find a table, and by the time you do, your food could be cold.

The Island Grill (it's actually a section inside the Windjammer Café), for casual dinner (no reserva-tions needed), with a grill and open kitchen.

Johnny Rockets, a retro 1950s all-day, all-night diner-style eatery, has hamburgers, malt shakes (at extra cost), and jukebox hits, with both indoor and outdoor seating.

Promenade Café: for Continental breakfast, all-day pizzas, and speciality coffees (provided in paper cups).

Sprinkles, located on the Royal Promenade, is for round-the-clock ice cream and yogurt, pastries, and coffee.

ENTERTAINMENT. The stunning 1,350-seat Palace Showlounge spans five decks, with only a few slim pillars and almost no disruption of sight lines – an example of fine design and shipbuilding.

The ship also carries an array of cabaret acts, who regularly travel the cruise ship circuit. Strong cabaret acts perform in the main showlounge, while others perform in the Maharaja's Lounge, also the venue for adult-only late-night comedy. The best shows are the Ice Spectaculars.

SPA/FITNESS. The Vitality at Seas Spa is reason-ably large, and measures 15,000 sq ft (1,400 sq m). It includes an aerobics room, fitness center, treatment rooms, and men's and women's sauna/steam rooms. Another 10,000 sq ft (930 sq m) of space features a Solarium (with sliding glass-dome roof) to relax in after you've exercised.

Aft of the funnel is a 32.8ft (10m) rock-climbing wall, with five climbing tracks. It's a great buzz being 200ft (60m) above the ocean while the ship is mov-ing. Other sports facilities include a roller-blading track, a dive-and-snorkel shop (equipment rentals available), a full-size basketball court, and a nine-hole, par 26 golf 'course.'

Fifty Years of Victory
★★★★

Size:	Boutique Ship
Tonnage:	23,439
Lifestyle:	Standard
Cruise Line:	Various expedition operators
Former Names:	*Ural*
IMO Number:	9152959
Builder:	Baltic Works, St Petersburg (Russia)
Original Cost:	n/a
Entered Service:	Jul 2009
Registry:	Russia
Length (ft/m):	523.6/159.6
Beam (ft/m):	98.4/30.0
Draft (ft/m):	36.3/11.0
Propulsion/Propellers:	nuclear reactors (2)/3 propulsion motors (75,000 hp)
Passenger Decks:	6
Total Crew:	140
Passengers (lower beds):	132

Passenger Space Ratio (lower beds):	177.5
Passenger/Crew Ratio (lower beds):	0.9
Cabins (total):	66
Size Range (sq ft/m):	148.5–367.0/13.8–34.1
Cabins (for one person):	0
Cabins (with private balcony):	0
Cabins (wheelchair accessible):	0
Wheelchair accessibility:	None
Cabin Current:	110 volts
Elevators:	1
Casino (gaming tables):	0
Slot Machines:	0
Swimming Pools:	1
Hot Tubs (on deck):	0
Self-Service Launderette:	Yes
Dedicated Cinema/Seats:	No
Library:	Yes
Onboard currency:	US$

Nuclear-powered, this is the ultimate Arctic expedition ship

OVERVIEW. An advanced vessel of the *Arktika*-class of icebreaking ships, *Fifty Years of Victory* is an outstanding polar expedition cruise ship that carries adventurous, hardy outdoors types of mature years. It is powered by two nuclear reactors, providing 75,000hp, and carries enough fuel to power it for four years. Experienced lecturers are carried on each sailing.

THE SHIP. This dramatic, incredibly impressive vessel (*Let Pobedy* in Russian, or *50 Years of Victory* or *Fiftieth Anniversary of Victory*) is the world's largest and most powerful icebreaker, capable of breaking through ice up to 8ft (2.5m) thick. While the noise created by the ice-crushing capability of this marine machine is intense, it is all part of the great adventure.

There are more crew members than passengers, giving a most impressive passenger/space ratio. The ship is comfortable, and it carries a fleet of Zodiac inflatable landing craft, as well as two helicopters for passenger use, and expedition leaders. The crew is experienced in challenging conditions.

Fifty Years of Victory typically leaves from its northern Russian base city of Murmansk before heading across the Barents Sea. Approaching the North Pole – 90° north and 1,000 miles (1,600km) from the closest tree – aboard a Russian icebreaker is the ultimate prize of a true Arctic Expedition voyage. It's really one of the most spectacular voyages to be made by ship.

The ship has a library that is stocked with books about polar exploration, nature, and wildlife. Because there are so few voyages to the North Pole,

Berlitz's Ratings		
	Possible	Achieved
Ship	500	367
Accommodation	200	143
Food	400	260
Service	400	273
Entertainment	100	80
Cruise Experience	400	306
OVERALL SCORE		
1429 points out of 2000		

places sell out quickly. Yellow parkas and rubber boots are provided, but you should take waterproof trousers and thermal wear.

Gratuities to staff are at your discretion, but a suggestion is about $10 per day, per person. Note that the ship will be withdrawn from service after the 2018 Arctic season.

ACCOMMODATION. There are two 'suite' grades and three cabin grades. The suites have a spacious bedroom and separate lounge room, while the bathroom has a tub. Suites also have a coffee-making machine, and fresh fruit is replenished daily. All suites/cabins have windows that open. Each has private bathroom facilities (with shower), TV/DVD player, and a decent amount of storage space. Only two cabins (46 and 48) have obstructed views.

DINING. The dining room operates in a single, open seating, so you sit with whomever you wish. Expect the food to be carbohydrate-rich, hearty fare that will provide the energy you need for the adventures ahead.

ENTERTAINMENT. There isn't any as such: dinner and conversation among all participants being the main event each day, as well as evening recaps, and, of course, wildlife spotting.

SPA/FITNESS. Facilities include a sauna, fitness center, basketball, and indoor volleyball court. There is a small 'dip' pool at the stern, underneath the helicopter deck.

Fram
★★★+

Size:	Small Ship	Passenger/Crew Ratio (lower beds):	3.3
Tonnage:	11,647	Cabins (total):	127
Lifestyle:	Standard	Size Range (sq ft/m):	113.0-415.5/10.5-38.6
Cruise Line:	Hurtigruten	Cabins (for one person):	0
Former Names:	none	Cabins (with private balcony):	6
IMO Number:	9370018	Cabins (wheelchair accessible):	2
Builder:	Fincantieri (Italy)	Wheelchair accessibility:	Fair
Original Cost:	€68.6 million	Cabin Current:	110 volts
Entered Service:	Apr 2007	Elevators:	2
Registry:	Norway	Casino (gaming tables):	No
Length (ft/m):	374.0/114.0	Slot Machines:	No
Beam (ft/m):	66.2/20.2	Swimming Pools:	0
Draft (ft/m):	16.7/5.1	Hot Tubs (on deck):	2
Propulsion/Propellers:	diesel (4.6MW)/2	Self-Service Launderette:	No
Passenger Decks:	6	Dedicated Cinema/Seats:	No
Total Crew:	75	Library:	No
Passengers (lower beds):	254	Onboard currency:	Norwegian krona
Passenger Space Ratio (lower beds):	45.8		

Expedition-style cruising in a modern, minimalist ship

OVERVIEW. Designed to operate in polar waters, *Fram* sails from Reykjavik, Iceland, operating Greenland and Spitzbergen cruises from May through September, and winter cruises to Antarctica. It suits mature adults who like exploring independently.

THE SHIP. *Fram's* design reflects Norwegian and Greenlandic culture, using an extensive mix of wool, leather, and oak. The interior decor is decidedly Inuit. The few public rooms include the Quilac observation lounge, an Internet café, board room, and a small shop. There is no walk-around promenade deck. Hurtigruten doesn't have a great culture of hospitality and service, so many passengers feel they are traveling with a ferry company rather than a cruise line. The crew to passenger ratio is low, which does not equate to a high level of service or attention to detail.

In Antarctica, the ship is a fairly capable expedition vessel, but it can still get stuck in heavy pack-ice. MV *Fram* was assisted in January 2013 by the British Royal Navy's ice patrol ship HMS *Protector*. An Expedition Leader organizes everything to do with a specific voyage. Expedition specialists provide daily lectures. Boots are provided; they come in European sizes – so it helps to know yours before you go.

Life on board is very relaxed, so formal attire is never needed. Smoking is allowed only on the open deck – and not at all when *Fram* is in port. The ship operates in Norwegian and English. There are no safety deposit boxes. Hurtigruten operates a no-tipping-required policy. All in all, the ship should provide a

Berlitz's Ratings		
	Possible	Achieved
Ship	500	355
Accommodation	200	130
Food	400	242
Service	400	246
Entertainment	100	72
Cruise Experience	400	269
OVERALL SCORE		
1314 points out of 2000		

fine expedition-style experience in a modicum of comfort.

ACCOMMODATION. There are 13 price categories (too many), according to size and location. The good thing is that no cabins have obstructed views. The largest accommodation is one Owner's Suite, which consists of a bedroom, living room, and bathroom with Jacuzzi tub. Six cabins at the aft of the ship, overlooking the stern and the ship's wake, have a shared balcony. There are several price grades for the standard cabins, which typically have one bed, and a sofa that converts to a fold-down bed, or two pull-down sofa beds; there's little room and a few shelves.

DINING. Restaurant Imaq, the main dining room, is located at the stern, and connects to the main lobby via an arcade. Local cuisine and recipes, including bison meat and fresh fish, are featured. However, several meals are of the self-help buffet variety only. An extra-charge bistro and self-serve buffet is available for snacks. Dessert items are particularly good. Alcohol prices are very high.

ENTERTAINMENT. There isn't any. Guides and lecturers organize talks and informative briefings based on the cruise area.

SPA/FITNESS. Saunas are located one deck above the exercise area. There are no other spa facilities other than a small, but well-equipped exercise room.

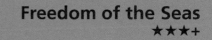

Freedom of the Seas
★★★+

Size:	Large Resort Ship
Tonnage:	154,407
Lifestyle:	Standard
Cruise Line:	Royal Caribbean International
Former Names:	none
IMO Number:	9304033
Builder:	Kvaerner Masa-Yards (Finland)
Original Cost:	$590 million
Entered Service:	Jun 2006
Registry:	The Bahamas
Length (ft/m):	1,112.2/339.0
Beam (ft/m):	183.7/56.0
Draft (ft/m):	27.8/8.5
Propulsion/Propellers:	diesel-electric (75,600kW)/3 pods (2 azimuthing, 1 fixed) (42,000kW)
Passenger Decks:	15
Total Crew:	1,360
Passengers (lower beds):	3,701

Passenger Space Ratio (lower beds):	41.7
Passenger/Crew Ratio (lower beds):	2.7
Cabins (total):	1,817
Size Range (sq ft/m):	153.0–2,025.0/14.2–188.1
Cabins (for one person):	0
Cabins (with private balcony):	842
Cabins (wheelchair accessible):	32
Wheelchair accessibility:	Best
Cabin Current:	110 volts
Elevators:	14
Casino (gaming tables):	Yes
Slot Machines:	Yes
Swimming Pools:	2
Hot Tubs (on deck):	6
Self-Service Launderette:	No
Dedicated Cinema/Seats:	No
Library:	Yes
Onboard currency:	US$

A large floating theme park – good for the whole family

OVERVIEW. *Freedom of the Seas* is a lively large resort ship, with tasteful decor and many bars and lounges. It is certainly a fine ship for young, active families with children, as long as you don't mind lines when signing up for popular activities such as the Flowrider surf area, rock-climbing wall, and full-size boxing ring.

THE SHIP. *Freedom of the Seas* (with sisters *Independence of the Seas* and *Liberty of the Seas*) is an extension of the highly successful *Voyager*-class of ships, introduced in 1999. For this ship, the length and beam were extended, enabling an increase in cabins and passenger capacity, and a combined pool area 43 percent larger than the *Voyager*-class – but with 500 more passengers (after a 2015 refit, another 134 passengers), yet the same number of elevators. The ship is the length of 37 London double-decker buses.

Perhaps the 'wow' factor (particularly for younger cruisers) is its connection with water, including its 40ft x 32ft (12.2 x 9.7m) Flowrider body/board surfing zone aft. This wave simulator creates a wall of water, flowing at 35,000 gallons per minute.

There's also an H2O Zone forward of the funnel, an interactive water-themed play area with a pool fed by a waterfall, two hot tubs, water cannons, spray fountains, water jets, and ground gushers; at night, it all morphs into a colorfully lit Sculpture Garden. Twin central pools consist of a main and a sports pool, with grandstand-style seating and competitive games.

There are 16 bars and lounges to enjoy, and a whole promenade of shops and munching and drink-

Berlitz's Ratings		
	Possible	Achieved
Ship	500	394
Accommodation	200	142
Food	400	235
Service	400	278
Entertainment	100	73
Cruise Experience	400	270
OVERALL SCORE		
1392 points out of 2000		

ing spots along an indoor mall-like environment called the Royal Promenade. The promenade is four decks high, and some interior-facing cabins have great views into it. It is home to fashion, jewelry and perfume shops, a general store, logo shop, Promenade Café, Ben & Jerry's ice cream outlet, a Book Nook, a 'classic' barber shop (A Close Shave, with a razor shave 'experience' that costs over $70), a pizzeria, and a Bull and Bear (English pub).

The forward section of it leads into a large nightclub – Pharaoh's Palace – usually for late-night adult-only comedy. One deck down from the Royal Promenade is a large Casino Royale (gaming tables and slot machines), The Crypt disco, Schooner Bar (piano bar), Boleros (Latin hangout), and a photo gallery, while forwardmost is the Arcadia Theatre.

FAMILIES. For children of six months to 17 years of age (teens get their own chill-out room) there's Adventure Ocean (on Deck 12). Kids will love this ship and all the fun activities and sports activities – not to mention meeting other youngsters and making new friends.

ACCOMMODATION. There is a wide range of suites and cabins in several categories and price grades, from a Presidential Family Suite that can sleep up to 14 to twin-bed two-person interior cabins, and the interior cabins that look into the Royal Promenade. The price you pay depends on the size, grade, and location. There are many family-friendly cabins, good for reunions, but no solo-occupancy cabins. All outside-view cabins have even numbers; all interior cabins have odd numbers.

Presidential Family Suite. Located in the aft section, this suite comprises five rooms. These include two master bedrooms, each with twin beds that convert to a queen-size bed and bathroom with tub/shower (the toiletries cabinets are the same as in all other cabins); two other very small bedrooms that can sleep four; private balcony with sand-colored rubberized decking (not teak), with loungers, tables, chairs, a bar, and a view aft – although part of the balcony is overlooked by balconies on the decks above, and there is a lot of wasted space aft of the balcony because it doesn't extend to the very stern. There's also a lounge with two sofa beds and bar. The suite can accommodate eight to 14, located aft, at the opposite end of the ship to the showlounge. Size: 2,025 sq ft (188 sq m) including balcony. It's pleasant enough, but pretty cramped, and with plain ceilings. It could be good value for a large family, if everyone gets on well in a confined space.

Owner's Suite. Sleeps up to five. Size: 506 sq ft (46 sq m) plus balcony: 131 sq ft (12 sq m).

Royal Suite. Sleeps up to four. Size: 1,406 sq ft (130.6 sq m) plus balcony: 377 sq ft (35 sq m). Includes a black baby grand piano.

Grand Suite. Sleeps up to four. Size: 381 sq ft (35.3 sq m) plus balcony: 89 sq ft (8.2 sq m).

Junior Suite. Sleeps up to four. Size: 277 sq ft (25.7 sq m) plus balcony: 65 sq ft (6 sq m).

Superior ocean-view cabin. Sleeps two (some rooms sleep three or four). Size: 202 sq ft (18.7 sq m) plus balcony: 42 sq ft (3.9 sq m).

Deluxe ocean-view cabin. Sleeps two (some rooms sleep three or four). Size: 173 sq ft (16.0 sq m) plus balcony: 46 sq ft (4.2 sq m).

Interior (promenade-view) cabin. These cabins, on three decks, are interior-facing but they have bay windows that allow occupants to look into the Royal Promenade.

Interior cabin. Sleeps two (some rooms sleep three or four). Size: 160 sq ft (14.8 sq m).

Family ocean-view cabin. Located at the front of the ship, it contains two twin beds (convertible to queen-size), plus sofa and/or Pullman beds, sitting area; bathroom, with shower. Accommodates six, and has 48ins (122cm) round windows. Size: 265 sq ft (24.6 sq m).

DINING. The large main dining room is set on three levels. Each has a theme and different name – Leonardo, Isaac, and Galileo – but all have the same menus and food. A dramatic staircase connects the three levels, but huge support pillars obstruct the sight lines from many seats. When you book, choose from one of two seatings – tables are for 4–12 – or My Time Dining (eat when you want, during dining hours).

The place settings, porcelain, and cutlery are of good quality. However, the menu descriptions make the food sound better than it is, and the selection of breads, rolls, fruit, and cheese is poor. Overall, meals are rather hit and miss – in fact it's unmemorable. Also, if you want lobster or a decent filet mignon (steak), you will be asked to pay extra.

Other dining options. Make reservations in these extra-cost venues as early as possible to avoid disappointment.

Chops Grille for premium steaks, chops, and special seafood, set in a great location. Open for dinner only; reservations required and a cover charge applies.

Sabor: for 'authentic' Mexican specialty cuisine. Open for dinner only and reservations required; cover charge appplies.

New American steakhouse: featuring dry-aged steak options (at extra cost).

Giovanni's Table: for Italian cuisine.

Casual eateries.

Promenade Café: for Continental breakfast, sandwiches, and coffees (in paper cups); Cupcake Cupboard, for cupcakes; Sorrento's, for pizzas and Italian cakes; Sprinkles Ice Cream Parlor, for round-the-clock ice cream and yoghurt, pastries, and coffee.

Windjammer Café: this is a really large, sprawling venue for casual buffet-style, self-help breakfast (this tends to be the busiest time of the day), lunch, and light dinners (but not on the last night of the cruise); it's often difficult to find a table, and, by the time you do, your food could be cold.

Jade 'Restaurant' (it's actually a section of the Windjammer Café), for casual Asian-themed food.

Johnny Rockets, a retro 1950s all-day, all-night diner-style eatery that serves hamburgers, hot dogs, and other fast-food items, malt shakes, and sodas (at extra cost) with indoor and outdoor seating. All indoor tables have a mini-jukebox (dimes are provided for you to make your selection of vintage records). The waitresses are all-singing and all-dancing. There's a cover charge.

ENTERTAINMENT. The 1,350-seat Arcadia Theater spans three decks at the forward end of the ship (it actually spans five decks – including the orchestra pit and scenery storage space). A well-designed showlounge, it has only a small number of pillars to disrupt the sight lines to the stage.

SPA/FITNESS. The large Steiner-operated Vitality at Sea Spa and Fitness Center includes a large aerobics room, fitness center (stairmasters, treadmills, stationary bikes, weight machines, and free weights), several treatment rooms, men's and women's sauna/steam rooms, and relaxation areas. Some exercise classes are free, but some cost extra.

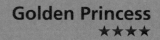

Golden Princess
★★★★

Size:	Large Resort Ship
Tonnage:	108,865
Lifestyle:	Standard
Cruise Line:	Princess Cruises
Former Names:	none
IMO Number:	9192351
Builder:	Fincantieri (Italy)
Original Cost:	$450 million
Entered Service:	May 2001
Registry:	Bermuda
Length (ft/m):	951.4/290.0
Beam (ft/m):	118.1/36.0
Draft (ft/m):	26.2/8.0
Propulsion/Propellers:	diesel-electric (42,000kW)/2
Passenger Decks:	13
Total Crew:	1,100
Passengers (lower beds):	2,624
Passenger Space Ratio (lower beds):	41.4

Passenger/Crew Ratio (lower beds):	2.1
Cabins (total):	1,312
Size Range (sq ft/m):	161.4–764.2/15.0–71.0
Cabins (for one person):	0
Cabins (with private balcony):	720
Cabins (wheelchair accessible):	28
Wheelchair accessibility:	Best
Cabin Current:	110 and 220 volts
Elevators:	14
Casino (gaming tables):	Yes
Slot Machines:	Yes
Swimming Pools:	3
Hot Tubs (on deck):	9
Self-Service Launderette:	Yes
Dedicated Cinema/Seats:	No
Library:	Yes
Onboard currency:	US$

A comfortable, informal, family-friendly large ship

OVERVIEW. *Golden Princess*, with its bold, forthright profile, provides a wide variety of choices and 'small-ish' rooms to enjoy – a veritable playground for the whole family.

THE SHIP. *Golden Princess*, sister to *Grand Princess* and *Star Princess*, has a racy 'spoiler' at the stern that is an observation lounge with aft-facing views by day, and a discotheque by night. The ship has a rather flared snub-nosed bow and a galleon-like transom stern.

There is a good sheltered faux teak promenade deck – it's actually painted steel – which almost wraps around (three times round is equal to one mile) and a walkway that goes to the enclosed bow of the ship. The outdoor pools have various beach-like surroundings, plus a large poolside movie screen. One lap pool has a pumped 'current' to swim against.

High atop the stern of the ship is a ship-wide glass-walled lounge, with spectacular views from the extreme port and starboard side windows; it's a good place to read a book in the daytime, but at night it becomes a disco/nightclub. The Sanctuary is adult passengers only; it has plush padded lounge chairs, two private massage cabanas, and dedicated Serenity Stewards.

There is plenty of space inside the ship and a wide array of public rooms. The passenger flow is well thought-out, with minimal congestion. The decor is attractive and warm, with lots of earth tones.

The main lobby, La Piazza, often has live entertainment; an International Café for (extra-cost) coffees,

Berlitz's Ratings		
	Possible	Achieved
Ship	500	370
Accommodation	200	147
Food	400	250
Service	400	285
Entertainment	100	76
Cruise Experience	400	292
OVERALL SCORE		
1420 points out of 2000		

fresh cookies, pastries, panini, and tapas; and Vines, a wine bar. The ship has a non-glitzy interior design and colors.

There is a Wedding Chapel, with a web-cam to relay ceremonies via the Internet. The ship's captain can legally marry (American) couples, thanks to the ship's Bermuda registry and a special dispensation (this should, however, be verified when in the planning stage, and may vary according to where you reside).

The large casino, on Deck 7, has more than 260 slot machines, plus blackjack, craps, and roulette tables for the more serious gamers. The wood-paneled Wheelhouse Bar is finely decorated with memorabilia and ship models tracing part of parent company P&O's history. There is an Internet café – which isn't a café, though it does have computer workstations.

The automated telephone system is frustrating to use, and luggage delivery is inefficient. Lines can form at the passenger services desk, and for open-seating breakfast and lunch. There is a charge for using the washers and dryers in the self-service launderettes (coins are needed).

FAMILIES. A two-deck-high playroom and teen room is located in the forward section of the ship, and a video games room is located at the opposite end of the ship. There is a host of trained counselors. Many cabins have additional upper berths (there are 609), which are good for families. Group babysitting services are available for an hourly charge.

ACCOMMODATION. There are six principal types of cabins and configurations but a bewildering number of price categories. The price depends on grade, size, and location.

(a) The largest, most lavish suite is the Grand Suite (B748), at the stern. It has a large bedroom with a queen-size bed, huge walk-in closets, a large bathroom with full-size tub and separate shower enclosure, toilet, and washbasin, and a hot tub (accessed from the bedroom), a lounge with sofa bed, dining table and chairs, wet bar and refrigerator, a guest bathroom, and a large private balcony.

(b/c) Suites (with a semi-private balcony) have a separate living room with sofa bed and a bedroom (with a TV in each). The bathroom is quite large and has both a tub and shower stall. The mini-suites also have a semi-private balcony, and a separate living and sleeping area (with a TV in each). The bathroom is also spacious, with both a bathtub and separate shower enclosure. Passengers occupying the best suites receive greater attention, including priority embarkation and disembarkation. But some of the most expensive accommodation has only semi-private balconies that can be overlooked, so there is no privacy (suites C401, 402, 409, 410, 414, 415, 420, 421, 422, 423, 424, and 425 on Caribe Deck in particular). Also, the extremely large suites D105 and D106 (Dolphin Deck) have balconies that can be seen from above.

(d/e/f) The standard interior and outside-view cabins (the outsides come either with or without private balcony) are of a functional, practical, design, although almost no drawers are provided. They are very attractive, with warm, pleasing decor and fine soft furnishing fabrics.

Two family suites consist of two suites with an interconnecting door, plus a large balcony. These can sleep up to 10 (if at least four are children), or up to eight adults.

The views from most outside cabins on Emerald Deck are obstructed by lifeboats. Some cabins can accommodate a third and fourth person in upper berths. However, in such cabins, the lower beds cannot then be pushed together to make a queen-size bed.

Cabins with balconies on Dolphin, Caribe, and Baja decks are overlooked by passengers on balconies on the deck above; they are, therefore, not at all private. However, perhaps the least desirable balcony cabins are the eight located forward on Emerald Deck, as the balconies don't extend to the side of the ship and can be passed by walkers and gawkers on an adjacent walkway (so occupants need to keep their curtains closed most of the time). Cabin attendants

have many cabins to look after (typically 20), which cannot translate to fine personal service.

DINING. For 'formal' meals there are three principal dining rooms (Bernini, Canaletto, and Donatello). There are two seatings in one restaurant, and the others have 'anytime dining' where you choose your time and companions. All are split into multi-tier sections in a non-symmetrical design that breaks what are quite large spaces into many smaller sections, for better ambience. Each dining room has its own galley. While four elevators go to Fiesta Deck for Canaletto and Donatello, only two go to Plaza Deck 5 for Bernini, which can mean long wait problems at peak times, particularly for anyone in a wheelchair). Note that 15 percent is added to all beverage bills, including wines, coffees, etc.

Other dining options. There are two extra-cost dining venues: Sabatini's and Crown Grill. Sabatini's features Italian-style pizzas and pastas, with a variety of sauces, as well as Italian-style entrées, including tiger prawns and lobster tail. Sabatini's is by reservation only, for lunch or dinner on sea days only. Crown Grill has a viewable galley, and features premium-quality steaks and grilled seafood items. Reservations are required and a cover charge applies in both restaurants, but it's worth it for food that is cooked to order.

A poolside hamburger grill and pizza bar (no extra charge) offer casual bites. Other casual meals can be taken in the 24-hour Horizon Court, with large ocean-view windows and direct access to the two main swimming pools and Lido Deck, and outdoor seating. Plastic plates are provided instead of trays.

ENTERTAINMENT. The 748-seat Princess Theater spans two decks and has comfortable seating on both main and balcony levels. It has a nine-piece orchestra. Princess Cruises prides itself on its glamorous and colourful, all-American production shows.

The Vista Lounge is a second entertainment venue and multi-function room. It presents cabaret acts at night, and lectures, bingo, and horse racing during the day.

Explorers, is a third entertainment lounge that features cabaret acts and dance bands, and it has a decent-sized dance floor. Many other lounges and bars have live music, and there are male dance hosts as partners for women traveling alone.

SPA/FITNESS. The Lotus Spa is a complex that surrounds one of the swimming pools at the forward end of the ship. It comprises a large fitness room with all the high-tech workout machinery, an aerobics room, sauna and steam rooms, beauty salon, treatment rooms, and a relaxation area.

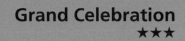

Grand Celebration
★★★

Size:	Mid-size Ship
Tonnage:	47,262
Lifestyle:	Standard
Cruise Line:	Bahamas Paradise Cruise Line
Former Names:	*Grand Celebration, Celebration*
IMO Number:	8314134
Builder:	Kockums (Sweden)
Original Cost:	$130 million
Entered Service:	Mar 1987/Jun 2008
Registry:	Panama
Length (ft/m):	732.6/223.3
Beam (ft/m):	92.5/28.2
Draft (ft/m):	25.5/7.8
Propulsion/Propellers:	diesel (23,520kW)/2
Passenger Decks:	10
Total Crew:	620
Passengers (lower beds):	1,502
Passenger Space Ratio (lower beds):	31.4

Passenger/Crew Ratio (lower beds):	2.4
Cabins (total):	751
Size Range (sq ft/m):	184.0/17.1
Cabins (for one person):	0
Cabins (with private balcony):	10
Cabins (wheelchair accessible):	14
Wheelchair accessibility:	Fair
Cabin Current:	110 and 220 volts
Elevators:	8
Casino (gaming tables):	Yes
Slot Machines:	Yes
Swimming Pools:	3
Hot Tubs (on deck):	2
Self-Service Launderette:	Yes
Dedicated Cinema/Seats:	No
Library:	No
Onboard currency:	Euros

A child-friendly ship for low-cost party cruises to the Bahamas

OVERVIEW. This ship is a water-taxi to fun in The Bahamas.

THE SHIP. *Grand Celebration*, now more than 25 years old, has extremely short bows. It also has a distinctive, large, swept-back wing-tipped blue funnel just aft of the center of the ship. The swimming pools are smaller than one would expect, and the open deck space is extremely limited (think crowded).

It has a double-width indoor promenade and a good selection of public rooms, including a large (Paradice – cute spelling!) casino, Internet center, and several lounges and bars. There is no walk-around open promenade deck.

Children are divided into three age groups: Kruzers (ages 3–7); Club Chill (8–12); and Vibe (13–17).

ACCOMMODATION. There are several accommodation grades, and several price categories: suite with balcony; junior suite with balcony; outside-view; and interior cabins. The cabins are quite standard, are of fairly generous proportions, except for the interior cabins, which are quite small. A 24-hour room service menu is provided. The best living spaces are in 10 suites, each of which has much more space, its own private balcony, a larger bathroom and more closet, drawer, and storage space.

Berlitz's Ratings

	Possible	Achieved
Ship	500	282
Accommodation	200	116
Food	400	207
Service	400	234
Entertainment	100	60
Cruise Experience	400	227

OVERALL SCORE
1126 points out of 2000

DINING. There are two dining rooms: the 550 seat Admiralty Club and the 450-seat Steller Prime. They are cramped when full, and extremely noisy. There are tables for four, six, or eight (none for two). The decor is bright and extremely colorful. Dining is in two seatings. Meals for vegetarians and special children's menus are available, as is a snack at midnight.

The presentation of the dishes is simple, and few garnishes are used. Some meat and fowl dishes are disguised with gravies and sauces. There is much use of canned fruit and jellied desserts. This is strictly banquet catering, with all its standardization and production cooking. For casual meals, there's the 280-seat, self-serve Ocean View Buffet.

ENTERTAINMENT. Legends Grand Theater is the venue for large-scale, high-volume production shows (Legends in Concert). Almost every lounge/bar onboard has live bands and musical units, so there's always plenty of live music in the evening.

SPA/FITNESS. The Indulgence Spa is located on the ship's uppermost deck. It has a gymnasium with muscle-pumping equipment, men's and women's changing rooms, and saunas. The beauty salon is elsewhere. Massages, facials, pedicures, and beauty treatments cost extra.

Grande Mariner
★★

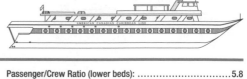

Size:	Boutique Ship
Tonnage:	99
Lifestyle:	Standard
Cruise Line:	Blount Small Ship Adventures
Former Names:	none
IMO Number:	8978643
Builder:	Blount Industries (USA)
Original Cost:	$8 million
Entered Service:	Jun 1998
Registry:	USA
Length (ft/m):	183.0/55.7
Beam (ft/m):	40.0/12.1
Draft (ft/m):	6.5/1.9
Propulsion/Propellers:	diesel (1,044kW)/2
Passenger Decks:	3
Total Crew:	17
Passengers (lower beds):	91
Passenger Space Ratio (lower beds):	0.99

Passenger/Crew Ratio (lower beds):	5.8
Cabins (total):	50
Size Range (sq ft/m):	72.0–96.0/6.6–8.9
Cabins (for one person):	9
Cabins (with private balcony):	0
Cabins (wheelchair accessible):	0
Wheelchair accessibility:	None
Cabin Current:	110 volts
Elevators:	0
Casino (gaming tables):	No
Slot Machines:	No
Swimming Pools:	0
Hot Tubs (on deck):	0
Self-Service Launderette:	No
Dedicated Cinema/Seats:	No
Library:	Yes
Onboard currency:	US$

A US coastal cruise ship with basic food and facilities

OVERVIEW. This ship is best for mature-age couples and solo travelers who enjoy nature and wildlife up close, who wouldn't dream of cruising in the mainstream sense aboard warehouse-size ships, and who don't necessarily demand a high standard of service. It's a basic, no-glitz vessel, providing an all-American cruise experience, albeit at a high price, and is not for children.

THE SHIP. *Grande Mariner* is the second of two almost identical Blount-built vessels. Like sister ship *Grande Caribe*, it has stabilizers. During emergency drill, passengers are taught how to use fire extinguishers – a useful piece of training.

The ship's shallow draft enables it to cruise into off-the-beaten-path destinations well out of reach of larger ships. It also has a retractable navigation bridge – practical for those low bridges along inland waterways. An underwater video camera allows passengers, while seated in comfort in the lounge, to view on large-screen TV monitors what a scuba diver might see underneath the ship. Underwater lights, which attract fish and other marine life, are fitted. There are two 24-passenger launches, one of which is a glass-bottomed boat, and snorkeling equipment.

There is one lounge/bar, located on a different deck to the dining room. The style is casual – no jackets or ties – by day and night. An electric stairway chairlift is provided for those with restricted mobility. Gratuities (high at the suggested $10–15 per person, per day) are pooled and shared by all the staff.

Berlitz's Ratings

	Possible	Achieved
Ship	500	160
Accommodation	200	67
Food	400	190
Service	400	190
Entertainment	100	35
Cruise Experience	400	192
OVERALL SCORE		
840 points out of 2000		

ACCOMMODATION. The cabins are all extremely small, relatively utilitarian units, with very little closet space but just enough drawers. The very small bathrooms have new vacuum toilets. The twin beds convert to queen-size beds, with good storage space under them. There is no room service menu, and only soap is supplied – bring your own toiletries. Each cabin has its own air conditioner, so passengers don't have to share air with the rest of the ship. Refreshingly, there are no cabin keys. Be prepared for noise from the generators.

DINING. The dining room seats all passengers in one open seating, so you dine with whomever you wish, making new friends each day – it is also good for small groups. The tables convert to card tables for use between meals. Passengers should bring their own alcohol, as the company doesn't sell it aboard ship. Effervescent, young American waitresses provide the service, although there is little finesse.

A hand-held colonial bell is rung to summon passengers to the dining room.

ENTERTAINMENT. There is no formal entertainment, so conversation with fellow passengers in the ship's lounge/bar becomes the diversion each evening. If that isn't appealing, take a good book.

SPA/FITNESS. There are no facilities.

Grandeur of the Seas
★★★+

Size:	Mid-size Ship
Tonnage:	73,817
Lifestyle:	Standard
Cruise Line:	Royal Caribbean International
Former Names:	*none*
IMO Number:	9102978
Builder:	Kvaerner Masa-Yards (Finland)
Original Cost:	$300 million
Entered Service:	Dec 1996
Registry:	The Bahamas
Length (ft/m):	916.0/279.6
Beam (ft/m):	105.6/32.2
Draft (ft/m):	25.5/7.6
Propulsion/Propellers:	diesel-electric (50,400kW)/2
Passenger Decks:	11
Total Crew:	760
Passengers (lower beds):	1,950
Passenger Space Ratio (lower beds):	37.8

Passenger/Crew Ratio (lower beds):	2.5
Cabins (total):	975
Size Range (sq ft/m):	158.2–1,267.0/14.7–117.7
Cabins (for one person):	0
Cabins (with private balcony):	212
Cabins (wheelchair accessible):	14
Wheelchair accessibility:	Good
Cabin Current:	110 and 220 volts
Elevators:	9
Casino (gaming tables):	Yes
Slot Machines:	Yes
Swimming Pools:	2 (1 w/sliding glass dome)
Hot Tubs (on deck):	6
Self-Service Launderette:	No
Dedicated Cinema/Seats:	No
Library:	Yes
Onboard currency:	US$

Family-friendly mid-size ship with multiple-choice dining

OVERVIEW. *Grandeur of the Seas* features a varied collection of artworks including several sculptures, principally by British artists, with classical music, ballet, and theater themes. Huge murals of opera scenes adorn several stairways.

THE SHIP. *Grandeur of the Seas* (sister ships: *Enchantment of the Seas*, *Legend of the Seas*, *Rhapsody of the Seas*, *Splendor of the Seas*, and *Vision of the Seas*) has an attractive contemporary profile, with a single funnel located well aft – almost a throwback to some ship designs used in the 1950s. The ship also has a nicely rounded stern. A large Viking Crown Lounge, a trademark of Royal Caribbean International (RCI) ships, sits between funnel and mast at the top of the atrium lobby, and overlooks the forward section of the swimming pool deck, with access provided from stairway off the central atrium. This, together with the forward mast, provides three distinct focal points of the ship's exterior profile. There is a walk-around promenade deck outdoors, but there are no cushioned pads for the tacky plastic sunloungers.

While not as large as some of the newer ships in the fleet, *Grandeur of the Seas* is perhaps more suited to couples and families with children that don't need all the bells and whistles, but want to cruise with up-to-date facilities and have multiple dining choices for more convenience. In 2012, Royal Caribbean added some of the dining options found on the larger ships, and enhanced the overall onboard experience by adding, for example, ship-wide Wi-Fi (it costs extra if

Berlitz's Ratings	Possible	Achieved
Ship	500	379
Accommodation	200	142
Food	400	240
Service	400	262
Entertainment	100	75
Cruise Experience	400	272
OVERALL SCORE		
1370 points out of 2000		

you use it), flat-screen televisions in all cabins, and finger-touch digital 'wayfinder' direction screens.

A seven-deck high atrium lobby, called the Centrum, is the real focal point within the ship, and *the* social meeting place. In the most recent makeover, the whole area was revamped, and new features were added. On its various levels it houses an R Bar (for some creative cocktails), several passenger service counters, an art gallery, Casino Royale (for table gaming and slot machines – and viewing the theatrical glass-covered underfloor exhibits), the popular Schooner Bar, with its nautical-theme decor and maritime art, Café Latte-tudes (for coffee), and library. Aerial entertainment happens in the Centrum, too.

There is a good use of tropical plants throughout the public rooms, which helps counteract the otherwise rather plain and clinical pastel wall colors.

Niggles include charges for shuttle buses in many ports of call; the high cost of bottled water; and receipts that provide an extra line 'for additional gratuity,' when a gratuity has already been added.

ACCOMMODATION. There are numerous price grades, including several grades for suites. The price depends on size, and location, with location and grade perhaps more important since so many of the cabins are of the same, or a very similar size. All are well appointed and have pleasing decor, best described as Scandinavian Modern, with good wood and color accenting. There are, however, a huge number of interior (no-view) cabins.

Royal Suite. This is the largest accommodation, located directly aft of the navigation bridge on the starboard side. It has a separate bedroom with king-size bed, walk-in closet, and vanity dressing area, living room with queen-size sofa bed, baby grand piano, refrigerator and wet bar, dining table, entertainment center, and large private balcony. The bathroom has a whirlpool tub, separate shower enclosure, two washbasins, and toilet.

Owner's Suites. These suites are at the forward end of the ship, just behind the navigation bridge. They have a queen-size bed, separate living area with queen-size sofa bed, vanity dressing area, refrigerator, and wet bar. The bathroom has a full-size tub, separate shower enclosure, toilet, and two washbasins.

Royal Family Suites. These suites include two bedrooms with twin beds that convert to queen-size beds, living area with double sofa bed and Pullman bed, refrigerator, two bathrooms (one with tub), and private balcony. They can accommodate eight, and so might suit families.

Grand Suites. These have twin beds that convert to a queen-size bed, vanity dressing area, lounge area with sofa bed, refrigerator, and a bathroom with tub, plus a private balcony.

Superior Suites. These suites, including two suites for the disabled, have twin beds that convert to a queen-size bed, vanity dressing area, lounge area with sofa bed, refrigerator, plus private balcony, and a bathroom with tub. Although they are called suites, they really are little more than larger standard cabins with a balcony.

Other grades. All standard cabins have twin beds that convert to a queen-size bed, ample closet space for a one-week cruise, and a good amount of drawer space, although under-bed storage space is not good for large suitcases. The bathrooms have nine mirrors. Plastic buckets are provided for Champagne or wine and are really tacky.

All accommodation grades include a hairdryer. The room service menu is really minimal, with only the most basic selection – there are no hot items for breakfast, for example.

DINING. The 1,171-seat Great Gatsby Dining Room is spread over two decks, with both levels connected by a grand, sweeping staircase. When you book, choose one of the two seatings for dinner or 'My Time Dining' – so you can eat when you want, during dining room hours. A neat Champagne terrace bar sits forward of the lower level of the two-deck-high dining room.

The menu descriptions make the food sound better than it is, and the selection of breads, rolls, fruit, and cheese is poor. Overall, meals are rather hit and miss – in fact it's unmemorable. Also, if you want lobster or a decent filet mignon (steak), you will be asked to pay extra.

Other dining options. A cavernous, 790-seat, glass-walled Windjammer Café is a casual, eatery for self-serve breakfast, lunch and dinner buffet items. Note that there are no cups and saucers for tea – only paper cups or plastic mugs, and only plastic plates are provided (so hot food doesn't stay hot long).

For decent (extra-cost) Seattle's Best espresso/cappuccino, head for Caffe Latte-tudes on Deck 6.

In the 2012 makeover, extra dining options were added. These include Giovanni's Table, an Italian trattoria (a service charge applies); Izumi (located in a delightful spot just forward of the funnel) for pan-Asian cuisine including hot-rock cooking (service charge and à-la-carte menu pricing apply); Park Café outdoor market; Chops Grille steakhouse; and Chef's Table, an exclusive hosted event (it is located on the starboard side aft, within the dining room) with a five-course, wine-paired menu; worth it for celebrating a birthday or special event, perhaps.

ENTERTAINMENT. The 875-seat Palladium Theater is the ship's principal showlounge. It is located at the forward part of the ship, and is used for big production shows. It has excellent sight lines from 98 percent of the seats.

Another showlounge, the 575-seat South Pacific Lounge, is used for smaller shows and cabaret acts, including smutty late-night adult-only comedy.

SPA/FITNESS. The Vitality at Sea spa is aft of the funnel and spans two decks. Facilities include a gymnasium with all the latest muscle-pumping exercise machines, aerobics exercise room, sauna and steam rooms, a beauty salon, and a clutch of private massage/body treatment rooms. The spa is staffed and operated by specialist Steiner Leisure.

For the sporting, there is activity galore – including a rock-climbing wall with several separate climbing tracks. It is located outdoors at the aft end of the funnel (just behind the Vitality at Sea spa). A jogging track (outside on Deck 10) takes you around most of the ship.

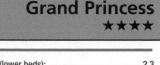

Grand Princess
★★★★

Size:	Large Resort Ship
Tonnage:	108,806
Lifestyle:	Standard
Cruise Line:	Princess Cruises
Former Names:	none
IMO Number:	9104005
Builder:	Fincantieri (Italy)
Original Cost:	$450 million
Entered Service:	May 1998
Registry:	Bermuda
Length (ft/m):	951.4/290.0
Beam (ft/m):	118.1/36.0
Draft (ft/m):	26.2/8.0
Propulsion/Propellers:	diesel-electric (42,000kW)/2
Passenger Decks:	13
Total Crew:	1,100
Passengers (lower beds):	2,600
Passenger Space Ratio (lower beds):	41.8

Passenger/Crew Ratio (lower beds):	2.3
Cabins (total):	1,300
Size Range (sq ft/m):	161.4–764.2/15.0–71.0
Cabins (for one person):	0
Cabins (with private balcony):	710
Cabins (wheelchair accessible):	28
Wheelchair accessibility:	Best
Cabin Current:	110 and 220 volts
Elevators:	14
Casino (gaming tables):	Yes
Slot Machines:	Yes
Swimming Pools:	3
Hot Tubs (on deck):	9
Self-Service Launderette:	Yes
Dedicated Cinema/Seats:	No
Library:	Yes
Onboard currency:	US$

A multi-choice large ship for informal family cruising

OVERVIEW. Whether *Grand Princess* provides a genuinely relaxing holiday is a moot point, but with many choices and 'small' rooms to enjoy, it is an extremely well-designed ship – particularly for families with children. The odds are that you'll have a fine time, in a controlled, well packaged way.

THE SHIP. *Grand Princess* was first in a series of *Grand*-class ships, whose interior design and configuration evolved with each new ship in the series. It has a flared dolphin-like bow and a galleon-like transom stern. The ship was refreshed following an extensive 2011 refit. There is a good sheltered faux teak promenade deck – it's actually painted steel – which almost wraps around, and a walkway that goes right to the enclosed, protected bow. The outdoor pools have various beach-like surroundings. One lap pool has a pumped 'current' to swim against.

Unlike the outside decks, there is plenty of space inside the ship – but also plenty of passengers – and a wide array of public rooms, with many 'intimate' (this being a relative word) spaces. The decor is attractive and warm, with lots of earth tones, and an extensive collection of art complements the interior design and colors well.

Four areas center on swimming pools, one of which is two decks high and can be covered by a retractable glass dome. The former Skywalkers Nightclub was repositioned to a lower deck (Deck 15, aft of the funnel) in 2011, and is now called One5 (cute).

Berlitz's Ratings

	Possible	Achieved
Ship	500	370
Accommodation	200	147
Food	400	249
Service	400	284
Entertainment	100	76
Cruise Experience	400	291
OVERALL SCORE		
1417 points out of 2000		

Other facilities include a Piazza Atrium (always a good place to sit, watch, and meet others), with an integral International Café, Vines wine bar (including tapas and sushi items and wines for purchase); and Leaves Tea Lounge and Library (with 'tea sommelier' to create personalized 'artisan' teas). There's a Wedding Chapel with a web-cam to relay ceremonies via the Internet. The ship's captain can legally marry US citizens, due to the ship's Bermuda registry and a special dispensation.

Another neat feature is the motion-based 'virtual reality' room with its enclosed motion-based rides. There is an excellent library/computer room, and a separate card room. Youngsters have a two-deck-high playroom, teen room, and trained counselors.

Gamblers should enjoy the large casino, with more than 260 slot machines with dolphin-shaped handles; there are blackjack, craps, and roulette tables.

Ship enthusiasts will savor the wood-paneled Wheelhouse Bar, decorated with memorabilia and ship models tracing part of the history of sister company P&O.

The dress code has been simplified to formal or smart casual. Gratuities are automatically added to your account, and tips for children are charged at the same rate. If you want to pay less, you'll have to line up at the reception desk.

ACCOMMODATION. There are six types of cabins and configurations, but there is a bewildering choice of price categories. Many cabins have additional upper berths (there are 609 of them), which is good for families with children. Many balcony cabins overhang the ship's lower hull section.

(a) The plushest accommodation is the Grand Suite, with a hot tub accessible from both the private balcony and from the bedroom, two bedrooms, lounge, two bathrooms, a huge walk-in closet, and lots of drawer and storage space.

(b/c) Suites, with a semi-private balcony, have a separate living room with sofa bed, and bedroom – with a TV set in each. The bathroom is quite large and has both a tub and shower stall. The mini-suites also have a private balcony, and a separate living and sleeping area, with a TV set in each. The differences between the suites and mini-suites are basically in the size and appointments. Passengers in both receive priority attention, including speedy embarkation and disembarkation. However, the most expensive accommodation has only semi-private balconies that can be seen from above (suites C401, 402, 409, 410, 414, 415, 420, 421/422, 423, 424, and 425 on Caribe Deck). Suites D105 and D106 (Dolphin Deck) are extremely large, but their balconies can be seen from above.

(d/e/f) Both interior and outside-view cabins – the outsides come either with or without private balcony – are functional and practical, although there are almost no drawers. They are attractive, with warm, pleasing decor and fine soft furnishing fabrics. The tiled bathrooms have a good amount of open shelf storage space for toiletries.

There are also two family suites. These consist of two suites with an interconnecting door, plus a large balcony, and can sleep up to 10 (if at least four are children), or up to eight adults.

Most outside cabins on Emerald Deck have views obstructed by lifeboats. Sadly, there are no cabins for solo travelers. Your name is placed outside your suite or cabin – making it simple for delivery service personnel but compromising privacy. Some cabins can accommodate a third and fourth person in upper berths – but in such cabins, the lower beds cannot then be pushed together to make a queen-size bed.

Perhaps the least desirable balcony cabins are the eight located forward on Emerald Deck, as the balconies do not extend to the side of the ship and can be passed by walkers and gawkers on the adjacent Upper Promenade walkway. Also, passengers occupying some the most expensive suites with balconies at the stern may experience some vibration during certain ship maneuvers.

The cabin bath towels are small, and drawer space is limited. There are no butlers – even for the top-grade suites. Cabin attendants have many cabins to look after (typically 20), which cannot translate to fine personal service.

DINING. For formal meals, there are three main dining rooms, Botticelli (504 seats), Da Vinci (486), and Michelangelo (486). There are two seatings in one restaurant, while the other two have 'anytime dining' where you choose when, and with whom, you want to eat. All three split into multi-tier sections in a non-symmetrical design that breaks what are quite large spaces into many smaller sections. Each dining room has its own galley. While four elevators go to Fiesta Deck for the Botticelli and Da Vinci restaurants, only two go to Plaza Deck 5 for the Michaelangelo Restaurant – this can cause long waits at peak times, especially for wheelchair users.

Other dining options. There are several informal dining areas, open for lunch and dinner. The food is mostly prepared and cooked to order, and so there is much more taste, and it is perhaps worth paying the extra cost to get better food.

Sabatini's is an extra-cost, reservations-required Italian eatery, with colorful tiled Mediterranean-style decor. It has Italian-style pizzas and pastas, with a variety of sauces, as well as Italian-style entrées that including tiger prawns and lobster tail.

Crown Grill is an extra-cost steakhouse – featuring premium American steaks and seafood in a welcoming setting, with plenty of space around diners' tables. There's a cover charge (worth it), and reservations are required.

Painted Desert is an open area that features 'Southwestern' American food for lunch or dinner (sea days only).

The poolside hamburger grill and pizza bar (no additional charge) are additional dining spots for casual bites, while extra charges apply if you order items to eat at either the coffee bar/patisserie, or the caviar/ Champagne bar.

Other casual meals can be taken in the Horizon Court buffet – open 24 hours a day, with large ocean view on port and starboard sides and direct access to the two main swimming pools and Lido Deck. Oval, plastic plates are used (there are no trays).

ENTERTAINMENT. The 748-seat Princess Theater spans two decks and has comfortable seating on both main and balcony levels. Princess Cruises has long been known and liked for its traditional colourful Hollywood-style (rather than Las Vegas-style) production shows.

The Vista Lounge, a second entertainment lounge, presents cabaret acts at night, and lectures, bingo, and horse racing during the day. Explorers, a third lounge, can also host cabaret acts and dance bands.

SPA/FITNESS. The Lotus Spa is a large complex that surrounds one of the swimming pools at the forward end. It comprises a large gymnasium with all the usual equipment, an aerobics room, sauna and steam rooms, salon, ocean-view treatment rooms, and a relaxation area. It is operated by Steiner Leisure.

Hamburg
★★★+

Size:	Small Ship	Passenger/Crew Ratio (lower beds):	2.4
Tonnage:	14,903	Cabins (total):	205
Lifestyle:	Standard	Size Range (sq ft/m):	139.9–339.0/13.0–31.5
Cruise Line:	Plantours Cruises	Cabins (for one person):	2
Former Names:	*Columbus*	Cabins (with private balcony):	2
IMO Number:	9138329	Cabins (wheelchair accessible):	2
Builder:	MTW Schiffswerft (Germany)	Wheelchair accessibility:	Fair
Original Cost:	$69 million	Cabin Current:	220 volts
Entered Service:	Jul 1997/Jun 2012	Elevators:	2
Registry:	The Bahamas	Casino (gaming tables):	No
Length (ft/m):	472.8/144.1	Slot Machines:	No
Beam (ft/m):	70.5/21.5	Swimming Pools:	1
Draft (ft/m):	16.8/5.1	Hot Tubs (on deck):	0
Propulsion/Propellers:	diesel (10,560kW)/2	Self-Service Launderette:	No
Passenger Decks:	6	Dedicated Cinema/Seats:	No
Total Crew:	170	Library:	Yes
Passengers (lower beds):	408	Onboard currency:	Euros
Passenger Space Ratio (lower beds):	36.5		

A small ship for worldwide port-intensive cruising

OVERVIEW. This ship will appeal to youthful-minded German-speaking couples and solo travelers seeking good value for money on a first cruise, aboard a ship with contemporary, comfortable, and unpretentious surroundings, and good itineraries, at a very modest price.

THE SHIP. *Hamburg* has an ice-strengthened hull, useful for cold-weather cruise areas. While it's a comfortable, trendy ship, the swimming pool is small – it's really a 'plunge' pool – as is the open deck space, and there is no walk-around promenade deck outdoors.

The delightful Palm Garden doubles as an observation lounge and has four Internet-connect computers. Shipwide Wi-Fi is also available. The fit and finish of the interiors is a little utilitarian – the mottled gray walls are somewhat cold, but a contrast to the splashes of color found in carpeting and other decorative touches.

ACCOMMODATION. The standard cabins are really small. All but 10 cabins have lower berths. Except for two forward-facing suites, there are only two balcony cabins, and no room service except for accommodation designated as suites. There are several single-occupancy cabins. Note that 16 cabins on Deck 4 have lifeboat-obstructed views. The cabin decor is bright and upbeat, and there's a good amount of closet and shelf space. All cabins have a minibar/refrigerator, flat-screen TV, personal safe, and hairdryer.

Berlitz's Ratings		
	Possible	Achieved
Ship	500	339
Accommodation	200	136
Food	400	267
Service	400	278
Entertainment	100	60
Cruise Experience	400	256
OVERALL SCORE		
1336 points out of 2000		

There are eight suites, each at least double the size of a standard cabin and each with a curtained partition between its lounge and sleeping areas. Two suites at the bows each have a narrow private verandah, a bedroom and lounge area separated by a curtain, two TV sets, and an excellent amount of storage space.

DINING. There's one large main dining room, at the stern, with large ocean-view windows on three sides. All passengers can be seated in a single seating, at assigned tables, although breakfast is open seating. There are just two tables for two, but other tables can accommodate up to 16. The unstuffy cuisine is good, though the choice is small. Themed dinners make dining a treat. Breakfast and lunch can also be taken in the bright, but casual, setting of the self-serve Palm Garden, which doubles as a comfortable observation lounge. Light dinners can also be taken there; a small dance floor adds another dimension.

ENTERTAINMENT. The showlounge is a single-level, H-shaped room, with banquette and individual seating in tub chairs, and a bar, which is located at the back of the room. Because the apron stage is in the center of the room, the sight lines from many seats aren't good.

SPA/FITNESS. A fitness room is located forward on the uppermost deck of the ship. There's a sauna on the lowest passenger deck, next to the beauty salon. Massage and facial treatments are available.

Hanseatic
★★★★★

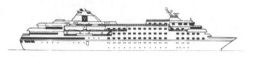

Size:	Boutique Ship
Tonnage:	8,378
Lifestyle:	Luxury
Cruise Line:	Hapag-Lloyd Expedition Cruises
Former Names:	*Society Adventurer*
IMO Number:	5321679
Builder:	Rauma Yards (Finland)
Original Cost:	$68 million
Entered Service:	Mar 1993
Registry:	The Bahamas
Length (ft/m):	402.9/122.8
Beam (ft/m):	59.1/18.0
Draft (ft/m):	16.1/4.9
Propulsion/Propellers:	diesel (5,880kW)/2
Passenger Decks:	7
Total Crew:	122
Passengers (lower beds):	184
Passenger Space Ratio (lower beds):	45.5

Passenger/Crew Ratio (lower beds):	1.5
Cabins (total):	92
Size Range (sq ft/m):	231.4–470.3/21.5–43.7
Cabins (for one person):	0
Cabins (with private balcony):	0
Cabins (wheelchair accessible):	2
Wheelchair accessibility:	None
Cabin Current:	220 volts
Elevators:	2
Casino (gaming tables):	0
Slot Machines:	0
Swimming Pools:	1
Hot Tubs (on deck):	1
Self-Service Launderette:	No
Dedicated Cinema/Seats:	Yes (160)
Library:	Yes
Onboard currency:	Euros

A delightful, small, and stylish expedition ship for discovery

OVERVIEW. *Hanseatic* provides destination-intensive, nature cruises and expeditions in elegant but unstuffy surroundings at a suitably handsome price that ensures good food and service. It is at its best in the Arctic and Antarctic, but passengers should be wary of the difficult conditions for shore landings in these areas.

THE SHIP. *Hanseatic*, operated by Hapag-Lloyd Expedition Cruises, was designed for worldwide expedition-style cruises in contemporary, but quite luxurious, surroundings. It is extremely environmentally friendly, and is one of few ships that allow you to tour the engine room. It has a fully enclosed bridge and an ice-hardened hull with the highest passenger vessel ice classification, plus a helicopter pad and the very latest in high-tech navigation equipment.

A fleet of 14 Zodiac inflatable craft, each named for a famous explorer, is used for in-depth shore landings (including one named David Fletcher, the celebrated expedition leader who spent 16 years working with the British Antarctic Expedition – he loves being aboard *Hanseatic*). These craft provide the ship with tremendous flexibility in itineraries, with excellent possibilities for up-close wildlife viewing in natural habitats. Rubber boots, parkas, boot-washing and storage rooms are provided. For warmer climes, a Bike Box, with 10 bicycles for passenger use at no charge, is offloaded in each port the ship is alongside, where possible.

Inside, the ship is equipped with fine-quality luxury fittings and soft furnishings, and exudes a

Berlitz's Ratings		
	Possible	Achieved
Ship	500	444
Accommodation	200	172
Food	400	348
Service	400	346
Entertainment	100	87
Cruise Experience	400	361
OVERALL SCORE		
1758 points out of 2000		

microclimate of good taste. There is a choice of several public rooms – most located aft, with accommodation forward. All are well furnished and decorated, and all have high ceilings, which help to make the ship feel much larger than its actual size. The library/observation lounge provides a good selection of hardback books in English and German, including many geographical, travel, wildlife, and archaeology titles; it has a sunken bar, and a warm, inviting atmosphere, and two Internet-access computer stations. A large lecture hall, with excellent audio-visual facilities, on a lower deck, can accommodate almost all passengers.

The passenger count is generally kept to about 150, which means plenty of comfort, no lines, and lots of space. In passageways and suites/cabins, 400 large, framed, black-and-white photographs depict wildlife and expedition experiences. Bouillon is always served at 11am.

Safety is paramount, particularly in Antarctica, and here the ship excels with professionalism, pride, and skilled seamanship. Most of each day is taken up with being ashore, and evenings consist mainly of dinner and daily recaps. Lectures, briefings, and the amount of information provided about the itinerary, ports of call, and expedition landings are excellent. Well-qualified lecturers and naturalists accompany each cruise, and a discreet crew and service staff are hallmarks of this ship.

Hanseatic operates in two languages, English and German, though many staff speak several languages;

the ship caters well to both sets of passengers. All port taxes, insurance, staff gratuities, and Zodiac trips are included. A relaxed ambience and informal dress code prevail.

Hapag-Lloyd publishes its own excellent handbooks (in both English and German) on expedition regions such as the Arctic, Antarctica, Amazonia, and the South Sea Islands, as well as exclusive maps.

There are few negatives. The ship is marketed mainly to German and English speakers, so other nationalities may find it hard to integrate.

ACCOMMODATION. There are no bad cabins, and accommodation is priced in seven grades. The all-outside cabins, located in the forward section, are large and very well equipped, and include a separate lounge area next to a large picture window (which has a pull-down blackout blind as well as curtains).

All furniture is in warm woods such as beech, and everything has rounded edges. Wood trim accents the ceiling perimeter, and acts as a divider between bed and lounge areas. Each cabin has a minibar, flat-screen interactive TV with Internet access, when available, and wireless keyboard. A complete infotainment system includes movies and audio tracks on demand at no extra charge. There's a separate bedside three-channel radio, two locking drawers, a retro alarm clock, and plenty of closet and drawer space, as well as two separate cupboards and hooks for all-weather outerwear. One useful feature of all cabins is a blue night/safety light, nicely hidden in each bathroom. A privacy curtain between the cabin door and the sleeping area of the cabin would be useful – you can be seen from the hallway when the cabin door is opened.

All cabin bathrooms have a large shower enclosure with curved glass wall, toiletries cabinets, hairdryer, and bathrobe. There are only two types of cabins; 34 have double beds, others have twin beds. The bath-size towels are large, bed linens and pillowcases are 100 percent cotton, and individual cotton-filled duvets are provided. Laundry, dry cleaning, and pressing services are available.

Suites and cabins on Bridge Deck have impeccable butler service and in-cabin dining privileges, plus stationery and a larger flat-screen TV. Free soft drinks in the refrigerator are replenished daily, but all liquor costs extra. Bulgari and Crabtree & Evelyn amenities are provided.

DINING. The 186-seat Marco Polo restaurant is elegant, warm, and welcoming, with large picture windows on two sides as well as aft. There is one seating for dinner, and open seating for breakfast and lunch, although many passengers like to be seated at their 'regular' table. On embarkation day, waiters introduce themselves after the meal, so hungry passengers won't be delayed by small talk.

The cuisine and service are absolutely first-rate, but are slightly more informal than, for example, aboard the larger *Europa*, which is at or close to the same price level. Top-quality ingredients are always used, and most items are bought fresh when available. In some ports, passengers can go shopping with the chef to source local, regional ingredients and fresh fish.

The meals are very creative and nicely presented, each being appealing to the eye as well as to the palate. There is always an outstanding selection of breads, cheeses, desserts, and pastry items. In the Arctic or Antarctic, table setups are often minimal, due to possible movement of the ship – stabilizers can't be used in much of the Antarctic – so cutlery is provided and changed for each course. Three types of sugar are presented when coffee or tea is ordered – it should never be placed on the table during meal service.

Other dining. An alternative dining spot is the Bistro Lemaire, with 74 seats and leather-topped tables indoors, as well as copious seating at outdoor tables. An informal, open-seating, self serve (or waiter service) buffet-style eatery by day, it changes into a second dining room at night, with themed dinners and barbeques featuring region-specific food. Reservations are required – you make them in the morning of the day you want to dine there – but there is no extra charge and no tipping.

The Bistro features several different breakfast themes: the well-named Zodiac breakfast (quick and easy before Zodiac landing); Small Hanseatic Breakfast; Big Hanseatic Breakfast; Gourmet Breakfast; and Healthy Breakfast. Each cruise also includes a full Viennese teatime, as well as a daily teatime with a selection of cakes, pastries, and finger sandwiches befitting a Viennese coffeehouse.

ENTERTAINMENT. There is no showlounge as such, although there is a lecture room. Entertainment is certainly not a priority aboard this ship, but the itinerary and destinations are the main show. There is no formal entertainment – except on some summer cruises, when a small classical music ensemble might be on board – nor does the ship normally carry a band.

SPA/FITNESS. The spa facilities include a decent-size gymnasium (with up-to-date cardio-vascular and muscle-toning equipment, treadmills, and exercycles) and sauna, all located forward on the Sun Deck in an area that also includes a solarium and hot tub. There's also a cosmetics/make-up room. Massage is available in a rather clinical room within the medical facility, on a lower deck.

Harmony of the Seas
NYR

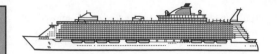

Size:	Large Resort Ship	Passenger Space Ratio (lower beds):	41.4
Tonnage:	227,700	Passenger/Crew Ratio (lower beds):	2.2
Lifestyle:	Standard	Cabins (total):	2,747
Cruise Line:	Royal Caribbean International	Size Range (sq ft/m):	96.8-2,389.6/9.0-222.0
Former Names:	none	Cabins (for one person):	15
IMO Number:	9682875	Cabins (with private balcony):	2,000
Builder:	STX France (France)	Cabins (wheelchair accessible):	46
Original Cost:	$1.35 billion	Wheelchair accessibility:	Best
Entered Service:	May 2016	Cabin Current:	110 volts
Registry:	Bahamas	Elevators:	24
Length (ft/m):	1,187.9/362.1	Casino (gaming tables):	Yes
Beam (ft/m):	234.5/71.5	Slot Machines:	Yes
Draft (ft/m):	30.0/9.1	Swimming Pools:	3
Propulsion/Propellers:	diesel-electric/3 pods	Hot Tubs (on deck):	10
	(2 azimuthing, 1 fixed)	Self-Service Launderette:	No
Passenger Decks:	16	Dedicated Cinema/Seats:	No
Total Crew:	2,394	Library:	Yes
Passengers (lower beds):	5,496	Onboard currency:	US$

The new largest family-friendly resort ship in the world

OVERVIEW. Longer than the first two Oasis-class ships (which, when built, were the largest cruise ships in the world, Allure of the Seas and Oasis of the Seas) by 7ft (2.15m), Harmony of the Seas is now officially the largest resort ship in the world – and absolutely stunning for families with children. It is a benchmark for self-contained resorts with propellers.

Berlitz's Ratings		
	Possible	Achieved
Ship	500	NYR
Accommodation	200	NYR
Food	400	NYR
Service	400	NYR
Entertainment	100	NYR
Cruise Experience	400	NYR
OVERALL SCORE		
NYR points out of 2000		

THE SHIP. No matter what your entertainment and activity interests are, this ship should really turn you on – and then some. It includes some of the wow-factor high-tech whiz-kid gismos and gadgets, and stimulating features found aboard *Anthem of the Seas* (2015), *Quantum of the Seas* (2014), and *Ovation of the Seas* (2016). While the uppermost exterior decks have quite a lot of space, there's little room for sunbathing quietly or reading a book on deck (unless you occupy suite-grade accommodation, in which case there is the adults-only Suite Sundeck, located forward). Much of the open deck space is taken up by water parks, fountains, and sports activities. Sadly, there's not a hint of teak decking.

As aboard the *Oasis*-class ships, the inner 'city' is divided into seven neighborhoods: Central Park (over which three triple-deck-high waterslides twist and turn; you'll also find a Rising Tide Bar, Dazzles, a Trellis Bar, Chops Grille, and 150 Central Park), Boardwalk (for Starbucks, the Boadwalk Dog House, Johnny Rockets, Sabor/Sabor Bar, and a children's carousel), the Royal Promenade (where you'll find the Boot and Bonnet Pub, Sorrentos, Boleros, and the Bionic Bar – with bartenders you can't talk to,

although you can order a wide variety of cocktails from the brands and ingredients provided... and you'll still have to tip), the Pool and Sports Zone, Entertainment Place and Youth Zone, plus a Vitality at Sea Spa and Fitness Center. The most popular strolling areas are the Boardwalk and Central Park, both open to the air, and the indoor Royal Promenade.

In all, there are 37 bars, and more than 20 restaurants, cafés, and other eateries to choose from, but some are exclusively dedicated to Pinnacle members, certain suite accommodation grades, and SeaPass gold card holders; this is all part of the 'pay more, get more' system of class distinction. There's also a large casino, plus blackjack, craps, Caribbean Stud poker, and 450 slot machines, plus a player's club and poker room.

WOWbands (you wear them on your wrist), using RFID technology, can provide access to your accommodation (a 'normal' key card is also provided) and make on-board reservations and purchases easy. Super-high-speed Internet enables video streaming, Skyping, and social media sharing (at a price).

FAMILIES. For children Kid's Avenue – located forward – leads to several age-specific playrooms just aft of the Solarium on Deck 14. Meanwhile, teenagers have The Living Room (chill-out room for teens only) and Fuel, a teen disco.

DreamWorks Animation Studios provides interactive shows featuring characters from *Shrek*, *Kung Fu Panda*, *Madagascar*, and *How to Train Your Dragon*.

ACCOMMODATION. From the smallest cabin (for solo occupancy) to the largest (Presidential Suite, with baby grand piano), there is a wide range of cabins and larger suites to suit all tastes, including 'Royal Family Suites,' 'Loft Suites,' and family cabins. All suites and balcony cabins have floor-to-ceiling sliding glass doors. Some 15 'Studio' category cabins are designed for solo occupancy (something new for RCI). Over 690 have a third/fourth bed – useful for families with small children. Interior cabins have virtual balconies (you can turn this feature off if you wish), and solo travelers get more choice than normal on a cruise. All cabins have a mini bar.

On the down side, the cabin numbering system is a little awkward to get used to. Also, cabin doors open outwards (towards you), as in many European hotels. In many lower grade rooms, closet access is awkward. Most of the standard cabins are dimensionally challenged, but manageable for a week.

CUISINE. Spanning three decks, Opus (formerly the main dining room) is split into three different venues (American Icon Grill, Chic, and The Grande) for 'Dynamic Dining' (eat when you want within restaurant hours). Each venue has its own menus: American Icon Grill, Silk (for Asian fusion cuisine), and The Grande (for a more formal dining and dressy experience).

You can choose the 'Classic' option if you want to dine at one of two fixed times for dinner (you change 'restaurants' each night, together with your waiter and tablemates), or Dynamic Dining, which allows you to dine when you want (in an open seating arrangement).

Other dining options (some cost extra).

150 Central Park – for the most exclusive, cooked-to-order cuisine.

Central Park Café for deli-style sandwiches, salad items, paninis, crêpes, and hearty soups.

Chef's Table – six-course degustation meal (think two hours minimum) with paired wines (open for dinner, reservations required).

Chops Grille – a 'signature' steakhouse featuring large, premium-quality steaks and other grilled food items (open for dinner, reservations required).

Giovanni's Table – a casual Italian trattoria with rustic decor; open for lunch and dinner (reservations required and there's a cover charge for dinner).

Izumi Hibachi and Sushi – for Japanese-style dishes.

Rita's Cantina – featuring quasi-Mexican fare; no tablecloths.

Vintages – a nice, sociable wine bar with cheese and tapas (at à-la-carte prices).

Windjammer Marketplace is the rather large self-serve casual buffet-style eatery, with several different sections featuring different food types, salad bar, etc. The venue can be extremely crowded due to the number of passengers carried.

Other snacking spots on The Boardwalk or along the Royal Promenade: Boardwalk Dog House, Donut Shop, and Ice Cream Parlor.

ENTERTAINMENT. The 1,380-seat Royal Theater (main showlounge) spans three decks. Reservations for shows can be made up to three months ahead (there is no charge).

Adult-only (smutty) comedy is featured in 'The Attic Comedy Club.'

A 750-seat Aqua Theater, located outside at the ship's stern with a 6,000-sq-ft (560-sq-m) stage, is a stunning combination show theatre, sound stage, and events space (some great viewing places can be found high in the aft wings of the ship on both sides). The stern has some 'overhang,' to accommodate the venue.

SPA/FITNESS. The Steiner Leisure operated Vitality at Sea Spa facilities (set low down forward on Decks 5 and 6) include a large fitness center (cardio and resistance equipment) and beauty salon, while an extra-cost Thermal Suite pass allows you access to men's and women's saunas, steam rooms, and heated tiled relaxation loungers, plus a 60-seat Vitality Café for extra-cost 'health' drinks and snacks.

Sporting activities include two Flowriders for body surfing, a zipline that careers over The Boardwalk (and its inner balcony cabins), and three water slides that career over Central Park. There's also a Sports Pool, Harmony Dunes (mini-golf), a Sports Court, two rock climbing walls (aft), and an ice skating rink – which, aboard sister ships Allure of the Seas and Oasis of the Seas – has proven to be extremely popular with children.

Hebridean Princess
★★★★+

Size:	Boutique Ship	Passenger/Crew Ratio (lower beds):	1.3
Tonnage:	2,112	Cabins (total):	30
Lifestyle:	Luxury	Size Range (sq ft/m):	144.0–340.0/13.4–31.6
Cruise Line:	Hebridean Island Cruises	Cabins (for one person):	10
Former Names:	Columba	Cabins (with private balcony):	4
IMO Number:	6409351	Cabins (wheelchair accessible):	0
Builder:	Hall Russell (Scotland)	Wheelchair accessibility:	None
Original Cost:	n/a	Cabin Current:	240 volts
Entered Service:	1964/May 1989	Elevators:	0
Registry:	Great Britain	Casino (gaming tables):	No
Length (ft/m):	235.0/71.6	Slot Machines:	No
Beam (ft/m):	46.0/14.0	Swimming Pools:	0
Draft (ft/m):	10.0/3.0	Hot Tubs (on deck):	0
Propulsion/Propellers:	diesel (1,790kW)/2	Self-Service Launderette:	No
Passenger Decks:	5	Dedicated Cinema/Seats:	No
Total Crew:	38	Library:	Yes
Passengers (lower beds):	50	Onboard currency:	UK£
Passenger Space Ratio (lower beds):	42.2		

This English country inn afloat is the real McCoy

OVERVIEW. This charming little ship has a warm, totally cosseted, traditional Scottish country house ambience and a stately home service that's unobtrusive but always at hand when you need it. It suits mature-age adult couples and solo travelers who enjoy learning about the natural sciences, geography, history, gardening, art, architecture, and enjoy a very small ship with almost no entertainment.

Berlitz's Ratings	Possible	Achieved
Ship	500	410
Accommodation	200	174
Food	400	349
Service	400	342
Entertainment	100	84
Cruise Experience	400	319
OVERALL SCORE		
1678 points out of 2000		

THE SHIP. Small and old can be chic and comfortable. *Hebridean Princess*, originally one of three Scottish ferries built for David MacBrayne Ltd – although actually then owned by the British government – was skillfully converted into a gem of a cruise ship in order to operate island-hopping itineraries in Scotland, together with the occasional jaunt to Norway and an occasional sailing around the UK coast. It was renamed in 1989 by the Duchess of York, and underwent a facelift in 2015.

There is an outdoors deck for occasional sunbathing and alfresco meals, as well as a bar where occasional formal cocktail parties are held when weather conditions are right. There is no walk-around promenade deck, although there is an open deck atop ship. The ship carries two Zodiac inflatable runabouts (*Calgary* and *Kiloran*) and two Hardy shore tenders (*Sanda* and *Shona*).

Use of the ship's small boats, speedboat, a dozen or so bicycles, and fishing gear are included in the price, as are entrance fees to gardens, castles, other attractions, and the occasional coach tour, depending

on the itinerary. The destination-intensive cruises have very creative itineraries, and there's plenty to do, despite the lack of big-ship features. Specialist guides, who give daily talks about the destinations to be visited and some fascinating history and the local folklore, accompany all cruises.

What passengers appreciate is the fact that the ship does not have photographers or some of the trappings found aboard larger ships. They also love the fact that there is no bingo, art auctions, or mindless parlor games.

The principal public room inside the ship is the charming Tiree Lounge, which has a real brick-walled inglenook fireplace, plus a very cozy bar with a wide variety of whiskies – the selection of single malts is excellent – and cognacs for connoisseurs. Naturally, the ship specializes in Scottish spirits.

Agatha Christie's Inspector Hercule Poirot would be very much at home here, particularly in the Tiree Lounge. Who needs megaships when you can take a retro-cruise aboard this little gem? Direct bookings are accepted.

Hebridean Princess has UK officers and an excellent Lithuanian service crew; all are discreet and provide unobtrusive service. This little ship remains one of the world's best-kept travel secrets, although Queen Elizabeth II chartered the ship for a family-only celebration of her 80th birthday in 2006, and again for a family holiday in 2010, which raised its profile.

A roughly polished gem, it is especially popular with single passengers. More than half the passengers are repeaters. Children under nine are not accepted. Despite the shortcomings of the ship itself, it's the food that rates highly.

If you cruise from Oban, you can be met at Glasgow station (or airport) and taken to/from the ship by private motor coach. Passengers are piped aboard at embarkation by a Scottish bagpiper – a neat touch. All drinks (except premium brands, which incur a small charge), soft drinks, and bottled Scottish mineral water are included in the fare, as are gratuities – the company requests that no additional gratuities be given.

Although this vessel is strong, it does have structural limitations and noisy engines that cause some vibration. However, the engines do not run at night because the ship anchors before bedtime, providing soul-renewing tranquility – except for the sound of a single generator. The ship doesn't have an elevator, so anyone with walking disabilities may find it challenging – and there may be several tender ports on each itinerary. It is often cold and very wet in the Scottish highlands and islands, so take plenty of warm clothing for layering.

ACCOMMODATION. All cabins have different color schemes and names – there are no numbers, and, refreshingly, no door keys, although cabins can be locked from the inside. No two cabins are identical – they are individually created, with delightfully eclectic curtains, sweeping drapes over the beds, and lots of cushions. They really are quite different from almost all other cruise ships, and come in a wide range of configurations (some with single, some with double, some with twin beds), including four with a private balcony – a private and self-indulgent bonus.

All cabins have a private bathroom with bath or shower. All have a refrigerator, ironing board with iron, trouser press, brass clock, and tea/coffee-making set – there's something magical about getting up in the morning, making fresh tea in your cabin using mineral water and organic teas, and sitting outside on a protected balcony watching Scotland's islands come and go. All seems right with the world.

Cabins have Victorian-style bathroom fittings, many of which are gold-plated, and some have brass cabin portholes or windows that actually open. Three of the newest cabins are outfitted in real Scottish Baronial style. All towels and bathrobes are 100 percent cotton, as is the bed linen. Some cabins in the front of the ship are subject to noise from the anchor being weighed each morning.

Each cabin has Villeroy and Boch china, fair trade coffee, organic teas, and fresh milk – not the irradiated long-life milk or chemical milk found aboard many ships these days.

DINING. The Columba Restaurant has ocean-view windows and tables laid with crisp white linen and classic white Schonwald china. There is a single seating at assigned tables. Some chairs have armrests, while some do not. While days are casual, dinner means jackets and ties, and formal attire typically twice per cruise.

The cuisine is extremely creative, and at times outstanding – and about the same quality and presentation as *SeaDream I* and *SeaDream II*. Menus offer just one meat and one fish dish (a different fish each day), plus an alternative, casual option. Fresh ingredients are sourced and purchased locally, supporting Scottish suppliers – a welcome change from the mass catering of most ships. Although there are no flambé items – the galley has electric, not gas, ranges – what is created is beautifully presented and of the highest standard. Just remember to save space for the desserts.

The breakfast menu is standard each day, although you can always ask for any favorites, and each day there's a specialty item, plus a help-yourself buffet table. Try the porridge and a 'wee dram' (Scotch whisky – single malt, of course) – it's lovely on a cold morning, and it sets you up for the whole day.

Not to be missed is the exclusive theatrical treat 'a tasting o' haggis wi' bashed neeps an champit tatties,' accompanied by bagpipe music and an 'address to the haggis' ceremony, traditionally given by the captain. Although there is waiter service for most things, there is also a good buffet table display during breakfast and luncheon. Wines are provided at lunch and dinner, although an additional connoisseur's list is available for those seeking fine vintage wines. Highly personal and attentive service from an attentive staff completes the picture.

ENTERTAINMENT. The Tiree Lounge is the equivalent of a main lounge aboard this very small ship. Dinner is the entertainment of the evening. Occasionally, there might be after-dinner drinks, poetry readings, and an occasional storyteller, but little else (passengers neither expect nor need it).

SPA/FITNESS. There is no spa, as the ship is too small. The only concessions to fitness are an exercycle and treadmill.

Hebridean Sky
★★★+

Size:	Boutique Ship	Passenger Space Ratio (lower beds):	37.5
Tonnage:	4,280	Passenger/Crew Ratio (lower beds):	1.6
Lifestyle:	Premium	Cabins (total):	53
Cruise Line:	Noble Caledonia	Size Range (sq ft/m):	234.6–353.0/21.8–32.8
Former Names:	Sea Explorer, Corinthian II, Island Sun,	Cabins (for one person):	0
	Sun, Renaissance VII, Regina Renaissance,	Cabins (with private balcony):	4
	Renaissance VII	Cabins (wheelchair accessible):	0
IMO Number:	8802882	Wheelchair accessibility:	None
Builder:	Nuovi Cantieri Appaunia (Italy)	Cabin Current:	110 volts
Original Cost:	$25 million	Elevators:	1
Entered Service:	Dec 1991/May 2016	Casino (gaming tables):	No
Registry:	Marshall Islands	Slot Machines:	No
Length (ft/m):	297.2/90.6	Swimming Pools:	0
Beam (ft/m):	50.1/15.3	Hot Tubs (on deck):	1
Draft (ft/m):	12.9/2.9	Self-Service Launderette:	No
Propulsion/Propellers:	diesel (5,000kW)/2	Dedicated Cinema/Seats:	No
Passenger Decks:	5	Library:	Yes
Total Crew:	66	Onboard currency:	UK£
Passengers (lower beds):	111		

For life enrichment in a comfortable small-ship environment

OVERVIEW. This really intimate little ship is very comfortable and totally inviting, and operates warm-weather cruises in regions devoid of large cruise ships. It suits mature adults who like to discover small ports in a relaxed lifestyle combined with good food and service, and itineraries that enable you to 'get away from it all, but in comfort.'

THE SHIP. *Hebridean Sky* has a smart profile and handsome styling, with twin flared funnels and a 'ducktail' (or sponson) stern to provide fairly decent stability and seagoing comfort. This ship was purchased by Noble Caledonia in 2014. It has a narrow teak walk-around promenade deck outdoors, and a decent amount of open deck space.

A baby shore tender hangs off the aft deck and acts as ship-to-shore transportation.

The interior design is elegant, with polished wood-finish paneling throughout. There is also a very small book and video library. Although Hebridean Sky is not up to the standard of a Seabourn or Silversea ship, it will provide a good cruise experience at a moderate cost. Gratuities are appreciated but not required.

ACCOMMODATION. The cabins are quite spacious and combine highly polished imitation rosewood paneling with lots of mirrors and hand-crafted Italian furniture, lighted walk-in closets, and vanity

Berlitz's Ratings		
	Possible	Achieved
Ship	500	353
Accommodation	200	156
Food	400	267
Service	400	282
Entertainment	100	60
Cruise Experience	400	271
OVERALL SCORE		
1389 points out of 2000		

mirrors. In fact, there are a lot of mirrored surfaces in the decor, as well as just about everything you need, including a TV set and DVD player, a refrigerator, and free soft drinks and bottled water. The beds are fixed, so there's no under-bed storage space.

The bathrooms are extremely compact; they have real teakwood floors and marble vanities, and shower enclosures. None have tubs, not even the Owner's Suite. Cabins with balconies have glass panels topped with a polished wood railing.

DINING. The dining room operates in an open-seating arrangement, so you sit where you like, with whom you like, and at what time you like. It is small but quite smart, with tables for two, four, six, and eight. The meals are self-service, buffet-style cold foods for breakfast and lunch, with hot foods chosen from a table menu and served properly, and sit-down service for dinner. The food quality, choice, and presentation are all very good.

ENTERTAINMENT. There is no formal entertainment in the main lounge, the venue for all social activities. However, six pillars obstruct the sight lines to the small stage area, so it's not easy to see the speaker/lecturer.

SPA/FITNESS. Sports-related facilities include an aft platform, and Zodiacs for close-in coastal visits.

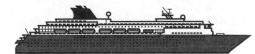

Horizon
★★★+

Size:	Mid-size Ship
Tonnage:	47,427
Lifestyle:	Standard
Cruise Line:	CDF Croisieres de France
Former Names:	*Pacific Dream, Island Star, Horizon*
IMO Number:	8807088
Builder:	Meyer Werft (Germany)
Original Cost:	$185 million
Entered Service:	May 1990/Apr 2012
Registry:	Malta
Length (ft/m):	682.4/208.0
Beam (ft/m):	95.1/29.0
Draft (ft/m):	23.6/7.2
Propulsion/Propellers:	diesel (19,960kW)/2
Passenger Decks:	10
Total Crew:	620
Passengers (lower beds):	1,442
Passenger Space Ratio (lower beds):	32.8
Passenger/Crew Ratio (lower beds):	2.0
Cabins (total):	721
Size Range (sq ft/m):	172.2–500.5/16–46.5
Cabins (for one person):	0
Cabins (with private balcony):	68
Cabins (wheelchair accessible):	4
Wheelchair accessibility:	Good
Cabin Current:	110 and 220 volts
Elevators:	7
Casino (gaming tables):	Yes
Slot Machines:	Yes
Swimming Pools:	2
Hot Tubs (on deck):	3
Self-Service Launderette:	No
Dedicated Cinema/Seats:	No
Library:	Yes
Onboard currency:	Euros

This is a family-friendly casual ship for French-speakers

OVERVIEW. This ship is quite suited to young (and young at heart) French-speaking couples, solo travelers, and families with children of all ages who want a first cruise experience in a smart, almost elegant ship, with plenty of public rooms, a lively atmosphere, and a French cruise experience.

THE SHIP. *Horizon* was originally built for and owned and operated by Celebrity Cruises. Although now around 25 years old, it still has a fairly contemporary, though angular, profile that gives the impression of power and speed thanks to its blue hull (the hull itself was designed by mega-yacht designer Jon Bannenberg). CDF Croisières de France took over the ship – from Pullmantur Cruises – in April 2012.

The exterior pool deck features one large pool and another for children, plus a couple of hot tubs, and in-built shower enclosures.

Inside, there is a similar interior layout to its sister ship, *Pullmantur Cruises' Zenith*, with decor that is quite restrained, even elegant. The feeling is one of uncluttered surroundings, and the ship features some interesting artwork. Soothing, pastel colors and high-quality soft furnishings are used throughout the interiors. The decks are named after colors (cobalt, turquoise, indigo, etc.).

An elegant Art Deco-style hotel-like lobby, reminiscent of Miami Beach hotels, has a two-deck-high ceiling and a spacious feel, and is the contact point for the reception desk, shore excursions, and onboard accounts counters.

Berlitz's Ratings

	Possible	Achieved
Ship	500	353
Accommodation	200	140
Food	400	236
Service	400	264
Entertainment	100	61
Cruise Experience	400	258
OVERALL SCORE		
1312 points out of 2000		

The principal deck that houses many of the public entertainment rooms (located two decks above the lobby, has a double-width indoor promenade, which is good for strolling and people-watching. There is a decent-size library. Other facilities include a large Zephyr Lounge Bar; a Piano Bar; a Café Moka – for coffee and chat; and an Internet center. A large, elegantly appointed Monte Carlo Casino has its own bar.

CDF Croisières de France changed some of the public rooms and open areas, and added splashes of bright colors, motifs, and new signage – all tailored to its French-speaking family clientele. Expect to find an abundance of children during the peak holiday periods, when the passenger mix becomes younger. 'Inclusive' drinks packages are available at an additional cost per day.

Passenger niggles? Lines for embarkation, disembarkation, shore tenders, and for self-serve buffet meals. The doors to the public restrooms and the outdoor decks are very heavy. The public restrooms are clinical and need some refreshing. There are no cushioned pads for the poolside sunloungers.

FAMILIES. CDF Croisières de France has a good program for children and teenagers, with specially trained youth counselors, and a decent range of activities, although the children's play areas are not extensive (because this is a mid-size ship and not a large resort ship). Children under 3 travel free. All drinks are included, which makes things simpler for families with children.

ACCOMMODATION. There are several price grades, including outside-view suites and cabins, and interior cabins. Note that many of the outside-view cabins on the safety equipment deck have lifeboat-obstructed views.

Standard cabins. The outside-view and interior cabins have good-quality fittings with lots of wood accenting, are tastefully decorated and of an above-average size, with an excellent amount of closet and drawer space and reasonable insulation between cabins. All have twin beds that convert to a queen-size bed, and a good amount of closet and drawer space. The cabin soundproofing is quite good although this depends on location – some cabins are located opposite crew access doors, which can be busy and noisy. The bathrooms have a generous shower area, and a small range of toiletries is provided, although towels are a little small, as is storage space for toiletries. The lowest priced outside-view cabins have a porthole, but all others have picture windows.

Royal Suites. The largest accommodation is in two Royal Suites midships on Atlantic Deck (Deck 10), and forward on Marina Deck. These have a large private balcony and a separate bedroom and lounge, a dining area with glass dining table, plus media players and large television. The bathroom is also large and has a whirlpool tub with integral shower.

Another 20 suites, also on Atlantic Deck, are tastefully furnished, although they are really just larger cabins, not suites. They have generous drawer and other storage space, and a sleeping area (with European duvets on the beds), plus a lounge area, and decent bathrooms. All accommodation designated as suites suffers from noise generated on the swimming pool deck directly above.

DINING. Le Splendide Restaurant (the main dining room) features a raised section in its center. It has several tables for two, as well as for four, six, or eight (in banquettes), although the chairs don't have armrests. There are two seatings for dinner and open seating for breakfast and lunch, at tables for two, four, six, eight, or 10. The cuisine, its presentation, and service are quite decent, with menus overseen by Francis Leveque, chef of the Restaurant du Marché in Paris.

Other dining options. For informal meals, the Marché Gourmand has a traditional single-line self-service buffet for breakfast and lunch, and includes a pasta station, rotisserie, and pizza ovens. At peak times, the buffet is simply too small, too crowded, and noisy. It is also open (as Bistro Gourmand) for casual dinner between 6.30pm and 11pm.

The Terrace and Grill, located outdoors adjacent to the Bistro, serves typical fast-food items such as burgers and hot dogs.

ENTERTAINMENT. The two-level Broadway Theater, with main and balcony levels, has good sight lines from almost all seats, except where the railing at the front of the balcony level impedes sight lines. It has a large stage for this size of ship, and decent lighting and sound equipment.

The shows consist of a troupe of showgirl dancers, whose routines are reminiscent of high-school shows. Cabaret acts are the main feature; these include singers, magicians, and comedians, among others, and are very much geared to the family audience that this ship carries on most cruises. There is also plenty of live – and loud – music for dancing to in various bars and lounges, plus the Saphir Dance Club (disco). Participation activities tend to be quite amateurish.

SPA/FITNESS. The Salle de Fitness is located high in the ship, just aft of the funnel. It has a gymnasium with ocean-view windows and high-tech muscle-pump equipment, an exercise area, several therapy treatment rooms including a Rasul (mud treatment) room, and men's/women's saunas.

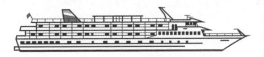

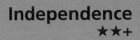

Independence
★★+

Size:	Boutique Ship
Tonnage:	2,300
Lifestyle:	Standard
Cruise Line:	American Cruise Lines
Former Names:	none
IMO Number:	1223608
Builder:	Chesapeake Shipbuilding (USA)
Original Cost:	n/a
Entered Service:	Jun 2010
Registry:	USA
Length (ft/m):	223.0/67.9
Beam (ft/m):	51.0/15.5
Draft (ft/m):	8.2/2.5
Propulsion/Propellers:	diesel/2
Passenger Decks:	4
Total Crew:	27
Passengers (lower beds):	97
Passenger Space Ratio (lower beds):	23.7

Passenger/Crew Ratio (lower beds):	3.5
Cabins (total):	52
Size Range (sq ft/m):	204.0–240.0/18.9–22.2
Cabins (for one person):	7
Cabins (with private balcony):	40
Cabins (wheelchair accessible):	1
Wheelchair accessibility:	None
Cabin Current:	110 volts
Elevators:	1
Casino (gaming tables):	No
Slot Machines:	No
Swimming Pools:	0
Hot Tubs (on deck):	0
Self-Service Launderette:	No
Dedicated Cinema/Seats:	No
Library:	Yes
Onboard currency:	US$

A small, personal US coastal ship for mature cruisers

OVERVIEW. This ship is for couples and solo travelers of mature years sharing a cabin and wishing to cruise in an all-American environment, with destinations more important than food, service, or entertainment. It is extremely expensive for what you get – although this is a new ship, and the cabins are larger and marginally better equipped than those in comparable ships.

Berlitz's Ratings

	Possible	Achieved
Ship	500	284
Accommodation	200	127
Food	400	210
Service	400	180
Entertainment	100	10
Cruise Experience	400	145

OVERALL SCORE
956 points out of 2000

THE SHIP. *Independence* is the fourth vessel in this cruise line's growing fleet (sister ships: *American Glory*, *American Spirit*, and *American Star*). The company builds the ships in its own shipyard in Chesapeake, Maryland. *Independence* is built specifically for coastal and inland cruising, in a casual, unregimented setting, to destinations unreachable by large cruise ships.

The uppermost deck is open – good for views – behind a forward windbreaker; plenty of sunloungers are provided, as is a small golf putting green.

The public rooms include an observation lounge, with views forward and to port and starboard side; a library/lounge; a small midships lounge; and an elevator that goes to all decks, including the outdoor sun deck.

Cruises are typically seven to 14 days long. The ship docks in the center, or within walking distance, of most towns and ports. The dress code is 'no ties casual.' There are no additional costs, except for gratuities and port charges, because it's all included – quite different from big-ship cruising.

ACCOMMODATION. There are five cabin price grades – four are doubles, one is for singles. All cabins have twin beds that convert to a king-size bed, a small desk with chair, flat-screen television, DVD player, and hanging space for clothes. All also have Internet access, a private (modular) bathroom with separate shower, washbasin and toilet (no cabin has a bathtub), windows that open, and satellite-feed TV sets. Rooms incorrectly designated as suites (23) have private balconies; although narrow, these do have two chairs and a small drinks table.

DINING. The dining salon, in the latter third of the vessel, has large, panoramic picture windows on three sides. Everyone eats in a single open seating, so you can get to know your fellow passengers. The cuisine is mainstream American: simple, honest food highlighting regional specialties. The choice of soups, appetizers, and entrées (mains) is limited. There is no wine list, although basic white and red American table wines are included. On the last morning of each cruise, Continental breakfast only is available.

ENTERTAINMENT. Dinner and after-dinner conversation with fellow passengers in the ship's lounge/bar form the entertainment each evening. Otherwise, take a good book.

SPA/FITNESS. There is a tiny fitness room with a few bicycles and other exercise machines.

Independence of the Seas
★★★+

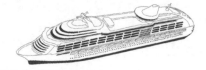

Size:	Large Resort Ship
Tonnage:	154,407
Lifestyle:	Standard
Cruise Line:	Royal Caribbean International
Former Names:	none
IMO Number:	9349681
Builder:	Kvaerner Masa-Yards (Finland)
Original Cost:	$590 million
Entered Service:	May 2008
Registry:	The Bahamas
Length (ft/m):	1,112.2/339.0
Beam (ft/m):	184.0/56.0
Draft (ft/m):	27.8/8.5
Propulsion/Propellers:	diesel-electric (75,600kW)/3 pods (2 azimuthing, 1 fixed)
Passenger Decks:	15
Total Crew:	1,397
Passengers (lower beds):	3,634

Passenger Space Ratio (lower beds):	42.0
Passenger/Crew Ratio (lower beds):	2.6
Cabins (total):	1,817
Size Range (sq ft/m):	149.0–2,025.0/13.8–188.1
Cabins (for one person):	0
Cabins (with private balcony):	842
Cabins (wheelchair accessible):	32
Wheelchair accessibility:	Good
Cabin Current:	110 volts
Elevators:	14
Casino (gaming tables):	Yes
Slot Machines:	Yes
Swimming Pools:	2
Hot Tubs (on deck):	6
Self-Service Launderette:	No
Dedicated Cinema/Seats:	No
Library:	Yes
Onboard currency:	US$

This ship has excellent family facilities and entertainment

OVERVIEW. This ship's 'wow' factor is its connection with water in its dramatic water theme park on the pool deck – recommended for families with children. There is, however, something for everyone.

THE SHIP. This *Freedom*-class ship is essentially split into three separate areas, rather like Disney's cruise ships: adults-only, family, and main.

The ship's 'wow' factor (particularly for children) is its connection with water in the design of a dramatic water theme park afloat. By day, an H2O Zone (in the center of the pool deck, has an interactive water-themed play area for families that includes water cannons and spray fountains, water jets and ground gushers; by night the 'water park' turns into a colorfully lit sculpture garden. Adjacent is a 'sports' pool – with grandstand-style seating – for the likes of jousting contests and other sports-related pool games, plus a 'main' pool.

There are 16 bars and lounges to enjoy, plus a whole promenade of shops and munching and drinking spots along an indoor mall-like environment called the Royal Promenade. This is four decks high, and some cabins have great views into it. The Royal Promenade is home to fashion, jewelry and perfume shops, a general store, logo shop, Promenade Café, Ben & Jerry's ice cream outlet, a Book Nook, a 'classic' barber shop called A Clean Shave (for a razor shave 'experience'), a pizzeria, and an English pub – the Dog & Badger. Look out for the stilt walkers and inflatable elephants when the circus is in town (promenades will be announced in the daily program).

Berlitz's Ratings

	Possible	Achieved
Ship	500	388
Accommodation	200	142
Food	400	235
Service	400	284
Entertainment	100	75
Cruise Experience	400	269

OVERALL SCORE
1393 points out of 2000

One deck below the Royal Promenade is a large Casino Royale (full of gaming tables and slot machines), The Raven disco, Schooner Bar (piano bar), Boleros Lounge (a Latin hangout), and a photo gallery and shop, while the forward section leads into the three-deck-high Alhambra Theatre.

A regulation-size ice-skating rink (Studio B) has real, not fake, ice, with 'bleachers'-style seating, and broadcast facilities. Outstanding Ice Follies shows are presented here, but note that a number of slim pillars obstruct clear-view arena stage sight lines.

Almost at the top of the ship is RCI's trademark Viking Crown Lounge, the cutely named Olive or Twist jazz lounge, and a Wedding Chapel (this is actually on the deck above). Other facilities include a cigar smoker's lounge, conference center, a concierge lounge (for suite occupants only), and a comfortable 3,600-book library – located at the aft end of the Royal Promenade, on Deck 7.

FAMILIES. Children are well catered to, with Adventure Ocean (on Deck 12) for kids of six months to 17 years of age (teens get their own chill-out room). Children will love this ship and all the fun activities and sports activities – not to mention meeting other kids. Adventure Ocean is where new friends are made easily.

ACCOMMODATION. There is a wide range of suites and cabins in several categories and different price grades, from a Presidential Family Suite that can sleep up to 14 to twin-bed two-person interior cabins, and interior cabins that look into an interior shopping/strolling atrium promenade. The price you pay depends on the size, grade, and location you choose. There are many family-friendly cabins, good for reunions, but no solo-occupancy cabins. All outside-view cabins have even numbers; all interior cabins have odd numbers.

Presidential Family Suite. Located in the aft section, it comprises five rooms. These include two master bedrooms, each with twin beds that convert to a queen-size bed and en suite bathroom with tub/shower (but the toiletries cabinets are the same as in all other cabins); two other small bedrooms that can sleep four; private balcony with sand-colored rubberized decking (not teak), with loungers, tables, chairs, a bar, and a decent view aft – although part of the balcony is overlooked by balconies on decks above, and there is a lot of wasted space aft of the balcony because it doesn't extend to the ship's edge. There's also a lounge with two sofa beds and bar. It can accommodate eight to 14 (that's odd numbers breathing in, even numbers breathing out!), located aft, at the opposite end of the ship to the showlounge. Size: 1,215 sq ft (113 sq m) plus balcony: 810 sq ft (75 sq m). It's a pleasant enough apartment, but nothing special – it actually feels cramped and the ceilings are plain – but it could be good value for a large family.

Owner's Suite. Sleeps up to five. Size: 506 sq ft (46 sq m) plus balcony: 131 sq ft (12 sq m).

Royal Suite. Sleeps up to four (and includes a black baby grand piano). Size: 1,406 sq ft (130.6 sq m) plus balcony: 377 sq ft (35 sq m).

Grand Suite. Sleeps up to four. Size: 381 sq ft (35.3 sq m) plus balcony: 89 sq ft (8.2 sq m).

Junior Suites. These sleep up to four, and measure 277 sq ft (25.7 sq m) plus balcony: 65 sq ft (6 sq m).

Superior ocean-view cabins. These measure 202 sq ft (18.7 sq m) plus balcony: 42 sq ft (3.9 sq m), and sleep two (some rooms sleep three or four).

Deluxe ocean-view cabins. These cabins measure 173 sq ft (16.0 sq m) plus balcony: 46 sq ft (4.2 sq m). They sleep two (some rooms sleep three or four).

Interior (promenade-view) cabins. These cabins, on three decks, are interior cabins, but with bay windows that allow occupants to look into the Royal Promenade. They sleep two.

Interior cabins. These no-view cabins measure 160 sq ft (14.8 sq m), and sleep two (some rooms sleep three or four).

Family ocean-view cabin. Located at the front of the ship, it has two twin beds (convertible to queen-size), sofa and/or Pullman beds, sitting area, and bathroom with shower. Accommodates six, and has 48ins (122cm) round windows. Size: 265 sq ft (24.6 sq m).

DINING. The huge Shakespeare-themed main dining room is set on three levels, each with a different name: King Lear, Macbeth, and Romeo and Juliet. A dramatic staircase connects all three levels, and fat support pillars obstruct many sight lines. All three dining rooms have the same menus and food. When you book, choose one of two seatings, or 'My Time Dining' (eat when you want, during dining-room hours). Tables are for four, six, eight, 10, or 12, and place settings, china, and cutlery are of good quality.

The menu descriptions make the food sound better than it is, and the selection of breads, fruit, and cheese is poor. Overall, meals are rather hit and miss – in fact it's unmemorable. Also, if you want lobster or a decent filet mignon (steak) you will be asked to pay extra.

Other dining options. Promenade Café: for Continental breakfast, all-day pizzas (Sorrento's), sandwiches, and coffee in paper cups or plastic mugs.

Windjammer Café: this is a large, sprawling venue for casual buffet-style, self-help breakfast (this tends to be the busiest time of the day), lunch, and light dinners (but not on the last night of the cruise); it's often difficult to find a table and by the time you do your food could be cold. This venue bears the brunt of many passenger complaints regarding poor, lukewarm food, and non-caring staff.

Jade 'Restaurant' (it's actually a section of the Windjammer Café) is the spot for casual Asian-themed food.

Portofino: a Euro-Italian specialty restaurant, open for dinner only. Reservations are required, and a there's a cover charge. The menu, which doesn't change during the cruise, includes antipasti, soup, salad, pasta, main dish, dessert, cheese, and coffee.

Chops Grille: an intimate specialty restaurant for steaks and seafood. There's a cover charge and reservations are required.

Johnny Rockets: a retro 1950s all-day, all-night diner-style eatery that serves hamburgers, hot dogs, and other fast-food, and malt shakes, with both indoor and outdoor seating. All indoor tables have a mini-jukebox; dimes are provided for you to make your selection of vintage records. The all-singing, all-dancing waitresses will knock your socks off, if you can stand the volume. There's a cover charge, and it's located near Adventure Ocean on the starboard side of Deck 12.

Sprinkles: for round-the-clock ice cream and yoghurt, pastries, and coffee.

ENTERTAINMENT. The 1,350-seat Alhambra Theater – the ship's stunning showlounge – is located at the forward end of the ship. It spans five decks in height, with only a few slim pillars and almost no disruption of sight lines. The room has a hydraulic orchestra pit and huge stage area, together with sonic-boom loud sound, and good lighting equipment.

SPA/FITNESS. A large Independence Day Spa includes an aerobics room, fitness center, private massage/body treatment rooms, men's and women's sauna/steam rooms, and relaxation areas. Some basic exercise classes are free, but the good ones such as yoga and personal training cost extra.

Insignia
★★★★

Size:	Small Ship	
Tonnage:	30,277	
Lifestyle:	Premium	
Cruise Line:	Oceania Cruises	
Former Names:	Columbus 2, Insignia, R One	
IMO Number:	9156462	
Builder:	Chantiers de l'Atlantique	
Original Cost:	$150 million	
Entered Service:	Jul 1998/Apr 2014	
Registry:	Marshall Islands	
Length (ft/m):	593.7/181.0	
Beam (ft/m):	83.5/25.5	
Draft (ft/m):	19.5/6.0	
Propulsion/Propellers:	diesel (18,600kW)/2	
Passenger Decks:	9	
Total Crew:	386	
Passengers (lower beds):	684	
Passenger Space Ratio (lower beds):	44.2	

Passenger/Crew Ratio (lower beds):	1.7
Cabins (total):	342
Size Range (sq ft/m):	145.3–968.7/13.5–90.0
Cabins (for one person):	0
Cabins (with private balcony):	232
Cabins (wheelchair accessible):	3
Wheelchair accessibility:	Good
Cabin Current:	110 and 220 volts
Elevators:	4
Casino (gaming tables):	No
Slot Machines:	No
Swimming Pools:	1
Hot Tubs (on deck):	2 (+ 1 thalassotherapy tub)
Self-Service Launderette:	Yes
Dedicated Cinema/Seats:	No
Library:	Yes
Onboard currency:	US$

This compact, contemporary ship is good for worldwide cruising

OVERVIEW. This ship is suitable for couples who like good food and style, but want informality, and interesting itineraries at a price well below what the luxury ships charge. Oceania Cruises provides a high level of food and service in an informal setting that's elegant yet comfortable and welcoming, with almost no announcements.

THE SHIP. *Insignia* was one of a series of almost identical ships built for the now-defunct Renaissance Cruises. The all-white ship has a large, square funnel, and a very pleasant lido and pool deck outdoors, with teak overlaid decking and high-quality lounge chairs. In 2014, the ship underwent a refurbishment program that included the addition of Barista's coffee bar (for *illy* coffees), installed completely new bathrooms for the Owner's Suites and Vista Suites, and updated the decor in all other cabins. Also added were a miniature golf course, shuffleboard courts, and other deck games.

Although there's no walk-around promenade deck outdoors, there is a jogging track around the perimeter of the swimming pool, and on the port and starboard side of a lower deck.

The interior decor is quite lovely, a throwback to the ship decor of the ocean liners of the 1920s and '30s, with dark woods and warm colors, all in fine taste – though a bit 'faux' in places. This includes detailed ceiling cornices, both real and faux wrought-iron staircase balustrades, leather-paneled walls, trompe l'oeil ceilings, rich carpeting in hallways, and many other interesting expensive-looking decorative

Berlitz's Ratings	Possible	Achieved
Ship	500	400
Accommodation	200	153
Food	400	310
Service	400	295
Entertainment	100	74
Cruise Experience	400	309
OVERALL SCORE		
1541 points out of 2000		

touches. The decor is reminiscent of an old-world country club.

The public rooms are spread over three decks. The reception hall has a staircase with an intricate wrought-iron balustrade, a scaled-down version of *Titanic*'s First-class staircase. A large Horizon Lounge is located high atop ship; it's a long bar with forward ocean views (at least for the barman), lots of seating, and a dance floor.

There are plenty of bars – including one in each of the restaurant entrances. Perhaps the nicest is Martinis, a lovely room reminiscent of Europe's grand hotels. It has an inviting marble fireplace, comfortable sofas, individual armchairs, and a dance floor.

The Library is a stunning Regency-style room, with a fireplace, a high, indented, trompe l'oeil ceiling, and an excellent selection of books, plus very comfortable wingback chairs with footstools, and sofas you could sleep on.

There may not be marble bathroom fittings, but the value for money is good. Note that a rather large 18 percent gratuity is added to bar purchases. The dress code is informal. *Insignia* started cruising again for Oceania Cruises in mid-April 2014 following a two-year charter to Hapag-Lloyd Cruises as *Columbus 2*.

ACCOMMODATION. There are nine cabin categories and price grades. The standard interior and outside-view cabins (the lowest four grades) are rather compact units – tight for two persons, particularly for longer cruises. They have twin beds or queen-size bed, with good under-bed storage areas, personal safe, vanity desk with large mirror, good closet and drawer space in rich, dark woods, 100 percent cotton bathrobe and towels, slippers, clothes brush, and shoehorn.

Suite occupants get Bulgari bathroom amenities and other goodies, complimentary shoeshine, cashmere throw blanket, bottle of Champagne on arrival, hand-held hairdryer, and priority restaurant reservations.

Owner's Suites (6). Measuring 968.7 sq ft (90 sq m), these are the most spacious accommodation. They are outstanding, decadent, and exclusive living spaces located aft overlooking the stern on Decks 6, 7, and 8. Each has extensive teak-floor private balconies that really are private and can't be overlooked from the decks above. Each has an entrance foyer, living room, separate bedroom (the bed faces the sea, which can be seen through the floor-to-ceiling windows and sliding glass door), CD player, fully tiled bathroom with Jacuzzi tub, and a small guest bathroom.

Vista Suites (4). Measuring 785.7 sq ft (73 sq m), these are located forward on Decks 5 and 6. They have extensive teak-floor private balconies that can't be overlooked from the decks above. The layout is similar to the Owner's Suites except that there is no guest bathroom.

Penthouse Suites (52). These measure about 322.9 sq ft (30 sq m). They are not really suites, but large cabins because the bedrooms aren't separate from the living areas. They have a good-size teak-floor balcony with sliding glass door (but with partial, and not full, balcony partitions) and teak deck furniture. The lounge area has a proper dining table and there is ample clothes storage space. The bathroom has a tub, shower enclosure, washbasin, and toilet.

Cabins with balcony. Cabins with private balconies (about 216 sq ft/20 sq m) comprise about two-thirds of all cabins. They have partial, not full, balcony partitions and sliding glass doors, and 14 cabins on Deck 6 have lifeboat-obstructed views and no balcony. The living area has a refrigerated minibar, lounge area with breakfast table, and a balcony with teak floor, two teak chairs, and a drinks table. The bathrooms, with tiled floors and plain walls, are compact, standard units, and include a shower stall with a strong, removable hand-held shower unit, hairdryer, toiletries storage shelves, and retractable clothesline.

Outside-view and interior cabins. These measure around 160–165 sq ft (14.8–15.3 sq m) and have twin beds (convertible to a queen-size bed), van-ity desk, small sofa and coffee table, and bathroom with a shower enclosure with a strong, removable hand-held shower unit, hairdryer, toiletries storage shelves, retractable clothesline, washbasin, and toilet. Although they are not large, they are quite comfortable, with decent storage space.

DINING. Flexibility and choice are what the dining facilities are about. There are four restaurants:

The Grand Dining Room has around 320 seats and a raised central section. There are large ocean-view windows on three sides, with prime tables overlooking the stern. The chairs are comfortable and have armrests.

Toscana Italian Restaurant has 96 seats, windows along two sides, and a set menu.

Polo Grill has 98 seats, windows along two sides, and a set menu including prime steaks and seafood.

The Lido Café, a self-serve buffet venue, has both indoor and outdoor seating; it is open for breakfast, lunch, and casual dinners (including Tapas on the Terrace). It has a small pizzeria and grill.

All restaurants have open-seating dining, so you can dine when you want, with whom you wish. Reservations are needed in Toscana Restaurant and Polo Grill, where there are mostly tables for four or six; there are few tables for two. Unlike other same-size ships in the same class, there's no extra charge. There is also a Poolside Grill outdoors. On days at sea, afternoon teatime is present in the Horizon Lounge, with formally dressed staff, cake display trolleys, and a selection of different teas.

ENTERTAINMENT. The Insignia Lounge presents (mini-show) entertainment, cabaret, lectures, and some social events. There is also live music in several bars and lounges.

SPA/FITNESS. A Lido Deck has a swimming pool and good sunbathing space, plus a thalassotherapy tub. A jogging track encircles the swimming pool deck (one deck above). The uppermost outdoors deck includes a golf driving net and shuffleboard court. The Canyon Ranch SpaClub consists of a beauty salon, three treatment rooms, men's and women's changing rooms, steam room (but no sauna), and a good range of body treatments. Note that an 18 percent gratuity is added for spa and beauty treatments and services.

Island Escape
★★+

Size:	Mid-size Ship
Tonnage:	40,132
Lifestyle:	Standard
Cruise Line:	Island Cruises
Former Names:	*Viking Serenade, Stardancer, Scandinavia*
IMO Number:	8002597
Builder:	Dubigeon-Normandie (France)
Original Cost:	$100 million
Entered Service:	Oct 1982/Apr 2009
Registry:	Bahamas
Length (ft/m):	623.0/189.8
Beam (ft/m):	88.6/27.0
Draft (ft/m):	23.6/7.2
Propulsion/Propellers:	diesel (19,800kW)/2
Passenger Decks:	10
Total Crew:	540
Passengers (lower beds):	1,504
Passenger Space Ratio (lower beds):	26.6

Passenger/Crew Ratio (lower beds):	2.7
Cabins (total):	757
Size Range (sq ft/m):	143.1–398.2/13.3–37.0
Cabins (for one person):	0
Cabins (with private balcony):	5
Cabins (wheelchair accessible):	3
Wheelchair accessibility:	None
Cabin Current:	110 volts
Elevators:	5
Casino (gaming tables):	Yes
Slot Machines:	Yes
Swimming Pools:	1
Hot Tubs (on deck):	0
Self-Service Launderette:	No
Dedicated Cinema/Seats:	No
Library:	Yes
Onboard currency:	UK£

This is a laid-back, family-friendly, no-frills ship

OVERVIEW. This is so-called 'all-inclusive' cruising in comfortable, unpretentious surroundings that are dated but comfortable, with a totally relaxed ambience that appeals to anyone looking for a casual first cruise with plenty of life and entertainment, food that is quantity rather than quality, and a modest price. In summer the ship operates one-week cruises specifically for the British family market.

Berlitz's Ratings

	Possible	Achieved
Ship	500	270
Accommodation	200	106
Food	400	200
Service	400	233
Entertainment	100	53
Cruise Experience	400	173

OVERALL SCORE
1035 points out of 2000

THE SHIP. *Island Escape*, originally built for a cruise-ferry service between New York and Freeport, Bahamas, was extensively reconstructed in 1991 to become a full-fledged cruise ship. Today it is run by Island Cruises, which itself is owned and operated by Thomson Cruises, part of the TUI group. This is the company's most laid-back ship.

It has only a token bow, a fairly decent amount of open deck and sunbathing space, and a pool (more a 'dip' pool) with a sliding glass dome that can be used in case of inclement weather. It suffers from having an extremely boxy, angular shape with a short, stubby funnel, and has a 'sponson' skirt that goes around the stern at the waterline – this is required for stability reasons.

Inside, the accommodation is mostly located forward, while the public rooms are mostly in the aft third of the ship. There is a decent number of public rooms and facilities, including six bars, and a lounge/discotheque is cantilevered around the funnel with good ocean views. The decor employs tasteful colors and furnishings of decent quality, though some have seen better days. Other facilities include an Internet-connection center, and a coffee/pastry shop with three Internet computer stations. The ceilings in many public areas and accommodation hallways are quite low – a legacy of the ship's original role as a cruise-ferry.

Vacations can be extended with a 'cruise-and-stay' package, with special pricing to make an extended break more affordable. If you book two cruises back-to-back, some entertainment may be repeated for the second week. Children should enjoy themselves with Palmy, a character they can eat with, and there are well-supervised activities.

Background music is played almost everywhere inside the ship and on deck around the pool, making it difficult to find quiet spots to relax, chill out, or simply read a book. Passenger participation events tend to be quite amateurish. Standing in line for embarkation, disembarkation, shore tenders, and for self-serve buffet meals can be frustrating.

In March 2013, the ship became an 'all-inclusive' product, with drinks, gratuities and service charges included, which makes it easier for families with children – no worries. However, the drink brands are poor. Cruise-and-stay vacations were introduced at the same time. In my professional view, this ship does what it says on the tin, but there are actually many extra charges (for example, if you want better-quality drink brands, a bottle of water, a safe deposit box, or a sandwich in the coffee bar).

Niggles include the fact that excursions and bingo cards are expensive.

ACCOMMODATION. There are just six categories, so choosing the right one shouldn't be difficult. The price will depend on grade, size, and location. The cabins, however, are quite small, with little closet space, so take as few changes of clothes as possible. They are moderately appointed with soft furnishings that are very cheerful, with upbeat colors.

Almost all cabins have twin beds that can be pushed together to form a queen-size bed; some cabins have an L-shaped arrangement, with immovable beds. All grades have a TV set, telephone, and three-channel radio, dressing table, and mirror. There are many interior cabins, and drawers and other storage space is extremely limited. If you'd like more space, it's best to go for one of the suite categories. Room service is available 24 hours a day, at extra cost.

The cabin bathrooms are really small, so you can expect to dance with the shower curtain, and only some of the accommodation designated as suites have a bathtub. Eleven outside-view cabins have even numbers, and all interior cabins have odd numbers. Also, if you are cruising with young children, there's almost no space for baby strollers. If, after looking at the deck plans, you want to book a specific cabin number, it currently costs extra.

Some cabins have extra Pullman upper berths – good for families with young children. An in-cabin room service menu is available, but all items cost extra.

Island Suite. Towards the aft on the port side, this is the largest accommodation. Although it doesn't have a balcony, it's relatively spacious. There's a walk-in closet, and minibar/refrigerator. The bathroom has a tub and shower.

Club Suites. Five other cabins with balconies at the stern are designated as suites. These have great views over the wash created by the ship's propellers, although they may be subject to a little occasional vibration. A tub and shower are provided in the marble-clad bathroom, and there's a walk-in closet in the sleeping area, and minibar/refrigerator and entertainment center in the living room. Additionally, another two suites (without balcony or bathtub) are located in the forward third of the ship one deck lower than the aft-facing suites, but with the same facilities.

DINING. The Island Restaurant, the main dining room, has ocean-view windows on two sides, and upbeat decor. There are tables for two to eight. Open for breakfast, lunch, and dinner, you serve yourself from the buffets. Although there is much repetition of salad items for lunch, there are plenty of main dish and dessert choices. There is a variety of British-style food on the menus.

Other dining options. Oasis is a smaller, more intimate, quieter restaurant, one deck below the Island Restaurant. This à-la-carte, extra-cost dining spot, with seats for two or four, is open only for dinner (reservations required), with full waiter service for all courses. The wine list is typical of a high-street eatery, with European prices that provide decent value for money.

The ceiling is low in both venues, which provides a sense of intimacy, but the noise level is intense.

For breakfast, lunch, and dinner – in fact, 24 hours a day – there is another place to go: the Beachcomber Café. It's really casual, and ideal for grabbing a bite to eat while taking the sun on the open decks. Again, it's a self-serve buffet, with food being constantly refreshed. Tea and coffee are provided at a beverage station, with plastic cups and mugs. Additionally, there's Café Brazil for pastries, extremely sinful cakes and pastries, and a range of espresso and cappuccino coffees, all at extra cost.

ENTERTAINMENT. The Ocean Theater is a single-level showlounge, with banquette and individual seating surrounding a thrust stage. Although it is a comfortable room, several pillars obstruct sight lines from some seats.

A resident troupe of young, enthusiastic singer/dancers provide the low-budget revue-style 'shows' that are, at best, amateurish, with weak recorded tracks but lots of color. Also, visiting cabaret acts – typically strong singers, magicians, and smutty comedians – are presented, both in their own shows and as the middle of a 'pie' that includes the ship's resident troupe.

There is a ship's band, and several small musical units and pianists provide live music for dancing and listening in the bars and lounges. There's a also throbbing disco.

SPA/FITNESS. The Ship Shape Hair and Beauty Spa is surprisingly good for the size of the ship. There are treatment rooms for massage, separate saunas and changing rooms for men and women, and a large beauty salon. The gymnasium is quite large and contains lots of muscle-pumping equipment. It is located just aft of the main swimming pool on the port side of the ship.

The spa is run by concessionaire Harding Brothers, and treatments offered include massages, aromatherapy facials, manicures, pedicures, and hair treatments.

Island Princess
★★★★

Size:	....	Mid-size Ship
Tonnage:	....	91,627
Lifestyle:	....	Standard
Cruise Line:	....	Princess Cruises
Former Names:	....	none
IMO Number:	....	9230402
Builder:	....	Chantiers de l'Atlantique (France)
Original Cost:	....	$360 million
Entered Service:	....	Jun 2003
Registry:	....	Bermuda
Length (ft/m):	....	964.5/294.0
Beam (ft/m):	....	105.6/32.2
Draft (ft/m):	....	26/7.9
Propulsion/Propellers:	......	gas turbine + diesel (40,000kW)/2
Passenger Decks:	....	11
Total Crew:	....	900
Passengers (lower beds):	....	1,974
Passenger Space Ratio (lower beds):	....	46.4
Passenger/Crew Ratio (lower beds):	....	2.1
Cabins (total):	....	987
Size Range (sq ft/m):	....	156–470.0/14.4–43.6
Cabins (for one person):	....	0
Cabins (with private balcony):	....	727
Cabins (wheelchair accessible):	....	20
Wheelchair accessibility:	....	Good
Cabin Current:	....	110 volts
Elevators:	....	14
Casino (gaming tables):	....	Yes
Slot Machines:	....	Yes
Swimming Pools:	....	2
Hot Tubs (on deck):	....	5
Self-Service Launderette:	....	Yes
Dedicated Cinema/Seats:	....	No
Library:	....	Yes
Onboard currency:	....	US$

A comfortable contemporary ship for mature-age cruisers

OVERVIEW. The layout is user-friendly aboard this rather pleasant, pencil-slim ship.

THE SHIP. *Island Princess* has an instantly recognizable funnel due to two jet engine-like pods that sit high up on its structure, but these really are mainly for decoration. Four diesel engines provide the generating power. Electrical power is provided by a combination of four diesel and one gas turbine (CODAG) unit; the diesel engines are located in the engine room, while the gas turbine unit is located in the ship's funnel housing. The ship also has three bow thrusters and three stern thrusters.

Island Princess has two decks full of public rooms, lounges, and bars instead of just one. Sensibly, there are three major stair towers for passengers with plenty of elevators for easy access.

A large 'Movies Under the Stars' screen is located in the second of two pool areas on the open deck just forward of the funnel. Adults using the 'Sanctuary' area have their own splash pool. Walkers will like the ship's full walk-around exterior promenade deck.

Despite the ship's size, it's actually easy to find one's way around quickly – due to good design and its practical layout. Facilities include a flower shop where you can order flowers and Godiva chocolates for cabin delivery – nice for a birthday or anniversary – a pleasant cigar and cognac lounge (Churchill Lounge), and a Martini bar (Crooners). The casino has a London theme, and both gaming tables and slot machines.

Berlitz's Ratings		
	Possible	Achieved
Ship	500	379
Accommodation	200	144
Food	400	255
Service	400	290
Entertainment	100	77
Cruise Experience	400	292
OVERALL SCORE		
1437 points out of 2000		

An AOL Internet Café is conveniently located on the top level of the four-deck-high lobby. Adjacent is the Wedding Chapel, with a live web-cam to relay ceremonies via the Internet. The captain can legally marry American couples, thanks to the ship's registry and a special dispensation. The Wedding Chapel can host renewal of vows ceremonies, for a fee.

This ship has lots of nooks and crannies – so you can hide away and just read a book if you want to. Also, at the forward end of Decks 10 and 11, doors open onto a large observation terrace. There are also several self-service launderettes.

Niggles include the fact that the forward elevators go between Decks 15 and 7, but you will need to change elevators to get down to the dining rooms on Deck 5 (strangely, the 'panoramic' elevators go only between Decks 5 and 8; passengers do find this a trifle confusing, but it's all about the way the layout and flow has to work – from a designer's point of view, that is).

ACCOMMODATION. There are numerous price categories, in six types: 16 suites with balcony (470 sq ft/43.6 sq m); 184 mini-suites with balcony (285–302 sq ft/26.4–28 sq m); eight mini-suites without balcony (300 sq ft/27.8 sq m); 527 outside-view cabins with balcony (217–232 sq ft/ 20.1–21.5 sq m); 144 standard outside-view cabins (162 sq ft/15 sq m); 108 interior cabins (156 sq ft/144.5 sq m). There are also 20 wheelchair-accessible cabins (217–374 sq ft/20.1–34.7 sq m).

Almost all outside-view cabins have a private balcony. Some cabins can accommodate a third, or third and fourth person. Some cabins on Emerald Deck (Deck 8) have a view obstructed by lifeboats. The decor is earth tones. All cabins have a personal safe, hair dryer, small 'fridge, television, and premium-quality bedding.

Suites (16). Each has a private balcony. All suites are located on either Deck 9 or Deck 10. In a departure from many ships, *Island Princess* doesn't have any suites or cabins with a view of the stern. There are four Premium Suites, located sensibly in the center of the ship, adjacent to a bank of six elevators. Farther aft are six other suites (Veranda Suites).

All Accommodation. Suites and cabins have a refrigerator, personal safe, TV set with audio channels, hairdryer, satellite-dial telephone, and twin beds that convert to a queen-size bed (there are a few exceptions). All accommodation has a bathroom with shower enclosure and toilet. Accommodation designated as suites and mini-suites (there are seven price categories) have a bathtub and separate shower enclosure, and two TV sets.

All passengers receive turndown service and chocolates on pillows each night, bathrobes on request, and toiletry kits. Most outside-view cabins on Emerald Deck have views obstructed by lifeboats. There are no cabins for solo travelers. Nor are there butlers – even for the top-grade suites. Cabin attendants have too many cabins to look after (typically 20).

DINING. The two main dining rooms, Bordeaux and Provence, are in the forward section of the ship on the two lowest passenger decks. Both are almost identical – the ceilings are quite low, and have plenty of intimate alcoves and cozy dining spots, with tables for two, four, six, or eight. There are two seatings for dinner (or you can opt for 'Anytime' Dining in the Bordeaux Restaurant), while breakfast and lunch are on an open-seating basis; you may have to wait for some while at peak times.

Other dining options. There are two extra-charge restaurants: Sabatini's and the Bayou Café, both enclosed and both requiring reservations. Sabatini's, with colorful tiled Mediterranean-style decor, has Italian-style pizzas and pastas, with a variety of sauces, as well as Italian-style entrées including tiger prawns and lobster tail, all provided with flair and entertainment by the waiters. The food is both creative and tasty. There is a cover charge for lunch or dinner on sea days only.

The Bayou Café, open for lunch and dinner, has a cover charge that includes a Hurricane cocktail. It evokes the charm of New Orleans' French Quarter, with wrought-iron decoration, and features Cajun/Creole cuisine. Platters include Peel 'n' Eat Shrimp Piquante, Sausage Grillades, Oysters Sieur de Bienville. Popular entrées include premium steaks, Seafood Gumbo, and Chorizo Jambalaya, plus Alligator Ribs, Corn Meal Fried Catfish, Blackened Chicken Brochette, and Red Pepper Butter Broiled Lobster. Desserts include sweet potato pie and banana whiskey pound cake. The venue has a small stage, with baby grand piano and live jazz is part of the evening dining scenario.

Horizon Court, a casual 24-hour eatery, is in the forward section of Lido Deck with superb ocean views. Self-serve counters provide food for breakfast and lunch buffets, and bistro-style casual dinners are available each evening. Sadly, there's just not enough seating for the number of passengers using the facility.

Also, La Pâtisserie, in the reception lobby, is a coffee, cakes, and pastries spot and good for informal meetings. There's also a pizzeria, hamburger grill, and an ice cream bar (extra charge for the ice cream).

ENTERTAINMENT. The Princess Theater is two decks high, and, unusually, there is much more seating in the upper level than on the main floor below. Princess Cruises prides itself on its colourful Hollywood-style production shows.

A second entertainment venue, the Universe Lounge, is more for cabaret-style features. It also has two levels, and three separate stages, enabling non-stop entertainment to be provided without constant set-ups. Some 50 of the room's seats are equipped with a built-in laptop computer. The room is also used for cooking demonstrations (it has a full kitchen set), and other participation activities.

Princess Cruises always provides plenty of live music in bars and lounges, with a wide mix of light classical, jazz, and dance music, from solo entertaining pianists to showbands, and volume is normally kept to an acceptable level.

Those craving education can learn aboard ship with the ScholarShip@Sea program, which includes about 20 courses per cruise (six on any given day at sea). Although all introductory classes are free, fees apply if you want to continue any chosen subject in a smaller setting. There are four core subjects: culinary arts, visual/creative arts, photography, and computer technology. A full culinary demonstration kitchen set is built into the Universe Lounge (it's also used for wine tastings), and there's a pottery studio with kiln.

SPA/FITNESS. The Lotus Spa is located aft on one of the ship's uppermost decks. It contains men's and women's saunas, steam rooms, changing rooms, relaxation area, beauty salon, aerobics exercise room, and gymnasium with aft-facing ocean views, with high-tech muscle-pumping, cardiovascular equipment. There are several large rooms for individual treatments.

Sports enthusiasts will find a nine-hole golf putting course, two computerized golf simulators, and a sports court.

Island Sky

★★★★+

Size:	Boutique Ship	Passenger/Crew Ratio (lower beds):	1.7
Tonnage:	4,280	Cabins (total):	59
Lifestyle:	Standard	Size Range (sq ft/m):	234.6–353.0/21.8–32.8
Cruise Line:	Noble Caledonia	Cabins (for one person):	0
Former Names:	Sky, Renai II, Renaissance VIII	Cabins (with private balcony):	4
IMO Number:	8802894	Cabins (wheelchair accessible):	0
Builder:	Nuovi Cantieri Appaunia (Italy)	Wheelchair accessibility:	None
Original Cost:	$25 million	Cabin Current:	110 volts
Entered Service:	Dec 1991/May 2004	Elevators:	1
Registry:	The Bahamas	Casino (gaming tables):	No
Length (ft/m):	297.2/90.6	Slot Machines:	No
Beam (ft/m):	50.1/15.3	Swimming Pools:	0
Draft (ft/m):	12.9/2.9	Hot Tubs (on deck):	1
Propulsion/Propellers:	diesel (5000kW)/2	Self-Service Launderette:	No
Passenger Decks:	5	Dedicated Cinema/Seats:	No
Total Crew:	66	Library:	Yes
Passengers (lower beds):	122	Onboard currency:	UK£
Passenger Space Ratio (lower beds):	35.0		

A delightful small ship for life-enrichment cruises

OVERVIEW. This comfortable, intimate ship operates in areas devoid of large cruise ships. Although not quite matching the standard of Seabourn or Silversea ships, it provides a fine cruise experience at a moderate cost. It suits seasoned travelers who like a relaxed lifestyle, good food and service, and an itinerary that promises 'get away from it all, but in comfort.'

THE SHIP. *Island Sky* has contemporary mega-yacht looks and handsome styling, with twin flared funnels that give it a smart profile, and a 'ducktail' (sponson) stern that provides stability and seagoing comfort. This ship was originally built as one of a series of eight similar ships for the now-defunct Renaissance Cruises. It was completely refurbished in 2010.

There is a narrow teak walk-around promenade deck outdoors, and a reasonable amount of open deck and sunbathing space. The ship has a fleet of Zodiac inflatables for shore landings.

Inside, the interior design is elegant, with polished wood-finish paneling throughout. There is a very small library with two Internet-connect workstations. Gratuities are included, as are house wine, beer, and soft drinks during lunch and dinner.

ACCOMMODATION. The spacious cabins combine highly polished imitation rosewood paneling

Berlitz's Ratings

	Possible	Achieved
Ship	500	397
Accommodation	200	161
Food	400	317
Service	400	307
Entertainment	100	70
Cruise Experience	400	317
OVERALL SCORE		
1569 points out of 2000		

with lots of mirrors and hand-crafted furniture, lighted walk-in closets, three-sided vanity mirrors – in fact, there are a lot of mirrored surfaces in the decor – and just about everything you need, including a refrigerator, a TV set and player, and Wi-Fi access. The bathrooms are extremely compact; they have real teakwood floors and marble vanities, and shower enclosures, but none have tubs, not even the Owner's Suite. All were replaced in a 2010 refit.

DINING. The dining room operates with open seating for all meals. Small, but quite smart, it has tables for two, four, six, and eight. You sit where you like, with whom you like, and at what time you like. The meals are self-service, buffet-style foods for breakfast and lunch, with hot foods chosen from a table menu and served properly. The dining room operation works well. The food quality, choice, and presentation are all very decent.

ENTERTAINMENT. There is no formal entertainment in the main lounge, the venue for all social activities. Six pillars obstruct sight lines to the small stage area.

SPA/FITNESS. Facilities include an aft platform, and Zodiac inflatable craft.

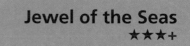

Jewel of the Seas
★★★+

Size:	Large Resort Ship	Passenger/Crew Ratio (lower beds):	2.4
Tonnage:	90,090	Cabins (total):	1,055
Lifestyle:	Standard	Size Range (sq ft/m):	165.8–1,216.3/15.4–113.0
Cruise Line:	Royal Caribbean International	Cabins (for one person):	0
Former Names:	none	Cabins (with private balcony):	577
IMO Number:	9228356	Cabins (wheelchair accessible):	14
Builder:	Meyer Werft (Germany)	Wheelchair accessibility:	Good
Original Cost:	$350 million	Cabin Current:	110 volts
Entered Service:	Jun 2004	Elevators:	9
Registry:	The Bahamas	Casino (gaming tables):	Yes
Length (ft/m):	961.9/293.2	Slot Machines:	Yes
Beam (ft/m):	105.6/32.2	Swimming Pools:	2
Draft (ft/m):	27.8/8.5	Hot Tubs (on deck):	3
Propulsion/Propellers:	gas turbine (39,000kW)/2 azimuthing pods	Self-Service Launderette:	No
Passenger Decks:	12	Dedicated Cinema/Seats:	Yes/40
Total Crew:	858	Library:	Yes
Passengers (lower beds):	2,110	Onboard currency:	US$
Passenger Space Ratio (lower beds):	42.9		

This large resort ship is for family-friendly casual cruising

OVERVIEW. This ship is best suited to young-minded adult couples, solo travelers, and families with children of all ages – toddlers to teenagers – who like to mingle in a large ship setting with plenty of city-like life and high-energy entertainment. The food is acceptable, stressing quantity rather than quality, unless you pay extra to dine in the specialty restaurant.

Berlitz's Ratings		
	Possible	Achieved
Ship	500	380
Accommodation	200	141
Food	400	242
Service	400	279
Entertainment	100	74
Cruise Experience	400	271
OVERALL SCORE		
1387 points out of 2000		

THE SHIP. *Jewel of the Seas* is a streamlined, contemporary ship, with a two-deck-high wraparound structure (Viking Crown Lounge) in the forward section of the funnel. Along the starboard side, a central glass wall protrudes, giving great views – cabins with balconies occupy the space directly opposite on the port side. The gently rounded stern has nicely tiered decks, which gives the ship an extremely well-balanced look.

As aboard almost all new cruise ships today, the navigation bridge is of the fully enclosed type. In the very front of the ship is a helipad, which also acts as a viewing platform. Pod propulsion power is provided.

Inside, the decor is contemporary, yet elegant, bright and cheerful, designed for young, active types. The artwork is quite eclectic and provides a spectrum and a half of color works. The interior focal point is a nine-deck high atrium lobby with glass-walled elevators that travel through 12 decks, face the sea, and provide a link with nature and the ocean. The Centrum, as the atrium is called, has several public rooms connected to it: the guest relations and shore excursions desks, a lobby bar, a Champagne bar, a small library, Royal Caribbean Online (an Internet center with 12 computers), a Concierge Club, and a Crown & Anchor Lounge. A great view can be had of the atrium by looking down through the flat glass dome high above it.

Other facilities include a large Schooner Bar that houses maritime art in an integral art gallery, and a rather large, noisy, and colorful Casino Royale. There's also a small dedicated screening room for movies (with space for two wheelchairs), as well as a 194-seat conference center, and a business center.

This ship also contains a Viking Crown Lounge, a large structure set around the base of the ship's funnel. It functions as an observation lounge during the daytime, with views forward over the swimming pool. In the evening, the space morphs into a high-energy dance club, as well as a more intimate and relaxed entertainment venue for softer mood music and 'black box' theater.

The very comfortable *Jewel of the Seas* offers more space, more comfortable public areas and several more intimate spaces, slightly larger cabins, and more dining options than most of the larger ships in the Royal Caribbean International fleet. A 15 percent gratuity is automatically added to all bar and spa bills.

Niggles? There are no cushioned pads for sun-loungers, and the deck towels are quite thin and small. It is virtually impossible to escape background music anywhere (it's even played in the hallway outside your cabin).

FAMILIES. Youth facilities include Adventure Ocean (it's on Deck 12), an 'edutainment' area with four separate age-appropriate sections for junior passengers: Aquanaut Center (for ages 3–5); Explorer Center (6–8); Voyager Center (9–12); and the Optix Teen Center (13–17). There is also Adventure Beach, with splash pool and water slide; Surfside, with computer lab stations with entertaining software; and Ocean Arcade, a video games hangout.

ACCOMMODATION. There's a wide range of suites and standard outside-view and interior cabins to suit different tastes, requirements, and depth of wallet, in 10 different categories and numerous price groups. There are 14 wheelchair-accessible cabins, eight of which have a private balcony.

Apart from the largest suites (six Owner's Suites), which have king-size beds, almost all other cabins have twin beds that convert to a queen-size bed. All cabins have rich but faux wood cabinetry, including a vanity desk with hairdryer, faux wood drawers that close silently (hooray), television, personal safe, and three-sided mirrors. Some cabins have ceiling-recessed, pull-down third and fourth berths, although closet and drawer space would be extremely tight. Some cabins have interconnecting doors, allowing families with children to cruise together in adjacent cabins. Audio channels are available through the TV set, so you can't switch off its picture while listening. Data ports are provided in all cabins.

Many 'private' balcony cabins aren't very private, as they can be overlooked by anyone standing in the port and starboard wings of the Solarium, and from other locations.

Most cabin bathrooms have tiled accenting and a terrazzo-style tiled floor, and a shower enclosure in a half-moon shape (it is rather small, however, considering the size of some passengers), Egyptian cotton towels, a small cabinet for toiletries and a small shelf. There is little space to stow toiletries for two or more.

The largest accommodation consists of a family suite with two bedrooms. One bedroom has twin beds that convert to a queen-size bed, while a second has two lower beds and two upper Pullman berths, a combination that can sleep up to eight persons – this would be suitable for large families.

Occupants of accommodation designated as suites also get the use of a private Concierge Lounge, where priority dining room reservations, shore excursion bookings, and beauty salon/spa appointments can be made.

DINING. Tides – the main dining room – spans two decks; the upper deck level has floor-to-ceiling windows, while the lower deck level has picture windows. It is a fine, but inevitably noisy dining hall and eight huge, thick pillars obstruct the sight lines.

It seats 1,222, and the decor has a cascading water theme. There are tables for two to 10, in two seatings for dinner. Two small private dining rooms (Illusions and Mirage) are located off the main dining room. There is an adequate wine list, with moderate prices.

Menu descriptions make the food sound better than it is, and the selection of breads, rolls, fruit, and cheese is poor. Overall, meals are rather hit and miss – in fact it's unmemorable. Additionally, if you want lobster or a decent filet mignon (steak) you will be asked to pay extra.

Other dining options. Extra-cost venues include Portofino, with 112 seats, offers Italian cuisine, and Chops Grille Steakhouse, with 95 seats and an open 'show' kitchen, serves premium meats in the form of chops and steaks. Both have food that is of a better quality than in the main dining room and are typically open 6–11pm. There is a cover charge, and reservations are required.

Casual breakfasts, lunches, and dinners can be taken in the self-serve, buffet-style Windjammer Café, which can be accessed directly from the pool deck. It has about 400 seats, and 'islands' for specific food types, and indoor and outdoor seating. Additionally, there is Seaview Café, open for lunch and dinner. You can choose from the self-serve buffet, or from the menu for casual, fast-food seafood items including fish sandwiches, fish 'n' chips, as well as non-seafood items such as hamburgers and hot dogs.

ENTERTAINMENT. Facilities include the three-level Coral Theater, the ship's large showlounge, with 874 seats, including 24 wheelchair stations. The sight lines are good from most seats due to steep tiers. A second entertainment venue is the Safari Club, which hosts cabaret shows, late-night adult comedy, and dancing to live music. All the ship's entertainment is upbeat – so much so that it's virtually impossible to get away from music and noise.

SPA/FITNESS. The Day Spa health and fitness facilities have themed decor, and include a 10,176-sq-ft (945-sq-m) solarium with whirlpool and counter current swimming under a retractable glass roof, a gymnasium with many cardiovascular machines, a 50-person aerobics room, sauna and steam rooms, and private massage/body treatment rooms. The facility is staffed and operated by Steiner Leisure.

For the sports-oriented, there are activities galore – including a 30ft (9m) -high rock-climbing wall with five separate climbing tracks. It's free, and all safety gear is included, but you'll need to sign up.

Other sports facilities include a nine-hole miniature golf course, and an indoor/outdoor country club with computer-controlled golf simulator, a jogging track, and basketball court. Want to play pool? You can, thanks to two special tables whose gyroscopic technology adjusts to the movement of the ship.

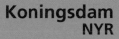

Koningsdam
NYR

Size:	Large Resort Ship	Passenger/Crew Ratio (lower beds):	2.5
Tonnage:	99,500	Cabins (total):	1,331
Lifestyle:	Standard	Size Range (sq ft/m):	127.0-1,291.1/11.7-120.0
Cruise Line:	Holland America Line	Cabins (for one person):	12
Former Names:	none	Cabins (with private balcony):	912
IMO Number:	n/a	Cabins (wheelchair accessible):	27
Builder:	Fincantieri (Italy)	Wheelchair accessibility:	Good
Original Cost:	$520 million	Cabin Current:	110 volts
Entered Service:	May 2016	Elevators:	12
Registry:	The Netherlands	Casino (gaming tables):	Yes
Length (ft/m):	983.5/299.8	Slot Machines:	Yes
Beam (ft/m):	114.8/35.0	Swimming Pools:	3 (1 w/sliding glass dome)
Draft (ft/m):	22.9/7.0	Hot Tubs (on deck):	5
Propulsion/Propellers:	diesel/2 azimuthing pods	Self-Service Launderette:	No
Passenger Decks:	12	Dedicated Cinema/Seats:	No
Total Crew:	1,025	Library:	Yes
Passengers (lower beds):	2,650	Onboard currency:	US$
Passenger Space Ratio (lower beds):	37.7		

Family-friendly ship with a good mix of modern and Dutch traditional

OVERVIEW. The first of what Holland America Line calls its 'Pinnacle'-class ships is a natural extension of the company's fleet, and includes a few more up-to-date features while maintaining the company's heritage.

THE SHIP. The exterior profile is not exactly handsome, but the single large funnel tries hard to balance the upper structure. The ship's name honors the first Dutch king in more than a century – King Willem-Alexander. It's the company's largest ship to date.

There is a complete walk-around exterior teak promenade deck, with hardwood steamer-style sunloungers, and a jogging track is located in the forward third of the ship and around its mast. Exterior glass elevators provide fine ocean views from any one of 10 decks. One of the two swimming pools outdoors can be used in inclement weather because of a retractable sliding glass roof. Two hot tubs, adjacent to the pools, are bridged by a bar. There's also a small pool for children.

Facilities (on two decks) include the Queen's Lounge (a lecture and demonstration room); a Culinary Arts Center, where cooking demonstrations are held; a large casino; and the Crow's Nest, an observation lounge and library; the Explorations Café; a shopping street; card room; art gallery; and meeting rooms.

FAMILIES. Club HAL's KidZone provides an area devoted to children's facilities, with extensive programming for different age groups (5–17), with one counselor for every 30 children. Free ice cream is provided at certain hours, plus hot hors d'oeuvres in bars.

Berlitz's Ratings

	Possible	Achieved
Ship	500	NYR
Accommodation	200	NYR
Food	400	NYR
Service	400	NYR
Entertainment	100	NYR
Cruise Experience	400	NYR
OVERALL SCORE		
NYR points out of 2000		

ACCOMMODATION. There are 35 different price categories for seven accommodation grades. Some 32 family-together cabins (222–231 sq ft/20.6–21.4 sq m) are a new feature for HAL. Also new are 12 single-occupancy cabins (127–172 sq ft/11.7–16.0 sq m). There's also the Grand Pinnacle suite (1,290 sq ft/119.8 sq m); two Neptune Spa suites and 43 Neptune suites ranging from 465–855 sq ft (43.1–79.4 sq m); 14 Signature suites (up to 400 sq ft/37 sq m); and Vista suites (260–356 sq ft/24.1–33 sq m).

DINING. The ship has a main dining room on two levels, with two seatings at set times. The dining room's focal point is a wine tower spanning two decks. HAL can provide Kosher meals (if ordered when you book).

Extra-cost dining includes: Pinnacle Grill, for premium steaks and grilled seafood items. Tamarind, for Asian 'fusion' cuisine; it includes a sushi bar. Canaletto, for Italian-style cuisine. Sel de Mer, a French-style seafood brasserie. Culinary Arts Center – a dinner bistro.

The Grand Dutch Café offers pastries and coffee, while for casual eating, the extensive Lido Café has indoor-outdoor seating and ocean views. Salad, stir-fry, and sushi sections are included, among others.

ENTERTAINMENT. The circular World Stage showlounge features a 270-degree LED-surround backdrop.

SPA/FITNESS. The Greenhouse Spa is a good-sized facility, including a hydrotherapy pool, unisex thermal suite, beauty salon, treatment rooms, and a large gym.

L'Austral
★★★★

Size:	Small Ship
Tonnage:	10,944
Lifestyle:	Premium
Cruise Line:	Ponant
Former Names:	none
IMO Number:	9502518
Builder:	Fincantieri (Italy)
Original Cost:	€110 million
Entered Service:	May 2011
Registry:	Wallis & Fortuna
Length (ft/m):	465.8/142.0
Beam (ft/m):	9.0/18.0
Draft (ft/m):	15.4/4.7
Propulsion/Propellers:	diesel-electric (4,600kW)/2
Passenger Decks:	6
Total Crew:	140
Passengers (lower beds):	264
Passenger Space Ratio (lower beds):	41.4

Passenger/Crew Ratio (lower beds):	1.5
Cabins (total):	132
Size Range (sq ft/m):	226.0–581.2/21.0–54.0
Cabins (for one person):	0
Cabins (with private balcony):	125
Cabins (wheelchair accessible):	3
Wheelchair accessibility:	Fair
Cabin Current:	110 and 220 volts
Elevators:	3
Casino (gaming tables):	No
Slot Machines:	Yes
Swimming Pools:	1
Hot Tubs (on deck):	0
Self-Service Launderette:	No
Dedicated Cinema/Seats:	No
Library:	Yes
Onboard currency:	Euros

A contemporary ship and style to suit French speakers

OVERVIEW. *L'Austral* is best suited to young-minded couples and solo travelers who enjoy sophisticated facilities in a relaxed but chic, premium, yacht-like environment quite different to most cruise ships, with very good food and decent service.

THE SHIP. One of four almost identical sister ships (the others are *Le Boréal, Le Lyrial,* and *Le Soléal*) catering to French speakers, *L'Austral* (South Wind) is a gem of contemporary, uncluttered design and chic details. With a dark gray hull and sleek white superstructure, it looks like a large private yacht rather than a traditional cruise ship. The passenger/space ratio, a healthy 53.5, decreases if the 40 suites that convert into 20 are all occupied by two persons.

L'Austral has a smart 'sponson' skirt built-in at the stern for operational stability, and carries a fleet of 12 Zodiac landing craft for soft expedition voyages. For Antarctic voyages, passenger numbers are kept to a maximum of 199. The ship does not, however, have boot storage lockers.

There is some sunbathing space outdoors forward of the funnel and around the small pool – aft of the casual eatery one deck below – together with one shower enclosure. Aft of the funnel is an outdoor bar (Copernico) and grill, but seating is limited.

Almost all public rooms are aft, with accommodation located forward; the elevators go to all decks except the uppermost one (Deck 7). The decor is minimalist and super-yacht chic – relaxing and pleasant, with lots of browns and creams and a splash of

Berlitz's Ratings		
	Possible	Achieved
Ship	500	406
Accommodation	200	155
Food	400	291
Service	400	301
Entertainment	100	74
Cruise Experience	400	300
OVERALL SCORE		
1527 points out of 2000		

red here and there. Glitz is entirely absent, although there are many reflective surfaces and the overall feeling of the decor is cool rather than warm.

The focal point is the main lobby, with a central, circular seating and tiled floor surround; its small central section spans two decks. The other flooring is wood, which can be noisy. The lower decks of the main stairway are made of faux gray wood, while the upper decks are carpeted – a strange combination that somehow works.

This is all-inclusive cruising – except for spa treatments – with drinks, table wine for lunch and dinner, bottled mineral water, port charges, and Zodiac excursions on expedition-style cruises all included in the fare. The crew is English- and French-speaking, with many hotel service staff from Asia. How delightful – cruise tickets are provided in a proper document pouch and sent to you (so, no digital frustration).

Passenger niggles? There's no outside walking or jogging deck. The interior stairways are a quite steep and have short steps. The restaurant is noisy. The entertainment system is not user-friendly and internet connection is slow and expensive. Overall, it's difficult for French-speaking and non-French-speaking passengers to mix.

ACCOMMODATION. Of the 132 suites/cabins, there are three Prestige Suites with 301 sq ft plus a 54-sq-ft balcony (28 plus 5 sq m). Forty of the 94 deluxe cabins – 200 sq ft plus a 43-sq-ft balcony (18.6 plus 4 sq m) – can be combined into 20 larger suites, each with two bathrooms, and separate living area and bedroom. All cabinetry is made in elegant dark woods. A real plus is that there are no interior (no-view) cabins – all cabins have a view of the outside, and cabin insulation is good.

Each deluxe and standard cabin has a large ocean-view window, two beds that convert to a queen-size bed, and a long vanity desk with good lighting. Facilities include a TV set, DVD player, refrigerator, and personal safe. The marble-appointed bathrooms have large, rather heavy hand-held shower hoses. Amenities include a minibar, personal safe, hairdryer, bathrobe, and French bathroom products. Wi-Fi costs extra.

All other cabins have good-size beds, although the corners of the bed frames are square, so you need to be careful when passing between the bed and the storage units – these are quite large, with two deep drawers. Other facilities include refrigerator, television, wall mirror, good-size wardrobe-style closet (armoire) with personal safe, and a vanity desk with drawer and a small shelf.

The small cabin bathrooms (the entrance door is only 20.5ins/52cm wide) also have a sliding partition window that enables you to see through the cabin to the ocean, and a deep, half-size tub/shower combination. The lip between floor and bathroom is just over 6ins (15cm) high. L'Occitane products are provided.

There are no shelves for toiletries, but there are two drawers under the washbasin – although they are not very practical. A separate cubicle houses the vacuum toilet. Balconies have faux wood decking and a fine (real) wood handrail, although solid paneling obstructs views when seated and makes the cabin seem dark – glass panels would have been nicer; the balconies are also narrow. The closet space is quite good, although the doors, with excellent white leather handles, are wide – at 31ins (79cm), they are wider than the cabin door, and can't be opened without first closing the bathroom and toilet doors that are directly opposite.

Good-quality bed linen, overlays, and cushions are provided, although there is no choice of pillows.

DINING. The main restaurant is chic but not pretentious. It accommodates all passengers in an open-seating arrangement and has two integral wine display cabinets (not temperature-controlled). The chairs are square and have thin armrests and low backs – but they look good. And the food? While appetizers and main course items are reasonably good but nothing special, the cakes and desserts are delightful.

A casual indoor/outdoor Grill (although there is no actual grill) has seating for up to 130, with self-serve buffet set-up for breakfast and lunch, and a 'fast grill' dinner in an alfresco setting. But the layout is disjointed, and the port and starboard sides are separated by two elevators. There are two main buffet display units (one for cold food, one for hot), and a separate table set-up for bread, and an active cooking station (eggs for breakfast, pasta dishes at lunchtime).

Veuve-Clicquot is the Champagne chosen by Ponant, a perfect example of French *savoir-faire*, and premium selections include Brut Carte Jaune, Rosé, and La Grande Dame varieties.

ENTERTAINMENT. French Line, the showlounge/ lecture hall, has amphitheater-style seating for 260, and a raised stage suited to concerts and cabaret. The production shows are weak, repetitive, and loud. The venue is also used for expert specialist lecturers, and expedition-style recaps. Two large pillars obstruct the sight lines from several seats.

SPA/FITNESS. The Yacht Spa facilities include a fitness room with starboard-side ocean views, adjacent kinetic wall, and a steam room, but there's no changing room. A wide range of massage and other body treatments are provided by Carita of Paris, which staffs and oversees the facility.

Le Boreal
★★★★

Size:	Small Ship	Passenger/Crew Ratio (lower beds):	1.5
Tonnage:	10,700	Cabins (total):	132
Lifestyle:	Premium	Size Range (sq ft/m):	226.0–581.2/21.0–54.0
Cruise Line:	Ponant	Cabins (for one person):	0
Former Names:	none	Cabins (with private balcony):	124
IMO Number:	9502506	Cabins (wheelchair accessible):	3
Builder:	Fincantieri (Italy)	Wheelchair accessibility:	Fair
Original Cost:	€115 million	Cabin Current:	110 and 220 volts
Entered Service:	May 2010	Elevators:	3
Registry:	Wallis & Fortuna	Casino (gaming tables):	No
Length (ft/m):	465.8/142.0	Slot Machines:	Yes
Beam (ft/m):	9.0/18.0	Swimming Pools:	1
Draft (ft/m):	15.4/4.7	Hot Tubs (on deck):	0
Propulsion/Propellers:	diesel-electric (4,600kW)/2	Self-Service Launderette:	No
Passenger Decks:	6	Dedicated Cinema/Seats:	No
Total Crew:	140	Library:	Yes
Passengers (lower beds):	264	Onboard currency:	Euros
Passenger Space Ratio (lower beds):	41.4		

This ship exudes French ambience and super-yacht chic

OVERVIEW. *Le Boréal* is best suited to young-minded couples and solo travelers who want some contemporary, sophisticated facilities and a chic yet relaxed yacht-like environment quite different to most cruise ships, with very good food and decent service. The ship is often chartered or part-chartered by 'premium' travel organizers, such as Abercrombie & Kent, Gohagen, and Tauck Tours, who prefer smaller ships.

Berlitz's Ratings		
	Possible	Achieved
Ship	500	406
Accommodation	200	155
Food	400	291
Service	400	301
Entertainment	100	74
Cruise Experience	400	300
OVERALL SCORE		
1527 points out of 2000		

THE SHIP. One of four almost identical new ships catering to French speakers, *Le Boréal* (North Wind) is a gem of contemporary design – chic and uncluttered. The ship has a smart 'sponson' skirt built-in at the stern for operational stability, and carries a fleet of 12 Zodiac landing craft for soft expedition voyages.

There is some sunbathing space outdoors forward of the funnel and around the small pool – aft of the casual eatery one deck below – together with one shower enclosure. Aft of the funnel is an outdoor bar/grill, but not much seating.

Almost all public rooms are aft, with accommodation located forward; the elevators go to all decks except the uppermost one (Deck 7). The decor is minimalist and super-yacht chic – relaxing and pleasant, with lots of browns and creams and a splash of red here and there. Glitz is entirely absent, although there are many reflective surfaces, and the overall feeling of the decor is cool rather than warm.

The focal point is the main lobby, with a central, circular seating and tiled floor surround; its small central section spans two decks. The other flooring is

wood, which can be noisy. The lower decks of the main stairway are made of faux gray wood, while the upper decks are carpeted – a strange combination that somehow works.

This is all-inclusive cruising – except for spa treatments – with drinks, table wine for lunch and dinner, bottled mineral water, port charges, and Zodiac excursions on expedition-style cruises all included in the fare. The crew is English- and French-speaking, with many hotel service staff from Asia. It's refreshing to note that cruise tickets and documents are provided in a proper ticket pouch and sent to you – so, there's no digital frustration, but much anticipation.

Passenger niggles? There's no outside walking or jogging deck. The interior stairways are a quite steep and have short steps. The restaurant is noisy. The entertainment system is not user-friendly, and Internet connection is slow and expensive. Overall, it's difficult for French-speaking and non-French-speaking passengers to mix.

ACCOMMODATION. Of the 132 suites/cabins, there are three Prestige Suites with 301 sq ft plus a 54-sq-ft balcony (28 plus 5 sq m). Forty of the 94 deluxe cabins – 200 sq ft plus a 43-sq-ft balcony (18.6 plus 4 sq m) – can be combined into 20 larger suites, each with two bathrooms, and separate living area and bedroom. All cabinetry is made in elegant dark woods. A real plus is that there are no interior (no-view) cabins – every cabin has an outside view, and the cabin insulation is good.

Each deluxe and standard cabin has a large ocean-view window, two beds that convert to a queen-size bed, and a long vanity desk with good lighting. Facilities include a TV set, DVD player, refrigerator, and personal safe. The marble-appointed bathrooms have heavy hand-held shower hoses. Amenities include a minibar, personal safe, hairdryer, bathrobe, and French bathroom products. Wi-Fi costs extra.

All other cabins have good-size beds, although the corners of the bed frames are square, so you need to be careful when passing between the bed and adjacent storage units – these are quite large, with two deep drawers. Other facilities include a refrigerator, television, wall mirror, good-size wardrobe-style closet (armoire) with personal safe, and a vanity desk with drawer and a small shelf.

The small cabin bathrooms (the entrance door is only 20.5ins/52cm wide) also have a sliding partition window that enables you to see through the cabin to the ocean, and a deep, half-size tub/shower combination. The lip between floor and bathroom is just over 6ins (16cm) high. L'Occitane products are provided.

There are no shelves for toiletries, but there are two drawers under the washbasin – although they are not really practical in use. A separate cubicle houses the vacuum toilet. Balconies have faux wood decking and a fine (real) wood handrail, although solid paneling obstructs views when seated and makes the cabin seem dark – glass panels would have been nicer; the balconies are also very narrow. The closet space is quite good, although the doors, with excellent white leather handles, are wide – at 31ins (79cm), they are wider than the cabin door, and can't be opened without first closing the bathroom and toilet doors, which are directly opposite.

Good-quality bed linen, overlays, and cushions are provided, although there is no choice of pillows.

DINING. The main restaurant, La Licorne, is chic but not pretentious. It accommodates all passengers in an open-seating arrangement and has two integral wine display cabinets (not temperature-controlled). The chairs are rather square and have very thin armrests and low backs – but they certainly look good. And the food? While appetizers and main course items are reasonably good but nothing special, the cakes and desserts are delightful.

La Boussole, an indoor/outdoor Grill (though there's no actual grill), has casual seating for up to 130, with a self-serve buffet set-up for breakfast and lunch, and a 'fast grill' dinner in an alfresco setting. But the layout is quite disjointed, and the port and starboard sides are separated by two elevators. There are two main buffet display units – one for cold food, one for hot – and a separate table set-up for bread, and an active cooking station (eggs for breakfast, pasta at lunchtime).

ENTERTAINMENT. French Line, the show lounge/lecture hall, has amphitheater-style seating for 260, and a raised stage suited to concerts and cabaret presentations. The production shows are weak, repetitive, and loud. The venue is also used for expert specialist lecturers and expedition-style recaps. Two large pillars obstruct the sight lines from several seats, however.

SPA/FITNESS. The Yacht Spa facilities include a fitness room with starboard-side ocean views, adjacent kinetic wall, and a steam room, but no changing room. A wide range of massage and body treatments are provided by Carita of Paris, which staffs and operates the facility.

Legend of the Seas
★★★+

Size:	Mid-size Ship
Tonnage:	69,472
Lifestyle:	Standard
Cruise Line:	Royal Caribbean International
Former Names:	none
IMO Number:	9070620
Builder:	Chantiers de l'Atlantique (France)
Original Cost:	$325 million
Entered Service:	May 1995
Registry:	The Bahamas
Length (ft/m):	867.0/264.2
Beam (ft/m):	105.0/32.0
Draft (ft/m):	23.9/7.3
Propulsion/Propellers:	diesel (40,200kW)/2
Passenger Decks:	11
Total Crew:	726
Passengers (lower beds):	1,804
Passenger Space Ratio (lower beds):	38.4

Passenger/Crew Ratio (lower beds):	2.4
Cabins (total):	902
Size Range (sq ft/m):	137.7–1,147.4/12.8–106.6
Cabins (for one person):	0
Cabins (with private balcony):	231
Cabins (wheelchair accessible):	17
Wheelchair accessibility:	Good
Cabin Current:	110 and 220 volts
Elevators:	11
Casino (gaming tables):	Yes
Slot Machines:	Yes
Swimming Pools:	2
Hot Tubs (on deck):	4
Self-Service Launderette:	No
Dedicated Cinema/Seats:	No
Library:	Yes
Onboard currency:	US$

A ship with refined European decor for mature-age cruisers

OVERVIEW. *Legend of the Seas* had a decent make-over in 2013, although the ship is certainly showing its age in many areas. However, the interior decor has been modified and now has a warmer feel to it than before.

THE SHIP. *Legend of the Seas* has a contemporary profile and a nicely tiered stern, although the stern was fitted with a 'duck-tail' in 2013 to aid stability. The pool deck amidships overhangs the hull to provide an extremely wide deck, while still allowing the ship to navigate the Panama Canal. With engines placed midships, there is little noise and no noticeable vibration, and the ship has an operating speed of up to 24 knots.

The outside light is brought inside in many places, with over 2 acres (8,000 sq m) of glass. There's a single-level sliding glass roof over the more formal setting of one of two swimming pools, providing an all-weather indoor-outdoor area called the Solarium. While not as large as some of the newer ships in the fleet, *Legend of the Seas* is perhaps more suited to couples and families with children that don't need all those bells and whistles, but want to cruise with up-to-date facilities and have multiple dining choices for more convenience. In a 2013 makeover, RCI added some of the dining options found on the larger ships, and enhanced the overall onboard experience by adding, for example, ship-wide Wi-Fi (it costs extra if you use it), flat-screen televisions in all cabins, and finger-touch digital 'wayfinder' direction screens.

Berlitz's Ratings

	Possible	Achieved
Ship	500	379
Accommodation	200	142
Food	400	240
Service	400	262
Entertainment	100	75
Cruise Experience	400	271
OVERALL SCORE		
1369 points out of 2000		

Inside, two full entertainment decks are sandwiched between five decks full of cabins, so there are plenty of public rooms to lounge and drink in. A seven-deck-high atrium lobby – called the Centrum, is the real focal point within the ship, and *the* social meeting place. In 2013, the whole area was revamped, and new features were added. On its various levels it houses an R Bar (for creative cocktails), several passenger service counters, an art gallery, Casino Royale (for table gaming and slot machines), the popular Schooner Bar, with its nautical-theme decor and maritime art, a 2,000-book library (outside of which is a bust of Shakespeare), and Café Latte-tudes (for coffee). Aerial entertainment happens in the Centrum, too.

Set around the base of the funnel is a Viking Crown Lounge – open day and night and also home to two extra-cost restaurants (Chops Grill and Izuma).

ACCOMMODATION. There are many different cabin price grades. Some cabins on Deck 8 also have a larger door for wheelchair access, while there are some cabins that are suitable for less-mobile passengers. This all makes this ship very accessible, when taken with its ample ramped areas and sloping decks.

All cabins have a sitting area and a queen-sized bed, and there is ample closet and drawer space. Generally, there is very little space around the bed, though, and the showers could have been better designed (bathrooms are mostly really small, too).

Those cabins with balconies have glass railings rather than steel/wood to provide less-intrusive sight lines.

The largest accommodation is the Royal Suite, which is beautifully designed, and nicely decorated, with a baby grand piano as a bonus.

DINING. The 1,050-seat Romeo and Juliet Dining Room has dramatic two-deck-high glass side walls, so many passengers both upstairs and downstairs can see both the ocean and each other in reflection; it is quite noisy when full, and would perhaps have been even better located at the stern. When you book, choose one of two seatings, or 'My Time Dining' (eat when you want, during dining room hours).

Overall, meals are rather hit and miss – in fact non-memorable. Also, if you want lobster or a decent filet mignon (steak), you will be asked to pay extra.

Part of the upper level has become The Chef's Table (an extra-cost venue for a more upscale culinary experience).

Other dining options. A large indoor-outdoor Windjammer Café, located forward (above the bridge), has good views on three sides from large ocean-view windows. A good-size snack area provides even more informal eating options. However, there are mainly large tables (fewer tables for two or four than before the 2013 refit), so be prepared for table sharing as part of the casual eatery experience (the food selection is, at best, adequate).

The Park Café (a bistro-style eatery that is part of the Solarium), Chef's Table, Chops Grille (for premium steaks and other meats), Giovanni's Table (for Italian fare), and Izumi Asian Cuisine (high atop the ship, with some fine views) were added in a 2013 makeover. These venues provide more dining choices (most at extra cost).

ENTERTAINMENT. That's Entertainment Theater seats 802 and is a single-level showlounge with tiered seating levels: sight lines are generally good from almost all seats. Strong cabaret acts are also presented here. A second entertainment lounge, the Anchors Aweigh Lounge, is where cabaret acts, including late-night adult comedy are presented. Other lounges and bars have live music for listening and dancing, and aerial entertainment is featured in the Centrum – the atrium lobby.

Entertainment throughout the ship is upbeat – in fact, it is difficult to get away from music and noise – but is typical of the kind of resort hotel found ashore in Las Vegas. There is even background music in all corridors and elevators, and constant music outdoors on the pool deck. If you want a quiet relaxing holiday, choose another ship.

SPA/FITNESS. The Vitality at Sea Spa and Fitness Center has a small fitness room, located on the port side of the ship, aft of the funnel, with a small selection of muscle-pumping equipment. There is also an aerobics studio, a beauty salon, and a sauna, as well as rooms for body pampering treatments. While the facilities are quite small compared with those aboard the company's newer ships, they are adequate for short cruises.

A rock-climbing wall, with several separate climbing tracks, is located outdoors at the aft end of the funnel.

Le Lyrial
★★★★

Size:	Small Ship	Passenger/Crew Ratio (lower beds):	1.5
Tonnage:	10,944	Cabins (total):	122
Lifestyle:	Premium	Size Range (sq ft/m):	226.0-710.4/21.0-66.0
Cruise Line:	Ponant	Cabins (for one person):	0
Former Names:	none	Cabins (with private balcony):	122
IMO Number:	9704130	Cabins (wheelchair accessible):	3
Builder:	Fincantieri (Italy)	Wheelchair accessibility:	Fair
Original Cost:	€105 million	Cabin Current:	110 and 220 volts
Entered Service:	Apr 2015	Elevators:	3
Registry:	Wallis & Fortuna	Casino (gaming tables):	No
Length (ft/m):	465.8/142.0	Slot Machines:	Yes
Beam (ft/m):	9.0/18.0	Swimming Pools:	1
Draft (ft/m):	15.4/4.7	Hot Tubs (on deck):	0
Propulsion/Propellers:	diesel-electric/2	Self-Service Launderette:	No
Passenger Decks:	6	Dedicated Cinema/Seats:	No
Total Crew:	140	Library:	Yes
Passengers (lower beds):	244	Onboard currency:	Euros
Passenger Space Ratio (lower beds):	44.8		

This is a small, chic, contemporary yacht-like French ship

OVERVIEW. *Le Lyrial* is best suited to young-minded couples and solo travelers who are looking for sophisticated facilities in a relaxed but chic yacht-like environment, that is different to most large cruise ships, with decent food and informal service.

THE SHIP. Le Lyrial (its name refers to the Lyra constellation in the northern hemisphere) has a smart 'sponson' skirt built-in at the stern for operational stability, and a fleet of 12 Zodiac landing craft is carried for shore landings and excursions during soft expedition and nature cruises.

There is some sunbathing space outdoors forward of the funnel and around the small pool – aft of the casual eatery on the deck below. Aft of the funnel is an outdoor bar/grill, but there's really not enough seating.

It's trendy and uncluttered, with contemporary mega-yacht chic decor, and, although it carries a few less passengers, it's the same size as sister ships L'Austral, Le Boreal, and Le Soleil. So, it is classed as a Boutique ship, and not a small ship. The decor is minimalist and super-yacht chic – relaxing and pleasant, with lots of blue and white. The focal point is the two-deck high main lobby, which has a central, circular seating area.

This is all-inclusive cruising – except for spa treatments – with drinks, wine for lunch and dinner, bottled mineral water, port charges, and Zodiac excursions on 'expedition-style' cruises included in the fare. Note, however, that the cruise line chooses the drinks and wine. It is refreshing that cruise tickets and documents are provided in a proper ticket pouch and sent to you.

Berlitz's Ratings

	Possible	Achieved
Ship	500	412
Accommodation	200	158
Food	400	295
Service	400	303
Entertainment	100	75
Cruise Experience	400	299
OVERALL SCORE		
1542 points out of 2000		

However, there's no outside walking or jogging deck. The interior stairways are steep and have short steps.

ACCOMMODATION. There are 122 suites/cabins. The largest accommodation includes eight suites of 45 sq mtr/484.3 sq ft (including an 8 sq m/86.1 sq ft balcony), one larger Owner's Suite measuring 67 sq m/721.2 sq ft (including a 12 sq m/21.5 sq ft balcony) and a Grand Deluxe Suite of 54 sq m/581.2 sq ft (including a 9 sq m/96.8 sq ft balcony). The cabin cabinetry is crafted in elegant woods. A real plus is that there are no interior cabins – each cabin has an outside view. Insulation is good, there is quality bed linen, a refrigerator, television, and L'Occitane products.

CUISINE. The main restaurant is chic but not pretentious. It accommodates all passengers in an open-seating arrangement. The chairs have thin armrests and low backs, but they look good. An indoor/outdoor Grill has casual seating for up to 130, with self-serve buffet set-up for breakfast and lunch and a 'fast grill' dinner in an alfresco setting.

ENTERTAINMENT. The show lounge has amphitheater-style seating for all passengers and a raised stage. It's also used for lectures and recaps. Two pillars block sight lines from several seats, however.

SPA/FITNESS. The Yacht Spa has a fitness room, kinetic wall and a steam room, but no changing room. A range of treatments are provided by Carita of Paris.

Le Ponant
★★★+

Size:	Boutique Ship	Passenger/Crew Ratio (lower beds):	2.1
Tonnage:	1,489	Cabins (total):	32
Lifestyle:	Premium	Size Range (sq ft/m):	145.3-164.6/13.5-15.3
Cruise Line:	Ponant	Cabins (for one person):	0
Former Names:	none	Cabins (with private balcony):	0
IMO Number:	8914219	Cabins (wheelchair accessible):	0
Builder:	SFCN (France)	Wheelchair accessibility:	None
Original Cost:	n/a	Cabin Current:	220 volts
Entered Service:	Jun 2009	Elevators:	No
Registry:	France	Casino (gaming tables):	No
Length (ft/m):	288.7/88.0	Slot Machines:	No
Beam (ft/m):	39.3/12.0	Swimming Pools:	0
Draft (ft/m):	13.1/4.0	Hot Tubs (on deck):	0
Propulsion/Propellers:	diesel/sail power/1	Self-Service Launderette:	No
Passenger Decks:	3	Dedicated Cinema/Seats:	No
Total Crew:	32	Library:	Yes
Passengers (lower beds):	64	Onboard currency:	Euros
Passenger Space Ratio (lower beds):	23.2		

Chic decor and relaxed cruising for French-speakers

OVERVIEW. *Le Ponant* is best suited to young-minded couples and solo travelers seeking contemporary, sophisticated facilities in a very relaxed but chic setting, with good food and service, no entertainment, and plenty of time for quiet relaxation.

THE SHIP. Ultra sleek, and very efficiently designed, this contemporary sail-cruise ship has three masts that rise 54.7ft (16.7m) above the water line, and electronic winches assist in the furling and unfurling of the sails. The total sail area measures approximately 16,140 sq ft (1,500 sq m). This captivating ship has plenty of room on its open decks for sunbathing. Although they have padded cushions, the off-white plastic sunloungers are still not at all elegant.

The interior design is clean, stylish, functional, and high-tech. Three public lounges have pastel decor, soft colors, and great flair. One price fits all. The ship is marketed mainly to young, sophisticated French-speaking passengers who love yachting and the sea. The company also has a four mega-yacht cruise ships. Gratuities are 'not required,' but they are expected. It's refreshing to find that cruise tickets and documents are provided in a proper ticket pouch and sent to you (so, there's no digital frustration, but much anticipation).

ACCOMMODATION. There are five cabins on Antigua Deck (the open deck) and 27 on Marie Galante Deck (the lowest deck). Crisp, clean blond woods and pristine white cabins have twin beds that convert to a double. There's a minibar, personal safe, and a bathroom. All cabins have portholes, artwork, and a refrigerator. There is limited storage, however, and few drawers – they are also very small. The cabin bathrooms are quite small, but efficient.

DINING. The lovely Karukera dining room has an open-seating policy. There is fresh fish daily, when available, and dinner is always treated as a true gastronomic affair. The chef goes out to buy local fresh food items, including fresh fish and fruit. Free wines are included for lunch and dinner, and the cuisine is, naturally, classic French. That Frenchness also means the selection of cheeses, breads, and breakfast croissants is good. There are free cappucinos and espressos. For casual breakfasts and luncheons, there is a charming outdoor café under a canvas sailcloth awning.

ENTERTAINMENT. There is no professional entertainment as such, although occasionally the crew may put on a little soirée. Dinner is the main event each evening, and, being a French product, dinner can provide several hours' worth of entertainment in itself.

SPA/FITNESS. There is no spa, fitness room, sauna, or steam room. However, for recreation, there are water sports facilities, and these include an aft marina platform from which you can swim, windsurfing, water-ski boating, and scuba and snorkel equipment. Scuba diving costs extra, charged per dive.

Berlitz's Ratings

	Possible	Achieved
Ship	500	371
Accommodation	200	152
Food	400	268
Service	400	282
Entertainment	100	70
Cruise Experience	400	228
OVERALL SCORE		
1371 points out of 2000		

Le Soleal
★★★★

Size:	Small Ship		Passenger/Crew Ratio (lower beds):	1.5
Tonnage:	10,944		Cabins (total):	132
Lifestyle:	Premium		Size Range (sq ft/m):	226.0–581.2/21.0–54.0
Cruise Line:	Ponant		Cabins (for one person):	0
Former Names:	none		Cabins (with private balcony):	125
IMO Number:	9641675		Cabins (wheelchair accessible):	3
Builder:	Fincantieri (Italy)		Wheelchair accessibility:	Fair
Original Cost:	€105 million		Cabin Current:	110 and 220 volts
Entered Service:	Jul 2013		Elevators:	3
Registry:	Wallis & Fortuna		Casino (gaming tables):	No
Length (ft/m):	465.8/142.0		Slot Machines:	Yes
Beam (ft/m):	9.0/18.0		Swimming Pools:	1
Draft (ft/m):	15.4/4.7		Hot Tubs (on deck):	0
Propulsion/Propellers:	diesel-electric (4,600kW)/2		Self-Service Launderette:	0
Passenger Decks:	6		Dedicated Cinema/Seats:	No
Total Crew:	140		Library:	Yes
Passengers (lower beds):	264		Onboard currency:	Euros
Passenger Space Ratio (lower beds):	41.4			

French ambience and small mega-yacht premium chic

OVERVIEW. *Le Soléal* is geared to young-minded couples and solo travelers who want semi-sophisticated facilities in a relaxed but stylish yacht-like environment quite different from most cruise ships, and are happy with reasonably good food and service. The ship is often chartered or part-chartered by 'premium' travel organizers, such as Abercrombie & Kent, Gohagen, and Tauck Tours, who prefer smaller ships.

Berlitz's Ratings		
	Possible	Achieved
Ship	500	406
Accommodation	200	155
Food	400	292
Service	400	301
Entertainment	100	74
Cruise Experience	400	302
OVERALL SCORE		
1530 points out of 2000		

THE SHIP. One of four almost identical sister ships catering mainly to French speakers, *Le Soléal* is contemporary – chic and uncluttered. With a dark gray hull and sleek white superstructure, the ship looks more like a large private yacht rather than a traditional cruise ship.

The ship has a smart 'sponson' skirt built in at the stern – this is for operational stability – and carries a fleet of 12 Zodiac landing craft for soft expedition voyages. There is some sunbathing space outdoors forward of the funnel and around the small pool – aft of a casual eatery located one deck below – together with a shower enclosure.

Almost all the public rooms are located in the aft section, with accommodation located forward; the elevators go to all decks except the uppermost one (Deck 7). The decor is minimalist and super-yacht chic – relaxing and pleasant, with lots of browns and creams and a splash of red here and there. However, there are many reflective surfaces, and the overall feeling of the decor is cool rather than warm and cosseting.

The focal point of the interior is the main lobby, with a central, circular seating and tiled floor surround; its small central section spans two decks. The other flooring is wood, which can be noisy. The lower decks of the main stairway are made · of faux gray wood, while the upper decks are carpeted – a strange combination that somehow works.

This is all-inclusive cruising – except for spa treatments – with drinks, table wine for lunch and dinner, bottled mineral water, port charges, and Zodiac excursions on expedition-style cruises included in the fare. The crew is English- and French-speaking, with many hotel service staff from Asia. It is, however, refreshing to note that cruise tickets and documents are provided in a proper ticket pouch and sent to you – so, there's no digital frustration, but much anticipation.

Passenger niggles? There's no outside walking or jogging deck. The interior stairways are a quite steep and have short steps. The restaurant is noisy. The entertainment system is not user-friendly and Internet connection is slow and expensive. Overall, it's difficult for French-speaking and non-French-speaking passengers to mix.

ACCOMMODATION. Of the 132 suites/cabins, there are three Prestige Suites with 301 sq ft plus a 54-sq-ft balcony (28 plus 5 sq m). Forty of the 94 deluxe cabins – 200 sq ft plus a 43-sq-ft balcony (18.6 plus 4 sq m) – can be combined into 20 larger suites, each with two bathrooms, and separate living area and bedroom. All cabinetry is made in elegant dark woods. A real plus is that there are no interior (no-view) cabins – every cabin has an outside view. Cabin insulation is also good, so you won't hear your neighbor easily.

The deluxe and standard cabins have a large ocean-view window, two beds that convert to a queen-size bed, and a long vanity desk with good lighting. Facilities include a TV set, DVD player, refrigerator, and personal safe. The bathrooms are marble-appointed, but they have very heavy hand-held shower hoses. Amenities include a minibar, personal safe, hairdryer, bathrobe, and French (L'Occitane) bathroom products. Wi-Fi costs extra.

All other cabins have good-size beds, although the corners of the bed frames are square, so be careful when passing between bed and an adjacent storage unit – it's quite large, with two deep drawers. Other facilities include a refrigerator, television, wall mirror, good-size wardrobe-style closet (armoire) with personal safe, and a vanity desk with drawer and a small shelf.

The small cabin bathrooms (the entrance door is only 20.5ins/52cm wide) also have a sliding partition window that enables you to see through the cabin to the ocean, and a deep, half-size tub/shower combination. The lip between floor and bathroom is just over 6ins (16cm) high. L'Occitane products are provided.

There are no shelves for toiletries, but there are two drawers under the washbasin – although they are not very practical. A separate cubicle houses the vacuum toilet. Balconies have faux wood decking and a fine (real) wood handrail, although solid paneling obstructs views when seated and makes the cabin seem dark – glass panels would have been nicer; the balconies are also narrow. The closet space is decent enough, although the doors, with nice white leather handles, are wide – at 31ins (79cm), they are wider than the cabin door, and can't be opened without first closing the bathroom and toilet doors that are directly opposite.

Good-quality bed linen, overlays, and cushions are provided, although there is no choice of pillows.

DINING. The main restaurant is chic but not pretentious – or even warm. It accommodates all passengers in an open-seating arrangement and has two integral wine display cabinets. The chairs are rather square and have very thin armrests and low backs – but they look good. And the food? While appetizers and main course items are reasonably good but nothing special, the cakes and desserts are delightful.

An indoor/outdoor Grill has casual seating for up to 130, with self-serve buffet set-up for breakfast and lunch, and a 'fast grill' dinner in an alfresco setting. The layout is disjointed, and port and starboard sides are separated by two elevators. There are two main buffet display units – one for cold food, one for hot, plus a separate table set-up for bread and an active cooking station (eggs for breakfast, pasta at lunchtime, for example).

ENTERTAINMENT. The showlounge, which doubles as a lecture hall, has amphitheater-style seating for 260, and a raised stage for concerts and cabaret-style entertainment. The production shows are weak, repetitive, and loud, but they do have a sort of French flair about them. The venue is also used for expedition-style recaps and lectures, but two large pillars obstruct the sight lines from several seats.

SPA/FITNESS. The Yacht Spa facilities include a fitness room with starboard-side ocean views, adjacent kinetic wall, and a steam room, but there is no changing room. A wide range of massage and body treatments are provided by Carita of Paris, which staffs and oversees the facility.

Liberty of the Seas
★★★+

Size:	Large Resort Ship	Passenger Space Ratio (lower beds):	42.0
Tonnage:	154,407	Passenger/Crew Ratio (lower beds):	2.6
Lifestyle:	Standard	Cabins (total):	1,815
Cruise Line:	Royal Caribbean International	Size Range (sq ft/m):	149.0–2,025.0/13.8–188.1
Former Names:	none	Cabins (for one person):	0
IMO Number:	9330032	Cabins (with private balcony):	842
Builder:	Kvaerner Masa-Yards (Finland)	Cabins (wheelchair accessible):	32
Original Cost:	$590 million	Wheelchair accessibility:	Best
Entered Service:	May 2007	Cabin Current:	110 volts
Registry:	The Bahamas	Elevators:	14
Length (ft/m):	1,112.2/339.0	Casino (gaming tables):	Yes
Beam (ft/m):	184.0/56.0	Slot Machines:	Yes
Draft (ft/m):	27.8/8/5	Swimming Pools:	2
Propulsion/Propellers:	diesel-electric (75,600kW)/3 pods	Hot Tubs (on deck):	6
	(2 azimuthing, 1 fixed)	Self-Service Launderette:	No
Passenger Decks:	15	Dedicated Cinema/Seats:	No
Total Crew:	1,397	Library:	Yes
Passengers (lower beds):	3,630	Onboard currency:	US$

A large resort ship for casual family-friendly cruising

OVERVIEW. *Liberty of the Seas* is a large, Las Vegas-style floating resort city. The facilities (such as public rooms, bars, and lounges) of the *Voyager*-class ships have been incorporated in this larger version, but with more conference and meetings facilities, Wi-Fi capabilities, and connectivity for cell phones.

THE SHIP. *Liberty of the Seas* is a fine ship for families with children. The ship's 'pod' propulsion system virtually eliminates vibration. The ship's 'wow' factor is the H2O Zone, a water-themed play area for families; by night it turns into a colorfully lit sculpture garden. Adjacent is a 'sports' pool. Two 16-person hot tubs are cantilevered 12ft (3.7m) over the ship's sides in an adults-only Solarium area.

There are 16 bars and lounges to enjoy, plus a whole promenade of shops, munching and drinking spots along the Royal Promenade. One deck down from the Royal Promenade is a large Casino Royale, The Catacombs disco, Schooner Bar, Boleros Lounge, and a photo gallery and shop, while the forward section leads into the three-deck-high Platinum Theater.

A regulation-size ice-skating rink called Studio B has real, not fake, ice, with bleachers seating, and good broadcast facilities. Outstanding Ice Follies shows are presented here, but note that a number of slim pillars obstruct clear-view arena stage sight lines.

Almost at the top of the ship is Royal Caribbean International's trademark Viking Crown Lounge, the Olive or Twist jazz lounge, and a Wedding Chapel. Other facilities include a cigar smoker's lounge, con-

Berlitz's Ratings		
	Possible	Achieved
Ship	500	389
Accommodation	200	141
Food	400	235
Service	400	283
Entertainment	100	74
Cruise Experience	400	267
OVERALL SCORE		
1389 points out of 2000		

ference center, a concierge lounge (for suite occupants only), and a comfortable 3,600-book library.

Liberty of the Seas is an exciting and very comfortable ship, with contemporary decor. However, there are only four banks of elevators (two forward and two aft) totaling 14, so if you have a cabin in the center of the ship, you'll need to walk in order to travel vertically between decks; and there are only two major passenger stairways – one forward, one aft.

FAMILIES. Children are well catered for, with Adventure Ocean (on Deck 12) for kids of six months to 17 years of age (teens get their own chill-out room). Children will love this ship and all the fun activities and sports activities.

ACCOMMODATION. There is a wide range of cabins in 14 categories and 21 price grades. There are many family-friendly cabins, which are good for family reunions.

Presidential Family Suite. Two master bedrooms each have twin beds that convert to queen-size, a private balcony, sofa bed, bar, private bathroom, bathtub, vanity, hairdryer, flat screen TV, and telephone. The suite has great views over the ship's stern, and occupants have access to the Concierge Club lounge and services. There is only one Presidential Family Suite, which can sleep up to 14, though it would be quite cramped with that number of occupants. Size: 1,215 sq ft (113 sq m) plus balcony: 810 sq ft (75 sq m), set with lounge area and dining table.

Royal Suite. Features a separate bedroom with king-size bed, private balcony, living room with queen-size sofa bed, and private bathroom. Size: 1,406 sq ft (131 sq m) plus balcony: 377 sq ft (35 sq m).

Royal Family Suite. Two bedrooms with twin beds that convert to queen-size beds (one room has third and fourth Pullman beds), a private balcony, two bathrooms, and living area with double sofa bed. Size: 588 sq ft (54.6 sq m) plus Balcony: 234 sq ft (21.7 sq m).

Owner's Suite. There's a queen-size bed, private balcony, separate living area with queen-size sofa bed, wet bar, vanity area, walk-in closet; bathroom with tub and shower, plus access to the Concierge Club lounge and attendant services. Sleeps up to five. Size: 506 sq ft (46 sq m) plus balcony: 131 sq ft (12.1 sq m).

Grand Suite. Two twin beds convert to queen-size. There's a private balcony, sitting area (some with sofa bed), vanity area, and bathroom with tub and shower. Access to the Concierge Club lounge and services. Sleeps up to four. Size: 381 sq ft (35.3 sq meters) plus balcony: 89 sq ft (8.2 sq m).

Junior Suite. Two twin beds convertible to a queen-size one, private balcony, sitting area (some with sofa bed), vanity area, and bathroom with tub and shower. Sleeps up to four. Size: 285.2 sq ft (26.5 sq m) plus balcony: 101 sq ft (9.3 sq m).

Superior ocean-view cabin. Two twin beds convertible to queen-size, a private balcony, sitting area (some with sofa bed), vanity area, and bathroom with shower. Sleeps two (three or four in some rooms). Size: 202 sq ft (18.7 sq m) plus balcony: 42 sq ft (3.9 sq m).

Deluxe ocean-view cabin. Same facilities as superior ocean-view cabins, but size is different: 173 sq ft (16.0 sq m) plus balcony: 46 sq ft (4.2 sq m).

Promenade cabin (interior, but overlooking the Royal Promenade). A view of the Royal Promenade with bay windows, two twin beds that convert to queen-size, and private bathroom. Size: 149 sq ft (13.8 sq m).

Promenade family cabin. Two twin beds convertible to a queen-size one, and private bathroom. Size: 300 sq ft (27.8 sq m).

Interior cabin. Two twin beds convertible to a queen-size one; private bathroom with shower. Sleeps two (some rooms sleep three or four). Size: 152 sq ft (14.1 sq m).

Family ocean-view cabin. Located at the front of the ship, with two twin beds (convertible to a queen-size one), sofa and/or Pullman beds, sitting area, and bathroom with shower. Accommodates six and has 48ins (122cm) round windows. Size: 265 sq ft (24.6 sq m).

All cabins have a private bathroom (with tub and shower, or shower only), vanity desk with hairdryer, minibar, safe, flat-screen TV, iPod dock, radio, and satellite telephone. A room service menu is provided. Suite occupants have access to a Concierge Lounge, for more personal service – this saves standing in line at the reception desk.

DINING. The main dining room is large and is set on three levels, each with a different name: Botticelli, Michelangelo, and Rembrandt. A dramatic staircase connects all three, but huge support pillars obstruct the sight lines. When you book, choose one of two seatings, or 'My Time Dining.' Tables are for four to 12.

The place settings, porcelain, and cutlery are of good quality. The menu descriptions make the food sound better than it is, however, and the selection of breads, rolls, fruit, and cheese is poor. Overall, meals are rather hit and miss – unmemorable, in fact. Also, if you want lobster or a decent filet mignon (steak), you will be asked to pay extra.

Other dining options. Promenade Café: for Continental breakfast, all-day pizzas (Sorrento's), sandwiches, and coffees (in paper cups).

Windjammer Café: this is a really large, sprawling venue for casual buffet-style, self-help breakfast (this tends to be the busiest time of the day), lunch, and light dinners (but not on the last night of the cruise); it's often difficult to find a table and by the time you do, your food could be cold.

Jade 'Restaurant' (it's actually a section of the Windjammer Café), for casual Asian-themed food.

Portofino: this is an upscale Euro-Italian restaurant, open for dinner only. Reservations are required, and there's a gratuity. Choices include: antipasti, soup, salad, pasta, main dish, dessert, cheese, and coffee (the menu does not change during the cruise).

Chops Grille: an intimate restaurant for steaks and seafood. Note that a cover charge applies.

Johnny Rockets: a retro 1950s all-day, all-night diner-style eatery that has hamburgers, hot dogs, and other fast-food items, plus malt shakes, with both indoor and outdoor seating (indoor tables have a mini-jukebox), and singing waitresses. There's a cover charge.

Sprinkles: for round-the-clock ice cream and yoghurt, pastries, and coffee.

ENTERTAINMENT. The Platinum Theater is a stunning, well-designed showlounge located forward, with only a few slim pillars and almost no disruption of sight lines. The showlounge has a hydraulic orchestra pit and huge stage areas, as well as superb lighting equipment.

A performance not to be missed is the Greatest Show at Sea Parade – a 15-minute extravaganza that bumbles along the Royal Promenade; it replicates the parade of stars and animals at a circus of yesteryear. This is when it's really good to have one of those interior-view atrium cabins. Otherwise, get a position early along the Royal Promenade.

SPA/FITNESS. The Steiner-operated Day Spa is large. It includes a large aerobics room, fitness center, treatment rooms, and sauna/steam rooms and relaxation areas. Some basic exercise classes are free, but others cost extra. Active types can go body-boarding, go boxing in the full-size boxing ring, go rock-climbing, in-line skating, jog, putt, swim, surf, or play in the golf simulators.

Louis Aura
★★+

Size:	Mid-size Ship
Tonnage:	16,916
Lifestyle:	Standard
Cruise Line:	Louis Cruises
Former Names:	*Orient Queen, Bolero, Starward*
IMO Number:	6821080
Builder:	A.G. Weser (Germany)
Original Cost:	n/a
Entered Service:	Dec 1968/Aug 2006
Registry:	Greece
Length (ft/m):	525.9/160.3
Beam (ft/m):	74.9/22.8
Draft (ft/m):	22.5/6.8
Propulsion/Propellers:	diesel (12,950kW)/2
Passenger Decks:	7
Total Crew:	400
Passengers (lower beds):	828
Passenger Space Ratio (lower beds):	26.3

Passenger/Crew Ratio (lower beds):	2.4
Cabins (total):	414
Size Range (sq ft/m):	111.9–324.0/10.4–30.1
Cabins (for one person):	0
Cabins (with private balcony):	0
Cabins (wheelchair accessible):	2
Wheelchair accessibility:	None
Cabin Current:	110 and 220 volts
Elevators:	4
Casino (gaming tables):	Yes
Slot Machines:	Yes
Swimming Pools:	2
Hot Tubs (on deck):	0
Self-Service Launderette:	No
Dedicated Cinema/Seats:	Yes/210
Library:	Yes
Onboard currency:	Euros

A traditional, small, casual ship for frugal cruisers

OVERVIEW. *Louis Aura* (ex-*Orient Queen*) will suit adult couples and solo travelers who want to cruise aboard a smaller ship, in modest but still comfortable surroundings, at a similarly modest price.

THE SHIP. The open deck and sunbathing space is very limited, and some of the decks are of plain, painted steel. On the aft decks, there's a clutter of wooden sun-loungers, and sun-shade umbrellas. Forward of the twin funnels is an enclosed sports facility. Aft of the mast is a solarium-style shielded housing, with a multi-level lounge/bar/disco that's adjacent to one of the ship's small swimming pools. The dress code is casual.

There's a decent choice of public rooms, including six bars, all with clean, contemporary furnishings, upbeat fabric colors, and a mix of traditional and fairly contemporary decor. However, the diesel engines tend to throb in some parts of the vessel and can be a little noisy, particularly for occupants of cabins on the lower decks close to the engine casing.

ACCOMMODATION. There are four Royal Suites, and 54 other 'suites' (they are not really suites, because there is no separate bedroom). The other cabins are very compact units that are moderately comfortable and decorated in soft colors. While closet space is limited, there are plenty of drawers, although they are metal and tinny.

Berlitz's Ratings		
	Possible	Achieved
Ship	500	273
Accommodation	200	94
Food	400	216
Service	400	244
Entertainment	100	55
Cruise Experience	400	206
OVERALL SCORE		
1088 points out of 2000		

The bathrooms are small, compact units, and the towels provided are not large. Toilets are of the gentle flush (non-vacuum) variety. Unfortunately, the soundproofing between the cabins is poor, and air conditioning is noisy.

The four Royal Suites have decent space. There is a king-size bed, vanity desk, closet, plenty of drawer and storage space, a lounge with a sofa that converts into an additional bed, drinks table, and two chairs. A large pillar obstructs movement. The bathroom has a small but deep tub with hand-held shower.

DINING. The 444-seat Mermaid Restaurant is cheerful, almost charming, and has some prime tables that overlook the stern. Seating is at tables for four to eight, in two seatings. The cuisine is Mediterranean, with some Greek specialties, while the wine list consists mainly of young wines.

Breakfast and lunch buffets are provided indoors at the casual self-serve Horizon Café, with outdoor seating at tables around the aft swimming pool, but space is tight.

ENTERTAINMENT. The 420-seat El Cabaret Show-lounge is a single-level room, and the shows are simply basic. There's also a nightclub.

SPA/FITNESS. There is a beauty salon and massage/body treatment room – on two different decks.

Maasdam
★★★+

Size:	Mid-size Ship
Tonnage:	55,451
Lifestyle:	Premium
Cruise Line:	Holland America Line
Former Names:	none
IMO Number:	8919257
Builder:	Fincantieri (Italy)
Original Cost:	$215 million
Entered Service:	Dec 1993/Dec 1993
Registry:	The Netherlands
Length (ft/m):	719.3/219.3
Beam (ft/m):	101.0/30.8
Draft (ft/m):	24.6/7.5
Propulsion/Propellers:	diesel-electric (34,560kW)/2
Passenger Decks:	10
Total Crew:	557
Passengers (lower beds):	1,266
Passenger Space Ratio (lower beds):	43.8

Passenger/Crew Ratio (lower beds):	2.2
Cabins (total):	632
Size Range (sq ft/m):	186.2–1,124.8/17.3–104.5
Cabins (for one person):	0
Cabins (with private balcony):	150
Cabins (wheelchair accessible):	6
Wheelchair accessibility:	Good
Cabin Current:	110 and 220 volts
Elevators:	8
Casino (gaming tables):	Yes
Slot Machines:	Yes
Swimming Pools:	2 (1 w/sliding glass dome)
Hot Tubs (on deck):	2
Self-Service Launderette:	Yes
Dedicated Cinema/Seats:	Yes/249
Library:	Yes
Onboard currency:	US$

This ship has Dutch-style decor for mature-age cruisers

OVERVIEW. Holland America Line (HAL) constantly fine-tunes its performance, and its regular passengers, almost all North American, find its ships comfortable and well run. HAL continues its strong maritime traditions and keeps its vessels clean and tidy, although the food and service components still let the rest of the cruise experience down.

THE SHIP. *Maasdam* (now well over 20 years old) is one of four almost identical ships, along with *Ryndam* (now *Pacific Eden*), *Statendam* (now *Pacific Aria*), and *Veendam*. Although the exterior styling is rather angular (some say boxy – the funnel certainly is), it is softened and balanced somewhat by the black hull. There is a full walk-around teak promenade deck outdoors – excellent for strolling, and, thankfully, there's no sign of synthetic turf. The sunloungers on the exterior promenade deck are wood, and have comfortable cushioned pads, while those at the swimming pool on Lido Deck are of white (sort of) plastic. There is good passenger flow throughout the public areas.

In the interiors of this 'S'-class ship, an asymmetrical layout helps to reduce bottlenecks and congestion. Most of the public rooms are concentrated on two decks, Promenade Deck and Upper Promenade Deck, which creates a spacious feel to the ship's interiors. In general, the interior styling is restrained, using contemporary materials combined with traditional woods and ceramics. There is, thankfully, little glitz anywhere.

Berlitz's Ratings

	Possible	Achieved
Ship	500	346
Accommodation	200	141
Food	400	247
Service	400	281
Entertainment	100	68
Cruise Experience	400	263
OVERALL SCORE		
1346 points out of 2000		

Some $2 million worth of artwork was assembled and nicely displayed to represent HAL's fine Dutch heritage and to present a balance between standard itineraries and onboard creature comforts. Several oil paintings of the line's former ships by Stephen Card, a former captain, adorn stairway landings. Also noticeable are the fine flower arrangements in the public areas and foyers – used to good effect to brighten up what to some is dull decor. Atop the ship, with forward-facing views that wrap around the sides, is the Crow's Nest Lounge. By day it is a decent observation lounge, with large ocean-view windows; by night it turns into a nightclub with extremely variable lighting.

The atrium foyer is three decks high, although its light-catching green glass sculpted centerpiece (*Totem* by Luciano Vistosi, composed of almost 2,000 pieces of glass) makes it look a little crowded, and leaves little room in front of the front office. A hydraulic glass roof covers the reasonably sized swimming pool/hot tubs and central Lido area – where the focal point is a large dolphin sculpture – so that this can be used in either fine or poor weather.

This ship has a large, relaxing Leyden Library, a card room, an Explorer's Lounge (good for afternoon tea and after-dinner coffee), an intimate Piano Bar, and a casino. The casino features gaming tables and slot machines. However, note that part of the casino is open, and passers-by can be subject to cigarette smoke (yes, smoking is still permitted), so non-smokers may find this unpleasant.

HAL's many repeat passengers seem to enjoy the fact that social dancing is always on the menu. In the final analysis, however, the score for this ship ends up a tad under what it could be if the food and food service staff were more memorable – more professional training might help.

Niggles? An escalator travels between two of the lower decks, one of which was originally planned to be the embarkation point, but it is almost pointless. The charge to use the washing machines and dryers in the self-service launderette is petty, particularly for suite occupants, who pay high prices for their cruises. The men's urinals in public restrooms are unusually high. Sadly, the ship is now looking decidedly tired and dated.

ACCOMMODATION. The accommodation ranges from small interior cabins to a large Penthouse Suite, in 17 price categories. The interior and outside standard cabins have twin beds that convert to a queen-size bed, and there is a separate living space with sofa and coffee table. Although the drawer space is generally good, the closet space is very tight, particularly for long cruises, although more than adequate for a seven-night cruise. Bathrobes are provided for all suites and cabins, as are hairdryers, and a small range of toiletries. The bathrooms are quite well laid out, but the tubs are small units better described as shower tubs.

On Navigation Deck, 28 suites have accommodation for up to four. These have in-suite dining as an alternative to the dining room, for private meals. These are spacious, tastefully decorated and well laid-out, and have a separate, good-size living room, a bedroom with two lower beds that convert to a king-size bed, dressing room, plenty of closet and drawer space (walk-in closet), marble bathroom with Jacuzzi tub, and separate toilet/washroom with bidet.

Penthouse Suite. The largest accommodation, this is located on the starboard side of Navigation Deck at the forward staircase. It has a king-size bed and vanity desk; large walk-in closet with superb drawer space; oversize whirlpool bath (it could seat four) and separate shower enclosure; separate washroom with toilet, bidet, and washbasin; living room with writing desk, large TV set, and full set of audio equipment; dressing room; large private balcony (with teak lounge chairs and drinks tables, dining table, and four chairs); minibar/refrigerator; and a pantry with large refrigerator, toaster unit, full coffee/tea-making facilities, and food preparation area. There's a separate entrance from the hallway, a guest toilet, and floor-to-ceiling windows.

DINING. The Rotterdam Dining Room, spanning two decks, is located aft. It is quite large, and has a grand staircase, panoramic views on three sides, and a music balcony. Both open seating and assigned seating are available, while breakfast and lunch are open seating – you'll be taken to your table by restaurant staff, when you enter. The waiter stations are very noisy for anyone seated near them.

Other dining options. The 66-seat Pinnacle Grill is located just forward of the balcony level of the main dining room on the starboard side. It serves Pacific Northwest cuisine such as Dungeness crab, Alaska salmon, halibut, and other regional specialties (reservations needed, cover charge applies). A Bulgari show plate, Rosenthal china, Riedel wine glasses, and Frette table linen are used. The Pinnacle Grill is a much better, more relaxed dining experience than the main dining room and worth it for that special celebration.

For less-formal evening eating, the Lido Buffet is open for casual dinners on all except the last night of each cruise, in an open-seating arrangement. Tables are set with crisp linens, flatware, and stemware. A set menu includes a choice of several entreés. It is also open for casual breakfasts and lunches. Again there is much use of canned fruits and packeted items, although there are several commercial low-calorie salad dressings. The beverage station, which is on a par with those found in family outlets ashore in the United States, lets it down. Additionally, a poolside 'Dive-In at the Terrace Grill' features signature burgers, hot dogs, and fries.

Passengers have to use the Lido Buffet on days when the dining room is closed for lunch, which is typically once or twice per cruise, depending on the itinerary.

ENTERTAINMENT. The Showroom at Sea, in the forward part of the ship, spans two decks, with banquette seating on both main and upper levels. It is basically a well-designed room, but the ceiling is low and the sight lines from the balcony level are quite poor. The production shows are passé, but individual cabaret acts are sometimes good.

SPA/FITNESS. The Ocean Spa is located one deck below the navigation bridge at the very forward part of the ship. It has ocean views and includes a gymnasium with all the latest muscle-pumping exercise machines, including an abundance of treadmills. There's also an aerobics exercise area, large beauty salon with ocean-view windows to the port side, several treatment rooms, and men's and women's sauna, steam room, and changing areas.

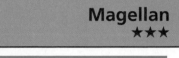

Magellan
★★★

Size:	Mid-size Ship	Passenger/Crew Ratio (lower beds):	2.2
Tonnage:	46,052	Cabins (total):	726
Lifestyle:	Standard	Size Range (sq ft/m):	189.2–420.0/17.0–39.0
Cruise Line:	Cruise and Maritime Voyages	Cabins (for one person):	0
Former Names:	*Grand Holiday, Holiday*	Cabins (with private balcony):	10
IMO Number:	8217881	Cabins (wheelchair accessible):	15
Builder:	Aalborg Vaerft (Denmark)	Wheelchair accessibility:	None
Original Cost:	$170 million	Cabin Current:	110 volts
Entered Service:	Jul 1985/Jun 2015	Elevators:	8
Registry:	The Bahamas	Casino (gaming tables):	Yes
Length (ft/m):	726.0/221.3	Slot Machines:	Yes
Beam (ft/m):	92.4/28.1	Swimming Pools:	3
Draft (ft/m):	25.5/7.7	Hot Tubs (on deck):	2
Propulsion/Propellers:	diesel (22,360kW)/2	Self-Service Launderette:	No
Passenger Decks:	9	Dedicated Cinema/Seats:	No
Total Crew:	660	Library:	Yes
Passengers (lower beds):	1,452	Onboard currency:	Euros
Passenger Space Ratio (lower beds):	31.7		

An informal, colorful, adults-only ship for British cruisers

OVERVIEW. This ship is best suited to British mature adults seeking a low-cost cruise experience. The passenger flow inside is good, although the ship has a high density and feels crowded in some areas.

THE SHIP. *Magellan* (formerly *Grand Holiday*) was originally built as a Carnival Cruise Line ship. It is a boxy, all-white vessel, although CMV have managed to soften its looks with a bow to stern stripe. The ship also has a short, rakish bow and a flat, stubby stern – typical of so many ships built in the 1980s. It does, however, have a distinctive swept-back wing-tipped funnel.

The salt-water swimming pools are quite small, as are the hot tubs, but the open deck and sunning space atop ship is decent. There is an exterior walking area, although it doesn't wrap around the front of the ship.

There are numerous public rooms on two main entertainment decks, and these flow from a wide indoor promenade. Strangely, the Neptune Observation Bar is aft. Still, you can see where you've been!

The good: escort to cabin when you embark; large public lounges and open spaces; friendly staff; non-glitzy decor; slot machines close to gaming tables in the casino. The not-so-good: no walk-around promenade deck outdoors, although the outdoor space itself is good; there are many slim pillars in public rooms; many of the low-back tub chairs have no back support.

ACCOMMODATION. There are just four cabin categories: Suite with balcony; Junior Suite with balcony; exterior cabins; and interior (no-view) cabins, in 15

Berlitz's Ratings		
	Possible	Achieved
Ship	500	289
Accommodation	200	123
Food	400	214
Service	400	241
Entertainment	100	64
Cruise Experience	400	225
OVERALL SCORE		
1156 points out of 2000		

different price grades. The standard cabins are plain but functional units that provide all you need, plus a vanity. TV sets are typically placed high in one corner and are not easy to watch. The bathrooms are practical, with decent-size shower enclosures.

DINING. There are two main restaurants: Kensington (in the center) and Waldorf (aft – with some nice ocean-view tables at the back). Both are large but feel cramped.

Remember that this really is banquet-style catering, so standardization and production cooking is the norm. In other words, don't expect too much in the way of quality, although several traditional British favorite dishes are part of the menu offerings. Although there is a decent wine list, there are no wine waiters.

Raffles Bistro is a self-serve buffet area that provides all the basics (except service), although its layout is old in style and makes the venue seem more like a canteen. Still, it's good for a quick meal when the ship is in port.

ENTERTAINMENT. The Magellan Show Lounge is the main venue for colourful, low-cost production shows and cabaret acts, but note that pillars obstruct the views from several seats. Most lounges and bars have live music, so there's always plenty of life.

SPA/FITNESS. The Jade Wellness Center is located on an upper deck, but the fitness room is on a different deck. Some fitness classes are free, while some may cost extra. Book early for massages, facials, or other beauty treatments, because time slots go quickly.

Marco Polo
★★+

Size:	Mid-size Ship
Tonnage:	22,080
Lifestyle:	Standard
Cruise Line:	Cruise and Maritime Voyages
Former Names:	*Aleksandr Pushkin*
IMO Number:	5112195
Builder:	VEB Mathias Thesen Werft (Germany)
Original Cost:	n/a
Entered Service:	Apr 1966/Apr 2008
Registry:	The Bahamas
Length (ft/m):	578.4/176.2
Beam (ft/m):	77.4/23.6
Draft (ft/m):	26.8/8.1
Propulsion/Propellers:	diesel(14,444kW)/2
Passenger Decks:	8
Total Crew:	356
Passengers (lower beds):	848
Passenger Space Ratio (lower beds):	26.0

Passenger/Crew Ratio (lower beds):	2.3
Cabins (total):	425
Size Range (sq ft/m):	93.0–484.0/8.6–44.9
Cabins (for one person):	many doubles are sold for single occupancy
Cabins (with private balcony):	0
Cabins (wheelchair accessible):	2
Wheelchair accessibility:	Fair
Cabin Current:	110 and 220 volts
Elevators:	4
Casino (gaming tables):	No
Slot Machines:	No
Swimming Pools:	1
Hot Tubs (on deck):	3
Self-Service Launderette:	No
Dedicated Cinema/Seats:	No
Library:	Yes
Onboard currency:	UK£

Modest ship, food, and service, for frugal cruisers

OVERVIEW. This is a comfortable ship with classic looks, and, with its deep draft, rides well in unkind sea conditions. It appeals to couples and solo travelers of mature years who enjoy visiting interesting destinations in the comfort of a ship that is unpretentious yet pleasing, without much entertainment or organized parlor games, but with plenty of old-world charm.

Berlitz's Ratings		
	Possible	Achieved
Ship	500	272
Accommodation	200	120
Food	400	198
Service	400	223
Entertainment	100	56
Cruise Experience	400	213
OVERALL SCORE		
1082 points out of 2000		

THE SHIP. Growing old gracefully, *Marco Polo* was built as one of five sister ships for the Russian/Ukrainian fleet. Originally designed in 1966 to re-open the Leningrad to Montreal transatlantic route, inoperative since 1949, it has a traditional 'real ship' profile, an extremely strong ice-strengthened hull, and huge storage spaces for long voyages.

The ship passed to Norwegian Cruise Line in 1998, and in 2007 to Greek owners. In 2008, it was operated under charter to Transocean Tours of Germany, which sub-chartered it to Cruise & Maritime Voyages, the UK's newest cruise line. It received a £3 million refit/refurbishment in 2009. It operates adults-only cruises from the UK (although during school vacation periods anyone 16 and over becomes an eligible passenger) with Tilbury (London International Cruise Terminal) as its home port.

Marco Polo is fitted with the latest navigational aids and biological waste treatment center, and carries 10 Zodiac landing craft for in-depth shore trips in eco-sensitive areas. There are two large, forward-facing open-deck viewing areas, and a helicopter pad. The teakwood-decked aft swimming pool/Lido Deck area is kept in good condition. Joggers and walkers can circle around the ship – not on the promenade deck, but one deck above, although this goes past vast air intakes that are noisy, and the walkway is narrow.

As soon as you walk aboard, you feel a warm, welcoming, homely ambience. There is a wide range of public rooms, most of which are arranged on one deck. A sense of spaciousness pervades, as most have high ceilings. The interior decor is quite tasteful, with careful use of mirrored surfaces and colors that do not clash but aren't boring. The subdued lighting helps maintain an air of calmness and relaxation.

Now more than 45 years old, the ship is still in decent shape. Indeed, it's in better shape than many ships only 10 years old, and its interiors are constantly being refurbished and refreshed. It operates well-planned destination-intensive cruises and offers really good value for money in very comfortable, unpretentious but tasteful surroundings, while an accommodating crew helps to make a cruise a pleasant, no-hassle experience. Gratuities are automatically applied to your onboard account.

Passenger niggles? There is no observation lounge with forward-facing views over the bows. There are many raised thresholds, so you need to be on your guard when walking through the ship and particularly when negotiating the exterior stairways, which could prove difficult for mobility-limited passengers.

ACCOMMODATION. The cabins, which come in various price grades, depending on location and size, are a profusion of different sizes and configurations. All are pleasingly decorated, practical units with good, solid, rich wood cabinetry, wood and mirror-fronted closets, adequate drawer and storage space, TV set, thin cotton bathrobe (upper grades only), and bathroom-mounted hairdryer and non-vacuum, non-noisy toilets. Carpets, curtains, and bedspreads are all nicely color-coordinated. Weak points include extremely poor sound insulation between cabins – you can probably hear your neighbors brushing their hair – and the fact that the bathrooms are small, with little storage space for toiletries, which is a particular issue during long cruises.

The largest accommodation is found in two suites: Dynasty and Mandarin, on Columbus Deck. These have a separate living room, and marble bathroom with tub/shower, walk-in closet, refrigerator, and a TV set/DVD unit. Slightly smaller are two Junior Suites on Pacific Deck. All suites have superior locations with forward-facing views over the ship's bow.

Also quite comfortable are the superior deluxe ocean-view cabins that have two lower beds (some can be converted to a queen-size bed), marble bathroom with tub/shower, and refrigerator.

Some cabins on Upper Deck and Sky Deck have lifeboat-obstructed views. It would be advisable to avoid cabins 310/312, as these are located close to the engine room doorway, and the noise level is considerable. No cabins have a balcony because the ship was built for long-distance ocean/sea crossings before they became popular.

DINING. The Waldorf, in the ship's center, is nicely decorated in soft pastel colors, practical in design, and functions well, but it has a low ceiling, is noisy, and the tables are very close together. There are two seatings, with tables for two to 10, and good place settings/china. The food itself is of a modest standard, and presentation, quality, and taste could certainly be improved. The wine and prices are reasonable, although most wines are young.

Other dining options. Marco's Restaurant is for informal self-serve breakfasts and lunches – there is seating inside as well as outdoors around the ship's single, aft swimming pool. On some evenings during each cruise, it also becomes an alternative dining spot for about 75 people. Reservations are required, but there is no extra charge. A 15 percent gratuity is added to all bar and wine accounts.

ENTERTAINMENT. The Ambassador Lounge is the principal venue for shows, cabaret acts, and lectures. A single-level room, it has banquette seating and fairly decent sight lines, although several pillars obstruct the view from some seats. Entertainment is low-key and low-budget, and consists of cabaret acts such as singers, magicians, and comedians. There's live music for social dancing and listening in several bars and cocktail lounges.

SPA/FITNESS. This is an older ship that was built when spa and wellbeing facilities were not really thought about. A Health Spa was added in a later refit. It is located aft on Upper Deck, and contains a gymnasium – it's not large, but there are a few treadmills, exercycles, and some muscle-toning equipment. There's also a beauty salon, a sauna, changing facilities, and treatment rooms for massages, facials, and other body-pampering treatments.

The spa is operated by Mandara Spa, and treatments have an Asian flavor – Indonesian facials, coconut body polish, aromatherapy massages, etc.

Marina
★★★★+

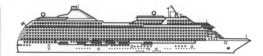

Size:	Mid-size Ship	Passenger/Crew Ratio (lower beds):	1.5
Tonnage:	66,084	Cabins (total):	629
Lifestyle:	Premium	Size Range (sq ft/m):	172.2–2,000/16.0–185.0
Cruise Line:	Oceania Cruises	Cabins (for one person):	0
Former Names:	none	Cabins (with private balcony):	593
IMO Number:	9438066	Cabins (wheelchair accessible):	6
Builder:	Fincantieri (Italy)	Wheelchair accessibility:	Good
Original Cost:	$530 million	Cabin Current:	110 and 220 volts
Entered Service:	Jan 2011/Jan 2011	Elevators:	6
Registry:	Marshall Islands	Casino (gaming tables):	Yes
Length (ft/m):	776.5/236.7	Slot Machines:	Yes
Beam (ft/m):	105.3/32.1	Swimming Pools:	1
Draft (ft/m):	24.2/7.4	Hot Tubs (on deck):	3
Propulsion/Propellers:	diesel-electric/2	Self-Service Launderette:	Yes
Passenger Decks:	11	Dedicated Cinema/Seats:	No
Total Crew:	800	Library:	Yes
Passengers (lower beds):	1,258	Onboard currency:	US$
Passenger Space Ratio (lower beds):	52.5		

Premium country club style for mature-age cruisers

OVERVIEW. *Marina* is really comfortable, although you will need to walk a little more than on many cruise ships. It will suit mature-age adults who appreciate quality and style, with plenty of space, plus excellent cuisine and service, in an informal setting with realistic pricing.

THE SHIP. Built in 55 blocks, *Marina* is the first newbuild for this growing small cruise line. Its profile is quite handsome, with a nicely rounded front and topped by a swept-back funnel. Able to cruise at a speed 25 percent faster than the other three ships in the fleet, it can operate cruises over longer distances.

Oceania Cruises has been careful to try to keep the warm and tasteful 'country house' decor style for which it has become known – the smaller ships were designed by the Scottish designer John McNeece – together with an uncomplicated layout that's easy to master quickly.

The interior focal point is the stunning wrought-iron and Lalique glass horseshoe-shaped staircase in the main lobby. Public rooms include nine bars and lounges. There is a 2,000-book library, set on the port side of the funnel housing. The Monte Carlo Casino has its own soft lavender-colored Casino Bar.

The Culinary Center, a cooking demonstration kitchen with 24 workstations run in conjunction with the US-based *Bon Appétit* magazine, incurs a fee for each of several cookery classes, but at least you get to eat your creations. An Artist's Loft hosts constantly changing artists – bring your own paint-

Berlitz's Ratings

	Possible	Achieved
Ship	500	442
Accommodation	200	179
Food	400	333
Service	400	316
Entertainment	100	82
Cruise Experience	400	327
OVERALL SCORE		
1679 points out of 2000		

brushes. If you like art, look for the genuine Picassos on board; there are 16 of them, including six in the casino.

The dress code is country club – no pyjamas or track suits, but no ties, either. Note that a rather large gratuity of 18 percent is added to bar and spa accounts.

In 2012, some of the modifications made when building its close sister *Riviera* were incorporated in its first drydocking. These include better lighting and deeper drawers in suites and cabins, teak decking, plus hand-held shower hoses in suites with bathtubs, and chandeliers in public rooms. Overall, a cruise aboard Marina is a very nice experience.

ACCOMMODATION. There are several price categories, with four suite grades: Owner's Suite; Oceania Suite; Vista Suite; and Penthouse Suite – and four cabin grades: concierge-level veranda cabin; veranda cabin; deluxe ocean-view cabin; and interior cabin. Price depends on size and location, but all have one thing in common – a good-size bathroom with tub, and separate (but small) shower enclosure, plus two toiletry cabinets.

Around 96 percent of all the accommodation onboard has teak-decked balconies. There's no tie rack in the closets, because the dress code is casual. The decor includes chocolate brown, cream, and white – earthy colors that don't jar the senses. All suites and cabins have dark wood cabinetry with rounded edges.

Standard veranda cabins. These measure 282 sq ft (26 sq m). Veranda and concierge-level cabins have a sitting area and teak balcony with faux wicker furniture. Concierge-level grades receive L'Occitane toiletries.

Penthouse Suites. These measure 420 sq ft (39 sq m) with living/dining room separate from the sleeping area, walk-in closet, and bathroom with a double vanity.

Oceania Suites. These measure about 1,030 sq ft (96 sq m) and have a living room, dining room, separate bedroom, walk-in closet, teak-decked balcony with Jacuzzi tub, main bathroom, and a second bathroom for guests.

Vista Suites. These range from 1,200 to 1,500 sq ft (111–139 sq m) and offer the same features as Oceania Suites but add floor-to-ceiling windows overlooking the bow.

Owner's Suite. At more than 2,000 sq ft (186 sq m), this spans the ship's entire beam. It is decked out in furniture, fabrics, lighting, and bedding from the Ralph Lauren Home collection with design by New York-based Tocar, Inc. It is outfitted with a Yamaha baby grand piano, private fitness room, laptop computers, Bose audio system, and a teak-decked balcony with Jacuzzi tub.

Suite-category occupants get extras such as Champagne on arrival, 1,000-thread-count bed linen, 42ins plasma TV sets, Hermès and Clarins bath products, butler service, en-suite delivery from any of the ship's restaurants, and priority check-in and early embarkation and priority luggage delivery. Amenities include Tranquility beds, Wi-Fi laptop computer, refrigerated minibar with unlimited free soft drinks and bottled water replenished daily, personal safe, writing desk, cotton bathrobes, slippers, and marble and granite bathroom.

Occupants of Owner's, Vista, Oceania, and Penthouse Suites can have in-suite course-by-course dining from any restaurant menu, making private dining possible as a change to being in the restaurants.

Some grades get access to an Executive Lounge or Concierge Lounge. These are great little hideaways, with sofas, Internet-connect computers, Continental breakfast items, soft drinks, and magazines. Self-service launderettes are on each accommodation deck – useful for long voyages.

DINING. Six open-seating dining venues provide plenty of choice, enough even for long cruises, although banquette seating in some venues does not evoke the image of premium dining as much as individual seating does. Also, it would be hard to describe some of the specialty dining venues as intimate. This is, however, a foodie's ship, with really high-quality ingredients and effectively fancy presentation. Particularly notable are the delicious breads, rolls, croissants, and brioches – all made on board from French flour and d'Isigny butter.

The Grand Dining Room has 566 seats, and a domed, or raised, central ceiling. Versace bone china, Christofle silver, and fine linens are used. Canyon Ranch Spa dishes are available for all meals.

Other dining options. French celebrity chef Jacques Pépin, Oceania's executive culinary director, has his first sea-going restaurant, Jacques, with 124 seats. It has antique oak flooring, antique flatware, and Lalique glassware, and offers fine dining in an elegant but informal setting, with roast free-range meats, nine classic French dessert items, and a choice of 12 AOC cheeses.

Polo Grill, with 134 seats, serves steaks and seafood, including Oceania's signature 32oz bone-in King's Cut prime rib. The setting is classic traditional steakhouse, with dark wood paneling and classic white tablecloths, although the tables are a little close together.

The 124-seat Toscana features Italian-style cuisine, served on Versace china.

Privée, with seating for up to 10 in a private setting, invites exclusivity for its seven-course dégustation menu.

La Réserve offers a choice of two seven-course small-portion dégustation menus (Discovery and Explorer), paired with wines. With just 24 seats, it's really intimate.

The Terrace Café is the casual self-serve buffet-style venue; outdoors, as an extension of the café, is Tapas on the Terrace – good for light bites (although the ceiling is low and it can be very noisy).

Red Ginger is a specialty restaurant, which offers 'classic and contemporary' Asian cuisine; the setting is visually refined, with ebony and dark wood finishes, but the banquette-style seating lets the venue down. Your waiter will ask you to choose your chopsticks from a lacquered presentation box.

The poolside Waves Grill, shaded from the sun, serves Angus beef burgers, fishburgers, veggie burgers, Reuben sandwiches, seafood, and other fast food, cooked to order.

Baristas coffee bar overlooks the pool deck and has excellent – and free – illy Italian coffee. However, in the bars the tonic mixed with gin and vodka is too sweet and of inferior quality.

ENTERTAINMENT. The 600-seat Marina Lounge spans two decks, with tiered amphitheater-style seating. It's more cabaret-style entertainment than big production shows, in keeping with the cruise line's traditions, which suits the passenger clientele just fine.

SPA/FITNESS. The Canyon Ranch SpaClub provides wellness and personal spa treatments. The facility includes a fitness center, beauty salon, several treatment rooms, thalassotherapy pool, and sauna and steam rooms. A jogging track is located aft of the funnel, above two of the specialty restaurants.

Mariner of the Seas
★★★+

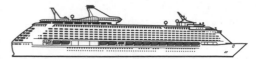

Size:	Large Resort Ship		Passenger Space Ratio (lower beds):	44.0
Tonnage:	137,276		Passenger/Crew Ratio (lower beds):	2.6
Lifestyle:	Standard		Cabins (total):	1,557
Cruise Line:	Royal Caribbean International		Size Range (sq ft/m):	151.0–1,358.0/14.0–126.1
Former Names:	none		Cabins (for one person):	0
IMO Number:	9227510		Cabins (with private balcony):	765
Builder:	Kvaerner Masa-Yards (Finland)		Cabins (wheelchair accessible):	26
Original Cost:	$500 million		Wheelchair accessibility:	Best
Entered Service:	Nov 2004		Cabin Current:	110 volts
Registry:	The Bahamas		Elevators:	14
Length (ft/m):	1,020.6/311.1		Casino (gaming tables):	Yes
Beam (ft/m):	155.5/47.4		Slot Machines:	Yes
Draft (ft/m):	28.8/8.8		Swimming Pools:	3
Propulsion/Propellers:	diesel-electric (75,600kW)/3 pods		Hot Tubs (on deck):	6
	(2 azimuthing, 1 fixed)		Self-Service Launderette:	No
Passenger Decks:	14		Dedicated Cinema/Seats:	No
Total Crew:	1,185		Library:	Yes
Passengers (lower beds):	3,114		Onboard currency:	US$

This large resort ship is for family-friendly casual cruising

OVERVIEW. This ship dwarfs many other cruise ships in size, but not in terms of personal service unless you happen to reside in a top suite. Royal Caribbean International (RCI) tries to provide a good standard of programmed service from its hotel service staff.

THE SHIP. *Mariner of the Seas* is a stunning, large, floating leisure resort. It has a healthy passenger/space ratio and extensive facilities such as a regulation-size ice-skating rink.

A four-deck-high Royal Promenade, 394ft (120m) long and the main interior focal point, is a good place to hang out or to arrange to meet someone. It has two internal lobbies that rise through 11 decks. Casual eateries, shops, and entertainment locations front this winding street and interior 'with-view' cabins look into it from above. The guest reception and shore excursion counters are located at the aft end of the promenade, as is an ATM machine.

Arched across the promenade is a captain's balcony. A stairway in the center of the promenade connects you to the deck below, where you'll find Schooner Bar and the colorful Casino Royale. Several shops line the Royal Promenade, including a jewelry store, gift shop, and liquor store.

There is a regulation-size ice-skating rink (Studio B), with real ice, and stadium-style seating for up to 900, plus high-tech broadcast facilities. Ice Follies shows are also presented here. Slim pillars obstruct clear-view arena stage sightlines, however. You can also read in the two-deck library, open 24 hours a day.

Berlitz's Ratings

	Possible	Achieved
Ship	500	390
Accommodation	200	141
Food	400	223
Service	400	267
Entertainment	100	74
Cruise Experience	400	264
OVERALL SCORE		
1359 points out of 2000		

Drinking places include an intimate Champagne Bar, Wig & Gavel Pub, a Sidewalk Café, Sprinkles, a sports bar, and a Connoisseur Club. Jazz fans might like the intimate Jazz Club. Golfers might also enjoy the 19th Hole, a golf bar, as they play the Explorer Links.

A TV studio is adjacent to rooms useable for trade show exhibit space, with a 400-seat conference center and a multimedia screening room seating 60. You can tie the knot in the Skylight Chapel, which has wheelchair access via an electric stairlift.

Passenger niggles: cabin bath towels and noisy (vacuum) toilets; few quiet places to sit and read – almost everywhere there is intrusive background music. If you have a cabin with an interconnecting door to another cabin, you'll be able to hear everything they do.

FAMILIES. Facilities for children and teenagers are quite extensive. Aquanauts is for 3–5-year-olds; Explorers (6–8); Voyagers (9–12). Optix is a dedicated area for teenagers, including a daytime club with computers, soda bar, disco with disc jockey and dance floor. Challenger's Arcade has the latest video games. Paint and Clay is an arts and crafts center for younger children. Adjacent to these indoor areas is Adventure Beach.

ACCOMMODATION. There is a wide range of cabin price grades, in four major groupings. Premium ocean-view suites and cabins, interior (atrium-view) cabins, ocean-view cabins, and interior cabins. Many cabins are of a similar size, and 300 have interconnecting doors.

Some 138 interior cabins have bay windows that look into the Royal Promenade. Regardless of the cabin grade you choose, all except the Royal and Owner's Suites have twin beds that convert to a queen-size unit, TV set, radio and telephone, personal safe, vanity unit, hairdryer, and private bathroom. However, you'll need to keep the curtains closed in the bay windows, because you can be seen easily from adjacent bay windows.

Royal Suite (Deck 10). At around 1,146 sq ft (107 sq m), the Royal Suite is the largest private living space, located almost at the top of the Centrum lobby on the port side. It has a king-size circular bed in a separate large bedroom, living room with an additional queen-size sofa bed, baby grand piano, refrigerator/wet bar, dining table and four chairs, expansive entertainment center, and a reasonably large bathroom.

Royal Family Suites. The four Royal Family Suites (two aft on Deck 9, two aft on Deck 8, each measuring around 574 sq ft/53 sq m) have two separate bedrooms. The main bedroom has a large vanity desk; the second, smaller, bedroom also includes two beds and third/fourth upper Pullman berths. There's a lounge with dining table and four chairs, wet bar, walk-in closet; and large bathroom with Jacuzzi tub, washbasin, and separate shower enclosure. These suites have large balconies with views over the ship's stern.

Owner's Suites. Ten slightly smaller but still desirable Owner's Suites (around 468 sq ft/43 sq m) are in the center of the ship, on both port and starboard sides, adjacent to the Centrum lobby on Deck 10. Each has a bedroom with queen-size bed or twin beds; lounge with large sofa; wet bar; bathroom with Jacuzzi tub, washbasin and separate shower enclosure. There's also a private balcony, although it's small.

Standard outside-view and interior cabins. All cabins have a private bathroom, as well as interactive TV and pay-per-view movies, including an X-rated channel. Cabin bathrooms really are compact, but at least they have a proper shower enclosure instead of a shower curtain.

Some accommodation grades have a refrigerator/minibar, although there is no space left because it is crammed with 'take-and-pay' items. If you take anything from the minibar/refrigerator on the day of embarkation in Miami, Florida, sales tax will be added to your bill.

Cabins with 'private balconies' aren't so private. The balcony decking is made of Bolidt – a sort of rubberized sand – and not wood, though the balcony rail is of wood. Cabin bath towels are small and skimpy. Room-service food menus are very basic.

DINING. The main dining room, with a seating capacity of 1,919, is set on three levels: Rhapsody in Blue, Top Hat and Tails, and Sound of Music, all offering exactly the same menus and food. A dramatic staircase connects all three levels, but huge, fat support pillars obstruct the sight lines from many seats. When you book, choose one of two seatings, or 'My Time Dining.' Tables are for four, six, eight, 10, or 12. The place settings, porcelain, and cutlery are of good quality.

Other dining options. Alternative dining options for casual and informal meals at all hours include: Promenade Café: for Continental breakfast, all-day pizzas, and specialty coffees – which are only available in paper cups. Windjammer Café: this is a really large, sprawling venue for casual buffet-style, self-help breakfast (this tends to be the busiest time of the day), lunch, and light dinners (but not on the last night of the cruise); it's often difficult to find a table and by the time you do your food could be cold. Island Grill: (actually this is a section within the Windjammer Café), for casual grilled meat and seafood items (no reservations necessary) featuring a grill and open kitchen. Portofino: the ship's upscale Italian restaurant, open for dinner only. Reservations are required, and there's a gratuity per person. The food and its presentation are better than the food in the dining room. The menu does not change throughout the cruise. Johnny Rockets, a retro 1950s eatery, has hamburgers, malt shakes (at extra cost), and jukebox hits, with both indoor and outdoor seating. Sprinkles, located on the Royal Promenade, is for round-the-clock ice cream and yogurt, pastries, and coffee.

ENTERTAINMENT. The 1,350-seat Savoy Showlounge is a stunning room that could well be the equal of many showrooms on land. It has a hydraulic orchestra pit and a huge stage area, and superb lighting equipment. *Mariner of the Seas* also has an array of cabaret acts. The best shows of all are the Ice Spectaculars. Note that RCI's entertainment is always upbeat. There is even background music in all corridors and elevators, and constant music outdoors on the pool deck.

SPA/FITNESS. The Vitality at Sea Spa is reasonably large, and measures 15,000 sq ft (1,400 sq m). It includes an aerobics room, fitness center, treatment rooms, and sauna/steam rooms. Another 10,000 sq ft (930 sq m) of space is devoted to a Solarium (with sliding glass-dome roof) to relax in.

On the back of the funnel is a 32.8ft (10m) rock-climbing wall, with five climbing tracks. It gives you a great buzz being 200ft (60m) above the ocean while the ship is moving. Other facilities include a roller-blading track, a full-size basketball court, and a nine-hole, par 26 golf course. A dive-and-snorkel shop provides equipment for rental, and diving classes.

Mein Schiff 1
★★★★

Size:	Mid-size Ship	Passenger/Crew Ratio (lower beds):	2.4
Tonnage:	77,713	Cabins (total):	962
Lifestyle:	Standard	Size Range (sq ft/m):	172.2-1,054/16.0-98.0
Cruise Line:	TUI Cruises	Cabins (for one person):	0
Former Names:	Celebrity Galaxy, Galaxy	Cabins (with private balcony):	430
IMO Number:	9106297	Cabins (wheelchair accessible):	8
Builder:	Meyer Werft (Germany)	Wheelchair accessibility:	Good
Original Cost:	$320 million	Cabin Current:	110 and 220 volts
Entered Service:	Dec 1996/May 2009	Elevators:	10
Registry:	Malta	Casino (gaming tables):	Yes
Length (ft/m):	865.8/263.9	Slot Machines:	Yes
Beam (ft/m):	105.6/32.2	Swimming Pools:	2
Draft (ft/m):	25.2/7.7	Hot Tubs (on deck):	4
Propulsion/Propellers:	diesel (31,500kW)/2	Self-Service Launderette:	No
Passenger Decks:	10	Dedicated Cinema/Seats:	Yes/200
Total Crew:	780	Library:	Yes
Passengers (lower beds):	1,924	Onboard currency:	Euros
Passenger Space Ratio (lower beds):	40.3		

Contemporary style for casual, family-friendly cruising

OVERVIEW. *Mein Schiff 1* is for German-speaking families with children who want to cruise aboard a ship with a contemporary environment, good itineraries and food, and European-style service from a well-trained crew that delivers a product that's fresh and surprisingly good. The product is worth more than the cruise fare charged when compared with several other large-ship cruise lines.

Berlitz's Ratings		
	Possible	Achieved
Ship	500	406
Accommodation	200	161
Food	400	282
Service	400	309
Entertainment	100	71
Cruise Experience	400	305
OVERALL SCORE		
1534 points out of 2000		

THE SHIP. *Mein Schiff 1*, originally built for Celebrity Cruises as *Galaxy*, was transferred in 2009 to newcomer TUI Cruises (part of TUI Travel – Europe's largest tour operator) specifically for German-speaking passengers, in a joint venture with Royal Caribbean Cruises, parent of Royal Caribbean International. The ship underwent a major conversion at that time. Its name ('My Ship') was suggested by several entrants to a magazine competition; the winner, whose name was drawn from a hat, was Oliver Krimmel, a Stuttgart designer.

This all-inclusive mid-size ship has just about all you need for an enjoyable and rewarding cruise experience, and provides competition for AIDA Cruises, whose ships, by comparison, lack a traditional dining room, and have few service staff. TUI Cruises has got the onboard product just about right for German-speaking passengers, with many more dining and eating choices and more class and style than AIDA's ships, and with better food and plenty of snappily dressed service personnel. With 10 bars, four restaurants, six bistros, and good facilities for families, *Mein*

Schiff 1 has become the benchmark for a high-value, full-service cruise vacation in Germany.

The ship has good tender-loading platforms. But, although there are more than 4.5 acres (1.8 hectares) of space on the open decks, it can appear to be a little small and cramped when the ship is full. Ten charming two-person cabanas can be rented on an upper, outside deck, with great ocean views, but insulated from the life that goes on around the ship.

Inside, a four-deck-high main foyer houses the reception desk and shore excursion station. There's a small, dedicated cinema, which doubles as a conference and meeting center with all the latest audio-visual technology, including simultaneous translation and headsets for the hearing-impaired.

Relaxation is a key element of the product, and *Mein Schiff 1* is equipped with individual hammocks in various locations, including on cabin balconies as well as in public areas. Additionally, 'Meditation Islands' are installed on deck: the ship's rail is fitted with mini-balconies, equipped with special blinds. Here, passengers are able to enjoy a private space for relaxation.

Making it even more user-friendly for families is the all-inclusive pricing introduced in 2010, though this excludes the extra-cost restaurants Richards Feines Essen, Blaue Welt Sushi Bar, and the Surf 'n' Turf Steakhouse and also excursions and spa treatments. The dress code throughout the ship is smart casual.

ACCOMMODATION. There are 10 price grades, depending on the size and location of your living space, but the accommodation is very comfortable throughout. Every cabin has its own Nespresso coffee machine, which takes pre-portioned packets of espresso coffee. The first two are included, but any additional packets cost €1 each. All accommodation grades are designated no-smoking.

Most suites with private balconies have floor-to-ceiling windows and sliding doors to balconies, and a few have outward opening doors. Suite-grade accommodation gets European duvets on the beds, instead of sheets and blankets. A balcony massage service is also available – it's worth it. Suite occupants get special cards to open their doors, plus priority service throughout the ship and for embarkation and disembarkation, free cappuccino/espresso coffees served by a butler, welcome Champagne, flowers, and picnic baskets as required. Suite occupants also get a private, 100-seat concierge lounge/bar and social venue (the 'X' Lounge) atop the ship, with great ocean views – a good place for reading a book during the day.

Penthouse Suites. These two suites, located amidships, are the largest. Each has its own butler's pantry, and an interconnecting door for linking to the suite next door.

Most of the Deck 10 suites and cabins are of generous proportions and beautifully equipped, and have balconies with full floor-to-ceiling partitions and large flat-screen TV sets. The Sky Deck suites are also excellent, and most of them have huge balconies; unfortunately, the partitions are not quite of the floor-to-ceiling type, so you can hear your neighbors. Also included are wall clock, large floor-to-ceiling mirrors, marble-topped vanity/writing desk, excellent closet and drawer space, and dimmer-controlled ceiling lights.

Standard outside-view/interior cabins. All of these are of a good size – larger than those aboard the ships of AIDA Cruises, for example – and come nicely furnished with twin beds that convert to a queen-size unit. The bathrooms are spacious and well equipped, and have generous-size showers, hairdryers, and space for personal toiletries. Baby-monitoring telephones are provided in all cabins. There are no cabins for occupancy by solo travelers.

DINING. Restaurants and bistros range from self-serve buffet style to service, with a focus on healthy eating. There is no pre-defined seating, so you can dine when you want, and with whomever you want – good for multi-generational families. The emphasis is on healthy food, including power food, brain food, soul food, erotic food, new food (quinoa, soya, and tofu dishes), including fresh fish.

The Atlantik Restaurant is a stunning, two-level dining hall – somewhat reminiscent of the dining halls aboard the ocean liners of the 1930s – with a grand staircase that flows between both levels and perimeter alcoves that provide more intimate dining spaces. However, there's one big difference, in that this restaurant has 6.5ft (2m) -wide trapeze bars built into its center. Tables are for two, four, six, eight, or 10.

Other dining options. Richards Feines Essen (Gourmet Restaurant) is an à-la-carte, reservations-only venue, with a calming, restful wood-laden interior, where high-quality fine dining and service are offered.

Surf 'n' Turf Steakhouse serves premium steaks and grilled seafood, with aged beef commanding different price points.

In a venue covered by a retractable glass dome, in the aft section of the ship, three eateries, combined with a communal bar, provide completely different food experiences: Bistro La Vela for Italian cuisine, including an 'active' pasta cooking station, and pizza; Gosch Sylt, for fresh fish and seafood; and Tapas y Mas, for tapas and other tasting dishes. This venue is a most popular place to meet the fashionable set.

Other dining spots around the ship include: La Vida Sana, for wellness cuisine; Blaue Welt (Blue World) Sushi Bar, on the upper level of the atrium; Vino, a wine-tasting bar; and a coffee lounge set around the atrium lobby, for specialty coffees and pastries.

For informal breakfasts and lunches, the two-level self-serve Anckelmannsplatz Buffet – the name comes from the road on which the TUI Cruises offices are located in Hamburg – is the place to go. There are several serving counters and 'active' food islands; the venue has warm wood-accented decor, and eight bay windows provide some prime seating spots. There are also two poolside grills – one located adjacent to the midships pools, the other wedged into an area aft of the swimming pool/hot tub cluster.

ENTERTAINMENT. The Theater is a 927-seat show-lounge spanning two decks, with seating on both main and cantilevered balcony levels. There are good sight lines from all seats. Production shows are excellent. It has a revolving stage, 'hard' curtain, and large fly tower.

SPA/FITNESS. The Spa and More, located at the front of the ship one deck above the navigation bridge, has 18,299 sq ft (1,700 sq m) of space. It includes a large fitness/exercise area with all the latest machines and exercise bikes; beauty salon; thalassotherapy pool; seven treatment rooms; and a Rasul room for Mediterranean mud and gentle steam bathing. Private 'spa suites' with fine, relaxing views are located above the ship's navigation bridge and can be rented for the morning, afternoon, or the whole day. Atop the ship at the front is a healthy FKK (Freikörperkultur) deck for naked sunbathing.

Mein Schiff 2
★★★★

Size:	Mid-size Ship	Passenger/Crew Ratio (lower beds):	2.4
Tonnage:	77,713	Cabins (total):	956
Lifestyle:	Standard	Size Range (sq ft/m):	172.2–1,054.0/16.0–98.0
Cruise Line:	TUI Cruises	Cabins (for one person):	0
Former Names:	*Celebrity Mercury, Mercury*	Cabins (with private balcony):	220
IMO Number:	9106302	Cabins (wheelchair accessible):	8
Builder:	Meyer Werft (Germany)	Wheelchair accessibility:	Good
Original Cost:	$320 million	Cabin Current:	110 and 220 volts
Entered Service:	Nov 1997/May 2011	Elevators:	10
Registry:	Malta	Casino (gaming tables):	Yes
Length (ft/m):	865.8/263.9	Slot Machines:	Yes
Beam (ft/m):	105.6/32.2	Swimming Pools:	3 (1 w/sliding glass dome)
Draft (ft/m):	25.2/7.7	Hot Tubs (on deck):	4
Propulsion/Propellers:	diesel (31,500kW)/2	Self-Service Launderette:	No
Passenger Decks:	10	Dedicated Cinema/Seats:	Yes/183
Total Crew:	780	Library:	Yes
Passengers (lower beds):	1,912	Onboard currency:	Euros
Passenger Space Ratio (lower beds):	40.6		

A large and stylish premium mid-size ship for the whole family

OVERVIEW. *Mein Schiff 2* is for German-speaking families with children who want to cruise aboard a ship with a contemporary environment, good itineraries, great food, and European-style service from a well-trained crew that delivers a cruise that's fresh and surprisingly good.

THE SHIP. *Mein Schiff 2*, originally built as *Mercury* for Celebrity Cruises, was transferred in 2011 to newcomer TUI Cruises (part of TUI Travel, Europe's largest tour operator) specifically for German-speaking passengers, in a joint venture with Royal Caribbean Cruises, parent of Royal Caribbean International. The ship underwent a major conversion at that time.

This all-inclusive mid-size ship has just about all you need for an enjoyable and rewarding cruise experience. There are 10 bars, four restaurants, six bistros, and good facilities for families with children.

The ship has good tender-loading platforms. But, although there are more than 4.5 acres (1.8 hectares) of space on the open decks, it can become crowded when the ship is full. Charming two-person cabanas can be rented on an upper, outside deck, with great ocean views, but insulated from shipboard life.

Inside, a four-deck-high main foyer houses the reception desk and shore excursion station. There's a small cinema, which doubles as a conference and meeting center, with the latest audio-visual technology, including simultaneous translation and headsets for the hearing-impaired. There's a large shopping center, including ultra-smart shops such as Swarovski, while cigar

Berlitz's Ratings	Possible	Achieved
Ship	500	406
Accommodation	200	161
Food	400	282
Service	400	309
Entertainment	100	71
Cruise Experience	400	306
OVERALL SCORE		
1535 points out of 2000		

smokers will appreciate the private club-like cigar lounge and bar.

The interior decor is at once contemporary in style, but with many restful colors and combinations throughout and nothing is garish – except, perhaps, for the starkly contrasting wallcovering of blood-red capillaries in the Blue World Bar.

Mein Schiff 2 has individual hammocks in various outdoor locations, including on some suite-grade balconies. 'Meditation Islands' are also installed on the open deck: the ship's rail is fitted with mini-balconies, equipped with special blinds, and created as spaces for private relaxation.

Making it even more user-friendly for families is the all-inclusive pricing, though this excludes spa treatments, excursions, and the extra-cost restaurants: Richards Feines Essen, Blaue Welt Sushi Bar, and Surf 'n' Turf Steakhouse. The dress code is smart casual.

FAMILIES. Younger children are well catered for, with a playroom and an outdoor paddling pool, while teens have their own adult-free chill-out lounge. There's also a character called Captain Sharky.

ACCOMMODATION. There are 10 price grades, depending on the size and location of your living space, but the accommodation is very comfortable. Every cabin has its own Nespresso coffee machine, which takes pre-portioned packets of espresso coffee. The first two are included, but any additional packets cost €1 each (free in suites). All accommodation grades are designated no-smoking.

Most suites with private balconies have floor-to-ceiling windows and sliding doors to large balconies – 12 have balconies measuring 258.3 sq ft (24 sq m), with a hammock, two sunloungers and a dining table, and a few have outward opening doors. Suite-grade accommodation gets European duvets on the beds instead of sheets and blankets. A balcony massage service is also available. Suite occupants get special cards to open their doors, plus priority service throughout the ship and for embarkation and disembarkation, free cappuccino and espresso coffees, welcome Champagne, flowers, and picnic baskets as required. Suite occupants also get keycard access to a private, 100-seat concierge lounge/bar and social venue – the 'X' Lounge, with a selection of cold food, including some rather nice caviar for breakfast.

Penthouse Suites. These two suites, located amidships, are the largest. Each has its own butler's pantry, and an interconnecting door to link it to the next door suite.

Most of the Deck 10 suites and cabins are generously proportioned, beautifully equipped, and have balconies with full or almost-full floor-to-ceiling partitions, and large flat-screen TV sets. Also included are a wall clock, large floor-to-ceiling mirrors, a well-stocked minibar, a marble-topped vanity/writing desk, excellent closet and drawer space, and large shower enclosure. Suite occupants get newspapers, chocolates, Champagne, and access to the exclusive X Lounge, next door to the Himmel und Meer Lounge. Look out for the phrase 'Wood Thrust Into Brine' in large letters above the bar – you'll have to look up to see it.

Standard outside-view/interior cabins. All of these are of a good size – larger than those aboard the ships of AIDA Cruises, for example – and come nicely furnished with twin beds that convert to a queen-size unit. The bathrooms are spacious and well equipped, and have generous-size showers, hairdryers, and space for toiletries. Baby-monitoring telephones and personal safes are provided in all cabins. A box containing three crystal-mineral stones provides special filtration for the ship's own bottled water. There are no cabins for occupancy by solo travelers.

DINING. Restaurants and bistros range from self-serve buffet style to service. There is no pre-defined seating. The emphasis is on healthy food, including power food, brain food, soul food, erotic food, and fresh fish. The Atlantik Restaurant is a lovely, two-level Art Deco grand dining hall with a grand staircase. Tables are for two, four, six, eight, or 10.

Other dining options. Richards Feines Essen (Gourmet Restaurant), a specialty dining venue, is à la carte and reservations only, with a restful wood-laden interior and high-quality fine dining and service. A dégustation menu and three specialty vegetarian menus are also available, and the wine list is extensive.

Surf 'n' Turf Steakhouse serves premium steaks and grilled seafood, with aged beef, displayed in a 'proving' or maturing cabinet – a cruise industry first.

In an area covered by a retractable glass dome in the aft section of the ship, three eateries and a communal bar provide very different food experiences (all included in the cruise price): Bistro La Vela for Italian cuisine, including an 'active' pasta cooking station with your choice of six pastas, and freshly made pizza; Gosch Sylt for fresh fish and seafood, with daily specials (it's hugely popular, so make a reservation early); and Tapas y Mas for tapas and other tasting dishes. This venue is a most popular place to meet the fashionable set, with both indoor and outdoor seating and bar.

Others include Blaue Welt (Blue World) Sushi Bar, on the upper level of the atrium; Vino, a wine tasting bar specializing in Austrian and German wines; Cliff 24, a 24-hour poolside grill with different food items throughout the day; and the TUI Bar, a coffee lounge set around the atrium lobby for specialty coffees and pastries, and a separate praline chocolate counter.

For informal breakfasts and lunches, the two-level self-serve Anckelmannsplatz Buffet is the place to go. There are several serving counters and 'active' food islands. There are also two poolside grills – one adjacent to the midships pools, the other wedged into an area aft of the swimming pool/hot tub cluster.

ENTERTAINMENT. The Theater is a 927-seat showlounge spanning two decks, with seating on both main and cantilevered balcony levels. There are good sight lines from all seats. The large-scale production shows are excellent.

SPA/FITNESS. The Spa and More, located at the front of the ship one deck above the navigation bridge, has 18,299 sq ft (1,700 sq m) of space. It includes a large exercise area with the machines and cycles; a beauty salon; a thalassotherapy pool; 15 treatment rooms; a Rasul room for mud and steam bathing; and a sauna.

Private 'spa suites', bookable for an hour or two, or half- or full-day, are extremely large, and include a steam/shower cabinet, thalassotherapy bath, two hydraulic massage/relaxation tables, relaxation seating, and great floor-to-ceiling windows. A balcony adjacent to the sauna is designated as an FKK (Freikörperkultur) deck for nude relaxation.

Mein Schiff 3
★★★★+

Size:	Large Resort Ship
Tonnage:	99,300
Lifestyle:	Standard
Cruise Line:	TUI Cruises
Former Names:	none
IMO Number:	9641730
Builder:	STX Europe (Finland)
Original Cost:	€390 million
Entered Service:	May 2014
Registry:	Malta
Length (ft/m):	967.8/295.0
Beam (ft/m):	118.1/36.0
Draft (ft/m):	26.2/8.0
Propulsion/Propellers:	diesel-electric (28,000kW)/2
Passenger Decks:	12
Total Crew:	1,000
Passengers (lower beds):	2,506
Passenger Space Ratio (lower beds):	39.7

Passenger/Crew Ratio (lower beds):	2.5
Cabins (total):	1,250
Size Range (sq ft/m):	182.9-581.2/17.0-54.0
Cabins (for one person):	0
Cabins (with private balcony):	1,033
Cabins (wheelchair accessible):	10
Wheelchair accessibility:	Good
Cabin Current:	110 and 220 volts
Elevators:	10
Casino (gaming tables):	Yes
Slot Machines:	Yes
Swimming Pools:	3 (1 w/sliding glass dome)
Hot Tubs (on deck):	4
Self-Service Launderette:	No
Dedicated Cinema/Seats:	Yes/200
Library:	Yes
Onboard currency:	Euros

This ship has it all for youthful German-speaking families

OVERVIEW. Named by German pop singer Helene Fischer when it debuted in June 2014, *Mein Schiff 3* is the new kid on the block for the rapidly expanding TUI Cruises. This new ship, for German-speaking families, takes the best parts of the all-inclusive brand further.

THE SHIP. Larger than *Mein Schiff 1* and *Mein Schiff 2*, this ship incorporates all the best of the previous two ships, and has added more facilities and tailored the design to its passengers' needs. Its new-generation propulsion system is stunningly quiet in operation, with absolutely no vibration anywhere.

A superb 82ft (25m) lap pool (long by cruise ship standards and half the length of an 'Olympic' sized pool) is featured outdoors – together with a large-scale movie screen and sports area for basketball and volleyball – while a second, indoor, pool and adjacent hot tubs provide plenty of choice for families with children.

High up on Deck 14 is what's known as the Blue Balcony, a 118.4-sq-ft (11-sq-m) glass-floored platform some 121.3ft (37m) above the sea, which gives the sensation of floating over the ocean.

Public rooms are plentiful, and include a really lovely music academy-style concert hall (auditorium), which has been designed to the highest acoustic specifications.

What makes a cruise aboard *Mein Schiff 3* really user-friendly for families is the all-inclusive pricing, though this excludes spa treatments, excursions, and

Berlitz's Ratings		
	Possible	Achieved
Ship	500	458
Accommodation	200	168
Food	400	327
Service	400	331
Entertainment	100	84
Cruise Experience	400	329
OVERALL SCORE		
1697 points out of 2000		

the extra-cost restaurants: Richards Feines Essen, Blaue Welt Sushi Bar, Fish House Gosch Sylt, and a Surf 'n' Turf Steakhouse, among others. The dress code is smart casual. But the real diamond in the crown is the two-deck high glass enclosure, which houses two different restaurants – with great views over the ship's stern (the back) – and a fine barista coffee lounge.

Mein Schiff 3 has a really comforting 'feel,' and boasts a number of outstanding passenger-friendly features, including: the longest swimming pool of any cruise ship; an ocean-connect museum (I call it an 'oceano-quarium'); water-dispenser units on each accommodation deck (special quartz crystals are provided in each cabin to add to the water pitcher for negative ion purification); vertical walls of living plants; a large meat-ageing (proving) cabinet adjacent to the Surf 'n' Turf Restaurant; smartphone food ordering for waiters (sent electronically to the kitchen, so the waiter is always at his station to attend to passengers); a Nespresso coffee machine in every cabin; large spa and wellness facilities; a large choice of (included and extra-cost) dining venues and eateries; and a completely enclosed shore-excursion information and booking room.

FAMILIES. Younger children are well catered for, with a playroom and an outdoor paddling pool, while teens have their own adult-free chill-out lounge. There's also a character called Captain Sharky (perhaps he's 'driving' the ship?).

ACCOMMODATION. About 82 percent of all cabins feature private balconies, and each one features a hammock – now a signature item for all ships in the TUI Cruises fleet. Likewise, every cabin comes with a Nespresso coffee machine.

Combination balcony cabins allow for interconnecting balconies, and a 'holiday home' package provides a *Mein Schiff 3* chef to prepare a barbecue on the balcony grill.

Spa accommodation is located near the spa and part of a package that includes a massage for two in one of the most extensive wellness spa environments at sea.

A Captain's Suite, at 581.2 sq ft (54 sq m), is the largest suite aboard ship, and is located near the navigation bridge. Meanwhile, each of the spacious Sea & Sky Suites has its own large roof terrace and private sunbathing (including a large hammock and upscale sunbeds) and shaded areas. Premium veranda cabins offer large, diagonal terraces, and there are three suite categories. Also, 10 cabins are designated as wheelchair-accessible.

Family-friendly suites sleep up to 6 (they come in three different types). One example measures about 452 sq ft (42 sq m), but there's also a huge balcony measuring 506 sq ft (47 sq m). The total adds up to a delightfully large 958 sq ft (89 sq m). All come with Xbox game consoles.

DINING. With a choice of 11 dining venues, there really is plenty of choice. The Atlantik Restaurant is the ship's main restaurant. It is divided into three sections, and focuses on three styles of food: Classic – for dishes such as steak with roasted shallots and a chili-chocolate reduction); Mediterranean – for choices including home-made pastas, grilled fish and lamb with herbs of Provence; and Eurasian – for items such as sweet-and-sour vegetables with fried jasmine rice. Five-course menus include home-made pastas, grilled fish or antipasti, as well as Asian dishes and is part of the inclusive offering.

Other dining options. At the aft of the ship, a 1,798-sq-ft (167-sq-m) multifaceted glass structure (nicknamed the 'diamond') spans two decks. Inside the 'diamond', are two restaurants that became extremely popular aboard the company's *Mein Schiff 1* and *Mein Schiff 2*: Richards Feines Essen for fine dining and the Surf 'n' Turf Steakhouse, which features a superb glass-enclosed meat dry-ageing cabinet.

Hanami (it means flower-watching – particularly cherry blossom) is a Japanese restaurant (try the shabu-shabu beef), which incorporates a sushi bar. The venue offers sushi creations and other specialties of Japanese cuisine, at an additional cost.

A real bakery, an adjunct of the self-serve buffet restaurant Anckelmannsplatz, features freshly baked (all day long) crispy rolls, panini, and cakes. Already appearing aboard *Mein Schiff 1* and *Mein Schiff 2*, the popular informal restaurant Fish House Gosch Sylt now has about 130 seats aboard *Mein Schiff 3* (versus 88 seats aboard *Mein Schiff 1* and *Mein Schiff 2*), and offers fresh fish and well-prepared seafood dishes, with daily specials listed on a blackboard.

The Day & Night Bistro provides regional and international snacks, including currywurst, around the clock, while in a modern coffee lounge a barista brews international coffees and presents *Mein Schiff*'s own hand-crafted pralines and chocolates.

ENTERTAINMENT. The Theater is the ship's show-lounge. It is a three-deck venue with 949 seats, and features colorful, razzle-dazzle production shows and major cabaret acts.

What is really innovative, however, is a stunning concert hall/movie theater called Klanghaus (literally: small music academy-style concert hall), which was developed in conjunction with renowned acoustics experts from leading opera houses and concert halls. It provides a really fine setting for live classical and jazz concerts, theatrical readings, lectures, and movies with surround sound.

Numerous bands, small musical units and solo musical entertainers provide live music in several of the lounge venues throughout the ship.

SPA/FITNESS. Sports facilities include a large arena in the aft section of the ship for volleyball, basketball, and football.

Mein Schiff 4
★★★★+

Size:	Large Resort Ship		Passenger/Crew Ratio (lower beds):	2.5
Tonnage:	99,300		Cabins (total):	1,250
Lifestyle:	Standard		Size Range (sq ft/m):	182.9-581.2/17.0-54.0
Cruise Line:	TUI Cruises		Cabins (for one person):	0
Former Names:	none		Cabins (with private balcony):	1,033
IMO Number:	9641730		Cabins (wheelchair accessible):	10
Builder:	Meyer Turku (Finland)		Wheelchair accessibility:	Good
Original Cost:	€390 million		Cabin Current:	110 and 220 volts
Entered Service:	May 2015		Elevators:	10
Registry:	Malta		Casino (gaming tables):	Yes
Length (ft/m):	967.8/295.0		Slot Machines:	Yes
Beam (ft/m):	118.1/36.0		Swimming Pools:	3 (1w/sliding glass dome)
Draft (ft/m):	26.2/8.0		Hot Tubs (on deck):	4
Propulsion/Propellers:	diesel-electric/2		Self-Service Launderette:	No
Passenger Decks:	12		Dedicated Cinema/Seats:	Yes/200
Total Crew:	1,000		Library:	Yes
Passengers (lower beds):	2,506		Onboard currency:	Euros
Passenger Space Ratio (lower beds):	39.7			

A delightful ship for youthful, German-speaking families

OVERVIEW. *Mein Schiff 4* is the sister ship to *Mein Schiff 3*, both belonging to the rapidly expanding TUI Cruises. The all-inclusive, premium ship features a wide choice of dining venues, has an excellent spa, and, for younger cruisers, there's an enthusiastic team of children's activity hosts.

THE SHIP. This new ship, for German-speaking families, takes the best parts of the all-inclusive brand further. Its new-generation propulsion system is extremely quiet in operation, with absolutely no vibration anywhere.

A superb 82ft (25m) lap pool (long by cruise ship standards and half the length of an 'Olympic'-sized pool) is featured outdoors – together with a large-scale movie screen and sports area for basketball and volleyball – while a second, indoor, pool and adjacent hot tubs provide plenty of choice for families with children.

High up on Deck 14 is what's known as the Blue Balcony, a 118-sq-ft (11-sq-m) glass-floored platform some 121ft (37m) above the sea, which gives the sensation of floating over the ocean.

There are numerous public rooms; these include a superb music academy-style concert hall (auditorium), which has been designed to the highest acoustic specifications.

What makes a cruise aboard *Mein Schiff 4* really user-friendly for families is the all-inclusive pricing, though this excludes spa treatments, excursions, and the extra-cost restaurants: Richards Feines Essen, Blaue Welt Su-

Berlitz's Ratings		
	Possible	Achieved
Ship	500	459
Accommodation	200	168
Food	400	327
Service	400	331
Entertainment	100	84
Cruise Experience	400	329
OVERALL SCORE		
1698 points out of 2000		

shi Bar, Fish House Gosch Sylt, and a Surf 'n' Turf Steakhouse, among others. The dress code is smart casual. But the real diamond in the crown is the two-deck high glass enclosure, which houses two different restaurants – with great views over the ship's stern (the back) – and a fine barista coffee lounge.

Mein Schiff 4, in keeping with sister Mein Schiff 3, feels really comfortable. It boasts a number of outstanding passenger-friendly features, including: the longest swimming pool of any cruise ship; an ocean-connect museum (I call it an 'oceano-quarium'); water-dispenser units on each accommodation deck (special quartz crystals are provided in each cabin to add to the water pitcher for negative ion purification); vertical walls of living plants; a large meat-ageing (proving) cabinet adjacent to the Surf 'n' Turf Restaurant; and smartphone food ordering for waiters (sent electronically to the kitchen, so the waiter is always at his station to attend to passengers). A Nespresso coffee machine is provided in every cabin. The spa and wellness facilities are large. A big choice of (included and extra-cost) dining venues and eateries gives passengers ample choices, and there is a completely enclosed shore-excursion information and booking room.

FAMILIES. Younger children are well catered for, with a playroom (called Ahoy) and an outdoor paddling pool, while teens have their own adult-free chill-out lounge. And do watch out for some character called Captain Sharky (perhaps he's 'driving' the ship?).

ACCOMMODATION. Each one of the cabins with a balcony (about 82 percent of all cabins) features a hammock – now a signature item for all ships in the TUI Cruises fleet. Likewise, every cabin comes with a Nespresso coffee machine.

Combination balcony cabins allow for interconnecting balconies, and a 'holiday home' package provides a *Mein Schiff 3* chef to prepare a barbecue on the balcony grill.

Spa accommodation is located near the spa and is offered as part of a package that includes a massage for two in one of the most extensive wellness spa environments at sea.

A Captain's Suite, at 581 sq ft (54 sq m), is the ship's largest suite; it is located near the navigation bridge. Meanwhile, each of the spacious Sea & Sky Suites has its own large roof terrace and private sunbathing (including a large hammock and upscale sunbeds) and shaded areas. Premium veranda cabins offer large, diagonal terraces, and there are three suite categories. Also, 10 cabins are designated as wheelchair-accessible.

Family-friendly suites sleep up to 6 (they come in three different types). One example measures about 452 sq ft (42 sq m), but there's also a huge balcony measuring 506 sq ft (47 sq m). The total adds up to a delightfully large 958 sq ft (89 sq m). All come with Xbox game consoles.

CUISINE. With a total of 11 dining venues (some at extra cost), there really is plenty of choice. The Atlantik Restaurant is the ship's main restaurant. It is included in the cruise fare, and is divided into three sections (each with a different menu): Classic – for dishes such as steak with roasted shallots and a chili-chocolate reduction; Mediterranean – for choices including home-made pastas, and Brasserie – for French style grilled fish and lamb with herbs of Provence. Note that several of the dining venues have both indoor and outdoor seating – slightly different to *Mein Schiff 3*.

Other dining options. At the aft of the ship, a 1,798-sq-ft (167-sq-m) multifaceted glass structure (nicknamed the 'diamond') spans two decks. Inside the 'diamond' are two restaurants that are extremely popular aboard the company's *Mein Schiff 1* and *Mein Schiff 2* – Richards Feines Essen for fine dining and the Surf 'n' Turf Steakhouse, which features a superb glass-enclosed meat dry-ageing cabinet.

Hanami (it means flower-watching – particularly cherry blossom) is a Japanese restaurant (try the shabu-shabu beef), which incorporates a sushi bar. The venue offers sushi creations and other specialties of Japanese cuisine at an additional cost.

A real bakery, an adjunct of the self-serve buffet restaurant Anckelmannsplatz, features freshly baked (all day long) crispy rolls, panini, and cakes. The popular informal restaurant Fish House Gosch Sylt has about 130 seats aboard *Mein Schiff 4*, and features fresh fish and well-prepared seafood dishes, with daily specials listed on a blackboard.

The Day & Night Bistro provides regional and international snacks, including currywurst, around the clock, while in a modern coffee lounge a barista brews international coffees and presents *Mein Schiff*'s own hand-crafted pralines and chocolates.

ENTERTAINMENT. The Theater is the ship's showlounge. A three-deck venue with 949 seats, it features colorful, razzle-dazzle production shows and major cabaret acts.

What is really innovative, however, is a stunning small concert hall/movie theater called Klanghaus, which was developed in conjunction with renowned acoustics experts from leading opera houses and concert halls. It provides a really fine setting for live classical and jazz concerts, theatrical readings, lectures, and movies with surround sound.

Numerous bands, small musical units, and solo musical entertainers provide live music in several of the lounge venues throughout the ship.

SPA/FITNESS. The Spa and Meer wellness and fitness facilities are really extensive, and include a large (co-ed) sauna, steam rooms, and several body-pampering treatment rooms. They also include a private (rentable) spa room for couples, with integral sauna, massage tables, shower, and relaxation areas.

Sports facilities include a large arena in the aft section of the ship for volleyball, basketball, and football. Sport bikes are also carried.

Minerva
★★★★

Size:	Small Ship	Passenger Space Ratio (lower beds):	33.9
Tonnage:	12,892	Passenger/Crew Ratio (lower beds):	2.1
Lifestyle:	Standard	Cabins (total):	190
Cruise Line:	Swan Hellenic Discovery Cruises	Size Range (sq ft/m):	139.9–360.6/13.0–33.5
Former Names:	Explorer II, Alexander von Humboldt, Saga Pearl, Minerva, Okean	Cabins (for one person):	0
		Cabins (with private balcony):	44
IMO Number:	9144196	Cabins (wheelchair accessible):	4
Builder:	Mariotti (Italy)	Wheelchair accessibility:	Fair
Original Cost:	n/a	Cabin Current:	220 volts
Entered Service:	Apr 1996/May 2008	Elevators:	2
Registry:	The Bahamas	Casino (gaming tables):	No
Length (ft/m):	436.3/133.0	Slot Machines:	No
Beam (ft/m):	65.6/20.0	Swimming Pools:	1
Draft (ft/m):	19.6/6.0	Hot Tubs (on deck):	0
Propulsion/Propellers:	diesel (6,960kW)/2	Self-Service Launderette:	Yes
Passenger Decks:	6	Dedicated Cinema/Seats:	No
Total Crew:	157	Library:	Yes
Passengers (lower beds):	380	Onboard currency:	UK£

A comfortable ship with a focus on discovery and learning

OVERVIEW. *Minerva* passengers, called 'Swanners', are couples and solo travelers of a mature age who seek to cruise off the beaten track in comfortable surroundings, and who don't need the highly organized entertainment provided by larger ships. This 'soft expedition' is highly valued for its excellent food, friendly service, and fine library. It is not recommended for children.

THE SHIP. Originally intended as a spy ship (*Okean*) for the Soviet navy, this vessel was built at the Nikolajev shipyard on the River Ingul in Ukraine. It had a stern ramp for launching submersibles for submarine tracking (now removed, but it does have a strong, 1989-built ice-strengthened hull. It was later converted for 'discovery' cruising and tailored to suit British tastes. The ship now operates for Swan Hellenic Discovery Cruises, part of the UK's All Leisure Group.

After an extensive refit in 2011–2, the ship's former angular profile has been improved. The refit included the addition of 32 wide balconies to existing cabins; remodeled bathrooms in all cabins; a new, large Orpheus (observation) Lounge above the navigation bridge; an extended Shackleton's Lounge; a larger, dedicated Internet-connect lounge; and an expanded library. The changes reflect the financial commitment of Swan Hellenic Cruises to its loyal clientele, and provide a better sense of space, more public rooms, and more comfort. There's ample open and shaded deck space too, particularly in the aft section, and there is also a new, wide teak walk-around promenade deck atop ship.

Berlitz's Ratings

	Possible	Achieved
Ship	500	336
Accommodation	200	145
Food	400	305
Service	400	303
Entertainment	100	77
Cruise Experience	400	280
OVERALL SCORE		
1446 points out of 2000		

Four rubber inflatable Zodiac craft are carried for excursions ashore, useful for inhospitable locations such as in Antarctica without landing piers or formal docking arrangements. The interior decor is homely and restrained, like a country house hotel, not in the slightest bit glitzy, for passengers with good taste, although cushions would be a welcome addition to the many sofas. Lectures and briefings take place in the Darwin Lounge, the main lounge. Fine wool carpets are laid in the passageways and public rooms, and the furniture is decidedly 'colonial' in style.

Perhaps the most appreciated and used public area is the excellent 5,000-book library with its classical 'armchair' decor and a fine range of reference books, many of academic standard. Shackleton's Lounge and Wheeler's Bar (in which is displayed fine glass-cased half-cut model of the SS *Caledonia*) exude a country-house atmosphere, and are good for socializing, as is the Orpheus Observation Lounge atop ship. The ship also has a small shop, and an in-port kiosk for basic items.

The ship absorbs passengers well and maintains a feeling of intimacy. A great benefit of a cruise with Swan Hellenic is the quality and diversity of the lecturers and guest speakers. The open space is very good for the size of the ship. Wine is included with lunch and dinner, as are shore excursions. All gratuities are also included, although port charges are extra.

While the ship is not new, and the cabins are small, the refurbishment added new features, and all cabin bathrooms were replaced. The food and service are extremely good, and so the score just tips the ship into the four-star category.

ACCOMMODATION. There are eight different cabin price grades, in 12 price categories. The price depends on grade and location rather than any great difference in size. Most standard cabins really are quite small, particularly when compared to the 'standard' cabin size on the latest ships today.

Owner's Suites (2). These Bridge Deck suites measure 372.4 sq ft (34.6 sq m). Facilities include a queen-size bed, bedside reading lights, an extra-large double closet and ample drawer space; separate lounge area with sofa, table and chair, and vanity table/writing desk, TV set with movie and audio channels, refrigerator, hairdryer, and binoculars; floor-to-ceiling patio doors leading to a private balcony (with green turf-covered deck); bathroom with bath/shower combination and toilet.

Deluxe Balcony Suites (22). These suites on Bridge Deck measure 336 sq ft (31 sq m), including an extra-large balcony. Facilities include twin beds or queen-size bed, two double closets and ample drawer space; separate lounge area with sofa, table and chair, and vanity table/writing desk, small TV set with movie and audio channels, refrigerator, hairdryer and binoculars; floor to ceiling patio doors and private balcony; bathroom with tub/shower and toilet.

Deluxe Balcony Suites. These new Sun Deck suites measure 340 sq ft (32 sq m), including a large balcony. Facilities include twin beds or queen-size bed, bedside reading lights, two double closets and ample drawer space; separate lounge area with sofa, table and chair, and vanity table/writing desk, TV set, refrigerator, hairdryer, and binoculars; large picture window; bathroom with bath/shower and toilet.

Standard outside-view or interior cabins. These 'standard' cabins are small (140 sq ft/13 sq m) when compared to the 182-sq-ft (17-sq-m) cabins aboard today's newest ships. Facilities include twin beds or queen-size bed, two double closets and ample drawer space; separate lounge area with sofa, table and chair, and vanity table/writing desk, TV set, refrigerator, hairdryer, and binoculars; large picture window or porthole, depending on deck and price category

(outside-view cabins only); bathroom with shower enclosure and toilet.

The bathrooms have a raised 'lip' to step over, are totally white, and have small shower enclosures (except for some suites, which have bathtubs and marble tiled floors).

All grades have a hairdryer, 100 percent cotton bathrobe, cotton duvets, binoculars, passenger list, direct-dial telephone, fresh fruit basket, and L'Occitane toiletries and soap, but bottled mineral water costs extra. All bathrooms have hygienic hand-held, flexible shower hoses, and large bath-size towels.

The TV set includes movie and music channels, although the quality leaves much to be desired. There is little space for hanging outerwear parkas and other gear for any of the 'soft' expedition-style cruises, and some cabins on B Deck aft are subject to noise and vibration from the ship's engines/generators.

DINING. The Swan Restaurant has open-seating dining, allowing you to eat with whomever you wish. The menus are quite extensive and feature many traditional British favorite dishes. The food itself is of a high quality. It's also creative, attractively presented, and has plenty of taste. The wine list is very decent (it includes the Chairman's Rothschild wine selection), and so is the special Champagne. The service staff are very pleasant, friendly, and willing.

Coffees and teas are available 24 hours a day from a beverage station in the self-serve Veranda Café, in which you can have casual breakfasts, luncheons, and dinners in an open-seating arrangement; for dinner items from the menu in the Swan Restaurant are available, in addition to lighter fare.

ENTERTAINMENT. Although there is a main lounge (Darwin Lounge), this is used principally for lectures, for classical music ensembles, and poetry readings. The ship has a small band and solo entertaining musicians to provide live music for dancing and listening.

SPA/FITNESS. There is a small fitness room on Aegean Deck, and a beauty salon, but no sauna or steam room. Massages and aromatherapy facials, manicures, pedicures, and hair beautifying treatments are available, provided by the Ocean Spa company.

Monarch
★★★

Size:	Large Resort Ship
Tonnage:	73,937
Lifestyle:	Standard
Cruise Line:	Pullmantur Cruises
Former Names:	Monarch of the Seas
IMO Number:	8819500
Builder:	Chantiers de l'Atlantique (France)
Original Cost:	$300 million
Entered Service:	Nov 1991/Apr 2013
Registry:	The Bahamas
Length (ft/m):	879.9/268.2
Beam (ft/m):	105.9/32.3
Draft (ft/m):	24.9/7.6
Propulsion/Propellers:	diesel (21,844kW)/2
Passenger Decks:	11
Total Crew:	858
Passengers (lower beds):	2,384
Passenger Space Ratio (lower beds):	31.0

Passenger/Crew Ratio (lower beds):	2.8
Cabins (total):	1,192
Size Range (sq ft/m):	118.4–670.0/11.0–62.2
Cabins (for one person):	0
Cabins (with private balcony):	62
Cabins (wheelchair accessible):	4
Wheelchair accessibility:	Fair
Cabin Current:	110 volts
Elevators:	11
Casino (gaming tables):	Yes
Slot Machines:	Yes
Swimming Pools:	2
Hot Tubs (on deck):	2
Self-Service Launderette:	No
Dedicated Cinema/Seats:	No
Library:	Yes
Onboard currency:	Euros

A modestly large, busy ship, good for a first cruise

OVERVIEW. This floating resort provides the basics for a well-tuned, but somewhat impersonal, short cruise experience for Spanish-speaking families. The range of facilities is decent enough, with consistently sound, highly programmed service from a reasonably attentive young staff. In April 2013, the ship was transferred from Royal Caribbean International to Pullmantur Cruises to operate family-friendly cruises for Spanish speakers, and renamed, simply, Monarch (ex-Monarch of the Seas).

Berlitz's Ratings		
	Possible	Achieved
Ship	500	302
Accommodation	200	117
Food	400	223
Service	400	260
Entertainment	100	64
Cruise Experience	400	245
OVERALL SCORE		
1211 points out of 2000		

THE SHIP. Monarch is almost identical in size and appearance to sister ship Sovereign, but actually has a slightly improved internal layout and better features in the public rooms. The ship, whose hull is painted a deep blue, has a lounge and bar that is wrapped around the blue funnel and provides a stunning view – it's a great place to sit and enjoy a decent coffee from one of its 320-plus seats. The open deck space itself, however, is very cramped when the ship is full, as aboard any large ship, although there seems to be plenty of it. There is a basketball court aft for sports lovers.

The interior layout is designed in a vertical stack, with most public rooms located aft, and the accommodation forward. There's a good array of spacious and elegant public rooms to play in, although the decor brings to mind the IKEA school of interior design. A spacious five-deck-high Centrum lobby has cascading stairways and two glass-walled elevators. You may be overwhelmed by the public spaces, but underwhelmed by the size of the cabins.

The ship has a good array of spacious, smart public rooms, including a conference room, library, and card players' room, plus a Monte Carlo Casino for the more serious gamers, as well as shops and an Internet-connect center. The decor is accented with wood paneling, and some bright color splashes. Children and teens are well catered for, and there's a whole team of youth activity staff, together with a range of rooms for children and teens, including a chill-out lounge and an open aft sundeck with a dance floor.

The dress code is ultra-casual. All gratuities and port taxes are included in the cruise fare. Passengers can embark at Panama's Colón, Colombia's Cartagena, or Venezuela's La Guaira on a seven-night year-round itinerary that also includes Aruba and Curaçao. Although Pullmantur Cruises markets this ship in Europe, it focuses more on Latin America, where it provides a visa-free alternative for many nationalities. This provides an opportunity for South Americans to cruise the Caribbean in their winter.

ACCOMMODATION. There are numerous categories, priced by grade, size, and location. Note that there are no cabins with private balconies.

Suites. Thirteen suites on Bridge Deck are fairly large and nicely furnished (the largest is the Royal Suite), with separate living and sleeping spaces. These provide more space, with better service and more perks than standard-grade accommodation.

Standard cabins. The standard outside-view and interior cabins are very small, although an arched window treatment and colorful soft furnishings give the illusion of more space.

Almost all cabins have twin beds that convert to a queen-size or double bed configuration, together with moveable bedside tables. However, when in a queen-bed configuration, the bed is flush against the wall, with access from one side only. All standard cabins have very little closet and drawer space. You should, therefore, pack only minimal clothing, which is all you really need for a short cruise.

All cabins have a private bathroom, with a shower enclosure, toilet, and washbasin.

DINING. The two large dining rooms, Claude's and Vincent's, are located off the Centrum lobby. There are tables for four, six, or eight, but none for two. There are two seatings, and the dining operation is well orchestrated, with emphasis on well-timed, programmed service. The cuisine is typical of mass banquet catering that offers standard fare comparable to that found in family-style eateries ashore. While menu descriptions are tempting, the actual food may be somewhat disappointing and unmemorable. Many items are pre-prepared ashore to keep costs down.

A decent selection of light meals is provided, and a vegetarian choice is also available. The selection of breads, rolls, and pastry items is good. The wine list is not extensive, but the prices are moderate.

For casual breakfasts and lunches, the Café is the place to go, although there are often long lines at peak times. On the aft of the upper level of the venue is a pizzeria.

ENTERTAINMENT. The Sound of Music is the principal showlounge; it has both main and balcony levels, with banquette seating, although sight lines from many of the balcony seats are poor.

A smaller entertainment venue, the April in Paris Lounge, is where cabaret acts, including late-night adult comedy are featured, as well as music for dancing.

The entertainment throughout is upbeat – in fact, it's difficult to get away from music and noise. There's even background music in all corridors and elevators, and constant music outdoors on the pool deck. If you want a quiet relaxing holiday, choose another ship.

SPA/FITNESS. The Spa del Mar features a gymnasium with aft-facing views and a selection of muscle-pumping equipment. There is also an aerobics studio, and classes are offered in a variety of keep-fit regimens, a beauty salon, and a sauna, as well as treatment rooms for pampering massages and facials. While the facilities aren't extensive, they're adequate.

For the sports-inclined, there is activity galore – including a rock-climbing wall with several separate climbing tracks. It is located outdoors aft of the blue funnel and wrap-around panoramic lounge.

MSC Armonia
★★★+

Size:	Mid-size Ship	Passenger Space Ratio (lower beds):	33.5
Tonnage:	65,542	Passenger/Crew Ratio (lower beds):	2.7
Lifestyle:	Standard	Cabins (total):	976
Cruise Line:	MSC Cruises	Size Range (sq ft/m):	139.9–236.8/13.0–22.0
Former Names:	European Vision	Cabins (for one person):	0
IMO Number:	9210141	Cabins (with private balcony):	224
Builder:	Chantiers de l'Atlantique (France)	Cabins (wheelchair accessible):	2
Original Cost:	$245 million	Wheelchair accessibility:	Good
Entered Service:	Jun 2001/May 2004	Cabin Current:	110 and 220 volts
Registry:	Italy	Elevators:	9
Length (ft/m):	902.2/275.0	Casino (gaming tables):	Yes
Beam (ft/m):	95.1/29.0	Slot Machines:	Yes
Draft (ft/m):	22.4/6.85	Swimming Pools:	2
Propulsion/Propellers:	diesel-electric (31,680kW)/ 2 azimuthing pods	Hot Tubs (on deck):	2
		Self-Service Launderette:	No
Passenger Decks:	10	Dedicated Cinema/Seats:	No
Total Crew:	721	Library:	Yes
Passengers (lower beds):	1,952	Onboard currency:	Euros

This is a comfortable large ship for pan-European cruisers

OVERVIEW. *MSC Armonia* will suit those comfortable with multilingual fellow passengers. It is best for adult couples and solo travelers, and families with children, who enjoy constant activity accompanied by lots of noise, late nights, and entertainment that is loud.

THE SHIP. As *European Vision*, the ship began its working life auspiciously, having been selected as a floating hotel to accommodate the leaders and staff of the G8 summit in 2001. When its owner, Festival Cruises, ceased operations in 2004, it was bought by MSC Cruises for €215 million and renamed *MSC Armonia*. The exterior deck space is barely adequate for the number of passengers carried. The Lido Deck surrounding the outdoor swimming pool also has whirlpool tubs and a large bandstand is set in raised canvas-covered pods. All sunloungers have cushioned pads.

In August 2014 the ship underwent a 'chop and stretch' operation which, added an 82ft (25m) midsection, almost 200 additional cabins, more public rooms, entertainment facilities and new shops (but no additional elevators), and more exterior deck space, which includes a large waterpark for children. Families with children will also find special kids' areas equipped with Chicco® and LEGO® products, and an energetic multilingual youth activity team.

Inside, the layout (and hence the passenger flow) is reasonably good, but slightly disjointed after the 'stretch.' The decks are named after European cities – eg Oxford Deck (with British public room names), Venice

Berlitz's Ratings		
	Possible	Achieved
Ship	500	381
Accommodation	200	153
Food	400	233
Service	400	294
Entertainment	100	55
Cruise Experience	400	270
OVERALL SCORE		
1386 points out of 2000		

Deck (with Italian names), and Biarritz Deck (with French names). The decor is 'European Moderne' and includes crisp, clean lines and minimalist furniture. The interior colors are good; nothing jars the senses, but rather calms them.

Facilities include Amadeus, a nightclub; Ambassador, a cigar smoking room with all the hallmarks of a gentleman's club; and Vivaldi, a piano lounge. The Goethe Library/Card Room has real writing desks – something many ships omit. There is an extensive Internet café, and an English pub, the White Lion. The Lido Casino has blackjack, poker and roulette games, plus an array of slot machines.

Standing in line for embarkation, disembarkation, shore tenders, and self-serve buffet meals is part of cruising aboard large ships. Announcements are in several languages.

Wheelchair-bound passengers should note that there is no access to the uppermost forward and aft decks, although access throughout most of the interior is good. The passenger hallways are a little narrow on some accommodation decks to pass when housekeeping carts are in place.

ACCOMMODATION. There are numerous categories, the price depending on the grade, size, and location you choose. These include 132 'suites' with private balcony (whose partitions are only of the partial and not the full type), outside-view cabins and interior (no-view) cabins.

Suite-grade accommodation – they are not true suites, as there's no separate bedroom and lounge – has more room, a larger lounge area, walk-in closet, wall-to-wall vanity counter, a bathroom with combination tub and shower, toilet, and private balcony with light. Bathrobes are provided. In general, the 'suites' are practical and nicely furnished. However, except for the very highest category, the bathrooms are plain, with white plastic washbasins and white walls, small shower enclosures, and mirrors that steam up.

Even the smallest interior cabins are acceptable, however, with enough space between two lower beds. All grades of accommodation have a TV, mini-bar/refrigerator, personal safe cleverly positioned behind a vanity desk mirror, hairdryer, and bathroom with shower and toilet. But standard grade cabins, at a modest 140 sq ft (13 sq m), are really small when compared to those in many other ships.

DINING. The principal dining room, the 610-seat Marco Polo Restaurant, has two seatings for dinner, and an open seating (meaning you'll be seated when you turn up when the dining room is open) for breakfast and lunch. However, during an open seating, you may well be seated with others with whom you may not be able to communicate very satisfactorily, given the wide mix of nationalities and languages on board.

In general, the cuisine is acceptable, but unmemorable. Even so, the menus are varied and the presentation is generally sound, and should prove a highlight for most passengers. Regional and seasonal specialties are also sometimes presented. The wine list has quite a wide variety of wines at fairly reasonable prices, although most of the wines are very young.

La Pergola, the most formal restaurant, features stylish Italian cuisine. It is assigned to all passengers occupying suite-grade accommodation, although others can dine in it too, on a reservations-only basis.

Other dining options. Chez Claude, on the starboard side aft, adjacent to the ship's funnel, is a grill area for fast food. La Brasserie is a casual, self-serve buffet eatery, open 20 hours a day (including a sit-down, casual dinner each evening with waiter service). The selections are quite standardized – ie minimal. Café San Marco, on the upper, second level of the main lobby, serves extra-cost Sagafredo coffees, and pastry items.

ENTERTAINMENT. La Gondola Theater, which is two decks high, is the main venue for production shows, cabaret acts, plays, and other theatrical presentations. It is a well-designed room, except for the fact that no space was allocated for a live showband. Consequently, production shows are performed to pre-recorded backing tracks. The sight lines from most seats are good, and four entrances allow easy access and exit. Seats for shows are on a first-come, first-served basis.

Other shows consist of cabaret acts such as singers, magicians, mimes, and comedy jugglers. A number of bands and small musical units provide live music for dancing or listening.

SPA/FITNESS. The Atlantica Spa has numerous body-pampering treatments, a gymnasium with ocean views, and high-tech, muscle-toning and strengthening equipment. A thermal suite has different kinds of steam rooms combined with aromatherapy infusions such as chamomile and eucalyptus, and a Rasul chamber provides a combination of two or three kinds of application mud and gentle steam shower. The spa, operated by the Italian concession OceanView, offers a wide range of wellbeing treatments. Gratuities to spa staff are at your discretion.

For active types, there's a simulated climbing wall outdoors aft of the ship's funnel, as well as a volleyball/basketball court, and mini-golf.

MSC Divina
★★★★+

Size:	Large Resort Ship	Passenger/Crew Ratio (lower beds):	2.5
Tonnage:	139,400 tons	Cabins (total):	1,751
Lifestyle:	Standard	Size Range (sq ft/m):	148.5–568.3/13.8–52.8
Cruise Line:	MSC Cruises	Cabins (for one person):	0
Former Names:	none	Cabins (with private balcony):	1,125
IMO Number:	9585285	Cabins (wheelchair accessible):	45
Builder:	STX France	Wheelchair accessibility:	Good
Original Cost:	$550 million	Cabin Current:	110 and 220 volts
Entered Service:	Jun 2012	Elevators:	17
Registry:	Panama	Casino (gaming tables):	Yes
Length (ft/m):	1,093.5/333.3	Slot Machines:	Yes
Beam (ft/m):	124.6/38.0	Swimming Pools:	3
Draft (ft/m):	27.72/8.4	Hot Tubs (on deck):	13
Propulsion/Propellers:	diesel-electric (40,000kW)/2	Self-Service Launderette:	No
Passenger Decks:	13	Dedicated Cinema/Seats:	No
Total Crew:	1,388	Library:	Yes
Passengers (lower beds):	3,502	Onboard currency:	Euros
Passenger Space Ratio (lower beds):	39.8		

A truly stunning, large family-friendly resort ship

OVERVIEW. This large, really elegantly attired resort ship has a trendy infinity pool and 'beach' zone, and will appeal to young adult couples, solo travelers, and families with children and teens who enjoy an urban Mediterranean lifestyle, with a mix of many European nationalities.

THE SHIP. *MSC Divina*, together with sister ship *MSC Preziosa*, are the largest ships yet for MSC Cruises. This ship features the latest in green-technology engines. Its exclusive area, the MSC Yacht Club, includes an expanded Top-Sail Lounge (an observation/lifestyle lounge and social meeting place), private sunbathing with integral dip pool, two hot tubs, and concierge services. Even more desirably, it has a private Yacht Club-only restaurant, Le Muse. Only Yacht Club-grade occupants are escorted to their cabins by their butlers. Housekeeping staff point passengers in the right direction, but no longer escort them to their cabins.

The interior decor is quite stunning. There are basically two decks full of public lounges, bars, and eateries, including a large two-deck-high theater-style showlounge, a nightclub/disco, library, card room, an Internet center, virtual-reality center, shopping gallery, and large casino (inhabited by many people who can smoke at the bar). Drinking places include a large number of lounges and bars, most with live music. One lounge in the aft section is for adults only, as is an aft swimming pool and relaxation deck. For a little music, the Golden Jazz Bar is a must (the walls are 'stoned').

Berlitz's Ratings		
	Possible	Achieved
Ship	500	421
Accommodation	200	162
Food	400	276
Service	400	308
Entertainment	100	76
Cruise Experience	400	308
OVERALL SCORE		
1551 points out of 2000		

Additionally, there are conference and small group meeting facilities.

The ship's focal point, however, is its gorgeous three-decks-high atrium lobby with shimmering Swarovski crystal stairways and elegant, Art Deco-influenced decor. The reception desk and financial services desk are located on the lower level, which also has a stage and seating in oh-so-comfortable oversized armchairs.

You can drive an F1 Ferrari racing car in a simulator, and experience seat-of-your pants rides in a 4D theater.

Niggles include the fact that all the lounges 'flow' into each other, and so the music from each one bleeds into the adjacent room.

FAMILIES. The ship is well designed to cater for families with children, who have their own play centers (a children's club and jungle adventure playground), youth counselors, and activity programs. Facilities include a water slide, video arcade, and a 4D cinema.

ACCOMMODATION. There are nine types of accommodation, in numerous cabin price grades. Included are two Royal Suites, three Executive/Family Suites, and a mix of outside-view (with or without balconies) and interior cabins. The price you pay depends on the grade, size, and location you choose.

The 'Yacht Club' exclusive accommodation consists of some 67 'suites', housed in a key-operated access only area of the ship, and comes with full butler service, interactive TV, minibar, personal safe, hairdryer, and satellite-link telephone. Included in the suites is number 16007 – the Sophia Loren Suite, in rich reds, specially designed lamps, and stunning photos of her great movie roles, together with a replica of the dressing table that Ms Loren uses in her home.

DINING. There are two main restaurants. The two-level Black Crab has 626 seats on one level and 529 on the other, and assigned tables and seating for dinner. The second is the 766-seat Villa Rossa Restaurant. The focus of the cuisine is on Mediterranean fare, with regional and seasonal fare when available. Light 'always available' choices are also provided. The ship makes all its pasta on board, and prides itself on its Italian flair.

Occupants of Yacht Club accommodation grades eat in Le Muse, a private, quite intimate restaurant that looks out onto the aft infinity pool area. The service here is less hurried and much more personalized.

Other dining options. These include Eataly, a seagoing version of a chain of the same name, with clear plastic chairs and clean, white diner-style decor.

Two large Lido-style self-serve buffet cafeterias (Calumet and Manitou – named after native Indian peace pipes and spirits; each has about 400 seats) are for breakfasts and lunches, and served, casual dinners. The buffets are open for up to 20 hours daily – so there's always something to eat whenever you're hungry).

Additional foodie-type places include La Cantina di Bacco (a wine bar and pizzeria), Piazza del Doge (for Italian pastries, coffees, and huge selection of gelato), an Italia Bar for coffees (the Italian Sagafredo brand is featured) and pastries, and Galaxy (an extra cost à-la-carte eatery located as part of the disco, it overlooks the entire mid-ship pool deck, and is good for a late-riser's brunch (featuring several trendy tapas-style dishes).

A Sports and Bowling Diner features a classic American food experience (including sandwiches and burgers).

ENTERTAINMENT. The 1,603-seat Pantheon Theater is spread over two decks. Because passengers really are multinational, the entertainment concentrates on shows that are highly visual, such as mime, magic, dancing, and acrobatics, and are performed to recorded music. A number of bands and small musical groups provide live music for dancing or listening in most lounges and bars.

SPA/FITNESS. The large Aurea Spa and Wellbeing Center houses a beauty salon, numerous body treatment rooms (with Balinese therapists and 21 types of massage), a bar (for fruit drinks and smoothies), relaxation room, solarium, and a gymnasium with great ocean views. A thermal suite contains two steam rooms and four saunas combined with herbal aromatherapy infusions. This is the first cruise ship to have a halotherapy (Himalayan salt crystal) bed for body detoxing. There's also a Shu Uemura Art of Hair Cabin. Gratuities to spa staff are at your discretion.

Sports facilities include basketball, tennis court, volleyball, a power-walking track, bowling, and shuffleboard.

MSC Fantasia
★★★★

Size:	Large Resort Ship
Tonnage:	137,936
Lifestyle:	Standard
Cruise Line:	MSC Cruises
Former Names:	none
IMO Number:	5515738
Builder:	STX Europe (France)
Original Cost:	$550 million
Entered Service:	Dec 2008
Registry:	Panama
Length (ft/m):	1,093.5/333.3
Beam (ft/m):	124.3/37.9
Draft (ft/m):	27.72/8.4
Propulsion/Propellers:	diesel-electric (40,000kW)/2
Passenger Decks:	13
Total Crew:	1,325
Passengers (lower beds):	3,274
Passenger Space Ratio (lower beds):	442.1

Passenger/Crew Ratio (lower beds):	2.5
Cabins (total):	1,637
Size Range (sq ft/m):	161.4-699.6/15-65
Cabins (for one person):	0
Cabins (with private balcony):	1,260
Cabins (wheelchair accessible):	43
Wheelchair accessibility:	Best
Cabin Current:	110 and 220 volts
Elevators:	14
Casino (gaming tables):	Yes
Slot Machines:	Yes
Swimming Pools:	3 (1 w/sliding glass dome)
Hot Tubs (on deck):	13
Self-Service Launderette:	No
Dedicated Cinema/Seats:	No
Library:	Yes
Onboard currency:	Euros

Comfort, space, and a Mediterranean lifestyle for families

OVERVIEW. This ship appeals to young adult couples, solo travelers, and families with children and teens – anyone who enjoys big ships, a big-city lifestyle, and a mix of nationalities, mostly European. You can drive an F1 Ferrari racing car in a simulator, and experience hair-raising, seat-of-your pants rides in a 4D theater. Note that only Yacht Club-grade occupants are escorted to their cabins by their butlers. Housekeeping staff point passengers in the right direction, but no longer escort them to their cabins.

THE SHIP. Built in 67 blocks, some more than 600 tons, *MSC Fantasia* is one of the largest ships built for a European cruise company. It is 33ft (10m) longer than the Eiffel Tower is high, and the propulsion power is the equivalent of 120 Ferraris. There are four swimming pools, one of which can be covered by a glass dome.

The interior design is an enlargement and extension of MSC's smaller *Musica-* and *Orchestra-*class ships, but with the addition of an exclusive area called the MSC Yacht Club for occupants of the 99 suites. This 'club' includes a Top-Sail Lounge, private sunbathing with integral dip pool, two hot tubs, and concierge services such as making dining reservations, and booking excursions and spa treatments.

If your wallet allows, it's worth paying extra to stay in one of the 'suites' in the Yacht Club accommodation. You'll get silver-tray room service by a team of well-trained butlers, a reserved (quieter) section of the Il Cerchio d'Oro restaurant, plus keycard access

Berlitz's Ratings		
	Possible	Achieved
Ship	500	416
Accommodation	200	162
Food	400	271
Service	400	306
Entertainment	100	77
Cruise Experience	400	306
OVERALL SCORE		
1538 points out of 2000		

to a members-only sundeck sanctuary area that includes its own bar and food counters, a small dip pool, two hot tubs, and expansive open but sheltered lounging deck. It's a world away from the hustle and bustle of the main pool decks and solarium on the decks below.

The interior decor is quite stunning. There are basically two decks full of public lounges, bars, and eateries, including a large two-deck-high theater-style showlounge, a nightclub/disco, library, card room, an Internet center, virtual reality center, shopping gallery, and large casino (inhabited by many people who can smoke at the bar). There's a big city-like environment in the shopping areas. The Monte Carlo Casino features blackjack, poker, and roulette games, plus an array of slot machines.

Drinking places include a pub-like venue and several comfortable lounges with live music. Note that 15 percent is added to all drinks/beverage orders. A neat mini-golf course is on the port side of the funnel, and a walking and jogging track encircles the two swimming pools.

Niggles include the fact that all the lounges 'flow' into each other, and so the music from each one bleeds into any adjacent room.

FAMILIES. The ship is designed to accommodate families with children, who have their own play centers (a children's club and jungle adventure playground), a teens arcade, youth counselors, and activity programs.

ACCOMMODATION. Eighty percent of cabins have an outside view, and 95 percent of these have a balcony – a standard balcony cabin will measure almost 172 sq ft (16 sq m), plus bathroom and balcony. There are 72 suites in a MSC Yacht Club VIP section; each measures 312 sq ft (29 sq m) and comes with full butler service. The price you pay depends on the grade, size, and location you choose.

In a 2011 refit, 28 Aurea Suites were created with direct access to the Aurea Spa. The spa suites come with amenities and 'extras,' including a non-alcoholic cocktail at the Aurea Spa Bar, unlimited access to the Thermal Suite (sauna and steam room) and a private consultation with the spa doctor. Also part of the price are a Balinese massage, a facial relax treatment using skin-firming cream, and a solarium session for full-body tanning.

A black marble floor leads to a magnificent Swarovski glass staircase that connects the concierge facilities between Decks 15 and 16 under a glass-domed ceiling.

DINING. There are four dining venues. The two-deck-high Red Velvet, the main restaurant, is in the aft section. It has a ship-wide balcony level, with a stairway to connect its two levels. The focus of the cuisine is on Mediterranean fare, with regional and seasonal fare when available. Light 'always available' choices are also provided. The ship makes all its pasta on board, and prides itself on its Italian flair.

Il Cerchio d'Oro is a single-level specialty restaurant, with a different menu each evening devoted to a different region of Italy. The Murano chandeliers are quite lovely, and definitely really worth noticing.

Other dining options. L'Etoile is a classic French restaurant, with decor reminiscent of the Belle Epoque era. Menus focus on one of three themes: the sea, the countryside, and the kitchen garden, and change seasonally. There's also an extra-charge Tex-Mex restaurant, El Sombrero, serving large portions of burritos, fajitas, enchiladas, tacos, tortillas, and more, together with a choice of several Mexican beers.

Casual breakfasts, lunches, and sit-down, served, but casual, dinners can be taken in the large self-serve L'Africana Café, a self-serve buffet-style eatery that is open 20 hours daily – so you can always find something to eat.

Another casual spot for people-watching is the Il Cappuccino coffee bar. Located two decks above the main reception area, it serves all types of coffees and teas, as well as fine chocolate delicacies.

La Cantina Toscana is a neat wine bar that pairs wines with food from several regions of Italy, in a setting that includes alcove seating, and L'Africana, which has a decor of dark African hardwoods.

A Sports and Bowling Diner features a classic American food experience (including sandwiches and burgers).

ENTERTAINMENT. L'Avanguardia, the main show-lounge, has 1,603 seats, and facilities that rival almost any to be found on land. Shows are highly visual, due to the multi-national passenger make-up. Additionally, live music is provided in most lounges by small musical groups and solo musicians.

SPA/FITNESS. The Aurea Spa has a beauty salon, several treatment rooms, and a gymnasium with great ocean views. A thermal suite contains different kinds of steam rooms combined with herbal aromatherapy infusions, in a calming Asia-themed environment. The spa is operated by OceanView, a specialist spa provider. Gratuities are not included, but left to your discretion.

Sports facilities include deck quoits, shuffleboard courts, large tennis/basketball court, mini-golf, and a jogging track.

MSC Lirica
★★★★

Size:	Mid-size Ship	Passenger/Crew Ratio (lower beds):	2.7
Tonnage:	65,542	Cabins (total):	988
Lifestyle:	Standard	Size Range (sq ft/m):	139.9–302.0/13.0–28.0
Cruise Line:	MSC Cruises	Cabins (for one person):	0
Former Names:	none	Cabins (with private balcony):	224
IMO Number:	9246102	Cabins (wheelchair accessible):	4
Builder:	Chantiers de l'Atlantique (France)	Wheelchair accessibility:	Good
Original Cost:	$266 million	Cabin Current:	110 and 220 volts
Entered Service:	Mar 2003	Elevators:	9
Registry:	Panama	Casino (gaming tables):	Yes
Length (ft/m):	902.2/275.0	Slot Machines:	Yes
Beam (ft/m):	95.1/29.0	Swimming Pools:	2
Draft (ft/m):	22.4/6.8	Hot Tubs (on deck):	2
Propulsion/Propellers:	diesel (31,680kW)/2 azimuthing pods	Self-Service Launderette:	No
Passenger Decks:	10	Dedicated Cinema/Seats:	No
Total Crew:	721	Library:	Yes
Passengers (lower beds):	1,976	Onboard currency:	Euros
Passenger Space Ratio (lower beds):	33.1		

This is a stretched, Euro-style, informal, family-friendly ship

OVERVIEW. *MSC Lirica* is best suited to young adult couples, solo travelers, and families with tots, children and teens who enjoy big-ship surroundings and facilities, and passengers of different nationalities and languages (mostly European). The decor has many Italian influences, including clean lines, minimalism in furniture design, and an eclectic collection of colors and soft furnishings that somehow work well together without any hint of garishness.

Berlitz's Ratings		
	Possible	Achieved
Ship	500	388
Accommodation	200	150
Food	400	236
Service	400	299
Entertainment	100	55
Cruise Experience	400	279
OVERALL SCORE		
1407 points out of 2000		

THE SHIP. *MSC Lirica*, sister to *MSC Opera*, was the first of a pair of new-builds for Mediterranean Shipping Cruises (MSC), Italy's largest privately owned cruise line. The ship's deep blue funnel is quite sleek; it has a swept-back design. The ship is fitted with an azimuthing pod propulsion system.

In 2015 the ship underwent a 'chop-and-stretch' operation, which added an 82ft (25m) mid-section, almost 200 additional cabins, more public rooms, entertainment facilities, and new shops (but no additional elevators), and more exterior deck space, home to a large waterpark for children. Families with children will also find special kids' areas equipped with Chicco® and LEGO® products, and an energetic multilingual youth activity team.

Inside, the layout (and passenger flow) is quite good with the exception of some congestion points – typically when first seating passengers exit the dining room and second seating passengers are waiting to enter.

An abundance of real woods and marble are used extensively in the interiors, and the standard of the fit and finish reflects MSC's commitment to high quality.

Facilities include a large main showlounge, a nightclub/disco, multiple lounges and bars, an Internet center, a virtual reality center, a children's club, and a shopping gallery named Rodeo Drive with stores that have an integrated bar and entertainment area, where you can shop, drink, and be entertained all in one convenient area. The Las Vegas Casino offers blackjack, poker, and roulette games, together with an array of slot machines. There is also a card room, but the integral library is small and disappointing, and there are no hardback books.

The ship is designed to accommodate families with children, who have their own play center, youth counselors, and activity programs. Anyone wheelchair-bound should note that there is no access to the uppermost forward and aft decks, although access throughout most of the interior is very good and there are also several wheelchair-accessible public restrooms. But passenger hallways are a little narrow on some decks for you to pass, when housekeeping carts are in place.

Some things that passengers find irritating: the ship's photographers always seem to be in your face; the telephone numbering system to reach such places as the information bureau (2224) and hospital (2360) are not easy to remember – single digit numbers would be better. Gratuities are extra, even though bar drinks already includes a 15 percent service charge added to all drinks/beverage orders.

ACCOMMODATION. There are several different price levels for accommodation, depending on grade and location: one suite category including 132 'suites' with private balcony, five outside-view cabin grades, and five interior cabin grades.

All cabins have a minibar and personal safe, satellite-linked television, several audio channels, and 24-hour room service. While tea and coffee are complimentary, snacks for room service incur a delivery charge of €2.50.

Accommodation designated as suites – they are not true suites, as there is no separate bedroom and lounge – has more room, a larger lounge area, walk-in closet, wall-to-wall vanity counter, a bathroom with combination tub and shower, toilet, and semi-private balcony with a light but partitions that are partial, not full. The bathrobes are 100 percent cotton. However, the suite bathrooms are very plain, with white plastic washbasins and white walls, and mirrors that steam up.

Some cabins on Scarlatti Deck have views obstructed by lifeboats, while those on Deck 10 aft (10105–10159) can be subject to late-night noise from the disco on the deck above.

DINING. There are two dining rooms: La Bussola Restaurant, and the smaller, slightly more intimate L'Ippocampo Restaurant, located one deck above. Both have large ocean-view picture windows at the aft end of the ship. There are two seatings for meals, in keeping with other ships in the MSC fleet, and tables are for two, four, six, or eight.

La Pergola is the most formal restaurant, offering stylish Italian cuisine. It is assigned to passengers in accommodation designated as suites, although other passengers can dine in it, too, on a reservations-only basis. The food and service are superior to that in the main dining room.

Other dining options. Casual, self-serve buffets for breakfast and lunch can be taken in Le Bistrot Cafeteria, which is also open for 20 hours a day, for sit-down, served, but casual, dinners each evening. For fast foods, there is also a grill and a pizzeria, both located outside, adjacent to the swimming pool and ship's funnel.

Coffee Corner, located on the upper, second level of the main lobby, is the place for coffees and pastry items – as well as for people-watching throughout the day and evening. Although there are windows, the view is not of the ocean, but of the stowed gangways and associated equipment.

ENTERTAINMENT. The Broadway Theater, the main showlounge, is located in the forward section. It has tiered seating set in a sloping floor, and sight lines are good from most seats. The room can also serve as a venue for large social functions. There is no separate bandstand, and the shows work with recorded music, with little consistency in orchestration and sound balance.

High-quality entertainment has not, to date, been part of MSC's offering. Hence, production shows and variety acts tend to be adequate at best. The Lirica Lounge, one deck above the showlounge, is the place for social dancing, with live music. For the young and lively set, there is The Blue Club, the ship's throbbing, ear-melting disco.

Additionally, live music is provided in most lounges by small groups and solo musicians.

SPA/FITNESS. The Lirica Health Center is located one deck above the navigation bridge at the forward end of the ship. The complex has a beauty salon, several private massage/body treatment rooms, plus a fitness center with ocean views and an array of cardio-vascular equipment. There's also a thermal suite, containing different kinds of steam rooms combined with aromatherapy infusions, available at extra cost.

The spa is operated by the Italian company Ocean-View, with European hairstylists and Balinese massage and body treatment staff. Gratuities to spa staff are not included, but left to your discretion.

MSC Magnifica
★★★★

Size:	Large Resort Ship	Passenger/Crew Ratio (lower beds):	2.5
Tonnage:	92,409	Cabins (total):	1,275
Lifestyle:	Standard	Size Range (sq ft/m):	150.6–301.3/14.0–28.0
Cruise Line:	MSC Cruises	Cabins (for one person):	0
Former Names:	none	Cabins (with private balcony):	827
IMO Number:	9387085	Cabins (wheelchair accessible):	17
Builder:	Aker Yards (France)	Wheelchair accessibility:	Good
Original Cost:	$360 million	Cabin Current:	110 and 220 volts
Entered Service:	Mar 2010	Elevators:	13
Registry:	Panama	Casino (gaming tables):	Yes
Length (ft/m):	963.9/293.8	Slot Machines:	Yes
Beam (ft/m):	105.6/32.2	Swimming Pools:	2
Draft (ft/m):	25.2/7.7	Hot Tubs (on deck):	4
Propulsion/Propellers:	diesel (31,680kW)/2	Self-Service Launderette:	No
Passenger Decks:	13	Dedicated Cinema/Seats:	No
Total Crew:	987	Library:	Yes
Passengers (lower beds):	2,550	Onboard currency:	Euros
Passenger Space Ratio (lower beds):	37.0		

This is a large, family-friendly ship with stylish, bright decor

OVERVIEW. This large resort ship is designed to accommodate families with children, who have their own play center, video games room, youth counselors, and activity programs. The interior layout and passenger flow are quite good, and decks are named after Mediterranean destinations such as Capri, Positano, Porto Venere, and Ischia. Some of the artwork is quite whimsical, but it suits the ship's contemporary design.

Berlitz's Ratings		
	Possible	Achieved
Ship	500	403
Accommodation	200	155
Food	400	242
Service	400	298
Entertainment	100	62
Cruise Experience	400	292
OVERALL SCORE		
1452 points out of 2000		

THE SHIP. *MSC Magnifica* is one of a quartet of the same class, the others being *MSC Musica*, *MSC Poesia*, and *MSC Orchestra*. The ship sports a dark blue funnel, which has a swept-back design that balances an otherwise large-ship profile. The hull itself has large circular porthole-style windows instead of square or rectangular ones. The ship is powered by diesel motors driving electric generators to provide power to two conventional propellers.

The interior decor has an abundance of Italian and general Mediterranean influences. These include clean lines, minimalism in furniture design, and a collection of colors, soft furnishings, and fabrics that work well together. Real wood and marble have been used extensively in the Italianate interiors, and the high quality reflects the commitment that MSC Cruises has in the vessel's future.

The focal point is a main three-deck-high lobby; it has a water-feature backdrop and a crystal (glass) piano on a small stage that appears to float on a pond. Facilities include a large main showlounge (Royal Theater), a nightclub, Atlantic City Casino, a disco that incorporates two bowling lanes, numerous lounges and bars (including L'Olimpiade sports/wine/food bar), a library, a card room, an Internet center, a 4D virtual-reality center, children's club, and a dedicated cigar lounge (Cuba Lounge) with specialized smoke extraction and stocking a selection of Cuban, Dominican, and Italian smokes.

One of the most popular venues is the Tiger Lounge/Bar. It features animal-themed decor and sumptuous but heavy chairs, and a long curvy bar. A shopping area, which includes an electronics store, is well integrated with bars and entertainment offerings in the main lobby, so you can shop, drink, and be entertained all in one convenient area.

Drinking places include a pub-like venue as well as several comfortable lounges with live music. Note that 15 percent is added to all bar drink prices. Although access throughout most of the interior is very good, wheelchair-bound passengers should note that accommodation hallways are narrow on some decks for you to pass when housekeeping carts are in place. Sadly, there is no walk-around open promenade deck.

ACCOMMODATION. There are numerous different price levels, depending on grade and location. Included are 18 'suites' with private balcony, minisuites, outside-view cabins, and interior cabins. Contrary to nautical convention, the cabin numbering system has even numbered cabins on the starboard side, and odd numbered cabins on the port side.

All cabins have high-quality Italian bed linen (400-count cotton for suites, 300-count cotton for all other cabins), a minibar, safe, satellite flat-screen TV, several audio channels, and 24-hour room service. Continental breakfast is complimentary in cabins from 7.30am to 10am, and room service snacks are available at extra cost at any other time.

Accommodation designated as 'suites' – they are not true suites, as there is no separate bedroom and lounge – also has more space, although they are small compared to suites on some other major cruise lines. They have a larger lounge area, walk-in closet, vanity desk with drawer-mounted hairdryer, a bathroom with combination tub and shower, toilet, and semi-private balcony with light. The partitions between each balcony are of the partial, not full, type. The bathrobes and towels are 100 percent cotton, and a pillow menu with a choice of five pillows is available.

Views from many cabins on Camogli Deck are obstructed by lifeboats. Some of the most popular cabins are those at the aft section of the ship, with views over the stern from the balcony cabins. The 17 cabins for the disabled are spacious and well equipped.

DINING. There are two principal dining rooms: L'Edera and Quattro Venti. Both are located aft – on different decks – with large ocean-view picture windows. There are two seatings for meals, at assigned tables for two to eight. Seating is both banquette-style and in individual chairs – although the chairs are slim and do not have armrests.

Other dining options. Casual, self-serve buffets for breakfast and lunch are set out in the Sahara Cafeteria (open 20 hours every day), where you can also enjoy sit-down and be served dinners in a casual setting each evening. There's also a pool deck fast-food eatery for burgers. Coffee/tea and pastries are available in several bars adjacent to the mid-ships atrium lobby.

Enclosed in the ship's center, on Amalfi Deck, Shanghai is a Chinese à-la-carte extra-cost restaurant. It's a popular place, and reservations are required.

L'Oesi is a reservation-required, extra-charge, à-la-carte dining spot that, by day, forms the aft section of the Sahara Cafeteria, complete with Moroccan-style decor. Dinners are cooked to order from the adjacent galley.

A Sports Bar is the venue for light-bite snack foods (examples: chicken breast and rocket salad; eggs stuffed with salmon roe; smoked salmon rosettes; assorted sole rolls – all at a small additional cost).

Silver trays full of late-night snacks are taken throughout the ship by waiters, and on some days, special late-night desserts, such as flambé items, are showcased in various lounges. Ice cream is made on board.

All sorts of coffees, available in the many bars and lounges, cost extra but are still good value.

ENTERTAINMENT. The Royal Theater is the large, principal show lounge, and the tiered seating spans three decks in the forward section of the ship, with good sight lines from most of the plush, comfortable seats. The room can also serve as a venue for large groups or social functions. All the large-scale production shows are performed to prerecorded music – there is no showband.

The L'Amethista Lounge is the place for social dancing and functions such as cooking demonstrations, with live music provided by a band. For the young and lively crowd, there's the ear-melting T32 disco. With its floor-to-ceiling windows, it is a quiet, pleasant place to relax and read during sea days.

Additionally, big-screen movies are shown on a mega-screen above the forward pool, just behind the ship's mast. Live music is provided in most bars and lounges.

SPA/FITNESS. The Aurea Spa is one deck above the navigation bridge at the forward end of the ship. The complex has a beauty salon, several treatment rooms offering massage and other body-pampering treatments, and a gymnasium with forward ocean views and an array of muscle-toning and strengthening equipment. There's also a Middle East-themed thermal suite, containing steam rooms and saunas with aromatherapy infusions, and a relaxation/hot tub room; there's an extra charge for using these facilities. Note that gratuities to staff are not included, but left to your discretion.

Sports facilities include table tennis, a tennis court, mini-golf course, golf practice net, two shuffleboard courts, and a jogging track.

MSC Musica
★★★★

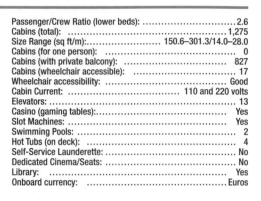

Size:	Large Resort Ship
Tonnage:	92,409
Lifestyle:	Standard
Cruise Line:	MSC Cruises
Former Names:	none
IMO Number:	9320087
Builder:	Aker Yards (France)
Original Cost:	$360 million
Entered Service:	Jul 2006
Registry:	Panama
Length (ft/m):	963.9/293.8
Beam (ft/m):	105.6/32.2
Draft (ft/m):	25.2/7.7
Propulsion/Propellers:	diesel (31,680kW)/2
Passenger Decks:	13
Total Crew:	987
Passengers (lower beds):	2,550
Passenger Space Ratio (lower beds):	36.2
Passenger/Crew Ratio (lower beds):	2.6
Cabins (total):	1,275
Size Range (sq ft/m):	150.6–301.3/14.0–28.0
Cabins (for one person):	0
Cabins (with private balcony):	827
Cabins (wheelchair accessible):	17
Wheelchair accessibility:	Good
Cabin Current:	110 and 220 volts
Elevators:	13
Casino (gaming tables):	Yes
Slot Machines:	Yes
Swimming Pools:	2
Hot Tubs (on deck):	4
Self-Service Launderette:	No
Dedicated Cinema/Seats:	No
Library:	Yes
Onboard currency:	Euros

Lively Italian decor and good style for family cruising

OVERVIEW. *MSC Musica* suits young adult couples, solo travelers, and families with tots, children, and teens who enjoy big-ship surroundings and a noisy, big-city lifestyle, with different nationalities and languages, mostly European. The ship is designed to accommodate families with children, who have their own play center, video games room, youth counselors, and activity programs.

Berlitz's Ratings		
	Possible	Achieved
Ship	500	403
Accommodation	200	155
Food	400	242
Service	400	298
Entertainment	100	62
Cruise Experience	400	289
OVERALL SCORE		
1449 points out of 2000		

THE SHIP. *MSC Musica* is an extension and evolution of the slightly smaller (and earlier) *MSC Lirica* and *MSC Opera*. The ship's deep blue funnel is sleek, and features a swept-back design that carries the MSC logo in gold lettering. The overall profile is quite well balanced. The hull has large circular porthole-style windows instead of square or rectangular windows. From a technical viewpoint, the ship is powered by diesel motors driving electric generators that provide power to two conventional propellers.

Real wood and marble have been used extensively in the ship's interiors, and the high quality reflects the commitment that MSC Cruises has in the cruise industry.

The interior focal point is a main three-deck-high lobby, with a water-feature backdrop and a crystal (glass) piano on a small stage that appears to float on a pond. Other principal facilities include a large main show lounge, a nightclub, disco, numerous lounges and bars (including a wine bar), library, card room, an Internet center, virtual-reality center, children's club, and cigar lounge with specialized smoke extraction

and a selection of Cuban, Dominican, and Italian (Toscana) smokes.

A shopping gallery has an integrated bar and entertainment area that flows through the main lobby, which is not only convenient, with everything all in the one place, but also has something of a city feel. The expansive San Remo Casino has blackjack, poker, and roulette games, and an array of slot machines for entertainment.

Drinking places include a pub-like venue as well as several comfortable lounges with live music. A gratuity of 15 percent is added to all drinks/beverage orders. Some of the artwork is whimsical, but fishermen will appreciate the stuffed head from a blue marlin caught by Pierfrancesco Vago, president of MSC Cruises in 2004; it weighs 588lbs (267kg) and stands at the Blue Marlin Bar on the pool deck. And do check out the 'restroom with a view' – the toilets have a great ocean view, if you leave the door open.

Although access throughout most of the interior of the ship is very good, anyone who is wheelchair-bound should note that the passenger hallways are a narrow on some decks. There is no walk-around open promenade deck.

Although the interior layout (and passenger flow) is good, a congestion point occurs when first-seating passengers exit the two main dining rooms and passengers on the second seating are waiting to enter.

ACCOMMODATION. There are several price levels, depending on grade and location. There are suites with private balcony, mini-suites, outside-view cabins, and interior (no-view) cabins. Contrary to nautical convention, the cabin numbering system has even-numbered cabins on the starboard side, and odd-numbered cabins on the port side.

All cabins have a minibar and personal safe, satellite flat-screen TV with audio channels, and 24-hour room service. Continental breakfast is complimentary from 7.30 to 10am, but room service snacks cost extra at any other time.

Accommodation designated as 'suites' – they are not true suites, as there is no separate bedroom and lounge – also has more room, although they are small compared to suites on some on other cruise lines. They have a larger lounge area, walk-in closet, vanity desk with drawer-mounted hairdryer, and a bathroom with combination tub and shower. There is a semi-private balcony with light, but the partitions between each balcony are of the partial, not full, type. The suite bathrooms are plain, with white plastic washbasins and white walls, and mirrors that steam up.

Many cabins on Forte Deck have views obstructed by lifeboats. Cabins on the uppermost accommodation deck (Cantata Deck) may be subject to the noise of sunloungers being dragged across the deck above when it is set up or cleaned early in the morning. Some of the most popular cabins are those at the aft end of the ship, with views over the ship's stern from the balcony cabins (on Virtuoso, Adagio, Intermezzo, and Forte decks). The 17 cabins for the disabled are spacious and well equipped.

DINING. There are two main dining rooms, L'Oleandro and Le Maxim's, both located aft, with large ocean-view picture windows. There are two seatings for meals, and tables are for two, four, six, or eight. Seating is both banquette-style and in individual chairs; the chairs, however, are slim and lack armrests. All dining venues are managed by Italians.

Passengers occupying accommodation designated as suites and deluxe grades are typically assigned the best tables in the quietest sections of Le Maxim's restaurant, which is quieter than L'Oleandro, the main dining room.

Other dining options. Gli Archi Cafeteria (a section of which forms the reservations-only Il Giardino) is the place for casual, self-serve buffets for breakfast and lunch and for sit-down, served, but casual, dinners each evening – it's actually open for 20 hours daily – so there's always something available. There's also an outside fast-food eatery on the pool deck for burgers and other grilled food items. Several bars adjacent to the midships atrium lobby, serve extra-cost Segafredo Italian coffees, or tea, and pastries.

Il Giardino is an à-la-carte dining spot that costs extra and requires reservations.

Kaito is a Japanese sushi bar with counter and table seating and a menu that has a fine array of extra-cost à-la-carte sashimi pieces, nigiri and temaki sushi and maki rolls, tempura and teriyaki items, and a choice of several types of cold or hot sake, and Japanese beer. Reservations are needed and à-la-carte pricing is in effect.

Enoteca Wine Bar, a very creative wine bar, provides a selection of famous regional Italian cheeses, hams, honey, and wines in a relaxing and entertaining bistro-style setting.

Silver trays full of late-night snacks are taken throughout the ship by waiters, and, on some days, special late-night desserts, such as flambé items, are showcased in various lounges like the Il Tucana Lounge. The ship makes ice cream freshly on board.

ENTERTAINMENT. The Teatro La Scala, the large, principal showlounge, is in the ship's forward section. It has tiered seating on two levels, and the sight lines are good from most of the plush, comfortable seats. The room can also serve as a venue for large groups or social functions.

High-quality entertainment has not, to date, been a priority for MSC Cruises. Production shows and the variety acts could be better. However, due to the multi-national passenger mix, almost all entertainment needs to be visual rather than vocal. There is no space for a showband in the showlounge, and so all shows are performed to pre-recorded tracks.

The Il Tucano Lounge, aft of the showlounge, is the place for social dancing and functions such as cooking demonstrations, with live music provided by a band. Another nightclub, the Crystal Lounge, provides music for social dancing. The young and lively crowd have the ear-melting G32 disco; with its floor-to-ceiling windows, it is a quiet, pleasant place to relax and read by day.

Big-screen movies are shown on a large screen above the forward pool, just behind the ship's mast.

SPA/FITNESS. The Aloha Beauty Farm is located one deck above the navigation bridge at the forward end of the ship. The complex has a beauty salon, several treatment rooms offering massage and other body-pampering treatments, and a gymnasium with forward ocean views and an array of high-tech, muscle-toning, and strengthening equipment. There's also a Middle East-themed thermal suite, containing steam rooms and saunas with aromatherapy infusions, and a relaxation/hot tub room; it costs extra to use these facilities.

The spa is run as a concession by Steiner Leisure, with European hairstylists and massage/body treatment staff. Gratuities to spa staff are at your discretion.

Sports facilities include table tennis, a tennis court, mini-golf course, golf practice net, two shuffleboard courts, and a walking/ jogging track.

MSC Opera
★★★★

Size:	Mid-size Ship	Passenger/Crew Ratio (lower beds):	2.9
Tonnage:	65,000	Cabins (total):	1,071
Lifestyle:	Standard	Size Range (sq ft/m):	139.9–302.0/13.0–28.0
Cruise Line:	MSC Cruises	Cabins (for one person):	0
Former Names:	none	Cabins (with private balcony):	232
IMO Number:	9240464	Cabins (wheelchair accessible):	4
Builder:	Chantiers de l'Atlantique (France)	Wheelchair accessibility:	Good
Original Cost:	$266 million	Cabin Current:	110 and 220 volts
Entered Service:	Mar 2004	Elevators:	9
Registry:	Italy	Casino (gaming tables):	Yes
Length (ft/m):	902.2/275.0	Slot Machines:	Yes
Beam (ft/m):	95.1/29.0	Swimming Pools:	2
Draft (ft/m):	22.4/6.8	Hot Tubs (on deck):	2
Propulsion/Propellers:	diesel (31,680kW)/2 azimuthing pods	Self-Service Launderette:	No
Passenger Decks:	10	Dedicated Cinema/Seats:	No
Total Crew:	721	Library:	Yes
Passengers (lower beds):	2,142	Onboard currency:	Euros
Passenger Space Ratio (lower beds):	30.3		

This large family-friendly ship has European style and flair

OVERVIEW. *MSC Opera* suits young adult couples, solo travelers, and families with tots, children, and teens who enjoy big-ship surroundings and a noisy, big-city lifestyle, with different nationalities and languages, mostly European. The ship is designed to accommodate families with children, who have their own play center, video games room, youth counselors, and activity programs.

Berlitz's Ratings		
	Possible	Achieved
Ship	500	404
Accommodation	200	155
Food	400	234
Service	400	298
Entertainment	100	62
Cruise Experience	400	285
OVERALL SCORE		
1438 points out of 2000		

THE SHIP. *MSC Opera* was the second of the new ships built for MSC Cruises, Italy's largest privately owned cruise line – the first was *MSC Lirica*, which had almost 100 fewer cabins than *MSC Opera*. The deep blue funnel is quite sleek, and features a swept-back design that carries the MSC logo. Although similar in size and structure to *MSC Lirica*, there are many modifications, mostly in technical spaces, and an improved layout in public rooms.

Between May and July 2015 the ship underwent a 'chop-and-stretch' operation, which added an 82ft (25m) mid-section, almost 200 additional cabins, more public rooms, entertainment facilities and new shops (but no additional elevators), and more exterior deck space, which houses a large waterpark for children. Families with children will also find special kids' areas equipped with Chicco® and LEGO® products, and an energetic multilingual youth activity team.

All decks are named after well-known operas. The interior layout and passenger flow are quite good, except for a couple of points of congestion, typically when the first seating exits the dining room and passengers on second seating are waiting to enter. The decor has many Italian and other Mediterranean influences, including clean lines, minimalist furniture, and a collection of colors, soft furnishings, and fabrics that work well together, and without any hint of garishness. Real wood and marble have been used extensively in the interiors, and the fit and finish are good.

Facilities include the ship's main showlounge, a nightclub/disco, several lounges and bars, an Internet center with 10 terminals, a virtual-reality center, a children's club, a shopping gallery named Via Conditti with shops that have an integrated bar and entertainment area, so that you can shop, drink, and be entertained conveniently all in the one place. The Monte Carlo Casino provides blackjack, poker, and roulette games, together with an array of slot machines. There is also a card room, but the integral library is small, uncared for, and disappointing, and there are no hardback books.

Drinking places include the Sotto Vento Pub (under the showlounge) and the La Cabala lounge. A 15 percent gratuity is added to all drinks/beverage orders. The ship is designed to accommodate families with children, who have their own play center, youth counselors, and programming.

Anyone who is wheelchair-bound should note that there is no access to the uppermost forward and aft decks, although access throughout most of the interior of the ship is very good, and there are several wheelchair-accessible public restrooms. In passenger hallways it can be a squeeze to get past housekeeping carts at certain hours.

Minor niggles include the in-your-face photographers; constant music in every lounge; and the fact that standing in line for embarkation, disembarkation, shore tenders, and for self-serve buffet meals is an inevitable aspect of cruising aboard all large ships. There is no forward observation lounge.

ACCOMMODATION. There are several different price levels, depending on grade and location: one suite category including 172 'suites' with private balcony, five outside-view cabin grades, and five interior cabin grades. The cabin numbering system has even-numbered cabins on the starboard side, and odd-numbered cabins on the port side – contrary to nautical convention.

All cabins have a minibar and personal safe, satellite TV, several audio channels, and 24-hour room service. Tea and coffee are complimentary, but snacks delivered by room service cost extra.

Accommodation designated as suites – they are not true suites, as there is no separate bedroom and lounge – has more room, a larger lounge area, walk-in closet, wall-to-wall vanity counter, a bathroom with combination tub and shower, toilet, and semi-private balcony with a light but partitions between each balcony that are partial, not full. Cotton bathrobes are provided. The suite bathrooms are very plain, with white plastic washbasins and white walls, and mirrors that steam up.

Some cabins on Othello Deck and Rigoletto Deck have views obstructed by lifeboats, while those on Turandot Deck aft (10192–10241) may be subject to late-night and early-morning noise from the cafeteria on the deck above. Cabins on the uppermost accommodation deck are subject to deck chairs and tables being dragged across the deck, when it is set up or cleaned early in the morning.

DINING. There is one principal dining room, La Caravella Restaurant, with large ocean-view picture windows in the aft section of the ship. There are two seatings for meals, in keeping with other ships in the MSC Cruises fleet, and tables are for two, four, six, or eight.

L'Approdo Restaurant is assigned to all passengers occupying accommodation designated as suites, although other passengers can dine in it, too, on a reservations-only basis. As you might expect, the food and service are superior to that in the main dining room.

Other dining options. Casual, self-serve buffets for breakfast and lunch can be taken in Le Vele Cafeteria, although the serving lines on both port and starboard sides are quite cramped, and the food is quite basic, or at the pool deck outside the fast food eatery, with grill and pizzeria. Le Vele is also open for sit-down, served, but casual, dinners each evening – it's actually open for 20 hours a day – so even in the middle of the night you can find something to eat. Extra-cost coffee/tea and pastries are served in the Aroma Café, on the upper level of the two-deck-high atrium lobby, but annoying videos constantly play on TV sets in the forward section of the area.

ENTERTAINMENT. The 713-seat Teatro dell'Opera is the ship's main showlounge, located in the forward section of the ship. It has tiered seating set in a sloping floor, and the sight lines are good from most seats, which are plush and comfortable. The room can also serve as a venue for large social functions. There is no separate bandstand, and the shows use recorded music, so there's little consistency in orchestration and sound balance.

High-quality entertainment has not, to date, been a priority for MSC Cruises. As a result, production shows and variety acts tend to be amateurish at best when compared to those on some other major cruise lines.

The Opera Lounge, one deck above the show lounge, is used extensively for social dancing, and features a live band. Meanwhile, for the young and lively set, there is the Byblos Discotheque, the ship's throbbing, ear-melting club. A number of bands and musical groups provide live music in the various bars and lounges.

SPA/FITNESS. The Opera Health Center is one deck above the navigation bridge at the forward end of the ship. The complex has a beauty salon, several treatment rooms offering massage and other body-pampering treatments, as well as a gymnasium with ocean views and an array of high-tech, muscle-toning, and strengthening equipment. There's also a thermal suite, containing different kinds of steam rooms combined with aromatherapy infusions, at extra cost.

The health center is operated by the excellent Italian company OceanView, with European hairstylists and Balinese massage and body-treatment staff. Gratuities are not included, and are at your discretion.

Outside on deck, sports fans will appreciate a neat eight-hole mini-golf course that wraps around the funnel, while a walking/jogging track encircles the two swimming pools in the center of the ship.

MSC Orchestra
★★★★

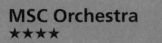

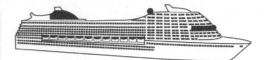

Size:	Large Resort Ship	Passenger/Crew Ratio (lower beds):	2.6
Tonnage:	92,409	Cabins (total):	1,275
Lifestyle:	Standard	Size Range (sq ft/m):	150.6–301.3/14.0–28.0
Cruise Line:	MSC Cruises	Cabins (for one person):	0
Former Names:	none	Cabins (with private balcony):	827
IMO Number:	9320099	Cabins (wheelchair accessible):	17
Builder:	Aker Yards (France)	Wheelchair accessibility:	Good
Original Cost:	$360 million	Cabin Current:	110 and 220 volts
Entered Service:	May 2007	Elevators:	13
Registry:	Italy	Casino (gaming tables):	Yes
Length (ft/m):	963.9/293.8	Slot Machines:	Yes
Beam (ft/m):	105.6/32.2	Swimming Pools:	2
Draft (ft/m):	25.2/7.7	Hot Tubs (on deck):	4
Propulsion/Propellers:	diesel-electric (40,4000kW)/2	Self-Service Launderette:	No
Passenger Decks:	13	Dedicated Cinema/Seats:	No
Total Crew:	987	Library:	Yes
Passengers (lower beds):	2,550	Onboard currency:	Euros
Passenger Space Ratio (lower beds):	36.2		

This large, family-friendly ship has elegant, chic decor

OVERVIEW. *MSC Orchestra* will suit young adult couples, solo travelers, and families with tots, children, and teens who enjoy big-ship surroundings and a noisy, big-city lifestyle, with different nationalities and languages, mostly European. The ship accommodates families with children, who have their own meeting and play centers, video games room, youth counselors, and fun programs.

Berlitz's Ratings	Possible	Achieved
Ship	500	403
Accommodation	200	155
Food	400	242
Service	400	298
Entertainment	100	62
Cruise Experience	400	291
OVERALL SCORE		
1451 points out of 2000		

THE SHIP. The ship's deep blue funnel is sleek, and features a swept-back design that carries the MSC logo in gold lettering. The overall profile is quite well balanced. The hull has large circular porthole-style windows instead of square or rectangular windows. From a technical viewpoint, the ship is powered by diesel motors driving electric generators to provide power to two conventional propellers.

MSC Orchestra is a sister to *MSC Musica* and *MSC Poesia*, though the fabrics and furnishings used in the ship's interiors are nicer and softer. Among the numerous lounges and bars, the Out of Africa Savannah Lounge is stunning. A delightful four-piece classical ensemble regularly performs in the atrium lobby.

Plenty of real wood and marble have been used in the interiors, and the high quality reflects the commitment that MSC Cruises has in the vessel's future.

The focal point of the ship is the main three-deck-high lobby, with a water-feature backdrop and a crystal piano on a small stage that appears to float on a pond. Other facilities include a large main show lounge, a nightclub, disco, numerous lounges and bars (including a wine bar), library, card room, an Internet center, virtual-reality center, children's club, and cigar lounge with specialized smoke extraction and a selection of Cuban, Dominican, and Italian (Toscana) smokes.

A shopping gallery, which includes an electronics store, has an integrated bar and entertainment area that flows through the main lobby, so that you can shop, drink, and be entertained all in one convenient place. The expansive San Remo Casino has blackjack, poker, and roulette games, and an array of slot machines.

Drinking places include a pub-like venue as well as several comfortable lounges with live music. A 15 percent gratuity is added to all drinks/beverage orders. Some of the artwork is whimsical. And, speaking of whimsical, take a look at the 'restrooms with a view' – the men's/ladies' toilets adjacent to the forward pool deck bar have a great ocean view, and you can even watch the passing scenery while sitting on the toilet – if you leave the door open.

The themed decor has many Italian influences, including clean lines, minimalism in furniture design, and a collection of colors, soft furnishings, and fabrics that work well together, although it's a little more garish than one would expect.

Access throughout most of the interior of the ship is good, but wheelchair-bound passengers should note that the accommodation hallways are narrow on some decks for you to pass the housekeeping carts. Note that there is no walk-around open promenade deck.

Although the interior layout and passenger flow is good, a congestion point occurs when first seating passengers exit the two main dining rooms and second seating passengers are waiting to enter.

The MSC Cruises crew really does try their best to provide good service to a multi-national clientele, and the ship exudes a noticeable 'feel-good' factor.

ACCOMMODATION. There are several price levels, depending on grade and location. There are suites with private balcony, mini-suites, outside-view cabins, and interior (no-view) cabins. Contrary to nautical convention, the cabin numbering system has even-numbered cabins on the starboard side, and odd-numbered cabins on the port side.

All cabins have a minibar and personal safe, satellite flat-screen TV with audio channels, and 24-hour room service. Continental breakfast is complimentary from 7.30 to 10am, but room-service snacks cost extra at any other time.

Accommodation designated as 'suites' – they are not true suites, as there is no separate bedroom and lounge – also has more room, although they are small compared to suites on some on other cruise lines. They have a larger lounge area, walk-in closet, vanity desk with drawer-mounted hairdryer, and a bathroom with combination tub and shower. There is a semi-private balcony with light, but the partitions between each balcony are of the partial, not full, type. The suite bathrooms are plain, with white plastic washbasins and white walls, and mirrors that steam up.

Many cabins on Forte Deck have views obstructed by lifeboats. Cabins on the uppermost accommodation deck (Cantata Deck) may be subject to the noise of sunloungers being dragged across the deck above when it is set up or cleaned early in the morning. Some of the most popular cabins are those at the aft end of the ship, with views over the ship's stern from the balcony cabins (on Virtuoso, Adagio, Intermezzo, and Forte decks). The 17 cabins for the disabled are spacious and well equipped.

DINING. There are two main dining rooms, Villa Borghese Restaurant and L'Ibiscus, located in the aft section of the ship, and with large ocean-view picture windows. There are two seatings for dinner, and open seating for breakfast and lunch. Tables are for two to eight, as well as some alcove banquette-style seats. Anyone occupying upper-grade accommodation typically gets the better tables in quieter areas.

Other dining options. Shanghai Chinese Restaurant makes a change from the main restaurants. This was the first real Chinese restaurant aboard any cruise ship – mainly because of the challenges of providing high-temperature wok and deep fryer preparation. Dim sum steamed dishes are also served, typically for lunch. The food embraces four main cuisines – Beijing, Cantonese, Shanghai, and Szechuan – and there's Tsing Tao beer.

The Four Seasons Restaurant offers extra-cost à-la-carte Italian cuisine in a garden-like setting with fine china, and a menu reflecting regional and seasonal fare. Food is cooked to order, so it tends to taste better than the meals in the main dining room. Reservations are required, and there's a cover charge.

La Piazzetta Café is open 20 hours a day for casual, self-serve buffet-style breakfasts and for sit-down, served dinners in a relaxed environment.

ENTERTAINMENT. Covent Garden is the ship's stunning large showlounge. The Opera Lounge, one deck above, is the place for social dancing, with live music. The G32 disco is for the more energetic. A large poolside movie screen provides moviegoers with more choices. All the activities are provided by energetic multilingual cruise staff. Also, live music is provided in almost all bars and lounges.

SPA/FITNESS. The Orchestra Health Center, operated by the Italian company OceanView, includes a beauty salon, several treatment rooms offering massage and other body-pampering treatments, and a fitness center with ocean views and high-tech muscle-toning equipment.

There's also a thermal suite, containing different kinds of steam rooms combined with aromatherapy infusions, at extra cost. There's a neat juice and smoothie bar opposite the reception desk. Gratuities are at your discretion.

For the sports-minded, there is deck quoits, as well as shuffleboard courts, tennis and basketball courts, mini-golf, and a jogging track.

MSC Poesia
★★★★

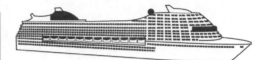

Size:	Large Resort Ship	Passenger/Crew Ratio (lower beds):	2.6
Tonnage:	92,490	Cabins (total):	1,275
Lifestyle:	Standard	Size Range (sq ft/m):	150.6–301.3/14.0–28.0
Cruise Line:	MSC Cruises	Cabins (for one person):	0
Former Names:	none	Cabins (with private balcony):	827
IMO Number:	9303073	Cabins (wheelchair accessible):	17
Builder:	Fincantieri (Italy)	Wheelchair accessibility:	Good
Original Cost:	$360 million	Cabin Current:	110 and 220 volts
Entered Service:	Oct 2008	Elevators:	13
Registry:	Panama	Casino (gaming tables):	Yes
Length (ft/m):	963.9/293.8	Slot Machines:	Yes
Beam (ft/m):	105.6/32.2	Swimming Pools:	2
Draft (ft/m):	26.2/8.0	Hot Tubs (on deck):	4
Propulsion/Propellers:	diesel (58,000kW)/2	Self-Service Launderette:	No
Passenger Decks:	13	Dedicated Cinema/Seats:	No
Total Crew:	987	Library:	Yes
Passengers (lower beds):	2,550	Onboard currency:	Euros
Passenger Space Ratio (lower beds):	36.2		

This is a delightful large, informal, family-friendly ship

OVERVIEW. *MSC Poesia* will suit young adult couples, solo travelers, and families with tots, children, and teens who enjoy big-ship surroundings and a noisy, big-city lifestyle, with many different nationalities and languages, mostly European. The ship is designed to accommodate families with children, who have their own play centers, video games room, and youth counselors, and plenty of activity programs.

Berlitz's Ratings		
	Possible	Achieved
Ship	500	403
Accommodation	200	155
Food	400	242
Service	400	298
Entertainment	100	62
Cruise Experience	400	292
OVERALL SCORE		
1452 points out of 2000		

THE SHIP. *MSC Poesia* is a sister ship to *MSC Musica* and *MSC Orchestra*. The ship's deep blue funnel is sleek, and has a swept-back design that carries the MSC logo in large lettering. The hull has large circular porthole-style windows instead of square or rectangular windows. From a technical viewpoint, the ship is powered by diesel motors driving electric generators to provide power to two conventional propellers.

The interior layout and passenger flow are good – with the exception of a couple of points of congestion, typically when the first seating exits the two main dining rooms, and passengers on the second seating are waiting to enter.

The interior focal point is a main three-deck-high lobby, which has a grand water-feature backdrop and a crystal (glass) piano on a small stage that appears to float on a pond. Other facilities include a large main showlounge, a nightclub, disco, numerous lounges and bars – including a wine bar – library, card room, Internet center, virtual-reality center, children's club, and cigar lounge with spe-

cialized smoke extraction and a selection of Cuban, Dominican, and Italian (Toscana) smokes.

The musically themed decor has many Italian influences, including clean lines, minimalism in furniture design, and a collection of colors, soft furnishings, and fabrics that work well together, although it's a little more garish than one would expect.

Real wood and marble have been used extensively in the interiors, and the high quality reflects the commitment that MSC Cruises has in the vessel's future.

A shopping gallery, which includes an electronics store, has an integrated bar and entertainment area that flows through the main lobby, so that you can conveniently shop, drink, and be entertained all in the one place. The expansive Casino Royale has blackjack, poker, and roulette tables, and an array of slot machines.

Drinking places include several comfortable lounges – all with live music. A 15 percent gratuity is added to all drinks/beverage orders. A mini-golf course is on the port side of the funnel, while a walking/jogging track encircles an upper level above the two swimming pools.

Some of the artwork is whimsical. Do check out the 'restroom with a view' – the men's/ladies' toilets adjacent to the Blue Marlin pool deck bar have a great ocean view, and you can even watch the passing scenery while sitting on the toilet, if you leave the door open.

Although access throughout most of the interior of the ship is good, wheelchair-bound passengers should note that the passenger hallways are a little narrow on some decks for you to pass when housekeeping carts are in place. There is no walk-around open promenade deck.

ACCOMMODATION. There are several price levels, depending on grade and location. Included are 18 'suites' with private balcony, mini-suites, outside-view cabins, and interior cabins. Contrary to nautical convention, the cabin numbering system has even-numbered cabins on the starboard side, and odd-numbered cabins on the port side.

All cabins have a minibar and personal safe, satellite flat-screen TV with audio channels, and 24-hour room service. Continental breakfast is complimentary from 7.30 to 10am; room-service snacks cost extra at any other time.

Accommodation designated as 'suites' – they are not true suites, as there is no separate bedroom and lounge – also has more room, although they are small compared to suites on some on other cruise lines. They have a larger lounge area, walk-in closet, vanity desk with drawer-mounted hairdryer, and a bathroom with combination tub and shower. There is a semi-private balcony with light, but the partitions between each balcony are of the partial, not full, type. The suite bathrooms are plain, with white plastic washbasins and white walls, and mirrors that steam up.

Many cabins on Forte Deck have views obstructed by lifeboats. Cabins on the uppermost accommodation deck (Cantata Deck) may be subject to the noise of sunloungers being dragged across the deck above when it is set up or cleaned early in the morning. Some of the most popular cabins are those at the aft end of the ship, with views over the ship's stern from the balcony cabins on four of the aft decks. The 17 cabins for the disabled are spacious and well equipped.

DINING. There are two principal dining rooms, both of them located aft (on different decks), with large ocean-view picture windows. There are two seatings for meals, as aboard other ships in the MSC Cruises fleet, and tables are for two to eight; seating is both banquette-style and in individual armless chairs.

Other dining options. Kaito is a delightful, extra-cost Japanese restaurant, with a sushi bar and an extensive à-la-carte menu. Reservations are needed, but the cuisine is worth the extra cost.

A Tex-Mex Restaurant is an extra-cost à-la-carte dining spot, and reservations are necessary.

The Wine Bar (Enoteca) provides a selection of famous regional cheeses, hams, and a variety of wines in a bistro-style setting that is relaxing and entertaining.

The Villa Pompeina Cafeteria is for casual, self-serve buffets for breakfast and lunch and for sit-down, served, but casual, dinners (it's actually open for 20 hours a day, so there's always something available to eat, even in the middle of the night). Outside, there's a fast-food eatery on the pool deck for burgers and other grilled fast-food items. Extra-cost Segafredo coffees, together with a variety of teas and pastry items are also available in several bars adjacent to the atrium midships lobby.

Silver trays full of late-night snacks are taken throughout the ship by waiters, and, on some days, special late-night desserts, such as flambé items, are showcased in various lounges.

ENTERTAINMENT. The Teatro Carlo Felice is the ship's principal showlounge; it is in the forward section of the ship, with tiered seating on two levels, and the sight lines are good from most of the plush, comfortable seats. The room can also be a venue for large group meetings or social functions. There is no showband, so all shows are performed to pre-recorded music tracks.

Almost all the entertainment is more visual than vocal, owing to the multi-national passenger mix,

Another large lounge (Zebra Bar), aft of the showlounge, is the place for social dancing and functions such as cooking demonstrations. Live music here is provided by a band.

Big-screen movies are shown on a large screen above the forward pool, just behind the ship's mast. Live music is provided in the various bars and lounges throughout the ship.

SPA/FITNESS. The Poesia Health Center is run by OceanView, an Italian spa specialist. The complex features a beauty salon, several treatment rooms offering massage and other body-pampering treatments, and a gymnasium with forward ocean views and an array of high-tech, muscle-toning, and strengthening equipment. There's also a Middle East-themed thermal suite, containing steam rooms and saunas with aromatherapy infusions, and a relaxation/hot tub room; it costs extra to use these facilities.

The spa is run as a concession by Steiner Leisure, with European hairstylists and massage/body-treatment staff. Gratuities to spa staff are at your discretion.

Sports facilities include table tennis, a tennis court, mini-golf course, golf practice net, two shuffleboard courts, and a jogging track.

MSC Preziosa
★★★★+

Size:	Large Resort Ship	
Tonnage:	140,000 tons	
Lifestyle:	Standard	
Cruise Line:	MSC Cruises	
Former Names:	none	
IMO Number:	9595321	
Builder:	STX France	
Original Cost:	$760 million	
Entered Service:	Mar 2013	
Registry:	Panama	
Length (ft/m):	1,093.5/333.3	
Beam (ft/m):	124.6/38.0	
Draft (ft/m):	27.72/8.4	
Propulsion/Propellers:	diesel-electric (40,000kW)/2	
Passenger Decks:	13	
Total Crew:	1,390	
Passengers (lower beds):	3,502	
Passenger Space Ratio (lower beds):	39.9	

Passenger/Crew Ratio (lower beds):	2.5
Cabins (total):	1,751
Size Range (sq ft/m):	148.5–568.3/13.8–52.8
Cabins (for one person):	0
Cabins (with private balcony):	1,125
Cabins (wheelchair accessible):	45
Wheelchair accessibility:	Good
Cabin Current:	110 and 220 volts
Elevators:	16
Casino (gaming tables):	Yes
Slot Machines:	Yes
Swimming Pools:	3 (1 w/sliding glass dome)
Hot Tubs (on deck):	13
Self-Service Launderette:	No
Dedicated Cinema/Seats:	No
Library:	Yes
Onboard currency:	Euros

A fine, large, family-friendly ship designed for Europeans

OVERVIEW. This large resort ship, a close sister to *MSC Divina*, *MSC Fantasia*, and *MSC Splendida*, will appeal to young-at-heart adult couples, solo travelers, and families with children and teens enjoying an urban lifestyle, with a mix of mostly European nationalities and style.

THE SHIP. *MSC Preziosa* was originally ordered by the Libyan government-owned shipping company GNMTC (the contract was signed by Captain Hannibal Muammar Gaddafi – fifth eldest son of Muammar Gaddafi) before Europe-based cruise line MSC Cruises acquired the hull and configured the ship as the fourth in its *Fantasia*-class. It has the very latest in green-technology engines.

Outside on the expansive main pool deck, there is a main swimming pool, together with a whole Aqua Park with raised sections, hot tubs, and numerous water features. Slightly forward of the pool deck is a family swimming pool; it's open well into the late evening, and can be covered by a sliding glass dome in case of inclement weather.

Facilities for all passengers include a large three-deck-high theater-style showlounge, a nightclub/disco, library, card room, an Internet center, a 4D virtual-reality center, multi-deck shopping gallery, a large Millennium Star Casino with gaming tables and an array of slot machines and a nicely-shaped stairway, and, in the aft section, an 'infinity' pool that overlooks the stern, and 'beach club' area. Drinking places include numerous lounges and bars (including a trendy 'Green Sax' jazz lounge/bar), most with

Berlitz's Ratings		
	Possible	Achieved
Ship	500	420
Accommodation	200	162
Food	400	276
Service	400	308
Entertainment	100	78
Cruise Experience	400	308
OVERALL SCORE		
1552 points out of 2000		

live music. One lounge in the aft section of the ship is for adults only.

An area called the MSC Yacht Club – an exclusive community of 'suite-grade' accommodation, including a Top-Sail Lounge – has an observation/lifestyle lounge and social meeting place, private sunbathing with integral dip pool, hot tubs, and concierge services for making dining reservations, booking excursions and spa treatments, and arranging private parties. A marble floor leads to a shiny Swarovski glass staircase that connects the concierge facilities between Decks 15 and 16 under a glass-domed ceiling.

FAMILIES. The ship is designed to cater well for families with children, who sail free and have their own extensive collection of play centers, including a children's club and jungle adventure playground, plus two water slides in an area called the Doremi Castle Aqua Park, youth counselors, and activity programs tailored to specific age groups. One coveted feature is a 394ft (120m) -long Vertigo water slide, with twists and turns and a 30ft (9m) transparent section that shoots off the side of the ship. Riders travel at an average speed of about 20ft (6m) per second. Note that only children over about 47.2ins (120cm) tall are allowed on the slide.

ACCOMMODATION. If the budget allows, it's worth paying extra to stay in one of the 'suites' in the Yacht Club accommodation. You'll get silver-tray room service by a team of well-trained butlers, who

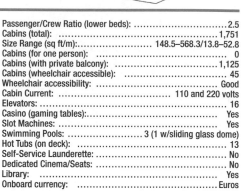

are good. The suites have a minibar, interactive TV, personal safe, hairdryer, and satellite-link telephone.

DINING. There are two main restaurants – Golden Lobster, on Deck 5 – and L'Arabesque, on Deck 6. There are two seatings for dinner, and open seating for breakfast and lunch. Tables are for two, four, six, or eight, and include some cozy alcove banquette seating (although it's challenging for waiters to serve these alcove tables properly). Both restaurants feature Mediterranean cuisine.

Occupants of Yacht Club-grade accommodation have their own intimate La Palmeraie Restaurant, with rather Moorish decor, Moroccan-style arches, and hanging brass lamps. Dining is in an open-seating arrangement.

Other dining options. A 115-seat Eataly Restaurant – a specialty dining spot (together with a 30-seat Ristorante Italia) – provides tastes of Italy, the 'slow food' way, with a choice of 18 items. A popular Turin-based chain (founded in 2007 by Oscar Farinetti), Eataly places its major emphasis on local artisanal producers, food education, accessibility and affordability, and sustainable sourcing and production. The chairs in the Ristorante Italia section of the Eataly Restaurant, however, are see-through plastic, and grossly uncomfortable.

The Galaxy Restaurant is an extra-charge venue that sits high above the main pool, and has great views. It has a trendy vibe (it forms part of the disco), and the food – Mediterranean fusion fare, including steaks and seafood items – is good.

Casual serve-yourself buffet-style meals can be taken in the huge Inca and Maya buffet venue (open 20 hours daily) for breakfasts and lunches, and waiter-served dinners in a relaxed, but always busy, setting. A bakery corner provides freshly baked breads and rolls throughout the day.

A Sports and Bowling Diner features a classic American food experience, including sandwiches and burgers.

ENTERTAINMENT. The 1,600-seat Platinum Theater is the ship's vast showlounge – it's really more like a concert theatre and auditorium. It is spread over three decks, and there are good sight lines from almost all seats except for a few rows at the back on port and starboard sides. It is a well-designed room, except for the fact that no space is allocated for a live showband.

The shows concentrate more on visual entertainment such as mime, magic, dancing, and acrobatics, because the clientele is so multinational. Productions are performed with recorded music (known as a 'click-track'), and introductions are done at breakneck speed by the multilingual cruise director.

There is live music in almost all the other lounge/bar venues – one of the most popular of which is the Golden Jazz Bar.

SPA/FITNESS. The Aurea Wellbeing Center is large and houses a beauty salon, body treatment rooms, and a gymnasium with great ocean views. A thermal suite contains different kinds of steam rooms combined with herbal aromatherapy infusions, in a calming Asia-themed environment. Features include a Shu Uemura Art of Hair cabin, a vintage barbershop, and a Himalayan salt crystal 'bed.' The spa is operated by OceanView, a specialist spa provider, and most of the therapists are from Bali.

Sports facilities include deck quoits, shuffleboard courts, large tennis/basketball court, mini-golf, and a jogging track.

MSC Sinfonia
★★★+

Size:	Mid-size Ship
Tonnage:	55,452
Lifestyle:	Standard
Cruise Line:	MSC Cruises
Former Names:	*European Stars*
IMO Number:	9210153
Builder:	Chantiers de l'Atlantique (France)
Original Cost:	$245 million
Entered Service:	Apr 2002/Mar 2005
Registry:	Italy
Length (ft/m):	902.0/275.0
Beam (ft/m):	95.1/29.0
Draft (ft/m):	22.4/6.8
Propulsion/Propellers:	diesel (31,680kW)/2 azimuthing pods
Passenger Decks:	10
Total Crew:	721
Passengers (lower beds):	1,960
Passenger Space Ratio (lower beds):	33.1

Passenger/Crew Ratio (lower beds):	2.7
Cabins (total):	980
Size Range (sq ft/m):	139.9–236.8/13–22
Cabins (for one person):	0
Cabins (with private balcony):	224
Cabins (wheelchair accessible):	2
Wheelchair accessibility:	Good
Cabin Current:	110 and 220 volts
Elevators:	9
Casino (gaming tables):	Yes
Slot Machines:	Yes
Swimming Pools:	2
Hot Tubs (on deck):	2
Self-Service Launderette:	No
Dedicated Cinema/Seats:	No
Library:	Yes
Onboard currency:	Euros

This is a large Euro-style, informal, family-friendly ship

OVERVIEW. *MSC Sinfonia* is best for adult couples and solo travelers, and families with children, who enjoy lots of activity, accompanied by lots of noise and late nights, in a setting that exudes Mediterranean family vacation values.

THE SHIP. *MSC Sinfonia* is a sister ship to *MSC Armonia*, with a decor that's decidedly 'European Moderne.' The international mix of passengers adds to the overall ambience of the cruise experience.

The exterior deck space is barely adequate for the number of passengers carried. The Lido Deck surrounding the outdoor swimming pool also has whirlpool tubs and a large bandstand is set in raised canvas-covered pods. All sunloungers have cushioned pads.

Between January and March 2015, the ship underwent a 'chop-and-stretch' operation, which added an 82ft (25m) mid-section, almost 200 additional cabins, more public rooms, entertainment facilities and new shops (but no additional elevators), and more exterior deck space, which houses a large waterpark for children. Families with children will also find special kids' areas equipped with Chicco® and LEGO® products, and an energetic multilingual youth activity team.

The interior decor is described as 'European Moderne,' which seems to include crisp, clean lines, and minimalist furniture design – including some chairs that look interesting but are totally impractical. However, the interior colors are good; nothing jars the senses, but rather calms them, unlike the effect aboard many ships.

Berlitz's Ratings

	Possible	Achieved
Ship	500	379
Accommodation	200	149
Food	400	233
Service	400	295
Entertainment	100	55
Cruise Experience	400	271
OVERALL SCORE		
1382 points out of 2000		

Standing in line for embarkation, disembarkation, shore tenders, and self-serve buffet meals is an inevitable aspect of cruising aboard large ships. Announcements are in several languages.

Wheelchair-bound passengers should note that there is no access to the uppermost forward and aft decks, although access throughout most of the interior is good. Also, passenger hallways are a little narrow on some accommodation decks to pass when housekeeping carts are in place.

The company keeps prices low by providing air transportation that may be at inconvenient times, or that involves long journeys by bus. In other words, be prepared for a little discomfort in getting to and from your cruise in exchange for low cruise rates. Note that 15 percent is added to all drinks and beverage orders.

Families with children will find plenty to keep them occupied, including special kids' areas equipped with Chicco® and LEGO® products, and an energetic multilingual youth activity team.

ACCOMMODATION. There are numerous categories, the price depending on the grade, size, and location you choose. These include 132 'suites' with private balcony (whose partitions are only of the partial, and not the full, type), outside-view cabins, and interior (no-view) cabins.

Suite-grade accommodation – they are not true suites, as there's no separate bedroom and lounge – has more room, a larger lounge area, a walk-in closet, a wall-to-wall vanity counter, a bathroom with combination tub and shower, and toilet, and a private balcony with light. Bathrobes are provided. In general, the 'suites' are practical and nicely furnished. However, except for the highest category, the bathrooms are very plain, with white plastic washbasins and white walls, small shower enclosures, and mirrors that steam up.

Standard grade cabins, at a modest 140 sq ft (13 sq m), are quite small when compared to those on many other ships, but they are reasonably comfortable, with plenty of space between two lower beds. All grades of accommodation have a TV, minibar/refrigerator, personal safe cleverly positioned behind a vanity desk mirror, hairdryer, and bathroom with shower and toilet.

DINING. There are two main dining rooms, the 610-seat Il Galeone Restaurant and the Il Covo Restaurant; both have two seatings and share the same menu. The cuisine is reasonably sound, and, with varied menus and good presentation, should prove a highlight for most passengers. The wine list has a wide variety of wines at fairly reasonable prices, although almost all are very young.

Other dining options. La Terrazza is a casual, self-serve buffet eatery that is open 20 hours a day, including sit-down, waiter-served dinners in a very relaxed setting. The selections are very standardized and could be better. Café del Mare, adjacent to one of two swimming pools and the ship's funnel, is a grill area for burgers and other fast-food items.

Extra-cost coffee/tea and pastries are available in Le Baroque Café, set around the upper level of the two-deck-high atrium lobby. It's a good location for people-watching, but annoying music videos are constantly played on TV monitors in the forward sections.

ENTERTAINMENT. The two-deck-high Gondola Theater is the main showlounge; it is the venue for production shows, cabaret acts, plays, and other theatrical presentations. Entertainment consists mainly of visual shows, because of the mix of nationalities carried onboard. Other shows consist of singers, magicians, mime artists, and comedy jugglers.

The ship carries a number of bands and small musical units that provide live music for dancing or listening to in various lounges and bars throughout the ship.

SPA/FITNESS. The spa features a gymnasium with ocean views, and high-tech, muscle-toning, and strengthening equipment. A thermal suite has different kinds of steam rooms combined with aromatherapy infusions such as chamomile and eucalyptus, and a Rasul chamber provides a combination of two or three kinds of application mud and a gentle steam shower. The spa, operated by the Italian concession OceanView, offers a wide range of body-pampering wellbeing treatments.

For active types there's a simulated climbing wall outdoors aft of the ship's funnel, as well as a volleyball/basketball court, and mini-golf.

MSC Splendida
★★★★

Size:	Large Resort Ship	Passenger/Crew Ratio (lower beds):	2.4
Tonnage:	137,936	Cabins (total):	1,637
Lifestyle:	Standard	Size Range (sq ft/m):	161.4–699.6/15–65
Cruise Line:	MSC Cruises	Cabins (for one person):	0
Former Names:	none	Cabins (with private balcony):	1,260
IMO Number:	9359806	Cabins (wheelchair accessible):	43
Builder:	Aker Yards (France)	Wheelchair accessibility:	Good
Original Cost:	$550 million	Cabin Current:	110 and 220 volts
Entered Service:	Jul 2009	Elevators:	14
Registry:	Panama	Casino (gaming tables):	Yes
Length (ft/m):	1,093.5/333.3	Slot Machines:	Yes
Beam (ft/m):	124.6/38.0	Swimming Pools:	3 (1 w/sliding glass dome)
Draft (ft/m):	27.2/8.4	Hot Tubs (on deck):	13
Propulsion/Propellers:	diesel (40,000kW)/2	Self-Service Launderette:	No
Passenger Decks:	13	Dedicated Cinema/Seats:	No
Total Crew:	1,313	Library:	Yes
Passengers (lower beds):	3,274	Onboard currency:	Euros
Passenger Space Ratio (lower beds):	42.1		

A large, family-friendly ship with tasteful, elegant decor

OVERVIEW. *MSC Splendida* will appeal to young adult couples, solo travelers, and families with children and teens who enjoy big ships with a mix of nationalities, mostly European. Children appreciate Virtual World's five white-knuckle 4D rides in a 10-seat thrill room. It all feels rather like a European city center, and is full of large and small rooms, nooks and crannies, and places to play in.

Berlitz's Ratings		
	Possible	Achieved
Ship	500	414
Accommodation	200	161
Food	400	271
Service	400	306
Entertainment	100	77
Cruise Experience	400	305
OVERALL SCORE		
1534 points out of 2000		

THE SHIP. A sister ship to *MSC Fantasia*, *MSC Splendida* is a stunning ship, and one of the largest ships built for a European cruise company. It is 33ft (10m) longer than the Eiffel Tower is high, and the propulsion power is the equivalent of 120 Ferraris. There are four swimming pools, one of which can be covered by a glass dome.

The interior includes an exclusive area called the MSC Yacht Club for the occupants of some 99 'suites.' This 'club' includes a Top-Sail Lounge (with butler service, canapés, and bite-sized food items), private sunbathing with an integral dip pool, two hot tubs, and concierge services for making dining reservations, and booking excursions and spa treatments.

If your budget allows, it's worth paying extra to stay in one of the 'suites' in the Yacht Club accommodation. You'll get silver-tray room service by a team of butlers, a reserved (quieter) section of the Villa Verde Restaurant, and keycard access to a members-only sundeck sanctuary area that includes its own bar and food counters, a small dip pool, two hot tubs, and expansive open but sheltered lounging deck. It's

a world away from the hustle and bustle of the main pool decks and solarium on the decks below.

The ship's interior decor is quite stunning. There are basically two decks full of public lounges and bars (most with live music), and eateries, including a large two-deck-high theater-style showlounge (The Strand), a nightclub/disco (The Aft Lounge), library, card room, an Internet center, virtual-reality center, extensive shopping gallery (that has the feel of a city), and large casino (inhabited by many who can smoke at the bar). The Royal Palm Casino features blackjack, poker, and roulette games, plus an array of slot machines.

The ship is well designed to accommodate families with children. A 15 percent gratuity is added to all drinks/beverage orders.

Niggles include the fact that all the lounges 'flow' into each other, and so the music from each one bleeds into the adjacent room. Note that only Yacht Club-grade occupants are escorted to their cabins by their butlers. Housekeeping staff point passengers in the right direction, but no longer escort them to their cabins.

ACCOMMODATION. Eighty percent of the cabins are outsides, and 95 percent of these have a balcony – the standard balcony cabin is almost 172 sq ft (16 sq m), plus bathroom and balcony. It's worth paying extra to stay in one of the 72 'suites' (each 312 sq ft/29 sq m) in the Yacht Club area at the top, front end of the ship. Here, you'll get silver-tray room service, a reserved section of the Villa Verde restaurant, plus access to a 'members only' sundeck sanctuary area that includes its own bar and food counters, small 'dip' pool, two hot tubs, and open lounging deck. It's very different from the hustle and bustle of the main pool decks.

In a 2011 refit, 28 Aurea Suites (from former Yacht Club accommodation) were created, with direct access to the Aurea Spa. The spa suites include unlimited access to the sauna and steam room, a private consultation with the spa doctor, a Balinese massage, a facial relax treatment, and a solarium session.

The Yacht Club has its own serene concierge lounge, small library, and reception desk. A Svarovski glass stairway leads to the Yacht Club suites, and a private elevator accesses the Aurea Spa, located one deck below. The lounge has its own galley and dedicated chef.

DINING. La Reggia is the ship's main restaurant. It spans two decks, and has two seatings for dinner, and an open seating for both breakfast and lunch. Tables are for two, four, six, or eight, and there's some alcove banquette seating on both the main and balcony levels. A second restaurant, the single-level Villa Verde, is for occupants of suite-grade accommodation and has panoramic windows at the stern of the ship.

Other dining options. L'Olivo is an Italian/Mediterranean extra-cost à-la-carte venue. It is located in a smaller, more intimate setting aft, overlooking a small pool and relaxation area. The food is cooked to order, and dining here is a pleasant, unhurried experience. Reservations are required.

Santa Fe is an extra-cost, L-shaped Tex-Mex restaurant with food items cooked to order.

Bora Bora Cafeteria is a large casual self-serve lido buffet-style eatery. It is open 20 hours a day, for breakfast and lunch, and for sit-down, casual, waiter-served dinners each evening.

ENTERTAINMENT. The Strand Theater has plush seating in tiers for as many as 1,700, and good sight lines. Because of the multi-national background of passengers, the shows concentrate on more visual entertainment such as mime, magic, dancing, and acrobatics, and are performed with recorded music – because there is no orchestra pit. Live music for dancing and listening to is provided by a number of bands and soloists throughout the ship.

SPA/FITNESS. The Aurea Spa (16,000 sq ft/1,485 sq m) has a beauty salon, well-equipped treatment rooms, and a large gymnasium with ocean views. Included is a large thermal suite, and saunas. The decor is welcoming and restful. The spa is run by Ocean-View. Gratuities to spa staff are at your own discretion. Sports facilities include deck quoits, large tennis/basketball court, mini-golf, and a jogging track.

National Geographic Endeavour
★★+

Size:	Boutique Ship	Passenger/Crew Ratio (lower beds):	1.7
Tonnage:	3,132	Cabins (total):	62
Lifestyle:	Standard	Size Range (sq ft/m):	191.6–269.1/17.8–25.0
Cruise Line:	Lindblad Expeditions	Cabins (for one person):	14
Former Names:	*Caledonian Star, North Star, Lindmar, Marburg*	Cabins (with private balcony):	0
IMO Number:	6611863	Cabins (wheelchair accessible):	0
Builder:	A.G. Weser Seebeckwerft (Germany)	Wheelchair accessibility:	None
Original Cost:	n/a	Cabin Current:	110 and 220 volts
Entered Service:	1966/Jun 2009	Elevators:	0
Registry:	The Bahamas	Casino (gaming tables):	No
Length (ft/m):	292.6/89.20	Slot Machines:	No
Beam (ft/m):	45.9/14.0	Swimming Pools:	1
Draft (ft/m):	20.3/6.2	Hot Tubs (on deck):	0
Propulsion/Propellers:	diesel (3,236kW)/1	Self-Service Launderette:	No
Passenger Decks:	6	Dedicated Cinema/Seats:	No
Total Crew:	64	Library:	Yes
Passengers (lower beds):	113	Onboard currency:	US$
Passenger Space Ratio (lower beds):	27.7		

A very small older ship, for nature and wildlife cruises

OVERVIEW. *National Geographic Endeavour* and its type of soft exploration cruising are best suited to adventurous, hardy types who enjoy being with nature and wildlife in some of the world's most interesting places, but cosseted aboard a small, modestly comfortable ship. Specialized lecturers accompanying each cruise make this a real life-enrichment experience.

THE SHIP. Renamed in 2005, the former *Endeavour* was built as a stern factory fishing trawler for North Sea service. Today, *National Geographic Endeavour* is a tidy and well-cared-for discovery-style cruise vessel operating 'soft' expedition cruises. There is an open-bridge policy for all passengers. It carries 10 Zodiac landing craft for excursions, and has a helicopter pad and an enclosed shore tender. A steep aft stairway leads down to the landing craft platform. This small ship has a reasonable number of public rooms and facilities, including a lecture room/lounge/bar/library, where videos are also stocked for in-cabin use. There's a good book selection.

This likeable, homey ship runs well organized, destination-intensive cruises, at a very reasonable price. It attracts loyal repeat passengers who don't want to sail aboard ships that look like apartment blocks. The itineraries include Antarctica, where this ship has been operating since 1998.

The interior stairways are a little steep, as is the exterior stairway to the Zodiac embarkation points.

Berlitz's Ratings

	Possible	Achieved
Ship	500	199
Accommodation	200	94
Food	400	194
Service	400	216
Entertainment	100	60
Cruise Experience	400	209

OVERALL SCORE
972 points out of 2000

Noise from the diesel engines can be irksome, particularly on the lower decks. Recommended gratuities are $10 per person, per day.

ACCOMMODATION. There are five categories of cabins: one suite category and four non-suite categories. The all-outside-view cabins are compact, but reasonably comfortable, and they are decorated in warm, muted tones. All cabins have a minibar/refrigerator, video player, and a decent amount of closet and drawer space – though it's tight for long voyages. The bathrooms are tight, with little space for storing toiletries. Four 'suites' are basically double the size of a standard cabin, and have a wood partition separating the bedroom and lounge area. The bathroom is still small, however.

DINING. The open-seating dining room is small and charming, but the low-back chairs are not comfortable. The cuisine is reasonably high quality, with fresh ingredients, but not a lot of choice. Salad items lack variety, as do international cheeses. Service is attentive and friendly.

ENTERTAINMENT. The main lounge is the venue for lectures, slide shows, and occasional film presentations. There are no shows.

SPA/FITNESS. There is a small fitness room and a tiny sauna.

National Geographic Explorer
★★+

Size:	Boutique Ship
Tonnage:	6,471
Lifestyle:	Standard
Cruise Line:	Lindblad Expeditions
Former Names:	*Lyngen, Midnatsol II, Midnatsol*
IMO Number:	8019356
Builder:	Ulstein Hatlo (Norway)
Original Cost:	n/a
Entered Service:	1982/Jun 2008
Registry:	The Bahamas
Length (ft/m):	367.4/112.0
Beam (ft/m):	54.1/16.5
Draft (ft/m):	15.0/4.5
Propulsion/Propellers:	diesel/2
Passenger Decks:	6
Total Crew:	70
Passengers (lower beds):	148
Passenger Space Ratio (lower beds):	43.7

Passenger/Crew Ratio (lower beds):	2.1
Cabins (total):	81
Size Range (sq ft/m):	n/a
Cabins (for one person):	14
Cabins (with private balcony):	13
Cabins (wheelchair accessible):	1
Wheelchair accessibility:	None
Cabin Current:	110 volts
Elevators:	1
Casino (gaming tables):	No
Slot Machines:	No
Swimming Pools:	0
Hot Tubs (on deck):	0
Self-Service Launderette:	No
Dedicated Cinema/Seats:	No
Library:	Yes
Onboard currency:	US$

A small, sturdy ship for nature and wildlife cruises

OVERVIEW. *National Geographic Explorer* suits hardy, adventurous types who enjoy being with nature and wildlife in some of the most interesting and occasionally inhospitable places on earth, cosseted aboard a small but comfortable ship.

THE SHIP. Originally built as *Midnatsol* for Hurtigruten, the ship was purchased by Lindblad Expeditions in 2007 and extensively refitted and outfitted well for expedition-style cruising, with some really good facilities and expedition equipment.

The ship has an ice-strengthened hull and is quite stable due to the stabilizers, so movement is minimized. Twin funnel uptakes are located almost at the very stern – an unusual design. There is little outdoor deck space, but it's not needed in cold-weather areas.

The main facilities include a lecture room and bistro bar with espresso machine adjacent to the restaurant, and boot-washing stations. An expedition voyage aboard this ship is all about learning and exploration. The dress code is totally casual; layered clothing and sturdy outerwear is recommended. Gratuities to staff are not included in the price.

ACCOMMODATION. The price you pay depends on size and location. The cabins are small, as are the bathrooms, although they are nicely designed, practical units. Some have a fixed queen-size bed configuration,

Berlitz's Ratings

	Possible	Achieved
Ship	500	265
Accommodation	200	110
Food	400	195
Service	400	232
Entertainment	100	60
Cruise Experience	400	215
OVERALL SCORE		
1077 points out of 2000		

others have twin beds (some can be pushed together, some are fixed). There are several cabins for single occupancy. The tiled bathrooms have shower enclosures, and small shelves for toiletries. Suites have two washbasins, premium bedding, and feather-fluffy duvets.

There is a decent supply of electrical outlets and an ethernet connection for laptops. Closet doors arc of the sliding type instead of the outward opening type, to minimize noise and banging when the ship is in tough weather conditions. Naturally, a National Geographic Atlas is provided.

DINING. There is one main dining room, as well as areas for self-serve buffet-style food. The food is hearty and fairly healthy, although you should not expect to find fresh greens in some of the more out-of-the-way areas.

ENTERTAINMENT. Lectures, briefings, and recaps, plus after-dinner conversation with fellow participants are the main entertainment – if you're not too tired after exhausting days of landings and other adventures.

SPA/FITNESS. Thcrc arc two body treatment rooms – with skylights, for wildlife-inspired wellness, facials, and massage, including a special 'ice-bear massage', as well as a fitness/workout room.

National Geographic Orion
★★★★+

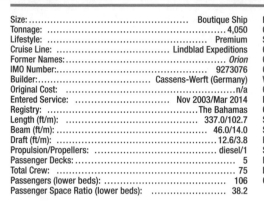

Size:	Boutique Ship
Tonnage:	4,050
Lifestyle:	Premium
Cruise Line:	Lindblad Expeditions
Former Names:	*Orion*
IMO Number:	9273076
Builder:	Cassens-Werft (Germany)
Original Cost:	n/a
Entered Service:	Nov 2003/Mar 2014
Registry:	The Bahamas
Length (ft/m):	337.0/102.7
Beam (ft/m):	46.0/14.0
Draft (ft/m):	12.6/3.8
Propulsion/Propellers:	diesel/1
Passenger Decks:	5
Total Crew:	75
Passengers (lower beds):	106
Passenger Space Ratio (lower beds):	38.2

Passenger/Crew Ratio (lower beds):	1.4
Cabins (total):	53
Size Range (sq ft/m):	175.0–345.0/16.3–32.1
Cabins (for one person):	0
Cabins (with private balcony):	9
Cabins (wheelchair accessible):	0
Wheelchair accessibility:	None
Cabin Current:	110 and 220 volts
Elevators:	1
Casino (gaming tables):	No
Slot Machines:	No
Swimming Pools:	0
Hot Tubs (on deck):	1
Self-Service Launderette:	No
Dedicated Cinema/Seats:	Yes/98
Library:	Yes
Onboard currency:	Australian $

For Australia-based 'soft' expedition and adventure cruising

OVERVIEW. This pocket-sized ship is enjoyed by mature couples and single travelers who like learning about nature and wildlife in an up-close-and-personal way. Cruising is really the wrong word for this type of eco-travel; it's more like having a magic carpet whisk to you to destinations most people have never heard of – particularly on the spectacular Papua New Guinea or Kimberley region itineraries.

Berlitz's Ratings

	Possible	Achieved
Ship	500	409
Accommodation	200	161
Food	400	308
Service	400	300
Entertainment	100	84
Cruise Experience	400	329

OVERALL SCORE
1591 points out of 2000

THE SHIP. The former *Orion* (Orion Expedition Cruises) was acquired in 2013 by Lindblad Expeditions, renamed *National Geographic Orion*, and transferred to the new operator in March 2014, when it became part of the Lindblad Expeditions/National Geographic fleet. More snorkeling gear and enough diving gear for 24 diving program participants was added, together with an ROV (remote operated vehicle) able to descend up to 1,000ft (305m).

National Geographic Orion (according to one myth, Neptune was Orion's father, while Queen Eurayle of the Amazon was his mother) features nature- and wildlife-rich expedition-style cruises in high-quality surroundings, in the company of other like-minded travelers. It has all the comforts of home, as well as specialist equipment for expedition cruising. Although small, it has stabilizers, bow and stern thrusters for maximum maneuverability, and a fleet of 10 heavy-duty Zodiac inflatable landing craft and a fishing boat, BeeKay. There is also an aft marina platform for swimming off.

There is no swimming pool, nor is one needed, but there is a hot tub set amid an open deck, which

also houses a bar and a small rock garden/water feature. All outdoor tables, chairs, and real steamer-style sunloungers are made of tropical hardwood.

The interior decor is warm and inviting, providing a cozy, cosseting, yet contemporary environment. Public rooms include an observation lounge and library (plus a nautical chart table and a self-serve beverage station), which opens onto a walk-around open promenade deck; it also connects with the small Health Spa.

Other public rooms include The Lounge (main lounge), a boutique, and a dedicated Cosmos Lecture Hall with surround sound system for lectures and movies. National Geographic provides stunning photographic images of the oceans as part of the artwork. Typically, an expedition leader and marine biology lecturers are carried on each expedition.

The reception desk is manned 24 hours a day, and there's an Internet-connect computer. Some rooms are clustered around a glass-walled atrium and the single elevator. A 'mud room,' complete with boot-washing stations, is adjacent to a Zodiac/tender loading platform on the port side.

This is about as far away from big cruise ships as you can get, with well-planned itineraries to some of the southern hemisphere's most remote regions, including the islands of Papua New Guinea, Australia's Kimberly region, 'Wild' Tasmania, and Antarctica's McMurdo Sound and Ross Sea regions. If you want magic moments in soft adventure travel, wrapped in the comfort of some fine, contemporary surroundings and good food, it would be hard to beat *Orion*. But make sure you can walk well – some expeditions are quite demanding.

When the ship operates in Australian waters – on Kimberly itineraries, for example – an Australian sales tax is added to all wine and beverage accounts. Drinks really should be included with this kind of product. However, bottled water *is* provided for all passengers at no charge.

ACCOMMODATION. There are four suite grades, and two cabin grades; the facilities in all of them are top-rate. All have twin beds that convert to a queen-size bed, a TV infotainment system, a mini-refrigerator, ample closet space, and a small personal safe.

The marble-clad bathroom has a small toiletries cabinet, single washbasin, and a large shower enclosure, with a retractable clothesline. Toiletries are by Escada. All the cabinetry was custom-made, and the bathrooms were fitted individually, which is rare in today's modular-fit world.

There are 13 suites, nine with a small 'French' balcony (meaning you can just about step out onto it), four Owner's Suites, six balcony suites, two Deluxe Suites, and one odd-shaped but delightful Junior Suite. These have more space, and some share a narrow communal balcony (meaning there is no partition between them), as well as having a sofa, glass drinks table, and good-size vanity desk. Only the four Owner's Suites have a bathtub; all other suites/cabins have large shower enclosures.

All cabins display black-and-white photographs of yachts, by Beken of Cowes.

DINING. The Restaurant has ocean-view picture windows, artwork based on the astrological signs, and operates one open seating. Its low ceiling, however, makes it rather noisy. The cuisine is extremely good and varied, and, in addition to an à-la-carte menu, each dinner includes a four-course signature menu by one of Australia's new breed of high-profile chefs, Serge Dansereau, of The Bathers' Pavilion in Sydney.

While portions are not large, they are colorful and creative. You can expect to find Tasmanian oysters, crocodile, emu, and kangaroo among the offerings. Place settings include Bauscher china and Hepp silverware.

The ship carries a decent range of mostly Australian wines.

Delphinus Outdoor Café, an open deck aft of the Leda Lounge, serves as an alfresco dining spot for casual breakfasts, lunches, and occasional barbecue dinners.

Continental breakfast and afternoon tea are also served in the Galaxy Lounge. Espressos and cappuccinos are available at no extra charge in two lounges/ bars and restaurant, and do try the delicious brownies on the bar counter.

The Filipino service staff are warm and communicate well with passengers.

ENTERTAINMENT. There is no formal entertainment, although the ship typically carries an entertaining duo. Each evening, lecturers provide daily recaps and fascinating, in-depth talks on marine or plant biology.

SPA/FITNESS. The Health Spa consists of a fitness center, sauna, shower enclosure, and a private treatment room (for massages). A beauty salon is located two decks below.

The ship carries a range of personal beauty products used on board and also for sale; creams, oils, and other ingredients are mixed by the therapist and tailored to your own needs.

Nautica
★★★★

Size:	Small Ship
Tonnage:	30,277
Lifestyle:	Premium
Cruise Line:	Oceania Cruises
Former Names:	R Five
IMO Number::	9200938
Builder:	Chantiers de l'Atlantique
Original Cost:	£150 million
Entered Service:	Dec 1998/Nov 2005
Registry:	Marshall Islands
Length (ft/m):	593.7/181.0
Beam (ft/m):	83.5/25.5
Draft (ft/m):	19.5/6.0
Propulsion/Propellers:	diesel (18,600kW)/2
Passenger Decks:	9
Total Crew:	386
Passengers (lower beds):	684
Passenger Space Ratio (lower beds):	44.2

Passenger/Crew Ratio (lower beds):	1.7
Cabins (total):	342
Size Range (sq ft/m):	145.3–968.7/13.5–90.0
Cabins (for one person):	0
Cabins (with private balcony):	232
Cabins (wheelchair accessible):	3
Wheelchair accessibility:	Good
Cabin Current:	110 and 220 volts
Elevators:	4
Casino (gaming tables):	Yes
Slot Machines:	Yes
Swimming Pools:	1
Hot Tubs (on deck):	2
Self-Service Launderette:	Yes
Dedicated Cinema/Seats:	No
Library:	Yes
Onboard currency:	US$

This premium ship has traditional decor, for mature-age cruisers

OVERVIEW. *Nautica* is best suited to couples who like good food and style, but want informality and interesting itineraries, all at a very reasonable price.

THE SHIP. *Nautica*, almost identical to *Insignia* and *Regatta*, is an all-white ship with a large, square white funnel, and a very pleasant Lido and Pool Deck outdoors, with teak overlaid decking and high-quality lounge chairs.

In 2014, the ship underwent a refurbishment program that included the addition of Barista's coffee bar (for illy coffees), new bathrooms for the Owner's Suites and Vista Suites, and updated decor in all other cabins. Also added were a miniature golf course, shuffleboard courts, and other deck games.

The interior decor is a delightful throwback to the ocean liners of the 1920s and 1930s, with dark woods and warm colors, all carried out in fine taste, although a little fake in places. This includes detailed ceiling cornices, both real and faux, wrought-iron staircase railings, leather-paneled walls, trompe l'oeil ceilings, rich carpeting in hallways with an Oriental rug-look center section, and many other interesting and expensive-looking decorative touches. It feels like a comfortable traditional country club.

The public rooms are spread over three decks. The lobby has a staircase with intricate wrought-iron railings. A large observation lounge, the Horizon Bar, is high atop ship.

There are plenty of bars, including one in each of the restaurant entrances. Perhaps the nicest is

Berlitz's Ratings

	Possible	Achieved
Ship	500	400
Accommodation	200	153
Food	400	308
Service	400	295
Entertainment	100	74
Cruise Experience	400	308
OVERALL SCORE		
1538 points out of 2000		

the casino bar/lounge, a beautiful room reminiscent of London's grand hotels and includes a Martini bar. It has an inviting marble fireplace, comfortable sofas, and individual chairs.

The Library is a grand Regency-style room, with a fireplace, a high, indented, trompe l'oeil ceiling, and an excellent selection of books, plus very comfortable wingback chairs.

Gratuities are automatically added to your onboard account. Accommodation designated as suites pay more, for the butler. An 18 percent gratuity is added to bar and spa accounts.

ACCOMMODATION. There are six cabin categories, and several price grades, including three suite price grades, five outside-view cabin grades, and two interior cabin grades. All of the standard interior and outside-view cabins – the lowest four grades – are very compact units, and tight for two persons. They have twin beds or queen-size bed, with good under-bed storage areas, personal safe, vanity desk with large mirror, good closet and drawer space in rich, dark woods, cotton bathrobe and towels, slippers, clothes brush, and shoehorn. TV sets carry a major news channel, where obtainable, plus a sports channel and round-the-clock movie channels.

About 100 cabins qualify as 'Concierge Level' accommodation, and occupants get extra goodies such as enhanced bathroom amenities, complimentary shoeshine, tote bag, cashmere throw blanket, bottle of Champagne on arrival, hairdryer, priority restaurant reservations, priority embarkation, and dedicated check-in desk.

Owner's Suites. The six Owner's Suites, measuring 962 sq ft (89.3 sq m), are the most spacious accommodation. They are fine, large living spaces located aft overlooking the stern on Decks 6, 7, and 8 – they are, however, subject to movement and vibration. They have teak-floor private balconies that really are private and can't be overlooked. Each has an entrance foyer, living room, separate bedroom (the bed faces the sea, which can be seen through the floor-to-ceiling windows), fully tiled bathroom with tub, and a small guest bathroom.

Vista Suites. There are four, each around 786 sq ft (73 sq m), and located forward on Decks 5 and 6. They have teak-floor private balconies that can't be overlooked. Each has an entrance foyer, living room, separate bedroom with similar layout to that in the Owner's Suites, CD player plus audio discs, and a fully tiled bathroom with Jacuzzi tub.

Penthouse Suites. There are 52 of these – though they are not suites at all, but large cabins (the bedrooms aren't separate from the living areas). They measure around 323 sq ft (30 sq m) and have a good-size teak-floor balcony with sliding glass door (but with partial, and not full, balcony partitions) and teak deck furniture. The lounge area has a proper dining table, and there is ample clothes storage space. The bathroom has a tub, shower enclosure, washbasin, and toilet.

Cabins with balcony. Cabins with private balconies (around 216 sq ft/20 sq m) comprise about two-thirds of all cabins. They have partial, not full, balcony partitions and sliding glass doors, and 14 cabins on Deck 6 have lifeboat-obstructed views and no balcony. The living area has a refrigerated minibar, lounge area with breakfast table, and a balcony with teak floor, two teak chairs, and a drinks table. The bathrooms, with tiled floors and plain walls, are compact, standard units, and include a shower stall with a strong, removable hand-held shower unit, hairdryer, toiletries storage shelves, and retractable clothesline.

Outside-view and interior cabins. These measure around 160–165 sq ft (14.8–15.3 sq m) and have twin beds that convert to a queen-size bed, vanity desk, small sofa and coffee table, and bathroom with a shower enclosure with a strong, removable hand-held shower unit, hairdryer, toiletries storage shelves, retractable clothesline, washbasin, and toilet. Although they are not large, they are quite comfortable, with decent storage space.

Some suites/cabins located at the stern may suffer from vibration and noise, particularly when the ship is proceeding at, or close to, full speed, or maneuvering in port.

DINING. Flexibility and choice are what the dining facilities aboard the Oceania ships are all about. There are four different restaurants:

The Grand Dining Room has around 340 seats and a raised central section, but the problem is the noise level: it's atrocious when the dining room is full – the effect of the low ceiling height. Being located at the stern, it has large ocean-view windows on three sides – prime tables overlook the stern. The chairs are comfortable and have armrests. The menus change daily for lunch and dinner.

Other dining options. The Toscana Italian Restaurant has 96 seats, windows along two sides, and a set menu plus daily chef's specials.

The cozy Polo Grill has 98 seats, windows along two sides, and a set menu including prime steaks and seafood.

The Terrace Café has both indoor and outdoor seating. It is open for breakfast, lunch, and casual dinners, with tapas (Tapas on the Terrace) and other Mediterranean food. As the ship's self-serve buffet restaurant, it incorporates a small pizzeria and grill. There are basic salads, a meat-carving station, and a reasonable selection of cheeses.

All restaurants have open-seating dining, so you can dine when you want, with whom you wish. Reservations are needed in Toscana Restaurant and Polo Grill but there's no extra charge; there are mostly tables for four or six, and few for two. There is also a Poolside Grill Bar. All cappuccino and espresso coffees cost extra.

The food and service staff is provided by a respected maritime catering company with an interest in Oceania Cruises. This certainly is a foodie's ship, with really high-quality ingredients, and a wide selection of dining venues. Particularly notable are the delicious breads, rolls, croissants, and brioches – all made on board from French flour and d'Isigny butter.

On sea days, an elegant tea is presented in the Horizon Lounge, with formally dressed staff, cake trolleys, and an excellent array of cakes and scones. Sadly, teabags – not loose tea – prevail.

ENTERTAINMENT. The Nautica Lounge has entertainment, lectures, and some social events. There is little entertainment because of the intensive nature of the itineraries. However, there is live music in several bars and lounges.

SPA/FITNESS. The Lido Deck has a swimming pool, and good sunbathing space, plus a thalassotherapy tub. A jogging track circles the swimming pool deck, but one deck above. The uppermost outdoors deck includes a golf driving net and shuffleboard court. The Canyon Ranch SpaClub consists of a beauty salon, three treatment rooms, men's and women's changing rooms, and steam room (but no sauna). An 18 percent gratuity applies to massages and treatments.

Navigator of the Seas
★★★+

Size:	Large Resort Ship	Passenger Space Ratio (lower beds):	44.0
Tonnage:	137,276	Passenger/Crew Ratio (lower beds):	2.6
Lifestyle:	Standard	Cabins (total):	1,643
Cruise Line:	Royal Caribbean International	Size Range (sq ft/m):	151.0–1,358.0/14.0–126.1
Former Names:	none	Cabins (for one person):	0
IMO Number:	9227506	Cabins (with private balcony):	779
Builder:	Kvaerner Masa-Yards (Finland)	Cabins (wheelchair accessible):	26
Original Cost:	$500 million	Wheelchair accessibility:	Best
Entered Service:	Dec 2002	Cabin Current:	110 volts
Registry:	The Bahamas	Elevators:	14
Length (ft/m):	1,020.6/311.1	Casino (gaming tables):	Yes
Beam (ft/m):	155.5/47.4	Slot Machines:	Yes
Draft (ft/m):	28.8/8.8	Swimming Pools:	3
Propulsion/Propellers:	diesel-electric (75,600kW)/3 pods	Hot Tubs (on deck):	6
	(2 azimuthing, 1 fixed)	Self-Service Launderette:	No
Passenger Decks:	14	Dedicated Cinema/Seats:	No
Total Crew:	1,185	Library:	Yes
Passengers (lower beds):	3,286	Onboard currency:	US$

A colorful, fun-filled large resort ship for family-friendly cruising

OVERVIEW. *Navigator of the Seas* provides a host of facilities, rather like a small town, with plenty of entertainment for all ages, yet it offers a healthy amount of space per passenger. The food focuses on quantity rather than quality, unless you are prepared to pay extra in a specialty restaurant.

THE SHIP. The first ship in the Royal Caribbean International (RCI) fleet to receive 'virtual balconies' for all interior (no-view) cabins – a neat feature installed during a 2013/4 revitalization, which also added 81 cabins, but no extra elevators; a digital photo kiosk was also added, meaning no more photo walls, or lines.

A stunning four-deck-high Royal Promenade is the main interior focal point; it's a fun place to hang out or meet friends. The length of two American football fields, it has two 11-deck-high internal lobbies. Cafés, shops, and entertainment locations line this 'street,' and interior 'with-view' cabins look into it from above (it's an imaginative piece of design work).

The horizontal atrium promenade includes the Two Poets (a 'traditional' pub), a Champagne Bar, a Sidewalk Café (for Continental breakfast, all-day pizzas, specialty coffees, and desserts), Ben & Jerry's (for round-the-clock ice cream and yoghurt), a sports bar, several shops – for jewelry, gifts, liquor, perfumes, wine, and souvenirs, and Boleros (for Latin music and nightlife). Guest reception and shore excursion counters are located at the aft end of the promenade, as is an ATM machine. At times, street entertainers appear, and parades are staged; at other times it's dif-

Berlitz's Ratings		
	Possible	Achieved
Ship	500	392
Accommodation	200	141
Food	400	223
Service	400	267
Entertainment	100	75
Cruise Experience	400	264
OVERALL SCORE		
1362 points out of 2000		

ficult to walk through the area, as it can be filled to the brim with tacky shopping items.

Arched across the promenade is a captain's balcony, and in the center of the promenade a stairway connects you to the deck below, where you'll find the Schooner Bar (a piano lounge common to all RCI ships) and a flashy Casino Royale. Gaming includes blackjack, Caribbean stud poker, roulette, and craps, plus 300 slot machines.

There's a regulation-size ice-skating rink (Studio B), with real ice, with 'bleacher' seating for up to 900, and the latest in broadcast facilities. A fine two-deck library is open 24 hours a day.

Other drinking places include the intimate Connoisseur Club – for cigars and cognacs. There is a TV studio ('Studio B') with high-tech broadcast facilities, located adjacent to rooms that can be used for trade show exhibit space, with a conference center seating 400 and a multimedia 60-seat screening room.

FAMILIES. Facilities for children and teenagers are quite extensive (actually, they are larger than aboard the sister ships); Aquanauts is for 3–5-year-olds; Explorers is for 6–8-year-olds; Voyagers is for 9–12-year-olds. Optix is a dedicated area for teenagers, including a daytime club with several computers, a soda bar, and a dance floor. Challenger's Arcade has an array of video games. Paint and Clay is an arts and crafts center for younger children. Adjacent is Adventure Beach, an area for all the family to enjoy; it includes swimming pools, a water slide, and outdoor game areas.

ACCOMMODATION. There is a wide range of cabin price grades, in four major groupings: premium ocean-view suites and cabins, interior (atrium-view) cabins, ocean-view cabins, and interior cabins (which now have 'virtual balconies' projected on a formerly blank wall – a really neat feature). Many cabins are of a similar size (good for incentives and large groups), and 300 have interconnecting doors (good for families).

Some 138 interior cabins have bay windows that look into the Royal Promenade. Regardless of which cabin grade you choose, all except for the Royal Suite and Owner's Suite have twin beds that convert to a queen-size unit, TV set, radio and telephone, personal safe, vanity unit, hairdryer, and private bathroom. However, you'll need to keep the curtains closed in the bay windows if you are scantily clad, because you can be seen easily from adjacent bay windows.

Royal Suite (Deck 10). At around 1,146 sq ft (107 sq m), the Royal Suite is the largest private living space, located almost at the top of the Centrum lobby on the port side. It is a nicely appointed penthouse suite, whose occupants must share the rest of the ship with everyone else, except for access to their own exclusive Concierge Club. It has a king-size circular bed in a separate large bedroom that can be fully closed off, a living room with an additional queen-size sofa bed, baby grand piano, refrigerator/wet bar, dining table and four chairs, expansive entertainment center, and a reasonably large bathroom.

Royal Family Suites. Four Royal Family Suites (two aft on Deck 9, two aft on Deck 8, each measure around 574 sq ft/53 sq m) each have two separate bedrooms (one includes two beds and third/fourth has upper Pullman berths). The lounge has a dining table and four chairs, wet bar, walk-in closet, and a large bathroom with Jacuzzi tub, washbasin, and separate shower enclosure. The suites have large balconies with views out over the ship's wash aft.

Owner's Suites. Ten slightly smaller but still desirable Owner's Suites (around 468 sq ft/43 sq m) are in the center of the ship, on both port and starboard sides, adjacent to the Centrum lobby on Deck 10. Each has a separate bedroom with queen-size or twin beds, lounge with large sofa, wet bar, and bathroom with Jacuzzi tub, washbasin, and separate shower enclosure. There's also a small private balcony.

Standard outside-view and interior cabins. All cabins have a private bathroom, as well as interactive TV and pay-per-view movies, including an X-rated channel. Cabin bathrooms really are compact, but at least they have a proper shower enclosure instead of a shower curtain.

DINING. The Sapphire (main dining room) has a total capacity of 1,889. It consists of three levels (a dramatic stairway connects them all), but the menu is the same on all three. Huge, fat support pillars obstruct sight lines from a number of seats. However, the ambience is good and there's always a good buzz when the ship is full and dinner is in progress.

When you book, choose one of two seatings – or 'My Time Dining' (eat when you want during dining room hours). Tables are for four, six, eight, 10, or 12. The place settings, china, and cutlery are of good quality. Two small private wings serve small groups: La Cetra and La Notte, each with 58 seats.

Other dining options. Chops Grille is for premium steaks, ribs, veal chops, and seafood; a cover charge applies, but it's worth it.

There's also Portofino, the ship's upscale Euro-Italian restaurant. It's open for dinner only, and a cover charge applies.

Sabor, added during the 2014 refit, features Mexican cuisine. A cover charge applies, and reservations are required (it's located on a lower deck in what was formerly The Dungeon disco).

Giovanni's Table is a popular Italian family-style eatery.

Windjammer Café is a really large, sprawling venue for casual buffet-style, self-help (always busy) breakfast, lunch, and light dinners (except for the last night of the cruise). It's often difficult to find a table, and, by the time you do, your food could be cold.

The Island Grill (a section of Windjammer Café), for casual dinners (no reservations needed), has an open kitchen. Johnny Rockets, a retro 1950s all-day, all-night diner-style eatery, has hamburgers, malt shakes (at extra cost), and jukebox hits, with both indoor and outdoor seating.

Promenade Café: for Continental breakfast, all-day pizzas, and specialty coffees, which are provided in paper cups.

ENTERTAINMENT. The 1,350-seat Metropolis Theater is a stunning showlounge, located at the forward end of the ship. It has Art Nouveau-themed decor, and spans three decks, with only a few slim pillars, and good sight lines from most seats. Production shows are presented here by a large cast and a live band. There's also an array of up-and-coming cabaret acts and late-night adults-only comedy.

SPA/FITNESS. The ShipShape health spa is reasonably large, and measures 15,000 sq ft (1,400 sq m). It includes an aerobics room, fitness center (with stairmasters, treadmills, stationary bikes, weight machines, and free weights), treatment rooms, and men's and women's sauna/steam rooms. Another 10,000 sq ft (930 sq m) of space is devoted to a Solarium (with sliding glass-dome roof) for relaxation.

Nieuw Amsterdam
★★★★

Size:	Large Resort Ship		Passenger Space Ratio (lower beds):	41.1
Tonnage:	86,700		Passenger/Crew Ratio (lower beds):	2.2
Lifestyle:	Premium		Cabins (total):	1,053
Cruise Line:	Holland America Line		Size Range (sq ft/m):	170.0–1,318.6/15.7–122.5
Former Names:	none		Cabins (for one person):	0
IMO Number:	9378450		Cabins (with private balcony):	708
Builder:	Fincantieri (Italy)		Cabins (wheelchair accessible):	30
Original Cost:	$400 million		Wheelchair accessibility:	Good
Entered Service:	Jul 2010		Cabin Current:	110 and 220 volts
Registry:	The Netherlands		Elevators:	14
Length (ft/m):	935.0/285.0		Casino (gaming tables):	Yes
Beam (ft/m):	105.6/32.2		Slot Machines:	Yes
Draft (ft/m):	25.5/7.8		Swimming Pools:	2 (1 w/sliding glass dome)
Propulsion/Propellers:	diesel-electric (34,000kW)/		Hot Tubs (on deck):	5
	2 azimuthing pods		Self-Service Launderette:	No
Passenger Decks:	12		Dedicated Cinema/Seats:	Yes/170
Total Crew:	929		Library:	Yes
Passengers (lower beds):	2,106		Onboard currency:	US$

Dutch decor, traditions, and comfort for entire families

OVERVIEW. The ship is designed to appeal to younger, more vibrant, multi-generational holidaymakers. Neat little tented cabanas on the aft deck provide private shaded space. They are filled with goodies such as Champagne, chocolate strawberries, bathrobes, fresh fruit, and chilled towels for two adults and two children.

THE SHIP. *Nieuw Amsterdam* is a *Vista*-class ship, sister to *Eurodam*, *Noordam*, *Oosterdam*, *Westerdam*, and *Zuiderdam*. It is named after the Dutch name for New York City, and the interior design reflects the great metropolis. The ship, the latest in a line of Holland America Line (HAL) ships to carry this name, has two upright 'dustbin lid' funnels in a close-knit configuration. The twin working funnels are the result of the slightly unusual machinery configuration; the ship has, in effect, two engine rooms – one with three diesels, and one with two diesels and a gas turbine. There's a pod propulsion system, so there's no vibration.

There is a complete walk-around exterior teak promenade deck, with teak steamer-style sunloungers. A jogging track outdoors is located around the mast and the forward third of the ship. Exterior glass elevators, mounted midships on both the port and starboard sides, provide fine ocean views from any one of 10 decks. One of the two centrally located swimming pools outdoors can be used in inclement weather because of a retractable sliding glass roof. Two hot tubs, adjacent to the swimming pools, are abridged by a bar. There's also a small swimming pool for children.

Berlitz's Ratings		
	Possible	Achieved
Ship	500	384
Accommodation	200	150
Food	400	270
Service	400	274
Entertainment	100	70
Cruise Experience	400	285
OVERALL SCORE		
1433 points out of 2000		

There are two entertainment/public room decks, the most dramatic space being a showlounge spanning four decks in the forward section. Other facilities include a winding shopping street with several boutique stores and logo shops, a card room, an art gallery, photo gallery, and several small meeting rooms. The large casino is equipped with an array of gaming paraphernalia and slot machines, and you have to walk through it to get from the restaurant to the showlounge.

Explorations – perhaps the most popular public room – is a combination coffee bar (where coffees and other drinks cost extra), lounge, extensive library, and Internet-connect center, all within an attractive, open 'lifestyle' environment – it's popular for relaxation and reading, although noise from the coffee machine can interrupt concentration.

On other decks (lower down), you'll find the Queen's Lounge, which is part lecture room and part Culinary Arts Center and bar, where culinary demonstrations and cooking classes are held. There are also a number of other bars and lounges, including an Explorer's Lounge (live string and piano music is appropriate for cocktails in the evenings, when warm hors d'oeuvres are provided). The ship also has a small movie-screening room.

The information desk in the lobby is small and somewhat removed from the main passenger flow on the two decks above it. Many pillars obstruct the passenger flow and lines of sight throughout the ship. There are no self-service launderettes – something that families with children miss, although special laundry packages are available.

Gratuities are automatically added to your onboard account. Passenger niggles? These include noisy cabin air conditioning, as the flow can't be regulated or turned off.

FAMILIES. Club HAL's KidZone provides a whole area dedicated to children's facilities and extensive programming for different age groups (five to 17), with one counselor for every 30 children. Free ice cream is provided at certain hours, plus hot hors d'oeuvres in all bars. Some cabins have interconnecting doors.

ACCOMMODATION. There are 24 price categories: 16 outside-view and eight interior. The views from some cabins on the lowest accommodation deck (Main Deck) are obstructed by lifeboats. Some cabins that can accommodate a third and fourth person have very little closet space, and only one personal safe. Occupants of suites get exclusive use of the Neptune Lounge and concierge service, priority embarkation and disembarkation, and other benefits. In many of the suites/cabins with private balconies, the balconies are not so private and can be overlooked from various public locations.

Penthouse Verandah Suites (2). These offer the largest accommodation (1,318 sq ft/123 sq m, including balcony). These have a separate bedroom with a king-size bed; there's also a walk-in closet, dressing room, living room, dining room, butler's pantry, minibar and refrigerator, and private balcony. The main bathroom has a large whirlpool tub, two washbasins, toilet, and plenty of storage space for toiletries. Personalized stationery and free dry cleaning are included, as are hot hors d'oeuvres and other goodies daily.

Deluxe Verandah Suites (60). These suites measure 563 sq ft (53 sq m). They have twin beds that convert to a king-size bed, vanity desk, lounge area, walk-in closet, minibar and refrigerator, and bathroom with full-size tub, washbasin, and toilet. Personalized stationery and complimentary dry cleaning are included, as are hot hors d'oeuvres and other goodies.

Verandah Suites (100). Actually they are cabins, not suites, and measure 284 sq ft (26 sq m). Twin beds can convert to a queen-size bed. There is also a lounge area, minibar, and refrigerator, while the bathroom has a tub, washbasin, and toilet. Floor-to-ceiling windows open onto a private balcony.

Outside-view cabins. Standard outside cabins (197 sq ft/18 sq m) have twin beds that can convert to a queen-size bed. There's a small sitting area; the bathroom has a tub/shower combination. Interior cabins are slightly smaller (183 sq ft/17 sq m).

DINING. The 1,045-seat Rembrandt Dining Room spans two decks at the stern, with seating at tables for two, four, six, or eight on both main and balcony levels. It provides a traditional HAL dining experience, with friendly service from smiling Indonesian and Filipino stewards. Both open seating and assigned seating are available for dinner, while breakfast and lunch are open seating – you'll be seated by restaurant staff when you enter.

HAL can provide Kosher meals (if requested when you book), although these are prepared ashore, then frozen, and brought to your table sealed in their original containers.

The 148-seat Pinnacle Grill is a more upscale dining spot, with higher-quality ingredients and better presentation than in the larger main dining room. On Lower Promenade Deck, it fronts onto the second level of the atrium lobby; tables along its outer section are open to it and can suffer from noise from the Atrium Bar one deck below, though these tables are good for those who like to see and be seen. Pacific Northwest cuisine is featured, with items such as sesame-crusted halibut with ginger-miso, and an array of premium-quality steaks. The wine list includes some fine wines from around the world, including many gorgeous Bordeaux reds. Reservations are required, and there is a cover charge.

Other dining options. For casual eating, there is an extensive Lido Café, an eatery that wraps around the funnel, with indoor-outdoor seating and ocean views. It includes several sections including a salad bar, Asian stir-fry and sushi section, deli sandwiches, and a separate dessert buffet, although lines can form for made-to-order items such as omelets for breakfast and pasta for lunch.

Also, a poolside 'Dive-In at the Terrace Grill' features multi-choice signature burgers (with special Dive-In sauce), hot dogs, and fries. On certain days, barbecues and other culinary specialties are available poolside.

ENTERTAINMENT. The 867-seat Mainstage Lounge is the venue for Las Vegas-style revues and major cabaret shows. The main floor level includes a bar in its aft section. Spiral stairways at the back of the showlounge connect all levels. Stage shows are best seen from the upper levels, from where the sight lines are quite good.

SPA/FITNESS. The Greenhouse Spa, a large, two-deck-high health spa, is located directly above the navigation bridge. Facilities include a solarium, hydrotherapy pool, and a unisex thermal suite – incorporating a Laconium (gentle sauna), Hammam (mild steam), and Chamomile Grotto (small aromatic steam room).

There is a beauty salon, 11 private massage/body treatment rooms (including one for couples), and a large gymnasium with floor-to-ceiling windows on three sides and forward-facing ocean views, and the latest high-tech muscle-toning equipment. Sports enthusiasts can enjoy a basketball court, volleyball court, and a golf simulator.

Nippon Maru
★★★★

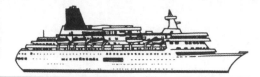

Size:	Small Ship
Tonnage:	22,472
Lifestyle:	Standard
Cruise Line:	Mitsui OSK Passenger Line
Former Names:	none
IMO Number:	8817631
Builder:	Mitsubishi Heavy Industries
Original Cost:	$59.4 million
Entered Service:	Sep 1990
Registry:	Japan
Length (ft/m):	546.7/166.6
Beam (ft/m):	78.7/24.0
Draft (ft/m):	21.4/6.5
Propulsion/Propellers:	diesel (15,740kW)/2
Passenger Decks:	7
Total Crew:	230
Passengers (lower beds):	408
Passenger Space Ratio (lower beds):	55.0

Passenger/Crew Ratio (lower beds):	2.5
Cabins (total):	204
Size Range (sq ft/m):	150.6–430.5/14.0–40.0
Cabins (for one person):	6
Cabins (with private balcony):	27
Cabins (wheelchair accessible):	2
Wheelchair accessibility:	Fair
Cabin Current:	100 volts
Elevators:	5
Casino (gaming tables):	Yes
Slot Machines:	No
Swimming Pools:	1
Hot Tubs (on deck):	4 (Japanese baths)
Self-Service Launderette:	Yes
Dedicated Cinema/Seats:	Yes/54
Library:	Yes
Onboard currency:	Japanese Yen

Modern styling for Japanese-speaking, mature-age cruisers

OVERVIEW. *Nippon Maru* is really for Japanese-speaking couples and solo travelers who want very comfortable surroundings combined with decent food and good service, all at a reasonable cost.

THE SHIP. *Nippon Maru* had an ambitious four-month refit in 2009–10, when a new hydraulic tender loading platform was created. Deck extensions created space for more public rooms such as a new dining room for suite-class and deluxe-grade passengers, a piano lounge, and a health/fitness facility.

The interior's focal point is an atrium lobby that spans six decks. Public rooms include a show-lounge, piano lounge, a 54-seat screening room/lecture room (Mermaid Theater), a gaming corner with give-aways rather than cash prizes, and a Chashitsu tatami room within the Horizon Lounge. The Neptune Bar has probably the most extensive assortment of Scotch whiskies (including many rare single malts) at sea.

ACCOMMODATION. The newer suites, on Deck 6, are large and have a separate sleeping and living areas. A sofa, two chairs, and coffee table occupy one section of the lounge; there is also a writing desk with Nespresso machine and tea-making facilities. The two beds can be pushed together. The bathroom includes a 'washlet,' (a toilet with a built-in water spray for washing – very popular in Japan), but the step into the bathroom is high, at 8ins (21cm). Slippers and bathrobes are provided. Nine suites include

Berlitz's Ratings		
	Possible	Achieved
Ship	500	377
Accommodation	200	147
Food	400	307
Service	400	301
Entertainment	100	78
Cruise Experience	400	288
OVERALL SCORE		
1498 points out of 2000		

two with huge balconies. Suites and deluxe-grade cabins are nicely decorated, and the living area has a table and two chairs, and two beds; there's also a personal computer.

All standard cabins have blond wood cabinetry and good drawer space. Many have a third (or third and fourth) pull-down upper Pullman berth. Tea-making sets are provided, as is a good range of personal toiletry items.

DINING. The Mizuho dining room, which seats around 320, serves both traditional Japanese cuisine and Western dishes. There is one open seating. The ship is known for its high-quality food. A premium dining room, Kasuga, has been added for suite- and deluxe-grade occupants; adjacent is the excellent Shiosai sushi bar – always with some very high-quality sashimi and sushi.

ENTERTAINMENT. The Dolphin Hall has a proscenium-arched stage, wooden dance floor, and seating on both the main and balcony levels of this two-deck-high room. There's social dancing, with gentlemen hosts available as partners, and a rich program of lecturers and musicians.

SPA/FITNESS. The Terraké Spa includes beauty and nail treatment rooms, three body treatment rooms, and a small fitness room. There's a traditional Japanese Grand Bath (one for women, one for men, open until 1am), with washing stations and a sauna. Adjacent is a sports massage room.

Noordam
★★★★

Size:	Mid-size Ship	Passenger Space Ratio (lower beds):	42.7
Tonnage:	82,318	Passenger/Crew Ratio (lower beds):	2.3
Lifestyle:	Premium	Cabins (total):	959
Cruise Line:	Holland America Line	Size Range (sq ft/m):	170.0–1,318.6/15.7–122.5
Former Names:	none	Cabins (for one person):	0
IMO Number:	9230115	Cabins (with private balcony):	641
Builder:	Fincantieri (Italy)	Cabins (wheelchair accessible):	28
Original Cost:	$400 million	Wheelchair accessibility:	Good
Entered Service:	Feb 2006	Cabin Current:	110 volts
Registry:	The Netherlands	Elevators:	14
Length (ft/m):	935.0/285.0	Casino (gaming tables):	Yes
Beam (ft/m):	105.6/32.2	Slot Machines:	Yes
Draft (ft/m):	25.5/7.8	Swimming Pools:	2 (1 w/sliding glass dome)
Propulsion/Propellers:	diesel-electric (34,000kW)/	Hot Tubs (on deck):	5
	2 azimuthing pods	Self-Service Launderette:	No
Passenger Decks:	11	Dedicated Cinema/Seats:	Yes/170
Total Crew:	820	Library:	Yes
Passengers (lower beds):	1,924	Onboard currency:	US$

A family-friendly ship with traditional Dutch decor

OVERVIEW. *Noordam* features a wide range of public rooms with a reasonably intimate atmosphere, and the overall feel of the ship is quite homely and comforting, with fresh flowers everywhere, as well as some nicely showcased Dutch artifacts from the 16th and 17th centuries.

THE SHIP. *Noordam*, with 35 cabins more than its close sisters *Oosterdam*, *Westerdam*, and *Zuiderdam*, is one of the *Vista*-class ships in the Holland America Line (HAL) fleet, designed to appeal to multi-generational holidaymakers. The twin working funnels are the result of the slightly unusual machinery configuration; the ship has, in effect, two engine rooms. A pod propulsion system is provided, so there's no vibration.

There is a complete walk-around exterior teak promenade deck, with teak steamer-style sunloungers. A jogging track outdoors is located around the mast and the forward third of the ship. Exterior glass elevators provide fine ocean views from any one of 10 decks. One of two swimming pools outdoors has a retractable sliding glass roof. Two hot tubs, adjacent to the swimming pools, are abridged by a bar. There's also a small swimming pool for children.

The intimate lobby – the ship's central spot – spans three decks, and is topped by a rotating Waterford Crystal globe of the world. Adjacent are interior and glass-walled elevators with exterior views. The information desk (on the lobby's lowest level) is small and somewhat removed from the main passenger flow on the two decks above it.

Berlitz's Ratings		
	Possible	Achieved
Ship	500	383
Accommodation	200	150
Food	400	270
Service	400	274
Entertainment	100	70
Cruise Experience	400	285
OVERALL SCORE		
1432 points out of 2000		

The interior decor is bright in many areas, and the ceilings are particularly noticeable. A large collection of artwork is a standard feature, and the pieces reflect the history of the former Dutch East Indies.

There are two whole entertainment/public room decks, the most dramatic space being a showlounge spanning four decks in the forward section. Other facilities include a winding shopping street with several boutique stores and logo shops, card room, an art gallery, photo gallery, and several small meeting rooms. The large casino is equipped with an array of gaming paraphernalia and slot machines, and you have to walk through it to get from the restaurant to the showlounge.

Explorations is a combination coffee bar (where coffees and other drinks cost extra), lounge, extensive library, and Internet center – it's a popular area for relaxation and reading, although noise from the coffee machine can interrupt concentration.

On other decks (lower down), you'll find the Queen's Lounge and bar, which acts as a lecture room a Culinary Arts Center, where cooking demonstrations and cooking classes are held.

Gratuities are automatically added to your onboard account. Passenger niggles? These include noisy cabin air conditioning – the flow can't be regulated or turned off, the only regulation being for temperature control. Also, several pillars obstruct the passenger flow and lines of sight throughout the ship. There are no self-service launderettes, although special laundry packages are available.

FAMILIES. Club HAL's KidZone provides a whole area dedicated to children's facilities and extensive programming for different age groups (five to 17), with one counselor for every 30 children. Free ice cream is provided at certain hours, plus hot hors d'oeuvres in all bars. Some cabins have interconnecting doors.

ACCOMMODATION. There are numerous price categories: 16 outside-view and eight interior. The views from some cabins on the lowest accommodation deck (Main Deck) are obstructed by lifeboats. Some of the cabins that can accommodate a third and fourth person have very little closet space, and only one personal safe. Occupants of suites get exclusive use of the Neptune Lounge and concierge service, priority embarkation and disembarkation, and other benefits. In many of the suites/cabins with private balconies, the balconies are not so private and can be overlooked from various public locations.

Penthouse Verandah Suites (2). These offer the largest accommodation (1,318 sq ft/123 sq m, including balcony). These have a separate bedroom with a king-size bed, walk-in closet, dressing room, living room, dining room, butler's pantry, minibar and refrigerator, and private balcony. The main bathroom has a large whirlpool tub, two washbasins, toilet, and plenty of storage space for toiletries. Personalized stationery and free dry cleaning are included, as are hot hors d'oeuvres and other goodies daily.

Deluxe Verandah Suites (60). These suites measure 563 sq ft (53 sq m). They have twin beds that convert to a king-size bed, vanity desk, lounge area, walk-in closet, minibar and refrigerator, and bathroom with full-size tub, washbasin, and toilet.

Verandah Suites (100). Actually they are cabins, not suites, and measure 284 sq ft (26 sq m). Twin beds can convert to a queen-size bed. There is also a lounge area, minibar, and refrigerator, while the bathroom has a tub, washbasin, and toilet. Floor-to-ceiling windows open onto a private balcony.

Outside-view cabins. Standard outside cabins (197 sq ft/18 sq m) have twin beds that can convert to a queen-size bed. There's a small sitting area, while the bathroom has a tub/shower combination.

Interior cabins. At 183 sq ft (17 sq m) these are just slightly smaller than the outside-view ones.

DINING. Located at the stern, the 1,045-seat Vista Dining Room is two decks high, with seating at tables for two, four, six, or eight on both main and balcony levels. It provides a traditional HAL dining experience, with friendly service from smiling Indonesian and Filipino stewards. Both open seating and assigned seating are available for dinner, while breakfast and lunch are open seating – you'll be seated by restaurant staff when you enter.

Kosher meals are available (if requested when you book), although these are prepared ashore, then frozen, and brought to your table sealed in their original containers.

Other dining options. The 148-seat Pinnacle Grill is an upscale dining venue, with better-quality ingredients and presentation than in the main dining room. It fronts onto the second level of the atrium lobby on Lower Promenade Deck; tables along its outer section are open to it and can suffer from noise from the Atrium Bar one deck below, though these tables are good for those who like to see and be seen. Pacific Northwest cuisine is featured, with items such as sesame-crusted halibut with ginger-miso, and an array of premium-quality steaks. The wine list includes some fine wines from around the world, including many gorgeous Bordeaux reds. Reservations are required, and there is a cover charge.

For casual eating, go to the Lido Café, an eatery that wraps around the funnel, with indoor-outdoor seating and ocean views. It includes several sections including a salad bar, stir-fry and sushi section, deli sandwiches, and a dessert buffet, although lines can form for made-to-order items.

Also, a poolside 'Dive-In at the Terrace Grill' features multi-choice signature burgers (with special Dive-In sauce), hot dogs, and fries.

ENTERTAINMENT. The 867-seat Vista Lounge is the venue for Las Vegas-style revues and major cabaret shows. The main floor level has a bar in its starboard aft section. Spiral stairways at the back of the lounge connect all levels. Stage shows are best seen from the upper levels, from where the sight lines are decent.

SPA/FITNESS. The Greenhouse Spa, a large, two-decks-high health spa, is located directly above the navigation bridge. Facilities include a solarium, hydrotherapy pool, unisex thermal suite – a unisex area incorporating a Laconium (gentle sauna), Hammam (mild steam), and Chamomile Grotto (small aromatic steam room), a beauty salon, 11 private massage/therapy rooms (including one for couples) for body-pampering treatments, and a large gymnasium with floor-to-ceiling windows on three sides and forward-facing ocean views, and the latest high-tech muscle-toning equipment. Sports enthusiasts can enjoy a basketball court, volleyball court, and a golf simulator.

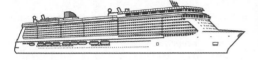

Norwegian Breakaway
★★★★

Size:	Large Resort Ship
Tonnage:	144,017
Lifestyle:	Standard
Cruise Line:	Norwegian Cruise Line
Former Names:	none
IMO Number:	9606912
Builder:	Meyer Werft (Germany)
Original Cost:	€600 million
Entered Service:	Apr 2013
Registry:	The Bahamas
Length (ft/m):	1,066.2/325.0
Beam (ft/m):	133.0/40.5
Draft (ft/m):	27.8/8.5
Propulsion/Propellers:	diesel-electric (79,800kW)/ 2 azimuthing pods
Passenger Decks:	15
Total Crew:	1,651
Passengers (lower beds):	4,028

Passenger Space Ratio (lower beds):	35.7
Passenger/Crew Ratio (lower beds):	2.4
Cabins (total):	1,994
Size Range (sq ft/m):	96.8-1,022.6/9.0-95.0
Cabins (for one person):	59
Cabins (with private balcony):	1,252
Cabins (wheelchair accessible):	40
Wheelchair accessibility:	Good
Cabin Current:	110 volts
Elevators:	16
Casino (gaming tables):	Yes
Slot Machines:	Yes
Swimming Pools:	5
Hot Tubs (on deck):	9
Self-Service Launderette:	No
Dedicated Cinema/Seats:	No
Library:	No
Onboard currency:	US$

Über-casual, multi-choice floating playground for the whole family

OVERVIEW. *Norwegian Breakaway* really is a ship for young, trendy, and edgy urbanites. It provides families with children, single parents, couples, and solo travelers with a mountain of entertainment choices, in an environment that is a pure playground for an active, entertaining cruise vacation.

THE SHIP. *Norwegian Breakaway* has a more streamlined and a better, more balanced profile than its slightly larger sister, *Norwegian Epic*, with a less boxy look to its front upper forward section. The colorful, signature artwork on the lower front section of the hull depicting the city of New York was created by Peter Max, the popular American illustrator and graphic artist.

Families with children really enjoy the pool deck facilities such as the Aqua Park, with five huge water slides, a large rock-climbing wall and rappelling wall, and a rope and scaffold-like walking course – with a small section that extends over the side of the ship. Aft is a large movie screen with amphitheater-style seating in an adults-only area called Spice H20.

Despite the ship's size, however, the open deck space for sunbathing is rather tight, and made smaller by the 'exclusive' 'Haven' area in the forward section, whose suites-only occupants (pay more, get more) are given enough sunbathing space, bar, pool, and hot tubs, all in a beach-club-like setting. The rest of the ship shares multiple pools and water-fun exterior decks, designed for families and children.

Lower down, on an outdoor promenade deck, a 'Waterfront' boardwalk-style outdoor area with

Berlitz's Ratings		
	Possible	Achieved
Ship	500	391
Accommodation	200	149
Food	400	248
Service	400	275
Entertainment	100	86
Cruise Experience	400	285
OVERALL SCORE		
1434 points out of 2000		

bar and eateries brings you more in contact with the sea. It forms part of the outdoor experience, and away from the hubbub of the family-friendly sun/sports action deck atop the ship.

Inside, the decor is decidedly more traditional and provides a more restful, relaxed feel and ambience – although this is all relative, and it's still rather upbeat and jazzy.

Careful planning and time management will be needed to make the most of this large resort ship and all it has to offer. It's really worth spending time to decide what you want to get out of your cruise vacation before you board the ship, which sort of negates the 'freestyle' aspect of a large resort ship cruise, although it is still all about choice.

Most of the public rooms, shops, entertainment spots, the large casino (gaming tables and slots), and a number of the 12 bars and 17 themed dining venues are located on Decks 6, 7 and 8 – a three-deck area complex called 678 Ocean Place.

A venue that proved popular aboard other Norwegian Cruise Line (NCL) ships is Bliss Ultra Lounge, a decadent venue (think late-night SoHo, minus the muggers).

The ship's home port is New York. Indeed, *Norwegian Breakaway* is the largest cruise ship ever to homeport in the Big Apple. Gratuities (called a 'service charge') are charged to your onboard account, or you can pre-pay online. Bar purchases incur a 15 percent gratuity; spa treatments are an eye-popping 18 percent.

FAMILIES. Facilities for kids and teens are pretty large and varied, and are spread over two decks; there's Splash Academy for kids and a separate Entourage space for teens. Nickelodeon is the family entertainment brand on all cruises, as part of NCL's children's programming.

Splash Academy is close to the family-friendly accommodation and provides areas for three age groups. Babies and toddlers have their own play space and parent-involving activities. At the Splash Academy reception area, tablet-based electronic registration allows parents to swipe their keycard and input a password to sign in their children.

Just past the reception area, the 3–5-year-olds (Guppies) have their own bright space, complete with child-sized furniture. In a separate zone, 6–9-year-olds (Turtles) have building block activity centers, an interactive dance mat with corresponding large video screen, game stations, and a video-viewing lounge.

Upstairs, 10–12-year-olds (Seals) get a multipurpose dance space with a touch-screen jukebox, moveable tables for activities, and bean bags for lounging; an activity zone includes arts and crafts items, and a 'hang out' area stocked with the latest video games.

Entourage, for ages 13–17 (Dolphins), has air hockey, foosball, and an arcade with five separate large-screen areas for video games while lounging on sofas. It becomes a teen nightclub with a dance floor and video jukebox at night.

ACCOMMODATION. Having learned a lot from its innovative big sister *Norwegian Epic*, NCL has made some sensible changes that should please many of its regulars. The 'wavy' cabin design has been modified, and the former separated bathroom has been reworked into a more traditional design, which is much more practical.

The Haven. The more exclusive accommodation is located in a two-deck-high section called The Haven – a 'ship within a ship.' It consists of 42 suites on Decks 15 and 16 forward, and includes a private restaurant, a cocktail bar, and a concierge desk area for relaxing, drinking, and making reservations for dining, entertainment, and the spa. There is a private pool, changing areas, two hot tubs, gym, saunas, two private massage rooms, and sun deck with bar. The Haven occupants get 24-hour butler service, and in-suite, white-tablecloth dining service. Suite occupants get a platinum key card and priority reservations for all the restaurants, spa, and entertainment venues.

The top suites within The Haven are two contemporary, apartment-style Deluxe Owner's Suites. These include an elegant living room and dining area with wet bar. The bedroom has a king-size bed with pillow-top mattress that faces floor-to-ceiling windows and a large wraparound private balcony. The bathroom has a large bathtub, two washbasins, and a shower. Deluxe Owner's Suites can be joined to Owner's Suites to create a grand suite that can sleep up to eight.

The 21 two-bedroom Family Villas have two bathrooms and two bedrooms. The living room and dining area includes a single sofa bed, writing desk, and bar. The master bedroom has a king-size bed, floor-to-ceiling windows, and a private balcony. The master bath includes an oversize oval tub that looks out to the sea. The second bedroom includes a double sofa bed and bathroom.

Also in The Haven are 17 Courtyard Penthouses, with a king-size bed, living and dining area, a single sofa bed, writing desk, and ample storage spaces. On other (non-Haven) decks throughout the ship are eight aft-facing penthouses and 10 forward-facing penthouses.

Other accommodation. There are 15 Spa mini-suite rooms and 28 Spa balcony cabins, all with easy access to the adjacent spa and its facilities. While most outside-view cabins have a balcony, some have only windows, but all have flat-screen televisions, satellite-linked telephone, and private bathroom. There are also 42 Family 'suites' with ocean views.

Balcony suites/cabins have rich wood-look paneling with warm tones and accent colors. Each balcony cabin has a king-size bed that can be made into twins, with a pillow-top mattress set against a chestnut leather headboard cushioned and tufted to make reading and sitting up in bed more comfortable. There's a lighted recess above the bed for books, magazines, tablet computers, or electronic reading devices. Each room has a sofa bed with additional storage. A built-in 26ins flat-screen television is mounted on the wall and tilts, so that it can be seen from the sofa or the bed. Underneath the television is another recessed nook to hold cruise information, books, and magazines. A vanity area has shelving and abundant storage space. LED lighting surrounds the perimeter of the ceiling to give the room warmth. There is also a full-size closet that is easily accessible with sliding doors. The cabins are energy-efficient, and key card access controls the lighting.

The balcony bathroom features a contemporary, clean design, ensuring more generous and comfortable space. There are several rich-wood shelves to help reduce clutter and keep everything within easy reach. There's an enclosed vanity unit underneath the washbasin that hides the trash bin, along with more storage. The built-in washbasin is size-generous and has an easy-to-use faucet. A private shower with a shaving bar for ladies completes the picture. Mini-suite bathrooms get a rain shower plus a hand-held shower hose.

There are 59 studio (single-occupancy) cabins. They are colorful, hip, trendy, and capsule-hotel small, with minimalist design – especially for closet space. Still this is a neat way to cruise solo – just don't bring many clothes

The many interior cabins also have one or two additional upper berths, while the lower beds are twins that convert to a queen-size bed – good for families with young children.

Note that room service breakfasts (other than coffee/tea and continental breakfast) incur a 'convenience' charge of $7.95 per order (except for occupants of The Haven, for whom they are free).

DINING. There are many food-themed restaurants (the largest of which, Savor and Taste, are like main dining rooms), dining venues, and casual eateries to choose from. This means that you'll need to make reservations in whichever venue you want to eat, so you'll need to be prepared for a bit of planning and waiting – just like you would ashore. However, if you want to see a show in the evening, then your dining time will really be dictated by the time of the show, which rather limits your choice. The good news is that the wall-based touch-screen reservations systems work well, so you see instantly how long you may have to wait if your chosen restaurant is fully booked.

Other dining options. The Manhattan Room is the equivalent of a main restaurant, and is included in the fare; it is large, with an integral dance floor and large ocean-view windows aft. Other dining venues (Cagney's Steakhouse and Moderno Churrascaria) are located one deck above, and have a view into the Manhattan Room.

Because the lifeboats hang over the side of the ship's hull, and not inboard (as is normal), a whole promenade deck has become an oceanfront extension of the eateries on the *inside*, thus creating a New York sidewalk-style experience, called The Waterfront.

Inside, 678 Ocean Place (meaning Decks 6, 7, and 8) connects with several interior extra-cost dining venues as well as the extensive Breakaway Casino, cigar smoking room, and several entertainment venues. These include Moderno Churrascaria, a Brazilian-style steakhouse with tableside carved meat service by 'passadores,' and a salad bar; Cagney's Steakhouse, a classic American steakhouse, with open kitchen; La Cucina, for Italian family food with a focus on Tuscany, with inside seating; or for alfresco eating on The Waterfront, Maltings (bar) and Ocean Blu by Geoffrey Zakarian – NCL's first à-la-carte all-seafood and raw bar eatery, designed and overseen by the popular Food Network chef. The ingredients and techniques that he employs in his land-based establishments are featured here.

Other venues include Le Bistro, for classic French-style cuisine; a 96-seat Teppanyaki restaurant with 12 flat-top grills and a lot of show, plus a Japanese rock garden with bamboo plants and bonsai trees; and Cirque Dreams and Dinner, a big-top, circus-like dining spot with a Cirque Dreams and Dinner show (a lively, action-filled supper club). All are extra-cost, and reservations are required.

Casual eateries, at no extra cost, include O'Sheehan's Neighborhood Bar & Grill, a sports bar and popular fast-food joint, with a big screen for sporting events, miniature bowling alley, pool and air hockey tables, and interactive games; the Atrium Café and Bar, for coffees and pastries; and Shanghai's Noodle Bar, for Chinese-style noodle dishes. The Ice Cream Bar signature item is a ship-specific sundae (Breakaway Sundae or Getaway Sundae), with nine scoops of ice cream in up to three flavors, topped with 'everything under the sun.'

The Garden Café is an extremely large, self-serve buffet, with indoor and outdoor seating. It's open round the clock. Many different counters provide themed and ethnic food varieties, and there's a special section for kids, too.

ENTERTAINMENT. The two-deck-high Breakaway Theater, located at the front of the ship, is a fine large showlounge, where all the major production shows and mainline cabaret acts are presented.

Spiegel Tent is a two-deck-high domed Cirque-like space, combining a show with dinner, similar to the Teatro ZinZanni dinner theater in Seattle. It's a mix of in-your-face street theatre, acrobatics, and Berlin-style 'foodertainment,' with lots of clowning and satire during a two-hour show. There's a cover charge.

Meanwhile, the popular Blue Man group, first introduced aboard *Norwegian Epic* to great acclaim and very entertaining for the whole family, forms part of the offering here, too.

Celebrity look-alike shows are presented in the Manhattan Room. These conjure up the likes of Elvis, Janet Jackson, Madonna, Neil Diamond, Tina Turner, and others. They are produced by Legends in Concert, a Las Vegas company that has provided shows for The Strip for over 25 years.

Jazz and blues devotees should enjoy the Fat Cats Jazz & Blues Club – an intimate room that's often standing room only – when the live jazzers are jammin' away in a really cool place.

SPA/FITNESS. The spa and fitness center is spread over two decks and houses a warehouse-size gymnasium. The complex includes an extra-cost thermal suite (herbal rainshowers, saunas and steam rooms, and relaxation area with hot-tile beds), a salt room, a beauty salon, and multiple body-treatment rooms, including massage rooms for couples.

Norwegian Dawn
★★★+

Size:	Large Resort Ship	Passenger/Crew Ratio (lower beds):	2.3
Tonnage:	91,740	Cabins (total):	1,238
Lifestyle:	Standard	Size Range (sq ft/m):	142.0–5,350.0/13.2–497.0
Cruise Line:	Norwegian Cruise Line	Cabins (for one person):	0
Former Names:	none	Cabins (with private balcony):	511
IMO Number:	9195169	Cabins (wheelchair accessible):	20
Builder:	Meyer Werft (Germany)	Wheelchair accessibility:	Best
Original Cost:	$400 million	Cabin Current:	110 volts
Entered Service:	Oct 2002	Elevators:	12
Registry:	The Bahamas	Casino (gaming tables):	Yes
Length (ft/m):	964.9/294.1	Slot Machines:	Yes
Beam (ft/m):	105.6/32.2	Swimming Pools:	3
Draft (ft/m):	26.9/8.2	Hot Tubs (on deck):	2
Propulsion/Propellers:	diesel-electric/2 azimuthing pods	Self-Service Launderette:	No
Passenger Decks:	11	Dedicated Cinema/Seats:	No
Total Crew:	1,069	Library:	Yes
Passengers (lower beds):	2,476	Onboard currency:	US$
Passenger Space Ratio (lower beds):	36.7		

This large casual ship is for lively, family-friendly cruising

OVERVIEW. Plenty of choices, including many dining options, add up to a very attractive holiday package, particularly suitable for families with children, in a contemporary floating leisure center that provides ample facilities for you to have an enjoyable time. Despite the company's name, Norwegian Cruise Line (NCL), there's almost nothing Norwegian about this product, except for some senior officers.

THE SHIP. *Norwegian Dawn*, sister to *Norwegian Star*, was built in 64 sections and has a pod propulsion system, so there's no vibration. In 2011, some 58 additional suites/cabins were added, making the ship more crowded.

Facilities include a large Dawn Club Casino gaming area, an Internet café with 24 computers, a 1,150-seat showlounge, a 3,000-book library, a card room, a writing and study room, a business center, conference and meeting rooms, and a large retail shopping complex.

A non-changeable per-person service charge is automatically added to your account daily for staff gratuities; 15 percent is also added for bar charges, and a whopping 18 percent for spa treatments.

FAMILIES. A good deal of space is devoted to children's facilities such as the T-Rex Kids' Center and Teen Club. All are tucked well away from adult recreation areas, at the aft end. Children of all ages will get to play in a superb wet 'n' wild space-themed water park, complete with large pool, water slide,

Berlitz's Ratings

	Possible	Achieved
Ship	500	367
Accommodation	200	145
Food	400	240
Service	400	273
Entertainment	100	67
Cruise Experience	400	275
OVERALL SCORE		
1367 points out of 2000		

and paddle pool. There's a room full of cots for toddlers to use for sleepovers, and even the toilets are at a special low height. Teens, too, are well catered for, and get their own cinema (with DVD movies), a disco with dance floor, and their own hot tub. Some cabins have interconnecting doors – good for families with children.

ACCOMMODATION. Although the suites and junior suites are quite spacious, the standard interior and outside-view cabins are very small when compared to those of other major cruise lines such as Carnival or Celebrity, particularly when occupied by three or four persons; the bathrooms, however, are decently sized and have large shower enclosures. There are many different price grades.

Garden Villas. The largest living spaces, Vista and Horizon, sit high atop the ship in a pod located forward of the funnel, and overlook the main swimming pool and recreation deck. These villas are stunning and have huge glass walls and landscaped private roof gardens for outdoor dining – with whirlpool tubs and huge private sunbathing areas. Each has three bedrooms and bathrooms, and a large living room overlooking the Lido/Pool Deck. These units have their own private elevator access and private stairway. Each measures 5,350 sq ft (497 sq m) and can be combined to create a huge, double-size 'house' measuring 10,700 sq ft (994 sq m), including a private outdoor Italian garden. Butler service is provided.

Owner's Suites. Located in the very front of the ship, each measures 750 sq ft (70 sq m). Two are nestled under the enclosed navigation bridge wings on Deck 11, and the other two are in the equivalent space on the deck below. If you don't need the entertaining space of the Garden Villas, these suites are delightful living spaces. However, they can suffer occasionally from noise generated in Spinnaker's nightclub/disco on the deck above. Each Owner's Suite can also be interconnected to a Penthouse Suite and balcony cabin – useful for large families, when parents value privacy.

Penthouse Suites. Each measures 366 sq ft/34 sq m. Penthouse Suites on Deck 11 can be interconnected to a children's cabin with double sofa bed and a pull-down Pullman-style bed, separate bathroom, and shower enclosure.

Romance Suites. Each measures 288 sq ft (27 sq m).

Mini-Suites. These measure 229 sq ft (21 sq m).

All suites are well furnished, most in rich cherry wood, although closet space in some of the smaller units is tight. Some suites have extras including a trouser press, and a full range of personal toiletries. Suites also get butlers, who can serve all meals en suite from the menus of several dining venues.

Many cabins have third- and fourth-person pull-down berths or trundle beds.

A small room service menu is available; non-food items cost extra, and a 15 percent service charge and a gratuity are added to your account. Bottled water is placed in each cabin, but you are charged if you open the bottle.

DINING. With Freestyle Dining, you can choose which restaurant to eat in, at what time, and with whom (no assigned dining rooms, tables, or seats). While this is fine in theory, in practice it means that you have to make reservations for a specific time, so 'freestyle dining' actually turns out to be programmed dining.

Other dining options. There are three principal dining rooms, plus a number of other themed eateries, giving a wide choice (some cost extra and require advance reservations). Two entire decks are filled with 10 restaurants and eateries. NCL's dress code states that 'jeans, T-shirts, tank tops, and bare feet are not permitted in restaurants.'

Venetian: the first main dining room (seats 472) offers traditional dining (open 5.30pm–midnight). It is located aft, with good views over the stern (at least in the daytime), although 14 pillars obstruct the sight lines from some seats. The room has a baby grand piano. For a quieter table, choose one of two wings in the forward section near the entrance/steps.

Aqua: the second main dining room seats 344 and offers traditional six-courses from 5.30pm to midnight.

Impressions: the third main dining room, seating 236, offers lighter cuisine from 5.30pm to midnight.

The waiter stations are too close to the tables and are very noisy.

Bamboo (a Taste of Asia): a Japanese/Thai/Chinese restaurant, with 140 seats, has a sit-up conveyor-belt style sushi/sashimi bar, sake bar, show galley, and separate room with a teppanyaki grill.

Le Bistro: a French restaurant with 72 seats, serving nouvelle cuisine. The decor includes four Impressionist paintings on loan from the private collection of the chairman of Star Cruises, NCL's parent company, although they don't really match the room's decor. There's a cover charge and also a line for you to add an extra gratuity – cheeky. But it's the best food on board and worth the extra cost.

Blue Lagoon: a food court-style eatery with 68 seats serves hamburgers, fish and chips, pot pies, and wok-fast dishes.

Garden Café: an indoor/outdoor self-serve buffet (seats 490). It includes 'action stations' with made-to-order omelets, waffles, fruit, soups, ethnic specialties, and pasta.

Salsa: a Spanish tapas eatery and bar (seats 112) with a selection of hot and cold tapas and authentic entertainment, located on the second level of the atrium lobby.

La Trattoria: located inside the indoor/outdoor buffet (seats 162); serves pasta, pizza, and other Italian fare.

Cagney's Steak House: arranged atop the ship seats 112, incorporates a show kitchen, and serves excellent US prime steaks and seafood. Be prepared for large portions. Reservations are required, and a cover charge applies.

Other eating/drinking spots include the Pearly Kings, an English pub for draft beer and perhaps a game of darts; Havanas, a cigar and cognac lounge; Java, an atrium lobby café and bar (hot and frozen coffees, teas, and pastries); a Beer Garden (grilled foods); a Gelato Bar (ice cream); and a Gym and Spa Bar (health food snacks and drinks).

ENTERTAINMENT. The 1,037-seat Stardust Theater is the venue for colorful Las Vegas-style production shows and major cabaret acts. It is designed in the style of an opera house, spans three decks, and has a steeply tiered main floor and port and starboard balconies. The production shows are very colorful, high-energy, razzle-dazzle shows with extensive use of pyrotechnics, lasers, and color-mover lighting. They're not particularly memorable, but they are very entertaining.

SPA/FITNESS. Wellness devotees should enjoy the two-deck-high El Dorado health spa complex, operated by the Steiner-owned and Hawaii-based Mandara Spa. Located at the stern, it has large ocean-view windows on three sides. There are many facilities and services, almost all at extra cost, including Thai massage in the spa, outdoors on deck, in your cabin, or on your private balcony.

Norwegian Epic
★★★★

Size:	Large Resort Ship	Passenger Space Ratio (lower beds):	37.1
Tonnage:	155,873	Passenger/Crew Ratio (lower beds):	2.4
Lifestyle:	Standard	Cabins (total):	2,100
Cruise Line:	Norwegian Cruise Line	Size Range (sq ft/m):	850.3–100.1/79–9.3
Former Names:	none	Cabins (for one person):	128
IMO Number:	9410569	Cabins (with private balcony):	1,415
Builder:	STX Europe (France)	Cabins (wheelchair accessible):	42
Original Cost:	$735 million	Wheelchair accessibility:	Good
Entered Service:	Jun 2010	Cabin Current:	110 volts
Registry:	Panama	Elevators:	16
Length (ft/m):	1,080.7/329.4	Casino (gaming tables):	Yes
Beam (ft/m):	133.0/40.5	Slot Machines:	Yes
Draft (ft/m):	28.5/8.6	Swimming Pools:	5
Propulsion/Propellers:	diesel-electric (79,800kW)/	Hot Tubs (on deck):	9
	2 azimuthing pods	Self-Service Launderette:	No
Passenger Decks:	15	Dedicated Cinema/Seats:	No
Total Crew:	1,730	Library:	Yes
Passengers (lower beds):	4,200	Onboard currency:	US$

An epic-sized, family-friendly, multiple-choice resort ship

OVERVIEW. *Norwegian Epic* is a blast for youthful adults and kids alike. It's all about lifestyle – bistro eateries, lots of dining choices, color and noise, the perceived über-chic South Beach nightlife at sea, stuffed with entertainment.

THE SHIP. *Norwegian Epic* is an example of 'all-exclusive' cruising, and is a throwback to the days when First Class, Cabin Class, and Tourist Class meant passengers could not access certain areas of the ship – the 'pay more, get more' philosophy.

Norwegian Epic is slightly larger than *Queen Mary 2*. Its profile isn't very handsome because several decks above the navigation bridge make it look really top-heavy, like a square lump of cheese. But the two side-by-side funnels – between which is a 60ft (18m) -wide rock-climbing wall – bring some semblance of balance. The ship is about 30 percent wider than the Norwegian *Jewel*-class ships.

The pool deck has an Aqua Park, with three major water slides – one involves inner tubes that give you a spin before spitting you out into a big bowl, reminiscent of a washing machine. Aft is a large movie screen with amphitheater-style seating, and a nightclub within an area called Spice H2O, which also includes a sun deck. However, despite the ship's size, the open deck space for sunbathing is extremely small and cramped – much diminished by the 'exclusive' Courtyard block in the forward section, whose occupants do have enough sunbathing space.

The three lowest passenger decks contain the main

Berlitz's Ratings		
	Possible	Achieved
Ship	500	386
Accommodation	200	145
Food	400	248
Service	400	275
Entertainment	100	85
Cruise Experience	400	285
OVERALL SCORE		
1424 points out of 2000		

entertainment venues, restaurants and other dining venues, show lounges, and a large casino. Some spaces open to two or three decks in height to create an illusion of space – like mini-atriums, but the overall flow is disjointed and invites congestion, particularly around a casino walk-through area. A dramatic three-deck-high chandelier in the lobby is the largest at sea.

Two escalators do nothing to diminish congestion – they even encourage gridlock at peak times. Sandwiched between these three lower entertainment decks and the upper entertainment decks are seven decks mainly comprised of accommodation. Something new for Norwegian Cruise Line (NCL) is a bridge viewing room, just behind the navigation bridge.

NCL extracts more money with a number of 'exclusive' experiences, including a members-only POSH Beach Club, above the more exclusive Courtyard area atop the ship. This has a Miami South Beach vibe and includes four pay-extra experiences: (1) POSH Vive, 6–9am, when you can participate in yoga classes and treatments in private cabanas; (2) POSH Rehab until noon, so you can recover from a hard night, with Bloody Marys and chill-out music; (3) POSH Sol, noon–6pm, when you can lounge on day beds and enjoy a beach-themed atmosphere; and (4) Pure POSH, echoing Caesar's Palace in Las Vegas, where you can drink and dance under the stars.

Other ship features include a novel Ice Bar, a chill-out hangout inspired by the original ice bars and ice hotels of Scandinavia. In this frozen chamber of iced vodka, the centerpiece is a giant ice cube that glows and changes color. The Ice Bar accommodates 25 passengers, who are given fur coats, gloves, and hats because the room's temperature does not rise above –8°C (around 17°F). Naturally, there's a cover charge, but it includes two drinks. Svedka vodka and Canada's Inniskillin ice wine are featured.

Then there's Halo, an über-bar, where garden and courtyard villa occupants, who pay a premium for much better accommodation, have exclusive access, although other passengers can use it by paying a cover charge. This bar sits at the top of the ship on Deck 16 and showcases art and jewelry, 'modeled' by shop staff.

Spice H2O is a tiered pool, stage, and movie screen complex for adults only, at the stern. It's a smaller version of the Aqua Theater aboard Royal Caribbean International's *Oasis*-class ships. With all-day-long music and a huge screen, different themes prevail: (1) Sunny Spice 8am–11am, including spicy drinks and breakfast; (2) Daytime Aqua Spice with sun and water and Chinese take-away food; (3) Evening Sunset Spice, with a perfect sunset every day; and (4) All Spice at night, offering a show of aqua ballet and dancing. A Beyond the Velvet Rope package for all clubs is available at extra cost.

It's a big ship, but elevators are only forward and aft (none in the middle of the ship), which is tough for mobility-limited passengers. Yet *Norwegian Epic* has more elevators than the much larger *Oasis of the Seas*.

A 'ship within a ship' two-deck complex provides a private courtyard/pool area, men's and women's steam rooms, concierge lounge, and private dining rooms and lounge for those willing to pay more for exclusivity.

Niggles include the cigarette smokers in the casino, a walk-through area.

The ship sails on alternating seven-day eastern and western Caribbean itineraries during the winter season, and operates Mediterranean cruises in summer.

A non-changeable per person service charge is automatically added to your account daily; 15 percent is also added for bar charges, and a whopping 18 percent for spa treatments.

FAMILIES. Family-friendly cabins are within easy access to the Kid's Crew facilities, in two zones: for Kids 2–9, and tweens of 10–12. Nickelodeon is the family entertainment brand on all cruises. Activities include: Slime Time Live, an interactive game; Nick Live, with poolside entertainment; Character ('Pajama Jam') breakfast, at extra charge; and meet and greet. There's also a Nickelodeon in-cabin TV channel.

ACCOMMODATION. There are many different accommodation price levels and accommodation grades, including what the company claims as the first 'Loft Suites' at sea – although upstairs/downstairs suites have been available for years aboard ships such as *Saga Ruby* and the now-withdrawn *QE2*. In true nautical tradition, even-numbered cabins are on the port side (red carpet), with odd-numbered cabins on the starboard side (blue carpet).

The Courtyard Suites (Decks 16 and 17) are located in the 'block of cheese' in the forward section called The Haven, above the navigation bridge. There are six courtyard 'villas' – two face forward, while six overlook the central pool section, although none has a private balcony. Occupants, however, have access to a four-deck gated-community style grouping of facilities, including a Concierge Lounge, private courtyard and pool, his-and-her steam rooms, and private sunbathing areas – so no need to go to the rest of the ship underneath you, except to disembark or go out to the entertainment decks to play, or escape.

All outside-view suites/cabins have a 'private' balcony, curved walls in a 'wave' shape for a contemporary look and feel, LED lighting, backlit domed ceiling, comfortable sofa seating (except standard cabins), vanity desk, and minibar. A palette of soft, warm colors in each cabin melds beautifully with walnut- and rosewood-colored veneers and stark white surfaces. See-through (no-privacy) bathrooms have a separate toilet; tub or tub/shower combination, and separate vanity washbasin (few people like the see-through toilet).

Although they are about the same size as current standard industry cabins, there's an efficient use of space, achieved by separating the toilet and shower unit to either side of the entryway, and by curving the bulkheads and furniture to give the cabins a more open, wavy, and contemporary feel. However, space at the foot of the bed is poor. Also, you'll need to grab a towel before you step into the shower, because they are in a different location – adjacent to a tiny washbasin.

Eight Spa Suites have private key-card entry to the adjacent Mandara Spa, and complimentary 24-hour access to the inner Thermal Spa. These have more space and larger balconies.

Solo travelers can try one of the 128 studio cabins, many of which interconnect – reminiscent of a capsule hotel. A small window looks out into the passageway. On Decks 11 and 12, these are priced for single occupancy, although they can be occupied by two persons (and two toothbrushes only), since there is a double bed. They measure 100 sq ft (9.3 sq m); occupants have access to a common lounge with hostess, and free espressos/cappuccinos. In interior cabins and studio categories, the bed faces the cabin door, so there's no privacy.

DINING. There are certainly plenty of dining choices. With 21 restaurants, and eateries, it will take some planning in order to eat where you want, when you want (there is no 'main' dining room as such). So, just like in any city or town, you choose where to eat – unless, of course, there are no tables available (this is possible at peak times, when everyone wants to see a show simultaneously), and you must wait for a table. There is also no Lido self-service buffet. Instead, different food outlets have been created in numerous locations – 11 are included in the cruise fare, the others require a per-person cover or à-la-carte charge. Because gratuities are automatically added to your account, if you change dining venues, there's no need to think about tips.

Cagney's Steakhouse & Churrascaria (skewered meats presented by tableside 'gauchos') has 276 seats and a central self-help salad bar.

Taste, on Deck 5, is touted as a European retro-chic restaurant with brick detailing and floor-to-ceiling velvet curtains. The menu includes traditional and contemporary cuisine for breakfast, lunch, and dinner.

The Manhattan Room, located aft, is two decks high and reminiscent of an elegant Art Deco supper club, with dance floor and live Celebrity Look-Alike shows. It's the closest thing to a main dining room and has a spectacular glass window wall aft.

La Cucina is from Tuscany. It's at the front of the ship, providing great ocean views, one deck above the navigation bridge.

The 124-seat Le Bistro serves French cuisine; there has been a Le Bistro aboard all NCL ships since the first one was installed aboard the now-scrapped *Norway*.

Multiple Asian-themed venues include Shanghai's for Chinese dishes and noodle bar specialties with an open kitchen and 133 seats; the 20-seat Wasabi for sushi and sakes; and a showy, food-chopping Teppan-yaki Grill, with 115 seats.

The Epic Club and Courtyard Grill, in the Courtyard Villas complex, is exclusive to suite and villa occupants and split between an elegant, private club-style restaurant with a large wine display and a casual outdoor area for breakfast and lunch. It can accommodate 127.

O'Sheehan's neighborhood-style sports bar and grill is open 24 hours (no extra charge). It is adjacent to a bowling alley, though I'm not sure why – it disturbs the ambience.

Café Jardin (Garden Café) is a large self-serve buffet, with 728 seats; it is like an English country garden conservatory – but with a French name and ocean views. It includes 'action' stations where chefs prepare pasta and other items. The outdoor seating area, the Great Outdoors, looks over the Aqua Park. A section for children, the Kids Café, has low-height tables and seats.

ENTERTAINMENT. The two-deck-high Epic Theater, at the front of the ship, presents major production shows and mainline cabaret acts. Another entertainment venue is the Bliss Ultra Lounge, a decadent venue that contains a bowling alley or two – there's another one in Sheehan's on the deck above. This is where late-night comedy and some cabaret acts are presented.

Celebrity look-alike shows, conjuring up the likes of Elvis, Janet Jackson, Madonna, Neil Diamond, and Tina Turner, are part of the entertainment. These shows are produced by Legends in Concert, the Las Vegas company that has provided shows for The Strip for over 25 years.

Spiegel Tent is a two-deck-high Cirque-like space, combining a show with dinner, similar to the Teatro ZinZanni dinner theater in San Francisco and Seattle. It's a mix of in-your-face street theater, acrobatics, and Berlin-style 'foodertainment', with lots of clowning and satire during a two-hour show. There's a cover charge.

As part of NCL's creative Check In, Rock Out program, guitar enthusiasts can, for a daily fee, rent a real Gibson guitar and a set of headphones to play in the comfort of their cabin.

SPA/FITNESS. The Smile Spa and Pulse Fitness Center complex is possibly the largest at sea (31,000 sq ft/2,880 sq m). Operated by the Steiner-owned Mandara Spa, it is in the center of the ship, and some of the 24 treatment rooms have no view. The Fitness Center has port-side ocean views; the aerobics room has no view.

Sports facilities include six bowling lanes in two venues (O'Sheehan's Neighborhood Bar & Grill and Bliss Ultra Lounge), a full-size basketball court, volleyball, soccer, dodge ball, a batting cage, bungee trampoline, a 24ft (7.3m) -tall climbing cage called the spider web, and an abseiling wall. Walkers should note that only 2.2 laps around the walking track equals 1 mile.

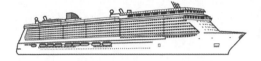

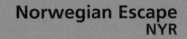

Norwegian Escape
NYR

Size:	Large Resort Ship
Tonnage:	164,600
Lifestyle:	Standard
Cruise Line:	Norwegian Cruise Line
Former Names:	none
IMO Number:	9677076
Builder:	Meyer Werft (Germany)
Original Cost:	€700 million
Entered Service:	Oct 2015
Registry:	Bahamas
Length (ft/m):	1,097.7/334.6
Beam (ft/m):	136.1/41.5
Draft (ft/m):	27.8/8.5
Propulsion/Propellers:	diesel-electric/2 azimuthing pods
Passenger Decks:	15
Total Crew:	1,651
Passengers (lower beds):	4,266
Passenger Space Ratio (lower beds):	38.5
Passenger/Crew Ratio (lower beds):	2.5
Cabins (total):	2,174
Size Range (sq ft/m):	96.8–1,090.0/9.0–101.0
Cabins (for one person):	82
Cabins (with private balcony):	1,571
Cabins (wheelchair accessible):	47
Wheelchair accessibility:	Good
Cabin Current:	110 volts
Elevators:	16
Casino (gaming tables):	Yes
Slot Machines:	Yes
Swimming Pools:	5
Hot Tubs (on deck):	9
Self-Service Launderette:	No
Dedicated Cinema/Seats:	No
Library:	Yes
Onboard currency:	US$

A multi-choice, über-casual playground for the entire family

OVERVIEW. *Norwegian Escape* really is a ship for young and trendy urbanites. In fact, it's a ship built around splash-tastic waterslides. It provides families with children, single parents, couples, and solo travelers with a mountain of entertainment choices, in an environment that is a pure playground for an active, entertaining cruise vacation.

THE SHIP. *Norwegian Escape* (close sister to *Norwegian Breakaway and Norwegian Getaway*) has a more streamlined, balanced profile than its slightly larger sibling ship, *Norwegian Epic*, with less of a less boxy look to its forward section, and a better Passenger Space Ratio (more space per passenger). The hull artwork is designed by marine wildlife artist and champion of ocean conservation, Guy Harvey, featuring an underwater scene of marine wildlife.

Norwegian Escape is cool, but the ambience is South Beach in heat, with all the hype and volume to prove it. It has some really good outdoor features for active types (including a jungle-like rope trek high above the aft decks). Families with children can enjoy extensive pool deck facilities including the Aqua Park (larger than the ones on Norwegian Breakaway, Norwegian Epic, and Norwegan Getaway), with multiple water slides and a rock-climbing wall and rope walk (more for adult kids). Aft is a large movie screen with amphitheater-style seating. But, despite the ship's size, the open deck space for sunbathing is really tight, made smaller by the 'exclusive' 'Haven' area in the forward section,

Berlitz's Ratings		
	Possible	Achieved
Ship	500	NYR
Accommodation	200	NYR
Food	400	NYR
Service	400	NYR
Entertainment	100	NYR
Cruise Experience	400	NYR
OVERALL SCORE		
NYR points out of 2000		

whose suites-only occupants (pay more, get more) are given their own sunbathing space, bar, pool, hot tubs, and beach-club-like setting. The rest of the ship shares multiple pools and water-fun exterior decks, designed for families and children. Still, the pool deck is where all the family action takes place, particularly on sea days. Kids will love it, especially the little ones, because Sponge Bob is in the wading pool.

Lower down, on an outdoor promenade deck, a 'Waterfront' boardwalk-style outdoor area with bar and eateries brings you more in contact with the sea. It forms part of the outdoor experience, and away from the hubbub of the family-friendly sun/sports action deck atop the ship.

Careful planning and time management will be needed to make the most of this large resort ship and all it has to offer. It's worth spending time to decide what you want to get out of your cruise vacation before you board the ship, which sort of negates the 'freestyle' aspect of a large resort ship cruise. You'll be sharing the ship with about 4,000 others, so there's no doubt it will be a lively travel experience.

Most of the public rooms, shops, entertainment spots, the casino, and a number of the bars and themed dining venues are located on decks 6, 7 and 8 – a three-deck indoor-outdoor complex called 678 Ocean Place. This includes Tobacco Road, named for a Miami icon that closed in 2014 after 102 years in business. Elements of the original Tobacco Road include the original iconic neon sign, memorabilia, and photographs that showcase Miami's history and happenings over the past century.

Norwegian Escape's year-round homeport is Miami Gratuities are charged to your onboard account, or you can pre-pay on-line. Bar purchases incur a 15 percent gratuity; spa treatments are 18 percent.

FAMILIES. Facilities for kids and teens are spread over two decks (Splash Academy for kids and a separate Entourage space for teens). There's also a nursery for children under two years of age.

Splash Academy is located adjacent to family-friendly accommodation and provides areas for three age groups. Babies and toddlers under three will also have their own dedicated play space and parent-involving activities. At the Splash Academy reception area, tablet-based electronic registration allows parents to swipe their keycard and input a password to sign in their children.

Just past the reception area, the three- to five-year-olds (Guppies) have their own brightly decorated space, complete with child-sized furniture. In a separate zone, six- to nine-year-olds (Turtles) have building block activity centers, an interactive dance mat with corresponding large video screen, video game stations, and a screening lounge.

Upstairs, 10- to 12-year-olds (Seas) get a multipurpose dance space with a touch-screen jukebox, moveable tables for activities, and bean bags for lounging. An activity zone includes arts and crafts items, and a 'hang out' area stocked with the latest computer games.

Entourage, the dedicated space for ages 13–17 (Dolphins) has air hockey, foosball, and an arcade with five separate large-screen areas to play computer games while lounging on sofas. It becomes a teen nightclub with a dance floor and video jukebox in the evenings. Adjacent is a video arcade and an outdoor eatery.

Nickelodeon family entertainment brand is now on all cruises, as part of NCL's children's programming. Activities include: Slime Time Live, an interactive game; Nick Live, with poolside entertainment; Character breakfast, at extra charge; and meet and greet. There's also a Nickelodeon in-cabin TV channel. So, expect to see Sponge Bob, Dora the Explorer, Patrick Star, and Diego as part of the family-themed entertainment.

ACCOMMODATION. There is an almost endless variety of accommodation grades and suite/cabin types, shapes, and sleeping capacities, so you'll need to decide what you are looking for or are comfortable with. Note that the cabin doors open outwards (towards you) rather than inwards, as is more traditional. Also, when music is being played late at night in the lobby, cabins located above it may suffer from volume levels that are quite intrusive, despite some generally good soundproofing.

The Haven. The more exclusive accommodation is located in a two-deck-high section called The Haven – really a 'ship within a ship.' It consists of 42 suites on decks 15 and 16 forward, and includes a private restaurant, a cocktail bar, and a concierge desk where passengers can relax, have a drink, and make dining, entertainment, and spa reservations through the dedicated concierge. There is a private pool (with a deep end for swimming and a shallow area for relaxing), changing areas, two hot tubs, gym, saunas, two private massage rooms, and sun deck with bar. The Haven occupants have private access to the spa and fitness center, as well as 24-hour butler service, and in-suite, white-tablecloth dining service. Suite occupants get a platinum key card (better recognition in the rest of the ship – who said the 'class' system was dead?) and priority reservations for all the restaurants, spa, and entertainment venues.

The top suites within The Haven are two Deluxe Owner's Suites, with their contemporary skyscraper apartment look – including an elegant living room and dining area with wet bar. The bedroom has a king-size bed with pillow-top mattress that faces floor-to-ceiling windows and an extra-spacious wraparound private balcony. The bathroom has an oversize tub, two vanity sinks, and a luxury shower. The Deluxe Owner's Suites can be joined to the Owner's Suites, creating one grand suite that can sleep up to eight.

The two-bedroom Family Villas have two bathrooms and two bedrooms, with a separate living room and dining area that includes a single sofa bed, writing desk, and bar. The master bedroom has a king-size bed, floor-to-ceiling windows, and a private balcony. The master bath includes an oversize oval tub with sea views. The second bedroom includes a double sofa bed and bathroom.

Also in The Haven are Courtyard Penthouses, with a king-size bed, living and dining area, a single sofa bed, writing desk, and ample storage spaces. On other (non-Haven) decks throughout the ship are eight aft-facing penthouses and 10 forward-facing penthouses.

Other accommodation. There are Spa mini-suite rooms and Spa balcony cabins, all with easy access to the adjacent spa and its facilities. While most outside-view cabins have a balcony, some have only windows, but all have flat-screen televisions, satellite-linked telephone, and private bathroom. There are also many Family 'suites' with ocean views.

Balcony suites/cabins have rich wood-look paneling with warm tones. Each has a queen-size bed that can be made into twins, with a pillow-top mattress. There's a lighted recess above the bed for books, magazines, tablets, mobiles, or other items. Each room has a sofa bed with additional storage. A built-in 26-ins flat-screen television is mounted on the wall and tilts for viewing from the sofa or the bed. Underneath the television is another recessed nook to hold cruise information, books, and magazines. A built-in vanity area has shelving and decent storage space. There's also a full-size closet with sliding doors. The cabins are energy-efficient, with key card access to control lighting in the room.

The balcony bathroom features a contemporary, clean design, with generous and comfortable space. An enclosed under-washbasin vanity hides the trash bin. A private shower with a shaving bar for ladies completes the picture. Mini-suite bathrooms get a rain shower plus a hand-held shower hose.

There are 59 studio (single-occupancy) interior-only cabins. They are colorful, hip, trendy, and small, with a minimalist design – especially the closet space. Still this is a neat way to cruise solo – just don't bring many clothes.

Many interior cabins also have one or two additional upper berths, while lower beds are twins that convert to a queen-size bed – good for families with young children.

Note that room service breakfasts incur a 'convenience' charge of $7.95 per order (free for occupants of The Haven).

DINING. Freestyle Dining means no assigned dining rooms, tables or seats, so you can choose which restaurant to eat in, at what time, and with whom. In practice, the wealth of choices means that you'll need to make reservations in whichever venue you want to eat, so you'll need to be prepared for a bit of planning and waiting – just like you would ashore. But, if you want to see a show in the evening, then your dining time will really be dictated by the time of the show, which rather limits your choice.

Other dining options. There are three main dining rooms: Savor, Taste, and the Manhattan Room. Other dining venues (Cagney's Steakhouse and Moderno Currascaria) are located one deck above, and have a view into the Tropicana Room.

The Waterfront is a boardwalk-style outdoor area with bar and eateries, while Geoffrey Zakarian's 678 Ocean Place (meaning decks 6, 7, and 8) connects it with several interior extra-cost dining venues as well as the extensive Breakaway Casino, cigar smoking room, and several entertainment venues. These include Moderno Churrascaria (Brazilian-style steakhouse with table-side carved meat service by passadores and a salad bar); Cagney's Steakhouse (classic American steakhouse, with open kitchen); La Cucina (Italian family food with a focus on Tuscany, with inside seating); or for alfresco eating on The Waterfront, Maltings, and Ocean Blu by Geoffrey Zakarian (designed and overseen by US TV's Food Network's celebrity chef of the same name). Zakarian uses fresh-as-possible ingredients and techniques that he employs in his land-based establishments.

Other venues include Le Bistro, for classic French-style cuisine; a 96-seat Teppanyaki restaurant with 12 flat-top grills and a lot of show and noise, and The Illusionarium (a lively, magic-filled dinner show – South Beach meets handcuffs and magic wand). All are extra-cost, and reservations are required.

Casual eateries, at no extra cost (except Wasabi – a sushi bar), include O'Sheehan's Neighborhood Bar & Grill, a sports bar and popular always open fast-food joint, with a big screen for sporting events, miniature bowling alley, pool and air hockey tables, and interactive games; Margaritaville – a Jimmy Buffet-themed eatery; the Atrium Café and Bar, for coffees, pastries and music; and Shanghai's Noodle Bar, for Chinese-style noodle dishes. Perhaps in a tribute to Man vs Food (the U.S. television 'food' show), the Ice Cream Bar signature item is a ship-specific extra-cost sundae (Breakaway Sundae or Getaway Sundae), with nine scoops of ice cream in up to three flavors topped with 'everything under the sun.'

The Garden Café is an extremely large, self-serve buffet, with indoor and outdoor seating. It's open round the clock. Many different counters provide themed and ethnic food varieties, and there's a special section for kids

ENTERTAINMENT. The two-deck-high Getaway Theater, located at the front of the ship, is a stunning showlounge, where the major production shows and mainline cabaret acts are presented. A specially produced version of seven-time Tony-award nominated *Legally Blonde* is one of the highlights, while Burn the Floor is a fast-paced and exciting dance show. Both are really cool productions.

What's also notable: The Illusionarium and its Grand Master Magic Show with Dinner, all set in a circular room with a dome that is a dinner show-only magic theatre-in-the-round. And Grammy Experience at Sea is a small venue featuring headline name musical artists.

Another entertainment venue is the Bliss Ultra Lounge, a decadent venue that contains a bowling alley or two, as well as other diversions.

NCL has always been at the forefront for creativity in entertainment.

SPA/FITNESS. The Mandara Spa and fitness center, spread over two decks, houses a warehouse-size gymnasium. The complex includes an extra-cost thermal suite (herbal rainshowers, a snow grotto, saunas and steam rooms, and relaxation area with hot-tile beds), a beauty salon, and multiple body-treatment rooms, including massage rooms for couples. The fitness room has Technogym fitness and cardio equipment, which is linked to Apple devices.

The Sports Complex includes Aqua Park's five thrilling water slides, a multi-elevated rope course (there are more than 40 elements), The Plank (a platform extending over the ship's side), rock-climbing wall, a spider-web-like enclosed spiral climbing cage, a bungee trampoline, and a bocce ball court.

Norwegian Gem
★★★+

Size:	Large Resort Ship
Tonnage:	93,530
Lifestyle:	Standard
Cruise Line:	Norwegian Cruise Line
Former Names:	none
IMO Number:	9355733
Builder:	Meyer Werft (Germany)
Original Cost:	$390 million
Entered Service:	Oct 2007
Registry:	Panama
Length (ft/m):	964.8/294.1
Beam (ft/m):	105.6/32.2
Draft (ft/m):	26.9/8.2
Propulsion/Propellers:	diesel-electric/2 azimuthing pods
Passenger Decks:	12
Total Crew:	1,126
Passengers (lower beds):	2,394
Passenger Space Ratio (lower beds):	39.0

Passenger/Crew Ratio (lower beds):	2.1
Cabins (total):	1,197
Size Range (sq ft/m):	142.0–4,390.0/13.2–407.8
Cabins (for one person):	0
Cabins (with private balcony):	540
Cabins (wheelchair accessible):	27
Wheelchair accessibility:	Good
Cabin Current:	110 volts
Elevators:	12
Casino (gaming tables):	Yes
Slot Machines:	Yes
Swimming Pools:	2
Hot Tubs (on deck):	6
Self-Service Launderette:	Yes
Dedicated Cinema/Seats:	No
Library:	Yes
Onboard currency:	US$

A large, family-friendly ship with multiple eating venues

OVERVIEW. A multitude of choices, including many dining options, add up to a very attractive vacation package, highly suitable for families with children, in a floating leisure center that provides ample facilities for enjoyment.

THE SHIP. The design and layout of *Norwegian Gem* is similar to that of *Norwegian Pearl*, and there is a pod propulsion system for vibration-free cruising. The white hull has a colorful string of gems along its sides as a design. There are plenty of deck lounge chairs – more than the total of passengers. Water slides are included for the adult swimming pools. Children have their own pools at the ship's stern.

Inside the ship is an entertaining mix of bright, warm colors and decor that you probably wouldn't have in your home, and yet somehow they all work well.

The dress code is ultra-casual: no jacket and tie needed, although you are welcome to dress formally – but jeans are probably essential. Although service levels and finesse may be inconsistent, the level of hospitality aboard Norwegian Cruise Line (NCL) ships is good. There's plenty of lively music, constant activity, entertainment, and food that is mainstream and acceptable but nothing more – even when you pay extra to eat in the specialty dining spots.

There are 11 bars (including a 24-hour 'pub') and lounges, including Bar Central, four specialty bars: a Martini bar, a Champagne and wine bar, a beer and whiskey bar, and a cigar lounge; these inter-

Berlitz's Ratings		
	Possible	Achieved
Ship	500	369
Accommodation	200	145
Food	400	240
Service	400	272
Entertainment	100	66
Cruise Experience	400	275
OVERALL SCORE		
1367 points out of 2000		

connect with the lobby, yet have distinct personalities. The lobby houses a Java Bar, plus a two-deck-high movie screen, typically used to show sports events and Wii activities. One neat room is the Bliss Ultra Lounge & Night Club, at the aft end of the ship; it houses a 24-hours-a-day V-shaped sports bar and lounge complex, including a bowling alley with four real bowling lanes – the cost is $5 per person, including special playing shoes, and it is limited to six persons per lane. The lounge doesn't have many seats, but does have a couple of decadent beds.

The casino is typical of larger resort ship casinos, with plenty of gaming tables, slot machines, noise, and smoke. So, if you walk through the casino to get from the showlounge to other public rooms, you'll be subject to cigarette smoke. A new twist in the onboard casino scene has appeared, with poolside blackjack now established in its own 'open-air casino' on the pool deck.

The ship is full of revenue centers designed to help you part with even more money than you paid for your cruise ticket. Expect to be subjected to a stream of flyers advertising art auctions, 'designer' watches, gold and silver chain by the inch, and other promotions – and the cruise director's long program announcements three times a day.

A per person service charge that can't be changed is automatically added to your account daily; 15 percent is also added for bar charges, and a whopping 18 percent for spa treatments.

FAMILIES. Because NCL is all about cruising with families of all ages, much space is devoted to children's facilities, all thoughtfully tucked well away from adult recreation areas, at the aft end of the ship. Children of all ages can play in the wet 'n' wild space-themed water park (the Aqua Kid's Club), complete with large pool, water slide, and paddle pool. There's a 30ft by 19ft (9m by 6m) climbing wall at the funnel. Teens are well catered for, and have their own cinema, disco with dance floor, and hot tub. There's a room full of cots for toddlers to use for sleepovers. And Nickelodeon characters are onboard, so young ones can enjoy a Pajama Jam Breakfast.

More than 250 cabins have interconnecting doors – good for families with children. That means interior cabins can connect; outside-view cabins can connect; and outside-view and balcony cabins can connect. Also for families, many cabins also have third- and fourth-person pull-down berths or trundle beds.

ACCOMMODATION. There are many, many different price grades, from small interior cabins to lavish suites in a private courtyard setting.

Although they are nicely furnished and quite well equipped, the standard outside-view and interior cabins are quite small, particularly when occupied by three or four people. A small room service menu is available – all non-food items cost extra cost, and a 15 percent service charge is automatically added to your account. Bottled water is placed in each cabin, but you will be charged if you open the bottle.

The following suites, part of The Haven, are available:

Courtyard Villas/Garden Villas. Two Garden Villa Suites, each measuring 4,390 sq ft (408 sq m), and 10 Courtyard Villas share a private courtyard with its own small pool, hot tub, and small fitness room, and they have butler service. These units enjoy exclusivity – rather like accommodation in a gated community – where others cannot live unless they pay the asking price.

Deluxe Owner's Suites. The Black Pearl and Golden Pearl suites have stunning ocean views, and consist of a master bedroom with king-size bed, a dining/lounge area, a decent-size balcony, and access to a private courtyard.

Penthouse Suites. Located at the front of the ship, they have a partly private balcony under the navigation bridge.

DINING. There are two main dining rooms: the 304-seat Grand Pacific, with minimalist decor; and the 558-seat Magenta Restaurant. There are several other themed eating spots, giving a wide range of choice; some cost extra, and require advance reservations, particularly for dinner. All are part of NCL's Freestyle Dining – there are no assigned dining rooms, tables, or seats, so you'll need to plan your meals and times accordingly.

With 17 video screens located around the ship, you can check how busy each dining spot is and make a booking and find out whether, or how long, you'll need to wait for a table; pagers are also available, so you can go bar-hopping while you wait for a table in your chosen venue. The system generally works well, with colored bars to indicate whether a restaurant is 'full', 'moderately busy', or 'empty'. This has cut down the frustration of waiting a long time for a table, although on formal nights, when you may want to see the production shows, congestion certainly does occur. Note that NCL's dress code states that 'jeans, T-shirts, tank tops, and bare feet are not permitted in restaurants.'

Other dining options. Additional dining options, some of which cost extra, include Cagney's Steak House (serving steaks from 5oz to 48oz); Blue Lagoon (for trendy fast-food street snacks); Moderno Churrascaria (for Argentinian-style grilled meats), Le Bistro for classic French cuisine; Orchid Garden (an Asian-style eatery with sushi bar and Teppanyaki grill, where the chef puts on a display in front of you); La Cucina Italian Restaurant; O'Sheehan's Neighborhood Bar & Grill; Garden Café, a large self-serve buffet-style restaurant, for casual meals; Kids' Café; and Java Café, for extra-cost Lavazza coffee, in the lobby.

ENTERTAINMENT. The 1,042-seat Stardust Theater is the venue for colorful Las Vegas-style production shows and major cabaret acts. It is designed in the style of an opera house, spans three decks, and has a steeply tiered main floor and port and starboard balconies.

All the colourful, high-energy production shows are ably performed by the Jean Ann Ryan Company.

SPA/FITNESS. Wellness devotees should enjoy the two-deck-high Yin-Yang Health Spa complex, open until 10pm and operated by the Steiner-owned and Hawaii-based Mandara Spa. It is located in the front of the ship, with large ocean-view windows on three sides. There are many facilities and services to pamper you, and 18 treatment rooms. There's also a 37ft (11m) indoor lap pool, hydrotherapy pool, two sit-in deep tubs, aromatherapy and wellness centers, and mud treatment room.

The Body Waves fitness and exercise rooms are within the spa and have the latest Cybex muscle-pumping equipment. Most classes, such as Pathway to Yoga, Body Cycling Class, and Body Beat Class (cardio kick-boxing), cost extra.

Recreational sports facilities include a jogging track, golf driving range, and basketball and volleyball courts, as well as several levels of sunbathing decks, plus four bowling lanes, and a funnel-mounted rock-climbing wall.

Norwegian Getaway
★★★★

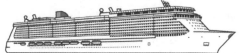

Size:	Large Resort Ship	Passenger/Crew Ratio (lower beds):	2.4
Tonnage:	145,655	Cabins (total):	1,994
Lifestyle:	Standard	Size Range (sq ft/m):	96.8-1,022.6/9.0-95.0
Cruise Line:	Norwegian Cruise Line	Cabins (for one person):	59
Former Names:	none	Cabins (with private balcony):	1,252
IMO Number:	9606912	Cabins (wheelchair accessible):	40
Builder:	Meyer Werft (Germany)	Wheelchair accessibility:	Good
Original Cost:	€600 million	Cabin Current:	110 volts
Entered Service:	Apr 2013	Elevators:	16
Registry:	The Bahamas	Casino (gaming tables):	Yes
Length (ft/m):	1,066.2/325.0	Slot Machines:	Yes
Beam (ft/m):	133.0/40.5	Swimming Pools:	5
Draft (ft/m):	27.8/8.5	Hot Tubs (on deck):	9
Propulsion/Propellers:	diesel-electric (79,800MW)/2	Self-Service Launderette:	No
Passenger Decks:	15	Dedicated Cinema/Seats:	No
Total Crew:	1,595	Library:	No
Passengers (lower beds):	3,929	Onboard currency:	US$
Passenger Space Ratio (lower beds):	37		

This is a multi-choice, super-casual playground for the family

OVERVIEW. *Norwegian Getaway* really is a ship for young and trendy urbanites. It's full of 'bling' and will provide families with children, single parents, couples, and solo travelers with a mountain of entertainment choices, in an environment that is a pure, lively playground for an active, entertaining cruise vacation. This is 'South Beach Miami' at sea – and then some!

THE SHIP. *Norwegian Getaway* (sister to *Norwegian Breakaway*) has a more streamlined, balanced profile than its slightly larger close-sister ship, *Norwegian Epic*, with a less boxy look to its forward section. Miami artist David 'LEBO' Le Batard provided the artwork on the hull, which depicts a whimsical mermaid holding the sun above the waves.

Norwegian Getaway is the coolest kid on the block. The ambience is pure South Beach in heat, with all the hype and volume to prove it, as well as some really great outdoor features for active types (including a jungle-like rope trek high above the aft decks). Families with children can enjoy extensive pool deck facilities including the Aqua Park, with multiple water slides and a rock-climbing wall and, rope walk (more for adult kids). Aft is a large movie screen with amphitheater-style seating. But, despite the ship's size, the open deck space for sunbathing is rather tight, and made smaller by the 'exclusive' 'Haven' area in the forward section, whose suites-only occupants (pay more, get more) are given extra sunbathing space, a bar, pool, and hot tubs, in a beach-club-like setting. The rest of the ship shares

Berlitz's Ratings		
	Possible	Achieved
Ship	500	395
Accommodation	200	149
Food	400	248
Service	400	274
Entertainment	100	87
Cruise Experience	400	285
OVERALL SCORE		
1438 points out of 2000		

multiple pools and water-fun exterior decks, designed for families and children. Still, the pool deck is where all the family action will be – particularly on sea days – and the kids will love it, especially the little ones, because Sponge Bob is in the wading pool.

Lower down, on an outdoor promenade deck, a 'Waterfront' boardwalk-style outdoor area with bar and eateries brings you more in contact with the sea. It forms part of the outdoor experience, away from the hubbub of the family-friendly sun/sports action deck atop the ship.

Inside, the decor is decidedly more traditional and provides a more restful, relaxed feel and ambience – although this is all relative and still rather upbeat. Careful planning and time management will be needed to make the most of this large resort ship and all it has to offer. So it's worth spending time to decide what you want to get out of your cruise vacation before you board the ship – which sort of negates the 'freestyle' aspect of a large resort ship cruise. You'll be sharing the ship with about 4,000 others, so there's no doubt it will be a lively travel experience.

Most of the public rooms, shops, entertainment spots, the casino, and a number of the bars and themed dining venues are located on Decks 6, 7 and 8 – a three-deck indoor-outdoor complex called 678 Ocean Place.

The ambience on board is lively, and invites plenty of social interaction. *Norwegian Getaway*'s homeport is Miami. Gratuities are charged to your onboard account, or you can pre-pay online. Bar purchases incur a 15 percent gratuity; spa treatments are 18 percent.

FAMILIES. Facilities for kids and teens are spread over two decks (Splash Academy for kids and a separate Entourage space for teens).

Splash Academy is located adjacent to the ship's family-friendly accommodation and provides areas for three age groups. Babies and toddlers under three will also have their own dedicated play space and parent-involving activities. At the Splash Academy reception area, tablet-based electronic registration allows parents to swipe their keycard and input a password to sign in their children.

Just past the reception area, the 3–5-year-olds (Guppies) have their own brightly decorated space, complete with child-sized furniture. In a separate zone, 6–9-year-olds (Turtles) have building block activity centers, an interactive dance mat with corresponding large screen, gaming stations, and a viewing lounge for movies, etc.

Upstairs, 10–12-year-olds (Seals) get a multipurpose dance space with a touch-screen jukebox, moveable tables for activities, and bean bags for lounging. An activity zone includes arts and crafts items, and a 'hang out' area stocked with the latest games.

Entourage, a dedicated space for ages 13–17 (Dolphins) has air hockey, football, and an arcade with five separate large-screen areas to play the latest computer games while lounging on sofas. In becomes a teen nightclub with a dance floor and jukebox in the evenings. Adjacent is a video arcade and an outdoor eatery.

Nickelodeon is the family entertainment brand on all cruises, as part of Norwegian Cruise Line's (NCL's) children's programming. Activities include: Slime Time Live, an interactive game; Nick Live, with poolside entertainment; Character breakfast, at extra charge; and meet and greet. There's also a Nickelodeon in-cabin TV channel. So, expect to see Sponge Bob, Dora the Explorer, Patrick Star, and Diego as part of the family-themed entertainment.

ACCOMMODATION. There is an almost endless variety of accommodation grades and suite/cabin types, shapes, and sleeping capacities, so you'll need to decide what you are looking for, or are comfortable with.

Aboard this ship, the cabin doors open *outwards* (towards you) rather than inwards, as is more traditional. Also, note that when music is being played late at night in the lobby, cabins located above it can suffer from intrusive volume levels, despite the generally good soundproofing.

The Haven. The more exclusive accommodation is located in a two-deck-high section called The Haven – really a 'ship within a ship.' It consists of 42 suites on Decks 15 and 16 forward, and includes a private restaurant, a cocktail bar, and a concierge desk where passengers can relax, have a drink, and make dining, entertainment, and spa reservations through the dedicated concierge. There is a private pool (with a deep end for swimming and a shallow area for relaxing), changing areas, two hot tubs,

gym, saunas, two private massage rooms, and a sun deck with bar. The Haven occupants have private access to the spa and fitness center, as well as 24-hour butler service, and in-suite, white-tablecloth dining service. Suite occupants get a platinum key card (better recognition in the rest of the ship – who said the 'class' system was dead?) and priority reservations for all the restaurants, spa, and entertainment venues.

The top suites within The Haven are two Deluxe Owner's Suites, with their contemporary skyscraper apartment look – including an elegant living room and dining area with wet bar. The bedroom has a king-size bed with pillow-top mattress that faces floor-to-ceiling windows and an extra-spacious wraparound private balcony. The bathroom has an oversize tub, two vanity sinks, and a luxury shower. The Deluxe Owner's Suites can be joined to the Owner's Suites, creating one grand suite that can sleep up to eight.

The 21 two-bedroom Family Villas have two bathrooms as well as two bedrooms. The separate living room and dining area includes a single sofa bed, writing desk, and bar. The master bedroom has a king-size bed, floor-to-ceiling windows, and a private balcony. The master bath includes an oversize oval tub that looks out to the sea. The second bedroom includes a double sofa bed and bathroom.

Also in The Haven are 17 Courtyard Penthouses, with a king-size bed, living and dining area, a single sofa bed, writing desk, and ample storage spaces. On other (non-Haven) decks throughout the ship are eight aft-facing penthouses and 10 forward-facing penthouses.

Other accommodation. There are 15 Spa mini-suite rooms and 28 Spa balcony cabins, all with easy access to the adjacent spa and its facilities. While most outside-view cabins have a balcony, some have only windows, but all have flat-screen televisions, satellite-linked telephone, and private bathroom. There are also 42 Family 'suites' with ocean views.

Balcony suites/cabins have rich wood-look paneling with warm tones. Each balcony cabin has a queen-size bed that can be made into twins, with a pillow-top mattress set against a chestnut leather headboard cushioned and tufted to make reading and sitting up in bed more comfortable. There's a lighted recess above the bed for books, magazines, mobiles, tablets, or electronic reading devices. Each room has a sofa bed with additional storage. A built-in 26-ins flat-screen television is mounted on the wall and tilts for viewing from the sofa or the bed. Underneath the television is another recessed nook to hold cruise information, books, and magazines. A built-in vanity area has shelving and decent storage space. There's also a full-size closet with sliding doors. The cabins are energy-efficient, using key card access to control lighting in the room.

The balcony bathroom features a contemporary, clean design, ensuring more generous and comfortable space. An enclosed vanity unit underneath the washbasin hides the trash bin, along with more storage. The built-in washbasin is size-generous. A private shower with a shaving bar for ladies completes the picture. Mini-suite bathrooms get a rain shower plus a hand-held shower hose.

There are 59 studio (single-occupancy) interior-only cabins (none has a sea view). They are colorful, hip, trendy, and small, with a minimalist design – especially the closet space. Still this is a neat way to cruise solo – just don't bring many clothes.

The many interior cabins also have one or two additional upper berths, while the lower beds are twins that convert to a queen-size bed – good for families with young children.

Note that room service breakfasts (other than coffee/tea and continental breakfast) incur a 'convenience' charge of $7.95 per order (free for occupants of The Haven).

DINING. Freestyle Dining means no assigned dining rooms, tables or seats, so you can choose which restaurant to eat in, at what time, and with whom. In practice, the wealth of choices means that you'll need to make reservations in whichever venue you want to eat, so you'll need to be prepared for a bit of planning and waiting – just like you would ashore. But, if you want to see a show in the evening, then your dining time will really be dictated by the time of the show, which rather limits your choice.

Other dining options. The Tropicana Room is the ship's equivalent of a main (included in the fare) restaurant; it is large, with an integral dance floor (for shows and dancing during dinner) and large ocean-view windows aft. Other dining venues (Cagney's Steakhouse and Moderno Churrascaria) are located one deck above, and have a view into the Tropicana Room.

The Waterfront is a boardwalk-style outdoor area with bar and eateries, while Geoffrey Zakarian's 678 Ocean Place (meaning Decks 6, 7, and 8) connects it with several interior extra-cost dining venues as well as the extensive Getaway Casino, a cigar-smoking room, and several entertainment and dining venues. These include Moderno Churrascaria, a Brazilian-style steakhouse with table-side carved meat service by passadores and a salad bar); the adjacent Cagney's Steakhouse, a classic American steakhouse, with open kitchen; La Cucina, for Italian family food with a focus on Tuscany, with inside seating; or, for alfresco eating on The Waterfront, Ocean Blu (designed and overseen by US TV's Food Network's popular Geoffrey Zakarian). The celebrity chef uses fresh-as-possible ingredients and techniques that he employs in his land-based establishments.

Other venues include Le Bistro, for classic French-style cuisine; a 96-seat Teppanyaki restaurant with 12 flat-top grills and a lot of knife show and noise,

and The Illusionarium – a combination magic show with dinner.

Casual (no-extra-cost) eateries (except Wasabi – an à-la-carte sushi bar), include O'Sheehan's Neighborhood Bar & Grill, a sports bar and popular always-open fast-food joint, with a big screen for sporting events, miniature bowling alley, pool and air hockey tables, and interactive games; the Atrium Café and Bar, for coffees, pastries, and music; and Shanghai's Noodle Bar, for Chinese-style noodle dishes. The Ice Cream Bar signature item is a ship-specific extra-cost sundae (Breakaway Sundae or Getaway Sundae), with nine scoops of ice cream in up to three flavors topped with 'everything under the sun.'

The Garden Café is an extremely large, self-serve buffet, with indoor and outdoor seating. It's open round the clock. Many different counters provide themed and ethnic food varieties, and there's a special section for kids

ENTERTAINMENT. Two-deck-high Getaway Theater, located at the front of the ship, is a stunning show-lounge where the major production shows and mainline cabaret acts are presented. A specially produced version of seven-time Tony-award nominated *Legally Blonde* is one of the highlights, while *Burn the Floor* is an excellent, fast-paced and exciting Latin dance show (it is presented in the Tropicana Room).

Really cool: The Illusionarium and its Grand Master Magic Show with Dinner. It's presented in a circular room with a large dome – a magic theater-in-the-round (think South Beach meets handcuffs and magic wand). The show is the result of collaboration between NCL's entertainment department and Broadway director/choreographer Patricia Wilcox, Tony Award-winning scenic designer David Gallo and veteran magician Jeff Hobson. Its design is inspired by the science fiction of Jules Verne, the artistry of legendary magicians such as Houdini, and by the supernatural. Whether you can get your water changed into wine remains to be seen.

Also, Grammy Experience at Sea is a small venue featuring headline-name musical artists.

SPA/FITNESS. The spa and fitness center, spread over two decks, houses a warehouse-size gymnasium. The complex includes an extra-cost thermal suite (herbal rain showers, saunas and steam rooms, relaxation area with hot-tile beds), a beauty salon, and multiple body treatment rooms, including massage rooms for couples.

The Sports Complex includes Aqua Park's five thrilling water slides, a multi-elevated rope course (there are more than 40 elements), The Plank (a platform extending over the ship's side), rock-climbing wall, a spider-web-like enclosed spiral climbing cage, bungee trampoline, and a nine-hole miniature golf course.

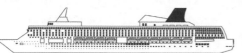

Norwegian Jade
★★★+

Size:	Large Resort Ship	Passenger Space Ratio (lower beds):	37.9
Tonnage:	93,558	Passenger/Crew Ratio (lower beds):	2.2
Lifestyle:	Standard	Cabins (total):	1,233
Cruise Line:	Norwegian Cruise Line	Size Range (sq ft/m):	142.0–4,390.0/13.2–407.8
Former Names:	Pride of Hawaii	Cabins (for one person):	0
IMO Number:	9304057	Cabins (with private balcony):	763
Builder:	Meyer Werft (Germany)	Cabins (wheelchair accessible):	27
Original Cost:	$390 million	Wheelchair accessibility:	Good
Entered Service:	May 2006/Mar 2008	Cabin Current:	110 volts
Registry:	The Bahamas	Elevators:	12
Length (ft/m):	964.8/294.1	Casino (gaming tables):	Yes
Beam (ft/m):	105.6/32.2	Slot Machines:	Yes
Draft (ft/m):	26.9/8.2	Swimming Pools:	2
Propulsion/Propellers:	diesel-electric (40,000kW)/ 2 azimuthing pods	Hot Tubs (on deck):	6
		Self-Service Launderette:	No
Passenger Decks:	12	Dedicated Cinema/Seats:	No
Total Crew:	1,076	Library:	Yes
Passengers (lower beds):	2,466	Onboard currency:	US$

Entertainment and a casual lifestyle for the whole family

OVERVIEW. *Norwegian Jade* best suits youthful adult couples, solo travelers, and families with children and teenagers who want upbeat surroundings, good facilities, a wide range of entertainment lounges and bars, and high-tech sophistication – all in a neat, highly programmed, and well-packaged cruise. But, although the initial fare seems very reasonable, the extra costs and charges can soon mount up.

Berlitz's Ratings		
	Possible	Achieved
Ship	500	367
Accommodation	200	145
Food	400	240
Service	400	273
Entertainment	100	66
Cruise Experience	400	276
OVERALL SCORE		
1367 points out of 2000		

THE SHIP. Built from 67 blocks, this is a sister ship to *Norwegian Jewel*. After service as *Pride of Hawaii*, it underwent a small transformation, gained a casino, and became *Norwegian Jade* for cruising in Europe and the Caribbean – though some interior decor elements from the ship's former life in Hawaii remain. The interior decor is decidedly bright and cheerful, and it has a pod propulsion system.

The ship's interior focal gathering place is Bar Central – three specialty bars (Magnum's Champagne/Wine Bar, Mixers' Martini/Cocktail Bar, and Tankard's Beer/Whiskey Bar) that are connected but have distinct personalities. They are located on the deck above the reception lobby. All told, there are a dozen bars and lounges. Other facilities include a casino, three meeting rooms, a chapel, card room, bridge viewing room, and the SS *United States* Library with original photography and material about America's last ocean liner.

The dress code is very casual; no jacket and tie are needed, although you are welcome to dress formally, if you wish. The ship is full of revenue centers de-signed to help you part with more of your money. You can expect to be subjected to a stream of flyers advertising daily art auctions, 'designer' watches, and many other promotions including poolside 'inch of gold' sales outlets.

A non-negotiable per person service charge is automatically added to your account daily; 15 percent is also added for bar charges.

Passenger niggles include waiting to use the interactive dining reservation screens in the public areas; lines for breakfast in the main dining spots, particularly before the shore excursions start; and poor service and hospitality in some areas.

FAMILIES. Children are well provided for, and have their own facilities, including a Kids' Club; teens have their own disco, the Wipe-Out Club. More than 250 cabins have interconnecting doors – good for families with children. That means interior cabins can connect; outside-view cabins can connect; and outside-view and balcony cabins can connect. Also for families, many cabins also have third- and fourth-person pull-down berths or trundle beds.

ACCOMMODATION. There are many, many different price grades, determined by size and location. Although they are nicely furnished and quite well equipped, the standard outside-view and interior cabins are quite small, particularly when occupied by three or four people.

A small room service menu is available; all non-food items cost extra, and a 15 percent service charge is added to your account. Bottled water is placed in each cabin, but a charge is made to your account, if you open the bottle.

Garden Villas. Two multi-room villas have great views over the pool deck and ocean. Each has a roof terrace and private garden, with open-air dining, hot tub, and private sunning and relaxation areas. They are among the most extravagant suites at sea today. Each has a living room with Bose audio-visual equipment (including a CD/DVD library), grand piano, wet bar, and refrigerator. Each has three bedrooms (king- or queen-size bed) with en suite bathroom and walk-in closet. Each Garden Villa measures approximately 4,390 sq ft (408 sq m), the ultimate in living space, exclusivity and privacy.

Courtyard Villas. 10 Courtyard Villas (up to 660 sq ft/61 sq m) share a private courtyard with its own small pool, hot tub, massage bed, and fitness room – all in a setting that is distinctly Asian. They also share a private Concierge Lounge with the two largest villas, as well as butler and concierge service. These units enjoy exclusivity, rather like accommodation in a gated community. The two Garden Villas each have three bedrooms with en suite bathroom, living room, dining room, and stunning views.

Owner's Suites. Each of these five units (approximately 1,195 sq ft/111 sq m) has a large bedroom with king-size bed and audio-visual entertainment center, and a living room with dining area. The bathroom has a tub, separate shower enclosure, and powder room. Some Owner's Suites can interconnect with Penthouse Suites.

Penthouse Suites. There are 24 of these, measuring up to 600 sq ft (56 sq m). They have a bedroom with queen-size bed, and living room with dining area. The bathroom has a tub/shower or separate shower enclosure. Some can be interconnect to a kid's room with double sofa bed and a Pullman bed with separate bathroom with shower.

All villas and suites have a private balcony, walk-in closet, rich cherry wood cabinetry, tea/coffee/espresso/cappuccino makers, plus butler and concierge service.

DINING. Freestyle Dining has no assigned dining rooms, tables, or seats, so you can choose which restaurant to eat in, at what time, and with whom. In practice, this means you have to make reservations for a specific time, so 'freestyle dining' turns out to be programmed dining. Ten restaurants and eateries are spread over two entire decks. Some are included in the cruise fare, others cost extra.

The two main restaurants, included in the cruise fare, are Alizar (310 seats) and Grand Pacific (486

seats). Other Norwegian Cruise Line specialty dining venues include Cagney's Steak House (176 seats), Blue Lagoon (a casual eatery serving American food and seating 94), and Le Bistro (a classic French restaurant, with 129 seats – check out the beautiful, and genuine, Van Gogh painting).

The 100-seat Moderno churrascaria is a Brazilian style steakhouse (with adjacent self-help salad bar). Jasmine Garden (including a sushi counter, sake bar, and a 32-seat Teppanyaki Grill for grilled food items and a knife show) has Southeast Asian cuisine. A 70-seat Papa's Italian Kitchen has a long wooden table that creates a farmhouse ambience. Self-serve buffet-style meals can be taken in the Garden Café and its outdoor section. Extra-cost Lavazza (Italian) coffees can be found in the Aloha Café.

You can make reservations through the Freestyle Dining information system; plasma screens showing waiting times for the various venues are located in high-traffic areas.

ENTERTAINMENT. The 1,042-seat Stardust Theater is the venue for colorful Las Vegas-style production shows and major cabaret acts. It is designed in the style of an opera house, spans three decks, and has a steeply tiered main floor and port and starboard balconies. Colorful, high-energy, razzle-dazzle production shows are ably performed by the Jean Ann Ryan Company.

Bands and solo entertaining musicians provide live music for listening and dancing to in several lounges and bars. Throughout the ship, loud music prevails. In Spinnakers Lounge, a nightclub located high atop the ship with great ocean views on three sides, a Pachanga Party (a Miami South Beach rave) is held during each cruise.

SPA/FITNESS. The two-deck-high Yin and Yang health spa complex, operated by the Steiner-owned Mandara Spa, is at the stern, with large ocean-view windows on three sides. There are many facilities and services, almost all costing extra. In addition, there is a 37ft (11m) indoor lap pool, hydrotherapy pool, two sit-in deep tubs, aroma-therapy and wellness centers, and mud treatment rooms, including one for couples. Spa treatments incur an 18 percent gratuity.

The fitness and exercise rooms, with Cybex muscle-pumping equipment, are located not within the spa, but at the top of the glass-domed atrium lobby. Included is a room for exercycle classes.

Recreational sports facilities include a jogging track, two golf driving nets (there's a golf pro shop, too), basketball and volleyball courts, paddle tennis, mini-golf, oversize chess, and several sunbathing decks.

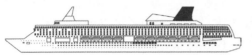

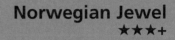

Norwegian Jewel
★★★+

Size:	Large Resort Ship	Passenger Space Ratio (lower beds):	39.3
Tonnage:	93,502	Passenger/Crew Ratio (lower beds):	2.1
Lifestyle:	Standard	Cabins (total):	1,188
Cruise Line:	Norwegian Cruise Line	Size Range (sq ft/m):	142.0–4,390.0/13.2–407.8
Former Names:	none	Cabins (for one person):	0
IMO Number:	9304045	Cabins (with private balcony):	540
Builder:	Meyer Werft (Germany)	Cabins (wheelchair accessible):	27
Original Cost:	$390 million	Wheelchair accessibility:	Good
Entered Service:	Aug 2005	Cabin Current:	110 volts
Registry:	Panama	Elevators:	12
Length (ft/m):	964.8/294.1	Casino (gaming tables):	Yes
Beam (ft/m):	105.6/32.2	Slot Machines:	Yes
Draft (ft/m):	26.9/8.2	Swimming Pools:	2
Propulsion/Propellers:	diesel-electric (40,000kw)/ 2 azimuthing pods	Hot Tubs (on deck):	6
		Self-Service Launderette:	No
Passenger Decks:	12	Dedicated Cinema/Seats:	No
Total Crew:	1,089	Library:	Yes
Passengers (lower beds):	2,376	Onboard currency:	US$

A large, casual ship for lively, family-friendly cruising

OVERVIEW. A multitude of choices, including many dining options, add up to a very attractive vacation package, highly suitable for families with children, in a floating leisure center that provides ample facilities for enjoyment. The dress code is very casual – no jacket and tie needed – although you are welcome to dress formally if you wish.

THE SHIP. *Norwegian Jewel*, assembled from 67 blocks, has a basic design and layout similar to that of *Norwegian Gem* and *Norwegian Pearl*, and a pod propulsion system. The white hull has a colorful, funky design on its sides featuring sparkling jewels. There are plenty of sunloungers – in fact, more than the number of passengers carried. Water slides are included for the adult swimming pools. Children have their own pools at the stern, out of sight of adult areas.

Inside the ship, you'll be met by an eclectic mix of colors and decor that you probably wouldn't have in your home, and yet somehow it works extremely well in this large resort ship setting designed to attract the young, active, and trendy.

There are 13 bars and lounges, including Bar Central, three specialty bars that are connected but have distinct personalities. Shakers Martini and Cocktail Bar is a 1960s-inspired lounge; Magnum's Champagne and Wine Bar recalls Paris of the 1920s and the liner *Normandie*; and Maltings Beer and Whiskey Pub is a contemporary bar with artwork themed around whiskey and beer production.

Berlitz's Ratings

	Possible	Achieved
Ship	500	365
Accommodation	200	145
Food	400	240
Service	400	273
Entertainment	100	66
Cruise Experience	400	276
OVERALL SCORE		
1365 points out of 2000		

Despite the company's name, there's little that's Norwegian about this product, except for some senior officers. There's plenty of lively music, constant activity, entertainment, and food that is mainstream and acceptable but nothing more, unless you pay extra to eat in the specialty dining spots. All this is delivered by a smiling, friendly service staff that lacks polish but is willing.

The ship is full of revenue centers designed to part you from your cash. Expect to be subjected to a stream of flyers advertising daily art auctions, 'designer' watches, and 'inch of gold/silver'. The initial cruise fare is reasonable, but extra costs soon mount up, if you want to sample more than the basics. A mandatory per-person service charge is added to your account daily; 15 percent is also added for bar charges, and a whopping 18 percent for spa treatments.

FAMILIES. A good deal of space is devoted to children's facilities, which are all tucked well away from adult recreation areas, at the aft end of the ship. Children of all ages get to play in a superb wet 'n' wild space-themed water park complete with large pool, water slide, and paddle pool. There's a room full of cots for toddlers to use for sleepovers, and even the toilets are at a special low height. Teens, too, are well catered for, and have their own cinema, disco with dance floor, and hot tub.

More than 250 cabins have interconnecting doors, which is good for families with children. That means interior cabins can connect; outside-view cabins can connect; and outside-view and balcony cabins can connect. Also for families, many cabins also have third- and fourth-person pull-down berths or trundle beds.

ACCOMMODATION. There are numerous accommodation price grades, so there's something for all tastes, from small interior cabins to lavish Penthouse Suites in a private courtyard setting – part of The Haven complex. Although they are nicely furnished and quite well equipped, the standard outside-view and interior cabins are quite small, particularly when occupied by three or four people.

A small room service menu is available; all non-food items are at extra cost, and a 15 percent service charge is added to your account. Bottled water is placed in each cabin, but you will be charged if you open the bottle.

Courtyard Penthouses/Suites. Two Garden Villas (each measures 4,390 sq ft/408 sq m), and 10 Courtyard Villas share a private courtyard with its own small pool, hot tub, massage bed, and fitness room – all in a setting that is distinctly Asian. They also share a private concierge lounge with the two largest villas, as well as butler and concierge service. These units enjoy exclusivity – rather like accommodation in a gated community – where others cannot live unless they pay the asking price. The two largest are duplex apartments, with a spiral stairway between the upper and lower quarters.

DINING. The ship's freestyle dining has no assigned dining rooms, tables or seats, so you can choose which restaurant to eat in, at what time, and with whom. In practice, this means you have to make reservations for a specific time, so 'freestyle dining' turns out to be programmed dining. Ten restaurants and eateries are spread over two entire decks. Some are included in the cruise fare, others cost extra.

There are two main dining rooms: the 552-seat Tsar's Palace, designed to look like the interior of Catherine the Great's St Petersburg palace in Russia, and the 310-seat Azura. There are also a number of other themed eating establishments, giving a wide range of choice – though some cost extra, and require advance reservations.

Computer screens around the ship enable you to check how long you'll have to wait for a table at each dining spot. Pagers are available, so you can go bar-hopping while you wait for a table. The system works well, although on formal nights when you may want to see the show, congestion can occur. Note: Norwegian Cruise Line's (NCL's) dress code states: 'jeans, T-shirts, tank tops, and bare feet are not permitted in restaurants.'

Other dining venues. Established favorites include: Cagney's Steakhouse (for fine steaks and seafood); Moderno Churrascaria (a Brazilian-style steakhouse for meat and seafood dishes); and Le Bistro (for fine classic French cuisine). In a 2014 refit, O'Sheehan's Neighborhood Bar and Grill was added, for homey pub food (and beer).

Chin Chin is an Asian eatery with a Teppanyaki Grill and sushi counter adjacent. La Cucina Italian Restaurant has a long wooden table running through the room to create the ambience of a Tuscan farmhouse.

The Garden Café is the large self-serve buffet eatery; it incorporates an ice cream bar, and Kid's Café, with its own kid-height counter, located opposite the children's play areas. For coffee, head to the Atrium Café in the lobby, and taste some of Buddy Valasco's cupcakes in Carlo's Bakery, adjacent.

ENTERTAINMENT. The Stardust Theater, seating 1,037, is the venue for colorful Las Vegas-style production shows and major cabaret acts. It is designed in the style of an opera house, spans three decks, and has a steeply tiered main floor and port and starboard balconies.

There are two or three production shows in a typical seven-day cruise, all ably performed by the Jean Ann Ryan Company. These are all very colorful, high-energy, razzle-dazzle shows with extensive use of pyrotechnics, lasers, and color-mover lighting. By the end of the evening, you may well be too tired to remember much about the shows, which are nevertheless very entertaining.

A number of bands and solo entertaining musicians provide live music for listening and dancing in lounges and bars. In Spinnakers Lounge, a nightclub, a Pachanga Party is held each cruise (a Miami South Beach rave).

SPA/FITNESS. Wellness devotees should enjoy the two-deck-high Bora Bora health spa complex, operated by the Hawaii-based Mandara Spa, located in the front of the ship with large ocean-view windows on three sides. There are many facilities and services to pamper you, almost all at extra charge, including Thai massage in the spa, outdoors on deck, in your cabin or on your private balcony.

In addition, there is a 37ft (11m) indoor lap pool, hydrotherapy pool, two sit-in deep tubs, aromatherapy and wellness centers, and mud-treatment rooms. There are 15 treatment rooms in all, including one specifically designed for couples, and heated tile loungers in a relaxation area.

The fitness and exercise rooms, with the latest Cybex muscle-pumping equipment, are located not within the spa, but at the top of the glass-domed atrium lobby. Included is a room for exercycle classes. Some classes, such as Pathway to Yoga, Body Cycling Class, and Body Beat Class (cardio kick-boxing), cost extra.

Recreational sports facilities include a jogging track, golf driving range, basketball and volleyball courts, as well as four levels of sunbathing decks.

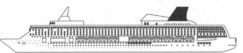

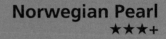

Norwegian Pearl
★★★+

Size:	Large Resort Ship	Passenger Space Ratio (lower beds):	39.0
Tonnage:	93,530	Passenger/Crew Ratio (lower beds):	2.2
Lifestyle:	Standard	Cabins (total):	1,197
Cruise Line:	Norwegian Cruise Line	Size Range (sq ft/m):	142.0–4,390.0/13.2–407.8
Former Names:	none	Cabins (for one person):	0
IMO Number:	9342281	Cabins (with private balcony):	540
Builder:	Meyer Werft (Germany)	Cabins (wheelchair accessible):	27
Original Cost:	$390 million	Wheelchair accessibility:	Good
Entered Service:	Dec 2006	Cabin Current:	110 volts
Registry:	Panama	Elevators:	12
Length (ft/m):	964.8/294.1	Casino (gaming tables):	Yes
Beam (ft/m):	105.6/32.2	Slot Machines:	Yes
Draft (ft/m):	26.9/8.2	Swimming Pools:	2
Propulsion/Propellers:	diesel-electric (39,000kW)/ 2 azimuthing pods	Hot Tubs (on deck):	6
		Self-Service Launderette:	No
Passenger Decks:	12	Dedicated Cinema/Seats:	No
Total Crew:	1,087	Library:	Yes
Passengers (lower beds):	2,394	Onboard currency:	US$

A casual, family-friendly ship with multi-choice dining options

OVERVIEW. Plenty of choices, including many dining options, add up to an attractive vacation package that is highly suitable for families with children, in a floating leisure center that provides ample facilities for enjoyment. The dress code is always casual – no jacket and tie needed – although you are welcome to dress formally if you wish.

THE SHIP. The ship's white hull has a colorful, funky design on its sides featuring sparkling jewels. There are plenty of sunloungers – in fact, more than the number of passengers carried. Water slides are included for the adult swimming pools. Children have their own pools at the stern, out of sight of adult areas.

Inside the ship, you'll be met by an eclectic mix of colors and decor that you probably wouldn't have in your home, and yet somehow it works extremely well in this large resort ship setting designed to attract the young, active, and trendy.

There are 13 bars and lounges, including Bar Central, three specialty bars that are connected but have distinct personalities. Shakers Martini and Cocktail Bar is a 1960s-inspired lounge; Magnum's Champagne and Wine Bar recalls Paris of the 1920s and the liner *Normandie*; and Maltings Beer and Whiskey Pub is a contemporary bar with artwork themed around whiskey and beer production.

Despite the company's name, there's little that's Norwegian about this product, except for some senior officers. There's plenty of lively music, constant activity, entertainment, and food that is mainstream

Berlitz's Ratings		
	Possible	Achieved
Ship	500	364
Accommodation	200	145
Food	400	240
Service	400	272
Entertainment	100	66
Cruise Experience	400	275
OVERALL SCORE		
1362 points out of 2000		

and acceptable but nothing more, unless you pay extra to eat in the specialty dining spots. All this is delivered by a smiling, friendly service staff that lacks polish but is willing.

The ship is, however, full of revenue centers designed to part you from your cash. Expect to be subjected to a stream of flyers advertising daily art auctions, 'designer' watches, and 'inch of gold/silver.'

The initial cruise fare is reasonable, but extra costs soon mount up if you want to sample more than the basics. A mandatory per person service charge is added to your account daily; 15 percent is also added for bar charges, and a whopping 18 percent for spa treatments.

FAMILIES. A good deal of space is devoted to children's facilities, which are all tucked well away from adult recreation areas, at the aft end of the ship. Children of all ages will get to play in a superb wet 'n' wild space-themed water park complete with large pool, water slide, and paddle pool. There's a room full of cots for toddlers to use for sleepovers, and even the toilets are at a special low height. Teens, too, are well catered for, and have their own cinema, disco with dance floor, and hot tub.

More than 250 cabins have interconnecting doors, which is good for families with children. That means interior cabins can connect; outside-view cabins can connect; and outside-view and balcony cabins can connect. Also for families, many cabins also have third- and fourth-person pull-down berths or trundle beds.

ACCOMMODATION. There are numerous accommodation price grades, so there's something for all tastes, from small interior cabins to lavish Penthouse Suites in a private courtyard setting – part of The Haven complex. Although they are nicely furnished and quite well equipped, the standard outside-view and interior cabins are quite small, particularly when occupied by three or four people.

A small room service menu is available; all non-food items are at extra cost, and a 15 percent service charge is added to your account. Bottled water is placed in each cabin, but you will be charged if you open the bottle.

Courtyard Penthouses/Suites. Two Garden Villas (each measures 4,390 sq ft/408 sq m), and 10 Courtyard Villas share a private courtyard with its own small pool, hot tub, massage bed, and fitness room – all in a setting that is distinctly Asian. They also share a private concierge lounge with the two largest villas, as well as butler and concierge service. These units enjoy exclusivity – rather like accommodation in a gated community – where others cannot live unless they pay the asking price. The two largest are duplex apartments, with a spiral stairway between the upper and lower quarters.

Deluxe Owner's Suites. Two suites are set high atop all other accommodation, have stunning ocean views, and consist of a master bedroom with king-size bed, a dining/lounge area, a decent-size balcony, and access to the private courtyard.

DINING. Freestyle Dining has no assigned dining rooms, tables or seats, so you can choose which restaurant to eat in, at what time, and with whom. In practice, this means you have to make reservations for a specific time, so 'freestyle dining' turns out to be programmed dining. Ten restaurants and eateries are spread over two entire decks. Some are included in the cruise fare, others cost extra.

The two principal dining rooms are the 304-seat Indigo, with its minimalist decor; and the 558-seat Summer Palace, plus eight other themed eating spots. The 17 video screens around the ship enable you to check how long you'll have to wait for a table at each dining spot. Pagers are available, so you can go bar-hopping while you wait for a table. The system works well, although on formal nights when you may want to see the show, congestion can occur. Norwegian Cruise Line's (NCL's) dress code states that 'jeans, T-shirts, tank tops, and bare feet are not permitted in restaurants.'

Other dining options. Note that some of these cost extra. Cagney's House (for fine steaks and seafood), Blue Lagoon (Asian street food), and Le Bistro (French cuisine) are NCL favorites. Mambo's is a contemporary spot with bright colors and tapas/Latin fare. Lotus Garden is an Asian eatery featuring a Teppanyaki Grill and sushi counter. A La Cucina Italian Restaurant is novel in that it has a long wooden table running through the room to create the ambience of a Tuscan farmhouse. For really casual (self-serve) buffet-style eating, there's the light, airy Great Outdoors. Finally, the Garden Café incorporates an ice cream bar, and Kid's Café, with its own kid-height counter, is wisely located opposite the children's play areas. For coffee, head to the Java Café in the lobby – it's a great place for people watching. Three of the specialty restaurants incur a cover charge, while others are free.

ENTERTAINMENT. The 1,037-seat Stardust Theater is the venue for colorful Las Vegas-style production shows and major cabaret acts. It is designed in the style of an opera house, spans three decks, and has a steeply tiered main floor and port and starboard balconies.

There are two or three production shows in a typical seven-day cruise, all ably performed by the Jean Ann Ryan Company. These are all very colorful, high-energy, razzle-dazzle shows with much use of pyrotechnics, lasers, and color-mover lighting. By the end of the evening, you may well be too tired to remember much about the shows, which are nevertheless very entertaining.

A number of bands and solo entertaining musicians provide live music for listening and dancing in lounges and bars. In Spinnakers Lounge, a nightclub, a Pachanga Party is held each cruise (a Miami South Beach rave).

SPA/FITNESS. Bodywaves is the name of the spa/fitness center. It is operated by the Hawaii-based Mandara Spa (Steiner Leisure), located in the front of the ship with large ocean-view windows on three sides. There are lots of facilities and services to pamper you, almost all at extra charge, including Thai massage in the spa, outdoors on deck, in your cabin or on your private balcony.

In addition, there is a 37ft (11m) indoor lap pool, hydrotherapy pool, two sit-in deep tubs, aromatherapy and wellness centers, and mud treatment rooms. There are 15 private massage/body treatment rooms, including one just for couples.

The fitness and exercise rooms, with the latest muscle-pumping equipment, are located not within the spa, but at the top of the glass-domed atrium lobby. Included is a room for exercycle classes. Some classes, such as Pathway to Yoga, Body Cycling Class, and Body Beat Class, cost extra.

Recreational sports facilities include a jogging track, golf driving range, basketball and volleyball courts, as well as four levels of sunbathing decks.

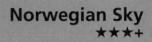

Norwegian Sky
★★★+

Size:	Large Resort Ship
Tonnage:	77,104
Lifestyle:	Standard
Cruise Line:	Norwegian Cruise Line
Former Names:	*Pride of Aloha, Norwegian Sky*
IMO Number:	9128532
Builder:	Lloyd Werft (Germany)
Original Cost:	$332 million
Entered Service:	Aug 1999/Jun 2008
Registry:	The Bahamas
Length (ft/m):	853.0/260.0
Beam (ft/m):	105.8/32.2
Draft (ft/m):	26.2/8.0
Propulsion/Propellers:	diesel-electric (50,000kW)/2
Passenger Decks:	12
Total Crew:	914
Passengers (lower beds):	2,002
Passenger Space Ratio (lower beds):	38.5

Passenger/Crew Ratio (lower beds):	2.1
Cabins (total):	1,001
Size Range (sq ft/m):	120.5–488.6/11.2–45.4
Cabins (for one person):	0
Cabins (with private balcony):	252
Cabins (wheelchair accessible):	6
Wheelchair accessibility:	Good
Cabin Current:	110 volts
Elevators:	12
Casino (gaming tables):	Yes
Slot Machines:	Yes
Swimming Pools:	2
Hot Tubs (on deck):	5
Self-Service Launderette:	No
Dedicated Cinema/Seats:	No
Library:	Yes
Onboard currency:	US$

A multi-choice ship for upbeat, family-friendly cruising

OVERVIEW. *Norwegian Sky*, a resort at sea, caters well to a multi-generational clientele, with lots of choices for dining and entertainment. It provides a fine, comfortable base from which to explore. The outdoor space is quite generous, including an extra-wide pool deck with two swimming pools and four hot tubs.

THE SHIP. In 2004 *Norwegian Sky* was 'Hawaiianized' and morphed into *Pride of Aloha* for Norwegian Cruise Line's (NCL's) Hawaii cruise operation, but withdrew from that market in 2008 and was transferred to NCL for short cruises in the Caribbean. The interior decor reflects its operating area, and the focal point is an eight-deck-high atrium lobby, with spiral sculptures and rainbow-colored sails.

Public rooms include a shopping arcade, children's playroom, Internet center with 14 terminals and coffee available from an adjacent bar, several lounges and bars, small conference room, the Mark Twain library, and Captain Cook's for cigars and cognac. Those with a black belt in shopping may seek out the Black Pearl Gem Shop.

The hustling for passengers to attend art auctions is aggressive and annoying, as is the constant bombardment for revenue activities and the daily junk mail that arrives at one's cabin door. There are many announcements – particularly annoying are those that state what is already written in the daily program. There is little connection to the sea from many public rooms. Passenger hallways are quite plain.

Berlitz's Ratings

	Possible	Achieved
Ship	500	365
Accommodation	200	145
Food	400	240
Service	400	266
Entertainment	100	74
Cruise Experience	400	272
OVERALL SCORE		
1362 points out of 2000		

A per-person service charge you can't change is added to your account daily; 15 percent is also added for bar charges, and a whopping 18 percent for spa treatments.

ACCOMMODATION. There are numerous price categories, including 13 for outside-view suites and cabins, and six for interior cabins. All the standard cabins have two lower beds that convert to a queen-size bed, a small lounge area with sofa and table, and a decent amount of closet space, but very little drawer space, and the cabins themselves are disappointingly small. However, each is decorated in colorful Hawaiian style, with an explosion of floral themes and vibrant colors.

More than 200 outside-view cabins have their own private balcony. Each cabin has a small vanity/writing desk, color TV set, personal safe, climate control, and a laptop computer connection socket. Audio can be obtained only through the TV set. Bottled water is placed in each cabin – but your account will be charged if you open it.

The largest accommodation is four Owner's Suites. Each has a hot tub, large teak table, two chairs, and two sunloungers outside on a huge, very private, forward-facing teakwood-floor balcony just under the ship's navigation bridge, with large floor-to-ceiling windows. Each suite has a separate lounge and bedroom. The lounge has a large dining table and four chairs, two two-person sofas, large TV set, DVD/CD unit, coffee table, queen-size pull-down Murphy's bed, guest closet, writing desk, wet bar with two bar stools, refrigerator and sink, several cupboards for glasses, and several drawers and other cupboards for storage. The bedroom, which has sliding wood half-doors that look into the lounge, has a queen-size bed (with European duvet) under a leaf-glass chandelier, vanity desk, TV, walk-in closet with plenty of hanging rail space, five open shelves, and large personal safe. The white-tiled bathroom, although not large, has a full-size tub with retractable clothesline, separate shower enclosure with glass doors, deep washbasin, and toiletries cabinets.

There are 10 Junior Suites, each with a private teak-decked balcony; these suites face aft in a secluded position and overlook the ship's wash. They have almost the same facilities as those in the Owner's Suites, except for the outdoor hot tub, and the fact that there is less space.

DINING. Freestyle Dining has no assigned dining rooms, tables or seats, so you can choose which restaurant to eat in, at what time, and with whom. In practice, this means you have to make reservations for a specific time, so 'freestyle dining' turns out to be programmed dining.

The main dining rooms – Palace Restaurant, with 510 seats, and Crossings Restaurant, with 556 seats – have tables for four, six, or eight and an open-seating arrangement. The cuisine in both includes regional specialties. However, it's best to have dinner in one of the specialty restaurants, as the food in these two large dining rooms is just so-so.

Other dining options. A smaller eatery, the 83-seat Plantation Club Restaurant, is an à-la-carte, light-eating option serving 'healthy' spa dishes and tapas. It has half-moon-shaped alcoves and several tables for two. The wine list is quite decent and well arranged, with moderate prices, although you won't find many good vintage wines. The cutlery is very ordinary and there are no fish knives.

For classic and nouvelle French cuisine, the 102-seat Bistro has an à-la-carte menu. The decor is inspired by royal and aristocratic gardens. For premium steaks and lamb chops, there's Cagney's Restaurant, with 84 seats, intimate seating alcoves, and good food, at extra cost.

Other eateries include Pacific Heights, a casual Pacific Rim/Asian Fusion eatery that has steaks plus local fish and seafood. Casual, self-serve buffet-style meals can be taken in the Garden Café.

ENTERTAINMENT. The 1,000-seat, two-deck-high (main and balcony levels) Stardust Theater is the venue for production shows and major cabaret acts, although the sight lines are quite poor from some seats. A number of bands and solo entertaining musicians provide live music for listening and dancing in several lounges and bars.

SPA/FITNESS. Body Waves is a large health/fitness spa – including an aerobics room and a separate gymnasium, and several treatment rooms. It is operated by Mandara Spa, headquartered in Honolulu but owned by Steiner Leisure. A whopping 18 percent gratuity is added to spa treatments.

Sports fans will appreciate the large basketball/ volleyball court, baseball-batting cage, golf-driving net, platform tennis, shuffleboard, and table tennis facilities. A sports bar, with baseball and surfing themes, has live satellite television coverage of sports events and major games on several TV screens. Joggers can take advantage of a walk-around indoor/outdoor jogging track.

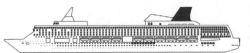

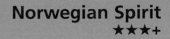

Norwegian Spirit
★★★+

Size:	Mid-size Ship
Tonnage:	75,338
Lifestyle:	Standard
Cruise Line:	Norwegian Cruise Line
Former Names:	*SuperStar Leo*
IMO Number:	9141065
Builder:	Meyer Werft (Germany)
Original Cost:	$350 million
Entered Service:	Oct 1998/May 2004
Registry:	Panama
Length (ft/m):	879.2/268.0
Beam (ft/m):	105.6/32.2
Draft (ft/m):	25.9/7.9
Propulsion/Propellers:	2 diesels (50,400kW)/2
Passenger Decks:	10
Total Crew:	948
Passengers (lower beds):	1,976
Passenger Space Ratio (lower beds):	38.1

Passenger/Crew Ratio (lower beds):	2.0
Cabins (total):	988
Size Range (sq ft/m):	150.6–638.3/14.0–59.3
Cabins (for one person):	0
Cabins (with private balcony):	374
Cabins (wheelchair accessible):	4
Wheelchair accessibility:	Good
Cabin Current:	240 volts
Elevators:	9
Casino (gaming tables):	Yes
Slot Machines:	Yes
Swimming Pools:	2
Hot Tubs (on deck):	4
Self-Service Launderette:	No
Dedicated Cinema/Seats:	No
Library:	Yes
Onboard currency:	US$

A mid-sized ship offering a casual, lively, active vacation

OVERVIEW. Because *Norwegian Spirit* is quite a stunning ship that features a wide choice of dining venues, keeping consistency of product delivery depends on the quality of the service staff. There are many extra-cost items in addition to the extra-charge dining spots.

THE SHIP. A full walk-around promenade deck outdoors is good for strolling and has lots of space, including a whole area devoted to children's outdoor activities and pool. Inside, there are two indoor boulevards and a stunning, two-deck-high central atrium lobby with three glass-walled lifts and ample space to peruse the shops and cafés that line its inner sanctum. The lobby itself is modeled after the lobby of Hong Kong's Hyatt Hotel, with little clutter from the usual run of desks found aboard other cruise ships.

The interior design theme revolves around art, architecture, history, and literature. The ship has a mix of both Eastern and Western design and decor details. Three stairways are each carpeted in a different color, which helps new passengers find their way around.

A 450-seat room atop the ship functions as an observation lounge during the day and a nightclub at night, with live music. From it, a spiral stairway takes you down to a navigation bridge viewing area, where you can see the captain and bridge officers at work.

There is a business and conference center – good for small groups – and a writing room, and a smoking room for those who enjoy cigars and cognac. A shopping concourse is set around the second level of the lobby.

Berlitz's Ratings		
	Possible	Achieved
Ship	500	362
Accommodation	200	145
Food	400	240
Service	400	274
Entertainment	100	66
Cruise Experience	400	274
OVERALL SCORE		
1361 points out of 2000		

The casino complex is at the forward end of the atrium boulevard on Deck 7 (not between show-lounge and restaurant as in most Western ships). This includes Maharajah's, a large general-purpose, brightly lit casino, with gaming tables and slot machines.

The dress code is extremely casual – no jacket and tie needed. With many dining choices, some of which cost extra, to accommodate different tastes and styles, your cruise and dining experience will largely depend on how much you are prepared to spend.

Standing in line for embarkation, disembarkation, shore tenders, and for self-serve buffet meals is an inevitable aspect of cruising aboard many ships. Note that a non-changeable per person service charge is added to your account daily; 15 percent is also added for bar charges, and a whopping 18 percent for spa treatments.

FAMILIES. Teens have their own huge video arcade, while younger children get to play in a wet 'n' wild aft pool (complete with pirate ship and caves) and two whirlpool tubs. Plus there's all the fun and facilities of Charlie's childcare center, which includes a painting room, computer learning center, and small cinema. Even the toilets are at a special low height, and there's a room full of cots for toddlers. Over 15,000 sq ft (1,400 sq m) is devoted to children's facilities – all tucked well away from adult recreation areas.

ACCOMMODATION. Three whole decks of cabins have private balconies, while two-thirds of all cabins have an outside view. Both the standard outside-view and interior cabins really are very small – particularly given that all cabins have extra berths for a third/fourth person – although the bathrooms have a good-size shower enclosure. So, take only the least amount of clothing you can manage with. All cabins have a personal safe, 100 percent cotton towels, and 100 percent cotton duvets or sheets. In cabins with balconies, the balconies are extremely narrow, and the cabins themselves are very small – the ship was originally constructed for three- and four-day cruises.

Choose one of the six largest Executive Suites (named Hong Kong, Malaysia, Shanghai, Singapore, Thailand, and Tokyo) and you'll have an excellent amount of private living space, with separate lounge and bedroom. Each has a large en suite bathroom that is part of the bedroom and opens onto it. It has a gorgeous mosaic tiled floor, kidney bean-shaped whirlpool tub, two sinks, separate shower enclosure with floor-to-ceiling ocean-view window, and separate toilet with glass door. There are TV sets in the lounge, bedroom, and bathroom. The Singapore and Hong Kong suites and the Malaysia and Thai suites can be combined to form a double suite – good for families with children. Butler service and a concierge come with the territory.

The 12 Zodiac Suites, each named after an astrological sign, are the second largest accommodation, and also have a butler and concierge. Each has a separate lounge, bedroom, and bathroom, and an interconnecting door to an ocean-view cabin with private balcony – good for families. All cabinetry features richly lacquered woods, large (stocked) wet bar with refrigerator, dining table with a top that flips over to reveal a card table, and four chairs, plus sofa, drinks table, and trouser press. The bedrooms are small but have a queen-size bed; there is a decent amount of drawer space, although the closet space is rather tight because it contains two personal safes.

A small room service menu is available; all non-food items cost extra, and both a 15 percent service charge and a gratuity are added to your account.

DINING. There are eight places to eat, two at extra cost, so you need to plan where you want to eat well in advance or you may be disappointed.

Windows Restaurant: the equivalent of a main dining room; it seats 632 in two seatings, is two decks high at the aft-most section, and has huge cathedral-style windows set in three sections overlooking the ship's stern and wake. Waiter stations are tucked neatly away in side wings, which help to keep down noise levels.

Other dining options. Note that some of these cost extra.

The Garden Room Restaurant: this venue has 268 seats.

Raffles Terrace Café: a large self-serve buffet restaurant with indoor/outdoor seating for 400 and pseudo-Raffles Hotel-like decor, with rattan chairs, overhead fans, etc.

Moderno Churrascaria: installed in a 2011 refit, this Brazilian steakhouse has passadors who serve skewered meats tableside. Reservations are required, and there's a cover charge.

Taipan: a Chinese Restaurant, with traditional Hong Kong-themed decor and items such as dim sum made from fresh, not frozen, ingredients. Cover charge, reservations needed.

Shogun Asian Restaurant: a Japanese restaurant and sushi bar, for sashimi, sushi, and tempura. A section can be closed off to make the Samurai Room, with 22 seats, while a traditional Tatami Room has seats for eight. There's also a teppanyaki grill, with 10 seats, where the chef cooks in front of you and displays his knife-juggling skills.

Maxim's: a small à-la-carte restaurant with ocean-view windows; fine cuisine in the classic French style. Cover charge applicable, reservations necessary.

Blue Lagoon Café: a small, casual street café with about 24 seats, featuring noodle dishes, fried rice, and other Southeast Asian cuisine. Adjacent is a street bar called The Bund.

In addition, The Café, in the atrium lobby, is a pâtisserie serving several types of coffees, teas, cakes, and pastries, at extra cost.

ENTERTAINMENT. The Moulin Rouge Show-lounge, with 973 seats, is the main venue. It is two decks high, with a main and balcony levels. The room has almost no support columns to obstruct the sight lines, and a revolving stage for Broadway-style reviews and other production shows – typically to recorded music since there's little space for an orchestra. The showlounge is also used as a large-screen cinema, and has excellent surround sound.

SPA/FITNESS. The Roman Spa and Fitness Center is on one of the uppermost decks, just forward of the Tivoli Pool. It has a gymnasium full of high-tech muscle-toning equipment, and aerobics exercise room, hair and beauty salon, and saunas, steam rooms, and changing rooms for men and women, as well as several treatment rooms, and aqua-swim pools that provide counter-flow jets (swimming against the current). The spa facility is operated by the Hawaii-based Mandara Spa, owned by Steiner Leisure.

The fitness and exercise rooms, with the latest Cybex muscle-pumping equipment, are located not within the spa, but at the top of the glass-domed atrium lobby. Included is a room for exercycle classes. Sports facilities include a jogging track, golf driving range, basketball and tennis courts, and there are four levels of sunbathing decks.

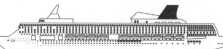

Norwegian Star
★★★+

Size:	Large Resort Ship	Passenger Space Ratio (lower beds):	39
Tonnage:	91,740	Passenger/Crew Ratio (lower beds):	2.1
Lifestyle:	Standard	Cabins (total):	1,174
Cruise Line:	Norwegian Cruise Line	Size Range (sq ft/m):	142.0–5,350.0/13.2–497.0
Former Names:	none	Cabins (for one person):	0
IMO Number:	9195157	Cabins (with private balcony):	
Builder:	Meyer Werft (Germany)	Cabins (wheelchair accessible):	20
Original Cost:	$400 million	Wheelchair accessibility:	Best
Entered Service:	Dec 2001	Cabin Current:	110 volts
Registry:	Panama	Elevators:	12
Length (ft/m):	964.9/294.1	Casino (gaming tables):	Yes
Beam (ft/m):	105.6/32.2	Slot Machines:	Yes
Draft (ft/m):	26.9/8.2	Swimming Pools:	3
Propulsion/Propellers:	diesel-electric (39,000kW)/	Hot Tubs (on deck):	5
	2 azimuthing pods	Self-Service Launderette:	No
Passenger Decks:	12	Dedicated Cinema/Seats:	Yes/151
Total Crew:	1,083	Library:	Yes
Passengers (lower beds):	2,348	Onboard currency:	US$

A fine family-friendly, multi-choice ship for active types

OVERVIEW. Many more choices, including lots of dining options, add up to a very attractive package, particularly suitable for families with children, in a very contemporary floating leisure center that really does provide ample facilities for enjoyment.

THE SHIP. *Norwegian Star*, a sister ship to *Norwegian Dawn*, has a pod propulsion system. A large structure located forward of the funnel houses a children's play center, and, one deck above, the two outstanding 'villa' suites. The hull is adorned with a decal consisting of a burst of colorful stars and streamers.

There are plenty of sunloungers. Water slides are included for the adult swimming pools, while children have their own pools at the ship's stern.

Facilities include an Internet café, a showlounge with main floor and two balcony levels, 3,000-book library, card room, writing and study room, business center, karaoke lounge, conference and meeting rooms, a large retail shopping complex, and a casino. With so many dining choices, some cost extra. The dress code is very casual – no jacket and tie needed, although you are welcome to dress formally if you wish. Although service levels and finesse are sometimes inconsistent, the level of hospitality is very good. But the hustling for passengers to attend art auctions is aggressive and annoying. Reaching room service tends to be an exercise in frustration.

A mandatory per person service charge is added to your account daily; 15 percent is also added for bar charges.

Berlitz's Ratings

	Possible	Achieved
Ship	500	376
Accommodation	200	145
Food	400	240
Service	400	272
Entertainment	100	67
Cruise Experience	400	273
OVERALL SCORE		
1373 points out of 2000		

FAMILIES. Children of all ages will get to play in a superb wet 'n' wild space-themed water park complete with large pool, water slide, and paddle pool. They also get their own dedicated cinema, in which movies are shown all day long, plus a jungle gym, painting area, and computer center. Even the toilets are at a special low height. Teens get their own cinema with movies, disco with dance floor, and whirlpool tub.

ACCOMMODATION. With many price grades, there is something for everyone. There are 36 suites, including two of the largest aboard any cruise ship, balcony-class standard cabins, outside-view cabins (no balcony), interior cabins, and 20 wheelchair-accessible cabins. Suites and cabins with private balconies have easy-to-use sliding glass doors.

All have a powerful hairdryer, and a tea- and coffee-making sets, rich cherry wood cabinetry, and a bathroom with a sliding door and a separate toilet, and shower enclosure and washbasin compartments. There is plenty of wood accenting in all accommodation, including wood frames surrounding balcony doors.

The largest accommodation is in two huge Garden Villas (Vista and Horizon), located high atop the ship in a pod that is located forward of the ship's funnel, and overlooks the main swimming pool. Each measures 5,350 sq ft (497 sq m) and can be combined to create a huge, double-size 'house.' These villas have huge glass walls and landscaped private roof gardens (one has a Japanese-style garden, the other a Thai-style garden) for outdoor dining (with whirlpool tubs, naturally), and huge private sunbathing areas that are completely shielded.

Each suite has three bedrooms, one with a sliding glass door that leads to the garden, and bathrooms. One bathroom has a large corner tub, and two washbasins set in front of large glass walls that overlook the side of the ship as well as the swimming pool, although most of the view is of the overlarge water slide, and a large living room with Yamaha baby grand piano, glass dining table, and eight chairs. These units have their own private elevator and private stairway.

There are many suites (the smallest measures 290 sq ft/27 sq m) in several different configurations. Some overlook the stern, while others are in the forward part of the ship. All are lavishly furnished, although closet space in some of the smaller units is tight.

Although the suites and junior suites are quite spacious, the standard interior and outside-view cabins are very small when compared to those of other major cruise lines such as Carnival or Celebrity, particularly when occupied by three or four people. The bathrooms, however, are of quite a decent size and have large shower enclosures. Some cabins have interconnecting doors – good for families with children – and many cabins have third- and fourth-person pull-down berths or trundle beds.

A small room service menu is available; all non-food items cost extra, and a 15 percent service charge are added to your account. Bottled water is placed in each cabin, but a charge is made if you open the bottle.

DINING. The ship offers 'Freestyle Dining,' which is all about choice. There are around 10 restaurants and casual dining venues to eat in, at what time, and with whom you wish. Some are at extra cost.

Versailles is a large (375-seat), ornate dining room, located aft and decorated in brilliant red and gold. It offers traditional six-course dining and has excellent views through windows that span two decks.

Aqua is a second large (374-seat), contemporary-styled dining room, offering lighter cuisine. It has an open galley, where you can view the preparation of pastries and desserts.

Cagney's Steakhouse: for (extra-cost, but well worth it) prime USDA steaks and grilled seafood items.

Moderno Churrascaria: a Brazilian-style steakhouse for meat and seafood dishes (adjacent is a Sugar Cane Mohito Bar).

Ginza Asian Restaurant: this includes a sit-up sushi bar (complete with moving sushi belt), à-la-carte Japanese Hot Rock Ishiyaki cuisine, the adjacent Teppanyaki Grill (for lots of show and go), and a Noodle bar for Chinese noodles, wok-fried dishes, and dim sum.

Le Bistro: a French restaurant, with 66 seats, serving nouvelle cuisine and six courses.

Market Café: a large indoor/outdoor self-serve buffet eatery, with almost 400ft (120m) of buffet counter space. 'Action Stations' has made-to-order omelets, waffles, fruit, soups, ethnic specialties, and pasta dishes. Outside on deck is Topsiders Grill, for burgers and hot dogs.

O'Sheehans Neighborhood Bar and Grill: for down-home comfort food and drinks.

La Cucina: for casual family-style Italian cuisine.

Other spots include the Red Lion, an English pub for draft beer and a game of darts; Havana Club cigar and cognac lounge; Atrium Café, a lobby bar-café for hot and frozen coffees, teas, and pastries; Bier Garten, a beer garden serving grilled foods; Spinkles, an ice cream bar; and Gatsby's wine bar.

ENTERTAINMENT. The Stardust Theater, seating 1,037, is the venue for colorful Las Vegas-style production shows and major cabaret acts. Two or three production shows are presented in a typical seven-day cruise, all ably performed by the Jean Ann Ryan Company. They're very entertaining if not particularly memorable.

A number of bands and solo entertainers provide live music for listening and dancing to in several lounges and bars.

SPA/FITNESS. The two-deck-high Barong health spa complex, operated by the Steiner-owned Mandara Spa, is at the stern, with large ocean-view windows on three sides. A gratuity of 18 percent is automatically added for spa and beauty treatments.

The many facilities and services, almost all cost extra, include Thai massage. There is an indoor lap pool measuring 37ft (11m), hydrotherapy pool, aromatherapy and wellness centers, 15 treatment rooms, and a juice bar.

The fitness and exercise rooms, with the latest equipment, are at the top of the atrium lobby. Recreational sports facilities include a jogging track, golf driving range, basketball and volleyball courts, as well as four levels of sunbathing decks.

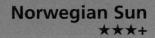

Size:	Mid-size Ship	
Tonnage:	78,309	
Lifestyle:	Standard	
Cruise Line:	Norwegian Cruise Line	
Former Names:	none	
IMO Number:	9218131	
Builder:	Lloyd Werft (Germany)	
Original Cost:	$332 million	
Entered Service:	Nov 2001	
Registry:	The Bahamas	
Length (ft/m):	853.0/260.0	
Beam (ft/m):	105.8/32.2	
Draft (ft/m):	26.2/8.0	
Propulsion/Propellers:	diesel-electric (50,000kW)/2	
Passenger Decks:	12	
Total Crew:	916	
Passengers (lower beds):	1,936	
Passenger Space Ratio (lower beds):	40.4	

Passenger/Crew Ratio (lower beds):	2.1
Cabins (total):	968
Size Range (sq ft/m):	120.5–488.6/11.2–45.4
Cabins (for one person):	0
Cabins (with private balcony):	252
Cabins (wheelchair accessible):	6
Wheelchair accessibility:	Good
Cabin Current:	110 volts
Elevators:	12
Casino (gaming tables):	Yes
Slot Machines:	Yes
Swimming Pools:	2
Hot Tubs (on deck):	5
Self-Service Launderette:	No
Dedicated Cinema/Seats:	No
Library:	Yes
Onboard currency:	US$

This is ultra-casual cruising in a family-friendly ship

OVERVIEW. What this offers is plenty of bars and lounges to play in, and multiple dining and snacking options. But the food in the large dining rooms is a weak point, and the ship is full of revenue centers, designed to help you part you from your money.

THE SHIP. *Norwegian Sun* is a close sister ship to *Norwegian Sky*, but with better finishing detail, an extra deck of balcony cabins, and additional cabins to accommodate the extra 200 crew needed for the Freestyle dining concept. The outdoor space is quite good, especially with its wide pool deck, with two swimming pools and four Jacuzzi tubs, and plenty of sunloungers, albeit arranged in camp-style rows.

A separate cabaret venue, Dazzles Lounge, has an extremely long bar. A large casino operates 24 hours a day. There's a shopping arcade, children's playroom, and a video arcade. Other facilities include a small conference room, library and beauty salon, a lounge for smoking cigars and drinking cognac, and an Internet café. You can expect to be subjected to a stream of flyers advertising daily art auctions, 'designer' watches, and other promotions, while 'artworks' for auction are strewn throughout the ship.

A mandatory per person service charge is added to your account daily; 15 percent is also added for bar charges, and a whopping 18 percent for spa treatments.

The standard interior and outside-view cabins are very small when compared to those of other major cruise lines.

Berlitz's Ratings

	Possible	Achieved
Ship	500	369
Accommodation	200	145
Food	400	240
Service	400	266
Entertainment	100	74
Cruise Experience	400	271
OVERALL SCORE		
1365 points out of 2000		

FAMILIES. Young passengers will find an array of facilities, which include a children's playroom called Kid's Corner for 'junior sailors' (ages 3–5); First Mates (6–9); Navigators (10–12); and Teens (13–17).

ACCOMMODATION. There are many, many different price categories, depending on size and location.

All standard outside-view and interior cabins have common facilities, such as two lower beds that can convert to a queen-size bed, a small lounge area with sofa and table, and a decent amount of closet and drawer space, although the cabins themselves are disappointingly small. Over 200 outside-view cabins have a private balcony. There are two Honeymoon/Anniversary Suites, each with a separate lounge and bedroom.

The largest accommodation? Two Owner's Suites, each with a hot tub, large teak table, two chairs and two sunloungers outside on a huge, private, forward-facing teak-floor balcony, located just under the navigation bridge, with floor-to-ceiling windows. There are a number of other suites, each with a private teakwood balcony. They share some facilities with the Owner's Suites, except for the outdoor hot tub and the fact that there's less space.

All cabins have tea-/coffee-making sets, a safe, satellite-linked telephone, and bathroom with bath or shower.

DINING. Freestyle Dining lets you choose which restaurant you would like to eat in, at what time, and with whom. Apart from two large dining rooms, there are a number of other themed eating establishments – although it would be wise to plan in advance, particularly for dinner. Some incur an extra charge. The dress code states that: 'jeans, T-shirts, tank tops and bare feet are not permitted in restaurants.'

The two main dining rooms – the 564-seat Four Seasons Dining Room and the 604-seat Seven Seas Dining Room – have tables for two, four, six, or eight. Sandwiched between the two (rather like a train carriage) is a third, 84-seat Italian Restaurant, Il Adagio, available as an à-la-carte (extra-charge, reservations-required) option, with window-side tables for two or four persons. Reservations are necessary.

Overall, the food is adequate, but lacks taste and presentation quality, although the menus make the dishes sound good. There's a reasonably decent selection of breads, rolls, cheeses, and fruits. The wine list is quite good and moderately priced, though the glasses are small.

Other dining options. Most are located on one of the uppermost decks, with great views from large picture windows, and include:

Le Bistro: a 90-seat dining spot for French-style meals, including tableside cooking. Reservations required.

Las Ramblas: a Spanish/Mexican style eatery serving tapas (light snack items).

Ginza: a Japanese Restaurant, with a sushi bar and a teppanyaki grill (show cooking in a U-shaped setting where you sit around the chef). Reservations required.

East Meets West: a Pacific Rim Fusion Restaurant, featuring à-la-carte California/Hawaii/Asian cuisine. Reservations are necessary for dinner.

Moderno Churrascaria: Brazilian steakhouse and salad bar, with tableside meat carving. Reservations required.

Garden Café: a busy 24-hour restaurant indoor/outdoor self-serve buffet-style eatery with fast foods and salads.

Although the menus make meals sound appetizing, overall the food is rather unmemorable, lacking taste, and mostly overcooked. However, the presentation is generally quite good. There is a reasonable selection of breads, rolls, and pastry items, but the selection of cheeses is very poor.

The wine list is well balanced, and there is also a connoisseur list of premium wines, although the vintages tend to be young. There are many types of beer (including some on draught in the popular Sports Bar & Grill).

There is no formal afternoon tea, although you can make your own at beverage stations (but it's difficult to get fresh milk, as non-dairy creamers are typically supplied). The service is, on the whole, adequate, nothing more.

A lavish chocoholics buffet is featured once each cruise – a firm favorite among Norwegian Cruise Line passengers.

ENTERTAINMENT. The Stardust Theater is a two-level showlounge with more than 1,000 seats and a large proscenium stage. However, the sight lines are obstructed in a number of seats by several slim pillars. Two or three production shows are presented in a typical seven-day cruise (all ably performed by the Jean Ann Ryan Company). These are very colorful, high-energy, high-volume razzle-dazzle shows with extensive use of pyrotechnics, lasers, and color-mover lighting.

The ship carries a number of bands and solo entertaining musicians. These provide live music for listening and dancing in several of the lounges and bars, including the loud Dazzles, home to musical groups.

SPA/FITNESS. Bodywaves, at the top of the atrium, is a large health/fitness spa (including an aerobics room and separate gymnasium), several treatment rooms, and men's and women's saunas/steam rooms and changing rooms.

There is an indoor-outdoor jogging track, a large basketball/volleyball court, baseball batting cage, golf driving range, platform tennis, shuffleboard and table tennis facilities, and sports bar with 24-hour live satellite TV coverage of sports events and major games.

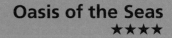

Oasis of the Seas
★★★★

Size:	Large Resort Ship
Tonnage:	222,900
Lifestyle:	Standard
Cruise Line:	Royal Caribbean International
Former Names:	none
IMO Number:	9383936
Builder:	Aker Yards (Finland)
Original Cost:	$1.5 billion
Entered Service:	Dec 2009
Registry:	The Bahamas
Length (ft/m):	1,181.1/360.0
Beam (ft/m):	216.5/66.0
Draft (ft/m):	30.0/9.1
Propulsion/Propellers:	diesel-electric (97,200kWW)/3 pods (2 azimuthing, 1 fixed)
Passenger Decks:	16
Total Crew:	2,164
Passengers (lower beds):	5,408

Passenger Space Ratio (lower beds):	41.6
Passenger/Crew Ratio (lower beds):	2.4
Cabins (total):	2,704
Size Range (sq ft/m):	150.6–1,523.1/14.0–141.5
Cabins (for one person):	0
Cabins (with private balcony):	1,956
Cabins (wheelchair accessible):	46
Wheelchair accessibility:	Good
Cabin Current:	110 volts
Elevators:	24
Casino (gaming tables):	Yes
Slot Machines:	Yes
Swimming Pools:	3
Hot Tubs (on deck):	10
Self-Service Launderette:	No
Dedicated Cinema/Seats:	No
Library:	Yes
Onboard currency:	US$

This huge floating resort is for families with boundless energy

OVERVIEW. The super-large *Oasis of the Seas* provides a fine all-round cruise and a wide range of choices for young adults and families with children. It's packed with innovative design elements, including a dramatic Central Park, a real park at sea. As might be expected, service is best in suite-class accommodation.

THE SHIP. *Oasis of the Seas*, the world's first cruise ship measuring over 200,000 tons – essentially a large block of apartments sitting on a white hull – is a benchmark for all floating self-contained resorts. It is no longer the world's largest cruise ship – at time of printing, its sister, *Allure of the Seas*, was almost 2ins (5cm) longer, and, in 2016, *Harmony of the Seas* will be even longer (the new 'largest cruise ship in the world'). However, the ships are almost identical.

It is a stunning ship and a credit to Royal Caribbean International's design team. There is a lot of outdoor and indoor/outdoor space for aqua-bathing and sports, although there's little actual space for sunbathing. There are several swimming pools, and an H2O Zone. Two large hot tubs hang over the ship's side.

Public spaces are arranged as seven 'neighborhoods': Central Park, the Boardwalk, the Royal Promenade, the Pool and Sports Zone, Vitality at Sea Spa/Fitness Center, Entertainment Place, and Youth Zone. The most popular are the Boardwalk and Central Park, both open to the air, and the indoor Royal Promenade.

The Boardwalk. With a design reminiscent of New York's Coney Island, the Boardwalk is home to trendy shops and an art gallery.

Berlitz's Ratings		
	Possible	Achieved
Ship	500	408
Accommodation	200	147
Food	400	236
Service	400	290
Entertainment	100	87
Cruise Experience	400	296
OVERALL SCORE		
1464 points out of 2000		

Eateries include the Boardwalk Donut Shop; Johnny Rockets, a burger/milk shake diner with jukeboxes; and a covered Seafood Shack for fish and seafood. **Central Park.** This space is 328ft (100m) long, and has 27 real trees and almost 12,000 plants, including a vertical 'living' plant wall. But, unlike its New York inspiration, it includes, at its lower level, a 'town center'. At night, it's a quiet, serene area – good for couples. Vintages wine (and tapas) bar is a good chill-out place, and there are several reservations-required, extra-charge dining venues; arguably the nicest is 150 Central Park, while Chops Grille and Giovanni's Table are also popular. If you are in a Central Park cabin, you'll need to take the elevator to get to the closest pool.

Central Park and the Boardwalk are open to the elements, so you might consider taking an umbrella, just in case it rains in the sunny Caribbean!

Royal Promenade. This is like a floating shopping mall, with casual food eateries (including a Starbucks at the forward end), shops with all kinds of merchandise, video screens, and changing color lights everywhere. Don't miss the 'Move On! Move On!' parade, a superb circus-like extravaganza including characters from DreamWorks' *Madagascar*. A hydraulic, oval-shaped Rising Tide Bar moves slowly through three floors and links the double-width Royal Promenade with Central Park.

The Pool and Sports Zone. Forward of the twin funnels is this fun area for families. An adults-only open-air solarium and rentable cabanas are part of the outdoor scene today (there are several). Two FlowRiders are located atop the ship around the aft exhaust mast, as are basketball courts and mini-golf. The ship also has a really long jogging track.

The Solarium. This is a most welcoming large, light-filled, and restful (despite the background music) space. High up, it is frequented by few children – so adults can 'escape' the Las Vegas-like atmosphere of much of the ship. In the casino, the roulette tables are all electronic and touch-buttony. There are also blackjack, craps, Caribbean Stud Poker, and 450 slot machines, plus a player's club and poker room – but this really can be a smoke-filled place, even in the 'no-smoking' area.

The Caribbean itinerary includes a 'private' beach day at Labadee, the company's leased island. RCI built its own 800ft (244m) pier, making it simple for you to access the ship and beach several times during the day-long stay. Do try the zipline – it's long, and a real blast. Other fun things: an alpine coaster, a beach club with 20 private cabanas, a large artisans' market, and a Haitian Cultural Center.

Passenger Niggles. Finding a sunlounger (they're so tightly packed together that there's little space to put one's belongings). Exterior wooden railings have mostly been replaced by fiberglass railings – particularly noticeable on the balconies.

Oasis of the Seas operates from a purpose-built $75 million Terminal 18 in Port Everglades (Fort Lauderdale), where the restroom facilities are minimal. Getting to the terminal can prove frustrating on embarkation day.

Disembarkation. If the two 'flybridge' gangways are working, disembarkation is relatively speedy, but, when only one is working, a line forms in the Royal Promenade, in which case it's better to sit somewhere until the line gets shorter. Disembarkation for non-US citizens can be appallingly slow.

ACCOMMODATION. There are numerous accommodation price grades, reflecting the choice of location and size. Suite occupants get access to a concierge lounge and associated services. There are many family-friendly cabins, good for family reunions, but no single-occupancy cabins. The cabin numbering system is awkward to get used to. Note that cabin doors open outwards (towards you), as in many European hotels. In many of the lower grade accommodation, closet access is awkward – often with small sofas in the way. Most cabins feel extremely small, given the size of the ship. All feature an iPod dock.

Some interior balcony cabins have either Central Park or Royal Promenade views from their curved interior balconies (four are wheelchair-accessible), plus 80 cabins with windows (no balconies) and Central Park views. But you'll need to keep your curtains closed for privacy, which rather defeats the object. Noise could be generated along the inner prom-

enades, particularly late at night with street parades and non-stop music.

Loft Suites. Although a few ships such as the now-withdrawn QE2, *Saga Rose,* and *Saga Ruby* had upstairs/downstairs suites, RCI introduced its version ('loft' suites) to the *Oasis*-class ships. These offer great views, with floor-to-ceiling, double-height windows, a lower living area plus a large balcony with sun chairs, and a stairway that connects to the sleeping area, which overlooks the living area.

There are 28 Loft Suites; 25 Crown Loft Suites measure 545 sq ft (51 sq m); three more spacious Royal Loft Suites measure 1,524 sq ft (141 sq m). Each sleeps up to six and has a baby grand piano, indoor and outdoor dining areas, a wet bar,, and an 843-sq-ft (78.3-sq-m) balcony with flat-screen TV, and Jacuzzi. Two large Sky Loft Suites measure 722 sq ft (67 sq m) and 770 sq ft (71 sq m), and a 737-sq-ft (68-sq-m) Crown Accessible Loft Suite includes an elevator to aid disabled passengers.

Standard cabins (balcony and non-balcony class). Electrical sockets are located below the vanity desk unit in a user-unfriendly position. Also, it's difficult to watch television from the bed.

Washbasins in non-suite-grade cabins are tiny and low, at just 30.5ins (77.5cm) above floor level. Be careful – it's easy to hit your head on the mirror above. Small soap bars are provided, with shampoo provided in a dispenser in the shower enclosure. The shower head is fixed. Although there is no soap dish or indentation in the washbasin surround for soap, useful touches include a blue ceiling bathroom nightlight.

Cabins are exposed to noise and whatever is happening on the Boardwalk, including rehearsals and sports activities in the Aqua Theater aft, bells from the carousel (whose animal figures took six weeks to carve), rowdy revelers late at night, plus screaming ziplining participants high above during the day, loud music from bands playing at one of the pools, and exceedingly loud announcements by the cruise director repeating what's already printed in the daily program.

Boardwalk-view balcony cabin occupants need to close their curtains for privacy at times. However, the curved balconies – good for storing luggage to free up space inside the cabin – connect you with the open air and provide a community feeling, as you look across at balconies on the opposite side. Almost all have a sea view aft (just); those close to the aft Aqua Theater can use their balconies for a great view of any shows or events. Boardwalk-level cabins have windows but no balcony – and actually the view is mainly of the top of things such as the carousel or beach hut-like structures. The best Boardwalk balcony cabins are, in my view, located above on Decks 8–12, but, for more privacy, book a sea-facing balcony cabin, not one overlooking the Boardwalk.

DINING. Spanning three decks, Opus (formerly the main dining room) was split into three different venues when 'Dynamic Dining' (eat when you want within restaurant hours) was introduced in 2015. Each venue has its own menus: American Icon Grill, Silk (for Asian fusion cuisine), and The Grande (for a more formal dining and dressy experience). There are tables of all sizes, including some for family reunions.

The menu descriptions make the food sound better than it is, and the selection of breads, rolls, fruit, and cheese is poor. Overall, meals are rather hit and miss – in fact it's unmemorable. Also, if you want lobster or a decent filet mignon (steak) you will be asked to pay extra.

Other dining options. Note that some of these are at extra cost.

150 Central Park: the most exclusive restaurant combines cutting-edge cuisine with interesting design. An observation window into the kitchen allows passers-by to watch the chefs in action, preparing the multi-course tasting menu (open for dinner only).

Chef's Table, on the upper level of the Concierge Lounge, offers a six-course meal with wine. It is hosted by the executive chef, but, with just 14 seats, trying to get a reservation is difficult.

Giovanni's Table is a casual Italian dining spot with a rustic feel. It features toasted herb breads, pizzas, salads, pastas, sandwiches, braised meat dishes, and stews.

Izumi Hibachi & Sushi features Japanese-style cuisine, including a Teppanyaki menu (a show grill featuring cooks with acrobatic knives).

Sabor Taqueria & Tequila Bar, for modern tastes of Mexico, while Wonderland Imaginative Cuisine features imaginative fare.

Vintage is a wine bar with a robust selection of wines, accompanied by cheese and tapas (with an à-la-carte item charge).

Central Park Café, a casual dining spot with a high level of variety and flexibility, is an indoor/outdoor food market with line-up counters and limited waiter service. Items include freshly prepared salads, made-to-order sandwiches, panini, crêpes, and hearty soups.

Other Boardwalk spots for snacking include: Boardwalk Dog House (for hot dogs, wieners, bratwurst, and sausages), the Donut Shop, and Ice Cream Shoppe.

Elsewhere, eateries include Sorrento's Pizzeria; Park Café (for salads and light bites); and Wipe Out Café.

For the sweet toothed, there's a 1940s-style Cupcake Shop (so if you're thinking of getting married, you could have a cupcake wedding cake). For lighter, more health-conscious fare, there's a self-serve section in the Solarium Bistro for breakfast and lunch – it's usually quieter, too.

The Windjammer Café is the (free) casual, self-serve eatery common to all RCI ships. No trays are provided – just oval plates; because they're plastic, it's impossible to get a hot plate. If you are disabled or have mobility difficulties, do ask for help. Unfortunately the venue is simply too small to handle the number of diners invading it at peak times – my advice is to try some of the other eateries to avoid the overcrowding. The food varies from quite acceptable to less than acceptable – fresh fruit tends to be hard and unripe. It's best to arrive early, when food has just been cooked and displayed. Although there's a decent enough variety, the quality of some of the meat is poor and overcooked.

Regular coffee is available free in many venues, but espresso and cappuccino (in paper cups) in Starbucks costs extra.

The longest waiting lines are usually for Johnny Rockets and Rita's Cantina. Check with RCI's website or your travel provider for the latest cover charges.

ENTERTAINMENT. The 1,380-seat main show-lounge (Opal Theater), spread over three decks, stages the popular musical Cats, an excellent, 90-minute-long production, just like a Broadway show, while Frozen in Time is a stunning, must-see ice show at the ice-skating rink.

The 750-seat Aqua Theater, located outside at the ship's stern with a 6,000-sq-ft (560-sq-m) stage, is a stunning combination show theatre, sound stage, and events space (some great viewing places can be found high in the aft wings of the ship on both sides). The ship's stern has some 'overhang,' to accommodate the venue. A DreamWorks Animation aquatic acrobatic and dive show is also presented.

SPA/FITNESS. The Vitality at Sea Spa includes a Vitality Café for extra-cost health drinks and snacks. Its fitness center includes 158 cardio and resistance machines, while an extra-cost thermal suite includes saunas, steam rooms, and heated tiled loungers. You can't just take a sauna for 10 minutes without paying for a one-day pass.

Oceana
★★★+

Size:	Mid-size Ship
Tonnage:	77,499
Lifestyle:	Standard
Cruise Line:	P&O Cruises
Former Names:	Ocean Princess
IMO Number:	9169550
Builder:	Fincantieri (Italy)
Original Cost:	$300 million
Entered Service:	Feb 2000/Nov 2002
Registry:	Bermuda
Length (ft/m):	857.2/261.3
Beam (ft/m):	105.6/32.2
Draft (ft/m):	25.9/7.9
Propulsion/Propellers:	diesel-electric (28,000kW)/2
Passenger Decks:	10
Total Crew:	850
Passengers (lower beds):	1,950
Passenger Space Ratio (lower beds):	39.7

Passenger/Crew Ratio (lower beds):	2.2
Cabins (total):	975
Size Range (sq ft/m):	158.2–610.3/14.7–56.7
Cabins (for one person):	0
Cabins (with private balcony):	410
Cabins (wheelchair accessible):	19
Wheelchair accessibility:	Good
Cabin Current:	110 and 220 volts
Elevators:	11
Casino (gaming tables):	Yes
Slot Machines:	Yes
Swimming Pools:	4
Hot Tubs (on deck):	5
Self-Service Launderette:	Yes
Dedicated Cinema/Seats:	No
Library:	Yes
Onboard currency:	UK£

For family-friendly cruising in a comfortable environment

OVERVIEW. This ship is all about British-ness and will be comfortingly familiar for families with children who want to travel and take their British traditions and food with them. It is suited to adults of all ages and families with children of all ages, and offers excellent value for money to first-time cruisers.

THE SHIP. The all-white *Oceana* has a pleasing profile and is well balanced by its large funnel, which contains a deck tennis/basketball/volleyball court in its sheltered aft base. There is 93,000 sq ft (8,600 sq m) of open deck space and a wide, teakwood walkaround promenade deck outdoors. A great amount of glass area on the upper decks provides plenty of light and connection with the outside world. The ship underwent a few changes to make it more user-friendly for British passengers, although it does look quite tired in places.

There is a wide range of public rooms, with several intimate rooms and spaces, so that you don't feel overwhelmed by large spaces. The interior focal point is a four-deck-high atrium lobby with winding, double stairways and two panoramic glass-walled lifts.

The artwork is pleasant, particularly on the stairways, and helps make the ship feel smaller than it really is. The Monte Carlo Club Casino, while large, is not in the main passenger flow and therefore does not generate the walk-through factor found aboard so many ships. The most traditional room is the Yacht and Compass Bar, decorated in the style of a turn-of-the-century gentleman's club, with wood paneling and comfortable seating.

A traditional Captain's cocktail party is held in the four-deck-high main atrium, so you can come and go as you please.

The swimming pools are really quite small and will be crowded when the ship is full; also the pool deck is cluttered with white plastic chairs, which don't have cushioned pads. The rule about not leaving sunloungers unattended for more than half an hour is flouted by many passengers keen to keep their favored position.

While the ship's interior space is a non-smoking environment, smoking is permitted on cabin balconies and in designated spots on the open decks.

In the quest for increased onboard revenue, even birthday cakes are an extra-cost item, as are espressos and cappuccinos (fake ones, made from instant coffee, are available in the dining rooms), ice-cream and bottled water – items that can add up to a considerable amount. Expect to be subjected to flyers advertising daily art auctions, 'designer' watches, and other promotions. Gratuities are automatically charged to your onboard account.

FAMILIES. For children, there's the Treasure Chest (ages 2–5), The Hideout (ages 6–9), and, for older children (10–13), The Buzz Zone. P&O Cruises provides plenty of staff to look after the children, and many activities to keep them occupied. A night nursery is available 6pm–2am, with a per-child charge af-

Berlitz's Ratings

	Possible	Achieved
Ship	500	370
Accommodation	200	148
Food	400	245
Service	400	278
Entertainment	100	71
Cruise Experience	400	272
OVERALL SCORE		
1384 points out of 2000		

ter midnight. While many children don't like organized clubs, they will probably find they make new friends quickly during a cruise.

ACCOMMODATION. There are several different cabin grades, designated as: suites with private balcony, mini-suites with private balcony, outside-view twin-bedded cabin with balcony, outside-view twin bedded cabin, and interior twin-bedded cabins. Although the standard outside-view and interior cabins are a little small, they are well designed and functional in layout, and have earth tone colors accentuated by splashes of color from the bedspreads.

Many of the outside-view cabins have private balconies, and all have good soundproofing, although the balcony partition is not of the floor-to-ceiling type, so you can hear your neighbors clearly. Balconies are very narrow – just large enough for two small chairs – and there is no lighting. Many cabins have third- and fourth-person upper bunk beds – good for families with children, and all cabins have useful tea- and coffee-making facilities.

There is a reasonable amount of closet and abundant drawer and other storage space in all cabins; although this is adequate for a seven-night cruise, it could prove to be quite tight for longer. A refrigerator is also provided, and each night a chocolate will appear on your pillow. The cabin bathrooms are small but practical. Fortunately, the shower enclosure is a decent size, and there's a small amount of shelving for your toiletries, real glasses, and a hairdryer.

Also standard in all cabins: Slumberland 8ins (20cm) sprung mattresses, 10.5 tog duvets (blankets and pillows, if you prefer), Egyptian cotton towels, and tea/coffee-making facilities with specialty teas (long-life milk is provided).

Suites. The largest accommodation is in six suites, two on each of three decks at the aft of the ship, with a private balcony giving great views over the stern. Each of these suites – Orcades, Orion, Orissa, Orontes, Oronsay, and Orsova (all P&O ships of yesteryear) has a large balcony. Marble-clad bathrooms have two washbasins, a Jacuzzi tub, and a separate shower enclosure. The bedroom has wood accenting and detailing, indented ceilings, and TV sets in both bedroom and lounge areas, which also have a dining room table and four chairs.

DINING. There are two principal asymmetrically designed dining rooms, Adriatic and Ligurian, each seating about 500, located just off the two lower levels of the four-deck-high atrium lobby. One has open seating, and the other has two seatings. Each has its own galley, and is split into multi-tier sections, which help create a feeling of intimacy, although there is much noise from waiter stations adjacent to many tables. Open-seating breakfast and lunch are provided, while dinner is in two seatings.

The cuisine is decidedly British – sometimes adventurous, but always with plenty of curry dishes and other standard British comfort food dishes. Don't expect exquisite dining – this is unpretentious British hotel catering that is attractive and tasty, with some excellent gravies and sauces to accompany meals, and desserts that are always decent. The wine list is quite reasonable. A statement in the onboard cruise folder states that P&O Cruises does not knowingly purchase genetically modified foods, though it makes no mention of all those commercial American cereals provided.

The Plaza, a self-serve buffet, is located above the navigation bridge, with some commanding views. At night, this venue (with two food lines) is transformed into an informal dinner setting with sit-down waiter service. Do try the (extra-cost) Tasting Menu – a selection of small cosmopolitan dishes, with three different menus per cruise.

Outdoors on deck, the Horizon Grill has fast-food items for those who want to stay in their sunbathing attire.

For other informal eats, there is Café Jardin, with a Frankie's Bar & Grill-style menu serving Italian-inspired dishes; it is on the uppermost level of the four-deck-high atrium lobby.

Explorer's serves for cappuccinos, espressos, and pastries, and Magnums is a Champagne/caviar bar.

ENTERTAINMENT. There are two showlounges – Footlights Theatre, and Starlights – one forward, and one aft. Footlights is a superb 550-seat, theater-style showlounge, for production shows and theater events; movies can also be shown here. Starlights is a 480-seat cabaret-style lounge with bar.

There's a big emphasis on a decent quality of entertainment. There's a resident group of actors, singers, and dancers, who provide theater-style presentations including cut-down versions of well-known musicals. In addition, the ship features an array of cabaret acts, who regularly travel the cruise ship circuit. Classical concerts are scheduled for many cruises.

SPA/FITNESS. The Ocean Spa facilities are contained in a glass-walled complex on one of the highest decks aft and include a gymnasium, with high-tech muscle-pumping equipment, a combination aerobics/exercise class room, sauna, steam room, and several treatment rooms.

The spa is operated by Harding Brothers, a UK concession that provides the staff and range of beauty and wellness treatments.

One swimming pool is 'suspended' aft between two decks – it forms part of the spa complex. Two other (small) pools are located in the ship's center. Sports facilities include basketball, volleyball, badminton, and paddle tennis. Joggers can exercise on a walk-around open promenade deck. There's an electronic golf simulator – no need to bring your own clubs.

Ocean Diamond
★★★

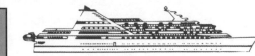

Size:	Boutique Ship	Passenger/Crew Ratio (lower beds):	1.4
Tonnage:	8,282	Cabins (total):	113
Lifestyle:	Standard	Size Range (sq ft/m):	183.0–398.0/17.0–37.0
Cruise Line:	Quark Expeditions	Cabins (for one person):	19
Former Names:	*Le Diamant, Song of Flower, Explorer Starship*	Cabins (with private balcony):	10
IMO Number:	7325629	Cabins (wheelchair accessible):	0
Builder:	KMV (Norway)	Wheelchair accessibility:	None
Original Cost:	n/a	Cabin Current:	220 volts
Entered Service:	1986/2012	Elevators:	2
Registry:	Wallis and Fortuna	Casino (gaming tables):	Yes
Length (ft/m):	407.4/124.2	Slot Machines:	Yes
Beam (ft/m):	52.4/16.0	Swimming Pools:	1
Draft (ft/m):	16.0/4.9	Hot Tubs (on deck):	1
Propulsion/Propellers:	diesel (5,500kW)/2 (CP)	Self-Service Launderette:	No
Passenger Decks:	6	Dedicated Cinema/Seats:	No
Total Crew:	144	Library:	Yes
Passengers (lower beds):	207	Onboard currency:	US$
Passenger Space Ratio (lower beds):	40		

'Soft' discovery cruising aboard a small, outdated ship

OVERVIEW. *Ocean Diamond* is for discovery-minded participants who enjoy a comfortable travel environment. It will provide a good base for learning and 'soft' expedition cruises, and there's a fairly decent amount of sheltered open-deck space.

THE SHIP. *Ocean Diamond* was originally built as the ro-ro vessel *Begonia* in 1974 and converted for cruising in 1986. Operated for many years by Radisson Seven Seas Cruises (now Regent Seven Seas Cruises), the ship was acquired in 2011 by Miami-based ISP (International Shipping Partners), who chartered it to Quark Expeditions. It was modified to operate 'soft' expedition cruises and has tall twin funnels (with a platform between them) that give a somewhat squat profile. If only the foredeck and bow could be a little longer, the ship would look less ungainly.

The interior decor is warm, with pastel colors accented by splashes of color. Good-quality soft furnishings and fabrics make the ship feel chic and comfortable. The crew is caring and tries hard to

Berlitz's Ratings	Possible	Achieved
Ship	500	271
Accommodation	200	121
Food	400	230
Service	400	230
Entertainment	100	56
Cruise Experience	400	337
OVERALL SCORE		
1141 points out of 2000		

make you feel at home during your cruise adventure.

ACCOMMODATION. There are 10 comfortable suites. All other accommodation grades are nicely equipped, but dated. However, all come with a good amount of closet and drawer space. Some cabins have bathtubs, but they are tiny – deep shower tubs would be a better description.

DINING. The dining room is quite charming and has warm colors, a welcoming ambience, and one seating, with no assigned tables. Tables are for two to six (some are subject to vibration at times).

ENTERTAINMENT. The well-tiered main lounge is ideal as a comfortable lecture hall, and there are good sight lines from almost all the banquette-style seats.

SPA/FITNESS. The health spa facility is compact and short on space, but is adequate, and includes a beauty salon and sauna.

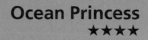

Ocean Princess
★★★★

Size:	Small Ship	Passenger/Crew Ratio (lower beds):	1.8
Tonnage:	30,277	Cabins (total):	344
Lifestyle:	Standard	Size Range (sq ft/m):	145.3–968.7/13.5–90.0
Cruise Line:	Princess Cruises	Cabins (for one person):	0
Former Names:	*Tahitian Princess, R Four*	Cabins (with private balcony):	232
IMO Number:	9187899	Cabins (wheelchair accessible):	3
Builder:	Chantiers de l'Atlantique (France)	Wheelchair accessibility:	Good
Original Cost:	$150 million	Cabin Current:	110 and 220 volts
Entered Service:	Nov 1999/Dec 2002	Elevators:	4
Registry:	Bermuda	Casino (gaming tables):	Yes
Length (ft/m):	593.7/181.0	Slot Machines:	Yes
Beam (ft/m):	83.5/25.5	Swimming Pools:	1
Draft (ft/m):	19.5/6.0	Hot Tubs (on deck):	3
Propulsion/Propellers:	diesel-electric (18,600kW)/2	Self-Service Launderette:	Yes
Passenger Decks:	9	Dedicated Cinema/Seats:	No
Total Crew:	373	Library:	Yes
Passengers (lower beds):	688	Onboard currency:	US$
Passenger Space Ratio (lower beds):	44.1		

This informal smaller ship is for mature-age cruisers

OVERVIEW. This ship is perhaps best suited to mature-age couples, and older singles who like to mingle in a small ship setting with pleasing, sophisticated surroundings and lifestyle, and are happy with reasonably good entertainment, and fairly decent food and service, all at an affordable price.

Note that this ship will be withdrawn from the fleet in March 2016; it will be extensively refurbished and then join the Oceania Cruises fleet as *Sirena* in late April 2016.

THE SHIP. *Ocean Princess* (known as *Tahitian Princess* until 2009) and sister ship *Pacific Princess* are an ideal size for smaller ports. The value for money is extremely good, and gives you a chance to cruise in comfort aboard a small ship with some interesting dining choices. There's very little entertainment, but it is not really needed in its main cruise areas such as Europe and Australasia. *Ocean Princess* is much more about relaxation than the larger ships in the Princess Cruises fleet.

The interior decor is stunning and elegant, a throwback to ship decor of the ocean liners of the 1920s and '30s. This includes detailed ceiling cornices, both real and faux wrought-iron staircase railings, leather- and cherry wood-paneled walls, trompe l'oeil ceilings, rich carpeting in hallways with an Oriental rug-look center section, and many other interesting and expensive-looking decorative touches. The overall feel is of an old-world country club. The staircase in the main, two-deck-high foyer

Berlitz's Ratings		
	Possible	Achieved
Ship	500	378
Accommodation	200	150
Food	400	252
Service	400	286
Entertainment	100	71
Cruise Experience	400	285
OVERALL SCORE		
1422 points out of 2000		

may remind you of the one in the movie *Titanic*.

The public rooms are spread over three decks. The reception hall has a staircase with intricate wrought-iron railings. The Nightclub, with forward-facing views, sits high in the ship and has Polynesian-inspired decor and furniture.

There are plenty of bars – including one in the entrance to each restaurant. Perhaps the nicest can be found in the casino bar/lounge, a beautiful room reminiscent of London's grand hotels and understated gaming clubs. It has an inviting marble fireplace, comfortable sofas, and individual chairs. There is also a large card room, which incorporates an Internet center, with eight stations.

The Library, a grand room designed in the Regency style by the Scottish interior designer John McNeece, has a fireplace, a high, indented trompe l'oeil ceiling, and an excellent selection of books, plus some comfortable wingback chairs with footstools, and sofas you can easily fall asleep on – it's the most relaxing room aboard.

There is no walk-around promenade deck outdoors, though there's a small jogging track around the perimeter of the swimming pool, and port and starboard side decks. There are no wooden decks outdoors; instead, they are covered by a sand-colored rubberized material. There is no sauna. Stairways, although carpeted, are tinny. To keep prices low, the air routing to get to and from your ship is often not the most direct. There is a charge for using machines in the self-service launderette, and you have to obtain tokens from the reception desk – a change machine in the launderette itself would be better.

Drinks prices are generally moderate, while beer prices are high. As with all Princess Cruises ships, 15 percent is added to bar and spa accounts, and a standard gratuity is added to your onboard account. To reduce the amount, you must visit the reception desk.

ACCOMMODATION. There are several different cabin types. All of the standard interior and outside-view cabins are extremely tight for two persons, particularly for cruises longer than seven days. Cabins have twin beds (convertible to a queen-size one), with good under-bed storage areas, personal safe, vanity desk with large mirror, good closet and drawer space in rich, dark woods, and a bathrobe. The infotainment television system carries a variety of programming, news, sports, and round-the-clock movies. The bathrooms, which have tiled floors and plain walls, are compact, standard units, and include a shower enclosure with a removable, strong handheld shower unit, hairdryer, cotton towels, toiletries storage shelves, and a retractable clothesline.

The suites/cabins with private balconies (66 percent of all suites/cabins, or 73 percent of all outside-view suites/cabins) have partial, and not full, balcony partitions, and sliding glass doors. Due to good design and layout, only 14 cabins on Deck 6 have lifeboat-obstructed views. The balcony floor is covered in thick plastic matting – teak would be nicer – and there's some awful plastic furniture.

Mini-Suites. These are in reality simply larger cabins than the standard varieties, as the sleeping and lounge areas aren't divided. While not overly large, the bathrooms have a good-size tub and ample space for storing toiletries. The living area has a refrigerated minibar, lounge area with breakfast table, and a balcony with two plastic chairs and a table.

Owner's Suites. Ten Owner's Suites, the most spacious accommodation, are fine, large living spaces in the forward-most and aft-most sections; particularly nice are those that overlook the stern, on Decks 6, 7, and 8. They have more extensive balconies that can't be overlooked by anyone from the decks above. There is an entrance foyer, living room, bedroom, CD player, bathroom with Jacuzzi tub, as well as a small guest bathroom. The bed faces the sea, which can be seen through the floor-to-ceiling windows and sliding glass door.

Be aware that all accommodation at the stern may suffer from vibration and noise, particularly when the ship is close to full speed, or maneuvering in port.

DINING. Flexibility and choice are what this mid-size ship's dining facilities are all about. There is a choice of four different dining spots, including a self-serve buffet:

The Club Restaurant has 338 seats (all with armrests), and a large raised central section. There are large windows on three sides, several prime tables overlooking the stern, and a small bandstand for occasional live dinner music. The noise level can be high, due to its single deck height ceiling. This restaurant is operated in two seatings, with dinner typically at 6pm and 8.15pm – the others have open dining hours.

Sabatini's Trattoria is an extra-charge, reservations-required Italian restaurant, with 96 seats (all with armrests), windows along two sides, and a set 'Bellissima' three-hour dégustation menu.

Sterling Steakhouse is an extra-charge, reservations-required American-style steak house with 98 seats (all with armrests), and windows along two sides. There's a set menu, plus the chef's daily specials. There are few tables for two.

The Lido Café has indoor and outdoor seating (white plastic patio furniture outdoor). It is open for breakfast, lunch, and casual dinners. As the ship's self-serve buffet restaurant, it incorporates a small pizzeria and grill. Basic salads, a meat-carving station, and a reasonable selection of cheeses are served daily. There is also a Poolside Grill and Bar for fast food items.

ENTERTAINMENT. The 345-seat Cabaret Lounge has a stage, and circular hardwood dance floor with banquette and individual tub chair seating, and raised sections on port and starboard sides. It is not large, and not really designed for production shows, so cabaret acts form the main focus, with mini-revue style shows presented by a troupe of resident singer/dancers in a potted version of what you might experience aboard the large ships of Princess Cruises.

A band, small musical units, and solo entertaining pianists provide live music for shows and dancing in the various lounges and bars before and after dinner.

SPA/FITNESS. A gymnasium has ocean-view windows, high-tech muscle-toning equipment and treadmills, steam rooms (no sauna), changing areas for men and women, and a beauty salon with ocean views. The spa is operated by Steiner, a specialist concession. A lido deck has a swimming pool, and good sunbathing space, while an aft deck has a thalassotherapy pool. A jogging track circles the pool deck, but one deck above. The uppermost outdoors deck includes a golf driving net and shuffleboard court.

Oosterdam
★★★★

Size:	Mid-sized Ship	Passenger Space Ratio (lower beds):	42.9
Tonnage:	82,305	Passenger/Crew Ratio (lower beds):	2.3
Lifestyle:	Premium	Cabins (total):	924
Cruise Line:	Holland America Line	Size Range (sq ft/m):	185.0–1,318.6/17.1–122.5
Former Names:	none	Cabins (for one person):	0
IMO Number:	9221281	Cabins (with private balcony):	623
Builder:	Fincantieri (Italy)	Cabins (wheelchair accessible):	28
Original Cost:	$400 million	Wheelchair accessibility:	Good
Entered Service:	Aug 2003	Cabin Current:	110 volts
Registry:	The Netherlands	Elevators:	14
Length (ft/m):	935.0/285.0	Casino (gaming tables):	Yes
Beam (ft/m):	105.6/32.2	Slot Machines:	Yes
Draft (ft/m):	25.5/7.8	Swimming Pools:	2 (1 w/sliding glass door)
Propulsion/Propellers:	diesel-electric (35,240kW)/	Hot Tubs (on deck):	5
	2 azimuthing pods	Self-Service Launderette:	No
Passenger Decks:	11	Dedicated Cinema/Seats:	Yes/170
Total Crew:	800	Library:	Yes
Passengers (lower beds):	1,918	Onboard currency:	US$

This is a contemporary, family-friendly ship with Dutch decor

OVERVIEW. *Oosterdam* offers a range of public rooms with a comfortable, intimate atmosphere. In keeping with the traditions of Holland America Line, there's a large collection of Dutch artwork and artifacts onboard.

THE SHIP. *Oosterdam* (sister ships: *Eurodam, Nieuw Amsterdam, Noordam, Westerdam,* and *Zuiderdam*) is one of a series of *Vista*-class ships, designed for younger, vibrant, multi-generational, family-oriented holidaymakers.

Twin working funnels are the result of the slightly unusual machinery configuration; the ship has, in effect, two engine rooms – one with three diesels, and one with two diesels and a gas turbine.

There's a complete walk-around exterior teak promenade deck, with teak steamer-style sunloungers. An outdoor jogging track is located around the mast and forward third of the ship. Exterior glass elevators, mounted midships on both port and starboard sides, provide ocean views. There are two centrally located swimming pools outdoors, and one can be used in poor weather thanks to its retractable sliding glass roof. Two whirlpool tubs, adjacent to the swimming pools, are abridged by a bar. Another smaller pool is available for children.

The intimate lobby spans just three decks, but it is topped by a beautiful, rotating Waterford crystal globe of the world. The interior decor is bright, yet comfortable. The ceilings are particularly noticeable in the public rooms. The cast-aluminum elevator doors are interesting – the design being inspired by

Berlitz's Ratings		
	Possible	Achieved
Ship	500	385
Accommodation	200	149
Food	400	261
Service	400	268
Entertainment	100	71
Cruise Experience	400	284
OVERALL SCORE		
1418 points out of 2000		

the Art Deco designs from New York's Chrysler Building.

There are two decks of entertainment/public rooms. A winding shopping street has several boutiques, and there's an Internet center, library, card room, art gallery, photo gallery, and several small meetings rooms. The casino is large, but you have to walk through it to get from the restaurant to the showlounge. Ice cream is free at certain hours, and a selection of warm hors d'oeuvres is provided in all bars.

On other decks, you'll find a Queen's Lounge, which acts as a lecture room and a Culinary Arts Center. There are also a number of other bars and lounges, including an Explorer's Lounge. The ship also has a small movie-screening room.

The information desk in the lobby is small and somewhat removed from the main passenger flow on the two decks above it. Many pillars obstruct passenger flow and lines of sight throughout the ship. There are no self-service launderettes – something families with children might miss, although special laundry packages are available.

FAMILIES. Children have KidZone, an indoor/outdoor facility, and Cub Hal for ages 5–12, with a number of dedicated youth counsellors (a ratio of one for every 30 children). Teenagers get to use WaveRunner, which includes a dance floor, special lighting effects, and a booming sound system. There's also a gaming room, and big-screen television for movies.

ACCOMMODATION. There are many price categories. Lifeboats obstruct the view from some cabins on Main Deck. Some cabins that can accommodate a third and fourth person have very little closet space, and only one personal safe. Suite occupants get exclusive use of the Neptune Lounge and concierge service, priority embarkation and disembarkation, and other benefits. In many of the suites/cabins with private balconies the balconies are not so private and can be overlooked from various public locations.

Penthouse Verandah Suites (2). These measure 1,318 sq ft (123 sq m), including balcony. Each has a separate bedroom with a king-size bed; there's also a walk-in closet, dressing room, living room, dining room, butler's pantry, mini-bar and refrigerator, and private balcony. The main bathroom has a large whirlpool tub, two washbasins, toilet, and plenty of storage space for toiletries. Personalized stationery and free dry cleaning are included, as are hot hors d'oeuvres and other goodies daily.

Deluxe Verandah Suites (60). These measure 563 sq ft (53 sq m). They have twin beds that convert to a king-size bed, vanity desk, lounge area, walk-in closet, minibar and refrigerator, and bathroom with full-size tub, washbasin, and toilet. Personalized stationery and complimentary dry cleaning are included, as are hot hors d'oeuvres and other goodies.

Verandah Suites (100). Actually, they are cabins, not suites, and measure 284 sq ft (26 sq m). Twin beds can convert to a queen-size bed; there is also a lounge area, minibar, and refrigerator, while the bathroom has a tub, washbasin, and toilet. Floor-to-ceiling windows open onto a private balcony.

Outside-view cabins. Standard outside cabins measure 197 sq ft (18 sq m) and have twin beds that convert to a queen-size bed. There's a small sitting area, while the bathroom has a tub/shower combination. The interior cabins are slightly smaller (183 sq ft/17 sq m).

Niggles include noisy air conditioning – the flow in cabins and bathrooms can't be turned off, and the only regulation is for temperature control.

DINING. The 1,045-seat Vista Dining Room is located aft. It spans two decks, and is quite a stunning room, with seating on both levels. Both open seating, and fixed seating are available for dinner, while breakfast and lunch are an open-seating arrangement (restaurant staff will seat you when you enter). There are tables for two, four, six, or eight. The waiter stations can be noisy for anyone seated adjacent to them. Live music is provided for dinner each evening. Once each cruise, there's a Dutch Dinner, and an

Indonesian Lunch. 'Lighter option' meals are always available for the nutrition- and weight-conscious. Kosher meals are also available; these are prepared ashore, frozen, and brought to your table sealed in their original containers.

Other dining options. The 130-seat Pinnacle Grill is more upscale, with higher-quality ingredients and better presentation than in the main dining room. It is on Lower Promenade Deck and fronts onto the second level of the atrium lobby. Pacific Northwest cuisine is featured, with items such as sesame-crusted halibut with ginger-miso, Peking duck breast with blackberry sauce, and an array of premium-quality steaks. There are fine table settings, china and silverware, and leather-bound menus. The wine bar offers mostly American wines. Reservations are needed, and there's a cover charge.

For casual eating, there's an extensive Lido Café, a self-serve eatery that wraps around the funnel housing and extends aft; there are also some fine views over the ship's central multi-deck atrium. Movement through the buffet area can be very slow, particularly at peak times. In the evenings, one side of this venue is turned into an extra-cost, 72-seat Canaletto Restaurant – a quasi-Italian informal eatery with waiter service.

Also, a poolside 'Dive-In at the Terrace Grill' features multi-choice signature burgers (with special Dive-In sauce), hot dogs, and fries, and, on certain days, barbecues and other culinary treats may be featured.

An extra-cost Windsurf Café in the atrium lobby (open 20 hours a day) serves coffee, pastries, snack foods, deli sandwiches, and, in the evenings, liqueur coffees.

ENTERTAINMENT. The 867-seat Vista Lounge is the venue for Las Vegas-style revues and major cabaret shows. The main-floor level has a bar in its starboard aft section. Spiral stairways at the back of the lounge connect all levels. Stage shows are best seen from the upper levels, from where the sight lines are quite good.

SPA/FITNESS. The Greenhouse Spa is a large, two-deck-high health spa, located directly above the navigation bridge. Facilities include a solarium, a hydrotherapy pool, and a unisex thermal suite, incorporating a Laconium, Hammam, and Chamomile Grotto. There is also a salon, 11 private massage/body-treatment rooms including one for couples, and a large gym with floor-to-ceiling windows, and the latest equipment. Sports enthusiasts can enjoy a basketball court, volleyball court, and golf simulator.

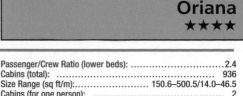

Oriana
★★★★

Size:	Mid-size Ship	Passenger/Crew Ratio (lower beds):	2.4
Tonnage:	69,153	Cabins (total):	936
Lifestyle:	Standard	Size Range (sq ft/m):	150.6–500.5/14.0–46.5
Cruise Line:	P&O Cruises	Cabins (for one person):	2
Former Names:	none	Cabins (with private balcony):	118
IMO Number:	6821080	Cabins (wheelchair accessible):	8
Builder:	Meyer Werft (Germany)	Wheelchair accessibility:	Good
Original Cost:	£200 million	Cabin Current:	110 and 220 volts
Entered Service:	Apr 1995	Elevators:	10
Registry:	Bermuda	Casino (gaming tables):	Yes
Length (ft/m):	853.0/260.0	Slot Machines:	Yes
Beam (ft/m):	105.6/32.2	Swimming Pools:	3
Draft (ft/m):	25.9/7.9	Hot Tubs (on deck):	5
Propulsion/Propellers:	diesel (47,750kW)/2	Self-Service Launderette:	Yes
Passenger Decks:	10	Dedicated Cinema/Seats:	Yes/189
Total Crew:	760	Library:	Yes
Passengers (lower beds):	1,870	Onboard currency:	UK£
Passenger Space Ratio (lower beds):	36.9		

British decor, style, and food for adults-only cruising

OVERVIEW. Anyone cruising aboard *Oriana*, an adults-only ship, will get a well-organized cruise experience. It suits mature adults seeking to cruise aboard a large ship with the facilities of a small resort.

THE SHIP. Although now 20 years old, *Oriana* has a feeling of timeless elegance. There's a good amount of outdoor space, with enough (white plastic) sunloungers for all passengers, and there's an extra-wide, traditional walk-around outdoor promenade deck. The stern superstructure is nicely rounded, with several tiers that overlook a swimming pool and hot tub. In 2011, a refit transformed *Oriana* from a ship for family cruising to an adults-only ship – and, as such, much better suited to long cruises. Some 27 new cabins were added, which lowered the space ratio and crew to passenger ratio. A sponson skirt was added to the hull, as a stability aid. However, vibration at the stern still persists (it has been a problem for years).

Inside, the design provides good horizontal passenger flow and wide passageways, with decor that is gentle and welcoming. Of note are some fine, detailed ceiling treatments. The interior focal point is a four-deck-high atrium. It is quite elegant but not glitzy, and is topped by a dome of Tiffany glass. The many public rooms provide plenty of choice.

The L-shaped Anderson's Lounge – named after Arthur Anderson, founder of the Peninsular Steam Navigation Company in the 1830s – contains an attractive series of 19th-century marine paintings and is decorated in the manner of a fine London club.

Berlitz's Ratings		
	Possible	Achieved
Ship	500	392
Accommodation	200	155
Food	400	244
Service	400	294
Entertainment	100	77
Cruise Experience	400	285
OVERALL SCORE		
1447 points out of 2000		

Atop the ship and forward is the Crow's Nest, a U-shaped observation lounge with one small wing that can be closed off for small groups. A long bar includes a model of *Oriana* and others in a glass case. Two small stages are set into the forward port and starboard sections, each with a wooden dance floor. Smoking is permitted only on cabin balconies and in designated spots on the open decks.

The library is a fine room, with a good range of hardback books and a librarian, inlaid wood tables and bookcases crafted by Viscount Linley's company, and some comfortable chairs. By the second day of almost any cruise, the library will have been almost stripped of books by word-hungry passengers. Adjacent is Thackeray's, a reading/writing room named after the novelist William Makepeace Thackeray, a P&O passenger in 1844. Lord's Tavern, decorated with cricket memorabilia, is the most sporting place to pitch a beverage or two, or take part in a singalong. There's also a small casino with table games and slot machines, and, unusually for ships today, not only a small cinema/lecture room but also a large room for card players.

The carpeting throughout is of a high quality, much of it custom designed and made from 100 percent wool. Some fine pieces of sculpture add the feeling of a floating museum, and original artworks by all-British artists include several tapestries and sculptures.

There's a wide variety of mainly British entertainment. P&O Cruises has a successful program of theme cruises covering areas such as antiques, art appreciation, classical music, comedy, cricket, gardening, jazz, motoring, popular fiction, and Scottish dance.

Most cabin stewards and dining room personnel are from India, and provide service with a warm smile. However, in the quest for increased onboard revenue, even birthday cakes cost extra, as do real espressos and cappuccinos – fake ones, made from instant coffee, are available in the dining rooms. Ice cream and bottled water also cost extra.

ACCOMMODATION. With the change to an adults-only ship, the former children's playrooms were converted into additional cabins. There are various price categories, according to size and location.

There are eight suites, each measuring 500 sq ft (46 sq m), with butler service. Facilities include a separate bedroom with two lower beds convertible to a queen-size bed, walk-in dressing area, two double closets, and plenty of drawer space. The lounge area has a sofa, armchairs and table, writing desk, binoculars, umbrella, trouser press, iron and ironing board, two TV sets, DVD player, personal safe, hairdryer, and refrigerator. The bathroom has a whirlpool bath, shower, and toilet, and there's also a guest bathroom. All in all, the suites, and particularly the bathrooms, are disappointing when compared with similarly sized suites in other ships. The private balcony has two sunloungers, tables, and chairs. Suite occupants get priority embarkation and their own lounge in the Southampton cruise terminal.

Other balcony cabins (called outside deluxe) measure 210 sq ft (19 sq m). There is plenty of closet and drawer space. The bathrooms are somewhat disappointing and dated, and have a very small, plain washbasin. One would expect marble or granite units in these grades.

Standard interior cabins and outside-view cabins are well equipped, but compact. There is much use of rich, warm limed oak or cherry wood, which makes even the least-expensive interior cabin quite inviting. All cabins have good closet and drawer space, a small refrigerator, full-length mirror, and blackout curtains (essential for North Cape cruises). All cabins have premium Slumberland mattresses, duvets, and high-quality bedlinen. Some can accommodate a third or third/fourth person, so sharing with friends can make for an economical cruise. Satellite television typically includes BBC World. Cabin soundproofing could be better.

There are a number of cabins for passengers traveling alone. Solos who share a cabin should note that only one personal safe is provided in most twin-bedded cabins.

The modest-size standard cabin bathrooms have mirror-fronted cabinets, although the lighting is quite soft; all have a wall-mounted hairdryer. High-

quality toiletries are by Temple Spa; suite occupants get larger bottles and more choice.

DINING. Peninsular (located amidships) and Oriental (aft – it can only reached by the aft stairway) are the two restaurants, each with two seatings and with one galley between them. Both are moderately handsome, with tables for two, four, six, or eight. But in the aft dining room the noise level can be high at many tables, because of the room's position above the propellers, and vibration at almost any speed. The meals are mostly of the 'Middle-England' variety, and the presentation generally lacks creativity. Curries and other Indian-style dishes are heavily featured, particularly on luncheon menus. Afternoon tea is disappointing. The typical menu cycle is 14 days; anyone on a long voyage may find it quite repetitive.

Other dining options. Marco Pierre White's Ocean Grill (Marco Pierre White also has restaurants aboard *Adonia* and *Arcadia*) is a pleasant alternative dining spot. Reservations are required, and there's a per-person cover charge. The menu is uncomplicated, but preparation, presentation, and taste are all good. An adjacent Tiffany's Bar serves as a pre-dinner anteroom for drinks.

A 50-seat Sorrento's, added in 2011, features Italian fare and has ocean views from its upper-level location at the aft portside section of the buffet venue (mainly with outdoor seating).

The Conservatory is for casual self-serve breakfast and luncheon buffets, and 24-hour self-serve beverage stands, although the selection of teas is poor, and the coffee is … well, let's not talk about that.

ENTERTAINMENT. The Theatre Royal, a well-designed room, has a sloping floor and good sight lines from almost all seats. The fare is mainly British, from production shows staged by a resident company to top British 'names' and lesser artists. A second, smaller Pacific Lounge is a multi-function venue for cabaret acts, including late-night comedy, and can also act as a lecture room. However, pillars obstruct the stage from a number of seats.

Ballroom dance fans will appreciate the four good-sized wood dance floors aboard his ship. A professional dance couple acts as hosts and teachers (social dancing time is always included in the programming).

SPA/FITNESS. The Oasis Spa is reasonably large, and provides the latest alternative treatment therapies. A gymnasium has high-tech muscle-toning equipment. The unisex sauna is a large facility; there is also a steam room each for men and women, and several massage/body-treatment rooms, an aerobics room with wood floor, plus a relaxation area with hot tub.

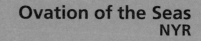

Ovation of the Seas
NYR

Size:	Large Resort Size	Passenger/Crew Ratio (lower beds):	3.2
Tonnage:	168,666	Cabins (total):	2,090
Lifestyle:	Standard	Size Range (sq ft/m):	101.1-799.7/9.4-74.3
Cruise Line:	Royal Caribbean International	Cabins (for one person):	34
Former Names:	none	Cabins (with private balcony):	1,571
IMO Number:	9682875	Cabins (wheelchair accessible):	34
Builder:	Meyer Werft (Germany)	Wheelchair accessibility:	Good
Original Cost:	$1.03 billion	Cabin Current:	110 and 220 volts
Entered Service:	May 2016	Elevators:	16
Registry:	Bahamas	Casino (gaming tables):	Yes
Length (ft/m):	112.2/339.0	Slot Machines:	Yes
Beam (ft/m):	134.5/41.0	Swimming Pools:	3
Draft (ft/m):	27.8/8.5	Hot Tubs (on deck):	4
Propulsion/Propellers:	diesel-electric/2 azimuthing pods	Self-Service Launderette:	No
Passenger Decks:	16	Dedicated Cinema/Seats:	No
Total Crew:	1,300	Library:	Yes
Passengers (lower beds):	4,180	Onboard currency:	US$
Passenger Space Ratio (lower beds):	40.3		

A high-tech, bling-filled cruise ship for the whole family

OVERVIEW. *Ovation of the Seas* is a sister ship to *Anthem of the Seas* and *Quantum of the Seas* – a trilogy of innovative ships designed to create the 'wow' factor and aimed particularly at families with children and at technology fans.

THE SHIP. *Ovation of the Seas* features an array of high-tech attractions, such as North Star, a large cherry-picker-like glass capsule (for 14 persons including the operator) that lifts you off the ship for a bird's-eye view. Located in the front section, just behind the ship's mast, it is complimentary (and wheelchair-accessible), but only operates at sea.

Also impressive is RipCord by iFly, a simulated skydiving experience in a two-storey vertical wind tunnel – ideal for a taste of skydiving, but in a safe, controlled environment. The unit uses a powerful air flow to keep you up – rather like a giant hairdryer underneath you. It is located aft of the ship's funnel housing, and accommodates 13 persons for each class; a turn in it includes two 'hovering in the air' experiences, instruction, and gear. You can book both attractions with interactive digital kiosks (adjacent to elevators) and tablets in public areas.

Meanwhile, a SeaPlex complex – located between the two funnels under the North Star – features a circus 'school,' and adrenalin-boosting bumper car rides, and also acts as a roller-skating rink and basketball court. Other active sports features include a rock-climbing wall, and a FlowRider surfing simulator.

Berlitz's Ratings		
	Possible	Achieved
Ship	500	NYR
Accommodation	200	NYR
Food	400	NYR
Service	400	NYR
Entertainment	100	NYR
Cruise Experience	400	NYR
OVERALL SCORE		
NYR points out of 2000		

Two70 o is an innovative multi-level venue at the stern that provides a casual living area by day, and at night becomes a stunning high-energy entertainment venue, with multiple dynamic robotic screens.

The decor is ultra-contemporary, rainbow colorful, and pretty jazzy to boot. The interior focal point is a three-storey-high Royal Esplanade, which includes Michael's Genuine Pub, Sorrento's pizza outlet, a Bionic Bar, Music Hall (a two-deck-high entertainment venue), plus several shops, a Schooner Bar, Boleros (Latin bar), Izumi (for Japanese-style cuisine), and the American Icon Grill.

This ship should be a fabulous cruise experience for the whole family, but, be warned: it's all about making reservations – lots of them – if you want to be sure not to miss out. High-speed wi-fi is extremely expensive, but all cabins come equipped with a USB socket for charging your digital items. Finally, this ship creates lines, so be prepared!

FAMILIES. For children and teenagers the facilities are on Decks 11 and 12. The Royal Babies and Tots Nursery is for tinies; Aquanauts is for 3–5-year-olds; Explorers is for 6–8-year-olds; and Voyagers is for 9–12-year-olds. Optix is the chill-out zone for teenagers. There's also Adventure Beach, an area for all the family, with swimming pools, a water slide, and game areas outdoors in the AquaPark. DreamWorks events and entertainment are featured, with live character appearances from *Shrek, Kung Fu Panda, Madagascar,* and *Barbie*. Unfortunately, the kids' pool is adjacent to a smoking area.

ACCOMMODATION. There are many different accommodation price grades and categories, with the price dependent on size and location. Every cabin has a view, whether real or virtual. 'Virtual' balconies – first introduced aboard *Navigator of the Seas* in 2013 – are a neat feature of the interior cabins; they can provide real-time ocean views, but you *can* turn them off. Optional wrist-bands (with RFID technology) provide access to your cabin, and act as your charge card (you have to take it off in order to give to the bartender), but they are uncomfortable to wear.

Standard cabins are about 9 percent larger than those aboard the Oasis-class ships. Note that suite-grade accommodation occupants can eat all their meals in the exclusive Coastal Kitchen. Also, note that most cabin doors open outwards into the hallway, and not inwards into the cabin.

Loft cabins (including a 975 sq ft/90.5 sq m Owner's Loft) vary in size and configuration, but measure about 502 sq ft (46.6 sq m) and are found at the ship's stern.

Inter-connecting family cabins are great for multi-generational groups. The 15 units consist of a junior suite, balcony cabin, and interior studio, linked through a shared vestibule. Together they create 575.8 sq ft (53.5 sq m) of living space with three bedrooms, three bathrooms, and a 216-sq-ft (20-sq-m) balcony.

There are 34 'studio' cabins (12 have real balconies; all have wall beds) for solo occupancy, a first for RCI. As there's no solo traveler supplement, they are priced in a new category.

Even the smallest bathroom is well designed, with touches such as a night light, and shower and vanity hooks, while cabins have bedside power outlets, and ample storage space.

Negatives include the fact that tablet-based infotainment systems don't answer questions, and the room service menu for breakfast is poor.

DINING. There are 18 restaurant and eatery choices (there's no single main dining room as such). You can go for the same table each night, if you choose the 'classic' option, part of the line's Dynamic Dining (a concept first introduced by Star Cruises). The 'classic' option means that you (together with your waiter and assistant waiter) will rotate each night between the four principal (free) restaurants).

The menu descriptions make the food sound better than it is, however, and the selection of breads, rolls, fruit, and cheese is poor. Overall, meals are rather hit and miss.

Some extra-cost restaurants require reservations, which can prove frustrating. Note that the menus are the same each night in most extra-cost restaurants, and service can be slow (there are no assistant waiters).

The following are complimentary (with tablecloths for dinner):

The Grande: with around 430 seats, the ship's most elegant restaurant (think Southern mansion hospitality) features classic dishes reminiscent of the days of the grand ocean liners of yesteryear.

Chic: this 434-seat restaurant serves 'contemporary' cuisine and sauces made from scratch.

Silk: this restaurant features pan-Asian cuisine, including a touch of spice. American Icon Grill: this 430-seat restaurant features many of America's favorite 'comfort food' dishes.'

Extra-cost venues:

Wonderland: based on the (real and imagined) elements of Fire, Ice, Water, Earth, and Dreams, this surreal 62-seat Alice in Wonderland-inspired venue offers food with a quirky touch thanks to ingredients such as Japanese bonito flakes.

Jamie's Italian: it's a 132-seat reservations-required tablecloth-free Euro-Italian bistro – and British celebrity chef Jamie Oliver's first restaurant at sea.

Chops Grille: for premium-quality steaks and grilled seafood (but an additional cost for dry-aged steaks and lobster, on top of the cover charge).

Chef's Table: this exclusive 16-seat venue (located within Chops Grille) is good for private parties, with wine-and-food pairing the specialty.

Izumi: a 44-seat Japanese-Asian fusion cuisine venue including hot-rock tableside cooking, sashimi, sushi, and sake.

Johnny Rockets: a retro 1950s all-day, all-night diner-style eatery (near the main pool) for hamburgers, extra-cost malt shakes, and jukebox hits (all tables feature a mini-jukebox). À-la-carte pricing applies.

For casual meals at no extra cost, the 860-seat Windjammer Marketplace is a self-serve buffet-style eatery. Other casual (included) spots include: The Café at Two700; SeaPlex Dog House, Sorrento's – for pizza slices and calzones – and Café Promenade.

ENTERTAINMENT. The Royal Theater spans three decks and seats 1,299. It is the principal showlounge for 'booked' shows and large-scale production shows by a resident troupe of singers and dancers (reservations advised).

SPA/FITNESS. The Vitality at Sea Spa facilities include a thermal suite (extra cost), beauty salon, barber shop, and gymnasium with Technogym equipment. Massage and other body-pampering treatments take place in 19 treatment rooms.

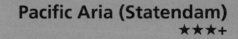

Pacific Aria (Statendam)
★★★+

Size:	Mid-size Ship
Tonnage:	55,819
Lifestyle:	Premium
Cruise Line:	Holland America Line
Former Names:	*Statendam*
IMO Number:	8919245
Builder:	Fincantieri (Italy)
Original Cost:	$215 million
Entered Service:	Jan 1993/Nov 2015
Registry:	Great Britain
Length (ft/m):	719.4/219.3
Beam (ft/m):	101.0/30.8
Draft (ft/m):	24.6/7.5
Propulsion/Propellers:	diesel-electric (34,560kW)/2
Passenger Decks:	10
Total Crew:	560
Passengers (lower beds):	1,260
Passenger Space Ratio (lower beds):	44.3

Passenger/Crew Ratio (lower beds):	2.2
Cabins (total):	630
Size Range (sq ft/m):	186.2–1,124.8/17.3–104.5
Cabins (for one person):	0
Cabins (with private balcony):	150
Cabins (wheelchair accessible):	6
Wheelchair accessibility:	Good
Cabin Current:	110 and 220 volts
Elevators:	8
Casino (gaming tables):	Yes
Slot Machines:	Yes
Swimming Pools:	2 (1 w/sliding glass dome)
Hot Tubs (on deck):	2
Self-Service Launderette:	Yes
Dedicated Cinema/Seats:	Yes/249
Library:	Yes
Onboard currency:	Australian $

A family-friendly ship with trendy decor and food for Australasians

OVERVIEW. This ship formerly sailed for Holland America Line (as *Statendam*). It was refurbished and 'Aussified' for its new role.

THE SHIP. The ship's exterior styling is rather angular, but it does have a full walk-around teakwood Promenade Deck outdoors – excellent for strolling and watching the water. A hydraulic glass roof covers the swimming pool, whirlpools, and central Lido area, so that they can be used in fine or poor weather. Aft is The Oasis, a quiet area for (adult-only) relaxation, with its own small (dip) pool.

Inside, an asymmetrical layout helps to reduce bottlenecks and congestion. Most public rooms are on two decks, which creates a spacious feel. Atop the ship, with forward-facing views that wrap around the sides, is The Dome, an observation lounge with large oceanview windows; by night it's a trendy nightspot.

The ship has a large, relaxing library and integral Internet-connect center. There's also a cards room, a Mix Lounge for relaxing in and for afternoon tea, an intimate Piano Bar, an indoor cinema, and a casino with gaming tables and slots (fruit machines).

FAMILIES. Children and teens have their own areas: Turtle Cove for 3–6-year-olds (even the little ones must be toilet-trained); Shark Shack for 7–10-year-olds; HQ Lounge for 11–14-year-olds; and Teen Lounge.

ACCOMMODATION. There are 23 cabin price grades (a lot for this size of ship), and 24 percent of all cabins have a balcony. The rooms range from small interior

Berlitz's Ratings		
	Possible	Achieved
Ship	500	346
Accommodation	200	140
Food	400	247
Service	400	279
Entertainment	100	68
Cruise Experience	400	264
OVERALL SCORE		
1344 points out of 2000		

cabins (with very little storage space) to cabins with balcony, to a seriously large Penthouse Suite.

All suite/cabin occupants benefit from shoeshine, express ironing, laundry, bathrobes and slippers, pillow menu, and yoga mat. Occupants of suite-grade accommodation also get a Nespresso coffee machine, iPod docking station pre-loaded with music, priority reservations for specialty dining venues, spa treatment bookings, and shore excursions.

DINING. The Waterfront restaurant is at the aft of the ship. It features open seating, with tables for two to 10, but note that tables near the waiter stations are noisy.

Other dining options. These include Angelo's (named for photographer Angelo Frontoni), for Italian cuisine, the extra-cost Salt Grill by Luke Mangan and adjacent Salt Grill bar, and Dragon Lady for extra-cost Asian-fusion cuisine. For more casual eating, head to The Pantry, which provides food court-style outlets.

ENTERTAINMENT. The Marquee Theater is the ship's showlounge, spanning two decks, with banquette seating. Large production shows are presented in the evening, with bingo games and quizzes in the daytime.

SPA/FITNESS. The Spa includes a gym with all the latest exercise machines. It has ocean views, an aerobics exercise area, a large beauty salon, several treatment rooms, and men's and women's sauna, steam room, and changing areas. The Edge features a high-adrenalin program that offers 20 different activities.

Pacific Dawn
★★★+

Size:	Mid-size Ship
Tonnage:	70,285
Lifestyle:	Standard
Cruise Line:	P&O Cruises (Australia)
Former Names:	*Regal Princess*
IMO Number:	8521232
Builder:	Fincantieri Navali (Italy)
Original Cost:	$276.8 million
Entered Service:	Aug 1991/Nov 2007
Registry:	Great Britain
Length (ft/m):	811.0/247.2
Beam (ft/m):	105.6/32.2
Draft (ft/m):	25.5/7.8
Propulsion/Propellers:	diesel (24,000kW)/2
Passenger Decks:	11
Total Crew:	725
Passengers (lower beds):	1,596
Passenger Space Ratio (lower beds):	44.0
Passenger/Crew Ratio (lower beds):	2.2
Cabins (total):	798
Size Range (sq ft/m):	193.7–592.0/18.0–55.0
Cabins (for one person):	0
Cabins (with private balcony):	148
Cabins (wheelchair accessible):	13
Wheelchair accessibility:	Fair
Cabin Current:	110 and 220 volts
Elevators:	9
Casino (gaming tables):	Yes
Slot Machines:	Yes
Swimming Pools:	2
Hot Tubs (on deck):	4
Self-Service Launderette:	Yes
Dedicated Cinema/Seats:	No
Library:	Yes
Onboard currency:	Australian $

This dated large ship is good for family-friendly cruising

OVERVIEW. *Pacific Dawn* has all the right facilities to provide a pleasant cruise in comfortable, modern surroundings, and a friendly staff will make you feel really welcome. Sunbathing space is a bit tight when the ship is full. But, overall, *Pacific Dawn* performs well and offers good value for money.

THE SHIP. There is no walk-around promenade deck outdoors – the only walking space being along the sides of the ship. Inside, the understated decor of soft pastel shades is highlighted by some colorful artwork. A striking, elegant three-deck-high atrium has a grand staircase with fountain sculpture. The Dome, an observation dome set high atop the ship, houses a multipurpose lounge/comedy club with live music.

FAMILIES. Children have their own play areas: Turtle Cove (ages 3–6); Shark Shack (ages 7–10); HQ (11–13); and HQ+ (14–17). Each age group has dedicated counselors to keep them occupied.

ACCOMMODATION. There are numerous different price grades, ranked by location and size. In a recent refit, some 282 cabins had upper berths fitted to accommodate two adults and two children. In general, the cabins are well designed, with large bathrooms and good soundproofing. All cabins have walk-in closets, refrigerator, personal safe, and TV set. Twin beds convert to queen-size beds in standard cabins. Lifeboats obstruct the view from the outside-view cabins for disabled passengers.

Berlitz's Ratings

	Possible	Achieved
Ship	500	313
Accommodation	200	135
Food	400	263
Service	400	276
Entertainment	100	72
Cruise Experience	400	271

OVERALL SCORE
1330 points out of 2000

The 14 most expensive suites, each with a large private balcony, are well equipped, and storage space is generous, adequate even for long cruises.

DINING. The Waterfront Restaurant has open seating for all meals. The food has good taste thanks to the use of fresh produce. A large 'always available' selection is combined with multiple daily additions; vegetable and potato side orders are always provided.

For more intimate dining, with food prepared to order, try the specialty venue Salt Grill by Luke Mangan. The fish specialties include barramundi and fresh oysters. There's a cover charge (A$40 for dinner, A$30 for lunch); reservations are needed. The downside is the intrusive background music.

There is a Trattoria (nominal fee) for informal meals; this is popular at lunchtime and in the afternoons. There's also an extra-cost patisserie, Charlie's Bar, in the spacious lobby.

ENTERTAINMENT. The Marquee Showlounge spans two decks. There's plenty of live music for the bars and lounges, with a wide mix of classical, jazz, and dance, from solo pianists to showbands. Several times each cruise, a stunning laser light and sound show is presented in the atrium.

SPA/FITNESS. The Aqua Spa and fitness center has a gymnasium, exercise room, steam room, and sauna.

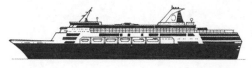

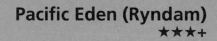

Pacific Eden (Ryndam)
★★★+

Size:	Mid-size Ship
Tonnage:	55,819
Lifestyle:	Premium
Cruise Line:	P&O Cruises Australia
Former Names:	*Ryndam*
IMO Number:	8919269
Builder:	Fincantieri (Italy)
Original Cost:	$215 million
Entered Service:	Nov 1994/Nov 2015
Registry:	Great Britain
Length (ft/m):	719.3/219.3
Beam (ft/m):	101.0/30.8
Draft (ft/m):	24.6/7.5
Propulsion/Propellers:	diesel-electric (34,560kW)/2
Passenger Decks:	10
Total Crew:	560
Passengers (lower beds):	1,260
Passenger Space Ratio (lower beds):	44.3

Passenger/Crew Ratio (lower beds):	2.2
Cabins (total):	630
Size Range (sq ft/m):	186.2–1,124.8/17.3–104.5
Cabins (for one person):	0
Cabins (with private balcony):	150
Cabins (wheelchair accessible):	6
Wheelchair accessibility:	Fair
Cabin Current:	110 and 220 volts
Elevators:	8
Casino (gaming tables):	Yes
Slot Machines:	Yes
Swimming Pools:	2 (1 w/sliding glass dome)
Hot Tubs (on deck):	2
Self-Service Launderette:	Yes
Dedicated Cinema/Seats:	Yes/249
Library:	Yes
Onboard currency:	Australian $

A good mid-size, family-friendly ship aimed at Australasians

OVERVIEW. This ship formerly sailed for Holland America Line (as *Ryndam*) and was refurbished and 'Aussified' for its new role.

THE SHIP. The ship's exterior styling is boxy, but it does feature a full walk-around teakwood Promenade Deck outdoors, which is excellent for strolling and whale-watching.

A hydraulic glass roof covers the swimming pool, whirlpools, and central Lido area, so that they can be used in any weather. Aft is The Oasis, a quiet area for (adult-only) relaxation, with a small (dip) pool.

Inside, an asymmetrical layout helps to reduce bottlenecks and congestion. Most public rooms are concentrated on two decks, which creates a spacious feel.

Atop the ship, with forward-facing views that wrap around the sides, The Dome is an observation lounge with large ocean-view windows by day; by night it's a trendy nightspot. The atrium foyer is three decks high, although its sculptured centerpiece, *Fountain of the Sirens* (a late 17th-century bronze piece by Willem de Groat), makes it a bit crowded.

The ship has a large, relaxing library, and integral Internet-connect center. There's also a room for card games, a Mix Lounge for relaxing in and for afternoon tea and after-dinner coffees), an intimate Piano Bar, an indoor cinema (and culinary center), and a casino with gaming tables and slots (fruit machines).

Children and teens have their own areas: Turtle Cove for 3–6-year-olds (even the littlest ones must be toilet-trained); Shark Shack for 7–10-year-olds; HQ Lounge for 11–14-year-olds; and Teen Lounge.

Berlitz's Ratings

	Possible	Achieved
Ship	500	347
Accommodation	200	140
Food	400	252
Service	400	281
Entertainment	100	68
Cruise Experience	400	265
OVERALL SCORE		
1353 points out of 2000		

ACCOMMODATION. There are 23 cabin price grades, and 24 percent of all cabins have a balcony. Cabins range from small interior cabins (with little storage space) to cabins with balcony, to a seriously large Penthouse Suite. All occupants benefit from shoeshine, express ironing, laundry, bathrobes and slippers, pillow menu, and yoga mat. Suite occupants also get a Nespresso coffee machine, iPod docking station pre-loaded with music, and priority reservations for specialty dining venues, spa treatments, and shore excursions.

DINING. The Waterfront restaurant is at the aft of the ship. It has open seating, with tables for two to 10; note that tables by the waiter stations are noisy.

Other dining options. These include Angelo's, for Italian cuisine, the specialty venue Salt Grill by Luke Mangan, or Dragon Lady for extra-cost Asian-fusion cuisine. For more casual eating, head to The Pantry, which provides an array of food court-style outlets.

ENTERTAINMENT. The Marquee Theater is the ship's showlounge; it spans two decks, with banquette seating. Large production shows are presented in the evening, with bingo games and quizzes in the daytime.

SPA/FITNESS. The Spa has a gym with all the latest machines, as well as an aerobics area, a beauty salon, several treatment rooms, and men's and women's sauna, steam room, and changing areas. The Edge features a high-adrenalin program with 20 different activities.

Pacific Jewel
★★★+

Size:	Mid-size Ship
Tonnage:	70,310
Lifestyle:	Standard
Cruise Line:	P&O Cruises (Australia)
Former Names:	Ocean Village Two, AIDAblu, A'RosaBlu, Crown Princess
IMO Number:	8521220
Builder:	Fincantieri Navali (Italy)
Original Cost:	$276.8 million
Entered Service:	Jul 1990/Dec 2009
Registry:	Great Britain
Length (ft/m):	805.7/245.6
Beam (ft/m):	105.8/32.2
Draft (ft/m):	26.9/8.2
Propulsion/Propellers:	diesel-electric (24,000kW)/2
Passenger Decks:	11
Total Crew:	621
Passengers (lower beds):	1,674

Passenger Space Ratio (lower beds):	42
Passenger/Crew Ratio (lower beds):	2.6
Cabins (total):	837
Size Range (sq ft/m):	193.7–398.2/18.0–37.0
Cabins (for one person):	0
Cabins (with private balcony):	198
Cabins (wheelchair accessible):	10
Wheelchair accessibility:	Fair
Cabin Current:	110 and 220 volts
Elevators:	9
Casino (gaming tables):	Yes
Slot Machines:	Yes
Swimming Pools:	2
Hot Tubs (on deck):	2
Self-Service Launderette:	Yes
Dedicated Cinema/Seats:	No
Library:	Yes
Onboard currency:	Australian $

This mid-size ship provides family-friendly Aussie cruising

OVERVIEW. *Pacific Jewel* is best suited to young Australian couples, single travelers, families, and single-parent families with children seeking a good-value-for-money first cruise in a large, casual ship setting, with appealing itineraries and destinations and a range of fun-filled activities. The young, vibrant staff members make passengers feel welcome.

THE SHIP. Originally ordered by Sitmar Cruises, this ship debuted in 1990 as *Crown Princess* but has since assumed many identities. It was moved to the A'Rosa Cruises brand and, as *A'Rosa Blu*, began operating cruises for the German-speaking family market in 2002. Two years later, it was refitted and renamed *AIDAblu* for AIDA Cruises, then became *Ocean Village Two* for the UK's Ocean Village brand. In 2009 it turned into *Pacific Jewel*, specifically for the Australian market.

It has a dolphin-like upper front structure made of lightweight aluminum alloy, originally designed to keep the weight down in line with stability requirements. It was designed by Renzo Piano, the renowned Italian architect behind the Centre Georges Pompidou in Paris and Japan's Kansai International Airport, Osaka. A large swept-back funnel, also made from aluminum alloy, is placed aft.

Facilities are in line with the tastes of young, active Aussie families, single parents with children, and single travelers. The interior layout is a bit disjointed, however. Some innovative and elegant styling is mixed with traditional features and a reason-

Berlitz's Ratings		
	Possible	Achieved
Ship	500	350
Accommodation	200	140
Food	400	261
Service	400	276
Entertainment	100	72
Cruise Experience	400	268
OVERALL SCORE		
1367 points out of 2000		

ably spacious interior layout. An understated decor of soft pastel shades is highlighted by splashes of color, as well as some colorful artwork.

The oval-shaped atrium lobby is three decks high and has a grand staircase as its focal point; it provides a good meeting and gathering point. Shops, bars, and lounges span out from the lobby on three decks. Other facilities include an Internet café, Mix Bar, and Charlie's Bar. Child-free areas include Oasis, a sunbathing quiet zone aft on Deck 10, and the Aqua Spa and Health Center.

There is no decent outdoor or indoor forward observation viewpoint, and no walk-around promenade deck outdoors, the only walking space being along the port and starboard sides of the ship. In fact, there's little contact with the outdoors, and sunbathing space is quite limited. Other niggles include the many support pillars throughout the public rooms; these obstruct sight lines and impede passenger flow.

P&O Cruises (Australia) scrapped automatic tipping from October 2010, so tips are at your discretion. P&O provides good value for money, particularly when compared to most land-based resorts in Australia. Some cruises have special themes, such as food and wine. The onboard product is playful and casual, and its delivery is highly targeted to the Australasian lifestyle. The crew are extremely friendly, and service is better than you can find in many parts of Australia.

FAMILIES. There is a good range of facilities for children, who are split into four age groups, with separate facilities and staff for each: Turtle Cove (ages 3–6); Shark Shack (ages 7–10); HQ (11–13s); and HQ+ (14–17s). A paddling pool for toddlers is included.

ACCOMMODATION. There are many differebt price categories, including mini-suites with private balconies, outside-view cabins and interior cabins, and special cabins for the disabled. Generally, accommodation on the higher decks will cost more because, aboard ship, location is everything. Occupants of mini-suites (there are 36) get more space, a larger bathroom, and premium bathroom amenities.

Single-parent families comprise an increasing number of today's cruise passengers, so a good number of two-bed cabins also have a third (or third/fourth) pull-down berth.

In general, the well-designed cabins have large bathrooms as well as decent soundproofing. Walk-in closets, refrigerator, personal safe, and color TV are provided in all of them. Twin beds convert to queen-size beds in most cabins. Bathrobes and toiletries are provided. Views from the outside-view cabins for the disabled are obstructed by lifeboats, as are those from some other cabins on the same deck (Deck 8).

Suites: The most expensive suites have a private balcony, and are quite well laid out to a practical design. The bedroom is separated from the living room by a heavy wooden door; there are TV sets in both rooms, and closet and drawer space are generous.

DINING. There are two principal restaurants, several decks apart: Plantation and The Waterfront. There are a few tables for two, but most are for four, six, or eight. Plantation is open 24 hours a day, while The Waterfront is open for à-la-carte breakfasts, lunches, and dinner at times given in the daily program. There's a neat table for 10 persons in the Wine Room, part of the Waterfront Restaurant, for use as a Chef's Table, complete with dégustation menu.

The Waterfront's menu is really varied and caters to the multicultural, multiethnic passenger mix. The food has great taste, thanks to the use of fresh Australian produce and meat and other items of Australian origin. It is perhaps best described as modern Australian fare. A large 'always available' selection is combined with multiple daily additions, plus vegetable and potato side orders ('sides' in Aussie-English).

Other dining options. For a treat or special celebration, extra-charge full service dining is available in the intimate bistro-style restaurant, Salt Grill by Luke Mangan (think: Sydney crab omelet with miso mustard broth). It is located forward of the main pools, on the starboard side, accessed by the forward stairway. The cover charge is worth it because the meals have more taste and neat flavor combinations.

La Luna, a small, casual deck restaurant adjacent to the aft pool and funnel, serves Asian-style cuisine.

For coffee, tea, chocolate, and sweet snacks during the day, and drinks in the evening, Charlie's Bar is an extra-cost patisserie/bar on the lower level of the spacious lobby.

ENTERTAINMENT. The Marquee Theatre, the venue for main entertainment events, spans two decks, with seating on both main and balcony levels. Several support pillars obstruct sight lines from a number of seats. There's plenty of colorful entertainment, including a song and dance troupe, and a good stable of Aussie cabaret acts. A high-energy acrobatic-and-dance deck show is provided for warm nights under the stars, on a stage and acrobatic archway fitted during one of the ship's refits.

Connexions (lounge/bar) is an adults-only comedy venue that doubles as a karaoke and live music venue. Also, if you like country and western music, hoedowns, and line dancing, you'll find your tastes are catered for.

SPA/FITNESS. The Aqua Spa and Health Club, an extensive wellness center, spans two decks and measures almost 14,000 sq ft (1,300 sq m); a staircase connects two levels. Located at the top of the ship at the forward stairway, it occupies the space in the 'dolphin head' section. With its curved surfaces, walking the treadmills or exercycling and facing out to sea (albeit on the port side) makes you feel you're doing so in the upper deck of a Boeing 747.

Panoramic saunas and Hammam steam room are on the lower level; a seven-day pass for the sauna and steam rooms costs extra. The reception area has a waterfall and cypress trees, and there are 11 treatment rooms for facials, massages (including hot stones and couples massage), manicure and pedicure, dry float and hydrobath. There is also a solarium, and a four-person relaxation room. It's a very nice spa facility.

The spa is operated by a specialist concession. Some exercise classes and health talks are free; others may incur a charge.

Pacific Pearl
★★★+

Size:	Mid-size Ship
Tonnage:	63,524
Lifestyle:	Standard
Cruise Line:	P&O Cruises (Australia)
Former Names:	Ocean Village, Arcadia, Star Princess, FairMajesty
IMO Number:	9048081
Builder:	Chantiers de L'Atlantique (France)
Original Cost:	$200 million
Entered Service:	Mar 1989/May 2010
Registry:	Great Britain
Length (ft/m):	810.3/247.0
Beam (ft/m):	105.6/32.2
Draft (ft/m):	26.9/8.2
Propulsion/Propellers:	diesel-electric (39,000kW)/2
Passenger Decks:	12
Total Crew:	514
Passengers (lower beds):	1,624
Passenger Space Ratio (lower beds):	39.1
Passenger/Crew Ratio (lower beds):	3.1
Cabins (total):	812
Size Range (sq ft/m):	182.9–398.2/17.0–37.0
Cabins (for one person):	0
Cabins (with private balcony):	64
Cabins (wheelchair accessible):	8
Wheelchair accessibility:	Good
Cabin Current:	220 volts
Elevators:	9
Casino (gaming tables):	Yes
Slot Machines:	Yes
Swimming Pools:	3
Hot Tubs (on deck):	2
Self-Service Launderette:	Yes
Dedicated Cinema/Seats:	No
Library:	Yes
Onboard currency:	Australian $

A dated, but very family-friendly ship for casual cruising

OVERVIEW. *Pacific Pearl* is best suited to young couples, solo travelers of all ages, and families with children and teenagers who like to mingle in a mid-size ship with plenty of life, music, and entertainment, and with food that is quantity rather than quality, and a price that's attractive.

THE SHIP. *Pacific Pearl* was originally designed and built as *FairMajesty* for Sitmar Cruises just as the company was absorbed into Princess Cruises. In 2003, after a refurbishment that brightened the interior passageways, public rooms, and dining spots, it morphed into *Ocean Village*, a trendy ship designed for younger couples and families.

Several new cabins were added during that refit. The casino was also relocated, displacing the library, and a former casino became an Internet center/bar. In 2010, the ship was transferred to P&O Cruises (Australia) to become *Pacific Pearl* for Australasian passengers, and further refurbished to suit Australian cruise tastes.

Pacific Pearl is a well-proportioned ship, with a decent amount of open deck and sunbathing space – and an adults-only quiet zone decks (The Oasis, with two hot tubs, but no shower) on the aft, tiered decks. On the open leisure deck are two pools, one with sloping steps, the other with vertical steps, and one has a sit-in 'splash' bar. An archway over the aft pool provides a platform for aerial acrobatic shows, and there's also a poolside screen for those important rugby games – and movies. An Oasis adults-only quiet zone with day beds, and a hot tub is located at the aft of Deck 8.

Berlitz's Ratings		
	Possible	Achieved
Ship	500	359
Accommodation	200	138
Food	400	262
Service	400	277
Entertainment	100	74
Cruise Experience	400	278
OVERALL SCORE		
1388 points out of 2000		

The interiors are quite elegant, with much attention paid to lighting. But they also include a few items that have a link with the past, such as the Art Deco stainless-steel balustrades and the soulless stainless-steel elevators. There aren't a lot of public rooms, although one nice feature is the fact that they have ceilings higher than the average for contemporary cruise ships. My favorite bar: Mix.

The focal point of the interior is a three-deck-high atrium lobby and a multi-deck dual staircase. The Dome, an observation lounge, sits atop the ship, forward of the mast. It is a lounge for cocktails; at night it turns into a night-spot/disco with a sunken, circular wooden dance floor.

For retail therapy, several shops are clustered around the second and third levels of the atrium lobby. Other facilities include a small casino, aft of the upper level of the two-deck-high showlounge, a Victorian pub called Oriana (with Fat Yak, Hoegaarden, Carlsberg, and Bulmers Cider on tap), Connexions Bar (for adult-only comedy, karaoke, and trivia quizzes), and Mix Bar, a more traditional cocktail bar/ drinking lounge with cool blue decor.

There's no full walk-around promenade deck outdoors, but open port and starboard walking areas stretch partly along the sides. There is, however, a walking track on the uppermost open deck.

Some cruises have special themes, such as food and wine. The onboard product is playful and casual; its delivery is highly targeted to the Australian lifestyle, and nobody does it better. The crew members are extremely friendly, and service is better than you can find in many parts of Australia. Also, hats off to P&O, who made tipping discretionary in 2010.

FAMILIES. The children's facilities and playrooms are quite extensive. At the aft of the ship, there's an indoor play area – Turtle Cove for 3–6-year-olds, and Shark Shack for 7–10-year-olds. An exterior aft deck has a paddling pool and games area. Tweens and teenagers have their own areas (HQ Club for ages 11–14, and HQ+ for 15–17s, including a good chill-out zone). A children's dinner is offered for ages 3–10, with babysitting available until 1am.

A number of cabins have third- and fourth-person berths – good for families with children, but the drawer and storage space is tight.

ACCOMMODATION. There are four basic types, mini-suites, outsides with balcony, outside-view, and interior, in 22 different price grades, depending on location and size. These include 36 mini-suites with small private balcony, walk-in closet, masses of storage space, and wood-floored bathroom with bathtub and shower. All other accommodation consists of standard outside-view and interior grade cabins, almost all of which are of a decent size. If you like to fall asleep with soft music playing, note that because music is available only through the TV set, you can't access any of the music channels without having a TV picture on.

Standard outside-view/interior cabins. All are equipped with twin beds that can, in most cases, be put together to form a queen-size bed. All have a good amount of storage, including wooden drawer units, plus some under-bed space for luggage, and a walk-in closet. Sound insulation between cabins could be better – TV sound late at night can be irritating. High-quality bed linen, duvets, and pillows are provided.

The bathrooms are of a modular design and have good-size shower enclosures and a retractable clothesline. None have tubs except for the mini-suites, as the ship was originally built for American passengers, who prefer showers. However, shower heads are affixed to the wall, denying you the ease of a flexible shower hose. Soap is provided.

Room-service items cost extra, and incur an additional delivery charge.

DINING. The main restaurant is the 812-seat, open-seating Waterfront; it has large ocean-view windows, sit-down, tablecloth dining, and tables for two, four, six, or eight persons. It has a high ceiling, and seating sections help divide the room into comfortable spaces, so it doesn't feel as large as it actually is.

The Waterfront's menu is really varied and caters to the multicultural, multiethnic passenger mix. The food has great taste, thanks to the use of fresh Australian produce and meat and other items of Austral-ian origin. It is perhaps best described as modern Australian fare. A large 'always available' selection, including vegetarian dishes, is combined with multiple daily additions, and vegetable and potato side orders are always provided. The food is straightforward, unfussy, and unpretentious, with little use of garnishes. The service is attentive, warm, and lighthearted. Bar snacks such as peanuts or crisps cost extra.

For more intimate dining and food prepared to order, try the specialty venue Salt Grill by Luke Mangan. This small dining spot with open kitchen serves really excellent New World cuisine. The steaks are extremely good, and the fish specialties include barramundi and fresh oysters. There's a cover charge (it's absolutely worth it), and reservations are needed; the downside is the intrusive, unnecessary vocal background 'music'.

Plantation is a self-serve buffet, open for breakfast, lunch, and dinner, but setting is limited. It's typically slow-going along straight buffet lines, so patience is needed. A wide selection of tea is provided at the smart beverage stations, as is coffee.

The Café, for coffees, hot chocolate, and chocolate snacks, is adjacent to the forward swimming pool. Charlie's, a neat little coffee bistro, located on the lowest lobby level opposite the reception desk, serves coffees, teas, pastries, and snacks (at extra cost). The pool has an ice cream bar.

ENTERTAINMENT. The Marquee Theatre is the venue for all principal entertainment events. A horseshoe-shaped room, with main and balcony levels (there's a bar at the back on the main level), it has adequate sight lines from most of the banquette-style seating, but the sight lines from the front-row seats on the upper level are obstructed by the required balcony railing.

Although the ship isn't young and doesn't have the latest bells and whistles, the stage has an excellent LED lighting backdrop. There is a good variety of entertainment, from production shows to cabaret-style acts and comedians. There is also live music throughout the many lounges and bars – in fact, there's no bar without music, so sitting down for a quiet drink or two isn't an option. Fans of country and western music, hoedowns, and line dancing are well catered for.

SPA/FITNESS. The attractive Aqua Spa facilities include a beauty salon, gymnasium, and an extra-cost thermal/relax area that includes a unisex sauna, steam room, herbal showers, and two body-shaped tiled hot beds. It is located on the lowest passenger deck.

It is wise to book treatments such as massages and facials as soon as possible after you embark, as time slots fill quickly. Some exercise classes are free, but most incur a charge.

Pacific Princess
★★★★

Size:	Small Ship	
Tonnage:	30,277	
Lifestyle:	Standard	
Cruise Line:	Princess Cruises	
Former Names:	R Three	
IMO Number:	9187887	
Builder:	Chantiers de l'Atlantique (France)	
Original Cost:	$150 million	
Entered Service:	Aug 1999/Nov 2002	
Registry:	Bermuda	
Length (ft/m):	593.7/181.0	
Beam (ft/m):	83.5/25.5	
Draft (ft/m):	19.5/6.0	
Propulsion/Propellers:	diesel-electric (18,600kW)/2	
Passenger Decks:	9	
Total Crew:	373	
Passengers (lower beds):	688	
Passenger Space Ratio (lower beds):	44.1	

Passenger/Crew Ratio (lower beds):	1.8
Cabins (total):	344
Size Range (sq ft/m):	145.3–968.7/13.5–90.0
Cabins (for one person):	0
Cabins (with private balcony):	232
Cabins (wheelchair accessible):	3
Wheelchair accessibility:	Good
Cabin Current:	110 and 220 volts
Elevators:	4
Casino (gaming tables):	Yes
Slot Machines:	Yes
Swimming Pools:	1
Hot Tubs (on deck):	3
Self-Service Launderette:	Yes
Dedicated Cinema/Seats:	No
Library:	Yes
Onboard currency:	US$

English country house decor for mature-age cruisers

OVERVIEW. *Pacific Princess* is good for mature adults who seek value for money aboard a comfortable small ship with plenty of dining choices and limited entertainment.

THE SHIP. *Pacific Princess* has an all-white hull, which makes the ship appear larger than it is – and a large, square-ish funnel. A Lido Deck has a swimming pool and good sunbathing space, while one of the aft decks has a thalassotherapy pool. A jogging track circles the swimming pool deck, but one deck above. The uppermost outdoors deck includes a golf driving net and shuffleboard court.

Although there is no walk-around promenade deck outdoors, there is a small jogging track around the perimeter of the swimming pool, and port and starboard side decks. Instead of wooden decks outdoors, these are covered by Bolidt, a sand-colored rubberized material. There is no sauna. The room service menu is extremely limited. Stairways, although carpeted, are tinny. In order to keep the prices low, often the air routing to get to/from your ship is not the most direct.

The interior decor is quite stunning and elegant, a throwback to ship decor of the ocean liners of the 1920s and '30s, executed in fine taste. This includes detailed ceiling cornices, both real and faux wrought-iron staircase railings, leather- and cherry wood-paneled wall, trompe l'oeil ceilings, and rich carpeting in hallways with an Oriental rug-look center section. The overall feel echoes that of an old-world country club. The staircase in the main, two-deck-high foyer recalls the staircase in the 1997 movie *Titanic*.

Berlitz's Ratings		
	Possible	Achieved
Ship	500	392
Accommodation	200	150
Food	400	252
Service	400	287
Entertainment	100	71
Cruise Experience	400	290
OVERALL SCORE		
1442 points out of 2000		

The public rooms are spread over three decks. The reception hall has a staircase with intricate wrought-iron railings. The Nightclub, with forward-facing views, sits high in the ship and has some Polynesian-inspired decor and furniture.

There are plenty of bars – including one in the entrance to each restaurant. Perhaps the nicest of all bars and lounges are in the casino bar/lounge that is a beautiful room reminiscent of London's grand hotels and understated gaming clubs. It has an inviting marble fireplace – in fact, there are three such fireplaces aboard – and comfortable sofas and individual chairs. There is also a large Card Room, which incorporates an Internet center with eight stations.

The Library is a beautiful, grand Regency-style room, with a fireplace, a high, indented, trompe l'oeil ceiling, and an excellent selection of books, plus very comfortable wingback chairs with footstools, and sofas you could sleep on; it's the most relaxing room aboard. There's very little entertainment, but it is not needed in the cruise areas featured. *Pacific Princess* is much more about relaxation than larger Princess ships.

As with all Princess Cruises ships, 15 percent is added to all bar and spa accounts – most drink prices are moderate, but beer prices are high. A standard gratuity is automatically added to onboard accounts – to reduce the amount, you'll need to go to the reception desk.

There is a charge – tokens must be obtained from the reception desk – for using the machines in the self-service launderette. A change machine in the launderette itself would be more user-friendly.

ACCOMMODATION. There is a variety of about eight different cabin types to choose from, with prices linked to grade, location and size.

All of the standard interior and outside-view cabins are extremely compact units, and extremely tight for two persons – especially for cruises longer than seven days. Cabins have twin beds or queen-size bed, with good under-bed storage areas, personal safe, vanity desk with large mirror, good closet and drawer space in rich, dark woods, and bathrobe. Color TVs carry a major news channel, where obtainable, plus a sports channel and several round-the-clock movie channels. The bathrooms, which have tiled floors and plain walls, are compact, standard units, and include a shower enclosure with a removable, strong hand-held shower unit, hairdryer, 100 percent cotton towels, toiletries storage shelves, and a retractable clothesline.

The suites/cabins that have private balconies (66 percent of all suites/cabins, or 73 percent of all outside-view suites/cabins) have partial, and not full, balcony partitions, and sliding glass doors. Thanks to good design and layout, only 14 cabins on Deck 6 have lifeboat-obstructed views. The balcony floor is covered in thick plastic matting – teak would be nicer – and some awful plastic furniture.

Mini-Suites (52). Units designated as mini-suites are in reality simply larger cabins than the standard varieties, as the sleeping and lounge areas are not divided. While not overly large, the bathrooms have a good-size tub and ample space for storing toiletries. The living area has a refrigerated minibar, lounge area with breakfast table, and a balcony with two plastic chairs and a table.

Owner's Suites (10). The most spacious accommodation onboard, these are fine, large living spaces in the forward-most and aft-most sections of the accommodation decks. Particularly nice are those that overlook the stern, on Decks 6, 7, and 8. They have bigger balconies that really are private and cannot be overlooked by anyone from the decks above. There is an entrance foyer, living room, bedroom, CD player, bathroom with Jacuzzi tub, as well as a small guest bathroom. The bed faces the sea, which can be seen through the floor-to-ceiling windows and sliding glass door.

All suites/cabins located at the stern may suffer from vibration and noise, particularly when the ship is proceeding at or close to full speed, or maneuvering in port.

DINING. There are four different dining spots – three restaurants and one casual self-serve buffet:

The Club Restaurant has 338 seats, all with armrests, and includes a large raised central section. There are large ocean-view windows on three sides, and some prime tables that overlook the stern, as well as a small bandstand for occasional live dinner music. However, the noise level can be high because of the single-deck-height ceiling.

Sabatini's Trattoria, an extra-cost Italian restaurant, has 96 seats (all chairs have armrests), windows along two sides, and a set 'Bellissima' three-hour dégustation menu.

The Sterling Steakhouse is an 'American steak house' with a good selection of large, prime steaks and other meats. It has 98 comfortable seats, all with armrests, and windows along two sides. It has a set menu, together with added daily chef's specials. There is a cover charge.

The Lido Café has seating for 154 indoors and 186 outdoors, with white plastic patio furniture. It is open for breakfast, lunch, and casual dinners. The ship's self-serve buffet restaurant, it is open 24 hours a day and has a small pizzeria and grill.

All restaurants have open-seating dining, so you dine when you want, although reservations are necessary for Sabatini's Trattoria and Sterling Steakhouse, where there are mostly tables for four or six – there are few tables for two. In addition, there is a Poolside Grill and Bar for fast food.

ENTERTAINMENT. The 345-seat Cabaret Lounge, in the forward part of the ship on Deck 5, is the main venue for entertainment events and some social functions. The single-level room has a stage, and circular hardwood dance floor with adjacent banquette and individual tub chair seating, and raised sections on the port and starboard sides. It is not a large room, and not really designed for production shows, so cabaret acts and local entertainment form the main focus. Mini-revue style shows with colorful costumes are presented by a troupe of resident singer/dancers in a potted version of what you might experience aboard the large ships of Princess Cruises. Inevitably, art auctions and bingo are pushed almost daily.

SPA/FITNESS. Facilities, which are located in the forward part of the ship on a high deck (Deck 9), include a gymnasium with ocean-view windows and some high-tech muscle-toning equipment and treadmills. There are steam rooms but no sauna, changing areas for men and women, and a beauty salon with ocean-view windows.

The spa is operated by Steiner, a specialist concession whose retail products are sold there. Some fitness classes, such as Stepexpress, Power Walk, Total Body Conditioning, Xpress Circuit, are free. Others, such as yoga and kick-boxing, cost extra, as do massage, facials, pedicures, and beauty salon treatments.

Pacific Venus
★★★★

Size:	Small Ship	Passenger/Crew Ratio (lower beds):	2.1
Tonnage:	26,518	Cabins (total):	238
Lifestyle:	Standard	Size Range (sq ft/m):	164.6–699.6/15.3–65.0
Cruise Line:	Venus Cruise	Cabins (for one person):	0
Former Names:	none	Cabins (with private balcony):	20
IMO Number:	9160011	Cabins (wheelchair accessible):	1
Builder:	Ishikawajima Heavy Industries (Japan)	Wheelchair accessibility:	Fair
Original Cost:	$114 million (13 billion yen)	Cabin Current:	110 volts
Entered Service:	Apr 1998	Elevators:	4
Registry:	Japan	Casino (gaming tables):	Yes
Length (ft/m):	601.7/183.4	Slot Machines:	Yes
Beam (ft/m):	82.0/25.0	Swimming Pools:	1
Draft (ft/m):	21.3/6.5	Hot Tubs (on deck):	1
Propulsion/Propellers:	diesel (13,636kW)/2	Self-Service Launderette:	Yes
Passenger Decks:	7	Dedicated Cinema/Seats:	Yes/94
Total Crew:	220	Library:	Yes
Passengers (lower beds):	476	Onboard currency:	Japanese yen
Passenger Space Ratio (lower beds):	55.7		

Comfortable decor and fine style for Japanese cruisers

OVERVIEW. *Pacific Venus* is best suited to Japanese-speaking couples and single travelers of mature years who appreciate very comfortable surroundings and good food and service, all at a moderate cost. The ship is often operated under charter to travel organizations, so drinks aren't always included in the fare; when operated by Venus Cruise, alcoholic drinks are not included.

THE SHIP. The company Venus Cruise is part of Japan Cruise Line, which is itself part of SHK Line Group, a joint venture between the Shin Nohonkai, Hankyu, and Kanpu ferry companies, which operate more than 20 ferries. There is a decent amount of open deck space aft of the funnel – good for deck sports – while protected sunbathing space is provided around a small swimming pool. All sunloungers have cushioned pads. The open walking promenade decks are rubber-coated steel – hardwood would be more desirable.

The base of the funnel is the site of a day/night lounge, which overlooks the pool; this is slightly reminiscent of Royal Caribbean International's funnel-wrapped Viking Crown lounges aboard its earlier ships. There is plenty of space per passenger. The decor is clean and fresh, with much use of pastel colors and blond woods, giving the interiors a feeling of warmth.

The dining rooms are located off Deck 7, which has a double-width indoor promenade, with high ceiling height. A three-deck-high atrium has a crystal chandelier as its focal point, and a white baby grand

Berlitz's Ratings		
	Possible	Achieved
Ship	500	388
Accommodation	200	147
Food	400	310
Service	400	310
Entertainment	100	75
Cruise Experience	400	301
OVERALL SCORE		
1531 points out of 2000		

piano sits on its lower level, close to the Reception Desk.

There are special rooms for meetings and conference organizers, for use when the ship is chartered. A piano salon has colorful low-back chairs, and a large main hall has a finely sculptured high ceiling and over 700 moveable seats. There's a 350-seat main lounge for cabaret shows and ballroom dancing, a small movie theater, and a library/writing room and card room. A casino gaming area is located as part of the Top Lounge set at the front of the funnel. Winners receive prizes instead of cash, under Japanese law. There's also a smoking room, Chashitsu (tatami mat) room and card room/mahjong room, free self-service launderettes on each accommodation deck, and two (credit card/coin) public telephone booths.

Overall, this company provides a well-packaged cruise in a ship that has a comfortable, serene environment. The dress code is relaxed, and no tipping is allowed.

The ship has two classes: Salon Class and Standard Class. Salon Class passengers pay more, but get suite-grade accommodation, eat in a private dining room, and are given extra perks and services, including a welcome embarkation basket, more toiletries, and priority tickets for shows and shore tenders.

ACCOMMODATION. There are five types: Royal Suites, suites, deluxe cabins, state cabins (in four price grades), and standard cabins. All are located from the uppermost to lowermost decks, respectively. All suites and cabins have an outside view, but few cabins have a private balcony.

The four Royal Suites (Archaic, Elegant, Modern, and Noble) are decorated in two different styles – one contemporary, one in a more traditional Japanese style. Each has a private balcony (with a drinks table and two chairs) with sliding door, an expansive lounge with large sofa and plush armchairs, coffee table, window-side chairs and drinks table, floor-to-ceiling windows, and a large flat-screen TV set, with separate DVD unit. The bedroom has twin beds or a queen-size one, vanity/writing desk, and a large walk-in closet with personal safe. Also provided are high-quality binoculars, camera tripod, humidifier, coffee/tea-making set, and free minibar set-up. The large bathroom has ocean-view windows, Jacuzzi tub, a separate shower enclosure, and his/her washbasins.

Sixteen other suites have private balconies (with teak table and two chairs), a good-size living area with vanity/writing desk, dining table, chair and curved sofa, separate sleeping area, and bathroom with deep tub slightly larger than the Royal Suites, and single large washbasin. There is ample lighted closet and drawer space (two locking drawers instead of a personal safe), and a DVD unit.

Some 20 deluxe cabins have large picture windows fronted by a large, curtained arch, a sleeping area with twin or queen beds, plus a daytime sofa that converts into a third bed.

So-called 'state' cabins, many with upper berths for third passengers, are in three price levels, and have decor that is best described as basic, with reasonable closet space but very little drawer space.

Standard cabins, however, are really plain, but can accommodate three persons – useful for families – although the drawer and storage space is a bit tight.

All accommodation grades have a tea set with electric kettle, TV set, telephone, and stocked minibar/refrigerator – all items included in the cruise price. Bathrooms have a hairdryer and lots of Shiseido toiletries, particularly in the suites. All room-service menu items cost extra – this is typical of all Japanese cruise ships – except for Salon Class suite-grade ac-commodation. All passengers receive a yukata (a Japanese-style light cotton robe). Suite occupants also get a plush bathrobe, and all accommodation grades have electric, automatic toilets (washlets) with heated seats.

DINING. The Primavera Restaurant is located aft, with ocean views on three sides, and a high ceiling. Passengers dine in one seating, and tables are for six, 10, or 12. The food consists of both Japanese and Western items; the menu is varied, and the food is attractively presented. For breakfast and lunch it includes a self-serve buffet, while dinner is typically a fully served set meal.

A separate, intimate 42-seat restaurant, Grand Siè-cle, is reserved for occupants of suite-grade (Salon Class) accommodation; it is tastefully decorated in Regency style, with fine wood-paneling and a detailed, indented ceiling. It has mostly tables for two (with plenty of space for correct service), better-quality chopsticks, nori seaweed, and better quality and variety of fine china. Cold and hot towels are provided, and the whole dining experience is far better than in the Primavera.

ENTERTAINMENT. Le Pacific Main Lounge is the venue for all shipboard entertainment and also functions as a lecture and activities room during the day. It is a single-level room with seating clustered around a thrust stage, so that entertainers are in the very midst of their audience.

On most cruises, special featured entertainers such as singers, instrumentalists, storytellers, and dance champions are brought on board from ashore.

SPA/FITNESS. Spa facilities comprise men's and women's Grand Baths, which include two bathing pools and health/cleansing stations. There are ocean-view windows, a steam room, a gymnasium with ocean-view windows (in a different location just aft of the funnel), and a sauna.

Japanese massage is available, as are hairdressing and barber services in the small salon, located on the lowest passenger-accessible deck of the ship.

Paul Gauguin
★★★★

Size:	Small Ship
Tonnage:	19,200
Lifestyle:	Premium
Cruise Line:	Paul Gauguin Cruises
Former Names:	none
IMO Number:	9111319
Builder:	Chantiers de l'Atlantique (France)
Original Cost:	$150 million
Entered Service:	Jan 1998/Jan 2010
Registry:	The Bahamas
Length (ft/m):	513.4/156.5
Beam (ft/m):	72.1/22.0
Draft (ft/m):	16.8/5.1
Propulsion/Propellers:	diesel-electric (9,000kW)/2
Passenger Decks:	7
Total Crew:	215
Passengers (lower beds):	332
Passenger Space Ratio (lower beds):	57.8

Passenger/Crew Ratio (lower beds):	1.5
Cabins (total):	166
Size Range (sq ft/m):	200.0–588.0/18.5–54.6
Cabins (for one person):	0
Cabins (with private balcony):	89
Cabins (wheelchair accessible):	1
Wheelchair accessibility:	Fair
Cabin Current:	110 volts
Elevators:	4
Casino (gaming tables):	Yes
Slot Machines:	Yes
Swimming Pools:	1
Hot Tubs (on deck):	0
Self-Service Launderette:	No
Dedicated Cinema/Seats:	No
Library:	Yes
Onboard currency:	US$

An elegant, cool ship for chic warm-weather cruising

OVERVIEW. *Paul Gauguin* is best suited to couples and solo travelers seeking specialized itineraries, good regional cuisine and service, and plenty of scuba and snorkeling opportunities. It suits those who are happy with almost no entertainment. Where the ship really shines is in its variety of water sports equipment, and its shallow draft that allows it to navigate and anchor in lovely little places that larger ships couldn't possibly reach.

Berlitz's Ratings		
	Possible	Achieved
Ship	500	393
Accommodation	200	167
Food	400	304
Service	400	320
Entertainment	100	71
Cruise Experience	400	285
OVERALL SCORE		
1540 points out of 2000		

THE SHIP. Built by a French company specifically to operate in shallow waters, *Paul Gauguin* is now under long-term charter to Pacific Beachcombers of Tahiti, who also own the Intercontinental Tahiti, Intercontinental Bora Bora Le Moana, Intercontinental Bora Bora, and Intercontinental Moorea. The ship cruises around French Polynesia and the South Pacific, and, while it could carry many more passengers, it is forbidden to do so by French law. It has a well-balanced, all-white profile, and a single funnel.

This smart ship also has a retractable aft marina platform, and carries two water-skiing boats and two inflatable craft for water sports. Windsurfers, kayaks, plus scuba and snorkeling gear, and dive helmets are available for your use; all except scuba gear are included in the cruise fare. Islands, beaches, and water sports are what *Paul Gauguin* is good at. Perhaps the best island experience is in Bora Bora. Its shallow draft means there could be some movement, as the ship is a little high-sided for its size.

Inside, there is a pleasant array of public rooms, and both the artwork and the decor have a real French Polynesia look and feel. The interior colors are quite restful, although a trifle bland, but the new deck and direction signage has been improved, and the ship was refreshed during a 2011 refurbishment. The 'tub' chairs in some of the public rooms are uncomfortable.

Expert lecturers on Tahiti and Gauguin accompany each cruise, and a Fare (pronounced *foray*) Tahiti Gallery features books, film, and other materials on the unique art, history, and culture of the islands. Three original Gauguin sketches are displayed under protective glass.

The dress code is totally relaxed – every day. The standard itinerary means the ship docks only in Papeete, and shore tenders are used in all other ports. There is little entertainment (and little needed), as the ship stays overnight in several ports. The high crew-to-passenger ratio translates to a high level of personalized service.

The ship has become a favorite of travelers to these climes, and the quiet, refined atmosphere on board makes it clubby, with passengers getting to know each other easily. Wi-Fi spots are provided, but Internet charges are high. Le Casino has blackjack and roulette tables, while slot players will find 13 machines in an adjacent area.

A cruise aboard *Paul Gauguin* is all about connecting with French Polynesia, and the ship carries lecturers to inform you about the life, history, and sea life of the region.

All in all, the ship will provide you with a delightful, intimate cruise and product that most will really enjoy. Gratuities are included. Soft drinks and mineral water are included in the cruise price. Note that if you fly out to Tahiti a day or so before the cruise and stay in a hotel, bugs (insects) are a problem encountered by many travelers, so it may be wise to take some insect repellent.

ACCOMMODATION. There are eight suite/cabin grades, priced according to location and size. The outside-view cabins, half of which have private balconies, are nicely equipped, although they are all strictly rectangular. Most have large windows, except those on the lowest accommodation deck, which have portholes. Each has queen- or twin-size beds convertible to queen, and wood-accented cabinetry with rounded edges. A minibar/refrigerator stocked with complimentary soft drinks, a DVD player, personal safe, hairdryer, and umbrellas are standard. A selection of L'Occitane toiletries is provided.

The marble-look bathrooms are large and pleasing and have a tub as well as a separate shower enclosure. All passengers are provided with 100 percent cotton bathrobes and cotton slippers. The two largest suites have a private balcony at the front and side of the vessel. Although there's a decent amount of in-cabin space, with a beautiful long vanity unit and plenty of drawer space, the bathrooms are disappointingly small and plain, and too similar to all other standard cabin bathrooms.

Butler service is provided in all accommodation designated as Owner's Suite, Grand Suites, and ocean-view 'A' and 'B' category suites.

DINING. L'Etoile, the main dining room, is open for dinner only, while La Veranda, an alternative dining spot, serves breakfast, lunch, and dinner. Both have open seating, which means you can choose when you want to dine and with whom. This provides a good opportunity to meet new people for dinner each evening. The chairs have armrests, making it more comfortable for a leisurely mealtime. The dining operation is well orchestrated, with cuisine and service of a reasonably high standard. Select wines and liquor are included

in the fare, while the limited selection of premium wines costs extra.

The 134-seat La Veranda Restaurant is one deck above L'Etoile. There is both indoor and outdoor seating. This is a self-serve buffet venue for breakfast and lunch. The breakfast buffets tend to be extremely repetitive (especially the boxed cereals), and lunch buffets are often a disappointment; there is, however, a decent selection of olive oils and sauces made on board. At night, the venue provides better, more creative fare, in very pleasant surroundings (reservations are required, but there's no extra charge, and the capacity is limited to 75 persons). La Veranda provides dinner by reservation, with alternating French and Italian menus; the French menus are provided by Jean-Pierre Vigato, chef of the Michelin one-star Apicius, in Paris.

An outdoor (but covered) Le Grill provides informal café fare on deck aft of the pool, with up 100 seats. Each evening it becomes Pacific Grill and serves Polynesian cuisine; although reservations are required there is no extra charge.

For something different, it is possible to have dinner on the Marina platform on certain nights (when it's calm, of course).

ENTERTAINMENT. Le Grand Salon is the venue for shows and cabaret acts. It is a single-level room, and seating is in banquette and individual tub chairs. Sight lines are quite good from most seats, although there are some obstructions. Don't expect lavish production shows (there aren't any), as the main entertainment consists of local Polynesian shows brought on board from ashore, plus the odd cabaret act. A piano lounge was added in a 2006 refit.

SPA/FITNESS. The Deep Nature Spa, on Deck 6 in the ship's center, is the wellbeing space. It includes a fitness centre with muscle-pumping and body-toning equipment (in a windowless room), a steam room, several treatment rooms, changing area (very small), and beauty salon. Spa/beauty services and staff are provided by Algotherm. There is no sauna, but use of the steam room is complimentary. Body-pampering treatments include various massages, aromatherapy facials, manicures, pedicures, and hairdressing services.

Pearl Mist
★★★+

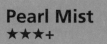

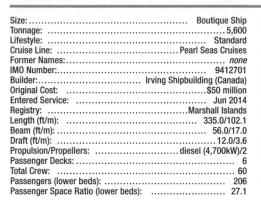

Size:... Boutique Ship	Passenger/Crew Ratio (lower beds): 3.4
Tonnage: 5,600	Cabins (total): 108
Lifestyle: .... Standard	Size Range (sq ft/m):..................... 302.0-580.0/28.0-53.8
Cruise Line: .... Pearl Seas Cruises	Cabins (for one person): 10
Former Names:.. none	Cabins (with private balcony): 108
IMO Number:... 9412701	Cabins (wheelchair accessible): 4
Builder:................................ Irving Shipbuilding (Canada)	Wheelchair accessibility: .... Fair
Original Cost: ....$50 million	Cabin Current: .... 110 volts
Entered Service: .... Jun 2014	Elevators: 1
Registry: ....Marshall Islands	Casino (gaming tables):...No
Length (ft/m): 335.0/102.1	Slot Machines: ....No
Beam (ft/m): 56.0/17.0	Swimming Pools: 0
Draft (ft/m): 12.0/3.6	Hot Tubs (on deck): 1
Propulsion/Propellers: ....diesel (4,700kW)/2	Self-Service Launderette: ....No
Passenger Decks:... 6	Dedicated Cinema/Seats: ....No
Total Crew: 60	Library: ....Yes
Passengers (lower beds): 206	Onboard currency: ....US$
Passenger Space Ratio (lower beds): 27.1	

This small ship specializes in US coastal and Caribbean cruises

OVERVIEW. *Pearl Mist* is best suited to couples and solo travelers of mature years who want to cruise in an all-American environment aboard a very small ship where the destinations are more important than food, service, or entertainment.

THE SHIP. American Cruise Lines ordered this ship from Ingalls shipyard in Canada, but had to complete the fitting out themselves in their company-owned shipyard in Chesapeake Bay, Maryland.

Pearl Mist was designed and built for international ocean-going cruises. Pearl Seas Cruises is an offshore outgrowth of the all-American company, American Cruise Lines (which has several coastal ships and rivership), based in Connecticut. But don't confuse the US's Pearl Seas Cruises with Australia's Pearl Sea Cruises.

Pearl Mist is designed to be a much more comfortable and upscale ship than the smaller ones belonging to American Cruise Lines (*American Glory*, *American Spirit*, and *American Star*). It has greater speed, the latest navigational technology and propulsion equipment, and better onboard facilities and service. It is meant to appeal to passengers who enjoy discovering ports in the company of like-minded people, away from the hunting grounds of crowded large resort ships.

Public rooms include two principal lounges, the Pacific Lounge, and the Atlantic Lounge; one is above, and the other is below the navigation bridge.

Other public rooms include a small Coral Lounge located just behind the mast; a library, and two small midship lounges. A single elevator goes to all decks,

Berlitz's Ratings		
	Possible	Achieved
Ship	500	361
Accommodation	200	148
Food	400	264
Service	400	285
Entertainment	100	67
Cruise Experience	400	272
OVERALL SCORE		
1397 points out of 2000		

including the outdoor sun deck. Shipwide Wi-Fi is complimentary, but internet access is patchy.

The ship cruises in the east coast waters of the US and Canada during the summer season and in the Caribbean during the winter season, from St. Martin. Gratuities are not included. Niggles: there is no laundry; some cabins (particularly aft) are extremely noisy; and there are no personal safes.

ACCOMMODATION. There are seven cabin price grades, but all accommodation grades are outside-view suites/cabins with private balcony (although the balcony is quite slender). All cabins feature twin beds that convert to king-size, and have high-quality bed linens; bathrooms have a walk-in shower. Some cabins can be interconnected, so a couple (partners or friends traveling together, for example) can have a bathroom each.

CUISINE. The single dining room – at the stern of the ship – accommodates all passengers at a set time in an open seating, so you can sit where and with whom you want. Complimentary cocktails and hors d'oeuvres are offered before dinner in the lounges.

ENTERTAINMENT. The Main Lounge is the venue for evening entertainment, lectures, and recaps, plus anything that is brought on board from ashore. However, it doesn't accommodate all passengers at once.

SPA/FITNESS. The small spa has a beauty salon; additionally, there is also one hot tub on deck.

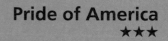

Pride of America
★★★

Size:	Large Resort Ship	Passenger Space Ratio (lower beds):	36.7
Tonnage:	80,439	Passenger/Crew Ratio (lower beds):	2.3
Lifestyle:	Standard	Cabins (total):	1,171
Cruise Line:	Norwegian Cruise Line	Size Range (sq ft/m):	129.1–1,377.8/12.0–128.0
Former Names:	none	Cabins (for one person):	4
IMO Number:	9209221	Cabins (with private balcony):	785
Builder:	Ingalls Shipbuilding (USA)/Lloyd Werft (Germany)	Cabins (wheelchair accessible):	21
Original Cost:	$450 million	Wheelchair accessibility:	Good
Entered Service:	Jul 2005	Cabin Current:	110 volts
Registry:	USA	Elevators:	10
Length (ft/m):	920.3/280.5	Casino (gaming tables):	Yes
Beam (ft/m):	106.6/32.2	Slot Machines:	Yes
Draft (ft/m):	26.25/8.0	Swimming Pools:	2
Propulsion/Propellers:	diesel-electric (32,000kW)/ 2 azimuthing pods	Hot Tubs (on deck):	0
		Self-Service Launderette:	No
Passenger Decks:	11	Dedicated Cinema/Seats:	No
Total Crew:	940	Library:	Yes
Passengers (lower beds):	2,186	Onboard currency:	US$

A large, family-friendly resort ship for Hawaii cruises

OVERVIEW. The ship suits first-time young couples, solo travelers, and families with children and teenagers who enjoy city nightlife and want contemporary, upbeat surroundings, plenty of entertainment lounges and bars, and high-tech sophistication – all in one well-packaged cruise vacation, with constant music, participation activity, and entertainment. But don't expect good service – most of the crew simply don't cut it.

Berlitz's Ratings		
	Possible	Achieved
Ship	500	370
Accommodation	200	148
Food	400	214
Service	400	206
Entertainment	100	68
Cruise Experience	400	237
OVERALL SCORE		
1243 points out of 2000		

at $12 per person ($6 for children aged 3–12) per day; this is pooled for all crew and provides payment when they are on vacation. You will be expected to provide gratuities. In addition, a 15 percent gratuity plus Hawaii's sales tax (because of the ship's US registry) is added to all bar (and 18 percent for spa treatment) accounts.

Although the islands are pleasant enough, a cruise aboard this ship is likely to test your patience.

THE SHIP. *Pride of America*, which sank during its dockside reconstruction at Germany's Lloyd Werft shipbuilders, sails on inter-island cruises, focusing on Hawaii's islands. The 85,850-sq-ft (7,975-sq-m) open deck space includes a sunbathing/pool deck inspired by Miami's South Beach – think Ocean Drive/Lincoln Mall – and an Art Deco area.

The stunning interior design is modeled after a 'Best of America' theme, with public rooms named after famous Americans. Facilities include the Capitol Atrium (a lobby spanning eight decks and said to be inspired by the Capitol Building and White House), a large casino, a conservatory complete with tropical landscaped garden and live exotic birds, SoHo Art Gallery (holding art auctions), Washington Library, and Newbury Shopping Center.

Six dedicated meeting rooms range in size from boardrooms for 10 people to an auditorium for up to 250. The ship has a mainly Hawaiian crew.

A non-changeable service charge (as distinct from a gratuity) for staff is added to your onboard account

ACCOMMODATION. About 75 percent of all cabins have outside views. There are also a large number of family-friendly interconnecting cabins; many cabins have third/fourth upper berths, and some family-friendly cabins can accommodate as many as six. Some suites have king-size beds, while most cabins have twin beds that can be placed together to make a queen-size bed. In 2013, four Studio-grade cabins were added, as were 24 'suites' and four interior (no-view) cabins (in the space previously used as a conference center). Butler and concierge service is provided for suite-grade occupants, who also get Lavazza espresso makers, Elemis bath products, private dining for breakfast and lunch, and other perks. A number of cabins are wheelchair-accessible – some are equipped for the hearing-impaired.

Grand Suites. Grand Suites have around 1,400 sq ft (130 sq m) of living space. They are located high atop the ship forward of the sun deck and offer sweeping views from a walk-around outdoor terrace, which includes a hot tub and large relaxation/sunbathing area.

There is a large living room with Bang & Olufsen entertainment center, wet bar, and separate dining room with dining table and six chairs. The master bedroom has a king-size bed, large bathroom, with whirlpool tub and separate shower enclosure; dressing area with flat-screen TV, and walk-in closet. At the entrance to the suite is a guest powder room.

Owner's Suites. Measuring around 870 sq ft (80 sq m), these are named after indigenous flowers in Hawaii such as Bird of Paradise, Gardenia, Orchid, and Plumeria. Each has a bedroom with king-size bed, walk-in closet, dressing area, and separate living room with Bang & Olufsen entertainment center. The bathroom has a whirlpool tub and separate shower enclosure. There is also a large private balcony with hot tub, outdoor dining facilities, and sun beds.

Deluxe Penthouse Suites. These measure around 735 sq ft (68 sq m). They have a separate bedroom with king-size bed and walk-in closet; the bathroom has a whirlpool tub, separate shower enclosure, two washbasins, and dressing area; the living room has a Bang & Olufsen entertainment center, wet bar, and private balcony.

Penthouse Suites. These measure 504–585 sq ft (47–55 sq m), and have a separate bedroom with king-size bed and walk-in closet; the bathroom has a whirlpool tub, separate shower enclosure, two washbasins, and dressing area; the living room has a Bang & Olufsen entertainment center, wet bar, and private balcony.

Family Suites. These measure around 360 sq ft (34 sq m). Each has a main bedroom with two twin beds that convert to a queen-size bed, a living room with double sofa bed and entertainment center, and den with single sofa bed. Another four family 'suites,' measuring 330–380 sq ft (30.5–35 sq m), have an interconnecting door between two cabins; there are thus two bathrooms.

Standard outside-view and interior cabins. Outside-view cabins have either a window or porthole, depending on location, twin beds that can convert into a queen-size bed, TV, satellite-dial telephone, and personal safe; the bathrooms have a built-in hairdryer.

DINING. Freestyle Cruising means you get a choice of several restaurants and informal eateries. Choose from two main dining rooms, and six other à-la-carte and casual venues (some cost extra).

Main restaurants include the 628-seat Skyline Restaurant – with decor inspired by the skyscrapers of the 1930s – and the 496-seat Liberty Dining Room, with two seatings.

Other dining options. The 106-seat Lazy J Texas Steak House is a contemporary steak house with Texas decor – the artwork includes Houston Space Center, Texas Rangers, and Dallas Cowboys.

East Meets West is an intimate 32-seat Pacific Rim/Asian Fusion restaurant with a sushi/sashimi bar and a Teppanyaki grill room with two tables (showmanship food is prepared in front of you). Jefferson's Bistro, seating 104, is the ship's 'signature' restaurant, with an à-la-carte menu of classic and nouvelle French cuisine. The decor is inspired by that of Thomas Jefferson's home in Monticello – Jefferson was the US ambassador to France from 1785 to 1789, before becoming America's third president.

Little Italy, a casual Italian eatery, serves pasta, pizza, and other popular light Italian fare. It has 116 seats.

Cadillac Diner accommodates 70 indoors and 36 outdoors, and is open 24 hours a day, with quirky Cadillac seats and a video jukebox. It's for fast food: hamburgers and hot dogs, fish and chips, pot pies, and wok dishes.

A Moderno Churrascarria (Brazilian steakhouse for meat delivered on a skewer by service staff dressed 'gaucho' style) was added in the 2013 refit, as was Cagney's Steak House – for prime American steaks and grilled seafood. A cover charge applies to both venues and reservations are required.

Aloha Café/Kids Café is an indoor/outdoor self-serve buffet-style eatery with a Hawaiian theme. A special section for children has counter tops at just the right height, as well as chairs and tables that have been shrunk to a child-friendly size.

Other eateries and bars include the Napa Wine Bar (wines by the glass), Pink's Champagne and Cigar Bar (inspired by Hawaii's Pink Palace Hotel on Waikiki Beach), the Gold Rush saloon (pub with karaoke, plus a darts board and bar billiards), and a John Adams Coffee Bar. Outdoor eateries and drinking places include the Key West Bar and Grill, and the Waikiki Bar.

ENTERTAINMENT. The Hollywood Theater seats 840 and stages large-scale production shows and local Hawaiian shows. A 590-seat cabaret lounge, the Mardi Gras Lounge, has cabaret entertainment, including late-night comedy.

SPA/FITNESS. The Santa Fe Spa and Fitness Center is decorated with artefacts from New Mexico. It is operated by Mandara Spa (owned by Steiner Leisure).

While some fitness classes are free, others cost extra. Massage facials, pedicures, and beauty salon treatments also cost extra.

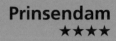

Prinsendam
★★★★

Size:	Mid-size Ship	Passenger/Crew Ratio (lower beds):	1.8
Tonnage:	38,100	Cabins (total):	419
Lifestyle:	Premium	Size Range (sq ft/m):	137.7–723.3/12.8–67.2
Cruise Line:	Holland America Line	Cabins (for one person):	3
Former Names:	Seabourn Sun, Royal Viking Sun	Cabins (with private balcony):	166
IMO Number:	8700280	Cabins (wheelchair accessible):	10
Builder:	Wartsila (Finland)	Wheelchair accessibility:	Best
Original Cost:	$125 million	Cabin Current:	110 volts
Entered Service:	Dec 1988/May 2002	Elevators:	4
Registry:	The Netherlands	Casino (gaming tables):	Yes
Length (ft/m):	674.2/205.5	Slot Machines:	Yes
Beam (ft/m):	91.8/28.0	Swimming Pools:	2
Draft (ft/m):	23.6/7.2	Hot Tubs (on deck):	4
Propulsion/Propellers:	diesel (21,120kW)/2	Self-Service Launderette:	Yes
Passenger Decks:	9	Dedicated Cinema/Seats:	Yes/101
Total Crew:	443	Library:	Yes
Passengers (lower beds):	835	Onboard currency:	US$
Passenger Space Ratio (lower beds):	45.6		

This very comfortable ship has a premium ambience

OVERVIEW. This ship is best suited to older adult couples and solo travelers who like to mingle in a mid-size ship operating longer cruises, in an unhurried setting with some eclectic, antique artwork, good food, and service from a smiling crew. It is a very comfortable vessel – smaller than other Holland America Line (HAL) ships, but more refined.

THE SHIP. *Prinsendam* is a well-designed ship with sleek lines, a sharply raked bow, and a well-rounded profile, with lots of floor-to-ceiling glass. Having started life as *Royal Viking Sun*, it was bought by Seabourn Cruise Line in 1998 and refitted as *Seabourn Sun*. In 2002, it was transferred to HAL as *Prinsendam*, and the color was changed from all white to dark blue (the hull) with a white superstructure. A 2007 refit added an Explorations Café and expanded the shopping arcade. In 2009 an aft deck, including 21 new cabins, was added.

Wide teakwood decks provide excellent walking areas including a decent walk-around promenade deck outdoors, but there's no jogging track. The swimming pool, outdoors on Lido Deck, is not large, but it is quite adequate, while the deck above has a croquet court and golf driving range. The interior layout is very spacious – it is even more ideal when no more than 600 passengers are aboard. Impressive public rooms and tasteful decor now reign. Two handrails – one of wood, one of chrome – are provided on all stairways, a thoughtful touch.

Berlitz's Ratings		
	Possible	Achieved
Ship	500	371
Accommodation	200	155
Food	400	266
Service	400	283
Entertainment	100	68
Cruise Experience	400	278
OVERALL SCORE		
1421 points out of 2000		

The Crow's Nest, the forward observation lounge, is an elegant, contemporary (at least in decor) space. Pebble Beach is the name of the electronic golf simulator room, complete with wet bar, with play possible on 11 virtual courses.

The Erasmus Library is well organized, although it's simply not large enough for long-distance cruising.

The Oak Room is the ship's cigar/pipe smoker's lounge; it has a marble fireplace, which sadly cannot be used due to United States Coast Guard regulations.

Whether by intention or not, the ship has a two-class feeling, with passengers in 'upstairs' Penthouse Suites and 'A' grade staterooms gravitating to the quieter Crow's Nest lounge, particularly at night, while other passengers go to the main entertainment deck.

The wide range of facilities includes a concierge, self-service launderettes (useful on long voyages), a varied guest lecture program, 24-hour information office, and true 24-hour cabin service for the discriminating passenger who demands spacious personal surroundings and good food and service, regardless of price. This ship operates mainly long-distance cruises in great comfort, and free shuttle buses are provided in almost all ports of call.

While *Prinsendam* isn't perfect, the few design flaws (for example: poorly designed bar service counters) are minor points. The elegant decorative features include Dutch artwork and memorabilia. Added benefits include a fine health spa facility, spacious, wide teakwood decks and many teak sunloungers.

There are only four elevators, so anyone with walking disabilities may have to wait for some time during periods of peak usage, such as before meals. This spacious ship shows signs of wear and tear in some areas, particularly in the accommodation passageways, despite recent refurbishments. The library is difficult for anyone in a wheelchair to enter. The shore tenders are thoughtfully air conditioned.

ACCOMMODATION. There are several accommodation grades, ranging from Penthouse Verandah Suites to standard interior cabins. All suites and cabins have undergone some degree of refurbishment since the ship was taken over by HAL in 2002.

Penthouse Verandah Suite. The Penthouse Verandah Suite (723 sq ft/67 sq m) is a most desirable living space, although not as large as Penthouse Suites aboard some other ships. It is light and airy, with two bathrooms, one of which has a large whirlpool tub with ocean views, and anodized gold bathroom fittings. The living room contains a large dining table and chairs, and large sofas. There is also a substantial private balcony, and butler service.

Deluxe Verandah Suites. There are 18 of these (eight on Sports Deck, 10 on Lido Deck). Located in the forward section, they have large balconies, two sofas, and large bar/entertainment center (minibar/refrigerator, color television, video and CD players). Bathrooms have separate toilet, sink and toiletries cabinets, connecting sliding door into the bedroom, large mirror, two toiletries cabinets, plenty of storage space, full bathtub, and anodized gold fittings. Each evening the butler brings different goodies – hot and cold hors d'oeuvres and other niceties. If you do choose one of these suites, it might be best on the starboard side where they are located in a private hallway, while those on the port side (including the Penthouse Verandah Suite) are positioned along a public hallway. The 10 suites on Lido Deck are positioned along private port and starboard side hallways.

Passengers in Penthouse and Deluxe Verandah Suites have a private concierge lounge, high tea served in the suite each afternoon, hors d'oeuvres before dinner (on request), complimentary laundry pressing and dry cleaning, private cocktail parties with captain, priority disembarkation, and more.

Other cabin grades. Most of the remaining cabins, spread over six other decks, are of generous proportions and have just about everything you would need. About 38 percent have a small, private balcony. All cabins have walk-in closets, lockable drawers, full-length mirrors, hairdryers, ample cotton towels, flat-screen TVs, and DVD players. A few cabins have third berths, while some have interconnecting doors – good for couples who want two bathrooms and more space or for families with children.

In all grades of accommodation, passengers receive a basket of fresh fruit, fluffy cotton bathrobes,

evening turndown service, and an HAL signature tote bag. Filipino and Indonesian cabin stewards and stewardesses provide unobtrusive personal service.

Four well-equipped, L-shaped cabins for the disabled are quite well designed, fairly large, and equipped with special wheel-in bathrooms with shower facilities and closets.

DINING. La Fontaine Dining Room wraps around the aft end of Lower Promenade Deck and has extensive ocean-view windows; along the starboard side is a second, smaller and quieter section. There is plenty of space around tables. A good number of window-side tables are for two persons, although there are also tables for four, six, or eight. Crystal glasses, Rosenthal china, and fine cutlery are provided.

There are two seatings for dinner, at assigned tables, and an open-seating arrangement for breakfast and lunch – you'll be seated by restaurant staff, when you enter. On most port days the restaurant is closed at lunchtime, which means using the self-serve buffet or ordering room service.

Other dining options. A small, quiet dining spot on the port side is the Pinnacle Dining Room, with 48 seats, wood-paneled decor that increases the feeling of intimacy and privacy, and fine ocean views. Table settings include Bulgari china, Riedel glassware, and Frette table linens. The venue specializes in fine steaks and seafood. Seating preference is given to suite occupants. Reservations are required, and there is a cover charge. There is a well-chosen wine list, although there's a great deal of emphasis on California wines, with prices that are quite high.

There is also a Lido Restaurant, for decent casual dining and self-serve buffet-style meals. At night, this eatery becomes the Canaletto (named after the famous Venetian artist).

Also, a Lido Deck poolside 'Dive-In at the Terrace Grill' features signature burgers, hot dogs and fries, and, on certain days, barbecues and other culinary treats may be featured.

ENTERTAINMENT. The Queen's Showlounge is an amphitheater-style layout, with a well-tiered floor, and both banquette and individual seating. While HAL isn't known for fine entertainment, what it does offer is a consistently good, tried and tested array of cabaret acts. There are male 'dance hosts,' who act as partners for women traveling alone.

SPA/FITNESS. The Greenhouse Health Spa includes six treatment rooms with integral showers, a Rasul chamber (for mud and gentle steam heat), a gymnasium with views over the stern, and separate sauna, steam room, and changing rooms for men and women. The spa is operated by specialist concession Steiner Leisure.

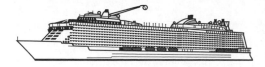

Quantum of the Seas
★★★★

Size:	Large Resort Ship	Passenger Space Ratio (lower beds):	40.3
Tonnage:	168,666	Passenger/Crew Ratio (lower beds):	3.2
Lifestyle:	Standard	Cabins (total):	2,090
Cruise Line:	Royal Caribbean International	Size Range (sq ft/m):	101.1-799.7/9.4-74.3
Former Names:	none	Cabins (for one person):	34
IMO Number:	9549463	Cabins (with private balcony):	1,571
Builder:	Meyer Werft (Germany)	Cabins (wheelchair accessible):	34
Original Cost:	$936 million	Wheelchair accessibility:	Good
Entered Service:	Oct 2014	Cabin Current:	110 and 220 volts
Registry:	The Bahamas	Elevators:	16
Length (ft/m):	1,145.0/348.0	Casino (gaming tables):	Yes
Beam (ft/m):	134.5/41.0	Slot Machines:	Yes
Draft (ft/m):	27.8/8.5	Swimming Pools:	3
Propulsion/Propellers:	diesel-electric (41,000kW)/	Hot Tubs (on deck):	4
	2 azimuthing pods	Self-Service Launderette:	No
Passenger Decks:	16	Dedicated Cinema/Seats:	No
Total Crew:	1,300	Library:	Yes
Passengers (lower beds):	4,180	Onboard currency:	US$

A high-energy, state-of-the-art, gizmo-filled family-friendly resort ship

OVERVIEW. *Quantum of the Seas* – a new class and type of smart ship for popular Royal Caribbean International (RCI) – has a slender profile (it was actually built in several huge sections and joined together). The ship is based in Tianjin (the port for Beijing), China, and the whole family will love it because it incorporates the very latest tech-intensive and creative features, and then some. You can even go flying aboard this ship! It's a lot of Royal Caribbean wow in an all-weather environment.

Berlitz's Ratings		
	Possible	Achieved
Ship	500	431
Accommodation	200	141
Food	400	298
Service	400	283
Entertainment	100	86
Cruise Experience	400	287
OVERALL SCORE		
1526 points out of 2000		

THE SHIP. *Quantum of the Seas* employs the latest in hydrodynamics, hull shape, low emissions, and, importantly, low fuel consumption, and technology. The stern slopes nicely – it looks like it could be the front! It contains the impressive Two70o – an innovative multi-level venue that is a casual living area by day and a stunning, high-energy entertainment venue by night, with dynamic screens and a huge video wall.

Several exciting features have been incorporated. North Star – quite the engineering marvel – is a 13-person (plus operator) glass capsule that lifts you off from the ship's uppermost deck and provides a bird's-eye view of all below you (including the sea) as it moves around. It's like a posh giant 'cherry picker' with attitude – and, lifting you almost 300ft (91m) above sea level (with an outreach of almost 135ft (41m), is quite a ride! Located in the front section of the ship, just behind the mast, it is complimentary (and wheelchair-accessible), but only operates at sea. A charge applies for booking for weddings or similar occasions.

The second stunner is RipCord by iFly – a simulated skydiving experience in a two-storey vertical wind tunnel that lets you experience the thrill of skydiving in a safe, controlled environment. The unit uses a powerful air flow to keep you up in the air and free-flying – like a giant hairdryer underneath you! It is located aft of the ship's funnel housing, accommodates 13 persons for each 75-minute class, including two 'hovering in the air' experiences, instruction, and gear. You can book both attractions with interactive digital kiosks (adjacent to elevators) and tablets in public areas.

Meanwhile, a SeaPlex complex – located just underneath the North Star offers a circus 'school' and adrenalin-boosting bumper-car rides, and acts as a roller-skating rink and basketball court. It's a veritable active interactive sporting venue that replaces the ice rinks of other large RCI ships. Other features include a rock-climbing wall, and a FlowRider surfing simulator.

The decor is stunningly colorful, contemporary, and jazzy. The interior focal point is the three-storey-high Royal Esplanade, which includes Michael's Genuine Pub, Sorrento's pizza outlet, a Bionic Bar, a two-deck-high entertainment venue called Music Hall, plus lots of shops, the Schooner Bar, Boleros (Latin bar), Izumi (for Japanese-style cuisine), and the American Grill. This where the action is day and night – note that it can be noisy.

Since mid-2015 *Quantum of the Seas* has been based year-round in Shanghai, China, and the principal language is Mandarin.

FAMILIES. For children and teenagers aboard this family-friendly, tech-smart ship the facilities are extensive – part of the Adventure Ocean program, with the facilities located *inside* the ship on Decks 11 and 12. The Royal Babies and Tots Nursery is for the really young ones; Aquanauts is for 3–5-year-olds; Explorers is for 6–8-year-olds; and Voyagers is for 9–12-year-olds. Optix is the chill-out zone for teenagers. There's also Adventure Beach, an area for all the family, which includes swimming pools, a water slide, and game areas outdoors in the AquaPark. DreamWorks entertainment is featured, with live character appearances from *Shrek*, *Kung Fu Panda* and *Madagascar* – not to mention *Barbie*.

ACCOMMODATION. There are many different price grades and categories for accommodation. The price you pay depends on the size and location you choose. Fortunately, every cabin aboard this ship has a view – whether real or virtual. 'Virtual' balconies were first introduced aboard *Navigator of the Seas* in a 2013 refit and are a neat feature of interior (no-view) cabins; they provide real-time ocean views, but you *can* turn them off, if you prefer. Although these cost more than standard interior cabins, they're worth it. Wrist-band RFID technology provides access to your cabin, and acts as your charge card, but it's not comfortable to wear.

Several new accommodation categories have been introduced aboard this ship. Standard cabins are about 9 percent larger than those aboard the Oasis-class ships. If you book suite-grade accommodation, you can eat all your meals in the exclusive Coastal Kitchen.

Loft cabins (including a 975 sq ft/90.5 sq m Owner's Loft) vary in size and configuration, but measure approximately 502 sq ft (46.6 sq m) and are located at the ship's stern, from where there are some great views.

Inter-connecting family cabins are really good for multi-generational groups, and highly sought after. The 15 units consist of a junior suite, balcony cabin, and interior studio, connected through a shared vestibule. Together they can create 575.8 sq ft (53.5 sq m) of living space with three bedrooms, three bathrooms, and a 216-sq-ft (20-sq-m) balcony.

There are studio cabins (12 have real balconies) for solo occupancy. As there's no supplement, they are priced in a new category for solo travelers.

Even the smallest bathroom is well designed, with thoughtful touches such as a night light, and shower and vanity hooks, while cabins have bedside power outlets, and ample storage space.

DINING. There are 18 restaurant and eatery choices (there's no main dining room as such), part of what the line calls Dynamic Dining. This means that you will need to make reservations in some venues, just like eating ashore – a concept first introduced by Star Cruises.

The following are complimentary, all with tablecloths for dinner:

The Grande: with 432 seats, the ship's most elegant restaurant (think Southern mansion hospitality) featuring classic dishes reminiscent of the days of the grand ocean liners of yesteryear. Menu examples: beef Wellington, chicken à l'orange, sole almondine.

Chic: this 434-seat restaurant features 'contemporary' cuisine and sauces made from scratch. Menu examples: rib-eye steak, lamb chops, and sea bass.

Silk: this 434-seat restaurant features pan-Asian cuisine, including a touch of spice. Menu examples: teriyaki steak, sake-glazed salmon, and lamb curry.

American Icon Grille: this 430-seat restaurant features many of America's favorite 'comfort food' dishes' including New England clam chowder, Southern buttermilk fried chicken, and New Orleans gumbo.

Extra-cost dining venues:

Wonderland: based on the elements Fire, Ice, Water, Earth, and Dreams, this surreal 62-seat Alice in Wonderland-inspired venue offers food with a quirky touch (such as the oddly shaped 'hoodie' chairs) thanks to ingredients including Japanese bonito flakes. I can just imagine the Mad Hatter's Tea Party here.

Jamie's Italian: it's a 132-seat reservations-required tablecloth-less Euro-Italian restaurant – and British celebrity chef Jamie Oliver's first restaurant at sea.

Chops Grille: for premium-quality steaks and grilled seafood (plus an integral Chef's Table).

Chef's Table: this exclusive 16-seat venue is good for private parties; wine-and-food pairing is the specialty.

Izumi: a 44-seat Japanese-Asian fusion cuisine venue including hot-rock tableside cooking, sashimi, sushi, and sake. The lantern lights fit perfectly into the decor.

Johnny Rockets: a retro 1950s all-day, all-night diner-style eatery (near the main pool) for hamburgers, extra-cost malt shakes, and jukebox hits (all tables feature a mini-jukebox). À-la-carte pricing applies.

For really casual meals at no extra cost, the 860-seat Windjammer Marketplace is a self-serve buffet-style eatery. Other casual (no extra cost) spots include: The Café at Two70o, SeaPlex Dog House, Sorrento's – for pizza slices and calzones, and Café Promenade.

ENTERTAINMENT. The Royal Theater spans three decks and is the principle showlounge for 'booked' shows and large-scale production shows by a resident troupe of singers and dancers.

Two70o is a stunning multi-level, glass-walled 'living' room (spanning almost three decks in height), located at the ship's stern, and includes a food-court-style marketplace, and sit-down eateries, including The Café @ Two70o. By night, the big venue morphs into the entertainment house, with Robo-screens and Bionic Bar featuring high-tech wizardry.

Music Hall is two-decks high a rock-'n'-roll joint, and will feature DJs and theme nights.

SPA/FITNESS. The Vitality at Sea Spa facilities include a thermal suite (extra cost), beauty salon, barber shop, and gymnasium with Technogym equipment. Massage and other body-pampering treatments take place in 19 treatment rooms.

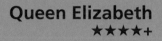

Queen Elizabeth
★★★★+

Size:	Large Resort Ship
Tonnage:	90,900
Lifestyle:	Premium/Standard
Cruise Line:	Cunard Line
Former Names:	none
IMO Number:	9477438
Builder:	Fincantieri (Italy)
Original Cost:	€634 million
Entered Service:	Oct 2010
Registry:	Bermuda
Length (ft/m):	964.5/294.0
Beam (ft/m):	105.9/32.3
Draft (ft/m):	26.2/8.0
Propulsion/Propellers:	diesel-electric (64,000kW)/ 2 azimuthing pods
Passenger Decks:	12
Total Crew:	1,005
Passengers (lower beds):	2,101

Passenger Space Ratio (lower beds):	43.2
Passenger/Crew Ratio (lower beds):	2.0
Cabins (total):	1,046
Size Range (sq ft/m):	152.0–1,493 sq.ft/14.0–138.5
Cabins (for one person):	9
Cabins (with private balcony):	820
Cabins (wheelchair accessible):	20
Wheelchair accessibility:	Good
Cabin Current:	110 and 220 volts
Elevators:	12
Casino (gaming tables):	Yes
Slot Machines:	Yes
Swimming Pools:	2
Hot Tubs (on deck):	5
Self-Service Launderette:	Yes
Dedicated Cinema/Seats:	No
Library:	Yes
Onboard currency:	US$

A delightful ship with interior decor that represents British heritage

OVERVIEW. *Queen Elizabeth*, a cruise ship that longs to be an ocean liner, suits mature adults and solo travelers, and families with children. It's pitched at traditionalists who like to dress more formally for dinner, and sail with a sense of style. Note that Berlitz's Ratings scores are the averages for both Grill Class and Britannia Class.

THE SHIP. *Queen Elizabeth,* named in the company's 170th year (the company began operations in 1840), is the second-largest Cunarder ordered in that long history. Although Cunard purports to offer a resolutely British experience, the marketing hype is undermined by the use of US dollars as the onboard currency, and trying to find British service staff is challenging. The Cunard red funnel is instantly recognizable.

Once inside, the ship feels instantly comfortable, rather like a mini-*QE2*. It has less somber colors than *Queen Victoria*, commendably little glitzy brass or chrome surfaces, and more of the look and feel of an ocean liner, including some gorgeous carpeting. The decor is classic and timeless.

Features include a majestic three-deck high Grand Lobby with a sweeping staircase, sculpted balconies and elegant decorative touches, and an adjacent Cunarders' Galleria floating museum, with memorabilia displayed in glass cabinets. The original Asprey silver model of *QE2* is in the Yacht Club, and there's a nice model of the original *Queen Elizabeth* in a cabinet on the upper level of the atrium.

Berlitz's Ratings

	Possible	Achieved
Ship	500	422
Accommodation	200	145
Food	400	300
Service	400	315
Entertainment	100	81
Cruise Experience	400	320
OVERALL SCORE		
1583 points out of 2000		

The Royal Arcade is a cluster of shops, selling goods connected with traditional and modern-day Britain, all set in an arcade-like environment; they include Hackett, Penhaligon's, and Aspinal of London.

The Library is a stunning two-deck-high wood-paneled 6,000-book facility serviced by full-time librarians, although there are few chairs in which to sit and read. Few ships today have such a fine library. There's also a bookshop selling maritime-related books, memorabilia, maps, and stationery.

Gratuities – called a Hotel and Dining charge, depending on your accommodation grade – are added to your onboard account daily.

Queen Elizabeth provides an elegant setting for a traditional cruise experience, with a wide choice of public rooms, bars, and lounges, and a mostly attentive staff. But, in the final analysis, the finesse is missing, and the ship's Princess Cruises-style cabins are below the standard expected.

ACCOMMODATION. There are three class categories of accommodation: Queens Grill; Princess Grill; and Britannia Club and Britannia Restaurant grade. So, it's all about location, location, location. Yet however much or little you pay, passengers all embark and disembark via the same gangway. Note that the air conditioning cannot be turned off in cabins or bathrooms.

Grand Suites. Four units, measuring 1,918–2,131 sq ft (178–184 sq m) and named Bisset, Charles, Illingworth, and Rostron (all former Cunard captains), are located aft, with great ocean views from their private wrap-around balconies, which contain a complete wet bar. Each has two bedrooms with walk-in closets; bathroom with tub and separate shower enclosure; lounge; and dining room with seating for six. In-suite dining from the Queens Grill menus is also available.

Master Suites. Two units, measuring 1,100 sq ft (102 sq m). Named Britten and Thomson, they are located in the center of the ship.

Penthouse Suites. Measuring 520–707 sq ft (48–65 sq m).

Queens Suites. Measuring 508–771 sq ft (47–72 sq m).

Princess Suites. Measuring 342–513 sq ft (32–48 sq m).

Balcony cabins. Measuring 242–472 sq ft (22–44 sq m).

Outside-view cabins. Measuring 180–201 sq ft (17–9 sq m).

Interior cabins. Measuring 151–243 sq ft (14–23 sq m).

All accommodation grades have both British three-pin (240-volt) sockets and American (110-volt) and European-style two-pin (220-volt) sockets. Penhaligon toiletries are supplied to all passengers, and a hairdryer is stored in the vanity desk units. Some cabins have nicely indented ceilings with suffused lighting.

The standard cabins (Grades C/D) are small, but functional, although the cabinetry is austere and lacks character. There's a lack of drawer space in a cabin supposedly designed for two persons – it's noticeable on long voyages; additional drawers are located under the bed, but these may prove challenging for some to use. The premium mattresses are excellent – as is the bed linen. European duvets are standard. The bathrooms are rather bland, like those found aboard the ships of Princess Cruises, with small washbasins, and little storage space for toiletries.

DINING. The 878-seat Britannia Restaurant – the name is taken from a former Cunard ocean liner of 1914–50 – is located aft. It is two decks high, with seating on both levels (stairways link both levels), and two seatings for dinner. An adjacent restaurant houses Britannia Club passengers, who get single-seat dining.

Exclusive dining (Queens Grill, Princess Grill). As with its sister ships, this one has two special Grill Class-only restaurants. These have a single-seating arrangement, providing a more intimate and exclusive dining experience than can be found in the two-seating main Britannia Restaurant.

The 142-seat Queens Grill (on the starboard side), with single-seating dining, is for those in suites and the top accommodation grades, and provides the best cuisine and service aboard the ship. The beloved Cunard Grill experience includes alfresco dining in The Courtyard, a courtyard terrace protected from

the wind, and access for Grill Class passengers only to an exclusive lounge and bar to their own upper terrace deck.

The 132-seat Princess Grill (on the port side), with single-seating dining, is for passengers in middle-class accommodation grades.

Other dining options. The Verandah Restaurant is a beautiful à-la-carte specialty dining venue, available to all passengers. It has a bar and is on the second level of the three-deck high lobby. The decor and ambience recreate the Verandah Grill restaurant aboard the original *Queen Elizabeth* and *Queen Mary*. The classic French cuisine is exceptionally good and makes for a fine dining experience. Reservations are required, and there's a cover charge for lunch or dinner.

The Lido Café (on Deck 9) has panoramic views, indoor/outdoor seating for approximately 470, and operates a standard multi-line self-serve buffet arrangement. It's a bit downmarket for what is supposed to be a stylish ship – the original *Queen Elizabeth* didn't have such a facility – but then, this is today. At night, the venue is transformed into three distinct flavors: Asado (South American Grill); Aztec (Mexican cuisine); and Jasmine (Asian cuisine), each with a small cover charge.

For excellent Lavazza-family coffees from Luigi (the name given to the coffee machine), teas, and light bites, there's the Café Carinthia, one deck above the purser's desk and adjacent to the popular Veuve Clicquot Champagne bar.

For traditional British comfort food, the Golden Lion Pub offers fish and chips, steak and mushroom pie, a ploughman's lunch, and, of course, bangers (sausages) and mash, plus, there's a wide range of draft beers and lagers.

ENTERTAINMENT. The 830-seat, three-deck-high Royal Court Theatre is designed in the style of a classic opera house. It has 20 private boxes that can be reserved by anyone for special nights, and a special package includes Champagne, chocolates, and a ticket printed with name and box number – in the tradition of a real London West End theatre. There's a lounge for pre-show drinks.

SPA/FITNESS. The Cunard Royal Health Club and Spa includes a beauty salon, large gymnasium with high-tech muscle-pumping equipment and great ocean views; an aerobics area; separate changing rooms for men and women, each with its own ocean-view sauna; a Thermal Area with sauna and steam rooms (extra-cost day passes are available, if you don't book a treatment, or at a lower per-day cost for a multi-use pass); several body treatment rooms; a Rasul chamber for private Hammam-style mud/steam bathing; and a relaxation area. A 12.5 percent gratuity is added to all spa treatment prices.

Queen Mary 2
★★★★+

Size:	Large Resort Ship
Tonnage:	148,528
Lifestyle:	Luxury/Premium/Standard
Cruise Line:	Cunard Line
Former Names:	none
IMO Number:	9241061
Builder:	Chantiers de l'Atlantique (France)
Original Cost:	$800 million
Entered Service:	Jan 2004
Registry:	Bermuda
Length (ft/m):	1,131.8/345.0
Beam (ft/m):	134.5/41.0
Draft (ft/m):	32.6/9.9
Propulsion/Propellers:	gas turbine + diesel-electric (103,000kW)/ 4 pods (2 azimuthing, 2 fixed)
Passenger Decks:	12
Total Crew:	1,254
Passengers (lower beds):	2,620

Passenger Space Ratio (lower beds):	56.6
Passenger/Crew Ratio (lower beds):	2.0
Cabins (total):	1,310
Size Range (sq ft/m):	194.0–2,249.7/18.0–209
Cabins (for one person):	0
Cabins (with private balcony):	953
Cabins (wheelchair accessible):	30
Wheelchair accessibility:	Best
Cabin Current:	110 and 220 volts
Elevators:	22
Casino (gaming tables):	Yes
Slot Machines:	Yes
Swimming Pools:	2
Hot Tubs (on deck):	8
Self-Service Launderette:	Yes
Dedicated Cinema/Seats:	Yes/473
Library:	Yes
Onboard currency:	US$

A real sturdy ocean liner built for transatlantic crossings

OVERVIEW. *Queen Mary 2 (QM2)* offers the pleasures of crossing the North Atlantic comfortably on a regular schedule. It is really suited to couples and solo travelers who enjoy the cosmopolitan setting of a floating city at sea with an unequaled maritime heritage. Scores given are averaged for all accommodation grades.

THE SHIP. RMS *Queen Mary 2*, designated a Royal Mail Ship by the British Post Office, is the largest ocean liner ever built – in terms of gross tonnage, length, and beam, though not passengers carried. A powerful propulsion system allows it to go backwards faster than many cruise ships can go forwards. Taller than the Empire State Building, it was the first new ship to be built for Cunard Line since 1969. In addition to its scheduled transatlantic crossings, *QM2* operates an annual round-the-world cruise, and other, shorter cruises.

Almost everything about the liner is British in style, but with some American decor input and accents; even the four tender stations have London names: Belgravia, Chelsea, Kensington, and Knightsbridge. There is a wide walk-around promenade deck outdoors (the forward section is under cover from the weather). Three times around is 6,102ft (1,860m), or 1.1 miles (1.6km). Teak 'steamer' chairs adorn the walk-around deck, with plenty of room for walkers to pass. However, plastic sunloungers are provided on some other open decks.

Here's a deck-by-deck look at the facilities and public rooms, starting at the lowest deck and working our way upward, forward to aft:

Berlitz's Ratings

	Possible	Achieved
Ship	500	437
Accommodation	200	174
Food	400	308
Service	400	335
Entertainment	100	86
Cruise Experience	400	335
OVERALL SCORE		
1675 points out of 2000		

Deck 2: Illuminations (and integral planetarium), the Royal Court Theatre, the lower level of the six-deck-high atrium lobby, the purser's desk, Video Arcade, Empire Casino, Golden Lion Pub, and the lower level of the two-deck-high Britannia Restaurant.

Deck 3: the upper level of Illuminations and the Royal Court Theatre, the second level of the six-deck-high atrium lobby, Mayfair shops, Sir Samuel's, The Library Room, Champagne Bar, the upper level of the Britannia Restaurant, the Queens Room, and the G32 nightclub.

Decks 4/Deck 5/Deck 6: accommodation and the third, fourth, and fifth levels of the six-deck-high atrium lobby; at the aft end of Deck 6 are facilities for children, including an outdoor pool (Minnows Pool).

Deck 7: Canyon Ranch Spa, the Winter Garden, the sixth and uppermost level of the six-deck-high atrium lobby, the expansive Kings Court Buffet, Queens Grill Lounge, Queens Grill, and Princess Grill dining salons.

Deck 8 (forward): the upper level of the Canyon Ranch Spa, and the Library and Bookshop. The center section has accommodation. In the aft section are the specialty restaurant Todd English, Terrace Bar, and swimming pool outdoors.

Deck 9 (forward): the Commodore Club, Boardroom, and the Cigar Lounge (Churchills). The rest of the deck has accommodation and a Concierge Club for suite occupants.

Deck 10: accommodation only.

Deck 11 (forward): outdoor observation area. The rest of the deck comprises accommodation. The aft section outdoors has a hot tub and sunbathing space.

Deck 12 (forward): accommodation. The mid-section has an indoor/outdoor pool with sliding glass roof, and golf areas (Fairways), located just aft of the public restrooms. The aft section has the Boardwalk Café, dog kennels, and shuffleboard courts.

Deck 13: the Sports Centre, Regatta Bar, a splash pool, and extensive outdoor sunbathing space.

There are 14 lounges, clubs, and bars. An observation lounge, the delightful Commodore Club, has commanding views forward over the bows; light jazz is played in this room, which is connected to the Boardroom, and Cigar Lounge. Other drinking places include a Golden Lion Pub (pub lunches are served here, too), Sir Samuel's (wine bar), a nautically themed cocktail bar (The Chart Room), and a Champagne/Coffee Bar. Outdoor bars include the Regatta Bar and Terrace Bar. The G32 nightclub, which has a main and mezzanine level, is at the aft end of the ship, away from passenger cabins; it is named after the number designated to the ship by its French builder.

Illuminations, the first full-scale planetarium at sea, is a stunning multi-purpose showlounge that also functions as a 473-seat grand cinema and broadcast studio. As a planetarium, it has tiered seating rows, with 150 reclining seats, so you sit in a special area under a dome, which is 38ft (11.5m) in diameter and almost 20ft (6m) deep – this forms the setting for the night sky. It's worth reserving a seat for at least one of the several outstanding 20-minute programs. The venue also screens 3D movies.

There are five swimming pools, including one that can be enclosed under a retractable glass roof. A large area of open sunning space includes a sports bar at one end. Sports facilities include an electronic golf simulator, giant chess board, and a paddle-tennis court.

The ship's Library and Bookshop is the world's largest floating bookshop and the most popular public room on transatlantic crossings. Staffed by full-time librarians from Ocean Books, it features 10,000 books in several languages, in 150 book cabinets. It is a delightful facility, but there are few chairs, and the adjacent bookshop is quite small.

Children have their own spaces, with a dedicated play area, the Play Zone. English nannies supervise toddlers, while older children use The Zone.

ACCOMMODATION. Although there are four separate categories – Queens Grill, Princess Grill, Britannia Club, and Britannia – QM2 really operates as a two-class ship (Grill Class and Britannia Class); the restaurant to which you are assigned depends on your accommodation grade. You even get a different cabin breakfast menu, depending on whether you travel in Grill Class or Britannia Class accommodation.

All grades have a 20-ins (or larger) flat-screen TV, and all beds have European duvets. There's a mini-fridge, safe, and hand-held hairdryer. All bathrooms have toiletries supplied by Penhaligon. Other features include digital video on demand (English-, French-, and German-language movies are available), music on demand with 3,000 titles, and audio books on demand. One channel covers Cunard Line's eventful history since 1840.

Beware of cabins on deck 6 located under the Kings Court – they can be subject to noise from the casual eatery on the deck above, where almost constant trolley movement creates noise.

Balmoral/Sandringham Duplexes (Grade Q1). The largest stand-alone accommodation (2,249 sq ft/209 sq m) have superb views along the length of the ship's exterior. Upstairs is a bedroom with wood-framed king-size bed, and large (not-so-private) balcony; downstairs is a living room with sofa, coffee table, dining table, and writing desk. There are two marble-clad bathrooms with whirlpool bath, separate shower enclosure, toilet and bidet, and two washbasins.

Queen Elizabeth/Queen Mary Suites (Grade Q2). Measuring 1,194 sq ft (111 sq m), these are located just under the navigation bridge, with good views over the ship's long bows, with living and dining areas, and a large private balcony (but smaller than the Balmoral/Sandringham Duplex balconies). The master, marble-clad bathroom has a whirlpool tub and shower enclosure, and a second bathroom has a shower enclosure (no tub). Each suite has the convenience of private elevator access.

Duplex apartments (Grade Q2). There are three duplex apartments: Buckingham and Windsor (each 1,291 sq ft/120 sq m), and Holyrood (1,566 sq ft/145 sq m). Each has a gymnasium, balcony, butler and concierge service, and superb views over the stern.

Queen Anne/Queen Victoria Suites (Grade Q3). These two suites (796.5 sq ft/74 sq m) have the most commanding views over the ship's long bows. They consist of a bedroom with master, marble-clad bathroom with whirlpool tub and separate shower enclosure, separate living/dining area, and a second bathroom with a shower enclosure (no tub).

Penthouse Suites (Grade Q4). The six Penthouse Suites (758 sq ft/70 sq m) have a living and dining area, large private balcony, bedroom, and dressing room with master, marble-clad bathroom with whirlpool tub and separate shower enclosure.

Suites (Grade Q5/Q6). These 82 suites (506 sq ft/47 sq m) have a large private balcony, living area, dressing room, and marble-clad bathroom with whirlpool tub/shower. Beds can be arranged as king-size or twins.

Junior Suites (Grade P1/P2). There are 76 Junior Suites (381 sq ft/35 sq m). Each has a lounge area, large private balcony, and marble-clad bathroom with whirlpool tub and separate shower enclosure.

Beds can be arranged in a king-size or twin-bed configuration.

Deluxe/premium balcony cabins. These 782 cabins (248 sq ft/23 sq m) include a sitting area with sofa, and bathroom with shower enclosure. Beds can be arranged in a king-size or twin-bed configuration.

Standard outside-view/interior cabins. There are 62 outside-view cabins and 281 interior cabins measuring 194 sq ft (18 sq m). Beds can be arranged in a king-size or twin-bed configuration.

Atrium-view cabins. Each of these 12 interior cabins (194 sq ft/18 sq m) has an unusual view – into the six-deck high atrium lobby. Beds can be arranged as king-size or twins. An en-suite bathroom has a shower enclosure, washbasin, toilet, and toiletries cabinet.

Wheelchair-accessible cabins. There are 30 wheelchair-friendly suites and cabins in various categories. All have pull-down closet hanging rails, above-bed emergency pull-cord, and large, well-equipped bathrooms with roll-in showers and handrails. Facilities for blind passengers include Braille signs and tactile room signs. Eight wheelchair-accessible elevators service the dining areas. Additionally, 36 cabins accommodate deaf or hearing-impaired passengers. There are headsets in the Royal Theatre and Illuminations, and closed-caption TV.

DINING. There are 10 dining rooms and eateries (and seven galleys to service them), and all dining venues have ocean-view windows. The wines and Champagnes have been selected by Michael Broadbent, one of the world's top wine experts.

Britannia Restaurant. This main dining room seats 1,347, and spans the ship's beam. A lavish room almost three decks high, it has two grand sweeping staircases, so you can make your entry in style. Breakfast and lunch are open seating, while dinner is in two seatings, all with crisp linen and fine china. Vegetarian options are included on all lunch and dinner menus. One downside of open seating for breakfast or lunch is that each time you'll probably have a different waiter, who won't know your preferences. Also, if you are seated on the lower level underneath the balcony formed along the sides of the upper level, you may feel enclosed in an inferior space. It's better to get a table in the central well or on the upper level.

Queens Grill/Princess Grill. There are two Grill Rooms (the 200-seat Queens Grill and the 178-seat Princess Grill), which are small dining salons. Which you dine in depends on your accommodation grade and fare. Both are located aft and have, in theory, fine ocean-view windows – although walkers passing by on the exterior promenade deck can be distracting in the daytime. Canyon Ranch SpaClub recommendations and vegetarian options are provided on all lunch and dinner menus.

Todd English Restaurant. This 216-seat reservations-only restaurant is named after the American TV chef, whose Boston restaurant (Olives) has a fine reputation. With its Moorish decor, it serves his noted Mediterranean cuisine. The room has been designed with intimate detailing and overlooks the Pool Terrace, for alfresco dining. Food presentation from an à-la-carte menu is excellent, although overly fussy at times.

Kings Court. This truly nondescript, informal eatery has 478 seats and obnoxious daytime lighting, and is more suited to a land-based shopping mall. It offers self-serve breakfast and lunch. Breakfast is repetitive, but includes British traditional standards: eggs, bacon, kippers, and fried tomatoes. The lunch menu changes daily, and includes several popular Indian dishes. The pizzas, however, cannot be recommended – think cardboard with toppings. At least the beverage station now has real teaspoons.

At night, decorated screens transform Kings Court into four extra-cost dining venues: an Italian trattoria (La Piazza), Asian cuisine (Lotus), a British eatery (The Carvery) for roast meats, and a Chef's Galley; all have full sit-down tablecloth service (the 36-seat Chef's Galley has a live demonstration of your meal's preparation).

Comfort foods are served in the outdoors Boardwalk Café, weather permitting, while pub lovers can find traditional British fare in the popular Golden Lion Pub. You can also order from the restaurant menus and have breakfast, lunch, and dinner served in your own suite or cabin.

ENTERTAINMENT. The Royal Court Theatre, a lovely venue, has tiered seating for 1,094, though some sight lines are less than ideal. It stages lavish West End-style productions and hosts headline entertainers and cabaret acts. The Royal Academy of Dramatic Art (RADA) supplies a company of actors to give Shakespearean performances, lead acting workshops, and take part in street-theater performances.

SPA/FITNESS. Health Spa and Beauty Services are provided in a 20,000-sq-ft (1,850-sq-m) Canyon Ranch SpaClub, arranged on two decks. There's a thalassotherapy pool, whirlpool, and thermal suite (at extra cost, but waived if you buy a treatment). There are 20 body and skincare-treatment rooms.

Queen Victoria
★★★★+

Size:	Large Resort Ship	Passenger Space Ratio (lower beds):	44.5
Tonnage:	90,049	Passenger/Crew Ratio (lower beds):	2.2
Lifestyle:	Premium/Standard	Cabins (total):	1,016
Cruise Line:	Cunard Line	Size Range (sq ft/m):	143.0–2,131.3/13.2–198.0
Former Names:	none	Cabins (for one person):	9
IMO Number:	9320556	Cabins (with private balcony):	718
Builder:	Fincantieri (Italy)	Cabins (wheelchair accessible):	20
Original Cost:	$390 million	Wheelchair accessibility:	Good
Entered Service:	Dec 2007	Cabin Current:	110 and 220 volts
Registry:	Bermuda	Elevators:	12
Length (ft/m):	964.5/294.0	Casino (gaming tables):	Yes
Beam (ft/m):	105.9/32.3	Slot Machines:	Yes
Draft (ft/m):	26.2/8.0	Swimming Pools:	2
Propulsion/Propellers:	diesel-electric (64,00kW)/ 2 azimuthing pods	Hot Tubs (on deck):	5
		Self-Service Launderette:	Yes
Passenger Decks:	12	Dedicated Cinema/Seats:	No
Total Crew:	1,001	Library:	Yes
Passengers (lower beds):	2,023	Onboard currency:	US$

A pretend ocean liner that really suits traditional British tastes

OVERVIEW. *Queen Victoria*, a very comfortable, likeable cruise ship posing as an ocean liner, is best suited to a couples and solo travelers who enjoy traditional British ocean liner-style decor, world-wide itineraries, and dressing for dinner. Note that scores given in the Berlitz's Ratings box are the averages for all accommodation grades.

THE SHIP. *Queen Victoria* is aimed at the North American and British markets, but will appeal to any Anglophile, because Cunard is still a British experience, although it is to some extent marketing hype, since British staff is rather thin on the ground.

Basically a stretched, modified platform and layout as the Vista series of ships (examples: *Arcadia, Carnival Legend, Costa Atlantica, Costa Luminosa, Costa Mediterranea, Oosterdam*), the Cunard version has an additional passenger deck, a specially strengthened hull lengthened by 36ft (11m), giving the ship more of an 'ocean liner' feel. It also has a more traditional interior layout reminiscent of yesteryear's ocean liners.

The interior decor is 'traditional' in Cunard-speak, with many public rooms finely decorated in Edwardian/Victorian styles, with wrought-iron balustrades on staircases and in some bars. The three-deck-high Grand Lobby has a sweeping staircase and sculpted balconies. The Cunardia museum's glass cabinets display models of former Cunard Line ships, old menus, and daily programs.

The Royal Arcade houses a cluster of seven shops, including Harrods, Royal Doulton, and Wedgwood, set

Berlitz's Ratings

	Possible	Achieved
Ship	500	419
Accommodation	200	145
Food	400	299
Service	400	313
Entertainment	100	81
Cruise Experience	400	318
OVERALL SCORE		
1575 points out of 2000		

in an arcade-like environment.

The Library is a stunning two-deck-high wood-paneled 6,000-book facility with full-time librarians, but few chairs; the upper deck features eight internet-connect computer terminals.

A Golden Lion Pub is a must aboard a Cunarder, and this one lies along the starboard side. It's a good gathering place for karaoke, singalong, and quiz enthusiasts, plus it does tasty pub food.

The Commodore Club acts as a large observation lounge, with its ocean views on three sides, and late-night room for low-volume interactive entertainment.

The adjacent Churchill's Cigar Lounge, on the starboard side, is a smokers' haven.

Chart Room Bar, adjacent to the Britannia Restaurant, is a place for a quiet drink before dinner.

Hemispheres, positioned aft of the mast and adjacent to the Commodore Club, overlooks the wood-decked Pavilion Pool; this is the high-volume disco and themed nightclub.

There's also a casino (no smoking) on the port side of the lower level of the Royal Court.

A grand conservatory (Winter Garden) has a moveable glass wall to an open-air swimming pool. Rattan furniture and ceiling fans help to conjure up the area's colonial theme.

A per person, per day gratuity is charged to your onboard account, and a 15 percent gratuity is added to all bar and wine accounts. Gratuities – called a 'Hotel and Dining' charge – of $11.50–13.50, depending on accommodation grade – are automatically added to your account daily. The onboard currency is the US dollar – another reason to take the Britishness claims with a pinch of salt.

ACCOMMODATION. There are numerous price grades but just eight types of accommodation, ranging from ample to opulent.

Grand Suites. There are four, measuring 1,918–2,131 sq ft (178–197 sq m). They are located aft, with great ocean views from their private wrap-around balconies, which contain a complete wet bar. The suites have two bedrooms with walk-in closets; bathroom with bathtub and separate shower enclosure; lounge; and dining room (with seating for six). In-suite dining from the Queens Grill menus is also available.

Master Suites. Two, measuring 1,100 sq ft (102 sq m), located in the center of the ship (Deck 7).

Penthouse Suites. 25, measuring 520–707 sq ft (48–66 sq m).

Queens Suites. 35, measuring 508–771 sq ft (47–72 sq m).

Princess Suites. 61, measuring 342–513 sq ft (32–48 sq m).

Balcony cabins. 581, measuring 242–472 sq ft (22–44 sq m).

Outside-view cabins. 146, measuring 180–201 sq ft (17–19 sq m).

Interior (no-view) cabins. 143, measuring 151–243 sq ft (14–19 sq m).

All accommodation grades have both British three-pin (240-volt) sockets and American (110-volt) and European-style two-pin (220-volt) sockets. Penhaligon toiletries are supplied to all passengers, and a hairdryer is stored in the vanity desk units. Some cabins have nicely indented ceilings with suffused lighting. However, the flat-screen TV sets are small – not good for bedtime movie watching.

The regular cabins (Grades C/D) are small, but functional, although completely lacking in 'wow' factor. The cabinetry resembles that in an Ibis hotel – a bit austere and lacking character. There is a distinct lack of drawer space in a cabin supposedly designed for two persons; it's very noticeable on long voyages, and additional drawers located under the bed may prove challenging for some to use. The premium mattresses are, however, excellent, as is the bed linen; European duvets are standard.

The bathrooms are stunningly bland, with small washbasins, little storage space for toiletries, cold, tiled floors, and wall-mounted shower heads.

Added in 2015 were nine cabins for solo-occupancy.

DINING. Cunard is respected for its cuisine and service, with a wide variety of well-prepared and presented dishes. The Britannia Restaurant – the name is taken from a former Cunard ocean liner of 1914–50 (not from P&O Cruises' new *Britannia*) – is located in the aft section. It is two decks high, with seating on both the main level (two seatings for dinner, but open seating for breakfast and lunch) and balcony level. A horseshoe-shaped stairway links both levels. While the lower level diners have a good sea view through large picture windows, balcony diners get a promenade view. Waterford Wedgwood china is used, and there's a wide range of wines (and prices).

Queens Grill and Princess Grill, two Grill Class-only restaurants, provide exclusive dining. These have a single-seating arrangement, providing an intimate, exclusive dining experience than in the two-seating main Britannia Restaurant.

On the port side, the 142-seat Queens Grill is for passengers in suites and top category accommodation grades, and provides the best cuisine and service aboard. The Cunard Grill experience also includes alfresco dining in a seldom-used courtyard terrace (The Courtyard), suitably protected from the wind, and exclusive access for Grill Class passengers to an upper terrace deck, with dedicated staff as well as the Grills' lounge and bar.

On the starboard side, the 132-seat Princess Grill is for passengers in middle-class accommodation grades.

Other dining options. The 100-seat, reservations required, extra-cost Verandah Restaurant (formerly Todd English Restaurant) focuses on classic French cuisine. It is on the second level of the three-deck high lobby.

The Lido Café, on Deck 11, has good panoramic views, indoor/outdoor seating for 468, and offers a fairly standard multi-line self-serve buffet arrangement. For excellent, but expensive Lavazza-family coffees from Maria (the coffee machine), and light bites, there's Café Carinthia, located one deck above the purser's desk and adjacent to a Veuve Clicquot Champagne bar.

For traditional British pub food, the Golden Lion Pub serves fish and chips, steak and mushroom pie, ploughman's lunch, and bangers (sausages) and mash – particularly good at lunchtime – with a nice draft pint of bitter, naturally.

ENTERTAINMENT. The 830-seat, three-deck-high Royal Court Theatre is designed in the style of a classic opera house, complete with royal boxes.

SPA/FITNESS. The Cunard Royal Health Club and Spa has features including a beauty salon, large gymnasium and several body treatment rooms.

Radiance of the Seas
★★★+

Size:	Large Resort Ship	Passenger/Crew Ratio (lower beds):	2.5
Tonnage:	90,090	Cabins (total):	1,072
Lifestyle:	Standard	Size Range (sq ft/m):	165.8–1,216.3/15.4–113.0
Cruise Line:	Royal Caribbean International	Cabins (for one person):	0
Former Names:	none	Cabins (with private balcony):	578
IMO Number:	9195195	Cabins (wheelchair accessible):	14
Builder:	Meyer Werft (Germany)	Wheelchair accessibility:	Good
Original Cost:	$350 million	Cabin Current:	110 and 220 volts
Entered Service:	Apr 2001	Elevators:	9
Registry:	The Bahamas	Casino (gaming tables):	Yes
Length (ft/m):	961.9/293.2	Slot Machines:	Yes
Beam (ft/m):	105.6/32.2	Swimming Pools:	2
Draft (ft/m):	27.8/8.5	Hot Tubs (on deck):	3
Propulsion/Propellers:	Gas turbine (40,000kW)/2 azimuthing pods	Self-Service Launderette:	No
Passenger Decks:	12	Dedicated Cinema/Seats:	Yes/40
Total Crew:	858	Library:	Yes
Passengers (lower beds):	2,146	Onboard currency:	US$
Passenger Space Ratio (lower beds):	42.0		

This large, family-friendly ship is for casual-style cruising

OVERVIEW. *Radiance of the Seas* offers a decent amount of space, comfortable public areas, and slightly larger cabins than some Royal Caribbean International (RCI) ships for younger, active travelers. A grand amount of glass provides extensive views of the ocean. While the ship is delightful in many ways, the operation does suffer from having too few well-trained service staff.

Berlitz's Ratings		
	Possible	Achieved
Ship	500	377
Accommodation	200	139
Food	400	237
Service	400	279
Entertainment	100	74
Cruise Experience	400	273
OVERALL SCORE		
1379 points out of 2000		

THE SHIP. *Radiance of the Seas* was the first RCI ship to use gas and steam turbine power instead of the more conventional diesel or diesel-electric combination. Pod propulsion is provided. At the very front of the ship is a helipad, which also acts as a viewing platform for passengers.

This is a modern-looking ship, with a two-deck-high walk-around structure in the forward section of the funnel. Along the ship's starboard side, a central glass wall protrudes, giving great views – cabins with balconies occupy the space directly opposite on the port side. The gently rounded stern has nicely tiered decks. One of two swimming pools can be covered by a glass dome for use as an indoor/outdoor pool.

Inside, the decor is contemporary, yet elegant, bright, and cheerful. A nine-deck-high atrium lobby has glass-walled elevators that travel through 12 decks, face the sea, and provide a link with nature and the ocean, while a finger-touch digital 'wayfinder' system helps you find your way around. The Centrum (city center), as the atrium is called, is the social hub of the ship. It is nine decks high, and has many public rooms and facilities connected to it: the business services desks, a

Lobby Bar, Champagne Bar, Schooner Bar (the nautical-themed bar, with maritime art), Café Latte-tudes (for extra-cost coffees), Royal Caribbean Online (with a dozen Internet-connect computers), the flashy Casino Royale (for casino gamers and slot machine fans; it has a French Art Nouveau decorative theme and sports 11 crystal chandeliers), a Quill and Compass Pub, Concierge Lounge, and a Crown & Anchor Lounge. There's also a 194-seat conference center, and a business center. The Viking Crown Lounge (a trademark aboard all RCI ships) is a large structure set around the base of the ship's funnel. It functions as an observation lounge during the daytime, with views forward over the swimming pool.

Shipwide Wi-Fi is available for a fee. More Internet-access terminals are located in Books 'n' Coffee, a bookshop with coffee and pastries, located in an extensive area of shops.

The artwork is eclectic, providing a spectrum of color. It ranges from Jenny M. Hansen's *A Vulnerable Moment* glass sculpture to David Buckland's *Industrial and Russian Constructionism 1920s* in photographic images on glass and painted canvas, to a huge, multi-deck-high, contemporary bicycle-cum-paddle-wheel sculpture design suspended in the atrium.

FAMILIES. Youth facilities include Adventure Ocean, an 'edutainment' area with four separate age-appropriate sections for junior passengers: Aquanaut Center (for ages 3–5); Explorer Center (6–8); Voyager Center (9–12); and the Optix Teen Center (13–17). A Royal

Babies and Tots Nursery, for 6–36-month-olds, was added in 2011. There is also Adventure Beach, which includes a splash pool complete with water slide; Surfside, with computer lab stations with entertaining software; and Ocean Arcade, a gaming hangout.

ACCOMMODATION. There is a wide range of suites and standard outside-view and interior cabins in 10 different categories and numerous price groups.

Apart from the largest suites (six Owner's Suites), which have king-size beds, almost all other cabins have twin beds that convert to a queen-size bed, All cabins have rich (but faux) wood cabinetry, including a vanity desk with hairdryer, faux wood silent-close drawers, flat-screen television, personal safe, and three-sided mirrors. Some cabins have ceiling-recessed, pull-down berths for third and fourth persons, although closet and drawer space would be extremely tight for four persons, even if two were small children, and some have interconnecting doors – so families with children can cruise together in separate but adjacent cabins. Audio channels are available through the TV set, whose picture cannot be turned off while listening to an audio channel.

Many bathrooms have a terrazzo-style tiled floor, and a small shower enclosure in a half-moon shape, Egyptian cotton towels, a cabinet for toiletries, and a shelf. In reality, there is little space to stow toiletries for two (or more).

The largest accommodation consists of a family suite with two bedrooms. One bedroom has twin beds that convert to queen-size bed, while a second has two lower beds and two upper Pullman berths, a combination that can sleep up to eight persons. Many of the 'private' balcony cabins aren't very private, as they can be overlooked.

DINING. Cascades, the main dining room, spans two decks. The upper deck level has floor-to-ceiling windows, while the lower deck level has picture windows. It is a delightful, but noisy, dining hall, although eight thick pillars obstruct the sight lines. It seats 1,110, and has cascading water-themed decor, and a large glass mural. There are tables for two to 10. A small private dining room (the 30-seat Tides) is located off the main dining room. When you book, choose one of two seatings, or 'My Time Dining,' which enables you to eat when you want, during dining room hours.

The cuisine is typical of mass banquet catering that offers standard fare comparable to that found in American family-style restaurants ashore. Overall, meals are rather hit and miss – in fact it's non-memorable. Also, if you want lobster or a decent filet mignon (steak), you will be asked to pay extra.

Other dining options. Several optional dining venues/eateries were added during an extensive refurbishment in 2011:

Boardwalk Dog House, for hot dogs, wieners, brats, sausages, and a variety of toppings to split a long bun (open for lunch and dinner, no added cost).

Giovanni's Table, an Italian trattoria with Italian classics served family-style (open for lunch and dinner; a cover charge applies, and reservations are required).

Izumi features a sushi bar with hot-rock cooking (open for lunch and dinner; a cover charge applies, as well as additional à-la-carte menu item pricing, and reservations are required).

Park Café, an indoor/outdoor market for salads, sandwiches, soups, and pastries (open for breakfast, lunch and dinner; no added cost, but reservations are required).

Rita's Cantina, a casual indoor/outdoor eatery, for families by day, and adults by night. It offers Mexican cuisine. It is open for lunch and dinner, a cover charge applies, as well as à-la-carte menu item pricing, and reservations are required.

Chef's Table, a private experience co-hosted by the executive chef and sommelier for a wine-pairing dinner of five courses (open for dinner only; a cover charge applies, and reservations are required).

Samba Grill, a Brazilian churrascaria (steakhouse), for a variety of meats, chicken, and seafood brought to the table ready to slice and serve upon request (a cover charge applies; open for dinner only, and reservations are required).

ENTERTAINMENT. The three-level Aurora Theater has 874 seats, including 24 stations for wheelchairs, and good sight lines from most seats. The Colony Club hosts casual cabaret shows, including late-night adult comedy, and provides live music for dancing. The entertainment throughout is lively and upbeat, and background music pervades all corridors and elevators; there's also constant music on the pool deck.

SPA/FITNESS. The Day Spa fitness and spa facilities have themed decor, and include a gymnasium with numerous cardiovascular machines, a large aerobics room, sauna and steam rooms, and body pampering treatment rooms. All are located on two of the uppermost decks, forward of the mast, with access from the forward stairway.

A climate-controlled 10,176-sq-ft (945-sq-m) indoor/outdoor Solarium has a sliding glass roof that can be closed in cool or inclement weather.

Sports facilities include a 30ft (9m) rock-climbing wall with five separate climbing tracks, an exterior jogging track, a nine-hole miniature golf course with novel 17th-century decorative ornaments, and an indoor/outdoor country club with golf simulator, a jogging track, and basketball court. There are two specially stabilized pool tables (within the Bombay Billiard Club).

Regal Princess
★★★★

Size:	Large Resort Ship
Tonnage:	141,200
Lifestyle:	Standard
Cruise Line:	Princess Cruises
Former Names:	none
IMO Number:	9584724
Builder:	Fincantieri (Italy)
Original Cost:	€775 million
Entered Service:	May 2014
Registry:	Bermuda
Length (ft/m):	1,082.6/330.0
Beam (ft/m):	126.3/38.5
Draft (ft/m):	27.8/8.5
Propulsion/Propellers:	diesel-electric (52,000kW)/2
Passenger Decks:	17
Total Crew:	1,346
Passengers (lower beds):	3,560
Passenger Space Ratio (lower beds):	39.6
Passenger/Crew Ratio (lower beds):	2.6
Cabins (total):	1,780
Size Range (sq ft/m):	161.4-554.3/15-51.5
Cabins (for one person):	0
Cabins (with private balcony):	1,438
Cabins (wheelchair accessible):	36
Wheelchair accessibility:	Best
Cabin Current:	110 and 220 volts
Elevators:	14
Casino (gaming tables):	Yes
Slot Machines:	Yes
Swimming Pools:	2
Hot Tubs (on deck):	6
Self-Service Launderette:	Yes
Dedicated Cinema/Seats:	No
Library:	Yes
Onboard currency:	US$

This large, multi-choice family-friendly resort ship has style

OVERVIEW. *Regal Princess* is a sister to *Royal Princess*, which debuted in 2013. Princess Cruises delivers a consistent, well-packaged cruise vacation, with a good range of entertainment options, at an attractive price, which is why passengers come back again and again.

THE SHIP. Although large, the ship's profile is quite well balanced, and is an enhancement of the earlier range of *Grand*-class ships. In terms of practical design, the lifeboats are located outside the main public room areas, so they don't impair the view from balcony cabins. The ship features a complete walk-around promenade deck.

An over-the-water SeaWalk, an open deck glass-bottomed enclosed walkway (first introduced in 2013 aboard sister ship *Royal Princess*) on the starboard side extends almost 30ft (9.1m) beyond the vessel's edge and forms part of a lounge/bar venue. This is the place to go for dramatic (downward) views, including to the sea 128ft (39m) below, so you *can* 'walk' on water (well, over it). On the ship's port side is a SeaView bar.

There are two principal stair towers and elevator banks, plus some panoramic-view elevators in a third, central bank (these elevators do not go to all decks, however). The interior decor is warm and attractive, with an abundance of earth tones that suit both American and European tastes. One of the line's hallmark venues, the Piazza Atrium, has been significantly expanded compared to the older ships in the fleet. This area is the ship's multi-faceted social hub and combines a specialty dining venue, light meals,

Berlitz's Ratings		
	Possible	Achieved
Ship	500	415
Accommodation	200	161
Food	400	267
Service	400	295
Entertainment	100	83
Cruise Experience	400	306
OVERALL SCORE		
1527 points out of 2000		

snack-food items, pastries, beverages, entertainment, shopping, and guest services. It is larger than aboard any other Princess Cruises ship (except sister ship *Royal Princess*), and has a horseshoe-shaped flowing stairway and lots of mood lighting effects.

The base level includes a large International Café, for coffees, teas, panini, and pastries (and to see and be seen); Sabatini's, a Tuscan specialty extra-cost restaurant (located just off the atrium itself), with both regular and à-la-carte menus; and a gift shop. Upstairs, level two includes Alfredo's Pizzeria, Bellini's (a bar serving Bellini drinks) a photo gallery, reception, and shore excursion counters. On the third level, Crooners Bar has a piano and pianist entertainers; there's also a small Seafood Bar. The Piazza Atrium is all about food, entertainment, and passenger services, and is the social nerve center of the ship.

The company provides a number of gentlemen dance hosts on each cruise to act as partners for women traveling alone. Each accommodation deck houses a self-service launderette. One downside is the lack of a central stairway above the two main restaurants, which leads to severe crowding of the adjacent elevators.

ACCOMMODATION. There are six main types of accommodation and 35 price grades: (a) Grand Suite; (b) suites with balcony; (c) mini-suites with balcony; (d) deluxe outside-view balcony cabins; (e) outside-view cabins with balcony; and (f) interior cabins. Pricing depends on two things: size and location. Outside-view cabins account for about 81 percent of all accommodation, and all have a balcony; those located at the stern are the quietest and most sought-after.

All accommodation grades share energy-efficient lighting and key card readers that automatically turn off lights when occupants leave their cabins. All cabins get beds with upholstered headboards, wall-mounted TV sets, additional 220v electrical socket, turndown service and heart-shaped chocolates on pillows each night, bathrobes (on request, unless you are in suite-grade accommodation), and toiletries. A hairdryer is provided in all cabins and is sensibly located at the vanity desk unit in the living area. Bathrooms generally have a good amount of open shelf storage space for toiletries, and – in a first for Princess Cruises – all bathrooms have hand-held, flexi-hose showers, and shower enclosures larger than aboard other Princess ships (except sister *Royal Princess*).

Suite and mini-suite grade occupants have a dedicated concierge lounge (towards the aft on Deck 14) – useful for making dining, spa, and shore excursion reservations. They also get more amenities and larger TV sets, and suites get two washbasins.

Some of the most sought-after suites are located aft, occupying the corner (port and starboard) positions.

DINING. There are three 'formal' main dining rooms. You can choose either traditional two-seating dining (typically 6pm and 8.15pm for dinner), or 'anytime dining,' which allows you to choose when and with whom you want to eat. If you want to see a show in the evening, however, then your dining time will be dictated by the time of the show, which rather limits your choice.

Other dining options. Extra-cost, reservations-required Sabatini's, located adjacent to Vines Wine Bar on the lower atrium level, is an Italian restaurant with colorful Tuscany-themed decor. Named after Trattoria Sabatini, the 200-year-old institution in Florence, it serves Italian-style pasta dishes with a choice of sauces, as well as Italian-style entrées, including tiger prawns and lobster tail, all provided with flair and entertainment by energetic waiters. There's both a table-d'hôte and an à-la-carte menu. This venue, which is all about Tuscany, also hosts Italian wine tasting.

Ocean Terrace, located on the second level of the atrium lobby, is a seafood bar. International Café, on the lowest level of the Piazza Atrium, is the place for extra-cost coffees, pastries, panini, and more. Vines Wine Bar, adjacent to Sabatini's – a good place for a glass of extra-cost wine, and some tapas. This is really

a pleasant area in which to while away a late afternoon, trying out new wines.

Crown Grill is an extra-cost à-la-carte dining venue, adjacent to the Wheelhouse Bar, on the uppermost level of the three-deck-high atrium, and is the place to go for extra-cost steaks and seafood.

For casual meals, the self-serve buffet venue (Horizon Court) seats 900 indoors and 350 outdoors at the Horizon Terrace, and there are multiple active cooking stations. Sections of the eatery highlight specific themes, such as Mediterranean, Asian, and Italian cuisine; there's also a deli section. At night, the Horizon Bistro (aft) section is for casual dinners. Certain nights will feature special themes and foods, such as British pub food or Brazilian churrascarria (for steaks). Rotisseries, carvings, hibachi grill, and other active cooking station items are all part of the scenario.

The ship's bakery (well, part of it) comes out of the galley and into a separate area of the Horizon Court. Called the Horizon Bistro Pastry Shop, it offers freshly baked bread, croissants, pastry items, waffles, and other pastries throughout the day.

ENTERTAINMENT. The Princess Theater, the ship's main showlounge, is a two-deck-high venue for the large-scale production shows that Princess Cruises is renowned for. There's also a 'Princess Live' auditorium for stand-up comedy and other small-audience entertainment features. At the stern of the ship (on the same deck) is a Vista Lounge; this is also an entertainment venue, with a large dance floor. Meanwhile, on the subject of dancing, the ship has a number of gentlemen dance hosts on each cruise for women without partners.

SPA/FITNESS. The Lotus Spa is located forward on the lower level of the atrium, so it doesn't take away premium outdoor-view real estate space. Separate facilities for men and women include a sauna, steam room, and changing rooms; common facilities include a relaxation/waiting zone, body-pampering treatment rooms, and a gymnasium packed with the latest high-tech, muscle-pumping cardio-vascular equipment, and providing great ocean views. Some fitness classes are free, while others cost extra. Children and teens have their own fitness rooms adjacent to their age-related facilities.

Spa operator Steiner Leisure is in charge of and staffs the Lotus Spa. You can make online reservations for any spa treatments before your cruise, which could be a great time-saver, as long as you can plan ahead.

Regatta
★★★★

Size:	Small Ship
Tonnage:	30,277
Lifestyle:	Premium
Cruise Line:	Oceania Cruises
Former Names:	R Two
IMO Number:	9156474
Builder:	Chantiers de l'Atlantique
Original Cost:	£150 million
Entered Service:	Dec 1998/Dec 2003
Registry:	Marshall Islands
Length (ft/m):	593.7/181.0
Beam (ft/m):	83.5/25.5
Draft (ft/m):	19.5/6.0
Propulsion/Propellers:	diesel (18,600kW)/2
Passenger Decks:	9
Total Crew:	386
Passengers (lower beds):	684
Passenger Space Ratio (lower beds):	44.2
Passenger/Crew Ratio (lower beds):	1.7
Cabins (total):	342
Size Range (sq ft/m):	145.3–968.7/13.5–90.0
Cabins (for one person):	0
Cabins (with private balcony):	232
Cabins (wheelchair accessible):	3
Wheelchair accessibility:	Good
Cabin Current:	110 and 220 volts
Elevators:	4
Casino (gaming tables):	Yes
Slot Machines:	Yes
Swimming Pools:	1
Hot Tubs (on deck):	3
Self-Service Launderette:	Yes
Dedicated Cinema/Seats:	No
Library:	Yes
Onboard currency:	US$

This is an informal premium ship for mature-age cruisers

OVERVIEW. Oceania Cruises is a young company that aims to provide a high level of food and service in an informal setting that's elegant yet comfortable. *Regatta* suits couples who like really good food and style, but want informality with no formal nights on board, and interesting itineraries, all at a very reasonable price.

THE SHIP. *Regatta* was originally one of eight almost identical ships built for the now-defunct Renaissance Cruises. The exterior design manages to balance the ship's high sides by painting the whole ship white, with a large, square white funnel. Teak overlaid decking and high-quality lounge chairs help create a very comfortable Lido and Pool Deck.

In 2014, the ship underwent a refurbishment program that included the addition of Barista's coffee bar (for illy coffees), installed completely new bathrooms for the Owner's Suites and Vista Suites, and updated the decor in all other cabins. Also added were a miniature golf course, shuffleboard courts, and other deck games.

There is no walk-around promenade deck outdoors as such – there is, however, a small jogging/walking track, above the swimming pool.

The stunningly elegant interior decor is a throwback to the ocean liners of the 1920s and 1930s, with dark woods and warm colors, all carried out in fine taste – if a bit faux in places. It feels like an old-world country club.

The public rooms are spread over three decks. The reception hall has a staircase with intricate wrought-

Berlitz's Ratings

	Possible	Achieved
Ship	500	399
Accommodation	200	153
Food	400	308
Service	400	295
Entertainment	100	74
Cruise Experience	400	309

OVERALL SCORE
1538 points out of 2000

iron railings. A large observation lounge, the Horizon Bar, is located high atop ship. There are plenty of bars, including one in each of the restaurant entrances. Perhaps the nicest is the casino bar/lounge, a beautiful room reminiscent of London's grand hotels. It has an inviting marble fireplace, sofas, and chairs.

The Library is a grand Regency-style room, with a fireplace, a high, indented, trompe l'oeil ceiling, and excellent selection of books, plus very comfortable wingback chairs with footstools, and sofas you could sleep on.

The dress code is 'smart casual.' Gratuities are added at $10.50 per person, per day, and accommodation designated as suites have an extra $3 per person charge for the butler. A gratuity of 18 percent is added to bar and spa accounts.

Passenger niggles include all the inventive extra charges that can be incurred. What's really nice is the fact that there are almost no intrusive announcements.

ACCOMMODATION. There are six cabin categories, and 10 price grades (three suite price grades; five outside-view cabin grades; two interior cabin grades). All of the standard interior and outside-view cabins (the lowest four grades) are extremely tight for two people, particularly for cruises longer than five days. They have twin beds or a queen-size bed, with good under-bed storage areas, personal safe, vanity desk with large mirror, good closet and drawer space in rich, dark woods, 100 percent cotton bathrobe and towels, slippers, clothes brush, and shoehorn.

Certain cabin categories (about 100 of them) qualify as 'Concierge Level' accommodation, and occupants get extra goodies such as enhanced bathroom amenities, complimentary shoeshine, tote bag, cashmere throw blanket, bottle of Champagne on arrival, a hand-held hairdryer, priority restaurant reservations, and priority embarkation.

Owner's Suites (6). Measuring around 962 sq ft (90 sq m), these fine living spaces provide the most spacious accommodation onboard. Located aft overlooking the stern on Decks 6, 7, and 8, they are subject to more movement and some vibration. They have extensive teak-floor private balconies that really are private and cannot be overlooked by anyone. Each has an entrance foyer, living room, separate bedroom, CD player, fully tiled bathroom with Jacuzzi tub, and a small guest bathroom. The bed faces the sea, which can be seen through the floor-to-ceiling windows and sliding glass door.

Vista Suites (4). These measure around 786 sq ft (73 sq m), and are located forward on Decks 5 and 6. They have extensive teak-floor private balconies that can't be overlooked by anyone from the decks above. Each has an entrance foyer, living room, separate bedroom, CD player (with selection of audio discs), and fully tiled bathroom with Jacuzzi tub. The bed faces the sea, which is visible through the floor-to-ceiling windows and sliding glass door.

Penthouse Suites (52). Actually, these are large cabins rather than suites, as the bedrooms aren't separate from the living areas, but they measure around 323 sq ft (30 sq m). They have a good-size teak-floor balcony with sliding glass door – but with partial, not full, balcony partitions. The lounge area has a dining table, and there is ample storage space. The bathroom has a tub, shower, washbasin, and toilet.

Cabins with balcony. Measuring around 216 sq ft (20 sq m), these comprise about two-thirds of all cabins. They have partial, not full, balcony partitions, sliding glass doors, and only 14 cabins on Deck 6 have lifeboat-obstructed views. The living area has a refrigerated minibar, a lounge area with breakfast table, and a balcony with teak floor, two teak chairs, and a drinks table. The bathrooms, with tiled floors and plain walls, are compact, standard units, and include a shower stall with a strong, removable hand-held shower unit, hairdryer, toiletries storage shelves, and retractable clothesline.

Outside-view and interior cabins. These measure around 160–165 sq ft (14.8–15.3 sq m) and have twin beds that convert to a queen-size bed, vanity desk, small sofa, coffee table, and bathroom with a shower enclosure with a strong, removable hand-held shower unit, hairdryer, toiletries storage shelves, retractable clothesline, washbasin, and toilet. Although not large, they are quite comfortable, with a decent amount of storage space.

All suites/cabins located at the stern may suffer from vibration and noise, particularly when the ship is maneuvering in port.

DINING. Flexibility and choice are what the dining facilities aboard Oceania Cruises ships are all about. There are four different restaurants:

The Grand Dining Room has around 340 seats, and a raised central section, but the problem is the noise level – because of the low ceiling height, it's atrocious when the dining room is full. Being located at the stern, there are large ocean-view windows on three sides, and prime tables overlook the stern. The chairs are comfortable, with armrests. The menus change daily for lunch and dinner.

Toscana Italian Restaurant has 96 seats, windows along two sides, and a set menu plus daily chef's specials.

The cozy Polo Grill has 98 seats, windows along two sides and a set menu including prime steaks and seafood.

The Terrace Café has both indoor and outdoor seating. It is open for breakfast, lunch, and casual dinners, with some fine tapas and other Mediterranean dishes. As the self-serve buffet restaurant, it incorporates a small pizzeria and grill.

A poolside Waves Grill serves fishburgers, veggie burgers, and Reuben sandwiches, as well as Angus beef burgers, and hot dogs.

All restaurants have open-seating dining, so you can dine when you want, with whom you wish. Reservations are needed in the Toscana Restaurant and Polo Grill (but there's no extra charge), where there are mostly tables for four or six, and few tables for two. There is a Poolside Grill Bar.

The food and service staff is provided by a respected maritime catering company that also has an interest in Oceania Cruises. This is definitely a foodie's ship, with really high-quality ingredients. Particularly notable are the delicious breads, rolls, croissants, and brioches – all made on board from French flour and d'Isigny butter.

On sea days, afternoon tea is presented in the Horizon Lounge, with formally dressed staff, cake trolleys, and an array of cake and scones.

ENTERTAINMENT. The Regatta Lounge has entertainment, lectures, some social events, and a mix of production shows and cabaret acts.

SPA/FITNESS. A Lido Deck has a swimming pool, and good sunbathing space, plus a thalassotherapy tub. The uppermost outdoors deck includes a golf driving net and shuffleboard court. Canyon Ranch SpaClub consists of a beauty salon, three treatment rooms, changing rooms, and steam room (but no sauna). Note that an 18 percent 'gratuity' is added to your spa account.

Rhapsody of the Seas
★★★+

Size:	Mid-size Ship	Passenger/Crew Ratio (lower beds):	2.6
Tonnage:	78,491	Cabins (total):	1,000
Lifestyle:	Standard	Size Range (sq ft/m):	135.0–1,270.1/12.5–118.0
Cruise Line:	Royal Caribbean International	Cabins (for one person):	0
Former Names:	none	Cabins (with private balcony):	229
IMO Number:	9116864	Cabins (wheelchair accessible):	14
Builder:	Chantiers de l'Atlantique (France)	Wheelchair accessibility:	Good
Original Cost:	$275 million	Cabin Current:	110 and 220 volts
Entered Service:	May 1997	Elevators:	9
Registry:	The Bahamas	Casino (gaming tables):	Yes
Length (ft/m):	915.3/279.0	Slot Machines:	Yes
Beam (ft/m):	105.6/32.2	Swimming Pools:	2
Draft (ft/m):	24.9/7.6	Hot Tubs (on deck):	6
Propulsion/Propellers:	diesel-electric (50,400kW)/2	Self-Service Launderette:	No
Passenger Decks:	11	Dedicated Cinema/Seats:	No
Total Crew:	765	Library:	Yes
Passengers (lower beds):	2,000	Onboard currency:	US$
Passenger Space Ratio (lower beds):	39.2		

This modern ship is good for casual, family-friendly cruising

OVERVIEW. What makes *Rhapsody of the Seas* feel warm and cozy is the use of fine, light wood surfaces throughout its public rooms, plus the large array of potted plants. Throughout the ship, the artwork is upbeat and colorful, with a musical theme: classical, jazz, popular, and rock 'n' roll.

THE SHIP. This all-white ship, sister to *Vision of the Seas*, has a beautifully rounded stern and a single, slim funnel positioned at the very back of the ship. There is a reasonable amount of open-air walking space, although this tends to become cluttered with sunloungers.

The ship shares design features that make many, but not all, Royal Caribbean International (RCI) ships identifiable, including a domed Viking Crown Lounge, positioned above the Centrum – the ship's multi-level atrium.

There's a wide range of interesting public rooms, lounges, and bars, and the interiors have been cleverly designed to avoid congestion and aid passenger flow into revenue areas (a digital finger-touch 'wayfinder' system shows you the ship in relation to where you are standing).

The seven-deck high atrium lobby – called the Centrum – is the interior focal point, and the social hub of the ship. It houses an R Bar (for some interesting cocktails), several passenger service counters, an art gallery, and Café Latte-tudes (for coffee). Aerial entertainment happens in the Centrum, too. Close by is the superbly flashy Casino Royale, and the company's signature Schooner Bar, with its nautical-theme decor.

Berlitz's Ratings

	Possible	Achieved
Ship	500	385
Accommodation	200	147
Food	400	257
Service	400	250
Entertainment	100	63
Cruise Experience	400	270
OVERALL SCORE		
1372 points out of 2000		

Ship-wide Wi-Fi is provided (although there's a charge if you use it), as is a digital direction-finding system, electronic mustering, and a large outdoor poolside movie screen. Also, iPads in every cabin contain content about the ship's amenities and activities. Ship enthusiasts will like the chair fabric in the Shall We Dance Lounge, with its large aft-facing windows, and the glass case-enclosed mechanical sculptures.

FAMILIES. RCI caters to children really well with Adventure Ocean – a play area adjacent to a Royal Babies and Tots nursery – for babies of 6–36 months. Other ages are grouped as follows and have their own facilities and play areas: Aquanauts (3–5-year-olds); Explorers (6–8); Voyagers (9–12); Navigators (12–14); and Teens (15–17).

ACCOMMODATION. There are numerous accommodation grades, priced by size and location. The standard interior and exterior-view cabins are very small but have just enough functional facilities to make them acceptable for a one-week cruise (longer might prove confining). The decor is bright and cheerful, although the ceilings are plain; the soft furnishings make this home away from home look like the inside of a modern Scandinavian hotel – with minimalist tones, and splashes of color. Twin lower beds convert to queen-size beds, and there is a reasonable amount of closet and drawer space, but there is little room to maneuver between the bed and the desk/television unit.

The bathrooms are small but functional. The shower units are small, too, and there is no cabinet for toiletries. The towels should be larger and thicker. In the passageways, upbeat artwork depicts musical themes.

Choose a 'C' grade suite if you want spacious accommodation that includes a curtained-off sleeping area, a good-sized outside balcony with part, not full, partition, a lounge with sofa, two chairs and coffee table, three closets, plenty of drawer and storage space, television, and DVD player. The bathroom is large and has a full-size tub, integral shower, and two washbasins with two toiletries cabinets.

For the best accommodation, choose the Royal Suite. It resembles a Palm Beach apartment, and comes complete with a white baby grand piano. It has a separate bedroom with king-size bed, living room with queen-size sofa bed, refrigerator/minibar, dining table, entertainment center, and vanity dressing area. The decor is simple and elegant, with pastel colors, and wood-accented ceiling treatments. Located just under the starboard side navigation bridge wing, it has its own private balcony.

DINING. The two-level Aquarius Dining Room is attractive and works well as a large restaurant, although the noise level can be high. When you book, choose one of two seatings (fixed for dinner) for dinner or My Time Dining (eat when you want, during dining room hours).

The cuisine is typical of mass banquet catering that offers standard fare comparable to that found in American family-style restaurants ashore. Overall, meals are rather hit and miss – in fact non-memorable. Also, if you want lobster or a decent filet mignon (steak), you will be asked to pay extra.

Other dining options. A number of (extra-cost) venues were installed or refreshed during the ship's 2011–12 refit. Chops Grille is for premium steaks and other grilled meats and seafood. Izumi Asian Cuisine includes a sushi bar and features hot-rock cooking; it is open for lunch and dinner. A-la-carte menu pricing applies to both venues.

Chef's Table is a private experience co-hosted by the executive chef and sommelier for a five-course wine-pairing dinner (it's a little expensive, but worth it for a special occasion). Park Café is a casual no-charge market-style eatery for salads, sandwiches, soups, and pastries.

For casual cuisine, the Windjammer Café – located at the front of the ship with some commanding ocean views – is the self-serve buffet eatery.

A drinks package is available at all bars, in the form of cards or stickers. This enables you to pre-pay for a selection of standard soft drinks and alcoholic drinks, but the packages are not exactly easy to understand.

ENTERTAINMENT. The Broadway Melodies Theater is the principal showlounge. It is a large, but well-designed room with main and balcony levels, and good sight lines from most of the banquette seats.

Other cabaret acts are presented in the Shall We Dance Lounge, located aft, and include late-night adult comedy, as well as live music for dancing. A number of other bars and lounges have live music of differing types.

The entertainment, for which RCI always gets plenty of praise, is upbeat and colorful. However, it's difficult to escape from the background music provided everywhere – even in the passenger hallways and elevators, and outdoors on the pool deck.

SPA/FITNESS. The Vitality at Sea Spa and Fitness Center is set in a spacious environment on one of the aft uppermost decks. The decor has Egypt as its theme, with pharaohs lining an indoor/outdoor solarium pool. The spa is operated by Steiner, a specialist concession with staff providing a wide range of body treatments and hair care.

For the more sporty, there is a rock-climbing wall with several separate climbing tracks. It is located outdoors at the aft end of the funnel.

Riviera
★★★★+

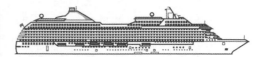

Size:	Mid-size Ship	Passenger/Crew Ratio (lower beds):	1.5
Tonnage:	66,084	Cabins (total):	629
Lifestyle:	Premium	Size Range (sq ft/m):	172.2–2,000/16.0–185.0
Cruise Line:	Oceania Cruises	Cabins (for one person):	0
Former Names:	none	Cabins (with private balcony):	593
IMO Number:	9438078	Cabins (wheelchair accessible):	6
Builder:	Fincantieri (Italy)	Wheelchair accessibility:	Good
Original Cost:	$530 million	Cabin Current:	110 and 220 Volts
Entered Service:	Jul 2012	Elevators:	6
Registry:	Marshall Islands	Casino (gaming tables):	Yes
Length (ft/m):	776.5/236.7	Slot Machines:	Yes
Beam (ft/m):	105.3/32.1	Swimming Pools:	1
Draft (ft/m):	24.2/7.4	Hot Tubs (on deck):	2
Propulsion/Propellers:	diesel-electric/2	Self-Service Launderette:	Yes
Passenger Decks:	11	Dedicated Cinema/Seats:	No
Total Crew:	800	Library:	Yes
Passengers (lower beds):	1,258	Onboard currency:	US$
Passenger Space Ratio (lower beds):	52.5		

A homey, comfortable, mid-size ship with a country club feel

OVERVIEW. This ship suits mature-age adults who appreciate refined quality and style, plenty of space and comfort (no lines), and excellent cuisine and service, in a semi-casual setting with realistic pricing. Oceania Cruises has succeeded in keeping the warm, tasteful country house decor style for which its ships are known, as well as an uncomplicated layout.

THE SHIP. *Riviera* is the second newbuild (close sister to *Marina*) for this popular, small premium-ship cruise line. Its profile is quite handsome, with a nicely rounded front, and is topped by a swept-back funnel. Able to cruise at a speed 25 percent faster than Oceania Cruises' smaller ships, *Nautica* and *Regatta*, the ship can operate a larger number of longer-distance cruises.

The interior focal point is a stunning wrought-iron and Lalique glass horseshoe-shaped staircase in the main lobby. Differences from *Marina* – there are reportedly 727 of them – include better steps on the main lobby staircase, a higher ceiling on one public deck, changes to drawer depth in cabins, a hand-held shower in suites with bathtub, and faster Internet speed.

Public rooms include nine bars and lounges. There is a 2,000-book library, set on the port side of the funnel housing, which also contains the staffed Oceania@Sea computer center, and Barista's coffee bar/lounge (serving the excellent illy brand Italian coffee). The ship also showcases a collection of fine Latin artwork by some of the most renowned artists from Cuba's Vanguard Movement (1927–50).

Berlitz's Ratings

	Possible	Achieved
Ship	500	442
Accommodation	200	179
Food	400	335
Service	400	316
Entertainment	100	82
Cruise Experience	400	328

OVERALL SCORE
1682 points out of 2000

A Monte Carlo Casino is located between two bars – the Grand Bar and Martinis, with its own soft lavender-colored Casino Bar. Martinis houses a beautiful special-edition Steinway baby grand piano. There are also three boutiques, and several dining venues. There aren't that many different lounges as such, because most are drinking venues.

A Culinary Center comprises a cooking demonstration kitchen and 24 workstations, with various classes run in conjunction with the US-based *Bon Appétit* magazine – there's a charge for these, but you get to eat your creations.

You can bring your paintbrushes to an Artist's Loft that has constantly changing artists. Other classes may include photography, needlepoint, scrapbooking, drawing, and quilting.

The dress code is 'elegant country club attire' – no pyjamas or track suits, but no ties either (so there's no tie rack in the closets). A gratuity of 18 percent is added to all bar and spa accounts.

ACCOMMODATION. There are 17 price categories, including four suite grades and four cabin grades. Price depends on size and location, but all have one thing in common – a good-sized bathroom with tub and separate shower enclosure, plus his 'n' hers toiletry cabinets. All suites/cabins have dark wood cabinetry with rounded edges. The decor includes chocolate brown, cream, and white – earthy colors that don't jar the senses. Around 96 percent of all accommodation has teak-decked balconies.

Standard veranda cabins. These measure 282 sq ft (26 sq m). Veranda- and Concierge-level cabins have a sitting area and teak balcony with faux wicker furniture. Concierge-level grades are supplied with L'Occitane toiletries.

Penthouse Suites. These measure 420 sq ft (39 sq m) with living/dining room separate from the sleeping area, walk-in closet, and bathroom with a double vanity.

Oceania Suites. These measure about 1,030 sq ft (96 sq m) and have a living room, dining room, separate bedroom, walk-in closet, teak-decked balcony with Jacuzzi tub, main bathroom, and a second bathroom for guests.

Vista Suites. These range from 1,200 to 1,500 sq ft (111–139 sq m) and offer the same features as Oceania Suites plus floor-to-ceiling windows overlooking the bow.

Owner's Suite. At more than 2,000 sq ft (186 sq m), this spans the entire beam of the ship (about 105ft/32m). It is decked out in furniture, fabrics, lighting, and bedding from the Ralph Lauren Home collection with design by New York-based Tocar Inc. It is outfitted with a Yamaha baby grand piano, private fitness room, laptop computers, Bose audio system, and a teak-decked balcony with Jacuzzi tub.

Suite-category occupants get niceties including Champagne on arrival, 1,000-thread-count bed linen, 42ins plasma TV sets, Hermès and Clarins bath amenities, butler service, and en suite delivery from any of the ship's restaurants. Amenities include Tranquility beds, Wi-Fi laptop computer, refrigerated minibar with unlimited free soft drinks and bottled water replenished daily, personal safe, writing desk, cotton bathrobes, slippers, and marble and granite bathroom. Priority check-in and early embarkation and priority luggage delivery are extra perks.

Occupants of Owner's, Vista, Oceania, and Penthouse Suites can have in-suite course-by-course dining from any restaurant menu, allowing private dining as a change from restaurant dining – a nice alternative on longer voyages.

Some grades get access to an Executive or Concierge Lounge. These are great little hideaways, with sofas, Internet-connect computers, Continental breakfast items, soft drinks, magazines, and more. Self-service launderettes are on each accommodation deck – useful for long voyages.

DINING. This really is a food lover's ship that uses high-quality ingredients and has a number of dining venues, providing plenty of choice, even for long cruises. However, banquette seating in some venues does not evoke the image of premium dining as much as individual seating does. Particularly notable are the breads, rolls, croissants, and brioches – all made on board from French flour and d'Isigny butter.

The Grand Dining Room has 566 seats, and a domed, or raised, central ceiling. Versace bone china, Christofle silver, and fine linens are used. Canyon Ranch Spa dishes are available for all meals.

Jacques, with 124 seats, is the second seagoing restaurant for French celebrity chef Jacques Pépin, Oceania's executive culinary director. It has antique oak flooring, antique flatware, and Lalique glassware, and provides fine dining in an elegant but informal setting, with roast free-range meats, nine classic French dessert items, and a choice of 12 AOC cheeses.

Polo Grill, with about 130 seats, serves steaks and seafood, including Oceania's signature 32oz bone-in King's Cut prime rib. The setting is classic traditional steakhouse, with dark wood paneling and classic white tablecloths, although the tables are close together.

Toscana is a 124-seat venue serving Italian-style cuisine (including some tasty desserts) and has Versace china.

Privée, with seating for up to 10 in a private setting, invites exclusivity for its seven-course dégustation menu.

La Réserve is the venue for wine and food, offering two different seven-course small-portion, wine-paired dégustation menus. With just 24 seats, it's also really intimate.

The Terrace Café is the ship's casual self-serve buffet-style venue. Outdoors, as an extension of the café, is Tapas on the Terrace, good for light bites – although the ceiling is low, so it can be very noisy.

Red Ginger is a specialty restaurant that offers 'classic and contemporary' Asian cuisine; the setting is visually refined, with ebony and dark wood finishes, but the banquette-style seating lets the venue down. You'll be asked by the waiter to choose your chopsticks from a lacquered presentation box.

The poolside Waves Grill, shaded from the sun, is for burgers (including fishburgers and veggie burgers), seafood, and other fast food, cooked to order. Baristas coffee bar overlooks the pool deck and has excellent, free illy Italian coffee – though, sadly, it's served in paper cups.

ENTERTAINMENT. The 600-seat Marina Lounge, spans two decks, with tiered amphitheater-style seating. It's more cabaret-style entertainment than big production shows, in keeping with the cruise line's traditions.

SPA/FITNESS. The Canyon Ranch SpaClub provides wellness and personal spa treatments. The facility includes a fitness center, beauty salon, several treatment rooms (including a couples room), sauna and steam rooms, and a large thalassotherapy pool. A jogging track is located aft of the funnel, above two of the specialty restaurants. All treatments incur an automatic 18 percent gratuity – almost one-fifth of the treatment price.

Rotterdam
★★★★

Size:	Mid-size Ship	
Tonnage:	59,855	
Lifestyle:	Premium	
Cruise Line:	Holland America Line	
Former Names:	*none*	
IMO Number:	9122552	
Builder:	Fincantieri (Italy)	
Original Cost:	$250 million	
Entered Service:	Dec 1997	
Registry:	The Netherlands	
Length (ft/m):	777.5/237.0	
Beam (ft/m):	105.8/32.2	
Draft (ft/m):	25.5/7.8	
Propulsion/Propellers:	diesel-electric (37,500kW)/2	
Passenger Decks:	12	
Total Crew:	600	
Passengers (lower beds):	1,404	
Passenger Space Ratio (lower beds):	42.6	

Passenger/Crew Ratio (lower beds):	2.3
Cabins (total):	702
Size Range (sq ft/m):	184.0–1,124.8/17.1–104.5
Cabins (for one person):	0
Cabins (with private balcony):	192
Cabins (wheelchair accessible):	25
Wheelchair accessibility:	Best
Cabin Current:	110 and 220 volts
Elevators:	12
Casino (gaming tables):	Yes
Slot Machines:	Yes
Swimming Pools:	2 (1 w/sliding glass door)
Hot Tubs (on deck):	2
Self-Service Launderette:	Yes
Dedicated Cinema/Seats:	Yes/235
Library:	Yes
Onboard currency:	US$

Dutch heritage and decor abound for senior-age cruisers

OVERVIEW. This is quite a contemporary ship for Holland America Line (HAL), with light, bright decor. It is extremely comfortable, with elegant decorative features. But these are marred by the poor quality of the dining room food and service, and a lack of understanding of what it takes to make the 'luxury' cruise experience touted in the company's brochures.

THE SHIP. This *Rotterdam* is the sixth HAL ship to bear the name, is capable of 25 knots – useful for longer itineraries. It has been built to look like a slightly larger but much sleeker version of the S-class ships, while retaining the graceful lines of its immediate predecessor, including a nicely raked bow and a more rounded exterior. Also retained are the familiar interior flow and design style, and twin-funnel.

Two decks – Promenade Deck and Upper Promenade Deck – house most of the public rooms, and are sandwiched between several accommodation decks. The layout is quite easy to learn, and the signage is good.

The interior decor is restrained, with much use of wood accenting. As a whole, the decor is extremely refined, with lots of the traditional ocean liner detailing so loved by frequent HAL passengers. A three-deck-high atrium has an oval, instead of circular, shape. Its focal point is a huge 'one-of-a-kind' custommade clock, based on an antique Flemish original that includes an astrolabe, an astrological clock, and 14 other clocks.

Berlitz's Ratings		
	Possible	Achieved
Ship	500	404
Accommodation	200	157
Food	400	267
Service	400	268
Entertainment	100	73
Cruise Experience	400	288
OVERALL SCORE		
1457 points out of 2000		

One room has a glass ceiling similar to that aboard a former *Statendam*. The Ambassador's Lounge has an interesting brass dance floor, similar to the dance floor that adorned the Ritz-Carlton room aboard the previous *Rotterdam*.

Instead of just two staircases aboard the S-class ships, *Rotterdam* has three – better from the viewpoint of safety, passenger accessibility, and evacuation. A pool, on the Lido Deck (between the mast and the ship's twin funnels), is covered by a glass dome.

Popcorn is available at the Wajang Theatre for moviegoers, while adjacent is the popular Java Café. The casino, located in the middle of a major passenger flow, has blackjack, roulette, poker, and dice tables alongside the requisite rows of slot machines.

HAL has a long legacy in Dutch maritime history. The $2 million worth of artwork here consists of a collection of 17th-century Dutch and Japanese artefacts, together with contemporary works specially created for the ship, although there seems little linkage between some of the items.

HAL's Signature of Excellence program has created 'Mix,' a new open area with comfortable sofa and armchair seating in small alcove-like setting adjacent to a shopping area. The trendy, upbeat space combines three specialty theme bars: Champagne (serving Champagne and sparkling wines from around the world), Martinis (in individual shakers), and Spirits & Ales (a sports bar with beer, baseball, and basketball). Microsoft Surface touch-screen technology enhances checkers and chess, air hockey, and other sports games.

With one whole deck of suites – and a dedicated, private Concierge Lounge, and preferential passenger treatment – the company has in effect created a two-class ship. Passenger niggles include inadequate room service, poor staff communication, and the charge to use the washing machines and dryers in the self-service launderette – petty and irritating, particularly for the occupants of suites, as they pay high prices for their cruises.

In a 2009 refit, 23 Veranda Deck cabins were converted into 'Spa Cabins,' while new lanai-style cabins were created on Lower Promenade Deck.

FAMILIES. The ship has allotted more space to children's and teens' play areas, although these really are token gestures by a company that traditionally doesn't cater well to children. However, grandparents do take their grandchildren with them – pleasing parents, who get a well-deserved break. Enhanced children's programming is brought into play, according to the number of children carried.

ACCOMMODATION. There are 17 categories, priced by grade, size and location. Accommodation is spread over five decks, and some cabins have full or partially obstructed views. Interestingly, no cabin is more than 144ft (44m) from a stairway, which makes it easier to get from cabins to public rooms. All cabin doors have a bird's-eye maple look, and hallways have framed fabric panels to make them less clinical.

All standard inside and outside cabins are tastefully furnished, with twin beds that convert to queen-size, though space is tight for walking between beds and vanity unit. There is a decent amount of closet and drawer space, but this will prove tight for longer voyages.

The fully tiled bathrooms are disappointingly small, particularly for long cruises, and have small shower tubs, utilitarian toiletries cupboards, and exposed under-sink plumbing. There is no detailing to distinguish them significantly from bathrooms aboard the S-class ships.

There are 36 full Veranda Suites on Navigation Deck, including four Penthouse Suites, which share a private Concierge Lounge and concierge to handle such things as special dining arrangements, shore excursions, and other requests – although strangely there are no butlers for these suites, as aboard many ships with similar facilities. Each suite has a separate steward's entrance and separate bedroom, dressing, and living areas. Suite passengers get personal stationery, complimentary laundry and ironing, cocktail-hour hors d'oeuvres, and other goodies, as well as priority embarkation and disembarkation. The Concierge Lounge, with its latticework teak detailing and private library is accessible only by private key-card.

Disabled passengers have a choice of 20 cabins, including two of the large Penthouse Suites that include concierge services. However, there are different cabin configurations, and it is wise to check with your booking agent.

DINING. The La Fontaine Dining Room seats 747, spans two decks, and has are tables for four, six, or eight, but only nine tables for two. Both open seating and assigned seating are available, while breakfast and lunch are open seating, where you'll be seated by restaurant staff when you enter. Fine Rosenthal china and good cutlery are provided.

Other dining options. Pinnacle Grill is an extra-cost 88-seat restaurant that is more upscale and more intimate than the main dining room. It also features higher-quality ingredients and better presentation than the main dining room. It is on Promenade Deck and fronts onto the second level of the atrium lobby. Pacific Northwest cuisine is featured, together with an array of premium-quality steaks. There are fine table settings, china and silverware, and leather-bound menus. The wine list consists mostly of American wines. Reservations are required and there's a cover charge – but the prime steaks are worth it.

For casual meals, the Lido Restaurant is a self-serve buffet venue. A section of this restaurant turns into the Canaletto Restaurant by night, when Italian dishes are featured (reservations are required and a cover charge applies).

Also, a Lido Deck poolside 'Dive-In at the Terrace Grill' features signature burgers, hot dogs and fries, and, on certain days, barbecues, and other culinary treats may be featured.

ENTERTAINMENT. The 577-seat Showroom at Sea is the venue for all production shows, the strongest cabaret, and other entertainment. It is two decks high, with seating on both main and balcony levels. The decor includes umbrella-shaped gold ceiling lamps made from Murano glass (from Venice), and the stage has hydraulic lifts and three video screens, as well as a closed-loop system for the hearing-impaired.

SPA/FITNESS. The Ocean Spa is one deck above the navigation bridge at the very forward part of the ship. It includes a gymnasium with all the latest muscle-pumping exercise machines, including an abundance of treadmills, with forward views over the ship's bows. There's an aerobics exercise area, large beauty salon with ocean-view windows to the port side, several treatment rooms, and men's and women's sauna, steam room, and changing areas.

Royal Clipper
★★★★

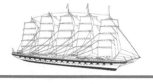

Size:	Boutique Ship	Passenger/Crew Ratio (lower beds):	2.1
Tonnage:	5,061	Cabins (total):	114
Lifestyle:	Premium	Size Range (sq ft/m):	100.0–320.0/9.3–29.7
Cruise Line:	Star Clippers	Cabins (for one person):	0
Former Names:	none	Cabins (with private balcony):	14
IMO Number:	8712178	Cabins (wheelchair accessible):	0
Builder:	De Merwede (Holland)	Wheelchair accessibility:	None
Original Cost:	$75 million	Cabin Current:	220 volts
Entered Service:	Oct 2000	Elevators:	0
Registry:	Luxembourg	Casino (gaming tables):	No
Length (ft/m):	439.6/134.0	Slot Machines:	No
Beam (ft/m):	54.1/16.5	Swimming Pools:	3
Draft (ft/m):	18.5/5.6	Hot Tubs (on deck):	0
Propulsion/Propellers:	diesel (3,700kW)/1	Self-Service Launderette:	No
Passenger Decks:	5	Dedicated Cinema/Seats:	No
Total Crew:	106	Library:	Yes
Passengers (lower beds):	228	Onboard currency:	Euros
Passenger Space Ratio (lower beds):	22.1		

This sail-cruise ship exudes character and charm

OVERVIEW. *Royal Clipper* best suits couples and solo travelers who would probably never consider a 'normal' cruise ship, but who enjoy sailing and the thrill of ocean and wind, but want a package that includes accommodation, food, like-minded companions, and interesting destinations, and not the bother of owning or chartering their own yacht. This is the bee's knees.

THE SHIP. The culmination of an owner's childhood dream, *Royal Clipper* is a stunning sight under sail. It's the world's largest true fully rigged sailing ship (it has five masts, whereas the company's two other, smaller ships (*Star Clipper* and *Star Flyer*) have four.

Royal Clipper's design is based on the only other five-masted sailing ship ever to be built, the 1902-built German tall ship *Preussen*, and has approximately the same dimensions, albeit 46ft (14m) shorter.

The construction time for this ship was remarkably short, because its hull had almost been completed (at Gdansk shipyard, Poland) for another owner, before becoming available to Star Clippers. It is instantly recognizable due to its geometric blue-and-white hull markings. Power winches, as well as hand winches, are employed in deck fittings, as well as a mix of horizontal furling for the square sails and hydraulic power assist to roll the square sails along the yardarm. The sail handling system, designed by the owner Mikael Krafft, is such that it can quickly be converted from a full rigger to a schooner.

Berlitz's Ratings		
	Possible	Achieved
Ship	500	401
Accommodation	200	157
Food	400	288
Service	400	296
Entertainment	100	80
Cruise Experience	400	312
OVERALL SCORE		
1534 points out of 2000		

Its masts reach 197ft (60m) above the waterline, and the top 19ft (5.8m) can be hinged over 90° to clear bridges, cable lines, and other port-based obstacles. Watching the sailors manipulate ropes, rigging, and sails is like watching a ballet – the precision and cohesion of a group of men, who make it all look so simple.

Passengers may be allowed to climb to special lookout points aloft, and on the bridge at any time – but they cannot go in the galley or engine room.

The ship has a large amount of open deck space and sunning space – something most tall ships lack – although, naturally, this is laid with rigging ropes. An aft marina platform can be lowered, so that passengers can use surfboards, sailing dinghies, take a ride on the banana boat, or go waterskiing or swimming. Snorkeling gear is available free, but there is a charge for scuba gear. You will be asked to sign a waiver if you use the water-sports equipment.

Inside, a midships atrium three decks high sits under one of the ship's three swimming pools, and sunlight streams down through a piano lounge on the uppermost level inside the ship and into the lower level dining room. A forward observation lounge is a real plus – it's connected to the piano lounge via a central corridor. An Edwardian library/card room includes a Belle Epoque fireplace. The Captain Nemo Club lets you observe fish and marine life when the ship is at anchor, through thick glass portholes; it's floodlit from underneath at night to attract the fish.

The ship operates cruises in the Grenadines and Lower Windward Islands of the Caribbean in winter and Mediterranean cruises in summer. Officers navigate using both traditional (sextant) and contemporary methods (advanced electronic positioning system).

This being a tall ship with true sailing traditions, there is, naturally, a parrot (it is sometimes kept in a large, gilded cage, but it may be seen around the ship on someone's shoulder); it's considered to be part of the crew. The ambience is extremely relaxed, friendly and unpretentious. The dress code is always casual (shorts and casual tops are the order of the day – yachting wear), with no ties needed ever.

The suites and cabins are, in general, smaller than aboard *Sea Cloud* and *Sea Cloud II*. I do not include the Windstar Cruises ships (*Wind Spirit*, *Wind Star*, *Wind Surf*), because they are not tall ships. *Royal Clipper*, however, is exactly that – a real, working, wind-and-sails-in-your-face tall ship.

This vessel is not for the physically impaired, or for children. The steps of the internal stairs are steep, as in most sailing vessels. Any gratuities you give are pooled and divided among all crew members. What gives the ship a little extra in the scoring department is the fact that many water sports are included in the price.

ACCOMMODATION. There are several accommodation grades, priced according to size, type and location: Owner's Suites (2), Deluxe Suites (14), and categories 1–6. All have polished wood-trimmed cabinetry and wall-to-wall carpeting, personal safe, full-length mirror, small TV set with audio channels and 24-hour text-based news, and private bathroom. All have twin beds (86 of which convert into a queen-size bed, while 28 are fixed queen-size beds), hairdryer, and satellite-linked telephone. The six interior cabins and a handful of other cabins have a permanently fixed double bed.

Most cabins have a privacy curtain, so that you can't be seen from the hallway when the cabin attendant opens the door – useful if you're undressed. Additionally, 27 cabins can sleep three.

Two Owner's Suites, located aft, provide the most lavish accommodation, and have one queen-size bed and one double bed, a living area with semi-circular sofa, large vanity desk, minibar/refrigerator, marble-clad bathroom with whirlpool bathtub, plus one guest bathroom, and butler service. They have an interconnecting door, so a combined super-suite can sleep eight.

The 14 'Deck Suites' have interesting names: Ariel, Cutty Sark, Doriana, Eagle Wing, Flying Cloud, France, Gloria, Golden Gate, Great Republic, Passat, Pommern, Preussen, and Thermopylae. However, they are not actually suites, as the sleeping area can't be separated from the lounge – they are simply larger cabins with a nicer interior, more storage space, and a larger bathroom. Each has two lower beds convertible to a queen-size one, small lounge area, minibar/refrigerator, writing desk, small private balcony, and marble-clad bathroom with combination whirlpool tub/shower, washbasin, and toilet. The door to the balcony can be opened, so that fresh air floods the room; note that there is a 12in (30cm) threshold to step over. There are no curtains, only roll-down shades for the windows and balcony door. The balcony itself typically has two white chairs and drinks table. The balconies are not particularly private, and most have ship's tenders or Zodiacs overhanging them, or some rigging obscuring the views.

Two other name cabins (Lord Nelson and Marco Polo) are located aft, but lack private balconies, although the facilities are similar.

The interior cabins and the lowest grades of outside-view cabins are extremely small and tight, with little room to move around the beds. So take only the minimum amount of clothing and luggage. When in cabins where beds are linked together to form a double bed, you need to clamber up over the front of the bed, as both sides have built-in storm barriers (this applies in inclement weather conditions only).

There is a small room service menu (all items cost extra).

DINING. The Dining Room is on several connecting levels (getting used to the steps is not easy), and seats all passengers at one seating under a three-deck-high atrium dome. You can sit with whom you wish at tables for four to 10. However, it is noisy, due to the numerous waiter stations. Some tables are badly positioned, so that correct waiter service is impossible; much reaching over has to be done in order to serve everyone.

One corner can be closed off for private parties. Breakfasts and lunches are self-serve buffets, while dinner is a sit-down affair with table service; the ambience is always friendly and lighthearted. The wine list consists of young wines, and prices are high. The cuisine, although perfectly acceptable, is nothing to write home about.

ENTERTAINMENT. There are no shows, nor are any expected by passengers aboard a tall ship such as this, where sailing is the main purpose. There is, however, live music, provided by a single lounge pianist/singer.

SPA/FITNESS. The Royal Spa is located on the lowest passenger deck and, although not large, incorporates a beauty salon, an extra-charge Moroccan steam room, and a small gymnasium.

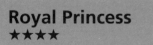

Royal Princess
★★★★

Size:	Large Resort Ship
Tonnage:	141,200
Lifestyle:	Standard
Cruise Line:	Princess Cruises
Former Names:	none
IMO Number:	9584712
Builder:	Fincantieri (Italy)
Original Cost:	€775 million
Entered Service:	Jun 2013
Registry:	Bermuda
Length (ft/m):	1,082.6/330.0
Beam (ft/m):	126.3/38.6
Draft (ft/m):	27.8/8.5
Propulsion/Propellers:	diesel-electric (52,000kW)/2
Passenger Decks:	17
Total Crew:	1,346
Passengers (lower beds):	3,560
Passenger Space Ratio (lower beds):	39.6
Passenger/Crew Ratio (lower beds):	2.6
Cabins (total):	1,780
Size Range (sq ft/m):	161.4-554.3/15-51.5
Cabins (for one person):	0
Cabins (with private balcony):	1,438
Cabins (wheelchair accessible):	36
Wheelchair accessibility:	Best
Cabin Current:	110 and 220 volts
Elevators:	14
Casino (gaming tables):	Yes
Slot Machines:	Yes
Swimming Pools:	2
Hot Tubs (on deck):	6
Self-Service Launderette:	Yes
Dedicated Cinema/Seats:	No
Library:	Yes
Onboard currency:	US$

This is a large, family-friendly, multi-choice contemporary resort ship

OVERVIEW. *Royal Princess* is a grand resort, a playground in which to roam when not ashore. Princess Cruises has taken the best features of its Grand-class ships, fine-tuned them to the latest passenger tastes, and included more hedonistic retreats and food venues. The company delivers a consistent and well-packaged cruise vacation at an attractive price, so passengers keep returning.

THE SHIP. *Royal Princess* has quite a streamlined look for its size. When the ship first debuted, there was no complete walk-around promenade deck. But, due to many passenger complaints, this has been changed, so now you can enjoy a complete walk-around deck. Also added in the retro-fit was an aft-deck swimming pool. Although this reduced some open deck space, it is now a much-appreciated facility. Lifeboats are located outside the main public room areas, so that they don't impair the view from balcony cabins.

One notable innovation are two 'over-the-water' Sea-Walks, top-deck glass-floor enclosed walkways (stiletto heels not advisable!) on both sides; these extend almost 30ft (9.1m) beyond the vessel's edge. Go there for dramatic views of the sea – some 128ft (39m) below.

For real escapees, an extra-cost adults-only retreat called The Sanctuary is larger than aboard the Grand-class ships and has more amenities. It includes four rentable cabanas, two extra-cost Lotus-Spa-operated 'couples' cabanas, and has its own retreat pool and relaxation areas (in both sunny and shaded positions). The adjacent Retreat area has grown in size, and so other passengers have less open deck space.

Berlitz's Ratings		
	Possible	Achieved
Ship	500	415
Accommodation	200	161
Food	400	268
Service	400	295
Entertainment	100	83
Cruise Experience	400	306
OVERALL SCORE		
1528 points out of 2000		

The Piazza Atrium is the ship's multi-faceted social hub. It combines specialty eateries, for light meals, snacks, pastries, beverages, entertainment, shopping, and passenger services all in one area, with multi-level horseshoe-shaped 'flowing' stairways, mood lighting effects, and a small dance floor.

The atrium's base level includes a large International Café, for coffees, teas, panini, and pastries; Sabatini's (adjacent to the atrium, not exactly in it), a Tuscan specialty extra-cost restaurant, with both regular and à-la-carte menus; and a gift shop. Upstairs, level two includes a 121-seat Alfredo's Pizzeria (pizzas are free), Bellini's (featuring Bellini drinks) a photo gallery, and the reception and shore excursion counters. On the third level is Crooners Bar, with solo pianist entertainers, and a small Seafood Bar. One serious design fault is the complete lack of a central stairway above the two main restaurants, which leads to severe crowding of the adjacent elevators.

FAMILIES. Children have their own playrooms (Pelicans, Shockwaves), teens-only chill-out room, pools, fitness and open deck areas, away from adult areas, plus a host of energetic, dedicated children's and youth counselors. There are good sports facilities for younger cruisers, too, so that they can be kept really active. Children can eat in a dedicated section of the Horizon Court buffet area equipped with kid-height tables and chairs. A total of 50 cabins have interconnecting doors – good for families with children. Children and teens have their own fitness rooms adjacent to their age-related facilities.

ACCOMMODATION. There are five main types of accommodation and a bewildering number of different price grades: (a) Grand Suite; (b) 40 suites with balcony; (c) 306 mini-suites with balcony; (d) 360 deluxe outside-view balcony cabins; (e) 732 outside-view cabins with balcony; and (e) 342 interior cabins. Pricing depends on two things: size and location. Outside-view cabins account for about 81 percent of all accommodation, and have a balcony; those located at the stern are the quietest and most sought-after. Note that some 68 cabins have lifeboat-obstructed views, and the 52 cabins on Deck 8 above the showlounge are subject to noise pollution from the shows until late in the evening.

All grades share energy-efficient lighting and key card readers that automatically turn off lights when occupants leave their cabins. All cabins have beds with upholstered headboards, wall-mounted TV sets, 220v electrical sockets, turndown service and heart-shaped chocolates on pillows each night, bathrobes (on request unless you are in suite-grade accommodation), and toiletries. A hairdryer is provided in all cabins, sensibly located at the vanity desk unit in the living area. Bathrooms generally have a good amount of open shelf storage space for toiletries.

Suite- and mini-suite-grade occupants have their own Concierge Lounge – useful for making dining, spa, and shore excursion reservations. They also have more amenities and larger TV sets, larger towels, and two washbasins.

Some of the most sought-after suites are located aft, occupying the corner (port and starboard) positions.

DINING. There are three 'formal' main dining rooms: Allegro, Concerto, and Symphony. You can choose either traditional two-seating dining (typically 6pm and 8.15pm for dinner), or 'anytime dining' – where you choose when and with whom you want to eat. However, if you want to see a show in the evening, then your dining time will be dictated by the time of the show, which limits your choice.

A 12-seat circular table is located within the Wine Cellar of the Allegro and Symphony dining rooms. This extra-cost, reservations-required venue is good for private functions and celebrations. Also available is a private Chef's Table Lumière, located within the Concerto dining room. It has a custom-made glass dining table and fine dining utensils. In both Allegro and Symphony, you can reserve a private table (at extra cost) for up to 12 in each venue's wine room, for meals that are paired with specific wines.

Other dining options. Extra-cost, reservations-required Sabatini's (Vines Bar is located adjacent), just off the lower atrium level, is an Italian restaurant with colorful Tuscany-themed decor. Named after Trattoria Sabatini, the 200-year-old institution in Florence, it serves Italian-style pasta dishes with a choice of sauces, all provided with flair and entertainment by energetic waiters. This venue also hosts Italian wine tasting.

Alfredo's is a sit-down pizzeria named after Alfredo Marzi, corporate chef for Princess Cruises; the venue specializes in 'authentic' family-friendly-size pizzas.

Ocean Terrace, located on the upper level of the three-deck-high atrium lobby, is a seafood bar. International Café, on the lowest level of the Piazza Atrium, is the place for extra-cost coffees, pastries, paninis, and more.

Vines Wine Bar is close to Sabatini's and provides an escape from all the noise and hubbub elsewhere – for a glass of extra-cost wine and tapas. It's a pleasant area in which to while away a late afternoon, trying out new wines.

Crown Grill is for all-American premium-quality steaks and grilled seafood. It is an extra-cost, reservations-required venue, located close to the aft stairway, and adjacent to the Wheelhouse Bar, which can be noisy at times.

For casual meals, the self-serve buffet venue Horizon Court (it seats 900 indoors and 350 outdoors at an adjacent Horizon Terrace) has multiple active cooking stations (but few beverage stations). Sections highlight specific themes, such as Mediterranean, Asian, and Italian cuisine; there's also a deli section. At night, the aft section becomes the Horizon Bistro, for casual dinners. Certain evenings feature special themes and foods, such as British pub food or as a Brazilian churrascaria (for carved meat dishes). A hibachi grill and other 'active' cooking stations (for regional specialties) are part of the scenario. It all translates to a more flexible large-scale eatery – but useful as a change to the main dining rooms. Additionally, Horizon Court has its own bakery.

Outside, the poolside Trident Grill (for hamburgers, hot dogs, and other fast-food grilled items during the day) becomes a traditional smokehouse barbecue in the evenings. Meanwhile, Mexican-style eats can be obtained from the Outrigger Bar.

ENTERTAINMENT. The 1,000 seat Princess Theater is the main showlounge. Two decks high, it is designed for the large-scale production shows that Princess Cruises is renowned for, and has good views from all seats – there are no pillars to spoil the view, which is an outstanding achievement in such a large room.

SPA/FITNESS. The Lotus Spa is large, and is forward on the lower level of the atrium, so it doesn't take away premium outdoor-view real estate space (it's adjacent to Sabatini's Italian Restaurant). Separate facilities for men and women include a sauna, steam room, and changing rooms; common facilities include a relaxation/waiting zone and body-pampering treatment rooms. A gymnasium packed with the latest high-tech, muscle-pumping cardio-vascular equipment is located aft on a higher deck.

Ruby Princess
★★★★

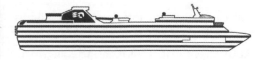

Size:	Large Resort Ship
Tonnage:	113,561
Lifestyle:	Standard
Cruise Line:	Princess Cruises
Former Names:	none
IMO Number:	1890038
Builder:	Fincantieri (Italy)
Original Cost:	$500 million
Entered Service:	Sep 2008
Registry:	Bermuda
Length (ft/m):	951.4/290.0
Beam (ft/m):	118.1/36.0
Draft (ft/m):	26.2/8.0
Propulsion/Propellers:	diesel-electric (42,000kW)/2
Passenger Decks:	15
Total Crew:	1,200
Passengers (lower beds):	3,114
Passenger Space Ratio (lower beds):	36.4

Passenger/Crew Ratio (lower beds):	2.5
Cabins (total):	1,557
Size Range (sq ft/m):	163–1,279/15.1–118.8
Cabins (for one person):	0
Cabins (with private balcony):	881
Cabins (wheelchair accessible):	25
Wheelchair accessibility:	Good
Cabin Current:	110 volts
Elevators:	14
Casino (gaming tables):	Yes
Slot Machines:	Yes
Swimming Pools:	3
Hot Tubs (on deck):	9
Self-Service Launderette:	Yes
Dedicated Cinema/Seats:	No
Library:	Yes
Onboard currency:	US$

This large, family-friendly resort ship has pleasant decor

OVERVIEW. This ship, among the best in the standard family market, is a veritable resort playground. Princess Cruises delivers a consistently fine, well-packaged vacation product, always with a degree of style, at a highly competitive price. Passenger flow is well thought-out, and, despite the ship's large capacity, there's little congestion.

THE SHIP. *Ruby Princess* has the same profile, interior layout, and public rooms as sister ships *Crown Princess* (2006) and *Emerald Princess* (2007). Accommodating over 500 more passengers than earlier half-sisters such as *Diamond Princess*, the outdoor deck space remains the same, as do the number of elevators.

The Sanctuary, an extra-cost adults-only retreat, is worth paying extra for in warm-weather areas. Located forward on the uppermost deck, it provides a 'private' place to relax and unwind. Attendants provide chilled face towels and deliver water and light bites; there are also two outdoor cabanas for private couples massage.

There's a good sheltered faux wood promenade strolling deck – it's actually painted steel – which almost wraps around the front and aft areas of the ship; three times round is equal to one mile. Movies Under the Skies and major sporting events are shown on a 300-sq-ft (28-sq-m) movie screen located at the pool forward of the large funnel structure.

The main public bars and lounges are located off a double-width promenade deck. The main lobby is the focal meeting point. Called The Plaza, it's like a town square, and includes a 44-seat International

Berlitz's Ratings

	Possible	Achieved
Ship	500	377
Accommodation	200	147
Food	400	249
Service	400	285
Entertainment	100	81
Cruise Experience	400	295
OVERALL SCORE		
1434 points out of 2000		

Café (patisserie/deli) and lots of nice cakes and pastries, and Vines, a combination wine/cheese and sushi/tapas counter.

The library is in a little corner adjacent to the wood-paneled Wheelhouse Bar. There are many other pleasant bars and lounges to enjoy, including Crooners, an intimate New York-style piano bar, with around 70 seats on the upper level of the lobby, but perhaps the nicest of all is Adagio's.

High atop the stern, with great views, is a ship-wide glass-walled disco pod (Skywalkers), which looks like an aerodynamic spoiler (it would make a great penthouse), but is a good place to read a book during the day.

The casino, Gatsby's, has over 260 slot machines (linked slot machines provide a combined payout), and blackjack, craps, and roulette tables for serious gamers.

FAMILIES. For children, there are several playrooms, a teen room, and a host of trained counselors. There are swimming and splash pools, hot tubs, and open deck area at the stern, away from adult areas. There are good netted-in areas; one section has a dip pool, while another has a mini-basketball court. The Wizard's Academy is an enrichment program from the California Science Center.

ACCOMMODATION. There are six main types of cabins and configurations: (a) Grand Suite, (b) suite, (c) mini-suite, (d) outside-view double cabins with balcony, (e) outside-view double cabins, and (f) interior (no-view) double cabins. These come in a multitude of different brochure price categories. Pricing depends on size and location. Two family suites have an interconnecting door, plus a large balcony. These can sleep up to 10, if at least four are children, or up to eight adults.

By comparison, the largest suite is slightly smaller, and the smallest interior cabin is slightly larger than the equivalent suites/cabins aboard *Golden*, *Grand*, and *Star Princess*. Almost all balcony suites and cabins can be overlooked both from the navigation bridge wing, as well as from the port and starboard sections of Skywalkers, high above the ship at the stern. Suites C401, 402, 404, 406, 408, 410, 412, 401, 405, 411, 415, and 417 on Riviera Deck 14, and D105 and D106 (Dolphin Deck 9) have only semi-private balconies that can be seen from above, so there is little privacy. Also, most outside-view cabins on Emerald Deck have views obstructed by lifeboats.

Some cabins can accommodate a third and fourth person in upper berths, but, in these, the lower beds can't be pushed together to make a queen-size bed.

Cabin bath towels are small, and drawer space is tight. There are no butlers – even for the top-grade suites, which are not large in comparison to similar suites aboard some other similarly sized ships. Suite-grade occupants get better service, personal amenities, and other perks.

The Grand Suite (A750), is the largest suite, and is located at the stern. It has a large bedroom with queen-size bed, huge walk-in closets, two bathrooms, a lounge with fireplace, sofa bed, wet bar and refrigerator, and a large private balcony on the port side, with a hot tub accessible from both balcony and bedroom.

The 28 wheelchair-accessible cabins measure 250–385 sq ft (23–35.7 sq m); but there's no mirror for dressing, and no full-length hanging space.

DINING. There are several dining options, including three main dining rooms, plus a Crown Grill, and Sabatini's Trattoria.

The three rooms for formal dining are Botticelli, Da Vinci, and Michelangelo. The Botticelli Dining Room has traditional two seating dining (typically 6pm and 8.15pm for dinner), while 'anytime dining' – where you choose when and with whom you want to eat – is offered in Da Vinci and Michelangelo. They are split into various sections in a non-symmetrical design that presents smaller sections for better ambience, and each restaurant has its own galley.

Other dining options. Sabatini's and Crown Grill, both requiring reservations and at extra charge, are open for lunch and dinner on days at sea. Sabatini's is a 132-seat Italian eatery with some painted scenes of Tuscan villas and gardens and colorful tiled Mediterranean-style decor; it is named after Trattoria Sabatini, the 200-year-old institution in Florence. It

has Italian-style pizzas and pastas, with a variety of sauces and Italian-style entrées – all provided with flair and entertainment by the waiters. It is also open for breakfast for suite/mini-suite occupants only, when it really is a quiet haven.

Crown Grill is a 138-seat restaurant featuring a good range of premium steaks, chops, and grilled seafood items (everything is cooked to order), and is located off the main indoor Deck 7 promenade. Seating is mainly in semi-private alcoves, and there's a show kitchen, so you can watch the action.

The 312-seat Horizon Court, with its indoor-outdoor seating, is open 24 hours a day for casual meals (on plastic plates), and has large ocean-view windows on both sides. The central display sections are often crowded.

Other casual eateries include a poolside hamburger grill and pizza bar, while extra charges apply if you order items to eat at the coffee bar/patisserie, or the caviar/Champagne bar.

The International Café, on Deck 5 in The Plaza, is the place for coffees and specialty coffees, pastries, light lunches, and delightful afternoon cakes, most at no extra cost.

For something different, try a private meal on your balcony: an Ultimate Balcony Dinner – an all-inclusive evening featuring cocktails, fresh flowers, Champagne, and a deluxe multi-course meal – or an Ultimate Balcony Breakfast; all served by a member of the dining staff. It costs $50 per person for dinner, or $32 per couple for the breakfast – superb value for money.

For an extra per-person charge, an exclusive dining experience showcases the executive chef in a mini-dégustation that includes appetizers in the galley. It is a fine dining experience that includes good wines paired with high-quality meat and seafood dishes, and creative presentation. You'll need three hours to enjoy this special dinner; the slow-cooked roast veal shank is outstanding.

ENTERTAINMENT. The Princess Theater spans two decks and has comfortable seating on both levels. It has $3 million worth of sound and light equipment, plus a live orchestra for backing colourful production shows and major cabaret acts. The ship has a resident troupe of singers and dancers, plus an army of audio-visual support staff.

SPA/FITNESS. The Lotus Spa is located forward on Sun Deck. Separate facilities for men and women include a sauna, steam room, and changing rooms; common facilities include a relaxation/waiting zone, body-pampering treatment rooms, and a gymnasium with high-tech muscle-pumping equipment, and great ocean views. Some fitness classes are free, while others cost extra.

Saga Pearl II
★★★+

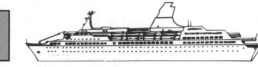

Size:	Small Ship	Passenger Space Ratio (lower beds):	40.7
Tonnage:	18,591	Passenger/Crew Ratio (lower beds):	1.8
Lifestyle:	Standard	Cabins (total):	258
Cruise Line:	Saga Cruises	Size Range (sq ft/m):	150.0–725.0/13.4–65.3
Former Names:	*Quest for Adventure, Saga Pearl II, Astoria, Arkona, Astor*	Cabins (for one person):	60
		Cabins (with private balcony):	40
IMO Number:	7904889	Cabins (wheelchair accessible):	0
Builder:	Howaldtswerke Deutsche Werft (Germany)	Wheelchair accessibility:	Fair
Original Cost:	$55 million	Cabin Current:	220 volts
Entered Service:	Dec 1981/May 2013	Elevators:	3
Registry:	The Bahamas	Casino (gaming tables):	No
Length (ft/m):	539.2/164.3	Slot Machines:	No
Beam (ft/m):	74.1/22.6	Swimming Pools:	2
Draft (ft/m):	20.0/6.1	Hot Tubs (on deck):	0
Propulsion/Propellers:	diesel (13,200kW)/2	Self-Service Launderette:	Yes
Passenger Decks:	8	Dedicated Cinema/Seats:	No
Total Crew:	252	Library:	Yes
Passengers (lower beds):	456	Onboard currency:	UK£

A comfortable small ship for discovery-style cruising

OVERVIEW. This ship is best suited to English-speaking couples, and solo travelers of mature years. Saga Cruises staff go out of their way to ensure you have an excellent time.

THE SHIP. *Saga Pearl II* is a traditional-looking cruise ship. A multimillion pound 2009 refit added a superb 3,000-book library, an array of balcony cabins, and new galleys. There is a good amount of open deck and sunbathing space, with some teakwood decks, polished wood railings, and cushioned pads for sunloungers. There is no walk-around promenade deck outdoors, but a small walking area under the lifeboats exists on both sides.

ACCOMMODATION. The accommodation consists of many different price categories, including several for solo travelers in single-occupancy cabins, and it is spread over four decks.

Grand Suites. Two Boat Deck suites (725 sq ft/65 sq m) provide really large spaces, and have just about everything needed for refined, private shipboard living. There's a separate bedroom with double bed, and a living room with sofa, dining table, and chairs. The tiled bathroom has a large tub, separate shower, and plenty of storage space for toiletries.

Suites. 34 suites (269 sq ft/25 sq m) have a separate bedroom with twin beds, and a living room with sofa, dining table, and chairs. The tiled bathroom has a large tub, separate shower enclosure, and plenty of space for toiletries.

Berlitz's Ratings

	Possible	Achieved
Ship	500	321
Accommodation	200	134
Food	400	262
Service	400	286
Entertainment	100	72
Cruise Experience	400	273
OVERALL SCORE		
1348 points out of 2000		

Outside-view cabins/interior cabins. The standard cabins (140 sq ft/13 sq m) are quite well appointed and decorated, and all are in crisp, clean colors – some might find them plain. The bathrooms are quite compact units, although there is a decent-size shower.

DINING. The Dining Room has ocean-view picture windows. It has dark wood paneling and restful decor. There's a single, open seating, at tables for four, six, or eight. Two small wings, each with one a 12-seat table, can be used for small groups. The wine list has a decent selection of wines from many regions. Self-serve buffets, for breakfast and lunch, and as a casual alternative to dinner in the Dining Room, can be taken in the Verandah Restaurant, which overlooks the aft pool and open deck area.

ENTERTAINMENT. The Discovery Lounge is the main entertainment space. It is a single-level room, although 14 pillars obstruct the sight lines from many seats. The stage also acts as the dance floor and cannot be raised for shows. The entertainment consists of cabaret-style performances. It can also be used as a lecture room.

SPA/FITNESS. The spa is located on the lowest passenger deck, and contains a sauna (but no steam room), solarium, indoor swimming pool, treatment rooms, and changing areas.

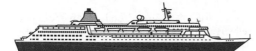

Saga Sapphire
★★★★

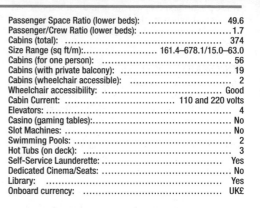

Size:	Small Ship	Passenger Space Ratio (lower beds):	49.6
Tonnage:	37,301	Passenger/Crew Ratio (lower beds):	1.7
Lifestyle:	Standard	Cabins (total):	374
Cruise Line:	Saga Cruises	Size Range (sq ft/m):	161.4–678.1/15.0–63.0
Former Names:	Bleu de France, Holiday Dream,	Cabins (for one person):	56
	SuperStar Aries, SuperStar Europe, Europa	Cabins (with private balcony):	19
IMO Number:	7822457	Cabins (wheelchair accessible):	2
Builder:	Bremer Vulkan (Germany)	Wheelchair accessibility:	Good
Original Cost:	$120 million	Cabin Current:	110 and 220 volts
Entered Service:	Jan 1982/Mar 2012	Elevators:	4
Registry:	The Bahamas	Casino (gaming tables):	No
Length (ft/m):	654.9/199.6	Slot Machines:	No
Beam (ft/m):	93.8/28.6	Swimming Pools:	2
Draft (ft/m):	27.6/8.4	Hot Tubs (on deck):	3
Propulsion/Propellers:	diesel (21,270kW)/2	Self-Service Launderette:	Yes
Passenger Decks:	10	Dedicated Cinema/Seats:	No
Total Crew:	415	Library:	Yes
Passengers (lower beds):	706	Onboard currency:	UK£

This is an elegant ship for British cruisers over 50

OVERVIEW. *Saga Sapphire* is best suited to couples and solo travelers, almost all British, seeking a holiday afloat in spacious, classy surroundings. It provides decent accommodation, good food, and friendly service, plus interesting itineraries and destinations. Passengers must be over 50, but spouses and partners can be as young as 45.

THE SHIP. *Saga Sapphire* was originally built as the fifth incarnation of *Europa* for Hapag-Lloyd Cruises, and was for many years the pride of the German cruise industry. It was originally to have twin side-by-side funnels, but the idea was dropped in favor of a single funnel. The ship is in remarkably fine shape, despite the fact that it is now just over 30 years old. Saga Cruises tailored the ship to British tastes when it took delivery in April 2012.

It has a deep blue hull and white upper structure, and a sponson stern, a kind of 'skirt' added in order to comply with the latest stability regulations. But it still maintains its moderately handsome, balanced profile. There is a really decent amount of open outdoor deck space. The ship has both outdoor and outdoor/indoor pools. While there is no walk-around outdoors promenade deck, there are half-length teak port and starboard promenades.

The interior focal point is a three-deck high lobby, which has a 'floating' fish sculpture. (I counted over 1,000 fish, including one red herring!) There is a good range of good-size public rooms, most of which have high ceilings, and wide interior stairways that create a feeling of spaciousness on a grand – but human

Berlitz's Ratings		
	Possible	Achieved
Ship	500	385
Accommodation	200	144
Food	400	274
Service	400	289
Entertainment	100	71
Cruise Experience	400	283
OVERALL SCORE		
1446 points out of 2000		

– scale. Contemporary yet restful colors have been applied to many public rooms and cabins, and subtle, hidden lighting is used throughout, particularly on the stairways. The public rooms are positioned aft in a 'cake-layer' stacking, with all the accommodation located forward, thus separating potentially noisy areas from quieter ones.

Facilities include a delightful observation lounge (The Drawing Room), and an integral, extensive library plus several Internet-connected computer stations (iPads can also be provided), chess and draught tables; light entertainment is presented here in the evenings, and yummy Lavazza coffees are available here at almost any time, with delightful cakes in mid-morning (free). Quirky table lamps are made from old clarinets and fishing rods.

For a delightful, neat hideaway, head to Cooper's, named after the British comedy-magician Tommy Cooper. There are numerous black-and-white photos on the wall of some of the UK's best-known comedians of yesteryear and today, including Spike 'Milligna' – the well-known typing error. The table lamps are topped by Tommy Cooper's trademark – a fez. Then there's Aviators – a cute little pre-dining room bar with models of those splendid Spitfire aircraft (from World War II), with, of course, Spitfire draft beer as the featured bar beverage.

The ship, which has some rather amusing and quirky artwork, provides an informal, relaxed, yet elegant setting, with many public rooms that have a high ceiling. Saga Cruises includes many things other UK-based operators charge extra for – that's why its cruises may appear to cost more – such as private car transfers to the ship (check brochure for details), all gratuities, shuttle buses in ports of call where possible, and newspapers in the library in each port of call, when available. Saga also provides excellent user-friendly port and shore excursion information booklets.

ACCOMMODATION. There is a wide range of suites and cabins (including many for solo travelers), in a multitude of price grades. All of the original cabins are quite spacious, and have illuminated closets, dark wood cabinetry with rounded edges, full-length mirrors, color TV/DVD player, minibar/refrigerator, personal safe, hairdryer, and good cabin insulation. They are also laid out in a very practical design. Some suites/cabins have table lamps made from old cameras such as the Kodak Brownie and similar 'box' cameras – delightfully quirky!

Most of the bathrooms (163 to be precise) have deep tubs (cabins without a bathtub have large shower enclosures), a three-head shower unit, two deep washbasins (not all cabins), large toiletries cabinet, and handsome toiletries – Citrus, created exclusively for Saga Cruises by Clarity, an organization that provides employment for blind persons.

The largest living spaces are the suites. However, because of their location – they were created from former bridge officers' cabins in a 1999 refit – they have lifeboat-obstructed views. Six other suites had private balconies added, and all provide generous living spaces. There is a separate bedroom with either a queen-size or twin beds, illuminated closets, and a vanity/writing desk. The lounge includes a wet bar with refrigerator and glass cabinets and large audio-visual center complete with large-screen TV set and DVD player. The marble-clad bathroom has a large shower enclosure, with retractable clothesline.

Even the standard, lower-priced cabins are very comfortable, the ship having been designed for long voyages.

DINING. Pole to Pole, the main restaurant, seats 620 diners and has ocean-view windows on two sides, yet still manages to have an intimate, clubby feel thanks to different areas styled to the theme of four continents: Africa, Asia, Europe, and the Americas. Both self-serve buffet and full-service meals are provided. There is open seating, so you can dine wherever you choose. For dinner, a number of tables can be reserved for fixed dining times when you book.

Other dining options. The Grill and Verandah, an indoor/outdoor venue, provides lighter, healthier grilled meals, with food cooked to order in a show kitchen. It's open for breakfast, lunch, and relaxed dinner. The 'spider's web' alcove seating partitions are novel – I haven't found any big spiders yet! One neat feature is a slicing machine to produce cold cuts of meat, so you know it's fresh.

Asian-fusion cuisine (Indian, Sri Lankan, and Thai) is served in the intimate 64-seat East to West restaurant, where the decor includes traditional wood carvings, reflecting the mood of the East. Adjacent is The Grill, specializing in steaks and seafood, in a room with an open kitchen.

The Beach, adjacent to the indoor/outdoor pool, provides fish and chips and other light British fare, traditional desserts, and ice cream (the machine is inside a blue-and-white-striped beach hut, and there are jars and jars of boiled sweets in a second beach hut – all very British and a pleasant throwback to yesteryear).

ENTERTAINMENT. The Britannia Lounge is the venue for major social events and shows. The sight lines are mostly good, although some thin pillars present problems from some seats – the room was originally built more for use as a single-level concert salon than a room for shows – but the setting is elegant. The shows consist of a small troupe of female dancers, plus a number of cabaret acts. There is live music for listening or dancing to in various bars and lounges. Male dance hosts are aboard each cruise for the many solo women passengers.

SPA/FITNESS. An area of about 8,611 sq ft (800 sq m) is host to a rather nice, homely retreat – an indoor wellness center. It includes an indoor swimming pool (few ships have them today). Adjacent facilities include a sauna and steam room, a fitness/exercise area, several treatment rooms, and a beauty salon. Sporting facilities include St Andrews, a crazy-golf course located outdoors atop ship in what was a former FKK – nude – sunbathing spot.

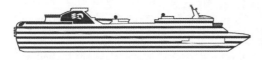

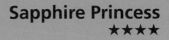

Size:	Large Resort Ship	Passenger/Crew Ratio (lower beds):	2.1
Tonnage:	115,875	Cabins (total):	1,337
Lifestyle:	Standard	Size Range (sq ft/m):	168–1,329.3/15.6–123.5
Cruise Line:	Princess Cruises	Cabins (for one person):	0
Former Names:	none	Cabins (with private balcony):	750
IMO Number:	9228186	Cabins (wheelchair accessible):	28
Builder:	Mitsubishi Heavy Industries (Japan)	Wheelchair accessibility:	Good
Original Cost:	$400 million	Cabin Current:	110 volts
Entered Service:	May 2004/May 2004	Elevators:	14
Registry:	Great Britain	Casino (gaming tables):	Yes
Length (ft/m):	951.4/290.0	Slot Machines:	Yes
Beam (ft/m):	123.0/37.5	Swimming Pools:	3
Draft (ft/m):	26.4/8.0	Hot Tubs (on deck):	9
Propulsion/Propellers:	diesel-electric (42,000kW)/2	Self-Service Launderette:	Yes
Passenger Decks:	13	Dedicated Cinema/Seats:	No
Total Crew:	1,238	Library:	Yes
Passengers (lower beds):	2,674	Onboard currency:	US$
Passenger Space Ratio (lower beds):	43.3		

A good multi-choice large ship for informal family cruising

OVERVIEW. *Sapphire Princess* is quite a grand playground in which to roam and play when you're not ashore. Princess Cruises delivers a fine, well-packaged holiday product, with some sense of style, at an attractive, highly competitive price, and this ship will appeal to those who really enjoy big-city life with all the trimmings.

THE SHIP. *Sapphire Princess* has an instantly recognizable funnel due to two jet engine-like pods that sit high up on its structure, but really are mainly for decoration. The ship is similar in size and internal layout to *Golden Princess*, *Grand Princess*, and *Star Princess*, although of a greater beam. Unlike its half-sister ships, all of which had a 'spoiler' containing a disco located aft of the funnel, this has been removed from both *Diamond Princess* and *Sapphire Princess*, being replaced by a more sensible aft-facing nightclub/disco, Skywalkers Nightclub.

Several areas focus on swimming pools. One has a giant poolside movie screen, one is two decks high and is covered by a retractable glass dome, itself an extension of the funnel housing, and one pool lies within The Sanctuary – an adults-only, extra-cost relaxation area.

The interiors were overseen and outfitted by the Okura Group, whose Okura Hotel is one of Tokyo's finest. Fit and finish quality is superior to that of the Italian-built *Golden Princess*, *Grand Princess*, and *Star Princess*. Unlike the outside decks, there is plenty of space inside the ship – but there are also plenty of passengers – and a wide array of public rooms, with many

Berlitz's Ratings

	Possible	Achieved
Ship	500	378
Accommodation	200	147
Food	400	250
Service	400	289
Entertainment	100	78
Cruise Experience	400	295
OVERALL SCORE		
1437 points out of 2000		

'intimate' (this being a relative term) spaces and places to enjoy. The passenger flow has been well thought-out, and there's little congestion.

The interior focal point is a piazza-style atrium lobby, with Vines (wine bar), an International Café (for coffee, pastries, panini, etc.) library/Internet-connect center, and Alfredo's sit-down pizzeria.

A Wedding Chapel has a live web-cam to relay ceremonies via the Internet. The ship's captain can legally marry American couples, due to the ship's Bermuda registry and a dispensation that should be verified in advance according to where you reside. Princess Cruises offers three wedding packages – Pearl, Emerald, and Diamond.

The Grand Casino is one of the largest casinos at sea, with over 260 slot machines (some of which are linked and may provide a combined payout), plus blackjack, craps, and roulette tables.

Other facilities include a library/computer room, and a card room. The wood-paneled Wheelhouse Bar is finely decorated with memorabilia and ship models tracing part of the history of sister company P&O. The Wake View Bar has a spiral stairway leading down to a great viewing spot for those who want to watch the ship's wake.

A high-tech hospital has live SeaMed telemedicine linkups to the Cedars-Sinai Medical Center in Los Angeles, with specialists available for emergency help.

The ship is full of revenue centers. Expect to be subjected to flyers advertising daily art auctions, designer watches, and the like.

The dress code is formal or smart casual – interpreted by many as jeans and trainers. Gratuities to staff are added to your account, with gratuities for children charged at the same rate. If you want to pay less, you can have these charges adjusted at the reception desk.

Lines form for many things aboard large ships, but particularly so for the information office, and for open-seating breakfast and lunch in the four main dining rooms. Long lines for shore excursions and shore tenders are also a fact of life, as is waiting for elevators at peak times, and embarkation and disembarkation – though an 'express check-in' option is available for embarkation if you fill in some forms 40 days before your cruise.

The many extra-charge items include ice cream and freshly squeezed orange juice. Yoga, group exercise bicycling, and kick-boxing classes cost extra. There's an hourly rate for group babysitting services, and a charge for using washers and dryers in the self-service launderettes.

FAMILIES. For youngsters and teenagers there is a two-deck-high playroom, teen room, and a host of specially trained counselors. Children have their own pools, hot tubs, and open deck area at the stern, away from adult areas.

ACCOMMODATION. Everyone receives turndown service and nightly chocolates on pillows, bathrobes on request, and toiletries. A hairdryer is provided in all cabins. All bathrooms are tiled and have a decent amount of open shelf storage space for toiletries.

Most outside cabins on Emerald Deck have views obstructed by the lifeboats. Sadly, there are no cabins for solo travelers. Your name is typically placed outside your suite or cabin – handy for delivery service personnel but eroding your privacy. Most balcony suites and cabins can be overlooked from the navigation bridge wing. There is 24-hour room service, though some menu items aren't available during early morning hours.

Note that cabins with balconies on Baja, Caribe, and Dolphin decks are overlooked by passengers on balconies on the deck above. Cabin bath towels are small, and drawer space is limited. There are no butlers, even for the top-grade suites – which aren't really large in comparison to similar suites aboard some other ships.

DINING. All dining rooms are located on one of two decks in the ship's center. There are five principal dining rooms with themed decor and cuisine: Sterling Steakhouse for steak and grilled meats, Vivaldi for Italian fare, Santa Fe for southwestern US cuisine, Pacific Moon for Asian cuisine, and International, the largest, located aft, with two seatings and 'traditional' cuisine. These offer a mix of two seatings and 'anytime dining' where you choose when and with whom you want to eat. All dining rooms are split into sections in a non-symmetrical design that breaks what are quite large spaces into many smaller sections, for better ambience and less noise pollution.

Specially designed dinnerware and good-quality linens and silverware are used. Note that 15 percent is added to all beverage bills, including wines.

Other dining options. Sabatini's is an informal eatery (reservations required; cover charge). It features an eight-course meal, including Italian-style pizzas and pastas, with a variety of sauces, as well as Italian-style entrées including tiger prawns and lobster tail. Its cuisine is prepared with better-quality ingredients and more attention to presentation and taste than the food in the other dining rooms.

A poolside hamburger grill and pizza bar (no additional charge) are additional dining spots for casual bites. You have to pay extra if you order items to eat at either the coffee bar/patisserie, or the caviar/Champagne bar.

Other casual meals can be taken in the Horizon Court, open 24 hours a day, with large ocean view on the port and starboard sides and direct access to the two principal swimming pools and Lido Deck.

ENTERTAINMENT. The Princess Theater, spanning two decks, has comfortable seating on both main and balcony levels. It has $3 million in sound and light equipment, plus a nine-piece orchestra.

Princess Cruises has glamorous all-American production shows, and the two or three shows on a typical seven-day cruise should not disappoint.

A second large entertainment lounge, Club Fusion, presents cabaret acts at night, and lectures, bingo, and horse racing during the day. A third entertainment lounge also hosts cabaret acts and dance bands. Most lounges and bars have live music, and a number of male dance hosts act as partners for women traveling alone.

SPA/FITNESS. The Lotus Spa is forward on Sun Deck – one of the uppermost decks. Separate facilities for men and women include a sauna, steam room, and changing rooms; common facilities include a relaxation/waiting zone, body-pampering treatment rooms, and a gymnasium packed with high-tech muscle-pumping equipment, and great views. Some fitness classes are free, while others cost extra.

The Lotus Spa is operated by Steiner Leisure (online reservations for any spa treatments are possible).

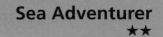

Sea Adventurer
★★

Size:	Boutique ship
Tonnage:	5,750
Lifestyle:	Standard
Cruise Line:	Quark Expeditions
Former Names:	*Clipper Adventurer, Alla Tarasova*
IMO Number:	7391422
Builder:	Brodgradiliste Uljanik, (Yugoslavia)
Original Cost:	n/a
Entered Service:	1976/2011
Registry:	The Bahamas
Length (ft/m):	328.0/100.0
Beam (ft/m):	53.2/16.2
Draft (ft/m):	15.2/4.6
Propulsion/Propellers:	diesel (3,884kW)/2
Passenger Decks:	5
Total Crew:	72
Passengers (lower beds):	122
Passenger Space Ratio (lower beds):	47.1

Passenger/Crew Ratio (lower beds):	1.4
Cabins (total):	61
Size Range (sq ft/m):	119.0–211.0/11.0-19.6
Cabins (for one person):	0
Cabins (with private balcony):	0
Cabins (wheelchair accessible):	0
Wheelchair accessibility:	None
Cabin Current:	220 volts
Elevators:	0
Casino (gaming tables):	No
Slot Machines:	No
Swimming Pools:	0
Hot Tubs (on deck):	0
Self-Service Launderette:	No
Dedicated Cinema/Seats:	No
Library:	Yes
Onboard currency:	US$

A hardy but dated expedition ship suited to polar regions

OVERVIEW. *Sea Adventurer* is a solidly built small ship that rides well. It has an ice-strengthened (A-1 ice classification), royal blue hull, and white funnel, bow-thruster, and stabilizers.

THE SHIP. *Sea Adventurer* is best suited to couples and solo travelers who enjoy nature and wildlife up close. However, even with an ice classification, the ship got stuck in an ice field in the Bellingshausen Sea in 2000. It also ran aground in 2010 in the Canadian Arctic. But all is now back to normal, helped by the ship's very tough, deep-draft hull.

There are 10 Zodiac rigid inflatable craft for landings and in-depth excursions, and a covered promenade deck. This cozy ship caters to travelers rather than mere passengers. The dress code is casual during the day, although at night many passengers wear jackets and ties. The public spaces are a little limited, with just one main lounge and bar. There is a small library, with high wingback chairs.

There is no observation lounge with forward-facing views, although there is an outdoor observation area directly below the bridge. Until 2015, the ship is operated under charter by Quark Expeditions, which provides its own expedition staff and experienced geologists. Naturalist lecturers accompany all cruise expeditions. Smoking is permitted only on the outside decks.

The passageways are narrow, and outer deck stairways are steep.

Berlitz's Ratings		
	Possible	Achieved
Ship	500	219
Accommodation	200	99
Food	400	190
Service	400	211
Entertainment	100	40
Cruise Experience	400	186
OVERALL SCORE		
945 points out of 2000		

ACCOMMODATION. There are seven grades of cabin, including a dedicated price for single occupancy. All cabins have outside views and twin lower beds, with private bathroom with shower, and toilet. The bathrooms are really tiny, although they are tiled, and have all the basics. Several double-occupancy cabins can be booked by single travelers, but special rates apply.

All cabins have a lockable drawer for valuables, telephone, and individual temperature control. Some have picture windows, while others have portholes. Two larger cabins (called suites in the brochure, which they really are not) are quite well equipped for the size of the vessel.

DINING. The dining room, with deep ocean-view windows, accommodates all passengers at a single seating. The food, a combination of American and Continental cuisine, is prepared freshly by chefs trained at some of America's finest culinary institutions. The food, however, is quite disappointing. There are limited menu choices, and far too much use of canned fruits and juices, particularly for breakfasts, which are repetitive. Casual, self-service breakfast and luncheon buffets are taken in the main lounge.

ENTERTAINMENT. After-dinner conversation in the lounge/bar is the main evening event.

SPA/FITNESS. There is a small sauna.

Seabourn Odyssey
★★★★★

Size:	Small Ship
Tonnage:	32,000
Lifestyle:	Luxury
Cruise Line:	Seabourn
Former Names:	none
IMO Number:	9417086
Builder:	Mariotti (Italy)
Original Cost:	$250 million
Entered Service:	Jun 2009
Registry:	Bahamas
Length (ft/m):	650.0/198.1
Beam (ft/m):	83.9/25.6
Draft (ft/m):	21.3/6.5
Propulsion/Propellers:	diesel-electric (23,040kwW)/2
Passenger Decks:	10
Total Crew:	330
Passengers (lower beds):	450
Passenger Space Ratio (lower beds):	71.1
Passenger/Crew Ratio (lower beds):	1.3
Cabins (total):	225
Size Range (sq ft/m):	295.0–438.1/27.5–133.6
Cabins (for one person):	0
Cabins (with private balcony):	199
Cabins (wheelchair accessible):	7
Wheelchair accessibility:	Good
Cabin Current:	110 volts
Elevators:	3
Casino (gaming tables):	Yes
Slot Machines:	Yes
Swimming Pools:	2
Hot Tubs (on deck):	6
Self-Service Launderette:	Yes
Dedicated Cinema/Seats:	No
Library:	Yes
Onboard currency:	US$

An elegant, upscale ship for well-traveled mature-age cruisers

OVERVIEW. This is a ship with a yacht-like ambience. Its strong points are the staff, high service levels, attention to detail, and the fitness/wellness facilities.

THE SHIP. Seabourn Odyssey, the first of a new series of ships for Seabourn, looks like an up-sized version of its three former (smaller) vessels – Seabourn Legend, Seabourn Pride, and Seabourn Spirit. However, this and sister ships Seabourn Quest and Seabourn Sojourn have passenger/space ratios that are among the highest in the cruise industry – so you will never feel that it's crowded.

There are two outdoor swimming pools, midships and aft; the aft pool is in a more secluded area, although there's not a lot of sunbathing space, and the sunloungers are of the steel-mesh variety. One of the most pleasing outdoor areas is the Sky Bar. But for stargazing, the hot tub located by the ship's bow is a delight. While real teak is used in most outdoor areas, Flexteak (faux teak) is used in some locations.

All accommodation areas are in the forward section, with most public rooms aft, so the accommodation is quiet, but you'll need to pass through several decks to get to some public rooms. An Observation Lounge, which has great views, is a well-laid-out, very comfortable room. The Marina, at the stern, has a staging area from which water sports are organized. The interior decor uses light woods, tame colors, and suitably rich soft furnishings to create a contemporary, restrained, and relaxing environment, which is

Berlitz's Ratings

	Possible	Achieved
Ship	500	434
Accommodation	200	178
Food	400	332
Service	400	343
Entertainment	100	81
Cruise Experience	400	333
OVERALL SCORE		
1701 points out of 2000		

good considering the low ceiling height in most public rooms.

Seabourn Square, a 'concierge lounge,' has a relaxed and club-like ambience designed to encourage sociability. The area includes a library, Internet-connect computers, an outdoor terrace, and a coffee bar that's particularly good for late-riser coffees and pastries. Wi-Fi is available throughout.

Drinks, wines with meals, and all gratuities are included, though premium brands and high-quality wines cost extra.

Passenger niggles include the high charge for Internet-connectivity. The ship's 'vertical stacking' layout is not particularly user-friendly. The cabin doors are rather narrow; doors within the cabins are of varying heights and sizes, and feel utilitarian. Most public rooms are of a single deck height, which doesn't create a good feeling of spaciousness, and support pillars are everywhere, as well as fire doors that protrude outside bulkheads instead of being integral to them.

ACCOMMODATION. There are several different grades of suites in many price categories, although the smaller 'suites' are really large cabins. However, the ship has many balcony cabins (about 90 percent, in fact), giving you plenty of personal privacy. Even the smallest cabin is a generous 269 sq ft (25 sq m). All cabins have a separate tub and shower enclosure in a granite bathroom setting, twin beds convertible to a queen-size bed, flat-screen TV plus CD and DVD player, minibar, vanity desk with hairdryer, world atlas, personalized stationery, and large walk-in closet with personal safe.

The interior designers have crafted homely, contemporary living spaces in the suites and cabins, although the walls are rather plain and unimaginative. It's good to see that the beds are high enough off the floor to enable even the largest suitcases to be stowed underneath. All drawers are fitted with soft gel, which means they are quiet – no more slamming contests with your next-door neighbor.

The cabins are bathed in soft earthy tones, although a splash of color wouldn't go amiss. The cabinetry has many seams and strips covering joints, which suggest that the ship's outfitters would benefit from a joinery course. It's also strange that several internal doors are of different sizes, widths, and heights. One neat, very creative feature is a leather-clad vanity stool/table that converts into a backgammon table.

Seabourn Suites and Veranda Suites are quite narrow, and feel cramped, with little space in the passageway between the bed and the opposite wall. However, the bathrooms are generously proportioned, with grey and chocolate-brown decor; there are two washbasins, a bathtub, and a separate shower enclosure.

Some size examples (excluding balcony): Grand Suites 1,135 sq ft (105 sq m), including two bedrooms; Signature Suites 819 sq ft (76 sq m); Wintergarden Suites 914 sq ft (85 sq m) – rather neat suites within a glass-enclosed solarium, set in front of the funnel, with a side balcony; Owner's Suites 611–675 sq ft (57–63 sq m); Penthouse Suites 436–611 sq ft (41–57 sq m); Veranda Suites 269–298 sq ft (25–28 sq m); and Seabourn Suites (295 sq ft (27 sq m).

Four 'Penthouse Spa Suites' were added in a 2013 refit. These are located directly above the spa itself (and connect to it via a spiral stairway), and measure between 688 sq ft (64 sq m) and 710 sq ft (66 sq m), including a balcony. The suites have a living and dining area with seating for four, a separate bedroom, walk-in closet, a bathroom with tub and shower, and balcony. Plus, there's free access to the spa's Serene Area.

DINING. There are three dining venues plus a poolside grill: The Restaurant has open-seating dining at tables for two to eight, with menus designed by American celebrity chef Charlie Palmer. It is a large venue that actually feels more clinical than classical with its white-on-white decor and double-height ceiling in its central section. The most-sought-after seats are located in the center, rather than along the port and starboard sides, which have a window, but low ceiling height.

Restaurant 2, with seating for around 50, features regional, seasonal cuisine and tasting menus, for a mini-dégustation. However, the ceiling height is rather low, which makes it feel cramped. The cuisine is contemporary, with a flirtation with fusion, where taste and flavors are what the experience is all about. This venue shares the same galley as the adjacent The Colonnade.

The Colonnade, located aft, has indoor/outdoor seating and is nicely decorated, although its free-flow design could be better; there's too little outdoor seating for the demand in warm-weather areas, when many passengers like to eat outdoors. During dinner, passengers who are dressed formally on designated formal nights have to share the space with those who are more casually dressed. The venue is also adjacent to one of the fine-dining restaurants.

The Patio Grill is located in a casual poolside setting outdoors – and is most enjoyable on balmy evenings, as a change to the air-conditioned interior dining venues. In addition, a 24-hour, in-suite menu offers the à-la-carte items served in the main dining room during dinner hours. Extra-cost Silver ($225) or Gold ($450) 'connoisseur' wine packages provide a choice of red and white vintage wines for a set amount – perhaps a good idea for a longer cruise.

ENTERTAINMENT. The Grand Salon is the main entertainment venue for shows, cabaret performances, social dancing, and for use as a cinema. However, the stage is small – large enough for a live band, but performers need to use the dance floor area – and the room has nine thick pillars that make it awkward to see anything at all, although the room has a gentle slope. In the central section, there's also a decorative steel ceiling grating, which is black, cold, and unappealing. It has banquette seating in the front and mid-section, and, strangely, sofa-style leather seating along the side walls to the rear, which means you actually sit with your back to the stage – a rather unhelpful arrangement (particularly for the performers)!

Another venue, The Club, is a large, cool, trendy but high-volume nightclub/disco with a wooden dance floor, large bar, and minimalist design. Located beneath the Grand Salon, it incorporates a comfortable casino.

SPA/FITNESS. The Spa at Seabourn, operated by Elemis, occupies the aft section of two decks. At 11,500 sq ft (1,068 sq m), it is quite large, and offers full services in a very pleasant setting that includes a two-deck-high waterfall at the entrance and seven indoor/outdoor treatment rooms. There's a Kneipp 'walk-in-the-water' experience, a thermal suite (for which a pass costs extra), and complete salon facilities, while a hot tub and relaxation area on the deck above are accessed by a spiral staircase. Separate saunas and steam rooms for men and women are provided, but they are extremely small. In the gymnasium, personal training sessions, yoga classes, mat Pilates, and body composition analysis are available at extra cost, but some basic exercise programs are free.

Seabourn Quest
★★★★★

Size:	Small Ship	Passenger/Crew Ratio (lower beds):	1.3
Tonnage:	32,000	Cabins (total):	225
Lifestyle:	Luxury	Size Range (sq ft/m):	295.0–438.1/27.5–133.6
Cruise Line:	Seabourn	Cabins (for one person):	0
Former Names:	none	Cabins (with private balcony):	199
IMO Number:	9483126	Cabins (wheelchair accessible):	7
Builder:	Mariotti (Italy)	Wheelchair accessibility:	Good
Original Cost:	$250 million	Cabin Current:	110 volts
Entered Service:	Jun 2011	Elevators:	3
Registry:	Bahamas	Casino (gaming tables):	Yes
Length (ft/m):	650.0/198.1	Slot Machines:	Yes
Beam (ft/m):	83.9/25.6	Swimming Pools:	2
Draft (ft/m):	21.3/6.5	Hot Tubs (on deck):	6
Propulsion/Propellers:	diesel-electric (23,040kW)/2	Self-Service Launderette:	Yes
Passenger Decks:	10	Dedicated Cinema/Seats:	No
Total Crew:	330	Library:	Yes
Passengers (lower beds):	450	Onboard currency:	US$
Passenger Space Ratio (lower beds):	71.1		

This is an elegant, inclusive ship for trendy cruisers

OVERVIEW. This ship's big attractions are its staff, service levels, and wellness facilities. Like its sister ships, *Seabourn Odyssey* and *Seabourn Sojourn*, it has one of the highest passenger space ratios in the cruise industry, so there's no sense of being crowded anywhere.

THE SHIP. *Seabourn Quest* has two small outdoor swimming pools, midships and aft; the aft pool is in a delightful area, although there's not a lot of sunbathing space, and the pool is just a 'dip' pool. One popular outdoor area is the Sky Bar – good for those balmy evenings in the right cruise areas. But for stargazing, the hot tub located by the ship's bow is a delight, and it's dimly lit and peaceful. By day it's a great place to sit and chill out when the ship is underway, watching the rest of the ship's lovely rounded front section of the ship and the navigation bridge.

All the accommodation areas are in the forward section, with most public rooms located aft, so the accommodation areas are quiet; however, you'll need to traverse through several decks to get to some of the public rooms. The Marina, at the stern, has a staging area from which water sports are organized. This was converted during 2013 to provide expedition equipment, Zodiac shore landing craft, a boot-washing station, and storage for boots and parkas – so that the ship could focus more on expedition-style cruising. Four suites were also added.

Seabourn Square, the focal social gathering point of the ship and 'concierge lounge,' has a relaxed, club-like ambience. The area includes a library, shops,

Berlitz's Ratings	Possible	Achieved
Ship	500	434
Accommodation	200	178
Food	400	332
Service	400	343
Entertainment	100	81
Cruise Experience	400	334
OVERALL SCORE		
1702 points out of 2000		

eight computers (Internet use is chargeable – at high cost – a major source of passenger complaints), an outdoor terrace, and a coffee bar. Its 'concierges' can provide in-port shopping tips, set up shore excursions, and make dinner reservations in ports of call, etc. There's a private diamond showroom, called The Collection. Drinks, wines with meals, and all gratuities are included, though premium brands and high-quality wines cost extra. Wi-Fi is available throughout the ship.

The 'vertical stacking' layout is not user-friendly. While real teak is used in most outdoor areas, Flex-teak (faux teak) is used in other areas. The cabin doors are narrow, and doors within the cabins are of varying heights and sizes, and feel utilitarian. Most public rooms are of a single deck height, so there's not such a good feeling of spaciousness, and support pillars are everywhere.

ACCOMMODATION. There are 13 grades of suites in many price categories – while the smaller 'suites' are really large cabins, not suites. However, there are many balcony cabins – good for personal privacy.

All cabins have a separate tub and shower enclosure in a granite bathroom setting, twin beds convertible to a queen-size bed, flat-screen TV plus CD and DVD player, minibar, vanity desk with hairdryer, world atlas, personalized stationery, and large walk-in closet with personal safe.

The interior designers have created very homely, contemporary living spaces in the suites and cabins, although the walls are rather plain and unimaginative. It's good to see that the beds are high enough off the floor to enable even the largest suitcases to be stowed underneath. All drawers are fitted with soft gel, which means they are quiet.

The suites are bathed in soft earthy tones – a splash of color wouldn't go amiss. The cabinetry has many seams and strips covering joints, which suggest that the ship's outfitters would benefit from joinery lessons. One neat, creative feature is a leather-clad vanity stool/table that converts into a backgammon table. The design of a 'cube table' that can be inserted under a glass-topped table when not being used as a footrest is a smart idea for making more space.

The Seabourn Suites and Veranda Suites are quite narrow, and feel cramped, with little space in the passageway between the bed and the opposite wall. However, the bathrooms are generously proportioned, with gray and chocolate-brown decor; there are two washbasins, a bathtub, and a separate shower enclosure.

Some size examples (excluding balcony): Grand Suites 1,135 sq ft (105 sq m), including two-bedrooms; Signature Suites 819 sq ft (76 sq m); Wintergarden Suites 914 sq ft (85 sq m) – rather neat suites within a glass-enclosed solarium, set in front of the funnel, with a side balcony; Owner's Suites 611–675 sq ft (57–63 sq m); Penthouse Suites 436–611 sq ft (41–57 sq m); Veranda Suites 269–298 sq ft (25–28 sq m); Seabourn Suites (295 sq ft (27 sq m).

Four 'Penthouse Spa Suites' were added in a 2013 refit. These are located directly above the spa itself (and connect to it via a spiral stairway), and measure between 688 sq ft (64 sq m) and 710 sq ft (66 sq m), including balcony. The suites have a living and dining area with seating for four persons, a separate bedroom, walk-in closet, a bathroom with tub and shower, and balcony. Plus, there's free access to the spa's Serene Area.

DINING. There are three venues, plus a Poolside Grill. The Restaurant has open-seating dining at tables for two, four, six, or eight, with menus designed by American celebrity chef Charlie Palmer. It is a large venue that actually feels more clinical than classical with its white-on-white decor and double-height ceiling in its central section. The most-sought-after seats are in the center rather than along the port and starboard sides, which have windows, but low ceiling height.

Restaurant 2, with around 50 seats, has regional, seasonal cuisine and tasting menus, perhaps for a mini-dégustation; however, the ceiling height is rather low, which makes the feeling cramped. The cuisine is contemporary, with a flirtation with fusion, where taste and flavors are what the experience is all about. This venue shares the same galley as the adjacent The Colonnade.

The Colonnade, located aft, has indoor/outdoor seating and is nicely decorated, although its free-flow design could be better; there's too little outdoor seating for the demand in warm-weather cruising areas, when many passengers like to eat outdoors. During dinner, passengers who are dressed formally on designated formal nights have to share the space with those who are more casually dressed. The venue is also adjacent to one of the fine-dining restaurants.

The Patio Grill is in a casual poolside setting outdoors – and most enjoyable on a balmy evening, as a change to the air-conditioned interior dining venues.

In addition, a 24-hour, in-suite menu offers the à-la-carte items served in the main dining room during dinner hours.

Extra-cost Silver ($225) or Gold ($450) 'connoisseur' wine packages provide a choice of red and white vintage wines for a set amount – perhaps a good idea for a longer cruise.

ENTERTAINMENT. The Grand Salon is the main entertainment venue for shows, cabaret performances, social dancing, and for use as a cinema. However, the stage is small – large enough for a live band, but performers need to use the dance floor area – and the room has nine thick pillars that make it awkward to see anything at all, although the room has a gentle slope. On the ceiling of the central section there is a decorative steel grating, which is black, cold, and unappealing. The room has banquette seating in the front and mid-section, and, strangely, sofa-style leather seating along the side walls to the rear, which means you actually sit with your back to the stage – a rather unhelpful arrangement.

Small production shows (remember this is a small ship) are performed well to pre-recorded tracks, and the audio equipment and sound dispersion are extremely good. Another venue, The Club, is a large, cool, trendy, but high-volume nightclub/disco with a wooden dance floor, large bar and minimalist design. Located beneath the Grand salon, it incorporates a comfortable casino.

SPA/FITNESS. The Spa at Seabourn, operated by Elemis, occupies the aft section of two decks, and is quite large, at 11,500 sq ft (1,068 sq m). It offers full services in a very pleasant setting that includes a two-deck-high waterfall at the entrance and seven indoor/outdoor treatment rooms, as well a Kneipp 'walk-in-the-water' experience, a thermal suite (for which a pass costs extra), and complete salon facilities, while a hot tub and relaxation area on the deck above are accessed by a spiral staircase. Separate saunas and steam rooms for men and women are provided, but they are very small. In the gymnasium, personal-training sessions, yoga classes, mat Pilates, and body-composition analysis are available at extra cost, but some basic exercise programs are free.

Seabourn Sojourn
★★★★★

Size:	Small Ship	Passenger/Crew Ratio (lower beds):	1.3
Tonnage:	32,000	Cabins (total):	225
Lifestyle:	Luxury	Size Range (sq ft/m):	295.0–438.1/27.5–133.6
Cruise Line:	Seabourn	Cabins (for one person):	0
Former Names:	none	Cabins (with private balcony):	199
IMO Number:	9417098	Cabins (wheelchair accessible):	7
Builder:	Mariotti (Italy)	Wheelchair accessibility:	Good
Original Cost:	$250 million	Cabin Current:	110 volts
Entered Service:	Jun 2010	Elevators:	3
Registry:	Bahamas	Casino (gaming tables):	Yes
Length (ft/m):	650.0/198.1	Slot Machines:	Yes
Beam (ft/m):	83.9/25.6	Swimming Pools:	2
Draft (ft/m):	21.3/6.5	Hot Tubs (on deck):	6
Propulsion/Propellers:	diesel-electric (23,040kW)/2	Self-Service Launderette:	Yes
Passenger Decks:	10	Dedicated Cinema/Seats:	No
Total Crew:	330	Library:	Yes
Passengers (lower beds):	450	Onboard currency:	US$
Passenger Space Ratio (lower beds):	71.1		

An upscale, elegant small ship for the well-traveled

OVERVIEW. This ship's big attractions are its staff and service levels, and the wellness facilities. Like its sister ships, *Seabourn Odyssey* and *Seabourn Quest*, it has one of the highest passenger/space ratios in the cruise industry, so you'll never get the feeling of it being crowded.

THE SHIP. *Seabourn Sojourn*, the second of Seabourn's three larger ships (the three former boutique-sized ships – *Seabourn Legend*, *Seabourn Pride*, and *Seabourn Spirit* – were sold to Windstar Crusies in 2014), has two small outdoor swimming pools, midships and aft; the aft pool is in a delightful area, although there's not a lot of sunbathing space. One of the most pleasing outdoor areas is the Sky Bar. But for stargazing, the hot tub located on the ship's foredeck is a peaceful delight.

All the accommodation areas are in the forward section, with most public rooms located aft, but you'll need to traverse through several decks to get to some of the public rooms. The Marina, at the stern, has a staging area from which water sports are organized.

Seabourn Square, the focal social gathering point of the ship, is a 'concierge lounge,' with a relaxed, club-like ambience. The area includes a library, shops, eight computers (Internet connection is chargeable), an outdoor terrace, and a coffee bar. Its 'concierges' can provide in-port shopping tips, set up shore excursions, and make dinner reservations in ports of call, etc. There's a private diamond showroom, called The Collection. Drinks, wines with meals, and all gratuities are included, though

Berlitz's Ratings		
	Possible	Achieved
Ship	500	433
Accommodation	200	178
Food	400	332
Service	400	343
Entertainment	100	81
Cruise Experience	400	334
OVERALL SCORE		
1701 points out of 2000		

premium brands and high-quality wines cost extra. Wi-Fi is available throughout the ship.

Minus points? The 'vertical stacking' layout is not really user-friendly. While real teak is used in most outdoor areas, Flexteak (faux teak) is used in other areas. The cabin doors are rather narrow, and doors within the cabins vary in height and size, and feel utilitarian.

Most public rooms are of a single deck height, so there's not such a good feeling of spaciousness, and support pillars are everywhere – Mariotti, the shipbuilder, should look at *Europa* to see that it's not necessary to have so many pillars.

ACCOMMODATION. There are several grades of suites in multiple price categories. The smaller 'suites' are really large cabins, and not true suites. However, there are many balcony cabins, for personal privacy (about 90 percent of all suites/cabins have them).

All cabins have a separate tub and shower enclosure in a granite bathroom setting, twin beds convertible to a queen-size bed, flat-screen TV plus CD and DVD player, minibar, vanity desk with hairdryer, world atlas, personalized stationery, and large walk-in closet with personal safe.

The interior designers have created very homely, contemporary living spaces in the suites and cabins, although the walls are rather plain and unimaginative. It's good to see that the beds are high enough off the floor to enable even the largest suitcases to be stowed underneath. All drawers are fitted with soft gel, which means they are quiet – no more slamming contests with your next-door neighbor.

The cabins are bathed in soft earthy tones, although a splash of color wouldn't go amiss. The cabinetry has many seams and strips covering joints, which suggest that the ship's outfitters would benefit from a joinery course. It's also strange that several internal doors are of different sizes, widths, and heights. One neat, very creative feature is a leather-clad vanity stool/table that converts into a backgammon table. The design of a 'cube table' that can be inserted under a glass-topped table when not being used as a footrest is a smart idea for making more space.

Seabourn Suites and Veranda Suites are quite narrow, and feel cramped, with little space in the passageway between the bed and the opposite wall. However, the bathrooms are generously proportioned, with gray and chocolate-brown decor; there are two washbasins, a bathtub, and a separate shower enclosure.

Some size examples (excluding balcony): Grand Suites 1,135 sq ft (105 sq m), including two-bedrooms; Signature Suites 819 sq ft (76 sq m); Wintergarden Suites 914 sq ft (85 sq m) – rather neat suites within a glass-enclosed solarium, set in front of the funnel, with a side balcony; Owner's Suites 611–675 sq ft (57–63 sq m); Penthouse Suites 436–611 sq ft (41–57 sq m); Veranda Suites 269–298 sq ft (25–28 sq m); Seabourn Suites 295 sq ft (27 sq m).

Four 'Spa Suites' were added in a 2013 refit. These are located directly above the spa itself (connected to it via a spiral stairway), and measure between 688 sq ft (64 sq m) and 710 sq ft (66 sq m), including a balcony. The suites have a living and dining area with seating for four, a separate bedroom, walk-in closet, a bathroom with tub and shower, and balcony. Occupants get free use of the 'Serene' relaxation area of the spa.

DINING. There are three venues, plus a poolside grill. The Restaurant has open-seating dining at tables for two, four, six, or eight, with menus designed by American celebrity chef Charlie Palmer. It is a large venue that actually feels more clinical than classical with its white-on-white decor and double-height ceiling in its central section. The most-sought-after seats are in the center rather than along the port and starboard sides, which have a window, but low ceiling height.

Restaurant 2, with around 50 seats, has regional, seasonal cuisine and tasting menus, perhaps for a mini-dégustation; however, the ceiling height is rather low, which makes the feeling cramped. The cuisine is contemporary, with a flirtation with fusion, where taste and flavors are what the experience is all about. This venue shares the same galley as the adjacent The Colonnade.

The Colonnade, located aft, has indoor/outdoor seating and is nicely decorated, although its free-flow design could be better; there's too little outdoor seating for the demand in warm-weather areas, when many passengers like to eat outdoors. During dinner, passengers who are dressed formally on designated formal nights have to share the space with those who are more casually dressed. The venue is also adjacent to one of the fine dining restaurants.

The Patio Grill is located in a casual poolside setting outdoors; it is at its most enjoyable on balmy evenings, as a change to the air-conditioned interior dining venues.

In addition, a 24-hour, in-suite menu offers the à la carte items served in the main dining room during dinner hours.

Extra-cost Silver ($225) or Gold ($450) 'connoisseur' wine packages provide a choice of red and white vintage wines for a set amount – perhaps a good idea for a longer cruise.

ENTERTAINMENT. The Grand Salon is the main entertainment venue for shows, cabaret performances, social dancing, and for use as a cinema. However, the stage is small – large enough for a live band, but performers need to use the dance floor area – and the room has nine thick pillars that make it awkward to see anything at all, although the room has a gentle slope. On the ceiling of the central section there is a decorative steel grating, which is black, cold, and unappealing. The room has banquette seating in the front and mid-section, and, strangely, sofa-style leather seating along the side walls to the rear, which means you actually sit with your back to the stage – a rather unhelpful arrangement (particularly for the performers)!

Small production shows (remember this is a small ship) are performed well to pre-recorded tracks, and the audio equipment and sound dispersion are extremely good. Just don't expect big ship entertainment, though.

Another venue, The Club, is a large, cool, trendy, but high-volume nightclub/disco with a wooden dance floor, large bar, and minimalist design. Located beneath the Grand salon, it incorporates a comfortable casino.

SPA/FITNESS. The Spa at Seabourn, operated by Elemis, occupies the aft section of two decks, and is quite large, at 11,500 sq ft (1,068 sq m). It offers full services in a very relaxing setting that includes a two-deck-high waterfall at the entrance and seven indoor/outdoor treatment rooms, as well as a thalassotherapy wave pool; there's also a thermal suite (a pass for this costs extra), and complete salon facilities, while a hot tub and relaxation area on the deck above are accessed by a spiral staircase. Separate saunas and steam rooms for men and women are provided, but they are extremely small. In the gymnasium, personal-training sessions, yoga classes, mat Pilates, and body-composition analysis are available at extra cost, but some of the basic exercise programs are free.

Sea Cloud
★★★★★

Size:	Boutique Ship	Passenger Space Ratio (lower beds):	39.5
Tonnage:	2,532	Passenger/Crew Ratio (lower beds):	1.1
Lifestyle:	Luxury	Cabins (total):	32
Cruise Line:	Sea Cloud Cruises	Size Range (sq ft/m):	102.2–409.0/9.5–38.0
Former Names:	Sea Cloud of Grand Cayman, IX-99, Antama,	Cabins (for one person):	0
	Patria, Angelita, Sea Cloud, Hussar	Cabins (with private balcony):	0
IMO Number:	8843446	Cabins (wheelchair accessible):	0
Builder:	Krupp Werft (Germany)	Wheelchair accessibility:	None
Original Cost:	n/a	Cabin Current:	220 volts
Entered Service:	1931/1979	Elevators:	0
Registry:	Malta	Casino (gaming tables):	No
Length (ft/m):	359.2/109.5	Slot Machines:	No
Beam (ft/m):	48.2/14.9	Swimming Pools:	0
Draft (ft/m):	16.8/5.1	Hot Tubs (on deck):	0
Propulsion/Propellers:	sail power + diesel (4,476kW)/2	Self-Service Launderette:	No
Passenger Decks:	3	Dedicated Cinema/Seats:	No
Total Crew:	60	Library:	Yes
Passengers (lower beds):	64	Onboard currency:	Euros

This is simply the most beautiful sailing ship in the world

OVERVIEW. *Sea Cloud* is the most romantic sailing ship afloat. It is best suited to couples and solo travelers (not children) who would probably never consider a 'normal' cruise ship, but who enjoy sailing aboard a real tall ship that is packaged to include accommodation, good food, like-minded companions, and interesting destinations. It operates under charter to various travel companies for much of the year, as well for individual bookings.

Berlitz's Ratings	Possible	Achieved
Ship	500	432
Accommodation	200	174
Food	400	341
Service	400	335
Entertainment	100	91
Cruise Experience	400	333
OVERALL SCORE		
1706 points out of 2000		

THE SHIP. *Sea Cloud* is a completely authentic 1930s barque whose 85th birthday is in 2016. It is the largest private yacht ever built – three times the size of Captain Cook's *Endeavour* – and a stunningly beautiful ship when under sail in both the Caribbean and European/Mediterranean waters. Its four masts are almost as high as a 20-story building, the main one being 178ft (54m) above the Main Deck, and, with its full complement of 30 sails (measuring some 32,292 sq ft (3,000 sq m) billowing in the wind, it really is a sight to behold.

This was the largest private yacht ever built when completed in 1931 by Edward F. Hutton for his wife, Marjorie Merriweather Post, the American cereal heiress. Originally constructed for $1 million as *Hussar* in the Germany's Krupp shipyard in Kiel, the steel-hulled vessel saw action during World War II as a weather observation ship, under the code name IX-99.

There is plenty of deck space (but lots of ropes on deck, and other nautical equipment), even under the vast expanse of white sail, and the Promenade Deck outdoors still has wonderful varnished sea chests. The decks themselves are made of mahogany and teak, and wooden steamer-style sunloungers are provided.

One of the most delightful aspects of sailing aboard this ship is its 'Blue Lagoon,' located at the stern. Weather permitting, you can lie down on the thick blue padding and gaze up at the stars and night sky – it's glorious, particularly when the ship is under sail, with engines turned off.

The original engine room, with diesel engines, is still in operation for the rare occasions when sail power can't be used. An open-bridge policy is the norm, except during poor weather or navigational maneuvers. Passengers are not, however, allowed to climb the rigging. This is because the mast rigging on this vintage sailing ship is of a very different type to more modern sailing vessels such as *Royal Clipper*, *Star Clipper*, *Star Flyer*, and *Sea Cloud II*.

In addition to its retained and refurbished original suites and cabins, some newer, smaller cabins were added in 1979 when a consortium of German yachtsmen and businessmen bought the ship and spent $7.5 million refurbishing it. The interiors exude warmth and are finely hand-crafted. There is much antique mahogany furniture, fine original oil paintings, gorgeous carved oak paneling, parquet flooring, and burnished brass everywhere, as well as some finely detailed ceilings. Marjorie Merriweather Post had been accustomed to the very finest things in life.

A cruise aboard the intimate *Sea Cloud* is really exhilarating. A kind of stately home afloat, it remains one of the world's best travel experiences. The activities are few, and so relaxation is the key, in a setting that provides fine service and style, but in an unpretentious way. The only dress-up night is the Welcome Aboard, and Farewell Dinners, but otherwise, smart casual clothing is all that is needed.

However, mini-skirts would be impractical because of the steep staircases in some places – trousers are more practical. Also bear in mind that a big sailing vessel such as this can heel to one side occasionally, so flat shoes are preferable to high heels.

White and red wines and beer are included for lunch and dinner, and soft drinks, espresso and cappuccino coffees are included at any time. Shore excursions are an optional extra, as are gratuities, which can be charged to your onboard account.

Although now aged 85 years – I doubt if any modern cruise ship will last this long – *Sea Cloud* is so lovingly maintained and operated that anyone who sails aboard it cannot fail to be impressed. The food and service are good, as is the interaction between passengers and mixed-nationality crew, many of whom have worked aboard the ship for many, many years. Once a cruise, a sailors' choir (made up of officers and crew members) sings seafaring songs. One bonus is the fact that the doctor on board is available at no charge for medical emergencies or seasickness medication.

Hamburg-based Sea Cloud Cruises also operates companion sailing ship, *Sea Cloud II*, with 23 sails.

ACCOMMODATION. Because *Sea Cloud* was built as a private yacht, there is a wide variation in cabin sizes and configurations. Some cabins have double beds, while some have twins (side by side or in an L-shaped configuration) that are fixed and cannot be placed together. Many of the original cabins have a fireplace, now with an electric fire.

All the cabins are very comfortable, but those on Main Deck (cabins 1–8) were part of the original accommodation. Of these, the two Owner's Suites (cabins 1 and 2) are really opulent, and have original Chippendale furniture, fine gilt detailing, a real fireplace, French canopy bed, and large Italian Carrara marble bathrooms with gold fittings.

Owner's Cabin Number 1 is decorated in white throughout, and has a French double bed, a marble fireplace, and Louis Philippe chairs; the bathroom is appointed in Carrara marble, with cut-glass mirrors, and faucets (taps) in the shape of swans. Owner's

Cabin Number 2, completely paneled in rich woods, retains the mahogany secretary used 60 years ago by Edward F. Hutton, its dark wood decor reminiscent of the 1930s.

Other cabins – both the original ones, and some newer additions – are beautifully furnished. All were refurbished in 1993 and are surprisingly large for the size of the ship. There is a good amount of closet and drawer space, and all cabins have a personal safe and telephone. The cabin bathrooms, too, are quite luxurious, and equipped with everything you might need, including bathrobes and hairdryer, and an assortment of toiletries. There is a 110-volt AC shaver socket in each bathroom, and toilets are of the 'quiet flush' type. The 'new' cabins are rather small for two persons, so it's best to take minimal luggage.

There is no cabin food or beverage service. Also, if you occupy one of the original cabins on Main Deck, you may be subjected to some noise when the motorized capstans are used to raise and lower or trim the sails. On one day each cruise, an 'open-house' cocktail party is held on the Main Deck, with cabins available for passengers to see.

DINING. The exquisitely elegant dining room, created from the original owner's living room/saloon, is in the center of the vessel, and also houses the ship's library. It has beautiful wood-paneled walls and a wood beam ceiling.

There is ample space at each table for open-seating meals. German chefs are in charge, and the high-quality cuisine is very international, with a good balance of nouvelle cuisine and regional dishes, although there is little choice, due to the size of the galley. There is always excellent seafood and fish, which are purchased locally, when available, as are most other ingredients.

For breakfast and lunch, there are self-serve buffets. Wines accompany lunch and dinner. Soft drinks and bottled water are included in the fare, while alcoholic drinks cost extra.

ENTERTAINMENT. A keyboard player/singer is available for the occasional soirée, but after-dinner conversation constitutes the main entertainment each evening.

SPA/FITNESS. There are no spa or fitness facilities. However, for recreation (particularly at night), there is the Blue Lagoon, an area of seating with blue cushioned pads at the very aft of the ship, where you can lie down and watch the heavens.

Sea Cloud II
★★★★★

Size:	Boutique Ship	Passenger/Crew Ratio (lower beds):	1.6
Tonnage:	3,849	Cabins (total):	47
Lifestyle:	Luxury	Size Range (sq ft/m):	215.2–322.9/20.0–30.0
Cruise Line:	Sea Cloud Cruises	Cabins (for one person):	0
Former Names:	none	Cabins (with private balcony):	0
IMO Number:	9171292	Cabins (wheelchair accessible):	0
Builder:	Astilleros Gondan, Figueras (Spain)	Wheelchair accessibility:	None
Original Cost:	DM 50 million	Cabin Current:	110 and 220 volts
Entered Service:	Feb 2001	Elevators:	0
Registry:	Malta	Casino (gaming tables):	No
Length (ft/m):	383.8/117.0	Slot Machines:	No
Beam (ft/m):	52.9/16.1	Swimming Pools:	0
Draft (ft/m):	17.7/5.4	Hot Tubs (on deck):	0
Propulsion/Propellers:	sail power + diesel (2,500kW)/2	Self-Service Launderette:	No
Passenger Decks:	4	Dedicated Cinema/Seats:	No
Total Crew:	60	Library:	Yes
Passengers (lower beds):	94	Onboard currency:	Euros
Passenger Space Ratio (lower beds):	40.9		

This fine tall ship provides exclusive sail-cruises for couples

OVERVIEW. This is just about as exclusive as it gets – sailing in the lap of luxury aboard one of the world's finest true sailing ships – although your experience will depend on which company is operating the ship (it may be under charter) when you sail, and what is included in the package.

THE SHIP. This three-mast tall ship (called a barque) is slightly longer and beamier than the original *Sea Cloud*, and has the look, ambience, and feel of a 1930s sailing vessel (think polished woods, brass elements, gold fittings, and marble fireplaces), while benefiting from the latest high-tech navigational aids. It complements the company's original, 1931-built *Sea Cloud* in almost every way, including its external appearance – except for a very rounded stern in place of the counter stern of the original ship.

The interior designers have managed to replicate the same beautiful traditional look and special decorative touches, so anyone who has sailed aboard *Sea Cloud* will feel instantly at home. Whether the modern materials used in this 15-year old ship will stand up to 85 years of use like those of the original remains to be seen, but it's certainly quality. The main lounge is truly elegant, with sofa and large individual tub chair seating around oval drinks tables. The ceiling is ornate, with an abundance of wood detailing, and an oval centerpiece is set around skylights to the open deck above. A bar is set into the aft port side of the room, which has audio-visual aids built in for lectures and presentations.

Berlitz's Ratings		
	Possible	Achieved
Ship	500	432
Accommodation	200	173
Food	400	339
Service	400	335
Entertainment	100	90
Cruise Experience	400	332
OVERALL SCORE		
1701 points out of 2000		

A treasured aspect of sailing aboard this ship is its 'Blue Lagoon', at the very stern – part of the Lido outdoor bar and casual dining area. Weather permitting, you can lie on thick blue padding and gaze up at the stars and warm night sky – it's a huge pleasure, particularly when the ship is under sail, with engines off.

In terms of interior design, degree of luxury in appointments, the passenger flow, fabrics, food, and service, the ceiling height of public rooms, larger cabins, great open deck space, excellent passenger/space ratio and crew per passenger ratio, there is none better than *Sea Cloud II*. I have sailed aboard both this and its sister vessel, and I can promise you a memorable sail-cruise experience.

A small water sports platform is built into the aft quarter of the starboard side (with adjacent shower), and the ship carries four inflatable craft for close-in shore landings, as well as snorkeling equipment.

There are three masts and up to 23 sails, measuring a billowing 32,292 sq ft/3,000 sq m. These are: flying jib, outer jib, inner jib; fore royal, fore topgallant, fore upper topsail, fore lower topsail, fore course; main royal staysail, main topgallant staysail, main topmast staysail; sky sail, main royal, main topgallant, main upper topsail, main lower topsail, main sail; mizzen topgallant staysail, mizzen topmast staysail; mizzen gaff topsail, mizzen upper gaff sail, mizzen lower gaff sail, middle gaff, upper gaff.

ACCOMMODATION. The decor in the cabins is very tasteful 1920s retro, with lots of bird's-eye maple wood paneling, brass accenting, and beautiful molded white ceilings. All cabins have a vanity desk, hairdryer, refrigerator (typically stocked with soft drinks and bottled water), and a combination TV/DVD unit. Comparisons are bound to be made, and if you have sailed aboard the original *Sea Cloud*, you may be disappointed with the smaller space and decoration of the equivalent cabins aboard this ship.

All cabins have a private bathroom with shower enclosure (or tub/shower combination), and plenty of storage space for products. Toilets are of the quiet, gentle flush type. The cabin current is 220 volts, although bathrooms also include a 110-volt socket for shavers.

There are two suites. Naturally, these have more space – but not as much space as the two Owner's Suites aboard *Sea Cloud* – and comprise a completely separate bedroom, with four-poster bed, and living room, while the marble-clad bathroom has a full-size tub.

There are 16 Junior Suites. These provide a living area and sleeping area with twin beds that convert to a queen-size bed. The marble-clad bathroom is quite opulent, and has a small tub/shower combination, with lots of cubbyholes to store toiletries.

DINING. The one-seating dining room is open-seating, so you can dine with whom you wish. It is decorated in a light, modern maritime style, with wood and carpeted flooring, comfortable chairs with armrests, and circular light fixtures. The gold-rimmed plates used for the captain's dinner – typically a candlelit affair – have the ship's crest embedded in the white porcelain; they are extremely elegant and highly collectible. The place settings for dinner, also often by candlelight, are green and white.

There is always excellent seafood and fish, purchased fresh, locally, when available, as are many other ingredients. For breakfast and lunch, there are self-serve buffets. These are really good, and beautifully presented – usually indoors for breakfast and outdoors on the Promenade Deck for lunch. Meal times are announced by the ringing of a bell.

European wines typically accompany lunch and dinner – mostly young vintages. Soft drinks and bottled water are included in the fare, while alcoholic drinks cost extra.

ENTERTAINMENT. There is a keyboard player/singer for the occasional soirée, but nothing else – nothing else is needed since the thrill of sailing is the entertainment. Dinner and after-dinner conversation with fellow passengers really becomes the main evening activity. So, if you are feeling anti-social and don't want to talk to your fellow passengers, take a good book or two.

SPA/FITNESS. There is a health/fitness area, with a small gymnasium, and sauna. Massage and facials are available.

SeaDream I
★★★★★

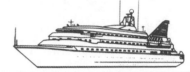

Size:	Boutique Ship	Passenger/Crew Ratio (lower beds):	1.1
Tonnage:	4,253	Cabins (total):	56
Lifestyle:	Luxury	Size Range (sq ft/m):	195.0–446.7/18.1–41.4
Cruise Line:	SeaDream Yacht Club	Cabins (for one person):	0
Former Names:	Seabourn Goddess I, Sea Goddess I	Cabins (with private balcony):	0
IMO Number:	8203438	Cabins (wheelchair accessible):	0
Builder:	Wartsila (Finland)	Wheelchair accessibility:	None
Original Cost:	$34 million	Cabin Current:	110 and 220 volts
Entered Service:	Apr 1984/May 2002	Elevators:	1
Registry:	Bahamas	Casino (gaming tables):	Yes
Length (ft/m):	343.8/104.8	Slot Machines:	Yes
Beam (ft/m):	47.9/14.6	Swimming Pools:	1
Draft (ft/m):	13.6/4.1	Hot Tubs (on deck):	1
Propulsion/Propellers:	diesel (3,540kW)/2	Self-Service Launderette:	No
Passenger Decks:	5	Dedicated Cinema/Seats:	No
Total Crew:	95	Library:	Yes
Passengers (lower beds):	112	Onboard currency:	US$
Passenger Space Ratio (lower beds):	37.9		

Informal, ultra-stylish cruising on a pocket-sized ship

OVERVIEW. *SeaDream I* is for sophisticated, well-traveled couples. Rejecting today's huge standard resort cruise ships, they are looking for a small ship with excellent food approaching gourmet standards, and fine European-style service in surroundings that border on the elegant and refined, while remaining informal.

THE SHIP. *SeaDream I* (and sister ship *SeaDream II*) were originally funded by about 800 investors, and operated under the Norske Cruise banner, and named *Sea Goddess I* and *Sea Goddess II*. They have an ultra-sleek profile, with deep blue hull and white superstructure, and the ambience of a private club. Purchased by SeaDream Yacht Club in 2001, they were completely refurbished, with many changes to public rooms and outdoor areas. Some new features were added to create contemporary, chic, and desirable, if aging, vessels.

A 'Top of the Yacht' bar, crafted in warm wood, was added to both ships. So were eight special alcoves set to the port and starboard sides of the funnel, equipped with two-person sunloungers with thick pads (and two equipped for one person); however, there is quite a bit of noise from the adjacent funnel. You are encouraged to sleep under the stars, if you wish, and cotton sleep suits are provided.

At the front part of the deck there are more sunloungers and a couple of large hammocks, as well as a golf simulator with a choice of 30 courses.

Inside, there is a feeling of unabashed but discreet sophistication. Elegant public rooms have flowers and

Berlitz's Ratings

	Possible	Achieved
Ship	500	430
Accommodation	200	173
Food	400	354
Service	400	369
Entertainment	100	84
Cruise Experience	400	346
OVERALL SCORE		
1756 points out of 2000		

potpourri everywhere. The main social gathering places are the lounge, a delightful library/living room with a selection of about 1,000 books, a piano bar – which can be more like a karaoke bar at times – and a small casino with two blackjack tables and five slot machines.

All drinks (including good-quality Champagne, but not premium drink brands and connoisseur wines), farmed caviar (sadly, American farmed Hackleback sturgeon malossol caviar, and not Russian caviar, whose supply today is challenging), and gratuities are included, but port charges and insurance are not.

ACCOMMODATION. There are four types, and six price categories (depending on location, size, and grade): Owner's Suite, Admiral Suite, Commodore Club Suite, and Yacht Club (standard) Cabin.

Owner's Suite. For the largest living space, go for the Owner's Suite. This measures a grand 490 sq ft (46 sq m). It's the only accommodation with a bathroom that has a full-size tub; there's also a separate shower enclosure and lots of space for toiletries.

Admiral Suite. Added in 2008–9, this suite occupies space previously devoted to the ship's boutique, and adjacent to the piano bar/library. It's a little smaller than the Owner's Suite, but is well laid out and extremely comfortable.

Commodore Club Suites. For larger accommodation, choose one of 16 Commodore Club Suites. These consist of two standard cabins with an interconnecting door, thus providing you with a healthy 380 sq ft (36 sq

m) of living space. One cabin is made into a lounge and dining room, with table and up to four chairs, while the other becomes your sleeping area. The advantage is that you get two bathrooms. One disadvantage is that the soundproofing between cabins could be better.

Yacht Club Cabins. Incorrectly called 'suites' in the brochure, the standard cabins are, more correctly, fully equipped mini-suites with an outside view through windows or portholes, depending on deck and price category. Each measures 195 sq ft (18 sq m), which is not large by today's cruise ship standards; however, it is large compared to cabins aboard many private motor yachts, and extremely large when compared to oceangoing racing yachts. The sleeping area has twin beds that can be put together to form a queen-size bed, positioned next to the window or porthole, so you can entertain in the living area without going past the sleeping area, as you must aboard the slightly larger Seabourn or Silversea ships. A curtain separates the sleeping and lounge areas. All cabinetry and furniture is of thick blond wood, with nicely rounded edges.

In the lounge area, a long desk has six drawers, plus a vertical cupboard unit that houses a sensible safe, refrigerator, and drinks cabinet stocked with your choice of drinks. There is also a 20-ins flat-screen television, CD and DVD player, and an MP3 audio player with more than 100 selections. The beds have the finest linens, including thick cotton duvets, and hypoallergenic pillows are also available. There's little room under the beds for luggage, although this can be taken away and stored.

One drawback is the fact that the insulation between cabins is not particularly good, although rarely does this present a problem, as most passengers are generally quiet, considerate types, who are allergic to noise. Incidentally, a sleep suit is supplied in case you want to sleep out on deck under the stars in one of the on-deck two-person beds.

When the ships became *SeaDream I* and *II*, all the bathrooms were totally refurbished. The cheerful decor is chic, with soft colors and large (beige) marble tiles. The former tiny sit-in bathtubs were taken out – these are missed by some passengers – and replaced by a multi-jet power glassed-in shower enclosure. A washbasin set in a marble-look surround and two glass shelves make up the facilities, and an under-sink cupboard provides further space for larger toiletries.

However, the bathrooms really are small, particularly for anyone of larger-than-average build. Also, the bathroom door opens inwards, so space inside is at a premium. The toilet is located in an awkward position, and, unless you close the door, you can see yourself in the mirror facing of the closets opposite the bathroom door.

DINING. The Restaurant is elegant and inviting, and has bird's-eye maple wood-paneled walls and alcoves showcasing beautiful handmade glass creations. It is cozy, yet with plenty of space around each table for fine service, and the ship provides a culinary celebration in an open-seating arrangement, so you can dine whenever, and with whomever, you want. Course-by-course meals can also be served on the open deck.

Tables can be configured for two, four, six, or eight. They are laid with a classic setting of a real glass base (show) plate, Porsgrund china, pristine white monogrammed table linen, and fresh flowers.

Candlelit dinners and leather-bound menus are part of the inviting setting. There's even a box of spare spectacles for reading the menu, should you forget your own.

The SeaDream Yacht Club experience really is all about good food. Only the freshest and finest quality ingredients are used. Fine, unhurried European service is provided. Additionally, good-quality Champagne is available whenever you want it, and so is caviar – American farmed Hackleback sturgeon malossol caviar, sadly, and not Russian caviar, whose purchase and supply today is limited. The ice cream, which is made on board, however, is excellent.

Everything is prepared individually to order for dinner, and the cuisine is extremely creative, and special orders are possible. You can also dine course by course in your suite for any meal, at any time during meal hours. The dining room isn't open for lunch, which disappoints those who don't want to eat outside, particularly in hot climates.

Good-quality table wines are included in the cruise fare for lunch and dinner. Real wine connoisseurs, however, will appreciate the availability of an extra wine list, full of special vintages and premier crus at extra cost. If you want to do something different with a loved one, you can also arrange to dine one evening on the open (but covered) deck, overlooking the swimming pool and stern – it is a rather romantic setting.

The Topside Restaurant is an informal open-air eatery with roll-down sides (in case of inclement weather), and is open for breakfast, lunch, or the occasional dinner. Teak tables and chairs add a touch of class.

ENTERTAINMENT. There is no evening entertainment as such (it's not needed), other than a duo or solo musician to provide music for listening and dancing to in the lounge. Dinner is the main event; DVDs are available to take to your cabin.

SPA/FITNESS. The holistic approach to wellbeing plays a big part in relaxation and body pampering aboard *SeaDream I*. The Asian Spa/Wellness Centre has three massage rooms, a small sauna, and steam shower enclosure.

SeaDream II
★★★★★

Size:	Boutique Ship	Passenger/Crew Ratio (lower beds):	1.1
Tonnage:	4,333	Cabins (total):	56
Lifestyle:	Luxury	Size Range (sq ft/m):	195.0–446.7/18.1–41.5
Cruise Line:	SeaDream Yacht Club	Cabins (for one person):	0
Former Names:	Seabourn Goddess II, Sea Goddess II	Cabins (with private balcony):	0
IMO Number:	8203440	Cabins (wheelchair accessible):	0
Builder:	Wartsila (Finland)	Wheelchair accessibility:	None
Original Cost:	$34 million	Cabin Current:	110 and 220 volts
Entered Service:	May 1985/Jan 2002	Elevators:	1
Registry:	Bahamas	Casino (gaming tables):	Yes
Length (ft/m):	343.8/104.8	Slot Machines:	Yes
Beam (ft/m):	47.9/14.6	Swimming Pools:	1
Draft (ft/m):	13.6/4.1	Hot Tubs (on deck):	1
Propulsion/Propellers:	diesel (3,540kW)/2	Self-Service Launderette:	No
Passenger Decks:	5	Dedicated Cinema/Seats:	No
Total Crew:	95	Library:	Yes
Passengers (lower beds):	112	Onboard currency:	US$
Passenger Space Ratio (lower beds):	37.9		

It's like having your own mega-yacht for stylish cruising

OVERVIEW. *SeaDream II* is best suited to sophisticated and well-traveled couples who are typically over 40 – in fact anyone looking for a small ship with excellent food approaching gourmet standards, and fine European-style service in surroundings that border on the elegant and refined while remaining trendy.

THE SHIP. *SeaDream II* (and sister ship *SeaDream I*) were originally funded by about 800 investors, and operated under the Norske Cruise banner as *Sea Goddess I* and *Sea Goddess II*. They have a sleek profile, with deep blue hull and white superstructure, and the ambience of a private club. After they were bought by SeaDream Yacht Club in 2001, they were completely refurbished, with many changes and several new features added to create what are contemporary, chic, and desirable, if aging, vessels. These ships are popular for small company charters, so you may find that the date and itinerary you want will not be available and you'll be asked to switch.

A 'Top of the Yacht' bar, crafted in warm wood, was added to both ships. So were eight special alcoves set to the port and starboard sides of the funnel, equipped with two-person sunloungers with thick pads (and two equipped for one person); however, there is noise from the adjacent funnel. You can sleep under the stars if you wish (cotton sleep suits are provided).

Inside, there is unabashed but discreet sophistication, and the public rooms have flowers everywhere. The main social gathering places are the lounge, a delightful library/living room with a selection of 1,000 books, a piano bar (more like a karaoke bar at times),

Berlitz's Ratings

	Possible	Achieved
Ship	500	428
Accommodation	200	173
Food	400	354
Service	400	369
Entertainment	100	84
Cruise Experience	400	344
OVERALL SCORE		
1752 points out of 2000		

and a small casino with two blackjack tables and five slot machines.

SeaDream II really is like having your own private yacht, in which hospitality, anticipation, and personal recognition are art forms practiced to a high level. The staff is delightful and accommodating, and the dress code is resort casual. Fine-quality furnishings and fabrics are used throughout, with marble and blond wood accents that make it warm. *SeaDream II* is a good choice for you if you don't like regular cruise ships, large ships, glitzy lounges, a platoon of people and kids running around, or dressing up – no tuxedos or gowns are allowed, and ties aren't needed. It's all about personal indulgence and refined, unstructured living at sea, in a casual setting akin to that on a private mega-yacht. One delightful feature of each cruise in warm-weather areas is a 'caviar in the surf' beach barbecue.

SeaDream I and *II* were the first of the mega-yacht-style ships when built, and none of the cabins has a private balcony – but anyway, yachts don't have balconies (they are too close to the waterline). Note that embarkation never starts before 3pm, in case you are eager to get aboard.

ACCOMMODATION. There are four types, and six price categories (depending on location, size, and grade): Owner's Suite, Admiral Suite, Commodore Club Suite, and Yacht Club (standard) Cabin.

Owner's Suite. For the largest living space, go for the Owner's Suite. This measures a grand 490 sq ft (46 sq m). It's the only accommodation with a bathroom that incorporates a real full-size tub; there's also a separate shower enclosure and lots of space for toiletries.

In all grades of accommodation, passengers receive personalized stationery, a personal email address, a 100 percent cotton sleep suit, Bulgari toiletries, 24-hour room service, and 'sweet dreams' chocolates.

Admiral Suite. Added in 2008–9, this suite occupies space previously devoted to the ship's boutique, adjacent to the piano bar/library. It's a little smaller than the Owner's Suite, but is well laid out and extremely comfortable.

Commodore Club Suites. For space larger than standard, choose one of 16 Commodore Club Suites. These consist of two standard cabins with an interconnecting door, thus providing you with a healthy 380 sq ft (36 sq m) of living space. One cabin is made into a lounge and dining room, with table and chairs, while the other is your sleeping area. The advantage is that you get two bathrooms. One disadvantage is that soundproofing between cabins could be better.

Yacht Club Cabins. Incorrectly called 'suites' in the brochure, the standard cabins are, more correctly, fully equipped mini-suites with an outside view through windows or portholes, depending on deck and price category. Each measures 195 sq ft (18 sq m), not large by today's cruise ship standards; however, it is large compared to cabins aboard many private motor yachts. The sleeping area has twin beds that can be put together to form a queen-size configuration; a curtain separates the sleeping and lounge areas. In the lounge area, a vertical cupboard unit houses a sensible safe, refrigerator, and drinks cabinet stocked with your choice of drinks. There is also a 20-ins flat-screen television, CD and DVD player, and an MP3 audio player with more than 100 selections. The beds have the finest linens, including thick cotton duvets; hypoallergenic pillows are also available. There's little room under the beds for luggage, although this can be taken away and stored. Note that the insulation between cabins is not particularly good, although rarely does this present a problem.

When the ships became *SeaDream I* and *II*, all the bathrooms were totally refurbished. The former tiny sit-in bathtubs were taken out and replaced by a multi-jet power glassed-in shower enclosure. Bulgari toiletries are provided. Gorgeously thick, plush, 100 percent cotton SeaDream-logo bathrobes and towels are also supplied. However, despite having been completely rebuilt, the bathrooms really are small, particularly for those of larger-than-average build. Also, the bathroom door opens inward, so space inside is at a premium.

DINING. The dining salon, called The Restaurant, is elegant and inviting. It is cozy, yet with plenty of space around each table for fine service, and the ship provides a floating culinary celebration in an open-seating arrangement, so you can dine whenever, and with whomever, you want. Course-by-course meals can also be served out on deck. Tables can be configured for two to eight. They are laid with a classic setting of a real glass base (show) plate, Porsgrund china, pristine white monogrammed table linen, and fresh flowers.

There's even a box of spare spectacles for reading the menu, in case you forget your own. You get close-to-impeccable personalized European service.

The SeaDream Yacht Club experience really is all about dining, and culinary excellence prevails, using the freshest and finest-quality ingredients possible. Fine, unhurried European service is provided. Additionally, good-quality Champagne is available whenever you want it, and so is caviar, albeit American farmed Hackleback sturgeon malossol caviar. The ice cream, which is made on board, is excellent.

In addition to the regular menus, some beautifully prepared and presented 'raw food' menu items have been introduced, in cooperation with Florida's Hippocrates Institute, with nothing cooked at a temperature of more than 115°F (46°C).

SeaDream II provides extremely creative cuisine. Everything is prepared individually to order, and special orders are possible. You can also dine course by course in your suite for any meal, at any time during meal hours. The dining room isn't open for lunch, which disappoints those who don't want to eat outside, particularly in hot climates.

Good-quality table wines are included in the cruise fare for lunch and dinner. Real wine connoisseurs, however, will appreciate the availability of an extra wine list, full of special vintages and premier crus at extra cost. If you want to do something different with a loved one, you can also arrange to dine one evening on the open (but covered) deck, overlooking the swimming pool and stern – a rather romantic setting.

The Topside Restaurant is an informal open-air eatery and has roll-down sides (in case of poor weather), and is open for breakfast, lunch, and the odd dinner.

ENTERTAINMENT. There is no evening entertainment as such, other than a musician to provide music for listening and dancing to in the lounge. Dinner is the main event, and DVDs are available.

SPA/FITNESS. The holistic approach to wellbeing plays a big part in relaxation and body pampering aboard *SeaDream II*. There are three massage rooms, a small sauna, and steam shower enclosure. The Spa, located in a private area, is operated as a concession by Universal Maritime Services. Massage on the beach is available when the ship stages its famous beach party.

For golfers, there's an electronic golf simulator, and choice of several courses to play. There is a small water sports platform at the stern. Equipment carried includes a water-ski boat, sailboat, wave runners (jet skis), kayaks, wake boards, snorkeling equipment, and two Zodiacs – all included in the price of a cruise. The sea conditions must be just right (minimal swell) for these items to be used, which, on average is once or twice during a typical seven-night cruise. Ten mountain bikes are also carried to be used on shore visits.

Sea Princess
★★★★

Size:	Large Resort Ship	Passenger/Crew Ratio (lower beds):	2.2
Tonnage:	77,690	Cabins (total):	1,008
Lifestyle:	Standard	Size Range (sq ft/m):	158.2–610.3/14.7–56.7
Cruise Line:	Princess Cruises	Cabins (for one person):	0
Former Names:	Adonia, Sea Princess	Cabins (with private balcony):	411
IMO Number:	9150913	Cabins (wheelchair accessible):	19
Builder:	Fincantieri (Italy)	Wheelchair accessibility:	Good
Original Cost:	$300 million	Cabin Current:	110 and 220 volts
Entered Service:	Dec 1998/Apr 2005	Elevators:	11
Registry:	Great Britain	Casino (gaming tables):	Yes
Length (ft/m):	857.2/261.3	Slot Machines:	Yes
Beam (ft/m):	105.6/32.2	Swimming Pools:	3
Draft (ft/m):	26.5/8.1	Hot Tubs (on deck):	5
Propulsion/Propellers:	diesel-electric (46,080kW)/2	Self-Service Launderette:	Yes
Passenger Decks:	10	Dedicated Cinema/Seats:	No
Total Crew:	850	Library:	Yes
Passengers (lower beds):	2,016	Onboard currency:	US$
Passenger Space Ratio (lower beds):	39.3		

This large, family-friendly ship has relaxing decor

OVERVIEW. *Sea Princess, like its sisters Dawn Princess and Sea Princess,* spends its time cruising in Australasian and South Pacific waters. As is the case aboard most large ships, you will be well attended if you live in the top-grade cabins; otherwise, you'll be one of a very large number of passengers.

THE SHIP. This all-white ship has a profile balanced by a large, swept-back funnel that contains a deck-tennis/basketball/volleyball court in its sheltered base aft. There is a wide, teak walk-around promenade deck outdoors, some real teak steamer-style deck chairs with cushioned pads, and 93,000 sq ft (8,640 sq m) of outdoors space. A large glazed area on the upper decks provides plenty of light and connection with the outside world.

Sea Princess absorbs passengers well and has a decent passenger/space ratio for a large ship. Some areas even have an intimate feel to them, which is what the interior designers intended. The interiors are attractive and welcoming with pastel colors and decor that includes countless wall murals and other artwork. There is a wide range of public rooms, including 13 bars, with several intimate rooms and spaces so that you aren't overwhelmed. A large, four-deck-high atrium lobby has winding, double stairways and two panoramic glass-walled elevators.

There is a library, a warm room with ocean-view windows and large buttery leather chairs for listening to CDs and audio books, a card room, and reading room. The artwork collection is good, particularly

Berlitz's Ratings

	Possible	Achieved
Ship	500	377
Accommodation	200	148
Food	400	247
Service	400	278
Entertainment	100	77
Cruise Experience	400	287

OVERALL SCORE
1414 points out of 2000

on the stairways, and helps make the ship feel smaller than it is. The Grand Casino is slightly out of the main passenger flow and so doesn't generate the 'walk-through' factor found aboard so many ships. Cyberspace is a lounge and Internet-connect room close to the pools on Riviera Deck.

Perhaps the most popular drinking venue is the Wheelhouse Bar, with decor that is a pleasing mix of traditional and modern, a bandstand and dance floor; it's like a gentleman's club, with its wood paneling and comfortable seating. For families with children, plenty of space is provided in The Fun Zone children's center, on the starboard side of the Riviera Deck.

One nice feature is the fact that the captain's cocktail party is normally held in the four-deck-high open-flow main atrium, so you can come and go as you please. In the quest for increased onboard revenue, even birthday cakes are now an extra-cost item, as are espressos and cappuccinos in the lobby café, though fake ones, made from instant coffee, are available in the dining rooms. Also at extra cost are ice creams, except in the restaurant, and bottled water; these can add up to a considerable amount on a long cruise.

There are a number of dead ends in the interior layout, so it could be more user friendly. The swimming pools are quite small for the number of passengers carried, and the pool deck is cluttered with plastic sunloungers. The digital voice announcing lift deck stops is annoying for many.

ACCOMMODATION. There are numerous different cabin price grades, designated as suites with private balcony, mini-suites with private balcony, outside-view twin-bedded cabins with balcony, outside-view twin-bedded cabins, and interior twin-bedded cabins. Although the standard outside-view and interior cabins are a little small, they are functional, and have earth tone colors accentuated by splashes of color from the bedspreads. Proportionately, there are quite a lot of interior cabins.

Many outside-view cabins have private balconies, and all seem to be quite well soundproofed, although the balcony partition is not of the floor-to-ceiling type, so you can hear your neighbors. The balconies are very narrow – just big enough for two small chairs – and there is no outdoor balcony light. Some cabins have third- and fourth-person upper bunk beds, which is good for families with children.

There is a reasonable amount of closet space and abundant drawer and other storage space in the cabins; although adequate for a seven-night cruise, it can prove challenging for longer cruises. Also provided are a TV set and refrigerator, and each night a chocolate will appear on your pillow. The cabin bathrooms are practical units, and come complete with all the facilities one needs – although, again, they really are tight spaces. Fortunately, they have a shower enclosure of a decent size, real glasses, a hairdryer, and a small amount of shelving for toiletries.

Suites. The largest cabins are six suites, two on each of three decks at the stern, each with its own large private balcony. These suites are well laid-out, and the large bathrooms have two washbasins, a Jacuzzi tub, and separate shower enclosure. The bedroom has generous amounts of wood accenting and detailing, indented ceilings, TV sets in the bedroom and lounge areas, and a dining table and four chairs.

Mini-Suites. These typically have two lower beds that convert into a queen-size bed. There is a separate bedroom/sleeping area with vanity desk, and a lounge with sofa and coffee table, indented ceilings, generous amounts of wood accenting and detailing, walk-in closet; the bathroom has a Jacuzzi tub and separate shower enclosure.

Standard outside-view/interior cabins. The cabin bathrooms are practical, but compact. They do, however, have a decent shower enclosure, real glasses, a hairdryer, and a small amount of shelving for toiletries.

The cabin-numbering system is quite illogical, with numbers going through several hundred series on the same deck. The room service menu is very limited.

DINING. Rigoletto and Traviata are the two main, asymmetrically designed, dining rooms, each one seating about 500 passengers; they are located adjacent to the two lower levels of the four-deck-high atrium lobby. Your cabin location determines which you are assigned to. Each has its own galley, and is split into multi-tier sections that help create a feeling of intimacy, although there is a lot of noise from the waiter stations. Breakfast and lunch have open seating, and dinner is in two seatings. The wine list is quite reasonable; 15 percent is added to all beverage bills, including wines.

Other dining options. Horizon Court is the ship's 24-hour casual, self-serve buffet. At night, this large room, which resembles a food court, can be transformed into an informal bistro dinner setting with waiter service. Reservations are necessary, and there may be a cover charge.

Outdoors on deck, with a sheltered view over the Riviera Pool, the Terrace Grill serves fast-food items to those who don't want to change from sunbathing attire. In the evening, the grill offers steaks, seafood, and a 'white sisters' mixed grill. There's a cover charge for dining under the stars.

For informal eats, Verdi's, on the uppermost level of the atrium lobby, serves steaks and seafood at extra cost. In addition, there's a patisserie for cappuccino/espresso coffees and pastries opposite the reception desk on the atrium's lowest deck, and a wine/caviar bar, Rendezvous, on Promenade Deck. Coffee or tea from any of the bars costs extra.

ENTERTAINMENT. The Princess Theater, located forward, is a 550-seat, theater-style showlounge, where the main production shows are staged and movies can be shown. The second theater, Vista Lounge, located aft, is a 480-seat lounge and bar for cabaret entertainment and lectures.

In addition, the ship has an array of cabaret acts. Although many are not what you would call headliners, they regularly travel the cruise ship circuit. Classical concerts are scheduled for many cruises throughout the year.

SPA/FITNESS. The Lotus Spa has facilities that are contained in a glass-walled complex located on Lido Deck – one of the highest decks, at the aft section of the ship. It includes a gymnasium with ocean views aft and to port, with all the associated high-tech muscle-pumping and body-toning equipment, a combination aerobics/exercise room, sauna and steam room, and several wellbeing treatment rooms. Some fitness and exercise classes may cost extra.

Forming part of the outside area of the spa complex, one swimming pool is 'suspended' aft between two decks. Two other pools are located in another area in the center of the ship, although they are not large for the size of the vessel. Sports facilities are located in an open-air sports deck positioned inside the funnel and adaptable for basketball, volleyball, badminton, or paddle tennis.

Joggers can exercise on the wraparound open Promenade Deck. There's also an electronic golf simulator – no need to bring your own clubs.

Serenade of the Seas
★★★+

Size:	Large Resort Ship	Passenger/Crew Ratio (lower beds):	2.4
Tonnage:	90,090	Cabins (total):	1,050
Lifestyle:	Standard	Size Range (sq ft/m):	165.8–1,216.3/15.4–113.0
Cruise Line:	Royal Caribbean International	Cabins (for one person):	0
Former Names:	none	Cabins (with private balcony):	577
IMO Number:	9228344	Cabins (wheelchair accessible):	14
Builder:	Meyer Werft (Germany)	Wheelchair accessibility:	Best
Original Cost:	$350 million	Cabin Current:	110 and 220 volts
Entered Service:	Aug 2003	Elevators:	9
Registry:	Bahamas	Casino (gaming tables):	Yes
Length (ft/m):	961.9/293.2	Slot Machines:	Yes
Beam (ft/m):	105.6/32.2	Swimming Pools:	2
Draft (ft/m):	27.8/8.5	Hot Tubs (on deck):	3
Propulsion/Propellers:	gas turbine (40,000kW)/2 azimuthing pods	Self-Service Launderette:	No
Passenger Decks:	12	Dedicated Cinema/Seats:	Yes/40
Total Crew:	858	Library:	Yes
Passengers (lower beds):	2,100	Onboard currency:	US$
Passenger Space Ratio (lower beds):	42.9		

This is a large resort ship for family-friendly casual cruising

OVERVIEW. *Serenade of the Seas* is a ship that all the family can enjoy, especially with the addition of a wider choice of restaurants and eateries (in a 2013 make-over).

THE SHIP. The ship uses gas and steam turbine power, as do sister ships *Brilliance of the Seas* and *Radiance of the Seas*, instead of the conventional diesel or diesel-electric combination.

As aboard all Royal Caribbean International (RCI) vessels, the navigation bridge is fully enclosed. In the very front of the ship is a heli-pad, which also acts as a viewing platform for passengers (it makes for a good photo opportunity). One of two swimming pools can be covered by a large glass dome. In 2013, a large poolside screen was added for movies in the open air.

Serenade of the Seas is a contemporary ship, and has a two-deck-high walk-around structure in the forward section of the funnel. Along the starboard side, a central glass wall protrudes, giving great views; cabins with balconies occupy the space directly opposite on the port side. The gently rounded stern has nicely tiered decks, which gives the ship a well-balanced look.

The interior focal point is the Centrum (city center), a nine-deck-high atrium lobby with glass-walled elevators (on the port side of the ship only) that travel through 12 decks, face the sea, and provide a link with nature and the ocean. In a 2013 makeover, the whole area was revamped, and new features added. Centrum is now the real focal point within the ship, and *the*

Berlitz's Ratings	Possible	Achieved
Ship	500	383
Accommodation	200	141
Food	400	242
Service	400	279
Entertainment	100	74
Cruise Experience	400	275
OVERALL SCORE		
1394 points out of 2000		

social meeting place. It houses an R Bar (for some creative cocktails), several passenger service counters, art gallery, and Café Latte-tudes (for coffees and specialty coffees). Close by is Casino Royale (for gamers and slot-machine lovers), and the Schooner Bar, with its nautical-themed decor and maritime art. Aerial entertainment takes place in the Centrum, too.

Other facilities include a delightful, but small, library. There's also a small dedicated screening room for movies, as well as a 194-seat conference center and a business center.

A Viking Crown Lounge, an RCI trademark, is set around the base of the funnel. It is an observation lounge by day, with views forward over the pool deck. In the evening, it morphs into a dance club, as well as a more intimate and relaxed entertainment venue for softer mood music.

Many 'private' balcony cabins aren't private, however, as they can be overlooked by anyone standing in the port and starboard wings of the Solarium, and from other locations. There are no cushioned pads for sunloungers, and the deck towels provided are small and thin. It is virtually impossible to escape background music.

FAMILIES. Children's facilities include Adventure Ocean, an 'edutainment' area with separate age-appropriate sections for junior cruisers: Aquanaut Center (for ages 3–5); Explorer Center (6–8); Voyager Center (9–12); and the Optix Teen Center (13–17). Royal Babies and Tots Nursery is for babies and toddlers aged 6–36 months old. Meanwhile, Adventure Beach, including a splash pool complete with water slide, is outdoors.

ACCOMMODATION. There is a wide range of suites and standard outside-view and interior cabins, in many different categories.

Apart from the largest suites (six Owner's Suites), which have king-size beds, almost all other cabins have twin beds that convert to a queen-size bed. All cabins have rich (but faux) wood cabinetry, including a vanity desk with hairdryer, faux wood drawers that close silently (hooray), a television, personal safe, and three-sided mirrors. Some cabins have ceiling-recessed, pull-down berths for third and fourth persons, although closet and drawer space is extremely tight for four people, even if two of them are children.

Most cabin bathrooms have tiled accenting and a terrazzo-style tiled floor, and a rather small shower enclosure in a half-moon shape, 100 percent Egyptian cotton towels, a small cabinet for toiletries, and a small shelf. In reality, there is little space to stow toiletries for two or more people.

The largest accommodation consists of a family suite with two bedrooms. One bedroom has twin beds that convert to a queen-size bed, while a second has two lower beds and two upper Pullman berths, a combination that can sleep up to eight people – this would suit large families.

Occupants of accommodation designated as suites also get the use of a private Concierge Lounge, where priority dining room reservations, shore excursion bookings, and beauty salon/spa appointments can be made.

DINING. Reflections, the main dining room, seats 1,096, at tables for two to 10 persons. With a water-themed decor, it spans two decks; the upper deck level has floor-to-ceiling windows, while the lower level has picture windows. It is a pleasant but inevitably noisy dining hall, reminiscent of those aboard the ocean liners of yesteryear, although eight thick pillars obstruct the sight lines.

Two small private dining rooms – Illusions with 94 seats and Mirage with 30 seats – are located off the main dining room. When you book, choose one of two seatings, or My Time Dining.

The cuisine is typical of mass banquet catering that offers standard fare comparable to that found in American family-style restaurants ashore. Menu descriptions make the food sound better than it is, and the selection of breads, rolls, fruit, and cheese is quite poor. Overall, meals are rather hit and miss – in fact they are rather non-memorable. Also, if you want lobster or a decent filet mignon (steak), you will be asked to pay extra.

Other dining options. During a 2013 makeover, several other restaurants and eateries were added or revamped, giving you more choice. These included:

Chops Grille (opposite the Schooner Bar): this venue features large-size premium-quality steaks and seafood items (a cover charge applies, and reservations are required). The food is cooked to order, and the menu doesn't change throughout the cruise.

Giovanni's Table (adjacent to Chops Grille): featuring Italian cuisine in a rustic setting (a cover charge applies, and reservations are required).

Izumi: an extra-cost Asian-style eatery with a sushi bar and hot-rocks cooking (it's open for lunch and dinner, with a small cover charge plus à-la-carte menu pricing).

Chef's Table: for a private experience, typically co-hosted by the executive chef and sommelier for a multi-course wine-pairing dinner (it's a little expensive, but worth it for a special occasion).

Park Café is a casual, no-charge market-style eatery for salads, sandwiches, soups, and pastries.

Informal breakfasts, lunches, and dinners can be taken in the self-serve, buffet-style Windjammer Café, accessed directly from the pool deck. It has islands dedicated to specific foods, and indoor and outdoor seating, but it gets crowded at peak times.

ENTERTAINMENT. Facilities include the three-level, 874-seat Tropical Theater, which also has 24 stations for wheelchairs, and good sight lines from most seats. Strong cabaret acts are also presented in this main showlounge.

A second entertainment venue is the Safari Club, for more casual cabaret shows, including late-night adult comedy. Entertainment is always upbeat – in fact, it is almost impossible to get away from music and noise. There is even background music in all corridors and elevators, and constant music on the pool deck. If you want a quiet holiday, choose another cruise line.

SPA/FITNESS. The Vitality Spa and Fitness center has themed decor. It includes a 10,176-sq-ft (945-sq-m) solarium, a gym with 44 cardiovascular machines, a 50-person aerobics room, sauna and steam rooms, and therapy treatment rooms. The climate-controlled 10,176-sq-ft (945-sq-m) indoor/outdoor Solarium, which provides facilities for relaxation, has a sliding glass dome roof that can be closed in cool or inclement weather conditions. It has Balinese-themed decor, and includes a whirlpool and counter-current swimming.

For the more sporting, there is activity galore – including a 30ft (9m) rock-climbing wall with five separate climbing tracks. It is located outdoors at the aft end of the funnel. Other sports facilities include a nine-hole miniature golf course, and an indoor/outdoor country club with golf simulator, a jogging track, and basketball court.

Serenissima
★★+

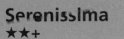

Size:	Boutique Ship	Passenger/Crew Ratio (lower beds):	2.1
Tonnage:	2,632	Cabins (total):	59
Lifestyle:	Standard	Size Range (sq ft/m):	66.0-236.8/6.1-22.0
Cruise Line:	Premier Cruises	Cabins (for one person):	0
Former Names:	Andrea, Harald Jarl	Cabins (with private balcony):	4
IMO Number:	5142657	Cabins (wheelchair accessible):	0
Builder:	Trondheims Mek (Norway)	Wheelchair accessibility:	None
Original Cost:	n/a	Cabin Current:	220 volts
Entered Service:	Jun 1960/Dec 2012	Elevators:	1
Registry:	Grenadines	Casino (gaming tables):	No
Length (ft/m):	286.7/87.4	Slot Machines:	No
Beam (ft/m):	43.6/13.2	Swimming Pools:	0
Draft (ft/m):	15.5/4.7	Hot Tubs (on deck):	1
Propulsion/Propellers:	diesel/2	Self-Service Launderette:	No
Passenger Decks:	5	Dedicated Cinema/Seats:	No
Total Crew:	55	Library:	Yes
Passengers (lower beds):	107	Onboard currency:	Euros
Passenger Space Ratio (lower beds):	24.5		

Dated but tough, casual little ship for coastal cruises

OVERVIEW. This intimate ship is best for cruising in coastal regions. It is suited to couples and solo travelers of mature years who enjoy nature and wildlife at close range, and who would not dream of cruising in the mainstream sense aboard ships with large numbers of people. This is for the hardy, adventurous types who don't need constant entertainment or parlor games.

Berlitz's Ratings		
	Possible	Achieved
Ship	500	253
Accommodation	200	109
Food	400	227
Service	400	241
Entertainment	100	54
Cruise Experience	400	211
OVERALL SCORE		
1095 points out of 2000		

THE SHIP. The 107-passenger *Serenissima* began her career as *Harald Jarl*, cruising the Norwegian coastline and fjords. Extensively renovated in 2003, she was renamed MS *Andrea* and began her career as a classic cruise ship (chartered by Noble Caledonia for a number of years).

In spring 2012 the ship was purchased by the owner of the Russian rivership *Volga Dream*, and renamed *Serenissima*. After a thorough renovation, this charming ship commenced cruise operations in April 2013. With her small size she is able to dock close to the heart of Europe's historic centers and is able to navigate into smaller, remote ports inaccessible to large resort ships.

Serenissima has a good amount of outdoors space (including a forward-viewing and observation platform), and the rather nice semi-covered aft area of the Boat Deck. The ship also now has stabilizers to counteract her well-known rolling motion.

ACCOMMODATION. Several different grades of cabins are arranged over five decks and, with the exception of the five interior cabins, all have either windows or portholes. Because of the nature of this eclectic ship, the cabins do vary in shape and size, giving the ship more character: from dimensionally challenged interior cabins of approximately 108 sq ft (10 sq m), to 'executive suites' of 273 sq ft (25.4 sq m), with small balconies, minibar, and other amenities. Two Owner's Suites are located at the front, directly under the navigation bridge, with forward-facing views, and measure 244 sq ft (22.7 sq m). Dedicated standard single-occupancy cabins range in size from 107 to 137 sq ft (9.9 to 12.7 sq m). The cabins are very nicely furnished, with blue and gold the predominant colors.

Cabin 407 is designated for mobility-limited passengers (an adjacent elevator serves Decks 3 to 6).

DINING. There is a cozy, one-seating Venice Restaurant, but the chairs do not have armrests, so lingering over a meal is not as comfortable as it could be. The food is tasty and well presented, and there is a good variety. Casual eats can be taken in the aft-facing open-deck Café.

ENTERTAINMENT. Really, with this kind of ship, it's the after-dinner conversation that creates most of the evening's entertainment, although there is usually a solo pianist or other musical unit.

SPA/FITNESS. A small fitness center has only a limited amount of equipment (treadmills, bicycles, and free weights), plus an adjacent massage room.

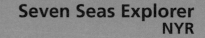

Seven Seas Explorer
NYR

Size:	Small Ship	Passenger/Crew Ratio (lower beds):	1.3
Tonnage:	56,000	Cabins (total):	375
Lifestyle:	Premium	Size Range (sq ft/m):	301.3-3,875.1/3,875.1-360.0
Cruise Line:	Regent Seven Seas Cruises	Cabins (for one person):	0
Former Names:	none	Cabins (with private balcony):	375
IMO Number:	9703150	Cabins (wheelchair accessible):	3
Builder:	Fincantieri (Italy)	Wheelchair accessibility:	Best
Original Cost:	$450 million	Cabin Current:	110 and 220 volts
Entered Service:	Jul 2016	Elevators:	6
Registry:	Bahamas	Casino (gaming tables):	Yes
Length (ft/m):	731.6/223.0	Slot Machines:	Yes
Beam (ft/m):	102.0/31.0	Swimming Pools:	1
Draft (ft/m):	23.0/7.0	Hot Tubs (on deck):	2
Propulsion/Propellers:	diesel-electric/2	Self-Service Launderette:	Yes
Passenger Decks:	10	Dedicated Cinema/Seats:	No
Total Crew:	542	Library:	Yes
Passengers (lower beds):	750	Onboard currency:	US$
Passenger Space Ratio (lower beds):	74.6		

This is an elegant and extremely spacious contemporary ship

OVERVIEW. This all-suite, all-balcony ship is the new flagship of Regent Seven Seas Cruises, although its exterior design is not particularly handsome. It is most suited to couples and solo travelers who appreciate space, creature comforts, and stylish surroundings.

THE SHIP. *Seven Seas Explorer* is another example of the evolution of small ships. Sadly, there's no wraparound outdoor promenade deck (although there is a jogging track atop ship). Inside, the main focus point is a two-deck high atrium lobby, with a grand stairway. Facilities include an Observation Lounge, Connoisseur Club (for cigar enthusiasts), library, card room, business center, and coffee bar (with illy Italian coffees).

So, is it the 'most luxurious ship ever built,' as claimed by this cruise line? No, although some aspects are certainly in keeping with the word luxury. It is, however, an extremely comfortable ship.

ACCOMMODATION. With 16 accommodation categories, the price you pay depends on the size, location, and features you want. All suites have a mini-bar replenished daily, walk-in closet, personal safe, hairdryer, marble-clad bathroom with bathtub or shower enclosure (or both), L'Occitane products, bathrobe and slippers, 24-hour room service, and balconies with teak decking.

The smallest accommodation units are Verandah Suites (approximately 215.2 sq ft/20 sq m, or 307 sq ft/29 sq m including balcony). The most expansive is the opulent 3,875 sq ft/360 sq m Regent Suite, which

Berlitz's Ratings		
	Possible	Achieved
Ship	500	NYR
Accommodation	200	NYR
Food	400	NYR
Service	400	NYR
Entertainment	100	NYR
Cruise Experience	400	NYR
OVERALL SCORE		
NYR points out of 2000		

spans the whole beam of the front of the ship on the uppermost deck. It has an in-built Spa Retreat, as well as a baby grand piano. However, unless you are on a long cruise and don't plan to go ashore much (if you do, you'll get a private car and driver), it may not be worth it.

CUISINE. Compass Rose Restaurant is the main dining room. It has over 30 tables for two, while the rest are for four or eight persons. The richly decorated Prime 7 is a premium-quality steakhouse. It is open for dinner only, reservations required. Pacific Rim features pan-Asian cuisine. The décor of La Verandah recalls Italian Riviera 1960s glamour. It's open for self-serve breakfast and lunch, and transforms into Sette Mari La Veranda, each evening.

The casual Pool Grill has open-air and glass-enclosed seating, with fine views.

You can also order meals in your suite 24 hours a day.

ENTERTAINMENT. The 694-seat Constellation Theater spans two decks. It is an amphitheatre-style showlounge with a thrust stage, and is the venue for production shows and cabaret acts, with music provided by a 9-piece showband. During the day, it also acts as a cooking school (extra cost), with 18 preparation stations. Live music is provided in various lounges.

SPA/FITNESS. The Canyon Ranch Spa Club is an open-air relaxation zone with its own dip pool. Facilities include a bocce court, shuffleboard, paddle tennis, a putting green, and a jogging track.

Seven Seas Mariner
★★★★+

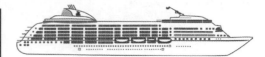

Size:	Small Ship	Passenger Space Ratio (lower beds):	67.9
Tonnage:	48,075	Passenger/Crew Ratio (lower beds):	1.6
Lifestyle:	Luxury/Premium	Cabins (total):	354
Cruise Line:	Regent Seven Seas Cruises	Size Range (sq ft/m):	301.3–2,002.0/28.0–186.0
Former Names:	none	Cabins (for one person):	0
IMO Number:	9210139	Cabins (with private balcony):	354
Builder:	Chantiers de l'Atlantique (France)	Cabins (wheelchair accessible):	6
Original Cost:	$240 million	Wheelchair accessibility:	Best
Entered Service:	Mar 2001	Cabin Current:	110 volts
Registry:	Bahamas	Elevators:	6
Length (ft/m):	713.0/217.3	Casino (gaming tables):	Yes
Beam (ft/m):	95.1/29.0	Slot Machines:	Yes
Draft (ft/m):	21.4/6.5	Swimming Pools:	1
Propulsion/Propellers:	diesel-electric (16,000kW)/	Hot Tubs (on deck):	3
	2 azimuthing pods	Self-Service Launderette:	Yes
Passenger Decks:	9	Dedicated Cinema/Seats:	No
Total Crew:	445	Library:	Yes
Passengers (lower beds):	708	Onboard currency:	US$

This is an all-inclusive premium ship for senior-age travelers

OVERVIEW. *Seven Seas Mariner* is best suited to well-traveled couples and solo travelers, typically over 50, who seek excellent itineraries, fine food, and good service, with some entertainment, all wrapped up in a contemporary ship that is elegant. Its passenger/space ratio is among the highest in the cruise industry.

THE SHIP. This was the first ship in the fleet to be given a pod propulsion system, replacing the traditional shaft and rudder. The ship was extensively refurbished in 2014.

There is a wide range of public rooms, almost all located under the accommodation decks. Three sets of stairways (forward, center, and aft) mean it is easy to find your way around. An atrium lobby spans nine decks, with the lowest level opening directly onto the tender landing stage.

Facilities include a very comfortable, large observation lounge, a small casino, a shopping concourse with 'open market' area, a garden lounge/promenade arcade, a large library (incorporating several computer workstations) and adjacent room with 14 Internet-connect computers, coffee lounge, card player's room, conference room, cigar-smoking lounge (Connoisseur Club), and a Park West art gallery (where silent auctions are held).

Seven Seas Mariner loses a few points because the dining service ranges from excellent to patchy and inconsistent.

Basic gratuities are included, as are all alcoholic and non-alcoholic beverages and table wines for

Berlitz's Ratings

	Possible	Achieved
Ship	500	428
Accommodation	200	177
Food	400	318
Service	400	310
Entertainment	100	82
Cruise Experience	400	325

OVERALL SCORE
1640 points out of 2000

lunch and dinner. Premium and connoisseur selections are available at extra cost, and Internet-connection charges are high. Shore excursions and pre- or post-cruise hotel stays are also included, depending on the itinerary.

ACCOMMODATION. There are several accommodation categories. *Seven Seas Mariner* was the cruise industry's first all-suites, all-balconies ship – though that's not technically correct, as not all accommodation has sleeping areas completely separated from living areas.

Most grades have private, marble-clad bathrooms with tub or half-tub, and suite entrances are neatly recessed away from the passenger hallways to provide quiet (refreshingly there's no music in the hallways, although there is some in the elevators).

Master Suites. The largest accommodation (1,580 sq ft/147 sq m), in two Master Suites, has two separate bedrooms, living room with TV/DVD and CD player, walk-in closet, dining area, two large marble-clad bathrooms with tub and separate shower enclosure, and two private teakwood-decked balconies. Butler service is provided, as is an illy espresso machine.

Mariner Suites. Six Mariner Suites (739 sq ft/69 sq m), on the port and starboard sides of the atrium on three separate decks, have a separate bedroom, living room with large audio-visual center, walk-in closet, dining area, large, marble-clad bathroom with tub and separate shower enclosure, and a good-size private balcony. Butler service is provided, as is an illy espresso machine.

Grand Suites. Two Grand Suites (707 sq ft/66 sq m) are located one deck above the ship's navigation bridge. The facilities are similar to those in Mariner Suites. Butler service is provided

Seven Seas Suites. There are eight of these spacious suites, with two on each of four decks. Six of them – the ones overlooking the ship's stern – are slightly larger (697 sq ft/65 sq m), and have very generous private balcony space and good wraparound views over the ship's stern and to port or starboard. The balconies, however, are only semi-private and can be partly overlooked. Another two are located just aft of the ship's navigation bridge. They are slightly smaller, at 600 sq ft (56 sq m), and have balconies. They have a separate bedroom, living room with audio-visual center, walk-in closet, dining area, and marble-clad bathroom with a combination tub/shower.

Horizon View Suites. The 12 Horizon Suites (627 sq ft/58 sq m) overlook the stern and have a very large balcony and good views. These suites have a separate bedroom, living room with TV/DVD, walk-in closet, dining area, and large marble-clad bathroom with a combination tub/shower. Butler service is provided.

Penthouse Suite. The 14 Penthouse Suites measure 449 sq ft (41.7 sq m) and have a bedroom that can be separated from the living area, and twin beds that convert to a queen-size bed. They are wide (highly desirable) rooms, located on the uppermost accommodation deck, and provide plenty of open space. The bathrooms are nicely appointed, and the balcony is quite large. Butler service is provided, as is an illy espresso machine.

Deluxe Suites. Concierge Suites and Deluxe Suites measure approximately 301 sq ft (28 sq m) and have twin beds that convert to a queen-size bed, small walk-in closet, marble-lined bathroom with combination tub/shower, vanity desk, hairdryer, TV/DVD, refrigerator (stocked with soft drinks and bar set-up on embarkation), and personal safe. In these suites, the sleeping area is separated from the living area only by partial room dividers, so the accommodation is therefore actually a cabin, not a true suite.

Six wheelchair-accessible suites are located as close to an elevator as one could possibly get, and provide ample living space, together with a large roll-in shower and all bathroom fittings located at the correct height.

DINING. Four dining venues all operate on an open-seating basis, so you can dine when and with whomever you choose. Reservations are required in two of the four venues. In general, the cuisine is good to very good, with creative presentation and a wide variety of food choices (Kosher meals can be provided).

The main dining room, the 570-seat Compass Rose Restaurant, has a light, fresh decor, and seating at tables for two, four, six, or eight – although tables for six or eight predominate. With a one-and-a-half deck height, the restaurant has a nice open feeling, and there's plenty of space around most tables for decent service to be provided.

Other dining options. The 80-seat Prime 7 Steakhouse is the smallest of the specialty dining venues. It features a range of superb USDA prime, dry-aged steaks as well as chops, oven-roasted half chicken, Alaskan king crab legs, and Maine lobster. It's the most intimate dining spot – though, again, the single-deck ceiling height makes it feel busy – and it can get noisy (call it lively ambience). There is seating for two, four, or six, and reservations are required.

Signatures is a 120-seat 'supper club' with ocean views along the room's port side. It is directed and staffed by chefs wearing the white toque and blue riband of Le Cordon Bleu, the prestigious culinary society for classic French cuisine. Doors open onto a covered area outdoors, with small stage and dance floor. Seating is at tables of two, four, or six, and reservations are required. However, the single-deck ceiling height robs the room of the grandeur that suits fine classic French cuisine best.

For more casual meals, La Veranda is a large self-serve indoor/outdoor café with seats for 450 and fresh, light decor. This eatery has several food islands and substantial counter display space. At night, it is transformed into Sette Mari – an Italian eatery with some excellent pasta-based dishes.

The outdoor Pool Grill and ice cream bar, adjacent to the swimming pool, is a popular eatery. It features a creative list of burgers (a choice of 11, to be exact), including Black Angus beefburger, Philly beefburger, southwestern beefburger, pesto beefburger, Portobello and feta cheese burger, Asian salmon burger, tofu veggie burger, roasted garlic teriyaki mushroom turkeyburger – and others – as well as various sandwiches.

ENTERTAINMENT. The Constellation Theater spans two decks and is delightful, with good sight lines from almost all seats. The proscenium stage also has a front thrust stage – useful for presenting more intimate cabaret acts – and an LED backdrop for dramatic show scenery images.

The Horizon Lounge, located aft, is a combination day lounge with bar, and the venue for afternoon tea and daily quizzes. A number of bands, small musical units, and solo pianists provide live music in lounges and bars.

There is also Stars nightclub, with an oval-shaped dance floor, and a stairway connecting it to the casino on the deck above.

SPA/FITNESS. Health and fitness facilities include an extensive health spa with gymnasium and aerobics room, beauty parlor, and separate changing, sauna, and steam rooms for men and women.

Sports devotees can play on the paddle-tennis court and in the golf driving and practice cages.

Seven Seas Navigator
★★★★+

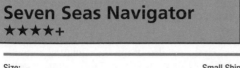
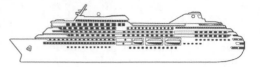

Size:	Small Ship	Passenger/Crew Ratio (lower beds):		1.5
Tonnage:	28,550	Cabins (total):		245
Lifestyle:	Luxury/Premium	Size Range (sq ft/m):		301.3–1,173.3/28.0–109.0
Cruise Line:	Regent Seven Seas Cruises	Cabins (for one person):		0
Former Names:	none	Cabins (with private balcony):		196
IMO Number:	9064126	Cabins (wheelchair accessible):		4
Builder:	T. Mariotti (Italy)	Wheelchair accessibility:		Good
Original Cost:	$200 million	Cabin Current:		110 and 220 volts
Entered Service:	Aug 1999	Elevators:		5
Registry:	Bermuda	Casino (gaming tables):		Yes
Length (ft/m):	559.7/170.6	Slot Machines:		Yes
Beam (ft/m):	71.5/21.8	Swimming Pools:		1
Draft (ft/m):	21.3.0/6.5	Hot Tubs (on deck):		2
Propulsion/Propellers:	diesel (13,000kW)/2	Self-Service Launderette:		Yes
Passenger Decks:	8	Dedicated Cinema/Seats:		No
Total Crew:	325	Library:		Yes
Passengers (lower beds):	490	Onboard currency:		US$
Passenger Space Ratio (lower beds):	58.2			

A mostly premium, all-inclusive ship for mature-age cruisers

OVERVIEW. This ship is best suited to well-traveled couples and solo travelers, typically over 50, who seek excellent itineraries, fine food, and good service, with some entertainment, all wrapped up in a contemporary ship that's elegant and comfortable. Designed for worldwide cruise itineraries, this is one of the upscale ships in the diverse Regent Seven Seas Cruises fleet.

THE SHIP. *Seven Seas Navigator* was built using a hull already constructed in St Petersburg, Russia, as the research vessel *Akademik Nikolay Pilyugin*. The superstructure was incorporated into the hull in an Italian shipyard – the result being that, in effect, a new ship was delivered in record time. The result is less than handsome – particularly at the stern – but it's large enough to be stable over long stretches of water, and there is an excellent amount of space per passenger. In 2009, a 'ducktail' stern was added to aid stability and buoyancy.

The interiors have a mix of classical and contemporary Italian styling and decor, with warm, soft colors and fine-quality soft furnishings and fabrics. Galileo's, a large piano lounge, has good views over the stern. A Navigator's Lounge has warm mahogany and cherry wood paneling and large, comfortable, mid-back tub chairs. Next door, cigars and cognac can be taken in the delightful Connoisseur's Club. An extensive library also has several computers with direct Internet access.

There is no walk-around promenade deck outdoors, although there's a jogging track high atop the aft section around the funnel housing. Two of the

Berlitz's Ratings

	Possible	Achieved
Ship	500	395
Accommodation	200	175
Food	400	307
Service	400	304
Entertainment	100	77
Cruise Experience	400	306
OVERALL SCORE		
1564 points out of 2000		

upper, outer decks are laid with green Astroturf, which cheapens the look of the ship – they would be better in teak. The ceilings in several public rooms, including the main restaurant, are quite low, which makes the ship feel smaller and more closed-in than it is. It suffers from a considerable amount of vibration, which detracts from the comfort level when compared with other vessels of the same size.

Basic gratuities are included in the fare, as are alcoholic and non-alcoholic beverages, plus table wines for lunch and dinner (premium wines are available at extra cost). Shore excursions and any pre- or post-cruise hotel stays are also included.

ACCOMMODATION. There are several different price grades, and the company markets this as an 'all-suites' ship. Even the smallest suite is quite large, and all have outside views (all were refreshed in 2012). Almost 90 percent of all suites have a private balcony, with floor-to-ceiling sliding glass doors, while 10 suites are interconnecting, and 38 have an extra bed for a third occupant. By comparison, even the smallest suite is more than twice the size of the smallest cabin aboard the world's largest cruise ships, Royal Caribbean International's *Voyager*-class ships.

All accommodation grades have a walk-in closet, European king-size bed or twin beds, wooden cabinetry with nicely rounded edges, plenty of drawer space, minibar/refrigerator stocked with complimentary soft drinks and bar set-up on embarkation, TV/DVD player, and personal safe. The marble-appointed bathroom has a full-size tub, as well as a separate shower enclosure, 100 percent cotton bathrobe and towels, and hairdryer. Balconies benefit from real teak decking.

The largest living spaces are in four Grand and Master Suites, with forward-facing views and double-length side balconies. Each suite has a completely separate bedroom with dressing table; the living room has a full dining room table and chairs for up to six persons, wet bar, counter and bar stools, large three-person sofa and six armchairs, an audio-visual console/entertainment center, and an illy coffee machine. Each suite has a large main, marble-clad, fully tiled bathroom with full-size tub and separate shower enclosure, a separate room with bidet, toilet, and washbasin, with plenty of space for toiletries. There is a separate guest bathroom.

Next in size are the superb Navigator Suites, which have a separate bedroom, walk-in closet, large lounge with minibar/refrigerator stocked with complimentary soft drinks and bar set-up on embarkation, personal safe, CD player, large TV/DVD player, and dining area with large table and four chairs. The marble-clad, fully tiled bathroom has a full-size tub with hand-held shower, plus a separate shower enclosure (although the door is only 18ins/45cm wide), large washbasin, toilet and bidet, and ample toiletries storage space.

Unfortunately, the Navigator Suites are located in the center of the ship, directly underneath the swimming pool deck. They are thus subject to early morning noise attacks – when deck cleaning is carried out – and chairs are dragged across the deck. You are also aware of pool deck stewards dragging and dropping sunloungers into place. Despite these disadvantages, the Navigator Suites are delightful living spaces.

Four suites aimed at passengers with physical disabilities have private balconies, and are ideally located adjacent to the elevators. However, while they are very practical, it is almost impossible to access the balcony because of the high threshold at the bottom of the sliding glass door.

DINING. The Compass Rose Dining Room has large ocean-view picture windows and open-seating dining, which means that you can choose your companions. There are a few tables for two, but most are for four, six, or eight persons. With a low ceiling height and noisy waiter stations, the overall feeling is cramped and unbecoming in terms of the lack of space and grace. Complimentary wines are served during dinner, and a connoisseur wine list is available at extra cost. The company also promotes 'heart healthy' cuisine.

Other dining options. La Veranda is the casual self-serve eatery for breakfast and lunch. Each evening, it is transformed into Sette Mari, for informal dining, and serves dinners with an emphasis on Italian cuisine (reservations required for dinner). Al fresco dining is also available.

The 70-seat Prime 7 is the place for steaks and seafood, is in an elegant setting for dinner only (reservations required). For fast food, there is a small outdoor Grill one deck above.

You can also dine in your cabin. There is a 24-hour room service menu and, during regular dinner hours, you can choose from the full dining room menu.

ENTERTAINMENT. The Seven Seas Lounge, a two-deck-high showlounge, has reasonable sight lines from most seats on both main and balcony levels, although pillars obstruct the views from some side balcony seats. Seven Seas Cruises has an eclectic entertainment program tailored to each ship. *Seven Seas Navigator* puts on both production shows and cabaret acts. Bands, small musical units, and solo pianist entertainers provide live music in several lounges and bars.

SPA/FITNESS. The spa, fitness center, and beauty salon are in the most forward part of the top deck. Canyon Ranch SpaClub operates the spa and beauty services as a concession, provides the staff, and sells its own beauty products. An 18 percent gratuity is included in treatment and beauty salon services prices.

Seven Seas Voyager
★★★★+

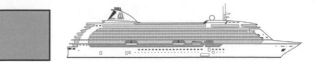

Size:	Small Ship	Passenger Space Ratio (lower beds):	59.8
Tonnage:	42,363	Passenger/Crew Ratio (lower beds):	1.6
Lifestyle:	Luxury/Premium	Cabins (total):	354
Cruise Line:	Regent Seven Seas Cruises	Size Range (sq ft/m):	356.0–1,399.3/33.0–130.0
Former Names:	none	Cabins (for one person):	0
IMO Number:	9247144	Cabins (with private balcony):	354
Builder:	T. Mariotti (Italy)	Cabins (wheelchair accessible):	4
Original Cost:	$240 million	Wheelchair accessibility:	Best
Entered Service:	Mar 2003	Cabin Current:	110 volts
Registry:	Bahamas	Elevators:	6
Length (ft/m):	669.2/204.0	Casino (gaming tables):	Yes
Beam (ft/m):	94.5/28.8	Slot Machines:	Yes
Draft (ft/m):	23.0/7.0	Swimming Pools:	1
Propulsion/Propellers:	diesel-electric (16,000kW)/	Hot Tubs (on deck):	3
	2 azimuthing pods	Self-Service Launderette:	Yes
Passenger Decks:	9	Dedicated Cinema/Seats:	No
Total Crew:	445	Library:	Yes
Passengers (lower beds):	708	Onboard currency:	US$

This is premium all-inclusive cruising with space and style

OVERVIEW. *Seven Seas Voyager* would be ideally suited to well-traveled couples and solo travelers, typically over 50, seeking excellent itineraries, fine food, and good service, with some entertainment, in a contemporary ship that's elegant and comfortable.

THE SHIP. *Seven Seas Voyager* was built in 32 blocks, with the same basic hull design as *Seven Seas Mariner*, with a few modifications. Following a 2013 multi-million dollar makeover, there is now a complete outdoor walk-around deck, and a forward observation area (both on Deck 12).

Inside, there is a decent range of public rooms, almost all located under the accommodation decks. Three sets of stairways mean it is easy to find your way around. An atrium lobby spans nine decks, with the lowest level opening directly onto the tender landing stage.

Facilities include five bars, a showlounge that spans two decks, an observation lounge, a casino, a shopping concourse, a large library, Internet-connect center (Club.com), business center (Coffee.com), card room, and small conference room. There is also a nightclub, Voyager, with an oval-shaped dance floor, a cigar-smoking lounge, the Connoisseur Club, for cigars and cognacs, and an 'art' gallery.

ACCOMMODATION. There are about a dozen different accommodation price grades. As the ship was built with a central corridor design, this has allowed for larger suites and bathrooms than aboard *Seven*

Berlitz's Ratings		
	Possible	Achieved
Ship	500	429
Accommodation	200	176
Food	400	324
Service	400	306
Entertainment	100	82
Cruise Experience	400	324
OVERALL SCORE		
1641 points out of 2000		

Seas Mariner. This is Regent Seven Seas Cruises' second 'all-suites, all-balconies' ship – although that's not strictly correct, as not all sleeping areas are completely separated from living areas.

All grades of accommodation have private, marble-clad bathrooms with tub, walk-in closet with personal safe, and most suite entrances are recessed away from passenger hallways (a central corridor), so as to provide extra quiet. All have a private balcony, although all except those in the Master Suites and Grand Suites measure only 50 sq ft (4.6 sq m); all have pleasing teak decking. Partitions are of the partial type, except for the Master Suites and Grand Suites, which have full floor-to-ceiling partitions, and are completely private.

Master Suites. Basically 1,162 sq ft (108 sq m), these two suites, 1100 and 1001, each expand to 1,403 sq ft (130 sq m) when paired with one Grand Suite via an interconnecting door, while 700 and 701 measure 1,335 sq ft (124 sq m). Each has two separate bedrooms, living room with TV/DVD player, walk-in closet with personal safe, dining area, two large marble-clad bathrooms, and private teakwood-decked balconies. These suites are directly under the navigation bridge. Butler service is provided, as is a Nespresso coffee machine. The bathrooms, which are open to the bedroom, have a stand-alone tub with integral shower, separate shower, toilet, bidet, and washbasin. The private balcony, with floor-to-ceiling partitions, has teak decking and deck furniture.

Grand Suites. These two suites (1104, 1005) are one deck above the navigation bridge and each is 876 sq ft (81 sq m). They are pleasant living spaces, with a separate bedroom, living room with TV/DVD player, walk-in closet, dining area, and two marble-clad bathing areas. One bathing area, which is open to the bedroom, although a curtain can be used to close it off, has a large five-sided sit-in tub placed in a glass-walled enclosure on the balcony – but with no access door to the balcony, which can be accessed only from the lounge/dining area. The second is a bathroom with separate shower enclosure, bidet, toilet, and washbasin. The suites have a private balcony with port or starboard views. There is also a guest toilet. Butler service is provided, as is a Nespresso coffee machine. The private balcony is similar to the one in a Master Suite.

Voyager Suites. Measuring 603 sq ft (56 sq m), these eight suites, on the port and starboard sides of the atrium on three decks, have a separate bedroom, living room with TV/DVD player, walk-in closet, dining area, large marble-clad bathroom with tub and separate shower enclosure, and a good-size private balcony with either port or starboard views. Butler service is provided. The balcony has teakwood deck, part partitions, and white plastic deck furniture.

Seven Seas Suites. Six spacious suites measuring 657 sq ft (61 sq m) are located aft overlooking the ship's stern and have a generous wraparound balcony. However, the balconies can be partly overlooked. They have teak decking, but white plastic deck furniture. Butler service is provided. Another four Seven Seas Suites, located amidships, measure a slightly smaller 545 sq ft (51 sq m), and have small balconies with either port or starboard views. They have a separate bedroom, living room with infotainment, walk-in closet, dining area, and large marble-clad bathroom with a combination tub/shower.

Penthouse Suites. There are 32 Category 'A' Penthouse Suites and 32 Category 'B' Penthouse Suites – Category 'A' Suites have the better location, but the size is the same at 370 sq ft (34.3 sq m). These have a sleeping area with dressing table and adjacent lounge area, walk-in closet, and bathroom with tub, washbasin, separate shower enclosure, and toilet. The balcony is accessed from the lounge. The balcony has teakwood deck, part partitions, and white plastic deck furniture. Butler service is provided.

Horizon Suites. The 29 Horizon Suites, measuring 522 sq ft (48.4 sq m), overlook the stern, with aft-facing views; some are sandwiched between the larger Seven Seas Suites. They have a separate bedroom, living room with TV/DVD player, walk-in closet, dining area, and a large marble-clad bathroom with a combination tub/shower. The good-size balcony has teakwood deck, part partitions, and white plastic deck furniture.

All other cabins. Categories C–H in the brochure, listed as Deluxe Suites and measuring 356 sq ft (33 sq m), have twin beds that convert to a queen-size bed (European duvets are standard), small walk-in closet, marble-lined bathroom with combination tub/shower, cotton bathrobe and towels, vanity desk, hairdryer, flat-screen infotainment center, refrigerator stocked with soft drinks and bar set-up on embarkation, and personal safe. The sleeping area is separated from the living area only by partial room dividers, and therefore they are cabins – albeit good-size ones – rather than suites.

Four wheelchair-accessible suites (761, 762, 859, and 860) are all as close to an elevator as one could possibly get, and provide ample living space, together with a large roll-in shower and all bathroom fittings at the correct height.

DINING. The 570-seat Compass Rose Restaurant is the main dining room. It has tables for two to 10, and dining is on an open seating basis, so you can dine with whomever you like, when you choose. In general, the cuisine is very good, and there's plenty of choice.

Other dining options. The 80-seat Prime 7 Steakhouse is the smallest of the specialty dining venues. It features a range of superb USDA prime, dry-aged steaks as well as chops, oven-roasted half chicken, Alaskan king crab legs, and Maine lobster. It's the most intimate dining spot – though, again, the single-deck ceiling height makes it feel busy – and it can get noisy. There is seating for two, four, or six, and reservations are required.

Signatures 'supper club' seats 120, and has ocean views along the room's port side. It is directed and staffed by chefs wearing the white toque and blue riband of Le Cordon Bleu, the prestigious culinary society for classic French cuisine. Seating is at tables of two, four, or six, and reservations are required.

For more casual meals, La Veranda is a large self-serve indoor/outdoor café with seats for 450, and fresh, light decor. This eatery has several food islands and substantial counter display space. At night, it is transformed into Sette Mari – an Italian eatery with some excellent pasta-based dishes.

The outdoor Pool Grill and ice cream bar, adjacent to the swimming pool, is a popular eatery. It features a creative list of burgers as well as various sandwiches.

ENTERTAINMENT. The stunning Constellation Showlounge spans two decks, and sight lines are very good from almost all seats. A troupe of 10 singers/dancers provides colorful mini-Las Vegas-style revues and production shows. Cabaret acts provide stand-alone evening shows. The ship carries a main showband, several small musical groups, and soloists.

SPA/FITNESS. For details of the Canyon Ranch SpaClub and other sporting facilities, see the listing for *Seven Seas Mariner*. An 18 percent gratuity is included in treatment and beauty salon services prices.

Silver Cloud
★★★★+

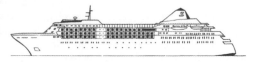

Size:	Small Ship
Tonnage:	16,927
Lifestyle:	Luxury
Cruise Line:	Silversea Cruises
Former Names:	none
IMO Number:	8903923
Builder:	Visentini/Mariotti (Italy)
Original Cost:	$125 million
Entered Service:	Apr 1994
Registry:	Bahamas
Length (ft/m):	514.4/155.8
Beam (ft/m):	70.62/21.4
Draft (ft/m):	17.3/5.3
Propulsion/Propellers:	diesel (11,700kW)/2
Passenger Decks:	6
Total Crew:	212
Passengers (lower beds):	296
Passenger Space Ratio (lower beds):	57.1

Passenger/Crew Ratio (lower beds):	1.4
Cabins (total):	148
Size Range (sq ft/m):	240.0–1,314.0/22.2–122.0
Cabins (for one person):	0
Cabins (with private balcony):	110
Cabins (wheelchair accessible):	2
Wheelchair accessibility:	Fair
Cabin Current:	110 and 220 volts
Elevators:	4
Casino (gaming tables):	Yes
Slot Machines:	Yes
Swimming Pools:	1
Hot Tubs (on deck):	2
Self-Service Launderette:	Yes
Dedicated Cinema/Seats:	Yes/306
Library:	Yes
Onboard currency:	US$

An all-inclusive, upmarket small ship for mature-age cruisers

OVERVIEW. *Silver Cloud* is an intimate sort of ship best suited to discerning and well-traveled couples, typically over 50, who seek a small ship with excellent food and fine European-style service in surroundings that border on the elegant. The passenger mix includes many nationalities, although the majority are North American. Children are sometimes seen aboard, although they are not really welcomed by most passengers.

THE SHIP. *Silver Cloud* has quite a handsome profile, with a sloping stern reminiscent of an Airstream trailer. The size is just about ideal for highly personalized cruising in an elegant environment. The vertical cake-layer stacking of public rooms aft and the location of accommodation forward ensures quiet cabins. There is a synthetic turf-covered (this doesn't equate with luxury) walk-around promenade deck outdoors, and a spacious swimming pool deck with teak/aluminum deck furniture. Little Silversea touches such as cold towels, water sprays, and fresh fruit provide poolside pampering on hot days.

The spacious interior is well planned, with elegant decor and fine-quality soft furnishings throughout, accented by the gentle use of brass fittings (some of substandard quality and now showing blotchy patches in several places), fine woods, and creative ceilings. In 2009, an extensive refit saw the addition of a proper observation lounge, with covered passageway to access it – so you don't have to go outside to do so. All suites were also refreshed.

Berlitz's Ratings

	Possible	Achieved
Ship	500	408
Accommodation	200	174
Food	400	333
Service	400	334
Entertainment	100	74
Cruise Experience	400	333
OVERALL SCORE		
1656 points out of 2000		

There is a business center as well as an audio and hardback book library, open 24 hours a day. An excellent amount of space per passenger means there is no hint of a line anywhere in this unhurried environment. Good documentation is provided before your cruise in a high-quality document wallet.

An elegant, announcement-free onboard ambience prevails, and there is no pressure or hype, and an enthusiastic staff to pamper you, including a high ratio of Europeans. All drinks, gratuities, and port taxes are included, and no further tipping is necessary – though it is not prohibited. This ship is ideal for those who enjoy spacious surroundings, excellent food, and some entertainment. It would be hard not to have a good vacation aboard this ship, albeit at a fairly high price.

Silversea Cruises has 'all-inclusive' fares, including gratuities, but charges extra for insurance. The fares do not, however, include vintage wines, or massage, or other personal services.

The onboard product delivered is good, particularly the cuisine and its presentation. Shuttle buses are provided in most ports of call, and all the little extras passengers receive make a cruise an extremely pleasant experience. The surroundings are very comfortable and contemporary without being extravagant, with open-seating dining and drinks included, and cold canapés and hot hors d'oeuvres served in the bars in the pre-dinner cocktail hour, a captain's welcome aboard, and a farewell cocktail party.

Niggles? Some vibration is evident when bow thrusters or the anchors are used, particularly in the forward-most cabins. The self-service launderette is not large enough for longer cruises. Crew facilities are minimal, leading to a high crew turnover, which undermines service.

ACCOMMODATION. There are seven price grades in this 'all-suites' ship. The all-outside-view suites, three-quarters of which have fine private teakwood balconies, have convertible queen-to-twin beds and are beautifully fitted out. They have large floor-to-ceiling windows, large walk-in closets, dressing table, writing desk, stocked minibar/refrigerator (no charge), and fresh flowers.

The marble-floor bathrooms have a tub, fixed showerhead, single washbasin, and plenty of high-quality towels. Personalized stationery, an eight-pillow menu from soft down to memory foam, bathrobes, and a range of Acqua di Parma bathroom products are provided in all suites.

All suites have televisions and DVD players, and top-grade suites also have CD players. However, the walk-in closets don't provide much hanging space, particularly for such items as full-length dresses, and it would be better for the door to open outward instead of inward. The drawers themselves are poorly positioned, but several other drawers and storage areas are provided in the living area.

Although the cabin insulation above and below each cabin is good, the insulation between cabins is not – a privacy curtain installed between entry door and sleeping area would be most useful. Light from the passageway leaks into the cabin, so it's hard to achieve a dark room.

Top-grade suites have teak balcony furniture, while other suites do not, but all balconies have teak floors. Suites with balconies on the lowest deck can suffer from sticky salt spray when the ship is moving, so the balconies need lots of cleaning. Each evening, the stewardesses bring plates of canapés to your suite – just right for a light bite with cocktails. In the Grand, Royal, Rossellini, or Owner's Suites, you get unobtrusive butler service from butlers certified by London's Guild of Professional Butlers.

DINING. The Restaurant provides open-seating dining in elegant surroundings. It has an attractive arched gazebo center and a wavy ceiling design as its focal point, and is set with fine Eschenbach china and well-balanced Christofle silverware. Meals are served in an open seating, which means you can eat when you like within the given dining room opening times, and with whom you like.

Standard table wines are included for lunch and dinner, and there is a 'connoisseur list' of premium wines at extra charge. All meals are prepared a la minute, with little of the pre-preparation that used to exist.

Other dining options. La Saletta, adjacent to the main dining room, is an intimate 24-seat specialty dining salon. Dégustation menus include dishes designed for Silversea Cruises by chefs from Relais Châteaux Gourmands, the cuisine-oriented division of Relais & Châteaux, paired with selected wines. Reservations are required, and there's a cover charge.

La Terrazza provides self-serve breakfast and lunch buffets and informal evening dining with different regional Italian dishes nightly. Both indoor and outdoor seating is at teakwood tables and chairs.

There is a 24-hour in-cabin dining service. Full course-by-course dinners are available, although the balcony tables in the standard suites are rather low for dining outdoors.

ENTERTAINMENT. The Showlounge hosts entertainment events and some social functions. The room spans two decks and has a sloping floor; banquette and individual seating are provided, with good sight lines.

Although Silversea Cruises places more emphasis on food than entertainment, what is provided is quite tasteful and not overbearing, as aboard some larger ships. A decent array of cabaret acts does the Silversea circuit, and small colorful production shows have been re-introduced.

Most of the cabaret acts provide intelligent entertainment that is generally appreciated by the well-traveled international clientele, and there's more emphasis now on classical music ensembles. A band provides live music in the evenings in The Bar, and Panorama Lounge.

SPA/FITNESS. The Spa at Silversea is quite small compared to those on other so-called luxury ships.

Facilities include a separate sauna for men and women, several treatment rooms, and a beauty salon. Massage and other body pampering treatments, facials, pedicures, and beauty salon treatments cost extra.

A separate gymnasium (formerly an observation lounge), located atop the ship, provides sea views.

Silver Discoverer
★★★★

Size:		Boutique Ship
Tonnage:		5,218
Lifestyle:		Standard
Cruise Line:		Silversea Cruises
Former Names: *Clipper Odyssey, Oceanic Odyssey, Oceanic Grace*		
IMO Number:		8800195
Builder:		NKK Tsu Shipyard (Japan)
Original Cost:		$40 million
Entered Service:		Apr 1989/May 2014
Registry:		Bahamas
Length (ft/m):		337.9/103.0
Beam (ft/m):		50.5/15.4
Draft (ft/m):		13.5/4.1
Propulsion/Propellers:		diesel (5,192kW)/2
Passenger Decks:		5
Total Crew:		52
Passengers (lower beds):		124
Passenger Space Ratio (lower beds):		42.0
Passenger/Crew Ratio (lower beds):		2.3
Cabins (total):		62
Size Range (sq ft/m):		182.9–258.3/17–24
Cabins (for one person):		0
Cabins (with private balcony):		8
Cabins (wheelchair accessible):		1
Wheelchair accessibility:		Fair
Cabin Current:		115 volts
Elevators:		1
Casino (gaming tables):		No
Slot Machines:		No
Swimming Pools:		1
Hot Tubs (on deck):		1
Self-Service Launderette:		No
Dedicated Cinema/Seats:		No
Library:		Yes
Onboard currency:		US$

A small expedition-style ship for discovery cruises

OVERVIEW. *Silver Discoverer* is liked by couples and solo travelers who seek nature and wildlife up close and personal, but in highly comfortable surroundings, and who wouldn't dream of cruising aboard anything larger.

THE SHIP. The ship has quite a smart, chic, mega-yacht-like profile, with a flared bow, square stern, and twin funnels that sweep up from each of the ship's sides. Designed in Holland and built in Japan, it tried to copy the *SeaDream* small ship/ultra-yacht concept, originally for the Japanese market. Operated by Japan's Showa Line, it wasn't suited to Japan's often choppy seas, so, after 10 years, it was sold to Clipper Cruise Line and managed by International Shipping Partners. In 2013 it was purchased by Silversea Cruises and renamed following a substantial refit and refurbishment program.

There are expansive areas outdoors for its size, and these excellent for viewing nature and wildlife. A small swimming pool is just a 'dip' pool, but there is a wide teakwood outdoor jogging track. Snorkeling equipment is available, as is a fleet of 12 Zodiacs for shore landings, and a glass-bottom boat for marine life exploration.

Inside, nothing jars the senses, as the interior design concept is balanced. The ambience is warm and intimate. There are, however, several pillars throughout the public areas, which spoil the decor and sight lines.

Berlitz's Ratings	Possible	Achieved
Ship	500	311
Accommodation	200	135
Food	400	319
Service	400	318
Entertainment	100	60
Cruise Experience	400	313
OVERALL SCORE		
1456 points out of 2000		

The ship concentrates on exploring regions such as Australia's Kimberley, the Russian Far East, and Bering Sea areas.

ACCOMMODATION. There are several cabin categories, and the all-outside cabins are tastefully furnished with blond wood cabinetry, twin- or queen-size beds, living area with sofa, personal safe, minibar/refrigerator, TV and three-sided mirror. All bathrooms have a deep, half-size tub. Some cabins have private balconies; but these are very small, with awkward door handles. The bathroom toilet seats are extremely high.

There is one suite, which is the size of two cabins. It provides more room, of course, with a lounge area, and more storage space.

DINING. The dining room has large ocean-view picture windows. It is quite warm and inviting, and all passengers eat in a single seating. The cuisine includes fresh foods from local ports where possible.

ENTERTAINMENT. There is no entertainment as such, although evening recaps, dinner and after-dinner conversation with fellow passengers in the ship's lounge/bar really is the entertainment.

SPA/FITNESS. There is a tiny beauty salon, and an adjacent massage/body treatment room. A small fitness room is located on a different deck.

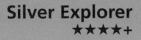

Silver Explorer
★★★★+

Size:	Boutique Ship	Passenger Space Ratio (lower beds):	46.0
Tonnage:	6,072	Passenger/Crew Ratio (lower beds):	1.1
Lifestyle:	Premium	Cabins (total):	66
Cruise Line:	Silversea Cruises	Size Range (sq ft/m):	172.2–785.7/16.0–73.0
Former Names:	Prince Albert II, World Discoverer, Dream 21,	Cabins (for one person):	0
	Baltic Clipper, Sally Clipper, Delfin Star,	Cabins (with private balcony):	6 + 14 French balconies
	Delfin Clipper, World Adventurer, Delfin Clipper	Cabins (wheelchair accessible):	0
IMO Number:	8806747	Wheelchair accessibility:	None
Builder:	Rauma-Repola (Finland)	Cabin Current:	110 and 220 volts
Original Cost:	$50 million	Elevators:	2
Entered Service:	Jul 1989/Jun 2008	Casino (gaming tables):	No
Registry:	Bahamas	Slot Machines:	No
Length (ft/m):	354.3/108.0	Swimming Pools:	0
Beam (ft/m):	51.1/15.6	Hot Tubs (on deck):	2
Draft (ft/m):	13.1/4.0	Self-Service Launderette:	No
Propulsion/Propellers:	diesel (4,500kW)/2	Dedicated Cinema/Seats:	No
Passenger Decks:	5	Library:	No
Total Crew:	111	Onboard currency:	US$
Passengers (lower beds):	132		

A small 'soft' expedition ship with some premium style

OVERVIEW. *Silver Explorer* is best suited to adventurous couples and solo travelers of mature years who enjoy seeing nature at close range, but want an extremely comfortable setting, plus good food and service.

THE SHIP. Twin swept-back outboard funnels highlight the semi-smart exterior design of this small specialist 23-year-old expedition cruise ship. It has a dark ice-hardened hull, carries a fleet of eight Zodiac inflatable landing craft for shore landings and exploration, and has one boot-washing station, the Mud Room, with six bays. There is no walk-around promenade deck outdoors.

The accommodation is located forward, with all public rooms aft, an arrangement that helps keep noise to a minimum in the accommodation areas. The interior has many European design elements, including warm color combinations. Public rooms include an observation lounge, large lecture room/cinema with bar, and library/Internet center.

This small expedition cruise vessel has many of the creature comforts of much larger vessels. It will provide a very comfortable expedition-style cruise experience in tasteful and elegant surroundings. All passengers receive a pre-cruise amenities package that typically includes a field guide, backpack, carry-on travel bag, and luggage tags.

ACCOMMODATION. There are six types of accommodation, and 11 price grades. The cabins –

Berlitz's Ratings		
	Possible	Achieved
Ship	500	395
Accommodation	200	172
Food	400	331
Service	400	329
Entertainment	100	57
Cruise Experience	400	327
OVERALL SCORE		
1611 points out of 2000		

quite large for such a small ship – are fitted out to a fairly high standard, with ample closet and drawer space. All have outside views and twin beds that convert to a queen-size bed, TV/DVD unit, telephone, hairdryer, refrigerator, and lockable drawer.

Although only six suites have a large private balcony (they're really not needed in cold-weather regions), another 14 cabins have glass doors that open onto a few inches of space outdoors. The suites have whirlpool bathtubs. The Owner's Suite has two rooms, linked by an interconnecting door, to provide a separate lounge, bedroom, and two bathrooms.

The sizes are: Owner's Suites 538 sq ft (50 sq m); Medallion Suites 358 sq ft (33 sq m); Grand Suites 650 sq ft (60 sq m); Silver Suites 431 sq ft (40 sq m); Veranda Suites 215 sq ft (20 sq m); Explorer Class 190 sq ft (28 sq m); Expedition Suites 431 sq ft (40 sq m).

DINING. The spacious dining room, with pastel-color decor, accommodates all passengers in one seating. Casual alfresco bites can be had at the outdoor grill.

ENTERTAINMENT. Daily recaps and after-dinner conversation make up the onboard entertainment.

SPA/FITNESS. Facilities include a small gymnasium, sauna, and treatment room for massage.

Silver Galapagos
★★★★

Size:	Boutique Ship	Passenger/Crew Ratio (lower beds):	1.3
Tonnage:	4,077	Cabins (total):	50
Lifestyle:	Standard	Size Range (sq ft/m):	231.4–282.0/21.5–26.2
Cruise Line:	Silversea Cruises	Cabins (for one person):	0
Former Names:	*Renaissance Three, Galapagos Explorer II*	Cabins (with private balcony):	24
IMO Number:	8708660	Cabins (wheelchair accessible):	0
Builder:	Cantieri Navale Ferrari (Italy)	Wheelchair accessibility:	None
Original Cost:	$20 million	Cabin Current:	110 volts
Entered Service:	Aug 1990/Sep 2013	Elevators:	1
Registry:	Ecuador	Casino (gaming tables):	No
Length (ft/m):	293.1/89.3	Slot Machines:	No
Beam (ft/m):	50.1/15.3	Swimming Pools:	0
Draft (ft/m):	11.9/3.6	Hot Tubs (on deck):	1
Propulsion/Propellers:	diesel (3,514kW)/2	Self-Service Launderette:	No
Passenger Decks:	5	Dedicated Cinema/Seats:	No
Total Crew:	72	Library:	Yes
Passengers (lower beds):	100	Onboard currency:	US$
Passenger Space Ratio (lower beds):	40.7		

A fine ship to use as a floating base in the Galápagos

OVERVIEW. *Silver Galápagos* operates two specific Galápagos cruise itineraries year-round from Baltra, Ecuador. It suits couples and solo travelers who want to cruise around the islands, but want to do so in comfortable, stylish surroundings.

THE SHIP. This is a comfortable and inviting ship, built as one of a series of eight similar small ships for the defunct Renaissance Cruises. While it is in good condition, maintenance could be better. Its looks are quite contemporary in the style of a mega-yacht. There is a wooden promenade deck outdoors. The limited number of public rooms have smart and restful, nonglitzy decor. The main lounge doubles as a lecture room, but perhaps it is the piano bar that provides the best place to relax after dinner in the evening. A doctor is carried at all times.

This ship (first operated by Silversea Cruises in 2013) provides a destination-intensive, refined, quiet, and relaxed cruise for those who don't like crowds or dressing up. Trained naturalist guides lead the shore excursions (included in the fare); the ship carries two glass-bottom boats, plus wetsuits and snorkeling equipment.

All drinks, bottled water, and soft drinks are included in the fare. Also included are guided visits to the islands. The brochure rates may or may not include the Galápagos Islands visitor tax, which must be paid in cash.

Sunbathing space is cramped. Plastic wood is everywhere (although it looks good). The service lacks finesse, but the crew is willing. The small library is attractive, but the book selection is poor.

Berlitz's Ratings		
	Possible	Achieved
Ship	500	368
Accommodation	200	157
Food	400	261
Service	400	297
Entertainment	100	50
Cruise Experience	400	282
OVERALL SCORE		
1415 points out of 2000		

ACCOMMODATION. This is located forward, with public rooms aft. Pleasant, all-outside suites have a large picture window, hand-crafted Italian furniture, and wet bar. All cabins have a queen-size bed, a sitting area, a minibar/refrigerator, TV, DVD player, and hairdryer. The small bathrooms have showers with a fold-down seat, real teakwood floors, and marble vanities.

DINING. The small, elegant and intimate dining room has open seating, and tables for two, four, six, and eight. The meals are dinner is à la carte, while lunch is buffet-style (sometimes on the open deck), with local Ecuadorian delicacies and meat.

ENTERTAINMENT. After-dinner conversation with fellow passengers forms the entertainment each evening, plus relaxation, of course.

SPA/FITNESS. There is a small sauna. Snorkel gear is also available.

Silver Shadow
★★★★★

Size:	Small Ship	Passenger/Crew Ratio (lower beds):	1.3
Tonnage:	28,258	Cabins (total):	194
Lifestyle:	Luxury	Size Range (sq ft/m):	287.0–1,435.0/26.6–133.3
Cruise Line:	Silversea Cruises	Cabins (for one person):	0
Former Names:	none	Cabins (with private balcony):	166
IMO Number:	9192167	Cabins (wheelchair accessible):	2
Builder:	Visentini/Mariotti (Italy)	Wheelchair accessibility:	Good
Original Cost:	$150 million	Cabin Current:	110 and 220 volts
Entered Service:	Sep 2000	Elevators:	5
Registry:	Bahamas	Casino (gaming tables):	Yes
Length (ft/m):	610.2/186.0	Slot Machines:	Yes
Beam (ft/m):	81.8/24.8	Swimming Pools:	1
Draft (ft/m):	19.6/6.0	Hot Tubs (on deck):	2
Propulsion/Propellers:	diesel/2	Self-Service Launderette:	Yes
Passenger Decks:	7	Dedicated Cinema/Seats:	No
Total Crew:	295	Library:	Yes
Passengers (lower beds):	388	Onboard currency:	US$
Passenger Space Ratio (lower beds):	72.8		

An all-inclusive premium ship for mature-age cruisers

OVERVIEW. This ship is best suited to discerning, well-traveled couples, typically over 50, who seek a small ship with excellent food that approaches gourmet standards, and fine service in surroundings bordering on the elegant and luxurious.

THE SHIP. *Silver Shadow* is one of the second generation of ships in the Silversea Cruises fleet, and slightly larger than *Silver Cloud* and *Silver Wind*, with a more streamlined forward profile and large, sleek single funnel. However, the ship's stern is not particularly handsome. There is a generous amount of open deck and sunbathing space, and aluminum/teak deck furniture is provided.

The company's many international passengers react well to the ambience, food, service, and the helpful staff. The cruise line's 'all-inclusive' fares, including gratuities and many things that cost extra aboard many rivals' ships, but the fares don't include vintage wines, massage, or other personal services.

Although the ship shows signs of wear, the on-board product is very good, particularly the cuisine and its presentation. Shuttle buses are provided in most ports of call, and all the little extras that passengers receive make this an extremely pleasant experience, in surroundings that are comfortable and contemporary without being extravagant, with open-seating dining and drinks included, cold canapés and hot hors d'oeuvres served in the bars in the pre-dinner cocktail hour, a captain's welcome aboard, and farewell cocktail party.

Berlitz's Ratings		
	Possible	Achieved
Ship	500	448
Accommodation	200	181
Food	400	341
Service	400	346
Entertainment	100	85
Cruise Experience	400	340
OVERALL SCORE		
1741 points out of 2000		

The swimming pool is surprisingly small, as is the fitness room, although it was expanded in 2007. The Humidor by Davidoff, the cigar lounge, has 25 seats and the style of an English smoking club. There is a Champagne bar and a four-terminal computer center (Wi-Fi costs extra).

Personalized Voyages enable you choose the port of embarkation and disembarkation and the length of cruise you want (minimum five days). While this adds flexibility, the onboard programming is already set, so you may be joining and leaving in the middle of a 'normal' cruise.

ACCOMMODATION. There are eight price grades in this all-suites ship. All suites have double vanities in the marble-floored bathrooms, which also have a tub and separate shower enclosure. All grades receive Silversea monogrammed Frette bed linen, an eight-pillow menu (from soft down to memory foam), 100 percent cotton bathrobes, a range of Acqua di Parma bathroom products, and personalized stationery. Stay in the Grand, Royal, Rossellini, or Owner's Suites and you get unobtrusive service from butlers certified by London's Guild of Professional Butlers.

Vista Suites. These 287-sq-ft (27-sq-m) suites don't have a private balcony. Instead there's a large window, twin beds that convert to a queen-size bed, sitting area, TV set and video player, refrigerator, writing desk, personal safe, cocktail cabinet, dressing table with hairdryer, and walk-in closet. The bathroom is marble-clad in gentle colors, and has two washbasins, a full-size tub, separate shower enclosure, and toilet.

Veranda Suites. Each of these suites (really Vista Suites plus a veranda) measures 345 sq ft (33 sq m) and has convertible twin-to-queen beds. They are well fitted-out with just about everything you would need, including large floor-to-ceiling windows, large walk-in closet, dressing table, writing desk, stocked minibar/refrigerator with all drinks are included in the fare, and fresh flowers. The marble-clad bathrooms have two washbasins, full-size tub, separate shower enclosure, and toilet.

Silver Suites. These measure 701 sq ft (65 sq m). These are much wider than the Vista Suites or Veranda Suites and have a separate bedroom, an entertainment center with CD player, TV/video player in both bedroom and living room, and much more living space that includes a large dining area with table and four chairs. The marble-clad bathrooms have two washbasins, full size tub, separate shower enclosure, and toilet.

Owner's Suites. These two suites, each measuring 1,208 sq ft (112 sq m), are much larger and include an extra powder room/toilet for guests, as well as more living space. There is a 200-sq-ft (18-sq-m) veranda, two bedrooms with queen-size beds, two walk-in closets, two living rooms, two sitting areas, separate dining area, an entertainment center with flat-screen plasma television in the living room and a TV set/video player player in each bedroom, plus telephones, refrigerators, cocktail cabinet, writing desk, and dressing tables with hairdryers. There are two marble-clad bathrooms, one with a full-size whirlpool tub and two washbasins, separate toilet, and separate shower, as well as a powder room for guests. Owner's Suites can be configured as one or two bedrooms.

Royal Suites. Stately accommodation can be found in two Royal Suites measuring either 1,312 sq ft (122 sq m) or 1,352 sq ft (126 sq m). These are two-bedroom suites, with two teakwood verandas, two living rooms, sitting areas, dining area, queen-size beds, an entertainment center with flat-screen plasma television in the living room and a TV/video player player in each bedroom, telephones, refrigerators, cocktail cabinet, writing desk, two closets, and dressing tables with hairdryers. There are two marble-clad bathrooms, one with a full-size whirlpool tub and two washbasins, separate toilet, and separate shower, as well as a powder room for guests. Royal Suites can be either a one- or two-bedroom configuration.

Grand Suites. There are two of these, one measuring 1,286 sq ft (119 sq m), and the other (including an adjoining suite with interconnecting door) 1,435 sq ft (133 sq m). These have two bedrooms, two large walk-in closets, two living rooms, Bang & Olufsen entertainment centers, and large, forward-facing, private verandas. These really are sumptuous

apartments that have all the comforts of home, and then some.

Disabled Suites. There are two suites for the physically disabled (535 and 537), both adjacent to an elevator and next to each other. Measuring a generous 398 sq ft (37 sq m), they are well equipped with an accessible hanging rail, and roll-in bathroom with roll-in shower unit.

DINING. The main dining room, The Restaurant, has open seating in elegant surroundings. Three grand chandeliers provide an upward focal point. Meals can also be served, course-by-course, in your suite, although the balcony tables are rather low for dining outdoors. The cuisine is very good, with a choice of formal and informal areas. Standard table wines are included for lunch and dinner, with an extra-cost 'connoisseur list' of premium wines. Once each cruise, there's a Galley Brunch when the galley is transformed into a large 'chef's kitchen.'

Other dining options. For something special, Le Champagne is a more intimate extra-cost venue that allows diners to sample highly specialized dégustation menus marrying international cuisine with vintage wines selection by Relais & Châteaux sommeliers. Reservations are needed, and the wines also cost extra.

For more informal meals, La Terrazza provides self-serve breakfast and lunch buffets; outdoor seating is at teakwood tables and chairs. The buffet design and set-up presents flow problems during breakfast, and 'active' stations for cooking eggs or pasta to order would help.

Adjacent to La Terazza is a wine bar and a cigar smoking room. A poolside grill provides a casual alternative daytime bistro-style eatery, for grilled and fast-food items, and becomes The Grill for evening dining, with food cooked on hot stones.

ENTERTAINMENT. The Showlounge, the venue for entertainment and some social functions, spans two decks and has a sloping floor; both banquette and individual seating are provided, with good sight lines from almost all seats.

Although Silversea Cruises places more emphasis on food than entertainment, what is provided is quite tasteful. A decent array of cabaret acts does the Silversea circuit, and small, colorful production shows have been reintroduced. More emphasis is placed on classical music ensembles. There is a band and several small musical units for live music in the evenings in The Bar, and the Panorama Lounge.

SPA/FITNESS. The Spa at Silversea health/fitness facility, just behind the Observation Lounge, high atop the ship, had a complete makeover in 2007. It includes a gymnasium, beauty salon, and separate saunas and steam rooms for men and women, plus several personal treatment rooms.

Size:	Small Ship
Tonnage:	36,009
Lifestyle:	Luxury
Cruise Line:	Silversea Cruises
Former Names:	none
IMO Number:	9437866
Builder:	Fincantieri (Italy)
Original Cost:	$250 million
Entered Service:	Dec 2009
Registry:	Bahamas
Length (ft/m):	642.3/195.8
Beam (ft/m):	86.9/26.5
Draft (ft/m):	20.9/6.4
Propulsion/Propellers:	diesel-electric (26,100kW)/2
Passenger Decks:	8
Total Crew:	370
Passengers (lower beds):	540
Passenger Space Ratio (lower beds):	66.6

Passenger/Crew Ratio (lower beds):	1.4
Cabins (total):	270
Size Range (sq ft/m):	312.1–1,614.6/29–150
Cabins (for one person):	0
Cabins (with private balcony):	258
Cabins (wheelchair accessible):	4
Wheelchair accessibility:	Best
Cabin Current:	110 volts
Elevators:	6
Casino (gaming tables):	Yes
Slot Machines:	Yes
Swimming Pools:	1
Hot Tubs (on deck):	4
Self-Service Launderette:	Yes
Dedicated Cinema/Seats:	No
Library:	Yes
Onboard currency:	US$

A stylish upper-class ship for sophisticated cruising

OVERVIEW. This ship suits discerning, well-traveled couples and solo travelers, typically over 50, who are looking for a smaller ship setting with fine food and European-style service in surroundings bordering on the elegant and luxurious without being extravagant. Shuttle buses are provided in most ports of call, and all the little extras passengers receive make a cruise an extremely pleasant experience.

Berlitz's Ratings		
	Possible	Achieved
Ship	500	443
Accommodation	200	181
Food	400	339
Service	400	347
Entertainment	100	85
Cruise Experience	400	340
OVERALL SCORE		
1735 points out of 2000		

THE SHIP. *Silver Spirit*, larger than *Silver Shadow* and *Silver Whisper*, is the newest 'all-inclusive' addition to the Silversea Cruises fleet – although 'all-inclusive' doesn't include the two specialty dining venues. It represents a substantial investment in new tonnage. Sharing its name with a famous Rolls-Royce car, *Silver Spirit* has a similar profile to the smaller *Silver Shadow* and *Silver Whisper*, with a nicely shaped stern with tiered aft decks, but exudes more style and provides more choice than the line's other ships.

Although there's a main pool and hot tub deck, there's little shade, and no hot tubs on any other deck. Also, because there are so many balcony suites/cabins, there's no walk-around outdoor promenade deck.

The interior layout has a cake-layer stacking of almost all the public rooms in the aft section, and the accommodation located forward, so there is minimal noise in passenger accommodation, although it means there are more stairs and no flow-through horizontal deck where passengers can parade. But regular Silversea Cruises passengers are used to

this arrangement, and it's good exercise. The decor is elegant and understated, but bland (muted colors), a mix of Art Deco and modern, but not contemporary.

The Observation Lounge, at the front of the ship with access from a central passageway, has fine ocean views, and is a very comfortable place to relax and read. A Panorama Lounge, at the stern, is a comfortable multi-function room. Non-smokers should note that smoking is allowed on the port side. A cigar lounge, with doors that open in to the casino, has a pleasing list of cigars. The casino has five blackjack tables, an American Roulette table, and 52 slot machines.

The company's 'all-inclusive' fares include gratuities, drinks with meals, and many things that cost extra on rivals' ships. Vintage wines, massage, and other personal services do cost extra, though. Passengers appreciate open-seating dining, cold canapés and hot hors d'oeuvres served in the bars in the pre-dinner cocktail hour, a captain's welcome aboard, and a farewell cocktail party.

The passenger mix includes many nationalities, which makes for a more interesting experience, although most passengers are North American. Children are sometimes seen aboard, but are not really welcomed by most people.

Passenger niggles include the lack of electrical sockets in the cabins; there are almost no shaded outdoor areas; the butler service is sometimes poor, not least because each butler has about 15 cabins to look after.

ACCOMMODATION. *Silver Spirit*, like other Silversea Cruises ships, has 'all-suites' accommodation. Some suites can accommodate a third person. Eight have interconnecting doors, so families and friends can be adjacent.

Accommodation consists of: two Owner's Suites, approx. 1,292 sq ft (120 sq m) for one bedroom and 1,614 sq ft (150 sq m) for two bedrooms; four Grand Suites in the front of the ship (990 sq ft/ 92 sq m for one bedroom and 1,302 sq ft/117 sq m for two bedrooms); two Royal Suites in the front of the ship, 26 Silver Suites (742 sq ft/69 sq m); 166 Midship Veranda Suites (376 sq ft/35 sq m); 50 Veranda Suites (376 sq ft/35 sq m); and 12 Vista Suites (312 sq ft/29 sq m). The Owner's, Grand, and Royal Suites all have interconnecting doors for an available second bedroom.

All provide personalized stationery, a menu with a choice of eight pillows from soft down to memory foam, bathrobes, and an array of Bulgari bathroom amenities. All have walk-in closets with personal safe, TV set, DVD unit, and vanity desk with hairdryer. Suite bathrooms are marble-clad, with marble and wood floors, and contain a toilet, one or two washbasins, a full-size tub, and a shower enclosure with a fixed 'rain shower' and a separate hand-held hose). Occupants of the Owner's Suites or Grand Suites receive unobtrusive service from 21 butlers certified by London's Guild of Professional Butlers.

The suites have recessed lighting in the ceiling – a nice touch that allows a little diffused mood lighting when needed. Balconies have sliding doors that can move if not securely locked when not in use. Non-smokers should be aware that Silversea Cruises allows smoking in cabins.

DINING. There are certainly plenty of dining choices. The Restaurant is the name of the ship's main dining room – a light, airy venue, although its design is quite disappointing – in particular because of its low ceiling height. It seats up to 456, and has an integral dance floor. This is all about open-seating dining in elegant surroundings, with unhurried, unobtrusive service. It is open for breakfast, lunch, and dinner; tables are set with fine china, silverware, and Riedel wine glasses. For complete privacy, meals can also be served, course-by-course, in your suite.

Other dining options. Le Champagne, adjacent to The Restaurant, is an intimate, extra-cost, reservations-required, dinner-only venue offering a six-course mini-dégustation menu based on Relais & Châteaux menus. Sadly, the banquette seating along the outer walls detracts from the otherwise very comfortable, uncluttered, intimate dining spot, which has a small walk-in wine room as its central, focal point.

Seishin Restaurant, also adjacent to The Restaurant, is an extra-cost reservations-required venue, with just 24 seats. It serves Kobe beef, sushi items, and Asian seafood, and an octagonal display counter is the focal point to the venue. It is open for dinner only, and there's a cover charge.

La Terrazza is the venue for self-serve buffet-style items for breakfast and lunch. Each evening, it turns into an Italian-themed dining spot, with waiter service and regional Italian cuisine cooked to order. Reservations are required for dinner (not open for lunch).

Stars Supper Club, with 58 seats and a dance floor, is designed in the manner of an English supper club of the 1920s to provide an intimate, club-like ambience and all-night entertainment – which means volume-intrusive. Reservations are required for dinner (not open for lunch).

The Pool Grill is a casual outside eatery serving steaks, seafood, and pizza. Meals are served on hot stones that act as plates, so you can't touch them, but this is more a casual eating novelty than proper dining.

Additionally, a lobby bar serves Lavazza Italian coffees, wines, spirits, and pastries.

ENTERTAINMENT. The Showlounge, in the aft section, has a main stage and two ancillary side stages. It seats about 320 passengers, and there are good sight lines from all seats but no beverage service. It's a lovely room, and seating consists of two-person love seats, and each has a small table for personal items. Production shows have been re-introduced, and these, together with cabaret acts, provide a balanced entertainment program.

SPA/FITNESS. The Spa at Silversea, with 8,300 sq ft (770 sq m) of space, is quite large for this size of ship, and includes a sanctuary for total relaxation and detox. Located at the stern of the ship, one deck below La Terrazza, it is a haven for me-time and personal treatments.

Silver Whisper
★★★★★

Size:	Small Ship
Tonnage:	28,258
Lifestyle:	Luxury
Cruise Line:	Silversea Cruises
Former Names:	none
IMO Number:	9192179
Builder:	Visentini/Mariotti (Italy)
Original Cost:	$150 million
Entered Service:	Jul 2001
Registry:	Bahamas
Length (ft/m):	610.2/186.0
Beam (ft/m):	81.8/24.8
Draft (ft/m):	19.6/6.0
Propulsion/Propellers:	diesel/2
Passenger Decks:	7
Total Crew:	295
Passengers (lower beds):	388
Passenger Space Ratio (lower beds):	72.8

Passenger/Crew Ratio (lower beds):	1.3
Cabins (total):	194
Size Range (sq ft/m):	287.0–1,435.0/26.6–133.3
Cabins (for one person):	0
Cabins (with private balcony):	166
Cabins (wheelchair accessible):	2
Wheelchair accessibility:	Good
Cabin Current:	110 and 220 volts
Elevators:	5
Casino (gaming tables):	Yes
Slot Machines:	Yes
Swimming Pools:	1
Hot Tubs (on deck):	2
Self-Service Launderette:	Yes
Dedicated Cinema/Seats:	No
Library:	Yes
Onboard currency:	US$

Inclusive cruising with space, style, and some good food

OVERVIEW. This ship suits discerning, well-traveled couples who like a small ship that provides good food and European-style service in elegant, highly comfortable surroundings. Silversea Cruises promotes its Italian Heritage theme, and its many international passengers respond well to the ambience, food, and the staff, most of whom go out of their way to please.

THE SHIP. *Silver Whisper*, which Russia's Vladimir Putin chartered in 2003 to host guests for the three-day celebrations of St Petersburg's 300th anniversary, is the second generation of vessels in the Silversea Cruises fleet. It is sister to *Silver Shadow*, and is slightly larger than the line's first two ships, *Silver Cloud* and *Silver Wind*, but with a more streamlined profile and a large, sleek single funnel.

The ship has 'all-inclusive' fares, including gratuities (although additional tips are not expected, they are not prohibited). The fares do not include vintage wines, or massage, or other personal services, but they do include many things that are extra-cost items compared with ships of some other cruise lines. The passenger mix includes many nationalities, although the majority of passengers are North American. Children are sometimes seen aboard, but not really welcomed by most passengers.

Only a few ships make it to a five-star Berlitz rating, but Silversea Cruises' emphasis on quality has earned it an enviable reputation, particularly for cuisine. Shuttle buses are provided in most ports of call, and all the little extras that passengers receive make

Berlitz's Ratings		
	Possible	Achieved
Ship	500	448
Accommodation	200	181
Food	400	341
Service	400	346
Entertainment	100	85
Cruise Experience	400	342
OVERALL SCORE		
1743 points out of 2000		

this ship an extremely pleasant experience. The surroundings are very comfortable and contemporary without being extravagant, there is open-seating dining with drinks included, cold canapés and hot hors d'oeuvres are served in the bars in the pre-dinner cocktail hour, and there's a captain's welcome aboard and farewell cocktail party.

Aluminum/teak deck furniture is placed by the swimming pool, but the pool itself is quite small. The Humidor, by Davidoff, a 25-seat cigar-smoking lounge, has been styled like an English smoking club. There's a wine bar and computer learning center.

ACCOMMODATION. This 'all-suites' ship has eight cabin price categories. All grades have double vanities in the marble-floored bathrooms, plus tub and separate shower enclosure. Silversea-monogrammed Frette bed linen is provided in all grades, as is an eight-pillow menu from soft down to memory foam, 100 percent cotton bathrobes, a fine array of Acqua di Parma bathroom amenities, and personalized stationery. In the Grand, Royal, Rossellini, or Owner's Suites, you get unobtrusive service from butlers certified by London's Guild of Professional Butlers.

Vista Suites. These suites measure 287 sq ft (27 sq m) and don't have a private balcony. Instead, there is a large window, twin beds that convert to a queen-size bed, sitting area, TV and video player, refrigerator, writing desk, personal safe, cocktail cabinet, dressing table with hairdryer, and walk-in closet. The bathroom is marble-clad in gentle colors, and has two washbasins, full-size tub, separate shower enclosure, and toilet.

Veranda Suites. Each of the Veranda Suites – which are really Vista Suites plus a veranda – measures 345 sq ft (32 sq m) and has convertible twin-to-queen beds. They are well fitted-out and have large floor-to-ceiling windows, large walk-in closet, dressing table, writing desk, stocked minibar/refrigerator (drinks included in the fare), and fresh flowers. The marble-clad bathrooms have two washbasins, full-size tub, separate shower enclosure, and toilet.

Silver Suites. The Silver Suites measure 701 sq ft (65 sq m). Much wider than the Vista Suites or Veranda Suites, they have a separate bedroom, an audio-visual entertainment center in both the bedroom and living room, and much more living space, including a large dining area with table and four chairs. The marble-clad bathrooms have two washbasins, full-size tub, separate shower enclosure, and toilet.

Owner's Suites. The two Owner's Suites, each 1,208 sq ft (112 sq m), are much larger units and include an extra bathroom for guests, plus more living space. There is a 200-sq-ft (18-sq-m) veranda, two bedrooms with queen-size beds, two walk-in closets, two living rooms, two sitting areas, separate dining area, an entertainment center with flat-screen plasma television in the living room and TV/DVD player in each bedroom, telephones, refrigerators, cocktail cabinet, writing desk, and dressing tables with hairdryers. There are two marble-clad bathrooms, one with a full-size whirlpool tub and two washbasins, separate toilet, and separate shower, plus a powder room for guests. Owner's Suites can be a one- or two-bedroom configuration.

Royal Suites. Stately accommodation can be found in two Royal Suites, measuring 1,312 sq ft (122 sq m) and 1,352 sq ft (126 sq m). These are two-bedroom suites, with two teakwood verandas, two living rooms, sitting areas, dining area, queen-size beds, an entertainment center with flat-screen plasma television in the living room and TV/DVD player in each bedroom, telephones, refrigerators, cocktail cabinet, writing desk, two closets, and dressing tables with hairdryers. There are two marble-clad bathrooms, one with a full-size whirlpool tub and two washbasins, separate toilet, and separate shower, as well as a powder room for guests. Royal Suites can be either a one- or two-bedroom configuration.

Grand Suites. There are two, one 1,286 sq ft (119 sq m) and the other, including an adjoining suite with interconnecting door, 1,435 sq ft (133 sq m). These have two bedrooms, two large walk-in closets, two living rooms, Bang & Olufsen entertainment centers, and large, forward-facing, private verandas. These are sumptuous apartments with all the comforts of home, and then some.

Disabled Suites. There are two adjacent suites for the physically disabled (535 and 537), both beside an elevator. They measure a generous 398 sq ft (37 sq m) and are well equipped with an accessible hanging rail, and roll-in bathroom with roll-in shower unit.

DINING. The main dining room, The Restaurant, offers open-seating dining in elegant surroundings. Three grand chandeliers provide an upward focal point. Meals can also be served, course-by-course, in your suite, although the balcony tables are rather low for dining outdoors. The cuisine is good throughout the ship, with a choice of formal and informal areas, although the cuisine and presentation don't quite match up to that of vessels such as the smaller Seabourn Cruise Line ships. Cristofle silverware is provided. Standard table wines are included for lunch and dinner, and there is an extra-cost 'connoisseur list' of premium wines.

Other dining options. As an alternative to the main restaurant, the extra-cost Le Champagne offers a more intimate, reservation-only dining spot. Here, passengers can enjoy highly specialized dégustation menus marrying international cuisine with vintage wines selected by Relais & Châteaux sommeliers.

La Terrazza is for self-serve breakfast and lunch buffets. The buffet design and set-up presents flow problems during breakfast, however, and 'active' stations for cooking eggs or pasta to order would help. In the evening, this room serves regional Italian cuisine, and has softer lighting to create a more intimate atmosphere.

Adjacent to the café is a wine bar and a cigar-smoking room. A poolside grill provides a casual alternative daytime dining spot; in the evening it turns into The Grill, with food cooked using the Black Rock (hot stone) method.

ENTERTAINMENT. The Showlounge spans two decks and has a sloping floor; both banquette and individual seating are provided, with good sight lines from almost all seats.

A decent array of cabaret acts does the Silversea circuit, most providing intelligent entertainment; colourful productions are also featured. Musically, more emphasis is placed on classical music ensembles. A band and small groups/ensembles perform in the evenings in The Bar and the Panorama Lounge.

SPA/FITNESS. The Spa at Silversea health/fitness facility, just behind the Observation Lounge, includes a gymnasium, beauty salon, separate saunas and steam rooms for men and women, plus several treatment rooms. A range of body-pampering services is offered to men and women. Massage and other treatments, facials, pedicures, and beauty salon treatments cost extra.

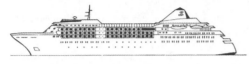

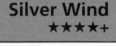

Silver Wind
★★★★+

Size:	Small Ship	Passenger/Crew Ratio (lower beds):	1.3
Tonnage:	17,400	Cabins (total):	151
Lifestyle:	Luxury	Size Range (sq ft/m):	240.0–1,314.0/22.2–122.0
Cruise Line:	Silversea Cruises	Cabins (for one person):	0
Former Names:	none	Cabins (with private balcony):	123
IMO Number:	8903935	Cabins (wheelchair accessible):	2
Builder:	Visentini/Mariotti (Italy)	Wheelchair accessibility:	Fair
Original Cost:	$125 million	Cabin Current:	110 and 220 volts
Entered Service:	Jan 1995	Elevators:	4
Registry:	Bahamas	Casino (gaming tables):	Yes
Length (ft/m):	514.4/155.8	Slot Machines:	Yes
Beam (ft/m):	70.62/21.4	Swimming Pools:	1
Draft (ft/m):	17.3/5.3	Hot Tubs (on deck):	2
Propulsion/Propellers:	diesel (11,700kW)/2	Self-Service Launderette:	Yes
Passenger Decks:	6	Dedicated Cinema/Seats:	Yes/306
Total Crew:	222	Library:	Yes
Passengers (lower beds):	302	Onboard currency:	US$
Passenger Space Ratio (lower beds):	57.6		

An all-inclusive small ship for the well-traveled

OVERVIEW. This ship is best suited to discerning, well-traveled couples, typically over 50, who seek a small ship with fine cuisine, European-style service, and surroundings that border on the elegant. An announcement-free ambience prevails, and there is no pressure or hype, and an enthusiastic staff knows how to pamper you.

THE SHIP. *Silver Wind* has a quite handsome profile, with a sloping stern reminiscent of an Airstream trailer. The size is just about ideal for personalized cruising in an elegant environment. The vertical cake-layer stacking of public rooms aft and the location of accommodation units forward ensures quiet cabins. There is a synthetic turf-covered (not quite equating with luxury) walk-around promenade deck outdoors – which should be upgraded to teak or Bolidt – and a fairly spacious swimming pool and sunbathing deck with teak/aluminum deck furniture. Little touches such as cold towels, water sprays, and fresh fruit provide poolside pampering on hot days.

The ship has had several makeovers (in 2003, 2009, and 2014), which have made it more user-friendly by adding a proper, if small, observation lounge with bookcases and a covered walkway to access it, as well as a relocated and enlarged health spa. The spacious interior is well planned, with elegant decor and fine-quality soft furnishings throughout, accented by brass fittings (some of sub-standard quality and showing blotchy patches in several), fine woods, and creative ceilings. There

Berlitz's Ratings		
	Possible	Achieved
Ship	500	410
Accommodation	200	174
Food	400	333
Service	400	333
Entertainment	100	74
Cruise Experience	400	334
OVERALL SCORE		
1658 points out of 2000		

is an excellent amount of space per passenger, and no hint of a line anywhere. There is a useful Internet center, a 24-hour library with hardback books and DVDs, and a cigar lounge.

Before your cruise, good documentation is provided in a high-quality document wallet and presentation box. Insurance, once included in the fare, now costs extra. All drinks, gratuities, and port taxes are included, and no further tipping anywhere on board is necessary (although not prohibited). Not included, however, are vintage wines, spa treatments, or other personal services. It would be hard not to have a good cruise aboard this ship, albeit at a fairly high price. The company's many international passengers like the ambience, food, service, and the staff, who generally go out of their way to please.

Shuttle buses are provided in most ports of call, and all the little extras that passengers receive aboard this ship makes it an extremely pleasant experience, in surroundings that are comfortable and contemporary without being extravagant, with open seating dining, cold canapés and hot hors d'oeuvres served in the bars in the pre-dinner cocktail hour, a captain's welcome aboard, and a farewell cocktail party.

Silversea Cruises has a defined product based on an Italian Heritage theme. While the past few years sometimes saw the delivery of a tarnished service, this has been recognized and Silversea Cruises is now polishing the silver again.

The passenger mix includes many nationalities, although most passengers are North American. Children are sometimes seen aboard.

Passenger niggles include the fact that some vibration is evident when bow thrusters or the anchors are used, particularly in the forward-most suites. The self-service launderette is poor and not large enough for longer cruises, when passengers like to wash their own small items. Crew facilities are minimal, so crew turnover is quite high, making it difficult to maintain consistency.

ACCOMMODATION. There are seven price grades. The all-outside suites, 75 percent with fine private teakwood-floor balconies, have convertible queen-to-twin beds, and are nicely fitted out. They include large floor-to-ceiling windows, large walk-in closets, dressing table, writing desk, stocked minibar/refrigerator (no charge), and fresh flowers. The marble floor bathrooms have a tub, fixed shower head, single washbasin, and plenty of high-quality towels. Personalized stationery, an eight-pillow menu from soft down to memory foam, bathrobes, and an array of Acqua di Parma bathroom amenities are provided in all suites.

In the Grand, Royal, Rossellini or Owner's Suites, you get unobtrusive service from butlers certified by London's Guild of Professional Butlers.

All suites have TV and DVD players (top-grade suites also have CD players). However, the walk-in closets don't provide much hanging space, particularly for such items as full-length dresses; it would be better for the door to open outward instead of inward. Drawers are poorly positioned, although several other drawers and storage areas are provided in the living area. Although the cabin insulation above and below each suite is good, insulation between them is not – a privacy curtain installed between entry door and sleeping area would be useful – and light from the passageway leaks into the suite, making it hard to achieve a dark room.

The top suite grades have teak balcony furniture, while others don't – but all balconies have teak floors. Suites with balconies on the lowest deck can suffer from sticky salt spray when the ship is moving, so the balconies need lots of cleaning. Each evening, the stewardesses bring canapés to your suite – just right for a light bite with cocktails.

DINING. The main dining room, The Restaurant, provides open-seating dining in elegant surroundings. It has a wood floor, an attractive arched gazebo center, and a wavy ceiling design as its focal point, and is set with fine Limoges china and well-balanced Christofle silverware. Meals are served in an open seating, which means you can eat when you like within the given dining room opening times, and with whom you like.

The cuisine/dining experience is good, with a choice of three dining salons. Standard table wines are included for lunch and dinner, but there is also a 'connoisseur list' of premium wines at extra charge. All meals are prepared as à-la-carte items, with almost none of the pre-preparation that used to exist. Special orders are also possible.

Other dining options. A specialty dining salon, the intimate 24-seat La Saletta, adjacent to the main dining room, has dégustation menus that include dishes designed for Silversea Cruises by chefs from Relais & Châteaux Gourmands (the cuisine-oriented division of Relais & Châteaux; these are paired with selected wines. Reservations are required, and there's a cover charge.

For more casual dining, La Terrazza offers self-serve breakfast and lunch buffets. In the evening it serves Italian regional dishes and has softer lighting, with both indoors and outdoors seating at teakwood tables and chairs.

There is a 24-hour in-cabin dining service; full course-by-course dinners are available, although the balcony tables in the standard suites are rather low for dining outdoors.

ENTERTAINMENT. The Showlounge is the venue for all entertainment events and some social functions. The room spans two decks and has a sloping floor; both banquette and individual seating are provided, with good sight lines from almost all seats.

Although Silversea Cruises places more emphasis on food than entertainment, what is provided is quite tasteful and not overbearing, as aboard some larger ships. A decent array of cabaret acts does the Silversea circuit. Most of the cabaret acts provide intelligent entertainment.

Also, more emphasis is now placed on classical music ensembles. There is also a band, as well as several small musical units for live music in the evenings in The Bar and the Panorama Lounge.

SPA/FITNESS. Although The Spa at Silversea facility isn't large, it underwent a sea change in 2007 with redesigned, more welcoming, decor, and an updated range of treatments and spa packages for both men and women. Massage and other body-pampering treatments, facials, pedicures, and beauty salon treatments cost extra.

Facilities include a mixed sauna for men and women, several treatment rooms, and a beauty salon. A separate gymnasium, formerly an observation lounge, located atop the ship, provides sea views.

SkySea Golden Era
NYR

Size:	Mid-size Ship	Passenger/Crew Ratio (lower beds):	2.0
Tonnage:	71,545	Cabins (total):	907
Lifestyle:	Standard	Size Range (sq ft/m):	168.9–1,514.5/15.7–140.7
Cruise Line:	SkySea Cruises	Cabins (for one person):	0
Former Names:	*Celebrity Century, Century*	Cabins (with private balcony):	386
IMO Number:	9072446	Cabins (wheelchair accessible):	8
Builder:	Meyer Werft (Germany)	Wheelchair accessibility:	Good
Original Cost:	$320 million	Cabin Current:	110 and 220 volts
Entered Service:	Dec 1995/May 2015	Elevators:	9
Registry:	Malta	Casino (gaming tables):	Yes
Length (ft/m):	807.1/246.0	Slot Machines:	Yes
Beam (ft/m):	105.6/32.2	Swimming Pools:	2
Draft (ft/m):	24.6/7.5	Hot Tubs (on deck):	4
Propulsion/Propellers:	diesel (29,250kW)/2	Self-Service Launderette:	No
Passenger Decks:	10	Dedicated Cinema/Seats:	No
Total Crew:	858	Library:	Yes
Passengers (lower beds):	1,814	Onboard currency:	Renminbi
Passenger Space Ratio (lower beds):	39.4		

A fairly modern ship with colorful decor for Chinese cruisers

OVERVIEW. *SkySea Golden Era* is for Chinese-speaking families with children and operates short cruises from Shanghai. A niggle is the overload of annoying announcements.

THE SHIP. The exterior profile is well balanced, despite a squared-off stern. With a decent passenger/space ratio, there is no sense of crowding.

There is a good amount of open deck space, a three-quarter, two-level teakwood promenade deck, and a walking/jogging track atop the ship. The atrium lobby is calm and refreshing, due to its high ceiling, and not at all glitzy. In fact, many of the public rooms have high ceilings, providing a sense of space. Anyone who likes gambling will find a large casino tightly packed with slot machines and gaming tables.

In 2015, the ship underwent an extensive makeover. During the refit, a trampoline at sea and mini-golf were added, together with a trendy ice bar, and many other items designed for active Asian cruisers.

FAMILIES. Children and teens have several playrooms and areas of their own.

ACCOMMODATION. There are numerous different grades. The price depends on the grade, size, and location. The wide variety of cabin types includes family cabins, and cabins for couples, with many different configurations for extended families. All cabins have wood cabinetry, personal safe, minibar/refrigerator, and interactive flat-screen TVs and entertainment systems, and beds have duvets. Suites with private balconies have

Berlitz's Ratings		
	Possible	Achieved
Ship	500	NYR
Accommodation	200	NYR
Food	400	NYR
Service	400	NYR
Entertainment	100	NYR
Cruise Experience	400	NYR
OVERALL SCORE		
NYR points out of 2000		

floor-to-ceiling windows and most have sliding doors.

DINING. A grand staircase connects the upper and lower levels of the two-level Grand Dining Room. Huge windows overlook the stern. The cuisine is almost totally for Chinese tastes. Tables are for two to 10.

Other dining options. Murano, a reservations-only specialty restaurant off the main lobby, is a fine-dining experience that takes about three hours, in a small, intimate setting – ideal for celebrating a birthday or anniversary, with refined service and an extensive wine list.

For casual meals, Islands is a large indoor/outdoor, tray-less self-serve buffet venue; there are four self-service lines, plus two grill-serving stations located adjacent to the swimming pools outdoors. A coffee house is situated to one side of the main lobby, and is an excellent place to meet for coffees, cakes, and pastry items.

ENTERTAINMENT. The Celebrity Theater is the ship's two-level, 1,000-seat showlounge/theatre, with balcony alcoves on two sides. It has a large stage and a split orchestra pit (hydraulic).

SPA/FITNESS. The fitness facility has 9,040 sq ft (840 sq m) of space dedicated to wellbeing and body treatments, all set in a calming environment. It includes a large fitness/exercise area, thalassotherapy pool, and 10 treatment rooms. The spa includes an acupuncture clinic, and a Rasul – a mud and gentle steam bathing room (an excellent facility for couples).

Sovereign
★★★

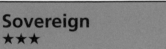

Size:	Large Resort Ship
Tonnage:	73,192
Lifestyle:	Standard
Cruise Line:	Pullmantur Cruises
Former Names:	*Sovereign of the Seas*
IMO Number:	8512281
Builder:	Chantiers de l'Atlantique (France)
Original Cost:	$183.5 million
Entered Service:	Jan 1988/Mar 2009
Registry:	Bahamas
Length (ft/m):	879.9/268.2
Beam (ft/m):	105.9/32.3
Draft (ft/m):	24.9/7.6
Propulsion/Propellers:	diesel (21,844kW)/2
Passenger Decks:	11
Total Crew:	820
Passengers (lower beds):	2,306
Passenger Space Ratio (lower beds):	31.7

Passenger/Crew Ratio (lower beds):	2.8
Cabins (total):	1,153
Size Range (sq ft/m):	118.4–670.0/11.0–62.2
Cabins (for one person):	0
Cabins (with private balcony):	62
Cabins (wheelchair accessible):	6
Wheelchair accessibility:	Fair
Cabin Current:	110 and 220 volts
Elevators:	13
Casino (gaming tables):	Yes
Slot Machines:	Yes
Swimming Pools:	2
Hot Tubs (on deck):	2
Self-Service Launderette:	No
Dedicated Cinema/Seats:	No
Library:	Yes
Onboard currency:	Euros

A busy, dated ship for casual, Spanish-speaking family cruising

OVERVIEW. This ship is best suited to Spanish-speaking families, young couples, and solo travelers seeking a first cruise at an all-inclusive price that even includes drinks. The high-density ship is well run and highly programmed, and is geared to families with children.

THE SHIP. *Sovereign* has a smart profile and nicely rounded lines. The ship, whose hull is painted a deep blue, has a lounge and bar that is wrapped around the blue funnel and provides a stunning view. Open deck space isn't generous, but there's a wide walk-around polished wood promenade deck. The interior layout is unusual in that most of the public rooms are located aft in a stack, like layers on a cake, with the accommodation situated forward.

There's an array of spacious public rooms, including a conference room, library, and card players' room, plus a Monte Carlo Casino. The decor is accented with wood paneling, and some bright color splashes. Children and teens are well catered for, and there's a whole team of youth-activity staff, together with a range of rooms for children and teens. The dress code is very casual. All gratuities and port taxes are included in the cruise fare.

ACCOMMODATION. There are 16 cabin price grades. Some cabins have interconnecting doors, which is useful for families.

Suites. Thirteen suites on Bridge Deck, the largest of which is the Royal Suite, are reasonably large and nicely furnished, with separate living and sleeping spaces.

Berlitz's Ratings

	Possible	Achieved
Ship	500	295
Accommodation	200	119
Food	400	225
Service	400	252
Entertainment	100	58
Cruise Experience	400	242

OVERALL SCORE
1191 points out of 2000

Standard cabins. The standard outside-view and interior cabins are very small, although arched windows and colorful soft furnishings give the illusion of more space. Almost all cabins have twin beds that convert to a queen-size or double-bed configuration. There is little closet and drawer space. All cabins have a private bathroom, with shower, toilet, and washbasin.

DINING. El Guardiana and El Duero, two dining rooms off the Centrum (lobby), have tables for four, six, or eight persons but none for two. Both have two seatings, with table wines included in the fare. An à-la-carte restaurant offers better menus at an extra cost. For casual meals and snacks, the two-level Buffet Panorama is open almost 24 hours a day, although it is usually congested at peak times.

ENTERTAINMENT. The Broadway Showlounge has both main and balcony levels, with banquette seating. On the stage is a video wall with 50 screens. A smaller venue for late-night dancing or chilling out is the Disco Zoom.

SPA/FITNESS. In the Spa del Mar, you'll find a gym with fine ocean views, full of cardiovascular equipment. There's also an aerobics studio, a salon, and sauna, as well as 11 treatment rooms, including one for couples' massages. An outdoor rock-climbing wall, located on the aft of the ship's blue funnel, has several climbing tracks.

Splendour of the Seas
★★★+

Size:	Mid-size Ship	Passenger/Crew Ratio (lower beds):	2.5
Tonnage:	69,130	Cabins (total):	902
Lifestyle:	Standard	Size Range (sq ft/m):	137.7–1,147.4/12.8–106.6
Cruise Line:	Royal Caribbean International	Cabins (for one person):	0
Former Names:	none	Cabins (with private balcony):	355
IMO Number:	9070632	Cabins (wheelchair accessible):	17
Builder:	Chantiers de l'Atlantique (France)	Wheelchair accessibility:	Good
Original Cost:	$325 million	Cabin Current:	110 and 220 volts
Entered Service:	Mar 1996	Elevators:	11
Registry:	Bahamas	Casino (gaming tables):	Yes
Length (ft/m):	867.0/264.2	Slot Machines:	Yes
Beam (ft/m):	105.0/32.0	Swimming Pools:	2 (1 w/sliding glass dome)
Draft (ft/m):	24.5/7.3	Hot Tubs (on deck):	4
Propulsion/Propellers:	diesel (40,200kW)/2	Self-Service Launderette:	No
Passenger Decks:	11	Dedicated Cinema/Seats:	No
Total Crew:	720	Library:	Yes
Passengers (lower beds):	1,804	Onboard currency:	US$
Passenger Space Ratio (lower beds):	38.3		

Try this lively mid-sized ship for family-friendly cruising

OVERVIEW. The ship's originally glitzy interior decor was toned down during a refurbishment in 2011.

THE SHIP. *Splendour of the Seas* has a contemporary profile that looks somewhat unbalanced – although it grows on you – and it does have a nicely tiered stern. The pool deck amidships overhangs the hull to provide an extremely wide deck, originally designed so that the ship could fit into the locks of the Panama Canal. With engines placed amidships, there's little noise and no noticeable vibration, and the ship has an operating speed of up to 24 knots.

New dining venues and lounges, 124 new balconies, remodeled cabins, and some upgraded technology were all part of the 2011 refurbishment, as were finger-touch digital 'wayfinder' screens to help you navigate your way around the ship.

The outside light is brought inside in many places, with more than two acres (8,000 sq m) of glass that provides contact with sea and air. There's a single-level sliding glass roof over the more formal setting of one of two swimming pools, providing a large, multi-activity, all-weather indoor/outdoor area, called the Solarium. The glass roof provides shelter for the Roman-style pool and good health and fitness facilities, and it slides aft to cover the miniature golf course when required – though both can't be covered at the same time.

Inside, two full entertainment decks are sandwiched between five decks full of cabins. A multi-tiered seven-deck-high atrium lobby, the ship's central social

Berlitz's Ratings		
	Possible	Achieved
Ship	500	370
Accommodation	200	140
Food	400	235
Service	400	256
Entertainment	100	75
Cruise Experience	400	270
OVERALL SCORE		
1346 points out of 2000		

point, has live acrobatics within its entertainment-based environment, plus an iconic 'R' Bar. The Centrum connects with a Viking Crown Lounge via glass-walled elevators. The Casino Royale (for gamers and slot-machine lovers), which has mirrored walls and lights flashing everywhere, is really expansive, glitzy, and always busy. The library, outside of which is a bust of Shakespeare, is a nice facility with more than 2,000 books. Ship-wide Wi-Fi is provided, for a fee. The ambience on board is lively, and invites plenty of social interaction.

Niggles include the fact that RCI charges for shuttle buses in some ports of call; the cost of bottled water is high; and receipts show an extra line 'for additional gratuity,' when a gratuity has been added automatically.

The ship will cease operating for Royal Caribbean International and will be transferred to Thomson Cruises (a division of TUI Cruises) in spring 2016. It will be modified to suit British family cruising tastes, and include British-Continental cuisine. Its name will also change to Thomsom Discovery.

FAMILIES. Royal Babies and Tots Nursery is available for young families, as are youth staff and special family-friendly programs.

ACCOMMODATION. There are many different cabin price grades, depending on size and location. All cabins have iPads, flat-screen TVs, a sitting area, and beds that convert to double configuration, and there is ample closet and drawer space, although there's not much space around the bed. Also, the showers could have been better designed. Cabins with balconies have glass railings rather than steel/wood to provide less intrusive sight lines.

The largest accommodation, the Royal Suite, is a fine living space. It is beautifully designed, finely decorated, and has a baby grand piano and whirlpool bathtub. Quiet sitting areas are located adjacent to the best cabins amidships.

Some cabins on Deck 8 have a larger door for wheelchair access in addition to the 17 cabins for the disabled, and the ship is very accessible, with ample ramped areas and sloping decks.

DINING. The King and I dining room has dramatic two-deck-high glass side walls, so many passengers on both levels can see both the ocean and each other in reflection. It would, perhaps, have been even better located at the stern, and it is quite noisy when full – call it atmosphere. When you book, choose one of two seatings, or My Time Dining, which allows you to eat when you want during dining room hours. So, what's the food like? It's similar to what you'd get in a high-class American family restaurant, but with better presentation, table settings, and service.

Other dining options. A Chef's Table offers wine-and-food-paired five-course dinners co-hosted by the executive chef and sommelier – a nice treat, but a hefty cover charge applies.

Chops Grille, added in 2011, is adjacent to the Viking Crown Lounge and features classic premium American steaks and grilled seafood – all cooked to order. There is a cover charge, and it's open for dinner only.

Izumi features pan-Asian cuisine, with items cooked on hot rocks, and a sushi bar (open for lunch and dinner). Individual items have à-la-carte pricing.

For casual meals, there's the Windjammer Café, a self-serve buffet venue (with good forward views, because it's located at the front of the ship). It can get a bit cramped when it's busy, however.

ENTERTAINMENT. The 802-seat 42nd Street Theater is a single-level showlounge with tiered seating levels. The sight lines are good from almost all seats. Strong cabaret acts are also presented here, and the orchestra pit can be raised or lowered as required. Other cabaret acts are featured in the Top Hat Lounge, and these include late-night adult comedy, as well as live music for dancing. A number of other bars and lounges have live music of differing types.

SPA/FITNESS. The Vitality Spa is located on Deck 9, aft of the funnel. It has a fitness center, with a small selection of high-tech muscle-pumping equipment and weights. There is also an aerobics studio, where classes in a variety of keep-fit regimes take place, plus a beauty salon, and a sauna, as well as rooms for such pampering treatments as massages, facials, etc.

While the facilities are small, they are adequate for the short cruises this ship operates. The spa is operated by Steiner Leisure. For the more sporting, there is a rock-climbing wall, with several separate climbing tracks – outdoors on the aft wall of the funnel. For golfers, there's 18-hole mini-golf, a 6,000-sq-ft (557-sq-m) miniature course, and lighting to enable play at night; the holes are 155 to 230 sq ft (14 to 21 sq m).

Star Breeze
★★★★+

Size:	Boutique Ship		Passenger/Crew Ratio (lower beds):	1.3
Tonnage:	9,975		Cabins (total):	106
Lifestyle:	Luxury		Size Range (sq ft/m):	277.0–575.0/25.7–53.4
Cruise Line:	Windstar Cruises		Cabins (for one person):	0
Former Names:	Seabourn Spirit		Cabins (with private balcony):	6
IMO Number:	8807997		Cabins (wheelchair accessible):	4
Builder:	Seebeckwerft (Germany)		Wheelchair accessibility:	None
Original Cost:	$50 million		Cabin Current:	110 and 220 volts
Entered Service:	Nov 1989/Apr 2015		Elevators:	3
Registry:	Bahamas		Casino (gaming tables):	Yes
Length (ft/m):	439.9/134.1		Slot Machines:	Yes
Beam (ft/m):	62.9/19.2		Swimming Pools:	1
Draft (ft/m):	16.8/5.1		Hot Tubs (on deck):	3
Propulsion/Propellers:	diesel (5,355kW)/2		Self-Service Launderette:	Yes
Passenger Decks:	6		Dedicated Cinema/Seats:	No
Total Crew:	160		Library:	Yes
Passengers (lower beds):	212		Onboard currency:	US$
Passenger Space Ratio (lower beds):	47.0			

This is a contemporary, handy-sized ship for mature-age cruisers

OVERVIEW. The intimate Star Breeze is best suited to sophisticated and well-traveled couples – typically over 50, but possibly younger – looking for a small ship with excellent food and fine European-style service. The ship's big advantage is being able to cruise where large cruise ships can't, thanks to its ocean-yacht size. You sail with only 100 other couples, creating a sense of intimate camaraderie.

Berlitz's Ratings

	Possible	Achieved
Ship	500	408
Accommodation	200	170
Food	400	327
Service	400	336
Entertainment	100	77
Cruise Experience	400	325
OVERALL SCORE		
1643 points out of 2000		

THE SHIP. This pleasantly appointed cruise vessel has sleek exterior styling, handsome profile with swept-back, rounded lines, and is an identical twin to *Star Pride*. It has two fine mahogany water taxis for use as shore tenders. An aft water sports platform and marina can be used in suitably calm warm-water areas. Water sports facilities include a small, enclosed 'dip' pool, sea kayaks, snorkel equipment, windsurfers, waterski boat, and Zodiac inflatable boats.

The sunloungers are now a steel mesh design. There is no walk-around promenade deck outdoors. There is only one dryer in the self-service launderette. Non-American passengers should note that almost all entertainment and activities are geared towards North American tastes, despite the increasingly international passenger mix.

A wide central passageway divides the port and starboard accommodation. Inviting, sumptuous public areas have warm colors. Fine-interior fixtures, fittings, artwork, and fabric combine to present an outstanding, elegant decor. For a small ship, there's wide range of public rooms. These include a main lounge that stages small cabaret shows, a nightclub, an observation lounge with bar, large, deep armchairs, and a cigar-smoking area complete with cabinet, cigar humidor, and small selection of good cigars. There is a small business center, small meeting room, and a small casino with roulette and blackjack tables, plus a few slot machines.

Not for the budget-minded, this ship is for those desiring supremely elegant, stylish, small-ship surroundings, but is perhaps rather small for long voyages in open waters.

Star Breeze provides a fine level of personal service and an utterly civilized cruise. All drinks except premium brands and connoisseur wines are included, as are gratuities, open-seating dining, and use of water sports equipment. Port charges and insurance are not included.

ACCOMMODATION. This is spread over three decks, with nine price categories. The all-outside cabins (called suites in brochure-speak) are comfortably large and beautifully equipped with everything one could reasonably need. Electric blackout blinds are provided for the large windows in addition to curtains. All cabinetry is made of blond woods, with softly rounded edges, and cabin doors are neatly angled away from the passageway.

All the suites have a sleeping area, with European duvets and Frette linens as standard. A separate lounge area has a Bose Wave audio unit, DVD player and flat-screen TV, vanity desk with hairdryer and personalized stationery, world atlas, minibar, and re-frigerator (stocked with soft drinks and two bottles of your favorite liquor when you embark). There's a large walk-in closet that illuminates automatically when you open the door, wooden hangers, electronic personal safe, umbrella, and wall-mounted clock and barometer.

Marble-clad bathrooms have one or two washba-sins, depending on the accommodation grade, a de-cent but not full-size tub (four suites have a shower enclosure only – no tub), plenty of storage areas, thick cotton towels, plush terrycloth bathrobe, de-signer soaps, and personal amenities.

In 2001, Seabourn added 36 French balconies to suites on two out of three accommodation decks. These are not balconies in the true sense of the word, but they do have two doors that open wide onto a tiny teakwood balcony that is just 10.6ins (27cm) wide. The balconies allow you to have fresh sea air, together with some salt spray.

Course-by-course in-cabin dining is available during dinner hours, and the cocktail table can be raised to form a dining table. There is 24-hour room service. Four Owner's Suites (King Haakon/King Magnus, each measuring 530 sq ft/49 sq m, and Amundsen/Nansen, each 575 sq ft/53 sq m), and two Classic Suites (King Harald/King Olav), each 400 sq ft (37 sq m), offer superb, private living spaces. Each has a walk-in closet, second closet, and full bathroom plus a guest toilet with washbasin. There is a fully secluded forward- or side-facing balcony, with sunloungers and wooden drinks table. The living area has ample bookshelf space including a complete edition of *Encyclopaedia Britannica*, large refrigerator/drinks cabinet, televi-sion, and DVD player, plus a second TV set in the bedroom. All windows, as well as the door to the balcony, have manually operated blackout blinds, and a complete blackout is possible in both bed-room and living room.

DINING. The AmphorA Restaurant is a part-marble, part-carpeted dining room with portholes and rest-ful decor. Open-seating dining means that you can dine when you want, with whom you wish.

The menus are creative and well balanced, with a wide selection of foods and regional cuisine. The food is artfully presented, with many items cooked to order. There is always a good selection of fruit and cheese.

Each day, basic table wine is included for lunch and dinner, but the decent bottles cost extra. The wine list is quite extensive, with prices ranging from moderate to high; many of the wines come from the smaller, more exclusive vineyards. The European din-ing room staff provides fine, unhurried service.

In addition, breakfasts and lunch buffets and cas-ual, themed candlelight dinners, including a '2' tast-ing menu, can be taken in the popular Veranda Café adjacent to the swimming pool.

The Star Bar provides an above-poolside setting for candlelit dining. It specializes in sizzling steaks and seafood.

ENTERTAINMENT. The Amundsen Lounge has a sloping floor that provides good sight lines from almost all seats. The shows are of limited scope, as dinner is usually the main event. You can, however, expect to see the occasional cabaret act. Singers also tend to do mini-cabaret performances in The Club, one deck above the showlounge, the gathering place for late-night drinkers.

SPA/FITNESS. The Spa is a small but well-equipped health spa/fitness center. It has sauna and steam rooms (separate facilities for men and wom-en), an equipment-packed gymnasium – but the ceil-ing height is low – and a beauty salon.

The spa is staffed and operated by concession Elemis by Steiner. Treatment prices equal those in an expensive land-based spa. The beauty salon has hair-beautifying treatments and conditioning.

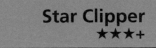

Star Clipper
★★★+

Size:	Boutique Ship	Passenger/Crew Ratio (lower beds):	2.3
Tonnage:	2,298	Cabins (total):	85
Lifestyle:	Standard	Size Range (sq ft/m):	95.0–225.0/8.8–21.0
Cruise Line:	Star Clippers	Cabins (for one person):	0
Former Names:	none	Cabins (with private balcony):	0
IMO Number:	9247807	Cabins (wheelchair accessible):	0
Builder:	Scheepswerven van Langerbrugge (Belgium)	Wheelchair accessibility:	None
Original Cost:	$30 million	Cabin Current:	110 volts
Entered Service:	May 1992	Elevators:	0
Registry:	Luxembourg	Casino (gaming tables):	No
Length (ft/m):	378.9/115.5	Slot Machines:	No
Beam (ft/m):	49.2/15.0	Swimming Pools:	2
Draft (ft/m):	17.7/5.6	Hot Tubs (on deck):	0
Propulsion/Propellers:	sail power + diesel (1,030kW)/1	Self-Service Launderette:	No
Passenger Decks:	4	Dedicated Cinema/Seats:	No
Total Crew:	72	Library:	Yes
Passengers (lower beds):	170	Onboard currency:	Euros
Passenger Space Ratio (lower beds):	13.5		

A real tall ship experience to put wind in your sails

OVERVIEW. This tall ship suits couples and solo travelers who would probably never even consider a 'normal' cruise ship, but who enjoy sailing and the thrill of ocean and wind, with everything packaged to include accommodation, decent food, like-minded companions, interesting destinations, and an almost unstructured lifestyle.

THE SHIP. *Star Clipper* is one of a pair of almost identical tall ships – its sister ship is *Star Flyer*, the first clipper sailing ship to be built for 140 years and the first commercial sailing vessel to cross the North Atlantic in 90 years. It is, first and foremost, a sailing vessel with cruise accommodation that evokes memories of the 19th-century clipper sailing ships. This is an accurate four-mast, barkentine-rigged schooner with graceful lines, a finely shaped hull and masts that are 206ft (63m) tall. Some amenities found aboard large cruise vessels are provided, such as air conditioning, cashless cruising, occasional live music, a small shop, and two pools to 'dip' in.

Breathtaking when under full sail, the ship displays excellent sea manners – heeling is kept to a very comfortable 6 degrees. This working sailing ship relies on the wind about 80 percent of the time. During a typical cruise, you may be able to climb the main mast to a platform 75ft (25m) above the sea and help with the ropes and sails at appropriate times – this could be an unnerving experience, if you're not used to heights, but it is exhilarating when the ship is moving under sail. One really neat chill-out pleasure is to lie in the netting at the front of the ship's bows, watching the

Berlitz's Ratings		
	Possible	Achieved
Ship	500	376
Accommodation	200	134
Food	400	249
Service	400	271
Entertainment	100	78
Cruise Experience	400	286
OVERALL SCORE		
1394 points out of 2000		

bow wake as it streams along the ship's sides.

A diesel engine is used as the main propulsion engine when the ship is not under sail (in poor wind conditions), and two generators supply electrical power and help desalinate 40 or so tons of seawater each day for shipboard needs. The crew performs almost every task, including hoisting, trimming, winching, and repairing the sails, helped by electric winches. Water sports facilities include a water-ski boat, sunfish, scuba and snorkel equipment, and eight Zodiac inflatables. Sports directors provide basic dive instruction for a fee.

Inside the vessel, classic Edwardian nautical decor throughout is clean, warm, intimate, and inviting. The paneled library has a fireplace and comfortable chairs. There are no lines and no hassle. Sailing a Square Rigger and other nautical classes are a part of every cruise, as is stargazing at night.

Depending on the itinerary and region, passengers may gather for 'captain's storytime,' normally held on an open deck area adjacent to the bridge, or in the bar – which, incidentally, has a collection of single malt whiskies. The captain may explain sailing maneuvers when changing the rigging or directing the ship as it sails into port, and note the important events of the day.

The sail-ship promotes total informality and provides a carefree sailing experience in an unstructured and relaxed setting at a fair price. Take minimal clothing: short-sleeved shirts and shorts for men, shorts and tops for women are the order of the day (smart casual at night). No jackets, ties, high-heeled shoes, cocktail dresses, or formal wear are needed. Take flat shoes because there are lots of ropes and sailing rig to negotiate on deck, not to mention the high thresholds to climb over and steps to negotiate – this is, after all a tall ship, not a cruise ship. The deck crew consists of real sailors, brought up with yachts and tall ships – most wouldn't set foot aboard a 'normal' cruise ship.

The steps of the internal stairways are short and steep, as in all sailing vessels, and so this ship cannot be recommended for anyone with walking disabilities. Also, there is no doctor on board, although there is a nurse.

For yachting enthusiasts, sailing aboard *Star Clipper* is like finding themselves in heaven, as there is plenty of sailing during a typical one-week cruise. The whole experience evokes the feeling of sailing aboard some famous private yacht, and even the most jaded passenger should enjoy the feel of the wind and sea close at hand. Just don't expect fine food to go with what is decidedly a fine sailing experience – which is what *Star Clipper* is all about. Note that a 12.5 percent gratuity is added to all beverage purchases.

For the nautically minded, the sailing rig consists of 16 manually furled sails, measuring a billowing 36,221 sq ft (3,365 sq m). These include: fore staysail, inner jib, outer jib, flying jib, fore course, lower topsail, upper topsail, lower topgallant, upper topgallant, main staysail, upper main staysail, mizzen staysail, main fisherman, jigger staysail, mizzen fisherman, and spanker. The square sails are furled electronically by custom-made winches.

ACCOMMODATION. There are six cabin price grades plus one Owner's Suite. Generally, the higher the deck, the more expensive a cabin. The cabins are quite well equipped and comfortable; they have rosewood-trimmed cabinetry and wall-to-wall carpeting, two-channel audio, color TV and DVD player, personal safe, and full-length mirrors. The bathrooms are very compact but practical units, and have gray marble tiling, glazed rosewood toiletries cabinet and paneling, some under-shelf storage space, washbasin, shower stall, and toilet. There is no 'lip' to prevent water from the shower from moving over the bathroom floor.

Individual European 100 percent individual cotton duvets are provided. There is no cabin food or beverage service.

The deluxe cabins (called 'deck cabins') are larger, and additional features include a full-size Jacuzzi tub or corner tub, flat-screen television and DVD player, and minibar/refrigerator. However, these cabins are subject to noise pollution from the same-deck Tropical Bar's music at night (typically until midnight), from the electric winches during sail maneuvers, and from noisy walkabout exercisers in the early morning.

The cabins in the lowest price grade are interior cabins with upper and lower berths, and not two lower beds – so someone will need to be agile to climb a ladder to the upper berth. A handful of cabins have a third, upper Pullman-style berth – good for families with children, but closet and drawer space will be at a premium with three persons in a cabin. Luggage can be stored under the bed, where extra-large.

DINING. The dining room is cozy and quite attractive. There are self-serve buffet breakfasts and lunches, together with a mix of buffet and à-la-carte dinners, generally with a choice of three entrées, in an open-seating environment.

The seating, mostly at tables of six, adjacent to a porthole or inboard, makes it difficult for waiters to serve properly – food is passed along the tables that occupy a porthole position. However, you can dine with whomever you wish, and this is supposed to be a casual experience, after all.

While cuisine aboard the ship is perhaps less than the advertised 'gourmet' excellence as far as presentation and choice are concerned, it is fairly creative – and there's plenty of it. Also, one has to take into account the small galley. Passenger niggles include repetitious breakfasts and lunchtime salad items, because lack of space prevents more choices. But most passengers are happy with the dinners, which tend to be good, although there is a lack of green vegetables. There's a good choice of bread rolls, pastry items, and fruit.

Tea and coffee is available 24 hours a day in the lounge – mugs, tea cups, and saucers are provided. There is no cabin food service.

ENTERTAINMENT. There are no shows as such, except for an occasional local folklore show from ashore, nor are any expected by passengers aboard a tall ship such as this. Live music is typically provided by a solo lounge pianist/singer. Otherwise, dinner is the main evening event, as well as 'captain's storytime,' recapping the day's events, and conversation with fellow passengers.

During the day, when the ship is sailing, passengers can learn about the sails and their repair, and the captain or chief officer will give briefings as the sails are being furled and unfurled. The closest this tall ship comes to any kind of 'show' is perhaps one provided by members of the crew, plus a few traditional sea shanties.

SPA/FITNESS. There are no fitness facilities, or beauty salon, although a masseuse provides Oriental massage. For recreation, the ship does have a water sports program. Facilities include kayaks, a water-ski boat, sunfish, scuba and snorkel equipment, and eight Zodiac inflatable craft. The use of scuba facilities costs extra.

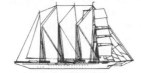

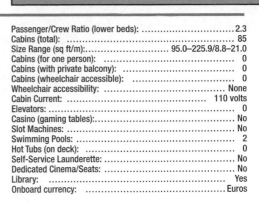

Star Flyer
★★★+

Size:	Boutique Ship	Passenger/Crew Ratio (lower beds):	2.3
Tonnage:	2,298	Cabins (total):	85
Lifestyle:	Standard	Size Range (sq ft/m):	95.0–225.9/8.8–21.0
Cruise Line:	Star Clippers	Cabins (for one person):	0
Former Names:	none	Cabins (with private balcony):	0
IMO Number:	8915433	Cabins (wheelchair accessible):	0
Builder:	Sheepswerven van Langerbrugge (Belgium)	Wheelchair accessibility:	None
Original Cost:	$25 million	Cabin Current:	110 volts
Entered Service:	Jul 1991	Elevators:	0
Registry:	Luxembourg	Casino (gaming tables):	No
Length (ft/m):	378.9/115.5	Slot Machines:	No
Beam (ft/m):	49.2/15.0	Swimming Pools:	2
Draft (ft/m):	17.7/5.6	Hot Tubs (on deck):	0
Propulsion/Propellers:	sail power + diesel (1,030kW)/1	Self-Service Launderette:	No
Passenger Decks:	4	Dedicated Cinema/Seats:	No
Total Crew:	72	Library:	Yes
Passengers (lower beds):	170	Onboard currency:	Euros
Passenger Space Ratio (lower beds):	13.5		

This proper sailing ship provides an antidote to cruise ships

OVERVIEW. The first clipper sailing ship to be built for 140 years, *Star Flyer* became the first commercial sailing vessel in 90 years to cross the North Atlantic. It suits those who would never consider a 'normal' cruise ship.

THE SHIP. *Star Flyer* is one of a pair of almost identical tall ships – its sister ship is *Star Clipper*. It is, first and foremost, a sailing vessel with cruise accommodation that evokes memories of the 19th-century clipper sailing ships. This is an accurate four-mast, barkentine-rigged schooner with graceful lines, a finely shaped hull, masts that are 206ft (63m) tall, and 16 manually furled sails totaling 36,221 sq ft (3,365 sq m). Some amenities found aboard large cruise vessels are provided, such as air conditioning, cashless cruising, live music, a small shop, and two pools to 'dip' in.

Breathtaking when under full sail, the ship displays excellent sea manners and relies on the wind about 80 percent of the time, and heeling is kept to a very comfortable 6 degrees.

During the cruise, you'll be able to climb the main mast to a platform 75ft (25m) above the sea and help with the ropes and sails at appropriate times. One really neat chill-out pleasure is to lie in the netting at the front of the ship's bows.

A diesel engine is used as the main propulsion engine when the ship is not under sail (in poor wind conditions), and two generators supply electrical power and help desalinate 40 or so tons of seawater each day for shipboard needs. Engine room visits

Berlitz's Ratings		
	Possible	Achieved
Ship	500	376
Accommodation	200	134
Food	400	249
Service	400	271
Entertainment	100	78
Cruise Experience	400	287
OVERALL SCORE		
1395 points out of 2000		

may be offered for anyone interested. Water sports facilities include a water-ski boat, sunfish, scuba and snorkel equipment, and eight Zodiac inflatables. Sports directors provide basic dive instruction for a fee.

Inside the vessel, classic Edwardian nautical decor throughout is clean, warm, intimate, and inviting. The paneled library has a fireplace and comfortable chairs. There are no lines and no hassle. Sailing a Square Rigger and other nautical classes are a part of every cruise, as is stargazing at night.

Depending on the itinerary and region, passengers may gather for 'captain's storytime,' normally held on an open deck area adjacent to the bridge, or in the bar – which, incidentally, has a collection of single malt whiskies. The captain may explain sailing maneuvers when changing the rigging or directing the ship as it sails into port, and notes the important events of the day.

The sail-ship promotes total informality and provides a carefree sailing experience in a totally unstructured and relaxed setting at a reasonable price. Take minimal clothing: short-sleeved shirts and shorts for men, shorts and tops for women are the order of the day (smart casual at night). No jackets, ties, high-heeled shoes, cocktail dresses, or formal wear are needed. Take flat shoes because there are lots of ropes and sailing rig to negotiate on deck, not to mention the high thresholds to climb over and steps to negotiate – this is, after all a tall ship, not a cruise ship.

The steps of the internal stairways are short and steep, as in all sailing vessels, and so this ship cannot be recommended for anyone with walking disabilities. Also, there is no doctor on board, although there is a nurse.

For yachting enthusiasts, sailing aboard *Star Flyer* is like finding themselves in heaven, as there is plenty of sailing during a typical one-week cruise. The whole experience evokes the feeling of sailing aboard some famous private yacht, and even the most jaded passenger should enjoy the feel of the wind and sea close at hand. Just don't expect fine food to go with what is decidedly a fine sailing experience – which is what *Star Flyer* is all about. Note that a 12.5 percent gratuity is added to all beverage purchases.

For the nautically minded, the sailing rig consists of 16 manually furled sails, measuring a billowing 36,221 sq ft (3,365 sq m). These include: fore staysail, inner jib, outer jib, flying jib, fore course, lower topsail, upper topsail, lower topgallant, upper topgallant, main staysail, upper main staysail, mizzen staysail, main fisherman, jigger staysail, mizzen fisherman, and spanker. The square sails are furled electronically by custom-made winches.

ACCOMMODATION. There are six cabin price grades plus one Owner's Suite. Generally, the higher the deck, the more expensive a cabin. The cabins are quite well equipped and comfortable; they have rosewood-trimmed cabinetry and wall-to-wall carpeting, two-channel audio, color TV and DVD player, personal safe, and full-length mirrors. The bathrooms are very compact but practical units, and have gray marble tiling, glazed rosewood toiletries cabinet and paneling, some under-shelf storage space, washbasin, shower stall, and toilet. There is no 'lip' to prevent water from the shower from moving over the bathroom floor.

Individual European 100 percent individual cotton duvets are provided. There is no cabin food or beverage service.

The deluxe cabins (called 'deck cabins') are larger, and additional features include a full-size Jacuzzi tub or corner tub, flat-screen television and DVD player, and minibar/refrigerator. However, these cabins are subject to noise pollution from the same-deck Tropical Bar's music at night (typically until midnight), from the electric winches during sail maneuvers, and from noisy walkabout exercisers in the early morning. The cabins in the lowest price grade are interior cabins with upper and lower berths, and not two lower beds – so someone will need to be agile to climb a ladder to the upper berth. A handful of cabins have a third, upper Pullman-style berth, which is good for families with children, although closet and drawer space will be at a premium with three people in a cabin.

DINING. The dining room is quite attractive, and has lots of wood and brass accenting and nautical decor. There are self-serve buffet breakfasts and lunches, together with a mix of buffet and à-la-carte dinners, generally with a choice of three entrées, in an open-seating environment.

The seating is mostly at tables of six, and either adjacent to a porthole or inboard; it makes it difficult for waiters to serve properly – so the food is passed along the tables that occupy a porthole position. However, you can dine with whomever you wish, and this is supposed to be a casual experience, after all.

While cuisine aboard the ship is perhaps less than the advertised 'gourmet' excellence as far as presentation and choice are concerned, it is fairly creative – and there's plenty of it. Also, one has to take into account the small galley. Passenger niggles include repetitious breakfasts and lunchtime salad items, because lack of space prevents more choices. But most passengers are happy with the dinners, which tend to be good, although there is a lack of green vegetables. There's a good choice of bread rolls, pastry items, and fruit.

Tea and coffee is available 24 hours a day in the lounge – mugs, tea cups, and saucers are provided. There is no cabin food service.

ENTERTAINMENT. There are no shows as such, except for an occasional local folklore show from ashore, nor are any expected by passengers aboard a tall ship such as this. Live music is typically provided by a solo lounge pianist/singer. Otherwise, dinner is the main evening event, as well as 'captain's storytime,' recapping the day's events, and conversation with fellow passengers.

During the day, when the ship is sailing, passengers can learn about the sails and their repair, and the captain or chief officer will give briefings, as the sails are being furled and unfurled. The closest this tall ship comes to any kind of 'show' is perhaps one provided by members of the crew, plus a few traditional sea shanties.

SPA/FITNESS. There are no fitness facilities, or beauty salon, although a masseuse provides Oriental massage. For recreation, the ship has a water-sports program. Facilities include kayaks, a water-ski boat, scuba and snorkel equipment, and eight Zodiac inflatable craft. The use of scuba facilities costs extra.

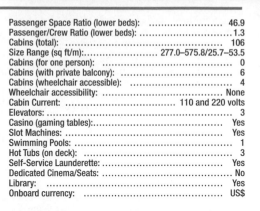

Star Legend
★★★★+

Size:	Boutique Ship
Tonnage:	9,961
Lifestyle:	Luxury
Cruise Line:	Windstar Cruises
Former Names:	Seabourn Legend, Queen Odyssey, Royal Viking Queen
IMO Number:	9008598
Builder:	Schichau Seebeckwerft (Germany)
Original Cost:	$87 million
Entered Service:	Mar 1992/May 2015
Registry:	Bahamas
Length (ft/m):	442.9/135.0
Beam (ft/m):	62.9/19.2
Draft (ft/m):	16.4/5.0
Propulsion/Propellers:	diesel (7,280kW)/2
Passenger Decks:	6
Total Crew:	160
Passengers (lower beds):	212
Passenger Space Ratio (lower beds):	46.9
Passenger/Crew Ratio (lower beds):	1.3
Cabins (total):	106
Size Range (sq ft/m):	277.0–575.8/25.7–53.5
Cabins (for one person):	0
Cabins (with private balcony):	6
Cabins (wheelchair accessible):	4
Wheelchair accessibility:	None
Cabin Current:	110 and 220 volts
Elevators:	3
Casino (gaming tables):	Yes
Slot Machines:	Yes
Swimming Pools:	1
Hot Tubs (on deck):	3
Self-Service Launderette:	Yes
Dedicated Cinema/Seats:	No
Library:	Yes
Onboard currency:	US$

A small, cozy, elegant ship for mature-age cruisers

OVERVIEW. *Star Legend* can cruise to places where large cruise ships can't, thanks to its ocean-yacht size. For a grand, small-ship vacation in fine surroundings, with just over 100 other couples as neighbors and excellent food that approaches gourmet standards, it's hard to beat. It is best suited to sophisticated, well-traveled couples, typically over 50, but possibly younger.

THE SHIP. *Star Legend* is a contemporary gem of a ship with a handsome profile, almost identical in looks and size to sisters *Star Breeze* and *Star Pride*, but younger and built to a higher standard, with streamline 'decorator' bars made by Mercedes-Benz located along the side of the upper superstructure and a slightly different swept-over funnel design. There is no walk-around promenade deck outdoors.

The ship has two fine mahogany water taxis for use as shore tenders. An aft water sports platform and marina can be used in suitably calm warm-water areas. Water sports facilities include a small, enclosed 'dip' pool, sea kayaks, snorkel equipment, windsurfers, water-ski boat, and Zodiac inflatable boats.

Inside, a wide central passageway divides port and starboard side accommodation. High-quality interior fixtures, fittings, and fabrics are combined in its sumptuous public areas to present an outstanding, elegant decor, with warm color combinations and some fine artwork. There is no glitz anywhere. The dress code, relaxed by day, is a little more formal at night.

All drinks, except premium brands and connoisseur wines, are included in the fare. Use of water sports

Berlitz's Ratings		
	Possible	Achieved
Ship	500	413
Accommodation	200	171
Food	400	327
Service	400	341
Entertainment	100	77
Cruise Experience	400	325
OVERALL SCORE		
1654 points out of 2000		

equipment is complimentary.

Niggles? The range of cigars offered is limited. The Club suffers from over-amplified music. Non-American passengers should note that almost all entertainment and activities are geared towards American tastes.

ACCOMMODATION. This is spread over three decks, and there are several price categories. All suites are comfortably large and comprehensively equipped. They are, for example, larger than those aboard the smaller *SeaDream I* and *SeaDream II*, but then the ship is also larger, with almost twice as many passengers.

All suites have a sleeping area with European duvets and Frette linens. A separate lounge area has a Bose Wave radio/CD unit, DVD player and flat-screen TV, vanity desk with hairdyer and personalized stationery, world atlas, minibar and refrigerator stocked with soft drinks and two bottles of your favorite liquor at embarkation, a large walk-in closet illuminated automatically when you open the door, digital personal safe, and wall-mounted clock and barometer. A full passenger list is provided – a rarity today – as are a fresh fruit basket, which is replenished daily, and flowers.

Marble-clad bathrooms have one or two washbasins, depending on accommodation grade, a decent but not full-size tub (four suites have a shower enclosure only – no bathtub), plenty of storage areas, thick cotton towels, plush terrycloth bathrobe, and designer soaps.

In 2001, 36 French (or 'Juliet') balconies were added to suites on two out of three accommodation decks. These are not balconies in the true sense, but have two doors that open wide onto a tiny teakwood balcony that is just 10.6ins (27cm) deep – just enough for toes. The balconies do allow you to have fresh sea air, however, together with some salt spray.

Four Owner's Suites (Ibsen/Grieg, each 530 sq ft/49 sq m, and Eriksson/Heyerdahl, each 575 sq ft/53 sq m), and two Classic Suites (Queen Maud/Queen Sonja, each 400 sq ft/37 sq m) are superb, private living spaces. Each has a walk-in closet, second closet, full bathroom plus a guest toilet with washbasin. There is a fully secluded forward- or side-facing balcony, with sun lounge chairs and wooden drinks table (Ibsen and Grieg don't have balconies). The living area has ample bookshelf space, including a complete edition of *Encyclopaedia Britannica*, large refrigerator/drinks cabinet, television and DVD player, plus a second TV set in the bedroom. All windows, as well as the door to the balcony, have manually operated blackout blinds, and a complete blackout is possible in both bedroom and living room.

DINING. The AmphorA Restaurant is a part-marble, part-carpeted dining room that has portholes and elegant decor. Open-seating dining means that you can dine when you want, with whom you wish.

The menus are creative and well balanced, with a wide selection of foods, including regional dishes.

The food is artfully presented, with many items cooked to order. The selection of fruit and cheese is good.

Each day, basic table wine is included for lunch and dinner, but the decent ones cost extra. The wine list is quite extensive, with prices ranging from moderate to high; many of the wines come from the smaller, more exclusive vineyards.

Breakfasts, lunch buffets, and casual, themed candlelight dinners can be taken in the popular Veranda Café, adjacent to the swimming pool, instead of in the dining room. The Star Bar provides an above-poolside setting complete with candlelit dining and specializing in steaks and seafood.

ENTERTAINMENT. The King Olaf Lounge is the venue for shows, cabaret acts, lectures, and most social functions. It has a sloping floor that provides good sight lines from just about every seat. This is a small, upscale ship, so the shows are of limited scope, because dinner is almost always the main event. You can, however, expect to see the occasional cabaret act.

Singers also tend to do mini-cabaret performances in The Club, one deck above the showlounge.

SPA/FITNESS. The Spa is a small, but well-equipped health spa/fitness center, located just aft of the navigation bridge. It provides sauna and steam rooms with separate facilities for men and women, an integral changing room, and a beauty salon.

Star Pride
★★★★+

Size:	Boutique Ship
Tonnage:	9,975
Lifestyle:	Luxury
Cruise Line:	Windstar Cruises
Former Names:	*Seabourn Pride*
IMO Number:	8797343
Builder:	Seebeckwerft (Germany)
Original Cost:	$50 million
Entered Service:	Dec 1988/May 2014
Registry:	Bahamas
Length (ft/m):	439.9/134.1
Beam (ft/m):	62.9/19.2
Draft (ft/m):	16.8/5.1
Propulsion/Propellers:	diesel (5,355kW)/2
Passenger Decks:	6
Total Crew:	160
Passengers (lower beds):	212
Passenger Space Ratio (lower beds):	47.09
Passenger/Crew Ratio (lower beds):	1.3
Cabins (total):	106
Size Range (sq ft/m):	277.0-575.0/25.7-53.4
Cabins (for one person):	0
Cabins (with private balcony):	6
Cabins (wheelchair accessible):	4
Wheelchair accessibility:	None
Cabin Current:	110 and 220 volts
Elevators:	3
Casino (gaming tables):	Yes
Slot Machines:	Yes
Swimming Pools:	1
Hot Tubs (on deck):	3
Self-Service Launderette:	Yes
Dedicated Cinema/Seats:	No
Library:	Yes
Onboard currency:	US$

A small, inclusive ship for compact, stylish cruising

OVERVIEW. *Star Pride* is best for sophisticated, well-traveled couples seeking an informal small ship experience. The ship's big advantage is being able to cruise where large cruise ships can't, thanks to its ocean-yacht size. You sail with only 210 others, creating a sense of intimate camaraderie.

THE SHIP. This pleasantly appointed, intimate cruise ship has sleek exterior styling, a handsome profile with swept-back, rounded lines, and is an identical twin to *Star Breeze*. It has two fine mahogany water taxis for use as shore tenders. An aft water sports platform and marina can be used in suitably calm warm-water areas. Water sports facilities include a small, enclosed 'dip' pool, sea kayaks, snorkel equipment, windsurfers, water-ski boat, and Zodiac inflatable boats.

There is no walk-around promenade deck outdoors. There is only one dryer in the self-service launderette. A wide central passageway divides the port and starboard accommodation. Inviting, sumptuous public areas have warm colors. Fine-quality interior fixtures, fittings, artwork, and fabric combine to present an outstanding, elegant, contemporary decor. For a small ship, there's a wide range of public rooms, all updated by new owner Windstar Cruises. These include a main lounge that stages small cabaret shows, a Compass Rose nightclub, The Yacht Club (observation lounge-cum-lifestyle lounge with coffee bar), and cozy armchairs. There is a small business center, a

Berlitz's Ratings	Possible	Achieved
Ship	500	408
Accommodation	200	170
Food	400	327
Service	400	335
Entertainment	100	77
Cruise Experience	400	324
OVERALL SCORE		
1641 points out of 2000		

small meeting room, and a small casino with roulette and blackjack tables, plus a few slot machines.

This ship is for those desiring elegant, stylish, but contemporary and informal boutique-ship surroundings, but it is rather small for long voyages in open waters.

Star Pride provides a fine level of service in a contemporary setting. All drinks except premium brands and connoisseur wines are included, as is open-seating dining, and the use of water sports equipment.

The ship was acquired by Xanterra Parks & Resorts, parent company of Windstar Cruises, and transferred in May 2014. Two sister ships *Star Breeze and Star Legend* joined the fleet in 2015.

ACCOMMODATION. This is spread over three decks, with several different price categories. The all-outside cabins (called suites in brochure-speak) are comfortably large and beautifully equipped with everything one could reasonably need. Electric blackout blinds are provided for the large windows in addition to curtains. All cabinetry is made of blond woods, with softly rounded edges, and cabin doors are neatly angled away from the passageway.

All suites have a sleeping area, with European duvets as standard. A separate lounge area has a Bose Wave audio unit, flat-screen TV, vanity desk with hairdryer, world atlas, minibar, and refrigerator. A large walk-in closet is illuminated automatically when you open the door; wooden hangers, electronic personal safe, umbrella, and wall-mounted clock and barometer are also provided. The decor is contemporary, but warm, in blues and beiges.

Marble-clad bathrooms have one or two washbasins, depending on the accommodation grade, a decent, but not full-size, tub (four suites have a shower enclosure only – no tub), plenty of storage areas, 100 percent cotton towels, bathrobe, and choice of personal amenities.

On two out of three accommodation decks, some 36 suites have a French balcony. These are not balconies in the true sense of the word, but they do have two doors that open wide onto a tiny teakwood balcony that is 10.6ins (27cm) wide (just enough for your feet). The balconies allow you to have fresh sea air, and salt spray.

Four Owner's Suites, each measuring between 530 sq ft (49 sq m) and 575 sq ft (53 sq m), and two Classic Suites, each 400 sq ft (37 sq m), offer superb, private living spaces. Each is named after a Windstar destination, for example, the Bora-Bora Suite. Each has a walk-in closet, second closet, full bathroom plus a guest toilet with washbasin. There is a fully secluded forward- or side-facing balcony, with sun-loungers and wooden drinks table. The living area has ample bookshelf space including a complete edition of *Encyclopaedia Britannica*, large refrigerator/drinks cabinet, main TV, plus a second TV set in the bedroom. All windows, as well as the door to the balcony, have manually operated blackout blinds, and a complete blackout is possible in both bedroom and living room.

DINING. The AmphorA Restaurant (whose name is derived from a vessel or container) is the main dining room; it has portholes and restful decor. The silverware is by Robbe & Berking. Open-seating dining means that you can dine when you want, with whom you wish.

The menus are creative and nicely balanced, with a good selection of contemporary cuisine and regional foods.

Each day, basic table wine is included for lunch and dinner, but the decent bottles of wine cost extra. The wine list is very good, with prices ranging from moderate to high; many of the wines come from the smaller, more exclusive vineyards.

In addition, relaxed breakfasts and lunch buffets and themed candlelight dinners can be taken in the Veranda/Candles Grill at the aft of the ship.

The Star Bar provides an above-poolside setting for candlelit dining. It specializes in sizzling steaks and seafood.

ENTERTAINMENT. The Magellan Lounge has a sloping floor that provides good sight lines from just about every seat. 'Production' shows are of limited scope, as dinner is usually the main event. You can, however, expect to see the occasional cabaret act. Non-American passengers should note that almost all entertainment and activities are geared towards North American tastes.

SPA/FITNESS. The Spa is a small but well-equipped health spa/fitness center. It has sauna and steam rooms (separate facilities for men and women), an equipment-packed gymnasium – but the ceiling height is low – and a beauty salon.

The spa is staffed and operated by concession Elemis by Steiner. Treatment prices equal those in an expensive land-based spa. The beauty salon has hair-beautifying treatments and conditioning. In the gymnasium, personal training sessions and some classes may be at extra cost.

Star Princess
★★★★

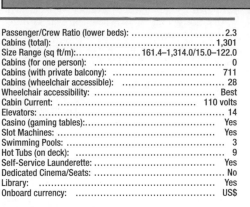

Size:	Large Resort Ship
Tonnage:	108,977
Lifestyle:	Standard
Cruise Line:	Princess Cruises
Former Names:	none
IMO Number:	9192363
Builder:	Fincantieri (Italy)
Original Cost:	$460 million
Entered Service:	Feb 2002
Registry:	Bermuda
Length (ft/m):	951.4/290.0
Beam (ft/m):	118.1/36.0
Draft (ft/m):	26.2/8.0
Propulsion/Propellers:	diesel-electric (42,000kW)/2
Passenger Decks:	13
Total Crew:	1,200
Passengers (lower beds):	2,602
Passenger Space Ratio (lower beds):	41.8

Passenger/Crew Ratio (lower beds):	2.3
Cabins (total):	1,301
Size Range (sq ft/m):	161.4–1,314.0/15.0–122.0
Cabins (for one person):	0
Cabins (with private balcony):	711
Cabins (wheelchair accessible):	28
Wheelchair accessibility:	Best
Cabin Current:	110 volts
Elevators:	14
Casino (gaming tables):	Yes
Slot Machines:	Yes
Swimming Pools:	3
Hot Tubs (on deck):	9
Self-Service Launderette:	Yes
Dedicated Cinema/Seats:	No
Library:	Yes
Onboard currency:	US$

This large, multiple-choice, resort ship is for the whole family

OVERVIEW. *Star Princess* is a grand resort playground, with many choices and 'small' rooms to enjoy. It is extremely well designed and competitively priced. The odds are that you'll have a fine time, in a controlled, well-packaged way.

THE SHIP. The design for this large cruise ship, whose sister ships are *Golden Princess* and *Grand Princess* (and slightly larger half-sister *Caribbean Princess*), presents a bold, forthright profile, with a racy 'spoiler' effect at its galleon-like transom stern (the 'spoiler' acts as a stern observation lounge by day, and a stunning disco by night).

There is a good sheltered faux teak promenade deck – it's actually painted steel – which almost wraps around (three times round is equal to one mile) and a walkway, which goes right to the ship's enclosed bow. The outdoor pools have various beach-like surroundings. One lap pool has a pumped 'current' to swim against.

Unlike the outside decks, there is plenty of space inside the ship – but there are also plenty of passengers – and a wide array of public rooms, with many 'intimate' (this being a relative word) spaces and places to play. The passenger flow has been well thought-out, and works well. The decor is attractive, with lots of earth tones, well suited to North American and European tastes.

Four areas center on swimming pools, one of which is two decks high and is covered by a glass dome, itself an extension of the funnel housing.

The Grand Casino has more than 260 slot machines;

Berlitz's Ratings

	Possible	Achieved
Ship	500	371
Accommodation	200	147
Food	400	247
Service	400	284
Entertainment	100	77
Cruise Experience	400	291

OVERALL SCORE
1417 points out of 2000

there are blackjack, craps, and roulette tables, plus other games. But the highlight could well be the specially linked slot machines that provide a combined payout.

Other facilities include a decent library/computer room, and a separate card room. Ship lovers should enjoy the wood-paneled Wheelhouse Bar, finely decorated with memorabilia and ship models tracing part of the history of sister company P&O; this ship highlights the 1950-built cargo ship *Ganges*. A sports bar, Shooters, has two billiard tables, as well as eight television screens.

The dress code is either formal or 'smart casual,' the latter interpreted by many as jeans and trainers. Daily per-person gratuities are automatically added to your account, for both adults and children. To have these charges adjusted, you'll need to line up at the reception desk.

Passenger niggles? The cabin bath towels are small, and drawer space is negligible. There are no butlers – even for top-grade suites. Cabin attendants have too many cabins to look after – typically 20 – which doesn't translate to fine personal service. The automated telephone system is frustrating, and luggage delivery is inefficient.

FAMILIES. For children, there is a two-deck-high playroom, teen room, and a host of specially trained counselors. Children have their own pool, hot tub, and open deck area at the stern, thankfully away from adult areas. There are good netted-in areas; one section has a dip pool, while another has a mini-basketball court.

ACCOMMODATION. There are six principal types of cabins and configurations: (a) grand suite, (b) suite, (c) mini-suite, (d) outside-view double cabin with balcony, (e) outside-view double cabin, and (f) interior double cabin. These come in 35 different price categories – the choice is bewildering. Note that the interior (no-view) cabins and standard ocean-view cabins are extremely small. Some cabins can accommodate a third and fourth person in upper berths, although the lower beds cannot then be pushed together to make a queen-size bed.

All cabins get turndown service and chocolates on pillows each night, bathrobes on request, and toiletry kits (larger for suite/mini-suite occupants). A hairdryer is provided in all cabins, sensibly located at the vanity desk unit in the living area. All bathrooms have tiled floors, and there is a decent amount of open shelf storage space for toiletries, although the plain beige decor is very basic and unappealing. Princess Cruises typically carries CNN, CNBC, ESPN, and TNT, when available, on the in-cabin television system.

Lifeboats obstruct most outside-view cabins on Emerald Deck. Your name is placed outside your suite or cabin in a documents holder – making it simple for delivery service personnel but privacy-insensitive. There is 24-hour room service, though some items on the menu are not available during early morning hours.

Almost all balcony suites and cabins can be overlooked both from the navigation bridge wing, as well as from the port and starboard sections of the ship's disco – located high above the ship at the stern. Cabins with balconies on Dolphin, Caribe, and Baja decks are also overlooked by passengers on balconies on the deck above. They are, therefore, not at all private. However, perhaps the least-desirable balcony cabins are eight ones located forward on Emerald Deck – the balconies don't extend to the side of the ship and can be passed by walkers and gawkers on the adjacent Upper Promenade walkway, so occupants need to keep their curtains closed most of the time. Also, passengers in some the most expensive suites with balconies at the stern may experience vibration during certain ship maneuvers.

DINING. For formal meals there are three principal dining rooms: Amalfi, with 504 seats; Capri, with 486 seats; and Portofino, with 486 seats. Seating is assigned according to your cabin location. There are two seatings in Amalfi, while Capri and Portofino offer 'anytime dining' – so you choose when and with whom you want to eat. All three are split into multi-tier sections in a non-symmetrical design that breaks them into small sections. Each dining room has its own galley.

While four elevators go to Fiesta Deck where the Amalfi and Portofino restaurants are located, only two elevators go to Plaza Deck 5 where the Capri Restaurant is located; this can cause long wait problems at peak times, particularly for anyone in a wheelchair.

Specially designed dinnerware (by Dudson of England), high-quality Frette Egyptian cotton table linens, and silverware by Hepp of Germany are used in the main dining rooms. Note that 15 percent is automatically added to all beverage bills, including wines.

Other dining options. There are two extra-charge restaurants: Sabatini's and Tequila's, both open for lunch and dinner on days at sea. Sabatini's, with colorful tiled Mediterranean-style decor, serves Italian-style pizzas and pastas, with a variety of sauces, plus Italian-style entrées including tiger prawns and lobster tail. All provided with flair and entertainment from by the staff of waiters. Reservations are required.

Tequila's features southwestern American' food (a cover charge applies for lunch or dinner) on sea days only. It is spread over the ship's entire width and two walkways intersect it, which means that it's a very open area, with people walking through it as you eat – not a comfortable arrangement. Reservations are needed.

A poolside hamburger grill and pizza bar (no additional charge) are dining spots for casual bites. But it costs extra to eat at the coffee bar/patisserie, or the caviar/ Champagne bar.

Other casual meals can be taken in the Horizon Court, open 24 hours a day. It has large ocean-view windows on port and starboard sides and direct access to the two main swimming pools and Lido Deck. There is no real finesse in presentation, however, as plastic plates (no trays) are provided.

ENTERTAINMENT. The Princess Theater is the showlounge; it spans two decks and has comfortable seating on both levels. It has $3 million worth of sound and light equipment, and a live showband to accompany the colourful production shows for which Princess Cruises is well known.

The Vista Lounge, a second entertainment lounge, has cabaret acts such as magicians, comedy jugglers, and ventriloquists at night, and lectures, bingo, and horse racing during the day. Explorers, a third lounge, can also host cabaret acts and dance bands. Various other lounges and bars have live music, and Princess Cruises has a number of male dance hosts as partners for women traveling alone.

SPA/FITNESS. The Lotus Spa has Japanese-style decor, and surrounds one of the swimming pools. You can have a massage or other spa treatment in an ocean-view treatment room. Some of the massage treatment rooms are located directly underneath the jogging track.

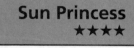

Sun Princess
★★★★

Size:	Mid-size Ship	Passenger/Crew Ratio (lower beds):	2.0
Tonnage:	77,499	Cabins (total):	975
Lifestyle:	Standard	Size Range (sq ft/m):	134.5–753.4/12.5–70.0
Cruise Line:	Princess Cruises	Cabins (for one person):	0
Former Names:	none	Cabins (with private balcony):	410
IMO Number:	9000259	Cabins (wheelchair accessible):	19
Builder:	Fincantieri (Italy)	Wheelchair accessibility:	Good
Original Cost:	$300 million	Cabin Current:	110 and 220 volts
Entered Service:	Dec 1995	Elevators:	11
Registry:	Great Britain	Casino (gaming tables):	Yes
Length (ft/m):	857.2/261.3	Slot Machines:	Yes
Beam (ft/m):	105.6/32.2	Swimming Pools:	3
Draft (ft/m):	26.5/8.1	Hot Tubs (on deck):	5
Propulsion/Propellers:	diesel-electric (28,000kW)/2	Self-Service Launderette:	Yes
Passenger Decks:	10	Dedicated Cinema/Seats:	No
Total Crew:	900	Library:	Yes
Passengers (lower beds):	1,950	Onboard currency:	Australian $
Passenger Space Ratio (lower beds):	39.7		

This family-friendly mid-sized ship has modern decor

OVERVIEW. *Sun Princess* absorbs passengers well, and has a quasi-intimate feel, with warm, welcoming decor.

THE SHIP. In November 2007, *Sun Princess* was assigned to Australia, operating cruises from Sydney, Melbourne, and Fremantle. The onboard currency became the Australian dollar, the entertainment was geared to Australian tastes, and other aspects of the cruise operation modified accordingly.

This all-white ship has a good profile, and is well balanced by its large funnel, which contains a deck tennis/basketball/volleyball court in its sheltered aft base. There is a wide, teakwood walk-around promenade deck outdoors, some real teak steamer-style deck chairs with royal blue cushioned pads, and 93,000 sq ft (8,600 sq m) of space outdoors. An extensive glass area on the upper decks provides plenty of light and connection with the outside world.

A wide array of public rooms includes several intimate rooms and spaces, so that you don't feel overwhelmed by large spaces. The interior focal point (and always a good place to arrange to meet others) is a pleasant four-deck-high atrium lobby with winding, double stairways, and two panoramic glass-walled elevators.

The main entertainment rooms are located underneath three decks of cabins. There is plenty of space, the traffic flow is good, and the ship absorbs people well. There are two showlounges, one at each end of the ship; one is a pleasant theater-style space,

Berlitz's Ratings		
	Possible	Achieved
Ship	500	377
Accommodation	200	148
Food	400	246
Service	400	278
Entertainment	100	75
Cruise Experience	400	284
OVERALL SCORE		
1408 points out of 2000		

where movies are also shown, and the other is a cabaret-style lounge, complete with bar.

The library is a warm, welcoming room with ocean-view windows, and it has six large buttery leather chairs for listening to audio CDs. There is a conference center for up to 300, as well as a business center. The collection of artwork is good, particularly on the stairways, and it helps to make the ship feel smaller than it is, although in places it doesn't always seem coordinated.

The most traditional room aboard (a standard on all Princess ships) is the Wheelhouse Lounge/Bar, decorated in the style of a late 19th-century gentleman's club, complete with wood paneling and comfortable seating. Its focal point is a large ship model from the P&O archives.

One nice feature is the captain's cocktail party; it is held in the four-deck-high main atrium, so you can come and go as you please. There's no standing in line to have your photograph taken with the captain, if you don't want to.

Niggles include the layout: there are a number of dead ends in the interior, so it's not as user-friendly as a ship this size should be. The cabin-numbering system is extremely illogical, with numbers going through several hundred series on the same deck. The walls of the passenger accommodation decks are very plain. The swimming pools are small for the number of passengers carried, and the pool deck is cluttered with white plastic sunloungers that lack cushioned pads.

ACCOMMODATION. There are many different cabin grades. Although the standard outside-view and interior cabins are small, they are well designed, with a functional layout, and are in earth tones accentuated by splashes of color from the bedspreads. Many of the outside-view cabins have private balconies, and all are quite well soundproofed, although the balcony partition is not floor-to-ceiling type, so you can hear your neighbors clearly. The balconies are very narrow, just large enough for two small chairs.

A 'reasonable' amount of closet and abundant drawer and other storage space is provided in all cabins – just about adequate for a seven-night cruise – as are a TV set and refrigerator. However, for longer voyages, the cabin closet space could prove to be much too small. Each night a chocolate will appear on your pillow.

The cabin bathrooms are practical, and come complete with all the details one needs, although they really are tight spaces, one-person-at-a-time units. They have a decent shower enclosure, real glasses, a hairdryer and bathrobe, and a small amount of shelving for toiletries.

The largest accommodation is in six suites, two on each of three decks at the stern, with large private balcony (536–754 sq ft/50–70 sq m, including balcony). They are well laid-out, and have large bathrooms with two washbasins, a Jacuzzi tub, and a separate shower enclosure. The bedroom has pleasing wood accenting and detailing, while the living area includes a dining room table and four chairs.

Mini-suites (374–536 sq ft/35–50 sq m) typically have two lower beds that convert to a queen-size bed. There is a separate bedroom/sleeping area with vanity desk, and a lounge with sofa and coffee table, indented ceilings with wood accenting and detailing, walk-in closet, and larger bathroom with Jacuzzi tub and separate shower enclosure.

Some are 19 wheelchair-accessible cabins, which measure 213–305 sq ft (20–28 sq m), in a mix of seven outside-view and 12 interior cabins.

DINING. There are two main dining rooms of asymmetrical design – Marquis and Regency – located adjacent to the two lower levels of the four-deck-high atrium lobby. Each seats around 500, has its own galley, and is split into multi-tier sections that help create a feeling of intimacy, although there is a lot of noise from the waiter stations adjacent to many tables. Breakfast and lunch are provided in an open-seating arrangement, while dinner is in two seatings.

On any given seven-day cruise, a typical menu cycle may include a Sailaway Dinner, Captain's Welcome Dinner, Chef's Dinner, Italian Dinner, French Dinner, Captain's Gala Dinner, and Landfall Dinner. The wine list is reasonable, but not good, and the company has, sadly, dispensed with wine waiters. Note that 15 percent is automatically added to all beverage bills, including wines.

Other dining options. For some really good meat, consider the extra-cost Sterling Steakhouse; there are four different cuts of Angus beef – Filet Mignon, New York Strip, Porterhouse, and Rib-Eye, first presented on a silver tray. There is also a barbecued chicken option, with baked potato or French fries as accompaniments. This is available as an alternative to the dining rooms between 6.30pm and 9.30pm, but, instead of being a separate, intimate room, it is located in a section of the Horizon Buffet, with its own portable bar and some decorative touches to set it apart from the regular buffet area.

The Horizon Buffet itself is open 24 hours a day, and, at night, has an informal dinner setting with sit-down waiter service. The buffet displays are, for the most part, fairly repetitious. There is no real finesse in presentation, however, as plastic plates are provided, instead of trays.

There is also a patisserie (for extra-cost cappuccino/espresso coffees and pastries), a wine/caviar bar, and a pizzeria (complete with cobblestone floors and wrought-iron decorative features), and a choice of six excellent pizzas.

ENTERTAINMENT. There are two showlounges, both theatre- and cabaret-style. The main one, the Princess Theater, has a sloping floor, with aisle-style seating that is well tiered, and with good sight lines to the raised stage from most of the 500 seats.

The 480-seat Vista Lounge, at the aft end, has cabaret entertainment, and acts as a lecture and presentation room. Princess Cruises has a good stable of regular cabaret acts to draw from, so there should be something for most tastes.

SPA/FITNESS. A glass-walled Lotus Spa is located in an aft area of Riviera deck, and includes a gymnasium with high-tech machines, several massage/body-treatment rooms, and a beauty salon. The facility is staffed and operated by a specialist spa concession.

Sports facilities are located in an open-air sports deck inside the funnel and adaptable for basketball, volleyball, badminton, or paddle tennis. Joggers can exercise on the walk-around open Promenade Deck.

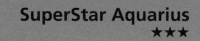

SuperStar Aquarius
★★★

Size:	Mid-size Ship	Passenger/Crew Ratio (lower beds):	1.7
Tonnage:	50,764	Cabins (total):	765
Lifestyle:	Standard	Size Range (sq ft/m):	139.9–349.8/13.0–32.5
Cruise Line:	Star Cruises	Cabins (for one person):	0
Former Names:	Norwegian Wind, Windward	Cabins (with private balcony):	74
IMO Number:	9008421	Cabins (wheelchair accessible):	11
Builder:	Chantiers de l'Atlantique (France)	Wheelchair accessibility:	Fair
Original Cost:	$240 million	Cabin Current:	110 volts
Entered Service:	Jun 1993/May 2007	Elevators:	10
Registry:	Bahamas	Casino (gaming tables):	Yes
Length (ft/m):	754.0/229.8	Slot Machines:	Yes
Beam (ft/m):	93.5/28.5	Swimming Pools:	1
Draft (ft/m):	22.3/6.8	Hot Tubs (on deck):	2
Propulsion/Propellers:	diesel (18,480kW)/2	Self-Service Launderette:	No
Passenger Decks:	10	Dedicated Cinema/Seats:	No
Total Crew:	889	Library:	Yes
Passengers (lower beds):	1,529	Onboard currency:	Hong Kong $
Passenger Space Ratio (lower beds):	33.1		

Family-friendly casual cruising that's good for gamblers

OVERVIEW. *SuperStar Aquarius* was transferred from Norwegian Cruise Line to the Star Cruises fleet in 2007 to operate overnight and short cruises from Hong Kong. The dress code is strictly casual. Several cabins are specially equipped for the hearing-impaired. All gratuities for staff are included.

THE SHIP. The exterior design emphasizes a clever and extensive use of large windows that help create a sense of open spaces, but the interior design has many smaller public rooms. There is no big atrium lobby, and the ceiling height is low.

Public rooms include bars and lounges, including Skyline Karaoke, which has five private karaoke rooms. There's a mahjong/card room, childcare center, video arcade, Genting Club for invited gaming guests, business meeting rooms, an Internet-connect center/library, cigar lounge, and a small boutique. There is a blue rubber-covered walk-around promenade deck outdoors. Outdoor stairways are numerous and confusing, while the carpeted steel interior stairwell steps are tinny.

ACCOMMODATION. There are 16 cabin price grades. No cabin includes the number '4' – which means 'die' in superstitious China. Most cabins have outside views and wood-trimmed cabinetry and warm decor with multi-colored soft furnishings, but there's almost no drawer space (although the closets have open shelves), so take minimal

Berlitz's Ratings		
	Possible	Achieved
Ship	500	296
Accommodation	200	119
Food	400	237
Service	400	247
Entertainment	100	60
Cruise Experience	400	233
OVERALL SCORE		
1192 points out of 2000		

clothing. All cabins have a sitting area. The bathrooms are small but practical.

There are 18 suites (12 with a private entrance and a small, private balcony), each with separate living room and bedroom, and plenty of closet and drawer space. Occupants of suites receive 'concierge' service. In addition, 16 suites and 70 cabins have interconnecting doors.

DINING. Freestyle Dining venues include the 280-seat Dynasty Restaurant, for Chinese family-style food. It has some prime tables at ocean-view window seats in a section that extends from the ship's port and starboard sides in half-moon shapes. There's also Spices Restaurant, an Asian specialty buffet venue with 180 seats; Oceana Barbeque, an outdoor buffet venue; Blue Lagoon, a 24-hour bistro, with 80 seats; and Mariner's Buffet, an international self-service buffet.

ENTERTAINMENT. The 700-seat Stardust Lounge is two decks high, but the banquette and individual tub chair seating is only on the main level. There is no live showband, only recorded music. High-volume razzle-dazzle shows are presented to a pre-recorded track, as well as special individual cabaret acts.

SPA/FITNESS. A gymnasium has high-tech muscle-toning equipment, reflexology lounge, and Oscar Hair and Beauty Salon. There's a ping-pong table, basketball/volleyball court, golf driving range, and a jogging track.

SuperStar Gemini
★★★

Size:	Mid-size Ship
Tonnage:	50,764
Lifestyle:	Standard
Cruise Line:	Star Cruises
Former Names:	*Norwegian Dream, Dreamward*
IMO Number:	9008419
Builder:	Chantiers de l'Atlantique (France)
Original Cost:	$240 million
Entered Service:	Dec 1992/Jan 2013
Registry:	Bahamas
Length (ft/m):	754.0/229.8
Beam (ft/m):	93.5/28.5
Draft (ft/m):	22.3/6.8
Propulsion/Propellers:	diesel (18,480kW)/2
Passenger Decks:	10
Total Crew:	889
Passengers (lower beds):	1,529
Passenger Space Ratio (lower beds):	33.1
Passenger/Crew Ratio (lower beds):	1.7
Cabins (total):	765
Size Range (sq ft/m):	139.9–349.8/13.0–32.5
Cabins (for one person):	0
Cabins (with private balcony):	74
Cabins (wheelchair accessible):	11
Wheelchair accessibility:	Fair
Cabin Current:	110 volts
Elevators:	10
Casino (gaming tables):	Yes
Slot Machines:	Yes
Swimming Pools:	1
Hot Tubs (on deck):	2
Self-Service Launderette:	No
Dedicated Cinema/Seats:	No
Library:	Yes
Onboard currency:	Hong Kong $

This casual, family-friendly ship is best for Asian nationalities

OVERVIEW. *SuperStar Gemini* is a mid-sized ship that is good for Asian families and couples looking for a general cruise experience in fairly contemporary surroundings.

THE SHIP. Although its funnel is large and square-ish looking, the ship has a profile that is quite well balanced; this is because it underwent a 'chop and stretch' operation, in which a new 131ft (40m) mid-section was added in 1998. This gave the ship not only more cabins, but more public rooms and places to play in.

The tiered pool deck aft is neat, as are the multi-deck aft sun terraces and all the fore and aft connecting exterior stairways. The overall exterior design emphasizes a clever and extensive use of large windows that create a sense of open spaces. However, there is no big atrium lobby, as one might expect.

The ship was highly successful for many years for Norwegian Cruise Line's younger, active sports-minded passengers, and now provides Star Cruises' passengers with a comfortable ship. Public rooms include a mahjong room, an activity center, several shops (including a duty-free store, a tea corner for premium teas, and a jewelry store), an Observatory Lounge (Karaoke Lounge), Genting Club, and Star Club (casino with gaming tables and slot machines).

ACCOMMODATION. There are several grades of cabins (the price you pay will depend on the grade,

Berlitz's Ratings		
	Possible	Achieved
Ship	500	296
Accommodation	200	119
Food	400	237
Service	400	247
Entertainment	100	60
Cruise Experience	400	235
OVERALL SCORE		
1194 points out of 2000		

size, and location you choose). Most cabins have outside views, wood-trimmed cabinetry and warm decor, with multi-colored soft furnishings. But there is almost no drawer space (the closets have open shelves). All cabins benefit from a sitting area, but this takes away any free space, making movement pretty tight. The bathrooms are small but practical.

DINING. There are plenty of choices when it comes to dining. The main full-service dining room is Bella Vista (the nicest of all the dining venues, with prime tables with ocean-view window seats); Dynasty (a self-serve Chinese buffet); Mariners Restaurant (a self-serve buffet); Oceana Barbecue (outdoors, for grilled specialties and buffet-style eats); and Blue Lagoon (a 24-hour à-la-carte venue).

ENTERTAINMENT. The Stardust Lounge is the ship's main showlounge. Two decks high, it is located in the center of the ship, with cabins in front of it, and other public rooms and dining spots behind it.

SPA/FITNESS. Spa/fitness facilities are located in the forward section of Sports Deck 12 (just aft of the observation lounge), and include a gymnasium with high-tech muscle-toning equipment, a beauty salon, several massage and associated treatment rooms, and men's and women's saunas and changing rooms.

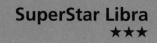

SuperStar Libra
★★★

Size:	Mid-size Ship
Tonnage:	42,276
Lifestyle:	Standard
Cruise Line:	Star Cruises
Former Names:	Norwegian Sea, Seaward
IMO Number:	8612134
Builder:	Wartsila (Finland)
Original Cost:	$120 million
Entered Service:	Jun 1988/Oct 2005
Registry:	Bahamas
Length (ft/m):	708.6/216.0
Beam (ft/m):	95.1/29.0
Draft (ft/m):	22.9/7.0
Propulsion/Propellers:	diesel (21,120kW)/2
Passenger Decks:	9
Total Crew:	700
Passengers (lower beds):	1,472
Passenger Space Ratio (lower beds):	28.0

Passenger/Crew Ratio (lower beds):	2.1
Cabins (total):	732
Size Range (sq ft/m):	109.7–269.1/10.2–25.0
Cabins (for one person):	0
Cabins (with private balcony):	0
Cabins (wheelchair accessible):	4
Wheelchair accessibility:	Fair
Cabin Current:	110 volts
Elevators:	6
Casino (gaming tables):	Yes
Slot Machines:	Yes
Swimming Pools:	2
Hot Tubs (on deck):	2
Self-Service Launderette:	No
Dedicated Cinema/Seats:	No
Library:	No
Onboard currency:	Hong Kong $

This casual, family-friendly Asian ship is good for gamers

OVERVIEW. This ship, which is based at Penang in Malaysia, is suited to couples and solo travelers seeking a short cruise in surroundings tailored specifically for them. It was built before balcony cabins came into vogue – so there aren't any.

THE SHIP. *SuperStar Libra* is an angular yet reasonably attractive ship that has a contemporary European cruise-ferry profile with a sharply raked bow and sleek mast and funnel added. It is quite well designed, with generally sound passenger flow. The interior decor, stressing corals, blues, and mauves, reminds you of sea and sky.

The lobby, two decks high, is pleasing without being overwhelming. There is a decent selection of public rooms, bars, and lounges, including an inviting wood-paneled Admiral's Lounge, a Star Club casino, a disco (Boomer's), and The Bollywood karaoke lounge. Gratuities are included in the fare.

The open decks are cluttered and badly dented, and scuffed panels in the accommodation hallways are unattractive. The steps on the stairways are quite tinny. The constant background music in the hallways is irritating. There is too much use of synthetic turf on the upper outdoors decks – this gets soggy when wet.

ACCOMMODATION. There are numerous suite/cabin price categories. No cabin includes the number '4' – which means 'die' in superstitious China. Although the cabins are of average size, they are

Berlitz's Ratings		
	Possible	Achieved
Ship	500	276
Accommodation	200	122
Food	400	227
Service	400	246
Entertainment	100	61
Cruise Experience	400	229
OVERALL SCORE		
1161 points out of 2000		

tastefully appointed and comfortable. Audio channels are available via the TV set, although the picture can't be turned off with the audio function on. The bathrooms are well designed, but the hairdryers are weak.

A suite or one of two upper-grade cabins offers a little more space, a lounge area with table and sofa that converts into another bed, European duvets, and a refrigerator (top categories only). The bathrooms also have a tub, shower, and retractable clothesline.

DINING. There are no assigned dining rooms, tables, or seats. Some eateries cost extra, including: the Four Seasons Restaurant, the principal dining room, serving Continental Cuisine; The Saffron; Two Trees Restaurant (exclusive lounge/restaurant); Taj by the Bay; Blue Lagoon for 24-hour casual refreshments; and Coconut Willy's, a poolside refreshment center.

ENTERTAINMENT. The 770-seat Stardust Lounge is the venue for shows and major cabaret acts, but 12 thick pillars obstruct many sight lines. The Galaxy of the Stars Lounge is for cabaret acts. A number of bands and solo entertaining musicians provide live music for listening and dancing in several lounges and bars.

SPA/FITNESS. There's a good gymnasium/fitness center, located around the mast and accessible only from the outside deck – not good when it rains.

SuperStar Virgo
★★★+

Size:	Mid-size Ship
Tonnage:	75,338
Lifestyle:	Standard
Cruise Line:	Star Cruises
Former Names:	none
IMO Number:	9141077
Builder:	Meyer Werft (Germany)
Original Cost:	$350 million
Entered Service:	Aug 1999
Registry:	Panama
Length (ft/m):	879.2/268.0
Beam (ft/m):	105.6/32.2
Draft (ft/m):	25.9/7.9
Propulsion/Propellers:	diesel (50,400kW)/2
Passenger Decks:	10
Total Crew:	1,225
Passengers (lower beds):	1,870
Passenger Space Ratio (lower beds):	41.7

Passenger/Crew Ratio (lower beds):	1.4
Cabins (total):	935
Size Range (sq ft/m):	150.6–638.3/14.0–59.3
Cabins (for one person):	0
Cabins (with private balcony):	390
Cabins (wheelchair accessible):	4
Wheelchair accessibility:	Good
Cabin Current:	240 volts
Elevators:	9
Casino (gaming tables):	Yes
Slot Machines:	Yes
Swimming Pools:	2
Hot Tubs (on deck):	4
Self-Service Launderette:	No
Dedicated Cinema/Seats:	No
Library:	Yes
Onboard currency:	Hong Kong $

A family-friendly ship for really casual cruising

OVERVIEW. This ship is best suited to couples, solo travelers, and families with children who want to cruise aboard a contemporary floating resort with decent facilities and many Asian dining spots, at a very attractive price.

THE SHIP. *SuperStar Virgo* was the second new ship ordered by Star Cruises for the Asian market. The all-white ship has a distinctive red-and-blue funnel with gold star logo, and decorative hull art. There are three classes of passengers. As you check in, you will be issued with a colored boarding card to denote Admiral Class passengers (yellow), Balcony Class (red), or World Cruisers (blue).

There is a walk-around promenade deck outdoors, good for strolling. Inside are two boulevards, and a stunning, large, two-deck-high central atrium lobby with three glass-walled elevators and space to peruse the shops and cafés.

The casino complex is at the forward end of the atrium boulevard on Deck 7. This includes a large general-purpose, brightly lit casino, called Oasis, with gaming tables and slot machines. There's a smaller members-only gaming club, as well as VIP gaming rooms, one of which has its own access to the upper level of the showlounge. The 450-seat Galaxy of the Stars Lounge is an observation lounge by day and a nightclub at night, with live music.

Three stairways are each carpeted in a different color, which helps new cruise passengers find their way around easily.

Berlitz's Ratings		
	Possible	Achieved
Ship	500	394
Accommodation	200	146
Food	400	258
Service	400	259
Entertainment	100	65
Cruise Experience	400	276
OVERALL SCORE		
1398 points out of 2000		

Other facilities include a business center with six meeting rooms, a large library and writing room, plus private mahjong and karaoke rooms, and a smoking room. A shopping concourse includes a wine shop.

Star Cruises has established a Southeast Asian regional cruise audience for its diverse fleet. *SuperStar Virgo* is good for the active local market, and is the most comprehensive ship sailing year-round in this popular region.

Lots of choices, more dining options, and Asian hospitality all add up to a very attractive holiday package particularly suitable for families with children, in a very contemporary floating resort that operates from Hong Kong (April–November) and Singapore (November–March). The dress code is ultra-casual (no jacket and tie needed), and the ship operates a no-tipping policy. While the initial cruise fare seems very reasonable, the extra costs and charges soon mount up if you want to indulge in more than the basics (pay more, get more). Although service levels and finesse are inconsistent, smile-rich hospitality is very good.

There are many extra-cost items in addition to the à-la-carte dining spots, such as for morning tea, afternoon tea, most cabaret shows (except a crew show), and childcare. Finding your way around many areas blocked by portable 'crowd containment' ribbon barriers can prove frustrating.

FAMILIES. Teens have their own huge video arcade, while younger children get to play in a wet 'n' wild aft pool (complete with pirate ship and caves) and two whirlpool tubs. Plus there's all the fun and facilities of Charlie's 24-hour childcare center, which includes a painting room, computer learning center, and small cinema. There's a room full of cots for toddlers to use for sleepovers, and even the toilets are at a special low height. About 15,000 sq ft (1,400 sq m) is devoted to children's facilities. On deck is the world's first stainless-steel water slide at sea. Installed in 2009, it cost $550,000, and is 330ft (100m) long. You can zoom along at up to 22ft (6.7m) a second due to its steep incline, from 35ft (10.7m) above the deck.

ACCOMMODATION. There are seven types of accommodation, in a number of different price categories. Three entire decks of cabins have private balconies, while two-thirds of all cabins have an outside view. Both the standard outside-view and interior cabins really are very small, particularly since all cabins have extra berths for a third/fourth person. So take the least amount of clothing you can – there's almost no storage space for luggage.

All cabins have a personal safe, cotton towels, and duvets or sheets. Bathrooms have a good-size shower enclosure, and include toiletries such as Burberry soap, conditioning shampoo, and body lotion.

For more space, choose one of 13 suites. Each has a separate lounge/dining room, bedroom, and bathroom, and an interconnecting door to an ocean-view cabin with private lit balcony.

The bedroom is small, completely filled by its queen-size bed; there is a reasonable amount of drawer space, but the drawers are very small. The closet space is rather tight – it contains two personal safes. A large en suite bathroom is part of the bedroom, and has a gorgeous mosaic tiled floor, tub, two basins, separate shower enclosure with floor-to-ceiling ocean-view window, and separate toilet with glass door. There are TV sets in the lounge, bedroom, and bathroom.

For even more space, choose one of the six largest suites (Boracay, Nicobar, Langkawi, Majorca, Phuket, and Sentosa) and you'll have a generous amount of private living space, with a separate lounge, dining area, bedroom, large bathroom, and private lit balcony. The facilities are similar to those in the suites already described. There are TV sets in the lounge, bedroom, and bathroom.

A small room service menu is available, with a 15 percent service charge plus a gratuity.

DINING. There's certainly no lack of choice, with eight venues, plus a café:

Bella Vista (perhaps the equivalent of a main dining room) seats over 600 in an open-seating arrangement, although in effect it operates two seatings. The aft section is two decks high, and huge cathedral-style windows are set in three sections overlooking the stern.

Mediterranean Buffet: this is a large self-serve buffet restaurant with indoor/outdoor seating for 400.

The Pavilion Room has traditional Cantonese Chinese cuisine, including dim sum at lunchtime.

The following are (extra-cost) à-la-carte dining spots:

Noble House: a Chinese Restaurant, with traditional Hong Kong-themed decor and items such as dim sum. There are also two small private dining rooms.

Palazzo: a beautiful, if slightly ostentatious Italian restaurant. It has fine food, and a genuine Renoir painting well protected by cameras and alarms.

Samurai: a Japanese restaurant and sushi bar (for sashimi and sushi). There are two teppanyaki grills, each with 10 seats, where the chef cooks in front of you.

The Taj: an Indian/vegetarian dining spot that offers a range of food in a self-serve buffet set-up.

Blue Lagoon: a casual 24-hour street café with noodle dishes, fried rice, and other Southeast Asian dishes.

Out of Africa: a casual karaoke café and bar, where coffees, teas, and pastries are available.

ENTERTAINMENT. The Lido showlounge, with 934 seats, is two decks high. It has main and balcony levels, with the balcony level reserved for VIP 'gaming club' members. The room has almost no support columns to obstruct the sight lines, and a revolving stage for revues and other production shows, usually with recorded music – there is no live showband. Kingdom of Kung-Fu, with a cast of 30, features the power and form of the Shaolin Masters in an action-packed martial arts show. The showlounge can also be used as a large-screen cinema, with superb surround sound.

In addition, local specialty cabaret acts are brought on board, as are revue-style shows complete with topless dancers. Bands and small musical units provide plenty of live music for dancing and listening in the various lounges.

SPA/FITNESS. The Roman Spa and Fitness Center is on one of the uppermost decks, just forward of the Tivoli Pool. It has a gymnasium full of high-tech muscle-toning equipment, plus an aerobics exercise room, hair and beauty salon, and saunas, steam rooms, changing rooms for men and women, several treatment rooms, and aqua-swim pools that provide counter-flow jets. There is an extra charge for use of the sauna and steam rooms.

Although there are several types of massages available, Thai massage is a specialty – you can have it in the spa, outdoors on deck, in your cabin or on your private balcony, space permitting. Sports facilities include a jogging track, golf driving range, basketball and tennis courts, and there are four levels of sunbathing decks.

Tere Moana
★★★★

Size:..	Boutique Ship	Passenger/Crew Ratio (lower beds): 1.8
Tonnage: 3,504		Cabins (total): 45
Lifestyle: .... Premium		Size Range (sq ft/m):.............. 193.7-296.0/18.0-27.5
Cruise Line: .... Paul Gauguin Cruises		Cabins (for one person): 0
Former Names:.. Le Levant		Cabins (with private balcony): 0
IMO Number:.. 9159830		Cabins (wheelchair accessible): 0
Builder:.............................. Leroux & Lotz (France)		Wheelchair accessibility: .... None
Original Cost: ....$35 million		Cabin Current: .... 110 and 220 volts
Entered Service: .... Jan 1999/Dec 2012		Elevators: 1
Registry: .... Wallis and Fortuna		Casino (gaming tables):.. No
Length (ft/m): 328.0/100.0		Slot Machines: .... No
Beam (ft/m): 45.9/14.0		Swimming Pools: 1
Draft (ft/m): 11.4/3.5		Hot Tubs (on deck): 0
Propulsion/Propellers: .... diesel (3,000 kW)/2		Self-Service Launderette: .... No
Passenger Decks:...................................... 5		Dedicated Cinema/Seats: .... No
Total Crew: 50		Library: .... Yes
Passengers (lower beds): 90		Onboard currency: .... US$
Passenger Space Ratio (lower beds): 38.9		

For yacht-chic and informal, very small-ship cruising

OVERVIEW. *Tere Moana* appeals to couples and solo travelers who want contemporary and sophisticated facilities in a very relaxed but chic, yacht-like small ship, with good food and service. Each cruise has life-enrichment lecturers aboard, as well as tour leaders.

THE SHIP. This is a sleek vessel with mega-yacht looks and a pencil-slim design. It has two slim funnels that extend over the port and starboard sides to carry any soot away from the vessel.

A stern 'marina' platform is used for scuba diving, snorkeling, or swimming. Two landing craft are carried for shore visits, as well as six inflatable craft for landings in the islands.

Inside, the vessel has contemporary, clean, and uncluttered decor, and all the facilities of a private yacht. The public rooms are quietly elegant, with much use of wood trim and accenting. Particularly pleasing is the wood-paneled library. There is one grand salon, which accommodates all passengers; it is used by day as a lecture room, and by night as the main lounge/bar.

This ship spends summers in the Mediterranean and winters in the Caribbean and Central America.

This is all-inclusive cruising, with all port charges, gratuities, and shore excursions included in the fare. The crew is almost entirely French.

The ship will start a new lease of life with Grand Circle Cruise Lines in May 2016.

Berlitz's Ratings

	Possible	Achieved
Ship	500	370
Accommodation	200	155
Food	400	269
Service	400	288
Entertainment	100	64
Cruise Experience	400	290
OVERALL SCORE		
1436 points out of 2000		

ACCOMMODATION. There are 45 ocean-view cabins, which the brochure incorrectly calls 'suites,' all being located midships and forward, in five price categories – a lot for such a small ship. Each cabin has a large ocean-view window, inlaid wood furniture and accenting, designer fabrics, two beds that convert to a queen-size bed, a TV set and DVD player, refrigerator, safe, and toiletry kits in the marble-appointed bathrooms, all of which have a shower with a circular door – nicer than a shower curtain. There are no bathtubs.

DINING. The Lafayette Restaurant is a warm, cozy wood-paneled room with round and oval tables, but no tables for two. The informal Panoramique Restaurant has a great view overlooking the stern, with both indoor and outdoor seating. Dining is in open seating. Free wines accompany lunch and dinner. The cuisine is, naturally, classic French.

ENTERTAINMENT. The Grand Salon accommodates all passengers. There are built-in video screens for showing movies, and the room has a small dance floor in its center.

SPA/FITNESS. There is a small fitness room, a steam room (there is no sauna), and a shower.

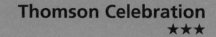

Thomson Celebration
★★★

Size:	Mid-size Ship	Passenger/Crew Ratio (lower beds):	2.4
Tonnage:	33,930	Cabins (total):	627
Lifestyle:	Standard	Size Range (sq ft/m):	140.0–430.0/13.0–40.0
Cruise Line:	Thomson Cruises	Cabins (for one person):	0
Former Names:	Noordam	Cabins (with private balcony):	26
IMO Number:	8027298	Cabins (wheelchair accessible):	4
Builder:	Chantiers de l'Atlantique (France)	Wheelchair accessibility:	Fair
Original Cost:	$160 million	Cabin Current:	110 and 220 volts
Entered Service:	Apr 1984/May 2005	Elevators:	7
Registry:	Malta	Casino (gaming tables):	Yes
Length (ft/m):	704.2/214.6	Slot Machines:	Yes
Beam (ft/m):	89.4/27.2	Swimming Pools:	2
Draft (ft/m):	25.9/7.9	Hot Tubs (on deck):	1
Propulsion/Propellers:	diesel (21,600kW)/2	Self-Service Launderette:	Yes
Passenger Decks:	10	Dedicated Cinema/Seats:	Yes/230
Total Crew:	520	Library:	Yes
Passengers (lower beds):	1,254	Onboard currency:	UK£
Passenger Space Ratio (lower beds):	27.0		

A family-friendly ship for a low-budget first cruise

OVERVIEW. This ship suits adult couples and solo travelers taking their first or second cruise, seeking a modern but not glitzy ship, and happy with a middle-of-the-road experience. It is exclusively chartered by Thomson Cruises, so most passengers will be British, typically over 55.

THE SHIP. *Thomson Celebration* has a nicely raked bow and a contemporary transom stern, but overall it looks squat. There is a good amount of open deck space and a walk-around promenade deck. It has a spacious interior design and several public lounges. The ship, however, is dated and can suffer from vibration. There are many interior cabins, and queuing is inevitable. Gratuities are included, linen changes are minimal, and the dress code is not enforced.

FAMILIES. Children have their own play areas and several children's clubs: Tots is for 3–5-year-olds; Team is for 6–8s; Tribe is for 9–12s. The clubs operate five days a week (not on embarkation or disembarkation days) and are supervised by qualified 'children's hosts.'

ACCOMMODATION. There are four grades: suite-grade, deluxe, outside, and interior. Four cabins with great forward-facing views are for the disabled. You can pre-book your preferred cabin for an extra fee. Cabins are adequately appointed and practically laid out. There is good counter but limited storage space and a small bathroom. Some cabins have bathtubs; others have shower enclosures only. Several cabins have king- or queen-size beds, although most have twins. In many

Berlitz's Ratings		
	Possible	Achieved
Ship	500	290
Accommodation	200	126
Food	400	226
Service	400	241
Entertainment	100	60
Cruise Experience	400	236
OVERALL SCORE		
1179 points out of 2000		

cabins, the layout is L-shaped, and beds can't be pushed together. Some cabins have additional upper berths.

Room service is provided 24 hours a day, at extra cost. Cabin insulation is poor. Some cabins on Mariner and Bridge Decks have lifeboat-obstructed views.

DINING. The 600-seat Meridian Restaurant has warm decor, and operates in an open-seating arrangement. Although there are a few tables for two, most are for four, six, or eight. Children have their own menu. Dessert items will usually be good quality, made for British tastes.

Other dining options. A small à-la-carte restaurant, Mistral's, is an intimate dining spot; reservations are required and there's a per-person cover charge. It has superior food and service. Kora La Restaurant was added in 2014 and features Asian cuisine. The Lido Restaurant is active 24 hours a day in an open-seating arrangement. Each week a themed buffet may be offered. However, self-serve buffets are quite repetitive. On Lido Deck, the outdoor Terrace Grill provides fast-food grilled items, pasta at lunchtime, and pizza.

ENTERTAINMENT. The two-deck-high, 600-seat Broadway Show Lounge is the venue for production shows. Several pillars obstruct sight lines. Liberties hosts quizzes, dancing, karaoke, and a disco. Musical units provide live music in several lounges and bars.

SPA/FITNESS. Oceans Health Club has an exercise room, gym, single-sex saunas, and treatment rooms.

Thomson Dream
★★★

Size:	Mid-size Ship	Passenger/Crew Ratio (lower beds):	2.5
Tonnage:	54,763	Cabins (total):	753
Lifestyle:	Standard	Size Range (sq ft/m):	129.1–425.1/12.0–39.5
Cruise Line:	Thomson Cruises	Cabins (for one person):	18
Former Names:	*Costa Europa, Westerdam, Homeric*	Cabins (with private balcony):	0
IMO Number:	7927984	Cabins (wheelchair accessible):	4
Builder:	Meyer Werft (Germany)	Wheelchair accessibility:	Fair
Original Cost:	$150 million	Cabin Current:	110 and 220 volts
Entered Service:	May 1986/Dec 2010	Elevators:	7
Registry:	Malta	Casino (gaming tables):	Yes
Length (ft/m):	797.9/243.2	Slot Machines:	Yes
Beam (ft/m):	95.1/29.0	Swimming Pools:	2
Draft (ft/m):	23.6/7.2	Hot Tubs (on deck):	2
Propulsion/Propellers:	diesel (23,830kW)/2	Self-Service Launderette:	Yes
Passenger Decks:	9	Dedicated Cinema/Seats:	Yes/237
Total Crew:	600	Library:	Yes
Passengers (lower beds):	1,506	Onboard currency:	UK£
Passenger Space Ratio (lower beds):	36.3		

This dated mid-size ship is for frugal, family-friendly cruises

OVERVIEW. *Thomson Dream* suits couples and solo travelers taking their first or second cruise, and families with children of all ages.

THE SHIP. *Thomson Dream* was originally *Homeric* for Home Lines; it was given an $84 million 'chop and stretch' in 1990 when bought by Holland America Line. The ship was acquired by Thomson Cruises in 2009, when it was refurbished. There are good teak outside decks, and a walk-around promenade deck, plus decent space for sunbathing. There is also a swimming pool deck, although the pool itself is small. The ship absorbs people well, with good passenger flow. There are several bars and lounges, plus lots of nooks and crannies to inhabit. Other facilities include a library/Internet lounge, card room, and shops. Niggles include poor maintenance of exterior areas, irritating announcements, expensive shore excursions, and the lack of an observation lounge.

FAMILIES. *Thomson Dream* allots a decent amount of space to children's facilities, which suits the increasing number of families who choose this ship. Some larger cabins have a sofa that turns into a bed.

ACCOMMODATION. There are several cabin price grades, including suites, mini-suites, outside-view cabins, and interior cabins, priced according to grade, size, and location. You can pre-book your preference for a per cabin fee of £42 (around $70). Except for suite-category cabins, each with king-size beds, separate lounge area, and bathroom with full size tub, most other cab-

Berlitz's Ratings		
	Possible	Achieved
Ship	500	304
Accommodation	200	122
Food	400	230
Service	400	248
Entertainment	100	61
Cruise Experience	400	241
OVERALL SCORE		
1206 points out of 2000		

ins are of a similar size. In general, they are fairly well equipped with decent storage space and good-size bathrooms. Soundproofing is poor. Most cabins have twin beds, but some have berths. There are four cabins for the disabled, located on higher decks, close to elevators.

DINING. The Orion Restaurant is a traditional dining room with port and starboard side portholes. Open-seating dining is the norm. The tables are close together and it can be loud. The cuisine is British-Continental but, although there's plenty of food, its quality is disappointing. However, it's all provided at a low price point – you get what you pay for.

Other dining options. The Grill is an extra-cost, à-la-carte steak and seafood restaurant, with white tablecloths and candlelight dining. Reservations are required. The Andromeda Restaurant and Sirens Restaurant provide meals in a self-serve buffet setting. The poolside Terrace Grill, open for lunch, features fast food such as barbecue items, pizzas, pasta, and salads.

ENTERTAINMENT. Facilities include the Atlante Theatre, a two-deck-high showlounge. Pillars obstruct some sight lines. A resident troupe of singers and dancers present colorful, high-energy production shows. The showlounge also presents cabaret acts. A number of musical acts provide live music in lounges and bars.

SPA/FITNESS. Oceans Spa includes a gym, saunas, and massage rooms. The facility is small, given the number of passengers carried. It is operated by Flair.

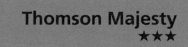

Thomson Majesty
★★★

Size:	Mid-size Ship	Passenger Space Ratio (lower beds):	27.9
Tonnage:	40,876	Passenger/Crew Ratio (lower beds):	2.4
Lifestyle:	Standard	Cabins (total):	732
Cruise Line:	Thomson Cruises	Size Range (sq ft/m):	118.4–374.5/11.0–34.8
Former Names:	*Louis Majesty, Norwegian Majesty,*	Cabins (for one person):	0
	Royal Majesty, Birka Queen	Cabins (with private balcony):	0
IMO Number:	8814744	Cabins (wheelchair accessible):	7
Builder:	Kvaerner Masa-Yards STX (Finland)	Wheelchair accessibility:	Fair
Original Cost:	$229 million	Cabin Current:	110 and 220 volts
Entered Service:	Sep 1992/May 2012	Elevators:	6
Registry:	Malta	Casino (gaming tables):	Yes
Length (ft/m):	681.1/207.6	Slot Machines:	Yes
Beam (ft/m):	91.8/28.0	Swimming Pools:	2
Draft (ft/m):	20.3/6.2	Hot Tubs (on deck):	2
Propulsion/Propellers:	diesel (21,120kW)/2	Self-Service Launderette:	No
Passenger Decks:	9	Dedicated Cinema/Seats:	No
Total Crew:	600	Library:	Yes
Passengers (lower beds):	1,462	Onboard currency:	UK£

A modestly stylish ship for casual, friendly cruising

OVERVIEW. This family-friendly ship provides good value for money. It absorbs passengers well and provides a very comfortable cruise experience in warm, crisp surroundings, with good food and decent hospitality from a really friendly crew.

THE SHIP. Smart and modestly stylish, *Thomson Majesty* is generally a well-designed vessel, ideally suited to Mediterranean cruising. Inside, it is quite pretty and warm, with lots of wood paneling, chrome/copper accents, reasonably discreet lighting, soothing colors, and no glitz. Wide passageways and high ceilings in some areas help provide a feeling of inner spaciousness.

ACCOMMODATION. There are several price grades. Almost all outside-view and interior cabins are on the small side, but quite comfortable; all have flat-screen TVs. The closets are really small, but luggage can be stored under the bed. The bathrooms are a little tight, although there's a generous amount of room in the shower enclosures.

Two large suites (901, 903) have a separate bedroom with walk-in closet and bathroom with combination tub and shower; there is a step of about 9ins (23cm). The lounge has a dining table, plus a sofa and chairs in the bay window. There are bay windows in both lounge and bedroom, and separate TV sets/DVD players; a tea/coffee-making set-up and late-afternoon snacks are provided. The Junior Suites (902–923) are smaller, but they do have a curtain separating lounge and bed-

Berlitz's Ratings		
	Possible	Achieved
Ship	500	313
Accommodation	200	130
Food	400	236
Service	400	253
Entertainment	100	61
Cruise Experience	400	246
OVERALL SCORE		
1239 points out of 2000		

room. Suite-grade bathrooms have a tub and shower combination. Room service food is available, at extra cost.

DINING. The main dining venues are the Seven Seas Restaurant, with 636 seats, and the Four Seasons Restaurant, with 266 seats, and both with open seating. The food, menu, creativity, and service are sound, with generous portions. The wine list is quite decent and reasonably priced.

Other dining options. The 56-seat Le Bistro restaurant serves Italian and Continental cuisine. No reservations are needed, but a cover charge applies.

Café Royale is an indoor self-serve buffet venue, with 112 seats. An outdoor grill, called Piazza San Marco, provides fast food such as burgers, hot dogs, pasta, and pizzas, while the Coffee Bar offers coffees and teas.

ENTERTAINMENT. The Royal Fireworks Lounge is the main showlounge; it has banquette seating and individual tub chairs. A second entertainment lounge, the Jubilee Lounge, is located aft of the Monte Carlo Casino. Several small musical units play in the ship's various lounges. Late-nighters might like to go to the real meeting place, Frame 52 – the ship's disco.

SPA/FITNESS. The Sana Wellness Center contains a small gymnasium with muscle-toning equipment, an aerobics area, men's and women's saunas, a beauty salon, and seven massage/body treatment rooms including one for couples.

Thomson Spirit
★★★

Size:	Mid-size Ship	Passenger/Crew Ratio (lower beds):	2.4
Tonnage:	33,930	Cabins (total):	627
Lifestyle:	Standard	Size Range (sq ft/m):	140.0–430.0/13.0–40.0
Cruise Line:	Thomson Cruises	Cabins (for one person):	0
Former Names:	Nieuw Amsterdam, Patriot, Nieuw Amsterdam	Cabins (with private balcony):	19
IMO Number:	8024014	Cabins (wheelchair accessible):	4
Builder:	Chantiers de l'Atlantique (France)	Wheelchair accessibility:	Fair
Original Cost:	$150 million	Cabin Current:	110 and 220 volts
Entered Service:	Jul 1983/May 2002	Elevators:	7
Registry:	Malta	Casino (gaming tables):	Yes
Length (ft/m):	704.2/214.6	Slot Machines:	Yes
Beam (ft/m):	89.4/27.2	Swimming Pools:	2
Draft (ft/m):	25.9/7.9	Hot Tubs (on deck):	1
Propulsion/Propellers:	diesel (21,600kW)/2	Self-Service Launderette:	Yes
Passenger Decks:	10	Dedicated Cinema/Seats:	Yes/230
Total Crew:	520	Library:	Yes
Passengers (lower beds):	1,254	Onboard currency:	UK£
Passenger Space Ratio (lower beds):	27.0		

This is a family-friendly, mid-size ship with acceptable food and service

OVERVIEW. *Thomson Spirit* is best suited to adult couples and solo travelers taking their first or second cruise, and families with children of all ages, all seeking a modern, nonglitzy ship with a decent array of public lounges and bars, and happy with a middle-of-the-road lifestyle, with food and entertainment that is acceptable rather than fancy.

THE SHIP. *Thomson Spirit*, originally built for Holland America Line (HAL), has a nicely raked bow and a contemporary transom stern, but overall the ship's angular exterior superstructure design makes it look squat and quite boxy. The exterior has an all-white hull and superstructure. There's a good amount of open teakwood deck space, particularly at the aft section of the ship, and the traditional outdoors teakwood decks include a walkaround promenade deck. Unfortunately, the ship has always suffered from poor build quality and excessive vibration, particularly aft.

HAL sold the ship to the publicly funded United States Lines in 2000, but that company sank in a sea of debt the following year. Carnival Corporation, which owns HAL, bought back the ship and chartered it to Louis Cruises, which in turn sub-chartered it to Thomson Cruises. *Thomson Spirit* has a sister ship in the slightly newer, 1984-built *Thomson Celebration* (formerly HAL's *Noordam*).

Thomson first operated cruises in the 1970s, but abandoned them, only to start cruise operations again in the mid-1990s using chartered, rather than wholly owned, ships. It has been a highly successful

Berlitz's Ratings		
	Possible	Achieved
Ship	500	295
Accommodation	200	125
Food	400	238
Service	400	249
Entertainment	100	60
Cruise Experience	400	241
OVERALL SCORE		
1208 points out of 2000		

venture, offering extremely good value for money, particularly for adult couples, and, occasionally, families with children.

Thomson Spirit has a fairly spacious interior design and layout, with little crowding and congestion; most public rooms (five bars and two lounges) are on a single deck. The color combinations do not jar the senses – most have splashes of color. There is much polished teakwood and rosewood paneling throughout the interiors. The Horizon Lounge, atop the ship, is an observation lounge by day and popular disco/nightclub by night.

This ship is quite acceptable for passengers wanting pleasant surroundings and an all-British ambience. However, many newer ships have more space, better facilities, and more options, so this ship loses a few points by comparison. Perhaps the best part of cruising aboard *Thomson Spirit* lies in the destinations and not the ship.

Hotel add-ons can extend a cruise vacation, and Thomson has a fine collection, depending on your needs, budget, and whether you are traveling with children or grandchildren. Because the ship is exclusive to Thomson Cruises, your fellow passengers are likely to be British.

Thomson owns its own airline, Thomson Airways, with airlift from almost a score of UK airports. With Thomson, you pay only for what you want. You can pre-book a window seat or a premium seat with more space than standard seats for an extra fee.

FAMILIES. Children have their own play areas at the aft of Bridge Deck. There are several children's clubs: Tots is for 3–5-year-olds, Team is for 6–8s, while Tribe is for 9–12s. The clubs operate five days a week (not on embarkation or disembarkation days) and are supervised by qualified 'children's hosts.'

ACCOMMODATION. There are four accommodation grades: suite-grade, deluxe, outside, and interior (no view). There are four large cabins, with fine forward-facing views, for the disabled. You can pre-book your preference for an extra per-cabin fee (and avoid any cabins with obstructed views).

Most cabins are quite small – below the industry standard of 170 sq ft (16 sq m). However, they are reasonably well appointed and practically laid out. Some have wood furniture, fittings, or accenting, good counter and storage space but little drawer space, a large dressing mirror, and private bathrooms that are adequate, but no more. Some cabins have full-size bathtubs, while others have showers. Several cabins have king- or queen-size beds, although most have twin beds. Some cabins also have additional berths for a third/fourth person (good for families with small children). Room service is available 24 hours a day (but costs extra). The cabin insulation is poor, and bathroom towels are small.

The largest accommodation is in the Presidential Suite. Small by comparison to suites aboard many other ships, it measures 430 sq ft (40 sq m) and is on the uppermost accommodation deck. It has a king-size bed, walk-in closet, wet bar, study and dining areas, TV set, DVD player, and stereo system. The bathroom includes a whirlpool tub, double sink unit, and a powder room.

DINING. The Compass Rose Restaurant is reasonably attractive, with ample space. Breakfast, lunch, and dinner (6–10.30pm) are served in an open-seating arrangement, so you may get a different table and waiters for each meal. Although there are a few tables for two, most are for four, six, or eight. Dinners typically include a choice of four entrées; a vegetarian entrée is also available daily. Children have their own menu, with 'home from home' dishes and small portions.

Other dining options. Dessert and pastry items are made to suit British tastes, although there is much use of canned fruits and jellies.

Sirocco's à-la-carte restaurant is an intimate dining venue; reservations are required, and a cover charge applies. It seats only 45 and has superior food and service and a quieter, more refined atmosphere than that of the main dining room. It is adjacent to the Compass Rose Restaurant, and best entered from the aft stairway.

For casual meals, the Lido Restaurant, is open 24/7, with open seating. Tables are set with crisp linens, flatware, and stemware for dinner, when the set menu includes a choice of four entrées. Each week a themed buffet – Chinese, Indian, or Mexican, depending on the cruise itinerary – may be offered for dinner. On Lido Deck, the outdoor Terrace Grill provides fast-food grilled items and pizza during the day.

ENTERTAINMENT. The 600-seat Broadway Show-lounge is two decks high (main and balcony levels) and is the venue for production shows and cabaret entertainment. Although Thomson is not known for high-quality shows, they are, in fact, good fun, and are professionally produced, while cabaret acts provide entertainment on evenings when there is no production show.

A second entertainment venue, High Spirits, is a multi-functional room for quizzes, dancing, and a late-night disco. A number of bands and musical units provide live music for dancing and listening to in several lounges and bars.

SPA/FITNESS. Oceans Health Club is atop the ship aft. It has good ocean views, and overlooks the aft pool and hot tub, on Bridge Deck. Facilities include an aerobics exercise room, a decent-size gymnasium with plenty of treadmills, exercycles, and other body-toning equipment, a men's and a women's sauna, but no steam room, and several treatment rooms.

You can have massages, aromatherapy facials, body wraps, manicures, pedicures, and other body-pampering treatments. The beauty salon is located close to the reception desk on the port side, in a completely different area from the health club.

Veendam
★★★+

Size:	Mid-size Ship
Tonnage:	57,092
Lifestyle:	Premium
Cruise Line:	Holland America Line
Former Names:	none
IMO Number:	9102992
Builder:	Fincantieri (Italy)
Original Cost:	$215 million
Entered Service:	May 1996
Registry:	Bahamas
Length (ft/m):	719.3/219.3
Beam (ft/m):	101.0/30.8
Draft (ft/m):	24.6/7.5
Propulsion/Propellers:	diesel-electric (34,560kW)/2
Passenger Decks:	10
Total Crew:	561
Passengers (lower beds):	1,348
Passenger Space Ratio (lower beds):	42.4

Passenger/Crew Ratio (lower beds):	2.2
Cabins (total):	674
Size Range (sq ft/m):	186.2–1,124.8/17.3–104.5
Cabins (for one person):	0
Cabins (with private balcony):	182
Cabins (wheelchair accessible):	8
Wheelchair accessibility:	Fair
Cabin Current:	110 and 220 volts
Elevators:	8
Casino (gaming tables):	Yes
Slot Machines:	Yes
Swimming Pools:	2 (1 w/ sliding glass dome)
Hot Tubs (on deck):	2
Self-Service Launderette:	Yes
Dedicated Cinema/Seats:	Yes/249
Library:	Yes
Onboard currency:	US$

Dutch heritage and decor for mature-age travelers

OVERVIEW. Holland America Line (HAL) is constantly fine-tuning its performance, and its regular passengers, almost all North American, find its ships very comfortable and well run. The company continues its strong maritime traditions, although the present food and service components still let down the rest of the cruise experience.

THE SHIP. *Veendam* is one of four almost identical ships, the others being *Maasdam*, *Pacific Aria (formerly Ryndam)*, and *Pacific Eden (formerly Statendam)*. The exterior styling is rather angular (some would say boxy – the funnel certainly is), although it is softened and balanced somewhat by the hull being painted black. A ducktail sponson stern was added in 2009 for better stability and ride characteristics. There is a full walk-around teakwood promenade deck outdoors – good for strolling, and there's no sign of synthetic turf anywhere. The sunloungers on the exterior Promenade Deck are wood, with comfortable cushioned pads, while those at the swimming pool on Lido Deck are white plastic.

In the interiors of this S-class ship, an asymmetrical layout helps to reduce bottlenecks and congestion. Most public rooms are concentrated on two decks, Promenade Deck, and Upper Promenade Deck, which creates a spacious feel to the interiors. In general, there's a restrained approach to interior styling, using a mixture of contemporary materials combined with traditional woods and ceramics. There's little glitz anywhere.

Berlitz's Ratings		
	Possible	Achieved
Ship	500	345
Accommodation	200	142
Food	400	251
Service	400	282
Entertainment	100	68
Cruise Experience	400	265
OVERALL SCORE		
1353 points out of 2000		

A $2 million artwork collection was assembled and displayed to represent HAL's fine Dutch heritage; it presents a balance between standard itineraries and onboard creature comforts. Also noticeable are the live flower arrangements, used to good effect to brighten up the otherwise dull decor.

Atop the ship is the Crow's Nest Lounge. By day it is an observation lounge, with large ocean-view windows; in the evening it's a nightclub with variable lighting.

A three-deck-high atrium foyer is quite appealing (and a good meeting place), although its sculpted centerpiece makes it look crowded, and leaves little room in front of reception. A hydraulic glass roof covers the reasonably sized swimming pool/whirlpools and central Lido area, so it can be used in all weather. The focal point here is a large dolphin sculpture.

There is a large, relaxing reference library. As part of its Signature of Excellence program, the ship received a new 'Mix' lifestyle area. This is a trendy, upbeat space combining three specialty theme bars in one central area: Champagne (serving Champagne and sparkling wines), Martinis (in individual shakers), and Spirits & Ales (a sports bar with beer and baseball/basketball). Microsoft Surface touch-screen technology is available for playing checkers and chess, air hockey, and other sports games.

A casino features gaming tables and slot machines. However, note that part of the Casino is open, and can be full of cigarette smoke (yes, smoking is still permitted here).

The service staff is Indonesian; although they are mostly quite charming, communication can occasionally prove frustrating, and service can be spotty and inconsistent.

An escalator travels between two of the lower decks (one was originally planned to be the embarkation point). The charge to use the washing machines and dryers in the self-service launderette is petty. The men's urinals in public restrooms are unusually high.

ACCOMMODATION. The accommodation ranges from small interior cabins to a large Penthouse Suite, in many different price categories. All cabin TV sets normally carry CNN.

The interior and outside-view standard cabins have twin beds that convert to a queen-size bed, and there is a separate living space with sofa and coffee table. Although the drawer space is generally good, the closet space is very tight, particularly for long cruises, but adequate for seven nights. The tiled bathrooms are compact but practical. Bathrobes, hairdryers, and a small range of toiletries are provided for all suites/cabins. The bathrooms are quite well laid out, but the tubs are small units better described as shower tubs. Some cabins have interconnecting doors.

On Navigation Deck, 28 suites can accommodate four persons and offer in-suite dining as an alternative to the dining room. They are spacious, tastefully decorated, and well laid-out, with a separate living room, bedroom with two lower beds that convert to a king-size bed, a good-size living area, dressing room, plenty of closet and drawer space, and marble bathroom with Jacuzzi tub.

The largest accommodation is the single Penthouse Suite, on the starboard side of Navigation Deck at the forward staircase. It has a king-size bed and vanity desk; large walk-in closet with superb drawer space; an oversize whirlpool bath that could seat four; separate shower enclosure; washroom with toilet, bidet, and washbasin; a living room with writing desk, large TV/infotainment system and DVD player; dressing room; large balcony with teak lounge chairs and drinks tables, dining table, and four chairs; a pantry with large refrigerator, toaster unit, full coffee/tea-making facilities, food preparation area, and a separate entrance from the hallway; a minibar/refrigerator; a guest toilet; and floor-to-ceiling windows.

DINING. The Rotterdam Dining Room spans two decks at the stern of the ship, and has two grand staircases to connect the two levels, panoramic views on three sides, and a music balcony. Both open seating and assigned-table seating are available, while breakfast and lunch are open-seating, though you'll be taken to a free table by restaurant staff when you enter. There are tables for two- to eight, and Rosenthal china and good-quality cutlery are provided. The waiter stations are very noisy for anyone seated near them.

Other dining options. The intimate Pinnacle Grill is located just forward of the balcony level of the main dining room on the starboard side. The 66-seat venue has Pacific Northwest cuisine such as fresh Alaskan salmon and halibut, and other regional specialties, plus a selection of premium steaks such as filet mignon from Black Angus beef. Reservations are needed, and a service charge applies. A Bulgari show plate, Rosenthal china, Riedel wine glasses, and Frette table linen are used. The extra cost is worth it for that special celebration.

For more casual evening eating, the dual-line, self-serve Lido Buffet is open for dinners on all except the last night of each cruise, in an open-seating arrangement. Tables are set with crisp linens, flatware, and stemware. A set menu is featured, with a choice of four entrées. This is also the place for casual breakfasts and lunches. Between 5.30–9pm, a section is transformed into Canaletto (reservations required) for casual Italian meals.

There is much use of canned fruits and packeted items, and several commercial low-calorie salad dressings. The choice of cheeses and crackers is poor.

You may need to eat in the Lido Buffet on days when the dining room is closed for lunch – typically once or twice per cruise, depending on the itinerary.

Also, a Lido Deck poolside 'Dive-In at the Terrace Grill' features signature burgers, hot dogs and fries, and, on certain days, barbecues and other culinary treats may be featured.

ENTERTAINMENT. The Showroom at Sea, at the forward part of the ship, spans two decks, with banquette seating on both the main and upper levels. It is basically a well-designed room, but the ceiling is low, and sight lines from the balcony level are quite poor.

SPA/FITNESS. The Ocean Spa is one deck below the navigation bridge at the very forward part of the ship. It includes a gymnasium with all the latest muscle-pumping exercise machines, including an abundance of treadmills. It has ocean views, an aerobics exercise area, a large beauty salon with ocean-view windows to the port side, several treatment rooms, a sauna, steam room, and changing areas.

Ventura
★★★★

Size:	Large Resort Ship
Tonnage:	116,017
Lifestyle:	Standard
Cruise Line:	P&O Cruises
Former Names:	none
IMO Number:	9333175
Builder:	Fincantieri (Italy)
Original Cost:	€535 million
Entered Service:	Apr 2008
Registry:	Bermuda
Length (ft/m):	951.4/290.0
Beam (ft/m):	118.1/36.0
Draft (ft/m):	27.8/8.5
Propulsion/Propellers:	diesel-electric (42,000kW)/2
Passenger Decks:	15
Total Crew:	1,239
Passengers (lower beds):	3,074
Passenger Space Ratio (lower beds):	37.7

Passenger/Crew Ratio (lower beds):	2.4
Cabins (total):	1,546
Size Range (sq ft/m):	134.5–534.0/12.5–49.6
Cabins (for one person):	18
Cabins (with private balcony):	880
Cabins (wheelchair accessible):	25
Wheelchair accessibility:	Good
Cabin Current:	220 volts
Elevators:	12
Casino (gaming tables):	Yes
Slot Machines:	Yes
Swimming Pools:	3
Hot Tubs (on deck):	6
Self-Service Launderette:	Yes
Dedicated Cinema/Seats:	No
Library:	Yes
Onboard currency:	UK£

A large, family-friendly ship aimed at British tastes

OVERVIEW. *Ventura* is mainly suited to British families with children as well as adult couples who are looking for a big-ship environment with comfortable but unstuffy surroundings and lots of options.

THE SHIP. *Ventura* is the P&O version of Princess Cruises' *Grand*-class ships, along with sister ship *Azura*. There are promenade walking decks to the port and starboard sides, underneath the lifeboats. You can't walk completely around, however; it's narrow in some places, and you have to weave past a number of deck lounge chairs. There are three pools: two on the pool deck, one of which can be covered by a glass-roofed skydome, and one at the stern.

Inside, a three-deck atrium is the focal social meeting point. Designed on a gateway theme, central to which are four towering black granite archways sourced from India, it's the place to see and be seen, and the best location to arrange to meet friends. The upper-deck public room layout is challenging, because you can't go from one end of the ship to the other without first going down, along, and up – poor for anyone with mobility problems.

Public rooms include a perfume shop, library, a Cruise Sales Centre, Fortunes Casino, and several bars, including The Exchange (an urban warehouse bar), and The Beach House (outside with great aft views and views along the ship's sides – over everyone's balcony), and Red bar. Check out the train that runs around the upper part of the upper bar of The Exchange.

Berlitz's Ratings

	Possible	Achieved
Ship	500	398
Accommodation	200	155
Food	400	249
Service	400	287
Entertainment	100	77
Cruise Experience	400	295

OVERALL SCORE
1461 points out of 2000

Passenger niggles include the constant push for on-board revenue, low passenger/space ratio, mediocre self-service buffet food, and a charge for shuttle buses in many ports.

Smoking is permitted only in designated spots on the open decks. Gratuities are automatically charged to your onboard account.

It's possible to get married on board, with the captain officiating.

FAMILIES. There are children's clubs for the under-twos up to 17 years, plus a rock 'n' roll school. Children will be pleased to find that, for 2–4-year-olds, Noddy is on board. Youngsters can also enjoy Scalextric at sea with Grand Prix-style track, 3D cinema, and interactive art classes. Family shore programs feature aqua and 'theme parks.' There's a useful Night Nursery for the under-fives.

ACCOMMODATION. There are many different accommodation price grades, according to size and location chosen, but really just the following types of accommodation: suite with balcony; family suite with balcony; outside-view twin/queen with balcony; outside-view twin/queen; and interior no-view cabin. More than one-third of all cabins are of the interior variety. Some have extra third/fourth berths that fold down from the ceiling. While the suites are quite spacious, they are small when compared to suites aboard some other cruise lines, such as Celebrity Cruises or Holland America Line. In 2013, 18 single-occupancy cabins were added (12 outside and six interior), in line with those aboard *Azura* – good news for solo travelers.

Standard in all cabins: bed runners, 10.5 tog duvets, Slumberland sprung mattresses, and Egyptian cotton towels. Basic tea/coffee-making facilities and packets of UHT milk, not fresh milk, are provided. The tea-making set-up is adequate, but getting fresh milk can sometimes be a problem. Bathrobes are available only for passengers occupying grades A, B, and D accommodation. There are UK three-pin sockets, plus US-style 110-volt sockets, for electrical devices.

Cabins have open closets (no doors = no money wasted), which actually provide easy access. Balcony cabins have teak patio furniture, and an outside light. The decent-quality personal toiletries are by Temple Spa.

Wheelchair-accessible cabins have a shower enclosure, except one (R415) that has a bathtub with integral shower. They are mostly in the front section. Note that the Bay Tree restaurant is aft, so be prepared for lots of waiting time at elevators. To take breakfast in the self-serve Waterside casual eatery, wheelchair users need to make their way across the decks containing the Beachcomber and Laguna pools and lots of deck chairs – not easy. Alternatively, room-service breakfast – typically cold items only – can be ordered. (Note that there is no room service breakfast on disembarkation day.)

DINING. P&O's marketing blurb claims there are 10 restaurants. There really aren't. There are five genuine restaurants (Bay Tree, Cinnamon, Saffron, The White Room, and East); the rest are more casual eateries.

The three main dining rooms, Bay Tree, Cinnamon, and Saffron, have standard à-la-carte menus. Bay Tree offers fixed seating dining, with assigned tables and typical seating times of 6.30pm or 8.30pm. In the other two, you can dine when you want, with whom you want, between 6pm and 10pm – P&O calls it Freedom Dining – although at peak times there can be long waiting times for a table.

Once or twice per cruise, additional special dinners are served in the main dining rooms, one being a 'Chaîne des Rôtisseurs' event. The ship's wine list is ho-hum average.

Other dining options. Specialty dining venues include the White Room, located high up on the ship above the children's play area, with a quarter of the tables on an open deck. It features modern European dishes by celebrity chef Marco Pierre White in an environment that is intimate and attentive but not stuffy – good for families. Reservations are needed, and there's a cover charge. The food is cooked to order, unlike in the main dining rooms. Occasionally,

Marco Pierre White sails aboard the ship, and holds cooking classes for up to eight participants in one of the ship's galleys.

For complete privacy, private balcony dining, with selections from the Marco Pierre White menu, is also available as a rather pricey (but perhaps worthwhile) extra-cost option.

The Waterside is a large, self-serve buffet 'seaside chic' dining spot, with indoor-outdoor seating, but the seating is rather poorly designed and cramped, and the food selection is poor (better for lunch than for breakfast or dinner).

On the same deck, adjacent to the forward pool, are Frankie's Grill and Frankie's Pizzeria.

Tazzine, a coffee lounge by day, turns into a cocktail bar in the evening.

The Beach House is a casual dining spot for families, open 24 hours. Marco's roof-side café serves gourmet pizzas, grills, and original ice cream flavors such as chocolate truffle and prune and Armagnac. Children's cutlery, bibs, and beakers are available.

East is an Asian fusion eatery on the main indoor promenade. In addition, 24-hour room service is available in cabins.

ENTERTAINMENT. P&O claims the 785-seat Arena Theatre, at the front of the ship and spanning two decks, is the largest showlounge aboard a UK-based cruise ship, but in fact the showlounge aboard *Queen Mary 2* is larger, with 1,094 seats, as is the Showlounge aboard *Independence of the Seas*. Havana, the main nightclub and entertainment venue, where movies are sometimes shown, is an activities room by day and a sultry Cuba-inspired club by night, but the sight lines are extremely poor from many seats.

A cool wall in the Cosmopolitan club lounge screens real-time footage of the world's seven most famous city skylines – Sydney, Paris, New York, Rio de Janeiro, Las Vegas, Hong Kong, and London.

SPA/FITNESS. The Oasis Spa is located forward, almost atop the ship. It includes a gymnasium, aerobics room, beauty salon, separate men's and women's sauna and steam rooms, and 11 treatment rooms. An internal stairway connects to the deck below, which contains an extra-charge Thermal Suite. Harding Brothers provide the spa staff and services. Treatments include special packages for couples, and the Silver-Spa Generation, as well as a whole range of individual treatments. Active types can take instruction in Cirque Ventura's activities, including juggling, acro-balancing, tight-wire walking, stilt walking, and clowning.

Viking Sky
NYR

Size:	Mid-size Ship	Passenger/Crew Ratio (lower beds):	1.7
Tonnage:	47,800	Cabins (total):	465
Lifestyle:	Premium	Size Range (sq ft/m):	312.1-1,668.4/29.0-155.0
Cruise Line:	Viking Cruises	Cabins (for one person):	0
Former Names:	none	Cabins (with private balcony):	465
IMO Number:	9650418	Cabins (wheelchair accessible):	2
Builder:	Fincantieri (Italy)	Wheelchair accessibility:	Good
Original Cost:	$400 million	Cabin Current:	110 and 220 volts
Entered Service:	May 2016	Elevators:	6
Registry:	Norway	Casino (gaming tables):	No
Length (ft/m):	745.4/227.2	Slot Machines:	No
Beam (ft/m):	94.5/28.8	Swimming Pools:	1
Draft (ft/m):	20.6/6.3	Hot Tubs (on deck):	1
Propulsion/Propellers:	diesel-electric / 2	Self-Service Launderette:	Yes
Passenger Decks:	9	Dedicated Cinema/Seats:	Yes/100
Total Crew:	545	Library:	Yes
Passengers (lower beds):	930	Onboard currency:	US$
Passenger Space Ratio (lower beds):	51.5		

A smart-looking premium ship for the experienced traveler

OVERVIEW. *Viking Sky* is a really handsome contemporary ship with Scandinavian character. It is for adults who want to experience destinations in comfort. There are numerous public areas and dining options for its size, plus an abundance of glass walls that help connect you with the sea on every level.

THE SHIP. The ship is powered by hybrid energy-efficient engines, solar panels, and equipment for minimizing air pollution. Viking Cruises focuses on enhancing the destination experience (rather than the ship being your only destination), so throughout the ship you'll find interactive stations that provide a wealth of destination information. The interior design leaves an uncluttered impression, so you won't find overly opulent surroundings – it's more Hyatt (premium) than Four Seasons (luxe).

A walk-around promenade deck is on a lower deck (Deck 2) so it's fairly well sheltered from any wind – good for a stroll. Meanwhile, on the largest upper open deck, a sliding glass dome covers the main pool deck on the deck below, just forward of the main pool; aft of the pool is a spacious Wintergarden, with wood cladding around its support pillars. There's also a large screen for poolside movies. A second pool (and adjacent hot tub) on the same deck, but at the aft of the ship, is an 'Infinity' pool that forms part of an alfresco casual eatery with fine ocean views, called the Aquavit Terrace.

One neat feature of all the sunloungers provided is that they come with a retractable footrest, while

Berlitz's Ratings		
	Possible	Achieved
Ship	500	NYR
Accommodation	200	NYR
Food	400	NYR
Service	400	NYR
Entertainment	100	NYR
Cruise Experience	400	NYR
OVERALL SCORE		
NYR points out of 2000		

the square drinks tables have a thick wood top – very smart and practical. Inside the ship, the main focal point is a delightful, elegant, rectangular atrium lobby that is three-decks high and features light woods and clean Scandinavian design that lets in plenty of natural light. There is an abundance of inviting seating on all levels.

An Explorer's Lounge spans two decks. It is a fine, comfortable observation lounge with great views, and incorporates a library, practical seating, and a deli counter called Viking Café – so it's rather like an all-in-one living space, or lifestyle lounge. The upper level is certainly reminiscent of the popular Polaris (observation) Lounge aboard the ships of the former Royal Viking Line, and includes glass cabinets displaying items connected with exploration and discovery, as well as models of historic ships.

Viking Cruises is the sister company of the well-established and highly experienced Viking River Cruises. It has certainly concentrated on devising itineraries that are very destination-rich and immersive, so the shore excursion program is focused much more on the cultural experience.

Overall, the company is positioned against Azamara Club Cruises and Oceania Cruises – with much larger shower enclosures, lower pricing, and with more included. *Viking Sky* is an almost all-inclusive ship, with the fare covering Wi-Fi, a shore excursion in each port of call, overnight stays in embarkation or disembarkation ports, and complimentary beer and wine with lunch and dinner.

ACCOMMODATION. There are just five types of accommodation categories (plus an Owner's Suite that is conveniently positioned adjacent to the Explorer's Lounge), but with many different prices according to deck and location. All have a private balcony (Viking calls them verandas).

Viking likes to keep things like interior decor simple – a philosophy that has worked very well for its river cruise division. It is comfortable and practical, but perhaps a little minimalist, which is typical of the Scandinavian approach.

All accommodation grades feature a *king*-size bed, and even the smallest cabin has a shower enclosure spacious enough to bathe in. If you like more space, the Explorer Suites, located at the very front or back of the ship, are the ones to go for; most of these have a wrap-around balcony.

DINING. There are several restaurants and eateries to choose from, all of which operate on an open-seating basis, so you can dine with whom you like, when you like, and all of which are included in the cruise price.

Most venues also have an alfresco option (in fact, there is a great emphasis on dining in the fresh air).

The main dining venue is called, with great simplicity, The Dining Room. It has a sliding glass wall that can open onto the wrap-around promenade deck aft, with a few tables for alfresco dining, weather permitting.

The cuisine is decidedly international, but with some 'always available' comfort classics. The focus is on regional and sustainably sourced ingredients.

Other dining venues. The first three of these are located on the deck below the Dining Room). Manfredi's Italian Restaurant features Italian food with a focus on Tuscany; its decoration includes real accordions (the national instrument of Italy).

The Chef's Table is for a food-and-wine-paired specialty dining experience. The Kitchen Table is an intimate venue for chef's selections at night, while during the daytime it can be used for cooking classes.

Viking Café is part of the Explorer's Lounge, on its lower level. World Café (Lido Café) also has an outdoor area known as the Aquavit Terrace (a term borrowed from the sister company's riverships). Adjacent is an 'infinity' pool and hot tub.

Additionally, complimentary specialty coffees and teas are available around-the-clock, as is 24-hour room service, while an afternoon 'High Tea' can be experienced in The Wintergarden.

ENTERTAINMENT. The 250-seat Star Theater is a single-deck-height showlounge, designed more for cabaret acts, recitals, and lectures than for large production shows. This is because most of the experience aboard this ship involves the destinations (including overnight visits in some), so there's little need for entertainment on a grand scale.

SPA/FITNESS. A rather nice facility, The Spa is located indoors, on the lowest passenger deck. It includes a beauty salon, fitness center, sauna, a 'snow' (ice grotto) room (with snowflakes), and a salt-water thermal pool, set against a very relaxing that backdrop includes glass-fronted fireplaces.

Viking Star
★★★★+

Size:	Mid-size Ship	Passenger/Crew Ratio (lower beds):	1.7
Tonnage:	47,800	Cabins (total):	465
Lifestyle:	Premium	Size Range (sq ft/m):	312.1-1,668.4/29.0-155.0
Cruise Line:	Viking Cruises	Cabins (for one person):	0
Former Names:	none	Cabins (with private balcony):	465
IMO Number:	9650418	Cabins (wheelchair accessible):	2
Builder:	Fincantieri (Italy)	Wheelchair accessibility:	Good
Original Cost:	$400 million	Cabin Current:	110 and 220 volts
Entered Service:	Apr 2015	Elevators:	6
Registry:	Norway	Casino (gaming tables):	No
Length (ft/m):	745.4/227.2	Slot Machines:	No
Beam (ft/m):	94.5/28.8	Swimming Pools:	1
Draft (ft/m):	20.6/6.3	Hot Tubs (on deck):	1
Propulsion/Propellers:	diesel-electric / 2	Self-Service Launderette:	Yes
Passenger Decks:	9	Dedicated Cinema/Seats:	Yes/100
Total Crew:	545	Library:	Yes
Passengers (lower beds):	930	Onboard currency:	US$
Passenger Space Ratio (lower beds):	51.5		

This handsome-looking premium ship is for the well-traveled

OVERVIEW. *Viking Star* is a very smart-looking contemporary ship (delightfully reminiscent of the former Royal Viking Line's *Royal Viking Star*) that exudes style, and is aimed squarely at adults who want comfort and some elements of luxe, but no glitz. It has a lot of public areas and dining options for its size, plus an abundance of glass walls that help connect you with the sea on every level and provides the feeling that you are cruising in a floating residence.

Berlitz's Ratings		
	Possible	Achieved
Ship	500	462
Accommodation	200	171
Food	400	338
Service	400	325
Entertainment	100	76
Cruise Experience	400	326
OVERALL SCORE		
1698 points out of 2000		

THE SHIP. The sleek, uncluttered design of this ship – powered by hybrid energy-efficient engines, solar panels, and equipment for minimizing air pollution – is focused on enhancing the destination experience (rather than the ship being your only destination), so throughout the ship you'll find interactive stations that provide a wealth of destination information. What you won't find is overly opulent surroundings – the result of design elements that are more Hyatt (premium) than Four Seasons (luxe), and approaching Europa 2's beautiful interior design.

A walk-around promenade deck is on a lower deck (Deck 2) and is fairly well sheltered from any wind – good for a stroll. On the largest upper open deck, a sliding glass dome covers the main pool deck (and adjacent rectangular hot tub with its fine geometric-design tile surround) on the deck below, just forward of the main pool; aft of the pool is a large screen for poolside movies. Another pool on the same deck, but at the aft of the ship, is an 'Infinity' pool (and adjacent tiled hot tub) that is cantilevered off the ship's stern; it is part

of the Aquavit Terrace, an alfresco casual eatery with fine ocean views. The sunloungers include a retractable foot rest, while square drinks tables have stylish thick wood tops.

Inside, it is clear that Viking uses space efficiently, and provides a restrained 'wow' factor. The main focal point is a stunning, elegant, rectangular atrium lobby called The Living Room. It is three decks high and features light woods and clean Scandinavian design that lets in plenty of natural light. There is an abundance of inviting seating on all levels, while a coffee bar, large lounge chairs, sofas, and low tables really do provide a spacious living room ambiance. The grand stairway is wide, with a huge LED backdrop screen that projects images of Norway; underneath it is a lichen garden.

The stair foyers have huge tapestry-style walls with scenes depicting the Battle of Stamford Bridge, which ended the Nordic reign in 1066. Walls adjacent to the elevators feature stone tablets of Nordic scenes.

At two decks high, the split-level Explorer's Lounge is a supremely comfortable observation lounge with fine views (and tactile seat decoration including animal pelts thrown over chairs and sofas, and an abundance of cushions). It incorporates a library, and Mamsen's – a deli counter featuring Nordic treats – including Norwegian waffles and fresh berries for a breakfast snack (the teacups and coffee mugs are the same as used in the Hagen family home). The whole room is like an all-in-one living space. The upper level is reminiscent of the Polaris Lounge (the observation lounge) aboard the ships of the former Royal Viking Line; it includes glass cabinets displaying items connected with exploration and discovery by Norwegians Roald Amundsen, Leif Erikson, and Thor Heyerdhl, and models of historic ships, and is a delightful spot to relax.

Viking Cruises is the first new start-up cruise line to build new ships since 1998, when Disney Cruise Line built two. It's the sister company of the well-established and highly experienced Viking River Cruises. Viking has concentrated on devising itineraries that are destination-rich and immersive, so the shore excursion program is more focused on cultural experience than most, and really learning about the destinations.

Despite an initial impression of Scandinavian minimalism, the interior designers have created a beautiful, cozy and warm home-like environment. There are lots of delightful, quirky details – in fact to find them all you'll need to take another cruise. You may not find flowers, but you find bonsai, arrangements of moss, bark, lichen, and other tactile items, including some beautiful fabrics and touchy-feely surfaces.

Viking Cruises appears to have positioned itself fairly and squarely against Azamara Club Cruises and Oceania Cruises, but with newer ships (and with much larger bathrooms and shower enclosures, for example), lower pricing, and with more things included. *Viking Star* is almost an all-inclusive ship. Together with extremely good value lead-in prices, these are all included: ship-wide Wi-Fi; a shore excursion in each port; overnight stays in embarkation or disembarkation ports; complimentary self-service laundry; specialty coffees and teas (served or self-serve 24/7); no extra charges for any restaurant or catery; 24-hour room service; stocked mini-bar (in most accommodation grades); and beer and wine with lunch and dinner. Viking Cruises really is the new game in town – and, straddling the line between premium-plus and luxury – is perhaps the best value in cruising today!.

ACCOMMODATION. There are just five accommodation categories (plus a superb Owner's Suite that is conveniently positioned adjacent to the Explorer's Lounge – it includes a master bedroom, lounge, dining area, walk-in closet, wet room, and private sauna), but many different prices, according to deck and location. All accommodation has a private balcony (or 'veranda'). Viking likes to keep things like interior decor simple – a philosophy that has worked very well for its river cruise division. It is comfortable and practical, but perhaps a little minimalist for some, which is typical of the Scandinavian design efficiency approach.

All accommodation grades feature a king-size bed, and even the smallest cabin has a shower enclosure spacious enough to bathe in. If you like more space, the Explorer Suites are the ones to go for; most of these have a wrap-around balcony.

DINING. There are several restaurants and eateries to choose from, all of which operate on an open-seating basis, so you can dine with whom you like, when you like, and all of which are included in the cruise price. Most also have an alfresco option (in fact, there is a great emphasis on dining in fresh air).

The principal dining venue is called, quite simply, The Dining Room (with tablecloths for all meals, and fine plates and cutlery that is of an ideal weight). It has a sliding glass wall that can open onto the wrap-around promenade deck aft, with some tables for al fresco dining, weather permitting.

The cuisine is decidedly international, but with some 'always available' comfort classics. The focus is on regional and sustainably sourced ingredients, with everything cooked from scratch (no pre-mixed sauces, soups, or bread purchased from outside sources).

Other dining venues. The first three of these are located on the deck below the main dining room (The Dining Room). Manfredi's Italian Restaurant features Italian food with a focus on Tuscany; its decoration includes real accordions (the national instrument of Italy), and photographs of Italian film stars (plus some amusing photographs of Italian chef Gaetano together with Torstein Hagen, chairman of Viking Cruises, and Manfredi d'Ovidio, chairman of Silversea Cruises).

The Chef's Table is for a specialty dining experience, where the food and wine are paired. The Kitchen Table is an intimate venue for chef's selections, while during the daytime the venue can be used for cooking classes.

Mamsen's (a sort of Norwegian deli) is part of the lower level of the Explorer's Lounge.

World Café is the ship's casual self-serve Lido Café – with open kitchen, and moveable glass doors that can open onto an outdoor area called the Aquavit Terrace (a term borrowed from the sister company's riverships) that is adjacent to the 'infinity' pool and hot tub.

Additionally, complimentary specialty coffees and loose-leaf teas are available around-the-clock, as is 24-hour room service, while an afternoon 'High Tea' can be taken in The Wintergarden. Do try one of the superb armagnacs, with vintages starting in 1935 – you'll find them in a hide-away bar called Torshavn.

ENTERTAINMENT. The 250-seat Star Theater is the ship's single-deck-height showlounge, designed more for cabaret acts, recitals, and lectures rather than large production shows. This is because most of the experience aboard this ship involves the destinations (including overnight visits in some), so there's little need for entertainment on a grand scale.

SPA/FITNESS. The Spa is expansive and beautifully designed. It includes a beauty salon, fitness center, 'snow' room, and salt water thermal pool (with swim-against-the-flow feature), in a relaxing backdrop. Separate male and female areas include a sauna, plunge bath, changing area, and a relaxation area. Operated by LivNordic, the whole spa area is precisely that – Nordic – and elegant, with well-trained staff, who don't push for sales of expensive bodycare items. However, pampering treatments are on the pricey side.

Vision of the Seas
★★★+

Size:	Mid-size Ship
Tonnage:	78,491
Lifestyle:	Standard
Cruise Line:	Royal Caribbean International
Former Names:	none
IMO Number:	9116876
Builder:	Chantiers de l'Atlantique (France)
Original Cost:	$275 million
Entered Service:	May 1998
Registry:	Bahamas
Length (ft/m):	915.3/279.0
Beam (ft/m):	105.6/32.2
Draft (ft/m):	24.9/7.6
Propulsion/Propellers:	diesel-electric (50,400kW)/2
Passenger Decks:	11
Total Crew:	735
Passengers (lower beds):	2,000
Passenger Space Ratio (lower beds):	39.2
Passenger/Crew Ratio (lower beds):	2.7
Cabins (total):	1,000
Size Range (sq ft/m):	135.0–1,270.1/12.5–118.0
Cabins (for one person):	0
Cabins (with private balcony):	229
Cabins (wheelchair accessible):	14
Wheelchair accessibility:	Good
Cabin Current:	110 and 220 volts
Elevators:	9
Casino (gaming tables):	Yes
Slot Machines:	Yes
Swimming Pools:	2
Hot Tubs (on deck):	6
Self-Service Launderette:	No
Dedicated Cinema/Seats:	No
Library:	Yes
Onboard currency:	US$

This good-looking ship has sleek lines and is very comfortable

OVERVIEW. *Vision of the Seas*, with its slim funnel placed at the very aft, is a ship that the whole family can enjoy, and offers a good choice of restaurants and eateries.

THE SHIP. *Vision of the Seas* shares the design features that make all Royal Caribbean International (RCI) ships identifiable. The ship's stern is beautifully rounded.

There are two swimming pools, the main pool, which also has a large movie screen, and an aft pool, which is within a Solarium indoor/outdoor area (with a retractable dome). There's a decent amount of open-air walking space, although this can become cluttered with sunloungers that would benefit from having cushioned pads. While not as large as the newer ships in the fleet, *Vision of the Seas* is perhaps more suited to couples and families with children that don't need all those bells and whistles, but want to cruise with up-to-date facilities and have multiple dining choices for more convenience. Enhancements made in the last refurbishment include ship-wide Wi-Fi (it costs extra to use it), flat-screen televisions in all cabins, and finger-touch digital 'wayfinder' direction screens.

A multi-level atrium lobby called the Centrum is the focal point within the ship, and *the* social meeting place. In a 2013 makeover, the whole area was revamped, and new features were added. On its various levels, it houses an R Bar (for some creative cocktails), several passenger service counters, an art gallery, and Café Latte-tudes (for coffee). Close by

Berlitz's Ratings		
	Possible	Achieved
Ship	500	379
Accommodation	200	142
Food	400	240
Service	400	262
Entertainment	100	75
Cruise Experience	400	271
OVERALL SCORE		
1369 points out of 2000		

are the flashy Casino Royale (for table gaming and slot machines), the popular Schooner Bar, with its nautical-theme decor and maritime art, and the Centrum shops. Aerial entertainment happens in the Centrum, too.

Other public rooms include the Library – with its decent array of books, and a neat wooden sculpture of something that looks like Tin Man from The Wizard of Oz.

Take time to look at some of the $6 million worth of artwork throughout the ship's interior – it's both colorful and creative.

ACCOMMODATION. There's a range of suites and cabin types to choose from, and the price you pay depends on the size, grade and location. All have a flat-screen television/infotainment system.

The many standard cabins are of an adequate size, and have just enough functional facilities to make them comfortable. Twin lower beds convert to queen-size ones, and there is a reasonable amount of closet and drawer space, but little room between the bed and desk. The bathrooms are small but functional, the shower units are very small, and there is no cabinet for personal toiletries.

Choose suite-grade accommodation for more space, including a curtained-off sleeping area, a good-size outside balcony with part-partition, lounge with sofa, two chairs and drinks table, three closets, plenty of drawer and storage space, and TV/infotainment system. The bathroom is large and has a full-size tub, integral shower, and dual washbasins/toiletries cabinets.

For the ultimate accommodation, choose the Royal Suite (think Palm Beach apartment), which has a white baby grand piano. It has a separate bedroom with king-size bed, living room with queen-size sofa bed, refrigerator/minibar, dining table, infotainment center, and vanity dressing area. Located just under the starboard-side navigation bridge wing is a private balcony.

DINING. The expansive Aquarius Dining Room spans two levels, with large ocean-view windows on two sides and a connecting stairway. Choose either one of two seatings (with fixed times for dinner), or My Time Dining, where you can eat when you want, during dining room hours.

So, what's the food like? It's like you'd get in a smart American family restaurant, although the menu descriptions make the food sound better than it is, and the selection of breads, rolls, fruit, and cheese is poor. Overall, meals are rather hit and miss – it's unmemorable. Also, if you want lobster or a decent filet mignon (steak), you will be asked to pay extra.

Other dining options. During the 2013 makeover, more restaurants and eateries were added, for greater choice. These included:

Chops Grille (opposite the Schooner Bar): featuring large-size premium-quality steaks and seafood items (a cover charge applies, and reservations are required).

Giovanni's Table (adjacent to Chops Grille): featuring Italian cuisine in a rustic setting (a cover charge applies, and reservations are required).

Izumi: an extra-cost Asian-style eatery with a sushi bar and hot-rocks cooking (it's open for lunch and dinner, with a small cover charge plus à-la-carte menu pricing).

Chef's Table (located in one corner of the lower level of the Aquarius main dining room): this is a private experience, typically co-hosted by the executive chef and sommelier for a multi-course wine-pairing dinner. It's a little expensive, but worth it for a special occasion.

Park Café is a casual no-charge market-style eatery for salads, sandwiches, soups, and pastries.

A drinks package is also available at all bars, in the form of cards or stickers. This enables you to pre-pay for a selection of standard soft drinks and alcoholic drinks, but the packages are not exactly easy to understand.

The Windjammer Café is the casual dining spot for self-serve buffets (open for all meals and late-night snacks). It is quite large, and, because it's positioned at the front of the ship, has fine ocean views.

ENTERTAINMENT. The Masquerade Theater, the ship's showlounge, is located forward and presents production shows and major cabaret performances. It is a large, but well-designed, room with main and balcony levels, and good sight lines from most of the banquette seating.

Other cabaret acts perform in the Some Enchanted Evening Lounge, located aft. These include late-night adult (smutty) comedy, plus live music for dancing. A number of other bars and lounges have live music of differing types.

The entertainment throughout is upbeat, and it's difficult to get away from it. There's even background music in all corridors and elevators, and constant music outdoors on the pool deck.

SPA/FITNESS. The Vitality at Sea Spa and Fitness Center, with its solarium and indoor/outdoor dome-covered pool, Inca- and Mayan-theme decor, sauna/steam rooms, and gymnasium, is for fitness buffs. Other facilities include a rock-climbing wall with several separate climbing tracks, located outdoors aft of the funnel.

Volendam
★★★★

Size:	Mid-size Ship	Passenger/Crew Ratio (lower beds):	2.5
Tonnage:	61,214	Cabins (total):	720
Lifestyle:	Premium	Size Range (sq ft/m):	113.0–1,126.0/10.5–104.6
Cruise Line:	Holland America Line	Cabins (for one person):	0
Former Names:	none	Cabins (with private balcony):	197
IMO Number:	9156515	Cabins (wheelchair accessible):	23
Builder:	Fincantieri (Italy)	Wheelchair accessibility:	Good
Original Cost:	$300 million	Cabin Current:	110 volts
Entered Service:	Nov 1999	Elevators:	12
Registry:	The Netherlands	Casino (gaming tables):	Yes
Length (ft/m):	781.0/238.00	Slot Machines:	Yes
Beam (ft/m):	105.8/32.2	Swimming Pools:	2 (1 w/ sliding glass dome)
Draft (ft/m):	25.5/7.8	Hot Tubs (on deck):	2
Propulsion/Propellers:	diesel-electric (37,500kW)/2	Self-Service Launderette:	Yes
Passenger Decks:	10	Dedicated Cinema/Seats:	Yes/205
Total Crew:	561	Library:	Yes
Passengers (lower beds):	1,440	Onboard currency:	US$
Passenger Space Ratio (lower beds):	42.5		

Dutch decor and heritage for mature-age cruisers

OVERVIEW. *Volendam* has the flow, artwork and comfortable feeling that repeat passengers will recognize from almost any ship in the Holland America Line (HAL) fleet.

THE SHIP. The ship's name is taken from the fishing village of Volendam, north of Amsterdam. The hull is dark blue, in keeping with all HAL ships. It has three main passenger stairways (better for safety and passenger flow). There is a glass dome-covered pool on the Lido Deck between the mast and the funnel; this is also one deck higher than the *Statendam*-class ships, with the positive result being that there is direct access between the aft and midships pools.

ACCOMMODATION. There is one Penthouse Suite, and 28 suites, with the rest of the accommodation a mix of outside-view and interior cabins, and balcony cabins ('mini-suites'). All standard interior and outside cabins are tastefully furnished, and have twin beds that convert to a queen-size bed, but space is tight. There are 28 full Verandah Suites on Navigation Deck, and one Penthouse Suite. Suite occupants share a private Concierge Lounge. Strangely, there are no butlers. Suite passengers get personal stationery, complimentary laundry and ironing, cocktail hour hors d'oeuvres and other goodies, as well as priority embarkation and disembarkation.

For the ultimate in accommodation, choose the Penthouse Suite. It has a large bedroom, living room with baby grand piano, and a dining room, dressing room, walk-in closet, butler's pantry, and private balcony – though the balcony is no larger than any other.

Berlitz's Ratings

	Possible	Achieved
Ship	500	392
Accommodation	200	154
Food	400	265
Service	400	268
Entertainment	100	71
Cruise Experience	400	278

OVERALL SCORE
1428 points out of 2000

Except for the Penthouse Suite, the bathrooms in suites and 'mini-suites' are not as spacious or opulent as one would expect. The 23 cabins for the mobility-limited have a roll-in shower enclosure for wheelchair users – none have bathtubs.

Although room service is adequate, it remains a weak point.

DINING. The 747-seat Rotterdam Dining Room is a traditional, grand room spread over two decks. Both open seating and fixed seating with assigned tables and times are available, while breakfast and lunch are open seating. Fine Rosenthal porcelain and good-quality cutlery are provided. Tables are for two, four, six, or eight.

Other dining options. The casual-dress Marco Polo Restaurant (Italian cuisine with a set menu and nightly specials) seats 88, and there is no charge, although reservations are required. The Lido Buffet is self-serve for breakfasts and lunches; it is also open for casual dinners in an open-seating arrangement. The Lido Deck poolside 'Dive-In at the Terrace Grill' features burgers, hot dogs and fries and on some days, barbecues.

ENTERTAINMENT. The Frans Hals Showlounge, spanning two decks, is basically a well-designed room, but the sight lines from the balcony level are poor.

SPA/FITNESS. The health spa facilities are decent, and include a gym, separate saunas and steam rooms, and several treatment rooms. There are practice tennis courts outdoors, as well as shuffleboard courts, a jogging track, and a full walk-around promenade deck.

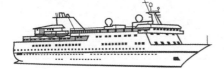

Voyager
★★★

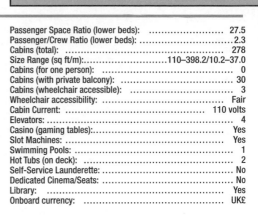

Size:	Small Ship	Passenger Space Ratio (lower beds):	27.5
Tonnage:	15,343	Passenger/Crew Ratio (lower beds):	2.3
Lifestyle:	Standard	Cabins (total):	278
Cruise Line:	Voyages of Discovery	Size Range (sq ft/m):	110–398.2/10.2–37.0
Former Names:	Alexander von Humboldt, Jules Verne,	Cabins (for one person):	0
	Walrus, Crown Monarch	Cabins (with private balcony):	30
IMO Number:	8985957	Cabins (wheelchair accessible):	3
Builder:	Union de Levante (Spain)	Wheelchair accessibility:	Fair
Original Cost:	$95 million	Cabin Current:	110 volts
Entered Service:	Dec 1990/Nov 2012	Elevators:	4
Registry:	Bahamas	Casino (gaming tables):	Yes
Length (ft/m):	494.4/150.7	Slot Machines:	Yes
Beam (ft/m):	67.6/20.62	Swimming Pools:	1
Draft (ft/m):	18.7/5.7	Hot Tubs (on deck):	2
Propulsion/Propellers:	diesel/2	Self-Service Launderette:	No
Passenger Decks:	7	Dedicated Cinema/Seats:	No
Total Crew:	240	Library:	Yes
Passengers (lower beds):	556	Onboard currency:	UK£

For discovery and learning aboard a cozy small ship

OVERVIEW. This modest-looking ship is best suited to adult couples and solo travelers seeking 'soft' adventure and enrichment-style cruising in a small ship.

THE SHIP. *Voyager*, bought at auction by the UK's All Leisure Group in 2009, underwent an extensive refurbishment and was tailored for the British cruise market in 2012. Its profile is somewhat angular, and it has a small, swept-back funnel.

On deck, the space is very limited, although there's more sunbathing space on the deck above. The swimming pool is really just a 'plunge' pool, and is flanked by two hot tubs. The focal point of the ship's social life is Harry's Bar Scotts Lounge – a high-ceilinged lifestyle lounge/bar, off to one side of which is a nicely revamped library. A separate bridge club is provided for card games.

ACCOMMODATION. There are several cabin price grades. There are 35 suites, 30 of which have a private balcony; 10 of these are located behind the navigation bridge. The sleeping area, which includes a small sofa and drinks table, and ample drawer space, can be curtained off from the lounge area, which includes a mini-fridge. There are two balcony doors (one each from the bedroom and the lounge). The bathrooms have a Jacuzzi tub/shower combination.

The standard cabins have all the basics, including twin beds that convert to a double, a small vanity desk

Berlitz's Ratings

	Possible	Achieved
Ship	500	276
Accommodation	200	116
Food	400	281
Service	400	284
Entertainment	100	51
Cruise Experience	400	240
OVERALL SCORE		
1248 points out of 2000		

and small chair, and flat-screen TV set. Bathrooms have a shower enclosure, toilet, and washbasin. There's not much closet and drawer space, and the soundproofing between cabins could be better. Cabins on the lowest decks have portholes, while those on upper decks have windows.

DINING. The 280-seat Discovery Restaurant is quite comfortable, with a slightly raised center section. Seating is at tables for two, four, six, or eight. It operates an open, one-seating arrangement, although there is often a long wait, due to the lack of available seating (particularly in colder weather areas, when the outdoor seating in The Veranda cannot be used). Adjacent to the restaurant is Explorer Grill, serving steaks. Alternatively, casual, buffet-style meals can be taken in the Veranda indoor-outdoor eatery, although in the indoor section, windows have obstructed views.

ENTERTAINMENT. The Darwin Lounge accommodates is a single-level lounge with mostly banquette seating for around 300, but the sight lines to the wooden dance floor/stage are poor.

SPA/FITNESS. A wellness center is located aft of the disco on the uppermost deck overlooking the stern, while a beauty salon is located several decks below, as is a small unisex sauna. There's a shuffleboard area on the topmost deck.

Voyager of the Seas
★★★+

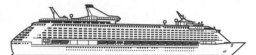

Size:	Large Resort Ship
Tonnage:	137,280
Lifestyle:	Standard
Cruise Line:	Royal Caribbean International
Former Names:	none
IMO Number:	9161716
Builder:	Kvaerner Masa-Yards (Finland)
Original Cost:	$500 million
Entered Service:	Nov 1999
Registry:	Bahamas
Length (ft/m):	1,020.6/311.1
Beam (ft/m):	155.5/47.4
Draft (ft/m):	28.8/8.8
Propulsion/Propellers:	diesel-electric (28,000kW)/ 2 azimuthing pods
Passenger Decks:	14
Total Crew:	1,176
Passengers (lower beds):	3,114
Passenger Space Ratio (lower beds):	44.0
Passenger/Crew Ratio (lower beds):	2.6
Cabins (total):	1,557
Size Range (sq ft/m):	151.0–1,358.0/14.0–126.1
Cabins (for one person):	0
Cabins (with private balcony):	757
Cabins (wheelchair accessible):	26
Wheelchair accessibility:	Best
Cabin Current:	110 volts
Elevators:	14
Casino (gaming tables):	Yes
Slot Machines:	Yes
Swimming Pools:	3
Hot Tubs (on deck):	6
Self-Service Launderette:	No
Dedicated Cinema/Seats:	No
Library:	Yes
Onboard currency:	US$

This large, family-friendly ship has many eating venue choices

OVERVIEW. In terms of sheer size, this ship presently dwarfs many others in the cruise industry, but in terms of personal service, the reverse is the case, unless you happen to reside in one of the top suites. This is impersonal city life at sea – it even has its own zip code, 33132-2028.

THE SHIP. The ship's exterior design is like an enlarged version of the company's *Vision*-class ships. With its larger proportions, it provides more facilities and options, yet manages to have a healthy passenger/space ratio. Embarkation and disembarkation take place through two access points, designed to minimize the inevitable lines at the start and end of the cruise – more than 1,500 people for each access point. A four-deck-high Royal Promenade, the interior focal point, is a good place to arrange to meet someone.

The entrance to one of three levels of the main restaurant, together with shops and entertainment locations are spun off from this 'boulevard,' while 'interior promenade-view' cabins, with bay windows, look into it from above. It houses a traditional English pub (the Pig 'n' Whistle), a Promenade Café (for Continental breakfast, pizzas, sandwiches, and coffees), Ben & Jerry's Ice Cream (at extra cost), Sprinkles (for round-the-clock ice-cream and yoghurt), and Scoreboard (a sports bar).

Several themed shops are featured here. It's a nice place to people-watch. It really is a cross between a shopping arcade and an amusement park. The chairman of Royal Caribbean International (RCI) even donated his own Morgan sports car to grace the Royal Promenade. Actually, the best view of it all is from one of the cabins

Berlitz's Ratings		
	Possible	Achieved
Ship	500	392
Accommodation	200	141
Food	400	222
Service	400	267
Entertainment	100	75
Cruise Experience	400	268
OVERALL SCORE		
1365 points out of 2000		

that look into it, or from a 'captain's bridge' that crosses above it. In the center, a stairway connects you to the deck below, for the Schooner Bar (a piano lounge) and the Casino Royale (large and full of flashing lights).

A second showlounge – Studio B, a regulation-size ice-skating rink that has real, not fake, ice – has arena seating for up to 900 and broadcast facilities. A number of slim pillars obstruct the sight lines, however. If ice-skating in the Caribbean doesn't appeal, you might visit the two-deck library, open 24 hours a day. A TV studio, part of Studio B, is adjacent to rooms that can be used for trade show exhibit space, with a 400-seat conference center. Many decks above, couples can tie the knot in the Skylight Chapel. Outdoors, the pool and open deck areas on Deck 11 provide a resort-like environment.

Drinking places include a neat Aquarium Bar, with 50 tons of glass and water in four large aquariums worth over $1 million; the intimate 52-seat Champagne Bar; and the Connoisseur Club – for cigars and cognacs. Jazz fans might appreciate High Notes, an intimate room atop the ship, or the Schooner Bar piano lounge. For golfers, there's the 19th Hole, a golf bar.

Although the ship is large, the cabin hallways have a warm and attractive feel. Expect lines at the reception desk and elevators, particularly at peak meal times. The theme-park, banquet-style regimentation is well organized, and excellent value for money for families. You will, however, need to plan what you want to do.

Because the fares are so reasonable, there's always a push for extra-revenue items, drinks packages, extra-cost dining, etc. In the end, you should have a decent cruise trip. Note that in 2014, *Voyager of the Seas* underwent 'Aussification' for its Australia 2014–15 season.

FAMILIES. Facilities for children and teenagers are quite extensive. Aquanauts is for ages 3–5; Explorers is for ages 6–8; and Voyagers for 9–12s. Optix, a dedicated area for teenagers, includes a daytime club with computers, soda bar, disk jockey, and dance floor. Challenger's Arcade has the latest video games. Virtual Submarine is a virtual-reality underwater center for all ages. Computer Lab has 14 computer stations loaded with fun and games. Paint and Clay is an arts-and-crafts center for younger children. Adjacent to these indoor areas is Adventure Beach, an area for all the family: it includes pools, a water slide, and game areas outdoors.

ACCOMMODATION. There is a range of cabin price grades, in four major groupings: premium ocean-view suites and cabins, interior (atrium-view) cabins, ocean-view cabins, and interior cabins. Many cabins are of a similar size and 300 have interconnecting doors. Some 138 interior cabins have bay windows that look into an interior horizontal atrium – a cruise industry first. Regardless of what cabin grade you choose, all except for the Royal Suite and Owner's Suite have twin beds that convert to a queen-size unit, TV, safe, vanity unit, and private bathroom. However, you'll need to keep the curtains closed in the bay windows if you are scantily clad, because you can be seen from adjacent bay windows.

Royal Suite. At around 1,146 sq ft (107 sq m), the Royal Suite is the largest private living space. It is located almost at the top of the Centrum lobby on the port side. It has a king-size circular bed in a separate large bedroom, a living room with a queen-size sofa bed, baby grand piano, refrigerator/wet bar, dining table, entertainment center, and a reasonably large bathroom.

Royal Family Suite. The four Royal Family suites (two aft on Deck 9, two aft on Deck 8, each measuring around 574 sq ft/53 sq m) have two bedrooms. The main bedroom has a large vanity desk; the second bedroom includes two beds and third/fourth upper Pullman berths. There's a lounge with dining table, wet bar, walk-in closet, and a big bathroom with Jacuzzi tub. The suites, aft, have large balconies with ocean views.

Owner's Suites. Ten slightly smaller but desirable Owner's Suites (around 468 sq ft/43 sq m) are in the center of the ship, adjacent to the Centrum lobby. Each has a bedroom with queen-size bed or twin beds, lounge with large sofa, a wet bar, and bathroom with Jacuzzi tub, washbasin, and separate shower enclosure. There's also a small private balcony.

Standard outside-view and interior cabins. All cabins have a private bathroom, as well as interactive TV and pay-per-view movies, including an X-rated channel. Cabin bathrooms are compact, but they do have a proper shower enclosure instead of a shower curtain.

Some accommodation grades have a refrigerator/minibar, although there is no space left, because it is crammed with 'take-and-pay' items. If you take anything from it on the day of embarkation in Miami, Florida, sales tax will be added to your bill.

Cabins with 'private balconies' aren't so private. If you have a cabin with a connecting door to another cabin, you'll probably be able to hear everything your next-door neighbors say and do. The bathroom toilets are very noisy. Room service food menus are basic.

DINING. The main dining room is extremely large and set on three levels, each with an operatic theme: Carmen, La Bohème, and Magic Flute. All three have exactly the same menus. Choose one of two seatings, or My Time Dining, which allows you to eat any time during dining room hours. Tables are for four, six, eight, 10, or 12. The place settings, china, and cutlery are of good quality. The menu descriptions make the food sound better than it is, however, and the selection of breads, rolls, fruit, and cheese is poor. Also, if you want lobster or filet mignon (steak), it costs extra.

Other dining options. Portofino: the ship's upscale Euro-Italian spot. It's open for dinner, reservations required, with a cover charge. The food is better than in the dining room, although the restaurant isn't large enough for everyone to try even once during a cruise.

Windjammer Café: this is a sprawling venue for buffet-style, self-help breakfast (this tends to be the busiest time of the day), lunch, and light dinners (but not on the last night). It's often difficult to find a table. Within this, Island Grill serves casual meat and seafood items (no reservations), from a grill and open kitchen.

Johnny Rockets: a retro 1950s all-day, all-night diner-style eatery that has hamburgers, malt shakes, and jukebox hits, with both indoor and outdoor seating. All indoor tables have a mini-jukebox with dimes provided and there are all-singing, all-dancing waitresses. There's a cover charge, whether you eat in or take out.

ENTERTAINMENT. The 1,347-seat La Scala Theater, a fine showlounge, is located at the front of the ship and spans the height of five decks, with almost no disruption of sight lines. The room has a hydraulic orchestra pit, together with superb lighting equipment.

In addition, the ship has an array of cabaret acts. The strongest acts are presented in the main showlounge, while others appear in the Cleopatra's Needle Lounge, also the venue for late-night adults-only comedy. Arguably the best shows are the Ice Spectaculars.

SPA/FITNESS. The Voyager Day Spa and Fitness Center is reasonably large. It includes an aerobics room, fitness center, treatment rooms, and single-sex sauna/steam rooms. Another 10,000 sq ft (930 sq m) of space is provided for a Solarium (with sliding glass-dome roof). Aft of the funnel is a 32.8ft (10m) rock-climbing wall, with five climbing tracks. Other sports facilities include a roller-blading track, a dive-and-snorkel shop (for equipment rental), a full-size basketball court, and a nine-hole, par 26 golf 'course.'

Westerdam
★★★★

Size:	Mid-size Ship	Passenger Space Ratio (lower beds):	41.9
Tonnage:	82,348	Passenger/Crew Ratio (lower beds):	2.3
Lifestyle:	Premium	Cabins (total):	958
Cruise Line:	Holland America Line	Size Range (sq ft/m):	170.0–1,318.6/15.7–122.5
Former Names:	none	Cabins (for one person):	0
IMO Number:	9226891	Cabins (with private balcony):	641
Builder:	Fincantieri (Italy)	Cabins (wheelchair accessible):	28
Original Cost:	$400 million	Wheelchair accessibility:	Good
Entered Service:	Apr 2004	Cabin Current:	110 volts
Registry:	The Netherlands	Elevators:	14
Length (ft/m):	935.0/285.0	Casino (gaming tables):	Yes
Beam (ft/m):	105.6/32.2	Slot Machines:	Yes
Draft (ft/m):	25.5/7.8	Swimming Pools:	2 (1 w/ sliding glass dome)
Propulsion/Propellers:	diesel-electric (35,240kW)/ 2 azimuthing pods	Hot Tubs (on deck):	5
		Self-Service Launderette:	No
Passenger Decks:	11	Dedicated Cinema/Seats:	Yes/170
Total Crew:	817	Library:	Yes
Passengers (lower beds):	1,916	Onboard currency:	US$

This contemporary, mid-sized ship has Dutch decor and crafts

OVERVIEW. *Westerdam* offers a range of public rooms with a reasonably intimate ambience, and the overall feel of the ship is quite cozy.

THE SHIP. *Westerdam* is one of what is known as a series of *Vista*-class vessels, whose sister ships are: *Eurodam, Nieuw Amsterdam, Noordam, Oosterdam,* and *Zuiderdam* – all designed to appeal to younger, active vacationers. It has two funnels, placed close together, one in front of the other, the result of the slightly unusual machinery configuration. The ship has, in effect, two engine rooms – one with three diesels, and one with two diesels and a gas turbine. Pod propulsion is provided, powered by a diesel-electric system (there's almost no vibration), and a small gas turbine in the funnel helps reduce emissions.

There's a complete walk-around exterior teak promenade deck, with teak steamer-style sunloungers. A jogging track is located around the mast and the forward third of the ship. Exterior glass elevators, mounted midships on both sides, provide ocean views. There are two centrally located swimming pools outdoors, one of which can be used in poor weather because it has a retractable sliding glass roof. Two whirlpool tubs, adjacent to the swimming pools, are abridged by a bar. Another smaller pool is for children; it incorporates a winding water slide that spans two decks in height. There is an additional whirlpool tub outdoors.

An intimate entrance lobby spans three decks, and is topped by a beautiful, rotating Waterford crystal

Berlitz's Ratings		
	Possible	Achieved
Ship	500	391
Accommodation	200	149
Food	400	261
Service	400	268
Entertainment	100	71
Cruise Experience	400	282
OVERALL SCORE		
1422 points out of 2000		

globe of the world. The interior decor is interesting; the ceilings are particularly noticeable in the public decor, the colors are muted and warm. The information desk in the lobby is small and removed from the main passenger flow.

There are two whole entertainment/public room decks. The most dramatic room is the showlounge, which spans three decks in the forward part of the ship. Other facilities include a winding shopping street with boutique stores and logo shops, an Internet center, a fine library, card room, an art gallery, photo gallery, and several small meeting rooms. The casino is large – one has to walk through it to get from the restaurant to the showlounge on one of the entertainments decks.

In a 2007 refit, an Explorations Café was added to the Crow's Nest (a HAL trademark observation lounge atop the ship). This encompasses the ship's library, a lounge area with fine ocean views, and a coffee shop.

On lower decks you'll find a Queen's Lounge and bar, which acts as a lecture room and a Culinary Arts Center. There are also a number of other bars and lounges, including an Explorer's Lounge. The ship also has a small movie screening room.

Niggles include several pillars that obstruct the passenger flow and lines of sight throughout the ship. Also, there are no self-service launderettes, although special laundry packages are available. Additionally, the air conditioning cannot be turned off in cabins or bathrooms.

FAMILIES. Children have KidZone, an indoor/outdoor facility, and Club HAL for ages 5–12, with a number of dedicated youth counselors. Teenagers get to use WaveRunner, which includes a dance floor, lighting effects, and a booming sound system. There's also a computer game room, and big-screen television for movies.

ACCOMMODATION. There are many price categories. From largest to smallest: **Penthouse Verandah Suites** (1,318 sq ft/123 sq m, including balcony); **Deluxe Verandah Suites** 563 sq ft/52 sq m); **Verandah Suites** (284 sq ft/26 sq m); **Outside-view cabins** (197 sq ft/18 sq m); Interior (no-view) cabins are slightly smaller, at 183 sq ft (17 sq m).

Lifeboats obstruct the view from some cabins on the lowest accommodation deck. Some cabins that can accommodate a third and fourth person have little closet space and only one personal safe. Some cabins have interconnecting doors. Occupants of suites get exclusive use of a Neptune Lounge and concierge service, priority embarkation and disembarkation, and other benefits. In many suites and cabins with private balconies the balconies aren't really private, as a lot of them can be overlooked.

DINING. Options range from full-service meals in the main dining room and à-la-carte restaurant to casual, self-serve buffet-style meals and fast-food outlets. The 1,045-seat Vista Dining Room is two decks high, with seating provided on both main and balcony levels, and is at the stern. Both open seating and assigned seating are available, while breakfast and lunch are open seating, where you'll be seated by restaurant staff when you enter.

There are tables for two, four, six, or eight. The waiter stations can be noisy for anyone seated adjacent to them. Fine Rosenthal porcelain and decent cutlery are used, but there are no fish knives. Live music is provided for dinner each evening. Once each cruise, a Dutch Dinner is held (hats are provided), as is an Indonesian Lunch. 'Lighter option' meals are available for the nutrition-conscious. HAL can provide Kosher meals, although these are prepared ashore, frozen, and brought to the table sealed in their original containers.

Other dining options. A 130-seat Pinnacle Grill is a more upscale dining spot with higher-quality ingredients than in the larger main dining room. It is on Lower Promenade Deck, and fronts onto the second level of the atrium lobby; a Pinnacle Bar was added in a 2007 refit. Pacific Northwest cuisine is served, plus an array of premium-quality steaks from hand-selected cuts of beef, shown to you at tableside. The wine bar offers mostly American wines. Reservations are required, and there's a cover charge (the steaks alone are worth it).

An extensive Lido Café wraps around the funnel housing and extends aft. It includes a pizzeria counter, a salad bar, Asian stir-fry counter, deli sandwiches, and a dessert buffet. Movement around the buffet area can be very slow, particularly at peak times. In the evenings, one side of this venue is turned into an extra-cost, 72-seat Canaletto Restaurant – a quasi-Italian informal eatery with waiter service.

Also, a poolside 'Dive-In at the Terrace Grill' features multi-choice signature burgers (with special Dive-In sauce), hot dogs and fries, and, on certain days, barbecues and other culinary treats may be featured.

Meanwhile, the Windsurf Café in the atrium lobby, open 20 hours a day for coffee, pastries, snack foods, deli sandwiches, and, in the evening, liqueur coffees.

ENTERTAINMENT. The 867-seat Vista Lounge is the main venue for Las Vegas-style revue shows and major cabaret presentations. It spans three decks in the forward section. The main floor level has a bar in its starboard aft section. Spiral stairways at the back of the lounge connect all levels. The upper levels have better sight lines.

SPA/FITNESS. The Greenhouse Spa, a large, two-deck-high health spa, is directly above the navigation bridge. Facilities include a solarium, hydrotherapy pool, and a unisex thermal suite – an area incorporating a Laconium, Hammam, and Chamomile Grotto. There's also a beauty parlor, 11 massage/therapy rooms, including one for couples, and a large gym with floor-to-ceiling windows, and the latest high-tech equipment.

Sports facilities include a basketball court, volleyball court, and golf simulator.

Wind Spirit
★★★+

Size:	Boutique Ship
Tonnage:	5,350
Lifestyle:	Premium
Cruise Line:	Windstar Cruises
Former Names:	none
IMO Number:	8603509
Builder:	Ateliers et Chantiers du Havre
Original Cost:	$34.2 million
Entered Service:	Apr 1988
Registry:	Bahamas
Length (ft/m):	439.6/134.0
Beam (ft/m):	51.8/15.8
Draft (ft/m):	13.4/4.1
Propulsion/Propellers:	(a) diesel-electric (1,400kW)/1; (b) sails
Passenger Decks:	5
Total Crew:	88
Passengers (lower beds):	148
Passenger Space Ratio (lower beds):	36.1
Passenger/Crew Ratio (lower beds):	1.6
Cabins (total):	74
Size Range (sq ft/m):	185.0–220.0/17.0–22.5
Cabins (for one person):	0
Cabins (with private balcony):	0
Cabins (wheelchair accessible):	0
Wheelchair accessibility:	None
Cabin Current:	110 volts
Elevators:	0
Casino (gaming tables):	Yes
Slot Machines:	Yes
Swimming Pools:	1
Hot Tubs (on deck):	1
Self-Service Launderette:	No
Dedicated Cinema/Seats:	No
Library:	Yes
Onboard currency:	US$

A modern sail-cruise ship with chic, contemporary style

OVERVIEW. This sail-cruise ship is ideally suited to youthful couples and solo travelers seeking contemporary facilities and some water sports in a relaxed but chic setting that's different from 'normal' cruise ships. It offers good food and service, and little in the way of entertainment, parlor games, structured activities, or ship's photographers to get in the way.

THE SHIP. *Wind Spirit*, an identical twin to *Wind Star*, is a sleek-looking craft that is part-yacht, part-cruise ship, with four masts that tower 170ft (52m) above the deck, and with computer-controlled sails. The masts, sails, and rigging alone cost $5 million, when the ship was built. A computer keeps the ship on an even keel via the movement of a water hydraulic ballast system of 142,653 gallons (540,000 liters), so there is no rolling over 6°. You may be under sail for less than 40 percent of the time, depending on the conditions and cruise area winds prevailing.

Because of the amount of complex sail machinery, there is little open deck space when the ship is full. At the stern is a small water sports platform that can be used when at anchor and only in really calm sea conditions. Water sports facilities include a banana boat, kayaks, sunfish sailboats, windsurf boards, water-ski boat, scuba and snorkel equipment, and four Zodiacs. You will be asked to sign a waiver, if you wish to use the water sports equipment.

The ship has a finely crafted interior with pleasing, blond woods, together with soft, complementary

Berlitz's Ratings	Possible	Achieved
Ship	500	360
Accommodation	200	160
Food	400	267
Service	400	271
Entertainment	100	73
Cruise Experience	400	262
OVERALL SCORE		
1393 points out of 2000		

colors and decor that is chic, even elegant, but a little cold. Note that the main lounge aboard this ship is of a slightly different design from that aboard *Wind Star*. Together with Wind Star, this ship had a makeover in 2012 – this included a complete refurbishment of cabins (including new lighting), Owner's Suite, and corridors together with The Restaurant, Veranda, Lounge, WindSpa, Library, Reception, and Pool Bar.

No scheduled activities help to make this a really relaxing, unregimented 'get away from it all' vacation. It allows you to cruise in very comfortable, contemporary surroundings bordering on the luxurious, in an unstructured environment – just right for seven idyllic nights in sheltered areas. It can, however, be disconcerting, when the vessel is in small ports alongside several gigantic cruise ships.

The swimming pool is just a tiny 'dip' pool. Be prepared for the whine of the generators, which are needed to run the air-conditioning and lighting systems 24 hours a day. You'll hear it at night in your cabin; it takes most passengers a day or two to get used to.

Beverage prices are a little high. The library is small and needs more hardback fiction. The staff, though friendly, is casual and a little sloppy at times in the finer points of service.

The dress code is casual, with no jackets and ties, even for dinner – the brochure states casual elegance. There are no formal nights or theme nights. Gratuities are charged at about $12 per person, per day, and 15 percent is added to bar and wine accounts.

ACCOMMODATION. All cabins are nicely equipped, have crisp, inviting decor, a minibar/refrigerator (stocked when you embark, but all drinks cost extra), 24-hour room service, personal safe, and plenty of storage space. A TV, with CNN when available, rotates so that it is viewable from the bed and the bathroom. There's also a DVD player and CD player. All cabins all have two portholes with outside views, and deadlights (steel covers that provide a complete blackout at night and can be closed in poor weather conditions). The decor is a pleasant mix of rich woods, natural fabrics and colorful soft furnishings, and hi-tech yacht-style amenities. A basket of fruit is replenished daily.

The bathrooms are compact units, designed in a figure of eight, with a teakwood floor in the central section. There is a good amount of storage space for toiletries in two cabinets, as well as under-sink cupboard space. A wall-mounted hairdryer is also provided. The shower enclosure (no cabins have bathtubs) is circular and has both a hand-held as well as a fixed shower. L'Occitane bathroom products are provided, as are a vanity kit and shower cap.

The lighting is not strong enough for the application of make-up – this is better applied at the vanity desk in the cabin, which has stronger overhead (halogen) lighting. Bathrobes and towels are 100 percent cotton.

DINING. The elegant AmphorA Restaurant (its name is derived from a vessel, or container) has ocean views from large, picture windows, a lovely wood ceiling, and wood-paneled walls. California-style nouvelle cuisine is served, with attractively presented dishes. Additionally, signature dishes created by master chefs Joachim Splichal and Jeanne Jones are offered daily. It's open seating, so you can dine when you want and with whomever you wish.

The service staff are mostly Indonesians and Filipinos, who struggle sometimes at communicating, although their service is pleasant. The selection of breads, cheeses, and fruits could be better. There is a big push to sell wines, but prices are extremely high, as they are for most alcoholic drinks, and even bottled water.

There is often casual dinner on the open deck under the stars, with grilled seafood and steaks. At the bars, hot and cold hors d'oeuvres appear at cocktail times.

Fancy something quiet and romantic? At no extra charge, a 'Cuisine de l'Amour' romantic dinner for two can be served to you in your cabin, complete with candle. The menu, with seductive-sounding selections, offers a choice of appetizer, a set soup, a choice of salad, and two entrée options, and a set dessert to finish.

ENTERTAINMENT. There is no showlounge, shows, or cabaret. However, these are not really needed, because a cruise aboard this high-tech sailing ship provides an opportunity to get away from all that noise and 'entertainment.' The main lounge, a corner of which houses a small casino, has a little dance floor, and, typically, a trio is there to play.

The main lounge is also used for cocktail parties and other social functions. Otherwise, it's down to more personal entertainment, such as a DVD in your cabin late at night – or, much more romantic, after-dinner hours spent outside strolling or simply lounging on deck.

SPA/FITNESS. A gymnasium (with a modicum of muscle-toning equipment, treadmills, and exercycles) and sauna are located at the aft of the ship, adjacent to the water sports platform. Special spa packages can be pre-booked through your travel agent before you arrive at the ship. Wellbeing massages, aromatherapy facials, manicures, pedicures, and hair-beautifying treatments all cost extra.

Wind Star
★★★+

Size:	Boutique Ship	Passenger/Crew Ratio (lower beds):	1.6
Tonnage:	5,350	Cabins (total):	74
Lifestyle:	Premium	Size Range (sq ft/m):	185.0–220.0/17.0–22.5
Cruise Line:	Windstar Cruises	Cabins (for one person):	0
Former Names:	none	Cabins (with private balcony):	0
IMO Number:	8420878	Cabins (wheelchair accessible):	0
Builder:	Ateliers et Chantiers du Havre	Wheelchair accessibility:	None
Original Cost:	$34.2 million	Cabin Current:	110 volts
Entered Service:	Dec 1986	Elevators:	0
Registry:	Bahamas	Casino (gaming tables):	Yes
Length (ft/m):	439.6/134.0	Slot Machines:	Yes
Beam (ft/m):	51.8/15.8	Swimming Pools:	1
Draft (ft/m):	13.4/4.1	Hot Tubs (on deck):	1
Propulsion/Propellers:	(a) diesel-electric (1,400kW)/1; (b) sails	Self-Service Launderette:	No
Passenger Decks:	5	Dedicated Cinema/Seats:	No
Total Crew:	88	Library:	Yes
Passengers (lower beds):	148	Onboard currency:	US$
Passenger Space Ratio (lower beds):	36.1		

A contemporary sail-cruise ship for smart casual cruising

OVERVIEW. *Wind Star* is suited to youthful couples and solo travelers who want contemporary facilities in a relaxed but chic setting.

THE SHIP. *Wind Star* is a long, sleek-looking craft that is part-yacht, part-cruise ship, with four masts towering 170ft (52m) above the deck, and with computer-controlled sails. The computer keeps the ship on an even keel via the movement of a water hydraulic ballast system of 142,653 gallons (540,000 liters), so there is no rolling over 6°. You may be under sail for less than 40 percent of the time, depending on the conditions and cruise area winds. Because of the amount of sail machinery, there is little open deck space when the ship is full. A small aft water sports platform can be used when at anchor. Water sports facilities include a banana boat, kayaks, sunfish sailboats, windsurf boards, water-ski boat, scuba and snorkel equipment, and four Zodiacs.

No scheduled activities help to make this a relaxing, unregimented 'get away from it all' vacation. Windstar offers cruising in very comfortable surroundings bordering on the luxurious, in an unstructured setting.

The swimming pool is really only a tiny 'dip' pool. Be prepared for the whine of the vessel's generators. You'll hear it at night in your cabin; it takes some passengers a day or two to get used to. Beverage prices are a little high. The library is small. The staff, though friendly, is a little sloppy at times in the finer points of service. The dress code is casual, with no jackets and ties. Gratuities are charged to your onboard account, and 15 percent is added to bar, wine and spa accounts.

Berlitz's Ratings

	Possible	Achieved
Ship	500	360
Accommodation	200	160
Food	400	267
Service	400	271
Entertainment	100	73
Cruise Experience	400	263
OVERALL SCORE		
1394 points out of 2000		

ACCOMMODATION. The cabins are nicely equipped, have crisp, inviting decor and a minibar/refrigerator (all drinks cost extra), 24-hour room service, safe, and plenty of storage. A TV rotates so that it is viewable from the bed and the bathroom. The bathrooms are compact with a circular shower enclosure (no cabins have bathtubs) and both a handheld as well as a fixed shower unit. L'Occitane toiletries are provided.

DINING. The AmphorA Restaurant is chic, and has ocean views. California-style cuisine is served, with attractively presented dishes. Open seating means you dine when and with whom you want to.

The service staff are mostly Indonesians and Filipinos, who struggle sometimes at communicating, although their service is pleasant. There is a big push to sell wines, although the prices are extremely high, as they are for most drinks – even bottled water is the highest in the industry, at $7 per liter bottle.

There is often casual dinner on the open deck under the stars, with grilled seafood and steaks. At the bars, hot and cold hors d'oeuvres appear at cocktail times. For something quiet and romantic, a 'Cuisine de l'Amour' dinner can be served to you in your cabin.

ENTERTAINMENT. There is no showlounge, so no shows. The main lounge, with a small casino, has a small dance floor, and, typically, a trio plays there.

SPA/FITNESS. A fitness room and sauna are located aft. Special spa packages can be pre-booked.

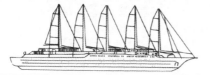

Wind Surf
★★★★

Size:	Small Ship	Passenger/Crew Ratio (lower beds):	1.9
Tonnage:	14,745	Cabins (total):	156
Lifestyle:	Premium	Size Range (sq ft/m):	188.0–500.5/17.5–46.5
Cruise Line:	Windstar Cruises	Cabins (for one person):	0
Former Names:	Club Med I	Cabins (with private balcony):	0
IMO Number:	8700785	Cabins (wheelchair accessible):	0
Builder:	Ateliers et Chantiers du Havre	Wheelchair accessibility:	None
Original Cost:	$140 million	Cabin Current:	110 and 220 volts
Entered Service:	Feb 1990/May 1998	Elevators:	2
Registry:	Bahamas	Casino (gaming tables):	Yes
Length (ft/m):	613.5/187.0	Slot Machines:	Yes
Beam (ft/m):	65.6/20.0	Swimming Pools:	2
Draft (ft/m):	16.4/5.0	Hot Tubs (on deck):	2
Propulsion/Propellers:	... (a) diesel-electric (1,400kW)/1; (b) sails	Self-Service Launderette:	No
Passenger Decks:	8	Dedicated Cinema/Seats:	No
Total Crew:	163	Library:	Yes
Passengers (lower beds):	312	Onboard currency:	US$
Passenger Space Ratio (lower beds):	47.2		

Elegant decor for smart-casual sail-cruising in comfort

OVERVIEW. This sail-cruise ship is a good choice for couples seeking informality (no jackets or ties), but who don't want the inconvenience of the workings of a real tall ship. It cruises in the Caribbean (Nov–Mar) and in the Mediterranean (May–Oct).

THE SHIP. *Wind Surf*, one of a pair of the world's largest sail-cruisers, is part-cruise ship, part-yacht – its sister ship operates as *Club Med II*. This is a larger, grander sister to the original three Windstar Cruises vessels. Five huge masts of 164ft/50m (rising 221ft/68m above sea level) carry seven triangular, self-furling Dacron sails, with a total surface area of 26,881 sq ft (2,497 sq m).

No human hands touch the sails – instead, everything is handled electronically by computer control from the bridge, which some might think is a little boring. Also, because European sailings take place at night, with days spent in port, there seems little point to having the sails, as you won't get to experience them.

A computer keeps the ship on an even keel via the movement of a water hydraulic ballast system of 266,800 gallons (1 million liters), so there is no heeling over 6°. When the ship isn't using the sails, four diesel-electric motors propel it at up to approximately 12 knots. The ship is very quiet when moving.

Swimming from the aft water sports platform isn't allowed. But extensive water sports facilities include windsurfers, sailboats, water-ski boats, scuba tanks, snorkels, fins, masks, and inflatable Zodiac motor-

Berlitz's Ratings

	Possible	Achieved
Ship	500	374
Accommodation	200	160
Food	400	280
Service	400	282
Entertainment	100	73
Cruise Experience	400	293
OVERALL SCORE		
1462 points out of 2000		

ized boats for water-skiing – all at no extra charge, except for the scuba tanks.

There are two saltwater swimming pools – little more than 'dip' pools. One is amidships on the uppermost deck; the other is aft, together with two hot tubs, and an adjacent bar. There are no showers at either of the pools, so passengers get into the pools or hot tubs while covered in oil or lotion, an unhygienic arrangement.

A meeting room can accommodate 30–60 people. The casino/main lounge has four blackjack tables, one roulette table, and 21 slot machines. It has an unusually high ceiling for the size of the ship.

A Yacht Club includes books and DVDs for in-cabin use and provides comfortable seating for relaxation or listening to music loaded for you on iPods available from reception. An espresso bar offers extra-cost Lavazza coffee drinks and deli sandwiches. Eight computers have Internet access, and there's Wi-Fi access.

Parts of the ship was refurbished in 2011, and so in late 2012 were public spaces including the Lounge, The Restaurant, Degrees, Veranda, Compass Rose, WindSpa, Yacht Club, and Pool Bar.

Hotel service is provided mostly by Filipino and Indonesian staff. Gratuities are charged to your onboard account, and 15 percent is added to bar and wine accounts, and to all spa treatments and services. The quality of food and its presentation is a definite plus, as is the policy of no music in passenger hallways or elevators.

ACCOMMODATION. There are just three price categories. Unusually, the cabin numbers (port side: even numbers; starboard side: odd numbers) are sequenced with lower numbers aft, while higher numbers are forward. All cabins are very nicely equipped, with crisp, inviting decor. They have a minibar/refrigerator (stocked when you embark, but all drinks are at extra cost), 24-hour room service, personal safe, a flat-screen TV set viewable from the bed (or sofa, depending on cabin configuration), DVD/CD player, plenty of storage space, and two portholes. DVDs and CDs are available from the library. There are six four-person cabins; 35 doubles are fitted with an extra Pullman berth, and several cabins have an interconnecting door – good for families. Spa Suite packages are available at extra cost. All cabins have Wi-Fi access, at extra cost.

The bathrooms are compact, designed in a figure of eight, with a teakwood floor in the central section. There is a good amount of storage space for toiletries in two cabinets, as well as under-basin storage space, and a wall-mounted hairdryer. The circular shower enclosure has both a hand-held and a fixed shower, so you can wash your hair without getting the rest of your body wet. The lighting is not strong enough for women to apply make-up – this is better applied at the cabin's vanity desk.

All but one of 31 suites have two bathrooms, a separate living/dining area, sleeping area that can be curtained off, two vanity/writing desks, and four portholes instead of two. There are two TV sets (one in the lounge, one in the sleeping area), video player and CD player, and Bose SoundDock for iPods. Popcorn for movie viewing is available from room service. Bathrooms have granite countertops, open shelving, toiletries cabinets, and magnifying mirror.

A further two Bridge Deck suites (around 495 sq ft/46 sq m) would be delightful for a honeymoon; each has a bedroom, separate living/dining room, and marble bathroom with Jacuzzi tub, two washbasins, and separate toilet, plus a walk-in closet.

Spa Suite packages, introduced in 2010, also include a queen-size bed with microfiber bed linen, bathrobes, an orchid flower arrangement, two bathrooms, a flat-screen TV with DVD player, and Bose SoundDock speakers for iPods; a pillow menu provides several choices, including a 'snore-no-more' hypoallergenic pillow.

Tea collections include wellbeing, herbal, or exotic teas. Brewing service includes contemporary porcelain tea-ware and is available from room service 24 hours a day. Berlitz tip: ask for it to be made with mineral water, not the standard chlorinated ship's water.

DINING. The AmphorA Restaurant (an ancient word meaning 'vessel' or 'container') seats 272 and has tables for two, four, or six. It has open seating with no pre-assigned tables, and is open only for dinner, typically 7.30–9.30pm. California-style nouvelle cuisine is served, with dishes attractively presented.

Other dining options. The 124-seat Degrees Bistro, a specialty dining venue, features Mediterranean cuisine. Located atop the ship, on Star Deck, it has picture windows on port and starboard sides, an open kitchen, and tables for two, four, or six. Reservations are required for dinner, although there's no extra charge.

The Veranda, amidships on Star Deck, has its own open terrace for informal, self-serve breakfast and lunch buffets. It really is very pleasant to be outside, eating an informal breakfast or lunch. Do try the bread pudding, available daily at lunch – the ship is famous for it, and each day has a variation on the theme.

The Compass Rose, an indoor/outdoor casual eatery, provides deli-style snack items plus some pastries and coffee for breakfast, lunch, and afternoon tea. At night, it turns into Candles for alfresco dining around the aft pool. A permanent outdoor barbecue offers fresh grilled items for breakfast and lunch.

Windstar Cruises food is generally very good, and geared toward American tastes. Europeans and other nationals should note that items such as bacon may be overcooked, and the choice of cheeses and teas is limited. Service in the dining room is also quite fast, geared towards those who haven't yet learned to unwind.

A nice feature is a 'Cuisine de l'Amour' romantic candlelight dinner for two, served in your cabin at no extra charge. The menu, with seductive-sounding selections, offers a choice of appetizer, a set soup, choice of salad, two entrée options, and a set dessert to finish.

Finally, there's quite an extensive room service menu.

ENTERTAINMENT. There is no showlounge as such (this is a yachting-style experience, after all), although the main lounge, which incorporates a small casino, serves as an occasional cabaret room. It has a small wooden dance floor, with music provided by a house band. The high-ceilinged room is also used for cocktail parties and other social functions.

SPA/FITNESS. The Health Spa has a unisex sauna (bathing suits required), beauty salon, and several treatment rooms for massage, facials, and body wraps. There is a decent gymnasium – on a separate deck, with ocean views – and an aerobics workout room. Unfortunately, the spa facilities are split on three separate decks, making them rather disjointed. Special spa packages can be pre-booked through your travel agent. The spa is operated by the UK's Onboard Spa Company.

Zaandam
★★★★

Size:	Mid-size Ship	Passenger/Crew Ratio (lower beds):	2.5
Tonnage:	61,396	Cabins (total):	720
Lifestyle:	Premium	Size Range (sq ft/m):	113.0–1,126.3/10.5–104.6
Cruise Line:	Holland America Line	Cabins (for one person):	0
Former Names:	none	Cabins (with private balcony):	197
IMO Number:	9156527	Cabins (wheelchair accessible):	23
Builder:	Fincantieri (Italy)	Wheelchair accessibility:	Good
Original Cost:	$300 million	Cabin Current:	110 volts
Entered Service:	May 2000	Elevators:	12
Registry:	The Netherlands	Casino (gaming tables):	Yes
Length (ft/m):	777.5/237.0	Slot Machines:	Yes
Beam (ft/m):	105.8/32.2	Swimming Pools:	2 (1 w/sliding glass dome)
Draft (ft/m):	25.5/7.8	Hot Tubs (on deck):	2
Propulsion/Propellers:	diesel-electric (37,500kW)/2	Self-Service Launderette:	Yes
Passenger Decks:	10	Dedicated Cinema/Seats:	Yes/205
Total Crew:	561	Library:	Yes
Passengers (lower beds):	1,440	Onboard currency:	US$
Passenger Space Ratio (lower beds):	42.6		

Dutch-style decor for cruisers of a mature age

OVERVIEW. Holland America Line's (HAL's) Signature of Excellence program provides passengers with more choice than on a standard ship. Music memorabilia is scattered throughout the ship, and includes instruments used by such diverse players as The Rolling Stones, David Bowie, and Bill Clinton. There's also a huge Dutch pipe organ complete with puppets that move in time to the music.

Berlitz's Ratings		
	Possible	Achieved
Ship	500	397
Accommodation	200	150
Food	400	260
Service	400	267
Entertainment	100	71
Cruise Experience	400	278
OVERALL SCORE		
1423 points out of 2000		

members of the rock band Queen; a Bently Les Paul-style guitar signed by artists including Carlos Santana, Eric Clapton, B.B. King, Robert Cray, Keith Richards, and Les Paul. Perhaps the ship should be called *Rockerdam*.

The Oasis outdoor relaxation areas aft of the funnel include a waterfall and family gathering areas. Explorations is an excellent combination of café, Internet connection center, and library. There are children's and teens' play areas. Popcorn is provided at the Wajang Theater for moviegoers, and this location incorporates a fully equipped kitchen for HAL's Culinary Arts program, which involves visiting chefs and interactive cooking and tasting demonstrations. The casino has blackjack, roulette, stud poker, and dice tables, and the requisite rows of slot machines. Adjacent is a sports bar.

THE SHIP. *Zaandam*'s hull is dark blue, in keeping with all HAL ships. Although similar in size to *Rotterdam*, this ship has a single funnel, and is a sister ship to *Volendam*.

It has three principal passenger stairways, which is so much better than two stairways from the viewpoints of safety, accessibility, and passenger flow. A glass-covered pool is located on the Lido Deck between the mast and the funnel.

The interior decor is restrained, with much traditional ocean liner detailing and wood accenting. The design theme of music includes fabrics, posters, and – believe it or not – real instruments. Most of this memorabilia was acquired from the 'Pop and Guitars' auction at Christie's in London in 1997. It includes a Fender Squire Telecaster guitar signed by Mick Jagger, Keith Richards, Charlie Watts, Ronnie Wood, and Bill Wyman of The Rolling Stones; a Conn saxophone signed on the mouthpiece by former US president Bill Clinton; an Ariana acoustic guitar signed by David Bowie and Iggy Pop; a Fender Stratocaster guitar signed in silver ink by the

The ship's focal point is a three-deck-high atrium, with the reception desk, shore excursions desk, photo shop, and photo gallery grouped around it. It also houses a real showpiece – a fancy 22ft (6.7m) -high pipe organ with puppets that move with the music. One of the largest such Dutch band organs ever built, it was custom-made for HAL in Hilversum in the Netherlands.

As on *Volendam*, the Lido Deck swimming pool is located one deck higher than on the *Statendam*-class ships, so that you can have direct access between the aft and midships pools (not so aboard the S-class ships). This has created more space for extra cabins on the Navigation Deck below.

With one whole deck of suites and a dedicated, private concierge lounge, the company has in effect created a two-class ship. The charge to use the washing machines and dryers in the self-service launderette is petty and irritating, particularly for the occupants of suites, who pay high prices for their cruises.

Communication in English with many of the staff, particularly in the dining room and buffet areas, can be frustrating. Room service is poor. Standing in line for embarkation, disembarkation, shore tenders, and for self-serve buffet meals is inevitable aboard large ships.

ACCOMMODATION. The range is comparable to that found aboard the similarly sized *Rotterdam*, and there are many different price categories. There is one Penthouse Suite, 28 suites, and 168 mini-suites, with the rest of the accommodation a mixture of outside-view and interior cabins. All passenger hallways now include pleasing artwork.

All standard interior and outside cabins are tastefully furnished, with twin beds that convert to a queen-size bed, though space is tight for walking between beds and vanity unit. There is a decent amount of closet and drawer space, but this will be tight for longer voyages. The fully tiled bathrooms are disappointingly small, particularly for long cruises, and have small shower tubs, utilitarian toiletries cupboards, and exposed under-sink plumbing. Occupants of the Verandah Suites and Penthouse Suite (this has a separate steward's entrance, but the balcony is no larger than that of any of other suite) share a private concierge lounge (Neptune Lounge, which is accessible only by private key card). Each suite has a separate bedroom, dressing, and living area. Strangely, there are no butlers for these suites, as aboard many other ships with similar facilities.

Other facilities include an audio-visual center with television and DVD player, wet bar with refrigerator, large bathroom with Jacuzzi tub, separate toilet with bidet, and a guest bathroom with toilet and washbasin.

Except for the Penthouse Suite, located forward on the starboard side, the bathrooms in the other suites and mini-suites are disappointingly not as spacious or opulent as one might expect. All outside-view suites and cabin bathrooms have a tub/shower, while interior cabins have only a shower. Some 23 cabins for the mobility-limited are, however, very spacious and have a large roll-in shower enclosure for wheelchair users (some also have a bathtub), and ramped access to the balcony.

DINING. The Rotterdam Dining Room, a grand, traditional room, spans two aft decks, with ocean views on three sides and an imposing staircase connecting the upper and lower levels. Both open seating and assigned seating are available, while breakfast and lunch are open seating, where you'll be taken to a table by restaurant staff when you enter. Tables are for two, four, six, or eight.

Live music is provided for dinner each evening; once each cruise, there's a Dutch Dinner (hats are provided), and an Indonesian Lunch. 'Lighter-option' meals are available for the nutrition- and weight-conscious. Fine Rosenthal china and cutlery are provided, but there are no fish knives.

Other dining options. The Pinnacle Grill features Pacific Northwest cuisine and seats 88. There's a cover charge, and reservations are required, although suite-grade occupants qualify for priority reservations.

The Lido Buffet is a casual, self-serve café for casual breakfasts and luncheons. A poolside grill, Terrace Café, has hamburgers, hot dogs, and other fast-food items. It's also open for casual dinners on several nights each cruise – in an open-seating arrangement. Tables are set with crisp linens, flatware, and stemware. The set menu includes a choice of four entrées.

Also, a Lido Deck poolside 'Dive-In at the Terrace Grill' features signature burgers, hot dogs, and fries, and, on certain days, barbecues and other culinary treats may be featured.

ENTERTAINMENT. The Mondriaan Show Lounge, at the forward part of the ship, spans two decks, with banquette seating on both main and upper levels. It is basically a well-designed room, but the ceiling is low, and the sight lines from the balcony level are quite poor.

SPA/FITNESS. The Greenhouse Spa facilities are quite extensive and include a gymnasium with good muscle-toning equipment, separate saunas and steam rooms for men and women, and several treatment rooms, each with a shower and toilet. Outdoor facilities include basketball and shuffleboard courts, a jogging track, and a full walk-around teakwood promenade deck for strolling.

Zenith
★★★+

Size:	Mid-size Ship	Passenger/Crew Ratio (lower beds):	2.0
Tonnage:	52,090	Cabins (total):	670
Lifestyle:	Standard	Size Range (sq ft/m):	172.2–500.5/16–46.5
Cruise Line:	Pullmantur Cruises	Cabins (for one person):	0
Former Names:	none	Cabins (with private balcony):	110
IMO Number:	8918136	Cabins (wheelchair accessible):	4
Builder:	Meyer Werft (Germany)	Wheelchair accessibility:	Good
Original Cost:	$210 million	Cabin Current:	110 and 220 volts
Entered Service:	Apr 1992/Jun 2007	Elevators:	7
Registry:	Malta	Casino (gaming tables):	Yes
Length (ft/m):	682.4/208.0	Slot Machines:	Yes
Beam (ft/m):	95.1/29.0	Swimming Pools:	2
Draft (ft/m):	23.6/7.2	Hot Tubs (on deck):	3
Propulsion/Propellers:	diesel (19,960kW)/2	Self-Service Launderette:	No
Passenger Decks:	10	Dedicated Cinema/Seats:	No
Total Crew:	670	Library:	Yes
Passengers (lower beds):	1,340	Onboard currency:	Euros
Passenger Space Ratio (lower beds):	37.3		

This family-friendly, casual ship is for French speakers

OVERVIEW. This ship is best suited to young (and young at heart) French-speaking couples, solo travelers, and families with children who want a first cruise experience in an elegant ship, with a lively atmosphere and plentiful food, at low cost.

THE SHIP. *Zenith* was formerly operated by Celebrity Cruises. Although now 20 years old, it still has a contemporary, though rather sharp, angular profile that gives the impression of power and speed. Inside there is elegant and restrained decor. The Art Deco-style hotel-like lobby has a spacious feel and the principal deck that houses has a double-width indoor promenade. There is a good-size library. Other facilities include a cigar-smoking lounge; an Internet-connect center; and the Plaza Café for coffee and (loud) chat. A large, elegant casino has its own bar. The hospitality and the range and variety of food have been tailored to its French-speaking family clientele. You will usually find a lot of smokers aboard.

FAMILIES. There is a good program for children and teenagers, with youth counselors, and lots of activities.

ACCOMMODATION. There are several different price grades, including outside-view suites and cabins, and interior cabins. Many outside-view cabins on one deck have lifeboat-obstructed views. All cabins have good-quality fittings and are tastefully decorated. They are of an above-average size, with an excellent amount of closet and drawer space. All have twin beds that convert to queen-size. Soundproofing is quite good, but

Berlitz's Ratings		
	Possible	Achieved
Ship	500	355
Accommodation	200	140
Food	400	233
Service	400	261
Entertainment	100	61
Cruise Experience	400	256
OVERALL SCORE		
1306 points out of 2000		

some cabins are located by noisy crew-access doors. Bathrooms have a generous shower area, although towels are small. The lowest-grade outside-view cabins have a porthole, but all others have picture windows, while suite accommodation is larger, but suffers from noise on the swimming pool deck above.

DINING. The Caravelle Dining Room has several tables for two, as well as for four, six, or eight (in banquettes). There are two seatings for dinner, and open seating for breakfast and lunch, at tables for two, four, six, eight, or 10. The cuisine and its presentation are more notable for quantity than quality.

For informal meals, the Windsurf Buffet has a single-line self-service buffet for breakfast and lunch. At peak times, the buffet is simply too small, too crowded, and very noisy. The Grill, located outdoors adjacent to the Windsurf Buffet, serves fast food such as pizzas.

ENTERTAINMENT. The two-level Showlounge has good sight lines from almost all seats. It has a large stage for this size of ship, and decent lighting and sound. The shows consist of a troupe of showgirl dancers, whose routines seem pretty amateurish. Cabaret acts are the main feature and are very much geared to a family audience. There is also plenty of live music in various bars and lounges, plus the inevitable discotheque.

SPA/FITNESS. The Spa has a gym with ocean-view windows and high-tech equipment, an exercise area, several therapy treatment rooms, and single sex saunas.

Zuiderdam
★★★★

Size:	Mid-size Ship
Tonnage:	82,305
Lifestyle:	Premium
Cruise Line:	Holland America Line
Former Names:	none
IMO Number:	9221279
Builder:	Fincantieri (Italy)
Original Cost:	$400 million
Entered Service:	Dec 2002
Registry:	The Netherlands
Length (ft/m):	935.0/285.0
Beam (ft/m):	105.6/32.2
Draft (ft/m):	25.5/7.8
Propulsion/Propellers:	diesel-electric (35,240kW)/ 2 azimuthing pods
Passenger Decks:	11
Total Crew:	800
Passengers (lower beds):	1,848

Passenger Space Ratio (lower beds):	44.5
Passenger/Crew Ratio (lower beds):	2.3
Cabins (total):	924
Size Range (sq ft/m):	185.0–1,318.6/17.1–122.5
Cabins (for one person):	0
Cabins (with private balcony):	623
Cabins (wheelchair accessible):	28
Wheelchair accessibility:	Good
Cabin Current:	110 volts
Elevators:	14
Casino (gaming tables):	Yes
Slot Machines:	Yes
Swimming Pools:	2 (1 w/ sliding glass dome)
Hot Tubs (on deck):	5
Self-Service Launderette:	No
Dedicated Cinema/Seats:	Yes/170
Library:	Yes
Onboard currency:	US$

Dutch heritage and decor aboard this family-friendly ship

OVERVIEW. This ship is designed to appeal to young, vibrant, family-oriented passengers, with a good array of public rooms, bars, and lounges.

THE SHIP. *Zuiderdam* is a sister ship to *Eurodam, Noordam, Oosterdam,* and *Westerdam,* and shares a common platform and hull shape. There are two funnels, placed close together, one in front of the other, and not side by side, as aboard the smaller *Amsterdam* and *Rotterdam.* This placement is because the ship has two engine rooms – one with three diesels, and one with two diesels and a gas turbine. Pod propulsion is provided, powered by a diesel-electric system, so there's almost no discernible vibration.

Several glass elevators provide fine ocean views. There are two centrally located swimming pools outdoors, and one of the pools can be used in inclement weather conditions due to its retractable glass-domed cover. Two whirlpool tubs, adjacent to the swimming pools, are abridged by a bar, while another (smaller) pool is provided for children.

The lobby space is small, and spans just three decks. It has a stairway, and the lobby's focal point is a large, 10ft (3m) -high transparent Waterford crystal 'seahorse.' The decor is extremely bright for a Holland America Line ship, with an eclectic color and pattern mix that assails you from all directions.

There are two entertainment/public room decks, the upper of which has an exterior promenade deck – something new for this traditional cruise line. Although it doesn't go around the whole ship, it's long

Berlitz's Ratings		
	Possible	Achieved
Ship	500	400
Accommodation	200	151
Food	400	261
Service	400	268
Entertainment	100	71
Cruise Experience	400	280
OVERALL SCORE		
1431 points out of 2000		

enough for walking. There is also a jogging track outdoors.

The most dramatic public room is the Vista Lounge, which spans three decks in the forward section of the ship. The casino is equipped with all the gaming paraphernalia and slot machines you can think of, and it is so large that you have to walk through it to get from the restaurant to the showlounge.

The Crow's Nest is a multi-function 'lifestyle' area, encompassing the ship's library, a lounge area with fine ocean views, and an Explorations Café.

Niggles include the fact that many of the 'private' balconies aren't so private, and can be overlooked from various public locations. Also, some pillars obstruct the passenger flow and lines of sight on the main public decks. It can sometimes be difficult to escape from smokers, and from those walking around in unsuitable clothing, clutching plastic sport drinks bottles.

FAMILIES. Children have KidZone, an indoor/outdoor facility, and Club HAL for ages 5–12, with a number of dedicated youth counselors and activity programs. Teenagers get to use WaveRunner, which includes a dance floor, special lighting effects, and a booming sound system. There's also a gaming room, and big-screen television for movies.

ACCOMMODATION. There are numerous accommodation price grades. The price you pay depends on the size, location, and grade you choose. From largest to smallest: **Penthouse Verandah Suites** (1,318 sq ft/122 sq m, including balcony); **Deluxe Verandah Suites** (563 sq ft/52 sq m); **Verandah Suites** (284 sq ft/26 sq m); **Outside-view cabins** (197 sq ft/18 sq m); Interior (no-view) cabins are slightly smaller, at 183 sq ft (17 sq m).

A number of cabins on the lowest accommodation deck, Main Deck, have views obstructed by lifeboats. Some cabins that can accommodate a third and fourth person have very little closet space, and there's only one personal safe. Audio channels are provided on the in-cabin TV system.

Each morning, an eight-page *New York Times* (Times Fax) is provided for each cabin. Fresh fruit is available on request. Shoe-shine service and evening turndown service are also provided, as is a small range of toiletries.

DINING. The 1,045-seat Vista Dining Room is aft. Spanning two decks, it is a charming room, with seating on the main and balcony levels. Both open seating (you may have to wait a considerable time for a table), and fixed seating (assigned tables and times) are available; you'll be taken to a table by restaurant staff when you enter. A traditional dining experience is provided, with friendly service from Indonesian and Filipino stewards, who access the galley – it's underneath the restaurant – by escalators.

Breakfast and lunch are an open-seating arrangement, so you'll be seated by restaurant staff. Tables are for two, four, six, or eight. The waiter stations can be noisy if you are seated adjacent to them. Live music is provided for dinner. Once each cruise, there's a Dutch Dinner (hats are provided), and an Indonesian Lunch. 'Lighter-option' meals are always available for the nutrition- and the weight-conscious. Holland America Line can provide Kosher meals, although these are prepared ashore, frozen, and brought to your table sealed in their original containers.

Other dining options. A 130-seat Pinnacle Grill is a more upscale dining spot with higher-quality ingredients cooked to order. Located on Lower Promenade Deck, it fronts onto the second level of the atrium lobby. The cuisine is Pacific Northwest, plus premium-quality steaks from hand-selected cuts of beef. The wine bar offers mostly American wines. Reservations are needed, and there's a cover charge (but the steaks are worth it).

For more casual eating, there's an extensive Lido Café, which includes a pizzeria/Italian specialties counter, salad bar, Asian stir-fry counter, deli sandwiches, and a separate dessert buffet. Movement through the buffet area can be very slow, particularly at peak times. In the evenings, one side of this venue is turned into an extra-cost, 72-seat Canaletto Restaurant – a quasi-Italian informal eatery with waiter service.

Also, a poolside 'Dive-In at the Terrace Grill' features multi-choice signature burgers (with special Dive-In sauce), hot dogs and fries, and, on certain days, barbecues and other culinary treats.

The Windsurf Café in the atrium lobby (open 20 hours a day) serves extra-cost coffees, pastries, snack foods, deli sandwiches, and, in the evenings, liqueur coffees.

ENTERTAINMENT. The 867-seat Vista Lounge is the venue for Las Vegas-style revue shows and major cabaret presentations. It spans three decks in the forward section, and the main floor level has a bar in its starboard aft section. Spiral stairways at the back of the lounge connect all levels. Stage shows are best seen from the upper levels, from where the sight lines are quite good.

SPA/FITNESS. The Greenhouse Spa is a large, two-decks-high health spa area, located directly above the navigation bridge at the front of the ship. Facilities include a solarium, and an extra-cost thermal suite – a unisex area incorporating a Laconium, Hammam, and Chamomile Grotto, while a Hydropool allows you to swim against a current. There's also a beauty parlor, 11 private body-treatment/massage and therapy rooms, including one for couples. A large gymnasium with floor-to-ceiling windows has the latest equipment.

Ship Ratings

Ship Name	Score	Stars
Adonia	1476	★★★★
Adventure of the Seas	1361	★★★+
Aegean Odyssey	1393	★★★+
AIDAaura	1347	★★★★
AIDAbella	1396	★★★+
AIDAblu	1397	★★★+
AIDAcara	1315	★★★+
AIDAdiva	1375	★★★+
AIDAluna	1380	★★★+
AIDAmar	1396	★★★+
AIDAprima	NYR	NYR
AIDAsol	1396	★★★+
AIDAstella	1396	★★★+
AIDAvita	1340	★★★+
Albatros	1197	★★★
Allure of the Seas	1466	★★★★
Amadea	1546	★★★★
American Star	1006	★★+
Amsterdam	1434	★★★★
Anthem of the Seas	1528	★★★★
Arcadia	1423	★★★★
Artania	1521	★★★★
Artemis	1296	★★★+
Astor	1296	★★★+
Asuka II	1663	★★★★★+

Ship Name	Score	Stars
Aurora	1460	★★★★
Azamara Journey	1555	★★★★★+
Azamara Quest	1554	★★★★★
Azura	1467	★★★★
Balmoral	1373	★★★+
Berlin	1219	★★★
Black Watch	1281	★★★+
Boudicca	1280	★★★+
Braemar	1275	★★★+
Bremen	1555	★★★★★+
Brilliance of the Seas	1376	★★★+
Britannia	1656	★★★★★+
Caledonian Sky	1591	★★★★★
Caribbean Princess	1430	★★★★
Carnival Breeze	1338	★★★+
Carnival Conquest	1322	★★★+
Carnival Dream	1337	★★★+
Carnival Ecstasy	1232	★★★
Carnival Elation	1237	★★★
Carnival Fantasy	1231	★★★
Carnival Fascination	1239	★★★
Carnival Freedom	1332	★★★+
Carnival Glory	1315	★★★+
Carnival Imagination	1235	★★★
Carnival Inspiration	1236	★★★

Ship Name	Score	Stars
Carnival Legend	1314	★★★★
Carnival Liberty	1305	★★★+
Carnival Magic	1317	★★★+
Carnival Miracle	1317	★★★+
Carnival Paradise	1234	★★★
Carnival Pride	1324	★★★+
Carnival Sensation	1229	★★★
Carnival Spirit	1320	★★★+
Carnival Splendor	1321	★★★+
Carnival Sunshine	1331	★★★+
Carnival Triumph	1302	★★★+
Carnival Valor	1301	★★★+
Carnival Victory	1295	★★★+
Carnival Vista	NYR	NYR
Celebrity Constellation	1491	★★★★
Celebrity Eclipse	1553	★★★★★
Celebrity Equinox	1553	★★★★★
Celebrity Infinity	1489	★★★★
Celebrity Millennium	1492	★★★★
Celebrity Reflection	1562	★★★★★
Celebrity Silhouette	1558	★★★★★
Celebrity Solstice	1544	★★★★
Celebrity Summit	1484	★★★★
Celebrity Xpedition	1331	★★★+
Celestyal Cristal	1239	★★★

Ship Name	Score	Stars
Celestyal Odyssey	1347	★★★+
Celestyal Olympia	1246	★★★
Club Med 2	1395	★★★+
Coral Princess	1439	★★★★
Costa Atlantica	1341	★★★+
Costa Deliziosa	1383	★★★+
Costa Diadema	1377	★★★+
Costa Fascinosa	1364	★★★+
Costa Favolosa	1367	★★★+
Costa Fortuna	1362	★★★+
Costa Luminosa	1362	★★★+
Costa Magica	1360	★★★+
Costa Mediterranea	1350	★★★+
Costa neoClassica	1229	★★★
Costa neoRiviera	1244	★★★
Costa neoRomantica	1239	★★★
Costa Pacifica	1355	★★★+
Costa Serena	1355	★★★+
Costa Victoria	1261	★★★+
Crown Princess	1427	★★★★
Crystal Serenity	1693	★★★★★
Crystal Symphony	1687	★★★★★+
Dawn Princess	1409	★★★★
Diamond Princess	1448	★★★★
Disney Dream	1520	★★★★

Ship Name	Score	Stars
Disney Fantasy	1522	****
Disney Magic	1445	****
Disney Wonder	1447	****
Emerald Princess	1442	****
Empress	1189	***
Enchantment of the Seas	1365	***+
Eurodam	1447	****
Europa	1852	******+
Europa 2	1860	******+
Explorer of the Seas	1360	***+
Fifty Years of Victory	1429	****
Fram	1314	***+
Freedom of the Seas	1392	***+
Golden Princess	1420	****
Grand Celebration	1126	***
Grande Mariner	840	**
Grandeur of the Seas	1370	***+
Grand Princess	1417	****
Hamburg	1336	***+
Hanseatic	1758	*****
Harmony of the Seas	NYR	NYR
Hebridean Princess	1678	*****+
Hebridean Sky	1389	***+
Horizon	1312	***+
Independence	956	***

Ship Name	Score	Stars
Independence of the Seas	1393	***+
Insignia	1541	****
Island Escape	1035	***
Island Princess	1437	****
Island Sky	1569	*****+
Jewel of the Seas	1387	***+
Koningsdam	NYR	NYR
L'Austral	1527	****
Le Boreal	1527	****
Legend of the Seas	1369	***+
Le Lyrial	1542	****
Le Ponant	1371	***+
Le Soleal	1530	****
Liberty of the Seas	1389	***+
Louis Aura	1388	***
Maasdam	1346	***+
Magellan	1156	***
Marco Polo	1382	***+
Marina	1579	*****+
Mariner of the Seas	1359	****
Mein Schiff 1	1534	****
Mein Schiff 2	1535	****
Mein Schiff 3	1597	*****+
Mein Schiff 4	1598	*****+
Minerva	1446	****

Ship Name	Score	Stars
Monarch	1211	***
MSC Armonia	1386	***+
MSC Divina	1551	*****+
MSC Fantasia	1538	****
MSC Lirica	1407	****
MSC Magnifica	1452	****
MSC Musica	1449	****
MSC Opera	1438	****
MSC Orchestra	1451	****
MSC Poesia	1452	****
MSC Preziosa	1552	*****+
MSC Sinfonia	1382	***+
MSC Splendida	1534	****
Natl. Geo. Endeavour	972	**+
Natl. Geo. Explorer	1077	***
Natl. Geo. Orion	1591	*****+
Nautica	1538	****
Navigator of the Seas	1362	***+
Nieuw Amsterdam	1433	****
Nippon Maru	1498	****
Noordam	1432	****
Norwegian Breakaway	1434	****
Norwegian Dawn	1367	***+
Norwegian Epic	1424	****
Norwegian Escape	NYR	NYR

Ship Name	Score	Stars
Norwegian Gem	1367	***+
Norwegian Getaway	1438	****
Norwegian Jade	1367	***+
Norwegian Jewel	1365	***+
Norwegian Pearl	1362	***+
Norwegian Sky	1362	***+
Norwegian Spirit	1361	***+
Norwegian Star	1373	***+
Norwegian Sun	1365	***+
Oasis of the Seas	1464	****
Oceana	1384	***+
Ocean Diamond	1141	***
Ocean Princess	1422	****
Oosterdam	1418	****
Oriana	1447	****
Ovation of the Seas	NYR	NYR
Pacific Aria	1344	***+
Pacific Dawn	1330	***+
Pacific Eden	1353	***+
Pacific Jewel	1367	***+
Pacific Pearl	1388	***+
Pacific Princess	1442	****
Pacific Venus	1531	****
Paul Gauguin	1540	****
Pearl Mist	1397	****

Ship Name	Score	Stars
Pride of America	1243	***
Prinsendam	1421	****
Quantum of the Seas	1526	****
Queen Elizabeth	1583	****+
Queen Mary 2	1675	*****+
Queen Victoria	1575	*****+
Radiance of the Seas	1379	***+
Regal Princess	1527	****
Regatta	1538	****
Rhapsody of the Seas	1372	***+
Riviera	1682	****+
Rotterdam	1457	****
Royal Clipper	1534	****
Royal Princess	1528	****
Ruby Princess	1434	****
Saga Pearl II	1348	***+
Saga Sapphire	1446	****
Sapphire Princess	1437	****
Sea Adventurer	945	**
Seabourn Odyssey	1701	*****
Seabourn Quest	1702	*****
Seabourn Sojourn	1701	*****
Sea Cloud	1706	*****
Sea Cloud II	1701	*****
SeaDream I	1756	*****

Ship Name	Score	Stars
SeaDream II	1752	*****
Sea Princess	1414	****
Serenade of the Seas	1394	****+
Serenissima	1095	**+
Seven Seas Explorer	NYR	NYR
Seven Seas Mariner	1640	*****+
Seven Seas Navigator	1564	*****
Seven Seas Voyager	1641	*****+
Silver Cloud	1656	*****+
Silver Discoverer	1456	****
Silver Explorer	1611	*****+
Silver Galapagos	1415	****
Silver Shadow	1741	*****
Silver Spirit	1735	******
Silver Whisper	1743	*****
Silver Wind	1658	*****+
SkySea Golden Era	NYR	NYR
Sovereign	1191	***
Splendour of the Seas	1346	****+
Star Breeze	1643	*****
Star Clipper	1394	****+
Star Flyer	1395	****+
Star Legend	1654	*****
Star Pride	1641	*****+
Star Princess	1417	****

Ship Name	Score	Stars
Sun Princess	1408	****
SuperStar Aquarius	1192	***
SuperStar Gemini	1194	***
Superstar Libra	1161	***
SuperStar Virgo	1398	****+
Tere Moana	1436	****
Thomson Celebration	1179	***
Thomson Dream	1206	***
Thomson Majesty	1239	***
Thomson Spirit	1208	***
Veendam	1353	****+
Ventura	1461	****
Viking Sky	NYR	NYR
Viking Star	1698	*****+
Vision of the Seas	1369	***+
Volendam	1428	****
Voyager	1248	***
Voyager of the Seas	1365	****+
Westerdam	1422	****
Wind Spirit	1393	****+
Wind Star	1394	****+
Wind Surf	1462	****
Zaandam	1423	****
Zenith	1306	****+
Zuiderdam	1431	****

Credits

Photo Credits

Aurora Expeditions 112
Aida 73
Alamy 191TL
All Leisure Holidays 91, 111
AWL Images 2/3
Ayako Ward 96, 97, 121, 174, 179, 183
Azamara Club Cruises 155
Carnival Cruises 29, 30, 34, 37, 57, 60, 76, 80, 84, 124, 128, 134, 135, 136
Celebrity Cruises 39, 59, 66, 68, 74, 127, 137, 138, 139, 176
Celestyal Cruises 54
Coral Princess Cruises 110
Corbis 23
Costa Crociere S.p.A 140, 141, 192
Crystal Cruises 45, 64, 85, 119, 157
Cunard Line 7, 14, 28, 71, 94, 120, 123, 132, 143, 182, 188
Disney Cruise Line 24T, 43, 44, 67, 69, 72, 79, 89, 108, 158
Douglas Ward 9, 10, 15, 22, 35, 40, 56, 65,

98, 101, 107, 109, 116, 151, 154, 156, 160, 162, 164, 166, 178, 180, 186, 189
Getty Images 1, 4/5
Hapag-Lloyd Cruises 8, 11, 17, 26, 36, 38, 41, 61, 82, 100, 102, 159, 172, 184, 190, 191TR, 191MR
Hebridean Island Cruises 63
Holland America Line 142
iStock 48, 55
Lindblad/Sisse Brimberg & Cotton Coulson 125
Louis Cruises 161
Ming Tang-Evans/Apa Publications 16
MSC Crociere S.A 20, 93, 95, 144, 145
NCL 50, 51, 78, 87, 105, 146, 147
P&O Cruises 24B, 104, 118, 148
Paul Gauguin Cruises 6, 163
Princess Cruises 70, 86, 150
Regent Seven Seas Cruises 19, 31, 32, 42, 165
Rex Features 114

Royal Caribbean International 75, 88, 90, 130, 152, 153
Sea Cloud Cruises 117
Sea Dream Yacht Club 52
Seabourn 167
Shutterstock 181
Silversea Cruises 53, 58, 92, 99, 122, 169, 170
Steve Dunlop Photographer/P&O Cruises 149
Viking Cruises 18, 168, 191ML

Cover Credits

Front cover: *MS Europa* in Fiji, Hapag-Lloyd Cruises; Back cover: *Seabourn Odyssey,* SeaBourn; Remy aboard *Disney Dream*, Disney CL; Penthouse Suite, *Seven Seas Explorer*, RSSC; Dancing aboard *Queen Elizabeth*, Douglas Ward; *Crystal Serenity*, Crystal Cruises

Insight Guide Credits

Distribution

UK
Dorling Kindersley Ltd
A Penguin Group company
80 The Strand, London, WC2R 0RL
sales@uk.dk.com

United States
Ingram Publisher Services
1 Ingram Boulevard, PO Box 3006
La Vergne, TN 37086-1986
ips@ingramcontent.com

Australia and New Zealand
Woodslane
14 Apollo St, Warriewood
NSW 2102 Australia
info@woodslane.com.au

Worldwide
Apa Publications (Singapore) Pte
7030 Ang Mo Kio Avenue 5
08-65 Northstar @ AMK
Singapore 569880
apasin@singnet.com.sg

© 2016 Apa Publications (UK) Ltd/
Douglas Ward
All Rights Reserved

Printed by CTPS-China

Berlitz Trademark Reg. U.S. Patent Office and other countries. Marca Registrada. Used under licence from the Berlitz Investment Corporation

First Edition 1984
Twenty-fourth Edition 2016

www.berlitzpublishing.com

Written by
Douglas Ward

Edited by
Sarah Clark and Clare Peel

Picture edit by
Tom Smyth

Production by
Rebeka Davies

Tell Us Your Thoughts

Dear Cruiser,

I hope you have found this edition of Berlitz Cruising and Cruise Ships both enjoyable and useful. If you have any comments or queries, or experiences of cruising that you would like to pass on, or perhaps some ideas for subjects that could be included in the future, I would be delighted to read them. With your help, I can improve and expand the guide in future editions.

The world of cruising is evolving fast and certain facts and figures may have changed since this guide went to print, so if you have found any outdated information in these pages, please do let me know and I will make sure it is corrected as soon as possible.

You can write to me by email at:
bertliz@apaguide.co.uk

Or by post to:
Berlitz Publishing
PO Box 7910
London SE1 1WE
United Kingdom

Thank you,
Douglas Ward

Index

A

Abercrombie & Kent 154
accommodations 9, 11, 25, 32, 35, 84, 127, 171, 174, 186
activities 7
 sports 36, 59, 77
adults-only cruises 30, 90, 165
AIDA Cruises 18, 154
alcohol 33, 55, 59
American Cruise Lines 112, 155
Antarctica 99, 100
Arctic 99, 101, 110
around-the-world cruises 118
Aurora Expeditions 155
Azamara Club Cruises 156

B

Baltic cruises 45
Blount Small Ship Adventures 112, 156
booking 27

C

cabins. See accommodations
cancellations 27
Caribbean cruises 43
Carnival Cruise Lines 132, 133
casinos 54
CDF Croisières de France 156
Celebration Cruise Line 156
Celebrity Cruises 133, 136
children 7, 9, 30, 106, 174
classes and lectures 91, 99
Club Med Cruises 157
coastal cruises 110
corporate cruising 109
Costa Cruises 133, 138, 178
Cruceros Australis 155
Cruise and Maritime Voyages 157
cruise lines 46, 132, 154. See also by name
cruise ships 9, 25, 36. See also sailing ships
 reviews and evaluations 183, 188
Crystal Cruises 157
cultural programs 91
Cunard Line 114, 133, 141
currency exchange 30

D

destinations 43
disabled travelers 96
disembarkation 55

Disney Cruise Line 30, 83, 158
dress codes 9

E

eco-cruising 176
embarkation 10
emergencies 179
entertainment 8, 68, 187
environmental issues 102, 176
etiquette 59
Etstur Cruises 158
excursions 50, 87
expedition cruises 36, 99, 159, 163, 165, 167

F

FAQs 26
food and drink 33, 58, 59, 61, 90, 107, 186. See also restaurants
Fred. Olsen Cruise Line 158
FTI Cruises 158

G

G Adventures 159
Galápagos Cruises 159
gay cruises 95
gentlemen hosts 90, 95
Grand Circle Cruise Line 159

H

hair salons 54
Hapag-Lloyd Cruises 118, 159
Hapag-Lloyd Expedition Cruises 159
health 40, 57, 90, 175, 180
 seasickness 39
Hebridean Island Cruises 160
Henna Cruises 160
Heritage Expeditions 160
Holland America Line 133, 142
Hurtigruten 160

I

Indian Ocean cruises 47
insurance 28
Internet 10, 30, 56
Island Cruises 161

L

laundry and dry cleaning 57, 175
libraries 57
Lindblad Expeditions 99, 112, 161

lost property 57
Louis Cruises 162
loyalty programs 29
luxury cruises 170

M

maiden voyages 109
mail 57
medical care. See health
Mediterranean cruises 45
MOPAS 162
MSC Cruises 133, 144

N

Noble Caledonia 162
Norwegian Cruise Line 18, 19, 133, 146
Norwegian fjords cruises 46
NYK Cruises 162

O

Oceania Cruises 162
Oceanwide Expeditions 163
One Ocean Expeditions 163

P

passports 8, 86
Paul Gauguin Cruises 163
Pearl Seas Cruises 112
pets 30
Phoenix Reisen 118, 163
piracy 181
Planatours Cruises 164
P&O Cruises 133, 147, 163
Ponant Cruises 164
prices 26
 discounts 27
 extras 10, 30, 31, 37, 94, 175
Princess Cruises 133, 148
problem solving 174
Pullmantur Cruises 164

Q

Quark Expeditions 165

R

Regent Seven Seas Cruises 165
religious services 58
repositioning cruises 31, 115
restaurants 9, 33, 61, 171, 175. See also food and drink
 captain's table 66
romantic cruises 92
room service 59
Royal Caribbean International 19, 133, 151

S

safety 41, 84, 178
 hygiene 39, 67
 lifeboat and muster drills 178, 179
Saga Cruises 165
sailing ships 116, 167, 169
Seabourn 166
Sea Cloud Cruises 165
SeaDream Yacht Cruises 166
seasonal cruises 29
security 10, 179
senior citizens 90, 165
shopping 37, 52
shore excursions 56
Silversea Cruises 167
smoking 40
solo travelers 28, 94
South Pacific cruises 49
spas and fitness 8, 9, 72
special needs cruising 96
Star Clippers 167
Star Cruises 167
Swan Hellenic Cruises 168
swimming pools 57, 59

T

telecommunications 10, 36, 56, 59
television 58, 59
theme and special interest cruises 105
Thomson Cruises 168
tickets 27
tipping 23, 30, 34, 56
transatlantic cruises 114
travel agents 8, 27
TUI Cruises 168

U

Un-Cruise Adventures 112, 168

V

Venus Cruise 168
Viking Ocean Cruises 19, 169
Voyages of Discovery 169
Voyages to Antiquity 169

W

weddings 92, 115
wheelchair users 97
Windstar Cruises 169

Y

youth programs 30